Leading Issues in
Economic Development

Leading Issues in Economic Development

SIXTH EDITION

GERALD M. MEIER
Stanford University

New York   Oxford
OXFORD UNIVERSITY PRESS
1995

For David, Daniel, Jeremy, Andrew
—Once more, thirty years later

Oxford University Press

Oxford   New York
Athens   Auckland   Bangkok   Bombay
Calcutta   Cape Town   Dar es Salaam   Delhi
Florence   Hong Kong   Istanbul   Karachi
Kuala Lumpur   Madras   Madrid   Melbourne
Mexico City   Nairobi   Paris   Singapore
Taipei   Tokyo   Toronto

and associated companies in
Berlin   Ibadan

Published by Oxford University Press, Inc.,

198 Madison Avenue, New York, New York 10016-4314

Oxford is a registered trademark of Oxford University Press

Library of Congress Cataloging-in-Publication Data
Leading issues in economic development /
[edited by] Gerald M. Meier.
—6th ed.
p. cm.   Includes bibliographical references and index.
ISBN 0-19-507180-8
1. Economic development.   I. Meier, Gerald M.
HD82.L3273 1995
338.9—dc20   94-13649

9 8 7 6 5 4 3 2

Printed in the United Stated of America
on acid-free paper

PREFACE

Two centuries after the Industrial Revolution, most of the world still has to contend with the daily pain of poverty. Why is this so? And what can be done about it?

This book concentrates on the latest thinking about policies to raise the standard of living for 80 percent of the world's population—the poverty-ridden peoples in less developed countries (LDCs). Over the past three decades—since the first edition of this book—there have been extraordinary changes in the development experience. This sixth edition is extensively revised in response to changes in the subject matter of development economics and new problems confronting the development community. Attention is now given to new growth theory, new institutional economics and problems of imperfect information and incomplete markets, new trade theory, models of household behavior, applied microeconomic studies, issues of gender, the environment, recent experience with policy reform, and political economy as related to governance.

I have, however, avoided writing the ordinary type of textbook, in favor of a distinctive kind of coursebook to illuminate the leading issues of economic development from a variety of viewpoints and different perspectives. Although ordinary textbooks in the subject now exist, I still doubt that a standard type of textbook can capture the range of thought and applications that are necessary to understand the problems and policies of development. Only by culling the most insightful readings from the diffuse field of development and bringing them into conceptual order can this be done. Interpreting development as a problem-solving and policy-oriented subject, I believe this eclectic approach best serves the student's needs.

Accordingly, the organization of this book presents material that combines the best analytical thought alongside instructive application. Unlike the organizaltion of an ordinary book of readings, I want to emphasize the importance of the interrelatedness of the selected readings on each issue—taken as a set—rather than any one particular reading. This is especially necessary for appreciating the relationships among the various materials that deal with analysis, policy implications, and the lessons of development experience. The section "Using This Book" (p. vii) describes the combination of Selected Readings and my Notes, Comments, and Exhibits.

Many of the Selected Readings are new, and there are new or revised Notes, Comments, and Exhibits. Throughout, the emphasis is on fundamental analytical principles and on empirical relationships within the main theme of how to improve the future quality of development policy making—both national and international.

I wish to express my appreciation to the authors and publishers who have granted permission to use excerpts from publications for which copyrights exist. Specific acknowledgment is given with each selection. Some parts of the original versions of the selected materials have been omitted out of consideration for relevance and to avoid repetition. In some instances, tables and diagrams have been renumbered, the footnotes have been deleted or renumbered. Some of the selections from an earlier (unenlightened) age fail to be gender-neutral; although I have not changed their original language, I do apologize for any male bias of other authors. Abstract male pronouns should be read in a gender-neutral sense.

Many revisions in this edition have been inspired by students at Stanford University and by lecture audiences in developing countries. The book is designed for them, and their appreciation means much to me. I hope this volume will prove of value to yet another generation of students concerned with the future of the developing world.

An extensive critique of the fifth edition by Professor Jere Behrman of the University of Pennsylvania has been helpful for my revision of this new edition. Three other anonymous readers also provided numerous and valuable suggestions.

For easing the laborious library process of preparing this edition, I am grateful to librarians at Stanford and Oxford, and for the assistance of Martin Gonzalez, Roberto Garcia, Elizabeth MacLean, and Gyoung-Gyu Choi. Ellen Kitamura inherited a disorganized manuscript that needed completion of several chapters and revisions. With exceptional efficiency—and good humor—she speedily processed the final typescript. Members of the World Bank, International Monetary Fund, and UNICEF have been generous in providing data, but are not responsible for my interpretation.

As previously, Herbert Addison has again been the most responsive and considerate of editors, while all others at Oxford University Press continue to make the thirty-year association an author's wish. Finally, I am grateful to the entire profession of development economists whose writings provide the foundation for this volume—especially the newer generation who have in this edition extended my own education in development.

Stanford   G.M.M.
April 1994

USING THIS BOOK

The materials in this book are designed to provide maximum flexibility of use for instructors and students. The subject of economic development is so large, and even controversial, that it cannot be encapsulated in an ordinary type of textbook. The different sections in the chapters therefore explore a variety of perspectives on issues of fundamental importance to developing nations.

Each chapter includes the following sections:

Chapter openings   A short introductory statement of the major themes of the chapter and a guide to the selections included.

Readings   Edited selections that present in succinct form the major contributions by development economists and practitioners on the central issues in economic development.

Notes   Connecting text that integrates or supplements the selections.

Comments   Further explanation of special topics and recommended readings.

Exhibits   Tables and charts drawn from research studies that provide empirical illustrations and data on topics under discussion.

Each section acquires added significance through its contextual position, and taken together within a chapter, the materials form a whole. Each chapter is self-contained, and the contents are designed to allow individual freedom of choice in deciding what chapters and selections to read and in what sequence.

ABBREVIATED CONTENTS

Chapter I.   The Challenge of Development   3

Chapter II.   Thinking About Development   67

Chapter III.   Dualistic Development   113

Chapter IV.   Domestic Financing of Development   161

Chapter V.   External Financing of Development   213

Chapter VI.   Human Resources   265

Chapter VII.   Industrialization and Agriculture: 1   327

Chapter VIII.   Industrialization and Agriculture: 2   395

Chapter IX.   Trade and Development   453

Chapter X.   Markets, Government, and Policy   513

                    Index   587

CONTENTS

ABBREVIATIONS   xix

I THE CHALLENGE OF DEVELOPMENT   **3**

I.A. WHAT IS ECONOMIC DEVELOPMENT?—NOTE   7
    Comment: Capabilities and Entitlements   *9*

I.B. MEASURES OF DEVELOPMENT   13

    I.B.1. Measurement of Key Indicators—Stern   13
    Comment: Relative Puchasing Powers   *17*
    Comment: Lorenz Curve and Gini Coefficient   *17*
    Comment: Inverted-U Hypothesis of Inequality   *20*
    Comment: Inequality and Growth   *22*

    I.B.2. Distributional Weights—Ahluwalia and Chenery   23

    I.B.3. Burden of Poverty—World Bank   25

    I.B.4. Why Does Absolute Poverty Persist?—Note   28

    I.B.5. The Environment Challenge of Development—Note   30
    Comment: Development and the Environment   *32*

I.C. HOW HAVE DEVELOPING COUNTRIES PERFORMED?   33

    I.C.1. Taiwan and South Korea—Scitovsky   33
    Comment: Success Stories   *42*

    I.C.2. Latin America—Naya   42
    Comment: Latin American Case Studies   *46*

    I.C.3. Sub-Saharan Africa—Overseas Development Institute   46
    Comment: Sub-Saharan Africa's Inferior Performance   *51*

    I.C.4. Lessons for Sub-Saharan Africa—Summers   52

    I.C.5. China—Burki   55
    Comment: Chinese Economic Reform   *59*
    Comment: Cross Country Empirical Comparisons   *59*

I.D. LEADING ISSUES—NOTE   62

II THINKING ABOUT DEVELOPMENT 67

II.A. HISTORICAL PERSPECTIVES 69

II.A.1. Sequence of Stages—Note 69
Comment: The "Take-Off" 71

II.A.2. Economic Backwardness in Historical Perspective—Gerschenkron 72

II.A.3. Why Are We So Rich and They So Poor?—Landes 74
Comment: Historical Studies 79
Comment: Transaction Costs, Institutions, and Historical Growth 80

II.A.4. Future Development in Historical Perspective—Note 80

II.B. ANALYTICAL PERSPECTIVES 86

II.B.1. Evolution of Development Economics—Note 86
Comment: Classical Growth Theory 89
Comment: Development Economics as a Special Subject 90

II.B.2. Neoclassical Analysis—Harberger 91
Comment: Total Factor Productivity 93

II.B.3. Structural Analysis—Chenery 95

II.B.4. The Imperfect Information Paradigm—Stiglitz 99
Comment: The New Market Failures Approach and Development 101

II.B.5. New Endogenous Growth Theory—Note 102

II.B.6. The New Institutional Economics and Development Theory—Bardhan 103

II.C. ALTERNATIVE PERSPECTIVES 107

II.C.1. Dependency Theories of Underdevelopment—Note 107
Comment: Varieties of Dependency Theory 110
Comment: Neostructuralism 110

III DUALISTIC DEVELOPMENT 113

III.A. THE LABOR SURPLUS ECONOMY 117

III.A.1. Labor Surplus on the Land—Nurkse 117

III.A.2. Choice of Techniques—Sen 119

III.B. INTERSECTORAL ANALYSIS 121

III.B.1. Lewis's Dual-Sector Model—Note 121

III.B.2. Effects of the Modern Sector on the Traditional—Lewis 125
Comment: Dual-Economy Models 128

III.B.3. Versions of Dualism—Note 129

III.B.4. Organizational Dualism—Myint 132

III.C. MIGRATION AND URBANIZATION 140

III.C.1. A Model of Rural–Urban Migration—Todaro 140

III.C.2. Migration and City Growth—Williamson 142
Comment: Econometric Studies of Migration 145

III.C.3. The Informal Sector—ILO Mission   146
    Comment: Studies of the Informal Sector   149

III.C.4. Reinterpretation of the Informal Sector—Livingstone   150
    Comment: Urban–Rural Wage Gap   151

III.D. THE LEWIS MODEL IN RETROSPECT—NOTE   153

IV DOMESTIC FINANCING OF DEVELOPMENT   161

IV.A. INVESTMENT REQUIREMENTS—NOTE   163

IV.B. SOURCES OF CAPITAL FORMATION—NOTE   167

IV.C. INFLATIONARY FINANCE AND ITS EFFECTS   174

IV.C.1. Financing by Money Creation—Goode   174

IV.C.2. Inflation and Development Policy—Johnson   179
    Comment: Monetarism versus Structuralism   183
    Comment: Stabilization Policy   184

IV.C.3. IMF Adjustment Policies—Frenkel and Khan   184

IV.D. NONINFLATIONARY FINANCE   188

IV.D.1. Private Saving—Srinivasan   188
    Comment: Hypotheses Regarding Household Savings   192

IV.D.2. Public Finance—Stern   194
    Comment: Taxation   197
    Comment: Fiscal Discipline   198

IV.E. FINANCIAL MARKETS AND DEVELOPMENT   199

IV.E.1. Organized and Unorganized Money Markets—Tun Wai   199

IV.E.2. Demand-Following or Supply-Leading Finance—Patrick   202

IV.E.3. Case Against Financial Repression—McKinnon   204
    Comment: Financial Liberalization   208

IV.E.4. The Design of Financial Systems—Collier and Mayer   210

V EXTERNAL FINANCING OF DEVELOPMENT   213

V.A. RESOURCE GAP AND FOREIGN-EXCHANGE GAP—NOTE   215
    Comment: Foreign-Exchange Constraint   215
    Comment: Capital Flight   216

V.B. PUBLIC FINANCIAL AID   221

V.B.1. Why Official Assistance?—Krueger   221

V.B.2. Does Aid Work?—Note   224
    Comment: Effects of Aid   226

V.B.3. Improving the Effectiveness of Aid—Note   226

V.B.4. The IMF and World Bank—Note   229

V.C. EXTERNAL FINANCE AND ENVIRONMENTAL MANAGEMENT—NOTE   231

V.D. EXTERNAL DEBT   233

V.D.1. Debt-Servicing Problems—IMF   233
    Comment: Growing Out of Debt   *239*

V.D.2. Country Risk Analysis—Note   241
    Comment: Econometric Default Functions   *244*

V.D.3. Debt Strategy—Note   244

V.E. PRIVATE FOREIGN INVESTMENT   247

V.E.1. Benefits and Costs of Private Foreign Investment—Note   247

V.E.2. Multinational Enterprises in Developing Countries—Note   256
    Comment: Evaluation of MNEs   *258*

V.E.3. Negotiating Foreign Investment—Note   259

V.E.4. Political Risk—Note   262

VI HUMAN RESOURCES   **265**

VI.A. DEVELOPMENT AS A GENERALIZED PROCESS OF CAPITAL
    ACCUMULATION—JOHNSON   269

VI.B. THE SUPPLY OF ENTREPRENEURSHIP—LEIBENSTEIN   273
    Comment: Entrepreneurial Performance   *275*

VI.C. POPULATION   276

VI.C.1. Population and Poverty—Note   276

VI.C.2. Population Growth—Birdsall   279
    Comment: Population–Economic Relationships   *284*
    Comment: Child Labor and Street Children   *285*
    Comment: Revisionist View of Population   *286*

VI.D. GENDER AND DEVELOPMENT   287

VI.D.1. Women in the Labor Force—ILO   287

VI.D.2. Women's Share of Poverty—Buvinic and Lycette   295

VI.D.3. Market Gender Discrimination—Collier   300

VI.D.4. Missing Women—Sen   302
    Comment: Gender-Aware Analysis   *304*

VI.E. NUTRITION AND HEALTH   305

VI.E.1. Nutrition Actions—Berg   305

VI.E.2. Health Policy—World Bank   307

VI.F. EDUCATION　　313

VI.F.1. Investment in Human Capital—Note　　313
Comment: Human Capital Theory　　316

VI.F.2. Educational Investment—Musgrave　　316
Comment: Education and Development　　320
Comment: Education and the Success Stories　　320

VI.F.3. Economic Impact of Education—Psacharopoulos　　322

VII INDUSTRIALIZATION AND AGRICULTURE: 1　　327

VII.A. STRUCTURAL TRANSFORMATION　　329

VII.A.1. Modeling Structural Transformation—Chenery and Syrquin　　329

VII.A.2. Elements of Structural Transformation—Tomich, Kilby, and Johnston　　333
Comment: Empirical Research on Structural Change　　338

VII.B. PROMOTING INDUSTRIALIZATION　　342

VII.B.1. External Economies and Industrialization—Rosenstein-Rodan　　342

VII.B.2. Linkage Effects and Industrialization—Hirschman　　346
Comment: Linkages　　349
Comment: Industrialization and the "Big Push" Revisited　　349

VII.B.3. Welfare Economics of Industry Promotion—Grossman　　350

VII.B.4. Industrialization via Import Substitution—Note　　355
Comment: Critique of ISI　　360

VII.B.5. Industrialization via Export Substitution—Note　　361
Comment: Small Manufacturing Enterprises　　363
Comment: Industrialization and the Environment　　363

VII.B.6. Government Interventions for Industrial Development—Lall and Kell　　364

VII.C. TECHNOLOGICAL PROGRESS　　368

VII.C.1. Appropriate Technology—Stewart　　368
Comment: Criteria of Technological Appropriateness　　371
Comment: Choice of Techniques by MNEs　　371
Comment: Technological Capability　　372

VII.C.2. Capital-Stretching Innovations—Ranis　　373

VII.C.3. Technology Transfer—Pack　　375

VII.D. PRIVATIZATION　　379

VII.D.1. Guide to Privatization Policy—Vernon　　379
Comment: State-Owned Enterprises and Privatization　　383

VII.E. AGRICULTURE–INDUSTRY INTERACTIONS　　385

VII.E.1. Industrialization and Agricultural Development—Bacha　　385

VII.E.2. Complementarity of Industry and Agriculture—Lewis　　390

VII.E.3. Overcoming the Weakness of Agriculture—Lewis　　391

VIII INDUSTRIALIZATION AND AGRICULTURE: 2 — 395

VIII.A. IMPORTANCE OF AGRICULTURE — 397

VIII.A.1. Agriculture's Contribution to Development—Note — 397

VIII.A.2. Role of Peasant Agriculture—Lele — 400
Comment: Food, Hunger, Famine — *404*

VIII.A.3. Urban Bias—Lipton — 405
Comment: Rural–Urban Terms of Trade — *408*
Comment: The Rural–Urban Divide — *409*
Comment: Green Revolution — *409*

VIII.B. MICROECONOMICS OF THE RURAL SECTOR — 411

VIII.B.1. Theory of Rural Organization—Stiglitz — 411

VIII.B.2. Labor Contractual Arrangements—Binswanger and Rosenzweig — 415
Comment: Contractual Choice Models — *418*

VIII.B.3. Land Tenure—Warriner — 419
Comment: Land Reform — *421*

VIII.B.4. Rural Credit Markets—Braverman and Gausch — 422

VIII.B.5. Agricultural Household Models—Singh, Squire, and Strauss — 424
Comment: Supply Functions and Price Responsiveness — *427*
Comment: Rural Labor Markets — *428*
Comment: Women in Rural Areas — *428*
Comment: Induced Technical and Institutional Change — *429*

VIII.C. DESIGNING AN AGRICULTURAL STRATEGY — 431

VIII.C.1. The Agricultural Transformation—Timmer — 431
Comment: Agricultural Strategies — *434*

VIII.C.2. Evaluation of Government Intervention—Stiglitz — 435

VIII.C.3. Price Policy Analysis—Timmer, Falcon, and Pearson — 438
Comment: Agricultural Pricing Policy — *443*
Comment: Rural Environmental Policy — *444*

VIII.C.4. The Case for a Unimodal Strategy—Johnston — 444

VIII.C.5. Strategic Priorities for Agriculture—Tomich, Kilby, and Johnston — 450

IX TRADE AND DEVELOPMENT — 453

IX.A. GAINS FROM TRADE VERSUS GAINS FROM GROWTH — 455

IX.A.1. Dynamic Comparative Advantage—Note — 455

IX.A.2. Trade as an "Engine of Growth"—Note — 458
Comment: Criticism of Neoclassical Trade Theory — *461*

IX.A.3. Trade as a Mechanism of International Inequality—Myrdal — 462
Comment: Terms of Trade and Unequal Exchange — *464*

IX.A.4. Conditions of Export-Led Development—Note — 465

IX.B. TRADE STRATEGY   470

   IX.B.1. Inward-Oriented Strategies—Balassa   470
     Comment: ERP and DRCs   474
     Comment: Infant-Industry Protection   475

   IX.B.2. New Protectionist Arguments—Greenaway   476
     Comment: New Trade Theory and LDCs   479

   IX.B.3. Superiority of Export-Oriented Policies—Krueger   479
     Comment: Dynamic Gains from Exports   483

   IX.B.4. Export Promotion: Lessons of Experience—Note   485

   IX.B.5. Taiwan's Trade Strategy—World Bank   488
     Comment: New Export Pessimism   490

   IX.B.6. Trade Policy Reform—World Bank   491
     Comment: Overvalued Exchange Rates and Trade Balance   493

   IX.B.7. Trade Liberalization and Exchange Rates—Corden   495
     Comment: Stabilization-cum-Liberalization Programs   499

IX.C. TRADE IN PRIMARY PRODUCTS   501

   IX.C.1. Impact of Agricultural Protection—World Bank   501

   IX.C.2. International Resource Bargaining—Note   502
     Comment: The Commodity Problem   505

IX.D. REGIONAL INTEGRATION AND DEVELOPMENT—NOTE   507

X. MARKETS, GOVERNMENT, AND POLICY   **513**

X.A. POLICY PRESCRIPTIONS   515

   X.A.1. Policy Reform Packages—Roemer and Radelet   515
   X.A.2. Policies for Economic Development—Fischer and Thomas   521
   X.A.3. Principal "Lessons"—Harberger   525
   X.A.4. Interaction of State and Markets—Thomas   529
   X.A.5. Neo-Structuralist Agenda for Development—Sunkel and Zuleta   531

X.B. MARKET FORCES AND DEVELOPMENT   536

   X.B.1. The Market Mechanism as an Instrument of Development—Johnson 536
   X.B.2. Market Failures—Note   540
   X.B.3. Steps to Making Markets Work—Perkins   542

X.C. GOVERNMENT INTERVENTIONS   548

   X.C.1. Role of the State—Stern   548

   X.C.2. The State and Industrial Strategy—Shapiro and Taylor   553
     Comment: Development Planning   556
     Comment: Governing the Market   557

   X.C.3. Social Benefit–Cost Analysis—Note   558
     Comment: Shadow Prices   561

X.D. POLITICAL ECONOMY OF GOVERNMENT FAILURE   562

X.D.1. Neoclassical Political Economy—Srinivasan   562

X.D.2. Rent-Seeking and DUP Activities—Note   565

X.D.3. Political Economy of Import Substitution—Findlay   567

X.D.4. Political Economy of Agricultural Policy—Bates   569
  Comment: Urban versus Rural Interests   575

X.D.5. Political Economy of Economic Liberalization—Lal   576
  Comment: Politics of Stabilization   578
  Comment: The Older Political Economy   578

X.E. IMPROVING THE QUALITY OF POLICY MAKING—NOTE   579

INDEX   587

ABBREVIATIONS

ASEAN	Association of Southeast Asian Nations
CACM	Central American Common Market
DRC	Domestic Resource Cost
DUP	Directly Unproductive, Profit-Seeking Activities
ECLAC	Economic Commission for Latin America and the Caribbean
EER	Effective Exchange Rate
ERP	Effective Rate of Protection
FAO	Food and Agriculture Organization of the United Nations
FDI	Foreign Direct Investment
GATT	General Agreement on Tariffs and Trade
GDP	Gross Domestic Product
GEF	Global Environmental Facility
GNP	Gross National Product
HDI	Human Development Index
HPAEs	High-Performing Asian Economies
IBRD	International Bank for Reconstruction and Development (World Bank)
ICOR	Incremental Capital–Output Ratio
ICP	International Comparison Project (Purchasing Power Parities)
IDA	International Development Association
IDB	Inter-American Development Bank
IFC	International Finance Corporation
ILO	International Labour Organisation
IMF	International Monetary Fund
ISI	Import-Substitution Industrialization
LAFTA	Latin American Free Trade Association
LDCs	Less Developed Countries
MDCs	More Developed Countries
MNE	Multinational Enterprise
MSC	Marginal Social Cost
MSV	Marginal Social Value
NGO	Nongovernmental Organization
NICs	Newly Industrializing Countries
NIEO	New International Economic Order
NPV	Net Present Value
NSB	Net Social Benefit
ODA	Official Development Assistance
OECD	Organization for Economic Cooperation and Development
OPEC	Organization of Petroleum Exporting Countries

PPP   Purchasing Power Parity
PSV   Present Social Value
SDRs   Special Drawing Rights
SITC   Standard International Trade Classification
SOEs   State-Owned Enterprises
TFP   Total Factor Productivity
UNCTAD   United Nations Conference on Trade and Development
UNDP   United Nations Development Programme
UNICEF   United Nations International Children's Emergency Fund
UNIDO   United Nations Industrial Development Organization
USAID   United States Agency for International Development
WHO   World Health Organization
WIDER   World Institute for Development Economics Research

Leading Issues in
Economic Development

CHAPTER I

The Challenge of Development

During the next hour—while we begin our study of economic development—more than 16,000 babies will begin their lives in the world. Of these, nearly 90 percent will be born in the developing world where average GNP per capita is only $800 compared with more than $19,000 in the industrial world.

In Asia, Africa, Latin America, the Caribbean, and the Middle East, they will join 14 million children who now die each year before reaching their fifth birthday. Most of these deaths are caused by chronic hunger and disease related to mass poverty.

They will join more than 190 million children under five who now suffer from serious malnutrition.

They will join over 130 million children of primary-school age not in school.

If they are girls, they will confront gender disparities, with female literacy rates still only two-thirds that of males, and with girls' primary enrollment only a little half that of boys.

An estimated 30 percent are likely to spend their entire lives in temporary shelters.[1]

Deplorable as the quality of life still is in the poor countries, the challenge of development has not gone unmet. We should recognize that in no other period in history has the condition of the world's poor improved as much as during the past four decades when the international community has made deliberate efforts to accelerate the economic development of poor countries. GNP per head has risen markedly in developing countries—by an annual average of nearly 3 percent from 1965 to 1980 and by 3.4 percent from 1980 to 1989. Average life expectancy increased by over one-third between 1960 and 1990, and is now 63 years. Adult literacy rates increased between 1970 and 1990, from 46 percent to 65 percent. Other nonmonetary indicators of food, nutrition, health, and education show marked progress, as can be noted in selection I.B.3 and Exhibit I.1.

Nonetheless, the challenge of development remains severe. See the balance sheet of progress and deprivation in Exhibit I.1. Of the world's people, nearly 80 percent are still in less developed countries (LDCs), earning less than 20 percent of world income.[2] Some 30 percent of the people in LDCs are in a condition of "absolute poverty"—what Robert McNamara, the former president of the World

---

[1]United Nations Development Programme, *Human Development Report 1992* (1992); author's correspondence with United Nations Population Division and UNICEF statistics and monitoring section. Also see Exhibit I.1.

[2]United Nations Development Programme, *Human Development Report 1991* (1991), p. 23.

EXHIBIT I.1. Balance Sheet of Human Development: Developing Countries

Progress	Deprivation
Life Expectancy	
Average life expectancy increased by over one-third during the past three decades; 23 countries have achieved a life expectancy of 70 years and more.	Of the 300 million people above the age of 60, only 20 percent have any form of income security.
Health and Sanitation	
In the developing world, more than 70 percent of the population has access to health services. Nearly 60 percent of the population has access to sanitation.	About 17 million people die every year from infectious and parasitic diseases, such as diarrhea, malaria, and tuberculosis. More than 80 percent of the 12–13 million HIV-infected people are in the developing world, and the cumulative direct and indirect cost of AIDS during the past decade was around $30 billion.
Food and Nutrition	
Between 1965 and 1990, the number of countries that met their daily per capita calorie requirements doubled—from about 25 to 50.	Some 800 million people still do not get enough food.
Education	
Primary school enrollment increased in the past two decades—from less than 70 percent to well over 80 percent. In the same period, secondary enrollment almost doubled—from less than 25 percent to 40 percent.	Nearly one billion people—35 percent of the adult population—are still illiterate, and the drop-out rate at the primary level is still as high as 30 percent.
Income and Poverty	
In South and East Asia, where two-thirds of the developing world's population live, the GNP growth averaged more than 7 percent a year during the 1980s.	Almost one-third of the total population, or 1.3 billion people, are in absolute poverty.
Children	
During the past 30 years, infant and under-five mortality rates were more than halved.	Each day, 34,000 young children still die from malnutrition and disease.
Women	
The secondary enrollment ratio for girls increased from around 17 percent in 1970 to 36 percent in 1990.	Two-thirds of illiterates are women.
Human Security	
With the end of the cold war, developing countries no longer have to serve as proxies for superpower rivalry, and in 1990, about 380,000 refugees returned to their homelands in Asia, Africa, and Latin America.	Internal conflicts afflict some 60 countries, and about 35 million people are refugees or internally displaced.
Environment	
The percentage of rural families with access to safe water has increased from less than 10 percent to almost 60 percent during the past two decades.	More than 850 million people live in areas that are in various stages of dsertification. The rate of tropical forest destruction is about the equivalent of one soccer field per second.

Source: United Nations Development Programme, *Human Development Report, 1993* (1993), p. 12.

Bank, defined as a "condition of life so degraded by disease, illiteracy, malnutrition, and squalor as to deny its victims basic human necessities." The World Bank's *Development Report 1992* observes that there are still over one billion people, one-fifth of the world's population, living on only one dollar a day.

Compounding the problem is the fact that future population growth is already assured. There are some 1.6 billion young people age 15 or under in the world, but 1.3 billion of them are in the poor countries.

For every 100 people now in the world's labor force, there will be 140 in the next two decades. Of this increase, 95 percent will be in poor countries. Where are the jobs to come from? Most of the world's people have nothing to sell but their labor. How can surplus labor in the poor countries be made more productive so as to earn higher incomes?

The future of Asia, Africa, and Latin America demands moral and humanitarian consideration. But for development practitioners it is a complex practical problem. As such, its diagnosis calls for economic analysis. And its solution calls for appropriate policy making.

The developing countries have to accelerate their economic growth rates, eradicate absolute poverty, reduce inequalities, and create more productive employment opportunities. Against the background of development experience, we shall examine the major analytic and policy issues raised by these challenges.

To begin our analysis, Chapter I attempts to clarify the meaning of "economic development." Section I.A. clarifies what is economic development and considers certain misconceptions about the objectives of development. The selections in I.B outline various dimensions and different measurements of economic development. We should become familiar with three common measures of economic development: per capita real income, per capita income corrected for purchasing power parities, and the components of a broader human development index.

Since the distribution of income in poor countries is generally highly unequal, many want a rise in income to be accompanied by less inequality. Section I.B also explains measures of inequality—the Lorenz curve and Gini coefficient—as well as posing the question of a trade-off between growth and equity.

Developing countries have become increasingly heterogeneous with differential rates and patterns of development performance, as can be seen in selections I.B.1 and I.B.2. The next selections (I.B.3 and I.B.4) focus on the burden of poverty—its extent and uneven spread. Relationships between poverty and the environment are then examined in Note I.B.5.

Turning to the differential performance records, section I.C compares the record of development performance in East Asia, Latin America, Sub-Saharan Africa, and China. The different records of success and failure will be evident.

In answer to this chapter's central question—Why isn't the whole world developed?—we shall conclude in Note I.D with a listing of the major constraints on a country's development. Our task in the rest of this book will be to analyze these constraints and focus on the design of appropriate policies to relax them. The overriding theme of our study will be that success in meeting the challenge of development depends in large part on improvement in the quality of policy making to accelerate development and reduce poverty.

First, however, we should now consider the initial questions: What is economic development? How do we measure development? How have developing countries performed?

I.A. WHAT IS ECONOMIC DEVELOPMENT?—NOTE

Although requiring careful interpretation, perhaps the definition that would now gain widest approval is one that defines economic development as the *process* whereby the *real per capita income* of a country increases over a *long period* of time—subject to the *stipulations* that the number of people below an "absolute poverty line" does not increase, and that the distribution of income does not become more unequal.

We emphasize *process* because it implies the operation of certain forces in an interconnected and causal fashion. In the following chapters, we examine the process of economic development as a form of progressive action—a working-out of certain principal forces that reveal the inner structure or "logic" of an economy's development. To interpret development in terms of a process involving causal relationships should prove more meaningful than merely identifying development with a set of conditions or a catalog of characteristics.

Economic development involves something more than economic growth. Development is taken to mean *growth plus change*: there are essential qualitative dimensions in the development process that extend beyond the growth or expansion of an economy through a simple widening process. This qualitative difference is especially likely to appear in the improved performance of the factors of production and improved techniques of production—in our growing control over nature. It is also likely to appear in the development of institutions and a change in attitudes and values.

Economic development is thus much more than the simple acquisition of industries. It may be defined as nothing less than the "upward movement of the entire social system,"[1] or it may be interpreted as the attainment of a number of "ideals of modernization," such as a rise in productivity, social and economic equalization, modern knowledge, improved institutions and attitudes, and a rationally coordinated system of policy measures that can remove the host of undesirable conditions in the social system that have perpetuated a state of underdevelopment.[2]

If our interest in the development of a poor country arises from our desire to remove mass poverty, then we should emphasize as the primary goal a rise in *per capita real income* rather than simply an increase in the economy's real national income, uncorrected for population change. For if the criterion were only an increase in real national income, then it would be possible for aggregate output to rise without a per capita improvement in living standards. Population growth may surpass the growth of national output or run parallel to it; the result would be falling, or at best constant, per capita income, and we would not consider this as economic development.

We also stress a *long period* of time because what is significant from the standpoint of development is a sustained increase in real income—not simply a short-period rise, such as occurs during the upswing of the business cycle. The underlying upward trend over decades—at least two or three decades—is the stronger indication of development. From this standpoint, a five-year development plan is only the start of the development process, and it remains to be seen whether there is the power to sustain the process so that per capita real income continues to rise over the longer period. There is a vital distinction between *initiating* development and the more difficult task of *sustaining* development over the longer run.

Although the increase in real income per head can be adopted as the primary goal, it is common to interpret economic development in terms of a number of subgoals or particular categories of the overall primary objective. Thus the alleviation of poverty and the diminution of economic inequality are generally stated objectives of development plans. Most students of development would undoubtedly qualify the primary goal by requiring that the absolute number of people below a minimum level of real income should diminish at the same time that real per capita income rises. Otherwise, it is conceivable that if there is population growth, the number of those living below a poverty line may actually have grown while there has been a rise in the average income of the population as a whole. When a dual economy exists—with a division between the modern money economy and the traditional

---

[1]Gunnar Myrdal, *Asian Drama* (1968), p. 1869.

[2]C. E. Black, *The Dynamics of Modernization* (1966), pp. 55–60.

indigenous economy—it is also possible for all of the increase in total income to occur in the modern economy,[3] and income per head might still rise, even though there had been no change in the indigenous economy. Judgment on the distribution of income is thus an integral part of the development problem.

A few of the many possible other subgoals may be the specification of a minimum level of consumption, a certain composition to the consumption stream, and a maximum level of unemployment that will be tolerated; the avoidance of marked disparities in the prosperity and growth of different regions within a country; and the diversification of the economy. Now, beyond equitable development, sustainable development—that is, development that lasts without making future generations worse off through environmental damage—is another challenge, as explained in I.B.5.

Owing to this variety of policy objectives, the emphasis on various dimensions of economic development will vary at different times and in different countries. We should, therefore, beware of interpreting economic development as meaning economic progress or an increase in economic welfare. An increase in real per capita income is not by itself a sufficient condition. Per capita real income is only a partial index of economic welfare because a judgment regarding economic welfare will also involve a value judgment on the desirability of a particular distribution of income. All observers would not, therefore, definitely say that economic welfare has increased even if per capita income has risen, unless the resultant distribution of income is also considered desirable.

Economic welfare poses not only the question of distributive justice, but also the prior questions of the composition of the total output that is giving rise to an increase in per capita real income, and the way in which this output is being valued. Whether a larger total output corresponds to individual preferences—let alone the more difficult test of collective choice—depends as much on what is produced and its quality as it does on the quantity produced. The valuation of the output may also be biased insofar as it is valued by market prices that do not reflect external diseconomies or social costs.

If such considerations of the composition, valuation, and distribution of aggregate output make it difficult to equate economic development with economic welfare, it is all the more unreasonable to claim that economic development means an increase in social welfare in general. Economic welfare is but a part of social welfare, and even if in the course of a country's development all the conditions necessary to promote economic welfare have been satisfied, this need not mean that social welfare has also been promoted. for the process of development has a profound impact on social institutions, habits, and beliefs, and it is likely to introduce a number of sources of tension and discord. Some aspects of human welfare might suffer if relations that were once personal become impersonal, the structure and functions of the family change, the stability in one's way of life is disrupted, and the support and assurance of traditional values disappear. Tensions also arise when the inequalities of income distribution, both among individuals and among regions in the developing country, tend to increase; when development creates "open unemployment" as well as employment; and when the pressures of excessive urbanization occur. In a fundamental sense, discords arise from the contrasts between the modern and the backward—from the superimposing of modern functions on traditional institutions.

In sum, even though it is conventional to begin with an increase in per capita real income as the best available overall index of economic development, we abstain from labeling this an increase in economic welfare, let alone social welfare, without additional considerations of various subgoals and explicit recognition of the value judgments regarding at least the composition, valuation, and distribution of the expanded output. The student of development must adopt such a cautious approach as a result of the strictures of welfare economics and the need for clarity on value premises in social research.

Even more, the policy maker must adopt such an approach because in many countries it has become only too painfully apparent that despite growth in aggregate output there can still be a larger number of people below the poverty line, rising unemployment, and greater income inequality. The quality of development is completely masked if the policy maker does not pierce the aggregate measure of gross national product (GNP) and consider its composition and distribution.

---

[3]The problem of dualistic development is discussed fully in Chapter III.

Instead of simply worshipping at the altar of GNP, development economists now attempt to concentrate more directly on the quality of the development process. This involves renewed emphasis on reducing the incidence of poverty—on giving more attention to improving the lives of the poorest of the world's poor. A 1992 operational directive from the World Bank's president states: "Sustainable poverty reduction is the overarching objective of the World Bank. It is the benchmark by which our performance as a development institution will be measured."[4]

To express the overall severity of poverty in a single measure or index, we need to measure the standard of living and determine what is a minimal standard of living. A consumption-based poverty line is then established. (For method of calculation, see the World Bank's *World Development Report 1990*, pp. 25–38.) Various interpretations, however, can be attached to the concept of poverty. Normally, both absolute and relative deprivation are essential ingredients of a common understanding of poverty. Absolute deprivation refers to the denial of an individual's basic needs.[5] Relative deprivation relates to interpersonal gaps in the income distribution within the poor country and to international gaps in standards of living.[6]

Attention to poverty and deprivation is in keeping with the view that people and the quality of their lives is at the center of the development challenge. We need a perspective of economic development that incorporates human development. The UNDP, for instance, empha-

sizes the concept and measurement of human development in terms of a Human Development Index (HDI). The HDI is based not only on real income, but also on social indicators of life expectancy, adult literacy, and years of schooling. Accordingly, a ranking of countries by the HDI can differ markedly from that by per capita income.

For the calculation of the HDI, see Exhibit I.2. Barbados is at the top of the developing countries, while among industrial countries the HDI rank is 1 for Canada, 2 for Switzerland, and 8 for United States.

The HDI measure goes beyond that of conventional growth. A country's economic growth is vital to sustain the welfare of its people, but growth is not the end of human development: it is one important means.

More important than mere growth in GNP is how growth is used to improve human capabilities, and, in turn, how people utilize their capabilities. Thus, Harvard's philosopher-economist Amartya Sen stresses that economic development should be interpreted as a process of expansion of the positive freedom that people enjoy. He observes that the real problems in LDCs are reduced lives, rather than low income as such, even though the latter contributes to the former. Sen interprets development as a process that expands the "entitlements" and "capabilities" of people to live in ways we have reason to value. Instead of concentrating on national product or aggregate income, he advocates that development economists should concentrate on entitlements of people and the capabilities these entitlements generate. His view is expanded in the Comment below.

In light of these reconsiderations of the meaning of development, we should not settle for any aggregate or even per capita index of development but must recognize the several dimensions of economic development. Instead of seeking development as an end, we might better view it as a means—as an instrumental process for overcoming persistent poverty and achieving human development.

---

[4]The World Bank's *World Development Report 1990* was devoted to the issue of poverty eradication.

[5]Literature on basic needs is now extensive. Most notable is Paul Streeten et al., *First Things First* (1981), which contains an extensive bibilography. For a critique of the basic needs approach, however, see T. N. Srinivasan, "Development, Poverty and Basic Human Needs: Some Issues," *Food Research Institute Studies* (1977).

[6]Illuminating considerations of the concept of deprivation are given by Amartya Sen, *Resources, Values and Development* (1984), and Partha Dasgupta, *An Inquiry into Well-being and Destitution* (1993).

Comment: Capabilities and Entitlements

In delimiting the nature of poverty, Amartya Sen has stated that

poverty is not just a matter of being relatively poorer than others in the society, but of not having some basic opportunities of material well-being—the failure to have certain minimum "capabilities." The criteria of minimum capabilities are "absolute" not in the sense that they must not vary from society to society, or over time, but people's deprivations are judged absolutely, and not simply in comparison with the

EXHIBIT I.2. HDI Ranking for Developing Countries

	HDI Value	HDI Rank	GNP Per Capita Rank	GNP Per Capita Rank Minus HDI Rank[a]		HDI Value	HDI Rank	GNP Per Capita Rank	GNP Per Capita Rank Minus HDI Rank[a]
Barbados	0.894	20	34	14	Morocco	0.549	111	101	−10
Hong Kong	0.875	24	22	−2	El Salvador	0.543	112	97	−15
Cyprus	0.873	26	30	4	Bolivia	0.530	113	119	6
Korea, Rep. of	0.859	32	36	4	Gabon	0.525	114	42	−72
Uruguay	0.859	33	53	20	Honduras	0.524	115	123	8
Trinidad and Tobago	0.855	35	46	11	Viet Nam	0.514	116	150	34
Bahamas	0.854	36	26	−10	Swaziland	0.513	117	96	−21
Argentina	0.853	37	43	6	Maldives	0.511	118	132	14
Chile	0.848	38	66	28	Vanuatu	0.489	119	93	−26
Costa Rica	0.848	39	75	36	Lesotho	0.476	120	124	4
Singapore	0.836	43	21	−22	Zimbabwe	0.474	121	118	−3
Brunei Darussalam	0.829	44	29	−15	Cape Verde	0.474	122	112	−10
Venezuela	0.820	46	55	9	Congo	0.461	123	100	−23
Panama	0.816	47	70	23	Cameroon	0.447	124	111	−13
Colombia	0.813	50	91	41	Kenya	0.434	125	146	21
Kuwait	0.809	51	28	−23	Solomon Islands	0.434	126	115	−11
Mexico	0.804	52	51	−1	Namibia	0.425	127	84	−43
Thailand	0.798	54	82	28	São Tomé and Principe	0.409	128	138	10
Antigua and Barbuda	0.796	55	40	−15	Papua New Guinea	0.408	129	108	−21
Qatar	0.795	56	20	−36	Myanmar	0.406	130	149	19
Malaysia	0.794	57	61	4	Madagascar	0.396	131	162	31
Bahrain	0.791	58	33	−25	Pakistan	0.393	132	140	8
Fiji	0.787	59	74	15	Lao People's Dem. Rep.	0.385	133	157	24
Mauritius	0.778	60	65	5	Ghana	0.382	134	133	−1
United Arab Emirates	0.771	62	10	−52	India	0.382	135	147	12
Brazil	0.756	63	52	−11	Côte d'Ivoire	0.370	136	117	−19
Dominica	0.749	64	62	−2	Haiti	0.354	137	141	4
Jamaica	0.749	65	87	22	Zambia	0.352	138	134	−4
Saudi Arabia	0.742	67	31	−36	Nigeria	0.348	139	145	6
Turkey	0.739	68	78	10	Zaire	0.341	140	160	20
Saint Vincent	0.732	69	77	8	Comoros	0.331	141	131	−10
Saint Kitts and Nevis	0.730	70	47	−23	Yemen	0.323	142	126	−16
Syrian Arab Rep.	0.727	73	94	21	Senegal	0.322	143	114	−29
Ecuador	0.718	74	102	28	Liberia	0.317	144	130	−14
Saint Lucia	0.709	77	57	−20	Togo	0.311	145	136	−9
Grenada	0.707	78	67	−11	Bangladesh	0.309	146	159	13
Libyan Arab Jamahiriya	0.703	79	41	−38	Cambodia	0.307	147	164	17
Tunisia	0.690	81	85	4	Tanzania, U. Rep. of	0.306	148	170	22
Seychelles	0.685	83	39	−44	Nepal	0.289	149	166	17
Paraguay	0.679	84	90	6	Equatorial Guinea	0.276	150	154	4
Suriname	0.677	85	48	−37	Sudan	0.276	151	137	−14
Iran, Islamic Rep. of	0.672	86	64	−22	Burundi	0.276	152	158	6
Botswana	0.670	87	58	−29	Rwanda	0.274	153	152	−1
Belize	0.666	88	69	−19	Uganda	0.272	154	168	14
Cuba	0.666	89	110	21	Angola	0.271	155	120	−35
Sri Lanka	0.665	90	128	38	Benin	0.261	156	142	−14
Oman	0.654	92	38	−54	Malawi	0.260	157	156	−1
South Africa	0.650	93	60	−33	Mauritania	0.254	158	127	−31

EXHIBIT I.2. (*continued*)

	HDI Value	HDI Rank	GNP Per Capita Rank	GNP Per Capita Rank Minus HDI Rank[a]		HDI Value	HDI Rank	GNP Per Capita Rank	GNP Per Capita Rank Minus HDI Rank[a]
China	0.644	94	143	49	Mozambique	0.252	159	173	14
Peru	0.642	95	98	3	Central African Rep.	0.249	160	135	−25
Dominican Rep.	0.638	96	107	11	Ethiopia	0.249	161	171	10
Jordan	0.628	98	99	1	Bhutan	0.247	162	165	3
Philippines	0.621	99	113	14	Djibouti	0.226	163	125	−38
Iraq	0.614	100	59	−41	Guinea-Bissau	0.224	164	167	3
Korea, Dem. Rep. of	0.609	101	109	8	Somalia	0.217	165	172	7
Mongolia	0.607	102	103	1	Gambia	0.215	166	144	−22
Lebanon	0.600	103	83	−20	Mali	0.214	167	155	−12
Samoa	0.596	104	105	1	Chad	0.212	168	161	−7
Indonesia	0.586	105	121	16	Niger	0.209	169	148	−21
Nicaragua	0.583	106	139	33	Sierra Leone	0.209	170	163	−7
Guyana	0.580	107	151	44	Afghanistan	0.208	171	169	−2
Guatemala	0.564	108	106	−2	Burkina Faso	0.203	172	153	−19
Algeria	0.553	109	72	−37	Guinea	0.191	173	129	−44
Egypt	0.551	110	122	12					

Note: "The HDI value for a country" is derived from 1991 and 1992 data on GNP per capita based on purchasing power parity, life expectancy, adult literacy, and mean years of schooling. The components are combined to arrive at an average deprivation index and to give a composite measure of human progress. The HDI does not measure absolute levels of human development but ranks countries in relation to each other for a particular period. A country's "HDI rank" is within the world distribution, according to how far the particular country has traveled from the minimum HDI value of 0 toward the maximum HDI value of 1. Countries with an HDI below 0.5 are considered to have a low level of human development, those between 0.5 and 0.8 a medium level, and those above 0.8 a high level.

For some countries—such as Angola, Gabon, Guinea, Namibia, Saudi Arabia, and the United Arab Emirates—the income rank is far ahead of the HDI rank, showing that they will have considerable potential for translating their income into improved well-being for their people.

For other countries—such as China, Colombia, Costa Rica, Cuba, Guyana, Madagascar, and Sri Lanka—the HDI rank is far ahead of their income rank, showing that they have made more judicious use of their income to improve the capabilities of their people. The highest positive difference between HDI and GNP ranks is for China (+49 places), and the highest negative difference is for Gabon (−72 places)—a striking demonstration of the differences between two development strategies.

For details of how the HDI is constructed, see United Nations Development Programme, *Human Development Report 1994* (1994), pp. 90–108. A critique of the HDI and its data base is given by T. N. Srinivasan, "Human Development: A New Paradigm or Reinvention of the Wheel?" *American Economic Review, Papers & Proceedings* (May 1994): 238–43.

[a] A positive figure shows that the HDI rank is better than the GNP per capita rank, a negative the opposite.

Source: United Nations Development Programme, *Human Development Report 1994* (1994), p. 94.

deprivations of others in that society. If a person is seen as poor because he is unable to satisfy his hunger, then that diagnosis of poverty cannot be altered merely by the fact that others too may also be hungry (so that this person may not be, relatively speaking, any worse off than most others). . . . A person's advantage is judged in this approach by his capabilities, viz., what he can or cannot do, can or cannot be. The relevant capabilities are of many different kinds (e.g., being free from starvation, from hunger, from undernourishment; participating in communal life; being adequately sheltered; being free to travel to see friends; and so on). The ranking of "capability vectors" can be used to rank people's advantages vis à vis others. But in the context of poverty analysis, it is a question of setting absolute standards of minimum material capabilities relevant for that society. Anyone failing to reach that absolute level would then be classified as poor, no matter what his relative position is vis a vis others. Poverty, in this view, is not ultimately a matter of incomes at all; it is one of a failure to achieve certain minimum capabilities. The distinction is important since the conversion of real incomes into actual capabilities varies with social circumstances and personal features.[1]

Sen has also maintained that the most important thematic deficiency of traditional development economics is its concentration on national product, aggregate income, and total supply of particular

[1] Amartya Sen, "A Sociological Approach to the Measurement of Poverty: A Reply to Professor Peter Townsend," *Oxford Economic Papers* (December 1985): 669–70.

goods rather than on the "entitlements" of people and the "capabilities" that these entitlements generate. Entitlement refers to the set of alternative commodity bundles that a person can command in a society using the totality of rights and opportunities that he or she has.

For an elaboration of entitlements and capabilities, see Amartya K. Sen, "Development: Which Way Now?" *Economic Journal* (December 1983), *Poverty and Famines: An Essay on Entitlement and Deprivation* (1981), *Choice, Welfare and Measurement* (1982), "Poor, Relatively Speaking," *Oxford Economic Papers* (July 1983), and *Commodities and Capabilities* (1985).

The case for a "capabilities-orientated" rather than a "goods-orientated" social welfare function is also argued by K. Griffin and J. Knight, "Human Development: The Case for Renewed Emphasis," *Journal of Development Planning* (1989).

I.B. MEASURES OF DEVELOPMENT

I.B.1. Measurement of Key Indicators*

Some basic statistics for the world's economies are set out in Table 1. These are drawn from the *World Development Report 1990,* with the exception of calculations of real GDP per capita provided by Summers and Heston (1988), which are based on purchasing power parity, The figures are presented with four aims in view:

(i) to illustrate the enormous diversity—aggregated blocs can be misleading;
(ii) to draw attention to the problems of income measurement;
(iii) to demonstrate that a perception of standard of living which is different from simply income gives rise to a very different picture; and
(iv) to report on how figures such as these have been used in the analysis of growth and development.

The countries are ranked in terms of income per capita as conventionally measured (World Bank 1990). It is immediately clear that we have a distribution which is fairly evenly spread over the spectrum of income per capita measured in this way. There are 12 countries with income per capita of between 100 and 200 (U.S. dollars per capita for 1988), 6 between 200 and 300, 9 between 300 and 400, 9 between 400 and 500, 18 between 1,000 and 2,000, 9 between 2,000 and 3,000, and so on. While it is true that there is a group of very rich countries (just 17 between 10,000 and 27,500) it is nevertheless misleading to see developing countries as a homogeneous group of poor countries called "the South," to be contrasted with the rich countries called "the North." That kind of simple dichotomy does not provide a plausible description of most of the relevant indicators of well-being and economic structure that one could imagine and does not, in my judgement, provide a helpful basis for modeling the world economy.

It must also be recognised that there is enormous variability within the countries. Many developing countries have groups which are colossally rich and, further, many of them have a substantial middle class whose conditions of life are very different from those of the poor. In countries as vast as India, China, and Brazil, regional as well as social variation can also be highly significant. China and India are, of course, the two most important examples in their own right, with a combined population of 1.9 billion in a total world population of around 5 billion, and one cannot think of them as just another drawing from a sample of world countries. They deserve special study.

The Summers and Heston (1988) recalculation of income per capita using an approach based on purchasing power parity (PPP) shows that the income figures must be treated with a good deal of circumspection. The adjustment for purchasing power parity is only one of the many problems associated with comparing income across countries, but making just this one change can have very substantial effects. Changes at the bottom end are particularly dramatic (although notice how Japan's ranking is lowered and Kuwait becomes the richest country—she was purchasing services at Indian and Pakistani prices). For example, China, India, and Pakistan are all ranked fairly closely under conventional national income measures, whereas in the Summers and Heston data the income per capita of Pakistan is more than 50 percent above that of India and the income per capita of China is more than twice that of Pakistan. . . .

There is much more to standard of living than income. The great variety of conditions in developing countries is further illustrated in some of the other dimensions summarised in Table 1. Further, the variations in the other indicators are far from perfectly correlated with income per capita whether measured in the standard or PPP manner. For example, infant mortality rates (in terms of deaths of children under one year of age per thousand live births) are, respectively, 31 and 21 for China and Sri Lanka (with conventionally measured income per capita of $330 and $420 respectively in 1988), whereas those for Brazil, Gabon, and Libya are 61, 101, and

*From Nicholas Stern, "Public Policy and the Economics of Development," *European Economic Review* 35 (1991): 243–50. Reprinted by permission.

TABLE 1. Basic Indicators

Country	GNP PC	RGDP	POP.	POP. Growth	IMOR	LEB	CSPC	PEDU	GDS	ODA	Growth
Low-Income Economies											
Mozambique	100	528	14.9	2.7	139	48	1,595	68	−15	70.6	—
Ethiopia	120	310	47.4	2.9	135	47	1,749	37	4	17.4	−0.1
Chad	160	254	5.4	2.4	130	46	1,717	51	−12	28.8	−2.0
Tanzania	160	355	24.7	3.5	104	53	2,192	66	−5	31.2	−0.5
*Bangladesh	170	647	108.9	2.8	118	51	1,927	59	3	8.2	0.4
Malawi	170	387	8.0	3.4	149	47	2,310	66	8	30.6	1.1
Somalia	170	348	5.9	3.0	130	47	2,138	15	3	42.9	0.5
Zaire	170	210	33.4	3.1	96	52	2,163	76	8	9.0	−2.1
Bhutan	180	—	1.4	2.1	127	48	—	24	—	14.0	—
Lao People's Dem. Rep.	180	—	3.9	2.6	108	49	2,391	111	21	14.4	—
Nepal	180	526	18.0	2.6	126	51	2,052	82	10	13.0	—
Madagascar	190	497	10.9	2.8	119	50	2,440	—	8	16.2	−1.8
Burkina Faso	210	377	8.5	2.6	137	47	2,139	32	−4	16.0	1.2
Mali	230	355	8.0	2.4	168	47	2,073	23	−4	22.0	1.6
Burundi	240	345	5.1	2.8	73	49	2,343	67	5	17.1	3.0
Uganada	280	347	16.2	3.2	101	48	2,344	70	5	8.4	−3.1
Nigeria	290	581	110.1	3.3	103	51	2,146	77	15	0.4	0.9
Zambia	290	584	7.6	3.7	78	53	—	97	14	12.0	−2.1
Niger	300	429	7.3	3.5	133	45	2,432	29	4	15.5	−2.3
Rwanda	320	341	6.7	3.3	120	49	1,830	67	6	11.0	1.5
*China	330	2,444	1,088.4	1.3	31	70	2,630	132	37	0.5	5.4
*India	340	750	815.6	2.2	97	58	2,238	98	21	0.8	1.8
*Pakistan	350	1,153	106.3	3.2	107	55	2,315	52	13	3.7	2.5
Kenya	370	598	22.4	3.8	70	59	2,060	96	22	9.4	1.9
Togo	370	489	3.4	3.5	92	53	2,207	101	14	14.7	0.0
Central African Rep.	380	434	2.9	2.7	102	50	1,949	66	−1	17.5	−0.5
Haiti	380	631	6.3	1.8	116	55	1,902	95	4	5.9	0.4
Benin	390	525	4.4	3.2	115	51	2,184	63	0	9.0	0.1
Ghana	400	349	14.0	3.4	88	54	1,759	71	6	9.1	−1.6
Lesotho	420	771	1.7	2.7	98	56	2,303	113	−73	26.3	5.2
*Sri Lanka	420	1,539	16.6	1.5	21	71	2,400	104	13	8.5	3.0
Guinea	430	452	5.4	2.4	143	43	1,776	30	19	10.3	—
Yemen PDR	430	—	2.4	3.0	118	51	2,298	—	—	7.2	—
Indonesia	440	1,255	174.8	2.1	68	61	2,579	118	25	2.1	4.3
Mauritania	480	550	1.9	2.6	125	46	2,322	52	10	18.4	−0.4
Sudan	480	540	23.8	3.1	106	50	2,208	49	7	7.8	0.0
Afghanistan	—	609	—	—	—	—	—	—	—	—	—
Myanmar	—	—	40.0	2.1	68	60	2,609	—	—	—	—
Liberia	—	491	2.4	3.2	130	50	2,381	35	—	—	—
Sierra Leone	—	443	3.9	2.4	152	42	1,854	—	17	—	—
Vietnam	—	—	64.2	2.4	44	66	2,297	102	—	—	—
Lower-Middle-Income Economies											
Bolivia	570	1,089	6.9	2.7	108	53	2,143	91	6	9.1	−0.6
Philippines	630	1,361	59.9	2.5	44	64	2,372	106	18	2.2	1.6
Yemen Arab Rep.	640	978	8.5	3.4	128	47	2,318	91	0	3.8	—
Senegal	650	754	7.0	3.0	78	48	2,350	60	9	11.4	−0.8
Zimbabwe	650	948	9.3	3.7	49	63	2,132	136	24	4.3	1.0
Egypt Arab Rep.	660	1,188	50.2	2.6	83	63	3,342	90	8	4.3	3.6
Dominican Rep.	720	1,753	6.9	2.4	63	66	2,477	133	16	2.5	2.7
Côte d'Ivoire	770	920	11.2	4.0	95	53	2,562	70	22	4.5	0.9
Papua New Guinea	810	1,374	3.7	2.4	61	54	2,205	70	21	10.8	0.5
Morocco	830	1,221	24.0	2.7	71	61	2,915	71	23	2.2	2.3
Honduras	860	911	4.8	3.6	68	64	2,068	106	11	7.3	0.6

14

TABLE 1. (*continued*)

Country	GNP PC	RGDP	POP.	POP. Growth	IMOR	LEB	CSPC	PEDU	GDS	ODA	Growth
Guatemala	900	1,608	8.7	2.9	57	62	2,307	77	8	2.9	1.0
Congo People's Rep.	910	1,338	2.1	3.5	117	53	2,619	—	20	4.1	3.5
El Salvador	940	1,198	5.0	1.3	57	63	2,160	79	6	7.7	−0.5
Thailand	1,000	1,900	54.5	1.9	30	65	2,331	95	26	1.0	4.0
Botswana	1,010	1,762	1.2	3.4	41	67	2,201	114	—	7.8	8.6
Cameroon	1,010	1,095	11.2	3.2	92	56	2,028	109	14	2.2	3.7
*Jamaica	1,070	1,725	2.4	1.5	11	73	2,590	105	19	6.0	−1.5
Ecuador	1,120	2,387	10.1	2.7	62	66	2,058	117	21	1.3	3.1
Colombia	1,180	2,599	31.7	2.1	39	68	2,542	114	22	0.2	2.4
Paraguay	1,180	1,996	4.0	3.2	41	67	2,853	102	23	1.3	3.1
Tunisia	1,230	2,050	7.8	2.5	48	66	2,994	116	19	3.2	3.4
Turkey	1,280	2,533	53.8	2.3	75	64	3,229	117	26	0.4	2.6
Peru	1,300	2,114	20.7	2.2	86	62	2,246	122	24	1.1	0.1
Jordan	1,500	2,113	3.9	3.7	43	66	2,991	—	−3	9.3	—
Chile	1,510	3,486	12.8	1.7	20	72	2,579	103	24	0.2	0.1
Syrian Arab Rep.	1,680	2,900	11.6	3.6	46	65	3,260	110	13	1.3	2.9
Costa Rica	1,690	2,650	2.7	2.3	18	75	2,803	98	26	4.0	1.4
Mexico	1,760	3,985	83.7	2.2	46	69	3,132	118	23	0.1	2.3
Mauritius	1,800	1,869	1.1	1.0	22	67	2,748	106	25	3.0	2.9
Poland	1,860	4,913	37.9	0.8	16	72	3,336	101	35	—	—
Malaysia	1,940	3,415	16.9	2.6	23	70	2,730	102	36	0.3	4.0
Panama	2,120	2,912	2.3	2.2	22	72	2,446	106	—	—	2.2
*Brazil	2,160	3,282	144.4	2.2	61	65	2,656	103	28	0.1	3.6
Angola	—	609	9.4	2.5	135	45	1,880	—	—	—	—
Nicaragua	—	1,989	3.6	3.4	60	64	2,495	99	—	—	−2.5
Upper-Middle-Income Economies											
South Africa	2,290	3,885	34.0	2.3	70	61	2,924	—	25	—	0.8
Algeria	2,360	2,142	23.8	3.1	72	64	2,715	96	31	0.3	2.7
Hungary	2,460	5,765	10.6	−0.1	16	70	3,569	97	28	—	5.1
Uruguay	2,470	3,462	3.1	0.6	23	72	2,648	110	14	0.5	1.3
Argentina	2,520	3,486	31.5	1.4	31	71	3,210	110	18	0.2	0.0
Yugoslavia	2,520	5,063	23.6	0.7	25	72	3,563	95	40	0.1	3.4
*Gabon	2,970	3,103	1.1	3.9	101	53	2,521	—	33	3.2	0.9
Venezuela	3,250	3,548	18.8	2.8	35	70	2,494	107	25	0.0	−0.9
Trinidad & Tobago	3,350	6,884	1.2	1.7	16	71	3,082	100	21	0.2	0.9
Korea	3,600	3,056	42.0	1.2	24	70	2,907	101	38	0.0	6.8
Portugal	3,650	3,729	10.3	0.7	14	74	3,151	124	21	0.2	3.1
Greece	4,800	4,464	10.0	0.5	12	77	3,688	104	11	0.1	2.9
Oman	5,000	7,792	1.4	4.7	38	64	—	97	—	—	6.4
*Libya	5,420	—	4.2	4.3	80	61	3,601	—	—	—	−2.7
Iran	—	3,922	48.6	3.0	64	63	3,313	114	—	—	—
Iraq	—	2,813	17.6	3.6	68	64	2,932	98	—	—	—
Romania	—	4,273	23.0	0.4	24	70	3,373	97	—	—	—
High-Income Economies											
Saudi Arabia	6,200	5,971	14.0	4.2	69	64	3,004	71	20	0.0	3.8
Spain	7,740	6.437	39.0	0.5	9	77	3,359	113	22		2.3
Ireland	7,750	5,205	3.5	0.5	7	74	3,632	100	27		2.0
Israel	8,650	6.270	4.4	1.7	11	76	3,061	95	10	2.8	2.7
Singapore	9,070	9.834	2.6	1.1	7	74	2,840	—	41	0.1	7.2
Hong Kong	9,220	9,093	5.7	1.5	7	77	2,859	106	33	0.0	6.3
New Zealand	10,000	8,000	3.3	0.8	11	75	2,463	107	26		0.8
Australia	12,340	8,850	16.5	1.4	9	76	3,326	106	23		1.7

(*continued*)

TABLE 1. (*continued*)

Country	GNP PC	RGDP	POP.	POP. Growth	IMOR	LEB	CSPC	PEDU	GDS	ODA	Growth
United Kingdom	12,810	8,665	57.1	0.2	9	75	3,256	106	17		1.8
Italy	13,330	7,425	57.4	0.2	10	77	3,523	95	23		3.0
Kuwait	13,400	14,868	2.0	4.4	15	73	3,021	94	15	0.0	−4.3
Belgium	14,490	9,717	9.9	0.0	9	75	—	100	21		2.5
Netherlands	14,520	9,092	14.8	0.5	8	77	3,326	115	23		1.9
Austria	15,470	8,929	7.6	0.0	8	75	3,428	101	27		2.9
United Arab Emirates	15,770	12,404	1.5	4.8	25	71	3,733	99	36	−0.1	—
France	16,090	9,918	55.9	0.4	8	76	3,336	113	21		2.5
Canada	16,960	12,196	26.0	0.9	7	77	3,462	105	23		2.7
Denmark	18,450	10,884	5.1	0.0	8	75	3,633	99	21		1.8
Germany Fed. Rep.	18,480	10,708	61.3	−0.1	8	75	3,528	103	26		2.5
Finland	18,590	9,232	5.0	0.5	6	75	3,122	101	27		3.2
Sweden	19,300	9,904	8.4	0.2	6	77	3,064	100	21		1.8
United States	19,840	12,532	246.3	1.0	10	76	3,645	100	13		1.6
Norway	19,990	12,623	4.2	0.3	8	77	3,223	95	28		3.5
Japan	21,020	9,447	122.6	0.6	5	78	2,864	102	33		4.3
Switzerland	27,500	10,640	6.6	0.3	7	77	3,437	—	31		1.5

GNP PC: GNP per capita (1988 $)
RGDP: Real GDP per capita as defined by Summers and Heston (1988)
POP.: Millions in mid-1988
POP. Growth: Average rate of growth 1980–88 (%)
IMOR: Infant mortality rate (per thousand live births), 1988
LEB: Life expectancy at birth (years), 1988
CSPC: Daily calorie supply (per capita), 1986
PEDU: Percentage of age group enrolled in primary education, 1987
GDS: Gross Domestic Saving (% GDP), 1988
ODA: Net Disbursement of Official Development Assistance (% GNP), 1988
Growth: Average annual growth rate of GNP per capita (%), 1965–88
Note: Asterisks denote countries whose specific statistics are discussed in the text. For technical information, see sources described.
Sources: World Bank, *World Development Report 1990* (1990), except RGDP; Summers and Heston (1988).

80, notwithstanding their incomes per capita of $2,160, $2,970, and $5,420. Life expectancies in China and Sri Lanka are 70 and 71, figures exceeded only by Jamaica among countries with income per capita less than $1,500, and by only a handful of countries with income per capita less than $5,000. The reasons for this high performance on this critical dimension appear to be closely associated with public action concerning food, education, health services, water supply, sanitation, and so on. . . .

There is a long history of using cross-section data of the type displayed in Table 1 to describe, or test theories of, growth. . . . Chenery and his collaborators (1986) have been particularly concerned with cross-country regressions "explaining" the rate of growth in the tradition of Solow (1957) and Denison (1967). More recently the wide availability of the Summers and Heston data together with a rekindling of interest in growth theory has generated a further spate of cross-country regressions, notably from Barro

(1989a, b). These have shown a worthy concern to bring in more theory and to take account of possible simultaneity.

The problems of simultaneity in this context are, in my view, almost insuperable—what *are* the exogenous variables? Problems of measurement are rampant as we have seen. And there is something about seeing China and Zaire as just two outcomes generated by the same underlying process that leaves me a little uncomfortable. Nevertheless the results can be suggestive and we give a flavour for some of them here (drawn from Barro 1989a, b). Growth is positively related to initial human capital. Growth is positively related to investment and the division between public and private appears unimportant. So-called "mixed economy" systems have slightly higher per capita growth rates than "free enterprise" economies but the difference is not statistically significant. An index of price distortions appears to be negatively associated with growth, as is initial GDP per capita and government consumption (as a share of GDP). Measures of political instability (proxied by figures on revolutions, coups, and political assassinations per capita per annum) are inversely related to growth although when these proxies are introduced the indicator for political freedoms (otherwise positive) becomes insignificant (thus the association between liberty and growth emphasized by Dasgupta [1990, pp. 27–28] must be treated with some circumspection). The shares in GDP of government spending on education and defence appear to be insignificantly related to the growth rate. In all these cases we are speaking about the signs of coefficients in a structural equation designed to explain a per capita growth rate (1960–85) where some simultaneities are taken into account.

References

Barro, R. J. (1989a). "Economic Growth in a Cross Section of Countries." National Bureau of Economic Research, Working Paper no. 3120, September.

Barro, R. J. (1989b). "Economic Growth in a Cross Section of Countries." University of Rochester Working Paper no. 201, September.

Chenery, H. B., S. Robinson, and M. Syrquin (1986). *Industrialisation and Growth: A Comparative Study*. Washington, D.C.: World Bank.

Dasgupta, P. S. (1990). "Well-Being and the Extent of Its Realisation in Poor Countries." *Economic Journal* 100:1–32.

Denison, E. F. (1967). *Why Growth Rates Differ: Post-War Experience in Nine Western Countries*. Washington, D.C.: Brookings Institution.

Solow, R. (1957). "Technical Change and the Aggregate Production Function." *Review of Economics and Statistics* 39:312–20.

Summers, R., and A. Heston (1990). "The Penn World Table (Mark 5): An Extended Set of International Comparisons, 1950–1987." National Bureau of Economic Research and University of Pennsylvania, April.

Comment: Relative Purchasing Powers

Intercountry comparisons of levels of income are often misleading when they are made by converting the incomes of the various countries into a common currency—say, the U.S. dollar—through the use of official exchange rates. These nominal exchange rates do not reflect the relative purchasing power of different currencies, and thus errors are introduced into the comparisons. The depression of per capita incomes is exaggerated by systematically understating those of poorer countries. Purchasing power parities (PPPs)—rather than exchange rates—are the correct converters for translating gross domestic product (GDP) from national currencies to dollars.

In recognition of comparative national price levels, studies by Irving Kravis and his associates have therefore attempted to adjust international comparisons for the real purchasing power parities of national currencies. See Irving B. Kravis, A. Heston, and R. Summers, *World Product and Income: International Comparisons of Real Gross Domestic Product*, 3 vols. (1975, 1978, 1982), and "Real GDP Per Capita for More than One Hundred Countries," *Economic Journal* (June 1978); and R. Summers and A. Heston, "The Penn World Table (Mark 5): An Expanded Set of International Comparisons, 1950–88," *Quarterly Journal of Economics* (May 1991).

Normally the purchasing power of the currency of an LDC tends to be greater than is suggested by its official exchange rate.

Exhibit I.3 shows the GDP per capita of developing countries relative to the United States (=100), based on PPPs. In countries where domestic prices are relatively low, the GDP per capita based on PPPs will be higher than that obtained from official exchange rates.

Exhibit I.4 compares income per head using market exchange rates with those on a PPP basis for a selection of developing countries in 1991.

Comment: Lorenz Curve and Gini Coefficient

The Gini coefficient is a single measure of relative poverty and the most frequently encountered in studies of income distribution. It is based on a curve fitted to percentile shares, which was developed by Lorenz and, not surprisingly, named after him—the Lorenz curve. Figure 1 illustrates this curve and a Gini coefficient that flows from it.

The vertical axis measures the percentage of income going to income recipients, who are arrayed in percentiles on the horizontal axis. Income recipients are ordered from the poorest to the richest,

EXHIBIT I.3. Gross Domestic Product Per Capita by Purchasing Power Parities (United States = 100)

	Low-Income Economies			Middle-Income Economies/Lower-Middle-Income	
	1987	1991		1987	1991
Mozambique	2.7	2.7	Bolivia	9.6	9.8
Tanzania	2.5	2.6	Côte d'Ivoire	9.1	6.8
Ethiopia	1.9	1.7	Senegal	7.9	7.6
Uganda	4.7	5.1	Philippines	10.8	11.0
Bhutan	2.8	2.8	Papua New Guinea	8.8	8.3
Guinea-Bissau	3.1	3.1	Cameroon	15.1	10.8
Nepal	4.8	5.1	Guatemala	14.4	14.4
Burundi	3.2	3.3	Dominican Rep.	15.5	13.9
Chad	2.9	3.3	Ecuador	17.8	18.7
Madagascar	3.6	3.2	Morocco	13.8	15.1
Sierra Leone	3.5	3.6	Jordan	29.3	22.0
Bangladesh	5.0	5.2	Tajikistan	11.9	9.9
Lao People's Dem. Rep.	8.3	8.7	Peru	19.7	14.1
Malawi	3.5	3.6	El Salvador	9.5	9.5
Rwanda	3.9	3.1	Congo	13.1	12.7
Mali	2.3	2.2	Syrian Arab Rep.	20.9	23.6
Burkina Faso	3.4	3.4	Colombia	23.7	24.7
Niger	3.9	3.6	Paraguay	14.9	15.5
India	4.6	5.2	Uzbekistan	12.1	12.6
Kenya	6.1	6.1	Jamaica	15.1	16.6
Nigeria	5.5	6.1	Romania	42.3	31.2
China	6.5	7.6	Tusinia	20.2	21.2
Haiti	6.7	5.5	Kyrgyzstan	14.2	14.8
Benin	7.3	6.8	Thailand	17.1	23.8
Central African Rep.	5.5	4.9	Georgia	24.7	16.6
Ghana	8.9	9.0	Azerbaijan	20.0	16.6
Pakistan	8.3	8.9	Turkmenistan	17.3	16.0
Togo	6.4	5.9	Turkey	21.0	21.9
Nicaragua	15.5	11.5	Poland	24.8	20.3
Sri Lanka	11.0	12.0	Bulgaria	31.1	22.5
Mauritania	6.9	6.3	Costa Rica	22.5	23.0
Honduras	8.5	8.2	Algeria	28.6	25.5
Lesotho	7.2	8.5	Panama	25.6	22.2
Indonesia	10.5	12.3	Armenia	24.3	20.8
Egypt, Arab Rep.	16.3	16.3	Chile	27.3	31.9
Zimbabwe	9.2	9.8	Iran, Islamic Rep.	22.1	21.1
Zambia	5.3	4.6	Moldova	23.1	21.0
			Ukraine	25.7	23.4
			Mauritius	40.8	50.5
			Czechoslovakia	35.0	28.4
			Kazakhstan	23.0	20.3
			Malaysia	26.5	33.4

	Upper-Middle-Income	
	1987	1991
Botswana	16.7	21.2
Lithuania	29.4	24.4
Hungary	31.9	27.5
Venezuela	36.3	36.7

EXHIBIT I.3. (*continued*)

	Low-Income Economies			Upper-Middle-Income	
	1987	1991		1987	1991
			Argentina	25.6	23.1
			Uruguay	30.4	30.1
			Brazil	26.0	23.7
			Mexico	31.4	32.4
			Belarus	29.7	31.0
			Russian Federation	35.2	31.3
			Latvia	37.2	34.1
			Trinidad and Tobago	42.5	37.9
			Estonia	45.8	36.6
			Portugal	35.9	42.7
			Oman	38.5	40.6
			Puerto Rico	44.7	49.3
			Korea, Rep.	28.6	37.6
			Greece	33.8	34.7
			Saudi Arabia	45.1	49.0

Source: World Bank, *World Development Report 1993* (1993), pp. 296–97.

moving from left to right. Thus in Figure 1, *OX* percent of the population (the poorest group) receives *a* percent of the income, and so on, giving the Lorenz curve, *L*. Complete equality would occur only if *a* percent of the population received *a* percent of the income, as indicated by the curve of complete equality, *E*. The curve of perfect inequality is *OGH*, with a right angle at *G*. This curve represents the case where one person has 100 percent of the income.

EXHIBIT I.4. Income Per Capita, Developing Countries, 1991

Country	GNP Per Capita at Market Exchange Rates	GDP Per Capita at Purchasing Power Parity
Ethiopia	120	370
Madagascar	210	710
Bangladesh	220	1160
Mali	280	480
India	330	1150
Kenya	340	1350
China	370	1680
Pakistan	400	1970
Indonesia	610	2730
Bolivia	650	2170
Philippines	730	2440
Guatemala	930	3180
Peru	1070	3110
Thailand	1570	5270
Costa Rica	1850	5100
Chile	2160	7060

Note: Measures of real GDP are based on an internationally comparable scale by using purchasing power parities instead of exchange rates as conversion factors. *PPP* is defined as the number of units of a country's currency required to buy the same amount of goods and services in the domestic market as one dollar would buy in the United States.

Source: World Bank, *World Development Report 1993* (1993), pp. 296–97. For an explanation of the technical calculation, see pp. 319–21.

FIGURE 1. The Lorenz curve.

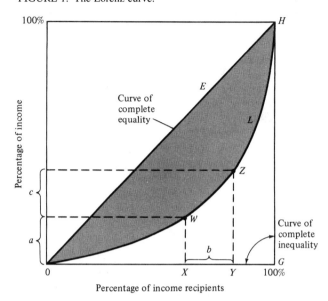

Percentage of income recipients

The shaded area in the figure, enclosed by the theoretical line of equality, E, and the observed Lorenz curve, L, is known as the concentration area (or area of inequality). The Gini coefficient is the ratio of this area to the total area under the line of equality. The simplest computation of the Gini proceeds by taking the sum of the areas under all trapezoids, such as $WXYZ$, and subtracting this from the area under E to give the concentration area. The required ratio then follows. As a measure of income concentration, the Gini coefficient ranges from 0 to 1—the larger the coefficient, the greater the inequality. Thus 0 represents perfect equality, and 1 represents perfect inequality.

For problems of data analysis, see Shail Jain, *Size Distribution of Income: A Compilation of Data* (1975), and Nanak Kakwani, *Income Inequality and Poverty* (1980).

For an illuminating application of the methodology of Gini coefficient analysis, see John C. H. Fei, Gustav Ranis, and Shirley W. Y. Kuo, *Growth with Equity: The Taiwan Case* (1979).

Comment: Inverted-U Hypothesis of Inequality

Much attention has been given to how the distribution of income changes in the course of development—in particular, to Simon Kuznets's "inverted-U hypothesis." In his early papers—"Economic Growth and Income Inequality," *American Economic Review* (March 1955) and "Quantitative Aspects of Economic Growth of Nations: VIII. Distribution of Income by Size," *Economic Development and Cultural Change* (January 1963)—Kuznets advanced the hypothesis that the secular behavior of inequality follows an inverted "U-shaped" pattern, with relative income inequality first increasing and then decreasing in the course of development. Although he was careful to indicate the limitations in the empirical evidence, Kuznets submitted that there is a long swing in the inequality characterizing the secular income structure: widening in the early phases of economic growth, when the transition from the preindustrial economy is most rapid; becoming stabilized for a while; and then narrowing in the later phases. Kuznets also observed that the size distribution of income in less developed countries was more unequal than in the developed countries during the years after World War II.

A careful reexamination of the relationship between the distribution of income and the process of development has been undertaken by Montek S. Ahluwalia, "Inequality, Poverty and Development," *Journal of Development Economics* (December 1976). But see A. Saith, "Development and Distribution: A Critique of the Cross-Country U-hypothesis," *Journal of Development Economics* (December 1983).

Although he stresses the deficiencies and limitations of income distribution data, Ahluwalia concludes from his multivariate regression analysis of cross-country data for 60 countries that

1. There is strong support for the proposition that relative inequality increases substantially in the early stages of development, with a reversal of this tendency in the later stages. This proposition holds whether we restrict the sample to developing countries or expand it to include developed and socialist countries. Furthermore, it appears that the process is most prolonged for the poorest group.
2. A number of processes occurring *pari passu* with development are correlated with income inequality and can plausibly be interpreted as causal. They are intersectoral shifts in the structure of production, expansion in educational attainment and skill level of the labor force, and reduction in the rate of growth of population. The operation of these processes appears to explain some of the improvement in income distribution observed in the later stages of development, but not the marked deterioration seen in the earlier stages.
3. The cross-section results do not support the stronger hypothesis that the deterioration in relative inequality reflects a prolonged absolute impoverishment of large sections of the population in the course of development. The cross-country pattern shows average absolute incomes of the lower-percentile groups rising as per capita GNP rises, although slower than for upper-income groups.
4. Finally, the cross-section results do not support the view that a faster rate of growth is systematically associated with higher inequality than can be expected, given the stage of development achieved.

Kuznets's inverted-U curve of income inequality is illustrated in Figure 1. Note that the more robust portion of the Kuznets curve lies to the right: income inequality falls with an increase in per capita income at higher levels of development. The variance around the estimated Kuznets curve is greatest, however, from low to middle levels of development.

The inverted-U result has been seriously questioned by S. Anand and S. M. R. Kanbur, "The Kuznets Process and the Inequality–Development Relationship," *Journal of Development Economics* (February 1993). Their study shows that the results are very sensitive to the measure of inequality and the choice of data set. By making different choices, one can get U relationships, inverted-U relationships, or no relationships at all.

FIGURE 1. Regression line: quadratic (the Kuznets curve).

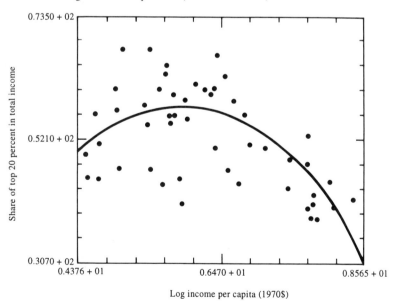

Log income per capita (1970$)

Note: This inverted-U relationship is based on Ahluwalia's sample of 60 countries. The inequality statistic is the share of the top 20 percent.

Source: Jeffrey G. Williamson, *Inequality, Poverty and Growth* (1991), p. 9.

For explanations of why a Kuznets curve should appear in the first place, we need to go beyond the data to analytical historical studies. For an insightful explanation of these historical studies, see Jeffrey C. Williamson, *Inequality, Poverty, and History* (1991), pp. 7–35.

Also of interest are G. S. Papanek and O. Kyn, "Flattening the Kuznets Curve," *Pakistan Development Review* (1987), and Irma Adelman, "What Is the Evidence on Income Inequality and Development?" in *Equity and Efficiency in Economic Development*, Donald J. Savoie and Irving Brecher, eds. (1992).

Comment: Inequality and Growth

It may be thought that by promoting higher saving rates by the rich, inequality of income is conducive to growth. There is no conclusive evidence, however, that saving is positively related to income inequality or that income inequality leads to higher growth. Figure 1 actually shows that, if anything, inequality in LDCs in recent decades is associated with slower growth. In many of the developing countries there has been no trade-off between growth and equity. Note the positions of Korea, Singapore, Taiwan, Hong Kong, and China in Figure 1.

Moreover, historical evidence of other countries over a longer period of time leads to the conclusion that rising inequality in a country has never historically played a critical role in making rising rates of nonhuman capital accumulation possible. Contradicting the growth–inequality trade-off, economic historian Jeffrey Williamson concludes that rising inequality accounted for little of America's nineteenth-century capital accumulation and for none of Britain's accumulation expenses during the first Industrial Revolution.[1] But rising inequality did play a critical role in making rising rates of human capital accumulation difficult.[2]

More equal income distributions have also contributed to rapid growth in East Asia through higher human capital formation from better heath and more education. A virtuous circle of equity and human capital growth has been established. See World Bank, *East Asian Miracle* (1993), chap. 5.

FIGURE 1. Income inequality and the growth of GDP in selected economies, 1965–89.

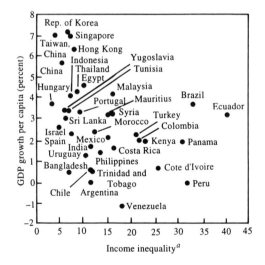

[a]The ratio of the income shares of the richest 20 percent and poorest 20 percent of the population. Data on income distribution are from surveys conducted mainly in the late 1960s and early 1970s.

Source: World Bank data.

[1] J. G. Williamson and P. H. Lindert, *American Inequality* (1980), chap. 12; J. G. Williamson, *Did British Capitalism Breed Inequality?* (1957).

[2] Jeffrey G. Williamson, *Inequality, Poverty, and History* (1991), p. 70.

EXHIBIT I.5. Income Distribution in Developing Countries Sorted by Ratio of Quintiles

| Country | Percentage Share of Household Income | | Ratio of Highest/ Lowest Quintile |
	Lowest Quintile	Highest Quintile	
Bangladesh	10.0	37.2	3.72
Morocco	9.8	39.4	4.02
Indonesia	8.8	41.3	4.69
India	8.1	41.4	5.11
Pakistan	7.8	45.6	5.85
Ghana	7.1	43.7	6.15
Philippines	5.5	48.0	8.73
Jamaica	5.4	49.2	9.11
Guatemala	5.5	55.0	10.00
Côte d'Ivoire	5.0	52.7	10.54
Venezuela	4.7	50.6	10.77
Malaysia	4.6	51.2	11.13
Sri Lanka	4.8	56.1	11.69
Peru	4.4	51.9	11.80
Colombia	4.0	53.0	13.25
Costa Rica	3.3	54.5	16.52
Botswana	2.5	59.0	23.60
Brazil	2.4	62.6	26.08

Source: World Bank, *World Development Report 1992* (1992), pp. 276–77. Data from various years in the 1980s.

I.B.2. Distributional Weights*

So long as economists were willing to assume the possibility of unrestricted transfers among income groups, they found no conflict in principle between the objectives of distribution and growth. Once it is recognized that large-scale transfers of income are politically unlikely in developing countries, however, it becomes necessary to evaluate the results of any development policy in terms of the benefits it produces for different socio-economic groups. . . .

An index of economic performance reflecting these objectives can be developed as follows. Assume a division of society into N socio-eco-

nomic groups, defined by their assets, income levels, and economic functions. For purposes of policy analysis, it is necessary to distinguish several poverty groups such as small farmers, landless laborers, urban underemployed, and others according to the similarity of their responses to policy measures. In order to illustrate the problem of evaluation, we will classify merely by income size into ordinarily ranked percentile groups.

Assuming a division by income level into quintiles, the rate of growth of income of each group, g_i, can be taken to measure the increase of its social welfare over the specified period. The rate of increase in welfare of the society as a whole can therefore be defined as a weighted sum of the growth of income in all groups:

$$G = w_1 g_1 + w_2 g_2 + w_3 g_3 + w_4 g_4 + w_5 g_5 \quad (1)$$

*From Montek S. Ahluwalia and Hollis B. Chenery, "The Economic Framework," in *Redistribution with Growth*, joint study by World Bank's Development Research Center and Institute of Development Studies at the University of Sussex, Oxford University Press, 1974, pp. 38–39. Reprinted by permission.

where G is an index of the growth of total social welfare and w_i is the weight assigned to group i.[1]

A summary measure of this type enables us to set development targets and monitor development performance not simply in terms of growth of GNP but in terms of the distributional pattern of income growth. The weights for each income class reflect the social premium on generating growth at each income level; they may be set according to the degree of distributional emphasis desired. As the weight on a particular quintile is raised, our index of the increase in social welfare reflects to a greater extent the growth of income in that group. Thus if we were only concerned with the poorest quintile we would set $w_5 = 1$ and all other $w_i = 0$, so that growth in welfare would be measured only by g_5. This approach is closely related to the more formal approach to welfare choices using explicit social welfare functions to measure improvements in welfare.

In these terms the commonly used index of performance—the growth of GNP—is a special case in which the weights on the growth of income of each quintile are simply the income share of each quintile in total income. The shortcomings of such an index can be seen from the following income shares for the different quintiles, which are typical for underdeveloped countries:

Quintiles	1	2	3	4	5	Total
Share in Total Income	53%	22%	13%	7%	5%	100%

The combined share of the top 40 percent of the population amounts to about three-quarters of the total GNP. Thus the rate of growth of GNP measures essentially the income growth of the upper 40 percent and is not much affected by what happens to the income of the remaining 60 percent of the population.

An alternative welfare principle that has considerable appeal is to give equal social value to a one-percent increase in income for any member of society. On this principle, the weights in equation (1) should be proportional to the number of people in each group and would therefore be equal for each quintile. Thus a one-percent increase in income in the lowest quintile would have the same weight in the overall performance measure as a one-percent increase in income for any other quintile, even though the absolute increment involved is much smaller for the lowest quintile than for the others.

When we use the growth of GNP as an index of performance, we implicitly assume that a dollar of additional income creates the same additional social welfare regardless of the income level of the recipient.[2] Given the typical income shares of the different quintiles, it follows that a one-percent growth in income in the top quintile is given almost eleven times the weight of a one-percent growth in the lowest quintile (in the preceding example) because it requires an absolute increment which is eleven times as great. In contrast to the GNP measure, the equal weights index gives the same weight to a one-percent increase in income in the lowest quintile as it does to a one-percent increase in the highest quintile. In this case a dollar of additional income in the lowest quintile is valued at eleven times a dollar of additional income in the highest quintile.

Many individuals (and some countries) may wish to define social objectives almost exclusively in terms of income growth of the lowest groups, placing little value upon growth in the upper-income groups beyond its contribution to national savings and investment. The welfare implications of such a ''poverty weighted'' index are stronger than those underlying either the rate of growth of GNP or the ''equal weights'' index, since it would be a welfare function based primarily on the lower-income groups.

Weighted indexes of the sort discussed above provide a very different evaluation of performance in many countries than is obtained from conventional measures. . . .

---

[1]This measure can be applied either to the income or the consumption of each group. When applied to income, the weight assigned should take account of the contribution made by each group to the financing of investment and government expenditure. For long-run simulations of policy an index based on consumption only is preferable.

[2]This statement has to be qualified to allow for the higher savings of the upper-income recipients and their greater contribution to future growth. In a more complete analysis, the increase in social welfare can be measured by the weighted growth of consumption rather than income.

EXHIBIT I.6. Poverty and Growth of Income Per Capita by Developing Region, 1985 and 1990, and Long- and Medium-Term Trends

Region	Headcount Index of Poverty[a]		Annual Percentage Change in Income per Capita	
	1985	1990	1970–92	1982–92
All developing countries	30.5	29.7	1.7	0.8
Sub-Saharan Africa	47.6	47.8	−0.2	−1.1
East Asia	13.2	11.3	5.3	6.3
South Asia	51.8	49.0	2.0	3.0
Eastern Europe	7.1	7.1	1.2	1.7
Middle East and North Africa	30.6	33.1	0.1	−1.6
Latin America and the Caribbean	22.4	25.2	1.1	−0.2

[a]Estimated share of the population consuming less than $32 per person per month at 1985 purchasing power parity prices.
Source: World Bank, *World Development Report 1993* (1993), p. 42.

I.B.3. Burden of Poverty*

The burden of poverty is spread unevenly—among the regions of the developing world, among countries within those regions, and among localities within those countries. Nearly half of the world's poor live in South Asia, a region that accounts for roughly 30 percent of the world's population. Sub-Saharan Africa accounts for a smaller, but still highly disproportionate, share of global poverty. Within regions and countries, the poor are often concentrated in certain places: in rural areas with high population densities, such as the Gangetic Plain of India and the island of Java, Indonesia, or in resource-poor areas such as the Andean highlands and the Sahel. Often the problems of poverty, population, and the environment are intertwined: earlier patterns of development and the pressure of rapidly expanding populations mean that many of the poor live in areas of acute environmental degradation.

The weight of poverty falls most heavily on certain groups. Women in general are disadvantaged. In poor households they often shoulder more of the workload than men, are less educated, and have less access to remunerative activities. Children, too, suffer disproportionately, and the future quality of their lives is compro-

*From World Bank, *World Development Report 1990* (New York: Oxford University Press, 1990), pp. 2, 26–29. Reprinted by permission.

mised by inadequate nutrition, health care, and education. This is especially true for girls: their primary enrollment rates are less than 50 percent in many African countries. The incidence of poverty is often high among ethnic groups and minorities such as the indigenous peoples in Bolivia, Ecuador, Guatemala, Mexico, and Peru and the scheduled castes in India.

In many but not all cases, low incomes go hand in hand with other forms of deprivation. In Mexico, for example, life expectancy for the poorest 10 percent of the population is twenty years less than for the richest 10 percent. In Côte d'Ivoire the primary enrollment rate of the poorest fifth is half that of the richest. National and regional averages, often bad enough in themselves, mask appallingly low life expectancy and educational attainment among the poorest members of society. . . .

Poverty is not the same as inequality. The distinction needs to be stressed. Whereas poverty is concerned with the absolute standard of living of a part of society—the poor—inequality refers to relative living standards across the whole society. At maximum inequality one person has everything and, clearly, poverty is high. But minimum inequality (where all are equal) is possible with zero poverty (where no one is poor) as well as with maximum poverty (where all are poor).

This report defines poverty as the inability to

attain a minimal standard of living. To make this definition useful, three questions must be answered. How do we measure a standard of living? What do we mean by a minimal standard of living? And, having thus identified the poor, how do we express the overall severity of poverty in a single measure or index?

The Poverty Line

All the measures are judged in relation to some norm. For example, we deem life expectancies in some countries to be low in relation to those attained by other countries at a given date. The choice of the norm is particularly important in the case of the consumption-based measures of poverty.

A consumption-based poverty line can be thought of as comprising two elements: the expenditure necessary to buy a minimum standard of nutrition and other basic necessities and a further amount that varies from country to country, reflecting the cost of participating in the everyday life of society. The first part is relatively straightforward. The cost of minimum adequate caloric intakes and other necessities can be calculated by looking at the prices of the foods that make up the diets of the poor. The second part is far more subjective; in some countries indoor plumbing is a luxury, but in others it is a "necessity."

The perception of poverty has evolved historically and varies tremendously from culture to culture. Criteria for distinguishing poor from nonpoor tend to reflect specific national priorities and normative concepts of welfare and rights. In general, as countries become wealthier, their perception of the acceptable minimum level of consumption—the poverty line— changes. . . .

Rather than settle for a single number, this chapter employs two: $275 and $370 per person a year. (The amounts are in constant 1985 PPP prices.) This range was chosen to span the poverty lines estimated in recent studies for a number of countries with low average incomes— Bangladesh, the Arab Republic of Egypt, India, Indonesia, Kenya, Morocco, and Tanzania. The lower limit of the range coincides with a poverty line commonly used for India.

How Much Poverty Is There?

Once the poor have been distinguished from the nonpoor, the simplest way to measure poverty is to express the number of poor as a proportion of the population. This *headcount index* is a useful measure, although it is often criticized because it ignores the extent to which the poor fall below the poverty line. The income shortfall, or *poverty gap*, avoids this drawback. It measures the transfer that would bring the income of every poor person exactly up to the poverty line, thereby eliminating poverty. . . .

The use of the upper poverty line—$370— gives an estimate of 1,115 million people in the developing countries in poverty in 1985. That is roughly one-third of the total population of the developing world. Of these, 630 million—18 percent of the total population of the developing world—were extremely poor: their annual consumption was less than $275, the lower poverty line. Despite these massive numbers, the aggregate poverty gap—the transfer needed to lift everybody above the poverty line—was only 3 percent of the developing countries' consumption. The transfer needed to lift everybody out of extreme poverty was, of course, even smaller—just 1 percent of the developing countries' consumption. Mortality for children under 5 averaged 121 per thousand for all developing countries, aggregate life expectancy was 62 years, and the overall net primary school enrollment rate was 83 percent. These figures hide considerable variation within and among countries. Table 1 sets out a detailed regional breakdown of these estimates. . . .

Nearly half of the developing world's poor, and nearly half of those in extreme poverty, live in South Asia. Sub-Saharan Africa has about one-third as many poor, although in relation to the region's overall population, its poverty is roughly as high. Table 1 also shows that both South Asia and Sub-Saharan Africa have low scores on several other social indicators; in Sub-Saharan Africa, in particular, life expectancy and primary school enrollment rates are alarmingly low, and under 5 mortality rates are alarmingly high. The Middle Eastern and North African countries have the next highest poverty, according to all the indicators. They are followed by Latin America and the Caribbean and by East Asia. China's overall performance is impressive, although the size of its population means that a relatively low headcount index still translates into large numbers of poor.

Although developing countries had made substantial progress in reducing poverty over the past three decades, there was only a slight im-

TABLE 1. How Much Poverty Is There in the Developing Countries? The Situation in 1985

Region	Extremely Poor			Poor (including extremely poor)			Social Indicators		
	Number (millions)	Headcount Index (percent)	Poverty Gap	Number (millions)	Heacount Index (percent)	Poverty Gap	Under 5 Mortality (per thousand)	Life Expectancy (years)	Net Primary Enrollment Rate (percent)
Sub-Saharan Africa	120	30	4	180	47	11	196	50	56
East Asia	120	9	0.4	280	20	1	96	67	96
China	80	8	1	210	20	3	58	69	93
South Asia	300	29	3	520	51	10	172	56	74
India	250	33	4	420	55	12	199	57	81
Eastern Europe	3	4	0.2	6	8	0.5	23	71	90
Middle East and North Africa	40	21	1	60	31	2	148	61	75
Latin America and the Caribbean	50	12	1	70	19	1	75	66	92
All developing countries	633	18	1	1,116	33	3	121	62	83

Note: The poverty line in 1985 PPP dollars is $275 per capita a year for the extremely poor and $370 per capita a year for the poor.
The headcount index is defined as the percentage of the population below the poverty line.
The poverty gap is defined as the aggregate income shortfall of the poor as a percentage of aggregate consumption.

provement in the aggregate incidence of poverty in the latter half of the 1980s. The number in poverty, therefore, increased at close to the rate of population growth (a compound annual rate of about 1.5 percent). The key challenge is to resume the more rapid rate of poverty reduction of earlier years. This will require higher economic growth rates during the rest of the 1990s and improved patterns of growth that benefit the poor.

EXHIBIT I.7. Poverty in Developing Countries, 1990

Country Groups	Higher Poverty Line[a]			Lower Poverty Line[b]		
	Number of Poor (million)	Headcount Index (percent)	Contribution to Total Poverty (percent)	Number of Poor (million)	Heacount Index (percent)	Contribution to Total Poverty (percent)
South Asia	562	49.0	49.8	287	25.0	44.7
India	(448)	(52.8)	(39.7)	(226)	(26.6)	(35.2)
East Asia	169	11.3	15.0	74	5.0	11.5
China	(128)	(11.3)	(11.3)	(63)	(5.6)	(9.8)
Africa, south of Sahara	216	47.8	19.1	152	33.6	23.7
North Africa and Middle East	73	33.1	6.5	53	24.0	8.3
Latin America	108	25.2	9.6	76	17.8	11.8
All developing countries	1,128	29.7	100.0	642	16.9	100.0

[a]Based on a poverty line of $370 (in 1985 international prices).
[b]Based on a poverty line of $275 (in 1985 international prices).
Source: World Bank data files.

EXHIBIT I.8. Rural and Urban Poverty in the 1980s

Region and Country	Rural Population as Percentage of Total	Rural Poor as Percentage of Total	Infant Mortality (per thousand live births)		Access to Safe Water (percentage of population)	
			Rural	Urban	Rural	Urban
Sub-Saharan Africa						
Côte d'Ivoire	57	86	121	70	10	30
Ghana	65	80	87	67	39	93
Kenya	80	96	59	57	21	61
Asia						
India	77	79	105	57	50	76
Indonesia	73	91	74	57	36	43
Malaysia	62	80	—	—	76	96
Philippines	60	67	55	42	54	49
Thailand	70	80	43	28	66	56
Latin America						
Guatemala	59	66	85	65	26	89
Mexico	31	37	79	29	51	79
Panama	50	59	28	22	63	100
Peru	44	52	101	54	17	73
Venezuela	15	20	—	—	80	70

Source: World Bank, *World Development Report 1990* (1990), p. 31.

I.B.4. Why Does Absolute Poverty Persist?—Note

In the 1970s, the then president of the World Bank, Robert McNamara, directed his staff to measure the rate of growth in per capita income in the LDCs from 1950 to 1970. They found that, on the average, income per person in the developing countries had increased over the period by 3.4 percent. This increase was a remarkably high historical rate of growth in per capita incomes. But at the same time, McNamara called world attention to the basic human needs of those in what he called "absolute poverty." He said that there will always be "relative poverty" in the sense of income differentials between richer and poorer, but he wanted the World Bank to focus on those in "absolute poverty—a condition of life so degraded by disease, illiteracy, malnutrition, and squalor as to deny its victims basic human necessities."[1] The Bank then identified approximately the lowest 40 per-

cent of the population in developing countries as being in absolute poverty—about 900 million with an average per capita income of less than US$100 a year.

Now, for the period since the 1970s, we can again note a substantial increase of 70 percent in the average person's level of consumption in developing countries. Average life expectancy has also risen notably from 51 to 63 years, and primary-school enrollment has reached 89 percent.[2] But the distressing fact remains: the total number in poverty has increased. As indicated in selection I.B.3, over 1 billion people remain below the poverty line of $370 (in 1985 PPP prices). Even more distressing is the fact that from 1985 to 1990, the increase in the total number of those below the poverty line was equal to the rate of population growth in that period. An additional 16 million people per year were consuming less than $1 per day in the years 1985

[1]R. S. McNamara, *Address to the Board of Governors* (Washington, D.C., World Bank, September 25, 1972), pp. 8–10.

[2]World Bank, *Implementing the World Bank's Strategy to Reduce Poverty* (1993), p. 3.

to 1990, an increase in the number of poor of nearly 8 percent over this five-year period. If this rate were to be maintained over the decade of the 1990s, approximately 1.3 billion people in the developing world will be consuming less than $1 a day (at 1985 prices) by the year 2000.[3] Two decades after McNamara's charge to the World Bank to attempt to reduce absolute poverty, the present president, Lewis Preston, has still had to proclaim that "no task should command higher priority for the world's policy makers than that of reducing global poverty." In many countries, the gains from growth have not been reaching the poor.

Why not? The answers relate in part to

- the rate of growth
- the pattern of growth
- the failure of governmental policies

A slow rate of growth increases the total number in poverty for two reasons: there is not only a weak "trickle down" effect, but even worse, when a country's growth is slow, its politicians need to gain political support. They then do so by in effect "buying" support through the granting of favors such as foreign-exchange allocations, import quotas, or subsidies. These rent-producing favors go to the nonpoor: businessmen, large farmers, trade unions, and the army.[4]

These inappropriate policies, in turn, tend to perpetuate a slow rate of growth. A vicious circle of slow growth and political favoritism then intensifies inequality and perpetuates poverty. A higher rate of growth is needed before politicians believe that they can afford to introduce policies that favor the poor.

The pattern of growth also matters in determining who are the beneficiaries of growth. The incidence of poverty can increase if the pattern of growth is urban biased, displaces unskilled labor, alters relative prices to the disadvantage of the poor, creates a gender gap, deteriorates

child welfare, and erodes traditional entitlements that have served as safety nets.[5]

Michael Lipton has analyzed why the poor remain poor in terms of urban bias that limits rural development and restricts the advancement of small farmers and landless laborers.[6] (See VIII.A.3.) The incidence of poverty is normally heaviest in the rural sector, and if growth does not increase productivity and real income in that sector, poverty persists.

The earnings of the poor can also lag, even with creditable growth rates, when technological forces are saving of unskilled labor. During periods of growth, the utilization of inappropriate capital-intensive and unskilled–labor-saving technology may intensify inequality.

The pattern of growth will also affect relative prices. Technical change and increasing productivity—and hence lower prices—are unlikely to be significant in those goods and services that predominate in the budgets of the poor. The most important of these is the price of food. So too is the cost of urban housing significant. In addition, inflation will hit the standard of living of the poor more than for higher-income groups. And on the income side, as growth occurs it is normal for the price of land, skilled labor, and capital to rise, but the poor do not own these assets.

Women in the less developed countries are especially prone to poverty. (See VI.D.) Their share of poverty is disproportionately large. In general, female-headed households are more susceptible to poverty. And the incidence of households headed by women is increasing rapidly in less developed countries. Moreover, discrimination against women is widespread, especially against women in poverty. Cultural, social, and legal obstacles confront women. So too do economic obstacles. Their entry into the labor market may be restricted. They confront discrimination in credit markets; they have limited access to capital and modern technology; and they are confined to low productive, labor-intensive work that offers only low earnings.

Poverty may also intensify when the traditional means of support and entitlements break down in the course of development. Traditional safety nets disappear with the breakup of the extended family, erosion of village economies, mi-

[3]Ibid., p. 7; Martin Ravillion et al., "New Estimates of Aggregate Poverty in the Developing World 1985–1990," World Bank Population and Human Resources Department, processed, p. 4. The World Bank's estimates are based on a universal poverty line to permit cross-country comparison and aggregation. The use of purchasing power parity prices allows the computation of a common set of prices in a common currency so that real international quantity comparisons can be made.

[4]Anne O. Krueger, *Political Economy of Policy Reform in Developing Countries* (1993).

[5]For an elaboration of some of these historical causes, see Jeffrey G. Williamson, *Inequality, Poverty, and History* (1991) pp. 105–9.

[6]Michael Lipton, *Why Poor People Stay Poor* (1976).

gration, and emphasis on "individualization" instead of "community." And the traditional support systems are not replaced by new transfer mechanisms that are adequate in time and amount.

At the same time as the forces in certain types of growth regimes can plunge some groups into poverty, governmental policies may be inadequate to lift them out of poverty. The major inadequacy is the lack of policies that create jobs. It can be argued that when the market-price system does not provide full employment, government should not ignore remedial action. When public deficiencies in nutrition, poor health, and lack of education perpetuate low productivity, governmental policies should not ignore investment in human resources. When public expenditures must be necessarily limited, governments should not direct their expenditures to the non-poor to the neglect of those in poverty. These same strictures apply to foreign aid donors and international lending agencies such as regional development banks and the World Bank.

We may conclude that with a given economic structure and policy environment, rapid growth is better than slow growth in eradicating poverty. But the economic structure and the policy environment do not remain constant.[7] Even with respectable rates of growth, the total number in poverty can increase. And it has done so in many countries because of the adverse changes in economic structure and the absence of appropriate policies by government. Growth does not help the poor unless it reaches the poor. Nor does government help unless the poor are the beneficiaries of public policies.

[7]Williamson, *Inequality, Poverty, and History*, p. 97.

I.B.5. The Environmental Challenge of Development—Note

Poverty is the worst form of pollution. But poverty in itself creates environmental problems. At the same time that policies need to be adopted to reduce poverty, care must also be taken to stop environmental degradation and achieve sustainable development.

Measures of net domestic product do not capture the loss or depletion of national environmental resources such as a nation's stock of water, soil, air, nonrenewable resources and wildlands. Although net domestic product allows for the depreciation of fixed capital, an ideal index would also deduct depreciation of the country's natural resource stocks as well—valued at accounting or shadow prices that reflect social benefits or social costs instead of simply market prices. If this were done, real domestic product would be lower than is currently estimated, and the rates of growth of net domestic product would also be lower than they are generally estimated.

Although measures of development performance based on national income data do not adequately reflect environmental damage, numerous examples can be cited. Not considering the amenity value of an unspoiled environment, but simply the environmental problems that damage the health and productivity of large numbers of people in the developing world, the World Bank cites such environmental problems as

- one-third of the world's population has inadequate sanitation, and 1 billion are without safe water
- 1.3 billion people are exposed to unsafe conditions caused by soot and smoke
- 300 to 700 million women and children suffer from severe indoor air pollution from cooking fires
- hundreds of millions of farmers, forest dwellers, and indigenous people who rely on the land and whose livelihoods depend on good environmental stewardship are being handicapped
- soil erosion can cause annual economic losses ranging from 0.5 to 1.5 percent of GNP
- one-quarter of all irrigated land suffers from salinization
- tropical forests—the primary source of livelihood for about 140 million people—are being lost at a rate of 0.9 percent annually[1]

Poverty does not allow people to husband their natural resources. Of necessity, marginal

[1]World Bank, *World Development Report 1992* (1992), pp. 2, 44.

land is farmed and forests are cleared. Labor intensive methods of production threaten the environment. New industries cannot afford pollution abatement technology. Rapid population growth places ever-increasing pressure on the environment.

Now, however, it is realized that proper environmental management may actually contribute to an alleviation of poverty. An increasing number of countries are seeking to establish programs for "sustainable development"—that is, a pattern of development that does not reduce production, but changes its quality so as to satisfy the needs of the present generation without compromising the ability of future generations to meet their own needs.[2]

To this end, economic policies need to be undertaken to protect and enhance farm and grazing land, promote environmentally sound farming practices, conserve energy, control pollution, develop appropriate technology, and foster research on biodiversity and tropical forestry. A more efficient use of natural resources can increase productivity and improve development performance.

But how can this be accomplished? The analytical principles of environmental economics provide a foundation for improved national environmental management. Environmental economics views the environment as composed of capital assets that produce a flow of services that can be valued in economic terms. Market failure and government failure, however, can distort the valuation of these services. Social benefits and social costs must be recognized, and the time profile of these benefits and costs considered. Essentially two approaches are possible—"command and control" or provision of incentives through the price system. To control pollution, for example, direct instruments may be employed, such as issuing permits or setting standards based on emissions. Alternatively, market-based instruments, involving taxes or tradable quotas on emissions, may be utilized to achieve a given emission reduction at the lowest possible cost.

The World Bank advocates policies that work with the grain of the market rather than against it, using incentives rather than regulations where

possible. The World Bank therefore recommends policies such as

- removing subsidies that encourage excessive use of fossil fuels, irrigation water, pesticides, and excessive logging
- clarifying rights to manage and own land, forests, and fisheries
- accelerating provision of sanitation and clean water, education (especially for girls), family planning services, and agricultural extension, credit, and research
- taking measures to enpower, educate, and involve farmers, local communities, indigenous people, and women so that they can make decisions and investment in their own long-term interest[3]

In shaping a country's development strategy, the government should ensure that the public sector provides appropriate policies that give incentives to the private sector for its involvement in promoting environmentally responsible development. Public-sector investments for infrastructure also need to be more environmentally responsible.[4]

A number of economists, however, are now questioning the meaning of sustainable development and are cautioning against an overemphasis on environmental problems based on faulty reasoning. For instance, a former chief economist of the World Bank states,

The argument that a moral obligation to future generations demands special treatment of environmental investments is fatuous. We can help our descendants as much by improving infrastructure as by preserving rain forests, as much by educating children as by leaving oil in the ground, as much by enlarging our scientific knowledge as by reducing carbon dioxide in the air. However much, or little, current generations wish to weigh the interests of future generations, there is every reason to undertake investments that yield the highest returns.

That means holding each investment, environmental and non-environmental, to a test of opportunity cost. Each project must have a higher return (taking

---

[2]A number of definitions of "sustainable development" have been offered, but all raise the philosophical issue of intergenerational justice. See J. Pasek, "Obligations to Future Generations: A Philosophical Note," *World Development* (April 1992): 513–22.

[3]World Bank, *World Development Report* (1992), pp. 2–3. The Bank also argues that many appropriate policies which are beneficial on macro- or microeconomic efficiency grounds would also be beneficial for environmental protection. They would produce less waste, use fewer raw materials, and promote resource-saving technological innovations.

[4]These policies are examined in some detail in World Bank, *World Development Report 1992*, especially chaps. 2–7.

account of both pecuniary and non-pecuniary benefits) than alternative uses of the funds. Once costs and benefits are properly measured, it cannot be in posterity's interest for us to undertake investments that yield less than the best return. At the long-term horizons that figure in the environmental debate, this really matters. A dollar invested at 10% will be worth six times as much a century from now as a dollar invested at 8%.[5]

Oxford's Wilfred Beckerman also contends that in contrast to the emphasis on the

alleged exhaustion of resources of the conventional kind—minerals or food supplies, the most important environmental problems in developing countries are local problems of access to safe drinking water or decent sanitation, and urban degradation. Furthermore there is clear evidence that, although economic growth usually leads to environmental deterioration in the early stages of the process, in the end the best—

and probably the only—way to attain a decent environment in most countries is to become rich.

Taking the main environmental indicators together, the exact point, or income level at which environmental conditions reach a stage when effective policies are introduced will depend on a host of variables, including technical, social and political variables. But as far as these components of the environment are concerned, it is fairly clear that the best way to improve the environment of the vast mass of the world's population is to enable them to maintain economic growth. Some developing countries may go through a transition period when population is still rising fast—particularly in the cities—and before environmental protection measures have been effectively implemented. But the strong correlation between incomes and the extent to which environmental protection measures are adopted demonstrates that, in the longer run, the surest way to improve your environment is to become rich.[6]

[5]Lawrence H. Summers, "Summers on Sustainable Growth," *The Economist*, May 30, 1992, p. 65.

[6]W. Beckerman, "Economic Growth and the Environment: Whose Growth? Whose Environment?" *World Development* (April 1992): 482–91.

Comment: Development and the Environment

A number of other issues that relate to the environment will be explored in other parts of this book. The topic is, however, new and subject to considerable controversy both at the conceptual and policy levels. National and local issues are also quantitatively and qualitatively different from international environmental concerns such as the threat of greenhouse warming.

For a basic approach to environmental economics, see A. Ulph, "A Review of Books on Resource and Environmental Economics," *Bulletin of Economic Research* (1989). The World Bank's *World Development Report 1992* (1992) contains an extensive bibliography, pp. 183–91. Also valuable is "Linking Environment to Development: Problems and Possibilities" [special issue], *World Development* (April 1992).

I.C. HOW HAVE DEVELOPING COUNTRIES PERFORMED?

I.C.1. Taiwan and South Korea*

South Korea and Taiwan not only grew very fast but did so without experiencing the customary great and increasing inequalities and the emergence of mass unemployment. Indeed, by the double criterion of growth and equity, they have been the most successful of all the developing countries.

Per capita GNP in real terms grew marginally faster in Taiwan than in Korea, at an average annual rate of 6.9 percent compared to Korea's 6.7 percent between 1965 and 1981 (Table 1). Taiwan also had slightly less unemployment, an even more egalitarian income distribution, and a much higher standard of living. Taiwan's GDP per capita was US$2,570 by 1981, whereas Korea's was US$1,697. In effect, Taiwan was six years ahead of Korea: Korea's per capita income in 1981 was about the same as Taiwan's in 1975.

But international comparisons, based on monetary estimates made in national currencies and then converted into a common currency at current exchange rates, are subject to notoriously wide margins of error. Indeed, two similar estimates, based on different data in slightly different ways, have yielded an eight- and a ten-year gap. Moreover, one must also bear in mind that Korea produces its lower GDP with greater effort. In 1980, the average length of the working week in Korea's manufacturing industries was in excess of fifty-nine hours, 16 percent longer than Taiwan's fifty-one-hour week. Correcting for that factor makes Taiwan's per capita GDP appear almost twice as high as Korea's. On the other hand, Koreans spend a much higher proportion of their lower GDP on private consumption: two-thirds as compared to Taiwan's one-half. Accordingly, the difference between the two countries' levels of living is not as great as the discrepancy between their per capita GDP would suggest.

Social indicators are sometimes more useful for assessing differences in levels of living than estimates in money terms. Those available for both countries are listed in Table 2; they suggest that Taiwan enjoys a considerably higher level

*From Tibor Scitovsky, "Economic Development in Taiwan and South Korea," *Food Research Institute Studies,* 19, no. 4 (1985): 215–64. Reprinted with permission.

TABLE 1. Average Annual Growth Rates in Real Terms, 1965–81 (percent)

	Korea	Taiwan
Population	1.9	2.3
Employment	3.4	3.7
Gross national product	8.7	9.4
Gross domestic product	8.6	9.4
Manufacturing output	20.6	15.5
Exports (quantum index)	26.0	18.9
GNP per capita = GDP per capita	6.7	6.9
Labor productivity[a]	5.2	5.4
Real wages in manufacturing	7.9	7.3
Consumers' expenditures per capita	5.5	5.2

[a]GNP per employed person.

of living than Korea. The only visible social indicator is the number of motorized vehicles (passenger cars and motorcycles) per household. It suggests that in Taiwan just about every household owns such a vehicle, while in Korea only one in twenty households does. . . .

None of the other social indicators is apparent; indeed, the tourist is likely not only to fail to notice Taiwan's greater prosperity but actually to get the impression that the difference between the two countries goes the other way around. Seoul, certainly, looks more affluent than Taipei, judging by the appearance of its main thoroughfares, the impressiveness of its commercial and office buildings, and the elegance of its stores and shopping areas. The explanation of the conflict between what the tourist sees and what the statistics show derives from the unequal distribution of income and of the things that income buys. All the social indicators of Table 2 are averages and indicate average tendencies; whereas the tourist is shown only the best, and his eye instinctively looks for the best. In an egalitarian society the best is not much better than the average, but the two differ greatly in a society with great inequalities.

Income distribution in both Taiwan and Korea is much more equal than in any other developing or newly industrializing country for which relevant statistics are available, but it is more egalitarian in Taiwan than in Korea. Inequalities in Korea are much the same as in the advanced

TABLE 2. Social Indicators

	Korea	Taiwan
Life expectancy at birth (years)	65	72
Infant mortality per 1,000 live births	37	25
Daily calorie intake per capita	2,785	2,805
Daily protein intake per capita (grams)	69.6	78
Residential floorspace per capita (m²)	9.5	15.7
Households with running water (percent)	54.6	66.8
Households with television sets (percent)	78.6	100.4
Households with passenger cars and motorcycles (percent)	5.8	108.4
Electric power consumption per capita (KWH)	914.8	2,131.2

industrial countries: somewhat less than in France and Italy, greater than in the United Kingdom and the Scandinavian countries, and just about the same as in the United States and Canada. Taiwan, on the other hand, is the most egalitarian of all capitalist countries, a finding that corresponds to the very small average size and limited dispersion of the size of Taiwan's business firms, and also explains the absence of an elite wealthy and numerous enough to support the elegant shops and finance the imposing office buildings that give Seoul its appearance of affluence (Table 3).

One more important difference between the two economies has been the much lower rate of inflation in Taiwan than in Korea. Between 1965 and 1981, the consumer price index rose three and one-half times in Taiwan, ten times in Korea, corresponding to average annual price infla-

TABLE 3. Gini Index of Inequality of Income Distribution

	1965	1970	1976
Korea	0.344	0.332	0.381
Taiwan	0.322[a]	0.293	0.289
Japan	0.380	0.420[b]	
United States		0.362[c]	
Brazil	0.520[d]	0.630	

[a]1966
[b]1971
[c]1972
[d]1960

Sources: The comparisons are based on Gini indexes of inequality: obtained for Taiwan from Kuo, Ranis, and Fei, *The Taiwan Success Story* (Boulder: Westview Press, 1981); for Korea from Park, *Human Resources and Social Development in Korea* (Seoul: Korea Development Institute, 1980), p. 289; and calculated for other countries from data in World Bank, *World Development Report 1982* (1982), pp. 158–59.

tion rates of 8 and 15 percent, respectively. Compared to other countries, Taiwan did about as well—or as badly—as Japan or the United States; Korea had more inflation than any of the industrial countries, but less than the major Latin American economies.

Similarities in Tradition and Background

Detailed analysis and comparison of the two countries' economic conditions and performance suggest that the similarities are due largely to similarities in their history and traditions. Korea's lag behind Taiwan is more than explained by the later date at which its growth policies began: the other differences are well accounted for by the two countries' divergent economic policies. Unexplained and puzzling is the close similarity in growth rates despite the very different ways in which the two countries went about promoting growth.

To begin with the similarities, both countries share a common Chinese tradition and Confucian philosophy. That explains, first of all, the great reverence and importance attached to learning in both countries and the very high educational and skill levels of their populations. They started from a very low level at the end of the war, especially in Korea where the literacy rate was 13.4 percent in 1945 (as against Taiwan's 21.3 percent by 1940), and where there was no large influx of a highly educated middle-class population such as benefited Taiwan in the late 1940s. Since then, illiteracy has been almost completely eradicated in both countries, and today Taiwan provides nine years and Korea six years of free and compulsory schooling. School enrollment rates at the primary and secondary levels are almost equally high in the two countries and only slightly lower than the average in the advanced industrial countries. That is especially impressive in Korea, where modernization started later, compulsory education ends sooner, and public expenditure on education is lower (averaging 3.5 percent of the GDP as against Taiwan's 4.5 percent), but where consumers make up for those disadvantages by paying for the greater part of their children's education out of their own pockets, bringing the total private and public expenditure on education to an astonishingly high 9 percent of the GNP.

A second condition of those countries' great economic success that can be traced back to their common tradition is the ability and willingness to work hard. Chinese tradition has many strands, but it seems to include a work ethic not unlike the Protestant and Jewish work ethics. The drive and ambition of Korean and Chinese businessmen, as well as their ability to work hard and long hours, are commented on by nearly every outside observer of the two economies. One is tempted to add the two countries' very long working week as a further manifestation of the work ethic, but in view of the very limited bargaining strength of their unions, it is hard to tell to what extent those long working hours are voluntary and to what extent they are imposed.

A third factor that probably also contributed to the two countries' economic success is the Chinese tradition in labor relations, which comprises both greater wage flexibility and greater employment stability than in Europe and America, and which was fully maintained and perhaps even strengthened under Japanese rule. Both countries adhere to the Chinese custom of paying bonuses to workers at major festivals and the end of the year; even if these constitute a much smaller proportion of the annual wage than they do in Japan, they nevertheless are likely to contribute to the two countries' high personal saving rate and to impart a measure of downward flexibility to wages. Again, relations between employer and employee are more permanent in the two countries than they are in the West, with employers under both moral and governmental pressure to take care of their workers even when business is slow.

Korea and Taiwan are also similar in that both were under Japanese rule, Korea for thirty-five years and Taiwan for fifty years, and that fact has facilitated their subsequent growth in at least two ways. First, the Japanese introduced the new, high-yielding strains of rice, established

agricultural research institutes, and generally did much to develop the two countries' farm productivity and food production; moreover, they built roads, railways, harbors, and whatever beginnings of industry the two countries had, thus providing an excellent start and base for subsequent development. A second and very important consequence of Japanese rule had to do with the confiscation of Japanese property when their rule came to an end. The Japanese acquired a sizable part of the land (21 percent of all arable land in Taiwan) and built most of the modern manufacturing plants in both countries, and since they owned all the large enterprises and most of the largest landed estates, the confiscation of their property by the liberating armies and its handing over to the new governments drastically reduced the inequality of private wealth holdings in both countries. In Korea, moreover, the Korean War destroyed much physical property, and since most of the loss was borne by the wealthy, that too helped to reduce inequalities of wealth.

Even more important in equalizing the distribution of wealth were the thorough land reforms in both countries, which not only distributed among small tenant farmers the large estates formerly held by the Japanese, but also forced the large indigenous landowners to sell all their land over three hectares (except in Korea's upland areas) at prices very much below market values. Korea's and Taiwan's land reforms were identical in almost every detail.

The stability of employment is another contributing factor in the equal distribution of income. Yet another important reason was the rise of farm families' earnings to the level of urban wage-earner families' incomes. In Taiwan, that came about largely through the operation of automatic market forces, aided by favorable circumstances. Impelled by high and rising labor costs in cities, an increasing proportion of new factories and offices was established in rural areas and offered additional employment opportunities to farmers and their families. The poorest farmers especially availed themselves of the opportunity: by 1975, 66 percent of their total earnings came from jobs off the farm. Nor was the corresponding percentage for all farm families much lower: 53.7 percent in 1975, rising to 72.7 percent in 1979. That is why, in contrast to most developing countries where mass migration into the cities depletes rural areas, Taiwan's rural population remained fairly stable, with members of farm families commuting or taking part-time jobs in nearby cities during off-peak seasons. The favorable circumstances that aided the process were a small, decentralized country, good roads, a mild climate, and a motorcycle in every family. Korea went out of its way to encourage a similar development but, perhaps for want of similarly favorable circumstances, had very limited success. It managed nevertheless to equalize rural and urban incomes through the costly expedient of a farm-price support program combined with subsidized low food prices for consumers.

Thanks to all those equalizing factors and influences, the degree of income inequality by the mid-1960s had fallen to just about the same level in the two countries. Since then, inequalities have declined yet further in Taiwan but increased in Korea, which explains why Taiwan is today the more egalitarian country.

Two additional similarities between the countries are the exceptionally generous economic aid both have received and the exceptionally heavy burdens of military expenditures they are saddled with: the first is an addition to economic resources, the second a drain on them. Both countries have also received substantial military aid from the United States in the form of military equipment, but since much of it seems to call for a larger defense establishment, military aid probably encourages domestic defense spending more than reduces it. Defense spending in Taiwan hovers around 10 percent of GNP; in Korea, thanks to an American military presence, it is 5 to 6 percent. But even that is much higher than the 3.8 percent average of industrial countries and the 3 percent average of newly industrializing countries. The annual aid Taiwan received until 1966 averaged 5.1 percent of GNP, just enough to finance the above-normal part of its defense spending.

Such a simple-minded calculation, of course, ignores that Taiwan would probably have spent as much on defense even if it had received no economic aid, and that aid may well have been crucial in the early 1950s for controlling inflation and securing the survival of the government of the Republic of China on Taiwan. But beyond assuring those initial conditions, aid cannot really be said to have accelerated growth.

Korea's situation is somewhat different. The aid it received exceeded defense expenditures, averaging 8.3 percent of GNP before 1965 and continuing, at a somewhat lower level, until 1972. The economy, however, was much more devastated by war than Taiwan's, and the aid to rebuild the war-torn country was more comparable to that received by Japan and Western Europe. . . .

One more similarity between the two countries worth mentioning here was their very limited imports of entrepreneurial skill and technical know-how in the form of direct foreign investments. In Taiwan, they constituted a mere 6.5 percent of fixed investment in manufacturing industries between 1967 and 1975; in Korea, they were equally insignificant until 1972, when they rose to about 20 percent, coming mainly from Japan and going mainly into textiles, electronics, and hotel business. The reasons for their limited need of direct foreign investment are obvious. Perhaps as part of their excellent educational systems and traditions of hard work and untiring application, both countries are well provided with native entrepreneurial skills, drive, and ambition. Moreover, they had no need for imported technical knowledge as long as they had previous experience. That, probably, is why in Korea the increase in foreign direct investment coincided with the decision to shift to more capital-intensive industries. Even at that stage, however, direct foreign investment in Korea was low compared to other developing countries, perhaps owing to the Koreans' preference for going it alone. They learned shipbuilding by employing Norwegians from closed-down Norwegian shipyards and gained their expertise in construction by contracting to do construction work abroad.

These similarities in the two countries' backgrounds help to explain not only their similar economic performances but also the exceptional nature of their success when compared to the record of other developing countries. To explain differences between the two countries themselves, one must look at their differing policies.

The Philosophy Behind Taiwan's Economic Policies

Taiwanese officials will occasionally say that their economic policy is to let market forces take their course. That, however, is a highly oversimplified and exaggerated statement. Taiwan has long had and still has plenty of economic controls, which are well used to implement the government's growth policies as set out in a succession of Four-Year Plans; one could hardly call the country's economy a hands-off, laissez-faire economy. Yet the Taiwanese also know how to press market forces into the service of their economic policies.

In the early 1960s, the Nineteen-Point Economic Financial Reform of the Third Four-Year Plan greatly encouraged investment by private enterprise. In Taiwan today, government does not have the strong ascendancy over private business it still has in Korea, and economic controls tend to be moderate and often make use of the market in a selective and quite sophisticated way. The Taiwanese, like the Koreans, have encouraged exports by creating an essentially free-trade, free-market regime for exports and export production; moreover, unlike the Koreans, they have shown great respect for the strength of market forces, manifest by the careful moderation of their policies when they aim at modifying or deflecting those forces and in the gradual, step-wise fashion in which they change economic controls and policies. Finally, while Korea's development weakened the pull of market forces, Taiwan's strenghtened it.

For a market economy to function properly, it must be competitive. Competition depends on the presence of many small firms and the absence of overwhelmingly large ones. In Taiwan, those conditions of competition and the proper functioning of markets are better fulfilled than in most other private enterprise economies, thanks partly to deliberate policies, and partly to fortuitous circumstances.

To begin with, heavy industries like steel, shipbuilding, and petrochemicals, whose great economies of scale render them natural monopolies in a small country, are publicly owned in Taiwan, probably more for lack of sufficient private resources and interest than for reasons of policy. Privately owned manufacturing firms were usually small in size and few in number in primitive economies, whose forced economic development in mid-twentieth century typically took the form of growth in the size rather than in the number of firms, owing partly to economies of scale and partly to its being so much harder for government to facilitate the establishment of new firms than the growth of already established ones.

Astonishingly enough, Taiwan managed to take the opposite route to development. Between 1966 and 1976, the number of manufacturing firms in Taiwan increased by 150 percent, while the average size of the individual enterprise, as measured by the number of employees, increased by only 29 percent. In Korea, where development took the more common route, the relation between those two changes goes the other way around. The number of manufacturing firms increased by a mere 10 percent, while the number of employees per enterprise increased by 176 percent.

The result of Taiwan's route of development was the much smaller size of private manufacturing enterprises and the more competitive spirit that goes with it. Not counting the very small firms with less than five employees, which are not registered in the Korean census, the average Taiwanese firm in 1976 was only half as big as the Korean, with 34.6 employees compared to 68.8 in Korea. Moreover, the very small firms, ignored by the Korean census, constituted 43 percent of all manufacturing firms in Taiwan, bringing the average size of all Taiwanese firms down to 27 employees. The disparity in firm size between the two countries seems even greater when one looks at their largest firms. In 1981, the $10 billion gross receipts of Hyundai, Korea's largest conglomerate, were three times as big as the $3.5 billion gross receipts of Taiwan's ten largest firms *combined.*

What explains this? There are at least four reasons for the faster increase in the number of Taiwanese firms. One is the immigration of overseas Chinese, who brought with them 30 percent of the total inflow of foreign capital and used it mostly for establishing independent enterprises of their own. A second is Taiwan's much higher personal saving rate, which generally makes it easier to secure the capital for establishing independent businesses. A third factor is probably the much smaller size of the average firm, which makes it easier and cheaper for newcomers to enter the market.

A fourth and possibly most important factor is Taiwan's policy of helping people with entrepreneurial inclinations and know-how but insufficient capital to establish themselves as independent businessmen. For the market to function well, labor, capital, and entrepreneurship must be somehow brought together. One usually thinks of the entrepreneur as the initiating and moving spirit, but real-life capital markets do not lend money to penniless entrepreneurs, and the capitalist owner of a small firm—as most firms are in Taiwan—can seldom afford to hire entrepreneurial talent. To remedy that situation, Taiwan has established forty-nine industrial parks and districts, some of them specialized (like the Youth Industrial Parks and the Science-Based Industrial Park), which provide infrastructure facilities, enable new investors to rent rather than buy land and buildings, and provide generous loans. In such areas, the technical skills of scientifically trained people are accepted as an important part (up to 50 percent) of their personal investment.

Those were the factors facilitating the establishment of new enterprise. Equally important for keeping alive the competitive spirit was the very slow growth of the average enterprise. Yet there is no evidence of official policy deliberately aimed at limiting either the size or the rate of growth of private firms. Indeed, Taiwan has many large private industrial groups, which, though much smaller in size than those in Korea, are sufficiently large and important to have contributed 30 percent of the country's total GDP in the 1980s. The explanation of the relatively slow growth of the size of firms, therefore, lies not in the presence of policies limiting but in the absence of policies encouraging their growth.

This brings us to the subject of monetary policy. The crucial difference between the two countries lay in their very different monetary policies. Taiwan's novel monetary policy was all-important for bringing about conditions favorable to the market economy's functioning as it should, although its effect on the size and growth of firms was an unintended side effect.

The rate of interest, or more correctly the structure of interest rates, is the one price or set of prices whose determination cannot be left entirely to the free play of market forces. Different countries pursue different monetary and interest-rate policies, yet there is a theoretically definable, though practically very hard-to-ascertain equilibrium or natural rate of interest that equates the demand for investable funds at full employment to the supply of full-employment savings; Taiwanese monetary policy may be said to have consistently tried to ascertain what the equilibrium interest rate was and to keep actual interest rates close to that equilibrium level. The beginnings of that monetary policy go back to the early 1950s, but since the same policy is still being adhered to today, and since it has profoundly affected and continues to affect many aspects of Taiwan's economy, a short account of it seems to be in order.

At a time when the universally approved and practiced policy in developing countries was to keep interest rates low to encourage capital accumulation and growth, Taiwan broke new ground and raised the interest rates paid to savers and charged to borrowers to levels almost unheard of at that time. . . .

A high interest-rate policy is, of course, a standard remedy for inflation, but totally unexpected was another effect that also followed Taiwan's adoption of the policy: the acceleration of capital accumulation and growth. Savings deposits accumulated very fast following the substantial raising of the interest paid on deposits, presumably because savers found the high interest rate so attractive that they stopped putting their savings into unproductive but price-increasing hoards of goods and real estate. They may also have increased their saving as a proportion of income. At the same time, however, that high deposit rates raised both the saving rate and the proportion of savings channeled into bank deposits, lending rates apparently were not high enough to reduce business' demand for investable funds to below the rate at which funds became available. In other words, the high deposit and loan rates instituted in Taiwan came close to but did not exceed the equilibrium rate of interest as defined earlier, which explains why raising interest rates raised the level of investment or capital accumulation.

In addition, the raising of interest rates is also likely to have rendered investment a more efficient and more effective engine of growth. For interest rates held below their natural level create excess demand for investable funds and so force the banks to ration credit. Credit rationing, however, usually favors large firms, the banks' established customers, or those whom government wants to favor, and these are not always the ones who earn the highest rate of return on their investments. Accordingly, credit rationing by bank or government policy is likely to crowd out some high-return investments that would not be crowded out if the interest rate were the main factor limiting the demand for credit. In other words, rationing credit by interest rates instead of by bank managers and government officials is almost certain to raise the average return on the total volume of investment, thereby further accelerating growth.

Those advantages of a carefully managed interest-rate policy in both containing inflation and promoting investment and growth have become well known in the literature of development economics, and the policy has been advocated for and imitated by other countries as well. . . . Taiwan's prolonged and consistent adherence to it has also had further advantages much less known but no less important. One is that high interest rates render profitable and encourage the use of labor-intensive methods of production. In developing countries where labor is plentiful but all else is scarce, that is an important advantage: it increases the employment of labor by creating more job opportunities for any given level of investment, and it raises labor's share in the national product. Taiwan is unique among developing countries in that its unemployment rate has been consistently and often much below 2 percent throughout the entire period under review. That excellent record must be credited, in large part, to its high interest-rate policy. Note that so-called Marxian (or structural) unemployment is minimized. In other developing countries such unemployment is due to manufacturing plants and equipment of such nature and quantity that employment for all those who seek it cannot be provided, however high the effective demand for output. That is the reason why stimulating demand has never been an effective employment policy in the developing world.

The high demand for labor due to Taiwan's encouragement and use of labor-intensive methods of production also raised wages and thus labor's share in the national product. Indeed, labor's share in Taiwan's national product has steadily risen, and property's share fallen over the past one and one-half decades, and since wage income is both lower on average and more evenly distributed than property income, that gradual shift in incomes away from capital and in favor of labor has been the main factor in explaining the diminution over time of income inequalities in Taiwan.

Having dealt with the two reasons why the choice of labor-intensive methods of production was an advantage, we can now discuss another advantage of Taiwan's high interest-rate policy that also has to do with income distribution.

. . . [In] today's newly industrializing economies, the typical lender is a small saver, the typical borrower is the corporation, often the large corporation, so that high interest rates favor the low-income saver and limit the profits of business enterprise. In other words, high interest rates transfer a large part of business profits to small savers in the form of interest on their savings, which supplements their wage and salary income. Accordingly, this is yet another factor that contributes to Taiwan's egalitarian income distribution.

One advantage of having high interest rates on savings deposits has already been dealt with: it encourages small savers to increase both their saving rate and the proportion of their savings that they put into bank deposits and so make available for productive use. Another advantage is that it limits profits, which restrains the rate at which the size of the individual enterprise grows. As already shown, the individual firm's size in Taiwan has grown very slowly and stayed small, which has helped to maintain competition.

Yet another advantage of small firms is that they render the always painful adaptation of the economy to changing circumstances a little more bearable. . . .

A final potential advantage of limited profits, mentioned here only for completeness' sake, is their tendency to keep entrepreneurs on their toes and so maintain their efficiency and initiative. Too high and secure profits, whether assured by monopoly advantage or government protection, can destroy entrepreneurial drive. In America, Europe, and Latin America, inefficiency, failure to innovate, and poor economic performance in general have often been traced to that factor. Ironically, in Korea there is no evidence that the large profits and fast accumulation of great fortunes that Korea's economic policies made possible had any unfavorable effects on the drive, stamina, and efficiency of Korea's businesses. Perhaps this is due to the Chinese cultural background.

EXHIBIT I.9. Korea: Egalitarian Distribution and Little Poverty

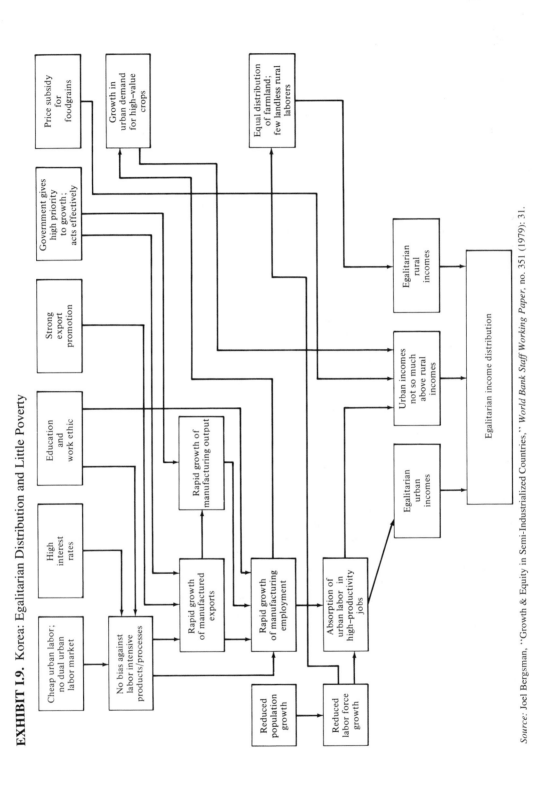

Source: Joel Bergsman, ''Growth & Equity in Semi-Industrialized Countries,'' *World Bank Staff Working Paper,* no. 351 (1979): 31.

EXHIBIT I.10. Changes in South Korea, 1965–91

	Share of Gross Domestic Product (percent) (from current price data)				
	1965	1973	1980	1989	1991
Gross domestic product	100.0	100.0	100.0	100.0	100.0
Total consumption	93.5	78.0	76.2	63.4	53.0
Gross domestic investment	15.1	24.5	31.7	34.5	39.0
Gross domestic saving	7.7	21.6	24.3	37.3	36.0

	Share of Labor Force (percent)			
	1965	1973	1980	1990
Agriculture	55.1	45.1	36.4	18.3
Industry	15.1	22.0	26.8	34.7
Services	29.8	32.8	36.8	47.0
Total	100.0	100.0	100.0	100.0

	Merchandise Exports Value at Current Prices (US$ millions)				
	1980	1987	1988	1989	1990	1991
Total exports f.o.b.	17,505	47,281	60,696	62,377	65,016	71,897

Source: World Bank, *Trends in Developing Economies* (1992), pp. 301–2.

EXHIBIT I.11. East Asia's Stellar Performance (average GNP per capita growth rate, in percent, 1965–90)

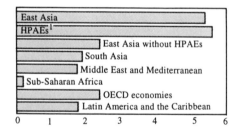

Exceptional Savings and Investment Rates (percent of GDP)

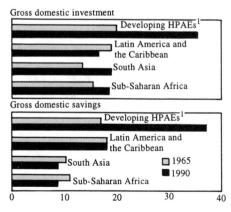

Note: The regional averages are unweighted.
[1]High performing Asian economies (HPAEs): Indonesia, Hong Kong, Japan, Malaysia, the Republic of Korea, Singapore, Taiwan Province of China, and Thailand.
Source: World Bank.

Comment: Success Stories

South Korea and Taiwan join Hong Kong and Singapore in being the success stories of East Asia. Only Japan has experienced, from 1955 to 1976, a period of economic growth comparable to the high rates experienced by South Korea and Taiwan over the past three decades. Moreover, no other economy has had so high a rate of real economic growth over so long a period.

Much of the success in South Korea and Taiwan may be attributed to appropriate policies undertaken by their governments. There is, however, a question of the extent to which government intervened in the economies. The common view is that reliance on markets and the prescriptions of neoclassical economics accelerated South Korea's growth. But for a contrary study, arguing that state intervention in South Korea was more extensive than is commonly recognized, see Robert Wade, *Governance of the Market* (1991). Wade argues that the state played an active role, with government strategies centrally determined and effectively implemented. For Wade, the political explanation for a successful interventionist policy lies in the authoritarian, corporatist state since 1949 in Taiwan, and from 1961 in South Korea. With a single-party-dominated executive, central state policy makers have had a high degree of autonomy. But there has been at the same time a corporatist alliance among the government leaders, an efficient bureaucracy, and local business interests. Government policies have therefore conformed in large part to market opportunities and have altered market signals to provide incentives to business.

See also Larry Westphal, "Industrial Policy in an Export-Propelled Economy: Lessons from South Korea's Experience," *World Development* (Summer 1990). For the government's role in providing information and technology, see H. Pack and L. E. Westphal, "Industrial Strategy and Technological Change: Theory versus Reality," *Journal of Development Economics* (1986), and G. White, ed., *Developmental States in East Asia* (1988).

The most important question arising from the success stories is the extent to which their success in policy making is transferable to other developing countries. For a critical view, see William Cline, "Can the East Asian Model of Development Be Generalized?" *World Development* (February 1982). This is related to the issue whether other developing countries can be major exporters the way the Asian NICs have been. This issue of the new export pessimism is discussed in Chapter IX.

Excellent studies are Walter Galenson, ed., *Economic Growth and Structural Changes in Taiwan* (1979); John C. H. Fei, Gustav Ranis, and Shirley W. Y. Kuo, *Growth with Equity: The Taiwan Case* (1979); E. S. Mason et al., *The Economic and Social Modernization of the Republic of Korea* (1980); A. Amsden, *Asia's Next Giant* (1989); Byung-Nak Song, *The Rise of the Korean Economy* (1990); Helen Hughes, ed., *Explaining the Success of East Asian Industrialization* (1988); Lawrence J. Lau, ed., *Models of Development*, rev. ed. (1990); Ezra Vogel, *The Four Little Dragons* (1991); Paul W. Kuznets, "An East Asian Model of Economic Development," *Economic Development and Cultural Change* (April 1988); Gustav Ranis, ed., *Taiwan: From Developing to Mature Economy* (1992); World Bank, *East Asian Miracle* (1993); and Cho Soon, *Dynamics of Korean Development* (1994).

I.C.2. Latin America*

A number of generalizations that describe and explain the differences in growth rates between Asia and Latin America have become quite common in academic and popular discussion. The first is perhaps the most general of all.

*From Seiji Naya et al., eds., *Lessons in Development: A Comparative Study of Asia and Latin America* (San Francisco: ICS Press, 1989), pp. 5–11, 252–53. Reprinted by permission.

GENERALIZATION 1: *In the late 1970s and through the 1980s, Asia has experienced rapid growth, while Latin America has stagnated.*

As early as the 1950s, it had seemed to many observers that some of the larger Latin American countries, in particular Brazil, Mexico, Argentina, and Venezuela, were poised for rapid long-term growth. Indeed, the term "NICs" was initially coined in reference to these Latin

American countries more than to the Asian NICs, and most Latin American countries started with higher per capita incomes than are now found in Asia outside the NICs. Therefore, the basic question that arises is why the growth of Latin American countries slowed.

GENERALIZATION 2: *The Asian countries identified in the 1960s as potential NICs succeeded, but those so identified in Latin America did not.*

Among the numerous explanations of this differential growth is that the Asian NICs have been united by a quasi-Confucian ethic. [Some would] argue that emphasis on a few Confucian values, such as loyalty, respect for elders, and a strong work ethic, was a key factor in the growth of the Asian NICs. This suggestion is similar to the religious and sociological explanations for the growth of the West in the last century. Certainly an observer is impressed with the continuation of traditional values in social and family life in many parts of Asia, continuation that may have contributed to the greater orderliness that is found there. This may be an important factor that has a bearing, for instance, on differences in industrial organization in Asia and the West. For example, it has been pointed out that the labor force of the Asian NICs exhibits more self-discipline than that of any other in the world economy. Yet the question of cultural influence is a complicated and technical one that needs to be (and is being) seriously addressed by cultural and political historians. It is not something on which economists can speak with comparative advantage.

Instead, the kind of explanation that the economist finds more appealing tends to be the following:

GENERALIZATION 3: *Asia has had more market-oriented and less-regulated economic policies than Latin America. There have been more incentives encouraging entrepreneurship and private initiative in Asia; there also has been greater confidence in and between the government and the private sector.*

This again is a broadly true statement that requires some qualification. The Asian NICs are well known for their policies emphasizing market- and private-sector development. At the same time, the policies of the Asian NICs (ex-cept Hong Kong's) are not laissez-faire policies, and in fact their governments do a great deal to determine the shape and direction of their economies' development. Chen proposes that this be called "neoclassical interventionism," since the policies adopted are based on neoclassical principles, with greater reliance on incentives and the market system. That is, the government intervenes, but only in a manner that—insofar as these policies are intended either to correct market distortions or achieve certain social goals—will facilitate the market system. The ASEAN-4 countries also have emphasized market-oriented policies, though less so than the Asian NICs.

On the other hand, the governments of the South Asian countries have traditionally intervened in every facet of the production process. Here the government, through its public enterprises, is a large producer of a wide range of goods. Several of these South Asian countries, like many Latin American ones, are in the process of easing regulations, but most are finding it a difficult task. How far, how fast, and in what order to liberalize are questions that must be further addressed. The task is made more difficult because in Latin America and South Asia, unlike in the NICs and the ASEAN-4 countries, there is a wariness and a mutual lack of confidence between the government and the private sector.

GENERALIZATION 4: *Asia has had more outward-looking trade and exchange-rate policies than Latin America.*

Despite extensive government intervention, trade regimes in the NICs have generally been left to market forces. In fact, Hong Kong and Singapore are virtually free-trade economies, while the level of protection in Taiwan is also very low. Although tariff levels are somewhat higher in Korea, they are still generally lower than those of other developing countries. Further, protected industries in Korea were required to become competitive and begin exporting within a short period of time. This meant that efficiency and competition have been promoted rather than suppressed.

One reason the NICs moved against the conventional wisdom and toward outward-looking policies was that their small markets and lack of natural resources made import–substitution policies untenable. Unlike the resource-rich larger countries in both Latin America and Asia, the NICs had few other options.

In contrast, most developing countries, including the Southeast Asian, South Asian, and Latin American countries, followed the economic wisdom of that time and allowed their industries to hide behind high tariff walls. This provided a quick spurt of growth that did not last once the domestic market was satiated. The large profits that were gained by inefficient domestic producers in a protected market invariably led to the creation of special-interest groups supporting the continuation of such policies. Because of the foreign exchange received from producing and exporting primary commodities, the ASEAN-4 and Latin American countries were able to sustain expensive import–substitution policies. However, such policies supported overvalued exchange rates, which discriminated against manufactured exports.

Further, commodity exporters were affected by the problem of booming sectors. With high commodity prices, other exporting industries were hurt by the appreciating domestic currencies. For example, the textile industry in Colombia went into crisis in the early 1980s despite efforts by the government to prevent revaluation of the domestic currency. . . .

More generally, there may have been a basic difference between parts of Asia and Latin America in their perceptions of export opportunities. For example, in Latin America the predominance of commodity exports and the low income elasticity of demand for commodities has generated more pessimism than has been the case in East or Southeast Asia. In contrast, despite the slower growth of world trade and the fact that the NICs and ASEAN-4 economies have faced at least as much, and possibly more, Western protectionism in the 1970s and 1980s than have Latin American economies, there seems to have been less "export pessimism" in Asia than in Latin America.

GENERALIZATION 5: *Asia has been more concerned with macroeconomic stability than Latin America, especially with respect to inflation and debt management.*

A few Asian countries have experienced repressed inflation and shortage and have not followed prudent borrowing or debt-management policies. Most of them, however, have adopted pragmatic policies and approaches with respect to debt management and inflationary expectations, in contrast to the less-restrained expenditure policies of Latin America. To this may be added the relatively higher rates of real saving in East and Southeast Asia than in Latin America. Furthermore, in contrast to many Latin American countries, saving rates have increased since 1970 in all East and Southeast Asian countries except the Philippines. Because of moderate levels of inflation, realistic interest rates, and the strong economic performance of the region, capital flight has not been a problem in Asia. . . .

The nominal growth of the Latin American economies in the 1960s and 1970s was financed by extensive borrowing, with the borrowed funds too often used not for productive investment but to pay for public sector consumption. The financial sectors of the Latin American countries were flooded by a large supply of capital available for borrowing in the 1970s, and the low or even negative real interest rates signaled the Latin American countries to borrow more rather than to produce for export.

Moreover, while economists in Asia would agree that high rates of real inflation are inimical to real economic growth due to the uncertainties and unanticipated transfers that inflation causes, the same may not be true of Latin America. Until only very recently, there has been relatively little consensus among Latin American economists and government officials with respect to economic policies, and there has not been the same sense of direction in Latin America with respect to macroeconomic policy that is found in the NICs. However, because of the serious distortions caused by inflation and hyperinflation (despite indexation of wages and prices), there is emerging a growing consensus among Latin American economists on the importance of lower inflation rates to support economic growth.

GENERALIZATION 6: *Efforts at regional cooperation succeed when they are not too ambitious; they should work to create trust and information capital.*

Latin America has the longest experience of regional cooperation beginning with the Central American Common Market (CACM) and the Latin American Free Trade Association (LAFTA) in the late 1950s and early 1960s. As the names suggest, these were ambitious attempts to form large markets with no tariff barriers. Asia has had a shorter history of regional cooperation. The Association of Southeast Asian Nations (ASEAN) was formed in 1967 without such ambitious goals. More recently, in 1985, the South Asian Association of Regional Cooperation (SAARC) was formed. These attempts at cooperation have taken different forms and have met with various degrees of success.

Efforts at regional cooperation can lead to more and better contacts, information, and channels of communication, all of which may reduce transaction costs and increase the stock of what may be called the "information capital" available to traders and potential traders. Such an invisible stock of trust or information capital can be very valuable. Bureaucracies may be needed to maintain this stock. While there is the danger that these new bureaucracies, once created, will develop lives of their own that are independent of their original purposes, the net gain may nevertheless be positive.

Attempts at integration often face the problem of intraregional trade expansion being limited by lack of complementarity in the export structures of the regional partners. Exports are often concentrated in primary products that are destined for Western markets. The question of how the structure of production can be expanded to allow for greater trade is central to most regional integration schemes. The Latin American experience clearly shows the problems of pursuing industrial programs of agreed-upon specialization, where regional production of certain goods is designated to selected countries. ASEAN's attempt at a regional industrial scheme also failed. Two major lessons that can be drawn from these experiences are the importance of a slow approach to integration as well as the need to maintain openness with the rest of the world.

GENERALIZATION 7: *Asia has had more political stability than Latin America.*

In the Asian countries, there have been few changes in government leadership in the past ten years and in some cases twenty years. for example, Lee Kuan Yew was the leader of Singapore's government for almost thirty years, and Suharto governed Indonesia for more than twenty years.

In addition to the generally long tenure of political regimes in Asia, the economic policies followed have generally reflected a pragmatism on the part of the government that, typically, has extended into the next regime despite differences in political ideology. For example, even when political coups occurred in Thailand in the 1970s and Korea in the 1980s, economic policies remained basically unchanged.

GENERALIZATION 8: *Latin America has had more of a trend toward democratization than Asia.*

Of course there are major exceptions to this. The large and vibrant Indian democracy thrives as it has done for half a century, democratic institutions continue in Sri Lanka even in the midst of civil war, and the Philippines experienced an important democratic revolution only a few years ago. At the same time, dictatorships continue in some Latin American countries. Yet for a variety of reasons, the last decade has witnessed a broad trend toward political democratization in Latin America. While Latin American economists (of all persuasions) seem frank enough to be highly critical of many aspects of the management of economic policies in their part of the world, they take some pride in these recent political trends. Asian economists on the other hand are sometimes a little complacent and self-congratulatory with respect to the economic successes in their region, and they may need to move increasingly toward improvements in the nature of their political institutions.

Each of the eight generalizations given above contains an important element of truth (although the reader is reminded of the difficulties that are involved in making large-scale comparisons and contrasts).

EXHIBIT I.12. GDP Average Annual Growth Rate (percent)

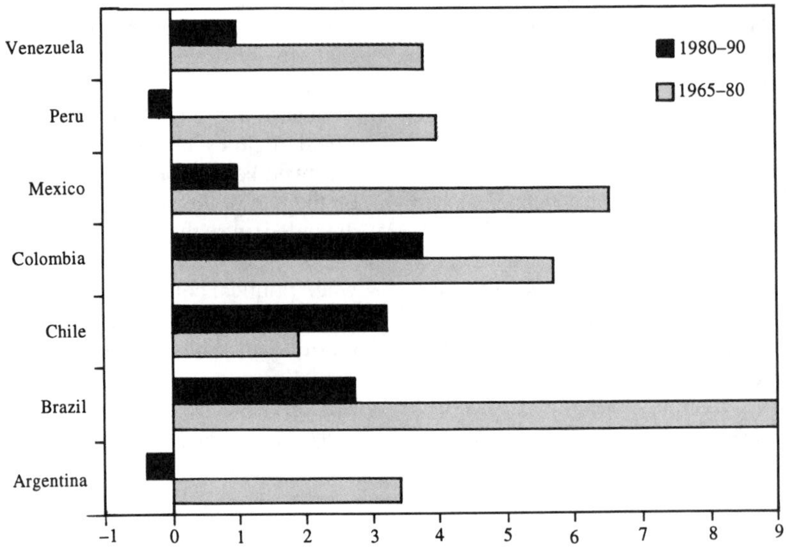

Comment: Latin American Case Studies

Although the 1980s represented a lost decade for Latin American countries, a number of countries are undertaking policy reforms in the 1990s that portend considerable improvement in their development performance. Notable are reforms in Bolivia, Costa Rica, Chile, Mexico, and Venezuela.

For some country studies, see R. Dornbusch and S. Edwards, eds., *Macroeconomics of Populism in Latin America* (1991); Stephan Haggard, *Pathways from the Periphery* (1991); John Williamson, *Latin American Adjustment: How Much Has Happened?* (1990); V. Corbo and J. de Melo, "Lessons from the Southern Cone Policy Reforms," *World Bank Research Observer* (1987); Jeffrey D. Sachs, *Social Conflicts and Populist Policies in Latin America* (1990); Eliana Cardoso and Ann Helwege, *Latin America's Economy* (1991); Victor J. Elias, *Sources of Growth: A Study of Seven Latin American Economies* (1992); Simon Teitel, ed., *Towards a New Development Strategy for Latin America* (1992); and Inter-American Development Bank's series of reports *Economic and Social Progress in Latin America* (annual), since 1961.

I.C.3. Sub-Saharan Africa*

The Record

Official estimates show that, on average, incomes in SSA are today no higher than 20 years ago and are well down over the last decade. There have also been comparatively large and persistent balance of payments and inflation problems, very low levels of saving and investment, and a declining productivity of investment. Table 1 summarizes some of the evidence and compares the African record with that of other low-income countries.

The economic comparisons are clearly to the

*From Overseas Development Institute, *Explaining Africa's Development Experiences*, Briefing Paper, June 1992. Reprinted by permission.

disadvantage of SSA. The comparatively poor record on export volumes, and the failure to diversify out of primary product exports, is arguably the most serious of these. The social indicators are better, showing improving mortality rates and school enrollments but even here, other low-income countries mostly made more progress, and the dietary comparison is particularly adverse. Progress with the enlargement of secondary school enrollments was a notable exception to these unfavorable comparisons. There are, however, concerns that in some SSA countries the quality of schooling has deteriorated and there is evidence of declining enrollment rates in recent years. . . .

There are, of course, large differences in the

TABLE 1. Comparative Indicators of Economic Performance

		Low-Income SSA	All-Low Income Countries
		SSA		
Economic Growth, 1980–89 (percent p.a.)				
Income (GNP) per capita		−1.2	−1.1	+0.7
Private consumption per capita		−2.2	−0.5	−0.5
Export volumes		−0.7	−1.8	+0.8
Prices (inflation rate)		+19.6	+30.2	+14.8
Structural Indicators				
Gross domestic savings as percent	1965	14	—	18
GDP	1989	13	—	26
Gross domestic investment as	1965	14	—	19
percent GDP	1989	15	—	28
Primary products as	1965	92	—	76
percent total exports	1989	89	—	48
Energy consumption	1965	72	—	125
per capita*	1989	73	—	330
Social Indicators (percent change 1965–89)				
Crude death rate		−32	−30	−39
Infant mortality rate		−32	−30	−37
Calorie supply per capita		−1	0	+13
Primary school enrollment		+55	+58	+60
Secondary school enrollment		+314	+292	+207

Note: * = kgs of oil equivalent.
Source: World Bank, various.

resource endowments, structures, performances and problems of African economies. There are major differences between the situations of oil-importing and exporting countries. The Franc Zone arrangements place most Francophone African countries in a special category. Countries in the Sahelian zone and the Horn of Africa have a special vulnerability to uncertain rainfall.

Figure 1 illustrates the wide spread of experiences by reference to the growth of per capita income in 1965–1990. Over that period substantial increases are shown for a number of countries, while in a slightly larger number, average incomes are today lower than they were a quarter of a century ago. The record is not uniformly bad. Yet strong performers like Botswana and Mauritius are distinguished more by their special circumstances than by their potential as role-

FIGURE 1. Change in per capita GNP, 1965–90 (percent per annum).

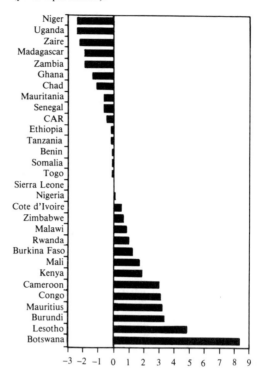

models. The more recent record has been worse and most of the countries listed in Figure 1 were unable to prevent declines in per capita incomes during the 1980s. Some of the worst performers, such as Sudan and Mozambique, are not included in the Figure; nor is it weighted by population. (Nigeria's stagnation and Zaire's decline far outweigh the growth of the smaller countries.) Yet there are many common characteristics and substantial similarities in experience; this paper is concerned with what the economies of SSA have in common rather than with the differences. . . .

Economic Policies

The poor quality of past economic policies is often blamed for SSA's unhappy experience, particularly policy biases which contributed to the poor export and balance-of-payments record. There was a tendency until the early 1980s to maintain fixed and over-valued exchange rates, with a two-fifths average real appreciation during the 1970s. Over-valuation reduced the profitability of exporting and this disincentive was compounded by other policy biases. A substantial proportion of export receipts was often withheld from producers as a result of export taxes (overt or covert) and the inflated costs of state monopoly marketing agencies. Exceptionally high levels of industrial protection also acted as a tax on exporters, by raising the cost of local inputs and biasing relative prices in favour of import substitution. Inadequate supporting services and a crumbling infrastructure often made things worse.

Implicit in the above was another common feature of the 1960s and 1970s: relative neglect of agriculture. To the pro-urban bias of import substitution, particularly in manufacturing, and the taxation of cash crops can be added, in some cases, price controls on foodstuffs, depressing the prices paid to farmers; underresourced inefficient research and extension services; and underinvestment in rural infrastructure.

"Financial repression" was another common feature: interest rates controlled at well below market levels; lending decisions based on political and other non-financial criteria; a variety of devices for capturing a disproportionate share of domestic credit to finance the deficits of the public sector. Such "repression" is blamed for holding back the development of financial systems, frustrating the credit requirements of private businesses, and contributing to low-productivity investment.

The large need of the public sector for bank credit reflected two further weaknesses: deteriorating fiscal balances and unprofitable public enterprises. The evidence indicates that governments were increasingly unable to meet even their recurrent expenditures from tax revenues, contributing to the deteriorating savings position, and to inflationary and balance-of-payments pressures. The number of public enterprises was greatly expanded and, while some of them performed well, they were the exceptions. The inefficiency of some—in the delivery of agricultural services, export marketing, banking, manufacturing, and retailing—further contributed to the poor economic record under examination.

Another common weakness was a preference in the 1960s and 1970s for the use of controls and discretionary powers rather than policy interventions which operate through market incentives. Controls over imports and prices, a multitude of licensing requirements, and other restrictions on economic life often had the effect of tying-up high-level manpower, created large opportunities for corruption, and spawned parallel (black) markets.

The economic role of the state was in these ways often expanded well beyond its capacity to perform efficiently. It seems likely that this over-expansion contributed to the serious decline in the productivity of investment which also occurred. It may also have undermined the state as an instrument for economic change, by widening the gap between the expectations created and the ability of governments to satisfy these expectations, alienating the people. Some of the chosen forms of intervention themselves hastened the decline of the state, by creating parallel markets, shrinking the tax base, and eroding those aspects of economic life within the control of the state.

Some governments failed notoriously to provide basic security for their peoples. Wars—civil and international—, political instability, and breakdowns of the rule of law have brought suffering to a multitude of Africans—displacing many, forcing others to retreat into the subsistence economy or to operate in the twilight zone of the parallel economy, contributing to the creation of burdensome armies.

The Effects of Personal Rule

Some of the policy weaknesses identified above were also in evidence in various Asian and Latin American countries. One of the features which has placed SSA into a special category, however, was the slowness of its governments to respond to the deteriorating economic results produced by these weaknesses. In many cases deficient policies were sustained for many years so the question arises, why was the policy response so slow? Why were policies harmful to the economy allowed to remain for so long even though governments' popularity, even legitimacy, was undermined by the resulting economic decline? Why were so many of the subsequent policy changes initiated from outside and why has progress with these reforms been slow? In the search for answers to these questions, political, historical, and cultural forces appear to be at least as important as the economic factors described above.

For many political scientists "personal rule" models of African political systems are particularly persuasive. They see the position of modern African rulers and their governments as maintained by patron-client relationships, largely based on familial and ethnic loyalties. Followers are rewarded with preferential access to loans, import licenses, contracts, and jobs. Institutional rules and constitutional checks are swept aside in the struggle to maintain power. The distinction between the public and private domains becomes blurred.

Governments which conform to this model are unlikely to care much about broad-based, long-term economic development. Indeed they are seen as destructive of it, with the pursuit of personal aggrandizement and short-term political advantage leading to economic irrationality. As rule becomes more personalized and power more concentrated, so policies are apt to become less predictable, more arbitrary. Manipulating the distribution of wealth becomes more important than its creation.

Despite its explanatory value, there are particularly large dangers of over-generalizing here and of appearing to denigrate all African governments. Nonetheless, the personal rule model appears able to predict and explain a number of the policy weaknesses described earlier:

- The proliferation of generally over-manned public enterprises and, more generally, the over-expansion of the state relative to the private sector to maximize opportunities for patronage.
- The preference for direct controls and discretionary actions over interventions that work impersonally through the market, for similar motives.
- Inward-looking import-substitution policies, to provide further opportunities for rewarding important urban groups; and the neglect of (politically unimportant) peasant farmers.
- Financial repression and politicized credit allocation mechanisms, in order to have cheap credit to offer to supporters.
- The persistence of anti-development policies long after their ill-effects have become apparent, because their primary function was to provide a system of rewards and maintain the ruler in power, rather than to promote development per se.

History and Social Structure

It is evident that personal rule and clientelist-based politics occur in many parts of the world but they do appear to have been particularly pervasive in Africa. If this is so, the question becomes why the region has offered such fertile soil for the growth of this style of politics. A full exploration of Africa's development experience thus requires reference to social structures, values, and historical experiences unique to SSA. . . .

Initial Conditions and Structural Weaknesses

Whatever the validity of these wider political and cultural factors, they do not alone explain Africa's development experience. Further explanations are provided by reference to other conditions at the time of independence, and to chronic weaknesses in the structures of its economies, in respect of which the average African economy was at a serious disadvantage relative to other developing countries at the beginning of the 1960s.

- Populations were largely illiterate and there were acute shortages of educated and trained personnel. Thus, in 1960 the proportion of people enrolled in tertiary education relative to the population aged 20–24 was less than half of one percent in 16 of the 18 SSA countries for which estimates are available, compared to 2 percent for all low-income countries taken together and 4 percent for middle-income countries. This has had serious and long-lived consequences for attempts at modernization, and for SSA's capacity to absorb and adapt modern technologies. Modern approaches to the determinants of economic growth place real importance upon such human and technological capacities.
- As another aspect of under-developed human resources, the relative absence of an indigenous entrepreneurial class equipped to employ modern know-how to the development of substantial productive firms.
- The heavy dependence on primary product exports induced by the colonial approach to development; the consequentially under-developed condition, and distorted nature, of the infrastructure of transport and communications, oriented towards trade with Europe rather than internal development.
- The tiny size of the domestic market for industrial goods (which today for a typical SSA country is about $\frac{1}{300}$ that of an average-size industrial country), operating as a major constraint upon industrialization (a constraint greatly aggravated by import–substitution strategies based on the home market).
- Market mechanisms operated poorly, due to the poverty of the economies, their small size, weak communications and infrastructure, low literacy, and scarcities of modern skills. These conditions created extensive dualism and much monopoly outside of traditional agriculture and marketing.

These initial conditions can, in turn, be seen as resulting in inflexible economic structures and a low economy-wide capability of adapting to changing needs. Combined with a predominantly primary production base, these conditions interacted with personal rule to reduce economic responsiveness. This helps explain the static composition of exports, and could be why the response of African economies to structural adjustment programmes has been sluggish by comparison with other developing economies.

In respect of most of the initial conditions just surveyed, the SSA situation was worse (often much worse) than was typical of countries in Asia and Latin America at a comparable stage, helping to answer the question, why Africa? With hindsight, absolutely and comparatively poor development performance could have been predicted, although that was not how it was seen at the time. It is therefore inappropriate to describe the SSA experience as one of ''failure.'' Sustained rapid development would have been extraordinary.

EXHIBIT I.13. Key Macroeconomic Ratios, 1960–90: Sub-Saharan Africa (annual average as percentage of GDP)

	1960–69	1970–74	1975–79	1980–84	1990
Gross Domestic Investment Total Sub-Saharan Africa	15.6	19.5	24.2	20.3	16.0
Gross Domestic Savings Total Sub-Saharan Africa	14.4	19.8	21.0	15.9	16.0
Private Consumption Total Sub-Saharan Africa	73.2	67.1	65.0	69.9	68.0
Public Consumption Total Sub-Saharan Africa	12.4	13.1	14.0	14.3	15.0
Exports of Goods and Nonfactor Services Total Sub-Saharan Africa	25.6	24.8	25.7	23.2	29.0
Imports of Goods and Nonfactor Services Total Sub-Saharan Africa	26.7	24.4	28.9	27.9	30.0

Note: Numbers are weighted averages.
Source: World Bank data.

EXHIBIT I.14. Sub-Saharan Africa, Basic Indicators

	Population (millions) Mid-1990	Area (thousand of square kilometers)	GNP Per Capita		Average Index of Food Production per Capita 1978–81 = 100 1988–90	Life Expectancy at Birth (years) 1990
			Dollars 1990	Average Annual Growth Rate (percent) 1965–90		
Mozambique	15.7	802	80	—	81	47
Tanzania	24.5	945	110	−0.2	88	48
Ethiopia	51.2	1,222	120	−0.2	84	48
Somalia	7.8	638	120	−0.1	94	48
Chad	5.7	1,284	190	−1.1	85	47
Malawi	8.5	118	200	0.9	83	46
Burundi	5.4	28	210	3.4	92	47
Zaïre	37.3	2,345	220	−2.2	97	52
Uganda	16.3	236	220	−2.4	95	47
Madagascar	11.7	587	230	−1.9	88	51
Sierra Leone	4.1	72	240	0.0	89	42
Mali	8.5	1,240	270	1.7	97	48

EXHIBIT I.14. (*continued*)

	Population (millions) Mid-1990	Area (thousand of square kilometers)	GNP Per Capita		Average Index of Food Production per Capita 1978–81 = 100 1988–90	Life Expectancy at Birth (years) 1990
			Dollars 1990	Average Annual Growth Rate (percent) 1965–90		
Nigeria	115.5	924	290	0.1	106	52
Niger	7.7	1,267	310	−2.4	71	45
Rwanda	7.1	26	310	1.0	77	48
Burkina Faso	9.0	274	330	1.3	114	48
Benin	4.7	113	360	−0.1	112	50
Kenya	24.2	580	370	1.9	106	59
Ghana	14.9	239	390	−1.4	97	55
Central African Rep.	3.0	623	390	−0.5	91	49
Togo	3.6	57	410	−0.1	88	54
Zambia	8.1	753	420	−1.9	103	50
Guinea	5.7	246	440	—	87	43
Mauritania	2.0	1,026	500	−0.6	85	47
Lesotho	1.8	30	530	4.9	86	56
Liberia	2.6	111	—	—	84	54
Suidan	25.1	2,506	—	—	71	50
Zimbabwe	9.8	391	640	0.7	94	61
Senegal	7.4	197	710	−0.6	102	47
Côte d'Ivoire	11.9	322	750	0.5	101	55
Cameroon	11.7	475	960	3.0	89	57
Congo	2.3	342	1,010	3.1	94	53
Botswana	1.3	582	2,040	8.4	75	67
Mauritius	1.1	2	2,250	3.2	100	70
Angola	10.0	1,247	—	—	81	46
Gabon	1.1	268	3,330	0.9	84	53
Sub-Saharan Africa	495.2 t	23,066 t	340 w	0.2 w	94 w	51 w

Note: t = total; *w* = weighted average.

Source: World Bank, *World Development Report 1992* (1992), pp. 218–19.

Comment: Sub-Saharan Africa's Inferior Performance

Several studies examine Africa's generally poor performance: Tony Killick, "Development Planning in Africa: Experiences, Weaknesses, and Prescriptions," *Development Policy Review*, 1 (May 1983), and "Explaining Africa's Post-Independence Development Experiences," ODI Working Paper 60 (January 1992); World Bank, *Sub-Saharan Africa: From Crisis to Sustainable Growth* (1989), and *The Long-Term Perspective Study of Sub-Saharan Africa* (1990); and Douglas Rimmer, ed., *Africa Thirty Years On* (1991).

Killick summarizes his argument in the following propositions:

1. Notwithstanding poor data and considerable inter-country differences, SSA's post-Independence record on economic growth, modernisation, macroeconomic management and, to a lesser extent, social welfare has been poor, when judged against the aspirations of its peoples and the achievements of other developing regions.

2. Explanations have been sought from different directions. As regards *economic explanations*, only modest weight has been given to two commonly asserted sources of difficulty: a hostile world environment and rapid population growth. Even the overhang of external debt, which is strongly linked with the stagnation of the 1980s, is seen primarily as reflecting domestic weaknesses. Poor export performance, and the factors contributing to that, have been given pride of place, including past exchange rate over-valuation and various other policy interventions which have biased incentives against exports. The declining productivity, and limited volume, of investment have also been stressed, as have the adverse consequences of fiscal weaknesses and the over-expansion of the economic role of the state.

3. Economic explanations only take us so far, however, for they leave unanswered the question why anti-developmental policies were adopted and allowed to remain in place for so long. To answer this we

looked at *political factors*. Political instability is one source of difficulty but we pay particular attention to "patrimonial" models of African politics. Such models seem able to predict quite a number of the policy weaknesses previously described, which increases their persuasiveness, although we point out the dangers of over-generalising about Africa's varied political reality. In any case, the patrimonial model still leaves us with the question, why Africa and not other regions?

4. This search thus led into the *historical and social* particularities of the continent, concluding that a conjuncture of demographic, social, and historical influences unique to SSA resulted in a situation ready-made for the spread of clientelist-based political systems. The fragility of post-Independence nation-states reinforced the incentive to use patronage and a centralised authoritarianism. These factors combined with the experiences of late colonialism and various intellectual influences to result in many of the policy choices which hindsight shows to have been anti-developmental.

5. We finally drew attention to other comparative disadvantages with which SSA entered the 1960s, in terms of the stock of human and inanimate capital, technological capacities, and institutional development which together define the region's *social capabilities* for rapid economic development. And we stressed the problems created by the smallness of the domestic market and the economic inflexibility which characterises most SSA economies.[1]

[1]Killick, "Explaining Africa's Post-Independence Development Experiences."

I.C.4. Lessons for Sub-Saharan Africa*

For the developing world as a whole, the past 25 years have seen unprecedented progress:

- Per capita income in low-income countries has nearly doubled over the last generation—growing faster than the United Kingdom during the Industrial Revolution, faster than the United States in its period of rapid growth as it came to economic maturity, and faster than Japan during its prewar growth spurt;
- Life expectancy has increased by ten years—twice the gain the United States could achieve by eliminating both cancer and heart disease; and
- Infant mortality rates have been nearly halved, child death rates have plummeted, and immunization rates have skyrocketed.

But this impressive overall performance conceals an extremely uneven pattern of progress. While some countries in East Asia have seen their incomes double and then double again, 36 nations are poorer today than they were a generation ago—19 of them in Sub-Saharan Africa. One in every two Africans lives in a nation that has lost ground over the last 25 years, compared with only one in 20 Asians or one in four Latin Americans, meaning social development has stagnated or even suffered reversals. In many

*From Lawrence H. Summers, "The Challenges of Development," *Finance & Development* (March 1992), pp. 6–8. Reprinted by permission.

African countries today, children are more likely to have their development stunted by lower birth weight, higher malnutrition, and poorer access to primary education than their siblings born in the late 1970s and early 1980s.

Why, in the face of so much progress, have 36 countries with a combined population of over half a billion people actually regressed? The World Bank's *1991 World Development Report* provides two explanations:

- First, national development failures are the fault of national policies—they cannot be blamed on a hostile international environment, or physical limits to growth; and
- Second, national policies have failed when governments thwarted progress, supplanting markets rather than supporting them.

Why Has Development Failed?

In searching for an answer to this difficult question, several reasons are often cited that seem to absolve national governments of responsibility. Perhaps the least plausible is a lack of foreign aid. Just look across continents—Africa received 8 percent of its income in foreign aid in 1989, much higher than the 1.7 percent for South Asia, 0.7 percent for East Asia, and 0.4 percent for Latin America. Eastern Europe dreams of, but does not expect to receive, 2 percent of its income in foreign assistance. True,

Africa is poor so its aid share in income looks big. But Africa received four times as much assistance per person as Asia in 1989, and Africa's share of world aid has risen even as it has fallen further behind.

What about terms of trade? Terms of trade have turned against some commodity exporters in recent years, and many are on the list of countries that have regressed. But this can hardly explain why some countries succeeded while others failed. A comparison is telling. In 1965, Thailand was poorer than Ghana, Uganda, and Niger, and even as late as 1970, was more dependent on commodity exports than Kenya or Côte d'Ivoire. Yet today, Thailand is emerging as a newly industrialized economy, with manufactures accounting for more than half of exports.

Despite all the complaints about declining terms of trade, African countries have not fared well in maintaining their share of the market. From 1970 to 1986, Ghana's share of cocoa exports slipped from 29 percent to 8 percent, Uganda's share of coffee exports fell by almost 50 percent, and Sudan's share of cotton exports dropped by more than half. If Africa had simply managed to maintain its share, it would have enjoyed an additional $10 billion in export revenues—a figure approaching its total foreign aid receipts.

What about debt? Africa's debt burden is crushing, and there is no realistic prospect of the debts being repaid. But those burdens are a consequence, not a cause, of the miserable return that has been earned on the investments that debt financed. In 1980, the ratio of debt to GNP was 49 percent in South Korea and 28 percent in Indonesia, compared to 9 percent in Nigeria, 29 percent in Ghana, 33 percent in Zaïre and 50 percent in Tanzania and Kenya. Debt did not stop these two Asian countries from prospering, and it need not have stopped any African nation. Of course, what is past is past, and as shall be indicated later on, there is a compelling case for debt reduction when and if countries undertake serious reforms in their policy environment.

Finally, what about inherent absolute physical limitations on nations' ability to provide for growth? In some cases of regress, Argentina for example, this clearly does not apply. Nor is it very persuasive in Africa. Agricultural yields per hectare have more than doubled over the last 30 years in the developing world, but they have risen by less than 30 percent in Africa. There is no question that with proper incentives for farmers and adequate infrastructures, Africa could greatly expand its food output.

Policies That Work

Where then can we turn for guidance? Certainly, there is one simple but often neglected lesson: War stops development. Almost all of the 36 countries that have lost ground over the last 25 years have been involved in a substantial military conflict. The Middle East is often thought of as the world's tinderbox; yet relative to population, Africans have three times as high a war fatality rate. In the last 30 years, wars have claimed nearly seven million victims, either directly or indirectly, by making the provision of food and basic social services difficult or impossible. Today, post-Cold War, the threat of "hot" war in Africa persists. Sub-Saharan African governments spend four times as much on the military as on health, and equal amounts on the military and education. By contrast, in East Asia, spending on both health and education far exceeds military outlays.

But what else does the development record have to offer? A review of the successes and failures suggests four key lessons about government policies. In essence: governments that fail do too much and do it badly; successful governments do less and do it better.

Sound macroeconomic policies with sustainable fiscal deficits and realistic exchange rates are a prerequisite to progress. Large government budget deficits absorb domestic saving and foreign funds that could otherwise be channeled to the private sector. They crowd out more productive investments, frequently placing the financial system under great strain. Often they induce rapid inflation, which exacerbates the deficit, creating a vicious cycle. Deficits also lead to overvalued exchange rates, thereby stifling exports, damaging domestic producers, and creating pressures for protectionism. Look at Zaïre and Thailand in the late 1980s. Thailand enjoyed stable rapid growth with low deficits, while Zaïre suffered large deficits and bore the consequences in terms of lost export competitiveness, reduced private investment, and slow growth.

If persistent government budget deficits are the surest route to economic failure, an artificially overvalued exchange rate must be the runner up. Overvaluation leads to the rationing of foreign exchange, which historically means that those in government and their friends skim off large rents. It creates pressure for layer after layer of controls on imports, capital flows, and even travel. It also destroys emerging export industries, perhaps the most important foundation for growth.

There is an easy and reliable way to identify unrealistic exchange rate policies: compare the official rate with the parallel market rate. Studies demonstrate that when the spread is wide, growth slows, returns on investment decline, and the prospect of financial crisis and capital flight increases. That a strong currency makes for a strong economy is a particularly damaging myth. The Asian success stories were all built around the export growth created by low, realistic, real exchange rates. In 1970, Indonesia's manufactured exports were less than Nigeria's and are now 36 times as large, and Malaysia's were three and a half times Kenya's and are now 52 times bigger.

A permissive rather than a prohibitive policy environment is essential for the private sector. The great debate over economic systems is now over. Almost no one disagrees that communism is the longest way from capitalism to capitalism. For all their faults, competitive markets are the best way man has yet found to get goods and services produced efficiently.

What does creating a permissive environment for the private sector entail? One thing it means is avoiding government monopolies or punitive regulations. The tremendous success of the Nigerians in abolishing agricultural marketing boards and moving toward a realistic exchange rate is clear. Output of a number of key export crops, including cocoa, has increased by more than 50 percent since low points reached in the mid-1980s. Indeed, the production of both rubber and cotton has quadrupled since 1986; soybean production and processing have risen even more.

A permissive environment also means allowing market forces to determine prices without price controls or large subsidies. Fertilizer policies in many African countries exemplify what is wrong with price controls—the resulting rationing implies that some well-connected farmers secure large amounts of fertilizer at low cost, while those less well-connected find fertilizer less available and more expensive.

Finally, a permissive environment is one where government seeks to reduce rather than increase the cost of doing business. That means lowering tariffs and quotas on crucial intermediate and capital goods. According to a recent study, investment costs are 50 percent higher in Africa than in South Asia, and this is just the cost of capital goods, with no account taken of the additional costs caused by the inefficient provision of infrastructure. The need for business to maintain their own capacity for generating electricity is an example.

Government has no business attempting to directly manage the production of private goods and services. Around the world, the record of public enterprise management is one of disaster. While it may be true in theory that a properly managed public enterprise can be as productive and efficient as a private one, the reality is that politics, usually of a virulent nature, intrudes, and efficiency is sacrificed. Public enterprise managers are rarely permitted to shed labor to produce at minimum cost. Moreover, procurement is often treated as a way of enriching contractors and procurement officers.

Nigeria appears to provide almost a textbook example of what can go wrong when the government gets directly into the business of producing goods and services. Between 1973 and 1990, the Nigerian public sector invested $115 billion, just about $1,000 for every citizen. Yet there is no growth to show for this investment. Why? Most of the investment was greatly overpriced for "non-commercial" reasons. In addition, most public sector assets are operating at capacity utilization of less than 40 percent. This is not to mention the $3 billion Ajaokuta Steel complex, which, after another $1 billion to complete, will then lose money even on a sunk cost basis.

It does not have to be this way. Look at the difference between oil refineries run by private firms and those that are public. Look at the difference between hotels maintained privately and publicly. Relying on the private sector to undertake major investments, Nigeria could have achieved the same output with up to $80 billion less investment over the last 18 years since the oil boom.

No country has ever developed without adequate provision of basic investment in infrastructure and in people. Governments that spread themselves too thin inevitably find themselves neglecting the tasks that only they can perform. Experience suggests that governments that stay out of the production business, as did many in East Asia, provide more effectively for schooling and health care and create better infrastructure foundations for private business.

Small amounts of public investment in key

sectors, such as agriculture, can make a huge difference. For example, small-scale relatively cheap irrigation schemes and the basic tasks of agricultural research and extension are neglected, while large outlays are allocated for fertilizer subsidies in many countries. Similarly, a classic pattern is overinvestment in new physical facilities and underinvestment in repair and maintenance.

Human investments are especially important. The two greatest threats to Africa's future are the investments that are being neglected in primary education and in food security. A child born in Mali, Niger, or Burkina Faso today is more likely to be malnourished while under five than to go to primary school on reaching six, and in at least 16 African countries, a child is more likely to die before the age of five than to attend secondary school. Ironically, the public sector workforce is often neglected even as employment expands. Teachers' real wages fell by two thirds over the last 15 years in Nigeria and by 13 percent in eastern and southern Africa from 1980 to 1985. It is hardly surprising that education deteriorates. In nations where the quality of education and health care is rising, the salaries of teachers and nurses are increasing as well. . . .

Can the next two decades be better than the last two? If African nations learn from worldwide experience and put into action the above-mentioned principles, there is no reason why living standards in Africa cannot double over the next generation. But there is one lesson to keep in mind: Takeoff takes longer than one expects but then happens faster than one expects.

I.C.5. China*

In 1978 China began a process of economic reforms that has brought about dramatic economic and social change in just over ten years. In 1980, Chinese planners set a target of quadrupling the country's industrial and agricultural output by the close of the century. Since 1976, China has achieved a GNP growth rate of over 8 percent a year and if this trend can be maintained the country will comfortably meet the target set for 2000. Between 1949 and 1976, China's output increased mostly through increased capital formation, made possible by a very high level of domestic savings; productivity increased slowly, if at all. But in more recent years, half or more of China's growth can be explained by rising total factor productivity. This signals a change from the past.

Will China be able to maintain the rate of growth of recent years? The answer depends in part on the country's ability to address a number of problems that have surfaced recently. Inflation has been increasing: it was estimated at 7.9 percent for 1987, but it increased to an annualized rate of 11 percent in the first quarter of 1988; more recently, estimates suggest a rate of close to 20 percent. Increases in prices have been much higher in major cities and for such commodities of daily use as pork, eggs, and vegetables. Reform inevitably tends to be inflationary in all circumstances, since it requires adjustments in relative prices, which in practice means that average prices are certain to rise. China's situation differs little from those of countries that have attempted deep restructuring of their economies. But what complicates matters in China is the country's size and the rapid move from a centrally controlled system to one in which the market has an increasing role to play. Future success will depend on whether China can do four things simultaneously: let growth result from productivity improvements rather than simply from capital formation; introduce fiscal discipline at all levels of government; control monetary expansion; and integrate quasi-autonomous provinces into a national market. In other words, reform has entered a new and critical phase.

Decentralization

The process of reform begun in 1978 needs to be seen in the context of China's earlier attempts to decentralize economic decision making. The reforms associated with the Great Leap Forward of 1958 had increased the authority of local governments over the supply of raw materials and over certain types of investment, and had given them responsibility for the great ma-

*From Shahid Javed Burki, "Reform and Growth in China," *Finance & Development* (December 1988), pp. 46–48. Reprinted by permission.

jority of enterprises formerly managed by central government ministries. The 1958 reforms also transferred responsibility for "unified balance" in the economy away from the State Planning Commission; the new system sought to achieve balance by aggregating decisions taken by individual production units. Later, when the failure of the Great Leap Forward led to some recentralization of economic management and controls, the central government did not completely reestablish its authority over local governments.

Another series of the decentralization measures was adopted in 1970 under the slogan of "delegating power to lower levels is a revolution." However, this attempt to relocate economic decision making away from the center did not proceed very far, since the country at that time was in the throes of the Cultural Revolution.

Nature of Current Reforms

The reforms undertaken since 1978 differ in two important ways from the earlier ones alluded to above. First, the approach adopted in December 1978 used the slogan *fangquan rangli*, or "delegate power and relinquish revenues." This way of thinking has had a profound economic and social impact over the years, particularly since it has allowed economic decision making to be influenced by the market. Decision making under this approach has thus meant more than shifting authority over economic decisions from central ministries to provincial bureaus. It has meant introducing producers and managers to some of the discipline of the market place.

Second, the post-1978 reforms have left a much larger share of revenue in the hands of producers and managers. Within limits not very strictly defined, these revenues can be used for investment, social development, and increases in wages and therefore in consumption. The state expects to control economic activity by regulating the market, not by directly controlling individual units of production.

The current reforms began, and have progressed farthest, in rural areas, but there is hardly a part of the economy left untouched by the new policies.

Agriculture

Agriculture supplies 30 percent of China's GDP and employs more than two thirds of the labor force. China's is the oldest surviving agricultural system in the world. Agriculture in China has always been more intensive than in other parts of the world. This has been made possible by the development of a sophisticated network of irrigation and by the adoption of new technologies. It is for these reasons that while China has less than 8 percent of the world's arable land, it provides food for about 22 percent of the world's population.

The combination of the age of the system and the intensity of cultivation created a unique set of problems that demanded action by the government, especially after the disruption caused first by the Great Leap Forward in 1958 and then by the Cultural Revolution which began in 1966. These left many unhappy legacies, among them the virtual elimination of the market for surplus agricultural output; dispersal of industrial capital all over the country, including those units critical for providing agriculture with inputs; and destruction of the educational system, including the closing down of agricultural research institutions. The Great Leap Forward and the Cultural Revolution encouraged provinces to become self-sufficient in food and to depend on indigenous agricultural technology.

In the late 1970s the Government responded to this situation by recreating markets for agricultural output, reestablishing agricultural research institutions, and importing modern technologies. Prices for farm products procured by the state have been raised sharply, while a much larger share of output may now be sold in the market, rather than handed over to the state. At the same time, the system of people's communes has been dismantled. (This highly structured system had been built up over the two decades since 1958, when land was collectivized and management of the production system was made the responsibility of a hierarchy of supervisors located at four different levels—counties, communes, production brigades, and production teams.)

Under the household responsibility system that has replaced the people's communes, land is leased to farming households; farmers are encouraged to manage cropping patterns according to their perception of market opportunities. Villages are also permitted to start nonagricultural activities as well as farming; some 80 million villagers have left farming altogether and entered the "town and village enterprise" sector of the economy.

Collective Enterprises

Collective enterprises have been encouraged to grow rapidly and some private entrepreneurs have been allowed to set up their own businesses. Rural and urban private sector employment grew from insignificant levels to 3.4 million in the five years between 1979 and 1984. The share of the collective and private sector in industrial output increased from 14 percent in 1979 to 40 percent in 1987.

This growth signifies a massive restructuring in the industrial sector, not only in terms of ownership and management but also in the mix of products produced and the geographic location of industries. For example, the province of Guangdong overtook Shanghai in its contributions to national industrial output since it was able to invest large amounts in light and consumer goods industries that were in demand at home and abroad.

State Enterprises

State enterprises had not performed well before the current series of reforms, and thus the Government began to loosen control over them. In 1981, an immense number of "economic responsibility systems," or *jingji zerenzhi*, were introduced, to provide managers within the state enterprises with incentives similar to those enjoyed by managers and owners of collective and private enterprises.

A new financial relationship between state enterprises and the Government has been shaped by reforms introduced between 1983 and 1985. Its centerpiece is a 55 percent tax on gross profits, with enterprises allowed to retain after-tax profits. Retained profits can be used for new investments and worker bonuses. Enterprises are now being permitted to buy equity in other enterprises, and this has led to the creation of "social joint stock companies." The highly centralized budgetary system has been replaced by a contractual revenue-sharing arrangement which fixes central government appropriations for a period of five years, leaving surpluses to be used by local governments or individual enterprise owners at their discretion.

Response of Output, Exports

The economy has responded vigorously to the reforms. Between 1980 and 1986, GDP increased at 10.5 percent a year, or almost twice as fast as in 1973–80 (Table 1). Agricultural production has expanded at a rate unprecedented in Chinese history, and at nearly three times the rate of 1973–80. In 1985, China produced 407 million tons of foodgrain, an amount that not only met domestic demand but also allowed significant exports. The output of the industrial sector grew by 12.5 percent a year.

Partly because of the greater freedom allowed private and collective enterprises, exports from China became competitive; they have risen at more than 13 percent a year in real terms since the beginning of the reform effort (Table 1). In 1987, China earned $39 billion in exports, as against $15 billion in 1979.

Living Standards

While the productive sectors of the economy were being reformed, the Government continued

TABLE 1. Key Indicators, China

	Shares of Gross Domestic Product (from current price data)			Annual Growth Rates (from constant price data)				
	1965	1980	1986	1965–73	1973–80	1980–86	1986	1987
Agriculture	39.1	32.0	30.7	2.8	2.8	7.9	3.4	4.7
Industry	37.5	48.0	46.2	12.1	8.6	12.5	11.4	16.5
Manufacturing	29.6	35.3	33.7	11.8	8.4	12.6	9.6	—
Services	23.3	20.0	23.1	11.7	3.4	9.4	5.4	−3.4
GDP	100.0	100.0	100.0	7.8	5.4	10.5	7.9	9.4
Exports	4.2	7.1	10.9	2.1	3.6	13.3	10.8	15.3
Imports	3.7	8.4	13.7	1.6	11.3	17.1	−13.2	−7.9

Note: — denotes data not available.
Source: World Bank

TABLE 2. Comparative Statistics

Country/Region	Crude Death Rate (per 1000)	Infant Mortality Rate (per 1000 live births)	Life Expectancy at Birth (years)	GNP Per Capita (1985 US$)
China: 1985	7	35	69	310
1950–55	31	236	34	—
India: 1985	12	89	57	270
Brazil: 1985	8	67	64	1,640
1985 Average				
Low-income countries	10	72	60	270
Middle-income countries	10	68	62	1,290

Note: — denotes data not available.
Sources: WDR 1987; China: The Health Sector (World Bank, 1988).

its efforts to alleviate poverty. China's accomplishments here are impressive. One measure of the country's achievement is the increase in life expectancy at birth. In 1955, life expectancy was estimated at 39 years; in 1985, as Table 2 shows, life expectancy had risen to 69 years, largely because of a sharp drop in infant mortality and in the incidence of communicable diseases.

Having significantly improved both its health and education standards, China has now begun to address a number of "second tier" problems. These include improving the standard of general education and dealing with health problems associated with urbanization, industrialization, and the aging of the population.

In 1986, the Government passed the "compulsory education law" under which nine-year universal education is to be achieved in stages: in the cities and coastal areas by 1990; in less-developed towns and villages by 1995; and in the more remote areas at a rate commensurate with the development of each area. These are ambitious targets. At present, for example, only 52 percent of children of lower secondary school age are attending school. This is a respectable figure for a developing country but far short of the goal adopted by the Government.

Further progress in health will be equally demanding of government resources and skilled manpower. China's health problems are those familiar in developed countries, but to address them, China has a level of income only one fortieth of that in the industrial world.

Questions

Even in the productive sectors where progress has been rapid, questions are being asked as to whether growth at such a pace can be sustained. For instance, if China chooses to remain self-sufficient in food, it will need to increase annual grain output per head of the population from the 400kg achieved in the mid-1980s to 500kg by the end of the century. (This is because as incomes rise and people consume more meat in their diets, more grain will be required as animal feed.) This increase will have to come from a sector that already uses land very productively and which is losing valuable agricultural land to urbanization and industrialization.

In the past, China relied more on export earnings than on foreign borrowings to generate the revenues required for investment. A second important question is whether a world in which trade is now expanding at a sluggish rate will be able to absorb large annual increases in Chinese merchandise exports.

A third question, receiving a great deal of attention in China, is whether it can sustain its current high rate of economic growth without addressing the problems that are created by severe transport and communication bottlenecks and by the shortage of electricity. In other words, China will have to reorient its growth strategy: perhaps allowing some food imports, so that land can be released to produce high-value crops for export; placing somewhat greater emphasis on using domestic markets as the engine of growth; and reviving national development programs for improving infrastructure.

EXHIBIT I.15. Key Indicators: China

National Accounts	Share of Gross Domestic Product (from current price data)						Growth Rate (percent per year) (from constant price data)				
	1965	1973	1980	1989	1990	1991	1965–73	1973–80	1980–91	1990	1991
Gross domestic product	100.0	100.0	100.0	100.0	100.0	100.0	8.5	5.3	9.6	5.1	6.7
Agriculture	38.2	32.3	30.4	26.6	28.4	28.4	2.7	2.2	5.7	7.5	3.0
Industry	35.0	40.7	44.7	40.7	39.5	39.5	11.7	8.9	11.1	5.7	13.0
Manufacturing	27.7	31.1	40.1	37.0	35.6	35.6	7.5	14.4	11.2	4.9	13.0
Services	26.8	27.0	24.9	32.7	32.1	32.1	21.1	5.4	11.7	2.2	1.0
Total consumption	75.2	70.2	67.8	61.9	57.6	60.8	7.3	5.0	7.5	−1.6	11.2
Private consumption	67.6	62.7	59.5	53.8	49.4	52.1	7.3	4.4	7.4	0.5	11.6
General government	7.6	7.5	8.3	8.2	8.2	8.7	7.0	9.5	8.7	−15.1	8.7
Gross domestic investment	24.0	29.0	32.2	38.7	38.9	36.0	12.9	8.9	12.5	5.2	−1.7
Fixed investment	—	—	24.0	25.9	25.1	27.0	—	—	—	—	—
Changes in stock	—	—	8.2	12.8	13.8	9.0	—	—	—	—	—
Gross domestic savings	24.8	29.8	32.2	38.1	42.4	39.2	12.4	8.1	12.4	16.4	−2.7

Other Indicators	Growth Rate (percent per year)		
	1965–73	1973–80	1980–91
Population	—	1.6	1.4
Labor force	2.4	2.5	2.1
Gross national income p.c.	−60.6	4.3	7.6
Private consumption p.c.	−61.1	2.7	5.9

Source: World Bank, *Trends in Developing Economies* (1992), p. 119.

Comment: Chinese Economic Reform

For an analysis of China's series of economic reforms and a discussion of the relevance of China's experience for other countries, see Neville Maxwell and Bruce McFarlane, *China's Changed Road to Development* (1984); Keith Griffin, ed., *Institutional Reform and Economic Development in the Chinese Countryside* (1984); Gene Tidrick and Chen Jiyuan, eds., *China's Industrial Reform* (1987); Dwight H. Perkins, *China: Asia's Next Economic Giant?* (1986); Carl Riskin, *China's Political Economy* (1987); D. H. Perkins and S. Yusuf, *Rural Development in China* (1984); World Bank, *China: Socialist Economic Development* (1983); Nicholas R. Lardy, *Agriculture in China's Modern Economic Development* (1983); Dwight Perkins, "Reforming China's Economic System," *Journal of Economic Literature* (June 1988); Bruce J. Reynolds, ed., *Chinese Economic Reform: How Far? How Fast?* (1988); D. Gale Johnson, *The People's Republic of China 1978–1990* (1990); and Nicholas R. Lardy, *Foreign Trade and Economic Reform in China, 1978–1990* (1992), and *China in the World Economy* (1994).

Comment: Cross-Country Empirical Comparisons

Quantitative comparisons of the development experiences of different countries now abound—from simple statistical tables to formal econometric models. For regression analysis of large samples of countries with the common objective of testing the significance of variables in explaining growth rates, see Hollis Chenery et al., *Industrialization and Growth: A Comparative Study* (1986). Chenery considers not only differences in factor inputs to explain differences in growth performance among different countries but also includes the structural variables of reallocation of labor and capital, growth of exports, capital inflow, and level of development. However, results are meaningful only if we assume that the underlying development process is similar and that we can isolate differences in explanatory variables. To do this it is helpful to stratify the sample.

Less technical are the numerous analytical stories or histories that compare country performance. Notable are the volumes of twin countries in the World Bank's multivolume study *Political Economy, Growth, and Poverty* in a number of countries. Also, Gustav Ranis and Syed Akhtar Mahmood compare three pairs of countries—Mexico and Colombia, Taiwan and South Korea, and the Philippines and Thailand—in their *Political Economy of Development Policy Change* (1992). Ranis and Mahmood are particularly concerned with the differential effects of policy actions in different countries.

Major questions arising from these comparative studies are: To what extent can differences in performance be explained by differences in initial conditions, domestic variables, and external variables? Above all, do differences in policies provide meaningful explanatory variables? And are the specific institutions and programs of the success stories transferable to other countries?

EXHIBIT I.16. Developing Countries: Economic Indicators (annual percentage change unless otherwise noted)

	Average 1988–90	1991	1992	1993
Developing Countries				
Real GDP	3.7	3.2	6.1	5.7
Consumer prices	69.0	42.7	46.3	40.7
Consumer prices (median)	9.2	9.3	7.9	5.9
Investment ratio (in percent of GDP)	24.1	23.3	24.3	24.4
Export volume	8.0	8.2	8.3	8.9
Terms of trade	0.1	−3.9	−1.6	0.6
Current account (in billions of U.S. dollars)	−17.8	−78.2	−47.1	−45.7
Debt (in billions of U.S. dollars)[a]	1,281.0	1,361.0	1,428.0	1,470.0
Debt (in percent of exports)[b]	125.6	126.3	122.7	114.0
Debt service (in percent of exports)	15.9	14.0	14.2	14.1
Africa				
Real GDP	2.6	1.5	2.0	3.3
Consumer prices	18.1	27.1	28.3	18.0
Consumer prices (median)	9.1	9.2	7.0	5.0
Investment ratio (in percent of GDP)	21.0	19.8	19.6	20.4
Export volume	4.5	2.1	2.7	4.6
Terms of trade	−0.9	−6.2	−6.0	−0.8
Current account (in billions of U.S. dollars)	−6.2	−3.5	−8.8	−7.1
Debt (in percent of exports)[b]	221.3	230.5	238.0	231.4
Debt service (in percent of exports)	25.3	25.9	30.8	28.6
Asia				
Real GDP	6.6	5.7	6.6	6.4
Consumer prices	13.4	8.9	8.1	7.4
Consumer prices (median)	8.4	8.6	7.7	6.5
Investment ratio (in percent of GDP)	30.2	30.3	31.1	31.3
Export volume	9.7	12.3	9.9	10.9
Terms of trade	−0.3	—	−0.4	0.3
Current account (in billions of U.S. dollars)	3.6	−3.5	−8.8	−7.1
Debt (in percent of exports)[b]	69.1	68.6	66.8	63.7
Debt service (in percent of exports)	9.8	8.1	7.8	7.5
Middle East and Europe				
Real GDP	2.7	—	9.9	8.6
Consumer prices	18.9	22.1	16.4	16.3
Consumer prices (median)	8.2	6.9	7.5	6.9
Investment ratio (in percent of GDP)	19.7	15.7	18.4	17.4
Export volume	7.2	3.1	6.9	6.4
Terms of trade	1.7	−12.4	−2.9	1.1

EXHIBIT I.16. (*continued*)

	Average 1988–90	1991	1992	1993
Current account (in billions of U.S. dollars)	−6.7	−50.5	−6.1	−3.4
Debt (in percent of exports)[b]	122.7	134.3	135.0	124.5
Debt service (in percent of exports)	14.8	13.6	12.6	12.3
Western Hemisphere				
Real GDP	0.4	2.8	2.7	2.0
Consumer prices	416.1	165.3	212.2	179.4
Consumer prices (median)	14.8	21.4	11.8	8.0
Investment ratio (in percent of GDP)	20.1	21.0	21.8	23.3
Export volume	6.2	4.5	7.1	6.5
Terms of trade	−0.1	−4.8	−2.0	1.9
Current account (in billions of U.S. dollars)	−8.5	−19.9	−23.9	−24.7
Debt (in percent of exports)[b]	252.0	265.1	256.4	232.2
Debt service (in percent of exports)	30.4	28.8	31.6	33.7

[a]End of period.
[b]Total debt at year-end in percentage of exports of goods and services in the year indicated (for 1988–90, in percent of 1990).
Source: International Monetary Fund, *World Economic Outlook* (January 1993), p. 17.

I.D. LEADING ISSUES—NOTE

Throughout this book, we will have to diagnose the disappointments that have been experienced in the development record. Why—two centuries after the Industrial Revolution—is 80 percent of the world's population still in less developed countries?

In his presidential address to the Economic History Association, Richard Easterlin asked, "Why isn't the whole world developed?"[1] He observed that development had spread from northern and western Europe and then on to some regions of recent settlement, but it had stopped short of being diffused to most of the world. Why was it not transmitted? Easterlin stated that development is a function of the rate of technological change—the introduction of new production techniques. The transfer of *technological change*, according to Easterlin, is an educational process. Thus the spread of development depends on the growth of science and the diffusion of modern education, which, in turn, depends on an incentive structure and new political conditions and ideological forces. Historically, the growth of formal schooling has led to a secular, rationalistic, and materialistic trend in intellectual thought that promoted development.

The question "Why isn't the whole world developed?" was answered quite differently in the pre–World War II period of *colonialism*, when many economists and anthropologists engaged in what Gunnar Myrdal has called "colonial apologetics." To them, the absence of development in the colonies could be attributed to the tropical climate, to overpopulation, to a lack of motivation on the part of the population, or to the colonials' simple contentment with their lot.

A number of achievements in the developing countries after World War II have dealt a severe blow to such an apologetic view. Neither Singapore nor Hong Kong—among the superperformers in development—has an ideal temperate climate. Nor are the climates of Ghana and the Ivory Coast different from each other, but the Ivory Coast was an "economic miracle," while Ghana retrogressed. As for population, South Korea and Taiwan—two superperformers in de-

velopment—are the second and third most densely populated countries in the world (after Bangladesh). Moreover, any number of examples can now be cited to prove that when incentives are offered through higher wages or higher prices, a supply of labor or productive activity responds positively.

During the period of colonialism, another rationalization of underdevelopment was offered by those who interpreted imperialism as a process by which the rich countries exploited the poor. A contemporary form of this line of thinking is offered by the school of dependency, which is especially prevalent in Latin America. This school asserts that the development countries "underdevelop" the less developed, that forces of international and national polarization retard development (more on this in Chapters II and IX).

Those who subscribe to the dependency school would contend that even after becoming politically independent the former colonies suffered from their colonial legacy and from neocolonialism. The balance sheet of colonialism is, however, complex. In a recent study of historical growth in a large number of countries, Yale's Lloyd Reynolds has made several telling points:

First, we cannot safely generalize about all colonies at all times. We cannot toss all the colonial powers into one basket. Japan has always been growth-oriented, in colonial areas as well as at home; and it is clear that Japanese rule helped to initiate intensive growth in both Korea and Taiwan. In the Philippines, too, intensive growth dates from their transfer from Spanish to American rule. The British were also typically growth-minded. But they tended to delegate much authority to local administrators; so policy varied from one country to the next and even in the same colony at different times. (The case of India, which did not achieve intensive growth during the colonial era, has tended to dominate the anti-colonial literature; but India is rather a special case, and most other British colonies did better.) . . . General statements which profess to apply to all colonial powers and to all periods of time clearly cannot be true.

Second, one should distinguish several different questions which can be asked about colonial rule. i. Did areas under colonial rule achieve a turning point and embark on intensive growth (rising per capita income)? Some did, and some did not. ii. Could these areas have grown more rapidly had the colonial powers made indigenous economic growth a prime objec-

[1]Richard Easterlin, "Why Isn't the Whole World Developed?" *Journal of Economic History* (March 1981): 1–17.

tive? Here the answer usually is "Yes, more could have been done than actually was done." But here again, one must distinguish among countries and time periods. In Britain's African colonies there was a clear progression from a relative lack of interest in economic advancement of "the natives" before 1914, to a more substantial interest and even some infusion of development and preparation for eventual independence from 1945–1960. For whatever reason, the two World Wars were distinct punctuation marks in colonial policy.

iii. Would these areas have developed faster before 1950 if they had been completely independent countries rather than colonies? Any answer to this counterfactual question is conjectural, especially for "countries" which did not exist before colonization. But the record of countries which never fell under colonial rule—Ethiopia, Afghanistan, Nepal, pre-1949 China—is not impressive. There is no magic in independence.

Colonial rule usually made several positive contributions. . . .

There are also negative items on the score card. . . .

The net score from adding these pluses and minuses varied widely among countries. We are not suggesting a generalized pro-colonial view, but urging rather a careful sifting of evidence on a country-by-country basis.[2]

When economists first turned to the challenge of development after World War II, many interpreted limited development in terms of *missing components* in the less developed countries. They looked at the history of a more developed country (MDC) and noted its resource deposits, literacy, supply of entrepreneurs, law and order, Protestant ethic, and the like. If an LDC was missing some of the elements in an MDC, its underdevelopment was attributed to the missing components. This is, however, a mechanistic approach that overlooks the interrelations among the elements and the evolution of the forces of development in an organic process. The missing-components approach also led to an overemphasis on favorable "initial conditions." As indicated in selection I.C.I. some of the success stories of development, such as Taiwan and South Korea, have actually begun with highly unfavorable initial conditions.

Furthermore, it was only too simple to say that the absence of a component constituted an *obstacle* to development. But the obstacles approach to development has been shown to be inadequate.[3] Different students of development have emphasized different "obstacles": natural (lack of resources), man-made (lack of law and order, lack of capital), objective (lack of resources), subjective (lack of entrepreneurship and risk taking, lack of a desire for change, contempt for material success), internal (all the factors so far named), and external (exploitation by a foreign power).

Albert Hirschman argues, however, that the concept of an "obstacle" is not very illuminating and that it is not possible to identify either a finite number of "reliable" hindrances to development or a hierarchy among them that would permit their neat arrangement into boxes marked "basic," "secondary," and so on. Moreover, it does not allow a reliable list; there is no absolute barrier to development. When an alleged obstacle appears in another context, it may not even have to be removed. Or an alleged obstacle in another context may actually be an advantage. As Hirschman shows, what is considered an obstacle in one country at one time may actually be accommodated or neutralized in another country at another time, or obstacles may turn out to be blessings in disguise. Many countries have demonstrated that if they lack a so-called prerequisite, they may invent their own substitutes, or the alleged prerequisite may prove to be dispensable:

We may simply be proven wrong in our belief that a certain resource, institution, or attitude needed to be created or eradicated for development to be possible. In other words, the requirements of development turn out to be more tolerant of cultural and institutional variety than we thought on the basis of our limited prior experience. Recent research shows this to be the case in various parts of the world.[4]

From the standpoint of this book's emphasis on development policy making, the major weakness with the obstacles approach to development is that it limits policy making. It forecloses the ability to perceive alternatives. It reduces the vision of different approaches to development. The very essence of policy making is to practice the art of the possible and to institute the feasible. The objective is not simply to replicate the

---

[2]Lloyd Reynolds, "The Spread of Economic Growth to The Third World: 1850–1980," *Journal of Economic Literature* (September 1983): 956–58.

[3]Albert O. Hirschman, "Obstacles to Development: A Classification and a Quasi-Vanishing Act," *Economic Development and Cultural Change* (July 1965): 385–93.

[4]Ibid., 389.

development of another country in an earlier period.

Although some of the foregoing views may be discussed in some selections in this book, our leading issues center on an analysis of the *constraints* on development and the need to relax them through the implementation of *appropriate policies*. On the basis of the logic of economic analysis and the evidence from development experiences, it would appear that the answer to the question ''Why isn't the whole world developed?'' can best be approached through an understanding of the restrictions on development and the pursuit of policies to overcome them.

From the preceding discussion of the development performance in various countries, three overriding questions emerge:

1. What have been the constraints on the *potential* rates of development in the LDCs?
2. Why have the *actual* rates of development been below the potential rates in most of these countries?
3. What policies in a strategy of development can raise growth rates, eradicate absolute poverty, and reduce inequality?

These questions will dominate much of the analysis in subsequent chapters.

Behind the disappointments in the statistical record of those countries that have not yet emerged from poverty lie four major constraints that have limited their attainable rate of development. The first stems from the low level of *savings*. The inability to mobilize sufficient domestic resources, or to supplement domestic resources with external resources, has continued to inhibit development. According to Ragnar Nurkse, a country is poor because it is poor.[5] This is represented by a ''vicious circle of poverty'' that runs from low real income to low savings to low investment to low productivity and then back to low real income. This vicious circle remains to be broken in some LDCs. An increase in the ratio of savings and investment to national income is still imperative in most LDCs. It is, however, disturbing that the rate of increase of capital formation has slowed down in many countries, and it is indeed questionable whether in many LDCs the domestic saving rate and capital inflow are now sufficiently high to sustain a satisfactory rate of development. Problems associated with the savings constraint are examined in Chapters III and IV.

The *foreign-exchange* constraint—or the deterioration in the capacity to import—is another acute limitation on a country's rate of development. The import demand of some LDCs has risen more than their capacity to import based on export earnings. And since the early 1970s, the stagnation of the world economy and the slowing down of world trade have contrasted with the buoyancy of overseas markets during the 1950s and 1960s. A new export pessimism has set in. Compounding the difficulties, the net inflow of foreign capital has slackened, debt servicing of amortization and interest on public foreign debt has risen markedly, and income payments of dividends and profits on private direct foreign investment have grown. In many countries the import surplus that can be supported by external financial resources has therefore diminished.

For many developing countries, the foreign-exchange constraint has persisted as a severe limitation on their development programs by making it impossible to fulfill import requirements; for some, the external-debt crisis has become acute. The problems of mobilizing external resources are discussed in Chapter V. Related trade strategies and policy implications with respect to import substitution and export promotion are considered in Chapter IX.

The third major constraint relates to the need for *human-resource development*. Policy issues centering on the need for social development are now critical, as analyzed in Chapter VI. It has become increasingly apparent that an improvement in the quality of human life cannot be simply awaited as an ultimate objective of development, but must be viewed as a necessary instrument of development. Beyond an increase in the quantity of productive factors, it is necessary to improve the quality of people as economic agents. If development is growth *plus* change, and change is social and cultural as well as economic, then the qualitative dimensions of development become extremely significant in terms of human-resource development. Without such change, the process of development will not become self-sustaining.

This qualitative change requires a greater emphasis on investment in human capital and on measures to modify social and cultural values. Recognizing that the problem of controlling population growth has now reached serious dimensions throughout most of the underdevel-

[5]Ragnar Nurkse, *Problems of Capital Accumulation in Poor Countries* (1953), p. 4.

oped world, many would also argue that population-control policies are essential to foster a rise in the standard of living in many poor countries. Unless this is done, it will be all the more difficult to improve the quality of the population, and the potential for development will not be realized.

The fourth bottleneck relates to the *agricultural sector*. Agriculture constitutes a large share of the GDP of developing countries. Agricultural commodities account for a considerable part of the value of their total exports. Agricultural development is therefore essential for economic growth, the accumulation of capital through savings and taxation, and the earning of foreign exchange. It must also support and complement industrial development by providing food for a growing nonagricultural labor force, raw materials for industrial production, and a growing home market for domestic manufacturers. The development record has demonstrated a close association between the agricultural performance and the overall growth rate of developing countries: in the ''high-growth'' developing countries, the average rates of increase in agricultural production have been considered higher than in the ''slow-growth'' countries.

For the majority of developing countries, however, agriculture has been a problem sector. A major restraint on the development rate has been the slow growth of their agricultural output in general and of food crops in particular. In many LDCs, the demand for food has grown faster than the production of food, and an increasing number of LDCs have become net importers of food. The neglect of the agricultural sector has been pervasive, and it underlies problems created by the population explosion, unemployment and underemployment, inequality, and absolute poverty. In Chapters VII and VIII, we stress the important role of agricultural improvements in the development process, and we examine the interactions between the industrial and the agricultural sectors.

These constraints—multiple in number and both internal and external to the developing country's economy—aggravate the problem of development. The problem is all the more complicated by the question of trade-offs that involve growth, employment, and equity. Is there a conflict between increasing output and increasing employment? Given that capital is a scarce resource, is the type of production that economizes on the use of capital per unit of output consistent with maximizing employment? Or

does output have to be sacrificed through use of inefficient labor-intensive methods of production in order to provide more employment? The conflict lies not so much with the relationship between current output and current employment, but with the relationship between current employment and the growth rate of employment and output in the future.

Another troublesome trade-off is between output and equity. Does social justice have to be sacrificed for greater output? Or is it possible to achieve what might be termed ''efficient equity''—that is, an improvement in the distribution of income and wealth, together with an increase in output? Does this also hold in intertemporal terms? In other words, is it possible to have both greater equality and greater output in the present period and in future periods as well? Or is it more probable that a country can have greater equity and greater output in the future only if it endures greater inequality in the present?

Although we do not minimize the significance of noneconomic factors in the process of modernization and the inherent problem of trade-off in objectives, we emphasize in this book the strategic economic-policy issues connected with the relaxation of the savings, foreign-exchange, agricultural, and human-resource constraints.

Given the constraints on its development, a country's success in attaining its potential rate of development depends on the government's willingness and ability to implement policies that will raise the actual rate of development up to the potential rate. In essence, the *super constraint* on the relaxation of the other constraints is the inadequate quality of national economic management.

Instead of saying that ''a country is poor because it is poor,'' it can now be said—on the basis of a comparison of the success stories and failures in the development record—that ''a country is poor because of poor policies.'' As summarized in Chapter X, the pursuit of appropriate policies, the stability of government, a strong commitment to development goals, and a capacity for efficient public management are essential. Only if these conditions are realized can the actual rate of development approach more closely the potentially attainable rate.

Various perspectives on the development record and development theories, to which we now turn, may begin to illuminate these leading issues as they relate to policy making.

EXHIBIT I.17.

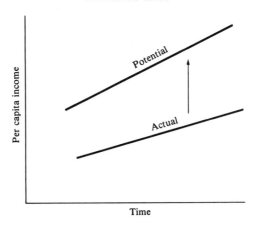

The potential rate of development of an economy is determined by the relaxation of four constraints: savings, foreign exchange, human resources, and agriculture. But the economy's actual rate is below the potential because of inappropriate policies. The "super constraint" is management—both private and public. Appropriate polices must be undertaken to mobilize resources, allocate the resources efficiently, and raise productivity. By so doing, the actual rate of development can be brought closer to the potential rate over time.

CHAPTER II

Thinking About Development

In attempting to understand the process of economic development, we shall have to think about it in various ways—by utilizing economic history, mainstream neoclassical economic analysis, structural analysis, and some more radical concepts. For country applications, we shall also have to engage in empirical and data analysis.

Although this chapter presents various approaches to development, the economics for development relies for the most part on the fundamental principles of mainstream economics—resource allocation, international trade theory, and the macroeconomics of monetary and fiscal policies. But the application of these principles has to be adapted to the particular conditions of developing countries. For considering the special problems of less developed countries (LDCs), development economics retains its position as a unique subdiscipline in economics.

If we are to appreciate fully the variety, complexity, and pervasiveness of development problems, we must be aware of their historical dimension. Historical perspective is one of the best safeguards against taking a superficial view of these problems. Section II.A, therefore, considers the relevance of historical experience to our understanding of the sources of development. It does so, in part, by focusing on W. W. Rostow's provocative application of a stages approach to the course of development. In II.A.2, Alexander Gerschenkron relates the degree of economic backwardness and the issue of "prerequisites" to historical cases of industrial development. Selection II.A.3 also offers a historical answer to the question of "why are we so rich and they so poor?" The note "Future Development in Historical Perspective" (II.A.4) places special emphasis on some of the differences between the earlier development of now advanced economies and present cases of development—differences that give rise to problems that we shall consider in detail in subsequent chapters.

Selections in Section II.B. trace changes in development thought over the past four decades since the modern subject of development economics emerged. Note II.B.1 provides a general survey of the evolution of the subject. In II.B.2, Arnold Harberger summarizes the neoclassical analysis of the determinants of economic growth. Hollis Chenery (II.B.3) and Joseph Stiglitz (II.B.4) offer some additional considerations relating the way in which structural elements and imperfect information and incomplete markets modify the neoclassical analysis. Section II.B. also examines the relevance of the new market failures approach, new endogenous growth theory (II.B.5), and new institutional economics (II.B.6) for development analysis.

In Section II.C, we consider some alternative perceptions outside the mainstream. Among them, the dependency school of thought (II.C.1) is very prominent as a radical critique. Although the school is more influential among sociologists and political scientists than economists, it remains a vigorous component of the Latin American school of development. The recent emergence of ''neostructuralism'' offers an instructive contrast between the neostructuralist paradigm and the mainstream neoliberal paradigm, as summarized at the end of the chapter.

II.A. HISTORICAL PERSPECTIVES

II.A.1. Sequence of Stages—Note

It has always been tempting to search for regularities in history, and many writers have adopted a unidirectional view of development in terms of some pattern of stages. As summarized by Simon Kuznets,

a stage theory of long-term economic change implies: (1) distinct time segments, characterized by different sources and patterns of economic changes; (2) a specific succession of these segments, so that *b* cannot occur before *a*, or *c* before *b;* and (3) a common matrix, in that the successive segments are stages in one broad process—usually one of development and growth rather than of devolution and shrinkage. Stage theory is most closely associated with a uni-directional rather than cyclic view of history. In the cyclic view the stages are recurrent; in a uni-directional view, a stage materializes, runs its course, and never recurs. Even in the process of devolution and decline, the return to a level experienced previously is not viewed as a recurrence of the earlier stage.[1]

The central question raised by Kuznets is: How can such a simple design be a summary description or an analytic classification of a vast and diverse field of historical change sufficiently plausible to warrant the formulation and persistence of many variants?

At one extreme, Adam Smith referred to the sequence of hunting, pastoral, agricultural, commercial, and manufacturing stages. At the other, Karl Marx related Hegel's thesis, antithesis, and synthesis to the Marxian stages of feudalism, capitalism, and socialism. Most recently, Walt Rostow attempted to generalize ''the sweep of modern economic history'' in a set of stages of growth, designated as follows: the traditional society, the preconditions for take-off, the take-off, the drive to maturity, and the age of high mass-consumption.[2]

Basic to Rostow's original analysis, in *The Stages of Economic Growth,* was his sketch of a dynamic theory of production that emphasized the composition of investment and the growth of particular sectors in the economy. This theory of production allowed Rostow to identify certain ''leading sectors,'' the growth of which is thought to be instrumental in propelling the economy forward. Rostow also indicated that a sequence of optimum patterns of investment can be postulated from a set of optimum sectoral paths determined by the level of income and population, by technology, by the quality of entrepreneurship, and by the empirical fact that deceleration is the normal optimum path of each sector. The actual course of investment, however, generally differs from these optima inasmuch as they are influenced not only by private choices, but also by the politics of governments and the impact of wars. Nonetheless, Rostow believes that, at any period of time, leading sectors can be identified,and the changing sequence of leading sectors plays an important role in Rostow's stages of growth. The sequence of stages suggests, in turn, that a succession of strategic choices is open to societies, and that political and social decisions about the allocation of resources are made in terms beyond the usual market processes. Of Rostow's five stages of growth, the most relevant for poor countries at present are the first three: the traditional society, the emergence of the preconditions for take-off, and the take-off.

The ''take-off'' is meant to be the central notion in Rostow's schema, and it has received the most critical attention. The take-off is interpreted as ''a decisive transition in a society's history''—a period ''when the scale of productive economic activity reaches a critical level and produces changes which lead to a massive and progressive structural transformation in economies and the societies of which they are a part, better viewed as changes in kind than merely in degree.'' The take-off is defined ''as requiring all three of the following related conditions'':

1. a rise in the rate of productive investment from, say, 5% or less to over 10% of national income (or net national product);
2. the development of one or more substantial manufacturing sectors, with a high rate of growth; and
3. the existence or quick emergence of a political, social, and institutional framework

[1]Simon Kuznets, ''Notes on Stage of Economic Growth as a System Determinant,'' in *Comparison of Economic Systems,* ed. Alexander Eckstein (1971), p. 243.

[2]W. W. Rostow, ''The Stages of Economic Growth,'' *Economic History Review* (August 1959) and *The Stages of Economic Growth* (1960); W. W. Rostow et al., *The Economics of Take-Off into Sustained Growth* (1963).

that exploits the impulses to expansion in the modern sector and the potential external economy effects of the take-off and gives to growth an ongoing character.[3]

Of the earlier proponents of stages, only Marx commands Rostow's explicit attention. Indeed, Rostow presents his analysis as an alternative to Marx's theory of modern history. Describing his system as "A Non-Communist Manifesto," Rostow poses his five stages of growth against Marx's stages of feudalism, bourgeois capitalism, socialism, and communism.

We can recognize some broad similarities between Rostow's analysis and Marx's sequence. Both are audacious attempts to interpret the evolution of whole societies, primarily from an economic perspective; both are "explorations of the problems and consequences for whole societies of building compound interest into their habits and institutions";[4] and both recognize that economic change has social, political, and cultural consequences.

From other viewpoints, however, there are fundamental differences. The basic Marxian problems of class conflict, exploitation, and inherent stresses within the capitalist process find no place in Rostow's analysis. Nor does Rostow reduce the complexities of man to a single economic dimension. Rostow recognizes that in terms of human motivation, many of the most profound economic changes must be viewed as the consequence of noneconomic human motives and aspirations. Instead of limiting human behavior to simply an act of maximization, Rostow interprets net human behavior "as an act of balancing alternative and often conflicting human objectives in the face of the range of choices men perceive to be open to them."[5] Rostow allows for the different facets of human beings, and interprets the total performance of societies as an act of balance in the patterns of choice made by individuals within the framework permitted by the changing setting of society. Rostow insists that although his "stages-of-growth are an economic way of looking at whole societies, they in no sense imply that the worlds of politics, social organization, and of culture are a mere superstructure built upon and derived uniquely from the economy."[6] On the

contrary, what most concerns Rostow is how societies go about making their choices and balances: "the central phenomenon of the world of post-traditional societies is not the economy—and whether it is capitalist or not—it is the total procedure by which choices are made."[7] Marx's assumption that a society's decisions are merely a function of who owns property is therefore rejected as inaccurate; instead, it is maintained that "one must look directly at the full mechanism of choice among alternative policies, including the political process—and indeed, the social and religious processes—as independent arenas for making decisions and choices."[8]

The implications of this broader view of human motivation become especially significant when Rostow's interpretation of post-traditional societies is contrasted with Marx's account of the postfeudal phase. Thus, Rostow concludes that his account of the break-up of traditional societies is

based on the convergence of motives of private profit in the modern sectors with a new sense of affronted nationhood. And other forces play their part as well, for example the simple perception that children need not die so young or live their lives in illiteracy: a sense of enlarged human horizons, independent of both profit and national dignity. And when independence or modern nationhood is at last attained, there is no simple, automatic switch to a dominance of the profit motive and economic and social progress. On the contrary there is a searching choice and problem of balance among the three directions policy might go: external assertion; the further concentration of power in the centre as opposed to the regions; and economic growth.[9]

This approach may have more immediate relevance for the problems now confronting many underdeveloped countries than Marx's narrower view that political behavior is dependent on economic advantage, and that the decisions of capitalist societies are made simply in terms of the free-market mechanism and private advantage.

Moreover, as Rostow observes, the Marxian sequence suffers by basing its categories on only one historical case: the British take-off and drive to maturity. Rostow reminds us that Marx presented his whole system before any society other than Britain experienced the take-off, and instead of revising his categories so as to be more applicable to other cases, Marx merely gener-

---

[3]Rostow, *Stages of Economic Growth*, pp. 36–40.
[4]Ibid., p. 148.
[5]Ibid., p. 149.
[6]Ibid., p. 2.

[7]Ibid., p. 150.
[8]Ibid.
[9]Ibid., p. 152.

alized and projected his interpretation of the British case. A concentration on the British case, however, misses the variety of experience in the evolution of different societies, and makes the Marxian analysis of the "march of history" unduly rigid and artificial. If for no other reason than that it draws on a far wider range of historical knowledge, and is thereby more comprehensive and less doctrinaire, Rostow's analysis can claim to be a superior alternative to the Marxian sequence.

Nonetheless, if Rostow's thesis is to assert with a high degree of generality that it is able to trace a structure of history in the form of a sequence of stages, then it must also answer a number of criticisms that have commonly been levied against stage-theorists. "Stage-making" approaches are misleading when they succumb to a linear conception of history and imply that all economies tend to pass through the same series of stages. Although a particular sequence may correspond broadly to the historical experience of some economies, no single sequence fits the history of all countries. To maintain that every economy always follows the same course of development with a common past and the same future is to overschematize the complex forces of development, and to give the sequence of stages a generality that is unwarranted. A country may attain a later stage of development without first having passed through an earlier stage, as stages may be skipped, and different types of economies do not have to succeed or evolve from one another. The sequence is also blurred inasmuch as frequently the stages are not mutually exclusive, and characteristics of earlier stages often become mixed with characteristics of later stages. Anyone who attempts to impose on economic history a one-way course of economic evolution is bound to be challenged, since it is difficult to accept one unique schema as the

only real framework in which the facts truly lie; the same facts can be arranged in many patterns and seen from many perspectives.[10] What matters, therefore, is how suggestive and useful Rostow's pattern is in providing answers to our questions as we attempt to make sense out of the past and make the future more predictable. This comes down to the question of the adequacy of Rostow's pattern in helping us isolate the strategic factors that make for change, especially those factors that constitute the necessary and sufficient conditions for determining the transition of an economy from a preceding stage to a succeeding stage.

In this respect, Rostow's efforts are more substantial than those by other proponents of stages. Recognizing the importance of the search for strategic factors, Rostow adopts an approach that is more analytic and related to a wider range of issues than any of the approaches of his predecessors. His argument abounds with terms such as "forces," "process," "net result," "inner logic"—all indicative of his desire to present an analytic, not merely a descriptive, set of stages. According to Rostow, the "analytic backbone" of his argument is "rooted in a dynamic theory of production," and he believes that his set of stages reveals a "succession of strategic choices" that confronts a country as it moves forward through the development process. On this basis, perhaps the most illumination can be gained from Rostow's analysis by interpreting each stage as posing a particular type of problem, so that the sequence of stages is equivalent to a series of problems that confronts a country in the course of its development.

[10]Although Rostow gives little attention to the problem, his analysis raises many questions related to basic social theory. In this connection, it is illuminating to consult Isaiah Berlin, *Historical Inevitability* (1954), especially sections 2, 8.

Comment: The "Take-Off"

Rostow has extended his analysis in *How It All Began* (1975) and *Why the Poor Get Richer and the Rich Slow Down: Essays in the Marshallian Long Period* (1970).

For a more detailed exposition of Rostow's general thesis, and criticisms levied against it, see the papers presented at the International Economic Association's conference, published in W. W. Rostow et al., *The Economics of Take-Off into Sustained Growth* (1963), and the review article by Albert Fishlow, "Empty Economic Stages?" *Economic Journal* (March 1965).

Several other critiques deserve special mention: K. Berrill, "Historical Experience: The Problem of Economic 'Take-Off,'" in *Economic Development with Special Reference to East Asia*, ed. K. Berrill (1964); Henry Rosovsky, "The Take-Off into Sustained Controversy," *Journal of Economic History* (June 1965); P. Baran and E. Hobsbawm, "The Stages of Economic Growth," *Kyklos* 14, no. 2 (1961); P. T. Bauer and Charles Wilson, "The Stages of Growth," *Economica* (May 1962); Goran Ohlin,

"Reflections on the Rostow Doctrine," *Economic Development and Cultural Change* (July 1961); and G.L.S. Shackle, "The Stages of Economic Growth," *Political Studies* (February 1962). But see Rostow's third edition of *The Stages of Economic Growth* (1991), especially the preface and Appendix B.

Of special interest is the Festschrift in honor of Rostow: C. P. Kindleberger and Guido di Tella, eds., *Economics in the Long View* (1982).

II.A.2. Economic Backwardness in Historical Perspective*

The map of Europe in the nineteenth century showed a motley picture of countries varying with regard to the degree of their economic backwardness. At the same time, processes of rapid industrialization started in several of those countries from very different levels of economic backwardness. Those differences in points—or planes—of departure were of crucial significance for the nature of the subsequent development. Depending on a given country's degree of economic backwardness on the eve of its industrialization, the course and character of the latter tended to vary in a number of important respects. Those variations can be readily compressed into the shorthand of six propositions.

1. The more backward a country's economy, the more likely was its industrialization to start discontinuously as a sudden great spurt proceeding at a relatively high rate of growth of manufacturing output.[1]

2. The more backward a country's economy, the more pronounced was the stress in its industrialization on bigness of both plant and enterprise.

3. The more backward a country's economy, the greater was the stress upon producers' goods as against consumers' goods.

*Reprinted by permission of the publishers from *Economic Backwardness in Historical Perspective* by Alexander Gerschenkron, Cambridge, Massachusetts: Harvard University Press, Copyright © 1962 by the President and Fellows of Harvard College.

[1]The "great spurt" is closely related to W. W. Rostow's "take-off" (*The Stages of Economic Growth*, Cambridge University Press, 1960, Chap. 4). Both concepts stress the element of specific discontinuity in economic development; great spurts, however, are confined to the area of manufacturing and mining, whereas take-offs refer to national output. Unfortunately, in the present state of our statistical information on long-term growth of national income, there is hardly any way of establishing, let alone testing, the take-off hypotheses.

4. The more backward a country's economy, the heavier was the pressure upon the levels of consumption of the population.

5. The more backward a country's economy, the greater was the part played by special institutional factors designed to increase supply of capital to the nascent industries and, in addition, to provide them with less decentralized and better informed entrepreneurial guidance; the more backward the country, the more pronounced was the coerciveness and comprehensiveness of those factors.

6. The more backward a country, the less likely was its agriculture to play any active role by offering to the growing industries the advantages of an expanding industrial market based in turn on the rising productivity of agricultural labor.

. . . [T]he differences in the level of economic advance among the individual European countries or groups of countries in the last century were sufficiently large to make it possible to array those countries, or group of countries, along a scale of increasing degrees of backwardness and thus to render the latter an operationally usable concept. Cutting two notches into that scale yields three groups of countries which may be roughly described as advanced, moderately backward, and very backward. To the extent that certain of the variations in our six propositions can also be conceived as discrete rather than continuous, the pattern assumes the form of a series of stage constructs. Understandably enough, this result obtains most naturally with regard to factors referred to in proposition 5, where quantitative differences are associated with qualitative, that is, institutional, variations.

. . .

Such an attempt to view the course of industrialization as a schematic stagelike process differs essentially from the various efforts in "stage making," the common feature of which was the assumption that all economies were supposed regularly to pass through the same individual stages as they moved along the road of economic progress. The regularity may have been frankly presented as an inescapable "law" of economic development.[2] Alternatively, the element of necessity may have been somewhat disguised by well-meant, even though fairly meaningless, remarks about the choices that were open to society.[3] But all those schemes were dominated by the idea of uniformity. Thus, Rostow was at pains to assert that the process of industrialization repeated itself from country to country lumbering through his pentametric rhythm. . . .

The point, however, is not simply that these were important occurrences which have just claims on the historian's attention. What matters in the present connection is that observing the individual methods of financing industrial growth helps us to understand the crucial problem of prerequisites for industrial development.

The common opinion on the subject has been well stated by Rostow. There is said to be a number of certain general preconditions or prerequisites for industrial growth, without which it could not begin. Abolition of an archaic framework in agricultural organization or an increase in the productivity of agriculture; creation of an influential modern elite which is materially or ideally interested in economic change; provision of what is called social-overhead capital in physical form—all these are viewed as "necessary preconditions," except that some reference to the multifarious forms in which the prerequisites are fulfilled in the individual areas are designed to take care of the "unique" factors in development. Similarly, the existence of a value system favoring economic progress and the availability of effective entrepreneurial groups basking in the sun of social approval have been regarded as essential preconditions of industrial growth.

These positions are part and parcel of an undifferentiated approach to industrial history. But their conceptual and empirical deficiencies are very considerable, even though it is by no means easy to bid farewell to this highly simplified way of viewing the processes of industrialization. It took the present writer several years before he succeeded in reformulating the concept of prerequisites so that it could be fit into a general approach premised upon the notion of relative backwardness. . . .

There should be a fine on the use of words such as "necessary" or "necessity" in historical writings. As one takes a closer look at the concept of necessity as it is appended to prerequisites of industrial development, it becomes clear that, whenever the concept is not entirely destitute of meaning, it is likely to be purely definitional: industrialization is defined in terms of certain conditions which then, by an imperceptible shift of the writer's wrist, are metamorphosed into historical preconditions.[4]

The recourse of tautologies and dexterous manipulations has been produced by, or at any rate served to disguise, very real empirical difficulties. After having satisfied oneself that in England certain factors could be reasonably regarded as having preconditioned the industrialization of the country, the tendency was, and still is, to elevate them to the rank of ubiquitous prerequisites of all European industrializations. Unfortunately, the attempt was inconsistent with two empirical observations: (1) some of the factors that had served as prerequisites in England either were not present in less advanced countries or at best were present to a very small extent; (2) the big spurt of industrial development occurred in those countries despite the lack of such prerequisites.

If these observations are not ignored or shrugged away, as is usually done, they quite naturally direct research toward a new question: in what way and through the use of what devices did backward countries *substitute* for the missing prerequisites? . . . It appears, on the one hand, that some of the alleged prerequisites were not needed in industrializations proceeding under different conditions. On the other hand, once the question has been asked, whole series of various substitutions become visible which could be readily organized in a meaningful pattern according to the degree of economic backwardness. . . . [I]t is easy to conceive of the capital supplied to the early factories in an advanced country as stemming from previously accumulated wealth or from gradually plowed-back profits; at the same time, actions by banks and

---

[2] See, for example, Bruno Hildebrand, *Die Nationalökonomie, der Gegenwart und Zukunft und andere gesammelte Schriften*, 1, Jena, 1922, p. 357.

[3] See Rostow, *The Stages of Economic Growth*, pp. 118ff.

[4] It is not surprising, therefore, to see Rostow at one point (p. 49) mix conditions and preconditions of industrial development very freely.

governments in less advanced countries are regarded as successful attempts to create *in the course* of industrialization conditions which had not been created in the "preindustrial" periods precisely because of the economic backwardness of the areas concerned. . . .

[T]he area of capital supply is only one instance of substitutions for missing prerequisites. As one looks at the various patterns of substitution in the individual countries, taking proper account of the effects of gradually diminishing backwardness, one is tempted to formulate still another general proposition. The more backward was a country on the eve of its great spurt of industrial development, the more likely were the processes of its industrialization to present a rich and complex picture—thus providing a curious contrast with its own preindustrial history that most often was found to have been relatively barren. In an advanced country, on the other hand, the very richness of its economic history in the preindustrial periods rendered possible a relatively simple and straightforward course in its modern industrial history.

Thus, the concept of prerequisites must be regarded as an integral part of this writer's general approach to the industrial history of Europe. At the same time, it is important to keep in mind the heuristic nature of the concept. There is no intention to suggest that backward countries

necessarily engaged in deliberate acts of "substitution" for something that had been in evidence in more advanced countries. Men in a less developed country may have simply groped for and found solutions that were consonant with the existing conditions of backwardness. In fact, one could conceivably start the study of European industrializations in the east rather than in the west of the Continent and view some elements in English industrial history as substitutions for the German or the Russian way of doing things. This would not be a very good way to proceed. It would make mockery of chronology and would be glaringly artificial. True, some artificiality also inheres in the opposite approach. It is arbitrary to select England as the seat of prerequisites. Yet this is the arbitrariness of the process of cognition and should be judged by its fruits.

The main advantage of viewing European history as patterns of substitutions governed by the prevailing—and changing—degree of backwardness lies, perhaps paradoxically, in its offering a set of predictabilities while at the same time placing limitations upon our ability to predict. To predict is not to prophesy. Prediction in historical research means addressing intelligent, that is, sufficiently specific, questions as new materials are approached.

II.A.3. Why Are We So Rich and They So Poor?*

In the beginning was Adam Smith, and he told us not to worry about economic growth: it would take care of itself. Left alone, people would sort things out, do what they did best, make appropriate choices to maximize return. The market would take care of the rest, rewarding reasons and quickness and knowledge and punishing the opposite. All of this, moreover, would work to the general advantage, augmenting the wealth of nations and leading them through a natural progression of stages from agriculture to industry to commerce. Long live the invisible hand! . . .

This "growth is natural" model (though no

one would have called it that) remained for well over 100 years the dominant paradigm; so much so, that it became an invisible given of economic thought in general, and more or less disappeared as a subject of inquiry. Insofar as some nations had trouble following this path—doing what comes naturally—the explanation was as Smith himself understood it: man and politics had gotten in the way.[1] In particular, the intervention of the state, however well meant, worked to hobble

*From David S. Landes, "Richard T. Ely Lecture," *American Economic Review, Papers and Proceedings* 80, no. 2 (May 1990): 1–13. Reprinted by permission.

[1]See, on this point, Smith's analysis of China's "stationary" state: the country "had probably long ago acquired that full complement of riches which is consistent with the nature of its laws and institutions. But this complement may be much inferior to what, with other laws and institutions, the nature of its soil, climate, and situation might admit of" (p. 95).

initiatives, distort the market, and cripple the invisible hand.

The same sense of complacency prevailed in regard to distribution. Clearly some nations were richer than others. But that was all right because it was in the nature of things. Of the three factors of production—land, labor, and capital—it was the first that made the difference. Land (which included resources under the land and climate above) was unequally distributed. That was God's work. Those nations more richly endowed with resources were, other things equal (the saving proviso of economic thinking), bound to be richer. As for the other two factors, labor and capital, the assumption was that, in the long run, these were homogeneous and equal. People were rational maximizers or could like putty be shaped to the role; and money was money, subject to appropriate rates of exchange. Both factors were assumed to be mobile and/or elastic, ready to move to opportunity—labor by migration or population change, capital by transfer or saving. Even knowledge and know-how were there for the buying. Only land was different, and there, given this natural inequality, it was in the interest of each nation to make the best of what it had. Here the Ricardian analysis of comparative advantage reinforced the Smithian model and the contentment that went with it. . . .

By the end of the nineteenth century, then, the Industrial Revolution that had begun in Britain had diffused throughout Europe and to European offshoots overseas. Not to Latin America, whose monied elites were long content to trade primary products for overseas manufactures (in those days, such things as wheat, meat, coffee, and copper; today much the same, plus cocaine); nor to European colonies or even free countries in Asia. Africa, especially sub-Saharan Africa, lay beyond the pale of awareness. And if one had asked a European economist about this, he would have described it once again as the natural order of things. The international division of labor had been modified by the diffusion of the new technologies. Britain was no longer the Workshop of the World which had expanded to include Europe and the United States. But specialization remained, and no European would have seen it as anything but rational and logical, inscribed in geography and, for many in that era, in the racial endowment. . . .

When non-Marxist, "mainstream" economists belatedly began looking at the question of growth and development in what we now call the Third World, they were no more inclined than the Marxists to jettison the classical paradigm. The Western experience was proof of what could be done, even by countries that seemed destined to serve as sources of primary products. Canada and Australia, even Argentina and Brazil: there was no reason why a nonindustrial country could not eventually create a balanced, diversified modern economy. What it needed was good government and good markets, and resources would flow to the areas of highest return. If some of these went to industry, say, food processing, why that was just fine, especially if such movement reflected true marginal rates of return and not distorted rewards. Staples theory (vent for surplus) was invented to explain this process, and it seemed to work well with a variety of economies in time and space, ranging from Canada (furs, timber, grain, minerals), to the United States (tobacco, cotton, grain), to Sweden (timber, copper, iron ore), and perhaps eventually to Argentina (hides, grain, frozen meat), and Brazil (gold, sugar, hardwoods, coffee), and even to medieval England (wool).

The trouble was that once the development bug bit, the poor countries of the twentieth century had no patience for the slow, selective, and contingent success of staples growth. On the contrary, they saw it as a trap. In this they were really no different from the follower countries of Europe in the eighteenth and nineteenth centuries. Like them, they were in a hurry, and if anything in a greater hurry, because they were poorer and, thanks to the demonstration effect, hungrier. (If you ask any of the follower countries today whether they are prepared to wait 100 years to catch up, they will express outrage. Yet that is how long it took Japan.) The primary producers of the twentieth century found that most staples were easily substitutable and subject to fierce competition in world markets; hence that staples income was uncertain and beyond their control. They also found, as nineteenth-century exporters had, that private revenue from staples exports enriched disproportionately a small fraction of the society, who more often than not were self-indulgent consumers of luxury imports, who preferred rents to the risks of market competition, and who therefore avoided engagement in a broader pattern of development.

At the same time, these would-be developers were not prepared to eschew industrialization, that is, to accept the apparent dictates of comparative advantage, because industry, especially heavy industry (above all, coal, steel, and machines), spelled power and Marxist theory told them that there could be no modernization without what Marx called Modern Industry. (In all this, they had the example of such earlier developers as the United States and Japan, which may have built their earliest gains on light industry but then shifted resources into such branches as metallurgy.)

The result was Third World development economics, which bore a strong resemblance to its intellectual predecessors of the nineteenth century (Hamilton, List, et al.), but modified, first by Marxian notions of the primacy, indeed the indispensability, of industry; of the superior if not sole legitimacy of government or collective ownership of the means of production, including peasant land; and of the importance of state planning and intervention; and second, by post-Marxian concepts and grievances of international exploitation and the penalties of inequality. . . .

So the picture is mixed; to the point where it is now commonplace to note that the Third World is a heterogeneous congeries of nations, rich and poor. Some of the distinction is based on the localized distribution of windfall staples wealth; some of it on real differences in the ability to absorb new technologies and grow. Whatever the source of the distinctions, one has the sense of a conceptual unity in course of dissolution. It is coming apart. Some countries are being "promoted," as it were, into the ranks of the advanced, industrial nations. Others are trying very hard and are still in midstream. Still others are for the moment getting nowhere.

In effect, we have the glass half-full, half-empty. Some would argue from success that all it takes is to get things right: wise policies; true prices. Others would argue from failure that getting things right is never an accident, and that some (many) may be condemned to persistent lateness and hence relative if not absolute failure.

What are the implications? Is it merely a question of optimists versus pessimists?

The question needs to be reformulated. We are talking about late development, of semi-industrial and preindustrial nations that want to catch up with a process of growth that began over 200 years ago. Well, does it make any difference to be a late developer? Or, to put it differently, does it pay to be late? . . .

The conventional wisdom has always been that lateness is an advantage; that the gap between what is and what can be is a tremendous opportunity; that the follower country can profit from the experience and knowledge of its predecessors and avoid their mistakes; and that by mobilizing resources and allocating them energetically to the right uses, it will in fact grow faster than its forerunners. This was the argument made by Alexander Gerschenkron in his seminal articles of 1951–52 on "Economic Backwardness in Historical Perspective."[2] Gerschenkron based his analysis on the European experience, on the comparison and contrast among Britain, Germany, and Russia in particular, and offered a "spurt" model of late growth. He noted, to be sure, that such spurts, when driven from above (i.e., by the state), could impose a heavy burden on the population, to the point of exhaustion; hence the Russian pattern of alternating surges and collapses. But given good judgment and management, there was no reason why a follower country could not catch and even surpass its predecessors. . . .

That was Europe in the nineteenth century. Some of the experience since then would seem to support the Gerschenkron thesis. Thus the high growth rates of such countries as Taiwan and [South] Korea (7 and 8 percent per capita over a period of decades) show that it can still pay to be late. These are economies that have passed very rapidly through an import-substitution phase to export-led growth, much of it in the newest, most technology-intensive branches. Who would have thought it possible?

On the other hand, the moderate success of others and failure of still more have led some to argue that lateness is now a growing handicap. The reasons for such a judgment are not far to seek:

1. The size of the gap. It is now a gulf and keeps widening. By the older paradigm, that only means bigger potential gains to change. On the other hand, the threshold costs are higher. Capital is not the biggest problem. Knowledge and know-how are more esoteric, even opaque, hence harder to come by. Two possibilities present themselves: (a) hire people; (b) train one's own people. The former is expensive, and the best usually have better things to do. So one makes do with less than best (LTB), which may

[2]See selection II.A.2.

be less than enough. The second is also expensive, not so much for the cost of training as for the permanent loss of talent. How ya gonna keep 'em down on the farm after they seen Paree, London, Cambridge, Berkeley, or what have you? Again, the best are the ones with the least incentive to return; again, one can settle for LTB, which may or may not be enough.

2. Staples are not what they used to be. The same technology that has produced this inequality of nations works to limit the market power of primary products by making them more substitutable. Take sugar, a commodity of unusual potency in economic history. There was a time, in the eighteenth century, when this luxury-become-necessity could provide the basis of French commercial prosperity and of the industrial growth of the western half of the country: fleets, ports, *fabriques*, all hanging on the cane crop of one island, Saint-Domingue. By the beginning of the nineteenth century, however, that was over: France had been cut off by war from overseas supplies and had learned to make sugar from beets; while other centers of cane cultivation had developed to replace what was now Haiti, lost to sugar and to France as a result of the world's first successful slave revolt.

One could tell similar stories about rubber, food crops, even rare minerals.

3. Lateness makes for bad politics. It creates uncomfortable pressures, which conduce to poor answers. This has always been true, but at one time these pressures were the exclusive concern of governing elites: the ordinary Frenchman of the late eighteenth or early nineteenth century was not aware of and could not have cared less about industrial and technological changes across the Channel. In the twentieth century, however, awareness has been enhanced by the demonstration effect, itself much reinforced by new media of communication; and political urgency has been aggravated by ideological conviction and commitment. Governments are expected to deliver, to their own members to begin with, to the populace thereafter.

Hence great haste, with much waste. Lateness is the parent of bad government. Economists have been quick to point to the adverse effects of bad government on development (indeed, some would call it the primary cause of development failure), but have said little about the sources of bad government itself, which they see as properly the matter of other disciplines. Yet bad government—or for that matter, any kind of government, good, bad, or indifferent—is not unrelated to economics. . . .

Government is clearly part of a larger social system that includes economic structures and relations. (Marxists, indeed, would go farther and say that it is the creature of class relations and interests.) Good government is not there for the wanting, or even for the knowing. It is not an act of will or fiat. It will not come about because someone appoints good counselors, even good economists—who may well be our students and who, like us, may or may not agree. (And even if they did, most politicians would say that business and the economy are too important to be left to the economists.) It takes time to create an effective, functional bureaucracy; also to establish a commitment to a larger national identity and purpose. European countries took centuries to do this; new nations have tried to establish the whole panoply of institutions in a matter of years or decades. It is no accident that the success stories of East Asia are of relatively homogeneous societies with a strong sense of historical and cultural identity.

For new nations, moreover, the process has been immensely complicated by the grievances stored up over years of subordination and humiliation; by egalitarian ideologies that deprecate private success while justifying public privilege; by the impatience to set things right and catch up . . . quickly, NOW; by the choice of the fast and meretricious over the slow and steady; by the ubiquity of the state, which distorts the reward pattern and makes it easier to get rich by politics than by industry, by connections than by performance; and by the interplay of private, rent-seeking interests that are only too-quick to exploit these possibilities.

4. Misdiagnosis and mistreatment. There's nothing that succeeds like success, and conversely. Lateness ideologized is like a malady that invites, even seeks out, bad therapy.

When Gerschenkron wrote about this problem, he offered the undisprovable thesis that nations would leap the gap between backwardness and development when they were ready. Today, by one definition, every nation is ready; and when things do not work out, they do not console themselves with the thought that they have been untimely. Rather they look for villains, whom they characteristically find outside themselves.

I need not go into the detail of these alleged sources of failure. They are familiar to all of us:

colonialism or neocolonialism, unequal trade, underdevelopment (a noun derived from a newly invented transitive verb, to underdevelop), peripherality, dependency.[3] There is some truth in all of these, and with will and good will, there is much that can be done to eliminate or mitigate their effects. On the other hand, they are more the symptoms than the explanation of development failure. There are few of these alleged sources of backwardness, for example, that do not apply to Korea or Taiwan, both formerly Japanese colonies, both deliberately pastoralized by their rulers. And many of them apply to the British colonies in North America, even to the early American republic, and to Meiji Japan. All of them reflect circumstances of inequality that yield to sovereignty and to performance: make a better, cheaper radio, TV, watch, etc., and the world will be happy to do business with you on equal terms.

What's more, even if this bill of indictment were true, it would not pay to dwell on it. It leads to self-pity, myopia, and counterproductive policies. At the extreme, it would suggest complete delinking and economic isolation. Also, there is nothing so self-defeating as the transfer of responsibility and blame to others, if only because there are limits to altruism. After an initial surge of guilt, generosity wanes; it is a wasting asset. Indeed, the greater the benefit to others of unequal arrangements, the less likely they are to surrender them. The market, like God, best helps those who help themselves.

5. Cultural factors. Values are an especially thorny problem for would-be developers, partly because, insofar as they are an impediment to growth, they are strongest in "traditional" societies; and partly because they tend to be reinforced by economic failure. To be sure, economists do not like these. They lie outside the purview of the discipline, and they always seem to get in the way. (Historians, on the other hand,

to say nothing of sociologists, have often cited them as explanations for exceptional economic performance in earlier periods [compare Max Weber and *The Protestant Ethic*]; or for Japanese achievements today.) They are often rejected as implicitly immutable, almost congenital (hence racist), although there is nothing to that effect in the argument. Or they are rejected for just the reverse, as epiphenomena that will yield easily to interest (in both senses of the word) and reason.

The truth, as so often, lies somewhere in between. Values and attitudes do change, but slowly, and their force and influence vary with circumstances. Many religious values operate, for instance, to impede the mobility and openness conducive to efficient allocation of resources and rational economic behavior. Worse yet, insofar as economic development entails changes in social structures and relations, vested cultural values, like vested material interests (they are in effect interests), can become a potent force for resistance, to the point of overturning governments and reversing the course of development. . . .

In the meantime, the struggle to pass from preindustrial to industrial, from "backward" to "advanced," goes on. By that I do not simply mean growth in income per head. That would be too easy. "Intensive growth," as it is sometimes called, can come about because nature has been kind, because new crops are more productive than old, because new land (including resources) becomes available, because relative prices change, because of outside developments and a free ride. But sustained growth is not possible without technological progress and gains in productivity. And that, history tells us, requires sooner or later the creation or assimilation of new kinds of knowledge and organization, which in turn depends on transformations within the society. External, enclave development will not do.

Such transformations require not only the absorption and adoption of new ways, but also, for many societies, the creation and acceptance of a new ethic of personal behavior. New ways demand and make new people. Time consciousness must become time discipline; the organization and character of work, the very relations of person to person, are transformed. These changes do not come easy. Historically they were often achieved by building on the more docile members of the society, the ones who

---

[3] The last three of these doctrines have come to us from Latin America, which, because it has been independent for a century and a half, has a special problem with the common recourse to neocolonialism as an excuse for failure. The difficulty is compounded by nature's bounty: these are lands generously endowed by nature that were able as a result to achieve considerable staples growth. At the turn of the century, Argentina, for example, was widely seen as a nation of unlimited possibilities, destined soon to take its place among the richest in the world. A half-century later, however, it was clear that none of these countries had done much to convert these earnings into balanced growth, including industry, so that the years of "follow-up" and catching-up were still ahead.

could not say no, that is, on women and children, and in that way creating a new labor force over a period of generations. This is still true. They have been most readily effected in those societies, like the Japanese, which had already developed appropriate time and work values before the coming of modern industry. Selection, then, is not a matter of chance or need or desire.

So the transition to modernity is necessarily a case-by-case process. Many try but few are chosen. Insofar as the transition is adventitious, superficial, or forced, moreover, it proves to be discouragingly fragile, at least in the early stages. (This is especially true of windfall staples growth: witness the experience of Côte d'Ivoire.) Small wonder that development is full of mistakes and disappointments, or that what seems like a breakthrough often slows or aborts.

References

Ayittey, George B. N. "The Political Economy of Reform in Africa," *Journal of Economic Growth*, Spring 1989, *3*, 4–17.

Bober, M. M. *Karl Marx's Interpretation of History*, 1st ed., 1927; Cambridge: Harvard University, 2nd ed., rev., 1968.

Crafts, N.F.R. *British Economic Growth during the Industrial Revolution*, Oxford: Clarendon, 1985.

Dong, Fureng. "Development Theory and Socialist Developing Economies," in Gustav Ranis and T. Paul Schultz, eds., *The State of Development Economics: Progress and Perspectives*, Oxford: Basil Blackwell, 1988.

Evans, F. T. "Wood since the Industrial Revolution: A Strategic Retreat?", *History of Technology*, 1982, *7*, 37–56.

Fagerberg, Jan. "Why Growth Rates Differ," in Giovanni Dosi et al., eds., *Technical Change and Economic Theory*, London and New York: Pinter, 1988.

Greenberg, Dolores. "Reassessing the Power Patterns of the Industrial Revolution: An Anglo-American Comparison," *American Historical Review*, December 1982, *87*, 1237–61.

Griffin, Keith, and John Gurley. "Radical Analyses of Imperialism, the Third World, and the Transition to Socialism: A Survey Article," *Journal of Economic Literature*, September 1985, *23*, 1089–1143.

Jones, Eric L. *Growth Recurring: Economic Change in World History*, Oxford: Clarendon, 1988.

Lipset, S. M. "Neoconservatism: Myth and Reality," *Society*, July–August 1988, 29–37.

McCloskey, Donald. "The Storied Character of Economics." *Tijdschrift voor Geschiedenis*, 1988, *101*, 643–54.

Marx, Karl. *Capital: A Critique of Political Economy*, Vol. 3, F. Engels, ed., Moscow: Foreign Languages Publishing, 1894/1962.

O'Brien, Patrick K., and Caglar Keyder. *Economic Growth in Britain and France 1780–1914: Two Paths to the Twentieth Century*, London: Allen & Unwin, 1978.

Patel, Surendra J. "Rates of Industrial Growth in the Last Century, 1860–1958," *Economic Development and Cultural Change*, April 1962, *9*, 316–30.

Roehl, Richard. "French Industrialization: A Reconsideration," *Explorations in Economic History*, July 1976, *13*, 233–81.

———. "British and European Industrialization: Pathfinder Pursued?", *Review* (Fernand Braudel Center, SUNY-Binghamton), 1983, *6*, 455–73.

Smith, Adam. *An Inquiry into the Nature and Causes of the Wealth of Nations*, 1st ed., 1776, New York: Modern Library, 1937.

Smith, Thomas. "Peasant Time and Factory Time in Japan," *Past & Present*, May 1986, *111*, 165–97.

Wrigley, E. A. *People, Cities and Wealth: The Transformation of Traditional Society*, Oxford: Basil Blackwell, 1987.

Comment: Historical Studies

No attempt can be made to do justice to the innumerable historical studies of development. A few, however, can be singled out: R. M. Hartwell, "The Causes of Industrial Revolution: An Essay in Methodology," *Economic History Review* 18 (1965); Richard A. Easterlin, "Is There a Need for Historical Research on Underdevelopment?", *American Economic Review* (May 1965); J. Hughes, *Industrialization and Economic History* (1970), pt. II; J. R. Hicks, *A Theory of Economic History* (1969); Lloyd G. Reynolds, *Economic Growth in the Third World, 1850–1980* (1985); D. Kumar and M. Desai, *The Cambridge Economic History of India*, vol. 2: *1757–1970* (1983); J. G. Williamson, "The Historical Content of the Classical Labor Surplus Model," *Population and Development Review*

(June 1985), and *Inequality, Poverty, and History* (1991); W. Arthur Lewis, *Tropical Development 1880–1913* (1970), and *The Evolution of the International Economic Order* (1977); Cynthia Taft Morris and Irma Adelman, *Comparative Patterns of Economic Development, 1850–1914* (1988), and "Nineteenth–Century Development Experience and Lessons for Today," *World Development* (September 1989); E. L. Jones, *Growth Recurring: Economic Change in World History* (1988); and Irma Adelman, "Prometheus Unbound and Developing Countries," in *Favorites of Fortune*, ed. Patricia Higonnet et al. (1991).

Comment: Transaction Costs, Institutions, and Historical Growth

Nobel laureate Douglass C. North emphasizes that institutional change is a central force affecting growth and development: *Institutions, Institutional Change and Economic Performance* (1990). North criticizes the neoclassical model for ignoring transaction costs and hence ignoring institutions. But, according to North, institutions—that is, formal rules, norms of behavior, and conventions, and their enforcement characteristics—determine the choices that individuals actually make in a complex structure of exchange that extends both in time and space. While "institutions are the rules of the game, organizations are the players." By creating the incentive structure in an economy, institutions thereby affect the kinds of skills and knowledge that political and economic organizations will acquire. Institutions that evolve to lower transaction costs thereby improve an economy's development performance.

So too are

> efficient markets a consequence of institutions that provide low-cost measurement and enforcement of contracts. Essential to efficiency over time are institutions that provide economic and political flexibility to adapt to new opportunities. Such adaptively efficient institutions must provide incentives for the acquisition of knowledge and learning, induce innovation, and encourage risk taking and creative activity. In a world of uncertainty, no one knows the correct solution to the problems we confront. Therefore, institutions should encourage trials and eliminate errors. A logical corollary is decentralized decision making that will allow a society to explore many alternative ways to solve problems. Institutions therefore must . . . also provide incentives to encourage decentralized decision making and effective competitive markets.[1]

North concludes that "if the constraints on development that exist in developing countries are overcome, it will be because the 'proper' organizations are put in place and their entrepreneurs carry out the necessary policies."[2] The lesson from history is that institutional innovation must occur in order to achieve sustainable development.

See also R. C. O. Matthews, "The Economics of Institutions and the Sources of Growth," *Economic Journal* (December 1986); "The Role of Institutions in Economic Development" [special issue], *World Development* (September 1989).

The selection "Organizational Dualism" (III.B.4) in Chapter III is also relevant in emphasizing the institutional importance of information and transaction costs.

[1]North, *Transaction Costs, Institutions, and Economic Performance*, p. 9.
[2]Ibid., p. 19.

II.A.4. Future Development in Historical Perspective—Note

"The historian is a prophet looking backwards"—this dictum is apt for the economic historian concerned with development. Rostow's analysis, for instance, presumes that the choices now confronting the poor countries may be revealed in the light of the stages of preconditions and take-off that the currently rich countries experienced in earlier centuries, and that historical perspective may contribute to the formulation of development policy. From this viewpoint, Rostow's analysis may be most instructive for many countries that have not yet passed successfully through the take-off stage; it may point up the similarities and differences between past and present take-offs, and suggest what policy implications flow from the differences.

With respect to the role of particular sectors of the economy, Rostow observes many problems and patterns familiar from the past. He submits that present take-offs depend, as in the past, on the allocation of resources:

to building up and modernizing the three non-industrial sectors required as the matrix for industrial growth: social overhead capital; agriculture; and foreign-exchange-earning sectors, rooted in the improved exploitation of natural resources. In addition, they must begin to find areas of modern processing or manufacture where the application of modern technique (combined with high income- or price-elasticities of demand) are likely to permit rapid growth-rates, with a high rate of plow-back of profits.[1]

It will be instructive to reconsider these conclusions after reading Chapters VII to IX in which questions not recognized by Rostow are raised. They are concerned with the allocation of investment resources and the role of industrialization.

Further, Rostow believes that for the presently underdeveloped nations, the inner mechanics of the take-off involve problems of capital formation, just as in the past. If their take-offs are to succeed, the underdeveloped countries

must seek ways to tap off into the modern sector income above consumption levels hitherto sterilized by the arrangements controlling traditional agriculture. They must seek to shift men of enterprise from trade and money-lending to industry. And to these ends patterns of fiscal, monetary, and other policies (including education policies) must be applied, similar to those developed and applied in the past.[2]

Again, this interpretation of the take-off should be critically reexamined after reading Chapter IV, in which a case is made against assigning as much importance as Rostow does to the role of capital accumulation. Rostow also notes some political and sociocultural similarities between past and present take-offs. As in the past, political interest groups range from defenders of the *status quo* to those prepared to force the pace of modernization at whatever cost. Above all, "there is continuity in the role of reactive nationalism, as an engine of modern-

ization, linked effectively to or at cross-purposes with other motives for remaking traditionalist society."[3]

Historical cases of successful take-offs also indicate a contemporary catalog of necessary social change:

. . . how to persuade the peasant to change his methods and shift to producing for wider markets: how to build up a corps of technicians, capable of manipulating the new techniques; how to create a corps of entrepreneurs, oriented not towards large profit margins at existing levels of output and technique, but to expand output, under a regime of regular technological change and obsolescence; how to create a modern professional civil and military service, reasonably content with their salaries, oriented to the welfare of the nation and to standards of efficient performance, rather than to graft and to ties of family, clan, or region.[4]

On the basis of foregoing similarities, Rostow regards the process of development now going forward in Asia, the Middle East, Africa, and Latin America as an analog to the stages of preconditions and take-off of other societies in earlier centuries. But there are also differences—in the kinds of problems now confronting poor countries, and in the manner in which some problems, although similar in kind to those of the past, are now expressed in different degrees of intensity and complexity. Especially significant is the fact that the poor countries now stand in a different relationship to rich countries than was true when the presently rich countries were poor. These differences are extremely important, and they deserve more attention than Rostow gives them. For insofar as most of these differences aggravate the problems of the take-off, they warn against letting the success stories of past take-offs lull us into too easy an interpretation of the development task. Nor should we equate the LDCs to the early stages of the presently developed countries. The persistence of underdevelopment in the world economy poses some refractory problems that were absent in earlier cases of successful development. If we recognize these differences, we may hesitate to join Rostow in concluding that in the end, the lesson of history is that "the tricks of growth are not all that difficult."[5]

In the first place, poor countries are at-

---

[1]W. W. Rostow, *The Stages of Economic Growth* (1960), p. 139.

[2]Ibid.

[3]Ibid., p. 140.

[4]Ibid.

[5]Ibid., p. 166.

tempting to accelerate their development from a lower economic level than was true for the presently rich countries at the time of their rapid rates of development. As Kuznets observes,

Output per capita is much lower in the underdeveloped countries today than it was in the presently developed countries at the date of entry—a period rather than a point of time—into modern economic growth, i.e., when growth of per-capita product (with an already high rate of population growth) began to accelerate, the shift toward non-agricultural sectors occurred, modern technology (modern by the times) was adopted, and so forth. However difficult the comparison of per-capita gross product at such distances of time and space, the weight of the evidence clearly suggests that, with the single and significant exception of Japan (the records for which are still to be fully tested), the pre-industrialization per-capita product in the presently developed countries, at least $200 in 1958 prices (and significantly more, in the offshoots overseas), was appreciably higher than per-capita product in underdeveloped countries in the late 1950s—certainly in most of Asia and Africa, and in a good part of Latin America.

Yet this statistical difference in aggregate output per capita is less important that what it represents. It implies that even today these underdeveloped countries still have such a low product per capita that they are not at the same stage as the presently developed countries were at their initial stage of modern economic growth. This seems to be the case despite access to modern technology and despite the existence of a modern sector within these countries (no matter how small). These underdeveloped countries are either at some earlier stage within the long-term trend of the presently developed countries—in terms of the Western European sequence perhaps at the period of city formation in the early Middle Ages; or, what is far more defensible, they are at some stage in a sequence of long-term growth separate and distinct from that of the Western European cradle of the modern economic epoch and are following a time and phase sequence that may be quite different.[6]

Not only do poor countries now confront the strategic policy issues of development from a level of per capita income absolutely lower than that in the advanced countries when they were developing, but their relative positions are also inferior to those of other countries—unlike the position of the early comers to development, which entered the industrialization process from a position of superior per capita income relative to other countries. The implications of attempting to develop rapidly from a lower level of per

capita income, and from a relative position that entails more pressures of backwardness, should receive a fuller treatment than Rostow's analysis provides.

Gerschenkron's suggestive analysis, outlined above, can provide a more profound understanding of these implications. We should examine, as does Gerschenkron, the processes of industrial development in relation to the degree of backwardness of the areas concerned on the eve of their great spurts of industrialization. Gerschenkron's approach has distinct advantages over Rostow's in maintaining that it is only by comparing industrialization processes in several countries at various levels of backwardness that we can hope to separate what is accidental in a given industrial evolution from what can be attributed to the historical lags in a country's development, and that it is only because a developing country is part of a larger area that includes more advanced countries that the historical lags are likely to be overcome in a specifically intelligible fashion.[7]

Another fundamental difference is that many of the poor countries have not yet experienced any significant degree of agricultural improvement as a basis for industrialization. The failure to have undergone an agricultural revolution makes the present problem of accelerating development far more difficult than it was for the now developed countries when they entered on their industrial revolutions. It is fairly conclusive that productivity is lower in the agricultural sector of underdeveloped countries than it was in the preindustrial phase of the presently developed countries. Although direct evidence of this is unavailable, it is indirectly confirmed by data suggesting that the supply of agricultural land per capita is much lower in most underdeveloped countries today than it was in presently developed countries during their take-off, and that there is a wider difference between per worker income in agricultural and nonagricultural sectors in the underdeveloped countries today than there was in the preindustrial phase of presently developed countries.

The more severe population pressures in the underdeveloped areas constitute another essential difference. Rates of population increase in these areas are higher than those that generally

[6]Simon Kuznets, "Notes on Stage of Economic Growth as a System Determinant," in *Comparison of Economic Systems*, ed. Alexander Eckstein (1971), pp. 254–55.

[7]Alexander Gerschenkron, *Economic Backwardness in Historical Perspective* (1962), p. 42. For the application of this general conception of a system of gradations of backwardness to particular countries, see chaps. 1, 4, 7, 8.

obtained during the Western cases of development in the past. Even though not all the poor countries are now densely populated, the rate of population growth is, or gives indications of soon becoming, a serious problem for most of them. And unlike the earlier cases, in which population growth was induced by, or at least paralleled, a higher rate of development, the present growth in population is simply the result of the introduction of public-health measures, which lower death rates. These act as an autonomous factor, quite unrelated to the rate of internal development. Moreover, unlike the European industrial countries that began lowering their birth rates before their sharpest declines in mortality, the poor countries now will not do so until long after their death rates have reached a modern low level. Given the fact that many poor countries are already experiencing population growth rates that are two to three times higher than those that confronted the currently rich nations when they were in their early phases of development, and that other poor countries may face a population problem in a relatively short time, the need to attain increases in production sufficient to outstrip potential increases in population is now more acute than it ever was in Western countries at the beginning of their industrialization.

Sociocultural and political differences also account for some obstacles to development that are now more formidable than in the past. Unlike the social heritage with which Western countries entered the take-off stage, the social structure and value pattern in many poor countries are still inimical to development. The structure of social relations tends to be hierarchical; social cleavages remain pronounced; and mobility among groups is limited. Instead of being allowed to achieve status by their own efforts and performance, individuals may have their status simply ascribed to them, according to their position in a system of social classification—by age, lineage, clan, or caste. A value system that remains "tradition-oriented" also tends to minimize the importance of economic incentives, material rewards, independence, and rational calculation. When the emphasis is on an established pattern of economic life, family obligations, and traditional religious beliefs, the individual may simply adopt the attitude of accepting what happens to exist, rather than attempting to alter it—an attitude of resignation rather than innovation. Within an extended-family system or a village community, individuals may resign themselves to accepting group loyalties and personal relationships that remain in a stable and tradition-dominated pattern, assigning little importance to material accomplishments and change. Even though they may have latent abilities, individuals may lack the motivations and stimulations to introduce change; there may not be sufficiently large groups in the society that are "achievement-oriented," concerned with the future, and believers in the rational mastery of nature. The positive value that the traditional way of life still holds for many of the people in a poor country inhibits the necessary orientation toward the future, and change either is resisted or, if accepted, is restricted to fringe areas.

In short, the cultural context in many poor countries may not yet be as favorable to economic achievement as it was in Western countries. This is not, of course, to assume simply that, because the West is developed, Western values and institutions are therefore necessary for development, and that Western cultural patterns must be imported into the poor countries. Many Western values and institutions may be only accidentally associated with Western development, and many values and institutions in poor countries are not obstacles to development. But although the West need not be imitated, some institutional changes and modifications in the value structure are necessary if the inhibiting institutions and values are to be removed. To allow poor countries to enter into the development process with a favorable cultural framework, as did the currently developed nations, there must be changes in their cultures so that new wants, new beliefs, new motivations, and new institutions may be created. Until these cultural changes are forthcoming, an acceleration of development will be more difficult to achieve than it was in the past.

If the degree of sociocultural development has been less than what occurred in the past, so too has there been a difference in political development. In many poor countries, the political foundations for developmental efforts are not yet as firm as they were in Western countries when they developed. Whereas the currently developed countries had already enjoyed a long period of political independence and a stable political framework before their periods of rapid economic development, most of the currently poor countries have only recently acquired a real measure of political independence. Political instability, undifferentiated and diffuse political structures, and inefficient governments are still only too prevalent. In some countries, government leadership has yet to be exercised by groups that do not have vested interests in preserving the *status quo;* in others, there is still a wide gap between the traditional mass and the modern elite, which controls the central structures of government and is the main locus of political activity.[8]

At the same time, the pressures on governments to accelerate development are now much greater than during nineteenth-century development. The revolution of rising expectations has called for active governments that are expected to institute development policies, if not a development plan. Government in the last half of the twentieth century has been held responsible for an economy's development, unlike the nineteenth-century period of *laissez faire.* And it is likely that in the twenty-first century, government policies will be instrumental in promoting development, even in market-type economies.

All these differences might be subsumed under a more general observation that it matters a great deal for the course of an individual country's development where that country stands relative to other countries. This has already been alluded to by Gerschenkron for European cases of development. With more direct reference to the problems of the presently poor countries, Paul Streeten has argued persuasively that the existence of advanced industrial societies makes a number of important differences to the development prospects of the less developed societies.[9]

On the one side, the coexistence of rich and poor countries now has a number of drawbacks for the less developed countries. A suggestive list follows.[10]

1. The most important difference is that advanced medical knowledge that can be borrowed from rich countries makes it possible to reduce the number of deaths cheaply and rapidly, without contributing to an equivalent reduction in the number of births—thereby presenting the LDCs with more difficult population problems than the now advanced countries faced in their preindustrial phase.

2. Modern technology in rich countries evolved under conditions of labor scarcity and has therefore been designed to save labor in relation to capital. But the transfer of labor-saving technology to LDCs, which is encouraged by attitudes toward modernization and by the prestige of Western technology, tends to aggravate the underutilization of labor in the LDCs.

3. The knowledge of organizations and institutions that prevail in the advanced countries may be ill-adapted to the needs of LDCs. The adoption of the trade-union structure, for example, may be inappropriate for conditions of labor surplus. Or public expenditure on social-welfare services developed in advanced industrial welfare states may be premature for LDCs. Or large-scale business enterprises may be undesirable in lesser developed economies. The transfer of inappropriate institutions to the LDCs may impede their development.

4. Technical progress in advanced economies has harmed the trade prospects of the less developed countries that depend on the export of primary products by facilitating the substitution of synthetics for natural products, by reducing the input of raw materials per unit of industrial output, and by shifting demand away from products with a high primary import content.

5. The land-rich or capital-rich countries that at one time served as an outlet for labor-surplus countries are no longer receptive to immigration; with accelerated population growth and the intensified underutilization of labor, the development pressures are thus all the greater. At the same time, the scarce resources of capital and skilled individuals are drained off to the rich centers and away from the poor peripheral countries.

Streeten has rightly emphasized that it is this coexistence of rich and poor countries, rather than the intentional or unintentional exploitation by means of colonialism or neocolonialism, that can have detrimental effects on development efforts. And he properly concludes that this coexistence sets limits on the ready transfer of the lessons of one historical setting to the entirely different present setting of poor countries vis-à-vis much more advanced countries.

Beyond the coexistence of rich and poor countries, we should recognize that the attempts of many poor countries to develop si-

---

[8]For a discussion of the difference between Western and non-Western political systems, see G. A. Almond and J. S. Coleman, eds., *The Politics of the Developing Areas* (1960).

[9]Paul P. Streeten, "The Frontiers of Development Studies: Some Issues of Development Policy," *Journal of Development Studies* (October 1967): 2–24.

[10]Streeten fully elaborates this list and some other differences in ibid., pp. 3–7.

multaneously may also intensify the task for any one of the LDCs. The policies adopted by each country in its effort to develop may hinder the development of another country. Thus the poor countries compete among themselves in attempting to increase their exports, attract private capital and skilled services, and foster industrialization by means of import-substitution policies, and in pursuing other restrictive nationalistic policies that have beggar-my-neighbor (usually a poor neighbor) effects.

Although these several differences now aggravate the problem of development, there are some dissimilarities that, on the other side, make the problems less difficult. Some advantages may accrue to presently poor countries from their position of being latecomers to development. Most helpful now may be the ability of the poor countries to draw on the accumulated stock of knowledge in countries that have already developed. Developing countries not only may acquire improved productive techniques and equipment, but also may benefit from the transfer of ideas in the realm of social techniques and social innovation as well as technology. As we have already seen, however, the value of this imitative ability is debatable, since it is still necessary to modify and adapt—not simply imitate—the technological and social innovations within the context of the borrowing country's environment. This problem receives fuller treatment in Chapter V. And aside from the requirements of readaptation, there remains the ultimate difficulty of having change accepted and integrated into the recipient society. We should not, therefore, accept too readily the view that by drawing on the lessons and experiences of countries that have developed earlier, the latecomers are in a position to telescope the early stages of development.

The existence of many advanced countries that have already reached a high level of development, which was not the case when these countries were in their preindustrial phase, may now, however, help to ease the development of poor countries by providing a flow of resources from the rich to the poor countries. Never in the past was there as much international concern as there is now with the desirability of increasing trade, technical assistance, private foreign investment, and the flow of public funds as objectives of development policy. But how effective foreign economic assistance may actually prove to be is, of course, another matter. Some judgment on this may be had from Chapter V.

Finally, there is now a strong conscious desire for development on the part of national leaders in many countries. The national interest in deliberate and rapid development, the willingness of national authorities to assume responsibility for directing their country's economic development, and the knowledge of a variety of policies that a government can utilize to accelerate development—all these give new dimensions to the role that the state may play in the development of emerging nations. Through governmental action, to a degree unknown in Western development, a more favorable environment for a take-off might be created. Nonetheless, as will be appreciated time and again in subsequent chapters, the mere act of development planning cannot be expected to remove the difficult choices and decisions that must be made to accelerate development.

Depending on how much importance we attach to each of the various differences between past and present conditions, we may reach contrasting conclusions as to whether conditions are more or less favorable now than in the past for the acceleration of development. But in the final analysis, what will determine whether a poor country will succeed is whether its government can implement effectively the policies that might make the country's development potential realizable, and whether its people are prepared to bear the costs that accelerated development will necessarily entail. Regardless of whether we interpret conditions in the currently poor countries as being on balance more or less favorable, we must not expect these countries to follow simply the historical patterns of presently developed countries. We must still give due weight to the severity of the particular problems confronting these countries. And we must determine what policies might now be most effective in removing the barriers to development. With the benefit of historical perspective, however, we should be better able to appraise the significance of these present-day development problems and their various policy implications.

II.B. ANALYTICAL PERSPECTIVES

II.B.1. Evolution of Development Economics—Note

Modern development economics arose in the late 1940s as an economic counterpart to the political independence of the emerging countries of Asia, Africa, and the Caribbean. Its influence spread rapidly to Latin America and other low-income areas. Regions that had been considered in the eighteenth century as "rude and barbarous," in the nineteenth century as "backward," and in the prewar period as "underdeveloped" now became the "less developed countries" or the "poor countries"—and the "emergent countries" and "developing economies."

But how was the development to be achieved? Although political independence can be legislated, economic independence cannot. An understanding of the forces of development was necessary, and the design of appropriate policies to support these forces was essential. To accomplish this, the creative participation of economists was needed.

The new development economics had some relation to the old growth economics of classical economists (Smith, Malthus, Ricardo)—a concern with the heavy variables of capital, population, and the objective of what Adam Smith termed the "progress of opulence" in the progressive state.[1]

But the new development economists went beyond their classical and neoclassical predecessors to consider the kinds of policies that an active state and the international community could adopt to accelerate a country's rate of development. And the new development economics, with its concern for economic theory and policy analysis, became more analytic than the prewar phase of colonial economics, which had been characterized by narrow institutional studies and economic anthropology.

The term "economic development" constituted a persuasive definition: an increase in real income per head as a desirable objective. During the 1950s and early 1960s, development policies emphasized the maximization of growth of GNP through capital accumulation and industrialization based on import substitution. In view of a distrust of markets and a belief in the pervasiveness of market failure, governments also turned to central planning. There was general optimism with respect to what could be accomplished by emphasizing planned investment in new physical capital, utilizing reserves of surplus labor, adopting import-substitution industrialization policies, embracing central planning of change, and relying on foreign aid. But there was pessimism regarding the external conditions of development—the international environment within which the national development process would have to progress—and the export of primary products: low price elasticities of demand, low income elasticities of demand, fluctuations in export revenue, deteriorating terms of trade—all these pessimistic views regarding primary-product exports reinforced the inward-looking import-substitution policies.[2]

Policy makers were adopting these policies not simply because of advice from economists, but also because of ideology and political economy.[3] Chapter X considers from the perspective of the new political economy the more general problem of why governments of developing countries do what they do—either in accordance with or contrary to professional economic advice. Nonetheless, much of the thinking in the new development economics could be appealed to in support of these policies. A "big push"[4]

[1]For more detailed reference to early growth economists, see G. M. Meier and R. E. Baldwin, *Economic Development: Theory, History, Policy* (1957); G. M. Meier, *Emerging from Poverty* (1984), chap. 5; William J. Baumol, *Economic Dynamics* (1959); Irma Adelman, *Theories of Economic Growth and Development* (1961); and Lionel Robbins, *Theory of Economic Development in the History of Economic Thought* (1968).

[2]See Jagdish Bhagwati, "Development Economics: What Have We Learned?" *Asian Development Review* 2, no. 1 (1984): 24–29.

[3]See, for example, Albert O. Hirschman, "Political Economy of Import Substituting Industrialization," *Quarterly Journal of Economics* (February 1968).

[4]P. N. Rosenstein-Roden, "Problems of Industrialization of Eastern and Southeastern Europe," *Economic Journal* (June–September 1943).

or "critical minimum effort"[5] was believed necessary to break out of a "low level equilibrium trap."[6] An increase in the proportion of national income invested above 10 percent was advocated for a "take-off," with industry as the leading sector.[7] "Balanced growth"—the synchronized application of capital to a wide range of industries—was advocated by Nurkse:

A frontal attack—a wave of capital investments in a number of different industries—can economically succeed while any substantial application of capital by an individual entrepreneur in any particular industry may be blocked or discouraged by the limitations of the preexisting market. . . . [T]hrough the application of capital over a wide range of activities, the general level of economic activity is raised and the size of the market enlarged. . . . [Balanced growth] is a means of getting out of the rut, a means of stepping up the rate of growth when the external forces of advance through trade expansion and foreign capital are sluggish or inoperative.[8]

Hirschman, however, advocated unbalanced growth in order to maximize induced decision making and to take advantage of forward and backward linkages in the production process.[9] Unlike the neoclassical economists, who assumed a smoothly working market-price system, some of the early development economists adopted a more structuralist approach to development problems. Structuralist analysis attempted to identify specific rigidities, lags, shortages and surpluses, low elasticities of supply and demand, and other characteristics of the structure of developing countries that affect economic adjustments to development policy. The structuralist view also was pessimistic about the responsiveness of agents to price signals and incentives. Instead of neoclassical flexibility and substitutability, the structuralist view emphasized low elasticities of supply and market imperfections that limit the mobility of factors and the responsiveness of agents. Myrdal, Prebisch, and Singer were especially prominent in reinforcing the pessimistic view with respect to exports of primary products.[10]

During the late 1960s and early 1970s came a second phase of development economics, which focused more directly on poverty and inequality. It was argued that growth in GNP is not a sufficient condition for the removal of poverty: income was not trickling down to the lowest income groups, and the number of people living in absolute poverty was increasing in many countries. The very meaning of development was questioned, and instead of worshiping at the altar of GNP, many economists added other dimensions to the objectives of development. The World Bank emphasized redistribution with growth.[11] The International Labor Organization (ILO) concentrated on basic human needs.[12] Much of the development literature turned from an emphasis on industrial development to one on rural development. Impressed by studies of human capital formation,[13] economists also shifted their attention from physical capital to human resources. And the concern with appropriate technology broadened the problem of what could or should be borrowed from the more developed countries.[14]

The most substantial change in the content of development economics came during the 1970s and 1980s—decades marked by the resurgence of neoclassical economics.[15] There was increasing criticism of policy-induced distortions and the nonmarket failures associated with the implementation of public policies. This led to a critique of comprehensive and detailed administrative controls. With the renewed attention to the application of neoclassical economics, price distortions were to be removed: "'Getting prices right' is not the end of economic development. But 'getting prices wrong' frequently

[5]Harvey Leibenstein, *Economic Backwardness and Economic Growth* (1957), chap. 8.

[6]Richard R. Nelson, "A Theory of the Low-Level Equilibrium Trap in Underdeveloped Economies," *American Economic Review* (December 1956): 894–908.

[7]W. W. Rostow, *The Stages of Economic Growth* (1960).

[8]Ragnar Nurkse, *Problems of Capital Formation in Underdeveloped Countries* (1953), pp. 13–15.

[9]Albert O. Hirschman, *The Strategy of Economic Development* (1958).

[10]Gunnar Myrdal, *Economic Theory and Underdeveloped Regions* (1957); Raúl Prebisch, "The Economic Development of Latin America and Its Principal Problems," *Economic Bulletin for Latin America* 7 (1950); Hans Singer, "Gains and Losses from Trade and Investment in Underdeveloped Countries," *American Economic Review* (May 1950).

[11]World Bank, *Redistribution with Growth* (1974).

[12]International Labor Organization, *The Basic Needs Approach to Development* (1977).

[13]T. W. Schultz, "Investment in Human Capital," *American Economic Review* (March 1961): 1–17.

[14]Frances Stewart, *Technology and Underdevelopment* (1977).

[15]I. M. D. Little, *Economic Development* (1982), chap. 9.

is."[16] It had long since become evident that economic rationality characterizes agents in the less developed countries as well as in the more developed.[17] Beyond the removal of price distortions, neoclassical economics advocated getting all policies right. Markets, prices, and incentives became central. Inward-looking strategies of development were to give way to liberalization of the foreign-trade regime and export promotion. Inflation was to submit to stabilization programs. State-owned enterprises were to be privatized. A poor country was now considered poor because of inappropriate policies, and good economics—that is, neoclassical economics—was good for the developing country.

In the 1950s, the pioneers in development had asked why underdeveloped countries were underdeveloped, and they formulated grand theories and general strategies. In contrast, the focus in the 1970s and 1980s became increasingly directed to the heterogeneity of the developing countries and to an explanation of differential rates of country performance. Analysis moved from highly aggregated growth models to disaggregated micro models. More emphasis was placed on applied research that was country-specific, based on empirical data, and on the application of neoclassical principles to policy issues. In an increasing number of countries, these changes in development thought produced an improvement in agricultural policies, a liberalization of the foreign-trade regime, and a professionalism in project appraisal.[18]

Instead of the earlier fascination with long-term optimizing models, more attention is now being given to micro aspects of the development process and to the shorter term period. And based on four decades of development experience, efforts are now being made to understand why certain policies were effective in a country,

while other policies were not, and why the same type of policy was effective in one country, but not in another. In this inquiry, the new political economy, based on neoclassical analysis of political markets, is becoming more significant (more on this in Chapter X).[19]

In contrast to the position of the early development economists, who eschewed the universal use of neoclassical economics and thought the "special case" irrelevant for development policy, many economists now emphasize the universality of neoclassical economics and dismiss the claim that development economics is a special subdiscipline in its own right. Hirschman, for instance, has written provocatively about the rise and decline of development economics.[20] So, too, does Kreuger state:

Once it is recognized that individuals respond to incentives, and that "market failure" is the result of inappropriate incentives rather than of nonresponsiveness, the separateness of development economics as a field largely disappears. Instead, it becomes an applied field, in which the tools and insights of labor economics, agricultural economics, international economics, public finance and other fields are addressed to the special questions and policy issues that arise in the context of development.[21]

Many other students of development, however, believe that an obituary of development economics is not in order. Thus Sen argues that there is still much relevance in the broad policy themes that traditional development economics has emphasized: (1) industrialization, (2) rapid capital accumulation, (3) mobilization of underemployed manpower, and (4) planning and an economically active state.[22] And Lewis recognizes that "the overlap between Development Economics and the Economics of the Developed is bound to be great, but there are also differences that are rather large, which is why each also has some tools of its own."[23]

Moreover, following Harberger's exposition of the neoclassical viewpoint (II.B.2), Chenery

[16]C. Peter Timmer, "Choice of Techniques in Rice Milling in Java," *Bulletin of Indonesian Economic Studies* (July 1973).

[17]The usual postulates of rationality and the principles of maximization or minimization have quite general applicability. For illustrative evidence, see P. T. Bauer and B. S. Yamey, *The Economics of Under-Developed Countries* (1957), pp. 91–101; W. J. Barber, "Economic Rationality and Behavior Patterns in an Underdeveloped Area: A Case Study of African Economic Behavior in the Rhodesias," *Economic Development and Cultural Change* (April 1960): 237–51; and W. O. Jones, "Economic Man in Africa," *Food Research Institute Studies* (May 1960): 107–34.

[18]Gerald M. Meier, "On Getting Policies Right," in *Pioneers in Development,* 2d ser., ed. Gerald M. Meier (1987), pp. 3–11.

[19]D. C. Collander, ed., *Neoclassical Political Economy* (1980).

[20]Albert O. Hirschman, "Rise and Decline of Development Economics," in *Essays in Trespassing* (1981).

[21]Anne O. Krueger, "Aid in the Development Process," *World Bank Research Observer* (January 1986): 62–63.

[22]Amartya K. Sen, "Development Which Way Now?" *Economic Journal* (December 1983).

[23]W. Arthur Lewis, "The State of Development Theory," *American Economic Review* (March 1984): 2.

(II.B.3) and Stiglitz (II.B.4) point up some limitations to the neoclassical approach for development economics.

Perhaps the issue of the relevance of neoclassical economics to developing countries can be best resolved by concluding that the task of development economists is made difficult not because they must start afresh with a completely new set of tools or because they confront problems that are wholly different from those in advanced countries, but because they must acquire a sense of the different assumptions that are most incisive for analyzing a problem within the context of a poor country. In particular, this calls for special care in identifying different institutional relations, in assessing the different quantitative importance of some variables, and in allowing some elements that are usually taken as givens—such as population, "state of the arts," institutions, and supply of entrepreneurship—to become endogenous variables in development analysis.

When reading selections in the following chapters, we should therefore be alert to the efforts being made to adapt our conventional way of thinking about economic problems to the particular context of developing countries. For some issues, the adaptation is made explicit: the key factors distinguishing the situation in a poor country from that in an advanced economy are recognized, and a new set of assumptions is explicitly adopted; for example, the existence of a subsistence sector, disguised unemployment, or an unorganized money market may require modification of the usual assumptions of macroanalysis. In other instances, some concepts are introduced out of consideration for the special conditions of poor countries—for instance, "social dualism," the structuralist view of inflation, or noneconomic criteria for investment. Whether these considerations of the relevance of conventional economic analysis are introduced explicitly or are only implicit, we should be aware that they constitute a major theme of this book. This problem of adapting our accepted tools and principles is, in a fundamental sense, an overriding general issue in development economics.

Comment: Classical Growth Theory

Prior to the neoclassical marginalist revolution in the 1870s, classical economists had been very much interested in economic growth—Adam Smith's "progressive state." According to Smith, the level of output per head, together with the growth of output, "must in every nation be regulated by two different circumstances: first by the skill, dexterity, and judgement with which its labor is generally applied; and, secondly, by the proportion between the number of those who are employed in useful labor, and that of those who are not so employed."

The major sources of growth are (1) growth in the labor force and stock of capital, (2) improvements in the efficiency with which capital is applied to labor through greater division of labor and technological progress, and (3) foreign trade that widens the market and reinforces the other two sources of growth.

Once begun, the growth process becomes self-reinforcing in the progressive state. As long as the growth in wealth favors profits, there are savings and additional capital accumulation, and hence further growth. And with capital accumulation, the demand for labor rises, and a growing labor force is absorbed in productive employment.

Smith also attributed overwhelming importance to the division of labor, in the broad sense of technical progress. The division of labor entails improved efficiency of labor, and increasing specialization leads to rising per capita income. By extending the division of labor, improvements in production reduce the amount of input per unit of output. According to Smith, however,

> the division of labor is limited by the extent of the market. . . . When the market is very small, no person can have any encouragement to dedicate himself entirely to one employment, or want of power to exchange all that surplus part of the produce for his own labor, which is over and above his own consumption, or such parts of the produce of other men's labor as he has occasion for.

The division of labor increases wealth, which, in turn, widens the market, enabling the division of labor to be carried further forward.

If capital accumulation, division of labor, and foreign trade are sources of a nation's economic growth, then—according to Smith—growth can be promoted through the extension of market institutions and the activity of competition.

Some of Smith's insights retain much relevance. To Smith and the modern economists, growth is the outcome of a logical process. Both search for some laws and generalizations. Modern economists emphasize, as did Smith, capital accumulation as a driving force in the growth process. So, too, do they concentrate on increasing productivity. They also point to the possibilities for development based on foreign trade. And at the forefront of development discussions, economists seek to find a proper division between reliance on the market-price system and dependence on governmental actions.

Among the classical economists, the development views of Thomas Malthus, David Ricardo, and John Stuart Mill are also significant.

From the 1870s to the 1930s, the theory of value and resource allocation dominated economic thought. Economic analysis turned its attention to the conditions that would make possible various optima rather than the conditions that would allow an economy to achieve ever-changing optima of ever-increasing range. Not the movement of aggregate output in the entire economy, but the movement of particular lines of production toward an equilibrium position became the neoclassicist's concern. To tighten up the economy and avoid inefficiency was the neoclassicist's objective. Rigorous analysis of individual markets and of price formation was the neoclassicist's hallmark. In *The Theory of Economic Growth* (1955), W. Arthur Lewis could therefore say that "no comprehensive treatise on the subject has been published for about a century. The last great book covering this wide range was John Stuart Mill's *Principles of Political Economy,* published in 1848."

For studies of the classical economists' views on economic growth, see Lionel Robbins, *The Theory of Economic Development in the History of Economic Thought* (1968); William J. Baumol, *Economic Dynamics* (1959); Irma Adelman, *Theories of Economic Growth and Development* (1961); G. M. Meier and R. E. Baldwin, *Economic Development: Theory, History, Policy* (1957); G. M. Meier, *Emerging from Poverty* (1984), chap. 5.; G. M. Meier, ed., *From Classical Economics to Development Economics* (1994).

Comment: Development Economics as a Special Subject

In the years following World War II, the subject of development economics was formulated in its own right. Investigating issues that went beyond the earlier growth economics of classical economists (Smith, Malthus, Ricardo), a "new development economics" began to be formulated by a number of economists. For the outstanding contributions made in the formative period of the 1950s, see Gerald M. Meier and Dudley Seers, eds., *Pioneers in Development* (1948). Also, H. W. Arndt, *Economic Development: The History of an Idea* (1989).

Several retrospective papers have considered the evolution of development thought over the past four decades. Most useful in tracing the changing views of development economists are Albert Hirschman, "The Rise and Decline of Development Economists," in *Essays in Trespassing* (1981); Ian Livingstone, "The Development of Development Economics," *O.D.I. Review,* no. 2 (1981); Amartya Sen, "Development: Which Way Now?" *Economic Journal* (December 1983); Jagdish Bhagwati, "Development Economics: What Have We Learned?" *Asian Development Review* 2 (1984); W. Arthur Lewis, "The State of Development Theory," *American Economic Review* (March 1984); and "The Methodological Foundations of Development Economics" [special issue], *World Development* (February 1986).

Although development economists now rely much more on standard neoclassical principles that apply to rich and poor countries alike, the subject of development economics still has sufficient distinctive characteristics to distinguish it as a special subdiscipline in economics. This distinction is recognized in two recent surveys of the subject. Nicholas Stern's "Survey of Development," *Economic Journal* (September 1989) is addressed to "economists and students of economics who do know the tools of their trade but not necessarily how they have been applied to and fashioned for the analysis of the economics of developing countries." Bliss also argues that

> general economic principles are precisely too general to give us insights into applications for less developed economies. Alone, the parts of economic theory and method that apply more or less universally tell us less than we need in particular application. To give them life they have to be enlarged and translated. When this is done a specialty is created. Development economics consists in part of the refinement of general economics to deal with questions which arise in the context of development, and partly of certain special ideas which have proved useful in studying developing countries.[1]

[1]Christopher Bliss, *Handbook of Development Economics* (1989), p. 1188.

II.B.2. Neoclassical Analysis*

While one must recognize that in the tradition of our profession, on the subject of the analysis of economic growth, there are and always have been many strands, I do not believe I am wrong in saying that in the late 1940s and early 1950s the Harrod–Domar model occupied centre stage. It was written about, talked about, extended, elaborated, and empirically applied. To me, its dominant characteristic as well as its ultimate flaw as a theory of growth was the assumption of a strict link between the growth of the capital stock on the one hand and the consequent growth of potential output on the other. If demand conditions were made right, said the model, the only bottleneck to growth was a lack of physical capital. In this sense physical capital accumulation was the only ultimate source of economic growth.

This, of course, left little scope (really none at all) for other factors and forces in the growth process. And I think there can be no doubt that this extreme vision of the world would not have gained the widespread acceptance that it did, were it not for another strand in the intellectual mainstream of the time—the notion that the less-developed economies were suffering from surplus labour. Labour was thought to be in surplus, not in the sense that there was a lot of it working with relatively little capital, resulting in relatively low marginal productivity and consequently low wages. Rather, the thought was that labour was in surplus in the much stricter sense that its marginal productivity was zero. Capital investment was critical not just for its own sake, as it were, but because it gave employment to labour that would otherwise be unemployed, and because that labour was paid, not out of its own marginal product, but out of the marginal product of capital.

The passage of the theory of growth out of this early stage took place at the hands of Solow, Kendrick, Denison, Abramovitz, and, before it was over, many, many others. I think of it as a two-pronged effort, one prong having its roots in theoretical analysis, the other being based more directly on empirical work. On the theoretical side we have the development of the concept of the aggregate production function, containing factors other than just physical capital. Increments to any factor would then cause increments to product, according to the marginal productivity of that factor. The interesting discovery at this second stage of development was that, when factor earnings (wage rates, returns per unit of capital, etc.) were used as measures of the contributions of productive factors to the process of economic growth, a substantial amount of growth, which ultimately came to be known as "the residual," remained unexplained.

The residual was initially thought of as a coefficient of technical advance (since it effectively measured the growth in output per unit of input), but it was quickly recognized to be a composite of the effects of many different forces:

(i) improvement in the quality of labour through education, experience and on-the-job training;
(ii) reallocation of resources from low-productivity to higher-productivity uses, either through normal market forces, or through the reduction of barriers or distortions;
(iii) exploitation of economies of scale;
(iv) improved ways of combining resources to produce goods and services, not just at the level of new machines or processes, but also by relatively mundane adjustments at the level of the factory or the farm.

The end result of this evolution is, at least in my opinion, a rather microeconomic view of the growth process. The basic equation of growth is

$$\Delta Y = \sum_i w_i \Delta L_i + \sum_j r_j \Delta K_j + R \quad (1)$$

where Y is national product, w_i is the unit labour cost (gross wage) of labour of type i, r_j is the unit return to capital of type j (which should be gross of taxes and may be gross of depreciation as well in the case where Y is defined as gross rather than net product), and R is still "the residual."

Labour and capital can be defined into very narrow categories for the purposes of equation (1). Labour may vary over age, sex, region, industry, experience, unionization, etc. Capital will have different categories, but there can nonetheless be substantial variation among them.

In the process of looking at economic growth

*From Arnold C. Harberger, "The Cost- Benefit Approach to Development Economics," *World Development,* Vol. 11, no. 10 (1983), pp. 864–66. Reprinted by permission from Elsevier Science Ltd. Oxford, England.

in a more microeconomic fashion we have, I believe, unhooked our view of growth from the concept of an aggregate production function. Working with an equation like (1) we simply do not need to appeal to such a function. We may find it convenient to think in terms of individual production functions in individual industries, but we need not do that either, for processes can differ greatly from firm to firm within an industry and from plant to plant within a firm. In the final analysis, one can simply interpret (1) as imputing to an increment of labour of category i a contribution to growth equal, at least, to its gross wage, on the ground that otherwise its employer would not have wanted to hire it. The two summations in equation (1) then tell us what to attribute as the contribution of labour and capital to growth under such an imputation. The residual, R, is what is left. R will tend to be small if the indices i and j run over many narrowly and well-defined categories; R will tend to be large if the indices i and j run over few and poorly defined categories.

Let me now try to link what has just been said with modern applied welfare economics or cost–benefit analysis. We know on the one hand that productive factors tend to get paid (in unsubsidized activities) at most their marginal product; we know, too, that many types of distortion (or divergence between social and private marginal product) can exist. Taxes are the most obvious and widespread of all distortions; they invariably introduce a wedge between the value of marginal product of a factor and the reward which that factor perceives. Other sources of distortion include (a) monopoly and oligopoly profits (which are really privately imposed and privately collected taxes); (b) economies of scale, which generate marginal productivity in excess of average productivity and, typically, in excess of factor remunerations (i.e., activities with economies of scale should typically be subsidized to correct for the distortion); (c) congestion in all its forms, including what Anne Krueger has called rent-seeking activity of all types [here the marginal social product of a resource or of an activity is less than its private marginal product, and the activity should typically be taxed (or a common-property resource properly priced) to correct for the distortion]; (d) pollution, contamination and their opposites which generate external benefits to particular activities.

Consider, then, that all of these items that create differences between the marginal social product and the marginal private product of a resource in a given activity, are summarized in a measure D_i, of the distortion applying there. Then let us express the growth of output by the equation

$$\Delta Y = \sum_i \Delta L_i(w_i + D_i)$$
$$+ \sum_j \Delta K_j(r_j + D_j) + R \quad (2)$$

In this framework we must think of labour and capital as classified into quite narrowly defined boxes. A 30-year-old engineer is more productive than a 30-year-old sweeper, so the labour force must be broken down by occupation. Education also plays a role, as those with more education tend to be more productive. Location can be relevant, too, for the wages of workers of a given type, age, education, etc. need not be the same in different regions. (In the U.S. there are significant differences between, say, Alaska and Mississippi; in India, the differences, particularly in agricultural wages, between, say, the Punjab and Bihar, are vast.) Industry is important as a characteristic of classification to the extent that distortions such as product taxes, product monopoly elements, factor monopoly elements (union wages in excess of the norm for equivalent workers), economies of scale, and other distoritons referred to above will vary from industry to industry. But in principle if even within an industry these distortions were to vary from factory to factory, then the criterion of classification ought to be narrowed down to the level of the factory.

Of course we never really do these things, but this is nonetheless the way to think clearly, in modern terms, about the process of economic growth. In principle, the first term of equation (2) takes into account the contribution to the growth of, say, GNP from the following sources among others:

(a) the employment of labour previously unemployed;
(b) the movement of labour from an activity with low wages to an activity with high wages;
(c) the movement of labour from an untaxed to a taxed activity (GNP grows and the government gains tax revenues);
(d) the increase in the labour force of an activity with economies of scale;
(e) the improvement that occurs when a worker's productivity is upgraded, be it through

education, experience, or on-the-job training;

(f) the improvement that occurs when, by reducing distortions, the government causes the use of labour to increase in activites with positive distortions.

With respect to capital, the relevant categories are different from those applying to labour. In general, the principal criteria relate to the tax status of the capital involved. This varies depending on whether the financing is in the form of equity (to the income from which the corporation income tax usually applies) or from debt (where it does not). It also varies depending on the nature of the asset; some assets are subject to property or real estate taxes; others are not. Of course, where excise taxes are involved, these create distortions between the private and the social marginal productivity of capital; hence wherever they are present the classification of capital (K_j) should include the criterion of the industry in which it is employed or the product it helps to produce.

The second term of equation (2) thus captures the contribution to economic growth stemming from

(g) new investible funds that are injected into the capital stock;

(h) the negative growth stemming from the depreciation or retirement of old components of the capital stock;

(i) the reallocation of capital between low-productivity and high-productivity uses;

(j) the movement of capital into activities with positive distortions (taxes, monopoly profits, economies of scale, or other positive externalities).

The message of all this is that with a simple and quite straightforward approach, fully rooted in neoclassical economic theory yet thoroughly capable of taking into account all sorts of distortions and market imperfections, we end up explaining most of what in the earlier modern macroeconomic analysis of growth, as represented by equation (1), would be stuck in the residual R.

In short, the current version of modern growth analysis, as represented in equation (2) embodies quintessential common sense. It is so simple that it hardly merits the term "theory," yet it is a theory, and a very powerful one in the sense that it helps one to interpret events and to make choices in many circumstances that arise as part of our daily experience in the real world. Above all it shows that the incredible complexity of the growth process is perfectly reasonable, perfectly plausible, perfectly consonant with common sense.

Comment: Total Factor Productivity

The measurement of total factor productivity (TFP) shows the efficiency with which all inputs are utilized in a production function. Whereas a partial productivity index measures the value of output per unit of input, the TFP index sums the partial productivities of all inputs in the production process.

Both input growth and TFP growth contribute to output growth simultaneously. The purpose of measuring TFP is to separate these two forces contributing to growth in output. The estimate of TFP change is derived from a production function that gives the maximum amount of output that can be produced with a given amount of input. The structure of production implied by the production function requires that the following accounting identity hold:

Percentage change in total factor productivity ≡ percentage change in output *minus* [percentage change in inputs *multiplied* by elasticity of output with respect to inputs].

The percentage change in output and in inputs between any two periods can be obtained from standard economic statistics.The elasticity of output with respect to each input—that is, the percentage increase in output that is achieved from a 1 percent increase in the input—can be obtained econometrically from the production function. The second term on the right-hand side of the identity therefore measures the percentage change in output made possible by the increase (or decrease) in inputs. Any increase (or decrease) in output that occurs in addition to this is due to TFP change. "TFP change" is often used synonymously with "technical change," as represented in Exhibit II.1 by a shift in the production function so that the efficiency with which all inputs are combined in production increases.

In a pioneering article—"Technical Change and the Production Function," *Review of Economics and Statistics* (August 1957)—Nobel laureate Robert Solow explained the neoclassical growth equation and showed how to segregate increases in output per head due to "technical change"(that is, a shift in the production function) from those due to changes in the availability of capital per head.

EXHIBIT II.1. Technical Change and the Production Function

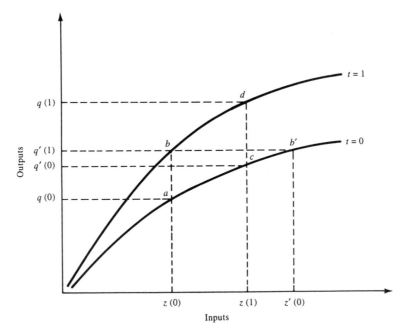

Exhibit II.1 depicts two production functions, each corresponding to a different level of technology: $t = 0$ and $t = 1$. A given level of technology, say at $t = 0$, implies that more output—for example, $q'(1)$ at production point b—cannot be produced without more inputs. To produce $q'(1)$ with technology $t = 0$, inputs would have to be increased to the level $z'(0)$ corresponding to production point b'.

If Total Factor Productivity or TFP increases, this means that greater output can be produced over time with given levels of inputs. Exhibit II.1 shows the production function to have shifted upward from $t = 0$ to $t = 1$. This shift represents a technical change, resulting in a larger amount of maximum output that can be produced at every level of inputs. It is now possible, for example, to produce the amount of output $q'(1)$ with the input level of $z(0)$ rather than $z'(0)$ at production point b. Thus the technical change represented by the shift in the production function means that the efficiency with which all inputs are combined in production increases. This is the definition of an increase in TFP.

EXHIBIT II.2. Sources of Growth
A. The Growth of GDP, Inputs, and TFP (percent)

Region, Group, or Economy	GDP			Capital			Labor			TFP		
	1960–73	1973–87	1960–87	1960–73	1973–87	1960–87	1960–73	1973–87	1960–87	1960–73	1973–87	1960–87
Developing economies												
Africa	4.0	2.6	3.3	6.3	6.3	6.3	2.1	2.3	2.2	0.7	−0.7	0.0
East Asia	7.5	6.5	6.8	9.8	10.7	10.2	2.8	2.6	2.6	2.6	1.3	1.9
Europe, Middle East, and North Africa	5.8	4.2	5.0	7.7	7.5	7.6	1.4	1.9	1.7	2.2	0.6	1.4
Latin America	5.1	2.3	3.6	7.4	5.6	6.3	2.5	2.8	2.6	1.3	−1.1	0.0
South Asia	3.8	5.0	4.4	8.0	7.2	7.7	1.8	2.3	2.1	0.0	1.2	0.6
Sixty-eight economies	5.1	3.5	4.2	7.4	7.1	7.2	2.2	2.4	2.3	1.3	−0.2	0.6

EXHIBIT II.2. (*continued*)

B. Percentage Share of Output Growth Accounted for by Factor Input Growth, Sample of World Economies, 1960–87

Region or Group	Capital	Labor	TFP
	1960–87		
Africa	73	28	0
East Asia	57	16	28
Europe, Middle East, and North Africa	58	14	28
Latin America	67	30	0
South Asia	67	20	14
Total	65	23	14

One method of analyzing the growth process is to estimate the contribution that the inputs of capital and labor make to growth in GDP. The sum of the contributions of the factor inputs does not account for overall growth. The residual in the estimated production function, or total factor productivity (TFP), accounts for the rest, as indicated above for different developing economies.

Source: World Bank, *World Development Report 1991* (1991), pp. 43, 45.

II.B.3. Structural Analysis*

There are two contrasting views of the way economic growth occurs. In the neoclassical tradition, GNP rises as the result of the long-term effects of capital formation, labor force expansion, and technological change, which are assumed to take place under conditions of competitive equilibrium. Shifts in demand and the movement of resources from one sector to another are considered relatively unimportant because labor and capital produce equal marginal returns in all uses.

In the second, broader view, economic growth is regarded as one aspect of the transformation of the structure of production that is required to meet changing demands and to make more productive use of technology. Given imperfect foresight and limits to factor mobility, structural changes are most likely to occur under conditions of disequilibrium; this is particularly true in factor markets. Thus a shift of labor and capital from less productive to more productive sectors can accelerate growth. Although this type of structural analysis has not received the same rigorous formulation as general equilibrium theory, it can provide a basis for empirical analysis.

*From Hollis Chenery, "Growth and Transformation," in Hollis Chenery, Sherman Robinson, Moshe Syrquin, *Industrialization and Growth*, Oxford University Press, New York, 1986, pp. 13–27, 27–32. Reprinted by permission.

When general equilibrium is not treated as axiomatic, the question of how much the reallocation of resources to sectors of higher productivity contributes to growth becomes an empirical one. It is likely to be more important for developing countries than for developed ones to recognize the potential of reallocation, for developing countries show more pronounced symptoms of disequilibrium in factor markets as well as more rapid change in the structure of production.

Some fundamental differences between the growth processes of developing or transitional economies and those of mature, industrial economies emerge from this survey. In particular, disequilibrium phenomena are shown to be more significant for the former than for the latter. Thus, although neoclassical theory is a useful starting point for the study of growth, it must be modified substantially if it is to explain the essential features of economies in the process of transformation.

The Sources of Growth

Measurement of the sources of economic growth has progressed greatly. The main objective has been to estimate the relative contributions of the growth of capital and labor inputs (corrected for quality changes) on the one hand and of total factor productivity on the other. There are now many studies of the industrial countries, covering much of the postwar period, that use variants of neoclassical theory. This methodology has also been applied to a growing number of semi-industrial countries, and therefore some of the differences in the growth processes of the two groups can be identified.

Because the study of the disequilibrium aspects of growth requires a more detailed model than that of equilibrium growth, the principal econometric efforts have tested the significance of these aspects in explaining differences in growth among countries. This work has established the importance of moving resources from lower-productivity to higher-productivity uses—for example, by expanding exports or by turning from agriculture to industry. These shifts are more important sources of growth in developing than in developed countries.

This empirical work suggests some answers to several questions of concern:

- How useful is the neoclassical methodology as applied to developing countries? Are there significant differences among groups of countries that should be taken into account?
- Which departures from the general equilibrium framework appear to be most significant? To what extent is more explicit analysis of the changing composition of demand and trade needed?
- Are there systematic variations with per capita income in the factors affecting growth that should be allowed for?

In considering these questions, it may be useful to contrast the assumptions underlying neoclassical and structural views of the sources of growth. Since the basic assumptions of neoclassical theory are well known, they can serve as a point of departure in explaining the hypotheses of the structural approach.

The most important distinction between the two views is between their systemic assumptions rather than between any one of their elements. Neoclassical theory assumes the efficient allocation of resources (Pareto optimality) over time from the point of view of both producers and consumers. At any given moment it is impossible to increase aggregate output by shifting labor and capital from one sector to another: reallocation takes place only as the economy expands. In contrast, the structural approach does not assume fully optimal resource allocation; consequently, there may be systematic variations in the returns to labor and capital in different uses.

Some of the assumptions that contribute to this basic distinction are outlined in Table 1. Maintaining equilibrium in the face of shifts in internal demands and in external trade is helped

TABLE 1. Alternative Views of Growth

Neoclassical Approach	Structural Approach
Assumptions	
Factor returns equal marginal productivity in all uses	Income-related changes in internal demand
No economies of scale	Constrained external markets and lags in adjustment
Perfect foresight and continuous equilibrium in all markets	Transformation of productive structure producing disequilibria in factor markets
Empirical Implications	
Relatively high elasticities of substitution in demand and trade	Low price elasticities and lags in adjustment
Limited need for sector disaggregation	Segmented factor markets
	Lags in adopting new technology
Sources of Growth	
Capital accumulation	Neoclassical sources plus:
Increase in labor quantity and quality	Reallocation of resources to higher-productivity sectors
Increase in intermediate inputs	
Total factor productivity growth within sectors	Economies of scale and learning by doing
	Reduction of internal and external bottlenecks

by high elasticities of substitution among both commodities and factors and by rapid responses to market signals. Neoclassical theory assumes that the economic system has sufficient flexibility to maintain equilibrium prices, whereas the structural approach identifies some conditions that make complete adjustment unlikely. One of the best documented sources of disequilibrium is the duality of the labor market—a duality which has been accentuated in many developing countries by a population growing too rapidly to be absorbed in the high-productivity sectors of the economy. The result is an elastic supply of unskilled labor concentrated in the agricultural and service sectors.

A second widely studied source of disequilibrium is the failure to reallocate resources efficiently to increase exports or replace imports. The factors contributing to a chronic balance of payments deficit include the tendency for import demands to expand more rapidly than total GNP, the lack of incentives for producers to enter new markets, and shortsighted policies that favor import substitution over export expansion. Whatever the factors limiting balance of payments adjustment in the past, there is little doubt that these factors have been a source of disequilibrium in many developing countries and have impeded growth.

Although the level of income in a hypothetical neoclassical economy is by definition higher than it would be under any set of disequilibrium assumptions, the growth potential of this economy may be less over time. Disequilibrium phenomena such as segmented factor markets and lags in adjustment imply a potential for accelerating growth by reducing bottlenecks and reallocating resources to sectors of higher productivity. This potential is likely to be greater in developing countries—which are subject to greater disequilibrating shocks and have greater market disequilibrium—than in developed countries. In addition, developing countries can take advantage of the more productive technology available from advanced countries. These two factors offer a plausible explanation for the acceleration of growth that has been noted in many industrializing countries.

In summary, the structural approach focuses on differences among sectors of the economy that may inhibit the equilibrating adjustments in resource allocation implied by neoclassical theory. Disequilibrium is more often mainifested by the differences in returns to labor and capital in different uses than by the shortages and sur-

pluses that indicate the complete failure of markets to clear. In contrast, neoclassical theory assumes that equilibrium is maintained over time, which limits the sources of growth to factors on the supply side.

Equilibrium Growth

The assumptions of competitive equilibrium that underlie neoclassical theory are a convenient starting point for growth analysis because they permit any group of inputs to be aggregated on the basis of their marginal productivities. For economywide studies, all primary inputs can be categorized as either capital or labor. Each of these can then be consolidated on the basis of its share in the total product. The difference between the growth of total output and the weighted average growth of capital and labor serves as a measure of the increase in total factor productivity for the economy as a whole. This procedure is sufficiently general to permit comparisons among studies using different methodologies, so long as they maintain the assumptions of competitive equilibrium.

Analyses designed to measure the importance of these three sources of growth have now been carried out for thirty-nine economies for several periods. They indicate that the growth of capital, labor, and productivity are of comparable importance for the sample as a whole but vary significantly with the structure of an economy and the effectiveness of its policies.

Disequilibrium Growth

Disequilibrium growth is characteristic of an economic system that exhibits significant departures from the neoclassical assumptions described above. It falls into the category of the "theory of second best," where for various reasons the optimal (equilibrium) solution is unattainable. In empirical terms, the main questions are whether one can identify the effects of disequilibrium in factor or product markets and incorporate them into an analysis of growth and development.

The growth characteristics of an inflexible economy are in general the opposite of those of neoclassical theory, which implicitly assumes a high degree of substitution among both commodities and factors of production. For example, a fixed coefficient model will almost automatically generate capital shortages and labor surpluses in a developing economy that has a relatively high growth of the labor force; yet this problem is virtually ruled out by neoclassical assumptions. Similarly, the growth of income produces a more than proportional rise in the demand for manufactured goods and a resulting tendency for manufactured imports to outrun exports. The structural adjustments through export expansion, import substitution, and capital inflows needed to maintain a balance of payments equilibrium will reduce growth unless they are carried out efficiently.

In each area of potential disequilibrium, the actual performance of developing countries lies somewhere between the extremes of flexibility and inflexibility assumed by the neoclassical and the input-output systems respectively. The next section tests the importance of disequilibrium factors by comparing the results of statistical studies that incorporate them with those that do not.

The Effects of Disequilibrium

To incorporate the effects of disequilibrium into the study of growth, I shall attempt to establish which of the seven factors suggested are of general significance for developing countries. Those shown to be important can then be studied in more detail for individual countries.

Several economists have done regression analyses of large samples of countries with the common objective of testing the significance of structural variables in explaining growth rates. . . .

The main factors tested were:

Neoclassical variables
    Growth of capital stock
    Growth of the labor force (or population)
    Improvements in the quality of labor (or a rise in the level of education)

Structural variables
    Reallocation of labor and capital
    Growth of exports
    Capital inflow (two-gap hypothesis)
    Level of development

Each study started from a version of the neoclassical growth formula and added other explanatory variables. Because analysts were forced to use proxies for the underlying factors, the regression coefficients in these equations cannot necessarily be identified with parameters in a specific model. The cross-country regression equations are of the general form

$$G_Y = a_0 + a_1(I/Y) + a_2G_L + a_3X_3 \\ + a_4X_a + a_5X_E + A_6X_F + a_7X_D$$

where

I/Y = the ratio of investment to GNP (a proxy for the growth of capital stock)
G_L = growth of the labor force
X_3 = a measure of increase in labor quality (or education)
X_A = a measure of the shift of labor or capital out of agriculture
X_E = a measure of the growth of exports
X_F = a measure of the balance of payments deficit
X_D = a measure of the level of development

The use of only the first two explanatory variables yields results that can be compared with the time-series estimates of neoclassical growth for individual countries.

In almost all cases the addition of structural variables substantially improved the explanation of differences in growth rates among developing countries.

Five conclusions emerge:

• The growth of capital is still the most important single factor, but its relative contribution is reduced from well over 50 percent of average growth in the neoclassical model to 30–40 percent in the structural formulations.
• The growth of the labor force is similarly reduced in importance; in some developing-country samples, it is no longer statistically significant. These findings are consistent with the evidence that many developing countries are characterized by surplus labor.
• The reallocation of capital and labor from agriculture to more productive sectors accounts for the 20 percent of average growth.
• The growth of exports makes a significant contribution to growth for all developing countries in the period 1964–73; however, it does not appear to have been significant before 1960. If both factor reallocation and export expansion are included in the same regression, the latter appears to be more important.
• The capital inflow (excess of imports over exports) shows a significant effect on growth in addition to its effects on investment and exports. This finding gives some support to the two-gap hypothesis that imports may constitute a limit to growth.

Structural Transformation

The structural transformation of the developing economy may be defined as the set of changes in the composition of demand, trade, production, and factor use that takes place as per capita income increases. A main thesis is that to understand country differences in sources and rates of growth, the transformation as a whole must be analyzed. More specifically, changes in demand and trade may affect the sources of growth as much as the changes in factor supply that have been stressed so far.

The central role of international trade in the structural transformation can be revealed only if the sectors that produce tradable commodities are isolated so that the relations between demand, trade, and productivity growth can be examined. Differences in resource endowments among countries are also manifested in variations in the patterns of trade over time.

II.B.4. The Imperfect Information Paradigm*

There is a widespread feeling that traditional neoclassical economic theory has little, if any, relevance to the problems of less developed economies. Some of the important developments in the theory during the past quarter of the century have provided considerable justification for that view. Though the Fundamental Theorem of Welfare Economics has shown rigorously that there is a set of conditions under which Adam Smith's conjecture concerning the invisible hand has some validity, the conditions required seem particularly inapplicable to the circumstances in which most LDCs find themselves. In particular, there is not the full set of markets—whether for risks, capital (futures), labor or products—that the theorem requires; information is far from perfect; the assumption of a fixed and known technology seems particularly incongruent with an attempt to understand the process by which LDCs adopt more advanced technologies and by which new technologies diffuse through the economy; and the first stages of development require the provision of infrastructure, which is a public good, and/or is characterized by strong non-convexities.

The problems I have listed are, of course, well recognized, and they are widely discussed under the rubric of "market failures." The liberal doctrines of the 1960s and early 1970s had it that a certain amount of tinkering by a benevolent government could remedy these deficiencies in the marketplace, and with these limited interventions, the market economy would function well, in the way that the classical theory had said it would all along.

To believers of neoclassical theory, the difference between LDCs and developed countries was a matter of degree: the market failures were perhaps more pronounced and thus stronger government intervention might be called for. To critics, the qualifications were of central importance.

Two developments during the past decade, however, have necessitated a reshaping of these views. The first is well known: many of the attempts by governments, both in LDCs and developed countries, to remedy the market failures which they saw have been less than successful. If markets do not work, but government interventions to remedy their deficiencies also do not work, where are we to go?

The second is perhaps not so well known: at the same time that the standard neoclassical theory was continually being refined, a number of economists were attempting to construct models of the economy using neoclassical tools of analysis, but introducing more realistic assumptions: they were concerned with investigating the causes and consequences of incomplete markets, imperfect information, and imperfect competition. In many cases, these studies were motivated by an attempt to provide models with a greater relevance to LDCs; but the models which worked well often also provided considerable insight into the kinds of macro-economic disequilibria observed in developed countries as well.

These two developments are not unrelated: the Economics of Information has focused on the information and incentive problems which are common both to public and private organizations; it has provided at least part of the rationale for Public Failures as well as Private Failures, and has provided a framework within which a more rational basis for the assign-

*From J. E. Stiglitz, "Economics of Information and the Theory of Economic Development," National Bureau of Economic Research Working Paper, no. 1566, February 1985 (processed), pp. 1–7, 25–26. Reprinted by permission.

ment of responsibilities to each sector can be made.

In this paper I wish to survey some of the more important applications of the economics of information to the theory of economic development, suggesting how the theory provides an explanation of phenomena which, within the traditonal neoclassical paradigm, appear irrational and/or inefficient; I wish to go on to show that the policy implications of the alternative paradigm may differ markedly from those of standard neoclassical theory.

Tenancy Relationships in Agriculture: Sharecropping

The prevalence of sharecropping in agriculture in less developed countries has always been somewhat of a puzzle to economists. Under sharecropping, a worker receives less than the value of his marginal product, and this seems to introduce an inefficiency. How could an inefficient system of land tenure be so persistent?

One natural answer was that it provided a means of risk sharing. Workers were more risk averse than landlords, and the sharecropping contract allowed the landlord to absorb more of the risk than he would if workers rented the land from the landlord. Thus, the prevalence of sharecropping contracts was related to one of the market failures described earlier, the absence of a complete set of risk markets, in which the worker could insure himself against the many risks which he faced.

It was subsequently shown, however, that transferring risk provided part, but only part, of the explanation of sharecropping: all the possibilities of risk sharing which sharecropping provided could be provided by combining wage and rental contracts, which seemingly lacked the inefficiencies associated with sharecropping.[1] I went on to show, however, that if there were no informational problems, there would, in fact, be no inefficiencies associated with sharecropping; the contract would specify precisely the amount of labor to be supplied by the worker. Cheung, having made a similar observation, argued that accordingly, if sharecropping is widely observed, it must be because of some advantage in transactions costs. While agreeing with the tenor

of that argument, it has always seemed to me that referring to transactions costs as an explanation is too easy and incomplete an answer. If the explanation of some important phenomena resides in the nature of the transactions costs, then transactions costs need to be the focus of the analysis, and a more detailed modeling of the structure of transactions costs and of the implications of alternative institutional structures for transactions costs is required. In a sense, my focus on information costs can be thought of as providing that detailed analysis. The information problems that I focused on were associated with monitoring the actions of the worker: it is prohibitively expensive, under most agricultural environments, to monitor perfectly the actions of the worker, to ensure that he acts in the interests of the landlord; for instance, that he weeds when and as much as he should. It is far less costly to monitor the output of the farm than the worker's input of effort. Moreover, because of the innumerable environmental factors which affect each farm (weather, pestilence, disease), which again cannot be perfectly monitored, by observing output one cannot make a perfect inference concerning the worker's input of effort.

If workers were risk neutral, then rental contracts would be employed. Rental contracts allow the worker to receive the full value of the marginal product of his efforts. But rental contracts force the worker to absorb all the risk.

On the other hand, with wage contracts the landlord absorbs all the risk, which is a good thing, given that the landlord is so much less risk averse than the worker. However, with a wage contract the worker has little incentive to work; to ensure that he performs requires a high level of monitoring. Though the costs of monitoring may not be too high for certain kinds of crops, for others these costs may make such contracts undesirable.

The equilibrium sharecropping contract is thus seen as a compromise: between the incentive properties of rental contracts and the risk properties of wage contracts.

Changes in the environment and in technology—in the degree of risk, in alternative means by which workers can divest themselves of risk or diversify out of the risk (outside uncorrelated income opportunities), in the degree of risk aversion (as the result of changes in wealth), and in the costs of monitoring—will alter the equilibrium contractual arrangement. Thus, the new theory provides not only an ex-

[1]J. E. Stiglitz, "Alternative Theories of Wage Determination and Unemployment in LDC's: The Labor Turnover Model," *Quarterly Journal of Economics,* Vol. 87 (May 1974), pp. 194–227.

planation of sharecropping, but also for the observed differences in land tenure systems, both over time and in different locations. Sharecropping is not seen as an inefficient, primitive method of land tenure, but as a rational solution to certain real problems facing these economies.

Indeed, this analysis of sharecropping has served as a prototype of a whole class of information problems known as "principal-agent problems." These are concerned with situations in which one individual (the agent) must take actions which affect another (the principal), where the agent has more information than the principal (the worker knows the weather better than the landlord), but the agent is risk averse. Principal-agent problems arise in labor markets (the employer-employee relationship) and in insurance markets. They are pervasive in all economies; understanding them provides considerable insight into a number of institutional arrangements, both in developed and less developed economies, and alters in a fundamental way the conclusions reached in standard neoclassical analysis.[2]

---

[2]I am limiting myself to a discussion of how information analysis affects the analysis of problems facing LDCs, but I should briefly mention how introducing these concerns alters the standard neoclassical results. First, the usual convexity assumptions are not, in general, satisfied: indifference curves and feasibility sets are not, in general, convex; competitive equilibrium may not exist, even when all the other strong assumptions of the standard theory obtain; when it does, it may have a quite different character than depicted in standard competitive models, as we have noted here, in the case of agricultural markets. (In other markets, the price paid or received may depend on the quantity traded, and there may be quantity rationing.) When competitive equilibrium exists, it will not, in general, be Pareto efficient; and it may not be possible to decentralize efficient resource allocations.

Conclusion

Traditional economic theory has ignored the central problems associated with costly information. When due attention is paid to these information theoretic considerations, the basic propositions of neoclassical analysis no longer remain valid: market equilibrium may not exist, even when all the underlying preferences and production sets are "well behaved"; when equilibrium exists, it is, in general, not Pareto efficient; it may not be possible to decentralize efficient resource allocations; the separation between efficiency and equity considerations which characterizes traditional neoclassical theory no longer obtains; market equilibrium may be characterized by an excess demand for credit or an excess supply of labor (that is, the law of supply and demand no longer holds). The theory which has been developed explicitly incorporating information theoretic considerations provides an explanation of phenomena about which traditional theory simply had nothing to say.

I have been particularly concerned with showing how this New Theory can provide insights into markets in less developed economies, to show how it can provide explanation for institutions which in neoclassical theory appear anomalous and/or inefficient. In some cases, it yields clear implications for policy, implications which are at variance with those emerging from traditional neoclassical analysis. In other cases, all we have obtained so far is a word of caution: information problems may give rise to public (governmental) failures just as they give rise to market failures. The analysis of the appropriate role of the government is far more complex than traditional analyses lead us to believe. But if we have learned this simple lesson, we may have learned a lot.

Comment: The New Market Failures Approach and Development

Joseph Stiglitz emphasizes the importance of the new market imperfections in LDCs. The earlier failures that development economists focused on were public goods and externalities. Now they should also recognize the risk and information imperfections that are even more pervasive in LDCs than in developed economies. See J. E. Stiglitz, "Alternative Tactics and Strategies for Economic Development," in *New Directions in Development Economics*, ed. A. K. Dutt and K. P. Jameson (1992).

In numerous other writings, Stiglitz propounds the thesis that market failures, particularly those related to imperfect and costly information, may provide insights into why the LDCs

> have a lower level of income and why so many find it difficult to maintain existing current differentials, let alone to catch up. What is at stake is more than just differences in endowments of factors, but basic aspects of the organization of the economy, including the functioning of markets. . . .
>
> The differences between LDCs and the more developed countries lies largely in matters of economic organization. . . . Markets are an important set of institutions in the organization of modern economies. We

need to remember that much of production in more developed economies is not, however, mediated through markets, but occurs within large corporations, each of which is the size of at least the smaller of the LDCs.

Market failures are particularly pervasive in LDCs. Good policy requires identifying them, asking which can be directly attacked by making markets work more effectively (and in particular, reducing government imposed barriers to the effective working of markets), and which cannot. We need to identify which market failures can be ameliorated through nonmarket institutions (with perhaps the government taking an instrumental role in establishing these nonmarket institutions). We need to recognize both the limits and strengths of markets, as well as the strengths, and limits, of government interventions aimed at correcting market failures.[1]

As we proceed through policy issues in subsequent chapters, we should keep in mind the possibilities of both market failures and nonmarket (government) failures. In Chapter X we shall give a summary assessment of the development role of markets and government.

[1]See Joseph E. Stiglitz "Markets, Market Failures and Development," *American Economic Review, Papers and Proceedings* (May 1989): 201–2. Also, Stiglitz, "Economic Organization, Information and Development," in *Handbook of Development Economics* vol. I, Hollis Chenery and T. N. Srinivasan (1988).

II.B.5. New Endogenous Growth Theory—Note

At various times in the history of thought, economists have stressed increasing returns as an endogenous explanation for economic growth. Adam Smith did so in emphasizing that growth in productivity was due to the division of labor, which depends upon the extent of the market. Alfred Marshall also emphasized that the role of "nature" in production may be subject to diminishing returns, but the role of "man" is subject to increasing returns. And again, in an earlier period, J. M. Clark also observed that "knowledge is the only instrument of production that is not subject to diminishing returns."[1] Allyn Young also related economic progress to increasing returns that were external to the firm as a result of the progressive division and specialization among industries and the use of roundabout methods of production.[2]

Nobel laureate Kenneth Arrow gave a dynamic interpretation to increasing returns by emphasizing "Learning by Doing."[3] This was an early attempt to render technological progress endogenous in growth models by making the productivity of a given firm an increasing func-

tion of cumulative aggregate investment for the industry. (Note that Arrow emphasized cumulative investment, not cumulative output.)

Most recently, new endogenous growth models have gone beyond Robert Solow's neoclassical growth model that exhibited diminishing returns to capital and labor separately and constant returns to both inputs jointly, and that left technological progress as a residual.[4] The new growth theory examines production functions that show increasing returns because of specialization and investment in "knowledge" capital. Technological progress and human capital formation are endogenized within general equilibrium models of growth. New knowledge is generated by investment in the research sector. The technological progress residual is accounted for by endogenous human capital formation. With knowledge being treated as a public good, spillover benefits to other firms may then allow aggregate investment in knowledge to exhibit increasing returns to scale. This in turn allows investment in knowledge capital to persist indefinitely and to sustain long-run growth in per capita income. A policy implication is that governments can promote growth by providing incentives to agents in the knowledge-producing, human capital–intensive sectors. Developing

[1]J. Maurice Clark, *Studies in the Economics of Overhead Costs* (1923), p. 120.

[2]Allyn A. Young, "Increasing Returns and Economic Progress," *Economic Journal* (December 1928): 527–42.

[3]Kenneth Arrow, "The Economic Implications of Learning by Doing," *Review of Economic Studies* (June 1962): 155–73.

[4]Robert M. Solow, "A Contribution to the Theory of Economic Growth," *Quarterly Journal of Economics* (February 1956): 65–94.

countries can also be aided by the international transfer of technology. See Paul M. Romer, "Increasing Returns and Long-run Growth," *Journal of Political Economy* (October 1986), and "Endogenous Technological Change," *Journal of Political Economy* (October 1990); and Robert Lucas, Jr., "On the Mechanics of Economic Development," *Journal of Monetary Economics* (January 1988).

In Romer's analysis, knowledge through investment in research displays increasing marginal productivity so that per capita income can continue to grow and the return to capital may continue to increase. In Lucas's analysis, endogenous technical change has a "growth effect" beyond simply the "level effect" (upward raising of the production function) of the earlier learning-by-doing models.

For developing countries, the implication of the new growth theory is to place more emphasis on human capital—even more than on physical capital, and to emphasize the benefit from the exchange of ideas that comes with an open economy integrated into the world economy.

It is also suggested by some empirical studies that the new endogenous growth models conform better to the evidence on diversity in growth rates among countries over the past three or four decades then does the neoclassical growth model. See Isaac Ehrlich, "The Problem of Development: Introduction," *Journal of Political Economy* (October 1990): S2–S3, S7; and Jati K. Sengupta, "Growth in NICs in Asia: Some Tests of New Growth Theory," *Journal of Development Studies* (January 1993): 342–57.

Human capital and increasing returns are also related to the question of convergence—that is, whether poor countries grow faster than rich countries. For an instructive empirical study, see Robert J. Barro, "Economic Growth in a Cross-Section of Countries," *Quarterly Journal of Economics* (May 1991): 407–43. Also, Costas Azariadis and Allan Drazen, "Threshold Externalities in Economic Development," *Quarterly Journal of Economics* (May 1990): 501–26.

In contrast to the critics of the Solow model, another study of cross-country variation in income explains much of the variation in terms of an augmented neoclassical production-function model that includes accumulation of human capital as well as physical capital, but maintains the Solow assumption of decreasing returns to scale in capital. Even when denying the new growth theory's emphasis on externalities to capital accumulation, the augmented Solow model can explain most of the international variation in income per capita by differences in saving, education, and population growth. See N. Gregory Mankiw, David Romer, and David N. Weil, "A Contribution to the Empirics of Economic Growth," *Quarterly Journal of Economics* (May 1992): 407–37. We are still left, however, with the challenge to understand the determinants of saving, population growth, and worldwide technological change that remain as exogenous variables in neoclassical growth models.

For an evaluation of different models of growth, see the symposium "New Growth Theory," *Journal of Economic Perspectives* (Winter 1994): 3–72.

II.B.6. The New Institutional Economics and Development Theory*

In recent years two strands of non-Walrasian economic literature have developed well-articulated endogenous theories of institutions, and they are both getting to be prominent in the new microeconomics of development. One is the transaction cost school, flowing out of the fa-

mous paper by Coase (1960), . . . The other school is associated with the theory of imperfect information. . . . Although there is some family resemblance between the two strands, there are important differences in their points of emphasis. But they both deny the validity of some of the principal results of mainstream economics. For example, one of the main pillars of Walrasian neoclassical economies—the separability of equity and efficiency—breaks down when transaction costs and imperfect information are im-

*From Pranab Bardhan, "The New Institutional Economics and Development Theory," *World Development* 17, no. 9 (1989): 1390–94. Reprinted by permission from Elsevier Science Ltd. Oxford, England.

portant; the terms and conditions of contracts in various transactions, which directly affect the efficiency of resource allocation, now crucially depend on ownership structures and property relations. Development economics, which deals with cases where market failure and incomplete markets (often the result of the substantive presence of transaction costs and information problems) are predominant, clearly provides hospitable territory for such institutional analysis.

According to the transaction cost school, institutions that evolve to lower these costs are the key to the performance of economies. These costs include those of information, negotiation, monitoring, coordination, and enforcement of contracts. When transaction costs are absent, the initial assignment of property rights does not matter from the point of view of efficiency, because rights can be voluntarily adjusted and exchanged to promote increased production. But when transaction costs are substantial, as is usually the case, the allocation of property rights is critical. In the historical growth process there is a trade-off between economies of scale and specialization on the one hand and transaction costs on the other. In a small, closed, face-to-face peasant community, for example, transaction costs are low, but the production costs are high, because specialization and division of labor are severely limited by the extent of market defined by the personalized exchange process of the small community. In a large-scale complex economy, as the network of interdependence widens the impersonal exchange process gives considerable scope for all kinds of opportunistic behavior (cheating, shirking, moral hazard) and the costs of transacting can be high. In Western societies over time, complex institutional structures have been devised (elaborately defined and effectively enforced property rights, formal contracts and guarantees, corporate hierarchy, vertical integration, limited liability, bankruptcy laws, and so on) to constrain the participants, to reduce the uncertainty of social interaction, in general to prevent the transactions from being too costly and thus to allow the productivity gains of larger scale and improved technology to be realized.

The imperfect–information theory of institutions is closely related to that of transaction costs, since information costs constitute an important part of transaction costs. But the former theory is usually cast in a more rigorous framework clearly spelling out assumptions and equilibrium solution concepts, drawing out more fully the implications of strategic behavior under asymmetric information, and sharply differentiating the impact of different types of information problems. Imperfect–information theory yields somewhat more concrete and specific predictions about the design of contracts, with more attention to the details of terms and conditions of varying contractual arrangements under varying circumstances, than the usual presentations of transaction cost theory.

The imperfect–information theory has been fruitfully used in modeling many key agrarian institutions which are seen to emerge as substitutes for missing credit, insurance, and futures markets in an environment of pervasive risks, information asymmetry, and moral hazard. It started with the literature on sharecropping, then on interlocking of transactions in labor, credit and land lease, on labor tying, on credit rationing, and so on. Radical economists have often cited some of these production relations as institutional obstacles to development in a poor agrarian economy, overlooking the microeconomic rationale of the formation of these institutions. Under a set of informational constraints and missing markets, a given agrarian institution (say, sharecropping or interlocking of contracts) may be serving a real economic function. Its simple abolition, as is often demanded on a radical platform, without taking care of the factors that gave rise to the institution in the first place, may not necessarily improve the conditions of the intended beneficiaries of the abolition program. There may be some important political lessons here from what can be called the economics of second-best reformism.

The transaction–cost and imperfect–information theories are equally murky on the mechanism through which new institutions and property rights emerge. One gets the impression that more efficient institutions and governance structures evolve as the parties involved come to appreciate the new benefit-cost possibilities. The literature is marked by a certain ahistorical functionalism and even vulgar Darwinism on this point. An institution's mere function of serving the interests of potential beneficiaries is clearly inadequate in *explaining* it, just as it is an incompetent detective who tries to explain a murder mystery only by looking for the beneficiary and, on that basis alone, proceeds to arrest the heir of the murdered rich man. One cannot get away from the enormity of the collective action problem that limits the ability of potential gainers to get their act together in bringing about institutional changes. There are two kinds of collective action problems involved here: one is the well known free-rider problem about sharing the costs of bringing about change, the other is a bargaining problem where disputes about sharing the potential benefits from the change may lead to a breakdown of the necessary coordination.

A related question is that of the presumed optimality of persistent institutions. The transaction–cost (as well as the imperfect–information) school often unthinkingly implies the application of the market analogy of competitive equilibrium to the social choice of institutions or the biological analogy of natural selection in the survival of the fittest institution. In fact transaction costs themselves, by raising barriers to entry and exit, reduce pressures from any social selection process; sunk costs and asset-specificity insulate internal governance structures from market forces. As Greenwald and Stiglitz (1986) have shown, the market equilibrium under imperfect information and incomplete markets is, in general, constrained Pareto inefficient; and, as Farrell (1987) has shown, with imperfect information even bilateral relationships may not be efficient on account of complexity of private bargaining.

In the recent development literature the institution of interlocking of transactions (in labor, credit, and land relations) has been rationalized as a device to save transaction costs and to substitute for incomplete or nonexistent credit and insurance markets. But one should not overlook that such interlocking itself may act as a barrier to entry for third parties and be a source of additional monopoly power for the dominant partner (usually the employer-creditor-landlord) in such transactions. Personalized interlocking of labor commitments and credit transactions (involving selective exclusion of others) also divides the workers and emasculates their collective bargaining strength vis-à-vis employers, who use this as an instrument of control over the labor process.

As we all know from experience, dysfunctional institutions often persist for a very long period. Akerlof (1984) has built models to show how economically unprofitable or socially unpleasant customs may persist as a result of a mutually sustaining network of social sanctions when each individual conforms out of fear of loss of reputation from disobedience. In such a system, potential members of a breakaway coalition fear that it is doomed to failure and thus failure to challenge the system becomes a self-fulfilling prophecy. . . .

The biological analogy of survival of the fit-test is particularly inappropriate as path dependence is assigned an important role in biological processes. To quote Gould (1980, p. 16): "Organisms are not billiard balls propelled by simple and measurable external forces to predictable new positions on life's pool table. . . . Organisms have a history that constrains their future in myriad, subtle ways. . . . Their complexity of form entails a host of functions incidental to whatever pressures of natural selection superintended the initial construction." The arguments against the operation of natural selection in social institutions are obviously much stronger. . . .

The neoclassical institutional economists focus their attention on allocative efficiency–improving institutions, whereas Marxists often emphasize how institutions change or do not change depending on considerations of surplus appropriation by a dominant class. In particular, progress toward a more productive institution may be blocked if it reduces the control of surplus by this class. (Even when historically valid, such a statement, of course, needs better microfoundations, showing how individuals within the class that could gain from the new institution are frustrated in their efforts by the aggregative necessity of retaining control for the whole class.) The emphasis on the effect of an institutional change on control of surplus by a particular class also suggests that the question of *efficiency–improving* institutional change cannot really be separated from that of *redistributive* institutional change. This is particularly true when issues of collective action, bargaining power, class capacity, mobilization, and struggle in the historical process are important. This means that the distinction Hayami and Ruttan (1985) make between the "demand" for institutional innovations (on the basis of changes in technological or demographic factors) and their "supply" (depending on political entrepreneurs undertaking the necessary collective action) may be somewhat artificial. In empirical analysis of actual institutional changes this may lead to a kind of "identification problem." For example, in English agricultural history did the (second) enclosure movement in the eighteenth century come about because enclosed farming was more efficient than open-field farming, or because the (prospective) redistributive effect of enclosures in favor of landowners made collective action on their part easier? In the example of Hayami and Kikuchi (1982) from agriculture in the Philippines in the mid-1970s, where the increase in population pressure on land brought about a new employer–employee relationship (the *gamma* system replacing the traditional *hunusan* system) lowering the wage rate, did it come about because the disequilibrium between labor productivity and wage "demanded" such a change, or because population pressure on land made collective action on the part of employers easier (or that on the part of laborers weaker), thus facilitating the "supply" side? . . .

A shift in the focus of attention from the efficiency aspects of an institution to the distributive aspects inevitably confronts us with the question of somehow grappling with the elusive concept of power and with political processes which much of neoclassical institutional economics would abhor. Marxists, of course, directly deal with these issues, but are often methodologically careless. The concept of power is often used in a question-begging way: differences in institutional arrangements are supposed to be explained by blanket references to differences in the power of the dominant class without an *independent* quantification of the latter. The literature—Marxist or non-Marxist—on a rigorous analysis of power is rather scanty in economics, compared with that in sociological and political theory. Game theorists have used the idea of bargaining power in dividing up the surplus in bargaining games, or the idea of power exercised as the Stackelberg leader taking the weaker party's reaction function as given, or as the ability to credibly precommit in noncooperative games—these are indirectly reflected in some of the models of the imperfect–information theory of institutions. In recent Marxist theoretical models in economics, two distinct forms of power relations have emerged: Roemer (1982) finds the primary locus of capitalist power in unequal distribution of property, whereas Bowles (1985, 1987) traces it to the political structures of control and surveillance at the point of production, both referring to a competitive economy. Roemer reiterates the well-known Samuelsonian proposition that in a competitive model it does not matter whether capital hires labor or labor hires capital, with the important modification that in either case the wealthy "exploit" (take advantage of) the poor. To Bowles, on the other hand, the locus of command in the production process is central to the functioning of the system. I find this distinction between domination in production and asset-based power somewhat overdrawn: who hires whom essentially depends on the capacity to be the residual claimant in production, and that in turn depends on the capacity to bear risks, the wealthy having obviously a larger risk-bearing capacity. But both these strands of Marxist theory serve as a reminder that in the transaction–cost and imperfect–information theories demonstrating the economic rationale of some existing institutions in terms of transaction costs and moral hazard, it is underemphasized that a more democratic organization of the work process (following Bowles) or a more egalitarian distribution of assets (following Roemer) might have significantly reduced (not eliminated) the informational constraints and Hobbesian malfeasance problems which form the staple of much of the principal-agent games in the literature.

References

Akerlof, G. (1984). *An Economic Theorist's Book of Tales.* Cambridge: Cambridge University Press.

Bowles, S. (1985). "The production process in a competitive economy: Walrasian, neo-Hobbesian and Marxian models." *American Economic Review* 75 (March): 16–36.

———. "Contested exchange: A microeconomic analysis of the political structure of the capitalist economy." Unpublished.

Coase, R. (1960). "The problem of social cost." *Journal of Law and Economics* 3 (October): 144.

Farrell, J. (1987). "Information and the Coase theorem." *Journal of Economic Perspectives* 1 (Fall): 113–129.

Gould, S. J. (1980). *The Panda's Thumb.* New York: Norton.

Greenwald B., and J. E. Stiglitz (1986). "Externalities in economies with imperfect information and incomplete markets." *Quarterly Journal of Economics* 101 (May): 229–64.

Hayami, Y., and M. Kikuchi (1982). *Asian Village Economy at the Crossroads: An Economic Approach to Institutional Change.* Baltimore: Johns Hopkins University Press.

Hayami, Y., and V. W. Ruttan (1985). *Agricultural Development: An International Perspective.* Baltimore: Johns Hopkins University Press.

Roemer, J. (1982). *A General Theory of Exploitation and Class.* Cambridge, Mass.: Harvard University Press.

II.C. ALTERNATIVE PERSPECTIVES

II.C.1. Dependency Theories of Underdevelopment—Note

Along with some elements of structuralism, dependency theories of underdevelopment have arisen in Latin America. Unlike the implications of neoclassical development economics, the dependency school argues that conditions of dependency in world markets of commodities, capital, and labor power are unequal and combine to transfer resources from dependent countries to dominant countries in the international system.[1] Historically, the dependent country was a colony and the dominant country the imperial power. Now asymmetrical power relationships are between the center (Western Europe, Britain, and the United States) and the periphery. Dependency results in underdevelopment of the periphery. Accordingly, it is contended that the development problems of the periphery are to be understood in terms of their insertion into the international capitalist system, rather than in terms of domestic considerations.

Being heavily represented by sociologists and political scientists, dependency theorists consider social and political factors neglected by economists. In general, dependency ideas combine variants of Marxism and nationalism. Instead of focusing on different commodities— primary products and industrial products—the dependency theorists emphasize the contrasting positions of dominant and dependent countries within the operation of the international system. Even if the LDC is industrializing and is not simply a primary producing country, nonetheless, it is argued that the advanced capitalist countries are still the chief gainers from any kind of international relationship with the LDC— whether in trade, investment, or technology. The advanced countries possess the dominant technology, hold a monopoly over R&D, and are the home of the multinational corporations. Even if industrializing, the LDC is still dependent on the superior power of the advanced countries, and the periphery is still exploited by the center. The underdevelopment of the periphery is a function of its external dependence as affected by the operation of transnational capitalism.

Chronic underdevelopment is ascribed to a Marxist theory of capitalism—not to precapitalist traditions or institutions. The present economic, social, and political conditions prevailing in the periphery are not the reflection of an "original" undeveloped state of affairs, but have been created by a historical international process: the same process of capitalism that brought development to the presently advanced capitalist economies resulted in the underdevelopment of the dependent periphery. The global system is such that the development of part of the system occurs at the expense of other parts. Underdevelopment of the periphery is the Siamese twin of development at the center.

The driving force in this process is a capital-seeking profit motive—which existed in the imperialistic period of capitalist merchants and capitalist bankers and is carried on in the present period of multinational corporations. As a Marxist analyst of Latin American affairs, André Gunder Frank, states: "It is capitalism, world and national, which produced underdevelopment in the past and still generates underdevelopment in the present."[2] Underdevelopment, according to Frank, is not simply nondevelopment, but is a unique type of socioeconomic structure that results from the dependency of the underdeveloped country on advanced capitalist countries. This results from foreign capital removing a surplus from the dependent economy to the advanced country by structuring the underdeveloped economy in an "external orientation" that is characterized by the export of primary commodities, the import of manufactures, and dependent industrialization.

Structural bottlenecks within the underdeveloped economy may also act as "mechanisms of dependence." The Chilean economist Osvaldo Sunkel focused on the peripheral country's stagnation of agriculture, its high commodity concentration of exports, its high foreign exchange content of industrialization, and its growing fiscal deficit—all of which intensified the need for foreign financing: "It is this aspect—the over-

---

[1] This note follows Gerald M. Meier, *Emerging From Poverty* (1984), pp. 196–202.

[2] André Gunder Frank, *Capitalism and Underdevelopment in Latin America* (1967), p. 11.

bearing and implacable necessity to obtain foreign financing—which finally sums up the situation of dependence: this is the crucial point in the mechanisms of dependence."[3]

Dependencistas further contend that the developing metropolis exploits the underdeveloped periphery in various ways—by biasing its structure of production toward the supplying of raw materials, by the external drain of foreign capital, and by thwarting autonomous national development. Center–periphery trade is also characterized by "unequal exchange." This may refer to deterioration in the peripheral country's terms of trade. It may also refer to unequal bargaining power in investment, transfer of technology, taxation, and relations with multinational corporations. Considering relations between multinational corporations and host countries, dependencistas commonly allege that the multinationals siphon off an economic surplus that could otherwise be used to finance domestic development, and that foreign investment causes both economic distortions and political distortions in the host society.

Some of the alleged economic distortions are that the multinational corporations use inappropriate capital-intensive technology that adds to the host country's unemployment, that they worsen the distribution of income, that they alter consumer tastes and promote a consumerism characteristic of developed societies, and that they centralize research and entrepreneurial decision making in the home country so that subsidiaries and affiliates of the multinational are not integrated with the local economy.

Political distortions, it is claimed, arise when the multinational brings the laws, politics, and foreign policy of the parent country into the subsidiary country. Multinationals may even reduce the ability of the government to control the economy, and they may structure the international system of finance and trade to respond to their multinational needs to the detriment of host authorities.

A more Marxist analysis of unequal exchange has been presented by Samir Amin, an Egyptian economist who has specialized in African economies. Amin also analyzes world capitalism in terms of two categories—center and periphery. Capitalist relations in the periphery are introduced from outside, and peripheral formations are fundamentally different from those of the center because the periphery's exporting sector dominates over the periphery's economic structure as a whole, which is subjected to and shaped by the requirements of the external market. The economies of the periphery "are without any internal dynamism of their own."[4] Dominated by "absentee" metropolitan bourgeoisie, the peripheral country is a mere appendage to the central economy. The development of the center causes underdevelopment of the periphery and its dependence on the center.

Within the dependent economy, it is also claimed that an internal colonialism or internal polarization occurs parallel to the international polarization. Sunkel states:

The evolution of the global system of underdevelopment–development has, over a period of time, given rise to two great polarizations which have found their main expression in geographical terms. First, a polarization of the world between countries: with the developed, industrialized, advanced, "central northern" ones on the one side, and the underdeveloped, poor, dependent, and "peripheral southern" ones on the other. Second, a polarization within countries between advanced and modern groups, regions, and activities, and backward, primitive, marginal and dependent groups, regions, and activities. The main difference between [the two structures] is that the developed one, due basically to its endogenous growth capacity, is the dominant structure, while the underdeveloped structure, due largely to the induced character of its dynamism, is a dependent one.[5]

The Brazilian sociologist, Fernando Henrique Cardoso, also claims that

as a result [of investment by multinational corporations] in countries like Argentina, Brazil, Mexico, South Africa, India, and some others, there is an internal structural fragmentation connecting the most "advanced" parts of their economies to the international capitalist system. Separate although subordinated to these advanced sectors, the backward economic and social sectors of the dependent countries then play the role of "internal colonies."[6]

The relationships of internal polarization are based on a neo-Marxist analysis of classes that focuses on mechanisms of social and economic

---

[3]Osvaldo Sunkel, "National Development Policy and External Dependence in Latin America," *Journal of Development Studies* (October 1969): 31.

[4]Samir Amin, *Unequal Development: An Essay on the Social Formations of Peripheral Capitalism* (1976), p. 179.

[5]Osvaldo Sunkel, "Transnational Capitalism and National Disintegration in Latin America," *Social and Economic Studies* (March 1973): 132–76.

[6]Fernando Henrique Cardoso, "Dependent Capitalist Development in Latin America," *New Left Review* (July 1972): 90.

exploitation: the working class is maintained subordinate to the bourgeoisie, and the latter are in turn subordinate to the imperialist centers. The modern dominant groups within the dependent underdeveloped structures derive their high incomes from their association with activities linked to the developed structures and from internal exploitation of the backward, marginal, and dependent groups. The advanced groups are more integrated economically—and also culturally and socially—with the developed structures than with the marginalized population of their own countries. The elites, capitalists, and some workers are part of the internal system; others are marginalized.

Economic power also has political correlates: dominant countries may bring political pressures to bear on the dependent countries, and political alliances may emerge between foreign interests and the upper strata within the dependent country. Thus, the very process of transnational integration of some classes produces at the same time national disintegration. Internal polarization and class conflict are reflections of the international polarization and the disparities among nations. In *Dependency and Development in Latin America*, Cardoso and Faletto emphasize the political setting of development:

Economic power is expressed as social domination, that is, in politics. Through the political process, one class or economic group tries to establish a system of social relations that will permit it to impose its view on the whole society, or at least it tries to establish alliances to ensure economic policies compatible with its own interests and objectives.[7]

And in their preface to the same book:

We conceive the relationship between external and internal forces as forming a complex whole whose structural links are not based on mere external forms of exploitation and coercion, but are rooted in coincidences of interest between local dominant classes and international ones, and, on the other side, are challenged by local dominated groups and classes.[8]

Policy Inferences

What policy inferences are to be drawn from dependency theory? How is dependency to be reversed and underdevelopment overcome? Answers naturally differ according to the different interpretations of dependency. But all who argue that dependency relations characterize the international economy unite in rejecting the "developmentalist" or "modernization" themes discussed by mainstream neoclassicists. The diffusion model of development spreading from the modern capitalist sector to the traditional sector is rejected. So too is it denied that industrialization per se will reverse dependency.

To reverse dependency, most dependencistas argue that it is necessary to change the internal production structures, which give rise to the mechanisms of dependence, and to change the institutional order.

If capitalism underdevelops peripheral countries, then some dependencistas conclude that there can be no development unless there is transformation at the world level to an international socialist system. Autonomous development is only possible by constructing paths toward socialism, through the emergence of new social groups with new ideological goals.

Others, however, focus on remedies for the unequal power relations between center and periphery. They believe the adverse effects on the periphery can be minimized through affirmative policy measures taken by the periphery, such as regional economic integration, international commodity agreements, and the development of indigenous technology.

Still others advocate a more extreme "delinking" from the international system that would go beyond previous inward-looking policies of import substitution to "collective self-reliance." As Amin concludes, "So long as the underdeveloped country continues to be integrated in the world market, it remains helpless . . . [and] the possibilities of local accumulation are nil."[9] He therefore advocates a new development strategy, which he divides into three complementary aspects: (1) the choice of a "self-reliant" development based on the principle of relying on one's own resources, (2) the priority given to cooperation and economic integration between the countries of the Third World ("collective self-reliance"), and (3) the demand for a New International Economic Order based on higher prices for raw materials and the control of natural resources, access for the manufactures of the Third World to the markets of the developed countries, and the acceleration of the transfer of technologies.

[7]Fernando Henrique Cardoso and Enzo Faletto, *Dependency and Development in Latin America* (1979), p. 19.

[8]Ibid., p. xvi.

[9]Samir Amin, *Accumulation on a World Scale* (1975), p. 131.

Comment: Varieties of Dependency Theory

We consider other aspects of dependency theory in connection with foreign investment and multi-national corporations in Chapter V. In Chapter IX, the discussion of international trade as a mechanism of international inequality is also related to dependency theory.

There is a plurality of dependency views: different meanings are accorded the concept of *dependence*, and different analyses are offered to explain underdevelopment as a result of the interplay between internal and external structures.

Varieties of dependency theory can be identified in the following works: Paul Baran, *The Political Economy of Growth* (1957); Samir Amin, "Underdevelopment and Dependency," *Journal of Modern African Studies* 10 (1972), and *Unequal Development* (1976); Fernando Henrique Cardoso and Enzo Faletto, *Dependency and Development in Latin America* (1979); André Gunder Frank, *Capitalism and Underdevelopment in Latin America* (1967), *Dependent Accumulation and Underdevelopment* (1979), and *Critique and Anti-Critique: Essays on Dependence and Reformism* (1984); C. Furtado, *Development and Underdevelopment* (1978); T. Dos Santos, "The Structure of Dependence," *American Economic Review* (May 1970); O. Sunkel, "National Development Policy and External Dependence in Latin America," *Journal of Development Studies* (October 1969); Immanuel Wallerstein, "Dependence in an Interdependent World," *African Studies Review* 17 (1974), and *The Capitalist World Economy* (1979); Ronald H. Chilcote, *Theories of Development and Underdevelopment* (1984); Enmer L. Bacha, "An Interpretation of Unequal Exchange from Prebisch-Singer to Emmanuel," *Journal of Development Economics* 5 (1978); Keith Griffin and John Gurley, "Radical Analyses of Imperialism, the Third World, and the Transition to Socialism," *Journal of Economic Literature* (September 1985); Cristobal Kay, ed., *Latin American Theories of Development and Underdevelopment* (1989); and Robert Pakenham, *The Dependency Movement* (1992).

Some critical discussions of dependency theory are Sanjaya Lall, "Is 'Dependence' a Useful Concept in Analyzing Underdevelopment?" *World Development* (November–December 1975); P. J. O'Brien, "A Critique of Latin American Theories of Dependency," in *Beyond the Sociology of Development*, ed., I. Oxaal et al. (1975); Alec Nove, "On Reading André Gunder Frank," *Journal of Development Studies* (April–July 1974); Sheila Smith, "The Ideas of Samir Amin: Theory or Tautology?" *Journal of Development Studies* (October 1980); and David Booth, "Marxism and Development Sociology," *World Development* 13 (July 1985).

A number of country studies contradict the dependency thesis: Robert Kaufman et al., "A Preliminary Test of the Theory of Dependency," *Comparative Politics* (April 1975); David Ray, "The Dependency Model and Latin America: Three Basic Fallacies," *Journal of Inter-American Affairs and World Studies* (February 1973); Patrick J. McGowan, "Economic Dependency and Economic Performance in Black Africa," *Journal of Modern African Studies* 14 (1976); and Patrick J. McGowan and Dale L. Smith, "Economic Dependency in Black Africa: An Analysis of Competing Theories," *International Organization* (Winter 1978).

Some literature on the sociology of development now focuses on "modes of production" and "forms of exploitation." This approach is especially influential in the study of peasants and trends in rural social structure. See Harold Wolfe, ed., *The Articulation of Modes of Production* (1980); David Goodman and Michael Redclift, *From Peasant to Proletarian* (1981); and John Harriss, ed., *Rural Development: Theories of Peasant Economy and Agrarian Change* (1982).

Comment: Neostructuralism

During the late 1980s and early 1990s, a revised version of Latin American structuralism emerged in a number of writings on "neostructuralism." These writings are characterized by an attempt to redefine the role of the nation-state and policy design so as to promote higher rates of growth, equity, and regional autonomy in Latin America.

The neostructuralists' paradigm can be contrasted with the neoliberal paradigm as is done in the following comparison by the neostructuralists' author Ricardo French-Davis in "An Outline of a Neostructuralist Approach," *CEPAL Review*, no. 34 (April 1988), p. 40:

Neoliberal paradigm	*Neostructuralist paradigm*
1. An adjustment is quicker and more benign in a liberalized economy. Tends towards theoretical propositions which work with marginal changes in a homogeneous economy.	1. Adjustments are slow and/or may produce disequilibria in a heterogeneous national economy; the costs of the transition greatly affect the final equilibrium, depending on what course the adjustment process has followed.
2. A static comparative analysis; focuses on microeconomic efficiency, while failing to give sufficient consideration to the macroeconomic effects on employment, distribution, and productive investment.	2. The analysis takes the dynamics of adjustment processes into consideration; the search for macroeconomic efficiency predominates and takes into account the effects on the rate of utilization of production resources and on physical and human capital formation.
3. Tends to consider just one disequilibrium at a time, which is assumed to be the result of ill-advised public policies; Pareto's optimum state is regarded as attainable.	3. Acknowledges the existence of many different disequilibria and maintains that a number of them are of a structural origin. The quest for efficiency is seen within the context of a real ''sub-optimal'' (''second-best'') world.
4. Only one policy tool is used for each problem to be analyzed, although this is not seen as precluding the application of economic policy packages.	4. Considers the simultaneous application of a package of policies to deal with a group of problems, establishing priorities as regards the timing and intensiveness of each policy.
5. Economics is a science which provides the same answers for the same problems in each case, regardless of the historical, political, and economic contexts of the analysis.	5. The answers may vary, according to the point in time concerned and the prevailing institutional structure.
6. Economic liberalization ensures the deconcentration of political power. Extensive economic freedom is postulated as a pre-condition for full political freedom.	6. Selective economic regulation and an improved distribution of power buttress one another. Excessive economic freedom is conducive to concentration among small groups.
7. Advocates economic internationalism and assumes that there is a trend towards the obsolescence of the nation-State. The main unit of analysis is the microeconomic unit.	7. The main unit of analysis is the nation-State. Attention is focused on the deliberate (as opposed to spontaneous) maximization of national social well-being.

See also O. Sunkel, ed., *Developments from Within: Towards a Neostructuralist Approach for Latin America* (1992), and articles by S. Bitar, R. French-Davis, and O. Rosales in *CEPAL Review* (April 1988).

In our final chapter, we shall consider the extent to which there is now some convergence of views on several strategic issues in the policy recommendations of neostructuralists and orthodox neoclassicists.

CHAPTER III

Dualistic Development

Having considered in Chapters I and II the general context of developmental problems and some approaches to their analyses, we are now ready to turn directly to a more detailed examination of the development process. We begin by focusing on an outstanding characteristic of LDCs—that of "dualism." In many LDCs, a modern commercialized industrial sector has developed alongside a traditional subsistence agricultural sector, resulting in what is termed a *dual economy*. Dualism motivates asymmetries in organization and production between sectors. The contrasts in organization and production between the advanced exchange sector and the backward indigenous sector are among the most striking—and puzzling—characteristics of a poor country.

If we are to identify the structural relationships involved in the development process, we must understand the dual structure of the modern and traditional, and we must consider how the acceleration of a country's development will entail a higher rate of structural transformation. As an economy develops, its structure is transformed in terms of the pattern of production, composition of demand, foreign trade, and employment. Changes in economic structure are associated with transformation of the supply and use of resources that accompany the rise in income. Attention to structural transformation requires us to study the interactions among sectors. We therefore explore in this chapter several questions about dualism: What conditions have given rise to a dual economy? In what sense is a dual economy also a labor surplus economy? How can the absorption of the indigenous economy into an expanding modern economy be accomplished?

Underemployment is commonly believed to be a dominant feature of densely populated, underdeveloped countries, and the labor force is continually increasing with population growth. It is therefore important to consider how dualism relates to the problem of providing higher productivity employment opportunities for the currently underemployed workers and for those joining the labor force. Through dual-sector models, this chapter focuses on the macrodynamics of the supply and demand for labor and the movement of labor to higher productivity activities.

There has been much confusion about the phenomena of unemployment, underemployment, and disguised unemployment in the traditional sector of a poor country. The selections in section III.A are therefore designed to clarify the effects of a dualistic structure on employment by examining the concept of the "labor surplus economy."

Several models of development have focused on the structural transformation of a dual economy (section III.B). Prominent among them is the Fei–Ranis model of a labor surplus economy, which is characterized by the coexistence of a relatively large and overwhelmingly stagnant agricultural sector, in which institutional forces determine the wage rate, and a relatively small but growing commercialized sector, in which competitive conditions shape the labor market. In such a labor surplus dualistic economy, labor is not scarce, whereas capital is extremely so. Development therefore requires that

> the center of gravity must continually shift towards industry through the continuous reallocation of labor from the agricultural to the industrial sector: the related criterion of "success" in the development effort is thus a rate of industrial labor absorption sufficiently rapid to permit the economy to escape from the ever-threatening Malthusian trap.[1]

Perhaps the most celebrated of the labor surplus models is Nobel laureate Arthur Lewis's analysis in "Economic Development with Unlimited Supplies of Labor." The Note (III.B.1) summarizes this model, emphasizing the interaction between an advanced "capitalist" sector and an indigenous "noncapitalist" sector in a developing economy, and indicating how resources can be drawn into the modern exchange system through capital accumulation in the expanding capitalist sector. The Lewis model is helpful in explaining the mechanism by which the proportion of domestic savings in the national income increases during the course of development. As the model explains, growth in the modern capitalist sector turns on the higher than average propensity to save from profit income, as well as on the rise of the share of profits in the national income in the early stages of development. The traditional noncapitalist sector, in turn, serves as a reservoir from which the expanding capitalist sector draws labor. The model therefore has significant policy implications for labor absorption and for the employment problem—a problem to which we return frequently in subsequent chapters.

It will be illuminating to reexamine Lewis's dual-sector model in light of the more than four decades of development experience since Lewis first formulated his model. A prominent feature of development experience has been the extensive rural–urban migration of labor, as examined in section III.C. We need to identify the determinants of migration and understand migrant experience in urban locations. The model by Michael Todaro, presented in selection III.C.1, emphasizes a migration function that hypothesizes that the relevant urban income is the present value of expected earnings (that is, a rational calculation by an individual migrant that allows for the probability of the migrant obtaining urban employment). In a distorted labor market, growing urban unemployment is consistent with equilibrium in this model, and rural–urban migration is assumed to occur until there is equality between the actual rural wage and the expected urban wage. Although the specific character of the probability function for urban employment can be questioned, the migration function is analytically useful in explaining why policies that are devoted only to raising urban labor demand cannot be relied on to reduce urban unemployment.

The high rate of population growth has also been the main cause of the high density of land occupation in the rural areas; this growth in turn, has been an underlying factor in the high rate of migration from rural to urban areas in many countries. The accelerated rural–urban labor migration has produced extremely high rates of growth of the active population in urban areas that have far exceeded the growth of urban employment opportunities, culminating in rising levels of urban unemployment. Given the limited employment opportunities in the modern sector of urban areas, an increasing share of the urban labor force has become unemployed or has drifted into the tertiary sector, or what has come to be called the "informal sector." As unemployment and underemployment have been transferred from the rural sector, the absorption of labor in the informal sector has become in many respects an extension into the urban areas of the traditional rural subsistence economy.

As discussed in selection III.C.3, an ILO Mission to Kenya has given considerable emphasis to the role of the informal sector. In almost every area of Kenyan activity, there appears to be a sharp and analytically significant dualism between the protected, organized, large-scale, foreign-influenced, formal sector and the unprotected, unorganized, small-scale, family-based, essentially self-reliant, informal sector. The Mission argued that to infer the growth of total employment, let alone the volume of unemployment, from the growth of employment in the formal sector can be very misleading. It has become a general phenomenon in the urban areas of the LDCs that the number of people in the informal

---

[1]John C. H. Fei and Gustav Ranis, *Development of the Labor Surplus Economy* (1964), p. 3.

sector has increased absolutely and as a proportion of the labor force. The size of urban areas has commonly doubled within a decade, and with such high urban growth rates, unemployment and underemployment have also risen.

To reexamine the problem of labor absorption, we need to consider what has gone wrong with the Lewis model of labor transfer—why urban unemployment has increased and why the labor reservoir in the noncapitalist sector still remains so large after more than four decades of developmental effort. Section III.D. examines how some important conditions of the Lewis model have failed to be fulfilled in reality and indicates ways by which the explanatory power of the model could be improved. Specifically, it suggests that the analysis give more attention to the interrelationships between the rural and urban sectors, to the existence of an informal (nonmodern, noncapitalist) sector alongside the organized (modern, capitalist) sector in urban areas, and to the need for improving the quality of employment in the informal sector as well as the quantity of employment throughout the economy. Organized and informal subsectors are within both the rural and the urban sectors, giving the economy the characteristic of ''double dualism.'' Unemployment and underemployment are not confined to the rural areas, but comparable problems of open unemployment, inadequate incomes, and low productivity have also arisen in urban areas.

The plea is for a set of interrelated policy measures rather than partial measures. An entire set of policies is now needed that will concentrate on employment in the urban informal sector and the rural sector, as well as on demand in the urban formal sector. The underutilized labor reservoir in the traditional sector and open unemployment in the urban area are problems in their own right. Employment problems, however, pervade the economy, and pervasive policies are therefore needed.

Subsequent chapters will also discuss the employment problem, especially in connection with structural transformation, the transfer of technology, income distribution, education, and trade expansion. From a comprehensive analysis of the employment problem, we should become aware that the objectives of greater utilization of labor, diminution of poverty, and improved income distribution are complementary, not competitive goals.

III.A. THE LABOR SURPLUS ECONOMY

III.A.1. Labor Surplus on the Land*

The concept of surplus farm labor has attracted increasing attention in the underdeveloped countries, especially in Asia. The simplest definition of it implies that some labor could be withdrawn from subsistence farming without reducing the volume of farm output. In technical terms, the marginal productivity of labor is believed to be zero. If this is true, it has some far-reaching implications. But is it true? Is it even conceivable? Some economists have had serious doubts on this score. It must be admitted that the idea of "disguised unemployment," as it is usually called, has sometimes been carelessly formulated and inadequately substantiated.

The subject must be viewed in relation to the general population problem. The crucial fact is that world population has doubled in the last hundred years. About two-thirds of the increase has taken place in the underdeveloped areas, chiefly in Asia, largely through a fall in death-rates. This has been part of the uneven impact of Western civilization on the rest of the world. Now in the poorer countries as a rule the majority of the population works in agriculture to start with, for basic and obvious reasons. Just as food is the major item of consumption in low-income communities, so the struggle for food takes up most of their time and resources. In such countries rapid population growth naturally leads, and in some has already led, to excess population on the land.

Consider for a moment the effects of population growth in a community of peasant cultivators. Numbers are increasing while land, capital and techniques remain unchanged. Alternative employment opportunities may be lacking because of the rigid social structure, and may actually be decreasing because of the decline of traditional handicraft industries due to the competition of imported manufactures.

With the growing pressure of people on the land, farms become smaller and smaller. What is more, farms are divided and subdivided into tiny strips and plots. Accordingly it seems to me

that agricultural unemployment in densely populated peasant communities may be said to take at least two basic forms: (1) underemployment of peasant cultivators due to the small size of farms; (2) unemployment disguised through fragmentation of the individual holding. . . .

To the extent that the labor surplus is absorbed—and concealed—through fragmentation, it cannot be withdrawn without bad effects on output unless the fragmentation is reversed and the holdings are consolidated. Over a limited range the marginal productivity of labor might be zero without any such reorganization. It could be zero over a much wider range if the remaining factors of production were appropriately reorganized, which would require for one thing a consolidation of plots. Appropriate reorganization of the other factors of production is clearly a necessary and a reasonable pre-requisite for purposes of policy as well as analysis.

There are a number of empirical studies that tend to confirm this general picture. The evidence can never be entirely satisfactory in a matter such as this where some things, including the weather, would have to be held constant and others subjected to a reorganization which may necessitate a revolutionary change in rural life, bringing inevitably other changes with it. Nevertheless the connection between over-population and fragmentation goes a long way to make the existence of surplus farm labor plausible.

On a theoretical view of the matter it is clear that excess population can be so great in relation to land and capital that the marginal productivity of labor is reduced to zero. There are, however, two reasons why some economists have found this idea difficult to accept. First, anyone trained in Western economics would have to ask: Who would employ these people if their product is zero? Or else one might ask: How can these marginal people live, what do they eat, if they really produce nothing?

The answer to the first question is that in many countries the wage-labor system, which Western economists are apt to take for granted, hardly exists. The prevailing condition in subsistence farming is one of peasant family labor.

*From Ragnar Nurkse, "Excess Population and Capital Construction," *Malayan Economic Review,* October 1957, pp. 1, 3–5. Reprinted by permission.

The answer to the second question—How can they live?—is that they live by sharing more or less equally in the total product of the farm, which includes the product of intramarginal labor and of any land and capital goods the peasants may own. The product from these factors goes into the same pot and the members of the household eat out of that same pot. These institutional arrangements are foreign to the economies of business enterprise, and so the conditions which they make possible may seem paradoxical.

If this sharing of food is considered a little further the ultimate limit to the multiplication of people on the farms becomes starkly plain.[1] If the average total product per person falls below the physical level of subsistence, the outcome is the Malthusian state of starvation cutting down numbers or at least checking their further increase. At the point where this average product equals the physical subsistence level, the marginal product of labor may well be zero or even negative.[2] Still, it need not be as low as zero. Conversely, if and when labor's marginal product is zero, the average product need not be as low as the physical subsistence level; it may be a little above that level.

In any case, excess population necessarily implies that the marginal product is less than the average. In this state of affairs further population growth brings down the average level of consumption. Why? Because the additional labor contributes less than the average worker previously, and so it pulls down the average product per head. If the average product is as low as we know it to be, it does not seem far-fetched to suppose that in some cases the marginal product of labor may be zero. The upshot of the argument does not, of course, depend on its being exactly zero, although this is a convenient case on which to concentrate the analysis. The essential point is that the marginal workers live, in effect, on a subsidy if their own contribution to output is less than their intake of food and other necessities.

The relationship between total product and total population is illustrated in the accompanying diagram (Figure 1). Average product per head is reflected in the slope of the vector from the origin to any point on the curve. The marginal product is reflected in the slope of the curve itself at any given point. The average product per head reaches a maximum at A (where the angle AOL is largest) and declines thereafter as population increases further. The marginal product becomes zero at B (where the average product measured by the angle BOM may still be substantial). If population increases beyond M, the marginal product becomes negative and the average product continues to fall. If we suppose that the average product at N represents the absolute physical minimum of subsistence, then population cannot increase beyond N. This supposition is of course purely arbitrary and illustrative. Actually the physical subsistence level of average product per head may lie, not in the range of negative marginal productivity, but conceivably at B or somewhere between A and B where marginal product is still positive. The diagram merely illustrates the possibilities and does not, of course, tell us what actually happens.

It must be conceded that this view of the matter is essentially that of "optimum population" theory (in the diagram the optimum size of population is OL). Now this theory has sometimes been criticized as being an unrealistic exercise in comparative statics. It assumes that nothing changes except the number of people—and, in response thereto, the volume of total product. It abstracts from, and ignores, any connections that may exist between population size on the one hand and, say, the state of techniques or the volume of capital on the other hand. It holds all

---

[1] The analysis concentrates on the subsistence farm sector. The reader should bear in mind that even the most backward economy usually contains other sectors also, including export production, commerce, government and even some industrial activity.

[2] Professor J. E. Meade has shown this very clearly in his book, *The Theory of International Economic Policy;* Vol. II, *Trade and Welfare,* issued under the auspices of the Royal Institute of International Affairs, London, Oxford University Press, 1955, Chapter 6 and Appendix 1.

FIGURE 1.

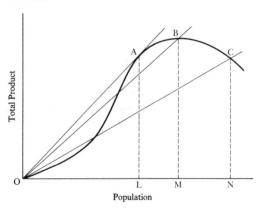

Population

other things constant. Is this not bound to lead to a distorted view of reality?

The criticism may be perfectly valid with regard to population trends in the Western world. But if we consider Asia over the last hundred years, I am not sure that the objection has much force. I began by saying that the population explosion in Asia, due largely to the fall in death-rates, reflects the *uneven* impact of Western civilization. The point is precisely that while population has doubled, other things such as techniques, capital supplies and cultivable land have remained *too much the same*. Therein lies the whole problem. Of course, there has been some advance in these other things too, but not nearly at the same rate as in population. In Asia there has been nothing like the advance that accompanied population growth in the West. In this state of affairs it seems to me that the "optimum population" approach, questionable though it may be in the West, has a good deal of validity in the East. The economic problem of the East has been largely a consequence of dynamic population growth in an otherwise relatively static environment.

"Optimum population" theory directs attention chiefly to the variation of *average* product as the size of population varies. We have found it at least equally important to consider the *marginal* product. The question might be asked: Why this obsession with the margin? Why not stress the obvious fact of a low general level of productivity? The answer is that the marginal approach is useful here because of the need to take away some labor from current production for work on capital construction.

III.A.2. Choice of Techniques*

Unemployment is often not "visible." It may be "disguised" as a result of a particular task being performed by more labour than is necessary (given the technique and the productive resources). As Professor Nurkse puts it, "the marginal productivity of labour, over a wide range, is zero." Thus labour can be taken away from these occupations without affecting production.

The concept of "disguised unemployment" is actually less simple than it looks, and we must say a few words on it to avoid any possible misunderstanding. We may ask if "marginal productivity of labour, over a wide range, is zero," why is labour being applied at all? Does it not go against rational behaviour? In Figure 1, curve Y gives the relationship between labour and output, given the technique and the supply of other productive factors. If OL_2 is the amount of labour that is applied and the marginal productivity becomes zero at point L_1, then L_1L_2 is the relevant range. But what is the point of applying labour beyond L_1?

This confusion arises because of not distinguishing between *labour* and *labourer*. It is not that too much labour is being spent in the production process, but that too many labourers are spending it. Disguised unemployment thus normally takes the form of smaller number of work-ing hours per head per year; for example, each of three brothers shepherding the sheep every third day. It is thus the marginal productivity of the *labourer*, so to say, that is nil *over a wide range* and the productivity of *labour* may be just equal to zero at the margin. It may also take the form of lower intensity of work with people "taking it easy," e.g., the peasant having time to watch the birds while working. If a number of labourers went away, the others would be able to produce about the same output working *longer* and *harder*. There is no contradiction between disguised unemployment and rational behaviour. In a family-based peasant economy unemployment will naturally put on this disguise. A piece of land that can be cultivated fully by two, may actually be looked after by four, if a family of four working men having no other em-

*From A. K. Sen, *Choice of Techniques,* Basil Blackwell, 1960, pp. 13–16. Reprinted by permission.

FIGURE 1.

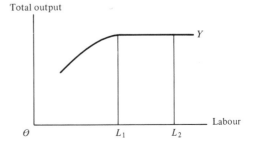

ployment opportunity happens to own it. All this is represented in Figure 2. The south represents the number of labourers, the east the number of labour-hours spent and the north the product. The marginal product of labour becomes *nil* with OL_1 labour-hours and labour is not applied beyond this point. The working population being OP_2, each puts in tan a hours of work. Tan b represents the "normal" working hours per labourer. So the job can be done by OP_1 labourers keeping normal hours. In this sense P_1P_2 population is surplus. Thus while marginal productivity of *labour* is nil at point L_1 only, that of the *labourer* is *nil over the range P_1P_2*. This represents the volume of "disguised unemployment."

A further difficulty with the concept of disguised unemployment is that any shift of labour from the rural area will lead to some reorganization of the techniques of production in that area. The *organization* of production may change considerably and thus the concept of zero marginal productivity, from the point of view of strict theory, becomes difficult to apply. The contrast between a movement *along* the

FIGURE 2.

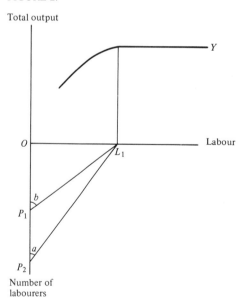

Total output

productivity curve and a *shift* of the curve as a result of a change of the supply of other factors of production (e.g., "organization") is relevant in this connection. But actually from the point of view of operational policy these conceptual complications need not be very important. The point is that we are in a position to remove a considerable part of the rural labour force away from the rural area without affecting the rural output appreciably.

A more real difficulty will arise if it is found that at the given supply of capital and land, marginal productivity of labour is not *in fact* nil. In this case, when some of the rural labourers move out, some real investment (and not merely more "organization") is necessary to keep the output constant. The "opportunity cost" of labour can be measured by the amount of investment that has to be put in to keep rural output constant as a labourer moves out. This is a measure of the cost in *stock* terms. In terms of *flow*, the opportunity cost can be measured (*a*) as the amount of alternative rural output sacrificed per year as a result of drawing a labourer away from the rural area, or (*b*) as the amount of alternative output sacrificed per year as a result of putting in the compensatory investment to make good the above loss of rural output rather than using that amount of investment in some other field.

It is in fact possible that even in some of the so-called "overpopulated" areas scarcity of capital has led to such a substitution of capital by labour that the marginal product of labour is not zero; thus a withdrawal of labour *will* reduce the rural output somewhat. Rural techniques of production in some of the underdeveloped countries are so primitive and labour-intensive that this will not be very surprising. It is, however, likely that in this case a relatively small amount of investment may make good the loss of rural output and the opportunity cost in terms of the necessary increase in the capital *stock* or in terms of the resulting loss of *flow* of alternative output, i.e., in sense (*b*), may be rather small. Thus, while labour in some of these economies may not be "free," it is likely to be cheap—cheaper than the conventionally measured opportunity cost, sense (*a*), suggests.

III.B. INTERSECTORAL ANALYSIS

III.B.1. Lewis's Dual-Sector Model—Note

When a dual economy exists, the ultimate question for the country's future development is how the modern exchange sector is to expand while the indigenous sector contracts. This requires an analysis of the interrelationships between the two sectors. Sir W. Arthur Lewis has offered a perceptive analysis of this problem.[1] This note summarizes Lewis's model and assesses its relevance for contemporary problems of development.

Lewis analyzes the process of economic expansion in a dual economy composed of a "capitalist" sector and a "noncapitalist" sector. The capitalist sector is defined as that part of the economy that uses reproducible capital, pays capitalists for the use thereof, and employs wage labor for profit-making purposes. Capitalist production need not be restricted to manufacturing; it may also be in plantations or mines that hire labor and resell its output for a profit. The capitalist sector may also be either private or public; again, the distinguishing feature of the capitalist sector is the hiring of labor and the sale of its output for a profit, which can be undertaken by public enterprise as well as private. The subsistence sector is that part of the economy that does not use reproducible capital and does not hire labor for profit—the indigenous traditional sector or the "self-employment sector."[2] In this sector, output per head is much lower than that in the capitalist sector; given the available techniques, the marginal productivity of a laborer in agricultural production may be zero as a limiting case. As a result of institutional arrangements, such as the family farm or communal holdings of land, members of the farm labor force consume essentially the average product of the farm's output, even though the marginal product of some farm laborers may be well below the average product.

A fundamental relationship between the two sectors is that when the capitalist sector expands, it draws labor from the reservoir in the noncapitalist sector. For countries that have experienced high rates of population growth and are densely populated, it is assumed that the supply of unskilled labor to the capitalist sector is unlimited. Labor is "unlimited" in the sense that when the capitalist sector offers additional employment opportunities at the existing wage rate, the numbers willing to work at the existing wage rate will be greater than the demand: the supply curve of labor is infinitely elastic at the ruling wage. According to Lewis, one condition for this is that the ruling wage of the capitalist sector exceeds the earnings in the noncapitalist sector of those who are willing to transfer themselves. The other condition is that any tendency that the transfer may set in motion for earnings per head to rise in the noncapitalist sector must initially be offset by the effect of increases in the labor force (natural increase, immigration, or greater female participation).[3] A large component of the unlimited supply of labor from the noncapitalist reservoir of labor is composed of those who are in disguised unemployment in agriculture and in other overmanned occupations, such as domestic service, casual odd jobs, or petty retail trading. Another source of labor is women who transfer from the household to commercial employment, and the labor force has also grown as a result of the population increase. The large

[1]W. Arthur Lewis, "Economic Development with Unlimited Supplies of Labour," *The Manchester School* (May 1954): 139–91, "Unlimited Labour: Further Notes," *The Manchester School* (January 1958): 1–32, and "Reflections on Unlimited Labor," in *International Economics and Development, Essays in Honor of Raúl Prebisch,* ed. Luis Eugenio Di Marco (1972).

[2]The characterization of this traditional agricultural sector as the "self-employed" sector is suggested by Kazushi Ohkawa, "Balanced Growth and the Problem of Agriculture—with Special Reference to Asian Peasant Economy," *Hitotsubashi Journal of Economics* (September 1961): 13–25.

Lloyd Reynolds has also proposed that a four-sector model would be more relevant—with the "traditional sector" divided into the rural sector and the urban trade-service sector, and with both an industry subsector and a government subsector in the "modern sector." The urban trade-service sector employs people with little skill and little initial capital, and there is relative freedom of entry. For a discussion of the different production functions in these four sectors, see Lloyd G. Reynolds, "Economic Development with Surplus Labor: Some Complications," *Oxford Economic Papers* (March 1969): 89–103. Reynolds's urban trade-service sector bears some resemblance to the "informal sector" discussed in selection III.C.3.

[3]Lewis, "Reflections on Unlimited Labor," p. 77.

pool of unskilled labor enables new industries to be created or old industries to expand in the capitalist sector without encountering any shortage of unskilled labor.

In considering the sources of finance for development, Lewis realized that the bulk of the finance, even with foreign aid, has to come from increases in private domestic saving. The problem is to elucidate how this comes about. History indicates that in the present-day developed countries, increased savings came from a rising share of profits in national income. But what caused this increase in the share of profits? Lewis maintains that neoclassical economics is of no help in understanding a long-term rise in the savings propensity. In contrast, he recalls,

As I was walking down a road in Bangkok one morning in August 1952, it suddenly occurred to me that all one needed to do was to drop the assumption— then usually (but not necessarily) made by neoclassical macroeconomists—that the supply of labor was fixed. Assume instead that it was infinitely elastic, add that productivity was increasing in the capitalist sector, and one got a rising profits share.[4]

The wage that the growing capitalist sector has to pay is determined in Lewis's model by what labor earns in the subsistence sector. Peasant farmers will not leave the family farm for wage employment unless the real wage is at least equal to the average product on the land.[5] Capitalist wages, as a rule, will have to be somewhat higher than subsistence earnings in order to compensate labor for the cost of transferring and to induce labor to leave the traditional life of the subsistence sector. (Lewis observes that there is usually a gap of 30 percent or more between capitalist wages and subsistence earnings.) At the existing capitalist wages, however, the supply of labor is considered to be perfectly elastic.

This situation is illustrated in Figure 1, where OA represents subsistence earnings, OW the real wage rate in the capitalistic sector, and WS the perfectly elastic supply of labor. Given a fixed amount of capital at the outset, the demand for labor is initially represented by the marginal productivity schedule of labor, N_1D_1 in Figure 1. If we assume profit maximization, capital will then

FIGURE 1.

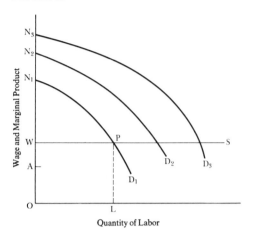

Quantity of Labor

be applied up to the point where the current wage equals the marginal productivity of labor. If OW is the current wage, the amount of labor employed in the capitalistic sector is OL; beyond L, workers earn whatever they can in the subsistence sector. The total product N_1PLO in the capitalist sector will then be divided between wages in the amount $OWPL$ and the capitalists' surplus, or profits, in the amount WPN_1.

As in classical models, Lewis assumes that all wages are consumed and that profits are the only source of savings. The rate of growth is therefore equal to the product of the rate of profit and the propensity to save out of profits. A rise in the economy's savings ratio results from an increase in the share of profits brought about by the relative expansion of the capitalist sector.

In tracing the process of economic expansion, Lewis emphasizes that the key to the process is the use of the capitalist surplus. The driving force in the system is generated by the reinvestment of the capitalist surplus in creating new capital. As the capitalist sector expands, labor withdraws from the subsistence sector into wage employment; the surplus then becomes even larger; there is still more reinvestment of profits; and the process continues, progressively absorbing surplus labor from the subsistence sector.

Figure 1 illustrates this process by the outward shift of the demand for labor, from N_1D_1 to N_3D_3 over time. When some of the initial surplus WPN_1 is reinvested, the amount of fixed capital increases, and the schedule of the marginal productivity of labor is then raised to the level of, say, N_2D_2. Both the capitalist surplus and capitalist employment are now larger. Further investment then raises the marginal produc-

[4]W. Arthur Lewis, "Development Economics in the 1950s," in *Pioneers in Development*, ed. Gerald M. Meier and Dudley Seers (1984), p. 132.

[5]Even though the marginal product of labor is zero in disguised unemployment, a member of the extended family shares in the total product and receives approximately the average product.

tivity of labor to, say, N_3D_3. And so the process continues.

The growth in capitalist profits is crucial in this process, and the share of profits in the national income is of strategic importance. This will be determined by the share of the capitalist sector in the national output and by the share of profits in the capitalist sector. As the capitalist sector expands, and the wage–price ratio remains constant, the share of profits in national income increases. And since the major source of savings is profits, savings and capital formation also increase as a proportion of the national income.

Barring a hitch in the process, the capitalist sector can expand until the absorption of surplus labor is complete, and the supply function of labor becomes less than perfectly elastic. Capital accumulation has then caught up with the excess supply of labor; beyond this point, real wages no longer remain constant but rise as capital formation occurs, so that the share of profits in the national income will not necessarily continue to increase, and investment will no longer necessarily grow relative to the national income.

Of particular significance is the possibility that the expansion process might be cut short by a rise in real wages and a reduction in profits that halt capital accumulation before the excess labor supply is completely absorbed. This may be due to a rise in average product in the subsistence sector because the absolute number of people in this sector is being reduced without a fall in total output, labor productivity happens to increase in the subsistence sector, or the terms of trade turn against the capitalist sector.

If, for instance, the capitalist sector produces no food, and the demand for food rises as the capitalist sector expands, then the price of food will rise in terms of capitalist products—that is, the terms of trade turn against the capitalist sector. In order to keep the real income of workers constant, capitalists then have to pay out to labor a larger part of their product as wages, thereby reducing their profits.

To analyze these possibilities, Lewis presents his model in three versions. In the first version, the economy is closed and there is no trade between the two sectors. The capitalist sector is self-contained, except that it imports labor. The first turning point that limits expansion of the capitalist sector then comes only when the labor supply ceases to be infinitely elastic and the wage starts rising through pressure from the noncapitalist sector. There is, however, no rea-

son to believe that the capitalist wage will rise endogenously as soon as the capitalist sector begins to grow. How soon this will happen depends on the number of workers who are transferred from the noncapitalist sector, the effect of this transfer on consumption per head in the noncapitalist sector, and the extent to which the labor force in the noncapitalist sector is replenished through population increase, greater participation of women in the labor force, or immigration.

In the second version, the economy is also closed, but the capitalist sector depends on trade with the noncapitalist sector for food or raw materials. There may then be an additional turning point if the capitalist sector suffers from adverse commodity terms of trade, even if the labor reservoir still exists. Although the commodity terms of trade worsen for the capitalist sector, the profit margin need not fall if productivity in the capitalist sector is rising sufficiently rapidly.

What will happen to profits depends on a race among productivity in the two sectors, real wages, and the commodity terms of trade. If real wages are constant, the increase in productivity accrues to profits, so the product-wage—that is the ratio of wages to value added—falls, the investment ratio rises, and the share of the capitalist sector in national income grows.

The third version postulates an open economy whose capitalist sector trades either with the labor reservoir or with the outside world.[6]

The possibility that industrialization can be inhibited by a deterioration in the terms of trade for the industrial sector points up the extreme importance of providing an agricultural surplus for consumption in the expanding industrial sector. This is one of several reasons why agricultural output must expand along with industrial development. This problem, together with other relationships between industry and agriculture, will be discussed more fully in Chapters VII and VIII.

It should, of course, be recognized that if the country earns sufficient foreign exchange, the capitalist sector could overcome the agricultural constraint on its further expansion by importing the necessary food and raw materials from overseas instead of being limited by domestic agricultural output. But if export earnings are insufficient, then the failure of exports to keep pace

---

[6]For details of these versions of the model, see Lewis, ''Reflections on Unlimited Labor,'' pp. 83–94.

with needed imports will constrain the rate of growth of output.

Once the reservoir of surplus labor is exhausted, the labor market is integrated, with a uniform wage determined endogenously by demand and supply, as in neoclassical theory. Lewis initially takes the wage as given and determines employment, whereas the neoclassical theory takes employment as given and determines the wage. The Lewis and neoclassical approaches are thus complementary in being two limiting polar cases in the course of development.

Although the Lewis model highlights some basic relationships in dualistic development, its applicability has been questioned on several counts. Some critics believe that the model rests on the existence of disguised unemployment in the noncapitalist sector, and they contend this is unrealistic. The strict interpretation of disguised unemployment is that the marginal productivity of labor, over a wide range, is zero; that is, labor is redundant or in surplus and can be withdrawn without any loss of output, even if no change in production techniques or in use of other productive resources occurs. But the existence of disguised unemployment is not necessary for the expansionary process that Lewis describes; all that the model needs is the fact that the supply of labor exceeds demand at the current wage. It therefore makes no difference whether the loss of noncapitalist output is zero or positive, so long as it is less than the value added by the labor in the capitalist sector, to which it is transferred.

Moreover, although Lewis refers to the zero marginal productivity of labor as a limiting case, he means by this the marginal product of a *man,* not the marginal product of a *manhour:*

For example, in many countries the market stalls (or the handicraft industries) are crowded with people who are not as fully occupied as they would wish to be. If ten percent of these people were removed, the amount traded would be the same, since those who remained would do more trade. This is the sense in which the marginal product of men in that industry is zero. It is a significant sense, and its significance is not diminished by pointing out that the fact that others have to do more work to keep the total product constant proves that the marginal product of manhours is positive.[7]

This interpretation of zero marginal productivity of labor is similar to that offered by A. K. Sen in selection III.A.2.

[7]Ibid., p. 79.

It is difficult to estimate empirically the amount of surplus labor. Lewis simply states:

Nobody denies that in the overpopulated countries handicraft workers, petty traders, dock workers, domestic servants, and casual workers have a lot of spare time on their hands, and that most of them (except the domestic servants) would be glad to exchange extra work for extra income at the current rate. Neither does anybody deny that there is much seasonal unemployment in agriculture. The dispute is confined to the situation on small family farms at the peak of the agricultural season, in some parts of Asia and the Middle East.

I do not believe that the productivity of a manhour is zero in agriculture, domestic service, petty retailing, handicrafts, or any other part of the noncapitalist reservoir. Nevertheless, I have seen nothing in the now vast literature of underemployment to alter my belief that in India or Egypt one could mobilize a group equal to, say, ten per cent of the unskilled noncapitalist labor force without significantly reducing the output of the noncapitalist sectors from which they were withdrawn.[8]

Another type of underemployment that characterizes some LDCs may, however, create more difficulties for the Lewis analysis. A type of "traditional" underemployment arises when sociocultural determinants of the division of labor between men and women in the traditional sector leave the men underemployed. In some African economies, for instance, it is common practice for the men to clear and prepare the land for cultivation, while the women do the routine work of sowing and cultivating. The men are left in surplus supply in agriculture, but they then frequently become migrant laborers in the exchange sector. As temporary immigrants from the traditional sector, they might work in industry or mining on a seasonal basis, or even for a year or two, and then return to their peasant farms. The migration of labor for short periods might have only a negligible effect on agricultural output, but several studies have shown that adult manpower cannot be spared from the traditional system of agriculture for more than two or three years without reducing output.[9] This special situation of temporary labor migration does not conform to a precise interpretation of disguised unemployment. It is more enlighten-

[8]Ibid., pp. 81–82.

[9]W. J. Barber, *The Economy of British Central Africa* (1961), pp. 72–73; Guy Hunter, *The New Societies of Tropical Africa* (1962); W. Elkan, "Migrant Labor in Africa: An Economist's Approach," *American Economic Review, Papers and Proceedings* (May 1959): 188–97; W. Watson, *Tribal Cohesion in a Money Economy* (1959).

ing to analyze the labor supply as a case of joint supply, whereby workers are being supplied jointly to the advanced sector and the traditional sector over a period of time. An important part of this problem is to determine whether and for how long an individual will offer his labor for wage employment in the wage sector.[10]

The case of a migrant labor force, however, poses special problems that cannot be adequately analyzed in Lewis's model.

Another difference is that even if an unlimited supply of unskilled labor is assumed to exist, it is generally true that in poor countries skilled labor is in very short supply. Lewis recognizes this problem, but discounts its importance by considering it to be only a temporary bottleneck that can be removed by providing the facilities for training more skilled labor. This will, however, at best involve a time lag.

Moreover, can we assume, as Lewis does, that a capitalist class already exists? A major obstacle to development in many countries still may be the absence of a capitalist class with the necessary ability and motivation to undertake long-term productive investment. We must confront the problem of how a class of private capitalists is to emerge, or else we must rely at the outset on the presence of foreign capitalists or a class of state capitalists. The analysis of the behavior in the capitalist sector may have to be modified, according to which type of capitalist class exists.

Further, it is assumed that whatever the capitalist sector produces, it can sell; no allowance is made for a problem of aggregate demand. But why should this be true if the output is to be sold within the capitalist sector itself, or if the product is an export good? The remaining alternative—that the capitalist sector sells to the noncapitalist sector—presents a special difficulty. For then productivity must rise in the noncapitalist sector in order to ensure an adequate market for the output of the capitalist sector. But if real wages rise in the noncapitalist sector, the supply-price of labor to the capitalist sector will then be higher, profits will be reduced, and the expansionary process may stop before all the surplus labor is absorbed.

Despite these restrictions on its direct applicability, the Lewis model retains high analytic value for its insights into the role of capital accumulation in the development process. What is clearly of prime significance is the way investment becomes a rising proportion of national income and the economy undergoes a structural transformation that involves the reallocation of labor between sectors and the potential acceleration of growth.

Lewis wanted his model to explain rising savings and profit ratios, and he states that

the chief historical example on which the model was based was that of Great Britain where . . . net saving seems to have risen from about 5 per cent before 1780 to 7 per cent in the early 1800s, to 12 per cent around 1870, at which level it stabilized. A similar rise is shown for the United States [between the 1840s and 1890s]. . . . Similar changes can be found since the second world war for many less-developed countries such as India or Jamaica.[11]

Along with the expansion of the capitalist sector and the rise in investment, the model also indicates that—short of the model's turning points—labor will be continually absorbed from the reservoir of the noncapitalist sector, and that disguised unemployment or underemployment of surplus labor will continually diminish.

---

[10]See E. J. Berg, "Backward-Sloping Supply Functions in Dual Economies—The African Case." *Quarterly Journal of Economics* (August 1961): 468–92.

[11]Lewis, "Reflections on Unlimited Labor," p. 75.

III.B.2. Effects of the Modern Sector on the Traditional*

A number of writers have expressed surprise and disillusionment that the rapid expansion of modern sectors that has occurred in LDCs has not

*From W. Arthur Lewis, "The Dual Economy Revisited," *The Manchester School,* Vol. 37, Basil Blackwell, 1979, pp. 212–17. Reprinted by permission.

"trickled down" to bring equal prosperity to the traditional sectors.

Actually, there is no reason to expect the traditional always to benefit from expansion of the modern. There are forces working for benefit and forces working for loss; the net result will vary from case to case.

Expansion of the modern sector may benefit the traditional in four ways, each of which has its loss counterpart: through provision of employment, through sharing physical facilities, through modernisation of ideas and institutions, and through trade.

The first medium is employment. The modern sector employs persons who move over from the traditional sector. They earn more in the modern sector, have better opportunities for their children, and rise at least a notch in social status.

A good deal of the "benefit" of development takes the form of creating a middle class, widely defined as the occupational categories lying between the landed gentry and the unskilled urban proletariat. If this is a benefit, it should be taken into account when assessing the progress of development.

These are part of the gains to the modern sector from its own expansion. The traditional sector shares in that some of its people move into the modern sector with its opportunities, earn money and send remittances home. The extent of the gain depends a great deal on how much population pressure the traditional sector is feeling. At one extreme the country is underpopulated, and the modern sector is getting labour only by exercising force of some kind;[1] while at the other extreme population is increasing at 3 percent per annum in an already overcrowded countryside. Where population is scarce the expansion of the modern sector is frequently predatory—not only in that labour is taken by force, but also in that the relative shortage of adult males in their prime disrupts the village economy and village life in general. At the other extreme, where population is dense, expansion of the modern sector throws a lifeline to the traditional sector. In this case people will pour out of the traditional sector faster than the modern sector can absorb them, and unemployment will increase no matter how rapidly modern sector employment may increase.

To continue with the effects of expansion of the modern sector, we have summarised the second set as "the sharing of physical facilities." The modern sector builds for itself infrastructure (railways, roads, ports, hospitals, water supplies, electricity, etc.) which is used also by the traditional sector, on payment of marginal cost or

less. The modern sector is also taxed to pay for schools, public health services, etc., and the traditional sector normally (though not inevitably) gets more of these services than it pays for. To tax its developed sectors and subsidise its underdeveloped sectors is one of the most powerful ways that a government can use to ensure that the benefits of development trickle down. Statisticians measuring changes in the distribution of income try to assess these non-cash benefits when dealing with developed countries, but tend to overlook their importance when dealing with LDCs.

The third set of effects of the expansion of the modern sector is the modernisation of ideas and institutions in the traditional sector. New technologies raise output; girls are allowed to attend school; land tenure systems are revised; farmers are introduced to co-operative agricultural institutions and so on. Alas the new ideas are not always appropriate—so we get inappropriate technology; or even if appropriate, ideas need to be introduced more gradually in line with other changes—so we get an outpouring of university graduates into an economy which cannot as yet absorb them. That social change entails inappropriate as well as appropriate changes seems to be inevitable.

The last set of effects of the expansion of the modern sector has to do with trade between the two sectors. There may be no such trade. Theoretically the modern sector could be self-contained, with its own factories, mines, and farms. Or, more likely, it may export part of its product to the outside world in return for needed imports. This latter type of enclave development has been very common; for example, Asian plantation economies exported (say) rubber, and imported rice and cloth for their workers. It is one reason why there was so much scope for import substitution in the third quarter of our century.

If the modern sector depends on the traditional for part of its needs (e.g., food, raw materials), its continued expansion will depend on similar expansion of the commodities in the traditional sector. Otherwise the terms of trade will move against it. However, the effects on the modern sector of rising productivity in the traditional sector move in opposite directions. The product-wage rises in the modern sector as traditional productivity rises, but this is countered by improved terms of trade, and the net effect on the product-wage may be in either direction.

Benefits are not confined to changes in the

[1]Slavery, indentured labour, prohibiting the small farmers from growing profitable cash crops on their own (e.g., coffee in Kenya), levying taxes payable only in cash, where cash can be had only through working for wages, etc.

terms of trade; changes in the volume of trade are also important. Thus in India industrial production rises in years of good harvests and falls in years of bad harvests; because industrial production depends partly on the availability of raw materials and partly on the farmers' income (marketable surplus). The condition for this is a highly elastic supply of industrial goods, due to existence of idle productive capacity, whether in factories or in the handicrafts sector. With a low elasticity of supply for industry a good harvest would ruin the farmers and might (through unemployment) ruin some industrial workers too.

Now in small countries it is unlikely that expansion of the modern sector will be choked off by an adverse movement in the terms of trade since it can buy and sell on the world market at constant terms of trade. Hence this possibility is important only for closed or very large economies. The other side of this coin is that the traditional sector's terms of trade are not improved by the expansion of the modern sector, a proposition of some importance when used to illuminate the world economy as a whole, and the factoral terms of trade between MDCs and LDCs. Insofar as the commodities that LDCs export are a small part of their agricultural output, these commodities are available at constant prices in terms of foodstuffs. (For further analysis see my Wicksell Lectures, 1969, *Aspects of Tropical Trade 1883–1965*. Also my *The Evolution of the International Economic Order*, 1978.)

The traditional sector may also be damaged by buying imports from the modern sector (or from abroad). Textbooks on international trade theory are concerned with all the assumptions one has to make for it to be true that such trade must benefit both parties. Since this set of assumptions does not always hold in LDCs, especially in their traditional sectors, an influx of imports may damage the economy even if paid for by exports.

Most of the literature of international trade theory assumes that the distribution of productive resources remains unchanged as between countries, and only goods flow; whereas the development process is much affected by the migration of capital, entrepreneurship, skills, unskilled labour, and technology, over a long period of time—and this yields very different results. The dynamic aspect of the effect of modern upon traditional sectors is most easily understood in the light of growth pole theory. Essentially, when an industrial centre begins to

grow there are economies of scale and economies of propinquity which make it attractive to more and more newcomers. It grows by underselling and destroying its rivals. It therefore attracts unto itself the skills, capital, and entrepreneurship of other areas, which tend to wind down correspondingly.

This polarisation of growth is a commonplace of economic history. It is now working powerfully in LDCs, where a small number of towns is growing at 5 to 10 percent per annum, at the expense of the rest of the economy. . . .

We must not overplay the likelihood that the expansion of the modern sector will damage the traditional sector within the same country. It may do so, but we have also seen half a dozen reasons why benefits may exceed losses. Each case must be looked at separately.

The moral for policy makers is of course not to rely on "trickle down" to benefit the traditional sector, but to attack the problems of that sector directly. The great majority of economists writing on this subject since 1940 have advocated strong measures to raise agricultural output, including land reform, agricultural extension, irrigation, cheap credit, etc.; and have indeed (rightly or wrongly) bolstered their case by arguing that this would also stimulate industrialisation by providing a wider market. Nowadays a bogus history of economic thought floats around in which the economists of the fifties were rooting for industry to the neglect of agriculture, but this was not so. The economics of the 1950s was obsessed by balanced growth, arguing that development of industry alone would be constrained by the farmers' poverty, and that development of agriculture alone would turn the terms of trade against agriculture and bankrupt the farmers. As it happened most governments neglected agriculture for reasons of their own, but this was in spite of and not in accordance with economists' advice.

Nowadays the real difficulty in the way of agricultural transformation is not ideological but technological. We know how to raise agricultural output in tropical areas with adequate rainfall or access to irrigation water, but arid lands have low yields, and in the absence of water do not respond to fertilisers or to the potential of high yielding varieties. Somewhere between 500,000,000 and 600,000,000 live in these arid lands, on the fringes of the great Asian and African deserts. This is where the real poverty is in LDCs, and the numbers are increasing rapidly. When people say "there has been such rapid growth of output, coupled with such rapid growth of poverty" they are putting together two half sentences which have little to do with each other. Rapid growth has contributed to the rise of unemployment in the towns but this is a fraction of the poverty into which the people of the arid lands are locked. To unlock this prison is the greatest challenge to development.

Comment: Dual-Economy Models

For instructive summaries of Lewis's dual-sector model, see Ronald Findlay, "On W. Arthur Lewis' Contribution to Economics," *Scandinavian Journal of Economics* 82 (1980), and Gustav Ranis and John C. H. Fei, "Lewis and the Classicists," in *The Theory and Experience of Economic Development,* ed. Mark Gersovitz (1983).

Lewis responded to criticisms of his first article, "Economic Development with Unlimited Supplies of Labour," in subsequent papers: "Unlimited Labour: Further Notes," *The Manchester School* (January 1958), "Employment Policy in an Underdeveloped Area," *Social and Economic Studies* (September 1958), "Unemployment in Developing Countries," *World Today* (1967), "Reflections on Unlimited Labor," in *International Economics and Development, Essays in Honor of Raúl Prebisch,* ed. Luis Eugenio Di Marco (1970), "Development and Distribution," in *Employment, Income Distribution and Development Strategy,* ed. A. Cairncross and M. Puri (1976), and "The Dual Economy Revisited," *The Manchester School* (September 1979).

Other models of a dual economy have been offered by John C. H. Fei and Gustav Ranis: "A Theory of Economic Development," *American Economic Review* (September 1961), *Development of the Labor Surplus Economy: Theory and Policy* (1964), and "A Model of Growth and Employment in the Open Dualistic Economy: The Cases of Korea and Taiwan," *Journal of Development Studies* (January 1975).

In their two-sector model, Ranis and Fei considered disguised unemployment to exist in the agricultural sector when the marginal physical product of labor is less than its average product, which is the institutional wage under the extended-family system in agriculture. When labor has a marginal product of zero, it is termed "redundant labor." In the Ranis–Fei model, the horizontal supply curve to the capitalist sector is then considered to end when the redundant labor force in the agricultural sector is taken up and a relative shortage of agricultural goods appears, so that the terms of trade turn against the capitalist sector, which is trading with the agricultural sector. This upward trend in the labor supply curve is later accentuated by a rise in the agricultural real wage traceable to the removal of disguised unemployment and the commercialization of agriculture, so that real wages become determined by competitive market forces, not by the nonmarket institutional average product.[1] When the marginal product is equal in the capitalist and noncapitalist sectors, the analysis then becomes the same as in the usual neoclassical one-sector economy.

Lewis's 1954 article presents two models: Model A, which is dynamic but for a closed economy, and Model B, which is for an open economy but is static. To emphasize alternative trade strategies, such as export of manufactures or import substitution in food, we should examine dynamic models of open dual economies. See, for instance, P. K. Bardhan, *Economic Growth, Development and Foreign Trade* (1970), and Ronald Findlay, *International Trade and Development Theory* (1973), pt. 2. We consider in detail the open economy in Chapters V and IX.

---

[1]For an excellent survey of dualism, see Gustav Ranis, "Analytics of Development: Dualism," in *Handbook of Development Economics,* ed. Hollis Chenery and T. N. Srinivasan (1988), vol. 1, 4.

Among many applications of dual economy models, see Gustav Ranis, "The Dual Economy Framework: Its Relevance to Asian Development," *Asian Development Review* (1984), and Louis Putterman, "Dualism and Reform in China," *Economic Development and Cultural Change* (1992).

III.B.3. Versions of Dualism—Note

While Lewis's two-sector model of a dual economy retains a central position in development literature, other versions of dualism have been presented. An early version was that of "social dualism." J. H. Boeke and other Dutch economists, in their studies of Indonesian development during the colonial and early postcolonial periods, emphasized

the clashing of an imported social system with an indigenous social system of another style. . . . In a dual society one of the two prevailing social systems, as a matter of fact, always the most advanced, will have been imported from abroad and have gained its existence in the new environment without being able to oust or to assimilate the divergent social system that has grown up there, with the result that neither of them becomes general and characteristic for that society as a whole. Without doubt the most frequent form of social dualism is to be found where an imported western capitalism has penetrated into a precapitalistic agrarian community and where the original social system—be it not undamaged—has been able to hold its own, or expressed in opposite terms, has not been able to adopt the capitalistic principles and put them into full practice.[1]

Arguing against Boeke's interpretation of social dualism, Benjamin Higgins states that "dualism is for Boeke virtually synonymous with 'Eastern.'" Dualism arises from a clash between "East" and "West," and the Eastern, or precapitalist, sector is alleged by Boeke to have characteristics that contradict Western neoclassical economics—backward-sloping supply curves of effort and risk taking, limited wants, absence of profit seeking, aversion to capital, lack of elasticity of supply, and absence of organization and of discipline. Because of these differences between Eastern and Western economies, Western economic theory is claimed to be inapplicable to less developed areas.

Higgins offers a powerful dissent to this argument.[2] And the resurgence of neoclassical economics in the practice of development policy over the past few decades presents a convincing rebuttal to the assertions of social dualism.[3] Studies of the microeconomics of the traditional sector provide abundant evidence of the utility and profit-maximization behavior of the "household-firms" in the traditional sector.[4] Households do allocate their labor, land, and capital in order to equate the marginal contribution of these resources to the household utility from the alternative uses of subsistence production and cash-earning activities. In response to a higher price or wage, households also increase their supply of cash crops or wage labor. When carefully analyzed, the behavior of peasant households appears as a rational response to their environment.

Several writers have suggested that the labor employment problems of a poor country are due to the existence of "technological dualism"—that is, the use of different production functions in the advanced sector and the traditional sector.[5] In this interpretation, dualism is associated with "structural unemployment" or "technological unemployment"—a situation in which productive employment opportunities are limited, not because of lack of effective demand, but because of resource and technological restraints in the two sectors.

The traditional rural sector is said to have the following characteristics: it is engaged in peasant agriculture and handicrafts or very small industries; the products can be produced with a wide range of techniques and alternative combinations of labor and capital (improved land)—that is, the sector has variable technical coefficients of production; and the factor endowment is such that labor is the relatively abundant fac-

[1] J. H. Boeke, *Economics and Economic Policy in Dual Societies* (1953), pp. 3–5.

[2] Benjamin Higgins, "The 'Dualistic Theory' of Underdeveloped Areas," *Economic Development and Cultural Change* (January 1956): 99–115, and "Jan Boeke and the Doctrine of 'The Little Push,'" *Bulletin of Indonesian Economic Studies* (December 1984): 55–69.

[3] I. M. D. Little, *Economic Development* (1982), pt. III; Albert O. Hirschman, "Decline of Development Economics," in *Essays in Trespassing* (1981).

[4] See selection III.B.4.

[5] As an alternative to Boeke's sociological theory of dualism, the theory of technological dualism has been emphasized by Benjamin Higgins, *Economic Development*, rev. ed. (1968), pp. 17–20, 296–305. The theory of technological dualism incorporates the "factor proportions problem," as discussed by R. S. Eckaus, "The Factor Proportions Problem in Underdeveloped Areas," *American Economic Review* (September 1955). Earlier references include Joan Robinson, *The Rate of Interest and Other Essays* (1952), pp. 110–11, and M. Fukuoka, "Full Employment and Constant Coefficients of Production," *Quarterly Journal of Economics* (February 1955).

tor, so that techniques of production are labor intensive (in the sense that relatively large amounts of labor and relatively small amounts of capital are used).

In contrast, the modern sector is composed of plantations, mines, oil fields, or large-scale industry; there is either in fact, or entrepreneurs believe there is, only a very limited degree of technical substitutability of factors, so that production is characterized by fixed technical coefficients; and the production processes in this sector are relatively capital intensive. This situation can be represented by a production function, as in Figure 1, where the points a, b, c, and so on denote the fixed combinations of factors—capital (K) and labor (L)—that would be used to produce the outputs q_1, q_2, q_3, and so on, irrespective of what the relative factor prices might be.[6] The line OE, joining the points a, b, c, and so on represents the expansion path of this sector, and its slope is equal to a constant, relatively capital-intensive factor ratio.

Only when capital and labor are actually available in proportions equal to the fixed capital–labor ratio is it possible that both factors can be fully utilized simultaneously. If the actual factor endowment is to the right of line OE—say, at point F—there must then be some unemployment of labor in this sector. To produce an output of q_1 the sector will use OK_1 units of capital and OL_1 units of labor; even though OL_2 units of labor are available, the excess supply of labor will have no effect on production techniques, and L_1L_2 units of labor will remain in excess supply, regardless of the relative factor prices of capital and labor. Only if the capital stock were to increase in the amount indicated by the length of the dashed line FF could the redundant labor be absorbed in this sector. Failing a sufficient accumulation of capital, the excess labor supply will simply remain unemployed, or must seek employment in the traditional sector.

[6]Units of capital (K) are measured on the vertical axis, and units of labor (L) on the horizontal axis. The curve q_1 is an isoquant representing a certain level of output; as drawn, the output q_1 can be produced only with the unique combination of factors at point a (OK_1 of capital and OL_1 of labor). The curves q_2, q_3, and so on represent different levels of output, with output increasing along the expansion line OE. Output can be increased, however, only by increasing the use of K and L in the constant proportions given by the slope of OE.

FIGURE 1.

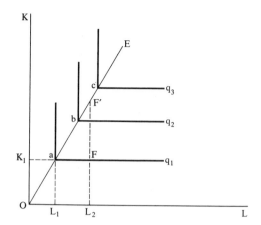

It is interesting to note that Marx had a similar view of the problem of unemployment. According to Marx, the amount of employment offered by capitalists depends on the amount of capital in existence, and there is unemployment because there is insufficient capital to employ all the potential available labor. If A represents the total labor available, and N the amount of employment required to work the existing stock of capital at its normal capacity, then $(A - N)$ is Marx's "reserve army of unemployed labor."[7]

Having in mind the different production functions in the two sectors, we may now summarize the argument that technological dualism has intensified the problem of employment in dual economies. In many countries, the advanced sector was initially developed by an inflow of foreign capital. As foreign enterprises operated under efficient management with modern production techniques, output in this sector expanded. At the same time, however, population was growing—in some cases, at a rate considerably in excess of the rate at which capital was accumulating in the advanced sector. And since production processes in this sector were capital intensive, and fixed technical coefficients were used, this sector did not have the capacity to create employment opportunities at a rate sufficient to absorb the greater labor force. While investment and output expanded in the advanced sector, capital accumulation was slow relative to population growth, and labor became a redun-

[7]Robinson, *Rate of Interest*, pp. 110–11, n. 2.

dant factor in this sector. Entry into the traditional rural sector was then the only alternative open to surplus labor.

As the labor supply increased in the traditional sector, it may have been possible initially to bring more land under cultivation, but eventually land became relatively scarce. Labor increasingly became the relatively abundant factor, and since technical coefficients were variable in this sector, the production process became ever more labor intensive in the traditional sector. Finally, all available land became cultivated by highly labor-intensive techniques, and the marginal productivity of labor fell to a low level. Thus with continuing population growth, the limited availability of capital caused a surplus of labor to arise in the traditional rural sector. Given the labor surplus, there was no incentive in the traditional sector to move along the production function toward higher capital–labor ratios and thereby achieve an increase in output per worker.

Further, it is contended that over the longer run, technological progress did not ease this situation. For in the modern sector, technological progress favored more capital-intensive techniques, so that it was all the more difficult to increase employment opportunities in this sector as investment and output expanded. At the same time, there was no incentive in the rural sector to introduce labor-saving innovations (even if it were assumed that the technical possibilities were known and the necessary capital was available).

Although the theory of technological dualism indicates why factor endowments and the differences in production functions have resulted historically in the rise of underemployment of labor in the traditional sector, its empirical relevance can certainly be questioned. Has production in the advanced sector actually been carried on with fixed coefficients? Even if an advanced, capital-intensive process was initially imported, was there subsequently no adaptation to the abundant labor supply? Was technical progress actually labor saving in the advanced sector? And does technological dualism now help to explain the greater degree of unemployment and underemployment in countries with lagging growth rates? These questions call for empirical studies beyond the highly impressionistic statements contained in this summary of the theory of technological dualism.

Fragmented or compartmentalized factor markets may also have the characteristic of dualism—"wage dualism" in the labor market and "financial dualism" in the capital market. "Financial dualism" means that capital funds are provided to larger size firms in the modern sector on easier terms than they are offered to small economic units in the traditional sector. Firms in the modern sector have access to financial institutions and can borrow at relatively low interest rates from the "organized" capital market. In contrast, institutional sources of credit are not developed for peasant farmers or handicraft workers in the traditional sector, and they must borrow at high interest rates from the "unorganized" capital market. The gap in interest rates tends to be larger the more underdeveloped are the domestic credit market and the financial institutions in a country.[8] Financial dualism may cause an allocation of excessive capital to the modern sector relative to the traditional sector.

In contrast, "wage dualism"—that is, the existence of a higher level of wages in the modern sector than in the traditional sector—may discourage the expansion of the modern sector and distort the allocation of resources in the opposite direction from that caused by financial dualism. There may be genuine economic differences in the two sectors that can explain wage differentials, such as differences in skills and in costs of living, higher wages in the modern sector to induce the head of a family to move with dependents to a permanent home near the new place of work, or willingness of large-scale firms in the modern sector to pay higher wages to obtain a regular labor force. But beyond these genuine differences, there may be certain factors that arbitrarily widen the wage differential between the modern and the traditional sectors and distort the allocation of labor between the two. An artificial widening can result from various government regulations on labor and minimum-wage rates or from the action of trade unions in the modern sector.

Finally, and in a more illuminating fashion, the various versions of dualism—technological, financial, wage—can be incorporated into a more comprehensive framework of "organizational dualism," as is done by Hla Myint in the next selection.

[8]For a fuller elaboration of "financial dualism," see Hla Myint, *Economic Theory and the Underdeveloped Countries* (1971), pp. 324–31.

III.B.4. Organizational Dualism*

What is the common factor behind the different versions of dualism and how far can we incorporate these different types of dualism into a general conceptual framework embracing the underdeveloped economy as a whole? We may further ask: What are the precise policy implications, if any, of the phenomenon of dualism?

Dualism is characterized by the wide price differentials for apparently the same product or factor of production in the traditional and the modern sectors. Most writers on dualism tend to identify these price differentials as signs of "market imperfections" and "distortions" in the allocation of resources between the two sectors. For them, therefore, the main policy implication of dualism is to correct these market imperfections and distortions. But this amounts to forcing the rich and suggestive concept of dualism into the straitjacket of the conventional neoclassical two-sector model. In order to study the distortions, the neoclassical two-sector model adopts as its frame of reference the "perfect competition model" which implicitly assumes that the organizational framework of the economy is already fully developed. I believe that dualism is pre-eminently a phenomenon of an underdeveloped organizational framework, characterized by an incomplete development, not only of the market network but also of the administrative and fiscal system of the government. I regard this underdevelopment of the market and non-market organization as a different type of phenomenon from the "imperfections" of an already fully developed market system and, therefore, I have always been uneasy about identifying the dual economy with the neoclassical two-sector model. Where dualism is an important factor behind an observed price differential, the habit of identifying it automatically with "price distortions" frequently leads to misguided policies to "correct" these alleged distortions which may not only introduce policy-induced distortions but also may aggravate dualism by repressing the normal development of appropriate economic institutions.

*From Hla Myint, "Organizational Dualism and Economic Development," *Asian Development Review,* Vol. 3, No. 1 (1985), pp. 25–42. Reprinted by permission.

Organizational Dualism: A Stylized Picture

We may adapt the "circular flow"-type diagram depicting the transactions between the different sectors of an economy for our purpose of illustrating the degree of tightness or looseness of the organizational framework of that economy. The usual circular flow diagram is concerned with the level of economic activity and the proportions in which it flows between the different sectors, on the assumption that the connecting pipelines are free flowing. For our purpose, we are interested not so much in the level of economic activity as in the functioning of the connecting pipelines themselves: on the question which of them are free flowing and which of them are clogged up, creating the weak links between the sectors concerned and segmenting the economy.

For convenient exposition, we may begin with a stylized picture of a fully organized economy where the pipelines connecting all the sectors are free flowing.

First, we have the sector consisting of business firms, which buys labor services from the wage-household sector, which in return buys consumer goods from the business firms. The wage households may be regarded as completely specialized consuming units and the business firms as completely specialized producing units. We then introduce a third sector, the financial institutions, which collects the savings from the households and business firms and in return provides them with loans. Our stylized picture is completed by bringing in the government sector, which collects taxes from the households and the business firms and in return provides them with appropriate public services. The government's fiscal and administrative machinery is assumed to be fully developed and is able to finance public expenditure both by borrowing from the financial institutions and by taxation. Its decisions concerning taxation and expenditure are assumed to be determined by its policy choices alone, and are not limited by administrative constraints. In Figure 1, which provides a stylized picture of a fully organized economy, all the sectors are connected by solid lines to indicate that the marketing and transaction costs, the administrative costs and the information costs have been kept as low as existing technology permits

FIGURE 1. A fully organized economy: stylized anatomy of a developed country.

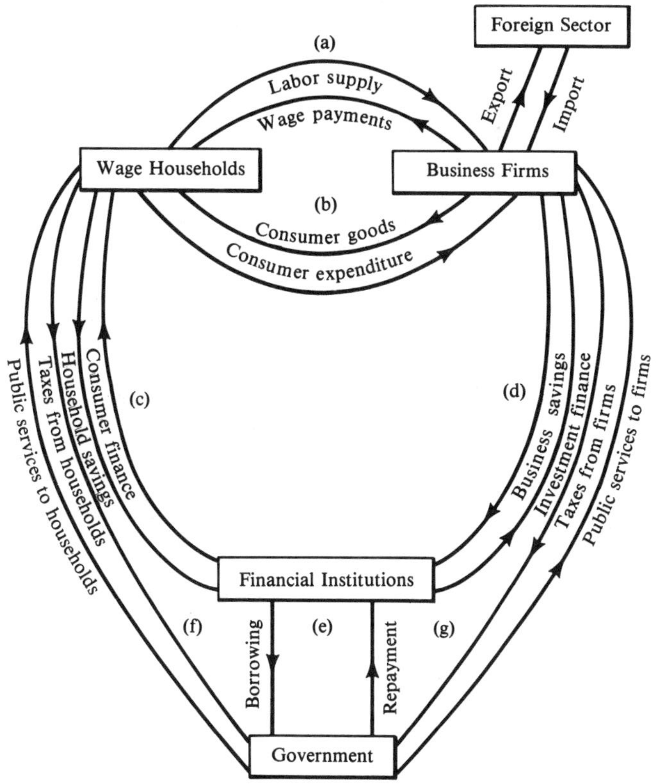

by the full development of the organizational framework.

Our stylized picture of a fully organized economy may be regarded as a crude attempt to represent the organizational framework which characterizes an advanced industrial economy. Accepting this as an approximate representation, it is necessary to point out that a fully organized economy in this sense is not the same as the "perfect competition" model in the usual sense. Both models work with a minimum of "frictions" in terms of transaction and information costs. But while the "perfect competition" model excludes the monopolistic distortions, the fully organized economy attempts to depict the economic organization of an advanced industrial country which may be subject to various distortions introduced by big business corporations, labor unions, and government policies. The real point is that these distortions are introduced in a well-organized manner and without observable price discrepancies. Thus, a monopolist firm may charge a uniform price for its product in all

parts of the country, only that this price happens to be above the marginal cost of the product. Similarly, a labor union may insist on "wage parity" for all its members, even if some of its members are less productive than others.

We can now go on to construct our stylized picture of an underdeveloped economy with organizational dualism (Figure 2).

The modern sector may be regarded as a miniature replica of the fully organized economy which we have just described. We may, therefore, represent it by a box containing the constituent sectors, namely, the wage households, the business firms, the financial institutions, and the government, omitting the solid lines connecting the sectors. The modern sector is loosely connected by the broken lines with another box representing the "traditional sector." This consists of a large number of peasant farmers and other small-scale units. We may describe these small scattered economic units as "household firms" since they partake of the character of both wage households and business firms. The

FIGURE 2. Organizational dualism: anatomy of an underdeveloped country.

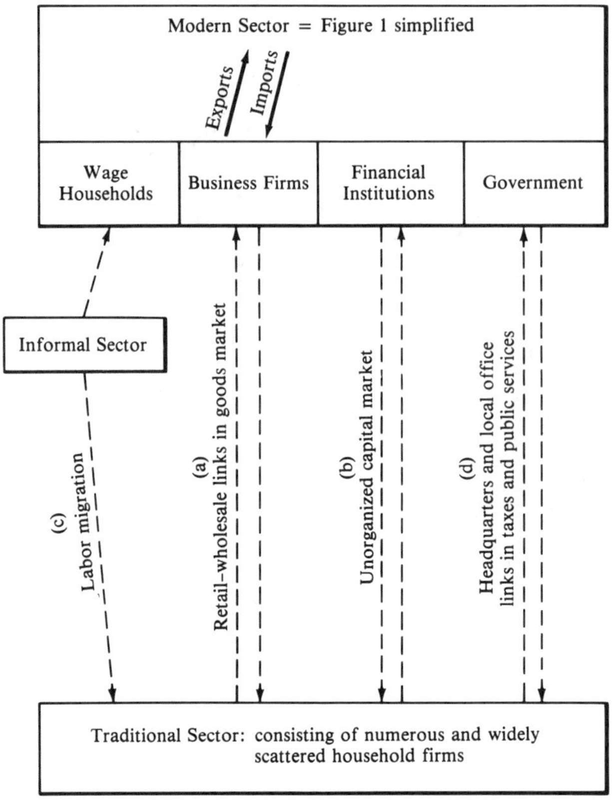

household firms maximize their utility like the ordinary wage households; but while the budget constraint of ordinary households is their wage income, the budget constraint of household firms is the amount of land, labor, and other productive resources possessed by each family. These resources are then deployed to maximize household utility, directly through subsistence production and indirectly through cash earning activities which provide the income to buy consumption goods. The household firms also maximize their "profits" like the ordinary business firms in that they allocate their resources to equate the marginal returns in the alternative uses given by subsistence production, cash crop production, and off-farm wage labor. But unlike business firms which sell the whole of their output, household firms retain a part of their output for their own consumption.

From this analysis of the behavior of household firms in the traditional sector, you will gather that I regard their incomplete entry into the exchange economy, not as a sign of "irra-

tionality" but merely as the result of applying the ordinary maximizing behavior to their local economic circumstances. These include the local prices at which they can buy and sell, the local opportunities for off-farm work, and the risks of price changes in cash crops. The local economic circumstances of a given household firm will depend on the transport costs, transaction costs, information costs, and insurance costs it has to face; that is, on the effectiveness of the organizational links which connect it with the modern sector and the outside world.

Before we go on to the loose organizational links connecting the modern and the traditional sectors, a word of caution would be in order. We should not equate the modern sector entirely with the manufacturing industry in the urban areas and the traditional sector with peasant agriculture. Some of the business firms in the modern sector may be plantation and mining enterprises located in the countryside. Conversely, some of the small economic units, which organizationally belong to the traditional sector, may be located in towns and be concerned with handicraft industries and other non-agricultural activities. These non-agricultural, small economic units are shown separately as the "informal sector" in Figure 2.

The Anatomy of the Dual Economy

Figure 2 depicts the loose organizational links shown by the broken lines connecting the modern and the traditional sectors. They illustrate the four types of dualism: (a) in the goods market; (b) in the capital market; (c) in the labor market; and (d) in the administrative and fiscal machinery of the government.

The Goods Market

In any underdeveloped country, the markets for final products are likely to be more developed than the markets for the factors of production, and the least developed part of the market system is the market for capital in the traditional sector. Even so, the organization of the goods market is incompletely developed and this may be gauged by three types of price differentials: (i) the differential between the retail buying and selling prices for the peasant farmers at village level and the wholesale prices of these commodities in the cities; (ii) the regional differences in the price of the same commodity; and (iii) the seasonal price variations of the agricultural products which form a large part of the total national output.

The broken lines (a) connecting the modern and traditional sectors in Figure 2 depict the incomplete development of the wholesale-retail chain in the market for goods. Even in a well-organized economy, the farm-gate price at which the peasant farmers can sell their produce will be less than the wholesale price (or f.o.b. price in the case of exports). The differential will be made up of various items of "marketing costs," such as the cost of collecting the produce in small quantities from a large number of geographically scattered farmers, sorting and "bulking up" the produce, and transporting it to the marketing centers or exporting points. Similarly, in the reverse direction, we would expect the retail village-level prices at which the peasant farmers can buy to be higher than the wholesale (or the c.i.f.) prices of these commodities by the marketing costs. In an underdeveloped economy with higher transport and market-ing costs, the retail-wholesale price differential will be wider than in a developed economy with a more effective market organization.

Further, with any given degree of under-development of the market system, the whole-sale-retail price differential will be greater for the peasant households located in the remoter districts and the peripheral parts of the market system than for those which are situated nearer to the marketing centers. Thus, the prevalence of subsistence production in the traditional sector in many underdeveloped countries may be explained in terms of these two types of differential marketing and transport costs rather than in terms of "economic irrationality" and "sociological dualism."

The Capital Market

Let us now go on to "financial dualism" which is manifested in the wide gap in the levels of interest rates in the organized and the unorganized capital markets. This differential in the interest rates may be partly accounted for in terms of the differences in transaction and information costs of lending at the wholesale and retail levels, analogously to our analysis of the goods market. But now we shall have to add the insurance premium for differential risks. The administrative costs to a bank of processing large loans to a small number of large business firms with established creditworthiness is clearly much less than the administrative costs of lending the same sum total of money in small amounts to a large number of small borrowers. Moreover, the information costs of assessing the creditworthiness of the small borrowers would be prohibitive. Thus, it is not surprising that the modern-type banks with heavy overhead costs in opening branches have not penetrated very far into the unorganized capital market of the traditional sector. The interest differentials between the organized and the unorganized markets might have been reduced if the money-lenders, with their lower overheads and a more intimate knowledge of local conditions, had been permitted to become full-fledged middle-men, borrowing wholesale from banks and lending retail to small borrowers. But this has rarely happened since the moneylenders have limited access (or are debarred by regulations from having access) to the modern banking system. Being obliged to rely largely on their own financial resources, the interest rates charged by the moneylenders are not only higher than those in the organized market but also tend to show wide dispersions around a high average rate, reflecting local circumstances. Thus, the unorganized capital market tends to be highly fragmented.

The high transaction and information costs restricting the flow of funds from financial institutions to the traditional sector are depicted by the broken lines (b) in Figure 2. The broken line in the reverse direction is added to show that the transactions and information costs are equally high in the collection of small savings from the traditional sector and that the small savers are likely to receive lower rates of interests on their savings after deducting these costs. This is why they tend to hoard gold and jewelry rather than lend their savings to organized financial institutions.

The Labor Market

Let us now turn to dualism in the labor market, shown by the contrast between the high wages in the modern sector and the low level of earnings in the traditional sector. At first sight, it looks as though my approach to dualism, in terms of weak organizational links and differential transaction, transport, and information costs, has broken down completely when applied to the labor market. One cannot seriously maintain that the higher wages in the modern sector are due to the cost of migration from the countryside to the towns. On the contrary, despite all these costs, including the cost of waiting to get a job, migrant labor has flooded into towns, lured by the prospect of high wages. It has gone either to the "informal sector" as a staging post or directly to the modern sector, adding to the open unemployment there. It seems that in the labor market, at least, distortions in the usual sense are more important than dualism in my sense as the explanation of the wage differentials. These distortions include not only the distortions within the labor market, such as the minimum wage laws and collective bargaining, but also the distortions introduced by high protection and subsidies given to the modern manufacturing sector which enable it to pay high wages out of artificially inflated profits.

But the wage differential in the labor market serves to bring to the surface one genuine element of dualism in my sense, which I have so far treated implicitly. Dualism is characterized by the price differential for the "same" com- modity or factor of production in the two sectors. But what do we mean by the word "same"? If we interpret it strictly to mean a homogeneous product or factor, then in a "frictionless" economy, all price differentials for the same article will be price distortions. So far my argument has been that, even if we could assume the products and the factors of production in the modern and the traditional sectors to be homogeneous in a strict sense, the price differentials in the two sectors may not be genuine price distortions because of the various costs required to overcome the "frictions" in an underdeveloped economic framework. Dualism in the labor market brings out another important source of the price differential, namely, the quality of the product or factor of production is not homogeneous in a strict sense. The unskilled labor in the modern sector is not the same as the raw labor from peasant agriculture. Thus, even if we would remove all the artificial distortions in the labor market, wages in the modern sector will tend to be higher than in the traditional sector. The differences in the costs of living in the towns and countryside may be important, but labor will be employed at a higher wage rate in the modern sector only if its productivity is higher than the wage necessary to cover the higher cost of living.

The qualitative differences in labor in the modern and the traditional sectors contribute to the wage differentials between these sectors in two ways. First, there are information costs of selecting and recruiting the right type of person with the appropriate physical and mental qualities for employment on a regular basis in the modern sector. Second, having found the right type of person, it would be necessary to retain him by paying an appropriate quality premium according to his ability and experience. In an underdeveloped economy with a patchy information network and inadequate facilities for training and education to transform the raw labor from the traditional sector into suitable material for a regular wage economy, large elements of labor market dualism would remain even if we could eliminate all the artificial wage distortions. Thus, it is in the interest of business firms in the modern sector to pay higher wages for the "same" type of labor to retain a stable force of experienced workers than it would be for business firms in the advanced countries which can draw upon a larger pool of experienced workers. As we shall see, these qualitative differences are also important elements in understanding dualism in other markets, and we cannot fully understand some types of dualism without bringing in the qualitative differences in the *same* commodity produced by large and small-scale economic units.

The Administrative and Fiscal Machinery of the Government

Finally, we come to dualism in the administrative and fiscal machinery of the government. We have seen that in the private sector business firms and banks located in the modern sector have to operate through a series of middlemen making up the retail-wholesale links to reach the myriad small economic units widely scattered in the traditional sector. Similarly, the headquarters of the government, located in the modern sector, has to operate through a series of its own "middlemen" making up the "retail-wholesale links" in the administration via the district and township offices to get at the small economic units at the village level. Just as we have illustrated the incomplete development of the retail-wholesale links in the goods market and capital market by the broken lines (a) and (b) in Figure 2, we may also illustrate the dualism in the administrative and fiscal apparatus of the government by the broken lines (d) in Figure 2. In an underdeveloped country, the effectiveness of general administration tends to decrease as we move away from the headquarters to the remoter peripheral areas. This is paralleled by the dualism in the fiscal apparatus. Normally, the government finds it difficult to tax the small economic units in the traditional sector, except by imposing customs duties on imports and taxes on exports of peasant products. In the reverse direction, the government would have to incur a large differential in administrative costs to provide the traditional sector with the same level of public services as the modern sector for familiar reasons, such as the scattered nature of the recipients of services and poor transport and communications, and the difficulties of attracting teachers and doctors to the rural areas. Thus, even if the government were to spend the same amount per head in providing public services to the rural and the urban population (which, of course, it never does in practice), the quality of these services would be distinctly poorer in the traditional sector compared with the modern sector. Therefore, dualism in the government's administrative and fiscal machinery must be recognized as an essential element in the total picture of dualism, imposing an organizational constraint on the capacity to implement policy. . . .

Dualism and Distortions

The "Lewis model" (though perhaps not Lewis himself) tends to encourage the habit of treating the traditional sector as a "black box" which exists merely to provide "unlimited supplies of labor" to the modern sector. Our model of organizational dualism serves to show that the amount of "surplus labor" available from the traditional sector is determined not only by the land-man ratio and agricultural technology but will also depend significantly on the development of the organizational framework in the traditional sector. The labor-market dualism, which the exponents of the "Lewis model" regard as the essence of the dual economy model, is after all only one element in the total picture of organizational dualism. The members of a peasant household in deciding whether to migrate to the town will weigh this possibility against the alternative economic opportunities in the traditional sector, viz., that of using available labor in cash crop production, subsistence production, and off-farm work in the locality. This means that although dualism represents an underdeveloped organizational framework, there is some interaction among the different types of dualism in the markets for goods, capital, and labor. . . .

By now it should be obvious, in general terms, why the neoclassical two-sector model is so ill-adapted to cope with dualism which is pre-eminently a phenomenon of an underdeveloped organizational framework characterized by an incomplete development not only of the market system but also of the administrative and fiscal system of the government. However, let me add some specific points of contrast to illustrate the difference between the two concepts.

First, with the given resources and technology, the neoclassical two-sector model will be on its production possibility frontier in the absence of distortions, because it is implicitly assumed that there are no organizational or institutional constraints on production. Now even if we could equate the X sector with the "traditional sector" and the Y sector with the "modern sector," an underdeveloped economy would not be on its production possibility curve after the distortions are removed. Rather, it would be on a lower curve which we may call the production feasibility curve because of additional constraints imposed by the underdeveloped organizational framework. Further, the "frictions" in the form of transport, transaction, and information costs are not uniformly distributed in an underdeveloped economy; they occur in a well-defined pattern, showing a higher degree of concentration along the weaker links connecting the modern and the traditional sectors and also within the traditional sector itself. Thus, if we permit ourselves to draw a production feasibility curve for a dual economy, with the X coordinate measuring the output of the traditional sector and the Y coordinate measuring the output of the modern sector, the gap between this curve FF and the conventional production possibility curve PP will become wider as we move in the direction of increasing the output of the traditional sector X (Figure 3).

The neoclassical production possibility curve PP is drawn on the assumption that the existing technology is "costlessly" embodied in the production functions for the two commodities. But the traditional sector producing X will suffer from a wider "technology gap" because of the greater costs of transmitting and diffusing the existing technological knowledge to a large number of small producers scattered within this sector. This is the formal reason why the gap between the production possibility curve PP and the production feasibility curve FF will become wider as we move along FF in the direction of increasing the output of X in the traditional sector.

FIGURE 3. Production possibility and feasibility curves.

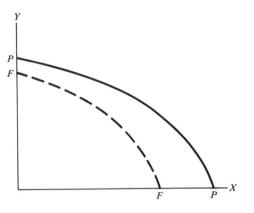

X = Traditional sector
Y = Modern sector
PP = Production possibility curve
FF = Production feasibility curve

Second, the neoclassical model also assumes that the production functions for both sectors are equally well developed. It is only on this basis that we can deduce a distortion in the factor markets when the two sectors face a different set of factor prices so that, geometrically speaking, the two production functions are not tangential to each other. But the traditional sector in a dual economy does not have a coherent production function in the ordinary sense. As we have seen, the household firms in the traditional sector maximize their utility or income by allocating the resources they each possess relatively to the prices of factors and products they each face in their own localities. These local prices will vary from place to place. Thus, it is not only that interest rates are higher and wages are lower on the average in the traditional sector compared with those in the modern sector, but there is also a wider range of dispersion around the average levels in the traditional sector. This indicates that the traditional sector tends to be broken up into a large number of narrow and segmented local markets. Thus, strictly speaking, there is no such thing as *the* production function for the traditional sector in the same sense as there is the production function for a given commodity X. This means that we cannot really draw a production possibility curve for a dual economy model. This is why a diagram such as Figure 3 should be treated with caution.

Finally, the neoclassical model is concerned with two entirely different commodities. Therefore, one would expect that they would be produced by two different technologies and that even with a uniform set of factor prices, they would be produced with different factor proportions. On the other hand, the notion of "technological dualism" focuses attention on the different scale of production and factor proportions adopted in the modern and traditional sectors and regards this as a problem requiring attention. Here, the problem arises, not because the two sectors are producing two entirely different commodities but because they are producing the same or a similar commodity. This type of dualism can be seen in "bimodal" agriculture where large-scale farming and peasant farming coexist, producing the same crop, and in some primary export products, such as rubber, where plantations and smallholders produce the same export product. To some extent, it also occurs in the manufacturing industry for a wide range of consumer goods, with large factories producing more expensive and better quality products and small handicraft industries producing cheaper and lower quality products.

The problem raised by technological dualism has not been clearly defined by its exponents but may be interpreted in two ways. First, we may regard it as consisting in the technological backwardness of small-scale producers because of the greater costs of transmitting and diffusing the available technological knowledge among a large number of widely scattered small producers. This can be subsumed under the general heading of the underdeveloped organizational framework. But the problem here is not merely a matter of improving the information network to transmit better technology; it must also include a wider range of improvements in marketing and credit facilities to provide the small producers with the necessary economic incentives to adopt the better technology. Second, we

may interpret the problem of technological dualism as consisting in the adoption of excessively capital-intensive and large-scale methods of production induced by government policies of providing subsidized capital and foreign exchange to encourage sophisticated modern industry. In this case, the problem arises from policy-induced distortions in the capital market which should be corrected. Thus, the concept of technological dualism does not introduce any new analytical issues into my analysis. But it has the useful purpose of reminding us that dualism means not only the coexistence of a modern and a traditional sector within the same economic system but also frequently within the same industry. This provides us with the final reason why dualism cannot be forced into the neoclassical two-sector model.

III.C. MIGRATION AND URBANIZATION

III.C.1. A Model of Rural–Urban Migration*

I would like to set forth briefly a theoretical framework which yields some important insights into the causes and mechanisms of rural-urban migration in tropical Africa. I believe that the model can usefully serve two purposes: first, to demonstrate why the continued existence of rural-urban migration in the face of rising levels of urban unemployment often represents a rational economic decision from the point of view of the private individual; and second, to demonstrate how such a theoretical framework can be used in an analysis and evaluation of alternative public policies to alleviate the growing urban unemployment problem.

The basic behavioural assumption of the model is that each potential migrant decides whether or not to move to the city on the basis of an implicit, "expected" income maximisation objective. There are two principal economic factors involved in this decision to migrate. The first relates to the existing urban-rural real wage differential that prevails for different skill and educational categories of workers. The existence of large disparities between wages paid to urban workers and those paid to comparably skilled rural labourers has long been recognised as a crucial factor in the decision to migrate. The increasing divergence between urban and rural incomes has arisen both as a result of the relative stagnation of agricultural earnings (partly as a direct outgrowth of post-war bias toward industrialisation at the expense of agricultural expansion) and the concomitant phenomenon of rapidly rising urban wage rates for unskilled workers.

The second crucial element, which for the most part has not been formally included in other models of rural-urban migration, relates to the degree of probability that a migrant will be successful in securing an urban job. Without introducing the probability variable it would be

extremely difficult to explain the continued and often accelerated rate of migration in the face of sizeable and growing pools of urban unemployed. Arguments about the irrationality of rural peasants who unwittingly migrate to urban areas permeated by widespread unemployment are as ill-conceived and culture-bound as earlier assertions that peasant subsistence farmers were unresponsive to price incentives. The key, in my opinion, to an understanding of the seemingly paradoxical phenomenon of continued migration to centres of high unemployment lies in viewing the migration process from an "expected" or permanent income approach where expected income relates not only to the actual wage paid to an urban worker, but also to the probability that he will be successful in securing wage employment in any given period of time. It is the combination and interaction of these two variables—the urban-rural real income differential and the probability of securing an urban job—which I believe determine the rate and magnitude of rural-urban migration in tropical Africa.

Consider the following illustration. Suppose the average unskilled or semi-skilled rural worker has a choice between being a farm labourer (or working his own land) for an annual average real income of, say, 50 units, or migrating to the city where a worker with his skill or educational background can obtain wage employment yielding an annual real income of 100 units. The more commonly used economic models of migration, which place exclusive emphasis on the income differential factor as the determinant of the decision to migrate, would indicate a clear choice in this situation. The worker should seek the higher-paying urban job. It is important to recognise, however, that these migration models were developed largely in the context of advanced industrial economies and, as such, implicitly assume the existence of full employment or near-full employment. In a full employment environment the decision to migrate can in fact be predicated solely on securing the highest-paying job wherever it becomes available. Simple economic theory would then

*Michael P. Todaro, "Income Expectations, Rural-Urban Migration and Employment in Africa," *International Labour Review,* Vol. 104, No. 5 (November 1971), pp. 391–95, 411–13, Copyright © International Labour Organisation 1971.

indicate that such migration should lead to a reduction in wage differentials through the interaction of the forces of supply and demand, both in areas of out-migration and in points of in-migration.

Unfortunately, such an analysis is not very realistic in the context of the institutional and economic framework of most of the nations of tropical Africa. First of all, these countries are beset by a chronic and serious unemployment problem with the result that a typical migrant cannot expect to secure a high-paying urban job immediately. In fact, it is much more likely that upon entering the urban labour market the migrant will either become totally unemployed or will seek casual and part-time employment in the urban traditional sector. Consequently, in his decision to migrate the individual in effect must balance the probabilities and risks of being unemployed or underemployed for a considerable period of time against the positive urban-rural real income differential. The fact that a typical migrant can expect to earn twice the annual real income in an urban area than he can in a rural environment may be of little consequence if his actual probability of securing the higher-paying job within, say, a one-year period is one chance in five. In such a situation we could say that his actual probability of being successful in securing the higher-paying urban job is 20 percent, so that his ''expected'' urban income for the one-year period is in fact 20 units and not the 100 units that the fully employed urban worker receives. Thus, with a one-period time horizon and a probability of success of 20 per cent it would be irrational for this migrant to seek an urban job even though the differential between urban and rural earnings capacity is 100 percent. On the other hand, if the probability of success were, say, 60 percent, so that the expected urban income is 60 units, then it would be entirely rational for our migrant with his one-period time horizon to try his luck in the urban area even though urban unemployment may be extremely high.

If we now approach the situation more realistically by assuming a considerably longer time horizon, especially in view of the fact that the vast majority of migrants are between the ages of 15 and 23 years, then the decision to migrate should be represented on the basis of a longer-term, more permanent income calculation. If the migrant anticipates a relatively low probability of finding regular wage employment in the initial period but expects this probability to increase over time as he is able to broaden his urban contacts, then it would still be rational for him to migrate even though expected urban income during the initial period or periods might be lower than expected rural income. As long as the present value of the net stream of expected urban income over the migrant's planning horizon exceeds that of the expected rural income, the decision to migrate is justified.

Our model attempts to demonstrate the conditions under which the urban-rural ''expected'' income differential can act to exacerbate the urban *unemployment* situation even though urban *employment* might expand as a direct result of government policy. It all depends on the relationship between migration flows and the expected income differential as expressed in an ''elasticity of migrational response'' term.

Since the elasticity of response will itself be directly related to the probability of finding a job and the size of the urban-rural real income differential, the model illustrates the paradox of a completely urban solution to the urban unemployment problem. Policies which operate solely on urban labour demand are not likely to be of much assistance in reducing urban unemployment since, in accordance with our expected income hypothesis, the growth of urban employment *ceteris paribus* also increases the rate of rural-urban migration. If the increase in the growth of the urban labour force caused by migration exceeds the increase in the growth of employment, the level of unemployment in absolute numbers will increase and the unemployment rate itself might also increase. This result will be accentuated if, for any increase in job creation, the urban real wage is permitted to expand at a greater rate than rural real income. A reduction or at least a slow growth in urban wages, therefore, has a dual beneficial effect in that it tends to reduce the rate of rural-urban migration and increase the demand for labour.

A second implication of the above model is that traditional methods of estimating the ''shadow'' price of rural labour to the urban sector will tend to have a downward bias if the migration response parameter is not taken into account. Typically, this shadow price has been expressed in terms of the marginal product of the rural worker who migrates to the city to secure the additional urban job. However, if for every additional urban job that is created more than one rural worker is induced to migrate, then the opportunity cost will reflect the combined loss of agricultural production of all those induced to migrate, not just the one who is fortunate enough to secure the urban position. It also follows that whenever there are sizeable pools of the urban unemployed, traditional estimates of the shadow price of urban labour will reflect an upward bias.

III.C.2. Migration and City Growth*

What explains the timing and the extent of the transition from a traditional rural to a modern urban society? Why does city growth speed up in early development and slow down in later stages? What role does migration play in the process, and do migrants make rational location decisions? Do urban labor markets serve to absorb urban immigrants quickly? Are rural emigrants driven by "push" conditions in the countryside or by "pull" conditions in the cities? Is the Third World "overurbanized"?

Despite a century and a half of debate, social scientists are still uncertain about the quantitative sources of the urban transition, how it can be influenced by policy, and if so whether it should be influenced by policy. While successful industrialization clearly fosters urbanization, what accounts for the "explosive" city growth in the Third World since the 1950s? The two principal hypotheses advanced in the literature are that rapid city growth and urbanization can be explained primarily by (1) unusually rapid rates of population growth pressing on limited farm acreage, pushing landless labor into the cities and (2) economic forces pulling migrants into the cities. In the contemporary developing world these latter forces include domestic policies that distort prices to favor cities (e.g., the domestic terms of trade have been twisted to "squeeze" agriculture); cheap energy prior to the first OPEC shock favoring the growth of energy-intensive urban sectors, thus creating urban jobs; the diffusion of technology from the developed world, which favors modern, large-scale urban industries; foreign capital flows into urban infrastructure, housing, power, transportation, and large-scale manufacturing—further augmenting the growth of cities in the Third World; and the liberalization of world trade since the late 1950s, which has stimulated demand for manufacturing exports produced in Third World cities.

Most demographers favor the first hypothesis. Exploding numbers of people must be employed, and a marginal agriculture with quasi-fixed arable land stocks cannot offer sufficient employment for the Malthusian glut created by the demographic transition. Marginal survival by hawking urban services may be the only way a social system can absorb the population glut, and squalid urban living conditions have been an attribute of early stages of industrialization since Engels wrote of Manchester in the 1840s. The demographer, writing in the shadow of Malthus, is likely, therefore, to favor a causal sequence running from a population boom, to labor pushed off the land, to city immigration, and thus to rapid urban growth under squalid living conditions. This view has also had a profound influence on economists' thinking about development. It is central to Lewis's (1954) labor surplus model—a model that also worked well for the classical economists developing their paradigms of growth during the British industrial revolution. It is also central to the Todaro (1969) thesis that rising immigration to the city is associated with high and even rising rates of urban unemployment. On the other hand, most economists now tend to favor the second hypothesis; that is, an emphasis on those economic forces which contribute to urban pull. . . .

This neo-Malthusian pessimism was given theoretical rationalization in 1969 with the appearance of Michael Todaro's model of labor migration and urban unemployment. Not surprisingly, the Todaro model took the profession by storm. After all, it had very attractive ingredients:

The idea that migrants compare expected gains with the current costs of being unemployed represented rather standard theory. The model's appeal lay rather in the fact that it fitted well with three prevalent stereotypes: high wages in the modern sector; presumptions of mass unemployment; permissive or overly generous policies and/or articulate, militant labor movements. (Kannappan 1985, p. 703)

*From J. G. Williamson, "Migration and Urbanization," in *Handbook of Development Economics*, ed. Hollis Chenery and T. N. Srinivasan (Amsterdam: North Holland, 1988), vol. 1, pp. 426–27, 443–46. Reprinted by permission.

The hypothesis is simple and elegant. Perhaps the most effective illustration can be found in Corden and Findlay (1975), reproduced in Figure 1. There are only two sectors analyzed in the figure, and labor is the only mobile factor there, but it is sufficient to illustrate the point. Under the extreme assumption of wage equalization through migration, and in the absence of wage rigidities, equilibrium is achieved at E (the point of intersection of the two labor demand curves, AA' and MM'). Here wages are equalized at $w_A^* = w_M^*$, the urbanization level is $O_M L_M^*/L$ (the share of the total labor force, L, employed in urban jobs, $O_M L_M^*$), where M denotes urban manufacturing and A denotes agriculture. Wages are never equalized in the real world, of course, and so the model incorporates the widely held belief that the wage in Third World manufacturing is pegged at artificially high levels, say at $\overline{w}_M$. If for the moment we assume unemployment away, then all of those who fail to secure the favored jobs in manufacturing would accept low-wage jobs in agriculture at w^{**}. The model now allows for a wage gap between the two sectors.

Figure 1 makes it clear that the level of city employment would be choked off by the high wage in manufacturing, but would city immigration also fall off? Not necessarily. Indeed, the model was originally motivated by concerns with urban unemployment, as well as by the coexistence of dramatic city growth, unemployment, *and* the expansion of the informal urban service sector where, it was alleged, low-wage underemployment prevailed. Todaro explains this apparent conflict (e.g., immigration in the face of urban unemployment and underemployment at very low wages) by developing an ex-

pectations hypothesis which, in its simplest form, states that the favored jobs are allocated by lottery, that the potential risk-neutral migrant calculates the expected value of that lottery ticket, and then compares it with the certain employment in the rural sector. Migration then takes place until the expected urban wage is equated to the rural wage. Given $\overline{w}_M$, and a wage in informal urban services so low that it can be taken as zero, at what rural wage would the migrant be indifferent between city and countryside? If the probability of getting the favored job is simply the ratio of employment in manufacturing, L_M, to the total urban labor pool, L_U, then the expression

$$w_A = (L_M/L_U)\,\overline{w}_M$$

indicates the agriculture wage at which the potential migrant is indifferent about employment location. This is in fact the qq' curve in Figure 1.[1] The equilibrium agriculture wage is given by w_A, and those unemployed or underemployed in the city (e.g., the size of the informal service sector plus those without any work at all) is thus given by L_{US}.

The new equilibrium at Z in Figure 1 seems to offer an attractive explanation for some of the stylized facts of Third World labor markets. It yields a wage gap, $\overline{w}_M - w_A$, and urban low-wage employment or unemployment, L_{US}. Moreover, when the dynamic implications of the model are explored, it turns out that an increase in the rate of manufacturing job creation need not cause any diminution in the size of the low-wage informal service sector. Indeed,

as long as the urban-rural [wage gap] continues to rise sufficiently fast to offset any sustained increase in the rate of job creation, then ... The lure of relatively high permanent incomes will continue to attract a steady stream of rural migrants into the ever more congested urban slums. (Todaro 1969, p. 147)

Nor has Todaro changed his view since 1969. A decade later he stated that city immigration in the Third World is

the major contributing factor to the ubiquitous phenomenon of urban surplus labor and as a force that continues to exacerbate already serious urban unemployment problems caused by growing economic and

FIGURE 1. The Todaro model according to Corden and Findlay.

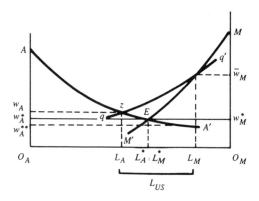

[1]The qq' curve is a rectangular hyperbola with unitary elasticity. The elasticity of the labor demand curve MM' is assumed to be less than unity in figure 1, an assumption motivated by empirical evidence available for the Third World.

structural imbalances between urban and rural areas. (Todaro 1980, p. 362)

Furthermore, the model makes some firm assertions about how urban labor markets work and how immigrants are absorbed into that labor market. First, it asserts that immigrants earn lower incomes than non-immigrants, the latter having first claim to the favored jobs. Second, it asserts that immigrants have a higher incidence of unemployment. Third, it implies that wages are lower in informal service sector employment than in industrial employment. Fourth, it implies that immigrants earn less in the cities when they first arrive, than they earned in the rural areas they left.

Critique: How Do Urban Labor Markets Really Work?

There are five critical assumptions of the Todaro model which lead to its dramatic results. Each of these seems restrictive, or at the very least deserve far more research.

First, as Willis (1980, p. 396) points out, job allocation rules are not likely to obey the simple lottery mechanism embedded in the Todaro model. The literature on job search has grown considerably since 1969, and it all emphasizes the role of investment in the search. In contrast, there is no such explicit investment in the Todaro model, except for the actual decision to migrate. In fact, recent evidence from the Third World suggests that unskilled immigrants do not engage in long job searches, and that overt urban unemployment is an attribute of the skilled rather than the unskilled (Yap 1976, 1977; Papola 1981). Indeed, this fact has encouraged the development of two-stream migration models and explicit attention to labor heterogeneity.

Second, there is no attention to informal sector labor market behavior in the Todaro model. In particular, we need to know far more about the sources of labor demand. After all, wages do clear that labor market, they are responsive to demand and supply, and they certainly do not settle to zero.

Third, there has been little evidence marshalled in support of the modern sector rigid-wage assumption (Montgomery 1985). This statement holds true for trade union pressure and minimum wage legislation. After all, wage differentials between urban formal and informal sectors could be explained just as well by ap-pealing to firm-specific training costs (Mazumdar 1973, 1976; Stiglitz 1974).

Fourth, there is the issue of discount rates and rational migrants. What matters to Todaro's migrants is the present value of expected urban earnings compared with the present value of expected rural earnings. Given modern sector wages double those of rural wages, given some unemployment duration before a migrant secures the modern sector job, and given some discount rate, how long a time horizon would a potential migrant have to have before present values were equated? Cole and Sanders (1985, p. 485) have made that calculation where discount rates are allowed to vary between 5 and 15 percent. They conclude: "If one must assume very long time horizons, in some cases greater than 50 years, an alternative explanation of migration may be in order" (Cole and Sanders 1985, p. 485).

Fifth, and perhaps most important, the model abstracts from many additional influences on the potential migrant's decision. This is the thrust of much of Stark's recent work on risk aversion, relative deprivation, and cooperative family games (Stark, 1984).

This debate is not merely academic nit-picking, since conflicting policy morals may emerge from the Todaro model and an alternative model which relaxes these critical assumptions. One of the first morals likely to be reversed is that ''underemployment'' in the informal service sector is socially unproductive. A second moral likely to be reversed is that rapid job creation in the modern sector fosters increasing urban unemployment. However, an important third moral is likely to remain unchanged; namely, development strategies should continue their recent emphasis on rural growth (Fields 1980, p. 390).

References

Cole, W. E., and R. D. Sanders (1985). ''Internal migration and urban employment in the Third World.'' *American Economic Review* 75: 481–94.

Corden, W., and R. Findlay (1975). ''Urban unemployment, intersectoral capital mobility and development policy.'' *Economica* 42: 59–78.

Fields, G. S. (1980). ''Comment,'' in R. A. Easterlin, ed., *Population and Economic Change in Developing Countries*. Chicago: University of Chicago Press.

Kannappan, S. (1985). "Urban employment and the labor market in developing nations." *Economic Development and Cultural Change* 33: 669–730.

Mazumdar, D. (1973). "Labor supply in early industrialization: The case of the Bombay textile industry." *Economic History Review* 26: 477–96.

———. (1976). "The urban informal sector." *World Development* (August): 655–79.

Montgomery, M. (1985). "The impacts of urban population growth on urban labor markets and the costs of urban service delivery: A review." Office of Population Research, Princeton University.

Papola, T. S. (1981). *Urban Informal Sector in a Developing Economy.* New Dehli: Vikas Publishing House.

Stiglitz, J. (1974). "Wage determination and unemployment in LDCs." *Quarterly Journal of Economics* 88: 194–227.

Stark, O. (1984). "Rural-to-urban migration in LDCs: A relative deprivation approach." *Economic Development and Cultural Change* 32: 475–86.

Todaro, M. (1969). "A model of labor migration and urban unemployment in less developed countries." *American Economic Review* 59: 138–48.

———. (1980). "Internal migration in developing countries: A survey." in R. A. Easterlin, ed., *Population and Economic Change in Developing Countries.* Chicago: University of Chicago Press.

Willis, R. J. (1980). "Comment." in R. A. Easterlin, ed., *Population and Economic Change in Developing Countries.* Chicago: University of Chicago Press.

Yap, L. (1976). "Rural-urban migration and urban underemployment in Brazil." *Journal of Development Economics* 3: 227–43.

———. (1977). "The attraction of cities: A review of the migration literature." *Journal of Development Economics* 4: 239–64.

Comment: Econometric Studies of Migration

The key question of what determines rural-urban migration can be explored further in studies that set forth probabilistic job-search models and in empirical investigations of migration functions. Field studies and econometric analyses indicate the importance of the economic motive in the decision to migrate. Econometric estimates of migration functions have also demonstrated that the probability of urban employment, independent of the differences in actual rural and urban wages, contributes significantly to the explanation of variance among time periods and subgroups of the rural population in rates of urban migration.

In an excellent survey of numerous studies, however, Yap indicates several problems with the econometric functions that limit their usefulness for prediction.[1]

The basic form of the migration function is as follows:

$$\overline{M}_{ij} = f(Y_i, Y_j; U_i, U_g; Z_i, Z_j; d_{ij}; C_{ij})$$

The specification is usually log linear. Typical independent variables used to explain migration from place i to place j ($\overline{M}_{ij}$) include wage or income levels (Y), unemployment rates (U), the degree of urbanization (Z) for the population in areas i and j, the distance between i and j (d_{ij}), and the friends and relatives of residents of i in the destination j (C_{ij}). Population in areas i and j is sometimes included.

Limitations of these studies are: (1) the level of demographic and geographic aggregation masks different patterns of migration; (2) the migration variable used in some of the studies presents conceptual and econometric difficulties; and (3) the independent variables are often poorly measured, especially the income estimates.

According to Stark and Bloom,

> Recent empirical research on the economics of labor migration has benefited a great deal more from the development of new econometric techniques than from new theoretical ideas. The techniques that have substantially improved our ability to use micro data sets in the estimation of relatively standard models of labor migration include techniques for the analysis of qualitative dependent variables, techniques that

[1] L. Y. L. Yap, "The Attraction of Cities: A Review of the Migration Literature," *Journal of Development Economics* 4 (1977): 239–64.

correct for sample selection bias, and techniques for the analysis of longitudinal and pseudo-longitudinal data. At the micro level, most empirical studies have attempted to test simple microeconomic models of migration according to which individuals (or families) make locational decisions primarily by comparing their income opportunities at alternative locations. The key feature of recent studies of this type is their focus on the estimation of structural, as opposed to reduced-form, models of the migration decision.[2]

In his *The Migration of Labor* (1991), Stark extends portfolio investment theory to migration and to the remittance of earnings. Under this theory, migration decisions are ordered by family needs for stable income levels, provided by a diversified portfolio of laborers, both male and female, and the need to jointly insure the family's well-being. In brief, group decision making and objectives, rather than the wishes of individual migrants, determine migration patterns and remittance flows. Viewed in light of portfolio investment theory, families allocate their labor assets over geographically dispersed and structurally different markets to reduce risk. Research indicates that after migration, family members pool and share their incomes. This pooling, or co-insurance, covers risks of losing income in individual markets and allows the family to smooth its consumption.

As Yap concludes, additional empirical research on migration would be useful to define the migration rate appropriately, adjust for simultaneous equation biases, and include more policy variables to provide more predictive value.

[2]Oded Stark and David E. Bloom, "The New Economics of Labor Migration," *American Economic Review* (May 1985): 176–77.

EXHIBIT III.1. Urban Population, Major Areas and Regions, 1950–2000 (thousands)

	1950	1960	1970	1975	1980	1990	2000
World Total	724,147	1,012,084	1,354,357	1,560,860	1,806,809	2,422,293	3,208,028
More developed regions	448,929	572,730	702,876	767,302	834,401	969,226	1,092,470
Less developed regions	275,218	439,354	651,481	793,558	972,408	1,453,067	2,115,558

Source: United Nations, *Patterns of Urban and Rural Population Growth*, ST/ESA/Ser. A/68.

III.C.3. The Informal Sector*

The popular view of informal-sector activities is that they are primarily those of petty traders, street hawkers, shoeshine boys and other groups "underemployed" on the streets of the big towns. The evidence suggests that the bulk of employment in the informal sector, far from being only marginally productive, is economically efficient and profit-making, though small in scale and limited by simple technologies, little capital and lack of links with the other ("formal") sector. Within the informal sector are employed a variety of carpenters, masons, tailors and other tradesmen, as well as cooks and taxi-drivers, offering virtually the full range of basic skills needed to provide goods and services for a large though often poor section of the population.

Our analysis lays great stress on the pervasive importance of the link between formal and informal activities. We should therefore emphasise that informal activities are not confined to employment on the periphery of the main towns, to particular occupations or even to economic activities. Rather, informal activities are the way of doing things, characterised by—

1. ease of entry;
2. reliance on indigenous resources;
3. family ownership of enterprises;
4. small scale of operation;

*From ILO Mission, *Employment, Incomes, and Equality: A Strategy for Increasing Productive Employment in Kenya*, Geneva, 1972, pp. 5–8, 503–8. Copyright 1972, International Labour Organisation, Geneva. Reprinted by permission.

5. labour-intensive and adapted technology;
6. skills acquired outside the formal school system; and
7. unregulated and competitive markets.

Informal-sector activities are largely ignored, rarely supported, often regulated and sometimes actively discouraged by the Government.

The characteristics of formal-sector activities are the obverse of these, namely—

1. difficult entry;
2. frequent reliance on overseas resources;
3. corporate ownership;
4. large scale of operation;
5. capital-intensive and often imported technology;
6. formally acquired skills, often expatriate; and
7. protected markets (through tariffs, quotas and trade licenses).

Our strategy of a redistribution from growth aims at establishing links that are at present lacking between the formal and the informal sectors. A transfer of incomes from the top income groups to the working poor would result in new types of labour-intensive investments in both urban and rural areas. This should not only generate demand for the products of the informal sector but also encourage innovations in labour-intensive techniques in this sector. The various policies which we recommend in other parts of the report are intended to reduce risk and uncertainty on the part of those employed in the informal sector and to ensure a dynamic growth of this large segment of the Kenyan economy.

There are marked contrasts between the relative security and income levels of those with wage-earning jobs in the bigger firms and those self-employed in the informal sector. These sharp inequalities inevitably create strong ambitions to migrate to the towns, to strive for higher education, to search for a job. As long as extreme imbalances persist, so will unemployment, since large differentials will always attract a margin of job seekers to hover in the towns, near the chances of the good jobs, in the hopes of snapping one up. This explains why the analysis of inequality is fundamental to the explanation of employment problems in Kenya.

But unemployment is not only the result of imbalance in differentials and opportunities. Even with perfect equality, unemployment could arise. Fast rates of population growth, of urbanisation and school expansion inevitably make it more difficult to absorb the growing labour force and reduce the time that might otherwise be available for structural adjustments. Here a second set of imbalances arise—dynamic imbalances relating to the structure of economic growth in the economy and to the constraints upon it. Rapid growth is needed, but rapid growth can itself generate imbalances which will frustrate its continuation—most notably a shortage of foreign exchange, of domestic savings, of skills and entrepreneurship, of demand or of the political support needed to keep the system workable. For this reason our report is not merely concerned with alleviating unemployment, poverty and gross inequality, but with economic growth on a pattern which can be sustained in the future, and which generates wider and more productive employment opportunities in the process. . . .

The Relation Between the Formal and Informal Sectors

The process of economic transformation and growth in Kenya has been marked by growing inequalities in the distribution of wealth and income among Africans. The usual explanation is the traditional–modern division of the economy, in which the westernised modern sector is the source of dynamism and change and the traditional sector slowly withers away. This view does not correspond to the reality of Kenya; we reject it for that reason, and because it ignores the dynamism and progressive elements indigenous to the Kenyan economy. We have considerable evidence to refute a view that attributes the sources of economic and social change almost exclusively to outside forces.

Furthermore, the traditional–modern analysis focuses only on the positive effects of the westernisation of the Kenyan economy and ignores the negative effects. In particular, it ignores inter-sectoral dynamics, which are the key to the employment problem. The accumulation of wealth in a small part of the modern sector is the consequence of the concentration of political power in that sector, and has given rise to the development of an impoverished and economically deprived modern sub-sector. The slums of Nairobi, Mombasa and to a lesser extent other urban areas are completely modern and due to the differences of wealth and income between different sectors of the economy. These differences draw migrants toward the concentrations, and bring about the modernisation of almost the entire economy, but not the spread of wealth.

Because of the slow growth of high-wage employment, migration to urban areas by income seekers has led to the growth of a low-income periphery. This low-income sector is peripheral both literally and figuratively. In Nairobi it sprang up, and continues to grow, just outside the borders of the wealthy urban zone, to supply goods and services to the fortunate few inside that zone and to its own population. Figuratively, it is peripheral in that it has only fortuitous and restricted access to the sources of wealth.

Characteristics and Dynamics of the Informal Sector

We describe these two urban sectors as being the ''formal'' and the ''informal'' sector. This designation is not intended to contribute to an academic proliferation of labels; we merely seek an analytical terminology to describe a duality that avoids the bias against the low-income sector inherent in the traditional-modern dichotomy. Both sectors are modern; both are the consequence of the urbanisation that has taken place in Kenya over the last 50 years. We might have used the terms ''large-scale'' and ''small-scale,'' but those terms are purely descriptive and tell us nothing about why one sector is large-scale and the other is small-scale. An explanation of this is central to explaining and solving the employment problem in Kenya. One important characteristic of the formal sector is its relationship to the Government. Economic activities formally and officially recognised and fostered by the Government enjoy considerable advantages. First, they obtain the direct benefits of access to credit, foreign exchange concessions, work permits for foreign technicians, and a formidable list of benefits that reduce the cost of capital in relation to that of labour. Indirectly, establishments in the formal sector benefit immeasurably from the restriction of competition through tariffs, quotas, trade licensing and product and construction standards drawn from the rich countries or based on their criteria. Partly because of its privileged access to resources, the formal sector is characterised by large enterprise, sophisticated technology, high wage rates, high average profits and foreign ownership.

The informal sector, on the other hand, is often ignored and in some respects helped and in some harassed by the authorities. Enterprises and individuals within it operate largely outside the system of government benefits and regulation, and thus have no access to the formal credit institutions and the main sources of transfer of foreign technology. Many of the economic agents in this sector operate illegally, though often pursuing similar economic activities to those in the formal sector—marketing foodstuffs and other consumer goods, carrying out the repair and maintenance of machinery and consumer durables and running transport, for example. Illegality here is generally due not to the nature of the economic activity but to an official limitation of access to legitimate activity. Sometimes the limitations are flouted with virtual abandon, as in the case of unlicensed *matatu* taxis; sometimes the regulations are quite effective. The consequence is always twofold: the risk and uncertainty of earning a livelihood in this low-income sector are magnified, and the regulations ensure a high quality of services and commodities for the wealthy few at the expense of the impoverished many.

The formal-informal analysis applies equally well to the agricultural sector. The parallels are obvious and striking. The division between favoured operators with licences and those without in urban areas is reproduced in agriculture between those who grow tea and coffee with official sanction and those who do so illegally. Similarly, with other agricultural products such as beef, there are those whose wealth enables them to conform to and benefit from standards officially laid down, while others can make a livelihood only by contravening the regulations. In the agricultural sector extension services take the place of the industrial estates and of loans from the Industrial and Commercial Development Corporation in the urban areas: farmers whose wealth and income allow them to conform to bureaucratic criteria benefit. Perhaps the most striking rural-urban parallel is with illegal rural squatters, who move unofficially on to land scheduled for resettlement and face a continual danger of eviction. Their similarity to urban squatters is obvious—both are irresistibly drawn to real or perceived sources of wealth, despite legal restrictions of access.

These characteristics of the informal sector, both agricultural and non-agricultural, result in low incomes for those who work in it. A natural consequence of these low incomes is that monetary exchanges within the informal sector are different in quality from those in the formal sector. A most important consequence of a low income is the primacy of risk and uncertainty. The loss a small farmer or a small entrepreneur can bear is disproportionately smaller than that which can be borne by a wealthy operator, particularly when the former has no access to institutionalised sources of credit. As a consequence, the entrepreneur in the informal sector must act continually to protect himself against risk. Accordingly he establishes semi-permanent relations with suppliers and buyers, frequently at the expense of his profits. For the same reason he may be hesitant to innovate, particularly in agriculture, for he cannot take the chance of failure. These characteristic behavioural responses are not inherent in the informal sector; they are adaptive responses to low income.

Despite the vitality and dynamism we see in the informal sector, we do not delude ourselves that it will develop successfully under present conditions. Although it has the potential for dynamic, evolutionary growth, under the existing nexus of restrictions and disincentives, the seeds of involutionary growth have been sown. Unlike the determinants of growth of the formal sector, the determinants of growth of the informal sector are largely external to it. The relevant question is not whether the informal sector is inherently evolutionary or involutionary, but what policies should be followed to cause evolutionary growth. Irrespective of policy changes, the informal sector will grow in the next 15 years. If policy continues as at present, the growth will be involutionary and the gap between the formal and informal sectors will widen. The employment problem will then be worse.

Comment: Studies of the Informal Sector

The concept of the informal urban sector was introduced by Keith Hart, with the distinction between wage and self-employment as the essential difference between the formal and the informal sectors; see Keith Hart, "Informal Income Opportunities and Urban Unemployment in Ghana," *Journal of Modern African Studies* (March 1973). As noted in the preceding selection, the ILO identifies the informal sector by a variety of other characteristics. For analytic purposes, it may be most incisive to define the informal sector as simply that sector in which the return to labor, whether or not in the form of wages, is determined by forces of demand and supply.

For studies of the informal sector, see Dipak Mazumdar, "The Urban Informal Sector," *World Development* (August 1976); Stephen Guisinger and Mohammed Irfan, "Pakistan's Informal Sector," *Journal of Development Studies* (July 1980); Peter Lloyd, The *"Young Towns"* of Lima: Aspects of Urbanization in Peru (1980); "Third World Migration and Urbanization: A Symposium" *Economic Development and Cultural Change* (April 1982); Oded Stark, "On Modelling the Informal Sector," *World Development* (May 1982); and ILO, *The Urban Informal Sector in Asia: An Annotated Bibliograph* (1992).

A later study of the informal sector in Nairobi (Kenya) found that the informal sector can be dichotomized into a dynamic entrepreneurial subsector, where a firm commitment has been made by the operators to their enterprises, and a relatively stagnant group—"the community of the poor"—engaged in menial employment with subsistence returns to their efforts. William J. House, "Nairobi's Informal Sector: Dynamic Entrepreneurs or Surplus Labor?" *Economic Development and Cultural Change* (January 1984).

In conformity with the potential expressed in the early ILO Mission Report (III.C.3), House concludes (p. 298):

> While critics of the ILO report on Kenya painted a very bleak picture of the informal sector, we have shown that they were far too pessimistic. A sizable part of the sector, the intermediate, has succeeded in expanding and accumulating capital assets despite an often aggressively negative attitude toward their activities by public authorities. The potential for increased incomes and employment opportunities referred to by the ILO is being realized in this subsector. Investment induces significant increases in incomes and, because of the labor intensity of the technology employed, improved job opportunities. Furthermore, linkages to the formal sector by way of subcontracts in general appear as benign rather than exploitive.
>
> On the other hand, significant numbers live in the community of the poor. Forty-two percent of proprietors and perhaps as many as fifty percent of employees receive less than the legal minimum wage. Within this group a considerable proportion receive incomes which fall below the minimum required to satisfy the barest of basic household needs.

III.C.4. Reinterpretation of the Informal Sector*

The informal/microenterprise sector turns out to be quite a heterogeneous set of activities, many of them in trade and services, so that it is unwise to make blanket judgments, completely positive or negative, regarding its potential contribution to development: rather, one should assess its various roles and consider in what ways its contribution can be enhanced.

The quantitative importance of the sector within the urban and rural economy shows that it is capable of substituting for large-scale units, both large-scale factories and "modern" small-scale enterprises. This is despite the pursuit of microeconomic and sectoral policies which are generally biased against microenterprises. Even if special small-industry development programs exist, the basic industrial development strategy pursued in Kenya and other African countries has been one of import-substituting industrialization, usually centering on large-scale, capital-intensive industry, often foreign-owned and using imported technologies. Other macroeconomic policies are well-known: duty-free import of capital goods (but taxed imports of microenterprise capital goods, treated as consumer goods) assisting large-scale units but competing with potential small-scale capital goods production; special depreciation provisions, subsidized real interest rates and special access to finance; and overvalued exchange rates, apart from direct support measures. A particular feature of SSI promotional programs and assistance measures, moreover, is usually a complete absence of technology improvement and product development components. With more even-handed macroeconomic and sectoral policies—including positive measures to promote linkages between large- and small-scale industry, and to upgrade microenterprise products and technologies—it should be possible to shift the boundary of production between large-scale and small-scale production.

A principal reason why informal sector producers are able to substitute for larger enterprise is that, in a market dominated quantitatively by low-income consumers, they offer cheap and "appropriate" goods and demand only a very low supply price for their services.

One form of "appropriateness" is to make goods last longer, hence the share of repair services of all kinds within the sector. Cheap but risky and uncomfortable transportation is another example.

This aspect has led some economists to suggest that informal sector manufacturing has no long-run development role, inevitably to be replaced by factory production as incomes rise. This neglects the time scale involved: only when development has proceeded far enough to substantially raise the supply price of labor will informal sector production modes become uneconomic. Even Asian countries with significantly higher per capita incomes than most African countries continue to have substantial informal sectors.

The sector expands not through the growth of individual enterprises but through an increase in the number of establishments, each employing only one or two persons. Given the numbers to be absorbed, and the inability of the formal sector to absorb them, labor is sufficiently cheap to make 1–2 person enterprises competitive. Informal sector enterprises represent a means of providing employment rather than potential developing firms (though not exclusively).

A substantial portion of rural Kenyan households are "divided": nonfarm self-employment and farm employment both contribute to rural household viability, even though family members may need to work in urban areas to secure the former. Household-based nonfarm activities also provide supplementary income to maintain viability. The substantial proportion of such "divided households" in rural Kenya implies a relatively favorable return to labor in the informal sector, but may in turn cause labor shortages and lower productivity in agriculture. It would be desirable to raise technology to improve productivity simultaneously in both sectors.

Disdain for the informal sector is produced by frequent reference to marginal activities such as shoe shining, car washing, or selling discarded whisky bottles. Evidence from an actual study of shoe shining in Nairobi (Elkan et al., 1983) puts a different perspective on this. Although House clearly places shoe shiners within his "community of the poor," Elkan found average

*From Ian Livingstone, "A Reassessment of Kenya's Rural and Urban Informal Sector," *World Development* 19, no. 6 (1991): 667–68. Reprinted by permission from Elsevier Science Ltd. Oxford, England.

net earnings in the trade to be around KShs600 a month, noting that this was "a good deal higher than had been expected." The significant finding, however, was that the chief customers were Kenyans, not tourists, and not even well-to-do Kenyans, but an intermediate category of "shop assistants, office clerks, and civil servants of the lower grades, none of whom have servants but all of whom like to look smart." This suggests that, rather than being a marginal occupation and a form of disguised unemployment, shoe shining has a natural place in the market economy of Kenya at its present stage of development. Many other "informal sector activities," of course, will have a much more important place in that economy, and the whole set of activities will basically reflect the level of income in the population. Thus in Asian developing economies, the urban and rural informal sectors may be much richer in content. Conversely, it is evident that in other African countries, where rural incomes and rural purchasing power are much lower than Kenya, the informal sector is thin. This wide variation was observed also within one country, in different districts of Kenya.

Part of the dichotomy, in fact, between the formal and informal sectors arises out of a corresponding income dichotomy between the mass of consumers making use of informal sector goods and services (and, of course, some mass-produced factory goods) and a wealthy class largely patronizing the formal sector. In some cases there may be a clear element of price discrimination involved, reflecting the effect of income levels. Thus a short taxi ride in the "formal" sector across Nairobi for the tourist or middle-class Kenyan will cost the same as an 80-mile ride from Nairobi to Embu in an "informal sector" taxi, even when the city taxi is considerably more ramshackle. Much of the service sector in Kenya and other developing countries (prostitution is an example) is characterized by price discrimination and segmented markets. However, informal manufacturing may be similarly if less obviously based on price discrimination, by supplying rough-and-ready goods such as furniture, household utensils, and garments for the mass market, while leaving the often much *smaller* quality market to the formal sector. Low-income consumers do not simply consume less: they consume goods and services which serve similar purposes but at a much lower price—informal sector taxis, local beer instead of canned beer, charcoal instead of electricity, simple houses instead of expensive houses, and less hygienic eating houses and food kiosks instead of modern hotels. There are, indeed, usually two price levels depending on the income category of the consumer.

The sharper the division between income categories, the clearer will be the gap between formal and informal producing sectors: also because a larger poor sector provides the necessary source of ultra-cheap labor. It is not a coincidence that much of the early literature on the informal sector focused on Kenya, and less so on West African countries such as Nigeria, and that the issue was taken up subsequently by the Latin American countries especially. In many Asian countries there is more of a spectrum than a dichotomy, but there remains a complex set of low-priced activities which reflect the general level of incomes, as these evolve over time, in each country. It is especially this level of income difference which produces differences in the content of the typical African economy and many of the Asian economies at the present time.

Reference

Elkan, W., T. C. I. Ryan, and J. T. Mukui (1983). "The economics of shoe shining in Nairobi." *African Affairs* 18, no. 323.

Comment: Urban–Rural Wage Gap

Despite extensive migration, the wage in the modern formal sector remains higher than a market clearing level. In the Todaro model, sticky industrial wages, notwithstanding urban unemployment, but flexible farm wages, jointly account for the wage gap. Other explanations are also possible.

First, considering real wages instead of only nominal wages, we may note that urban real wages, after allowing for the higher cost of living in cities and the in-kind payments to farm workers, may not be a great deal higher than rural wages.

Another explanation is based on institutional differences between the two sectors—the prevalence of trade unions, government employment, and minimum wage legislation in the formal urban sector.

These urban labor market distortions might thereby account for both rising unemployment and increased wage gaps.

A "labor turnover model" has also been used as a partial explanation of the wage gap: Joseph E. Stiglitz, "Alternative Theories of Wage Determination and Unemployment in LDCs: The Labor Turnover Model," *Quarterly Journal of Economics* (May 1974). Stiglitz observes that turnover costs (hiring and training) are greater in the urban sector than in the rural sector. He also postulates that the turnover rate is a decreasing function of the wage rate in the urban sector relative to the wage rate in the rural sector; therefore, it pays each competitive firm in the urban sector to offer more than the rural wage.

Another partial explanation by Stiglitz relies on the "efficiency wage model": Joseph E. Stiglitz, "Alternative Theories of Wage Determination and Unemployment in LDCs: The Efficiency Wage Model," in *The Theory and Experience of Economic Development*, ed. M. Gersovitz et al. According to this model, it is rational for a profit-maximizing firm to pay higher wages because higher wages, up to a point, lead to lower labor costs. Stiglitz submits that this happens because higher wages lead to (1) lower quit rates (the labor turnover model), (2) greater productivity on the job (the efficiency wage–productivity model), and (3) obtaining a higher quality labor force (efficiency wage–quality model).

To correct the effects of the urban–rural wage gap, economists often advocate a wage subsidy to encourage employers to use more labor-intensive techniques and hire more laborers in the modern sector. In project appraisal (X.C.3), as we shall see in Chapter X, labor should also be given a shadow wage that is lower than the market wage in the urban sector. According to the Stiglitz models, however, these policy recommendations may be wrong if government policy induces more migration to the urban sector with consequent unemployment, or if wage subsidies shift to workers in the form of higher real wages.

For an illuminating testing of these hypotheses, see Timothy J. Hatton and Jeffrey G. Williamson, "What Explains Wage Gaps Between Farm and City? Exploring the Todaro Model with American Evidence, 1890–1941," *Economic Development and Cultural Change* (January 1992). Also, Subbiah Kannappan, *Employment Problems and the Urban Labor Market in Developing Nations* (1983), and Janet L. Yellen, "Efficiency Wage Models of Unemployment," *American Economic Review, Papers and Proceedings* (May 1984).

III.D. THE LEWIS MODEL IN RETROSPECT—NOTE

The Lewis dual-sector model was first presented in 1954, but in light of the more than four decades of development experience it is now instructive to revisit the model and reassess its policy implications. In 1954, the model was forward looking, designed to indicate "what might be"—a theory of how an unlimited supply of labor might be absorbed from a rise in the savings ratio and capital accumulation in the modern sector.

True, over the intervening decades, some of the model's implications have turned out to have been realized empirically. Taiwan and South Korea are successful examples. Many other LDCs, however, are still left with severe problems of labor utilization. And, although the Lewis model made an increase in the savings ratio a central requirement for accelerated development, some countries have not been successful in overcoming surplus labor despite high savings and investment ratios. India, for example, has realized high savings ratios of 20 percent or greater, but its growth has been slow and the optimistic implications of the Lewis model have not been realized in practice. Although physical capital accumulation may be considered a necessary condition of development, it has not proved sufficient.

On the basis of development experience since 1954, we can now recognize deviations from the Lewis model and focus on future policy—what "ought to be" instead of "what might be" (as in 1954) and "what has been" (as in the past development record).

Deviations from the Lewis Model

Although Lewis's two-sector model did not so intend it, the capitalist sector in his model has, in practice, become identified with industry or the urban sector, while the noncapitalist sector has become identified with agriculture or the rural sector. It may be more preceptive, however, to recognize that in actuality a "double dualism" has arisen within poor countries. Not only is there rural–urban dualism, but within each of the two sectors are two subsectors, which might be termed the "organized" and the "informal" subsectors. The organized subsector in the urban sector is composed of wage earners in formal employment, is characterized by modern management and modern techniques of production, and is protected by governmental policies.

As noted in selection III.C.3, the informal subsector, in contrast, is composed of the self-employed and small-scale traditional crafts and services, all unprotected by governmental policies. Employment opportunities in the informal subsector are created by supply; necessity drives people to work in every conceivable way. Workers in the informal subsector may actually be working long hours at extremely difficult physical labor, but their productivity is very low, and their meager income is variable and frequently shared with others. With the extensive rural–urban migration, and the incapacity of the urban organized subsector to absorb the migration, the informal subsector of the city has acted as a sponge for the surplus labor. In most LDCs, the number in the urban informal subsector has risen not only absolutely, but also as a proportion of the total labor force. In urban centers, such as Calcutta or Bombay, it is estimated that one-half or more of the work force is in the informal subsector.

In the rural sector, a similar subdivision is evident. The organized sector comprises plantations, estates, and mines with modern management, advanced techniques of production, and wage employment. Widespread, however, is the informal subsector, in which production is still of the traditional subsistence variety, with production for household consumption.

As we saw in selection III.B.1, the essence of the Lewis model is that wages in the modern sector are based on the average product of labor in the traditional rural sector, but are somewhat higher—for unskilled labor, normally about 50 percent above the income of subsistence farmers—in order to attract labor into the modern sector and compensate for the higher cost of urban living and any nonpecuniary disadvantages. Lewis believed that this higher wage rate "brings the modern sector as much labor as it wants without at the same time attracting much more than it can handle."[1] Furthermore, the

---

[1] W. Arthur Lewis, *Development Planning* (1966), pp. 77–78, 92, and "Unemployment in Developing Areas," in *A Reappraisal of Economic Development*, ed. A. H. Whiteford (1967), p. 5.

model postulates that wage rates should not rise with increasing productivity, but that capital formation and technical progress in the capitalist sector should raise the share of profits in the national income. To the extent that the profit ratio rises, there should then be capital-widening investment in the industrial sector, so that the demand for labor continues to rise and more industrial workers are employed at a constant real wage. Finally, after the surplus labor is absorbed, wages begin to rise.

In actuality, however, the real income gap between the modern and the rural sectors has been much greater than allowed for in the Lewis model. The wage rate in the modern sector has been higher than that needed to cover the cost of transfer and the higher urban costs of living. And the differential above rural income has widened. The wage level in the industrial sector has risen in spite of open unemployment and before the surplus labor of the rural sector has been absorbed. It has also continued to rise in many of the LDCs, although the average product in agriculture may have been even stagnant in some economies. Instead of Lewis's suggested 50 percent differential, the average real wage for workers outside of agriculture has commonly been two to four times greater than the average family income in the traditional sector.

Most important, the inflow of labor to the modern sector has actually been "more than it can handle"; contrary to what is to be expected from the Lewis model, an exceedingly high rate of unemployment and underemployment has materialized in the modern sector. Those formerly in disguised unemployment in the rural sector have, in effect, transferred into visible unemployment and underemployment in the modern sector.

The reasons for this can be found in some of the actual deviations from the conditions of the Lewis model and in some structural distortions that have been perpetuated by inappropriate policy measures.

The rate of urbanization has indeed been high. The amenities and public services of the urban area are attractive in themselves to labor from the rural sector. But the strongest inducement has been the widening income difference between urban wages and rural income at the same time as rural employment opportunities have not expanded. Fundamentally, it can be submitted that the employment problem in the urban area has been the result of a premature increase in the industrial wage level combined with a premature reduction in agricultural employment. To a lesser extent, but still significantly in some countries, labor has been released from the very labor-intensive indigenous handicraft industries that cannot compete with the growth in new manufacturing activities. "Rationalization" of labor practices in the tertiary sector has also tended to increase the supply of labor to the urban industrial sector.

As already noted, the urban wage level has not been controlled by real earnings in agriculture. Urban wages have commonly risen to two to four times higher than agriculture earnings. Urban wages have risen independently through the wages policies of the government and trade unions. Trade union pressures have increased in many countries, and labor-supported governments have shown some sympathy to such pressures. Moreover, the monopolistic structure of many product markets has facilitated the passing on of higher wages in the form of higher prices. In several countries, union pressure in crucial sectors of the economy—for instance, in the oil, copper, and bauxite industries—has been instrumental in setting a pattern of wage increases in other sectors.

More significantly, governmental policies have been directly instrumental in raising urban wages. The public sector is frequently the largest sector of wage employment and the only sector that is highly organized. Wages in the public sector have risen rapidly and have commonly acted as the base for a wider pattern of wage increases.

In newly independent countries, the salary scales became basically those that were paid to expatriates during the earlier colonial period; but this scale does not now conform to the utilization of the domestic supply of labor, and it puts undue pressure on the wage structure. Nor can the heightened expectations from the extension of education be fulfilled. Furthermore, minimum-wage regulation has been influential in raising urban wages and has had a great impact on the total wage structure in a developing country. The minimum wage in a dominant industry is frequently negotiated with the government on the basis of "an ability to pay" criterion, but this wage tends to spread through other industries. The increase in the minimum wage will have considerable effect in raising the whole wage scale, since the wages being received by most of the unskilled workers are at or near the current minimum wage. The generalization of a minimum wage may then become highly unrealistic because it is oblivious to conditions of supply and demand in the labor market, living standards in the traditional sector, and the effects on the wage structure as a whole. Workers who were only marginally useful—but nonetheless employed at the lower wage—become redundant when the minimum wage rises.

Minimum-wage policies for unskilled labor have the effect of making the skilled–unskilled wage differential too narrow, as has happened in many African and Asian countries. Market forces of supply and demand are left to determine wages for skilled labor, but demand rises only slowly so that the market-determined wage for skilled labor also tends to rise slowly. If governments then insist that unskilled wages should increase independently of demand and supply conditions in the unskilled labor market, there is a likelihood that unskilled wages will increase faster than skilled wages, and that relatively low-wage labor will become overvalued.

In default of adequate profit taxation or another tax policy, governments have found it convenient in effect to ''tax'' companies—especially foreign companies—through wage increases. The government's policy of encouraging higher wages may initially be directed only at foreign companies in order to prevent ''excess'' profit repatriation and to raise the share of income for domestic factors. But the demonstration effect of higher wages in the foreign enterprises also causes a spread of higher wages to other enterprises.

At the same time as government policies have supported urban-wage increases, no particular attention has been given to the level of agricultural wages. The result has been a widening gap between the urban and the agricultural wage levels. Such a large differential has served to attract the disguised unemployed from the rural sector to the urban sector, but it has simultaneously kept industrial labor overpriced. Moreover, the differential between urban and rural wages has proceeded to widen in face of the substantial and growing urban unemployment and underemployment. With the rising expected wage, it has become increasingly difficult to absorb the excess supply of labor.

Although the Lewis model envisages sufficient capital-widening investment in the industrial sector to absorb the labor inflow, the actual result has been a substitution of capital for labor in the modern organized sector. Contrary to the model, wage rates in many LDCs have actually risen more rapidly than productiv-

ity. Real wages have risen at rates comparable to those in the advanced industrial countries. But whereas in the industrial countries, real wages have increased roughly in line with average national productivities, the rise of wages in the developing countries often implies an increase considerably faster than that in real national product per capita.

The consequence of this has been the use of more capital-intensive production methods either through the introduction of labor-saving machinery in response to rising wages or through improvement in personnel and production-management practices that have trimmed the labor requirements per unit of output.

Capital-intensive methods of production have also been subsidized by other price distortions—especially through too low a rate of interest and too low a price for foreign exchange. When interest rates in the urban sector do not reflect the true scarcity of capital, a bias is imparted to capital-intensive production methods. This is often intensified by inflation that lowers the real rate of interest below the nominal rate, possibly even to a negative real rate. So, too, is there a bias toward more advanced production techniques when the LDC's currency is overvalued in terms of foreign currency, and the true cost of importing machinery is thus undervalued. Governments have also lowered the relative price of producers' equipment by such measures as allowing duty-free importation of equipment, granting a preferential exchange rate, and making available foreign exchange for servicing loans from overseas machinery suppliers. When domestic enterprises are protected by tariffs and import quotas, the pressure to economize on capital is also less than it would be in more competitive markets.

It is most significant that the strategy of industrialization through import substitution has dominated the expansion of the urban industrial sector. In Chapter IX, we examine in some detail the policies used to promote the home replacement of imported final goods. At this point, we need only recognize that the attempt to industrialize by means of import substitution has generally been accompanied by inflation and an overvalued exchange rate. These policies have resulted in a distorted price structure in many LDCs: too low a rate of interest in the urban sector, too low a rate for foreign exchange, and too high a level of urban wages.

According to neoclassical analysis, the un-

FIGURE 1.

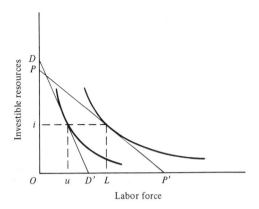

employment in less developed countries can be attributed to distorted factor prices. There exists some "natural" or "undistorted" set of factor prices that would reflect the opportunity cost of the various resources and would ensure full employment of all resources. Unemployment or underemployment, then, is due to various market imperfections that distort the factor prices and prevent full employment.

Figure 1 illustrates this. There is assumed to be substitutability in choice of techniques of varying labor and investment intensity. The slope of the price line PP' is the ratio of interest rate to wage rate. Full employment would occur with the price line of PP', given the limited investment resources Oi and labor supply OL. But distortions in capital and labor markets result in an actual price line of DD', representing too low a rate of interest and too high a wage rate. The factor market distortions then result in unemployment uL, given the limited investment resources Oi. The policy inference is "let the endowment speak," change factor prices, or subsidize and tax the factor markets to bring them into line with "undistorted" full-employment prices.[2]

The capital-intensive bias is also supported by a number of other measures. Employers tend to seek means of reducing their labor requirements when the government uses wage policies as a substitute for social legislation by requiring family allowances, pensions, licensing and health measures, or other fringe benefits bordering on social insurance. Officially required fringe benefits and wage supplements may commonly

[2]Frances Stewart, *Technology and Underdevelopment*, 2nd ed. (1978), p. 46.

amount to as much as 30 to 40 percent of the basic wage. When the employers are foreign enterprises, they are also likely to be simply imitating the advanced techniques of production known in the advanced country—techniques that are appropriate for the factor supply of the advanced country, but not for the labor surplus of the less developed country.

Contrary to the Lewis model, the expansion of the modern industrial sector also slowed down in many LDCs. Being based on import substitution, the industrial sector might be expected to have initially a substantial rate of growth as imports are replaced. But this may be a once-for-all expansion, with little subsequent reinvestment—unless the home market continues to grow, the process of import substitution can proceed from the final stages of production down through the production process to the replacement of intermediate goods, or the import-replacement industry is able to gain a competitive advantage in export markets. Such opportunities for the continual expansion of the modern sector have not materialized, and the capital-widening investment of the Lewis model, with an ever-expanding demand for surplus labor, has not been sustained.

At the same time as domestic policies have had the effect of subsidizing capital-intensive import-substitution industries, they have implicitly imposed a levy on domestic agriculture. This has gone against an expansion in labor-intensive agricultural output and a rise in rural employment.

For these various reasons, the employment problem remains a central problem of development.

Policy Implications

Lewis later recognized the unemployment problem and stated that

the most important ingredient in employment policy is to prevent too large a gap opening up between wages in the modern and earnings in the traditional sectors. So long as the traditional sector is not disturbed by a large income gap, it can hold and provide for all the people whom the modern sector is not yet ready to employ. . . .

Other ingredients are: measures to prevent excessive capital intensity; avoidance of an overvalued currency; adequate expenditure on developing the countryside; curbing the growth of a few large towns, in favor of developing more numerous small urban centers; and a population policy. . . . Deliberate action to substitute labor for machinery, in accordance with shadow pricing, even if confined to the public sector would go a long way toward eliminating open unemployment.[3]

An entire set of development policies that affect the demand and supply sides of the labor problem should now be of concern. Thus all the remaining chapters will concentrate on the formulation of a set of employment policies by treating the mobilization and allocation of investment resources, agricultural development, industrialization programs, and trade strategy.

At this point, however, it may be useful to offer some general principles underlying possible policy options for the better utilization of labor. Their validity will then be explored in greater detail in subsequent chapters.

1. If urban unemployment is to be reduced, policy measures must reduce the rural–urban drift. To this end, a reduction of urban–rural real income differentials would be most helpful; but this is probably the most difficult objective to achieve. According to some models of labor migration, the larger the gap between urban and rural nominal wages, the higher must be the urban unemployment rate before migration in excess of job opportunities ceases. As long as urban wages rise more rapidly than average rural incomes, rural–urban migration will continue, in spite of rising levels of urban unemployment. All policies that would redress the imbalance between urban and rural income levels would therefore be desirable—urban-wage restraint, adjustment of minimum-wage rates, revision of the tax structure, and a comprehensive national income and wages policy.

A number of institutional and political considerations, however, militate against the efficacy of these policies, and it is not realistic to expect any strong downward pressure on urban wages. An effective "wages policy" has proved difficult in the developed—let alone newly developing—countries.

2. If it is difficult to institute a "wages policy" that would increase urban employment, it is all the more important to emphasize the "supply side" of the problem. When the urban sector cannot absorb the inflow of labor from the rural sector, special consideration must be given to policies that will remove the causes of the rural "supply push" and help contain the labor force

in rural areas. Urban problems are in a fundamental sense rural problems; urban "pull" must be offset by lessening the "push" through rural development.

The modern sector must avoid producing what can be produced in the rural sector; for example, village handicraft employment should not be displaced if this entails the wasteful use of capital in the modern sector to produce an output that could be produced equally well by surplus labor. It is instructive that in Japan's case of successful development, both agriculture and village industry became more labor intensive. There may also be a considerably greater scope for rural-based industry involving simple technology and the processing of agricultural materials.

Beyond this, however, a full-scale program of rural development is needed to absorb and retain large amounts of manpower. If the rural–urban migration is to be reduced, it is necessary to modify policies that have turned the terms of trade against the agricultural sector. Ceiling prices on foodstuffs, export taxes or restrictions on primary products, and tariff protection on industrial inputs and consumer goods have acted as disincentives to agricultural producers, while they have artificially increased the urban–rural differential.

Efforts should also be made to disperse to the rural sector some of the amenities and public services now concentrated in urban areas. Readier access to such services as public utilities, health, education, and entertainment in the rural areas may amount to an increase in the rural social wage, and diminish the attractions of the city.

Of greatest consequence will be the type of strategy pursued for developing the agricultural sector. As elaborated in Chapter VIII, the most important factor influencing a developing country's ability to absorb a growing labor force into productive employment is whether a labor-using, capital-saving type of approach to agricultural development is followed (as in Japan and Taiwan). For most developing countries, the employment potential in rural modernization can be greater than that of the modern urban sector—provided that the countries avoid implicit taxation of agriculture and "unduly labor displacing" measures in agriculture.

3. If the previous strategy of industrialization by means of import substitution has resulted in "urban bias"—that is, distortions that favor the urban, import-substituting, modern sector at the

[3]Lewis, *Development Planning*, p. 83.

expense of the rural sector—then in the future, the promotion of nontraditional exports may allow a strategy of industrialization through export substitution that creates more employment, among other advantages. Chapter IX discusses various policies—notably those connected with trade policy and foreign investment—that are needed to make export substitution effective.

The distortions in the price structure also create divergences between domestic and international prices that inhibit the country's exports. To the extent that the comparative advantage of the country lies in labor-intensive commodities, the employment-intensity of trade can be raised by "getting prices right" and by establishing an efficient commodity composition of exports.

4. More effort is also needed to devise a range of technological choices that are superior to the country's indigenous traditional technology, but are not as advanced and labor saving as are the modern machines and equipment that have been imported from advanced industrial countries. As discussed in section VII.C, the transfer of "appropriate" technology has important consequences for employment in both the urban industrial sector and the rural agricultural sector.

The choice of a more labor-intensive production technique may, of course, conflict with other investment criteria; in particular, the maximum absorption of labor may yield only a low return per unit of capital and not maximize the future rate of growth in output.

The crucial consideration is the emphasis on devising new technology that is "capital stretching" in an efficient way; that is, the labor-intensive equipment should raise the labor–capital ratio without also raising the capital–output ratio. A more appropriate technology would in effect retain the essential quality of the tool element in physical equipment without the superfluous labor-saving appendages of the advanced technology of industrial countries.

To lessen the bias toward relatively capital-intensive techniques, it is again necessary to stress the removal of factor price distortions. Given that there is a positive elasticity of substitution of labor against capital,[4] it would be-

come less profitable to use capital-intensive technologies if interest rates were increased, foreign exchange became more expensive in terms of home currency, and the increases in urban wages were restrained.

5. As long as labor is induced to migrate from the rural sector and the manufacturing sector cannot absorb labor in sufficient quantities, it will be necessary for labor to seek employment in the tertiary sector. Labor has done so in many LDCs, and employment in services and commerce has actually risen more rapidly than in other sectors.

From the standpoint of providing an employment outlet, it is therefore advisable not to promote too rapid an increase in efficiency in employment practices in the service sector. As remarked by Galenson,[5] the pushcarts should not be too readily replaced by the supermarket; the bicycles, by the trucks; a casual but large labor force, by a permanent and stable but smaller labor force. The inefficient use of labor in the tertiary sector will not, of course, have the undesirable cost effects that would occur if this were done in the import-replacement or export sectors. In the production of nontradable commodities, it may therefore be important to be unimportant about seeking the least cost combination of factors when this would displace labor.

Emphasizing that "Asian countries will be forced to develop the labor-intensive sectors if jobs are to be created for the increasing waves of youngsters coming into the labor market," Oshima has stated that

the nonagricultural labor-intensive sector is very large, perhaps engaging two-thirds to three-fourths of the nonagricultural labor force. It is a sector that provides employment using the least amount of capital, in terms of capital efficiency uses the less scarce type of capital and saving, requires material inputs which are domestically produced, utilizes labor not appropriate for modern industries, and produces goods of the traditional type, consumed by lower-income families located in various parts of the country instead of being concentrated in the cities. It is an excellent complement to modern industrialization for underdeveloped countries where modern types of inputs and factors are scarce—whether these be capital and savings, skills, infrastructure, inputs, etc.[6]

---

[4]For a careful empirical study that suggests that considerable substitution possibilities exist in a number of manufacturing industries, see Howard Pack, "The Employment–Output Trade-Off in LDCs—A Microeconomic Approach," *Oxford Economic Papers* (November 1974).

[5]W. Galenson, "Economic Development and the Sectoral Expansion of Employment," *International Labour Review* (January–June 1963): 505–19.

[6]Harry T. Oshima, "Labor-Force 'Explosion' and the Labor-Intensive Sector in Asian Growth," *Economic Development and Cultural Change* (January 1971): 178.

6. Finally, more attention must be given to the "supply side" of the problem in terms of population-control policy and the "outputs" of the country's educational system. Growth in the labor force is a derivative of the population growth rate and the labor participation rate. But since there is about a 15-year lag between a decline in the birth rate and a decline in the labor force entry rate, any deceleration of population growth can have only long-run effects and is not a relevant instrument for short-term policy. Investment in human capital may, however, influence employment more readily. In this connection, some relevant points will be noted in Chapter VI, on human-resource development.

From even this summary listing of policy implications, it should be apparent that employment policies make sense only within the context of an overall development strategy. In contrast with the original formulation of Lewis's dual-sector model, more attention must now be given to the importance of human-resource development, the role of agriculture in transforming the production structure, qualitative changes in the development process beyond the quantitative aspects of economic growth, and the significance of markets and prices.

Effective policies to overcome the real resource gap in a poor country are still fundamental, as discussed in the next two chapters (IV and V). Beyond that, however, we must consider policies for human-capital formation (Chapter VI), agriculture-industry production transformation (Chapters VII and VIII), trade strategy (Chapter IX), and the respective roles of markets and governments (Chapter X).

CHAPTER IV

Domestic Financing of Development

We have seen that many economists believe that an increase in investment is a necessary, albeit not sufficient, condition for development. A central question then arises: How can investment be financed? This is not a question of where is the money coming from, but rather where are the real resources coming from to support real investment in the capital stock. For if financing development were only a matter of having more rupees or pesos, then India's or Mexico's central bank could create the domestic money; but this would lead only to inflation. What is needed to finance capital accumulation is more savings—that is, the release of resources from consumption, so that investment can be increased in real terms.

Even though labor may be abundant, the output of a less developed economy remains limited by a shortage of capital. From the perspective of production-function analysis, a country's growth in output depends on an increase in the quantity of inputs, improvements in the quality of inputs, and movement of resources from less productive to more productive activities (recall selection II.B.3). Considering an increase in the quantity of inputs, we emphasize in this chapter the mobilization of domestic resources to allow the formation of capital—that is, an increase in assets that generate an additional future stream of income. The mobilization of domestic resources, along with the mobilization of external resources (to be discussed in Chapter V), require policies that will facilitate the process of capital accumulation.

This chapter begins by focusing on the investment requirements to achieve a target rate of growth in national income (Note IV.A). This note clarifies various interpretations of the capital–output ratio in practice. We should also realize that in some countries there has been only a weak relation between the rates of saving and growth because the productivity of investment is as important—or even more so—than its volume.

The note in section IV.B. then outlines the various sources of capital formation—domestic and foreign, private and public. In examining these various sources of capital formation, we should assess each source from the wider perspective of how its contribution to the flow of resources for developmental purposes can be intensified.

Section IV.C. examines attempts to accumulate capital through inflationary financing. Particular attention is given to the effects of inflation on the rate and pattern of a country's development path. Beyond a very low rate, inflation is seen to be a hindrance to productive capital accumulation.

Section IV.C. also relates macroeconomic policy to problems of economic stabilization in developing countries, emphasizing the experience with adjustment policies.

Noninflationary methods of financing development are outlined in Section IV.D. Selection IV.D.1 examines the determinants of private saving, based on various hypotheses and empirical evidence.

The financing of government expenditure through taxation is then considered in IV.D.2. This section offers some basic principles for taxation and measures of tax reform. The need for fiscal discipline is also stressed.

Section IV.E. analyzes the influence of the financial sector on economic growth. Of increasing importance are the problems of financial development—the manner in which financial institutions and financial policies operate to mobilize savings, allocate loanable funds to investment, and affect a country's rate and pattern of development. Economic theory is generally conducted in "real" terms, such as national product in physical units, production functions, and capital–output ratios. For an understanding of the process of development, however, we must consider the way in which the financial superstructure and the real infrastructure interact.

The selections in section IV.E. ask some basic questions about the contribution of financial development to economic development. What are the alternative techniques available to each country for mobilizing its economic surplus and channeling capital flows? What are the relationships between finance and the rate and pattern of development? These general questions should help to place in perspective the empirical studies of particular financial institutions or the financial development of individual countries.

The selections in section IV.E. also analyze how financial reform may improve resource allocation and real economic growth. Of special concern is financial repression. Financial repression consists of an administratively determined nominal interest rate, which holds the real rate of interest (nominal rate minus inflation rate) below its free market equilibrium level. The central argument of the analysis of financial repression is that indiscriminate distortions of financial prices, including interest rates and foreign-exchange rates, reduce the real rate of growth and the real size of the financial system relative to nonfinancial magnitudes. This retards the development process by not allowing the financial sector to perform its proper functions in financial intermediation between savers and investors, and in efficient investment allocation. The policy prescription, therefore, is to raise institutional interest rates and reduce the rate of inflation. Financial deepening is also advocated; financial assets should grow at a faster rate than income. To do this, programs of financial liberalization have been advocated and implemented in several developing countries.

Nonetheless, because of capital market failures, government interventions in money and capital markets may still be advocated. Given our emphasis on appropriate policies, the essential problem is to determine what interventions are justified in financial markets.

IV.A. INVESTMENT
REQUIREMENTS—NOTE

Throughout the history of economic thought, the accumulation of real physical capital stock has been viewed as permitting more roundabout methods of production and greater productivity, thereby providing an additional future stream of income to society. As Adam Smith observed in *Inquiry into the Nature and Causes of the Wealth of Nations,* capital is the main determinant of "the number of useful and productive laborers" who can be set to work.[1] Labor is "put into motion" by capital. Capital accumulation allows population and the labor force to increase, provides workers with better equipment, and, most important, makes possible a more extensive division of labor. Capital accumulation serves to increase both total output and output per worker. An economy's rate of progress is proportional to its rate of investment:

When we compare, therefore, the state of a nation at two different periods, and find, that the annual produce of its land and labor is evidently greater at the latter than the former, that its lands are better cultivated, its manufactures more extensive, we may be assured that its capital must have increased during the interval between those two periods.[2]

In the early 1950s, Ragnar Nurkse also emphasized the lack of capital accumulation as being responsible for poverty. According to Nurkse, "a country is poor because it is poor." A vicious circle of poverty exists:

On the supply side, there is a small capacity to save, resulting from the low level of real income. The low real income is a reflection of low productivity, which in its turn is due largely to the lack of capital. A lack of capital is the result of the small capacity to save, and so the circle is complete.

On the demand side, the inducement to investment may be low because of the small buying power of the people, which is due to their small real income, which again is due to low productivity. The low level of productivity, however, is a result of the small amount of capital used in production, which in its turn may be caused at least partly by the small inducement to invest.

The low level of real income, reflecting low productivity, is a point that is common to both circles.

In addition to the circular relationships that plague the capital problem, there are, of course, matters of unilateral causation that can keep a country poor; for instance, lack of mineral resources, insufficient water or barren soil. Some of the poorer countries in the world today are poor partly for such reasons. But in all of them their poverty is also attributable to some extent to the lack of adequate capital equipment, which can be due to the small inducement to invest as well as the small capacity to save.[3]

It is, of course, possible to criticize the argument for a vicious circle of poverty by pointing out, as P. T. Bauer does, that if the circle were really so vicious, then there would be no developed countries because all began as underdeveloped, and there would be none of the progress that has been made by many underdeveloped countries.[4] But such a criticism implies a virtuous circle that resulted from a turning of the low savings into moderate savings and eventually into high savings, with a corresponding increase in investment and hence productivity and real income. The crucial issue is how the vicious circle is broken.

In Chapter III, W. Arthur Lewis was following the tradition of classical economists by also emphasizing growth of the capitalist sector in order to increase profits and saving and thereby investment. In presenting his model of a dual economy, Lewis contended that

the central problem in the theory of economic development is to understand the process by which a community which was previously saving and investing four or five percent of its national income or less, converts itself into an economy where voluntary saving is running at about 12–15% of national income or more. This is the central problem, because the central fact of economic development is rapid capital accumulation (including knowledge and skills with capital).[5]

According to Lewis,

All the countries which are now relatively developed have at some time in the past gone through a period

[3]Ragnar Nurkse, *Problems of Capital Formation in Underdeveloped Countries* (1953), p. 5.

[4]P. T. Bauer, *Dissent on Development* (1972), pp. 472–73.

[5]W. Arthur Lewis, "Economic Development with Unlimited Supplies of Labour," *The Manchester School* (May 1954): 139.

[1]Adam Smith, *Wealth of Nations* (1776), ed. R. H. Cambell and A. S. Skinner (1979), vol. 1, p. 343.

[2]Ibid.

of rapid acceleration, in the course of which their rate of annual net investment has moved from 5% or less to 12% or more. That is what we mean by an industrial revolution.[6]

Taking India as an example of a country in which the net investment rate in the early 1950s was perhaps 4 or 5 percent of national income and real income per capita was virtually stagnant, Lewis concluded that to achieve a 1.5 to 2 percent rise in the standard of living, a 12 percent net investment rate would be necessary—a figure achieved around 1960. In studies of the sources of growth in developing countries over the past three or four decades, it is common to attribute at least 25 to 50 percent of the increase in GDP to capital accumulation. The top growth performers have tended to have the highest rates of capital accumulation, while the worst performers have had the lowest rates of investment.[7]

In making projections of increases in real national output (Y), economists typically begin with an estimate of the rate of saving and the amount of net national output that may be expected from the investment to be made on the basis of the estimated savings. Numerous studies have tried to quantify the amount of capital required to increase output by 1 unit per annum in each sector of the economy and in the national economy as a whole. This amount is called the capital–output ratio, or capital coefficient. The marginal or incremental capital–output ratio (ICOR) estimates the amount of additional capital (ΔK) required to generate an increase in the national output (ΔY). The ICOR in LDCs typically range from 2:1 to 5:1. If, for example, we want to increase national output by 20, and we estimate the ICOR to be 4:1, then the required addition to the capital stock to be provided by new investment is 80. Such a calculation is based on the following identity:

$$\frac{\Delta Y}{Y} = \frac{I}{Y} \cdot \frac{1}{\Delta K/\Delta Y} = \frac{I}{Y} \cdot \frac{\Delta Y}{\Delta K}$$

Growth in national output is equal to the ratio of investment to output times the productivity of investment.

What, then, are the country's capital requirements? They will depend on the growth target in per capita income and the value of the ICOR ($\Delta K/\Delta Y$).

We may now write the target rate of growth in national income (G) as

$$G = \frac{\Delta Y}{Y} = \frac{S}{Y} \cdot \frac{\Delta Y}{\Delta K} \quad \text{or} \quad \frac{S}{Y} = G \cdot \frac{\Delta K}{\Delta Y}$$

If the growth target in national income (G) is equal to 5 percent, and the incremental capital–output ratio is 3:1, then the country will need a saving rate of 15 percent:

$$\frac{S}{Y} = G \cdot \frac{\Delta K}{\Delta Y} \quad \text{or} \quad 5\% \times (3{:}1) = 15\%$$

If population growth is 3 percent and the country simply wants to maintain its per capita real income, it will have to invest 9 percent of its national income.

If, however, population growth is 3 percent and the target of increase in per capita income is 2 percent, (so that per capita income doubles in 35 years), the country will have to save 15 percent of its income.

In general,

$$\frac{S}{Y} = (x + y)\% \cdot \frac{\Delta K}{\Delta Y}$$

where x is the population growth, and y is the target in per capita income. It follows that the capital requirements will be lower, the lower the population growth, and the lower the incremental capital–output ratio. In recent decades, however, population has been growing by more than 2 percent in many less developed countries, which has intensified the need for capital. In addition, there have been high rates of urbanization throughout the developing world because of population growth and rural–urban migration. Urbanization alone—not to mention a movement into more capital-intensive industries—puts more pressure on the need for capital accumulation.

In the simple calculations above, the capital–output ratio measures the productivity of investment. This can be done either in physical units or in value terms and by either the average or the marginal relation between capital and output. The average capital–output ratio of an economy is the stock of capital divided by the annual flow of output (K/Y); the incremental capital–output ratio (ICOR) measures the relation between increments to the capital stock and increase in output ($\Delta K/\Delta Y$ or $I/\Delta Y$). If an investment of $10,000 raises output by $2,500 a year

[6]W. Arthur Lewis, *The Theory of Economic Growth* (1955), p. 208.

[7]See A. K. Sen, "Development: Which Way Now?" *Economic Journal* (December 1983): 750.

into the future, then the capital–output ratio for that particular investment is 4:1. With fluctuations in income and with investment directed toward different sectors of the economy, the average capital–output ratio will differ substantially from the ICOR. From both time-series and cross-section data, there appears to be a strong inverse relation between the growth in output and the value of the ICOR.

In practice, the ICOR may be approximated in a rather crude fashion by simply taking

$$\frac{\Delta K}{\Delta \text{GDP}} = \text{ICOR}_t = \frac{I_{t-1}}{\text{GDP}_t - \text{GDP}_{t-1}}$$

where ΔK is net investment in the previous period and ΔGDP is increase in domestic output between the previous period and the present from national income statistics.

It should be noted, however, that many conceptual difficulties and statistical pitfalls surround the derivation and use of capital–output ratios. A definite causal relationship between the growth of capital and the growth of output cannot be so readily assumed as this discussion may imply. And it is misleading to suppose that the whole of any increase in output is due simply to capital accumulation. Even after it is decided which of the several possible definitions of "capital" and "output" are best to use, and some solution to the problem of valuation is accepted, there remain ambiguities. It is first necessary to distinguish between the average and the marginal capital–output ratios. Even though any change in the average ratio may be expected to be slow, the marginal ratio can vary a great deal more.

It is important to be clear whether all other productive factors that must cooperate with capital are also assumed to increase when capital increases. In an advanced economy, an adequate supply of cooperative factors is likely to exist. The institutional, political, and social prerequisites for development also are present. When using the incremental capital–output ratio under these conditions, it is reasonable to make a *mutatis mutandis* assumption that the supply of necessary factors other than capital is forthcoming. But in a poor country where the cooperative factors tend to be in short supply, and the other prerequisites for development may not yet exist, it is not legitimate to consider an increase in capital as a sufficient condition for an increase in output. Even though investment may be a necessary condition, output may not expand unless

conditions other than the increase in capital supply are also fulfilled. We must also consider explicitly the effect of other variables on output—for example, the supply of trained manpower, the number of entrepreneurs, institutional arrangements, and attitudes. To ignore these other variables or simply to assume that accommodating changes occur, and then to attribute to investment all the increment in output, is to take a too mechanical—and too easy—view of the changes that are necessary for an increase in output.

Exclusive attention to a capital–output ratio may also exaggerate the need for investment because output may be increased by changes in other factors without requiring a sizable amount of investment, or even any additional capital. If, for instance, unutilized capital exists, it is possible to raise output with the fuller utilization of the existing capital stock or without the investment of much more capital. Or there may be considerable opportunity to raise output by applying better methods of production to existing plants. To avoid taking either an overly optimistic view of what can be accomplished by capital accumulation alone, or an overly pessimistic view of how much investment is needed, we should guard against a too simple use of capital–output ratios.

For the purpose of clearly recognizing the changing of circumstances that may occur when additions to the capital stock are made, it is helpful to distinguish between the "net marginal capital–output ratio" and the "adjusted marginal capital–output ratio."[8] The net ratio interprets the marginal capital–output ratio as net of any changes in other factors; it considers the capital–output ratio with a *ceteris paribus* assumption—the supplies of all other factors are held constant. The adjusted ratio, however, refers to what the capital–output ratio would be if it were adjusted to a given specific increase in the supply of other factors; it assumes that investment is accompanied by changes in other output-yielding variables. For a given increment in output, the net marginal capital–output ratio would therefore be higher than the adjusted marginal capital–output ratio. Capital requirements will be underestimated if they are initially based on an adjusted marginal capital–output ratio, but

---

[8] Such a distinction is suggested by Harvey Leibenstein, *Economic Backwardness and Economic Growth* (1957), p. 178.

the other output-yielding factors do not actually accommodate themselves to the growth of capital as expected.

Even in the simplest (but most special) of cases—production coefficients fixed in all sectors and relatively small values for all the other variables that might affect output—the overall marginal capital–output ratio will still not be fixed, because sectoral output may vary with changes in demand. More generally, the overall ratio will vary according to a number of conditions, some of which may allow only a small additional income to be generated when there is more investment, while others may contribute to a large increment in output. Thus the following conditions will tend to make the capital–output ratio high: the sectoral pattern of investment is biased toward heavy users of capital, such as public utilities, public works, housing, industry rather than agriculture, and heavy industry rather than light industry; there is excess capacity in the utilization of capital; other resources are limited, and capital is substituted for these limiting factors; capital is long lived; the rate of technological and organizational progress is low; and investment is for completely new units of production, rather than simply for extensions of existing plant.

In contrast, the marginal capital–output ratio will be low when the composition of output is biased toward labor-intensive commodities; the average life of capital is shorter; the rate of technological and organizational progress is high; and some capital expenditure allows the fuller use of previously unutilized capacity, increases the productivity of labor, provides for capital-saving innovations, opens up new natural resources, or permits the realization of economies of scale.

From such considerations, we must conclude that the marginal capital–output ratio is unlikely to be constant over time. A projected ratio must be estimated over the period for which investment requirements are being calculated. And it may then turn out that there is a wide discrepancy between the actual ratio and the projected ratio.

Despite the statistical difficulties, this analysis does focus on the basic proposition that the growth rate of per capita income can be analyzed in three parts: a savings–income or investment–income ratio, additional income per unit of investment (the incremental capital–output ratio), and population growth rate. The importance of the rate of return on investment, or the efficient use of scarce capital, is attested to by the experience of a number of developing countries that have achieved creditable increases in their investment–income ratios but have not succeeded in attaining a notable increase in the growth rate of per capita income. For example, in Sub-Saharan Africa between 1965 and 1990 the growth rate in per capita GNP was only 0.2 percent, but the investment-income ratio was 15 percent in 1965 and 16 percent in 1990. In India, too, the investment-income ratio was as high as 17 percent in 1965 and 23 percent in 1990, but per capita GNP grew by only 1.9 percent annually between 1965 and 1990. Clearly, it is not sufficient merely to increase the amount of savings and investment: the resources must be invested productively.

IV.B. SOURCES OF CAPITAL FORMATION—NOTE

Whether it is financed from internal or external sources, by noninflationary or inflationary means, the accumulation of capital in any developing economy requires the mobilization of an economic surplus. If investment is to increase, there must be a growing surplus above current consumption that can be tapped and directed into productive investment channels. The different ways of financing capital formation will entail different institutional arrangements (for example, the plowing back of industrial profits into investment would imply a different institutional framework from that of financing through taxation by the state). It should be recognized, however, that the process of capital formation involves three essential steps: (1) an increase in the volume of real savings, so that resources can be released for investment purposes; (2) the channeling of savings through a finance and credit mechanism, so that investible funds can be collected from a wide range of different sources and claimed by investors; and (3) the act of investment itself, by which resources are used for increasing the capital stock.

The first requirement—an increase in the volume of real savings—is of fundamental importance if a higher rate of investment is to be achieved without generating inflation. This crucial step of mobilizing savings should not be confused, however, with the monetary financing of investment. The significance of financial institutions lies in their making available the means to utilize savings. As one study of the role of financial institutions concludes:

However poor an economy may be there will be a need for institutions which allow such savings as are currently forthcoming to be invested conveniently and safely, and which ensure that they are channelled into the most useful purposes. The poorer a country is, in fact, the greater is the need for agencies to collect and invest the savings of the broad mass of persons and institutions within its borders. Such agencies will not only permit small amounts of savings to be handled and invested conveniently but will allow the owners of savings to retain liquidity individually but finance long-term investment collectively.[1]

Although the existence of a more developed capital market and financial intermediaries will aid in the collection and distribution of investable funds, they in no way lessen the need for real saving. The rate of investment that it is physically possible to carry out is limited by saving, and a "shortage of capital"—in the sense of a shortage of real resources available for investment purposes—cannot be solved merely by increasing the supply of finance. Indeed, it is comparatively easy to introduce institutional arrangements to increase the supply of finance, and a lack of finance need not persist as a serious bottleneck. Once a sizable class of savers and borrowers comes into being, financial intermediaries are likely to appear, and lending institutions are readily created. But the creation of new financial institutions is no substitute for the necessary performance of real saving.

It is therefore important to be clear about the various sources from which the necessary savings can be mobilized to provide the wherewithal for capital expenditure. From internal sources, an increase of savings may be generated voluntarily through a reduction in consumption; involuntarily through additional taxation, compulsory lending to the government, or inflation; or finally, by the absorption of underemployed labor into productive work. From external sources, the financing of development may be met by the investment of foreign capital, restriction of consumption imports, or improvement in the country's terms of trade.

An increase in voluntary saving through a self-imposed cut in current consumption is unlikely when the average income is very low. At best, it can be hoped that when income rises, the marginal rate of saving may be greater than the average rate. Instead of relying on voluntary saving, the government will normally have to resort to "forced" saving through taxation, compulsory lending, or credit expansion. The efficacy of credit expansion and its resultant inflationary consequences are discussed in section IV.C.

Issues of taxation can be analyzed from two different perspectives—that of incentives and that of resources. If, as in supply-side economics, one believes that a lack of adequate incentives inhibits investment and growth, then the

---

[1] Edward Nevin, *Capital Funds in Underdeveloped Countries* (1961), p. 75.

tax system should be improved through the granting of additional concessions of various kinds. If, however, insufficient investment and low growth are attributed to a lack of resources, then the tax system should be designed to increase resources available for investment through additional taxation.

Emphasizing the shortage of resources in an LDC, rather than inadequate incentives, Kaldor has stated:

The importance of public revenue from the point of view of accelerated economic development could hardly be exaggerated. Irrespective of the prevailing ideology or the political color of particular governments, the economic and cultural development of a country requires the efficient and steadily expanding provision of a whole host of non-revenue-yielding services—education, health, communications systems, and so on, commonly known as "infrastructure"—which require to be financed out of government revenue. Besides meeting these needs, taxes, or other compulsory levies provide the most appropriate instrument for increasing savings for capital formation out of domestic sources. By reducing the volume of spending by consumers, they make it possible for the resources of the country to be devoted to building up capital assets. . . .

Ruling out inflation as a deliberate instrument, it may be asked: What are the most appropriate taxes that can be relied on for maximum revenue? The question does not admit of any general answer in the widely varying conditions of "underdeveloped" countries. The only feature that is common to them is that they all suffer from a shortage of revenue. This is partly because they have a low "taxation potential"—which may be defined as the maximum proportion of the national income that can be diverted for public purposes by means of taxation. But more important is the fact that the taxation potential in such countries is rarely fully exploited.[2]

A country's "taxation potential" depends on a variety of conditions: the level of per capita real income, the degree of inequality in the distribution of income, the relative importance of different sectors in the economy (cash crops, subsistence agriculture, mining, foreign trade), the political leadership, and the administrative powers of the government. It is generally true that in the lagging LDCs, the actual ratio of tax revenue to national income is less than in the more progressively developing countries and is less than their tax potential. In many countries,

it might be possible to increase the tax effort and approach closer to the tax potential, especially if more effective systems of progressive taxation were to be designed that recognized the inequality in the distribution of income, the taxable capacity of the agriculture sector, and the rising share of industrial and commercial wealth as development proceeds. The saving that is forced by additional taxation, however, will be less than the additional tax revenue to the extent that there is a restriction in private voluntary saving instead of a fall in consumption by the full amount of the tax.

To assess the tax performance of a developing country, we should go beyond a static index, such as the ratio of tax revenue to national income, and introduce more dynamic concepts, such as "tax elasticity" and "tax effort." The "tax elasticity" indicates the income elasticity of the tax system: if the marginal rate of taxation exceeds the average rate, there will be an automatic increase in the ratio of tax revenue to national income as income rises. The "tax effort" measures the political and administrative efforts to increase effective tax rates or the coverage of the tax system.[3]

There is only narrow scope in a poor country for the practice of compulsory saving through the practice of compulsory purchase of nonnegotiable government bonds. Of greater practical significance may be the operation of state marketing boards that have a statutory monopoly over export crops. These boards may compel native producers to save by purchasing the native's produce at prices below world prices.

Finally, another internal source of saving is represented by the "investible surplus" of underemployed labor. If this "investible surplus" is utilized in productive activity, the national output would be increased, and the required savings might be generated from the additional output. It should also be noted that the direct formation of capital through the use of underemployed labor can be obtained by what is termed the "unit multiplier" method.[4] If labor does have zero productivity in agriculture, it can be withdrawn and put to work on investment projects (construction, irrigation works, road

[2]Nicholas Kaldor, "Taxation for Economic Development," *Journal of Modern African Studies* 1, no. 1 (1963): p. 7, and "Will Underdeveloped Countries Learn to Tax?" *Foreign Affairs* (January 1963).

[3]For a fuller discussion, see Richard M. Bird, "Assessing Tax Performance in Developing Countries: A Critical Review of the Literature," in *Taxation and Economic Development,* ed. J. Toye (1978).

[4]James S. Duesenberry, "Some Aspects of the Theory of Economic Development," *Explorations in Entrepreneurial History* (December 1950): 65–67.

building, and the like) without a drop in agricultural output. Most of the payment of the additional wages will be directed toward foodstuffs, and agricultural income will rise. The higher income may then be taxed, and the tax revenue can finance the investment project. If taxes are levied in an amount equivalent to the additional wage-bill, there will be no change in consumption but income will have risen by the amount of the investment. When the investment projects are completed, there will be an increase in output, and some of this increase in income may also be captured through taxation. How much scope there is for this method of direct investment in kind depends on the ease with which labor can be attracted to investment projects, the degree to which labor can form capital directly without requiring additional investment expenditure, the absence of an adverse effect on agricultural output, and the capacity to offset the investment with taxation.

When we look to external sources of financing development, the capital assistance provided by foreign economic aid and the private investment of foreign capital are of most importance. Chapter V examines the contribution of foreign aid and private foreign investment. (See sections V.B and V.E.) Some contribution may also come from a restriction of consumption imports. Provided that there is not simply a switch in expenditure from imports to domestic consumption, the level of savings will rise. Imports of capital goods can then be increased, and this will represent a genuine addition to the rate of capital formation: the increase in the flow of investment goods imported is, in this case, matched by an increase in the flow of domestic income saved. If, however, consumers increase their domestic spending when they cannot import, then resources will be diverted from domestic capital production in favor of the increased domestic consumer spending, and the increase in imports of investment goods will be offset by reduced domestic investment. An increase in saving is therefore necessary if the restriction of consumption imports is to result in an increase in total net capital formation.[5]

A similar analysis applies to changes in the terms of trade. When export prices rise, the improvement in the country's commodity terms of trade makes it possible for the country to import larger quantities of capital goods. But again, this source of capital formation will not be fully exploited unless the increment in domestic money income due to the increase in export proceeds is saved. If the extra income merely increases consumer spending on home-produced or imported goods, the opportunity for new saving is lost. The extra resources made available by the improvement in the terms of trade must be withheld from consumption and directed into investment.[6] A corresponding increase either in voluntary saving or in taxation is necessary to give the country a command over additional imports of investment goods.

A special word should be added about consumption and capital formation. We have implied that present consumption is at the expense of future output; as usually stated, it is believed that restraints on consumption are needed to divert resources from the production of more consumer goods to capital accumulation. But is this always true? Can a case be made that in the context of a developing country, an increase in current consumption may actually lead to an expansion in future production?

When the level of living is as low as it is in an LDC, the distinction between consumption and investment becomes overdrawn insofar as private consumption may well have a positive marginal productivity. The reason is not that consumption will augment resources, but that a rise in consumption may improve labor quality and efficiency and hence allow better use to be made of the existing labor resources. The consumption of health-improving goods should improve the ability to work and increase the intensity of work. The greater consumption of foodstuffs that aid nutrition is especially significant, for it has now been established by medical scientists that improper food, especially a diet low in protein, can in itself impair the physical and mental development of children from birth.[7]

In an empirical study of the impact of components of "labor quality" on the growth of output, Galenson and Pyatt have demonstrated that an increase in consumption may improve labor quality. The components of labor quality examined were calories per head, investment in dwellings, higher education, health indicators, and social security benefits. Of these various

[5]See Ragnar Nurkse, *Problems of Capital Formation in Underdeveloped Countries* (1953), pp. 111–16.

[6]Ibid., pp. 97–103.

[7]National Academy of Sciences, National Research Council, *Pre-School Malnutrition, Primary Deterrent to Human Progress* (1966); N. S. Scrimshaw, "Infant Malnutrition and Learning," *Saturday Review,* 16 March 1968, pp. 64–68.

components, better diet was shown to have the greatest impact on labor productivity and growth of output.[8]

Certain policy implications follow from the view that private consumption may be productive. In its efforts to raise the community's marginal rate of saving, the government should put more emphasis on taxation and on business saving through profits rather than on individual saving through a curtailment of consumption. But there should at the same time be an improvement in the pattern of consumption, so that it might contribute as directly as possible to increasing efficiency. What is needed is a selective increase in consumption. Luxury consumption, for instance, should be taxed, and the import re-

[8]W. Galenson and G. Pyatt, *The Quality of Labour and Economic Development in Certain Countries* (1964), pp. 15–19, 87–88.

Another study has shown that in the rural areas of Asia, an insufficient intake of calories may result in inadequate work effort after the peak season. See Harry T. Oshima, "Food Consumption, Nutrition, and Economic Development in Asian Countries," *Economic Development and Cultural Change* (July 1967): 390–91. See also Food and Agriculture Organization, *Nutrition and Working Efficiency* (1962), and Gunnar Myrdal, *Asian Drama* (1968), pp. 1912–19. But Elliott J. Berg argues that under conditions of migrant labor and a joint-family system, higher income does not necessarily lead to better nutrition. He also contends that better nutrition is not sufficient to improve individual efficiency unless there are also present the necessary motivation and essential cooperative factors with labor ("Major Issues of Wage Policy in Africa," in *Industrial Relations and Economic Development,* ed. A. M. Ross [1966], pp. 190–96).

placement of consumer goods should be limited insofar as this policy has become suboptimal. There should, however, be an increase in consumption that favors the rural population if this will help overcome the agricultural bottleneck. In this connection, we should note Myint's observation that "incentive consumer goods" can be a useful means of encouraging peasants to enter the money economy: a rise in the aspiration to consume these goods may lead to the sale of a food surplus and may encourage better methods of production that will increase the food surplus in the future.[9]

In its most general terms, the principle that consumption can be productive raises the complex problem of specifying criteria for intertemporal efficiency in consumption, and then shaping policy instruments to meet these criteria. If we take the largest view, this brings us to the very frontier of multisectoral intertemporal models, where we should attempt to interrelate an optimal consumption policy with an optimal capital policy. The problem of the total amount of investment that can be made in the future then becomes a function of investment allocation and the pattern of consumption in the present period. We need not be overwhelmed at this point by the complexities of such a model, but we will return in Chapter X to the problem of optimal investment allocation.

[9]Hla Myint, *The Economics of the Developing Countries* (1964), p. 88.

EXHIBIT IV.1. Structure of Demand

	General Government Consumption		Private Consumption		Gross Domestic Investment		Gross Domestic Savings	
	1970	1991	1970	1991	1970	1991	1970	1991
Low-income economies	10 *w*	10 *w*	71 *w*	64 *w*	21 *w*	27 *w*	20 *w*	27 *w*
China and India	8 *w*	10 *w*	68 *w*	59 *w*	24 *w*	29 *w*	24 *w*	31 *w*
Other low-income	13 *w*	12 *w*	76 *w*	71 *w*	15 *w*	22 *w*	12 *w*	17 *w*
Mozambique	—	20	—	90	—	42	—	−10
Tanzania	11	16	69	96	23	22	20	−11
Ethiopia	10	21	79	78	11	10	11	0
Uganda	*a*	8	84	93	13	12	164	−1
Guinea-Bissau	20	17	77	85	30	30	3	−3
Nepal	*a*	10	97	85	6	19	3	5
Burundi	10	16	87	85	5	17	4	−1
Chad	27	20	64	97	18	8	10	−17
Madagascar	13	9	79	92	10	8	7	−1

The table header spanning row reads: Distribution of Gross Domestic Product (percent)

EXHIBIT IV.1. (*continued*)

| | Distribution of Gross Domestic Product (percent) | | | | | | | |
| | General Government Consumption | | Private Consumption | | Gross Domestic Investment | | Gross Domestic Savings | |
	1970	1991	1970	1991	1970	1991	1970	1991
Sierra Leone	12	11	74	85	17	11	15	4
Bangladesh	13	11	79	86	11	10	7	3
Lao People's Dem. Rep.	—	11	—	—	—	—	—	—
Malawi	16	14	73	77	26	20	11	9
Rwanda	9	20	88	78	7	13	3	1
Mali	10	12	80	82	16	23	10	6
Burkina Faso	9	17	92	79	12	23	−1	4
Niger	9	8	89	86	10	9	3	7
India	9	12	75	69	17	20	16	19
Kenya	16	17	60	63	24	21	24	19
Nigeria	8	13	80	65	15	16	12	23
China	8	9	64	52	28	36	29	39
Haiti	10	—	83	—	11	—	7	—
Benin	10	12	85	85	12	12	5	3
Central African Rep.	21	15	75	86	19	11	4	−1
Ghana	13	9	74	83	14	16	13	8
Pakistan	10	13	81	75	16	19	9	12
Togo	16	15	58	74	15	19	26	10
Guinea	—	10	—	76	—	18	—	14
Nicaragua	9	21	75	89	18	21	16	−10
Sri Lanka	12	10	72	77	19	23	16	13
Mauritania	14	9	56	81	22	16	30	10
Yemen, Rep.	—	28	—	70	—	13	—	2
Honduras	11	10	74	70	21	24	15	20
Lesotho	12	18	120	95	12	93	−32	−13
Indonesia	8	9	78	55	16	35	14	36
Egypt, Arab Rep.	25	10	66	83	14	20	9	7
Zimbabwe	12	21	67	61	20	22	21	18
Sudan	21	—	64	—	14	—	15	—
Zambia	16	10	39	78	28	13	45	12

Middle-income economies
  Lower-middle-income

Bolivia	10	15	66	77	24	14	24	9
Côte d'Ivoire	14	18	57	67	22	10	29	15
Senegal	15	13	74	78	16	14	11	9
Philippines	9	9	69	72	21	20	22	19
Papua New Guinea	30	24	64	63	42	29	6	13
Cameroon	12	14	70	71	16	15	18	15
Guatemala	8	6	78	84	13	14	14	10
Dominican Rep.	12	9	77	77	19	17	12	14
Ecuador	11	8	75	70	18	22	14	22
Morocco	12	15	73	68	18	22	15	17
Jordan	—	23	—	78	—	21	—	−1
Peru	12	5	70	82	16	16	17	13
El Salvador	11	11	76	88	13	14	13	1
Congo	17	22	82	58	24	11	1	20

(*continued*)

EXHIBIT IV.1. (*continued*)

| | Distribution of Gross Domestic Product (percent) | | | | | | | |
| | General Government Consumption | | Private Consumption | | Gross Domestic Investment | | Gross Domestic Savings | |
	1970	1991	1970	1991	1970	1991	1970	1991
Syrian Arab Rep.	17	—	72	—	14	—	10	—
Colombia	9	11	72	66	20	15	18	23
Paraguay	9	8	77	75	15	25	14	17
Jamaica	12	12	61	68	32	20	27	20
Romania	—	14	—	57	—	34	—	29
Namibia	—	27	—	64	—	14	—	9
Tunisia	17	16	66	66	21	23	17	18
Kyrgyzstan	—	16	—	50	—	34	—	34
Thailand	11	10	68	58	26	39	21	32
Turkey	13	17	70	66	20	20	17	17
Poland	—	20	—	58	—	21	—	22
Bulgaria	—	13	—	73	—	13	—	15
Costa Rica	13	16	74	61	21	23	14	22
Algeria	15	16	56	48	36	30	29	36
Panama	15	21	61	72	28	15	24	7
Chile	13	10	70	66	16	19	17	24
Iran, Islamic Rep.	16	13	59	77	19	20	25	10
Mauritius	14	12	75	65	10	28	11	23
Czechoslovakia	—	*a*	—	67	—	31	—	—
Malaysia	16	14	58	56	22	36	27	30
Upper-middle-income	**11** *w*	—	**66** *w*	—	**24** *w*	—	**23** *w*	—
Botswana	20	—	78	—	42	—	2	—
South Africa	12	21	63	58	28	16	24	21
Lithuania	—	16	—	63	—	21	—	21
Hungary	10	13	58	67	34	19	31	19
Venezuela	11	9	52	67	33	19	37	23
Argentina	10	4	68	81	22	12	22	15
Uruguay	19	13	83	70	*a*	13	−1	17
Brazil	11	*9*	69	*70*	21	*20*	20	*30*
Mexico	7	8	75	72	21	23	19	20
Belarus	—	*a*	—	71	—	30	—	—
Russian Federation	—	20	—	41	—	39	—	40
Latvia	—	10	—	46	—	34	—	43
Trinidad and Tobago	13	15	60	59	26	18	27	26
Gabon	20	17	37	41	32	26	44	42
Estonia	—	10	—	65	—	29	—	25
Portugal	14	—	67	—	26	—	20	—
Oman	13	35	19	38	14	17	68	26
Puerto Rico	15	15	74	64	29	16	10	22
Korea, Rep.	10	11	75	53	25	39	15	36
Greece	13	20	68	72	28	17	20	8
Saudi Arabia	20	—	34	—	16	—	47	—
Yugoslavia	18	*7*	55	72	32	*21*	27	*21*

EXHIBIT IV.1. (*continued*)

	Distribution of Gross Domestic Product (percent)							
	General Government Consumption		Private Consumption		Gross Domestic Investment		Gross Domestic Savings	
	1970	1991	1970	1991	1970	1991	1970	1991
Low- and middle-income	**11** *w*	—	**68** *w*	—	**23** *w*	**24** *w*	**21** *w*	—
Sub-Saharan Africa	12 *w*	15 *w*	73 *w*	71 *w*	17 *w*	16 *w*	16 *w*	14 *w*
East Asia and Pacific	9 *w*	10 *w*	66 *w*	55 *w*	26 *w*	35 *w*	25 *w*	36 *w*
South Asia	10 *w*	12 *w*	76 *w*	72 *w*	16 *w*	19 *w*	14 *w*	17 *w*
Europe and Central Asia	—	—	—	—	—	—	—	—
Middle East and North Africa	18 *w*	—	57 *w*	—	19 *w*	—	25 *w*	—
Latin America and Caribbean	10 *w*	13 *w*	70 *w*	—	21 *w*	19 *w*	20 *w*	—
Severely indebted	**10** *w*	—	**72** *w*	—	**22** *w*	**20** *w*	**21** *w*	—

Note: Countries in italics: no current estimates of GNP per capita.

Figures in italics: years other than those specified.

a = General government consumption figures are not available separately; they are included in private consumption, etc.; *w* = weighted average.

Source: World Bank, *World Development Report 1993* (1993), pp. 254–55.

IV.C. INFLATIONARY FINANCE AND ITS EFFECTS

IV.C.1. Financing by Money Creation*

A government finances its expenditures by money creation when it causes them to be covered by additional currency or bank deposits that are transferable and generally acceptable in domestic transactions. This form of finance neither reduces the amount of money held by residents, as taxation and domestic nonbank borrowing do, nor provides the government the means of paying for additional imports, as borrowing abroad does.

No elaborate demonstration is needed to show that government spending financed by net money creation results in an increase in aggregate spending. The process does not diminish the expenditures of enterprises and households, and the government spending will stimulate further increases in expenditures for goods and services and perhaps also the acquisiton of additional financial claims by those who receive the additional money as it is paid out and passes from hand to hand.

The increase in aggregate spending will result in some combination of additional output, higher prices, and larger imports in relation to exports. When idle productive capacity exists, increased spending may stimulate additional output up to the point at which capacity is fully used. While unemployed and underemployed people are numerous in many less developed countries and manufacturing plants frequently operate below their rated capacity, unused productive capacity is much smaller in most cases than may be supposed. Usually the unemployed lack needed skills, many idle plants cannot efficiently produce the goods that consumers want to buy, and other plants must import more materials and fuel to raise their output.

Inflation and balance-of-payments deficits are the most usual results of financing government expenditures by money creation. Since balance-of-payments deficits are constrained by the availability of foreign exchange reserves and ex-ternal credit (which are not increased), inflation will be the main effect when money creation is large and continuing.

Noninflationary Finance by Money Creation

A growing economy will require more money to facilitate its transactions and to serve as a liquid asset. The counterpart of the increased money stock may include lending to the government by the central bank and the commercial banks. If the increase in the money stock—and the counterpart in the form of loans and investments of the banking system—does not exceed the quantity that enterprises and households desire to hold at stable prices, money creation to finance the government will not be inflationary.

The relations can be clarified by reference to a consolidated, and condensed, balance sheet of the banking system, comprising the central bank and the commercial banks (deposit money banks).

Assets	*Liabilities*
Foreign assets (net claims on nonresidents)	Money Currency and coins Deposits
Domestic credit Claims on enterprises	Other deposits (quasi money)
Claims on households Claims on government (net) Other domestic assets (buildings, etc.)	Other liabilities Capital

Since the totals of assets and liabilities (plus capital) must always be equal, any bank net lending to government must be accompanied by an equivalent reduction in another asset—claims on nonresidents or on resident enterprises and households—or by an increase in liabilities— usually monetary liabilities in the form of currency and deposits. For convenience, foreign assets are shown net of the banking system's liabilities to nonresidents, and claims on government are net of government deposits.

*From Richard Goode, *Government Finance in Developing Countries,* The Brookings Institution, Washington, D.C., 1984, pp. 212–13, 215–22, 225–27. Reprinted by permission.

How much the banking system can lend to the government and other borrowers without causing inflation depends on how much money people are willing to hold at stable prices. That question has prompted a great deal of theorizing and quantitative analysis. Early versions of the quantity theory of money asserted that normally people wish to hold money balances equal to a constant fraction of their income. If other items in the consolidated balance sheet remain constant, that assertion implies that bank credit and money can increase at the same rate as real income without causing inflation. This version of behavior is now regarded as a special case, but it is a useful first approximation if no other information is available.

According to a more sophisticated formulation, the quantity of money that people wish to hold depends on income, wealth, the rate of return on other assets, and institutional factors, including the degree of monetization of the economy and payments practices. Also allowance has to be made for the current price level and any expected change in it.[1]

In condensed form this relation may be written algebraically as follows:

$$M/P = b(Y, P^*, W, r, F),$$

where M is money, P is the current price level, Y is real income, P^* is the expected rate of change in the price level, W is wealth, r is the rate of return on financial assets other than money, and F stands for other relevant factors mentioned above. The value M/P—often called real cash balances—is expected to vary positively with Y and W and negatively with P^* and r. In the special case in which P^* is zero (implying that no change in the price level is expected) and W, r, and F are unchanged, M/P varies only with Y.

Recently considerable effort has been devoted to studying the relationship between M/P and Y—real money balances and real income—in developing countries. Attempts have been made to isolate the relationship by statistically holding constant the estimated influence of certain other variables and assuming that wealth, the degree of monetization, and payments practices change so slowly that they can safely be ignored in an

analysis intended to cover no more than a few years. It has been hypothesized that money holdings are a luxury and hence will display an income elasticity above 1. Although findings differ, many statistical studies report elasticities between 1 and 2 (with respect to real per capita income), and some support can be adduced for a figure of the order of 1.5.

To see the relevance of the income elasticity of the demand for money for the question of the scope for noninflationary financing by money creation, it is necessary to combine the elasticity estimate with the ratio of money to income in a base period. This ratio differs among countries. In the majority of developing countries, the ratio of money (narrowly defined as currency plus demand deposits) to gross domestic product falls in the range 0.10 to 0.20. Combined with an income elasticity of 1.5, this implies that per capita money holdings will grow by an amount equal to 0.15 to 0.30 of an increase in per capita income. If, for example, real GDP per capita increases by 4 percent, real money holdings will increase by an amount equal to 0.6 percent to 1.2 percent of per capita GDP. In the absence of changes in any of the other relevant variables, the banking system can extend credit up to that amount without causing inflation. The ratio of money holdings to GDP tends to be somewhat higher in developed countries than in developing countries, but the income elasticity of the demand for money may be lower.

These figures illustrate a method of analysis and give an impression of possible orders of magnitude. A careful and detailed study would be needed to establish the basis for an estimate for a particular country. It appears, nevertheless, that in conditions that may be reasonably representative of those existing in developing countries, the amount of money that can be created annually without causing inflation—or adding to it—is only a small fraction of GDP. Furthermore, the government is not the only claimant for the credit counterpart of money creation. As the balance sheet of the banking system shows, the total has to be allocated among credit to domestic enterprises and households and net foreign assets as well as credit to government. In a growing economy, additional provision should normally be made for the nongovernmental uses. If the government attempts to appropriate the entire margin for noninflationary credit expansion, production and international trade will be handicapped or total credit expansion will exceed the noninflationary amount.

[1] Milton Friedman, "The Quantity Theory of Money—A Restatement," in Friedman, ed., *Studies in the Quantity Theory of Money* (University of Chicago Press, 1956), pp. 3–21; Ralph C. Bryant, *Money and Monetary Policy in Interdependent Nations* (Brookings Institution, 1980), pp. 53–57, and the references there cited.

Inflationary Finance

When financing of government expenditures by money creation exceeds the noninflationary limit, total spending in the country becomes greater than production valued at stable prices. Prices rise and the balance of payments tends to go into deficit. The noninflationary limit of money creation is not rigidly fixed, and there may be some delay in reactions. Especially if prices have been stable in the recent past, people may temporarily add to their money holdings, and many transactions may take place at the old prices for a time. The experience of inflation in most countries during the past decade, however, probably has made people sensitive to rising prices and has shortened the lags in adjustments.

The use of newly created money gives the government command over real resources, while the price rise reduces the purchasing power of each monetary unit. Broadly viewed, the holders of money involuntarily give up the equivalent of the real resources obtained by the government. Economists often call the process the imposition of an inflation tax and the resources so transferred the real revenue from the tax, though in a strict sense no tax is imposed.

If inflation had no effect on real income or the amount of money that people wish to hold in relation to income, prices would rise in proportion to the ratio of the actual money stock to the noninflationary stock. For example, if the noninflationary limit to money creation were a 6 percent increase in the money stock and the actual increase were 16.6 percent, the price level would rise by 10 percent ($116.6/106 = 1.1$). If all the new money were used by the government, it would obtain real resources equal to 15.1 percent of the initial money stock ($16.6/1.1 = 15.1$). To take another example, if government spending financed by money creation were equal to 112 percent of the initial stock and the noninflationary limit were 6 percent, prices would double and the government would gain real resources equivalent to 56 percent of the initial money stock. These figures, of course, reflect the assumption that, within the range under consideration, the ratio of money holdings to nominal income, hence the velocity of circulation of money, is constant.

Money holdings, however, will not remain constant in relation to income as inflation proceeds. Before long people will come to expect that prices will continue to rise and will adjust their behavior accordingly. In particular, they will recognize that they are suffering losses of purchasing power by holding money and will reduce their cash balances in relation to their income and wealth. In terms of the equation given earlier, P^* will no longer be zero but will be positive and will exert a negative influence on M/P, causing it to be smaller for any given values of the other variables. That is another way of saying that the velocity of circulation of money will increase. These adjustments will tend to accelerate the inflation and induce further adjustments that will perpetuate it.

The beginning of inflation does not immediately cause a flight from money. The use of money is a great convenience, and, as Keynes observed during the hyperinflations in several European countries after World War I, people will bear a cost before giving it up. Those who have studied cases of extreme inflation agree that, even after people come to understand what is occurring, they will continue to hold and use money. The function of money as a store of liquid wealth weakens first and may virtually disappear if rapid inflation persists. The use of money in current transactions continues in the face of prolonged and rapid inflation, though the velocity of circulation may become very high. Barter comes to be practiced, even in industrial countries, and foreign currency and other media of exchange (such as cigarettes) are used. Toward the end of a hyperinflation, domestic money is used only for small transactions or where creditors cannot prevent extinction of their claims by payment in depreciating money. Government claims are likely to be discharged in domestic money after its use becomes exceptional for other purposes.

The decline in the ratio of money to income reduces the real gain that the government can obtain from inflationary finance. To evaluate quantitatively the potential yield of financing by money creation, it would be necessary to know—or to guess—how people's expectations about inflation are formed and how these influence their money holdings. Expectations are not directly observable but may be inferred from behavior. In econometric studies, it has been assumed that people project into the future the price increases of the current period and the recent past. The value of P^* has been measured as an average of these rates (usually weighted exponentially so that the most recent period has the greatest influence on the estimate). Many studies have passed quickly over difficulties due to unstable expectations and adjustment lags and have estimated the sensitivity of money holdings to expected inflation (M/P to $P*$) on the assumption that inflation has been maintained at a steady rate long enough to condition expectations and for actual money holdings to be equated with desired holdings at that inflation rate. For simplicity, the studies usually have assumed that inflation has no effect on real income, wealth, or other variables that affect the demand for money and the inflation that will result from a given amount of money creation.

Even with such simplifying assumptions, estimates of the sensitivity of real money holdings to expected inflation differ widely. Most of the estimates indicate that in developing countries the amount of real resources obtainable from money creation increases up to steady-state inflation rates somewhere between 33 percent and 200 percent a year and declines at higher inflation rates. The size of these transfers in relation to income would depend on the ratio of money holdings to income in the absence of inflation. For a country in which the ratio is 15 percent at zero inflation, the maximum yield would range from about 2 percent to 11 percent of GDP. The width of the ranges suggests the uncertainty that surrounds the subject and the difficulty of using the analysis for policy purposes. Critics have argued that the figures greatly overstate the maximum potential yield of inflationary finance (and the range of values) but have not settled on other estimates.

A sudden and unexpected burst of inflation will be especially effective in diverting resources from money holders. Time is required for people to appreciate what is occurring and to adjust their money holdings. Hence the existence for a short time of inflation rates higher than those that would yield the maximum amount if steadily maintained does not necessarily indicate that the government would have gained more real resources from a smaller amount of money creation. It is also possible that the gains from continued but irregular inflation over a period of years will exceed those obtainable from a steady inflation rate equal to the average rate.[2]

In the preceding paragraphs, it has been implicitly assumed that the government obtains the proceeds of all money creation. In the usual

banking system, however, central bank lending to the government creates high-powered money (currency and deposits at the central bank), which serves as a reserve for commercial banks and allows them to expand their loans to enterprises. The banks and their customers will share in the real yield of inflation unless steps are taken to prevent this by raising reserve requirements against commercial bank deposits, requiring the banks to buy government securities, or other measures. The potential leakage to the banks and their customers will be greater the larger the proportion of the money stock consisting of commercial bank deposits as distinguished from currency.

The Impact of Inflation on the Budget

Inflation also affects tax revenue and government expenditures. These effects must be taken into account in evaluating the possible net fiscal contribution of financing by money creation.

In regard to tax revenue, two important factors are the elasticity of tax liabilities with respect to nominal income (that is, income in current prices) and the length of time between tax accrual and tax payment, or the collection lag. Inflation will reduce the real value of liabilities for specific taxes and all other taxes with an elasticity below 1. On the assumption that real income is not affected, inflation will have little if any impact on the real value of liabilities for broad sales taxes, the short-run elasticity of which is approximately 1. It will increase the real value of liabilities for taxes such as progressive income and profits taxes with elasticities above 1. Elasticities with respect to nominal income may differ from those with respect to real income. For example, an ad valorem excise tax on a luxury commodity may have a high elasticity in relation to changes in real income but an elasticity of approximately 1 in relation to changes in the price level and in nominal income. Delays in adjusting exchange rates often reduce the elasticity of import duties with respect to both nominal income and real income.

If tax liabilities are not indexed, the real value of tax collections will be reduced because of the collection lag. At any given inflation rate, the longer the lag, the greater the reduction in the real value of collections; and with any given lag, the faster the inflation, the greater the reduction. For example, if prices are rising by 1 percent a month, a three-month delay in tax collection will

[2]Harry G. Johnson, "A Note on the Dishonest Government and the Inflation Tax," *Journal of Monetary Economics*, Vol. 3 (July 1977), pp. 375–77.

reduce the real value of the payment by about 3 percent, a six-month delay, by almost 6 percent. With inflation at 5 percent a month, the loss of real value will be 13.6 percent with a three-month collection lag and 25.4 percent with a six-month lag. The characterization of a collection lag as long or short is rather arbitrary. In the context of inflation, perhaps a lag of more than three months may be considered long.

The Consequences of Inflation

Beyond its fiscal impact, inflation has far-reaching consequences. Even if everyone correctly anticipated inflation, it would cause inconvenience and additional transaction costs that would be associated with a reduction of money balances. It would also cause inefficiencies in production and distribution related to the premium on holding real assets rather than money claims. These are the only real social costs recognized by some econometric models, which assume that the actual and expected inflation rates are identical and that real income is not affected.

In reality, of course, people's ability to foresee inflation and to protect themselves against it differs greatly. Except perhaps in countries in which inflation has been going on at a rapid rate for a long time, there are many medium-term and long-term contracts that are fixed in money terms. Unanticipated inflation causes the real value of contractual receipts and payments to diverge from the expected value and brings about an arbitrary redistribution of income and wealth between creditors and debtors. It also distorts relative tax burdens. These effects are now widely recognized, and arrangements to mitigate them have been adopted in some countries. Nowhere, however, have the arrangements become so complete and effective that the redistributive effects of inflation are confined to a transfer of real purchasing power from money holders to the government and other recipients of the credit that is the counterpart of money creation.

There is no conclusive evidence that inflation either speeds or retards economic growth. Examples can be cited of rapid growth or of stagnation combined with inflation or with price stability. This, of course, does not prove that inflation has no effect on growth. Growth is the result of many factors, which in the aggregate may outweigh any influence that inflation exerts on the process.

It has been asserted that inflation promotes development by redistributing income from workers and peasants to capitalist entrepreneurs, thereby fostering saving and investment. Although such shifts of income may occur, especially in the early stages of inflation, they do not continue if inflation is prolonged. Wages come to be increased more frequently and at certain periods may advance more rapidly than prices. If agricultural prices do not keep pace with other prices, farmers resort to subsistence production and barter or migrate to cities. Holders of real estate, foreign currency, and speculative inventories often gain more than the owners and managers of productive enterprises.

Inflation, especially erratic inflation, distorts economic calculations and makes planning more difficult. This effect must be very harmful at high inflation rates. The loss of real income may not be accurately measured by available statistics, because price and output statistics may be unreliable in such conditions.

In the past, inflation must have retarded the development of financial intermediaries such as savings banks, building societies, and life insurance companies that collect and lend the savings of persons who have neither the knowledge nor the opportunity to make direct investments efficiently. Although this adverse effect is still present, it has become less serious in countries that have permitted the intermediaries to adopt indexing or flexible interest rates that compensate for inflation.

Perhaps the most harmful economic consequences of inflation actually are attributable to the bad policies that commonly accompany it. Governments frequently impose price controls in an effort to repress inflation or lessen the hardships that rising prices impose on consumers. Food prices and rents are especially likely to be regulated, and sometimes the controls are much more extensive. Although such controls may be tolerably effective for short periods and in special circumstances, they usually result in shortages, black markets, and inefficient production and distribution. Often urban transportation fares and public utility rates are held down, and public enterprises suffer losses, subsidies from the budget are needed, and service deteriorates.

The consequences of inflation for international trade and payments usually impose economic costs. Most theoretical and econometric treatments implicitly assume either a closed economy or a flexible exchange rate moving in step with the price level, but in fact there are no closed economies and the majority of developing countries maintain fixed exchange rates subject to periodic adjustments. Because of inertia and a desire to avoid price increases for imports and exports, governments usually do not move the exchange rate in proportion to inflation. Imports rise while exports fall, and quantitative restrictions on imports and foreign exchange controls must be instituted or tightened to contain the balance-of-payments deficit. For imports, shortages and black markets may become even more prevalent than for price-controlled domestic goods. The lack of imported materials, fuel, and spare parts may prevent factories, transportation systems, and farms from operating at capacity. Export production will be severely handicapped.

IV.C.2. Inflation and Development Policy*

The first question to be discussed is whether the mobilization of an economy's resources by development policy inevitably involves inflation. It is contended here that some degree of inflation—but a moderate degree only—is the logical concomitant of efficient economic mobilization. The argument rests on two propositions. One is that so long as inflation proceeds at a rate low enough not to disturb seriously the general confidence in the stability of the value of money its effects are primarily to redistribute incomes, and to do so to an extent that does not involve serious social consequences, rather than to produce significant misallocations of resources, such as those which occur when people come to expect inflation and seek to protect themselves from it by holding goods instead of money and by using political means to safeguard their real incomes. The other proposition is that, owing to the various rigidities and immobilities characteristic of any economy, but particularly of underdeveloped economies, upward movements of wages and prices can help to reallocate labour and resources and to draw labour out of traditional or subsistence sectors into the developing sectors of the economy. It is important to note that this proposition, like the first, presumes a general expectation of stability in the value of money, as a precondition for the offer of higher wages and prices to serve as an inducement to mobility.

The second proposition implies that some inflationary pressure in the economy will assist the task of mobilizing resources for development; the first implies that such inflationary pressure will not introduce offsetting distortions causing significant real losses to the economy as a whole, but will instead mainly involve transfers of income within the economy, the social consequences of which will be small enough to be acceptable. Efficient policy-making will therefore involve arriving at a trade-off between the mobilizing and redistributive effects of inflation that will involve some positive rate of inflation. The indicated optimum rate of inflation is likely to be significantly higher for an underdeveloped than for an advanced economy for two reasons: first, the sophisticated financial system of an advanced economy provides many more facilities for economizing on the use of money in face of expected inflation; and second, the superior mobility of resources of an advanced economy implies that the increase in total output achievable by inflationary means is relatively much smaller. Thus one might expect that whereas "tolerable" price stability in an advanced economy is frequently defined as a rate of inflation of no more than 1 to 2 percent a year, the tolerable degree of stability for an underdeveloped economy might be in the range of a 4 to 6 percent annual rate of price increase. (Harberger has suggested that a 10 percent annual rate of inflation represents the outside limit of inflation justifiable by this line of argument.)[1] This analysis, of course, relates to purely domestic considerations and ignores the balance-of-payments or exchange-rate implications of internal price trends.

The foregoing remarks relate to the question of inflation as a consequence or aspect of economic development policy, and to the argument that some degree of inflation is the necessary

*From Harry G. Johnson, "Is Inflation the Inevitable Price of Rapid Development or a Retarding Factor in Economic Growth?" *Malayan Economic Review*, Vol. 11, No. 1 (April 1966), pp. 22–28. Reprinted by permission.

[1]Arnold C. Harberger, "Some Notes on Inflation," in Werner Baer and Isaac Kerstenetzky (eds.), *Inflation and Growth in Latin America*, Homewood, Ill.: Irwin, 1964.

price of rapid development. It has been argued that a modest rate of inflation is a logical part of an efficient development policy, in the sense that the "price" may purchase gains in efficiency of resource allocation and utilization that outweigh the costs. The argument now turns to the second problem raised by the question, the effectiveness or otherwise of inflationary financing of development programmes.

The main theoretical arguments for inflationary development policies derive from two systems of economic thought, the Keynesian theory of income and the quantity theory of money. The Keynesian approach to the question (which derives from the Keynes of the *Tract* and the *Treatise* as much as from the Keynes of the *General Theory*) argues that inflation will promote growth in two ways: by redistributing income from workers and peasants, who are assumed to have a low marginal propensity to save, to capitalist entrepreneurs, who are assumed to have a high marginal propensity to save and invest; and by raising the nominal rate of return on investment relative to the rate of interest, thus promoting investment. Neither of these arguments, however, is either theoretically plausible or consistent with the facts, at least so far as sustained inflationary processes are concerned. Both rest on the arbitrary and empirically unsupported assumption that entrepreneurs realize that inflation is occurring, whereas the other members of the economy do not, or at least do not realize it fully. As to the first, the theoretical prediction is that all sectors of the economy the prices of whose services are upwards-flexible will come to anticipate inflation, so that no significant redistributions of income will take place; this prediction accords with the mass of the available evidence. As to the second, the theoretical expectation is that free-market interest rates will rise sufficiently to compensate holders of interest-yielding assets for the expected rate of inflation; this expectation also accords with the mass of the available evidence. This argument for inflation, therefore, is valid only under two possible sets of circumstances: first, in the early stages of an inflationary development programme, while the mass of the population (especially the workers and the savers) still has confidence in the stability of the value of money; and second, when inflationary financing is accompanied by governmental policies of holding down the wage and interest costs of business enterprise. Such policies would generate distortions in the allocation of resources, which might offset any benefits to growth from the inflationary policy; in particular, the contrary view has been argued that inflation will discourage the supply of saving for investment.

The quantity theory approach, on the other hand, adopts the more realistic assumption that in a sustained inflationary process the behavior of all sectors of the economy will become adjusted to the expectation of inflation, and that consequently the effect of inflation will be, not to redistribute income from workers or savers to capitalist entrepreneurs, but to redistribute it from the holders of money balances—who are the only losers from an inflation that is anticipated—to the monetary authorities who issue money the real value of which steadily depreciates. Inflation imposes an "inflationary tax" on holdings of money, which consists in the real resources that the holders of money have to forego each period in order to restore the real value of their money holdings. The presence of this tax, in turn, encourages the public to attempt to evade the tax by reducing their holdings of money, shortening payments periods, holding inventories of goods instead of cash, and so forth; these efforts involve a waste of real resources and a reduction of real income, representing the "collection cost" of the inflationary tax. On the other hand, the real resources collected by the inflationary tax are available for use in the development programme; and if they are used for investment, the inflationary policy may accelerate economic growth. It should be noted, however, that in the transitional stages of an inflationary development policy, or in the process of acceleration of such a policy, whatever contribution to growth there is may be outweighed by the increased waste of resources produced by the increase in the inflationary tax.

In practical experience, resort to the inflationary tax as a method of financing economic development is generally prompted by the inability of the developing country to raise enough revenue by taxation and by borrowing from the public to finance its development plans, either as a result of the low income and taxable capacity of the economy, or more commonly as a result of inability to command the necessary political consensus in support of the necessary sacrifices of current income. Unfortunately, the same characteristics of underdevelopment that limit the capacity to finance development by orthodox fiscal methods also place rather narrow limits on the possibility of financing development by inflation. In particular, underdevelopment implies a relatively smaller use of money than is common in advanced countries, and therefore a relatively smaller base on which the inflationary tax can be levied.

Before discussing this point in detail, it is appropriate to refer to a related question that figured large in the development literature of about a decade ago, the question of the extent to which development can be financed by monetary expansion without producing inflationary consequences. The answer, clearly, is that such financing can be safely pursued up to the limit set by the growth of demand for money consequent on the expected growth of the economy at stable prices, plus the growth of demand for money associated with the monetization of the subsistence sector (where relevant), minus the portion of the growth in the money supply that must be created against private debt. The magnitude of the resources that can be made available for financing development by this means, however, depends on the magnitude of the absolute increase in the money supply permitted by these factors or, to put it another way, on the rate of growth of the demand for money, the ratio of money to income, and the portion of the additional money that can be used to finance public spending. Thus, for example, with a rate of growth of demand for money of 6 percent, half of which can be used to finance public spending, the budget deficit financed by monetary expansion would be 3 percent of the initial money supply. If the ratio of money supply to national income were in the neighborhood of two-fifths, as is common in advanced countries, this would make 1.2 percent of national income available for development investment; if, on the other hand, the ratio of money supply to national income were in the lower neighborhood of one-fifth, as is common in underdeveloped countries, only one half of one per cent of national income would be available for development investment.[2] The difference in the order of magnitude of the money-to-income ratio explains both why budget deficits in underdeveloped countries are more frequently associated with inflation, and

why in such countries inflationary financing of development is more frequently resorted to, than in advanced countries.

In the same way as it limits the scope for noninflationary deficit financing of development, the restricted use of money in underdeveloped countries limits the extent to which inflation can make resources available for economic development through the inflationary tax. Ignoring the possibilities of noninflationary financing by monetary expansion due to the growth and monetization of the economy, the yield of the inflationary tax as a proportion of national income will be the product of the money-to-income ratio, the rate of inflation, and the proportion of the increase in the money supply captured for financing development. Thus, with the assumed money-to-income ratio of one-fifth and an assumed capture rate of one-half, a 10 percent rate of inflation would secure 1 percent of national income for the development programme, and so on. The money-to-income ratio, however, is not insensitive to the rate of inflation, but is on the contrary likely to decrease appreciably as the rate of inflation rises, thereby setting limits to the possibilities of development finance by these means. Further, it should be noted that insofar as development financing depends on a growth of demand for money resulting from monetization of the economy, inflation is likely to reduce that growth by inhibiting monetization, so further reducing the net amount of resources gathered for development finance through inflation. . . .

The circumstances in which inflation is resorted to in underdeveloped countries, however, are far from the most favorable conceivable, and their inflations are extremely likely to proceed in such a way, and to be accompanied by such other economic policies, as to exercise a serious retarding influence on economic growth. Specifically, inflationary financing may impede growth in three major ways, each contrary to the assumptions of the inflationary tax model.

In the first place, contrary to the assumption that prices throughout the economy adjust freely to inflation, the government of a developing country employing inflationary development policies is likely to be under strong political pressure to protect important sectors of the community from the effects of inflation, through control of food prices, rents, urban transport fares, and so on. Such controls inevitably distort the allocation of resources within the economy,

---

[2]The illustrative numbers used are derived from J. J. Polak, ''Monetary Analysis of Income Formation and Payments Problems,'' *International Monetary Fund Staff Papers*, November 1957, Table on p. 25.

and particularly their allocation to private investment in growth. Fixing of low prices for food inhibits the development of agricultural production and the improvement of agricultural technique; control of rents, on the other hand, may unduly foster the construction of new housing to accommodate those who cannot find rent-controlled housing or to enable landlords to evade rent controls. All these policies tend to promote urbanization, which involves expenditure on social overhead and may increase the numbers of the urban unemployed. Moreover, control of prices of food, and particularly of fares on state-owned transport facilities, may involve the state in explicit subsidies on the one hand and budget deficits on the other, so that the proceeds of the inflationary tax are wasted in supporting the consumption of certain sections of the population rather than invested in development. Such phenomena are widely observable in the underdeveloped countries of the world. . . .

Second, contrary to the assumptions of the inflationary tax model, inflation typically does not proceed at a steady and well-anticipated rate, but proceeds erratically with large politically determined variations in the rate of price increase. These variations in the rate of inflation divert a great deal of the effort of private business into forecasting and speculating on the rate of inflation, or hedging against the uncertainties involved. They also destroy the possibility of rational calculation of small margins of profit and undermine the incentives to strive constantly to reduce costs and improve performance, which striving is the key to the steady increase of productivity in the industrially advanced nations.

Finally, the inflationary tax model assumes either a closed economy or a country on a floating exchange rate system. In reality, countries—especially underdeveloped countries—are exposed to competition in and from the world economy, yet they display a strong propensity to maintain fixed exchange rates and to defend them to the limit of their exchange reserves, bor-

rowing powers, and ability to use exchange controls. In this kind of setting inflation introduces a progressive tendency toward exchange rate overvaluation, balance-of-payments difficulties, and resort to increasing protectionism, which in turn results in the diversion of resources away from export industries and toward high-cost import-substituting industries, and a consequent loss of economic efficiency. While the appearance of growth may be generated by the establishment of import-substitute industries, the reality may be lost in misallocation of resources produced by protectionism and the inefficiency of exchange control procedures. Moreover, eventually the increasing overvaluation of the currency is likely to force a devaluation, coupled with a monetary reform involving drastic domestic deflation. This experience, in addition to the immediate disturbing effects of deflation in interrupting the growth of the economy, has the long-run effect of damaging the stability and confidence of expectations on which the process of investing in the growth of the economy depends.

To summarize, this paper has argued the following propositions. First, an efficient development policy should plan on some modest degree of inflation as a means of more fully mobilizing the economy's resources; in this limited sense, inflation is an inevitable price of rapid development. Second, while a policy of financing development by deliberate inflation has strong attractions theoretically and politically, the possibilities of stimulating economic development by these means are quite limited. Third, inflationary development policies in practice are unlikely to achieve this stimulating effect, but on the contrary likely to retard economic growth, by distorting the allocation of resources and wasting the inflation-gathered development resources on consumption, by increasing uncertainty and reducing incentives for innovation and improvement, and through their balance-of-payments effects by fostering the inefficiencies of protectionism and exchange control.

EXHIBIT IV.2. Inflation

GDP Deflators	Average 1975–84	1985	1986	1987	1988	1989	1990	1991	1992
Developing countries	24.2	35.1	28.2	35.1	53.7	61.9	65.4	35.7	38.7
By Region									
Africa	17.1	14.5	15.1	16.8	21.3	21.9	16.9	32.2	40.2
Asia	7.7	6.8	8.3	9.2	13.8	11.5	7.6	8.5	7.4
Middle East and Europe	19.4	20.5	20.1	21.7	26.1	21.9	23.8	23.8	20.6
Western Hemisphere	58.9	130.5	86.6	124.6	245.0	363.3	478.9	135.8	169.9
By Analytical Criteria									
Fuel exporters	18.8	18.7	26.3	35.8	36.2	18.6	17.1	16.9	16.0
Nonfuel exporters	26.4	41.3	28.9	34.9	59.5	78.1	83.8	41.8	46.3
Market borrowers	35.9	61.9	41.8	55.1	94.7	122.8	131.7	50.3	59.7
Official borrowers	18.2	23.8	27.7	27.1	35.5	25.7	23.5	34.4	32.4
Countries with recent debt-servicing difficulties	42.0	81.7	62.8	83.6	143.0	183.7	226.6	92.4	111.2
Countries without debt-servicing difficulties	10.7	9.8	8.1	9.2	14.3	13.7	9.8	11.0	10.6

Source: International Monetary Fund, *World Economic Outlook* (May 1993): 139.

EXHIBIT IV.3. Average Annual Rate of Inflation (percent), Latin American Countries

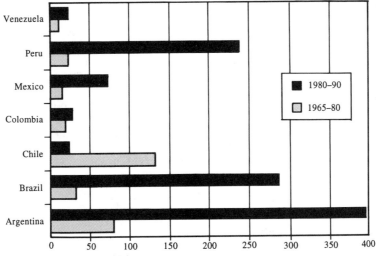

Source: World Bank and IMF data.

Comment: Monetarism versus Structuralism

In contrast to the monetarist view of inflation, a structuralist school has been influential in Latin America and has argued that inflation is unavoidable because of structural rigidities of supply and demand, in particular the inelasticity of the food supply and the inelasticity of exports. Thus cost-push inflation comes from having to undertake import-substitution policies, endure a rise in agricultural prices, deterioration of the terms of trade, and devaluation of the exchange rate. Structuralists believe that changes through import substitution, industrialization policies, and agrarian reform rather than orthodox monetary policies are necessary to achieve stability without sacrificing growth.

For readings on inflation in Latin America, consult Roberto de Oliveira Campos, "Two Views on Inflation in Latin America," in *Latin American Issues*, ed. Albert O. Hirschman (1961); Alfredo J. Canavese, "The Structuralist Explanation in the Theory of Inflation," *World Development* (July 1982);

Susan M. Wachter, *Latin American Inflation: The Structuralist–Monetarist Debate* (1976); and Vicente Galbis, "Inflation: The Latin Experience," *Finance and Development* (September 1982).

The structuralist and monetarist explanations of inflation are discussed together with a review of the theoretical and empirical evidence on inflation in LDCs, in C. H. Patrick and F. I. Nixson, "The Origins of Inflation in LDCs: A Selective Review," in *Inflation in Open Economies*, ed. M. Parkin and G. Zis (1976). See also Maxwell J. Fry, *Money and Banking in Economic Development* (1988), chap. 4, and Lance Taylor, *Varieties of Stabilization Experience: Towards Sensible Macroeconomics in the Third World* (1988).

Comment: Stabilization Policy

The adverse consequences of inflation, especially in Latin America, have prompted renewed emphasis on macroeconomic management to stabilize the economy. A number of policy lessons can be drawn from the experience of countries that have adopted policy reforms to reduce inflation.

Empirical studies based on both cross-country regressions and case studies show that a country's macroeconomic policies matter for its rate of long-run growth and development. Countries that manage short-run macroeconomic policies are able to grow faster. For summaries of the evidence see Stanley Fischer, "Role of Macroeconomic Factors in Growth," *Journal of Monetary Economics* (December 1993); Ross Levine and David Renelt, "A Sensitivity Analysis of Cross-Country Growth Regressions," *American Economic Review* (September 1992); and Richard N. Cooper, *Economic Stabilization in Developing Countries* (1991).

The orthodox approach to a stabilization program concentrates on a restrictive monetary policy and fiscal discipline. In contrast, heterodox stabilization policies include wage and price freezes, exchange rate pegging, and deindexation measures.

Latin American countries, such as Argentina, Brazil, Mexico, and Peru, introduced heterodox policies in the 1980s in the hope of breaking the self-fulfilling expectations of continued inflation. For some lessons from heterodox stabilization programs, see "Liberalization with Stabilization in the Southern Cone of Latin America" [special issue], *World Development* (August 1985), and Miguel A. Kiguel and Nissan Liviatan, "Progress Report on Heterodox Stabilization Programs," *Finance and Development* (January 1992). The latter argue that "the costs in terms of high interest rates, slow recovery of growth, and loss in external competitiveness—have been much higher than originally anticipated. Moreover, the removal of controls has proved difficult, there has been a loss in exchange rate flexibility, and the process of consolidating low inflation has been time-consuming" (p. 22).

If a country also wants to liberalize its foreign trade sector (by reducing import restrictions and providing incentives for exports), it is generally recommended that a stabilization program precede liberalization. This is because successful liberalization depends on credibility and on having a stable and competitive real exchange rate. See Vittorio Corbo and Jaime de Melo, "Lessons from the Southern Cone Policy Reforms," *World Bank Research Observer* (July 1987).

IV.C.3. IMF Adjustment Policies*

The principal objective of the International Monetary Fund (IMF), as defined by its articles of agreement, is the correction of balance-of-payments disequilibrium in member countries. The policies the IMF recommends to reduce the degree and duration of external and internal imbalances that give rise to balance-of-payments difficulties must, however, be set within the context of achieving and maintaining price stability and satisfactory rates of economic growth.

In analyzing IMF policies designed to achieve these multiple objectives, it is useful first to consider the circumstances in which the IMF is called upon to assist in designing an adjustment program and in providing temporary financial support for it. The need for a stabilization program, whether supported by the IMF or otherwise, arises when a country experiences a per-

*From Jacob A. Frenkel and Mohsin S. Khan, "Adjustment Policies and Economic Development," *American Journal of Agricultural Economics* (August 1990): 815–18. Reprinted by permission.

sisting imbalance between aggregate domestic demand (absorption) and aggregate supply, which is reflected in a worsening of its external payments position. As long as foreign financing is available, the relative expansion of domestic demand can be sustained for an extended period, although at the cost of a widening deficit in the current account of the balance of payments, a loss of international reserves, rising inflation, worsening international competitiveness, and a heavier foreign debt burden. However, this situation cannot last indefinitely. Eventually, the country would lose international creditworthiness, and the cessation of foreign credits would necessitate adjustment. This forced adjustment may be very disruptive for the economy. The aim of the IMF under these circumstances is to provide for an orderly adjustment, and the first task is to stabilize the economy—lower the rate of inflation, restore international competitiveness, reduce the current account deficit, and check the loss of international reserves—by correcting the macroeconomic imbalances that led to these problems. Once macroeconomic stability is assured, then policies to expand the productive capacity of the economy and improve the efficiency with which resources are utilized are more likely to be successful. Experience and theory both suggest that, to achieve adjustment with growth, such a pattern of sequencing of macroeconomic and structural policies is warranted.

Although growth is a central element in the IMF's objectives, it should be stressed that the IMF is not a development agency. Its mandate is to provide temporary financial support and not development aid. Consequently, the IMF does not possess a ''development paradigm'' as such. Nevertheless, by establishing macroeconomic equilibrium in the economy, the IMF sets the necessary foundation on which development is based. Furthermore, the IMF has increasingly emphasized structural reforms in its policy advice. While this change stems from the recognition that economic stability cannot be regained without basic institutional and economic change, such reforms have a direct bearing on long-term growth and the structural transformations that make up the development process. . . .

What then are the policies that would be considered to achieve balance-of-payment viability in the context of low inflation and improved growth performance? In general, most economists would tend to subscribe to the following set of measures typically included in IMF-supported adjustment programs:

(a) *Monetary restraint* aimed at reducing the growth of absorption and the rate of inflation. Generally speaking, a fall in the supply of credit will lower absorption directly through wealth effects and, by pushing up interest rates, cause the interest-sensitive components of aggregate demand to decline. The reduction in aggregate demand would tend to improve the current account of the balance of payments and put downward pressure on inflation. However, in curtailing monetary and credit expansion, care must be taken to prevent crowding the private sector out of the credit markets, so that government borrowing from the banking system, including the central bank, frequently must be restricted.

(b) *Interest rate policies* are employed to set rates at positive real levels, but not so high as to choke off investment and possibly cause the collapse of financial institutions. Thus in general there is a consensus that real interest rates should be positive but low.

(c) *Reduction in the fiscal deficit* through cuts in government expenditures and/or increases in taxes. Theory and substantial empirical evidence can be used to support the proposition that a reduction in the fiscal deficit tends to reduce aggregate demand. *Ceteris paribus*, this improves the balance of payments and reduces inflationary pressures in the economy. Furthermore, because developing-country governments rely heavily on bank financing of fiscal deficits, an improvement in the budgetary position reduces the amount of liquidity being injected into the system. For both these reasons—reducing the claim on resources in the economy and restricting monetary expansion—cutting the fiscal deficit becomes an essential, if not the most critical, element of an adjustment program. However, in choosing the method for reducing the deficit, the relationship between public and private saving and public and private investment also must be considered. For example, under some circumstances, an increase in public saving may lead to a partially offsetting fall in private saving. Also, private and public investment may be complementary to the extent that the public sector provides the necessary infrastructure; thus, reductions in public investment may have adverse effects on private investment and growth.

(d) *Exchange-rate action* to ensure a real exchange rate that would improve international competitiveness and create the incentive to expand the production of internationally tradable goods. The main theoretical aspects of devaluation are well known, but determining the appropriate change in the nominal exchange rate to achieve a target real exchange rate as well as predicting the effects of the policy are not easy tasks. Without a comprehensive general equilibrium model to specify relevant relationships among the exchange rate, trade and capital flows, and inflation, short-cut methods based on considerable judgments must be used. For example, it is common in developing countries to employ variants of purchasing power parity (PPP) calculations to assess the extent of the overvaluation of the domestic currency. It is assumed that a particular real exchange rate was "right" at some base period; and, using this as a target, nominal exchange-rate action and supporting policies (monetary, fiscal, incomes) to attain it are employed. This approach is susceptible to error and should be used with appropriate caution. By and large, the limited empirical evidence available supports the hypothesis that devaluation will work in the direction of improving competitiveness and the balance of payments. While it is sometimes argued that devaluation leads to a recession, there are doubts about the generality of this proposition.

(e) Policies to *reduce external debt* if it is perceived as currently unsustainable or to limit foreign borrowing if it is likely to become unsustainable in the future. To assist countries in a debt crisis situation, the IMF has undertaken a number of steps: providing additional financing from its own resources, facilitating rescheduling of the existing stock of debt, encouraging additional lending to the country from both official and private sources, and participating in market-based debt reduction schemes. All of these efforts are made with the idea that the country eventually will return to normal borrowing relations. In general, external-debt policies in IMF-supported programs are aimed at easing the liquidity problems of countries facing a debt problem and helping them maintain their long-run growth path.

(f) Introducing *structural reforms*, that is, financial sector reforms, producer pricing policies, trade liberalization, tax reforms, etc., to make the economy more flexible and efficient. Such structural reforms can help in the adjustment process by expanding productive capacity of the economy. Nevertheless, structural reforms are not without difficulties. First, by their very nature, distortions tend to be microeconomic,

and microeconomic policy measures suffer from certain theoretical weaknesses. Very soon one runs up against the propositions of the theory of the second best, and it is not always clear whether removing only some distortions will produce an increase in efficiency and welfare in the economy overall. Second, the issue of time lags is very relevant to the IMF as a short-term lender. Substantial time may be needed for structural policies to show positive benefits, and adequate foreign financing is usually essential in the interim to ensure that the adjustment is as costless as possible. Finally, there is the sequencing of reforms. Unfortunately, economic theory provides little guidance on the optimal sequence, and it is difficult to generalize from country-specific experiences. What does emerge from experience is that domestic goods and labor markets should be liberalized prior to trade liberalization. Similarly, it has been argued that the liberalization of the trade account of the balance of payments should precede that of the capital account because asset markets adjust more rapidly than goods markets. The opposite sequence could result in large capital movements that could adversely affect the real exchange rate and domestic monetary conditions. Sound theoretical and empirical reasons also suggest that macroeconomic stabilization should generally precede large-scale domestic financial sector liberalization to prevent interest rates from overshooting. Other than these broad lessons, little more can be deduced; accordingly, one needs to proceed on a case-by-case basis with the pace and sequencing of structural reforms. . . .

Establishing that IMF programs are conducive to macroeconomic stability is not the end of the story; the link between macroeconomic stability and long-run growth and development also must be shown. Linking macroeconomic stability to long-run growth is not easy. The economics profession lacks a fully satisfactory theory that directly relates macroeconomic policies and structural reforms to growth, other than through changes in the rate of capital formation. Therefore, macroeconomic policies are judged by their effects on investment, under the argument that policies with a favorable effect on investment are good for growth. But growth involves many factors other than physical investment. In general, growth of output will depend, *inter alia*, on growth of the labor force, changes in the efficiency of investment, changes in human capital (education, skills, and health), and technological developments. It is not known as yet how precisely economic policies of the type contained in IMF programs will affect these other determinants. There is presumption, supported by limited empirical evidence, that policies to achieve macroeconomic stability will affect growth in a positive fashion because they create a climate which is conducive to investment, increased domestic savings, and a larger flow of foreign financing, all of which will tend to raise the growth rate. Beyond these generalities, relatively little is known.

In the absence of a suitable theory to test, we conducted a purely statistical analysis of the relationship between long-run growth and macroeconomic stability. To this end, simple regressions were run relating the growth of real GDP to various indicators of macroeconomic stability using cross-section data for 101 developing countries averaged over the period 1973–88. These indicators were chosen arbitrarily because there is no generally accepted measure of macroeconomic stability. The following alternatives were included: inflation, the variance of inflation, the fiscal balance (as a percentage of GDP), the percentage change in the real exchange rate, and the variance of the real exchange rate.

These equations are not intended to explain growth; they should be interpreted only as simple tests of association. As such, one should not be overly concerned with the general lack of goodness-of-fit one observes in the estimated equations. With regard to the relationships themselves, there is uniform support for the hypothesis that growth and alternative measures of macroeconomic stability are positively related in this large sample of developing countries. The countries with higher average growth rates over the period 1973–88 also tended to have lower average rates of inflation, lower variance of inflation rates. better average fiscal positions, larger average depreciations of the real effective exchange rate, and lower variance of real effective exchange rates.

Taken at face value, the regressions confirm the view that countries that have adopted appropriate policies aimed at keeping the inflation rate low, not allowing overvaluation of the currency, and maintaining fiscal responsibility, and, furthermore, making these policies predictable, have also managed to attain higher long-run growth rates. One could, therefore, argue that to the extent that IMF policies establish macroeconomic equilibrium in the economy, they play a positive role in the growth and development process.

IV.D. NONINFLATIONARY FINANCE

IV.D.1. Private Saving*

The late Sir Arthur Lewis, in his celebrated paper on economic development with unlimited supplies of labor, argued that the

central problem of economic development is to understand the process by which a community which was previously saving and investing 4 or 5 percent of its national income or less converts itself into an economy where voluntary saving is running at about 12 to 15 percent of national income or more. This is the central problem because the central fact of economic development is rapid capital accumulation (including knowledge and skills with capital). (Lewis, 1954, p. 155)

If published international data are reliable, *the process* of conversion must be complete already! According to the IMF, the developing countries saved (and invested at home) 23.7 percent of their GDP during 1983–90 (IMF, 1991, table 12). Assuming capital consumption allowances of 10 percent, the implied net saving rate (i.e., ratio of net saving to net domestic product) is 15.3 percent. On the other hand, although the average annual rate of growth of GDP per capita in developing countries accelerated from about 2 percent in the 1950s to roughly 3.5 percent in the 1960s, since the oil shock of 1973, according to the World Bank data, the record is one of deceleration from 3.9 percent during 1965–73 to 2.5 percent during 1975–80 and 1.6 percent during 1980–89 (World Bank, 1991, table 1). This deceleration in per capita growth was not because of any acceleration in the rate of growth of population; on the contrary, there is some evidence of a *decline* in the latter from about 2.5 percent per annum during 1965–73 to about 2.1 percent during 1973–80. Thus the increasing rate of saving (and of investment, not including accumulation of human capital) has not resulted in any increase in the rate of growth of income. Of course, in a neoclassical model with *indefinitely* diminishing marginal returns to capital as capital accumulates relative to labor, the *steady-state growth* rate is independent of the investment rate. But even in that model during the transition to the steady-state, the investment rate influences the growth rate. As no developing country is likely to be in a steady-state by definition, either the link between increasing saving and development that Lewis postulated was not operative or the data on saving as well as income growth are unreliable, or both!

In Lewis's model the primary force that brought about an increase in the saving rate was the redistribution of income in favor of the classes that saved (which he viewed as the top decile of the income distribution) rather than growth of per capita incomes per se. The data on distribution of income are unavailable for many countries, and even where available, their conceptual basis, coverage, and reliability are known to be problematic. These problems notwithstanding, there is no evidence of a massive shift in the distribution of income in favor of the rich that would account for the observed increase in aggregate saving rates. Another influential strand in the early development literature placed the state at the center stage of the development process. The state in the paradigm, among other things, was to acquire an increasing share of national output (through taxation and surpluses of public enterprises) and to save and invest a substantial portion of what it acquired. Of course, if what has come to be known as Ricardian Equivalence holds, then the private sector in its saving decisions would take into account and offset the saving of the public sector, leaving the aggregate rate at the same level regardless of the extent of public sector activity. But even if one were to ignore Ricardian Equivalence for the reason that there is little empirical support for it in the data from developing countries (Haque and Montiel, 1989), public sector saving, if anything, does not appear to have increased significantly in the last four decades. In either case, one has to look for an explanation in the behavior of the private sector for the measured rise in aggregate saving rates.

Within the private sector, saving by households is usually distinguished from the saving (i.e., retained earnings) by corporate and unincorporated enterprises. If the analogue of Ricar-

*From T. N. Srinivasan, "Saving in the Development Process," in James H. Gapinski, ed., *The Economics of Saving* (Kluwer Academic Publishers, 1993), pp. 279–87. Reprinted by permission.

dian Equivalence holds, that the enterprise is merely a veil, then once again any changes in enterprise saving would be offset by household saving so that the aggregate saving in the private sector as a whole would remain unchanged. If capital markets are active and efficient with extensive financial intermediation taking place, an enterprise would have no incentive to retain and invest in itself a part of its earnings unless, of course, the returns to such investment are comparable to the best available in the market. The same applies to a household—its savings need not be invested in household enterprises (e.g., farm, household production of nonfarm products or service for the market, and the like). In particular, a household would not have to accumulate savings prior to investing in its enterprise or buying a house or consumer durable or any investment activity that is lumpy. It would instead borrow from the market and service the debt from future earnings. Thus the existence and efficiency of financial markets affect the saving and investment process.

The complete absence of a market for claims or resources available at different dates in the future, claims that can be traded for one another and for claims on current resources through arm's-length transactions among anonymous agents, is extreme. Equally extreme is the assumption of a complete set of markets for all such claims from here on for all dates into the indefinite future, the markets being competitive and efficient so that no opportunity for arbitrage remains in equilibrium. The real world is at neither extreme, the situation in the less-developed countries perhaps being closer to the former extreme and that in the industrialized world to the latter. This makes the analysis of saving in less-developed countries somewhat complex not only in theory but more so empirically. One has to account for the imperfect functioning of credit markets and allow for the possibility that intertemporal transactions such as saving, lending, and borrowing may involve agents known to each other and be combined with other transactions between the same two agents. The limited availability of financial intermediation means that the saving and investment decisions have to be considered jointly. For example, in the absence of a mortgage market, a decision to buy a house means a decision to accumulate the purchase price through prior savings. Also, given limited financial intermediation, household production opportunities through farm and nonfarm activities and transactions across generations within the same household, and so on, are likely to be much more important in household saving and investment decisions than in developed countries.

In the absence of opportunities to provide for one's retirement through the market for annuities and through nonmarket arrangements such as state-organized social security, individuals have to rely in part on their progeny or kin for old-age support. This means that fertility decisions would be made jointly with saving and investment decisions. This is not to imply that intergenerational transfers and implicit contracts are not important in developed countries.

Besides markets for dated claims on resources, the existence and the functioning of markets for risk are relevant for saving decisions. Indeed, one of the major motives for saving is the precautionary motive; households save and accumulate some assets that can be sold to maintain consumption in the future when there are adverse shocks to income. If insurance markets exist and function effectively, a household can smooth its consumption even though incomes are subject to random shocks by buying an insurance contract. Even if insurance markets do not exist, if the credit markets function well and a household has access to such markets, it can maintain consumption and tide over a temporary adverse shock in income by borrowing and expect to repay the debt when it experiences a favorable shock. The absence or imperfect functioning of credit markets will tend to reinforce the precautionary motive: The anticipated inability to borrow whenever an income fall is experienced in the future is an argument for accumulating assets when times are good. The absence of well-functioning credit markets thus affects the ability of a household to transfer resources over time as well as across uncertain states of nature relating to its income. Whether greater uncertainty about income, in a well-defined sense, leads to greater precautionary saving and analogously whether greater uncertainty about returns to investment increases saving are issues discussed in the literature. A large proportion of households in less-developed countries earn their incomes from agriculture directly or indirectly. Because agriculture is an inherently uncertain activity, the role of uncertainty in saving and investment decisions of households is particularly important in such countries.

Any credit transaction by definition involves an exchange separated by time. The possibility is real that the agent obligated to pay at a future date may renege, either because he did not put the resources received earlier to such use as would have generated the wherewithal to repay or because he willfully defaults in spite of having the ability to repay. Thus default risk and moral hazard have to be taken into account by a lender who cannot observe and monitor the actions of a borrower. Whether a creditor can get a loan contract enforced against a borrower and a borrower can ensure that he is left with some means of survival in the event of his inability to meet his obligations to the creditor depend on the legal system, particularly the laws relating to bankruptcy and limited liability. Also laws against usury or even charging of any interest would constrain the operation of credit markets. The legal system for enforcement of contracts is likely to be weak in the early stages of development. This weakness can inhibit saving because such savings lent to others are not safe.

Households in the aggregate would save if those who save actually save enough to offset the dissavings of other households. For example, if the population of households is stationary in number and age structure, and each household experiences the same income profile over its lifetime and optimally chooses a constant consumption stream whose present value equals that of its income at the market rate of interest, then in the aggregate there will be no net saving. Depending on the income profile, allowing the number of households to change or income profile to shift exogenously over time would generate saving. The simplest version of a model describing the optimal saving decision of an individual is one in which the individual lives for just two periods ($t = 1, 2$) and receives an exogenous income y_t in period t. His preference over consumption c_t ($t = 1, 2$) in the two periods is described by a concave utility function $u(c_1, c_2)$. He faces an exogenous interest rate r at which he can invest his savings (or borrow for financing his dissavings) in the first period. Thus his problem is to maximize $u(c_1, c_2)$ subject to the constraint $c_1 + Rc_2 = y_1 + Ry_2 \equiv w$, where $R = 1/(1 + r)$ and w is wealth or the present value of the income stream. Saving in the first period is ($y_1 - c_1$). At an optimum in which the individual consumes a positive amount in each period, the marginal rate of substitution—that is, the ratio u_2/u_1 of the marginal utilities $u_t(t = 1, 2)$—will equal R.

R is the price of future consumption relative to present consumption. It is also the present value (in terms of present income or consumption) or a unit of future income or the wealth per unit of future income. Thus an increase in the interest r, by decreasing R, makes future consumption c_2 cheaper relative to c_1. Thus, for given wealth, c_2 will go up. On the other hand, a decrease in R reduces wealth and thus would reduce c_2 as long as future consumption is normal. The net effect on c_2 of an increase in r is therefore ambiguous. If c_2 goes down, then clearly c_2R goes down, as R decreases with an increase in r. Even if c_2 goes up, if the elasticity of c_2 with respect to R is less than unity, the product c_2R will go down as r increases. Thus if c_2R goes down by more than the fall in wealth, then $c_1 = w - c_2R$ will go up and hence saving, $s_1 = y_1 - c_1$, will fall. If c_2R goes down by less than the fall in wealth or if it goes up, then c_1 will fall and saving will rise. All these events are well known. Leaving aside for a moment the facts that for a two-period model saving of period 1 is dissaved in period 2 and that whether there is net saving in the aggregate depends on whether there is growth in the population, its implications for policy, particularly in developing countries, are important for several reasons.

First, a very influential strand of the literature going back to Gurley and Shaw (1967), McKinnon (1973), and more recently Fry (1987) has argued that in many developing countries a policy of financial repression through ceilings on interest rates and requirements that commercial banks hold a specified proportion of their investment portfolio in the form of public debt and soon, discourages saving and that financial liberalization would increase saving. Such liberalization would almost certainly raise the *return* on saving but, as is clear from the two-period model, it is not certain in *theory* that it would raise the *volume* of saving. Whether the elasticity of saving with respect to the real interest rate is positive is an *empirical* question.

Second, if one moves away from the unrealistic assumption that the financial markets are well integrated, then the issue becomes even more complex. Lack of integration means that there would be a *distribution* of interest rates corresponding to different segments of the market. Once again, in theory, integrating and unifying such markets through policy may raise or lower the return to saving as compared with its mean value prior to integration, and even if it does go up, the aggregate volume of savings need not go up. One has to look to empirical analysis for answers.

Third, a feature of credit markets in developed as well as developing countries is the problem arising from information asymmetry between borrowers and lenders; the moral hazard in the use of borrowed funds and adverse selection of projects proposed to lenders for financing. A basic insight of the literature (Stiglitz and Weiss, 1981) on this problem is that equilibrium in such markets may well be characterized by quantitative rationing of credit rather than one of the interest rate adjusting to equate demand and supply. In developing countries, the rationing equilibrium arises both for reasons of moral hazard and adverse selection but also because the interest rate charged by formal institutions is often fixed by the government at a level below the market clearing level. However, informal credit arrangements, which in some countries are sufficiently extensive and organized to be termed *informal credit markets*, coexist with the formal institutions. Those who are denied credit altogether or are not given as much credit as they would like to have at the fixed formal sector interest rate turn to informal credit. Clearly, given this market segmentation, the spillover of demand from the formal to the informal market, and the possibility that informal credit transactions may be tied to transactions in other markets between the same agents, public policy intervention in the credit market, say for encouraging saving, might fail to do so or have other unintended and even deleterious consequences. This is just another illustration of the theory of the second best: If an initial equilibrium is characterized by distortions in several markets, intervening to remove one distortion while leaving others in place can be welfare worsening.

An implication of the possibility of an individual's being denied or rationed credit is that she cannot smooth consumption in the face of fluctuating income to the desired extent. In turn her consumption (and savings) would be more responsive to (responsive only to) current income (responsive in the case of her having no access to credit at all). A growing macroeconometric literature in the developed countries is testing the significance of liquidity constraints to smoothing of aggregate consumption. The simplistic assumption of these models, that the population of agents consists of two groups, one set of identical agents (the so-called life cycle or permanent income consumers) who are not li-

quidity constrained and another set, again of identical agents (the so-called Keynesian or current income consumers) who are constrained, is laughably extreme. Given the heterogeneity of agents and the range of possibilities of self-financing through purchases and sales of physical assets (land, farm animals, jewelry, and the like) that they have, it is unlikely that the popular but simplistic macroeconometric model would be appropriate for the analysis of aggregate saving behavior of households in developing countries.

Finally, in an economy open to foreign capital inflows, domestic investment can be financed in part by such inflows and, equally, part of domestic savings can be invested abroad. If the world capital market is well integrated and efficient so that investable capital freely moves across national boundaries seeking the highest return, there should be no correlation between domestic saving and domestic investment. Yet, puzzlingly, Feldstein and Horioka (1980) found such a correlation in their study of 21 countries over the period 1960–74. Since then, others have tried to reexamine and explain why the Feldstein–Horioka puzzle may not be a puzzle after all! The role of foreign capital in the context of development has been recognized from the early days of development economics. The then popular two-gap model (Chenery and Bruno, 1962) revolved around the twin roles of external capital, for example, in supplementing domestic savings in financing investment and in adding to export earnings in paying for imports. An issue that generated controversy and some empirical analysis in an attempt to resolve it was whether domestic saving was exogenous to foreign capital inflow so that a unit of inflow was translated into a unit of additional investment or whether it was endogenous so that a unit of inflow generated less (respectively more) than a unit of additional investment if it was a substitute (respectively complement) for domestic savings.

More recently the problem of capital flight from developing economies has been the focus of attention. Such flight is induced by public policies such as taxation and threats of expropriation that depress returns to domestic investment and make the returns riskier as well. Whether capital once flown out of a country can be induced to come back would depend on the credibility of policy reform. Credibility of proposed policy reform is achieved, of course, by definition if the government can (credibly!) precommit to pursuing reforms even when an incentive to deviate arises in the future. But such precommitment comes at the cost of flexibility to respond to unforeseen future events that might call for revising the reform program. The problem is the private sector's difficulty in distinguishing between flexibility and flip-flops in adherence to a reform program. At the very least, the private sector may take considerable time to be convinced of the seriousness of the government's intention to implement reforms and until then would have little or no response to reform. Thus flight capital might return, if at all, only after the credibility of the reform is established. Thus an empirical analysis that does not allow for this lag might wrongly conclude that private saving and portfolio choices do not respond to incentives.

To sum up, first, there are serious conceptual problems as well as measurement errors and biases in the data on saving, investment, and income of developing countries. . . . Second, although aggregate savings and investment rates seem to have increased significantly, the link between them and growth of income appears to be more complex than was originally thought. It was noted also that the interaction between household, corporate, and public saving depends on the extent to which households, in making their own saving decisions, allow for corporate decisions regarding earnings retention and the future tax implications of public decisions to accumulate (or retire) public debt. Also whether household saving responds positively to an increase in the rate of interest (or more generally to an increase in the rate of return to assets in which savings are invested) and whether households are constrained in their ability to smooth their consumption in the face of fluctuating income are primarily empirical issues, the former

depending on certain elasticity parameters and the latter on the existence and efficient functioning of the markets for credit and insurance.

References

Chenery, Hollis, and Michael Bruno (1962). "Development Alternatives in an Open Economy." *Economic Journal* 72: 79–103.

Feldstein, M. S., and C. Horioka (1980). "Domestic Saving and International Capital Flows." *Economic Journal* 90 (June): 314–29.

Fry, M. J. (1987). *Money, Interest, and Banking in Economic Development.* Baltimore: Johns Hopkins University Press.

Gurley, J. G., and E. S. Shaw (1967). "Financial Development and Economic Development." *Economic Development and Cultural Change* 15 (April): 257–65, 267–68.

Haque, Nadeem U., and P. Montiel (1989). "Consumption in Developing Countries: Tests for Liquidity Constraints and Finite Horizons." *Review of Economic Statistics* 71 (August): 408–15.

IMF (1991). *World Economic Outlook, May 1991.* Washington, D.C.

Lewis, W. A. (1954). "Economic Development with Unlimited Supplies of Labour." *The Manchester School* 22: 139–91.

McKinnon, R. I. (1973). *Money and Capital in Economic Development.* Washington, D.C.: Brookings Institution.

Stiglitz, J. E., and A. Weiss (1981). "Credit Rationing with Imperfect Information." *American Economic Review* 71: 393–410.

World Bank (1991). *World Development Report.* New York: Oxford University Press.

Comment: Hypotheses Regarding Household Savings

If savings and investment are so important for development, we should understand the determinants of saving. Various hypotheses deserve consideration.

In Keynesian national income analysis, personal saving is a function of personal disposable income (income after tax): as the level of personal disposable income rises, the average propensity to save (S/Y, where S is savings and Y is national income) also increases. This absolute income hypothesis has been modified to have the total level of saving increase with income, but at an ever decreasing rate. Different relationships between the average (S/Y) and marginal propensity to save ($\Delta S/\Delta Y$) have been postulated, and different estimates found in empirical studies.

Milton Friedman's "permanent income" hypothesis also finds some support in studies that indicate a strong marginal propensity to save out of permanent income. "Life cycle" hypotheses, however, do not have much empirical support, probably because in developing economies the households, farmers, and small enterprises are subject to severe fluctuations in income. These hypotheses are examined in Raymond F. Mikesell and James E. Zinser, "The Nature of the Savings Function in Developing Countries," *Journal of Economic Literature* (March 1973).

Some special features of developing countries also affect the rate of saving—notably, the informal credit markets, cultural factors, and financial repression.

Considering the role of informal credit markets in the generation of savings, we should note that in an LDC there is not the efficient functioning of credit and insurance markets such as is presumed for saving models in the more developed economies.

Hoff and Stiglitz argue that rural credit markets are neither perfectly competitive nor monopolized by informal money lenders. They indicate several features of these markets, such as

The formal and the informal sectors coexist, despite the fact that formal interest rates are substantially below those charged in the informal sector.

Interest rates may not equilibrate credit supply and demand: there may be credit rationing, and in periods of bad harvests, lending may be unavailable at any price.

Credit markets are segmented. Interest rates of lenders in different areas vary by more than plausibly can be accounted for by differences in the likelihood of default; and local events—a failure of a harvest in one area—seem to have significant impacts on the availability of credit in local markets.

There is a limited number of commercial lenders in the informal sector, despite the high rates charged.

In the informal sector interlinkages between credit transactions and transactions in other markets are common.

Formal lenders tend to specialize in areas where farmers have land titles.[1]

Given the wide range of developing economies and their different saving patterns, some analysts relate saving to a country's religious, cultural, and ethnic attributes. Such considerations for Taiwan were expressed in selection I.C.I.

These sociocultural elements also overlap with demographic variables involving age distribution (lower savings in younger households) and with rural–urban divisions (higher savings in rural households).

Although from our discussion of financial repression (section IV.E) some economists contend that a rise in the real interest rate would increase savings, others refer to econometric studies of interest-elasticity of savings that show low elasticities. Deaton, for instance, states that

there is no theoretical basis, whatsoever for this presumption. Changes in interest rates have both income and substitution effects, and can increase or decrease current consumption depending on the balance between the two. Higher (real) interest rates do indeed increase the incentive to postpone consumption and tend to make the planned consumption profile grow more rapidly over time, but the current starting point of that profile can move either up or down. There is also an enormous body of research, mostly but not exclusively in developed economies, that has singularly failed to show *any* empirical relation between interest rates and the rate of saving.[2]

For all the hypotheses regarding the determinants of savings, it is difficult to measure savings whether at the household level or macroeconomic aggregate level. Empirical tests are weak because the data are subject to biases, identification problems, and measurement errors. Before the hypotheses can be adequately tested, these data inadequacies need to be overcome.

For a more thorough survey of the theory and empirical evidence on saving in developing countries, see M. Gersovitz, "Saving and Development" in *Handbook of Development Economics*, vol. 1, ed. Hollis Chenery and T. N. Srinivasan (1988).

---

[1]K. Hoff and J. E. Stiglitz, "Introduction: Imperfect Information and Rural Credit Markets—Puzzles and Policy Perspectives," *World Bank Economic Review* (September 1990): 236–37.

[2]Angus Deaton, "Saving in Developing Countries: Theory and Review," *Proceedings of the World Bank Annual Conference on Development Economics* 1989: 87–88.

IV.D.2. Public Finance*

I have argued that both theory and experience tell us that there is an important role for government in crucial sectors of the economy. Any commitment of expenditure by the government has, however, to be financed, and any judgement of the appropriate size of the public sector must take into account its ability to raise revenue. We will review briefly here what experience and theory have to tell us about the ability of developing countries to tax. We shall see that developing countries now raise substantial amounts of tax revenue. Further, economic theory provides helpful guidance on how that revenue can be generated in a manner which is efficient, equitable, and consistent with administrative constraints.

Let us suppose here that taxation would provide the main source of revenue. There are a few countries for which aid is large in relation to national income but, with the exception of Bangladesh, they are generally rather small countries. In Africa, however, aid does remain very important, at least in comparison to savings. Borrowing (domestic or external) and the inflation tax have played a major part in public finances in some countries but again we may assume that their potential is limited in the longer term.

Non-tax revenue (for example, from oil royalties) is important for many countries and in most cases acts just like a tax. For analytical purposes we shall include it together with tax revenue for this discussion. In many countries non-tax revenue also comes from public-sector firms. In China, prior to the economic reforms, profits of public-sector enterprises were indeed the main source of revenue as was the case for Eastern Europe prior to the reforms. Interestingly, it does not seem to have been immediately appreciated in China that decentralisation of production decisions with profits going to private individuals requires a system of public finance to be put into place in order to substitute for the forgone profits. While my suggested guidelines for state activity assign a limited role to public firms, pricing policy for publicly provided goods and services is, and will remain, a crucial issue for many developing countries.

Similar principles apply as for indirect taxation and the effect on revenue of pricing policy is a key issue. We should also take a broad view of the relationship between government and community in providing and financing public services (see, e.g., Burgess and Stern 1991).

Generally speaking, then, the main source of finance for government expenditure will be government revenue. Writing in the early 1960s, Nicholas Kaldor posed in a famous article the question "Will underdeveloped countries learn to tax?" He pointed to tax revenues of 25–30 percent of GNP in developed countries and 8–15 percent in developing countries. Unfortunately in his enthusiasm to encourage developing countries to raise revenue in what he regarded as an efficient and equitable way, he appeared, in his role as adviser, to leave in his wake considerable social unrest. As a result his proposed tax reforms were rarely implemented—he paid, for example, insufficient attention to administrative problems and political opposition. Developing countries have, however, given their own answer to Kaldor's question. As Table 1 shows, developing countries now raise considerable fractions of GDP in tax revenue—15–20 percent. Further, the figures in the table understate the extent of taxation in the sense that they omit some local taxes as well as a number of sources of non-tax revenue—profits of marketing boards, government land sales, profits from public-sector firms, mineral royalties, and so on. Non-tax revenue has a larger share in total revenue in developing than developed countries. It comprises around 7 percent of GDP for developing countries bringing them close to, or in, the 25–30 percent range Kaldor mentioned (see Table 1).

The fact that many developing countries have been successful in raising revenue should not delude us into thinking that the problems of public finance are straightforward. Taxation does depend on a certain strength of government and a certain acceptance by the population of taxation. It appears, for example, that it has been possible for Chile to keep up government revenue (now around 30 percent of GDP), but not for Peru whose revenue has declined from around 17 percent in the late 1970s to less than 10 percent in the late 1980s. It has been argued that the reason for this is that the Chileans are like the Germans. While this is offered as a

*From Nicholas Stern, "Public Policy and the Economics of Development," *European Economic Review* 35 (1991): 262–67. Reprinted by permission.

TABLE 1. Source of Total Revenue by Geographical Area (percent of GDP, 1986–87)

Area	Average GNP Per Capita	Total Nontax	Total Tax	Income Taxes				Domestic Taxes				Foreign Taxes				Social Security	Wealth and Property	Other
				Total	Individual	Corporate	Other	Total	General Sales, Turnover, VAT	Excises	Other	Total	Import Duties	Export Duties	Other			
Industrial	13,477	6.26	31.22	10.96	8.45	2.37	0.14	9.43	5.58	3.02	0.83	0.72	0.70	0.01	0.01	8.90	1.11	0.10
Developing	1,241	6.50	18.05	5.52	2.08	3.29	0.40	5.20	2.46	2.06	0.68	5.13	4.32	0.62	0.20	1.30	0.45	0.50
Africa	614	4.93	20.29	6.86	2.30	4.31	0.33	5.11	3.09	1.55	0.47	6.73	5.60	0.96	0.20	0.78	0.42	0.32
Asia	749	4.57	14.84	4.46	2.37	2.64	0.09	4.55	1.59	2.23	0.72	5.46	4.82	0.48	0.15	0.04	0.16	0.18
Europe	3,424	8.90	20.02	5.33	2.99	1.63	0.72	6.08	2.96	2.18	0.94	2.68	2.67	0.00	0.01	4.64	0.66	0.95
Middle East	2,403	13.23	13.98	5.15	0.51	5.11	0.06	2.02	0.03	1.28	0.71	4.40	4.37	0.03	0.00	0.00	0.74	1.67
Western Hemisphere	1,634	5.05	17.15	4.41	1.48	2.38	0.67	6.13	2.41	2.82	0.89	3.40	2.54	0.50	0.36	2.18	0.57	0.66

Source: International Monetary Fund, *Government Finance Statistics Yearbook* (1989).

somewhat lighthearted suggestion, there does appear, for whatever reason, to be acceptance of taxation in Chile which is unusually high by Latin American standards. Further, governments must be in a position to control expenditure. Frequently there is extreme pressure on the government from a number of sources to increase that expenditure. For example, in Pakistan in the recent past military expenditure (comprising probably around one-quarter of the budget and 6 percent of GDP) has been very hard to control and the government has been sufficiently fragile that it has not felt confident in raising taxation. The upshot is substantial borrowing and public deficits which have reached worrying proportions (see Ahmad and Stern 1991).

Having seen that governments can raise revenue, we must ask what economic theory has to offer on how they should do it. Let me suggest the following seven principles, all of which are essentially based on theoretical results in public economics—see Ahmad and Stern (1989, 1990) for references. I emphasise them because in my experience it is common to encounter practices, approaches, and aphorisms directly counter to them. They focus on indirect taxes, the main source of revenue for most developing countries.

(i) Where possible, lump-sum taxes and transfers, or close approximations should be used to raise revenue and transfer resources. Examples are land taxes (although incentives to improve land must be considered) and subsidized (infra-marginal) rations. Rations can be quite large, for example, for urban households in China they may amount to ¼–½ of real income.

(ii) It can be very misleading to look at one set of tax tools in isolation from what is happening elsewhere in the tax system. For example, we should eschew simplistic rules such as allocating redistribution to the income tax and revenue raising to indirect taxes.

(iii) The focus of indirect taxation should be final consumption. This means that intermediate goods should not be taxed unless there is some difficulty in the way of taxing final goods or there are special distributional reasons for taxing these intermediates. This applies also to tariffs, which should be reduced as and when the revenue from final goods taxation can be built up. In the short term, it is generally preferable to replace quotas by tariffs so that the rent

from the quota is replaced by a direct flow to the government rather than accruing to those agents who allocate or receive the quota.

(iv) Public-sector prices should be set according to the same principles as indirect taxes: price equal to marginal social cost for intermediate goods (except for the cases noted in [iii] above) and marginal social cost plus a contribution to revenue in the case of final goods.

(v) The appropriate microeconomic criterion for the expansion of industries is profitability at shadow prices of the incremental output. Other indicators (such as effective protection rates or domestic resource costs) are reliable only where they coincide with shadow prices. Similarly a reform rule based on the other indicators, such as adjusting tariffs to move towards uniform protection, is incorrect.

(vi) Indirect taxes should be guided by a trade-off between efficiency and equity and in the absence of well-functioning schemes for income support there is no prescription for uniformity of indirect taxation.

(vii) There are important examples of externalities as a basis for taxation. These include road usage, energy consumption, tobacco, and alcohol. As with other taxes, income distribution and revenue effects elsewhere (and not simply marginal externality costs) should enter into the judgement of the appropriate tax.

In the long run an appropriate compromise between theory and administrative capabilities for indirect taxes might look as follows:

• a VAT with exemptions for food and a basic rate possibly supplemented by a luxury rate
• luxury excises on a few goods if the income tax system is weak
• no trade quotas; tariffs only where justified by well-substantiated learning arguments
• excises on petroleum, alcohol, and tobacco. . . .

One can ask whether tax systems in developing countries are generally moving in the direction which theory would suggest. Broadly speaking I would argue that, as far as indirect taxes are concerned, theory and practice are becoming increasingly harmonious. There is increasing dependence on VAT and domestic sales taxes on final goods and services. VAT systems have been introduced into over 20 developing countries and further introductions, especially in Asia and Africa, are planned. The importance of VAT in Latin America has been increasing over time. It now accounts for between 1 and 5 percent of GDP in Uruguay, Peru, Mexico, Guatemala, Colombia, and Argentina and for (around) 9 percent of GDP in Chile. VAT is also central in many countries outside Latin America including, for example, Turkey and Indonesia. At the same time the importance of trade taxes, and in particular import duties, has been declining worldwide, though dependence on this source of revenue in Africa is still uncomfortably high, representing close to 7 percent of GDP for Africa as a whole and being as high as 28 percent in Lesotho (International Monetary Fund 1989).

On direct taxes, however, there is little conformity between theory and the direction of change. Compared with the position in industrial countries, progressive individual income taxation and social security contributions are of minor importance in developing countries (and in a number of countries have been declining), where the bulk of income tax is collected in the form of corporation tax. Generally equity and efficiency considerations suggest an individual should be assessed on income from all sources put together. However, in developing countries it is common for people to have income from a number of sources and it is extremely difficult to put them together to find out what an individual's global income really is. In addition, there are difficulties with measuring correctly income from any particular source. Increasingly, then, developing countries are looking to tax income at source on a schedular basis, that is, there are individual schedules for different sorts of income.

References

Ahmad, E., and N. H. Stern (1989). "Taxation in developing countries." In H. B. Chenery and T. N. Srinivasan, eds., *Handbook of Development Economics*, Vol. 2 (Amsterdam: North-Holland), pp. 1005–92.

——— (1990). "Principles of taxation in developing countries." In M. FG. Scott, ed., *Public Policy and Economic Development: Essays in Honour of Ian Little* (Oxford: Oxford University Press), pp. 274–307.

——— (1991). *The Theory and Practice of Tax Reform in Developing Countries* (Cambridge: Cambridge University Press).

Burgess, R., and N. H. Stern (1991). "Social security in developing countries: What, why, who and how?" In E. Ahmad, J. Drèze, J. Hills, and A. K. Sen, eds., *Social Security in Developing Countries* (Oxford: Oxford University Press).

International Monetary Fund (1989). *Government Finance Statistics Yearbook*.

Comment: Taxation

The World Bank's *World Development Report 1988* (1988) presents a comprehensive examination of public finance in developing countries.

The role of the government as saver raises problems of taxation and the relative merits of alternative fiscal policies in developing countries. Tax reform is an important element of stabilization and adjustment programs. Problems of taxable capacity, tax effort, and tax elasticity can be studied in R. M. Bird and O. Oldman, eds., *Taxation in Developing Countries*, 4th ed. (1990); Charles E. McLure, "Taxation and the Urban Poor in Developing Countries," *World Development* (March 1977); J. F. Toye, ed., *Taxation and Economic Development* (1978); Stephen R. Lewis, Jr., *Taxation for Development* (1984), chap. 3; David M. G. Newbery and Nicholas Stern, eds., *Theory of Taxation for Developing Countries* (1987); and Richard Bird, *Tax Policy and Economic Development* (1992).

The appropriateness of different taxes for developing countries is often judged with reference to criteria such as (1) fruitfulness of revenue sources, (2) effects on resource allocation, (3) contribution to equity, and (4) ease of administration. For an empirical study of these criteria, see International Monetary Fund, *Taxation in Sub-Saharan Africa*, Occasional Paper No. 8 (October 1981). The Newbery and Stern volume, however, advances the analysis of tax reform by moving beyond traditional criteria of a "good tax system" to an analysis of tax policies in terms of their consequences—the gains and losses—for the economy.

Noteworthy empirical studies of tax issues and trends in developing countries have been undertaken by the Fiscal Affairs Department of the International Monetary Fund and reported in various issues of *IMF Staff Papers*.

Comment: Fiscal Discipline

Contrary to policies taken in the 1970s and 1980s, when many developing countries resorted to an easy fiscal policy to feed inflation in the hopes of thereby forcing savings and achieving higher growth rates, most governments now realize that fiscal restraint is a superior policy. From his review of the experiences of seventeen developing countries during "the public spending booms, crises and adjustment period" from about 1975 to 1988, Corden concludes that it is "plausible that poor economic management—which may be the result of an inability of government to resist pressure groups and generally ensure adequate macroeconomic controls—leads to a variety of policies that produce low growth. And high inflation, which is always unplanned and is a last resort tax imposed by default is clearly a symptom of poor management, as well as having directly adverse effects on growth."[1]

Fiscal discipline, in the sense of maintaining an inflation-adjusted budget deficit below 2 or 3 percent of GNP, is advocated not only to prevent inflation and ensuing balance-of-payments problems, but also to avoid the crowding out of private investment.

Beyond tight budget constraints, the exercise of fiscal discipline should also entail better control over the quality of public spending. This control calls for the proper setting of priorities, effective project appraisal (cost–benefit analysis), and efficient fiscal planning. At bottom, it requires clarity on what governments do best and what markets do best. This issue runs through all of our subsequent chapters and is summarized in the final chapter.

---

[1]W. Max Corden, "Macroeconomic Policy and Growth: Some Lessons of Experience," *Proceedings of the World Bank Annual Conference on Development Economics* (1990): 79. For a detailed investigation, see Ian M. D. Little et al., *Boom, Crisis, and Adjustment: The Macroeconomic Experience in Developing Countries* (1994).

IV.E. FINANCIAL MARKETS AND DEVELOPMENT

IV.E.1. Organized and Unorganized Money Markets*

The size of an organized money market in any country may be indicated by either or both of the following ratios, although neither measurement is perfect: the ratio of deposit money to money supply and the ratio of the banking system's claims (mostly loans, advances, and bills discounted) on the private sector to national income. . . .

The ratio of deposit money to money supply actually measures banking development of the money market. However, to the extent that the development of commercial banking is synonymous with the development of the money market, this ratio may be used as an indicator of the growth of a money market. In most underdeveloped countries, there are hardly any lending agencies of importance other than commercial banks. There are no discount houses or acceptance houses, and savings institutions (including life insurance companies) are in the early stages of development. . . .

Both ratios might be expected to be low in an underdeveloped country and high in a developed one. The ratio of deposit money to money supply should be higher in a more developed country because, with economic development, there is also development of the banking system. . . .

The structure of interest rates in the organized money markets of underdeveloped countries is usually more or less the same as in the developed ones. The short-term rate of interest is generally much below the long-term rate, as indicated by the spread between the government treasury bill rate and the government bond yield; the rate at which bills of exchange are discounted is also lower than the rate at which loans and advances are granted.

The lowest market rates are usually the call loan rates between commercial banks. The next lowest are those paid by commercial banks on short-term deposits, followed by the government treasury bill rate. Then come the rates at which commercial banks discount commercial paper, varying according to the type of security and the date of maturity. In most countries, especially in Asia, the government bond yield comes next, followed by the lending rates of commercial banks. . . .

In general, the level of interest rates in underdeveloped countries, even in organized money markets, is higher than in the more developed countries. The more notable difference between the two groups of countries, however, is that the range of interest rates is generally much wider in underdeveloped countries. The volume of loans granted at relatively low rates in an underdeveloped country is not very important, as only limited amounts of financial assets are available to serve as collateral for lending at low rates. It is usually the foreign business firms with longer experience and larger capital which are able to borrow at the lower rates. Most of the indigenous firms have to pay the higher rates; this is especially true where foreign banks occupy an important position in the banking system. . . .

In spite of the small direct dependence of commercial banks on the central banks for funds, the latter are able to influence market rates by changes in the bank rate because of their economic, and at times their legal, position in the domestic money market, with wide powers for selective credit control, open market operations, and moral pressures.

The general expectation is that the long-term trend of interest rates in underdeveloped countries, at least in the organized markets, should be downward. Generally speaking, in these countries the banking systems and with them the money markets are likely to develop at a faster rate than the other sectors of the economy. The long-term supply of loanable funds therefore tends to increase more rapidly than the long-term demand. Where, for one reason or another, the growth of banking has been restricted or the banking system subjected by law to many restrictions, including controls on interest rates

*From U Tun Wai, "Interest Rates in the Organized Money Markets of Underdeveloped Countries," *International Monetary Fund Staff Papers,* Vol. 5, No. 2 (August 1956), pp. 249–50, 252–53, 255, 258, 276–78; "Interest Rates Outside the Organized Money Markets of Underdeveloped Countries," ibid., Vol. 6, No. 1 (November 1957), pp. 80–83, 107–9, 119–25. Reprinted by permission.

and of the purposes for which loans may be granted (as in a number of countries in Latin America), the long-term trend of interest rates may, however, not be downward. . . .

In [the above] examination . . . of the interest rate structure and the lending practices of organized money markets in underdeveloped countries, . . . it was shown that these differed much less than might have been expected from those prevailing in most developed countries. In underdeveloped countries, however, unorganized money markets also play a very important role, and any study of credit conditions in these countries that is to be adequate must be extended to cover the unorganized as well as the organized markets. Efforts have often been made to repair the deficiences of the unorganized markets by government action designed to stimulate the development of cooperative credit or to provide credit through agricultural banks, etc.; it is convenient to include these government-sponsored institutions in a study of unorganized money markets in general.

Interest rates in the unorganized money markets of underdeveloped countries are generally very high in relation both to those in the organized money markets and to what is needed for rapid economic development. These high interest rates are caused by a disproportionately large demand for loanable funds coupled with a generally inelastic and limited supply of funds. The large demand stems from the special social and economic factors prevalent in the rural areas of underdeveloped countries. The low level of income leaves little surplus for saving and for the accumulation of capital for self-financing of agricultural and handicraft production. The uncertainty of the weather, which affects crop yields and incomes, causes an additional need for outside funds in bad years. A significant portion of the demand for loanable funds in rural areas is for financing consumption at levels much higher than are warranted by the low income of the peasant. . . .

The supply of loanable funds in the unorganized money markets is very limited and inelastic because the major source is the moneylender, and only very small quantities are supplied by indigenous bankers and organized institutions, such as cooperative credit societies and land mortgage banks. The moneylender in most cases is also a merchant or a landlord and therefore is willing to lend only at rates comparable with what he could earn by employing his capital in alternative uses which are often highly profitable. The lenders in the unorganized money markets do not have the facilities for mobilizing liquid funds available to commercial banks in organized markets and therefore the supply of funds is rather inflexible. Since the unorganized money markets are generally not closely connected with the organized money markets, there is little possibility of increasing the supply of loanable funds beyond the savings of the lending sector of the unorganized money markets. The limited supply of loanable funds indeed reflects the general shortage of capital in underdeveloped countries.

The disadvantages of the high rates of interest in the unorganized money markets are well known and include such important effects as ''dead-weight'' agricultural indebtedness, alienation of land from agriculturalists to moneylenders and the agrarian unrest that is thus engendered, and a general slowing down of economic development. . . .

The organized money markets in underdeveloped countries are less fully integrated than the money markets in developed countries. The unorganized money markets in underdeveloped countries are even more imperfect, and indeed it is questionable whether the existing arrangements should be referred to as ''markets.'' They are much less homogeneous than the organized markets and are generally scattered over the rural sector. There is very little contact between the lenders and borrowers in different localities. The usual textbook conditions for a perfect market are completely nonexistent: lenders and borrowers do not know the rates at which loans are being transacted in other parts of the country; the relationship between borrower and lender is not only that of a debtor and creditor but is also an integral part of a much wider socioeconomic pattern of village life and rural conditions.

In unorganized money markets, moreover, loans are often contracted and paid for not in money but in commodities; and the size of the average loan is very much smaller than in the organized money markets. Both borrowers and lenders in the two markets are often of quite different types. In the organized money markets, the borrowers are mainly traders (wholesale and retail) operating in the large cities and, to a less extent, manufacturers. Agriculturalists rarely account for a significant portion of demand except in those underdeveloped countries where export agriculture has been developed through plantations or estates. In the unorganized money markets, the borrowers are small agriculturalists, cottage industry workers, and some retail shop-keepers. The lenders in the organized money markets consist almost exclusively of commercial banks. In the unorganized markets, the suppliers of credit consist of a few financial institutions, such as cooperatives, private and government-sponsored agricultural banks, indigenous bankers, professional moneylenders, large traders, landlords, shopkeepers, relatives, and friends. Proper records of loans granted or repaid are usually not kept, and uniform accounting procedures are not adopted by the different lenders. Loans are granted more on a personal basis than in the organized money markets, and most of the loans granted by the moneylenders and by other noninstitutional sources are unsecured beyond the verbal promise of the borrower to repay.

The unorganized money market may be divided into three major parts: (1) a part in which the supply is dominated by indigenous bankers, cooperatives, and other institutions, and the demand by rural traders and medium-sized landords; (2) a part in which the demand originates mainly from small agriculturalists with good credit ratings, who are able to obtain a large portion of their funds from respectable moneylenders, traders, and landlords at high but reasonable rates of interest, that is, rates that are high in relation to those prevailing in the organized money market but not exorbitant by the standards of the unorganized money market; (3) a part in which the demand originates from borrowers who are not good credit risks, who do not have suitable collateral, and who in consequence are driven to shady marginal lenders who charge exorbitant rates of interest. . . .

Many explanations have been offered for the high interest rates that generally prevail in unorganized money markets. One theory is that interest rates are high there because they are determined by custom and have always been high. This might be called the theory of the customary rate of interest. . . .

The theory of customary rates is not satisfactory, however, because it does not explain how or why the custom of high rates developed. The true explanation has to be found in the economic and social conditions of underdeveloped countries, which cause the demand for loanable funds to be large in relation to the available supply. Some writers tend to explain the high rates of interest in terms of demand factors while others emphasize supply. . . .

The difference in the levels of interest rates between the organized and unorganized money markets stems partly from the basic differences between the sources of supply of funds in the two markets. In an organized money market, facilities for the expansion of credit are open to the commercial banks, which have the use of funds belonging to depositors. These banks are therefore able to charge relatively low rates of interest and yet make satisfactory profits for the shareholders. On the other hand, moneylenders in an unorganized money market have little influence on the supply of funds at their disposal and, furthermore, their supply price tends to be influenced by the alternative uses to which their funds can be put.

A number of institutional factors are also responsible for high rates of interest in unorganized money markets. The size of the loan is usually small and thus the fixed handling charges are relatively high. Defaults also tend to be larger in unorganized money markets. These higher defaults are due not so much to a lower standard of morality and willingness to repay debts as to the fluctuations in prices and incomes derived from agricultural products, which reduce the ability of the agriculturalists to repay debts at inopportune times. . . .

The list of causes of high interest rates could be extended to include other social and economic factors in underdeveloped countries—even to fairly remote factors, such as the system of land tenure which prevents land from being used as collateral. A general statement, however, is that interest rates in the unorganized money markets of underdeveloped countries are high because the economy is underdeveloped and the money market unorganized. . . .

Any program to bring down interest rates in unorganized money markets must be comprehensive and should be guided by the principle that interest rates can be lowered only by reducing the demand for loanable funds as well as by increasing the supply. . . .

A reduction in borrowing for productive purposes may not be desirable, especially as the amount of self-financing which can take its place is negligible. Such borrowing can be reduced in the long run only through an increase in savings from higher agricultural output and income. It is not sufficient that the ability of the farmer to save be increased. The willingness to save must also be created. The problem of cheap agricultural credit is inseparable from the whole problem of agricultural development, including such measures as increasing the use of fertilizers and proper seeds; making available adequate marketing facilities, including proper grading, transportation, and storage of crops; and providing an efficient agricultural extension service. . . .

Even if it is true that the cure for high rates of interest is to be found more on the demand side than on the supply side, the supply of credit should also be increased. Supply should be increased in such a way that legitimate credit needs are met at cheaper rates without encouraging borrowing for consumption. This can be achieved by increasing the supply of institutional credit while at the same time taking steps to discourage borrowing from noninstitutional lenders. In this connection, it could be argued that legislation regarding moneylenders which has had the effect of drying up noninstitutional credit may be a blessing in disguise—although in a manner different from that intended by legislators.

Increasing the supply of institutional credit is a difficult problem, but the efforts of governments have had a fair degree of success. One problem is that of getting the commerical banks to lend more to agriculture. . . .

One way of inducing the organized financial institutions to lend more to agriculture is by making agriculturalists more creditworthy and generally reducing the risks of lending by lessening the impact of some of the natural calamities (floods, plant and animal diseases); improving the human factor, i.e., reducing carelessness and increasing honesty; reducing the uncertainties of the market through crop insurance, stabilized agricultural prices, etc. The lenders might also take certain steps, such as spreading loans between different types of borrower and region and supervising the use of loans for productive purposes.

IV.E.2. Demand-Following or Supply-Leading Finance*

Typical statements indicate that the financial system somehow accommodates—or, to the extent that it malfunctions, it restricts—growth of real per capita output. For example,

It seems to be the case that where enterprise leads finance follows. The same impulses within an economy which set enterprise on foot make owners of wealth venturesome, and when a strong impulse to invest is fettered by lack of finance, devices are invented to release it . . . and habits and institutions are developed.[1]

Such an approach places emphasis on the demand side for financial services; as the economy grows it generates additional and new demands for these services, which bring about a supply response in the growth of the financial system. In this view, the lack of financial institutions in underdeveloped countries is simply an indication of the lack of demand for their services.

We may term as "demand-following" the phenomenon in which the creation of modern financial institutions, their financial assets and liabilities, and related financial services is in response to the demand for these services by investors and savers in the real economy. In this case, the evolutionary development of the financial system is a continuing consequence of the pervasive, sweeping process of economic development. The emerging financial system is shaped both by changes in objective opportunities—the economic environment, the institutional framework—and by changes in subjective responses—individual motivations, attitudes, tastes, preferences.

The nature of the demand for financial services depends upon the growth of real output and upon the commercialization and monetization of agriculture and other traditional subsistence sectors. The more rapid the growth rate of real national income, the greater will be the demand by enterprises for external funds (the saving of others) and therefore financial intermediation, since under most circumstances firms will be less able to finance expansion from internally generated depreciation allowances and retained profits. (The proportion of external funds in the total source of enterprise funds will

*From Hugh T. Patrick, "Financial Development and Economic Growth in Underdeveloped Countries," *Economic Development and Cultural Change*, Vol. 14, No. 2 (January 1966), pp. 174–77. Reprinted by permission.

[1] Joan Robinson, "The Generalization of the General Theory," in *The Rate of Interest and Other Essays* (London, 1952), pp. 86–87.

rise.) For the same reason, with a given aggregate growth rate, the greater the variance in the growth rates among different sectors or industries, the greater will be the need for financial intermediation to transfer savings to fast-growing industries from slow-growing industries and from individuals. The financial system can thus support and sustain the leading sectors in the process of growth.

The demand-following supply response of the growing financial system is presumed to come about more or less automatically. It is assumed that the supply of entrepreneurship in the financial sector is highly elastic relative to the growing opportunities for profit from provision of financial services, so that the number and diversity of types of financial institutions expand sufficiently; and a favorable legal, institutional, and economic environment exists. The government's attitudes, economic goals, and economic policies, as well as the size and rate of increase of the government debt, are of course important influences in any economy on the nature of the economic environment. As a consequence of real economic growth, financial markets develop, widen, and become more perfect, thus increasing the opportunities for acquiring liquidity and for reducing risk, which in turn feeds back as a stimulant to real growth.[2]

The demand-following approach implies that finance is essentially passive and permissive in the growth process. Late eighteenth and early nineteenth century England may be cited as a historical example. In fact, the increased supply of financial services in response to demand may not be at all automatic, flexible, or inexpensive in underdeveloped countries. Examples include the restrictive banking legislation in early nineteenth century France, religious barriers against loans and interest charges, and Gerschenkron's analysis of the abortive upswing of Italian industrial development in the 1880s "mainly, it is believed, because the modern investment bank had not yet been established in Italy."[3] In underdeveloped countries today, similar obstacles, together with imperfections in the operation of the market mechanism, may dictate an inadequate demand-following response by the financial system. The lack of financial services, thus,

in one way or another restricts or inhibits effective growth patterns and processes.

Less emphasis has been given in academic discussions (if not in policy actions) to what may be termed the "supply-leading" phenomenon: the creation of financial institutions and the supply of their financial assets, liabilities, and related financial services in advance of demand for them, especially the demand of entrepreneurs in the modern, growth-inducing sectors. "Supply-leading" has two functions: to transfer resources from traditional (non-growth) sectors to modern sectors, and to promote and stimulate an entrepreneurial response in these modern sectors. Financial intermediation which transfers resources from traditional sectors, whether by collecting wealth and saving from those sectors in exchange for its deposits and other financial liabilities, or by credit creation and forced saving, is akin to the Schumpeterian concept of innovation financing.

New access to such supply-leading funds may in itself have substantial, favorable expectational and psychological effects on entrepreneurs. It opens new horizons as to possible alternatives, enabling the entrepreneur to "think big." This may be the most significant effect of all, particularly in countries where entrepreneurship is a major constraint on development. Moreover, as has been emphasized by Rondo Cameron,[4] the top management of financial institutions may also serve as entrepreneurs in industrial enterprises. They assist in the establishment of firms in new industries or in the merger of firms (the advantages of economies of scale may be more than offset by the establishment of restrictive cartels or monopolies, however), not only by underwriting a substantial portion of the capital, but more importantly by assuming the entrepreneurial initiative.

By its very nature, a supply-leading financial system initially may not be able to operate profitably by lending to the nascent modern sectors.[5] There are, however, several ways in which new financial institutions can be made viable. First, they may be government institutions, using government capital and perhaps receiving direct government subsidies. This is exemplified not

[2]Cf. W. Arthur Lewis, *The Theory of Economic Growth* (London, 1955), pp. 267–86.

[3]Alexander Gerschenkron, *Economic Backwardness in Historical Perspective—A Book of Essays* (Cambridge, 1962) p. 363. See also Chapter 4.

[4]Rondo Cameron, "The Bank as Entrepreneur," *Explorations in Entrepreneurial History,* Series 2, Vol. I, No. 1 (Fall 1963), pp. 50–55.

[5]Except in the extreme case where inherent profit opportunities are very high, and supply-leading stimulates a major entrepreneurial effort.

only by Russian experience in the latter half of the nineteenth century, but by many underdeveloped countries today. Second, private financial institutions may receive direct or indirect government subsidies, usually the latter. Indirect subsidies can be provided in numerous ways. Commercial banks may have the right to issue banknotes under favorable collateral conditions; this technique was more important in the eighteenth and nineteenth centuries (national banking in Japan in the 1870s; wildcat banking in the United States) than it is likely to be in present underdeveloped countries, where this right is reserved for the central bank or treasury. Nonetheless, modern equivalents exist. They include allowing private financial institutions to create deposit money with low (theoretically, even negative) reserve requirements and central bank rediscount of commercial bank loans at interest rates effectively below those on the loans. Third, new, modern financial institutions may initially lend a large proportion of their funds to traditional (agricultural and commercial) sectors profitably, gradually shifting their loan portfolio to modern industries as these begin to emerge. This more closely resembles the demand-following phenomenon; whether such a financial institution is supply-leading depends mainly on its attitude in searching out and encouraging new ventures of a modern nature.

It cannot be said that supply-leading finance is a necessary condition or precondition for inaugurating self-sustained economic development. Rather, it presents an opportunity to induce real growth by financial means. It thus is likely to play a more significant role at the beginning of the growth process than later. Gerschenkron implies that the more backward the economy relative to others in the same time period (and the greater the forced-draft nature of the economic development effort), the greater the emphasis which is placed on what I here term supply-leading finance.[6] At the same time, it should be recognized that the supply-leading approach to development of a country's financial system also has its dangers, and they should not be underestimated. The use of resources, especially entrepreneurial talents and managerial skills, and the costs of explicit or implicit subsidies in supply-leading development must produce sufficient benefits in the form of stimulating real economic development for this approach to be justified.

In actual practice, there is likely to be an interaction of supply-leading and demand-following phenomena. Nevertheless, the following sequence may be postulated. Before sustained modern industrial growth gets underway, supply-leading may be able to induce real innovation-type investment. As the process of real growth occurs, the supply-leading impetus gradually becomes less important, and the demand-following financial response becomes dominant. This sequential process is also likely to occur within and among specific industries or sectors. One industry may initially be encouraged financially on a supply-leading basis and as it develops have its financing shift to demand-following, while another industry remains in the supply-leading phase. This would be related to the timing of the sequential development of industries, particularly in cases where the timing is determined more by governmental policy than by private demand forces. . . .

[6]Gerschenkron, *Economic Backwardness in Historical Perspective.*

IV.E.3. Case Against Financial Repression*

When governments tax and otherwise distort their domestic capital market, the economy is said to be financially "repressed."[1] Usury restrictions on interest rates, heavy reserve requirements on bank deposits, and compulsory credit allocations interact with ongoing price inflation to reduce the attractiveness of holding claims on the domestic banking system. In such

*From Ronald I. McKinnon, *Financial Liberalization in Retrospect: Interest Rate Policies in LDCs,* Center for Economic Policy Research Publication No. 74, Stanford University (July 1986), pp. 1–3, 5–9, processed. Reprinted by permission.

[1]Terminology introduced by Edward Shaw (1973) and McKinnon (1973). Further discussion of optimal financial management in a repressed economy is found in McKinnon and Mathieson (1981). A more general review of the literature on financial repression and liberalization can be found in Fry (1982).

a repressed financial system, real deposit rates of interest on monetary assets are often negative, and are difficult to predict when inflation is high and unstable. Thus, the demand for money—broadly defined to include saving and term deposits as well as checking accounts and currency—falls as a proportion of GNP.

But these monetary assets naturally dominate the financial portfolios of small savers in less developed countries. Thus Edward Shaw and I hyopthesized that repressing the monetary system fragments the domestic capital market with highly adverse consequences for the quality and quantity of real capital accumulation:

1. The flow of loanable funds through the organized banking system is reduced, forcing potential investors to rely more on self-finance;
2. Interest rates on the truncated flow of bank lending vary arbitrarily from one class of favored or disfavored borrower to another;
3. The process of self-finance within enterprises and households is itself impaired. If the real yield on deposits—as well as coin and currency—is negative, firms cannot easily accumulate liquid assets in preparation for making discrete investments. Socially costly inflation hedges look more attractive as a means of internal finance.
4. Significant financial deepening outside of the repressed banking system becomes impossible when firms are dangerously illiquid and/or inflation is high and unstable. Robust open markets in stocks and bonds, or intermediation by trust and insurance companies, require monetary stability.

Remedying financial repression is implicit in its definition. We suggested keeping positive and more uniformly high real rates of interest within comparable categories of bank deposits and loans by eliminating undue reserve requirements, interest ceilings, and mandated credit allocations on the one hand, while stabilizing the price level through appropriate macroeconomic measures on the other. Then, savers and investors would better "see" the true scarcity price of capital, and thus reduce the great dispersion in the profitability of investing in different sectors of the economy.

These strictures for liberalizing the financial system seem now like mere truisms to most economists—although not to politicians. Today, both the World Bank and the International Monetary Fund stress the importance of stabilizing the domestic price level, and increasing the flow of generally available loanable funds at close to market-clearing interest rates. From the perspective of the 1980s, those countries with substantially positive real interest rates and high real financial growth—such as Japan, Taiwan, and Singapore—are regarded as leading success stories.

In the 1980s, this new emphasis on the advantages of financial liberalization is quite remarkable. Well into the 1970s, many development economists had still favored the generation of "forced" saving through inflation—or through shifts in the internal distribution of income by such means as turning the internal terms of trade against agriculture in order to transfer an economic "surplus" to the industrial sector. Credit subsidies, at below market rates of interest, were once widely promoted as a means of stimulating socially desirable investments. Unless so manipulated or repressed, the financial sector was not viewed as a leading force in the development process.

Outside of the centrally planned economies, however, there is now widespread agreement that flows of saving and investment should be voluntary, and significantly decentralized in an open capital market at close to "equilibrium" interest rates. . . .

What lessons have been learned about financial repression in steady states—say over a decade or more? Countries that have sustained higher real rates of interest have generally had robust real financial growth leading to higher real economic growth. Some data on private holdings of "broad" money throw light on these issues. Table 1 presents ratios of the broad money supply (M2) to gross national product (GNP).[2] One noticeable characteristic is that even the slower-growing Asian countries (shown in the lower panel) tend to be more financially developed than typical Latin American countries (shown in the upper panel). However, both groups of slowly or erratically growing economies have fairly low ratios of M2 to GNP, averaging about 0.22.

In contrast, Table 2 shows financial development in the really rapid-growth economies—West Germany, Japan, South Korea, Taiwan, and Singapore. A high and rising M2/GNP ratio indicates a large real flow of loanable funds. Be-

---

[2]These ratios are taken from IMF, *International Financial Statistics,* various issues. The IMF defines M2 as money plus quasi-money plus deposits outside commercial banks. M2 is a stock tabulated as of 30 June for each calendar year, whereas GNP is the flow of output for that year.

TABLE 1. Bank Loanable Funds in Typical Semi-Industrial LDCs (ratio of M2 to GNP)

Country	1960	1965	1970	1975	1980	Mean 1960–80
Latin America						
Argentina	0.245	0.209	0.267	0.168	0.234	0.225
Brazil	0.148	0.156	0.205	0.164	0.175	0.170
Chile	0.123	0.130	0.183	0.099	0.208	0.149
Colombia	0.191	0.204	0.235	—	0.222	0.210
	Mean ratio of M2 to GNP for four Latin American countries					0.184
Asia and the Middle East						
India	0.283	0.262	0.264	0.295	0.382	0.297
Philippines	0.186	0.214	0.236	0.186	0.219	0.208
Sri Lanka	0.284	0.330	0.275	0.255	0.317	0.291
Turkey	0.202	0.223	0.237	0.222	0.136	0.204
	Mean ratio of M2 to GNP for four Asian countries					0.247

Source: International Monetary Fund, *International Financial Statistics* (various issues).

cause capital markets in these economies were dominated by banks, ratios of M2 to GNP encompass the main domestic flow of loanable funds in the system. By 1980 Japan, Taiwan, and Singapore had M2/GNP ratios of 0.75 or more. Only South Korea had a much lower ratio of M2 to GNP (0.34), and had to make up for this shortage of domestic loanable funds by borrowing heavily abroad. The other countries shown in Table 2 are now net international creditors.

Although a higher rate of financial growth is positively correlated with successful real growth, Patrick's problem [selection IV.E.2] remains unresolved: what is the cause and what is the effect? Is finance a leading sector in economic development, or does it simply follow growth in real output which is generated elsewhere? Perhaps individuals whose incomes grow quickly want financial assets simply as a kind of consumer good (i.e., an incidental outcome of the growth process). To disentangle these issues, Table 3 presents some data from a recent study on interest-rate policies in developing countries (IMF 1983). Pure data availability and membership of the IMF were the criteria on which countries were selected.

For any one country over time, the real interest rate can vary a great deal, even from positive to negative or vice versa. For the period from 1971 to 1980, the IMF calculated an average real interest rate for each country on a fairly common asset, usually a thirty-day deposit. Countries were then classified according to whether their average real interest rate was positive, mildly negative, or highly negative. Because most of these countries have fragmented interest-rate structures, a representative interest rate is not easy to select. Nevertheless the IMF managed to devise the three-way classification in Table 3.

Using this same sample of countries from the IMF study, real financial growth (which is not the same as measured personal saving) is shown to be positively correlated with real GDP growth in Figure 1. The left-hand panel of Figure 2 shows that those countries that maintain positive real rates of interest have higher growth in real financial assets, as might be expected. Most im-

TABLE 2. Bank Loanable Funds in Rapidly Growing Economies (ratio of M2 to GNP)

Country	1955	1960	1965	1970	1975	1980
Germany[a]	0.331	0.294	0.448	0.583	0.727	0.913
Japan	0.554[b]	0.737[b]	0.701[b]	0.863	1.026	1.390
South Korea	0.069	0.114	0.102	0.325	0.323	0.337
Taiwan	0.115	0.166	0.331	0.462	0.588	0.750
Singapore	—	—	0.542[b]	0.701	0.668	0.826

[a]As well as deposits and currency, the German series includes bank bonds sold directly to the public.
[b]The bias is downward because deposit information on specialised credit institutions was not collected.
Source: International Monetary Fund, *International Financial Statistics* (various issues).

TABLE 3. Selected Developing Countries Grouped According to Interest-Rate Policies: Growth of Real Financial Assets and Real GDP, 1971–80 (compound growth rates, percent per annum)

	Financial Assets[a]	GDP
1. Countries with Positive Real Interest Rates		
Malaysia	13.8	8.0
South Korea	11.1	8.6
Sri Lanka	10.1	4.7
Nepal	9.6	2.0
Singapore	7.6	9.1
Philippines	5.6	6.2
2. Countries with Moderately Negative Real Interest Rates		
Pakistan[b]	9.9	5.4
Thailand	8.5	6.9
Morocco	8.2	5.5
Colombia	5.5	5.8
Greece	5.4	4.7
South Africa	4.3	3.7
Kenya	3.6	5.7
Burma	3.5	4.3
Portugal	1.8	4.7
Zambia	−1.1	0.8
3. Countries with Severely Negative Real Interest Rates		
Peru	3.2	3.4
Turkey	2.2	5.1
Jamaica	−1.9	−0.7
Zaire	−6.8	0.1
Ghana	−7.6	−0.1

[a]Measured as the sum of monetary and quasi-monetary deposits with the banking sector, corrected for changes in the consumer price index.

[b]The period covered is 1974–80.

Source: International Monetary Fund, *Interest Rate Policies in Developing Countries,* Occasional Paper, no. 22, October 1983.

FIGURE 1. Selected developing countries: growth of real GDP and real financial assets, 1971–80.

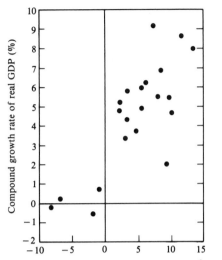

Compound growth rate of real financial assets[a] (%)

[a]As defined in Table 3.

Source: International Monetary Fund, *Interest Rate Policies in Developing Countries,* Occasional Paper, no. 22, October 1983.

portantly, the right-hand panel of Figure 2 shows a significant positive correlation between real rates of interest and real growth in GDP. . . .

With this kind of regression analysis, care must be taken in deciding which variables are exogenous and which endogenous. Positive correlations between growth in financial assets and growth in GDP do not show which way the causality operates. However, for the purposes of portfolio choice by individual investors, a case can be made for treating the real rate of interest as exogenous. Governments frequently intervene to set ceilings on nominal rates of interest on bank deposits, and at the same time they de-

termine the aggregate rate of price inflation; the real rate of interest, therefore, is very much determined by public policy. Thus the presumption is that nonrepressive financial policies, resulting in significantly positive real rates of interest, contribute to higher economic growth.

Any positive link between real rates of interest and personal saving, as measured in the GDP accounts, is much less apparent. The results of cross-country statistical studies linking inflation rates to aggregate saving have been quite ambiguous. This ambiguity is puzzling: shouldn't saving be discouraged as inflation erodes the real values of financial assets?

In an inflationary economy, real rates of interest on financial assets are usually negative. Because of inflation, however, the private sector is forced to abstain from current consumption. Individuals must keep adding to their nominal money balances in order to prevent their real balances from declining. But this inflation ''tax'' extracted by the government is classified in the GNP accounts as if it were private saving. However, real personal financial assets are not accumulating, and the flow of loanable funds to the private sector may be quite low—even though the flow of private ''saving,'' as measured in the GNP accounts, might be quite high.

FIGURE 2. Selected developing countries grouped according to interest-rate policies: growth of real financial assets and real GDP, 1971–80.

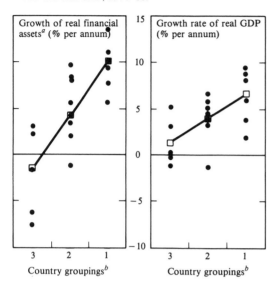

^{a}As defined in Table 3.
^{b}See Table 3 for specifications of these groupings.

Source: International Monetary Fund, *Interest Rate Policies in Developing Countries,* Occasional Paper, no. 22, October 1983.

Typically, therefore, systematic relationships cannot be derived from cross-sectional data between the flow of personal saving and real rates of interest, or between personal saving and inflation. From cross-country comparisons of "long-run" experiences over a decade or more, however, the positive correlation between real interest rates and real growth seems unambiguous.

Apparently the quality, if not the quantity, of investment improves significantly when interest rates are positive and financial intermediation is robust.

References

Fry, Maxwell J. (1982). "Models of Financially Repressed Developing Economies." *World Development* 10 (September).

McKinnon, Ronald I. (1973). *Money and Capital in Economic Development.*

McKinnon, Ronald I., and Donald Mathieson (1981). "How to Manage a Repressed Economy." *Princeton Essays in International Finance,* no. 145.

Shaw, Edward S. (1973). *Financial Deepening in Economic Development.*

Comment: Financial Liberalization

The policy implications of models of financial repression are that economic growth can be increased by removing interest rate ceilings and bringing the deposit rate of interest up to the free-market equilibrium rate, by eliminating selective or quantitative credit programs, and by ensuring that financial markets operate competitively with freedom of entry.

A number of developing countries have undertaken such policies of financial liberalization along with their stabilization programs (recall IV.C). According to the McKinnon analysis of financial repression, economic liberalization and monetary stabilization are complementary concepts. When inflation is high and uncertain, the full deregulation (liberalization) of markets in goods, financial capital, or labor services cannot work well. In determining how to bring domestic inflation under control in a liberalizing economy, the government must attempt to keep interest rates, exchange rates, and wage rates properly aligned during the process of disinflation.

This policy has proved difficult in a number of countries. The general case favoring financial liberalization has been called into question by a series of bank panics and bankruptcies in the Southern Cone of Latin America. See Carlos Diaz-Alejandro, "Good Bye Financial Repression, Hello Financial Crash," *Journal of Development Economics* (September–October 1985), and Vittorio Corbo and Jaime de Melo, eds., "Liberalization with Stabilization in the Southern Cone of Latin America" [special issue], *World Development* (August 1985).

From these country cases, it is clear that macroeconomic stabilization policies must precede deregulation of banks and other financial institutions. The developing country must also avoid overborrowing from abroad when a liberalization program appears to be successful. See Ronald I. McKinnon, "Monetary Stabilization in LDCs and the International Capital Market," Stanford Center for Research in Economic Growth (June 1986, mimeographed), and *The Order of Economic Liberalization* (1991); World Bank, *World Development Report 1989* (1989), chap. 9.

Contrary to the models of financial repression, however, the empirical evidence is ambiguous regarding whether a rise in real deposit rates has a positive effect on saving ratios. As discussed in

EXHIBIT IV.4. Saving and Investment Under a Financial Constraint

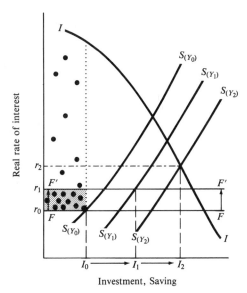

Investment, Saving

According to Maxwell Fry,

The essential common elements of the McKinnon-Shaw model are shown. Savings $S_{(Y_0)}$ at income level Y_0 is a function of the real interest rate.

F represents the financial constraint, taken here to consist simply of an administratively determined institutional nominal interest rate, which holds the real rate r below its equilibrium level.

Actual investment is limited to I_0, the amount of saving forthcoming at the fixed real interest rate r_0.

Nonprice rationing of investible funds must occur. This typically takes place on the basis of quality of collateral, political pressures, "name," loan size, and covert benefits to the responsible loan officers. These criteria can be counted on to discriminate inefficiently between investment opportunities. Indeed, there will be a preference for traditional, low yielding investments because these appear safest and simplest to finance. Interest rate ceilings discourage risktaking by the financial institutions; risk premia cannot be charged when ceilings are binding. This itself rations out a large proportion of potential investors.

Relaxing (raising) the financial constraint from F to F' increases saving and investment. It also rations out all those low yielding investments, illustrated by the dots in the shaded area, that were financed before. Hence, the average efficiency of investment increases. The level of income rises in this process and shifts the saving function to $S_{(Y_1)}$. Thus, the real rate of interest as the return to savers is the key to a higher level of investment, and as a rationing device to greater efficiency. The impacts on growth are multiplicative. The policy prescription is to raise institutional interest rates and/or reduce the rate of inflation.

Abolishing interest rate ceilings altogether produces the optimal result of maximizing investment and raising still further investment's average efficiency. This is shown by the equilibrium at I_2r_2, and a higher income level Y_2. Clearly, changes in the real interest rate trace out the saving function.

Source: Maxwell J. Fry, "Money and Capital or Financial Deepening in Economic Development?" *Journal of Money, Credit and Banking,* Vol. 10, No. 4 (November 1978), pp. 465–66 is reprinted by permission. © 1978 by the Ohio State University Press.

See also Fry, *Money, Interest and Banking in Economic Development* (1987).

IV.D.1, higher interest rates increase the benefits of saving but at the same time reduce the need for saving. The existence of informal curb markets in developing countries may also limit the influence of interest rates on saving.

A number of empirical studies conclude that the net response of savings to interest rates is small. See Rudiger Dornbusch and Alejandro Reynoso, "Financial Factors in Economic Development," in *Policymaking in the Open Economy*, ed., Dornbusch (1993), chap. 4; papers by Paul Collier and Colin Mayer, and Maxwell J. Fry in *Oxford Review of Economic Policy* 5 (1989); and Alberto Giovannini, "Saving and the Real Interest Rate in LDCs," *Journal of Development Economics* 18 (1985).

Even though the increase in savings and hence the quantity of investment may be small, there have been substantial gains in the quality of investment in countries that have undertaken financial liberalization. This result conforms to the better allocation of investment through the market instead of by government direction. Financial liberalization tends to be most effective in raising economic growth through higher productivity of investment.

For other discussions of how to pursue financial liberalization and inflation, see Ronald I. McKinnon and Donald J. Mathieson, *How to Manage a Repressed Economy*, Princeton Essays in International Finance, no. 145 (December 1981); Basant Kapur, "Alternative Stabilization Policies for Less Developed Countries," *Journal of Political Economy* (August 1976); S. Van Wijnbergen, "Interest Rate Management in LDCs," *Journal of Monetary Economics* (September 1983); and L. Taylor, *Structuralist Macroeconomics* (1983).

IV.E.4. The Design of Financial Systems*

The *World Bank Development Report* (World Bank, 1989) provides an excellent synthesis of current wisdom about the relationship between financial systems and economic development. The purpose of this article is to evaluate the proposals presented in that Report.

The Report addresses four sets of issues: macroeconomic policy to promote growth, the role of financial liberalization, government intervention in credit markets, and the design of financial systems. It puts forward the following blueprint for reform:

Reform should start by getting the fiscal deficit under control and establishing macroeconomic stability. The government should then scale down its directed credit programs and adjust the level and pattern of interest rates to bring them into line with inflation and other market forces. In the initial stage of reform the government should also try to improve the foundations of finance—that is, the accounting and legal systems, procedures for the enforcement of contracts, disclosure requirements, and the structure of prudential regulation and supervision. It should encourage managerial autonomy in financial institutions. If in-

stitutional insolvency is widespread, the government may need to restructure some financial institutions in the early stages of reform. (World Bank, 1989, p. 127)

The World Bank is clearly supportive of financial liberalization:

Studies suggest that rigid ceilings on interest rates have hindered the growth of financial saving, and reduced the efficiency of investment. . . . In most countries this overall rigidity has been compounded by a pattern of interest rates that failed to discriminate between borrowers on the basis of loan maturity, risk, or administration cost. Governments have often told banks to charge lower interest rates on loans to small borrowers and on loans of longer maturity. (pp. 128–29)

The World Bank is still more critical of government intervention in the allocation of credit: "the evidence suggests that directed credit programs have been an inefficient way of redistributing income and dealing with imperfection in the goods market" (p. 129). However, it notes that

reforms carried out against an unstable macroeconomic background can make that instability worse. Complete liberalization of interest rates in countries with high and unstable rates of inflation can lead to high real interest rates and wide spreads between lending and deposit rates (p. 127). In countries that

*From Paul Collier and Colin Mayer, "The Assessment: Financial Liberalization, Financial Systems, and Economic Growth," *Oxford Review of Economic Policy*, Vol. 5, No. 4 (1989). Reprinted by permission.

have not yet been restored to macroeconomic stability, governments may need to continue managing interest rates. (p. 129)

In particular, the World Bank suggests that, in the absence of macroeconomic stability, international capital flows can be detrimental. The premature opening of capital markets "can lead to volatile financial flows that can magnify domestic instability" (p. 131).

This conclusion is heavily influenced by the experience of the Latin American "Southern Cone" countries in which the liberalization of international capital movements coincided with excessive appreciation in the real exchange rate followed by capital flight.

In contrast, countries with reasonable macroeconomic stability were able to avoid the pitfalls of high real interest rates, fluctuations in real exchange rates, and insolvency among firms and banks. Some countries with considerable macroeconomic instability chose to liberalize gradually; they retained certain controls on interest rates and capital flows while encouraging greater competition and adjusting interest rates to reflect market conditions. These countries also avoided serious disruption and achieved rapid growth in their financial sectors. (p. 127)

On directed credit, the World Bank argues that

governments should attack the conditions that made directed credit appear desirable—imperfections in markets or extreme inequalities in income—instead of using directed credit programs and interest rate subsidies. With regard to interest rates, the aim should be to eliminate the difference between the subsidized rate and the market rate. (p. 129)

On the restructuring of financial systems,

liberalization should not be limited to the reform of the banking system but should seek to develop a more broadly based financial system that will include money and capital markets and non-bank intermediaries. A balanced and competitive system of finance contributes to macroeconomic stability by making the system more robust in the face of external and internal shocks. Active securities markets increase the supply of equity capital and longer-term credit, which are vital to industrial investment. (p. 130)

This article will consider the role of national governments and international organizations in the development process. It will suggest a life cycle of growth for which different policies are relevant at different stages. It will point to the central function of international agencies not only in financing early stages of growth but also in designing public institutions to administer de-velopment. In turn, a primary function of national governments is the establishment of private financial institutions capable of overseeing the development of corporate sectors.

Underlying the analysis of this paper is a control theory of finance. This points to a relation between capital market failures and the inability of lenders to ensure adequate rates of return. Lenders are exposed to bad borrowers and borrowers that fail to perform adequately. This leads them to limit the degree of control that borrowers can exert. For example, collateralized debt lending allows lenders to take possession of assets where default or violation of covenants has occurred.

In the absence of collateral, reputations are crucial to the elimination of capital market failures. Good reputations are associated with creditworthy institutions of high repute. In the economics literature, reputations encourage the provision of high quality goods and services and improve the operation of markets. The growth cycle involves a progressive transfer of reputations from international organizations to private corporations; more direct methods are impeded by inadequate reputations. In the process of establishing reputations, restrictions that prevent free access to capital markets may be needed. Efficiently administered, they allow governments of high repute to channel funds to profitable activities; inefficiently used, they inhibit entrepreneurship and permit corruption. That there may be "government failure" in the form of incompetence, negligence, and corruption does not justify reliance on market processes. There is a presumption that market failures are sufficiently serious in the financing of economic development that public intervention is required. Good government is crucial to the early stages of development and the challenge that economic development poses is finding the institutional arrangements that are associated with good government. . . .

The 1989 World Bank Development Report provides a valuable record of present thinking on finance and development. It mirrors the compromise view about financial liberalization that has emerged over the past decade: unrestrained financial liberalization can be damaging but, if properly sequenced, it can yield substantial benefits.

The basis for supporting financial liberalization is weak. The benefits of financial liberalization can at best be described as unproven. The relation of savings to interest rates is questionable and the benefits of improved resource allocation at higher interest rates seems to have more to do with the role of financial institutions than interest rates *per se*. Empirical studies that attempt to draw inferences from reduced form cross-sectional relations between real interest rates and growth rates in different countries for the effects of liberalization are particularly suspect. Even if the relation is valid then the direction of causation is unclear. It may merely reflect common independent factors (such as the rate of inflation), rather than an influence of interest rates on growth.

In contrast, there may be significant benefits of access to international markets for smoothing aggregate shocks and hedging risks. To date, developing countries have been unable to exploit these opportunities fully because of the sovereign risks to which investors have been exposed.

The extensive debate about financial liberalization has seriously distracted attention from the real issues associated with the design of financial institutions and markets. The World Bank attaches undue importance to securities markets in the development process. The role of securities markets can be expected to be concentrated in the financing of large well-established firms. As a consequence, their main contribution comes quite late in the development cycle. Instead, it is to banks that developing countries have to turn for the financing of growth.

But the more general criticism of the Report is that it does not fully acknowledge the implications of capital market failures. These failures are primarily associated with imperfect information. They create problems of underinvestment and capital rationing. Their resolution requires a greater degree of control by international agencies and governments than the financial liberalization literature suggests.

The first problem that developing countries face is devising macroeconomic policies that are consistent with the pursuit of economic growth. It is generally accepted that macroeconomic stability is a prerequisite for growth. But this suggests a passive role for government. The case for active management comes from the absence of adequate private sector institutions in the early stages of development. Inadequate managerial resources are one of the most serious constraints that developing countries face and as a consequence they should almost of necessity be concentrated in a small number of institutions.

In the first instance, governments are reliant on domestic financial resources. To relax the tight constraint that this imposes, international organizations should not only provide financial assistance but, more crucially, oversee the establishment of domestic public institutions that are capable of administering growth. In turn, governments are required to assist in the creation of intermediaries that are capable of financing and controlling corporations.

While establishing reputations, governments may limit private sector borrowing and lending by imposing capital controls. Furthermore, while developing private sector institutions, controls—in particular interest-rate ceilings— may be imposed on competition between institutions. At this stage, the economy will be characterized by a high proportion of intermediated bank finance, controls on the operation of financial institutions, exchange controls, and a high degree of central direction from government.

It is later, when a significant number of firms of high repute have been established, that liberalization can be considered. The first stage is to permit firms access to a broader set of domestic sources of finance. Securities markets can be used to augment and eventually substitute for finance available from banks. Controls on the operation of banks can be lifted and competition between financial institutions encouraged. Finally, once a country has established an international reputation, then free access to international capital markets can be permitted.

This is no more than a form of sequencing. What information and control theories do is to provide a basis on which to structure the design of financial systems. They point to the roles of government and international agencies in the development of financial systems. They bring out the hierarchical nature of the relation between different parties and the reasons why the restrictive control that is associated with these hierarchies is required. Finally, they point to the stage at which the elimination of these hierarchical arrangements and the liberalization of financial systems is warranted.

CHAPTER V

External Financing of Development

Most of the developing world still has to supplement domestic savings with finance from abroad. This chapter considers how to improve the process of transferring capital from rich to poor countries—whether the transfer is in the form of public financial aid, loans from private foreign banks, or private foreign investment.

As explained in V.A, an internal imbalance in the macroeconomy of a developing country—a resource gap—leads to an external imbalance in its balance of payments—a foreign-exchange gap. The foreign-exchange gap must be filled by a capital inflow from overseas through official development assistance, commercial bank loans, or private foreign investment (unless the deficit country is able to use foreign-exchange reserves to cover its external imbalance). External debt accumulates when the foreign loans are used to finance an excess of imports over exports plus interest payments on existing debt. The working out of the external debt will depend, in turn, on a reduction in the resource gap, lower interest rates, and a declining current account deficit. The working out of debt will be more prolonged the slower the growth rate of national output, the lower the debtor country's marginal saving rate, and the less productive its capital investment.

Section V.B focuses on issues that are of the most analytic and policy interest in the transfer of foreign aid. Public financial aid—that is, concessional finance or the "grant equivalent" in the capital inflow—has a twofold function. It supplements the LDC's low domestic savings, hence helping to fill the resource gap or "savings gap," and it provides additional foreign exchange, thereby helping to fill the "foreign-exchange gap."

In terms of policies, we should recognize the costs of aid to the donor countries as well as the benefits received through aid by the recipient countries. There is considerable controversy over the contribution that aid makes to development. Some economists dissent from the conventional view by arguing that, as an instrument of development, aid is generally of limited value.

With the emphasis now on policy reform, however, many see a new potential for positive links between the transfer of resources and constructive policy change. If, for instance, a policy dialogue between a developing country and donors is to result in a successful stabilization-cum-liberalization program, it may be necessary to underwrite measures of policy reform with foreign assistance.

Although not aid agencies, the International Monetary Fund (IMF) and World Bank are important international financial intermediaries that provide foreign exchange to developing countries under specified conditions. Selection V.B.4 outlines how the IMF and World Bank contribute to the financing of development.

In recent years the external debt problem of developing countries has become of intense concern. After the oil shock of the early 1970s, commercial banks became highly liquid with petrodollars in Eurocurrency deposits. A historically unique rise in commercial bank lending to governments of developing countries followed as cross-border sovereign lending to governments of developing countries grew. In the early 1980s, however, a debt crisis emerged, centering on the "MBA problem"— Mexico, Brazil, and Argentina. In 1992, the publicly guaranteed external debt of the developing countries amounted to nearly $1.5 trillion. Debt servicing (payment of interest and amortization) amounted to over 21 percent of the value of the low-income countries' exports and was nearly 32 percent for the developing countries of the Western Hemisphere. For severely indebted countries, their total external debt was over 46 percent of their GNP and was at a heavy discount on secondary markets. The economic burden of transferring the debt service was onerous for many countries, and for those that were politically fragile the difficulty was compounded. The large accumulation of debt—much of it of short or medium maturity—has raised fears of a crisis of liquidity, if not of solvency, for debtor nations. Problems of adjustment and debt strategy remain acute.

Section V.D focuses on issues of external debt, with particular attention to country risk analysis, as explained in V.D.2. This section on external debt explores some basic questions: Can a country grow with debt? Can it grow out of its debt? Is a country's external debt problem one of liquidity or solvency? Who should bear the risk of default? What are possible solutions to the debt problem?

Increasing attention is now being given to the potential for private foreign investment in developing countries. This interest is because of a desire in many countries to extend the market-price system and the private sector, to encourage more privatization programs, and to mitigate the external debt problem by attracting more private foreign capital. The desire to increase the equity to debt ratio on foreign capital is based on some relative advantage of foreign direct investment over foreign loans from the standpoint of balance-of-payments adjustment.

To attract a greater quantity—and improved quality—of private foreign investment, however, rationalization of public policy with respect to private foreign investment is still necessary. The discussion is Section V.E is concerned with policy measures that a host country might take to obtain a more substantial contribution to its development program from private foreign capital. To assess the potential contribution of private foreign investment, Note V.E.1 outlines the benefits and costs of various forms of private foreign investment, viewed from the standpoint of the recipient country's development program. As an agent of private foreign investment, the multinational corporation (MNC) merits special consideration, with particular attention to the nature of the bargaining process between host countries and foreign investors.

Unless foreign aid increases and commercial banks resume lending to developing countries, even greater reliance will have to be placed on private international capital markets for the necessary net resource flows to support development. This type of assistance requires increased financial integration of developing countries with global capital markets. With such integration, the issues raised in Section V.E will become all the more important—the benefit–cost analysis of private foreign investment, the operation of multinational corporations, and the bargaining process between multinationals and host governments.

V.A. RESOURCE GAP AND FOREIGN-EXCHANGE GAP— NOTE

To understand the necessity for external financing, we should recognize the relationship between national-income analysis and balance-of-payments analysis. If there is an internal macroimbalance between national expenditure and national saving, then there will also be an external imbalance in the balance of payments.

In national-income analysis, the uses of national income $(C + I + G + X - M)$ must equal the disposal of national income $(C + S + T)$, where C is consumption, I gross investment, G government expenditure, X exports, M imports, S gross saving, and T taxes.

Rearranging, we derive the fundamental relationship:

$$(I + G) - (S + T) = (M - X)$$

This relationship underlies many of the selections in this chapter. It states that when a country is spending more on investment and government expenditure than it is earning from the resources released through private savings and taxation, there will be a resource gap within the economy, and then imports will be greater than exports. The resource gap thus spills over into the balance of payments and creates a foreign-exchange gap. The only way to validate investment and government expenditures in real terms when insufficient resources are being released at home by savings and taxes is by importing goods and services. Foreign resources are then filling the domestic resource gap.

But when imports exceed exports, the country confronts a foreign-exchange gap that has to be filled. This can be done by losing foreign-exchange reserves or through external financing. For a developing country, the sources of external financing are foreign aid from government to government, cross-border sovereign lending by commercial banks, private foreign investment (foreign direct investment and portfolio investment), loans from the World Bank, and access to the country's drawing rights in the IMF. The financial inflow to fill the foreign-exchange gap allows the real capital transfer in the form of imports greater than exports.

For a developing country, it is common to have low private savings and negative government savings (i.e., $G > T$). If domestic investment is then to be high, the inflow of foreign capital will have to be large.

How large a capital inflow is needed? This amount depends on the target level of GNP. To support the target GNP, the gross capital inflow must cover the balance-of-trade deficit $(M - X)$ generated at that level of GNP, plus any servicing of external debt, outflow of interest, dividends, and profits on private foreign investment, capital flight, and the desired buildup of foreign-exchange reserves.

The net capital inflow will equal the gross capital inflow minus debt service outflow on private foreign investment, capital flight, and buildup of reserves. The net capital inflow is equivalent to the net resource transfer. And it is the net resource transfer that finances $(I + G)$ greater than $(S + T)$, or M greater than X, or national expenditure greater than national output. In other words, the external financing fills the resource gap and the foreign-exchange gap, thereby allowing national expenditure $(C + I + G)$ to be greater than the value of products produced domestically. Exhibit V.5 shows net resource flows in recent years to developing countries.

Comment: Foreign-Exchange Constraint

A two-gap analysis of capital requirements has been formulated by Hollis Chenery and Michael Bruno, ''Development Alternatives in an Open Economy,'' *Economic Journal* 72 (1962), and Hollis B. Chenery and Alan H. Strout, ''Foreign Assistance and Economic Development,'' *American Economic Review* (September 1966). According to this analysis, foreign capital fills both the savings gap and the foreign-exchange gap. In filling the savings gap, foreign capital provides an equivalent increment to the capital stock. If, however, the foreign-exchange constraint prevents the country from importing goods and services that are required to complement domestic capital in production, then the inflow of foreign capital will not only add additional capital but will also allow domestic capital that would otherwise be redundant to be utilized in production.

EXHIBIT V.1. Payments Balances on Current Account (billions of U.S. dollars)

	1985	1986	1987	1988	1989	1990	1991	1992
Developing countries	**−29.6**	**−50.7**	**−9.7**	**−28.7**	**−22.0**	**−21.3**	**−81.9**	**−78.4**
By Region								
Africa	−0.5	−9.4	−4.5	−9.6	−6.5	−2.3	−4.0	−7.8
Asia	−15.9	2.0	18.0	6.3	−4.5	−6.5	−6.6	−21.2
Middle East and Europe	−9.1	−24.8	−12.0	−13.8	−2.5	−5.6	−53.0	−15.8
Western Hemisphere	−4.1	−18.6	−11.1	−11.6	−8.4	−6.8	−18.4	−33.5
Sub-Saharan Africa	−3.4	−5.5	−6.1	−7.4	−6.2	−8.1	−8.7	−9.4
Four newly industrializing Asian economies	8.3	21.2	27.7	25.2	18.9	10.8	7.5	−1.5
By Predominant Export								
Fuel	−2.8	−39.4	−12.4	−29.6	−10.9	−4.2	−68.4	−45.7
Nonfuel exports	−26.8	−11.4	2.7	0.9	−11.1	−17.1	−13.5	−32.6
Manufactures	−9.9	2.6	18.8	17.6	7.4	0.3	6.3	−3.5
Primary products	−10.1	−11.1	−14.8	−12.5	−11.1	−10.5	−13.4	−20.2
Agricultural products	−7.8	−7.6	−11.2	−9.7	−9.4	−6.7	−9.8	−15.8
Minerals	−2.3	−3.5	−3.6	−2.7	−1.8	−3.8	−3.5	−4.4
Services and private transfers	−6.4	−5.1	−5.2	−5.9	−6.2	−5.5	−3.8	−2.6
Diversified export base	−0.4	2.3	3.8	1.7	−1.2	−1.4	−2.6	−6.3
By Financial Criteria								
Net creditor countries	11.2	5.5	14.7	5.0	13.5	13.4	−40.9	−16.8
Net debtor countries	−40.8	−56.2	−24.4	−33.7	−35.6	−34.7	−41.0	−61.6
Market borrowers	−13.4	−20.0	4.1	−0.1	−4.9	0.3	−20.1	−35.7
Diversified borrowers	−15.9	−19.4	−15.7	−18.5	−16.7	−24.7	−9.4	−14.5
Official borrowers	−11.5	−16.8	−12.8	−15.1	−13.9	−10.4	−11.5	−11.4
Countries with recent debt-servicing difficulties	−15.1	−40.4	−24.0	−29.9	−22.3	−19.8	−27.4	−42.6
Countries without debt-servicing difficulties	−25.7	−15.9	−0.4	−3.7	−13.2	−14.9	−13.5	−18.9

Source: International Monetary Fund, *World Economic Outlook* (May 1993), p. 164.

In neoclassical analysis, an increase in domestic savings should also relax the foreign-exchange constraint through the release of resources for import-substitute industries or for exports. In the two-gap analysis, however, this may not occur for structural reasons: there may not be sufficient domestic substitutes for necessary imports, there may be a fixed coefficient between imports and domestic output, and exports may face a highly inelastic demand.

Some fundamental theoretical formulations of the foreign-exchange constraint, two-gap analysis, and foreign capital requirements are presented in the following studies: R. McKinnon, "Foreign-Exchange Constraints in Economic Development" *Economic Journal* (June 1964); H. J. Bruton, "The Two-Gap Approach to Aid and Development: Comment," *American Economic Review* (June 1969); Vijay Joshi, "Saving and Foreign Exchange Constraints," in *Unfashionable Economics*, ed. Paul P. Streeten (1970); K. Dervis, J. de Melo and S. Robinson, "General Equilibrium Analysis of Foreign Exchange Shortages in a Developing Economy," *Economic Journal* (December 1981); Paul Mosley, "Aid, Savings and Growth Revisited," *Oxford Bulletin of Economics and Statistics* (May 1980); and Howard White, "The Macroeconomic Impact of Development Aid: A Critical Survey," *Journal of Development Studies* (January 1992).

Comment: Capital Flight

As seen in Note V.A, external finance increases a country's potential for greater investment, but this might be offset by capital flight from the country. The country's debt-servicing problems will also be aggravated by capital flight. The World Bank measures capital flight as a "net residual" by subtracting from the sources of foreign capital (external borrowing + foreign direct investment) the uses of foreign capital (current account deficit + increase in reserves). By this measure, a high stock of flight capital is a widespread phenomenon—not only from Latin America and the Caribbean, but even more so from Sub-Saharan Africa and the Middle East. According to the World Bank, at its peak during the 1980s global capital flight from developing countries amounted to nearly $80 billion per year, and the stock of capital flight amounted to $700 billion at the end of 1990, or 55 percent of the external debt stock at that time.[1]

Capital flight occurs when adverse repercussions are expected from overvalued real exchange rates, fiscal deficits financed by inflation, or policies of expropriation or high taxation on domestic assets. The political fragility of a developing economy also exacerbates uncertainty and induces an outflow of capital to a safe haven.

In the 1990s, capital flight reversed itself, with substantial return flows to Latin America. In 1992, capital inflows reached $36 billion. The Inter-American Development Bank attributes this turnaround to policy reforms in Latin American countries that have stabilized their economies, stimulated economic growth, and diminished currency risk. To the extent, however, that a large part of these new flows represent portfolio investment in a few Latin American countries, they are subject to considerable volatility.

[1] World Bank, *Global Economic Prospects and the Developing Countries* (1993): 24.

EXHIBIT V.2. Investment, Savings, and Resource Balance

	Distribution of Gross Domestic Product (percent)					
	Gross Domestic Investment		Gross Domestic Savings		Resource Balance	
	1970	1991	1970	1991	1970	1991
Low-income economies	**21** *w*	**27** *w*	**20** *w*	**27** *w*	**−1** *w*	**−1** *w*
China and India	**24** *w*	**29** *w*	**24** *w*	**31** *w*	**0** *w*	**1** *w*
Other low-income	**15** *w*	**22** *w*	**12** *w*	**17** *w*	**−4** *w*	**−6** *w*
Mozambique	—	42	—	−10	—	−52
Tanzania	23	22	20	−11	−2	−33
Ethiopia	11	10	11	0	0	−10
Uganda	13	12	164	−1	3	−13
Bhutan	—	—	—	—	—	−12
Guinea-Bissau	30	30	3	−3	−26	−33
Nepal	6	19	3	5	−3	−14
Burundi	5	17	4	−1	−1	−18
Chad	18	8	10	−17	−8	−25
Madagascar	10	8	7	−1	−2	−9
Sierra Leone	17	11	15	4	−2	−6
Bangladesh	11	10	7	3	−4	−7
Lao People's Dem. Rep.	—	—	—	—	—	−14
Malawi	26	20	11	9	−15	−11
Rwanda	7	13	3	1	−4	−11
Mali	16	23	10	6	−6	−16
Burkina Faso	12	23	−1	4	−12	−19
Niger	10	9	3	7	−7	−3
India	17	20	16	19	−1	−1
Kenya	24	21	24	19	−1	−1
Nigeria	15	16	12	23	−3	6
China	28	36	29	39	0	3

(continued)

EXHIBIT V.2. (*continued*)

| | Distribution of Gross Domestic Product (percent) | | | | | |
| | Gross Domestic Investment | | Gross Domestic Savings | | Resource Balance | |
	1970	1991	1970	1991	1970	1991
Haiti	11	—	7	—	−4	—
Benin	12	12	5	3	−6	−9
Central African Rep.	19	11	4	−1	−15	−12
Ghana	14	16	13	8	−1	−8
Pakistan	16	19	9	12	−7	−7
Togo	15	19	26	10	11	−9
Guinea	—	18	—	14	—	−4
Nicaragua	18	21	16	−10	−2	−31
Sri Lanka	19	23	16	13	−3	−10
Mauritania	22	16	30	10	8	−6
Yemen, Rep.	—	13	—	2	—	−11
Honduras	21	24	15	20	−6	−4
Lesotho	12	93	−32	−13	−44	−106
Indonesia	16	35	14	36	−2	1
Egypt, Arab Rep.	14	20	9	7	−5	−13
Zimbabwe	20	22	21	18	—	−4
Sudan	14	—	15	—	2	—
Zambia	28	13	45	12	17	−1
Middle-income economies						
Lower-middle-income						
Bolivia	24	14	24	9	0	−5
Côte d'Ivoire	22	10	29	15	7	5
Senegal	16	14	11	9	−5	−5
Philippines	21	20	22	19	1	−1
Papua New Guinea	42	29	6	13	−35	−16
Cameroon	16	15	18	15	2	0
Guatemala	13	14	14	10	1	−4
Dominican Rep.	19	17	12	14	−7	−3
Ecuador	18	22	14	22	−5	0
Morocco	18	22	15	17	−4	−6
Jordan	—	21	—	−1	—	−22
Peru	16	16	17	13	2	−3
El Salvador	13	14	13	1	0	−12
Congo	24	11	1	20	−23	9
Syrian Arab Rep.	14	—	10	—	−4	—
Colombia	20	15	18	23	−2	8
Paraguay	15	25	14	17	−1	−8
Jamaica	32	20	27	20	−4	0
Romania	—	34	—	29	—	−5
Namibia	—	14	—	9	—	−5
Tunisia	21	23	17	18	−4	−5
Kyrgyzstan	—	34	—	34	—	−1
Thailand	26	39	21	32	−4	−7
Turkey	20	20	17	17	−2	−3
Poland	—	21	—	22	—	0
Bulgaria	—	13	—	15	—	2
Costa Rica	21	23	14	22	−7	−1
Algeria	36	30	29	36	−7	6

EXHIBIT V.2. (*continued*)

| | Distribution of Gross Domestic Product (percent) | | | | | |
| | Gross Domestic Investment | | Gross Domestic Savings | | Resource Balance | |
	1970	1991	1970	1991	1970	1991
Panama	28	15	24	7	−3	−8
Chile	16	19	17	24	1	5
Iran, Islamic Rep.	19	20	25	10	6	−11
Mauritius	10	28	11	23	1	−5
Czechoslovakia	—	31	—	—	—	2
Malaysia	22	36	27	30	4	−5
Upper-middle-income	**24** *w*	—	**23** *w*	—	**−1** *w*	—
Botswana	42	—	2	—	−41	—
South Africa	28	16	24	21	−4	5
Lithuania	—	21	—	21	—	—
Hungary	34	19	31	19	−2	0
Venezuela	33	19	37	23	4	5
Argentina	22	12	22	15	*a*	2
Uruguay	*a*	13	−1	17	−1	4
Brazil	21	*20*	20	*30*	0	*0*
Mexico	21	23	19	20	−3	−3
Belarus	—	30	—	—	—	−1
Russian Federation	—	39	—	40	—	0
Latvia	—	34	—	43	—	10
Trinidad and Tobago	26	18	27	26	1	8
Gabon	32	26	44	42	12	16
Estonia	—	29	—	25	—	−4
Portugal	26	—	20	—	−7	—
Oman	14	17	68	26	54	10
Puerto Rico	29	16	10	22	−18	6
Korea, Rep.	25	39	15	36	−10	−3
Greece	28	17	20	8	−8	−9
Saudi Arabia	16	—	47	—	31	—
Yugoslavia	32	*21*	27	*21*	−5	*−1*
Low- and middle-income	**23** *w*	**24** *w*	**21** *w*	—	**−1** *w*	—
Sub-Saharan Africa	**17** *w*	**16** *w*	**16** *w*	**14** *w*	**−1** *w*	**−3** *w*
East Asia and Pacific	**26** *w*	**35** *w*	**25** *w*	**36** *w*	**−1** *w*	**−1** *w*
South Asia	**16** *w*	**19** *w*	**14** *w*	**17** *w*	**−2** *w*	**−3** *w*
Middle East and North Africa	**19** *w*	—	**25** *w*	—	**5** *w*	—
Latin America and Caribbean	**21** *w*	**19** *w*	**20** *w*	—	**−2** *w*	**−1** *w*
Severely indebted	**22** *w*	**20** *w*	**21** *w*	—	—	—

Note: Countries in italics: no current estimates of GNP per capita.
Figures in italics: years other than those specified.
a = General government consumption figures are not available separately; they are included in private consumption, etc.; *w* = weighted average.
Source: World Bank, *World Development Report 1993* (1993), pp. 254–55.

EXHIBIT V.3. Summary of External Financing (billions of U.S. dollars)

	1986	1987	1988	1989	1990	1991	1992	1993	1994	1995
Developing Countries										
Balance on current account, excluding official transfers	−60.9	−20.8	−40.7	−33.2	−26.7	−80.0	−87.5	−124.1	−124.7	−117.8
Change in reserves (− = increase)	−5.6	−48.2	1.8	−24.7	−42.5	−67.7	−52.0	−48.2	−22.9	−25.5
Asset transactions, including net errors and omissions	−7.2	8.6	−21.4	−7.8	−14.8	47.7	18.7	24.2	18.8	23.1
Total, net external financing	**73.7**	**60.4**	**60.3**	**65.8**	**84.0**	**100.0**	**120.8**	**148.1**	**128.8**	**120.2**
Non-debt-creating flows, net	26.9	35.5	26.5	30.5	31.2	20.1	54.1	66.7	67.7	59.9
Official transfers	14.0	16.0	15.8	16.3	15.1	−7.9	20.4	19.5	18.5	17.0
Direct investment	12.9	19.5	10.7	14.2	16.1	28.0	33.7	47.3	49.3	42.9
Reserve-related liabilities	−1.9	−2.7	−3.4	−1.0	−4.5	1.8	−0.6	1.2	−0.9	−2.1
Net credit from IMF	−2.2	−4.7	−4.1	−1.5	−1.9	1.6	−0.2	−0.3	—	—
Net external borrowing	48.7	27.5	37.2	36.2	57.3	78.1	67.4	80.2	62.0	62.4
Memorandum										
Balance on goods and nonfactor services in percent of GDP	−0.8	0.6	0.1	0.3	0.5	−1.0	−1.3	−1.8	−1.6	−1.2
Scheduled amortization of external debt	88.6	104.8	108.0	95.1	103.8	101.2	116.3	120.8	122.7	124.7
Gross external financing	162.2	165.2	168.4	160.9	187.8	201.3	237.1	268.9	251.6	244.9
Gross external borrowing	137.3	132.3	145.2	131.4	161.1	179.3	183.7	201.0	184.8	187.1
Exceptional financing	37.9	44.8	38.0	39.6	45.3	31.8	33.0	24.0	20.9	13.8
Arrears on debt service	7.6	5.1	11.4	15.0	16.5	−3.1	−5.1	6.5	—	—
Rescheduling of debt service	28.6	38.5	25.2	19.5	21.7	25.7	30.7	11.2	—	—
Net long-term borrowing from official creditors	31.5	30.7	20.8	21.7	35.7	27.6	38.1	33.6	5.9	14.0
Net borrowing from commercial banks	4.5	10.6	−1.1	3.7	25.8	35.4	11.3	13.7	38.0	17.2

Note: Projected estimates are given for 1994 and 1995.

Source: International Monetary Fund, *World Economic Outlook* (May 1994), p. 152.

V.B. PUBLIC FINANCIAL AID

V.B.1. Why Official Assistance?*

The next question is whether there is an economic (as opposed to humanitarian or political) rationale for official development assistance, concessional or otherwise. Critics of aid have alleged that, if profitable investments are available, private international capital markets will finance them. Insofar as the motive for aid is humanitarian, that is not a criticism (as long as aid does not impair development). Nonetheless, the bigger questions are whether world economic efficiency can be enhanced by official flows at market terms, and whether it can be increased by an official flow that could not be financed at market terms.

Clearly, a recipient's potential welfare could always be increased by a grant, whereas the donor's potential welfare might be reduced. The interesting questions are: (1) given optimal policies in recipient countries (those that maximize the economic welfare of their citizens), can foreign aid enhance worldwide efficiency and be in the economic self-interest, narrowly defined, of both donor and recipient? and (2) are there circumstances in which the answer to the first question is yes, but it would not pay the recipient to accept capital on commercial terms? These two questions are the subject of this selection. It is useful to start by assuming, first, that economic efficiency exists in a developing country, in the sense that, given resource constraints, domestic policies are consistent with efficient allocation of domestic resources; and, second, that aid is nothing more than a capital flow. The end of this selection will consider how to modify the analysis if aid is viewed as part of a bundled transfer of resources, including institution building, technical know-how, policy leverage, and capital.

Question 1. Could Official Flows Improve the Welfare of Both Donor and Recipient?

The answer to this question hinges on whether imperfections in the private international capital market preclude it from equalizing (risk-adjusted) rates of return between donor and recipient. If returns were higher in developing countries, the welfare of both donor and recipient could be improved through official flows. The recipient could service its debt and nonetheless have a higher future income stream than would otherwise be possible. Simultaneously, the donor could obtain a rate of return equal to or greater than that obtainable on other assets.

Consider, first, maximization of world welfare in the context of a simple two-factor neoclassical model. If the usual conditions for economic efficiency are met within individual countries, in the absence of capital flows free trade might fail to equalize factor returns. Gains in world efficiency could then be achieved by developing a means for capital to flow from low-return to high-return countries.

A first conclusion, therefore, is that official flows on commercial terms could not reduce world welfare. Indeed, they would normally be expected to increase world welfare if private financing were not available. This conclusion is based on the assumption that the development assistance permits incremental investments with real returns at least as great as the return to the donor, but for present purposes that is subsumed by the assumption of policy optimality in borrowing countries, even after they receive aid. Another underlying assumption is that behavior in the borrowing country is not influenced—or at least not negatively influenced—by the recipient of official development assistance. Since there is some basis for thinking that official development assistance is more likely to influence behavior positively (see below), this assumption does not alter the analysis.

Subject to these various qualifications, official flows on commercial terms would not reduce welfare but would increase it if they encouraged improved policies or if private markets failed to supply the capital instead, despite the higher real rates of return.

The remaining question is thus why the private international capital market might fail in this way. In the 1940s and 1950s, thinking on aid hardly addressed this question because the capital markets had broken down in the 1930s

*From Anne O. Krueger, "Aid in the Development Process," *World Bank Research Observer*, Vol. 1, No. 1 (January 1986), pp. 63–67. Reprinted by permission.

and during World War II. By the 1970s, however, they were functioning—if anything by providing too much capital.

After the debt crisis of the early 1980s, however, many analysts doubt whether private flows will resume, at least on a scale that could match the supply of profitable opportunities in developing countries. Some believe that there is a herd instinct among commercial bankers, who overlent in the 1970s and now will be irrationally unwilling to resume lending—even to countries that appear able to borrow and achieve the returns to service their debt (see Guttentag and Herring, 1984, for an elaboration of that view). Although other types of private capital may in the future partly compensate for reduced commercial bank lending, they are unlikely to do so to any great extent. This view, if correct, would certainly suggest that official flows at commercial terms could play a larger role than in the 1970s and increase world economic efficiency.

A second source of concern about developing countries' ability to use the private international capital market centers on the "debt overhang." For some developing countries, it is argued, current debts are so great relative to their existing income that increases in future earnings must be tapped to finance their existing obligations. Because foreigners correctly perceive this claim on future income, they will not lend even for new projects that would yield acceptable returns. This inability to insulate new claims from existing debts leaves countries in a vicious circle: they cannot restore creditworthiness without growth, and they cannot grow until creditworthiness is restored. The private capital market may thus fail despite the rational behavior of all participants, and there is a strong analytical case for official assistance on commercial terms.

Question 2. Why Concessional Aid?

Even though international commercial capital is available and there are projects that would yield the necessary returns, are there circumstances in which it would not pay anyone in the recipient country (including the government) to undertake the project at commercial terms? Most analysts of aid have focused on two reasons why this might be the case: the gestation or payout period of projects is too long, and the investor cannot fully capture the stream of returns.

Many investments by developing countries do have long gestation or payout periods. One obvious example is in the area of education projects, which occur over a period of a decade or more, followed by an even longer payout. In addition, some investments (in roads, ports, and power stations, for example) have such large indivisibilities that returns are low in their early years.

At a microeconomic level, if a project's repayments stream is not matched with the earnings stream it generates, an investor would not undertake it unless he had other earnings streams (or borrowing possibilities) to service his obligations in the project's early years. One could ask, of course, why the country could not refinance (or borrow more) to cover debt-servicing obligations in the years prior to high returns. In reality, the capital flows to developing countries have had a maturity structure of ten years or less (implicitly even less in the late 1970s, when the inflation premium in the nominal interest rate rose). At a macroeconomic level, therefore, poor countries may be unable to borrow at or near commercial terms to finance much of their infrastructural investment, despite adequate real rates of return in the long run.

A second, related difficulty is that many investments in the early stages of development entail public financing of activities that have significant externalities and for which user charges may not be appropriate. Roads are an example: with initially low utilization and negligible congestion costs, charging users is neither feasible (because collection costs exceed potential revenue) nor desirable (because the marginal cost of use is very low). And the government may not be able to finance the project on anything like commercial terms, even though incomes may be rising and increasing the tax base, because in a poor country only a fraction of incremental income is taxed.

These considerations would appear to have most relevance for the very poorest countries: the ones with high levels of illiteracy, rudimentary transport and communications systems, and low savings rates. It must be emphasized that this case for concessionality is based on the productivity of investment in these countries and is additional to the case based on need or humanitarian motives.

Question 3. What Kind of Aid as a "Bundle"?

This paper has so far treated aid purely as a capital flow. In practice, aid (and other capital,

EXHIBIT V.4. Official Development Assistance: Receipts

	Net Disbursement of ODA from All Sources								
	Millions of Dollars							Per Capita (dollars) 1991	As Percentage of GNP 1991
	1985	1986	1987	1988	1989	1990	1991		
Low-income economies	17,432 t	19,484 t	21,412 t	24,513 t	24,763 t	30,653 t	31,921 t	10.2 w	3.0 w
China and India	2,532 t	3,254 t	3,300 t	4,086 t	4,048 t	3,605 t	4,701 t	2.3 w	0.8 w
Other low-income	14,900 t	16,230 t	18,112 t	20,427 t	20,715 t	27,047 t	27,220 t	24.5 w	6.6 w
Middle-income economies	9,037 t	9,439 t	10,430 t	9,621 t	10,013 t	15,412 t	15,500 t	16.2 w	0.7 w
Lower-middle-income	7,049 t	8,087 t	9,027 t	8,257 t	8,533 t	13,629 t	13,639 t	24.3 w	1.8 w
Low- and middle-income	26,469 t	29,155 t	32,027 t	34,286 t	34,934 t	46,127 t	47,453 t	11.6 w	1.5 w
Sub-Saharan Africa	9,522 t	10,587 t	11,926 t	13,470 t	13,848 t	16,538 t	16,158 t	33.1 w	10.0 w
East Asia and Pacific	4,881 t	4,955 t	5,935 t	6,869 t	7,251 t	8,007 t	7,594 t	4.5 w	0.7 w
South Asia	4,244 t	5,474 t	5,307 t	6,236 t	6,101 t	6,030 t	7,488 t	6.5 w	2.1 w
Europe and Central Asia	247 t	403 t	458 t	359 t	207 t	1,307 t	1,896 t	20.6 w	1.0 w
Middle East and North Africa	4,710 t	4,474 t	4,700 t	3,670 t	3,517 t	9,747 t	9,300 t	38.1 w	2.3 w
Latin America and Caribbean	3,024 t	3,262 t	3,701 t	3,682 t	4,010 t	4,498 t	5,017 t	11.4 w	0.5 w
Severely indebted	3,633 t	3,851 t	4,166 t	3,544 t	3,373 t	5,976 t	6,488 t	14.9 w	0.6 w

Note: w = weighted average; t = total.
Source: World Bank, *World Development Report 1993* (1993), pp. 276–77.

EXHIBIT V.5. Total Net Resource Flows to Developing Countries

	Current $ Billion				1990 Prices and Exchange Rates			
	1970	1980	1990	1991	1970	1980	1990	1991
I. Official development finance (ODF)	8.9	34.3	69.9	72.8	39.1	54.2	69.9	70.4
1. Official development assistance (ODA)	7.9	27.3	52.7	55.8	34.7	43.1	52.7	54.0
Bilateral disbursements	6.8	19.5	39.2	41.8	29.9	30.8	39.2	40.4
Multilateral disbursements	1.1	7.8	13.5	14.0	4.8	12.3	13.5	13.5
2. Other ODF	1.0	7.0	17.2	17.0	4.4	11.1	17.2	16.4
Bilateral disbursements	0.3	2.2	7.0	7.0	1.3	3.5	7.0	6.8
Multilateral disbursements	0.7	4.8	10.2	10.0	3.1	7.6	10.2	9.7
II. Total export credits	2.7	17.2	4.7	3.1	11.9	27.2	4.7	3.0
Long-term	2.7	14.3	0.1	3.0	11.9	22.6	0.1	2.9
Short-term	—	1.8	4.5	—	—	2.8	4.5	—
III. Private flows	8.3	65.5	52.7	55.4	36.5	103.5	52.7	53.6
1. Direct investment (OECD)	3.7	11.2	26.9	28.4	16.2	17.7	26.9	27.5
in offshore centers	4.1	3.0	8.5	—	18.0	4.7	8.5	—
2. International bank lending	3.0	49.0	18.5	7.0	13.2	77.4	18.5	6.8
Short-term	—	26.0	9.0	7.0	—	41.1	9.0	6.8
3. Total bond lending	0.3	1.1	−3.2	9.0	1.3	1.7	−3.2	8.7
4. Other private	0.4	1.8	5.6	6.0	1.8	2.8	5.6	5.8
5. Grants by non-governmental organizations	0.9	2.4	4.9	5.2	4.0	3.8	4.9	4.8
Total net resource flows (I + II + III)	19.9	117.0	127.3	131.5	87.4	184.8	127.3	127.2

Source: OECD, *Developing Cooperation, 1992 Report* (1992), p. 78.

such as direct private investment) can be much more: donors may provide technical assistance with project design, know-how on organization and management, and so on. This assistance has undoubtedly been of great importance in many areas: the green revolution is perhaps the most visible and dramatic example.

For present purposes, however, one aspect of the aid bundle, the policy dialogue, deserves special attention. Recipients may be influenced in their choice of macroeconomic policies in the course of the dialogue, which can take many forms: discussion and persuasion, information on policy effectiveness and techniques for reform, support for reform efforts, and "conditionality"—that is, aid is given only if certain policies are changed. Regardless of the influence used, foreign assistance could certainly become a means of speeding policy reform in developing countries.

To the extent that donors have influence over recipients' policies, and are willing to use it, they may perform a function for which private capital markets seem ill-suited. Indeed, one might even imagine a world in which donor influence produced such improvement in world economic efficiency that they made large-scale private investment an attractive proposition. In this light, aid and private capital might well be more complementary than substitutes.

Reference

Guttentag, Jack M., and Richard J. Herring. "Commercial Bank Lending to Less Developed Countries: From Overlending to Underlending to Structural Reform." *Brookings Papers in International Economics,* Vol. 16 (June 1984): 1–52.

V.B.2. Does Aid Work?—Note

Foreign aid has been criticized by commentators on both the right and the left of the political spectrum. Some advocates of private enterprise and critics of governmental activities claim that the receipt of concessional resources from aid donors delays self-reliance on the part of the recipient country, substitutes for domestic saving, fosters *dirigisme*, and allows the postponement of needed policy reform. Others contend that

foreign aid is the source of the North–South confrontation, not its solution. The paramount significance of aid lies in this very important, perhaps momentous, political result. A further pervasive consequence of aid has been to promote or exacerbate the politicization of life in aid-receiving countries. . . . Aid increases the money, patronage, and power of the recipient governments, and thereby their grip over the rest of society. It thus promotes the disastrous politicization of life in the Third World.[1]

From the left come criticisms that aid perpetuates dependence, props up authoritarian and repressive regimes, and perverts domestic development.[2]

Despite these extreme views, most development economists would consider the question "Does aid work?" to be an empirical question that can be answered with only empirical evidence.

Reviewing aid experience, a former director of the Development Advisory Committee (DAC) of the OECD states:

It is obvious that the record of all development assistance by all donors up to now is mixed. It is easy enough to assemble a negative scorecard of mistakes, silly or counter-productive projects, and other failures. But there are some powerful counter points to be made.

First, there have been major and spreading achievements. Multifaceted aid from a number of donors was a catalyst—not the main force, but a strong, indispensable catalyst—for the remarkable improvement in South Asian food production that blossomed in the 1970s. In the case of South Asian agriculture, "success" (by no means complete) was achieved with a very thin spread of aid per capita. In other cases— South Korea and Taiwan, for example—very heavy concentrations of economic aid (in both cases, interestingly, for strategic reasons) have helped lay the base for burgeoning economic expansion. There also has been a good deal of progress—failures as well, but mainly significant, ramifying successes—in helping build such key development-promoting institu-

[1]Peter Bauer and Basil Yamey, "Foreign Aid: What Is at Stake?" *Public Interest* (Summer 1982): 53, 57.

[2]Teresa Hayter, *Aid as Imperialism* (1971).

tions as agricultural universities, technical institutes, and enterprise management training establishments in many countries. Directly and indirectly aid has contributed to the downward trend in birthrates that has begun to appear in certain countries, especially in Asia.

The list of on-balance successes could be many times longer. It constitutes no scientific proof that aid, overall, has had positive and significant net benefits. But it fortifies a strong suspicion that without aid in the 1960s and 1970s, Third World growth (which on average was strong) would have been slower, the outcomes for the poor would have been worse, social and political turbulence would have been greater, and less groundwork would have been laid for further advances. In particular, without aid, the poorest countries, where growth was slower, would have lagged more.[3]

On the question of whether aid substitutes for domestic savings, we need to consider the contentions that

(1) at a given level of income, the domestic saving rate in a recipient is less than it would be in the absence of aid; and (2) at a given level of income, investment is lower than it would be without aid. The first proposition asserts that the recipient will allocate its aid partly for present and partly for future income. The second proposition is more extreme, implying that aid is more than offset by increased domestic consumption.

The first proposition, that the marginal propensity to save is less than one, accords with economic theory and, therefore, is empirically testable. The second proposition, which essentially posits a negative propensity to save, is more extreme and is a priori impossible. Since government macroeconomic policy is a prime determinant of how an economy reacts to the receipt of aid, any outcome, in principle, is possible. Governments committed to the goal of economic growth would adjust macroeconomic policies to foster higher investment as a consequence of receiving aid. Alternatively, they might adjust policies in ways conducive to higher investment, and domestic savings would decline or domestic consumption rise in response to aid.[4]

A number of econometric studies have attempted to estimate the effects of aid on domestic saving rates. A study by Weisskopf reached the most negative conclusion: an estimate that about 23 percent of foreign-capital inflows were offset by declines in domestic sav-

ings.[5] Other studies, however, show different results, generally suggesting a positive marginal propensity to save, so that a part of aid might be offset by extra consumption.[6]

The most extensive study of the contribution of aid concludes that

most aid does indeed "work." It succeeds in achieving its developmental objectives (where those are primary), contributing positively to the recipient countries' economic performance, and not substituting for activities which would have occurred anyway. That is not to say that aid works on every count. Its performance varies by country and by sector.[7]

Aid agencies have also evaluated the effects of their aid to projects. A Development Advisory Committee report concluded that the findings of project evaluations show that about 33 percent of aid's capital projects are highly successful, 33 percent "can be judged satisfactory," and 33 percent are disappointing. Of these last, about 10 percent of the total have to be regarded as "a total loss."[8]

Evaluations of Work Bank projects completed in the 1970s (130 projects representing $10 billion of total investment) showed that 94 percent achieved their major objectives, including the minimum required economic rate of return of 10 percent. The 49 agricultural projects evaluated averaged an economic rate of return of 19.5 percent.[9] Even for the soft loans of the International Development Association (IDA), 80 percent of the projects achieved a rate of return of 10 per-

[3]John P. Lewis, "Development Assistance in the 1980s," in Overseas Development Council, *U.S. Foreign Policy and the Third World: Agenda 1982* (1982), pp. 102–8.

[4]Anne O. Krueger, "Aid in the Development Process," *World Bank Research Observer* (January 1986): 71.

[5]T. E. Weisskopf, "The Impact of Foreign Capital Inflow on Domestic Savings in Underdeveloped Countries," *Journal of International Economics* (February 1972).

[6]K. L. Gupta, "Foreign Capital and Domestic Savings," *Review of Economics and Statistics* (May 1970); Gustav Papanek, "The Effect of Aid and Other Resource Transfers on Savings and Growth in Less Developed Countries," *Economic Journal* (September 1972); J. Bhagwati and E. Grinols, "Foreign Capital Saving and Dependence," *Review of Economics and Statistics* (November 1976); Anne O. Krueger, Constantine Michalopoulos, and Vernon Ruttan, *The Impact of Development Assistance to LDCs* (1987), chap. 4; Paul Bowles, "Foreign Aid and Domestic Savings in Less Developed Countries: Some Tests for Casuality," *World Development* (June 1987); Paul Mosley, "Aid, Savings and Growth Revisited," *Oxford Bulletin of Economics and Statistics* (May 1980).

[7]Robert Cassen & Associates, *Does Aid Work? Report to an Intergovernmental Task Force* (1986), p. 11.

[8]OECD Development Advisory Committee, *Development Cooperation 1985 Review* (1985).

[9]A. W. Clausen, *Address to the Board of Governors of the World Bank* (September 1981).

cent or more. The Asian Development Bank and the Inter-American Development Bank (IDB) have also concluded that 60 percent of samples of their loans fully met their objectives, 30 percent partially did so, and less than 10 percent were marginal or unsatisfactory.

Comment: Effects of Aid

A number of illuminating studies allow additional interpretation of the effects of aid and an evaluation of its effectiveness: R. Ayres, *Banking on the Poor* (1983); P. T. Bauer, *Reality and Rhetoric* (1984); Brandt Commission, *Common Crisis* (1983); Hans W. Singer, "External Aid: For Plans or Projects?" *Economic Journal* (September 1965); Hans Singer et al., *Food Aid* (1987); Roger C. Riddell, *Foreign Aid Reconsidered* (1987); Paul Mosley, *Overseas Aid: Its Defense and Reform* (1987); Vernon W. Ruttan, "Why Foreign Economic Assistance?" *Economic Development and Cultural Change* (January 1989); Anne Krueger et al., *Aid and Development* (1989); Paul Mosley, Jane Harrigan, and John Toye, *Aid and Power* (1991); Howard White, "The Macroeconomic Impact of Development Aid: A Critical Survey," *Journal of Development Studies* (January 1992); and Howard Pack and Janet Rothenberg Pack, "Foreign Aid and the Question of Fungibility," *Review of Economics and Statistics* (May 1993). Also informative are the annual reports of the World Bank, African Development Bank, Asian Development Bank, Inter-American Development Bank, Development Advisory Committee of the OECD, and United States Agency for International Development.

Although failures in aid activities can be cited, these have been mainly in earlier decades of development assistance. With experience, the failures have diminished. Now donor agencies undertake better policy analysis, participate more actively in a policy dialogue with recipient governments, and recognize the necessary balance between the public and private sectors. Moreover, the end of the cold war has reduced the politicization of bilateral aid and has restored the central objective of aid—the reduction of poverty through efficient economic management.

V.B.3. Improving the Effectiveness of Aid—Note

What matters for securing the effective use of aid is not the specific form or the terms on which aid is rendered by the donor, but the extent to which aid is successfuly integrated by the recipient country into its development efforts. Clarity on the objectives of foreign assistance is the necessary first step in determining how much aid is needed by a recipient country. The essence of capital assistance is the provision of additional resources, but external assistance should add to—not substitute for—the developing country's own efforts. If financial assistance from abroad is to result in a higher rate of domestic investment, it must be prevented from simply replacing domestic sources of financing investment or from supporting higher personal consumption or an increase in nondevelopmental current expenditures by the government.

When foreign aid is available on a general-purpose basis, the allocation of the foreign capital is decisive in determining whether it contributes as much as possible to raising the growth potential of the recipient country. The efficient allocation of investment resources then depends on the application of investment criteria in terms of the country's entire development program, and domestic policy measures must be adopted to supplement the use of foreign assistance. Regardless of the amount of aid received, the formation of capital depends, in the last resort, on domestic action.

It is appropriate therefore to emphasize the necessity of self-help measures: unless recipient governments adopt policies to mobilize fully their own resources and to implement their plans, the maximum potential benefits from aid will not be realized. As the record of foreign assistance in several countries shows, external aid may be incapable of yielding significant results unless it is accompanied by complementary domestic measures, such as basic reforms in land-tenure systems, additional taxation, investment in human capital, and more efficient government administration.

There is now also a need to link aid to the inducement and support of policy reform in recipient countries. Stand-by arrangements with the IMF may be subject to conditionality—an agreed-on program of economic adjustment designed to reestablish a viable balance-of-payments position. Insofar as IMF financing is relatively short term, it has to be complemented by longer term concessional finance from other official sources.[1] A noteworthy effort to provide longer term support for policy reforms has come from the World Bank's structural adjustment loans. The catalytic potential of aid needs to be furthered without calling on donor countries to adopt an adversarial position toward recipient countries.

The donor as well as the recipient nations must also bear a responsibility for improving the aid relationship. Specifically, there are three major ways the donors might improve the quality of foreign assistance: by untying their aid, by giving more scope to program aid, and by operating more within a multilateral context.

Aid may be tied by both source and end use: the recipient country may not have the freedom to apply the aid to imports from sources other than the donor country, and the use of aid may be restricted *via* specification of commodities or projects. Aid-tying has a cost to the recipient countries; if it is tied by project as well as by source, the switching possibilities in the use of the aid are severely limited, and the costs of tying can be quite significant to the recipient country. Aid-tying is essentially a protectonist device, reducing the real value. The direct costs of tying aid can be estimated as the difference between the cost of importing from the tied source and the cost of importing the same commodities from the cheapest source.

In addition to the direct costs incurred, tying of aid may have significant indirect costs for the recipient country by causing a distortion of development priorities. The distortion in the allocation of investment resources can be especially deleterious by biasing the recipient's development program toward those projects that have a high component of the special import content allowed for under the conditions of the tied aid and by avoiding those projects with a large amount of "local costs" that cannot be covered by aid. "Double-tying"—by donor procurement and project restriction—can only too readily artificaly alter the relative priority of different projects and bias investment toward import-intensive projects.

To improve project performance, several common failings in project appraisal should be corrected. The recipient's capacity for administration and implementation should not be overestimated. The forecasting of effects on intended beneficiaries should be more precise. More attention should be given to incorporating realistic assessment of the time required for projects to become self-reliant and of the recurrent or maintenance needs and costs that may be involved. More understanding is needed of the human, social, and physical environment in which the project is to operate. More attention has to be given to the relation of a project to other projects and programs. Full recognition is also overdue of the complementary roles of project and nonproject finance, and of the need for their integration into a coherent framework of development finance.[2]

Although project-type loans have had most appeal to the donor countries, it can be argued that more development assistance should be on a general-program basis. It is first of all illusory to believe that aid for a certain project is financing only that particular project: it is impossible to limit the effects of aid to only the project to which the aid is ostensibly tied. Aid is fungible, and the aid is actually financing the marginal project that would not have been undertaken but for the receipt of aid. Moreover, the efficacy of any one project is a function of the entire investment program; what ultimately matters is how the recipient country allocates its total investment expenditures. When aid is limited to specific projects, it becomes difficult to provide more aid for education, agriculture, small-scale industry, and administrative services, which are not visible as large projects but are extremely important for development. Most significantly, it should be noted that the subsequent uses of the income generated from a project are of more importance than the initial benefits from the project. To determine the effectiveness of aid, it is necessary to consider not only the initial increment of income resulting from the receipt of aid, but also whether the increment in income is subsequently used to relax one of the constraints on development, or is instead dissipated in higher

[1]For elaboration of the case for loans to allow the dismantling of domestic direct control mechanisms and to finance an outward-looking strategy, see Anne O. Krueger, "Loans to Assist the Transition to Outward-Looking Policies," *World Economy* (September 1981): 271–82.

[2]Robert Cassen & Associates, *Does Aid Work? Report to an Intergovernmental Task Force* (1986), pp. 173–74, 314.

consumption or used to support a larger population at the same low per capita level of income. Insofar as the most effective use of aid depends on the operation of the whole set of development policies in the recipient country, program aid rather than project aid may be considered the more appropriate context from the start.[3]

The argument that the quality of development assistance can be improved by untying aid and shifting to nonproject aid is also an argument for extending the scale and range of aid efforts on a multilateral basis. In contrast to bilateral aid, multilateral aid has several distinct advantages: it is less influenced by the donor's interests; the undesirable effects of tying are more easily avoided; it can more readily harmonize with and improve the financial terms of aid (unlike bilateral aid, which allows one country to insist on hard terms, while another offers aid on soft terms); it facilitates coordination of aid programs among the various aid sources and with the development priorities of the recipient countries; and it provides the opportunity for more aid consortia and consultative group arrangements to bring together the aid donors assisting a group of developing countries. If regional integration can contribute to development, then attention should also be given to the means of distributing aid through regional development institutions. Aid programs can then avoid being piecemeal, and there can be more opportunity for the active participation of recipient countries in the aid process.

The success stories of foreign aid point up the case for "performance" as the criterion for allocating aid. The "performance criterion" would have a country qualify for aid according to its performance in accomplishing such objectives as raising its marginal rate of saving, lowering its incremental capital–output ratio, and reducing its balance-of-payments deficit.[4] The purpose of this criterion is to allow aid to exert positive leverage in having the recipient countries meet specified standards in their development policies and to ensure that the limited amount of aid is allocated to those countries where it will be most productive.

Several objections may be raised, however, to the "performance criterion" for aid allocation. It does not allow a country to qualify for aid simply on the basis of "need," which may be an essential part of any foreign-assistance program. The "performance criterion" is actually designed as a measure of the recipient country's progress toward a termination of external aid, but it may be argued that the transfer of resources from rich to poor countries should become a permanent feature of the international economy. Indeed, the performance criterion side-steps questions of equity: a country may reach a state of self-sustaining growth and thus not qualify for additional aid, but still have a per capita real income lower than another country that has not yet reached self-sustaining growth and is still receiving aid. Finally, the performance criterion might be interpreted as simply indicating that a country can absorb more capital, rather than that it needs aid; the fact that a country receives low marks on performance may be the very indication that it needs a larger component of aid in its capital inflow. It has been contended, for example, that many of the African countries require more aid proper.

Because the emphasis is now on the problems of absolute poverty, unemployment, and inequality, the performance criterion is less controlling of aid allocations than simpler evidence of need. Special consideration must now be given to the lowest income countries that are extremely vulnerable to foreign-exchange needs.

The use of income-distribution criteria and employment criteria may also improve the efficacy of foreign assistance. An expansion of lending activities in agriculture, education, and population sectors may support employment and income-distribution objectives. More generally, the emphasis on these objectives now requires a shift in the orientation of aid away from capital-intensive projects, investments in urban rather than rural areas, projects in the modern rather than the traditional and informal sectors, and larger rather than small projects.[5]

In order to ensure that aid trickles down and is more effective in reducing poverty, a number of suggestions can be offered. Donors could put a larger proportion of their aid into projects designed to eliminate poverty. Income-distribution effects should be considered in a wider range of projects. More aid could be concentrated on "self-targeting" goods and services—those

[3]Hans W. Singer, "External Aid: For Plans or Projects? *Economic Journal* (September 1965): 539–45.

[4]H. B. Chenery and A. M. Strout, "Foreign Assistance and Economic Development," *American Economic Review* (September 1966): 728–29.

[5]Cassen, *Does Aid Work?* pp. 64–66, 300.

consumed by the poor in particular. Donors should be more willing to cover local and recurrent costs. Greater attention should be given to including women in development policies. Donors could identify and make special efforts to target poverty groups.

Instead of imposing a rigid and quantitative interpretation of the performance criterion, it is more appropriate to interpret it as simply reemphasizing the necessity of self-help measures and the requirement that foreign aid should avoid supporting domestic policies that turn out to be counterproductive to the recipient country's development. From this viewpoint, the granting of program aid, the insistence on self-help measures, and the concern about "performance" are interdependent elements in the aid relationship—a relationship that is necessarily reciprocal with respect to donor and recipient behavior.

Just as the absence of complementary domestic policies may limit the effectiveness of aid, so may its impact be neutralized by changes in the other components of the total flow of resources from rich to poor countries. The total flow is affected by private foreign investment, export earnings, and the terms of trade, as well as by foreign aid. It is therefore essential to recognize the relationships among capital assistance, private foreign investment, and international trade. The contribution of international assistance will be greater if public loans and grants are not competitive with, but instead stimulate, private foreign investment. Public aid for economic overhead facilities can create opportunities for private investment, and the private investment can, in turn, ensure fuller use of these facilities and raise their financial and economic return. Similarly, policies should be pursued that will bolster export earnings so that the inflow of development capital will be able to do more than simply offset a weak trend of export earnings or a deterioration in the recipient country's terms of trade.

V.B.4. The IMF and World Bank— Note

The multilateral organizations for providing finance to developing countries are prominent sources of foreign public capital flows. Most important are the International Monetary Fund (IMF) and the World Bank. Regional development banks are also active (Asian Development Bank, Inter-American Development Bank, African Development Bank). The IMF and World Bank are influential in not only providing external finance but also in shaping the development policies of member countries. Established at the Bretton Woods Conference in 1944, both institutions have continued to evolve and expand their relationships with developing countries.

The IMF provides financing for balance-of-payments deficits, but subject to certain conditions on the drawing country's policies. Each member's quota in the Fund establishes its basic drawing rights of foreign exchange and standby arrangements or external finance. A member borrows in "tranches" from the Fund in proportion to its initial deposit or quota. The first tranche, equivalent to the country's initial deposit, is automatic, but the additional credit tranches are subject to conditions of adjustment policies imposed by the Fund to correct balance-of-payments deficits. In addition, the Fund has created at different times special facilities such as the Buffer Stock Financing Facility, Compensatory and Contingency Financing Facility, Enlarged Access Policy, Extended Fund Facility, and Enhanced Structural Adjustment Facility. Although the Fund is based on a uniformity principle (i.e., all member countries are to be treated equally), in effect, the special facilities favor the LDCs.

The World Bank originally concentrated on project lending to developing countries. These are loans for specifically approved purposes (a power plant, irrigation, education, etc.) and are of longer duration than the IMF's loans of three to five years for short-term balance-of-payments financing. The interpretation of projects has expanded, however, to overlap with programs. Moreover, the Bank has recently given more emphasis to "structural adjustment programs" and "special action programs." World Bank loans are at near-market rates and require government guarantees. As part of the World Bank group, however, the International Development Association (IDA) provides loans at concessional rates to the poorest countries.

When borrowing countries repay the IMF and service their debt to the Bank (payment of interest and amortization), the net transfer of resources to the developing countries will, of course, be reduced. In the late 1980s there was actually a significant net transfer of resources from the developing countries to the IMF and World Bank. In 1991, however, IMF disbursements were up and the net transfer from the Fund to developing countries was the equivalent of $1.1 billion. Projections of total net transfer from the World Bank group over the five-year period 1990 to 1994 amount to approximately $8.7 billion (1991 dollars), the equivalent of $2 per person in the developing world. This contrasts with total net transfers of $28.4 billion (1991 dollars) for the earlier period 1975 to 1980, amounting to $9 per person.[1]

The IMF's imposition of conditionality is controversial. Critics argue that Fund programs are inappropriate insofar as they are preoccupied with expenditure reduction and give too little attention to the supply side of production and to "adjustment with a human face." It is also alleged that the Fund impinges on the sovereignty of states, its programs are too small relative to financing needs and too short term, and a few major industrial countries are too influential in shaping Fund programs.[2]

Although it still emphasizes fiscal discipline, the Fund is responding to such criticisms by giving more attention to supply-side measures, being more flexible with respect to special conditions of individual countries, avoiding undue hardships from its programs, and cooperating more fully with recipient governments to have them voluntarily identify with the programs.[3]

Although in a less formal way than the Fund's imposition of conditionality, the World Bank also exercises influence over policies in borrowing countries through a "policy dialogue" for policy-based loans. The effectiveness of project lending depends not only on a project's technical and financial feasibility but also on the economic context in which the project is to be implemented. The quality of national economic management matters as to whether a project earns an acceptable economic rate of return. Hence the Bank's concern with macrostability, efficient resource allocation, and good governance. The Bank's attention to the recipient's economy necessarily widens when it grants a sectoral adjustment loan or a structural adjustment loan to transform a country's production structure. Frequently the imposition of sound policies calls for policy reform programs—especially for disinflation (macrostabilization), devaluation (a competitive real exchange rate), liberalization (removal of price distortions), and an outward-looking orientation, as discussed in Chapter X.

---

[1] World Bank data.

[2] Overseas Development Institute, *Briefing Paper*, April 1993.

[3] For an assessment of how effective Fund programs have been, see John Williamson, *Latin American Adjustment: How Much Has Happened?* (1990), and Tony Killick et al., "What Can We Know About the Effects of IMF Programmes?" *World Economy* (September 1992).

V.C. EXTERNAL FINANCE AND ENVIRONMENTAL MANAGEMENT—NOTE

If poverty is to be reduced, the central economic problem is to overcome the scarcity of nature. Will the limits of the environment constrain development? So far the problem has been avoided in the more developed countries through the application of knowledge—the only factor of production that is not subject to the law of diminishing returns. Now for poor countries that want to develop, it is bad economics to ignore environmental quality. Development needs environmental management. The World Bank's *World Development Report 1992* (1992) emphasized that the two are complementary, not competitive. Measures to improve the environment can also foster development: for example, to avoid soil degradation, deforestation, or loss of biodiversity is to support the development effort. To have higher rates of development is, in turn, to allow more effective environmental management.

Sustainable development is the objective—to meet the needs of the present generation without compromising the ability of future generations to meet their own needs. Sustainable development, however, requires three types of investment: (1) investment in human capital—the knowledge of people, (2) investment in natural capital—the resources of the country; and (3) investment in man-made physical capital to provide new and clean technologies.

How are these investments to be made? It would be a nearly hopeless task to try and establish new international agencies for financing investment in particular environmental projects. More relevant and feasible would be actions by the governments of the poor countries themselves, the World Bank group, and International Monetary Fund (IMF).

National governments can undertake policy reforms that would improve environmental control: for instance, imposition of fuel taxation, reduction of subsidies to energy, more efficient pricing of crops, reduction of pesticide subsidies. By establishing these honest prices that reflect scarcity and social value, governments can cause resources to be used more efficiently with less environmental damage. Such pricing reforms are costless to government; indeed, they

may be revenue enhancing or expenditure saving.

It is also possible for government to introduce new schemes to operate through the market and make the private sector more protective of the environment. These range from the creation of property rights to congestion charges, emission taxes, tradable permits, and use of performance bonds. When environmental neglect occurs because of market failure, there is a case for government to correct that failure with more direct measures of control (polluter pays, licenses, regulation).

What governments must realize is that their own policy failures and the market failures in their own economy can constrain their development more than the futurologist's concern over limited physical resources. As the World Bank's Report demonstrates, correction of these failures aids both development and the environment.

Moreover, when poor countries develop and poverty is alleviated, this effort will automatically produce some environmental improvement. This is because the poorest cannot afford to invest in the future but must eke out their subsistence in unskilled labor-intensive activities that have low productivity but a quick yield. Hence, soil and water depletion, deforestation, pollution, overgrazing, overfishing, and shorter fallow periods. As income per head rises, these environmentally damaging activities diminish.

On the other side, however, with development may come environmental harm from other sources—municipal waste with urbanization, pollution from heavier industries, greater demand for resource inputs. But the rising income also provides more government revenue and private saving for expenditures on environmental projects. The challenge is to translate this ability into action through information and incentives.

Reinforcing policy action by national governments, the World Bank and IMF can be effective catalysts in environmental management. To the extent that a poor country does not have sufficient financial resources, it must look abroad for the savings and foreign exchange to finance an environmental program. As one source, private foreign investment in environmental goods and services offers considerable potential, especially if host governments undertake policy reforms that are market friendly. Some debts to commercial banks can also be converted to debt-for-equity and debt-for-nature swaps. But the World Bank group and IMF will be mostly relevant in the immediate future for any sizable volume of financing—and what is equally important is their policy advice to governments. Through its project lending and structural adjustment loans, the Bank can take an integrated view of environmental problems that arise from a pattern of development which damages the environment.

Many types of development expenditures financed by the World Bank coincide with environmental management—for example, rural development programs, population programs, investment infrastructure. In its appraisal of projects to finance, the Bank is already giving more weight to environmental benefits or costs. To now add on special environmental projects will require additional funding. The Bank's request for additional capital from its member countries should be supported. The replenishment of the Bank's International Development Association (IDA) is especially needed for aiding the poorest countries where environmental stress tends to be especially severe.

In imposing conditionality on a member country's use of its drawing rights at the IMF, the Fund can include environmental conditions.

A structural adjustment loan from the World Bank and balance-of-payments support from the IMF are already subject to conditions on policy reform. These can be extended to take account of the environment's social value.

Global environmental problems, such as greenhouse warming, are more difficult to solve insofar as they raise questions of international standards and new international institutions—let along financing. Members of the World Bank, however, have agreed to increase the funding of the Global Environmental Facility (GEF) and to open it to universal membership. To enlist the full cooperation of the poor countries in global programs would, however, require much more financing than is likely to be forthcoming for the GEF.

National environmental management, in contrast, can be more readily financed through existing institutions. And the World Bank and IMF can be instrumental in transferring the necessary knowledge along with their financial resources. If this is accomplished, the return on investment in projects of environmental management can be high—not merely in husbanding natural resources but even more significantly in raising productivity and mobilizing additional resources. That is essential for sustainable development because during the time of the working lives of those born today, the world's population will almost double.

V.D. EXTERNAL DEBT

V.D.1. Debt-Servicing Problems*

Heavily indebted countries have faced especially severe adjustment problems in recent years. The unsustainably high levels of external debt and debt service facing many of these countries by the early 1980s were in many cases the culmination of long-standing domestic and external imbalances. These imbalances were then greatly exacerbated by the sharp increase in interest rates in international financial markets after 1978, the effects of the recession of 1980–82 on world trade, and the continued weakness of prices for many primary commodities. The impact of these developments was strengthened by a sharp cutback in the availability of external finance. Initially, heavy external borrowing to cushion the effects of global developments on domestic spending gave way in 1981–82 to increasing reluctance on the part of private creditors to continue to provide new financing at previous levels. For countries that had borrowed heavily, the task of adjustment was not simply to reduce absorption to meet a short-run inadequacy of foreign exchange, but to adjust the non-interest current account so that the ratios of external debt and debt service might diminish over time to more manageable levels. A necessary condition for achieving such an adjustment was the effective control of aggregate demand, but for highly indebted market borrowers such control has proved especially difficult.

To understand why this is so, one may observe, first of all, that in the case where most external debt consists of obligations of the public sector to commercial creditors, or the government has had to guarantee to take over private sector debt, high external debt means that an increase in world interest rates automatically and immediately creates a deterioration in the fiscal situation. The choices available to the government for dealing with this problem are fourfold: financing the increased deficit externally, financing it internally, cutting government expenditures (other than interest payments), or raising government revenues. The first option simply has the effect of worsening the future adjustment problem, unless accompanied by

simultaneous measures that will eventually reduce the fiscal and current account deficits. The second measure serves to crowd out financing for the private sector and in most countries (where government financing is through bank credit rather than securities) tends to be inflationary. The third alternative, cutting government expenditures, while often desirable from a structural point of view, is politically very difficult in any country and cuts tend to be centered in programs for which the political constituencies are weakest, such as government investment programs. Finally, increasing revenues is also politically difficult and, moreover, often hard to administer equitably and effectively, particularly if the tax is of a new type or if an overall tax reform is being attempted.

Of course, debt service has implications not only for the fiscal balance but also for the current account balance. To the extent that the additional interest payments must be recovered from foreign exchange earnings rather than additional borrowing, the rise in interest payments causes both an external transfer problem (how to raise net exports of goods and services to meet the additional interest payments) and an internal transfer problem (how to mobilize the additional domestic resources required for the transfer). When the debt service is payable by the public sector, the internal transfer problem is equivalent to the problem of dealing with the corresponding increase in government expenditures. To deal with the external transfer problem, an external adjustment must be made that involves some type of expenditure-switching or expenditure-reducing policy (exchange rate depreciation, cutting fiscal deficits, or direct controls). When no such adjustment is made—the problem being suppressed by additional external financing—a future external transfer problem of yet greater magnitude is created. To deal with the internal transfer problem, expenditure cuts, revenue increases, and additional financing (with both crowding-out and an inflation-tax element) can be used in some combination. If expenditure cuts and revenue increases are not carried out, inflation has often been the consequence. This explains, in part, the inflationary impetus that was observed in high-debt countries during the early 1980s. As shown in Figure 1, the debt-

*From International Monetary Fund, *World Economic Outlook 1987* (April 1987), pp. 84–86. Reprinted by permission.

FIGURE 1. Developing countries with recent debt-servicing problems: external debt, cumulative fiscal deficits, and inflation, 1979–86 (in percent).

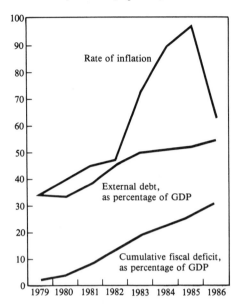

problem countries experienced a simultaneous rise in external indebtedness and fiscal deficits, and this led to an inflationary surge during the same period, which was most notable among major Latin American debtor countries.

The fiscal and balance of payments implications of dealing with a sudden, sharp rise in debt service obligations are mutually interactive. The inflationary impact of the increased fiscal deficit is exacerbated by the exchange rate depreciation (actual or implicit) that is necessary to effect the additional external transfer. This is not only because of the direct impact of the depreciation on domestic prices but also because of the effect on the fiscal deficit, since the (foreign and domestic) interest payments component of government expenditures is increased in proportion to the depreciation because domestic interest rates will tend to rise.

In the initial stage of the typical developments just described, there was also in many instances an increase in net capital outflows by residents, especially when the authorities initially resisted making adjustments in interest rates and exchange rates in response to changes in the economic environment. Such outflows, of course, eventually led to greater exchange rate movement than would otherwise have occurred, and also induced the authorities to raise interest rates

to high levels, thereby further increasing government interest costs. It might be added that increases in income and wealth taxes—one possible response to a weaker fiscal situation—also tended to induce capital flight.

All the factors just enumerated help explain why countries faced with debt-servicing problems found it difficult to sustain their growth performance. Increasing fiscal deficits in these countries led both to a crowding-out of private investment and to government expenditure cuts that reduced public investment programs. This is shown by the fact that gross capital formation declined more sharply in the early 1980s in debt-problem countries than elsewhere. The scarcity of foreign exchange available for imports led in many instances to quantitative restrictions; these, together with the depreciation of the real exchange rate, induced a decline in imports of intermediate and capital goods. The fall in net government saving was compounded by a fall in net saving of private residents retained domestically, as well as by a decline in the net inflow of foreign savings. The high inflation that occurred in a number of these countries reduced incentives for the productive use of investable funds, and incentives for productive investment were also damaged by the decline in economic activity and poor immediate prospects.

Under these circumstances, the countries with debt-servicing difficulties have faced an especially complex task in formulating a satisfactory adjustment package. There was initially an immediate need to achieve a sharp improvement in the current account as new financing dried up; the stabilization of the domestic economy was required to begin the process of reviving the confidence of domestic and foreign investors; and a policy setting for sustained growth in the longer term had to be established.

It has been evident for some time that the use of demand management instruments alone for reaching a current account target is biased toward a reduction in economic activity. It is thus necessary, in order to achieve an adequate growth performance, to employ additional measures to stimulate saving, investment, and the proper allocation of resources. At the same time, however, the efficacy of these measures is blunted if there has been no reduction in the drain on domestic saving created by the fiscal deficit and if high inflation has been permitted to prevail.

The problem of bringing a deeply entrenched

inflationary process to a halt consists in the fact that both firms and employees attempt to defend their real incomes by obtaining increases in prices and wages that are based on expectations of future inflation. The longer high inflation has prevailed, the greater will be the skepticism faced by the authorities when they announce anti-inflationary policies. Producers and workers would risk suffering large and hard-to-reverse falls in their real income if they acted on guidelines rather than on the behavior of others in the economy. Of course, explicit indexation of prices and wages merely institutionalizes this process. Under such conditions, one possible approach is to overshoot the required reductions in absorption in order to persuade economic agents of the seriousness of the anti-inflationary policy. This approach, however, can lead to a long and deep recession, even if accompanied by growth-oriented policies. An alternative strategy, designed to avoid such an outcome and attempted recently in several high-inflation countries (Argentina, Brazil, and Israel), is to impose a freeze on wages and prices, combined with a currency reform. Such ''heterodox'' policies can provide a useful breathing space, during which producers and employees can abstain with limited risk

from demanding higher prices and wages because they see other prices and wages remaining fixed. But this approach can succeed only if the necessarily limited period during which prices and wages are fixed is used to eliminate quickly the existing fiscal disequilibrium.

A final element in considering stabilization policies in countries with debt-servicing problems is the extent to which an unduly high level of external indebtedness hampers the design and implementation of a satisfactory set of adjustment measures. There may be instances where, because of past policy errors, the debt outstanding has become so large that eliminating outstanding arrears and meeting debt service obligations as they fall due make it impossible for an economy to increase its productive capacity at a rate sufficient to achieve long-term balance-of-payments viability. In such circumstances, it may be in the interest of both creditors and the debtor to restructure the debt in a way that permits the required long-term growth. It should also be added that it is equally in the interest of all concerned that the efforts of countries to reduce the relative burden of their external debt through export expansion be assisted by a liberalization of trade policies in creditor countries.

EXHIBIT V.6. Summary of External Debt and Debt Service (billions of U.S. dollars)

	1986	1987	1988	1989	1990	1991	1992	1993	1994	1995
External debt										
Developing countries	**1,036.6**	**1,154.3**	**1,171.7**	**1,201.5**	**1,290.0**	**1,364.3**	**1,407.3**	**1,488.5**	**1,546.1**	**1,608.8**
By Region										
Africa	169.8	192.8	200.3	209.9	224.6	230.5	224.1	228.2	228.4	232.5
Asia	281.8	315.4	324.5	329.9	362.0	403.3	428.9	467.1	494.0	524.7
Middle East and Europe	204.1	228.3	238.6	250.3	271.2	280.3	284.1	297.1	307.5	314.8
Western Hemisphere	380.9	417.8	408.3	411.4	432.2	450.3	470.2	496.2	516.2	536.7
By Financial Criteria										
Net creditor countries	57.9	63.8	62.1	59.7	54.0	66.2	73.4	78.0	84.7	88.0
Net debtor countries	978.6	1,090.5	1,109.6	1,141.8	1,235.9	1,298.1	1,333.9	1,410.5	1,461.4	1,520.8
Market borrowers	492.9	532.0	521.8	522.4	560.2	601.9	633.7	680.9	715.2	754.1
Diversified borrowers	274.1	319.3	334.5	354.1	390.3	403.8	411.6	429.3	434.5	448.3
Official borrowers	211.6	239.1	253.2	265.3	285.4	292.4	288.6	300.3	311.7	318.3
Countries with recent debt-servicing difficulties	628.0	696.9	705.7	724.9	771.6	792.3	803.9	837.2	860.5	886.4
Countries without debt-servicing difficulties	350.7	393.5	403.9	416.8	464.3	505.8	530.0	573.3	601.0	634.4

(continued)

EXHIBIT V.6. (*continued*)

	1986	1987	1988	1989	1990	1991	1992	1993	1994	1995
Debt-service payments										
Developing countries	**131.5**	**144.4**	**155.2**	**146.7**	**154.0**	**165.2**	**168.9**	**187.3**	**203.1**	**213.1**
By Region										
Africa	19.7	18.9	20.4	21.5	23.7	25.0	23.6	23.7	34.5	28.8
Asia	39.8	51.1	48.6	51.2	51.5	55.5	62.1	66.5	70.4	76.9
Middle East and Europe	22.2	24.0	25.6	28.4	34.8	32.4	25.4	26.2	34.3	37.7
Western Hemisphere	49.8	50.4	60.6	45.6	44.1	52.3	57.8	71.0	63.9	69.8
By Financial Criteria										
Net creditor countries	9.5	9.7	10.6	10.9	11.5	13.0	9.6	9.4	16.8	19.6
Net debtor countries	122.1	134.7	144.6	135.8	142.5	152.2	159.3	177.9	186.2	193.5
Market borrowers	74.0	83.8	89.9	76.3	74.2	83.4	93.5	108.4	102.9	112.4
Diversified borrowers	30.7	34.1	40.3	43.3	46.9	46.2	48.8	51.6	57.3	59.3
Official borrowers	17.4	16.8	14.5	16.2	21.4	22.6	16.9	17.9	26.1	21.9
Countries with recent debt-servicing difficulties	69.5	69.5	78.0	66.0	69.7	74.3	74.9	89.1	91.9	95.4
Countries without debt-servicing difficulties	52.6	65.2	66.6	69.8	72.8	77.8	84.3	88.7	94.3	98.2

Note: Projected estimates are given for 1994 and 1995.

Source: International Monetary Fund, *World Economic Outlook* (May 1994), p. 163.

EXHIBIT V.7. Seventeen Highly Indebted Countries, 1991

Country	Total Debt Outstanding (US$ millions)	Total Debt Service (US$ millions)	Interest Paid on Debt (US$ millions)	Ratio of Total Debt to GNP (percent)	Ratio of Interest to Exports (percent)
Argentina	63,707	7,121	3,699	49	25
Bolivia	4,075	323	138	85	15
Brazil	116,514	10,754	5,524	29	16
Chile	17,902	3,956	2,838	61	24
Colombia	17,369	3,644	1,431	43	14
Costa Rica	4,043	417	233	56	10
Côte d'Ivoire	18,847	1,445	586	223	16
Ecuador	12,469	1,106	504	114	15
Jamaica	4,456	703	233	156	10
Mexico	101,737	14,043	7,845	37	17
Morocco	21,219	2,289	1,169	80	14
Nigeria	34,497	3,375	2,259	109	17
Peru	20,708	1,186	572	43	13
Philippines	31,897	3,481	1,628	70	11
Uruguay	4,189	1,196	279	45	12
Venezuela	34,372	3,435	2,550	65	14
Yugoslavia	16,471	4,160	1,288	—	7

Debt-service ratios—interest and debt repayments during the year as a percentage of exports—have improved for most indebted countries in recent years. The debt-service ratio for the highly indebted countries fell from 45 percent in 1986 to 31 percent in 1991. The debt-service ratios for Sub-Saharan Africa, however, were not lower in 1991.

Net resource flows are indicated in Exhibit V.8. Exhibit V.11 shows the changing pattern of external finance, with a marked reduction in commercial bank loans but an increase in private foreign investment.

Source: World Bank, *World Debt Tables, 1992–93,* vol. 1, pp. 132–35.

EXHIBIT V.8. Aggregate Net Resource Flows and Net Transfers

	Net Flows on Long-Term Debt (millions of dollars)				Official Grants (millions of dollars)		Foreign Direct Investment in the Reporting Economy (millions of dollars)		Aggregate Net Resource Flows (millions of dollars)		Aggregate Net Transfers (millions of dollars)	
	Public and Publicly Guaranteed		Private Non-guaranteed									
	1980	1991	1980	1991	1980	1991	1980	1991	1980	1991	1980	1991
Low-income economies												
China and India												
Other low-income												
Mozambique	0	118	0	−3	76	752	0	23	76	889	76	879
Tanzania	348	193	15	0	485	688	0	0	848	880	804	847
Ethiopia	84	171	0	0	125	460	0	0	209	631	192	595
Uganda	60	111	0	0	62	253	0	1	122	365	118	341
Bhutan	0	5	0	0	2	28	0	0	2	33	2	31
Guinea-Bissau	66	28	0	0	37	60	0	0	103	88	102	85
Nepal	48	125	0	0	79	160	0	0	127	285	125	259
Burundi	35	59	0	0	39	126	0	1	74	186	72	171
Chad	3	93	0	0	22	106	0	0	25	199	25	194
Madagascar	319	150	0	0	30	352	0	14	349	516	322	447
Sierra Leone	54	46	0	0	24	33	−19	0	59	79	46	78
Bangladesh	594	614	0	0	1,001	1,070	0	1	1,595	1,685	1,548	1,532
Lao People's Dem. Rep.	37	45	0	0	16	54	0	0	53	99	52	96
Malawi	120	109	0	0	49	219	10	0	178	328	135	287
Rwanda	25	87	0	0	68	181	16	5	109	273	98	261
Mali	89	89	0	0	104	209	2	4	195	302	192	278
Burkina Faso	55	121	0	0	88	200	0	0	142	321	128	306
Niger	144	−32	79	−36	51	249	49	0	324	181	248	160
India	1,231	3,744	194	39	649	562	0	0	2,073	4,345	1,541	1,643
Kenya	433	104	−1	20	121	836	79	43	632	1,003	312	696
Nigeria	1,122	−225	388	−47	3	141	−740	712	773	581	−1,357	−1,836
China	1,927	5,669	0	0	7	262	0	4,366	1,934	10,298	1,616	7,342
Haiti	32	28	0	0	30	142	13	14	75	183	59	169
Benin	56	83	0	0	41	147	4	0	101	231	96	218
Central African Rep.	24	110	0	0	56	61	5	−5	85	166	85	161
Ghana	143	340	0	1	23	581	16	0	181	922	135	859
Pakistan	706	830	2	−22	482	429	63	257	1,254	1,494	1,000	876
Togo	82	46	0	0	15	92	42	0	139	139	119	99
Guinea	47	155	0	0	25	138	0	0	72	293	49	254
Nicaragua	221	−33	0	0	48	730	0	0	269	696	207	478
Sri Lanka	219	593	2	−3	161	200	43	98	425	887	377	737
Mauritania	113	17	0	0	61	97	27	0	201	113	165	93
Yemen, Rep.	542	80	0	0	335	87	34	0	910	167	900	139
Honduras	225	83	33	9	20	475	6	45	283	611	123	401
Lesotho	10	33	0	0	52	48	5	8	66	88	59	−72
Indonesia	1,611	1,434	2	1,519	109	300	180	1,482	1,902	4,735	−2,514	−1,056
Egypt, Arab Rep.	2,435	552	80	−50	165	3,355	548	253	3,229	4,110	2,813	3,451
Zimbabwe	93	152	0	80	127	231	2	0	221	462	133	210
Sudan	658	117	0	0	388	416	0	0	1,046	533	997	523
Zambia	416	89	−25	2	71	697	62	0	524	788	324	552

(continued)

EXHIBIT V.8. (*continued*)

| | Net Flows on Long-Term Debt (millions of dollars) | | | | Official Grants (millions of dollars) | | Foreign Direct Investment in the Reporting Economy (millions of dollars) | | Aggregate Net Resource Flows (millions of dollars) | | Aggregate Net Transfers (millions of dollars) | |
| | Public and Publicly Guaranteed | | Private Non-guaranteed | | | | | | | | | |
	1980	1991	1980	1991	1980	1991	1980	1991	1980	1991	1980	1991
Middle-income economies												
Lower-middle-income												
Bolivia	315	173	−3	−25	48	599	47	52	407	800	214	663
Côte d'Ivoire	896	175	224	371	27	264	95	46	1,241	856	670	309
Senegal	175	−2	−4	1	78	532	15	0	263	531	161	404
Philippines	1,161	290	152	149	59	400	−106	544	1,266	1,383	488	−381
Papua New Guinea	89	54	−25	25	279	280	76	0	418	359	163	227
Cameroon	480	277	18	−10	29	269	130	0	656	536	422	361
Guatemala	123	−77	−30	0	14	51	111	91	217	66	114	−85
Dominican Rep.	353	5	−7	−16	14	40	93	145	454	174	267	89
Ecuador	696	46	52	−21	7	56	70	85	825	166	349	−419
Morocco	1,138	336	50	0	75	553	89	320	1,353	1,209	685	26
Jordan	266	332	0	0	1,127	407	34	−12	1,427	727	1,348	422
Peru	289	46	0	−112	31	197	27	−7	347	124	−580	−269
El Salvador	92	120	−18	−5	31	114	6	25	111	255	34	147
Congo	486	−147	0	0	20	38	40	0	546	−109	503	−147
Syrian Arab Rep.	924	35	0	0	1,651	109	0	0	2,574	144	2,497	13
Colombia	766	−263	42	−9	8	51	157	420	974	199	553	−2,030
Paraguay	114	21	13	1	10	22	32	80	168	124	70	47
Jamaica	236	55	15	−6	13	248	28	127	292	424	57	59
Romania	1,973	281	0	0	—	—	0	40	1,973	321	1,641	315
Tunisia	342	378	10	−5	26	143	235	150	612	667	232	16
Thailand	1,143	306	678	2,706	75	220	190	2,014	2,087	5,245	1,576	3,412
Turkey	1,834	794	46	−319	185	1,147	18	810	2,083	2,432	1,545	−541
Poland	3,005	476	0	0	—	—	10	291	3,015	767	2,311	266
Bulgaria	217	−128	0	0	—	—	0	0	217	−128	193	−402
Costa Rica	359	160	14	0	0	83	53	142	425	385	235	140
Algeria	869	−1,321	0	0	77	79	349	0	1,295	−1,242	−830	−3,194
Panama	189	−73	0	0	6	89	−47	−62	149	−45	−174	−193
Chile	−34	109	2,123	616	9	97	213	576	2,312	1,398	1,307	−1,738
Iran, Islamic Rep.	−267	912	0	0	1	70	0	0	−265	982	−1,095	958
Mauritius	78	48	0	19	13	16	1	19	93	101	69	29
Czechoslovakia	0	374	0	0	—	—	0	600	0	974	0	643
Malaysia	889	41	223	451	6	57	934	3,455	2,052	4,003	524	837
Upper-middle-income												
Botswana	21	21	0	0	51	62	112	0	184	83	69	51
Hungary	728	781	0	0	—	—	0	1,462	728	2,243	92	760
Venezuela	1,133	920	656	0	0	5	55	1,914	1,844	2,839	47	505
Argentina	1,693	−791	1,162	0	2	40	678	2,439	3,535	1,688	1,593	−2,269
Uruguay	200	39	26	175	1	10	290	0	516	224	395	38
Brazil	4,472	−237	222	−124	14	46	1,911	1,600	6,618	1,286	−670	−4,545
Mexico	5,121	2,217	1,700	280	14	62	2,156	4,762	8,991	7,321	3,043	−556

EXHIBIT V.8. (*continued*)

	Net Flows on Long-Term Debt (millions of dollars)				Official Grants (millions of dollars)		Foreign Direct Investment in the Reporting Economy (millions of dollars)		Aggregate Net Resource Flows (millions of dollars)		Aggregate Net Transfers (millions of dollars)	
	Public and Publicly Guaranteed		Private Non-guaranteed									
	1980	1991	1980	1991	1980	1991	1980	1991	1980	1991	1980	1991
Trinidad and Tobago	187	−80	0	0	1	4	185	169	372	93	−157	−286
Gabon	−109	32	0	0	4	35	32	125	−73	192	−465	−32
Portugal	1,411	1,765	23	86	28	15	157	2,021	1,620	3,887	1,074	2,488
Oman	−81	49	0	0	157	3	98	0	174	51	−156	−105
Korea, Rep.	1,940	2,743	487	1,633	8	6	6	1,116	2,440	5,498	740	3,504
Yugoslavia	998	−1,247	1,211	−373	—	—	0	0	2,208	−1,620	1,131	−2,843

Source: World Bank, *World Development Report 1993* (1993), pp. 282–83.

Comment: Growing Out of Debt

A borrowing country proceeds through a sequence of growth-cum-debt phases. We have seen that when investment and government expenditures exceed savings and taxes, there is a real resource gap, which is filled by an excess of imports over exports in the current account. The external debt that finances the excess imports is the financial counterpart to the real resource transfer. A developing country will therefore proceed through stages in which the resource gap, then the debt, and finally the income level rise. In the later phase, the resource gap declines first, followed by the debt, while the income level continues to rise.

Although net capital income flow will cease when domestic savings equal required domestic investment, a gross capital inflow will continue until the resource surplus is greater than the amount needed to cover interest charges on accumulated debt. Once savings become greater than domestic investment plus the interest payments, the resource surplus can be utilized for amortization, and the debt will fall. The debt repayments are made by converting the excess of savings over investment into a surplus of exports over imports until the indebtedness is repaid.

In accordance with the debt-cycle hypothesis, Exhibit V.9 represents a country moving through stylized balance-of-payments and debt stages:

Stage I: Young debtor: characterized by a trade deficit; net outflow of interest payments; net inflow of capital; and rising debt.

Stage II: Mature debtor: characterized by a decreasing trade deficit; beginning of a surplus; net outflow of interest payments; decreasing net inflow of capital; and debt rising at diminishing rate.

Stage III: Debt reducer: characterized by a rising trade surplus; diminishing net outflow of interest payments; net outflow of capital; and falling net foreign debt.

Stage IV: Young creditor: characterized by a decreasing trade surplus, and then deficit; net outflow of interest payments, and then inflow; outflow of capital at decreasing rate; and net accumulation of foreign assets.

Stage V: Mature creditor: characterized by trade deficit; net inflow of interest payments; diminishing net flows of capital; and slow-growing or constant net foreign-asset position.

Dornbusch and Fischer have also illuminated the capacity of a country to grow out of its debt:

If the ratio of debt to exports continues to decline, the debt problem eventually becomes manageable as increased exports provide the earnings with which to meet debt payments. Conversely, a rising debt–export ratio would reflect a growing imbalance that would call into question the country's ability to maintain debt service. The question of the sustainability of debts can be viewed in terms of a simple equation describing the growth rate of the ratio of debt to exports.

$$\dot{v}/v = r - x - \alpha v$$

where v is the ratio of debt to exports; r, the real, or inflation adjusted interest rate; x, the growth rate of exports; and α, the non-interest surplus as a fraction of exports.

It is readily verified that the debt to export ratio declines if the growth rate of exports exceeds the real rate of interest, unless the country runs a non-interest deficit ($\alpha < 0$). But it is still the case that a sufficiently large non-interest surplus could compensate even for very high real rates of interest. The non-interest surplus would provide the foreign exchange earnings with which to cover interest payments on the debt. To create a non-interest surplus, a country has to reduce imports, increase exports, or both. Over time, such changes can be brought about by a change in the exchange rate. In the short run, though, the surest way to increase the non-interest surplus is to reduce the demand for imports both by devaluation and by restrictive domestic policies that tend to cause a recession.

If the growth rate of export earnings is high, because growth in the industrialized countries creates demand for export products of the debtor countries, and if interest rates are low (or only temporarily high), then the debt crisis is only temporary. Debtor countries can simply "grow out of their debts" by following a transitory period of restraint in which they avoid further debt build up by paying most of the interest out of trade surpluses generated through devaluation and domestic demand restriction, while export growth reduces the debt to export ratio. Conversely, if interest rates rise for a long period while export growth is reduced or even becomes negative, then large trade surpluses are required just to prevent the debt to export ratio from rising.[1]

[1]Rudiger Dornbusch and Stanley Fischer, "Third World Debt," *Science* 234 (November 1986): 838. Copyright 1986 by the AAAS.

EXHIBIT V.9. Balance-of-Payments Flows and Debt Stock During the Debt Cycle

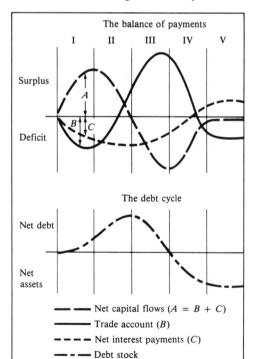

Source: World Bank, *World Development Report, 1985* (1985), p. 42.

V.D.2. Country Risk Analysis—Note

The increase in lending to governments of developing countries by private commercial banks has raised questions of country credit-worthiness. When banks engage in cross-border lending, they are obviously concerned about the capacity of the borrowing country to service the debt—that is, to pay interest and amortization in foreign currency. To appraise the credit-worthiness of the borrower, lenders engage in country risk analysis to determine the borrower's ability to generate sufficient foreign exchange to meet debt service obligations. For this analysis, there is no formula or one definitive approach: it depends on the analyst's perception of the country's development process and how this relates to the country's balance of payments. A debt service crisis—that is, the borrower cannot or will not repay on schedule—is in essence a balance-of-payments crisis, which, in turn, is a development crisis.[1] Country risk analysis therefore depends on an understanding of the development process and the way in which the course of development affects the balance of payments.

Even though the loan is ostensibly for a given project, it supports in reality the marginal project—the project that would not have been undertaken but for this loan. The loan helps to fill the savings gap and foreign-exchange gap by making more resources available for capital formation and by increasing the country's capacity to import. Because capital is fungible, the loan actually supports the country's development program and balance of payments instead of being limited to some given project. So, too, is the debt service on the loan a charge on the economy as a whole—a charge against the total use of resources. Provided that the social rate of return to capital in the least productive project is greater than the interest rate on the most expensive loan, there should be no debt service problem.

In practice, however, it is not operationally feasible to find the "marginal project" and to calculate whether the marginal return is greater than the marginal cost of borrowing. To circumvent this difficulty, the analyst must shadow price the project and undertake macroanalysis to analyze the ultimate effect of the loan on the total use of resources in the borrowing country.

When shadow pricing the project, the analyst corrects for price distortions to reflect true social costs—raising the rate of interest, lowering the wage rate, and increasing the cost of foreign exchange. Externalities are also calculated. Instead of focusing on simply the internal *financial* rate of return, the shadow pricing allows calculation of the internal *economic* rate of return. If, in addition, some judgment is made on the distribution of income, the internal *social* rate of return may be calculated. (This is explained in Chapter X.) This process of shadow pricing for the rate of return is equivalent to determining whether the effective rate of interest (nominal rate of interest corrected for inflation, aid-tying, and changes in terms of trade) is greater then the accounting rate of interest (social return to capital).[2]

Even though a project meets the social efficiency criterion based on shadow pricing, there is still the problem of whether the country can transfer a portion of the increased output and income into foreign exchange for debt servicing. To determine the capacity to service external debt, some analysts engage in ratio analysis, examining such ratios as debt outstanding/GNP, debt service/exports, imports/international reserves, imports/exports, and so forth. If the numerator in the fraction increases relative to the denominator, a debt crisis might be indicated. Ideally, one would like an index that would show the *risk* of a sharp fall in any kind of foreign-exchange inflow and a rise in import needs, compared with the *ability* to offset such risks by compressing imports rapidly, obtaining compensatory financing, or using international reserves. No one ratio captures this. Therefore, several ratios may need to be used as proxies. But again, neither the history of rescheduling cases nor the econometric analysis of default functions indicates a definitive number of ratios. A suggested list might include debt service/exports, debt service/debt outstanding, debt outstanding/exports, net transfer/imports, rate of growth of debt/rate

---

[1] Goran Ohlin, "Debts, Development and Default," in *A World Divided,* ed. Gerald K. Helleiner (1976), pp. 207–22.

[2] For details of evaluating foreign-capital inflows in a cost–benefit framework, see Deepak Lal, "The Evaluation of Capital Inflows," *Industry and Development,* no. 1 (1978): 2–19. In Chapter X, we consider project appraisal in greater detail.

of growth of exports, and imports/reserves. Increases in these ratios might be warnings of a debt crisis. But in past renegotiation cases, there has been large variance and dispersion in these ratios. Other factors must therefore be considered.

Beyond ratios, country risk analysis should monitor some "key performance indicators" that will indicate how national economic management is affecting the growth of the economy and the capacity to service the debt. The key performance indicators are (1) a rising ratio of savings to national income, (2) a rising ratio of taxes to income, (3) a decreasing ratio of incremental capital to output (less unutilized capacity), (4) a decreasing current account deficit, (5) high employment elasticity—that is, the rate of growth in employment relative to the rate of growth in output and (6) more equitable income distribution.

To realize positive changes in these performance indicators, the debtor country may have to undertake a set of policies, reflecting a higher quality of policy analysis and implementation. Price distortions will have to be removed: real interest rates raised, overvalued foreign-exchange rate corrected, wages brought closer to opportunity cost. The fiscal deficit must be reduced. Local capital markets may have to be deepened to mobilize local savings. The foreign-trade regime may have to be liberalized and the bias against exports removed. All these policies will affect the debtor country's performance. These policies are frequently suggested when the IMF imposes conditionality on a member country's access to drawing rights in the higher credit tranches or in stand-by arrangements. When the IMF imposes conditionality, this may also encourage commercial banks to provide longer term capital inflows.

This concentration on the policies necessary to improve the economy's performance in order to service the debt also illuminates other issues of debt servicing that are frequently confused.[3]

What is meant by the "burden" of the debt? This is usually related to the debt-servicing problem. There would, of course, be no problem of debt service if capital flowed into the country in sufficient amount to allow the developing country to meet interest and amortization payments on foreign obligations and to maintain its imports at a desired level. In reality, however, sooner or later—depending on the growth in new foreign borrowing, rate of interest, and amortization rate—the debt-servicing charges may require a net capital outflow from the debtor country. When the return flow of interest and amortization payments exceeds the inflow of new capital, the country becomes a "mature debtor" and confronts a transfer problem in servicing the debt. The country has to achieve sufficient self-sustaining growth to remove the resource gap and cover the net capital outflow. The country will have to generate an export surplus equal to its net outward transfer of interest on current account and amortization on capital account in its balance of payments.

The direct costs of debt service do not, however, constitute the burden of the debt—provided the social rate of return from the external capital exceeds the interest cost. True, part of the increased production from the use of the external resource inflow has to be repaid abroad, and this is a reduction that would not be necessary if the savings had been provided at home. But the reality is that the savings have been provided from overseas, and the foreign savers must receive some return. Of most importance to the borrowing country is that its economy has realized additional investment, and the benefits from this should exceed the direct costs of the foreign savings that made possible the capital formation. The direct costs of servicing the foreign debt out of additional income should not be a cause for concern.

Of genuine concern are the indirect costs. They arise when the debt-servicing country has to undertake burdensome policies of balance-of-payments adjustment to acquire sufficient foreign exchange for debt service. Domestic savings in the developing country will have to become sufficient to finance all domestic investment and, in addition, the interest cost of accumulated debt and the repayment of the principal of its loans. In order to convert the surplus of savings into the foreign exchange it needs for debt servicing, the developing country will have to generate an export surplus through expenditure-reducing and expenditure-switching policies in order to expand exports or reduce the demand for imports. This may require some combination of deflation, internal and external controls over resource allocation, and depreciation of the exchange rate. The adverse effects of

---

[3]This section is drawn from Gerald M. Meier, *International Economics* (1980), pp. 343–48.

these measures of balance-of-payments adjustment are the indirect costs of foreign borrowing, and they constitute the burden of debt servicing.

It might be thought that this burden can be avoided if the investment of foreign capital creates its own means of payment by directly expanding exports or replacing imports. The lender might also believe that if it lends for a project that earns foreign exchange or saves foreign exchange, there can be no transfer risk in debt servicing. But this is again to adopt the myopic and illusory view of project financing. Once we appreciate the relationship between total resource availabilities and resource uses, the interdependence of investments, and the principle that debt service is ultimately a charge on the economy as a whole, we can recognize that the transfer problem can still be solved without stipulating that the investment of foreign capital create its own means of payment by directly expanding exports or by replacing imports. Instead of committing the fallacy of misplaced concreteness, we should realize that debt capacity cannot be determined without appraising the country's development program as a whole. Analysis of the entire program is necessary for an assessment of the conditions under which the competing claims on total resources, on savings, and on foreign exchange can be adjusted in order to release the amount required for debt service. In the last analysis, it is not a matter of whether "the project" that the foreign loan is ostensibly intended to finance will be able to carry the cost of the loan—but the return on the marginal project or the ultimate effect on the total use of resources. If it is realized that the ability to create a sufficiently large export surplus depends on the operation of all sectors together, not simply on the use made of foreign capital alone, it is then apparent that a project financed by foreign borrowing need not itself make a direct contribution to the balance of payments. Indeed, even if foreign capital were limited to financing projects that earn or save foreign exchange, developments elsewhere in the economy may at the same time be affecting the supply of foreign exchange so adversely that the debt service problem is aggravated, even though the foreign capital has supposedly been directed to projects that ought to be able to carry the costs of the loans.

Instead of such a narrow balance-of-payments criterion for the allocation of investment, the basic test for the allocation of foreign capital, as for that of any investment, is that it should be invested in the form that yields the highest social marginal product. The allocation of capital according to its most productive use will also be the most favorable for debt servicing, because it maximizes the increase in income from a given amount of capital and thereby contributes to the growth of foreign-exchange availability. The export of particular commodities or services through which the interest is transferred abroad should then be determined by the principle of comparative costs. There are thus two principles determining debt capacity: the investment criterion of social marginal productivity and the trade criterion of comparative cost. To allocate foreign capital to a foreign-exchange project is to do violence to the separation of these two basic principles, and it is to settle for the easier, but misleading approach of project appraisal instead of country appraisal.

The elements that compose the analysis of a country's credit-worthiness can by synthesized in a country risk matrix (Table 1). The vertical scale illustrates the lender's appraisal of the borrowing country's balance-of-payments potential—that is, the country's potential to have a sufficient flow of foreign exchange to service its debt. Countries in the top row (numbered 1) have the highest potential, whereas countries at the lowest rating (numbered 5) have the least potential and can be expected to confront payment delays or defaults. Underlying the evaluation of balance-of-payments potential is the assessment of the key performance parameters. And behind these, in turn, lie the policies that the borrowing country would have to undertake to raise these performance parameters and to realize its balance-of-payments potential.

In the columns of Table 1, countries are ranked according to their capacity for national economic management. This involves a judgment on the borrowing country's ability and willingness (often a political matter) to undertake the policies that will allow the country to achieve its balance-of-payments potential. Countries in column A have the highest policy capability to undertake the measures that would allow debt servicing. All countries rated E or 5 would present the greatest country risk to the lender, whereas those rated A or 1 would be most credit-worthy, with the highest debt capacity. Japan and Zaire are simply illustrative of the relative ratings that the lender could make within the matrix. Ratings would, of course, change over time.

TABLE 1. Country Risk Matrix

Capacity for national economic management

Policies → Balance-of-payments potential		High A	B	C	D	Low E
	High 1	Japan				
	2					
	3					
	4					
	Low 5					Zaire

Comment: Econometric Default Functions

A number of econometric studies have attempted to identify the determinants of debt rescheduling. Discriminant analysis has been used to try to identify the characteristics of borrowing countries that presage rescheduling of their debt: Charles Frank, Jr., and William R. Cline, "Measurement of Debt Servicing Capacity: An Application of Discriminant Analysis," *Journal of International Economics* 1 (1971). Principal component analysis, logit analysis, and probit analysis have also been used to attempt to identify situations in which scheduling is likely. See Pierre Dhonte, "Describing External Debt Situations: A Roll-over Approach," *IMF Staff Papers* (March 1975); Gershon Feder and Richard E. Just, "A Study of Debt-Servicing Capacity Applying Logit Analysis," *Journal of Development Economics* 4 (1977); and Homi Kharas, "The Long-Run Creditworthiness of Developing Countries," *Quarterly Journal of Economics* (August 1984).

Variables found to be positively associated with rescheduling are debt service obligations at the time of rescheduling, ratio of imports to foreign reserves, stock of debt as a ratio of GNP, and stock of debt as a ratio to exports.

In a cross-section statistical model, higher income inequality was found to be a significant predictor of a higher probability of debt rescheduling. This is because political management becomes more difficult in economies with extreme inequality. See Andrew Berg and Jeffrey Sachs, "The Debt Crisis: Structural Explanations of Country Performance," *Journal of Development Economics* 29 (1988).

V.D.3. Debt Strategy—Note

How to deal with the external debt problem has prompted a wide-ranging debate with a variety of different views. The central issue that creditors have to confront, however, is whether to refinance or forgive a debt in order to avoid the debtor's repudiation of its existing debt.

In weighing whether to default on its inherited debt, the debtor country will balance the cost of continued debt servicing against the cost of defaulting. Defaulting entails the cost of losing future access to international capital markets, not being able to receive trade credits, having its assets possibly subject to assessment by the creditors, and suffering in general a loss of reputation.

The case for refinancing is based on the concept of defensive landing. Is it rational for a creditor to offer even more financing to a country that is already heavily in debt? The answer can be "yes" if the creditor believes that with the additional financing the debtor can grow and become creditworthy in the future, and if the creditor believes that it can defend the value of its existing claims by additional lending. In essence, as Paul Krugman observes, the creditor buys an option to collect in the future if the situation improves. New lending that reduces the interest burden, even if it is at a loss, may be worthwhile because it improves the expected value of the initial debt.

Krugman states:

Even under quite adverse circumstances this defensive lending argument can justify quite substantial increases in creditor exposure. To see why, consider the basic algebra of the situation. Let D be a country's outstanding debt, and d be the subjective discount that creditors place on that debt (which may be inferred from the secondary market price if that market is sufficiently well developed). Suppose that by relending part of the interest, and thus averting an immediate liquidity crisis, creditors can reduce the discount to some smaller amount d'. Such a program will have a cost—the expected loss on the new lending—and a benefit—the increase in the value of existing claims. The cost will be $d'L$, where L is the value of new lending; while the benefit will be $(d - d')D$. Thus a program of defense lending will be worth undertaking as long as

$$d'L < (d - d')D,$$

or

$$L/D < (d - d')/d'.[1]$$

The free-rider problem, however, creates a difficulty with defensive lending. For although the defensive lending by all the creditors would raise the expected value of their collective claims, it is still to the advantage of any single creditor not to lend more and simply gain from the collective claims on previous debt. Negotiating procedures and institutional arrangements have to guard against this problem.

Another difficulty with defensive lending is the determination of how much to lend and on what terms. Debtors will, of course, want the maximum amount, but lenders the minimum. In between, the negotiators will have to find a mutually beneficial arrangement that will allow the creditors to receive a positive resource transfer from the debtor, while the debtor prefers that amount of resource transfer from the debtor, while the debtor prefers that amount of resource transfer to its incurring the costs of default. Analysts have applied game theory and bargaining models to this problem.[2]

As an alternative to defensive lending, debt forgiveness—that is, creditors agree to accept less repayment than was specified in the original loan contracts—is another way to deal with the debt overhang problem. How can reducing the debt owed to it result in a benefit to a creditor? The answer lies in recognizing how a debt overhang can restrict growth in the debtor country and create disincentives for a transfer of resources to the creditor. To service a large debt, a country will have to undertake policies to expand its exports, reduce its imports, and restrain domestic demand. These measures are costly, and the country may avoid them when their benefit in the form of allowing the country to service its external debt accrues only to the creditor. The debt burden is excessive and acts like a high marginal tax rate on efforts to expand the country's foreign-exchange earnings. There may also be a disincentive for domestic investment and growth. The high initial debt may actually be counterproductive in the sense that the creditor has to discount previous loans so fast that an extra dollar of debt actually lowers expected debt service. If, however, the debt is reduced by forgiveness, there may be more of an incentive to service the smaller debt and undertake measures to stimulate the home economy.[3] By reducing the country's debt, creditors believe that they will increase the likelihood that the debtor will repay what remains.

Although debt forgiveness has its theoretical appeal, it too confronts operational difficulties. How much debt should be forgiven? By which creditors? And by what techniques?

According to one study, the amount of debt reduction should meet these criteria:

First, it should be sufficient to enable the country concerned to bring its stock of external liabilities down relative to its income and export capacity (a balance sheet test). Secondly, it should be sufficient to permit

[1]Paul Krugman, "Private Capital Flows to Problem Debtors," in *Developing Country Debt and Economic Performance,* ed. Jeffrey Sachs (1988), vol. 1, p. 303.

[2]For examples, see Jonathan Eaton and Mark Gersovitz, "Debt with Potential Repudiation," *Review of Economic Studies* (1981), and Jeremy Bulow and Kenneth Rogoff, "A Constant Recontracting Model of Sovereign Debt," *Journal of Political Economy* 97 (1989).

[3]This analysis can also be represented in terms of a debt-relief Laffer curve. See Stijn Claessens et al., "Market-Based Debt Reduction for Developing Countries," *World Bank Policy and Research Series* 16 (1990): 5.

part of a country's future income growth to accrue to domestic residents and not just to foreign creditors (a cash flow test). Thirdly, it should be sufficient to permit trade lines and interbank lines to be maintained on a voluntary basis with a medium-term perspective of voluntary lending for other purposes (a restored creditworthiness test).[4]

As for which creditors will participate in debt reduction, there is again a free-rider problem: part of the capital gains from reduced debt will accrue to nonparticipants. Some creditors will also not participate because they prefer financing a debt overhang for the time being with the expectation that they will benefit in the future from a favorable turn of events that will allow the debtor to finance the larger nominal debt at its full value. Nonparticipation creates a "prisoner's dilemma" in which it may well be to the collective advantage of all the creditors to forgive debt but no individual creditor has the incentive to do so.

Techniques to achieve debt reduction are various, ranging from voluntary market-based approaches to concerted negotiated agreements among all parties to the creation of a new International Debt Facility. Market-based schemes involve debt repurchases at a discount, and the retired debt is replaced with new obligations such as cash, exit bonds, or equity. In a buyback, the borrower repurchases a part of its external debt at a discount from a voluntary seller. Buybacks are the simplest form of debt reduction, but they raise the question of where the borrower's resources come from to finance the buyback—from the creditor government's own reserves, return of flight capital, proceeds of World Bank structural adjustment loans, or IMF loans. Under collateralization arrangements, inherited debt is exchanged for a new debt that has a reduced amount of principal or a lower rate of interest. The collateral can be in the form of deposits by the debtor or bonds, and it is the collateral that makes the reduced service on the new debt or the reduced principal possible. The conversion of debt into equity allows investors who have bought some of the debtor country's exter-

nal debt at a discount on the secondary market to redeem the debt for some domestic asset.

Summarizing the issue of financing versus forgiving a debt overhang, Krugman states that

the choice represents a tradeoff between the option value of a large nominal debt and the incentive effects of a debt that is unlikely to be repaid. Since good news is always possible, creditors would like to keep their claims high, so that if by some chance a country should turn out to be able to repay, they will not turn out to have forgiven debt unnecessarily. On the other hand, if a country is not going to be able to repay except in exceptional circumstances, it will have little incentive to try to adjust. Thus creditors may wish to forgive part of a country's debt to increase the likelihood that it will repay what remains. It is because of the tension between these two objectives that the issue of how much to rely on debt forgiveness and how much to rely on financing is a difficult one.[5]

In actual practice, a debt-rescheduling negotiation is likely to result in a combination of financing and forgiving. A notable example is the 1989 negotiation between Mexico and commercial banks that offered banks three options: (1) to swap Mexican debt for new long-term bonds at a 35 percent discount, with Mexico buying zero-coupon U.S. Treasury securities to guarantee the principal; (2) to switch from floating-rate debt, paying about 10 percent to new fixed-rate debt paying 6¼ percent, without any change in face value; and (3) to retain their present claims but make new loans to Mexico over the next four years by enough to raise those claims by 25 percent.

In any negotiation the participants will tend to have different objectives. Debtors have the option to default and they want the debt servicing and debt to be reduced. Commercial banks want greater repayments and they can walk away from additional involuntary lending. The IMF and World Bank are concerned with renewing economic growth in the debtor country and with political and economic stability. No general solution can be expected; instead, the outcome of country-by-country negotiations will depend on the various expectations of the participants and their bargaining power.

[4]WIDER Study Group Series No. 3, "Debt Reduction" (1989).

[5]Paul Krugman, "Financing vs. Forgiving a Debt Overhang," *Journal of Development Economics* 29 (1988): 267.

V.E. PRIVATE FOREIGN INVESTMENT

V.E.1. Benefits and Costs of Private Foreign Investment—Note

Considerable interest is now being shown in measures that might promote private foreign investment and allow it to make a greater contribution to the development of the recipient countries. In an attempt to stimulate larger flows of private capital to developing nations, several capital-exporting countries have adopted a range of measures that include tax incentives, investment guarantees, and financial assistance to private investors. International institutions are also encouraging the international flow of private capital; the International Finance Corporation (IFC), for instance, cooperates directly with private investors in financing new or expanded ventures.

Of far greater influence, however, than the measures adopted by capital-exporting nations or international organizations are the policies of the capital-recipient countries themselves. Controls exercised by the host country over the conditions of entry of foreign capital, regulations of the operation of foreign capital, and restrictions on the remittance of profits and the repatriation of capital are far more decisive in determining the flow of foreign capital than any policy undertaken by the capital-exporting country.

The central problem now is for the recipient country to devise policies that will succeed in both encouraging a greater inflow of private foreign capital and ensuring that it makes the maximum contribution feasible toward the achievement of the country's development objectives. The tasks of development require both more effective governmental activity and more investment on the part of international private enterprise. But the private investors must be aware of the developmental objectives and the priorities of the host country and understand how their investments fit into the country's development strategy. The contribution of private foreign capital has to be interpreted in terms beyond private profit. At the same time, the government must recognize that if risks are too high or the return on investment is too low, international private investment will be inhibited from making any contribution at all. Development planning requires the government to influence the per-

formance of private foreign investment, but in doing this, the government should appreciate fully the potential contribution of this investment and should devise policies that will meet the mutual interests of private investor and host country. This calls for more intensive analysis of the consequences of private foreign investment and for more thought and ingenuity in devising approaches that favor the mobilization of private foreign capital while ensuring its most effective "planned performance" in terms of the country's development program.

At present, the policies taken by the developing countries reveal a mixed picture of restrictions and incentives. On the one hand, the foreign investor's freedom of action may be restricted by a variety of governmental regulations that exclude private foreign investment from certain "key" sectors of the economy, impose limitations on the extent of foreign participation in ownership or management, specify conditions for the employment of domestic and foreign labor, limit the amount of profits, and impose exchange controls on the remission of profits and the repatriation of capital.

On the other hand, a progressive liberalization of policy toward private foreign capital has occurred during recent years. Many countries now recognize that an inflow of private capital may offer some special advantages over public capital, and a number of investment incentive measures have been recently adopted or are under consideration. These incentive devices include assistance in securing information on investment opportunities, the provision of supplementary finance, the establishment of economic overhead facilities such as in industrial estates, protective tariffs on commodities that compete with those produced by foreign investors, exemptions from import duties on necessary equipment and materials, the granting of exchange guarantees or privileges, tax concession schemes for the encouragement of desired new investments, and special legislation for the protection of foreign investments.

To remove the ambivalence that characterizes these policies, it is desirable to reexamine the role of private foreign capital more systematically by appraising the prospective benefits and costs of private foreign investment. Such an appraisal may then provide a more rational basis for determining the type of policy that is most appropriate for securing the maximum contribution from private foreign investment.

From the standpoint of national economic benefit, the essence of the case for encouraging an inflow of capital is that the increase in real income resulting from the act of investment is greater than the resultant increase in the income of the investor.[1] If the value added to output by the foreign capital is greater than the amount appropriated by the investor, social returns exceed private returns. As long as foreign investment raises productivity, and this increase is not wholly appropriated by the investor, the greater product must be shared with others, and there must be some direct benefits to other income groups. These benefits can accrue to (1) domestic labor in the form of higher real wages, (2) consumers by way of lower prices, and (3) the government through higher tax revenue. Beyond this, and most importantly in many cases, there are likely to be (4) indirect gains through the realization of external economies.

An increase in total real wages may be one of the major direct benefits from an inflow of foreign capital. This can be recognized in Figure 1, where the line *EG* illustrates the marginal productivity of capital in the capital-recipient country, given the amount of labor. If initially, the domestically owned capital stock is *AB,* the total output is *ABCE.* We assume that profits per unit of capital equal the marginal product of capital, and that total profits on domestic capital are *ABCD,* and total real wages are *CDE.* Let there now be an inflow of foreign capital in the amount of *BF.* Total output then increases by the amount *BFGC,* and the profits on foreign capital are *BFGH* of this amount. Since the profit rate on total capital has fallen, profits on domestic capital are reduced to *ABHI.* But the total real wages of labor are now *GIE,* with the increase in real wages amounting to *DCGI.* Although in this case, with a given marginal pro-

[1]Much of the following analysis is based on Sir Donald MacDougall, ''The Benefits and Cost of Private Investment from Abroad: A Theoretical Approach,'' *Economic Record* (March 1960): 13–35, and Paul Streeten, *Economic Integration,* 2nd ed. (1964), chap. 5.

FIGURE 1.

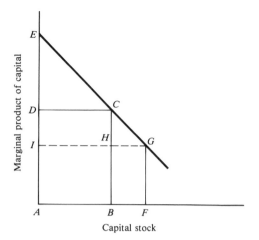

ductivity of capital schedule, most of labor's gain—the amount *DCHI*— is merely a redistribution from domestic capitalists, there is still a net increase in the real incomes of domestic factors, represented by the rise in real wages in the amount *CGH.*

For a developing country, the inflow of foreign capital may be significant in not only raising the productivity of a given amount of labor, but also allowing a large labor force to be employed. If, as was contended in the discussion of dualistic development in Chapter III, a shortage of capital in heavily populated poor countries limits the employment of labor from the rural sector in the advanced sector, where wages are higher, an inflow of foreign capital may then make it possible to employ more labor in the advanced sector. The international flow of capital can thus be interpreted as an alternative to labor migration from the poor country: where outlets for the emigration of labor are restricted, the substitution of domestic migration of labor into the advanced sector becomes the most feasible solution. The social benefit from the foreign investment in the advanced sector is then greater than the profits on this investment, for the wages received by the newly employed exceed their former real wage in the rural sector, and this excess should be added as a national gain.

Domestic consumers may also benefit from direct foreign investment. When the investment is cost reducing in a particular industry, consumers of the product may gain through lower product prices. If the investment is product improving or product innovating, consumers benefit from better quality products or new products.

In order that labor and consumers might enjoy part of their benefit from the higher productivity in enterprises established by foreign investors, the overseas withdrawal by the investors must be less than the increase in output. But even if the entire increase in productivity accrues as foreign profits, this requirement may still be fulfilled when the government taxes foreign profits. For many countries, taxes on foreign profits or royalties from concession agreements constitute a large proportion of total government revenue. The fiscal benefit derived from foreign investment is evident from the fact that the share of government revenue in the national product of countries that have received substantial foreign investment is considerably higher than in most of the other low-income countries.

The most significant contribution of foreign investment is likely to come from external economies. Direct foreign investment brings to the recipient country not only capital and foreign exchange, but also managerial ability, technical personnel, technological knowledge, administrative organization, and innovations in products and production techniques—all of which are in short supply. This ensures in the first instance that a project involving private foreign investment will be adequately formulated and implemented, unlike the situation that has frequently confronted public economic aid when the recipient country has not had the talent or inclination to undertake adequate feasibility studies and formulate projects that might qualify for public capital. The preinvestment survey, act of investment, and operation of the investment project are ensured in private foreign investment.

One of the greatest benefits to the recipient country is the access to foreign knowledge that private foreign investment may provide—knowledge that helps overcome the managerial gap and technological gap. The provision of this knowledge can be interpreted as "private technical assistance." The private technical assistance and the demonstration effects that are integral features of private foreign investment may spread and have beneficial results in other sectors of the economy. The rate of technological advance in a poor country is highly dependent on the rate of capital inflow. New techniques accompany the inflow of private capital, and by the example they set, foreign firms promote the diffusion of technological advance in the econ-

omy. In addition, foreign investment may lead to the training of labor in new skills, and the knowledge gained by these workers can be transmitted to other members of the labor force or these workers might be employed later by local firms.

Private foreign investment may also serve as a stimulus to additional domestic investment in the recipient country. This is especially likely through the creation of external pecuniary economies. If the foreign capital is used to develop the country's infrastructure, it may directly facilitate more investment. Even if the foreign investment is in one industry, it may encourage domestic investment by reducing costs or creating demand in other industries. Profits may then rise and lead to expansion in these other industries.

Since there are so many specific scarcities in a poor country, it is common for investment to be of a cost-reducing character by breaking bottlenecks in production. This stimulates expansion by raising profits on all underutilized productive capacity and by allowing the exploitation of economies of scale that had been restricted. When the foreign investment in an industry makes its product cheaper, another industry that uses this product benefits from the lower prices. This creates profits and stimulates an expansion in the second industry.

There is also considerable scope for the initial foreign investment to produce external investment incentives through demand creation in other industries. The foreign investment in the first industry can give rise to profits in industries that supply inputs to the first industry, in industries that produce complementary products, and in industries that produce goods bought by the factor-owners who now have higher real incomes. Similar effects may also follow from investment that is product improving or product innovating. A whole series of domestic investments may thus be linked to the foreign investment.

Against these benefits must be set the costs of foreign investment to the host country. These costs may arise from special concessions offered by the host country, adverse effects on domestic saving, deterioration in the terms of trade, and problems of balance-of-payments adjustment.

To encourage foreign enterprise, the government of the host country may have to provide special facilities, undertake additional public services, extend financial assistance, or subsidize inputs. These have a cost in absorbing governmental resources that could be used elsewhere. Tax concessions may also have to be offered and may have to be extended to domestic investment because the government may not be able to discriminate, for administrative and political reasons, in favor of only the foreign investor. Moreover, when several countries compete among themselves in offering inducements to foreign capital, each may offer more by way of inducement than is necessary; the investment may be of a type that would go to one country or another, regardless of inducements, but the foreign enterprise may "shop around" and secure extra concessions. Without some form of collective agreement among capital-receiving countries regarding the maximum concessions that will be made, the cost of "overencouraging" certain types of foreign investment may be considerable.

Once foreign investment has been attracted, it should be expected to have an income effect that will lead to a higher level of domestic savings. This effect may be offset, however, by a redistribution of income away from capital if the foreign investment reduces profits in domestic industries. The consequent reduction in home savings would then be another indirect cost of foreign investment. But it is unlikely to be of much consequence in practice, for it would require that foreign investment be highly competitive with home investment. In a poor country, it is more probable that foreign capital will complement domestic investment and will give rise to higher incomes and profits in other industries, as already noted.

Foreign investment might also affect the recipient country's commodity terms of trade through structural changes associated with the pattern of development that results from the capital inflow. If the inflow of capital leads to an increase in the country's rate of development without any change in the terms of trade, the country's growth of real income will then be the same as its growth of output. If, however, the terms of trade deteriorate, the rise in real income will be less than that in output, and the worsening terms of trade may be considered another indirect cost of the foreign investment. Whether the terms of trade will turn against the capital-receiving country is problematic, depending on various possible changes at home and abroad in the supply of and demand for exports, import-substitutes, and domestic com-

modities. It is unlikely, however, that private foreign investment would cause any substantial deterioration in the terms of trade. For if an unfavorable shift resulted from a rising demand for imports on the side of consumption, it would probably be controlled through import restriction. And if it resulted on the side of production, from a rising supply of exports owing to private direct investment in the export sector, the inflow of foreign capital would diminish as export prices fell, thereby limiting the deterioration in the terms of trade. Moreover, if the deterioration comes through an export bias in production, it is still possible that the factoral and the income terms of trade might improve even though the commodity terms of trade worsen, since the capital inflow may result in a sufficiently large increase in productivity in the export sector.

Of greater seriousness than the foregoing costs are those associated with balance-of-payments adjustments. Pressure on the balance of payments may become acute when the foreign debt has to be serviced. If the amount of foreign exchange required to service the debt becomes larger than the amount of foreign exchange being supplied by new foreign investments, the transfer mechanism will have to create a surplus on current account equal to the debit items on account of the payment of interest, dividends, profits, and amortization on the foreign borrowings.[2] When a net outflow of capital occurs, a reallocation of resources becomes necessary in order to expand exports or replace imports. To accomplish this, the country may have to endure internal and external controls or experience currency depreciation. The adverse effects of these measures of balance-of-payments adjustment must then be considered as indirect costs of foreign investment, to be added to the direct costs of the foreign payments.

The direct costs in themselves need not be a matter of great concern. For even though part of the increased production from the use of foreign capital has to be paid abroad in profits or interest—and this is a deduction that would not be necessary if the savings were provided at

---

[2]The length of time that elapses before this occurs will depend on the growth in new foreign investment, the rate of interest and dividend earnings, and the amortization rate. See E. D. Domar, "The Effects of Foreign Investment on the Balance of Payments," *American Economic Review* (December 1950): 805–26.

home—this is merely to say that the country must not expect to get an income from savings if it does not make the savings.[3] What is fundamental is that the country does have additional investment, and the benefits from this may exceed the direct costs of the foreign savings that made possible the capital formation.

The indirect costs, however, are rightly a cause of concern, insofar as the capital-receiving country may be unable or unwilling to endure a loss of international reserves and does not want to impose measures of balance-of-payments adjustment in order to find sufficient foreign exchange for the remittance of the external service payments. External measures—such as import quotas, tariffs, and exchange restrictions—may suppress the demand for imports, but they do so at the expense of productivity and efficiency. Internal measures of higher taxation and credit tightness involve the costs of reduced consumption and investment. And the alternative of currency devaluation may cause the country to incur the costs of a possible deterioration in its terms of trade, changes in income distribution, and necessary shifts of resources. To avoid, or at least minimize, these indirect costs, the role of private foreign investment must be related to the debt-servicing capacity of the host country. And this depends on the country's development program as a whole, since the ability to create a sufficiently large export surplus rests on the operation of all industries together, not simply on the use made of foreign investment alone (see section V.D).

In the past, there was a general tendency for poor countries to overestimate the costs of foreign investment and to discount the benefits, especially the indirect benefits. Now, however, there is a wider appreciation that within the context of a development program and with a careful appraisal of the prospective benefits and costs of foreign investment, policies may be devised to secure a greater contribution from the inflow of private capital. Instead of discouraging investment from abroad simply because it involves some costs, the developing countries are increasingly recognizing that they should attempt to devise policies that will encourage the maximum feasible contribution. Although the formulation of specific policies must depend on particular conditions in each country, we may at least suggest some of the principal considerations that might shape these policies.

In general, the attraction of private foreign investment now depends less on fiscal action, on which most countries have concentrated, and more on other conditions and measures that guarantee protection of the investment and provide wider opportunities for the foreign investor. If private foreign investment is to be encouraged, it is necessary to allay the investor's concern about the possibilities of discriminatory legislation, exchange controls, and the threat of expropriation. Investment guarantees may be utilized more effectively to lessen the investor's apprehension of nonbusiness risks. Either unilaterally or through bilateral treaties, governments can offer some assurances designed to reduce the likelihood of expropriation or of impairments of investors' rights and to assure investors of an adequate recourse if such impairments should occur. It has always been difficult to secure agreement by both investing and recipient countries on a uniform set of substantive rules, as in a multilateral investment charter. The World Bank has, however, succeeded in establishing the International Center for Settlement of Investment Disputes, which provides facilities for the settlement, by voluntary recourse to conciliation or arbitration, of investment disputes arising between the foreign investor and the host government.

Finally, along with guarantees against the occurrence of risk and measures for the adjustment of investment disputes, considerable attention is being given to the possibilities of providing guarantees under which the investors will be compensated for any loss they may suffer from other than normal business causes. Although such a guarantee is something of a measure of last resort, it does help to minimize the investor's risk and gives some advance assurance of a reliable "safety margin." Some capital-supplying nations have provided insurance coverage, but the insurance of investments in developing countries might be made more effective through the establishment of a multilateral investment insurance program, rather than participation in a number of bilateral programs.

While investment guarantees may help in removing "disincentives" to foreign investment, the attraction of private capital depends even more on positive inducements in the form of greater opportunities for profit making. The pri-

[3]See J. R. Hicks, *Essays in World Economics* (1959), p. 191.

vate investor's first concern is whether costs will be covered and a profit earned. Some developing countries offer special tax concessions that provide a tax holiday or reduce the rate of tax on profits, but these measures are not effective unless the investment yields a profit. The foreign investor is likely to be less interested in receiving an exemption after a profit is made than in being sure of a profit in the first instance. It is therefore most important to raise profit expectations. To do this, it may be necessary to undertake additional public expenditures, especially in developing the country's infrastructure and in ensuring a supply of trained labor. Yet rarely is a government willing to undertake expenditures expressly for the purpose of attracting foreign investment; instead of incurring the present cost of additional expenditures, most governments prefer to assist foreign investors through a future sacrifice in revenue. Although politically more feasible, tax concessions are not likely to be the most powerful inducements that the host country can offer to encourage a flow of investment.

At the same time, their use can be overdone. They involve a cost to the government not only in terms of a revenue forgone, but also in terms of equity and administrative costs. More importantly, the LDCs may offer excessive concessions in their efforts to attract foreign investment. If an investment is going to occur in one LDC or another (for example, in order to secure a raw material supply), but the LDCs compete with each other in offering concessions, then the LDCs are likely to overconcede.[4] When tax concessions are granted to existing investments, in order not to discriminate, there is simply a windfall. Moreover, the concessions are likely to attract the quick speculative type of foreign investment, which is in the country only to take advantage of the concessions and leaves as soon as they are withdrawn. Finally, if the benefits of foreign investment are realized for the host country during the early years of the investments, there is no case for prolonging the concessions beyond the relatively short period.

Developing nations are now mainly interested in having foreign enterprises contribute to their industrialization, rather than following the historical pattern of being directed to agriculture or mining. In most cases, however, the size of the domestic market has remained too small to offer much attraction. As a development program proceeds, domestic markets may widen, and this limitation will be reduced. Much can also be done to widen markets and establish a more substantial base for industry by promoting regional markets through arrangements for a common market or a free-trade association. The establishment of a customs union or free-trade area may have considerable potential for attracting investment to the development of manufacturing industry.

Even more significant than regional preferential arrangements would be a general preferential system by which developed countries granted preferences to all LDCs on their exports of manufactures and semimanufactures. Such a system may offer considerable attraction to private foreign investment, especially by inducing the transfer of production facilities required from the developed preference-granting countries to the less developed preference-receiving countries in order to turn labor and raw materials into saleable products and obtain the dual advantages of tariff-free or preferential market access and lower labor costs.

In considering measures to encourage foreign investment, a developing country does not want, of course, to seek foreign capital indiscriminately. The objective is to ensure that the investment supports activities from which the recipient nation may derive maximum national economic gain, as assessed through benefits and costs. To achieve the most effective utilization of foreign investments in terms of its entire development program, the country may have to adopt policies, such as preferential tax treatment or other incentives, that will attract private capital into activities where it will have the maximum catalytic effect of mobilizing additional effort. From this standpoint, it is especially important that policies affecting the allocation of foreign capital be based on an awareness of the external economies that can be realized from different patterns of investment. Beyond a consideration of the direct increase in

---

[4]See Dudley Seers, "Big Companies and Small Countries," *Kyklos* 16, fasc. 4 (1963): 601–3, and R. H. Green and Ann Seidman, *Unity or Poverty?* (1968), pp. 99–131.

Several studies indicate that tax incentive programs have not been effective. See, for example, Jack Heller and Kenneth M. Kauffman, *Tax Incentives for Industry in Less Developed Countries* (1963), pp. 60–66; M. C. Taylor, *Industrial Tax Exemption in Puerto Rico* (1957), pp. 143–49; and Peter Kilby, *Industrialization in an Open Economy: Nigeria, 1945–66* (1969), pp. 132–34.

income resulting from the investment and other short-term criteria, it is important to look to the more indirect and long-run possibilities—from the widening of investment opportunities to even the instigation of social and cultural transformations.

Finally, the recipient country may be well advised to emphasize a partnership arrangement between foreign and domestic enterprise. A joint international business venture that involved collaboration between private foreign capital and local private or public capital is a promising device for protecting international investment, integrating foreign investment into a development program and safe-guarding against an enclave type of investment, stimulating domestic management and investment and reducing the transfer burden and balance-of-payments difficulties.

The alternatives of a 100 percent foreign-owned enterprise and a joint venture are, however, only two of a number of possible arrangements for securing a mix of foreign capital, management, and technology. The major question is whether there are other means of transferring scarce managerial and technical knowledge without having to be in joint supply with capital, as in a foreign direct investment. As already noted, the cost for foreign equity capital is high, even post-tax. The host country may well consider this cost excessive for the foreign managerial and technical knowledge that it desires but cannot acquire through a direct foreign investment without the high payment for equity capital with which it is in joint supply. The new approach to foreign investment has therefore been to focus on alternative arrangements for securing capital, management, technology, and marketing capabilities without the foreign ownership and control that has commonly been associated with foreign direct investment. It may be possible to unbundle the inputs that come in the package of direct foreign investment and secure inputs that are more appropriate for the needs of the recipient country, or that cost less when they are not tied to equity capital.

The problem for the host country is to evaluate the benefits and costs of alternative arrangements for importing the investing firm's capabilities, and then to secure by inducements and regulations the best feasible alternative. The alternative arrangements span an entire spectrum. At one end of the spectrum is the traditional form of direct investment, involving 100 percent foreign equity ownership and no time

limit on the existence of the foreign-owned enterprise in the recipient country. This arrangement is appropriate for only those sectors where the mix of capital, technology, and management cannot be supplied in any other way and the investment continues to provide a properly discounted benefit–cost ratio greater than that of unity for an unlimited time period. Moving on from this arrangement, the host country may initially allow 100 percent ownership but then insist that any expansion of the enterprise occur through national participation. It may further limit the time of foreign control by requiring a national majority equity holding to emerge within a certain period. Moving still nearer to a dilution of foreign equity, the host country may insist at the very outset on a joint venture and may establish a limited time for any foreign equity participation. At the other end of the spectrum, the host country may exclude foreign equity altogether and seek the managerial and technological knowledge through contractual arrangements that allow the transfer of technical and managerial skills without being tied to equity capital. Licensing agreements, technical services agreements, engineering and construction contracts, management contracts, and production-sharing,[5] revenue-sharing, or profit-sharing agreements can prove to be of considerable benefit to a developing country—supplying the needed foreign knowledge at a lower cost than must be paid when the knowledge comes with equity capital.[6]

Some doubts, however, may be expressed whether the LDCs can indeed realistically expect to receive foreign technological and managerial knowledge without equity capital. This may prove difficult or impossible for the latest technology or research-and-development type of enterprise because the discoverer and owner of such technology normally wishes to retain control. But this does not apply to the older, more standardized types of technology. Assuming that

---

[5]A production-sharing agreement allows a national firm in the LDC to acquire imported equipment and technology in return for payment ''in kind'' by exporting its products for a number of years to a guaranteed market overseas.

[6]For a fuller discussion of these new forms of foreign investment, see Donald Lessard, *Financial Intermediation Beyond the Debt Crisis* (1985), 61–71; Charles Oman, *New Forms of Investment in Developing Country Industries* (1989); and Stijn Claessens, ''Alternative Forms of External Finance,'' *World Bank Research Observer* (January 1993).

the demand for such technical services should increase, then it can be expected that a supply of such services will be induced.

Similarly, it can be contended that a management contract is not an effective instrument for the discovery of investment opportunities, as distinguished from the actual operation of an investment. This may be true, but in the LDCs the discovery of investment opportunities is not as important as in more advanced countries; the crucial need is still much more for simply the adapting, imitating, widening, and deepening of existing methods of investment.

Finally, it may be doubted whether there will be sufficient motivation when there is no equity interest. But managerial fees can be graduated according to profits, and even other objectives, such as foreign-exchange savings, realized. Other incentive devices—short of ownership—can also be utilized.

In general, these contractual arrangements are extremely flexible devices for securing the transfer of the nonmonetary resources of management and technology; they may be adapted to widely diverse circumstances; and their utility in meeting a variety of objectives is becoming increasingly appreciated. This approach can be particularly efficacious when activities are reserved under a development program for public ownership or for majority ownership by local nationals, but there is still a need for seeking technical information or managerial services from abroad.

If the technical and managerial components of direct foreign investment can be secured through contractual nondirect investment devices without having to grant its supplier a controlling equity interest, and if financial aid is provided from foreign public sources of capital (either directly or indirectly through a development bank or development corporation), then the recipient LDC may benefit from an optimal mix of public financial aid and private technical assistance.

The potentialities for combining local public or private ownership with technical assistance from private foreign enterprise and capital assistance from public sources deserve considerable emphasis.

EXHIBIT V.10. Major Destinations of FDI to Developing Countries, 1991

Countries	US$ Millions	Share of Recipient GDP (percent)	Share of Recipient Gross Domestic Investment (percent)
All developing countries	35,895	1.1	4.5
Mexico	4,762	1.7	7.4
China	4,366	1.2	3.3
Malaysia	3,455	7.4	20.5
Argentina	2,439	1.9	15.1
Thailand	2,014	2.2	5.6
Venezuela	1,914	3.6	19.2
Brazil	1,600	0.4	2.0
Indonesia	1,482	1.3	3.6
Korea, Rep. of	1,116	0.4	1.0
Turkey	810	0.8	3.9

After averaging $13 billion a year from 1985 to 1989, and rising to $18 billion in 1990, foreign direct investment (FDI) into developing countries rose to nearly $36 billion in 1991. Asian countries received about 60 percent of the gross inflows and Latin America 28 percent.

Emerging markets in developing countries also received in 1992 another $37 billion of portfolio investment (in bonds, equities, and related securities). The increase in portfolio investment in the early 1990s was even greater than in FDI.

Sources: International Monetary Fund, *Balance-of-Payments Yearbook* (1992); World Bank, *World Debt Tables, 1993–94,* vol. 1 (1994).

EXHIBIT V.11. Long-Term Capital Flows to
LDCs

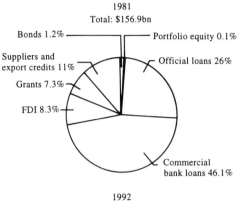

1981
Total: $156.9bn

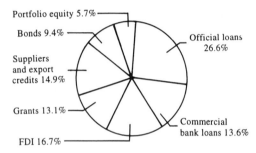

1992
Total: $229.2bn

The composition of external financing has changed markedly from 1981 to 1992. While official loans have remained the same percentage of the total, commercial bank loans have declined considerably since the debt problems of the 1980s, and FDI has increased, as have bonds and portfolio equity investment.

Source: World Bank.

EXHIBIT V.12. Real Aggregate Net
Resource Flows to Developing Countries,
1985–92

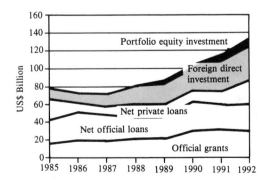

Note: All flows are deflated by the import unit value index at constant 1992 dollars, 1992 deflator is a World Bank staff estimate. Data for portfolio equity investment are World Bank estimates, available since 1989 only.

Source: World Bank, *World Debt Tables, 1991–92.*

V.E.2. Multinational Enterprises in Developing Countries—Note

The multinational enterprise (MNE)—with facilities in many countries and responsive to a common management strategy—has gained increasing prominence as an instrument for private foreign investment in developing countries. While the capital, technology, managerial competence, and marketing capabilities of an MNE can be utilized for a country's development, there is also a fear that the MNE may dominate the host country or impose excessive costs.

Criticism of the MNE is but the latest attempt to dispel complacency over the relevance of the neoclassical theory of international trade for development problems. As we shall see in Chapter VIII, critics of the neoclassical trade theory first attempted to discredit the theory's power to explain historical development by arguing that international trade had actually operated historically as a mechanism of inequality. After the establishment of the postwar international economic institutions, the argument shifted to a criticism of the alleged biases and deficiencies of the international institutions composing the Bretton Woods system. And now the MNE has become the object of criticism, with pessimistic warnings about future detriment to the developing countries if the MNE is not sufficiently regulated.

Does the evaluation of the operation of the MNE, however, call for more than a social benefit–cost analysis, such as outlined in Selection V.E.1? Why should the MNE be analyzed differently from direct investment from one home country to a host country? The essential question is what difference does the attribute of "multinationality" make to the analysis?

True, an MNE is likely to have the power of an oligopoly; but so too may some "simple" foreign enterprises or domestic independent companies. True, an MNE may be a vertically integrated enterprise that uses transfer prices for intrafirm trade; but so too may "simple" foreign investment from source country to a host country. True, an MNE may be involved in the costly process of import substitution; but so too may a simple foreign enterprise or a national firm. True, an MNE may be depleting too rapidly a wasting asset; but so too may other forms of investment that are not multinational in character. In assessing the contribution of a foreign investment by an MNE, we have to be clear on whether what is being assessed is the *investment project* per se, the *foreignness* of the investment, or some *alternative* institutional arrangement for acquiring the ingredients of the direct investment package.

The distinguishing feature of an MNE is that the range of its major decisions (finance, investment, production, research and development, and reaction to governmental policies) is based on the opportunities and problems that the MNE confronts in all the countries in which it operates. In utilizing its "global-scanning capacity" to determine its investment plan, worldwide sourcing strategies, and marketing based on expectations of returns and risk factors, the MNE concentrates on the total net worth of the investor's interests, not on that of an individual subsidiary alone.

Analyzing why a multinational undertakes foreign direct investment (FDI), Dunning has presented an eclectic theory that incorporates locational advantages, ownership-specific advantages, and internalization advantages.[1]

Locational advantages occur from foreign investment that seeks lower costs in the foreign country (frequently labor), a supply of natural resources as an input (such as bauxite in a vertically integrated aluminum industry), lower transportation costs, or a "tariff factory" if the foreign country raises tariffs, thereby inducing investment to jump over the tariff wall for production in the protected market.

Ownership advantages allow the foreign firm to appropriate rents if it innovates and produces differentiated products, giving the firm some monopoly element, or if the firm has some proprietary knowledge that others cannot duplicate.

Internalization advantages arise because the markets for human capital, knowledge, marketing and management expertise have high information costs and transaction costs. It is therfore administratively better to take out of the market those transactions that the market performs imperfectly and use an internal administrative method of allocation within the firms, instead of

---

[1]John Dunning, *Explaining International Production* (1988).

relying on the external market. The internalization of markets across boundaries leads to FDI. Compared with external markets, the firm's linkages, integration, transfer pricing, and economies of centralization allow costs to be reduced through FDI.

Based on location advantages, ownership advantages, and internalization advantages, FDI therefore allows the investor to profit from a comparative advantage in creating, exporting, and capturing private returns on information and new technologies.

Although these features of foreign investment associated with "multinationality" do not call for a different type of analysis from the general benefit–cost analysis already discussed, the multinational firm is characterized by some behavioral differences that broaden the reach and increase the intensity of both the benefits and the costs of foreign investment. As Caves has indicated,[2] a national branch of a multinational firm might behave differently from an equal-sized independent company for three reasons:

1. *Motivation.* The multinational firm maximizes profits from its activities as a whole, rather than telling each subsidiary to maximize independently and ignoring the profit interdependencies among them. The multinational firm also spreads its risks, and could therefore behave quite differently in an uncertain situation from an independent having the same risk-return preference function.
2. *Cognition and information.* Its corporate family relations give the multinational unit access to more information about markets located in other countries or to information to which it can attach a higher degree of certainty.
3. *Opportunity set.* The set of assets held by a multinational unit can differ from a national firm's in various ways, perhaps most notably in its skill in differentiating its product and its financial capacities.

Although Caves's analysis is concerned with the differences in market behavior between a national branch of a multinational firm and an equal-sized independent company, these behavioral differences are also relevant as between a multinational firm and a "simple" type of foreign enterprise in the developing country.

These behavioral differences can be especially significant in: first, promoting foreign investment; second, allowing the MNE to act as a unit of real economic integration; and third, endowing the MNE with greater bargaining power.

The growth of MNEs tends to promote more foreign investment because the MNE is less of a risk-averter when it operates in a number of countries, produces a number of products, practices process specialization, and enjoys greater maneuverability with respect to marketing opportunities and conditions of production than does a firm with a narrower range of activities.

Emphasizing the interrelations between output and input flows in international trade, Baldwin has stated:

When the international firm becomes economically viable in a particular industry, not only is it possible to transfer knowledge, capital, and technical and managerial labor across borders more efficiently, but these transfers tend to be economically feasible with smaller product markets than is the case when the optimum size of productive units is small. Moreover, because of the pecuniary and technological externalities that exist among intermediate sectors in a vertical product line, it may not be economically profitable from a private viewpoint to add a new product to a country's production list unless the international firm mechanism is utilized.[3]

The MNE is also a unit of integration in the world economy. The transmission of factors (capital, skills, technological knowledge, management) by the MNE, together with the MNE's economies of scale in R&D and marketing, make it a unit of real international integration. By its multinational operations and intrafirm transactions, the MNE transcends the national barriers to commodity trade and impediments to international factor movements. As a planning unit that makes resource-allocation decisions, the MNE becomes the mechanism for making effective the LDC's potential comparative advantage. The MNE provides the complementary resources of capital, technology, management, and market outlets that may be necessary to bestow an "effective" comparative advantage to the labor surplus factor endowment in the host country.

This can also be evaluated as efficient international production. The MNE views production as a set of activities or processes, and

[2]Richard E. Caves, *International Investment and Imperfect Markets,* Princeton University Special Papers in International Economics, no. 10 (November 1974), pp. 21–22.

[3]R. E. Baldwin, "International Trade in Inputs and Outputs," *American Economic Review, Papers and Proceedings* (May 1972): 433.

the global strategy of the MNE amounts in essence to the solution of activity models of production, with production processes in many countries. A competitive equilibrium solution to the programming problem is imposed within the MNE when it operates efficiently as a planning unit. Regulatory interference with the MNE will alter the equilibrium basis, and some processes formerly in operation may become inefficient to use. The likelihood for a labor surplus economy is that labor becomes unemployed for a lack of cooperating factors previously supplied by the MNE. Or if workers were formerly employed in a lower productivity occupation, there is a loss in real wages.

This interpretation of the MNE as an efficient technical and allocational unit of integration means that while intrafirm trade conforms to *corporate* advantage, it is also identical with the realization of *comparative* advantage. If the nation-state fragments the world economy through restrictions on commodity and factor movements and thwarts international economic integration, the MNE may serve a function complementary—rather than competitive—to that of the nation-state: the MNE may be the vehicle for evoking in practice the principle of comparative advantage in world trade, for trade in both outputs and inputs. The internal resource allocation in the MNE is a substitute mechanism for the market, but when the MNE realizes comparative advantage in processes and activities, its resource-allocation decisions will be more efficient than those in unintegrated markets that are characterized by imperfections and uncertainty. For global technical efficiency, the world economy is the territorial unit of international production (not the nation-state, which is a unit of international politics).

What, however, is the distribution of gains between the MNE and the host country? More pointedly, how might the net benefit for the host country be raised? This is the crucial question posed by the attribute of "multinationality." For multinationality instills foreign investment by an MNE with greater bargaining power because of its tendency to be of larger size, its capability to exercise wide options, and its capacity to avoid some forms of regulation that cannot reach beyond national jurisdiction.

These powers are especially suspect when they coalesce in the practice of transfer pricing. The host country may believe that transfer pricing allows the MNE to minimize taxes, escape from tariff charges, or be the means of remitting profits from a subsidiary to the parent company that would otherwise not be allowed by exchange restrictions.[4]

If the MNE is concerned with overall profit, not profit at any particular stage, then the dominant motivation behind the pricing structure in a vertically integrated operation is to gain maximum advantage vis-à-vis the different governmental rates of taxation and regulation of international capital flows. Transfer prices or cost-allocation techniques then acquire an artificial quality in the absence of "arms-length" transactions.

The developing country's desire to regulate transfer pricing is only a special instance of the general problem of how the bargaining process between the host government and the MNE distributes the fruits of the foreign investment—more technically, the extent to which the developing country can capture from the MNE a greater share of the MNE's quasi-rents on its supply of technological knowledge, management, and capital.

[4]For an analysis of the adverse effects of the transfer pricing mechanism, see Constantine Vaitsos, *Intercountry Income Distribution and Transnational Enterprises* (1974), chap. 6, and S. Lall, "Determinants and Implications of Transfer Pricing by International Firms," *Bulletin of the Oxford Institute of Economics and Statistics* (August 1973).

Comment: Evaluation of MNEs

For an evaluation of the role of multinational enterprises in LDCs, the following may be consulted: Paul Streeten, "The Multinational Enterprise and the Theory of Development Policy," *World Development* (October 1973), and "Costs and Benefits of Multinational Enterprises in Less Developed Countries," in *The Multinational Enterprise*, ed. J. H. Dunning (1971); Stephen Hymer, "The Multinational Corporation and the Law of Uneven Development," in *International Economics and World Order to the Year 2000*, ed. J. Bhagwati (1972), and "The Efficiency (Contradictions) of Multinational Corporations," *American Economic Review* (May 1970); Richard J. Barnet and Ronald E. Muller, *Global Reach* (1974); Raymond Vernon, *Sovereignty at Bay* (1971), and *Storm Over the Multinationals* (1977); Sanjaya Lall, *The Multinational Corporation* (1980); Theodore H. Moran et al., *Investing in Development: New Roles for Private Capital?* (1986); Rhys Jenkins, *The Transnational Corporation and Uneven Development* (1987); Mark Casson and Robert D. Pearce, "Multinational Enterprises in

LDCs,'' in *Surveys in Development Economics*, ed. Norman Gemmell (1987); G. K. Helleiner, ''Transnational Corporations and Direct Foreign Investment,'' in *Handbook of Development Economics*, ed. H. Chenery and T. N. Srinivasan (1989), chap. 27; and United Nations Center on Transnational Corporations, *Transnational Corporations in World Development: Trends and Prospects* (annual), and *World Investment Report* (annual).

V.E.3. Negotiating Foreign Investment—Note

The ultimate decision to invest will depend on the result of the foreign investor's negotiations with the host government. It is common to negotiate over the terms of entry, conditions of performance, and duration of the investment. Ideally, such negotiations should be based on a thorough cost–benefit analysis. More investment projects are now the outcome of a cost–benefit analysis in negotiations between the foreign investors and host governments, but, as yet, a comprehensive economic analysis is only approximated to various degrees in actual negotiations. Nonetheless, it is still desirable to have an ideal model in mind when negotiating. This type of model attempts to rationalize the mixture of incentives and restrictions that host governments place on foreign investment. It also may suggest arrangements that will give a higher payoff for both investor and host country.

Typical restrictions on FDI cover sectors of the economy from which a foreign investor is excluded; maximum percentage of foreign ownership; withholding and other taxes on profit and capital remittances; performance obligations, including minimum investment periods and/or required reinvestment of earnings; restricted access to local capital markets; discriminatory income taxes; foreign-exchange restrictions; restrictions on percentage of expatriate staff; and local content requirements.

On the other hand, there are investment incentives that can include direct financial inducements such as tax holidays, investment allowances, locating in free export zones, labor training subsidies; and, indirect economic benefits such as sheltering through protective tariffs and quotas, price floors and ceilings, granting of foreign-exchange guarantees or privileges.

The central problem now for a developing country is to devise policies that will succeed in both encouraging a greater inflow of private foreign capital and ensuring that it makes the maximum contribution feasible toward the achievement of the country's development objectives. Private investors must be aware, therefore, of the development objectives and the priorities of the host country and understand how their investments may contribute to the country's development strategy. The foreign investor has to be prepared to demonstrate the contribution of private foreign capital in terms beyond private profit. At the same time, the government must recognize that if risks are too high, or the return on investment is too low, FDI will be inhibited from making any contribution at all. The negotiation process should establish policies that will meet the mutual interests of private investor and host country.

Government as negotiator must go beyond political rhetoric. Foreign investor as negotiator must go beyond simply asking for a ''favorable climate.'' It is necessary to examine the role of private foreign capital more systematically by appraising the prospective benefits and costs of private foreign direct investment. Such an appraisal may then provide a more rational basis for determining the type of policy that is most appropriate for securing the maximum contribution from FDI.

In essence, the foreign investor must convince the host government that the increase in real income resulting from the investment project is greater than the resultant increase in the income of the investor. If the value added to output by FDI is greater than the amount appropriated by the foreign investor, social returns exceed private returns. The negotiating objective of the foreign investor is to convince the host country that the benefit–cost ratio of the FDI is greater than unity and to secure the most favorable conditions for entry and operation.

To this end, the foreign investor may point to a considerable list of benefits from the investment, as discussed in V.E.1: local value added, inflow of foreign exchange, creation of employment, infusion of skills, contribution of taxes and royalties, and the creation of external economies elsewhere in the economy beyond the investment project itself.

Offsetting these benefits, however, are the various costs, also discussed in V.E.1. The investor as negotiator must be aware of these costs in order to meet the objections of the government's negotiators. Governments are likely to point to costs such as concessions offered by the government to attract foreign investment, adverse effects on domestic saving, discouragement of domestic entrepreneurship, problems of balance-of-payments servicing, loss of domestic economic autonomy, inappropriate technology, and negative externalities.

The foregoing discussion indicates in a broad way the various benefits and costs of FDI. A more rigorous analysis, however, would require application of the techniques of project appraisal. This type of analysis values the time profile of the social benefits and social costs and uses shadow prices (accounting prices) that correct for market-price distortions and revalue the output or input according to a measure of its social worth in terms of social objectives. Shadow prices correct for price distortions: more "honest prices" are calculated for wages, inputs, foreign exchange, and interest rates to reflect their true value. The analysis also allows for the nonmarket effects of externalities that are not included in the calculation of a private rate of return. Social analysis may also give welfare weights to the benefits of employment creation or a more equitable distribution of income. These corrections make social benefit–cost analysis different from the private business discounted cash flow methods of investment appraisal. National economic profitability differs from private financial profitability; it is the former that matters to the host country. The objective then of social benefit–cost analysis of FDI is to determine if the social returns from the foreign investment exceed its social costs. The foreign investor should therefore be aware of how a calculation of net social benefit can be made. In Chapter X, we shall discuss the procedure of social benefit–cost analysis in more detail.

The following equation summarizes the calculation of net social benefit or national eco-

nomic profitability from a foreign-investment project:

$$NSB = [(P_s) \cdot (O)] - [P_s \cdot \text{inputs}] + [\text{net externalities} + \text{capital inflow} + \text{return to domestic investors} + \text{taxes and royalties}] - [D \text{ and } K \text{ repatriated in foreign exchange}],$$

where

NSB = Net Social Benefit
P_s = shadow (or accounting) price
O = output
D = dividends, interest, and profits
K = capital

Considering the stream of social benefits and social costs and discounting to the present, it would be in the best interest of the host government to allow entry if the present value of the NSB is greater than 0 at a social discount rate. The social discount rate reflects the time preference of society—that is, the community may be willing to wait for a longer payoff period on the investment than would a private investor. Mindful of future generations, society may value saving more than current consumption. Under these conditions, the social discount rate is less than the private market rate of interest.

Regarding the issue of termination of the investment, the government would be rational to insist on fade-out or divestment when the present value of NSB becomes less than 0, or when the NSB of a substitute domestic investment becomes greater than the NSB of the foreign investment.

In short, the criterion of present value of NSB says that a project should be undertaken as long as the sum of the future social returns minus social costs, discounted back to the present, is positive. The foreign investor should realize that project appraisal analysis may actually make the case for FDI even stronger than one based on simply private profit. When shadow prices are used and social benefits are included, the social net benefit may in some cases turn out higher than the private net benefit.

The negotiating process is also likely to focus on an entire spectrum of arrangements for securing foreign capital and scarce managerial and technical knowledge. The foreign investor may initially desire a wholly owned subsidiary for an unlimited time duration. The host government, however, may insist that after a certain period of time any expansion should be with local equity, or it may insist on a joint venture initially, or it may stipulate that the foreign investor should divest after a certain period of time.

At the other end of the range, the government may attempt to unbundle the package of inputs and secure each input separately at a lower cost in the form of technical collaboration agreements, licensing, and management contracts, instead of through one foreign-equity investment. The benefit–cost ratio of these contractual arrangements has to be compared with the benefits and costs of a foreign direct investment. Quasi-equity arrangements might also be considered in the form of production sharing, revenue sharing, or profit sharing.

Each of these alternative possibilities amounts to an alternative foreign investment proposal with a different production structure and concession terms. If the proposals are alternative, only the best alternative in the set will have a positive present value of *NSB*. In the negotiation process, the upper limit of concessions offered by the host government will lie just below the scarcity value to the host government of the services of the FDI. The lower limit to concessions will be just what is necessary to induce the FDI (net of rent, leaving only a normal return on investment).

Although countries may have nominal restrictions on the extent of foreign ownership, there is still the important issue of whether control can be exercised by the foreign investor even without majority ownership. Even with minority equity, the foreign investor may retain control, especially when the host country is short of technical and managerial expertise. Conceding management rights on paper may still mean that foreign management remains in control because it has the resources and abilities to make effective decisions. There may also be minority ownership by foreigners, but the local ownership can be so widely dispersed that the foreign owners retain managerial control. In some cases, control without majority ownership can be exercised through such devices as technical agreements and management contracts or by requiring more than a simple majority vote for decisions in certain key management areas. For the export of manufactures by multinationals from developing countries, minority ownership, technology contracts, management contracts, and marketing contracts may establish effective relationships between buying and selling firms even without majority ownership. It is also possible that, as has happened in Indonesia, foreign firms may respond to the pressure for greater localization

by increasing their debt-equity ratios and by maintaining control through long-term licensing and management contracts. Moreover, if majority ownership is not possible, a foreign enterprise may issue two classes of shares (i.e., voting and no-voting) so that the parent company can maintain management control even though it holds a minority equity position.

In sum, it is necessary to distinguish between de jure and de facto control. As Edith Penrose states,

Ownership wholly or in part is not a sufficient condition to assure control of a foreign enterprise. Stated in this bald form, there will probably be few who would not agree that the mere acquisition of shares is of little economic consequence without the ability and willingness to take advantage of the powers that ownership confers. If we assume that governments acquiring ownership interests in foreign companies want to exercise some effective control (as distinct from merely receiving their share of the distributive profits), we have then to inquire into their capacity to do so. . . .

One of the greatest sources of the power of multinational corporations lies in their knowledge, which includes technological knowledge, and knowledge of markets and finance, as well as of managerial skills. It follows that the only really effective way of reducing this power lies in the development of similar knowledge in the host country. The question then arises of whether the acquisition of equity control of foreign enterprises accelerates the acquisition of the relevant knowledge or makes possible a more effective use of the knowledge already in hand.[1]

Recognizing that control may be exercised without majority ownership, the foreign investor may find it advantageous in a negotiation to trade off reduced equity participation for increased effective control, a trade-off that may be preferable if increased equity participation (because it is highly visible) carries a greater perceived cost to the host government, but effective control does not because it is more difficult to discern, monitor, and regulate.[2] The foreign investor may find it advantageous to bargain, not for increased equity ownership, but for control over the variables critical to the success of its foreign subsidiary.

[1] Edith Penrose, "Ownership and Control: Multinational Firms in Less Developed Countries," in *A World Divided*, ed. G. K. Helleiner (1976), p. 154.

[2] Donald J. Lecraw, "Bargaining Power, Ownership, and Profitability of Transitional Corporations in Developing Countries," *Journal of International Business Studies* (Spring–Summer 1984): 41.

V.E.4. Political Risk—Note

Once entry is secured, and conditions of performance specified, the foreign investor still runs the risk of renegotiation, abrogation of some concessions, or changes in governmental policies. To assess the noncommercial risks, it is necessary to practice political risk analysis. A "political assessment function" has to be incorporated in an international firm to establish managerial contingencies generated by the political environment. Political events and political forces may cause a loss to the firm's cash flow or returns. Managers worry in a vague and general way about the investment climate, but this is an empty box that must be filled with content by more rigorous political risk analysis.

The political risk is not so much that of a dramatic revolution or macrochanges affecting ownership, but rather more of a microcharacter affecting operations. Revolutionary changes involving social and political upheaval that lead to nationalization or confiscation are relatively rare occurrences. If the negotiation process has resulted in a development contract with a payoff to each party, this arrangement can be the best guarantee against nationalization or expropriation as long as the government gains the benefits that it expected from the foreign investment. Political risk analysis can anticipate the coup or revolutionary type of widespread change by focusing on trends in the distribution of income, unemployment, asset distribution, ethnic and racial tensions, political participation, and political legitimacy. The major task of political risk analysis, however, is not to identify the relatively rare upheavals such as those that follow an election, as in Chile in 1971, or a revolution, as in Cuba in 1959, that may lead to the expropriation of most, if not all, foreign-owned firms. Instead, the major task of political risk analysis is to identify the politically generated managerial contingencies in routine policy making by the government.[1]

In most countries the impact of most political events varies from firm to firm and from project to project. It is of a microcharacter and normally affects operations rather than termination of ownership.[2] The most frequent political risk is a change in public policy that might entail partial divestment, price controls, changes in taxation, foreign-exchange remittance restrictions, local content rules, labor-law revisions, changes in tariffs and quotas. These policies do not relate to a general "investment climate," but are industry-specific, firm-specific, or even project-specific. They are far short of nationalization or confiscation, but they do affect cash flows and returns.

The object of political risk analysis should be to mitigate these noncommercial risks caused by political change. How can this be done? To meet the risk of changes in public policies that would have adverse impact on the firm, the investor should try to reduce exposure, share the risk with others, or create deterrent structures.[3] At the outset, the forestalling of political vulnerability is closely related to the bargaining power of the foreign investor. The degree of bargaining power is, in turn, dependent on certain characteristics of the investment project. These characteristics lead to certain likely outcomes independent of the ideology or political regime in the host country. The greater the firm's bargaining power, the less likely the investment will be vulnerable to political factors. A number of studies have determined those characteristics of an investment that will give the investor greater bargaining power and ensure less political vulnerability.[4] These are

- the bargaining power tends to be greater, the larger the size of the required fixed investment
- the higher the technical intensity of production

---

[1]Empirical studies by Stephen J. Korbin show that the number of major discontinuities that significantly affected the operations of foreign firms in the past three decades is limited. In the vast majority of instances, the impact of politics on firms varies widely, even given the same environmental scenario; it is a function of industry-, firm-, and even project-specific characteristics. The relationship between environment and firm varies in accordance with strategy, organizational structure, and managerial style. See Korbin, *Managing Political Risk Assessment* (1982).

[2]Ibid., p. 40.

[3]Theodore H. Moran, ed., *International Political Risk Assessment: The State of the Art* (1980), p. 8.

[4]For empirical studies, see Bryan Levy, "The Determinants of Policy in LDCs," *Journal of Development Economics* 28 (1988): 217–31; Donald J. Lecraw, "Bargaining Power, Ownership, and Profitability of Transnational Corporations in Developing Countries," *Journal of International Business Studies* (Spring–Summer 1984): 27–43; and Dennis J. Encarnation and Louis T. Wells, Jr., "Sovereignty on Guard: Negotiating with Foreign Investors," *International Organization* 39 (Winter 1985): 47–78.

- the higher the marketing intensity of production (marketing companies whose sales are determined to a large degree by brand identification and consumer loyalty occupy a strong position vis à vis host governments)
- the higher the managerial intensity of production
- the less the extent of competition among investors (more investors mean more alternatives for host authorities to choose from and more rivals to play off against one another, thereby increasing the strength of the host government).

These characteristics of the foreign firm and its investment projects may allow the foreign investor to gain more generous terms at the outset. Over time, however, to avoid increasing vulnerability during a long payback period, it is necessary to continue to demonstrate a high benefit–cost ratio to the host government. As long as the host country remains serious about accelerating its development, the continual beneficial economic performance of foreign investment will be the decisive determinant of the investment security. The ultimate source of security resides in the underlying community of interests between investor and host government. The protection of private foreign investment rests less in legal doctrines than in a benefit–cost analysis of the economic realities of the development process.

Renegotiation of an initial contract has become more frequent. This is because many developing countries have markedly increased confidence in their ability to alter the package of costs and benefits associated with foreign direct investment to their advantage. They prefer, therefore, regulation to expropriation.[5]

At the macro level, the most significant risk is that the country will have a balance-of-payments problem that causes the government to introduce trade controls or to depreciate its currency in terms of foreign exchange or to undertake deflationary monetary and fiscal policies. To anticipate such balance-of-payments difficulties in servicing foreign investment, the investor should undertake a country risk analysis similar to the matrix analysis previously explained in section V.D.2.

The ultimate objective of political risk analysis is to make political events less uncertain and to be better able to predict the impact of political events on the firm's operation or ownership. To do this, it is necessary to understand why the government does what it does. It is necessary to watch the political power of interest groups and their effect on policy making. As will be discussed in Chapter X, government policy makers frequently do not follow economic rationality, but pursue their own political rationality. Political risk analysis, therefore, must understand the government's political objectives, political resources, and the influence of various interest groups on public policy making.

[5]Nathan Fagree and Louis T. Wells, Jr., ''Bargaining Power of Multinationals and Host Governments,'' *Journal of International Business Studies* (Fall 1982): 9–23.

CHAPTER VI

Human Resources

Not only is it important to overcome the savings and foreign-exchange constraints, but it is also essential to focus on human-resource development. Indeed, human resource–rich countries have demonstrated that they can develop even if they are poor in natural resources. And if the faith in development through the accumulation of physical capital has waned, it has been replaced by a creed of investment in human capital. This chapter explores how improvement in the quality of people as productive agents must be a central objective of development policies.

We emphasize human capital because the knowledge embedded in human beings is the basis for achieving an increase in total factor productivity. Land, labor, and physical capital may be subject to diminishing returns, but knowledge is not. Alfred Marshall, first author of a major principles book, characterized the economic problem as being man over nature. As Marshall declared, ''although nature is subject to diminishing returns, man is subject to increasing returns. . . . Knowledge is our most powerful engine of production; it enables us to subdue nature and satisfy our wants.''

In accepting his Nobel Prize, the noted agricultural economist Theodore Schultz also stated that, while agricultural development is of paramount importance, ''the decisive factors of production in improving the welfare of poor people are not space, energy, and crop land; the decisive factor is the improvement in population quality.'' Stressing the economic value of human capital, he connected favorable economic prospects with an investment in health and education—two topics examined in this chapter.

More generally, this chapter inquires how the abilities and skills of people are to be improved, and their motivations and values modified in order to make them more suitable for development efforts. This is one of the most difficult questions we have encountered, and, yet, on its answer is likely to depend a country's success in achieving self-sustaining development.

Part of the difficulty in formulating policy to improve the ''human infrastructure'' within a less developed country is that economists have only recently begun to analyze this question systematically. Perhaps the greater part of the difficulty, however, is that an answer to the question entails not only economic analysis, but also sociological, psychological, and political considerations. The inherently multidisciplinary character of the answer has caused each discipline to acknowledge the question but to fall short of a satisfactory answer. This chapter, in concentrating on the economics of the problem, is not immune to this criticism, but it at least attempts to fashion the economic analysis so that it might suggest some links with other disciplines.

Selection VI.A emphasizes that development can be interpreted as a generalized process of capital accumulation, of which investment in human resources is a central element. Generalization of capital accumulation for diverse topics such as nutrition, health, education, and research involves the allocation of investment resources according to priorities set by the relative rates of return on alternative investments. The complementary role of entrepreneurship is examined in VI.B.

Before considering the policies related to the quality of the population, we should gain some perspective on the quantitative problem of population pressure. Section VI.C investigates the nature of the growth in population and its importance from the standpoint of affecting the quality of population. Nearly 95 percent of the growth in the world's population in the next 25 years will be in developing countries. Human-resource policies have to be implemented in the context of this rapid population growth. The exacerbation of the employment problem is direct. The effects of population growth on the quality of health facilities, nutrition, educational programs, and public services also make it necessary to acquire a better understanding of demographic problems. It is now especially apposite to investigate whether population growth worsens absolute poverty and the maldistribution of income. Do absolute poverty and the maldistribution of income contribute, in turn, to high rates of fertility? Furthermore, what are the socioeconomic correlates of declining fertility, and how might policy interventions affect these correlates in order to reduce the rate of population growth? If public policies can reduce mortality rates, can they also reduce fertility rates? These questions are examined in section VI.C.

Both the quantity and quality of population are influenced by the role of women in development. We emphasize in section VI.D gender-aware analysis in order to understand not only fertility rates, but how women are victims of poverty, the role of women in labor markets, women's role in household decision making, gender discrimination in other types of markets, and gender bias in development programs.

Section VI.E outlines some policies to improve nutrition conditions among the world's poor. Among the first to suffer from shortages or inadequacies of food are the children—a country's investment in the future. And children, along with their mothers, are numerically dominant in developing countries. In these areas, one-fifth of the population is under the age of 5 years, two-fifths are below the age of 15 years, while mothers and children together account for over two-thirds of the total population. The children are the most vulnerable group.

Especially tragic is the ill-health brought on or aggravated by malnutrition. Malnutrition adversely affects mental progress, physical growth, productivity, and the working life span. In cost-effectiveness terms—let alone fundamental human rights—there can be high returns from programs to reduce the incidence of malnutrition.

Poverty is the major cause of disease in developing countries, and many other policies besides medical facilities are needed to improve health conditions. Health policies must be related to the environment and to the ecological, cultural, and nutritional conditions that permit disease to thrive in poverty areas. As with technology, there is a need for an "appropriate" transfer of medical knowledge and medical technology; health programs have been only too often biased toward a small section of the urban population and to the over sophisticated "curative" treatment rather than providing more basic, widespread "preventive" treatment.

As analyzed in section VI.F, formal and informal education and training in both the modern and the traditional sectors are clearly necessary for the development of human resources. Cost–benefit analysis of the "returns" to education must incorporate the interactions between education and the economy, giving particular attention to education as an investment, the importance of rural education in a developing economy, and the interdependence of education, manpower requirements, and development. Although each individual commonly views his or her education as a consumption good, it is more appropriately viewed from the standpoint of the economy's development as an investment good: to the economist, human beings can be conceptualized as human capital or embodied savings. It is, then, an economic problem to determine how much the economy should invest in human capital and, of equal importance, what the composition of that investment should be. The selections in section VI.F therefore consider both the quantitative growth of education and the kind of education needed in a developing economy.

Although this chapter discusses population growth, nutrition and health, and education as separate topics, we should realize that all these elements of human-resource development are interrelated. And while fertility, nutrition, health, and education influence one another, so does each, in turn, affect income and human development. Moreover, within this social matrix, we must recognize various policy choices and assess what can be the contribution of government to human-resource development.

VI.A. DEVELOPMENT AS A GENERALISED PROCESS OF CAPITAL ACCUMULATION*

The contemporary interest in the economics of education, and more broadly in the economics of all processes connected with the augmentation and application of knowledge, represents a confluence of interests derived from concerns with widely divergent problems. These problems include such matters as the economic value of education, the contribution of education to past economic development in advanced countries, and the role of education and expenditure on increased education in the planned development of underdeveloped countries.[1]

The formulation of concern with the economics of education (in a broad sense) in these particular terms, while appropriate to the current state of economic research and thinking, is for this very reason both restrictive in its implications and likely to appear before much more time has passed as a transient stage in the evolution towards a more comprehensive formulation of economic development problems in terms of a broadly conceived concept of capital accumulation. . . .

Concentration on the role of human capital has already proceeded far enough to generate the beginnings of a counter-revolution. The general outlines of the counter-revolution are indeed already apparent. On the one hand, the recent emphasis on human capital formation in growth accountancy is based on the recognition that conventional measures of labour input fail to take account of improvements in the quality of labour and aims primarily at more accurate measurement of labour inputs. Application of the same criteria to inputs of capital suggests that the contribution of capital may also have been grossly underestimated, as a result both of understatement of the flow of capital services into production by the conventional equation of service flow with the depreciated value of capital stock, and of failure to measure accurately im-

provements in the performance characteristics ("quality") of capital equipment.[2] On the other hand, the evidence on rates of return to educational investment in the United States does not suggest that there has been serious general underinvestment in education there, while both casual empirical observation of underdeveloped countries and some detailed research on the relative returns to investments in education and material capital in them[3] suggest that at least in some cases the proportion of resources devoted to human capital formation may be too high rather than too low.[4] A rehabilitation of investment in material capital as a potent source of economic growth may therefore be in prospect. What is more important, while the process of increasing economic knowledge proceeds in phases of exaggerated concentration on one or another aspect of a problem, both the effect and the intent are to arrive at a unified and more powerful synthesis of explanations of economic phenomena. The contemporary phase, in which the concepts of human capital and of investment in it figure as corrections of emphasis in a system of economic ideas dominated by material capital, is bound to merge into one in which human and nonhuman capital are treated as alternative forms of capital in general. The desirability of achieving such a synthesis is not merely a matter of scientific economy and elegance, it is also a prerequisite for rational discussion and formulation of policy for economic growth in both advanced and underdeveloped countries. The purpose of this paper, accordingly, is to sketch the outlines of such a synthesis, in the form of a

*From Harry G. Johnson, "Towards a Generalised Capital Accumulation Approach to Economic Development," in OECD Study Group in the Economics of Education, *The Residual Factor and Economic Growth* (Paris, 1964), pp. 219–25. Reprinted by permission.

[1]Cf. T. W. Schultz, ed., "Reflections on Investment in Man," *Journal of Political Economy, Supplement,* October 1962, pp. 1–8.

[2]Cf. Zvi Griliches, "The Sources of Measured Productivity Growth: U.S. Agriculture, 1940–1960," *Journal of Political Economy,* August 1960.

[3]Arnold C. Harberger, *Investment in Man Versus Investment in Machines: The Case of India,* a paper prepared for the Conference on Education and Economic Development, University of Chicago, April 4–6, 1963. Harberger finds the rate of return on real investment in India to be substantially higher than the rate of return on investment in education.

[4]This proposition becomes almost a truism if the concept of investment in human capital formation is extended to include expenditures on improved health, whose effects on the rate of population increase constitute one of the major economic problems of underdeveloped countries.

generalised capital accumulation approach to economic development, and to discuss some of its implications for social and economic policy.

The essential elements of a generalised capital accumulation approach to economic development are already present in the literature of economics, and at least some applications of the approach (for example, the explanation of wage differentials) have been familiar to economists ever since economics became established as a separate subject of study. The foundations of it were explicitly laid in Irving Fisher's classic work on capital and income, and carried forward by F. H. Knight's work on the theory of capital; and the approach is exemplified, and its potency demonstrated, in the recent research of T. W. Schultz, Gary Becker, and others on human capital.[5] The essence of it is to regard "capital" as including anything that yields a stream of income over time, and income as the product of capital. From this point of view, as Fisher pointed out, all categories of income describe yields on various forms of capital, and can be expressed as rates of interest or return on the corresponding items of capital. Alternatively, all forms of income-yielding assets can be given an equivalent capital value by capitalising the income they yield at an appropriate rate of interest. By extension, the growth of income that defines economic development is necessarily the result of the accumulation of capital, or of "investment"; but "investment" in this context must be defined to include such diverse activities as adding to material capital, increasing the health, discipline, skill and education of the human population, moving labour into more productive occupations and locations, and applying existing knowledge or discovering and applying new knowledge to increase the efficiency of productive processes. All such activities involve incurring costs, in the form of use of current resources, and investment in them is socially worthwhile if the rate of return over cost exceeds the general rate of interest, or the capital value of the additional income they yield exceeds the cost of obtaining it. From the somewhat different perspective of planning economic development, efficient development involves allocation of investment resources according to priorities set by the relative rates of return on alternative investments.

The conception of economic growth as a process of accumulating capital, in all the manifold forms that the broad Fisherian concept of capital allows, is a potent simplification of the analytical problem of growth, and one which facilitates the discussion of problems of growth policy by emphasising the relative returns from alternative investments of currently available resources. The Fisherian concept of capital, however, and the approach to the analysis of production and distribution problems associated with it, are not as yet characteristic of the work and philosophical approach of the majority of economists, and to some the implications of the approach for policy with respect to human beings appear to be positively repugnant. Must economists instead employ a narrower concept of capital that identifies capital with material capital goods and equipment used in the production process, and distinguishes it sharply from labour? . . .

As already mentioned, the limitations of accumulation of material capital as an explanation of a prescription for growth have prompted the contemporary interest in human capital formation, and suggest a generalisation of the concept of capital accumulation to include investment in all types of capital formation. An important obstacle to such a generalisation is that the treatment of human beings as a form of capital, even if only conceptually, seems offensive to some economists as being contrary to democratic political philosophy. This reaction, however, involves a confusion of analytical approach and normative recommendations unfortunately only too common in discussions of economic problems with policy connotations. To recognise that important areas of socio-economic policy involve decisions analytically identical with decisions about investing in machines is not at all to imply that people should be regarded as no different from machines; on the contrary, refusal to recognise the investment character of a problem because people are involved may result in people receiving worse treatment than machines. One might, indeed, hazard the generalisation that democratic free-enterprise economies tend to make wasteful use of their human resources, precisely because people are not sufficiently regarded as socially productive assets.

Conception of economic growth as a generalised process of capital accumulation provides a unifying principle for the statistical explanation of past growth and the formulation of policy for future growth or plans for economic development. It does not, however—and cannot be expected to—dispose of any real problems, though it does clarify understanding of them. Instead, it transforms these problems into prob-

[5]Schultz, "Reflections on Investment in Man."

lems of the special characteristics of particular types of capital, or of the specification of efficient investment programmes.

From the point of view of economically relevant differentiations, items of capital can be classified in a variety of ways. One fundamental distinction to be drawn relates to the nature of the yield or contribution to economic welfare—the distinction between consumption capital, which yields a flow of services enjoyed directly and therefore contributing to utility, and production capital, which yields a flow of goods the consumption of which yields utility. The returns from production capital are directly observable, and therefore more amenable to measurement than the returns on consumption capital.

Another fundamental distinction relates to the form in which capital is embodied—here it seems necessary not only to distinguish capital embodied in human beings from capital embodied in non-human material forms, but also to distinguish between capital embodied in both human and non-human physical forms and capital embodied in neither, the latter category comprising both the state of the arts (the intellectual production capital of society) and the state of culture (the intellectual consumption capital of society). The significance of this distinction is closely related to a third distinction—one which is particularly relevant to policy problems—between types of capital according to whether the returns to investment in capital accumulation accrue to the investor or to others. Here it seems necessary to distinguish: (a) capital goods which render specific services to production or consumption by the owner; (b) human capital, the distinguishing characteristic of which is that, both inherently and by legal tradition, control over the use of the capital is vested in the individual embodying the capital, regardless of the source of finance of the investment in it; (c) social capital or collective capital, the distinguishing characteristic of which is that for reasons of inherent necessity or administrative convenience its services to production or consumption are not charged to individual users but are paid for by taxation of the community at large; (d) intellectual capital or knowledge, the distinguishing characteristic of which is that, once created it is a free good, in the sense that use of it by one individual does not diminish its availability to others.

All forms of capital other than capital goods rendering specific services to production or consumption raise serious problems for economic analysis measurement and policy formation. The fusion of human capital with the personality of its owner raises among other things the problem of how far expenditure on the creation of human capital should be accounted as investment, and how far it should be classed as consumption; while the vesting of control over the use of capital in the individual invested in, given the imperfection of markets for personal credit, poses the problem of how far education should be provided at public expense. The divergence of private and social costs and benefits inherent in free or subsidised education raises some particularly difficult problems in conjunction with the fact that educated people are especially mobile interregionally and internationally, so that resources devoted to education in poor countries may run substantially to waste in unilateral transfers of human capital to richer countries.[6] Social capital investment involves a similar separation of costs of investment from benefits, and a similar mixture of equity and efficiency considerations. Investment in knowledge raises the thorniest of all problems, since the zero marginal cost of knowledge to additional users implies that no system of recouping the cost of investment in knowledge-creation by charging for its use can be economically efficient. . . .

The distinctions discussed above do not include a distinction between natural resources (natural capital) and man-made capital. For most economic purposes, such a distinction is unnecessary—natural resources, like capital goods, can be appropriated, transferred, and invested in. Natural resources do, however, raise two sorts of special problems. First property rights in some range of natural resources are typically vested in society or the state; this poses the problem of ensuring efficient exploitation of these resources through appropriate accounting and charging for the use of the state's natural capital,

---

[6]Brinley Thomas has emphasised the economic absurdity of the contemporary migration pattern between advanced and underdeveloped countries, in which the advanced countries cream off the professional talent of the underdeveloped countries by immigration and attempt to replace it by their own experts supplied at great expense as part of development aid. See Brinley Thomas, "International Factor Movements and Unequal Rates of Growth," *The Manchester School of Economic and Social Studies,* January 1961. The ease of migration of educated people from underdeveloped countries, especially those in which English is the language of instruction, to advanced countries is a serious limitation on the potentialities of achieving economic development by educational investment and suggests the social desirability of devising means of obliging either the emigrants themselves or the countries receiving them to repay the social capital invested in them to their countries of origin.

a problem particularly important at the time when resources are first brought into use. Secondly, some kinds of natural resources, which are likely to be of particular importance to developing countries, are nonrenewable, and pose the problems of efficient depletion and exhaustion—of efficient capital decumulation, rather than accumulation. The problems of achieving economic development through the exploitation of depleting natural resources become particularly acute and politically highly charged when such exploitation is dependent on the participation of foreign capital and enterprise.

Conception of economic development as a generalised process of capital accumulation, in conjunction with recognition of economically significant differences between various types of capital, has important implications for the efficient programming of investment for economic development. These implications centre on the relationships of complementarity and substitutability in both production and consumption that may exist between types of capital provided by different investment processes, and the consequent desirability of aiming at both balanced investment in the production of complementary types of capital and the selection of the most efficient combinations of types of capital in the light of the relative costs of different kinds of investment. The complementarity between modern equipment and technology, a skilled labour force, and social overhead capital in the transportation and distribution systems is by now sufficiently recognised for development planning to aim at producing integrated investment programmes comprising investment in education and vocational training (manpower programmes) as well as investment in industrial and social overhead. For such comprehensive development investment programmes to maximise the contribution of investment to economic growth, however, recognition of complementarity must be allied with recognition of substitutability and analysis of rates of return on the total investment of capital in alternative programmes involving investment in capital goods, human capital, social capital and the acquisition of new knowledge.

Much of the literature on economic development assumes far too easily that low-wage labour is necessarily cheap industrial labour, ignoring the magnitude of the investments in human and social capital that may have to be made to convert rural workers into skilled industrial labour, and the possibility that investment of the same capital in agricultural improvement might yield far higher returns. On the other hand, there is a strong possibility, exemplified by the successful development of exports of some technologically fairly advanced products from otherwise underdeveloped countries, that the greatest comparative advantage for such countries lies in skilled-labour-intensive products, for the reason that a generally low-wage level makes the cost of investment in human capital low (especially forgone earnings and the cost of instruction and educational structures) by comparison with comparable costs in advanced countries. In addition, such countries may be able to catch up with the advanced countries far more rapidly in the accumulation of knowledge than in the accumulation of material capital.

Apart from its implications for planning for economic growth, a generalised capital accumulation approach to economic development points to the potential fruitfulness of research into and analysis of the efficiency of a wide range of processes and policies that involve the allocation of capital but are not usually thought of as concerned with investment. It has, for example, been amply demonstrated by empirical research that rates of return on investment in education vary widely between different levels of the education system; and there is good reason for doubting that existing educational systems are very efficient when considered as an industry producing extremely long-lived capital assets. The field of public health and medical care, viewed as an industry concerned with the repair and maintenance of human capital, also offers scope for economic analyses of rates of return on alternative investments. Institutional arrangements for supporting and rewarding fundamental and applied research, considered as an industry producing intellectual capital, provide an even greater challenge to economists. Within the traditional scope of economics, labour mobility, unemployment policy, and policy respecting the location of industry all demand the application of capital theory. Perhaps the most important area requiring rationalisation in terms of a broadened concept of capital accumulation, however, is the theory and practice of public finance. Not only do income tax systems typically make a very poor adjustment for the capital investment element in personal income, but the necessity of recouping by income and profits taxation the costs of investments in human capital customarily provided free or at a subsidised price to the people invested in creates disincentives to the efficient use and accumulation of all kinds.

VI.B. THE SUPPLY OF ENTREPRENEURSHIP*

We may distinguish two broad types of entrepreneurial activity: at one pole there is routine entrepreneurship, which is really a type of management, and for the rest of the spectrum we have Schumpeterian or "new type" entrepreneurship. (We shall refer to the latter as N-entrepreneurship.) By routine entrepreneurship we mean the activities involved in coordinating and carrying on a well-established, going concern in which the parts of the production function in use (and likely alternatives to current use) are well known and which operates in well-established and clearly defined markets. By N-entrepreneurship we mean the activities necessary to create or carry on an enterprise where not all the markets are well established or clearly defined and/or in which the relevant parts of the production function are not completely known. In both cases the entrepreneur coordinates activities that involve different markets; he is an intermarket operator. But in the case of N-entrepreneurship not all of the markets exist or operate perfectly and the entrepreneur, if he is to be successful, must fill in for the market deficiencies. To my mind one of the main obstacles to our understanding of the entrepreneurial role lies in the conventional theory of the production function. This theory seems so reasonable at first blush that we are likely not to notice the subtle assumptions it makes. The basic culprits are the following assumptions: that the complete set of inputs are specified and known to all actual or potential firms in the industry, and that there is a fixed relation between inputs and outputs. . . .

In its usual conception the production function is considered to be clearly defined, fully specified, and completely known. Where and to whom in the firm this knowledge is supposed to be available is never stated. In fact, there are great gaps of knowledge about the production function. Points on the production function refer to well-defined inputs. To the extent that they are not completely defined in actuality, the entrepreneur must in some way make up the deficiency. Suppose that to produce a certain commodity, a certain type of machine has to be employed. If no one in the country produces such a machine and if imports are barred, only entrepreneurs who have access to information on how to construct the machine can enter the industry. The potential entrepreneur has to make up for a market deficiency. But that is not his only major function.

Important inputs not well marketed are types of management and market knowledge. Even managers of the more routine type may not be available in well-organized markets in many developing countries. Where available, their capacities may be very difficult to assess. One of the important capacities of management is the ability to obtain and use factors of production that are not well marketed. In some countries the capacity to obtain finance may depend on family connections rather than on the willingness to pay a certain interest rate. A successful entrepreneur may, at times, have to have the capacity to operate well in the political arena connected with his economic activities.

The usual characteristics attributed to entrepreneurs involve gap-filling as one of their essential underlying qualities. For example, it may be thought desirable that entrepreneurs possess at least some of the capacities to search and discover economic opportunities, evaluate economic opportunities, marshal the financial resources necessary for the enterprise, make time-binding arrangements, take ultimate responsibility for management, be the ultimate uncertainty and/or risk bearer,[1] provide and be responsible for the motivational system within the firm, search and discover new economic information, translate new information into new markets, techniques, and goods, and provide leadership for the work group. In a world of perfect markets, if such a world were possible, each of these characteristics would be marketed as a specific service. Thus, some firms might specialize in the discovery of economic opportunities and sell this information to others. A similar remark could be made of each of the capacities mentioned above. The reason that this is not the case is because some inputs are inherently unmar-

*From Harvey Leibenstein, "Entrepreneurship and Development," *American Economic Review, Papers and Proceedings,* Vol. 58, No. 2, May 1968, pp. 72–75. Reprinted by permission.

[1]Schumpeter is very firm on the point that the entrepreneur is not a risk bearer or uncertainty bearer: "The one who gives credit comes to grief if the undertaking fails." Furthermore, in countries with highly developed stock markets some entrepreneurs can shift the risk by selling shares.

ketable, and some are difficult to market and are frequently unmarketed. For example, we cannot have a perfect market in risk-taking since, among other reasons, there is a "moral risk" problem in profit insurance. (The entrepreneur can intentionally do poorly and cash in on the policy.) Similarly, if the motivational system is the sum of all the human elements and their relations to each other within the firm rather than something specifically provided from outside the firm, then this element cannot be marketed. One of our basic points is that the conditions for perfect markets and the nature of some commodities are inconsistent with each other.

It is important to stress that entrepreneurial activities do not arise only because of market structure imperfections. This view gives too shallow an interpretation of the entrepreneurial role.[2] First, some gaps in markets are inherent in all cases. Second, and what is perhaps less apparent, is that the entrepreneur has to employ some inputs that are somewhat vague in their nature (but nevertheless necessary for production), and whose output is indeterminate. The provision of leadership, motivation, and the availability of the entrepreneur to solve potential crisis situations, the capacity to carry ultimate responsibility for the organizational structure and the major time-binding (implicit or explicit) contractual arrangements are of this sort. Third, and most important, the entrepreneur has to possess what might be called, for want of a better term, an "input-completing" capacity. If six inputs are needed to bring to fruition a firm that produces a marketable product, it does no good to be able to marshal easily five of them. The gap-filling and the "input-completing" capacities are the unique characteristics of the entrepreneur.

As we have defined the entrepreneur he is an individual or group of individuals with four major characteristics: he connects different markets, he is capable of making up for market deficiencies (gap-filling), he is an "input-completer," and he creates or expands time-binding, input-transforming entities (i.e., firms).

Entrepreneurship is frequently a scarce resource because entrepreneurs are gap-fillers and input-completers and these are scarce talents. Other things equal, the amount of gap-filling and input-completing required determines the degree of scarcity. Gap-filling is necessary because information about some inputs are unmarketable; and because private information about markets cannot always be proven and made public information. Of course, gap-filling will also be necessary where universalistic markets have not been developed, or where the inputs are, in principle, marketable but for some reason such markets have not arisen. For any given economic activity there is a minimum quantum of various inputs that must be marshaled. If less than this minimum variety is universalistically available, the entrepreneur has the job of stepping into the breech to fill the lack of marketable inputs; that is, he must be an input-completer. . . .

Although there is no universally accepted theory of development we can point to two important elements in the process: (1) Per capita income growth requires shifts from less productive to more productive techniques per worker, the creation or adoption of new commodities, new materials, new markets, new organizational forms, the creation of new skills, and the accumulation of new knowledge. (2) Part of the process is the interaction between the creation of economic capacity and the related creation of demand so that some rough balance between capacity growth and demand growth takes place. The entrepreneur as a gap-filler and input-completer is probably the prime mover of the capacity creation part of these elements of the growth process.[3]

We now know that development is not simply a process of physical and human capital accumulation in the usual sense. If that were all that were involved, then development would simply be a function of the willingness to save. Experience has shown that this is not the case. The work of Solow and others have shown that growth cannot be explained by the contributions of the increase in standard inputs. The work of

---

[2]A narrow "imperfect market" interpretation of the entrepreneurial role gives the impression that markets are perfectable, say by the elimination of monopolistic influences, and that by doing so, the significant aspects of the entrepreneurial role can be eliminated thereby. This is not the view taken in this paper. The ideas of this paper are not brought out fully by thinking that the entrepreneurs' role depends only on market imperfections.

[3]The basic idea is that firms do not operate on their production possibilities frontier. In part, the internal motivational state of the firm determines the degree to which actual output is less than the production possibilities frontier output. Thus, costs per unit of output are not minimized. The size of the difference between actual costs and true minimum costs offers opportunities for those entrepreneurs who think they can produce at lower costs.

Chenery and Strout emphasizes that the degree of capital absorption can be a significant constraint to growth in developing countries. The existence of and need for gap-filling and input-completing capacities could explain why standard inputs do not account for all outputs and why capital absorption should be a problem.

Economic planning experience in many countries reveals that there is frequently a considerable divergence between plan targets and results. This divergence may be partly explained by the fact that entrepreneurship is not a normal input whose contribution can be readily determined, predicted, planned for, or controlled. . . .

Comment: Entrepreneurial Performance

The literature on entrepreneurship divides on whether demand or supply conditions determine entrepreneurial performance. From the viewpoint of demand, it is believed that potential entrepreneurs are readily available but await a favorable environment to demand their latent abilities. From the viewpoint of supply, however, the specific skills and personal attributes of entrepreneurship are in short supply and must be cultivated.

For the various views, see Peter Kilby, ed., *Entrepreneurship and Economic Development* (1971); D. McClelland, *The Achieving Society* (1961); E. E. Hagen, "How Economic Growth Begins," in *Entrepreneurship and Economic Development*, ed. Peter Kilby (1971), chap. 6; M. Hashim Awad, "The Supply of Risk Bearers in Underdeveloped Countries," *Economic Development and Cultural Change* (April 1971); Peter Kilby, "An Entrepreneurial Problem," *American Economic Review* (May 1983); and Walter Elkan, "Entrepreneurs and Entrepreneurship in Africa," *Finance & Development* (December 1988).

Entrepreneurial ability as a form of human capital and the central role of entrepreneurship in a changing economy are emphasized by Theodore W. Schultz, *Restoring Economic Equilibrium: Human Capital in the Modernizing Economy* (1990).

VI.C. POPULATION

VI.C.1. Population and Poverty— Note

Few developmental problems evoke as much pessimism as does the rapid increase in population in poor countries. If economists value a higher rate of development, they still fear, as did John Stuart Mill, a growth in population that "treads close on the heels of agricultural improvement, and effaces its effects as fast as they are produced." It is not difficult to find a basis for this fear—in that a large part of the gain in aggregate income has been used simply to support a larger population at the same low per capita level of income.

This pessimistic outlook on population growth is as old as academic economics itself.[1] Long ago, economics was designated the "dismal science." Originally, this was because of the view of classical economists who, when considering the long-run development of an economy, could see only the eventual advent of a dismal "stationary state" in which the springs of economic progress would have evaporated, growth in output would no longer outstrip population growth, and wages would be at subsistence levels. So far, however, this pessimism has proved unfounded for industrial nations: the economic histories of these nations represent the success stories of economic progress— the achievement of a high rate of increase in real income, so that both population and per capita real income have been able to increase. Indeed, when some economists thought that the Great Depression of the 1930s might indicate a state of secular stagnation in mature industrial nations, they were concerned lest population growth in these countries actually be too slow. But although capital accumulation, technical progress, and the phenomenon of increasing returns to scale may have dispelled the shadow of Malthus from the few rich industrial countries, that shadow still hovers over the many poor agrarian countries.

In these countries, per capita income has remained pitifully low, and the alarming prospects of population growth have revived neo-Malthusian fears. Once again, there is widespread concern that economic betterment will be thwarted by excessive population pressure and that, unless acceptable means are found for checking population growth, the "revolution of rising expectations" must remain unfilled. It has become common to hear the development problem summarized as one of "increasing fertility of the soil and reducing the fertility of human beings."

Most development economists argue against the Malthusian view that population will eventually be limited by food production. They point to the fact that apart from drought areas, population nowhere appears yet to have approached the capacity of the land to support it. Whether or not adequate food production is achieved, however, depends a great deal on the government's making resources available, pursuing appropriate pricing policies, ensuring necessary research, and developing an infrastructure for transport, storage, and marketing.

Regarding the problem of malnutrition and hunger, this is, as noted in Chapter VIII, more a problem of poverty and inadequate income than a matter of inadequate global food supplies. In many countries where malnutrition is extensive, the food that is available would meet the food needs of all inhabitants if it were distributed according to need and not according to income. The population–food problem is solved when incomes suffice to buy adequate food at prices that provide adequate incentives to producers. From the viewpoint of global food policy, the rich countries are capable of generating surpluses of food for export. But to meet their increased demand for food grains by increased imports, the developing countries would have to export more, receive foreign aid, or borrow overseas. The great majority of developing nations will therefore have to satisfy most of their own production needs most of the time. To this end, cost-reducing innovations must continue to occur sufficient to outweigh the limitations of fixed land resources.

It is extremely important, however, to realize that the population problem is much more than a food problem; it has wider ramifications that

---

[1]The history of thought on population growth and development is traced by Lord Robbins, *The Theory of Economic Development in the History of Economic Thought* (1968), lecture II.

make it a general development problem. A high rate of population growth not only has an adverse effect on improvement in food supplies, but also intensifies the constraints on development of savings, foreign exchange, and human resources. Rapid population growth, which stems from high birth rates, tends to depress savings per capita and retards growth of physical capital per worker. The need for social infrastructure is also broadened, and public expenditures must be absorbed in providing these facilities for a larger population rather than in providing directly productive assets. Population pressure is also likely to intensify the foreign-exchange constraint by placing more pressure on the balance of payments. In some cases, the need to import foodstuffs will require the development of new industries for export expansion and/or import substitution. Possibly the most serious disadvantage to a high rate of population growth in a poor country is that it makes the human-resources constraint more difficult to remove. Larger numbers militate against an improvement in the quality of the population as productive agents. The rapid increase in school-age population and the expanding number of labor-force entrants put ever-greater pressure on educational and training facilities and retard improvement in the quality of education. Similarly, too dense a population aggravates the problem of improving the health of the population. With the concern over unemployment and inequality, students of population are now also asking whether population growth intensifies the extent of absolute poverty and the maldistribution of income.

In most developing countries, the working-age population has roughly doubled in the past 25 years. At expected growth rates, it will double again in the next 25 years. This growth clearly intensifies pressure on employment and the amount of investment available per labor market entrant.

That these disadvantages have become very real for many LDCs can be recognized if we contrast the demographic patterns of rich and poor countries. One striking difference is that a much higher percentage of the total population in poor countries is in younger age groups, and life expectancy is much lower than in rich countries. In most of the LDCs, 40 to 50 percent of the population is below 15 years of age, whereas in developed countries the corresponding figure is about 25 percent. If the economically productive age bracket is taken as 15 to 65 years,

the percentage of population in this category is considerably less in poor countries than in rich. This "bottom-heavy" age structure of population results in a high ratio of dependents to adult workers, which means the differentiation and productive power of the labor force are limited. Even worse, it means greater consumption and constitutes a major obstacle to an increase in savings in many LDCs. This high dependency ratio requires the economy to divert a considerable part of its resources, which might otherwise go into capital formation, to the maintenance of a high percentage of dependents who may never become producers or, if so, for only a relatively short working life.

Not only do most of the people in the world live in the less developed areas, but the concentration is increasing. In many LDCs, the populations are of the high-growth-potential type. In these countries, the simple application of modern public-health measures has allowed the death rate to fall spectacularly to the low levels of the rich countries, while birth rates have remained very high and resistant to change. If, as its true for many LDCs, the birth rate remains at a high level of about 40 per 1,000 while the death rate is reduced to about 10 per 1,000, then the population will double within a generation. With the declining death rates, the rates of natural increase have risen in the LDCs to 2, 3, or even 4 percent a year in regions of persistently high fertility. While the population in the rich countries, constituting 20 percent of the world's population, is growing at an average of only 1 percent or less, the population in the poor countries, amounting to 80 percent of the world's population, is growing at an average rate of 2.5 percent. Almost all the doubling times for populations in poor countries are more rapid than the world average. Selection VI.C.2 outlines the demographic situation well into the twenty-first century.

The population explosion that has been experienced during the past two decades in most of the LDCs is in marked contrast with the history of the presently rich industrial nations when they were in earlier phases of their development. In their nineteenth-century preindustrial phase, the countries of western Europe had a population growth that was generally less than half the rate now existing in the poor countries. Moreover, in the past the decline of the death rate in industrialized countries was due mainly to the development process itself—through such factors as improved diet, better housing, sanitation.

The death rates declined as part of the general evolution of Western society—induced by improvements in economic conditions and accompanied by changes in social attitudes that allowed birth rates to begin falling before death rates reached their low levels. Now, however, mortality rates are falling in poor countries not because of development, but because modern medical knowledge and scientific techniques of death control can be readily transferred from the rich countries and applied in nonindustrial areas. Modern medical and public-health advances have stimulated declines in mortality independently of economic development and social change.

A crucial question now is whether population-control policies can also stimulate declines in fertility,[2] without having to wait for higher levels of economic and social development to bring about a "normal" decline in fertility. Can family-planning programs be effective in the face of traditional beliefs and social institutions that have sustained fertility at a high level? Or can an adjustment of birth rates to the fall in death rates be induced only by long-run forces of development and the resultant changes in the traditional culture? Is the future of population growth essentially a question of the future of development?

This note has reversed the last question and emphasized that the very future of development is itself dependent on a reduction in heavy population pressures, lest it be increasingly difficult to remove the shortages of capital, foodstuffs, foreign exchange, and skills that now limit the rate of development. But the total discussion of this book can be interpreted as claiming that the potential for economic development is greater than the potential for population growth. To realize this potential as rapidly as possible, we must therefore recognize the beneficial effects that can come from declining fertility, and consider the inclusion of policies of family planning as a complement to other policies of development support. We must also give due weight to the belief that rapid population growth is a consequence as well as a cause of poverty. Declining fertility is highly correlated with a reduction in unemployment, improved status of women, better health care, more education, and greater income.

Many demographers believe that the time is dropping rapidly for the demographic transition from high to low birth and death rates. One major study of recent trends in natality in the LDCs concludes the following:

The data support the following conclusions about recent changes in natality in less developed regions:

1. A rapidly growing number of countries have been entering the demographic transition on the natality side especially since 1970.
2. Once a sustained reduction of the birth rate has begun, it proceeds at a much more rapid pace than it did historically in Europe and among Europeans overseas.
3. The "new" countries may reduce birth rates quite rapidly despite initially higher levels than existed historically in Western Europe.
4. Where available, the more refined measures of fertility, standardizing for differences in age structure, yield results similar to those for crude birth rates.
5. There is no direct evidence yet that current fertility reductions will terminate at levels significantly higher than those achieved in European countries and Japan.

Above observations are now based on the experience of many countries, though the precise extent of fertility decline is often clouded by defective data. There is now clear evidence of fertility reduction in the largest countries, dramatically rapid in China, and measurably in India and in Indonesia. Fertility reduction is now general in East Asia and in Latin America. As yet there is little evidence of this in tropical Africa or in the Moslem Middle East and Pakistan and Bangladesh.

The relationship between socioeconomic variables and fertility is clearly different within the different major cultural regions of the less developed world; quite different levels and kinds of development are associated with fertility reductions, for example, in East Asia and in Latin America. This confirms common sense and explains why efforts to relate socioeconomic measures and fertility "across the board" for all less developed countries have sometimes led to confusing results.

Finally, is there indeed a new or renewed demographic transition? The evidence suggests that there is. A rapidly growing number of countries of diverse cultural background have entered the natality transition since World War II and after a 25-year lapse in such entries. In these countries the transition is moving much faster than it did in Europe. This is probably related to the fact that progress in general is moving much faster in such matters as urbanization, education, health, communications and often per capita income. If progress in modernization continues, notably in the larger countries, the demographic transition in

---

[2]A general fertility rate is number of births per 1,000 women in reproductive ages 15 to 49.

the less developed world will probably be completed much more rapidly than it was in Europe.

It would be foolhardy, however, not to end on a word of caution. On any assumptions concerning the reduction of fertility that may occur with socioeconomic progress, it still follows that one may anticipate and must accommodate an enormous increase in the world population and that these increases will be greatest precisely in those countries economically least well-equipped to absorb the increase in numbers.[3]

[3]Dudley Kirk, "A New Demographic Transition?" in Study Committee, National Academy of Sciences, *Rapid Population Growth* (1971), pp. 145–46. Revised by the author for this edition.

VI.C.2. Population Growth*

Until the twentieth century, prosperity and population increase went hand-in-hand. In the eighteenth century, as living conditions began to improve steadily, world population growth accelerated slightly (to a then fast pace of 0.5 percent a year)—fastest in Europe and North America, where economic growth was taking hold.

In the twentieth century, world population growth accelerated dramatically, to 1 percent a year until almost 1950 and then to an unprecedented 2 percent, nearly doubling world population between 1950 and today. But population growth in the twentieth century has been concentrated where income is low; particularly since 1950, population growth has been concentrated in low-income developing countries. This delinking of population growth and prosperity occurred in part as improved health and communications brought mortality down even where gains in living standards were small. . . . A combination of continued high fertility and much reduced mortality has led to population growth of between 2 and 4 percent a year in most low- and middle-income countries (compared with 1 percent and less in most developed countries). Growth at 3 percent a year means that in 70 years population grows eightfold; at 1 percent a year it merely doubles.

For developing countries as a group, population growth rates have recently slowed somewhat, from a peak of 2.4 percent in 1965 to about 2 percent today. But further declines will not come automatically. Most families in developing countries (apart from China) now have at least four children, and rural families have five or more. In a few countries where fertility fell in the 1970s, there is evidence that it has leveled off recently, at still fairly high levels, while in much of Africa and Central America population growth rates are rising and could rise still further. Furthermore, population momentum means that growth rates in developing countries will remain high for several decades even if couples have fewer children; because of the large numbers of young people now entering childbearing age, absolute annual increases in population are likely to rise over 80 million people a year and remain that high well into the next century.

If the assumptions underlying the "standard" projections of the World Bank are correct, world population will rise from almost 5.2 billion today to almost 10 billion by the year 2050—the population of today's developed countries increasing from about 1.1 billion to 1.4 billion, and that of those countries now classified as developing increasing from 4.1 billion to 8.4 billion. By the time world population stabilizes (at over 11 billion in about 2150), the population of India would be 1.8 billion, making it the most populous nation on earth. Bangladesh, a country about one quarter the size of France, would have a population of 430 million. Sub-Saharan Africa and South Asia would account for about 50 percent of the world's inhabitants, compared with about 30 percent today.

In some respects the assumptions underlying these projections—including that fertility will fall to replacement level in some developing countries by 2005, and in all by 2045—are optimistic. Even with rapid income growth and advances in literacy in the next two decades, the poorer countries of Africa and South Asia are not likely to reach the income and literacy levels that triggered fertility declines in such countries as Brazil, the Republic of Korea, and Malaysia in the 1960s. Yet their fertitlity is projected to decline significantly. Even if it does, their pop-

*From Nancy Birdsall, "Population Growth," *Finance & Development* (September 1984), pp. 10–14. Reprinted by permission.

ulations will more than double in the next 50 years.

Alternative projections demonstrate two points: how much population growth there will be with even faster fertility decline than the "standard" projection allows for and how much of a difference a more rapid fertility decline could make. By the year 2050, for instance, Kenya, with an immediate and rapid decline in fertility, would have 70 million rather than 120 million people, compared with 18 million today. More rapid declines in mortality are also possible—but they would not boost population growth as the mortality declines of the 1950s and 1960s did. For most of the developing world, the time when declining mortality produced surges in population is passing rapidly. In part this is because mortality, although still high compared with developed countries, has already fallen considerably. In addition, declines in mortality affect population growth less when fertility is falling, as is and will be the case in most countries.

A Development Problem

There are three major reasons why rapid population growth slows development. First, it exacerbates the difficult choice between higher consumption now and the investment needed to bring higher consumption in the future. Per capita resources are lower the faster population grows, making investment in "population quality" difficult. Yet ultimately the key to development is more educated and skilled people. For example, in most developing countries, the high fertility and falling infant mortality of the mid-1960s mean that about 40 percent of populations are now aged 15 or younger. Many countries face a doubling or tripling of their school-age population by the end of the century. In Malawi, with rapid fertility decline could come savings of more than 50 percent as the numbers of children entering school by the year 2015 rise more slowly. School quality in Malawi (as in many other developing countries) is poor; the savings could be used to improve it.

Second, in many countries where populations are still highly dependent on agriculture, population growth threatens what is already a precarious balance between scarce natural resources and people. In part, the problem arises because rapid population growth slows the transfer of labor out of low-productivity agriculture into modern agriculture and other modern jobs. In many countries, much of the huge projected increases in the size of the labor force will have to be absorbed in agriculture, a difficulty which today's developed countries never faced. In Kenya, 70 percent of the labor force will probably still be working in agriculture as late as 2025, and the number of workers will be twice what it is today. The result is likely to be continuing low incomes for many families and, in some cases, stress on traditional agricultural systems and environmental damage that threatens the economic well-being of the poor.

Finally, rapid increases in population make it hard to manage the adjustments that are necessary to promote economic and social change. High fertility is a major contributor to rapid urban growth. Cities in developing countries are growing to unprecedented sizes. Such growth poses enormous new problems of management even to maintain—let alone improve—living conditions for city residents.

There are several reasons why population growth in developing countries is a greater economic burden today than it was in today's developed countries in their periods of economic transformation.

- Population growth is now much more rapid—in Europe and Japan in the nineteenth century, population growth seldom exceeded 1 percent a year.
- The large-scale emigration that occurred in nineteenth century Europe is not possible from today's developing countries. Nearly 45 percent of the increase in the population of the United Kingdom during 1846–1932 emigrated, compared with 0.5 percent of the increase in Asia between 1970 and 1980.
- Compared with Europe, Japan, and North America in their periods of fastest population growth, income in developing countries is still low, human and physical capital are less built up, and in some countries political and social institutions are less well established.
- Many developing countries whose economies are still largely dependent on agriculture can no longer draw on large tracts of unused land. In Japan and the United Kingdom by the 1880s, population growth in rural areas had ended; in much of Asia and Africa today, rural population growth still exceeds 2 percent a year (even taking into account migration to urban areas) implying a doubling of population size in rural areas every 40 years.

Countries in which education levels are already high, in which much investment in transport and communications systems is in place, and in which political and economic systems are relatively stable are well equipped to cope with rapid population growth. This is true whether or not their natural resources are limited or their countries already crowded—but these also tend to be the countries in which population is now slowing.

The problem of rapid population growth also affects countries with untapped natural resources, making it difficult to develop the human skills and administrative structures needed to exploit those natural resources. In Brazil, Ivory Coast, and Zaïre, for example, the development of unused land will require large complementary investments in roads, public services, and drainage and other agricultural infrastructure.

Where the amount of new land or other exploitable resources is limited—as in Bangladesh, Burundi, China, Egypt, India, Java in Indonesia, Kenya, Malawi, Nepal, and Rwanda—the short-run difficulties caused by rapid population growth are more obvious. Increases in agricultural yields are possible, and the expansion of manufacturing industry could provide exports to pay for extra food imports. But both solutions require costly investments, the development of new institutions, and numerous economic and social adjustments—all of which are easier if population is growing only slowly.

The consequences of high fertility also take their toll at the family level, particularly on children from families that are both large and poor. In Brazil, for instance, more than 60 percent of all children live in the poorest 40 percent of households that earn just 10 percent of the country's total income. From one generation to the next, an unequal distribution of income can be caused by, and contribute to, an unequal distribution of opportunities and skills, as large family size and low investments in children reinforce each other.

Need for a Public Policy

It is the poor, with little education, low and insecure income, and poor health and family planning services who have many children; yet it is also the poor who lose out as rapid population growth hampers development. It is this seeming paradox that provides the starting point for understanding the need for appropriate policies to reduce fertility. There are several good reasons why, from the point of view of poor parents, the economic costs of children are low, the economic (and other) benefits of children are high, and having many children makes economic sense.

- Where wages are low, income lost by the mother during a child's infancy may be easily recouped by the child later on.
- Where schooling opportunities are limited, the investment potential of children is not apparent. When schooling opportunities improve, and education becomes more clearly the key to future success for children (and their parents), parents want fewer, better-educated children.
- Given high mortality, parents may feel the need to have many babies to be sure that a few survive. Where boys are more important than girls—say, for security in old age—parents may need to have five children to be sure one son survives.
- For many poor parents, the need for support in their old age outweighs the immediate costs of children. For the rural poor, children are the best possible ''annuity'' for old age—not subject to theft, inflation, or the jealousies of neighbors. (Even land is an asset that may be difficult to manage without adult children once parents become old.)
- In some developing countries family systems encourage high fertility. For young women who have few other options, early marriage and many children may be the safest route to a satisfying adulthood and a relatively secure old age.
- Limited information about, and access to, modern and safe means of contraception encourage high fertility among the poor. . . .

If parents have many children in the hope of economic gain, the first step in reducing fertility is to relieve their poverty and reduce their uncertainty about their own future. In this sense, the persistence of high fertility in a changing world is a symptom of lack of access: to health services, which would reduce the need for many births to ensure against infant and child mortality; to education, which would raise parents' hopes for their children and would broaden a woman's outlook; to social security and other forms of insurance for old age; to consumer goods and social opportunities that compete with childbearing; and to family planning services, which provide the means to limit births.

Successful Experience

It was once assumed that reducing fertility in developing countries would require a typical sequence of economic advance: urbanization, industrialization, a shift from production in the household to factory production, and income growth to levels enjoyed by today's developed countries. This view seemed to be confirmed by the fertility declines of the 1960s, which were largely confined to the industrial economies of Korea, Singapore, and Hong Kong.

But fertility declines in many other countries, beginning in the late 1960s and spreading in the 1970s, have been related to a different kind of development: education, health, the alleviation of poverty, and government effort to assure widespread access to family planning services. Declines in birth rates since 1965 have been much more closely associated with adult literacy and life expectancy than with GNP per capita. And several countries that have supported family planning services have significantly lower fertility than the norm for their income level, including China, Colombia, Egypt, India, Indonesia, Korea, Sri Lanka, and Tunisia. (Countries with relatively high fertility given their income include Algeria and Morocco, most countries of Sub-Saharan Africa, and Venezuela.) In most of the low fertility countries, fertility has declined much faster than it did in today's developed countries—both because of the availability of more effective modern contraceptives and the rapid expansion of educational opportunities in the postwar period.

Within regions, differences among countries are due in part to population policy effort. Fertility has fallen faster and to lower levels in Colombia, where family planning programs received government support starting in the late 1960s, than in Brazil, a richer country where central government involvement is minimal. It has fallen more in Egypt and Tunisia, countries with demographic objectives, than in their richer neighbor, Algeria. It has fallen more in India than in Pakistan; per capita income is low in both, but in Pakistan population policy has received less sustained support over the past two decades. The pattern of decline shows that differences in income, religion, and culture do not tell the whole story. Education, access to family planning services, the status of women, and economic and social policies that bring opportunities to the majority of people all make a difference.

EXHIBIT VI.1. Population Projections by Region

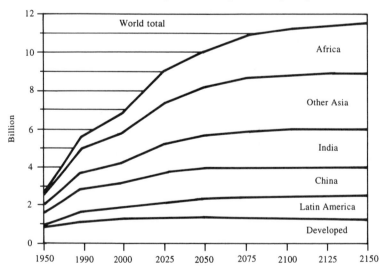

Population projections estimate an annual increase of nearly 100 million people for the next ten years. Africa and South Asia account for more than half of the population increases. By 2050, world population would be 10 billion. To encourage reduced family sizes, it is necessary to eliminate extreme poverty, improve health and education, and raise the status of women.

Source: United Nations Population Division, cited in United Nations Population Fund, *State of World Population 1992,* p. 6.

EXHIBIT VI.2. Measures of Demographic Change, 1950–90, by Region

Regions	Africa	Latin America	Asia	Except China	LDCs	Except China	More Developed Countries	World
Population in millions								
1950	224	165	1,292	737	1,684	1,129	832	2,516
1985	555	405	2,697	1,637	3,663	2,603	1,174	4,837
Percent annual population growth								
1950–55	2.12	2.73	1.96	2.04	2.04	2.13	1.28	1.79
1985–90	3.02	2.16	1.67	2.00	1.94	2.25	0.60	1.63
Crude birth rate per 1000								
1950–55	48.3	42.5	44.2	44.6	44.4	44.7	22.7	37.3
1985–90	45.2	29.7	26.0	31.1	29.4	33.9	15.1	26.0
Total fertility rate								
1950–55	6.47	5.86	6.07	6.04	6.12	6.12	2.80	4.94
1985–90	6.22	3.73	3.26	4.03	3.69	4.33	1.97	3.28
Crude death rate per 1000								
1950–55	27.1	15.4	24.8	24.6	24.2	23.8	10.1	19.6
1985–90	15.1	7.6	9.3	11.1	10.0	11.4	9.5	9.6
Life expectancy at birth								
1950–55	37.8	51.1	40.2	39.9	41.1	41.2	65.8	46.0
1985–90	51.3	65.7	62.0	57.1	59.1	54.9	74.0	61.1
Infant mortality rate per 1000								
1950–55	191	125	186	180	180	173	56	156
1985–90	101	56	68	92	79	98	14	71
Percent urban population								
1950	15.7	41.0	13.9	16.1	17.0	20.4	53.8	29.2
1985	29.7	68.9	24.9	27.7	31.2	35.5	71.5	41.0
Percent dependency under 15								
1950	42.4	40.5	36.7	39.1	37.9	40.0	27.8	34.5
1985	45.1	37.9	35.2	38.8	36.9	39.9	22.2	33.4
Percent dependency over 65								
1950	3.6	3.3	4.3	3.7	3.9	3.6	7.6	5.1
1985	3.1	4.5	4.7	3.9	4.2	3.8	11.2	5.9

Source: Allen C. Kelley, ''Economic Consequences of Population Change in the Third World,'' *Journal of Economic Literature* 26 (December 1988): 1690.

EXHIBIT VI.3. Average Number of Children per Woman

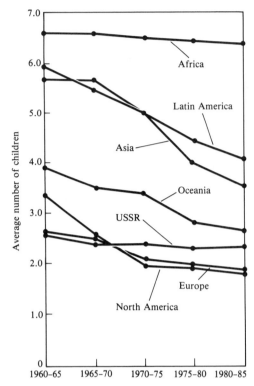

Source: United Nations Population Division, *World Population Prospects as Assessed in 1984* (October 1985), Table A-12.

Comment: Population–Economic Relationships

The major lines of research on the multiple relationships between population growth and economic development have been directed to analyzing the determinants and consequences of fertility and to making population an endogenous rather than an exogenous variable. The research can be further divided into micro- and macro-type research. An excellent survey of several research studies is presented by Nancy Birdsall, "Analytical Approaches to the Relationship of Population Growth and Development," *Population and Development Review* (March 1977; June 1977). Almost all studies of the determinants of fertility indicate a positive effect of infant mortality on fertility; that is, countries with high rates of infant mortality on the whole have high rates of fertility. Female education bears one of the strongest and most consistent negative relationships to fertility.

Another excellent review of population trends is Robert H. Cassen, "Current Trends in Population Change and Their Causes," *Population and Development Review* (March 1978). It indicates the importance of socioeconomic, cultural, and environmental factors in explaining fertility differences not only among countries, but also within countries. It suggests that the factors commonly associated with fertility decline—such "correlates of fertility decline" as education, urbanization, improved status of and wider employment opportunities for women, mortality decline, and increased practice of family planning—contribute to fertility differentials within countries, even in those in which the prevailing culture appears to give a disposition to high fertility.

Of particular interest in the macro-consequences studies is the attempt to compare the costs of a family-planning program with the projected savings realized in health or education costs. Usually, the savings in the latter are shown to "pay" for the former in this form of analysis. Such comparisons, however, necessitate assumptions about costs of launching family-planning programs, acceptor rates, and the relationship between acceptor rates and actual births averted, as well as assumptions about future costs in health, education, or other areas, and about the society's welfare function, which may value children per se in addition to capital goods.

A number of studies have considered the benefits and costs of population-control programs: A. J. Coale and E. M. Hoover, *Population Growth and Economic Development in Low-Income Countries* (1958); R. A. Easterlin, ed., *Population and Economic Change in Developing Countries* (1980); R. Easterlin et al., "Review Symposium: World Development Report 1984," *Population and Development Review* (March 1985); Timothy King et al., *Population Policies and Economic Development* (1974); Mark Perlman, "Population and Economic Change in Developing Countries," *Journal of Economic Literature* (March 1981); World Bank, *Population Change and Development* (1985) and *Population Growth and Policies in Sub-Saharan Africa* (1986); David Wheeler, *Human Resource Policies, Economic Growth and Demographic Change in Developing Countries* (1987); and Robert Cassen, ed., *Population and Development: Old Debates, New Conclusions* (1994).

Besides the macro-research involving benefit–cost analysis, there has been more research on how individual fertility decisions are affected by environmental changes. The "new economics of the household" treats the child as both a produced (investment) and a consumer good. Fertility is the result of rational economic choice within the household.

This economic model concludes that, for poor families in developing countries, children entail low net costs and, in the extreme case, may actually be a net benefit. In contrast, the literature dealing with macro-consequences concludes that high fertility entails a high net cost to poor societies. This theoretical gap between the low private and the high social costs of children has been a principal justification for government policies to reduce fertility. On the micro-models, see Theodore W. Schultz, ed., *Economics of the Family: Marriage, Children and Human Capital* (1974).

From models of household behavior a number of hypotheses have also been derived pertaining to the interrelationships among population growth, human capital, and economic development. Evidence supports the hypothesis that alterations in the returns to human capital associated with technical change lead simultaneously to increases in human capital investments and to reductions in fertility. See Mark R. Rosenzweig, "Population Growth and Human Capital Investments: Theory and Evidence," *Journal of Political Economy* (October 1990).

Comment: Child Labor and Street Children

The burden of poverty falls especially severely on children, not only through malnutrition, disease, and lack of education but also as child laborers and street children.

In developing countries, the majority of children are in households at the bottom of the income scale. Each day, 34,000 children still die from malnutrition and disease. In developing countries generally, children between the ages of 1 and 5 years are 12 to 15 times more likely to die than children born in developed countries.

The consequences of infant malnutrition endure even after the period of undernourishment is passed; malnutrition stunts growth, and there is evidence that it may retard intellectual development and limit the individual's learning abilities and educational achievement.

About 33 percent of the children of primary-school age in the developing countries are not enrolled in school. Of those who enter school, 60 percent will not complete more than three years of primary school.

Far removed from the classroom, the poor child is often a working child. The ILO and UNICEF estimate that hundreds of millions of children under 15 years of age are working at a fixed job. Some 17 million Indian children have gone straight from "swaddling clothes into working gear." In some Asian countries, child workers make up more than 10 percent of the labor force. In several African countries more than 20 percent of their children are working, and in some Latin American countries more than 25 percent. Child labor is by its nature in low-productivity jobs that yield only an irregular and inadequate income. Children are working long hours for low pay, sacrificing their health, education, and childhood.

See the annual report by UNICEF, *The State of the World's Children*, as well as Giovanni Andrea Cornia et al., *Adjustment with a Human Face* (1987); Elias Mendelievich, *Children at Work* (1979); Assefa Bequele and Jo Boyden, eds., *Combatting Child Labor* (1988); and William Myers, ed., *Protecting Working Children* (1990).

Comment: Revisionist View of Population

Recently a growing ''revisionist'' literature has contradicted the commonly accepted view that rapid population growth is a hindrance to development.

Instead of generalizing on adverse economywide repercussions of population growth, the revisionists claim that the repercussions vary according to time, place, and circumstance and must be studied empirically. The analysis is based on micro-individual or family-level decisions made in response to signals provided by the larger system. Microdecisions are presumed to maximize not only individual welfare, but also social welfare, unless there are substantial market failures.

A report by the National Research Council of the National Academy of Sciences, *Population Growth and Economic Development* (1986), emphasizes the ability of the market and institutions to adjust. The report also identifies positive as well as negative impacts of population growth and claims that the actual size of the net impact cannot be determined given current evidence.

For further consideration of the revisionist view, see Dominick Salvatore, ed., *World Population Trends and Their Impact on Economic Development* (1988); Nancy Birdsall, ''Economic Analyses of Rapid Population Growth,'' *World Bank Research Observer* (January 1989); and M. R. Rosenzweig and O. Stark, eds., *Handbook of Population and Family Economics* (1993).

Birdsall concludes:

> The long debate over population growth and development is entering a new phase. The emphasis is now on the interaction of rapid population growth with market failures. Research is concentrating on the quantitative importance of population growth in particular settings and time periods and among particular groups such as the poor, given likely market failures. The issue is whether population growth is so interlinked with other problems— such as poor macro-economic policies, weak political institutions, or such correctable market failures as poorly defined property rights—as to hardly merit specific attention; or whether the effects of population growth are large enough to justify special policies to reduce fertility.
>
> The issue warrants new empirical research for two types of economies: First are those in which it is likely that the social costs of high fertility exceed the private costs. Second are those economies in which market failures such as lack of property rights or distortions that discourage labor-using technology are likely to heighten any negative effect of rapid population growth.[1]

---

[1]Birdsall, ''Economic Analyses of Rapid Population Growth,'' p. 43.

VI.D. GENDER AND DEVELOPMENT

VI.D.1. Women in the Labor Force*

Rural women in the developing world, and particularly those who are poor, invariably work hard at a variety of tasks, with little time for leisure and little control over productive resources or even over their own income or labour. Yet they often must assume a large share of the responsibility for the survival of their families, through direct production for consumption, income earning, providing health care, etc. Women constitute a substantial part—in some countries the majority—of the agricultural labour force, including workers on plantations; they are engaged in home-based production of modern as well as traditional products, sometimes working for a contractor under the putting-out system; and many migrate from impoverished rural areas to work in the urban informal sector as traders, or in export processing zones as industrial workers.

Women in rural areas throughout the Third World are typically farmers. In Sub-Saharan Africa, subsistence farming is essentially a female activity, and women are the primary labourers on small farms, where they contribute two-thirds or more of all hours of work. Food production (as well as processing and often marketing) is essentially a female responsibility—a situation that also prevails in the Caribbean.

A more complex picture emerges in Asia. In India, while overall female labour force participation has been falling in the face of surplus labour, more and more women are becoming agricultural wage labourers because of growing landlessness. Between 30 and 40 percent of the agricultural labour force is composed of women. In Bangladesh, where women are still presumed to be secluded, they are increasingly seen in the fields, and poverty forces them to come forth for other hard work, such as road construction; these activities are in addition to their long-standing essential but largely invisible work behind compound walls in seed selection, processing, winnowing, and threshing. In China, the female labour force in rural areas has greatly increased

over the past 25 years, as women's participation in agricultural work and in many non-farm activities has been strongly encouraged, both to increase production and to combat discriminatory practices and prejudices. A new dimension is emerging with the recent shift toward family farming and the promotion of family-based domestic sidelines. In South-east Asian countries, such as Indonesia, women are very active in the rice fields, a crop which usually requires intensive farming.

In Latin America, women work more in agriculture than is commonly thought, even without counting such activities as processing done in the fields and services provided to field workers. Andean agriculture, often considered a male farming system, is in fact better characterised as a family farming system.

There is a large proportion of female labour in the plantation sector as well. Working as tea pluckers, as rubber tappers, or as casual workers on coconut plantations, women in Malaysia and Sri Lanka, for example, constitute more than half of the labour force; but they receive lower pay than men for the same work, face extra burdens because of inadequate child-care facilities and the long distances between home and work, and often see others collecting their pay. Despite a high rate of trade union membership on the part of women plantation workers, their particular needs and interests have seldom been given attention by the union leadership.

In addition to agricultural work, many women are engaged in home-based production, either full-time or in slack seasons to increase family income. In some cases such production is traditional; in others it is relatively new—particularly where traditional sources of production and income have been lost with modernisation and commercialisation; in still others it is the result of the promotion of ''income-generating activities'' designed to allow women to increase their cash income without disturbing their domestic responsibilities. Sometimes the result is a good income for women. In many cases, however, the returns to labour are very low. And at its worst, such home-based production definitely involves exploitation. . . . Secluded women in poor

*From International Labour Office, *World Labour Report* (Oxford University Press, 1987), pp. 251–55. Reprinted by permission.

households working at home rolling beedies (popular cigarettes) or crocheting lace for contractors under the putting-out system do not receive anywhere near the minimum wage, nor do they control their own labour, let alone the labour process or marketing. They constitute an invisible labour force, dependent on traders and intermediaries who control the work. Wages (or piece rate payments) may be very low, yet they account for a substantial proportion of the income of poor households. Data on such workers are very scanty, but the beedi industry in India alone employs between 2 and 3 million women. And this system has begun to encompass the manufacture of some modern products, such as electronics assembly units.

Access to and Control over Resources

Land is obviously the principal asset in rural areas: access to credit, extension services, technologies, and even cooperative organisations are generally linked to land titles. Yet even where women perform the bulk of agricultural work, as in much of Sub-Saharan Africa, they seldom have full title (but rather, land use rights). Where rights are collectively held, it is almost invariably the male head of household who participates in the peasant association. In family farming systems, women have even less access to basic assets. The provision of land rights and access to related resources (credit, technology, etc.) would alter the production relations, which are now characterised by the unequal bargaining position of the women. In many societies (particularly in Asia and Latin America), the process of agricultural growth and modernisation is leading to pauperisation and increasing landlessness, thus drawing more and more women into agricultural wage labour even where overall employment opportunities for women are shrinking. In North Africa and the Middle East, a little-heralded effect of male migration to the oil-producing countries of the region is the increase of female-headed households and women's participation in agricultural labour. And in Sub-Saharan Africa, while land in itself may be relatively abundant and accessible, women usually neither own nor control improved cultivable land. However, in many parts of the developing world women are beginning to organise themselves and to raise these issues within their communities and nations.

Forests are another resource that is very important to women in rural areas, as a source of fuel, food, fodder, and livelihood. Reduced access to forests, which may occur because of drought, deforestation, or changes in land tenure or forest policy, can have a devastating effect on family welfare. But it is the women who are most dependent on this resource, and whose work and income are at stake. When fuel is not readily available, families either have fewer cooked meals or have to work harder to find fuel or have to earn cash to buy fuel and/or cooked food.

There is increasing evidence that the income of household members is not automatically pooled, and that it does matter to family welfare who earns and, particularly, who controls "household" income. For example, a case-study in India has found that increasing women's wages has a visible effect on child nutrition. Therefore, increasing women's income and entitlement to or control over resources can be an important means of improving the welfare of households in rural areas.

Changing Division of Labour Between Men and Women

While domestic work is almost universally considered to be the domain of women, great variations are found in the division of labour between men and women in non-domestic activities (and even the domestic division may eventually change). Social and economic development affects men and women in specific ways, producing significant changes in the division of labour between men and women. In many developing countries great changes have occurred in agriculture during the past three decades, which have profoundly but differently affected the work of rural men and women in various income groups. The introduction of new technologies, changes in the agrarian structure, the spread of commodity production and growing inequality in rural areas have displaced women from many traditional activities, while at the same time increasing women's workload in certain agricultural tasks.

Labour mobility and the changing patterns of work and employment that accompany economic growth are often detrimental to women workers in rural areas. Modernisation has done away with many traditional income-earning opportunities, and rural development policies and programmes do not generally recognise women as producers. This is happening at a time when the incomes of poor households are dwindling, forcing women in many countries to provide for an increasing share of their family's needs. In the struggle for survival, women face great obstacles, such as their limited mobility due to family responsibilities and social and cultural restrictions. In Africa growing labour displacement towards cash crops is leaving rural women increasingly on their own to produce food with no means of improving productivity. The best arable land is usually allocated to cash crops. Yet concern is growing about falling per capita food production. This should logically lead to support for Africa's food producers—the rural women. ILO research has indicated that women's productivity can be increased by using improved technologies.

In green revolution areas in Asia, agricultural modernisation has increased the demand for casual labour while marginalising small tenants and dispossessing smallholders of their land. Male tasks have been more commonly mechanised than those of women, thereby decreasing male employment opportunities and income and pushing women into agricultural wage labour. Women are also seeking needed income in the informal sector or as home-based workers, or they may migrate to look for work elsewhere. Landlessness and poverty have dramatically increased the number of women working as casual labourers. Improved transport facilities and the spread of manufactured goods threaten many petty commodity trade activities undertaken by women and men without opening up new employment opportunities for women, as jobs in the modern sector are seldom available to them. Permanent or seasonal male out-migration in Asia, west and southern Africa is affecting farming practices. In Lesotho, for instance, the plight of migrant workers' families is such that the departure of able-bodied men to the mining industry in South Africa calls for additional work by women, and is hardly compensated by insecure and meagre migrant remittances. Strained family bonds and reduced household income are leaving women in a very vulnerable position. In Malawi about a quarter of rural households are headed by women, and this rate is even higher among the lowest income groups. Rural development programmes and extension services have failed to reach these women, who in the absence of male workers are unable to increase agricultural productivity. In some countries, such as Ghana, Malawi, and the Sudan, female-headed households constitute between one-fourth and one-third of all rural households,

while in other countries the proportion is estimated at between 5 and 20 percent (about 12 in Indonesia, 17 in Mauritania, and 13 in Panama, for instance).

Increasing rural poverty has also precipitated female out-migration as a means of supplementing family income. Export processing zones in Asia (e.g., in Malaysia, the Philippines, and Singapore) have increasingly attracted a young and docile female labour force for export-oriented industries relying on a cheap but intensive labour process.

Women as Industrial Workers

Rapid industralisation, while expanding employment opportunities, has not fully benefited working women, since they often lose traditional sources of income without getting new jobs. This has happened for example in such newly industrialised countries as Brazil, India, Mexico, and Nigeria. Various studies show that women are increasingly confined to home work (as in the textiles, clothing, and tobacco industries) and in marginal service jobs in the urban informal sector where employment is casual and irregular and where incomes are very low. It is also characteristic of most developing countries that mainly young unmarried women (in the 20–25 age group) obtain employment in the formal sector.

Why do certain employers prefer to recruit young unmarried women as employees? Some studies indicate that this preference is based less on the job requirements than on social perceptions. Women are supposed to have dexterity, speed, and endurance in certain assembly-line jobs in old industries such as clothing or new industries such as electronics. They are considered to be more disciplined and docile than male workers, and ready to accept low wages. In some cases young girls have been dismissed when they reached the legal age at which they would be entitled to adult wages.

The fact that women are concentrated in the traditionally "female industries" and in low-skilled jobs keeps their wages low, hinders their upward mobility, and makes them prone to long periods of unemployment in times of economic and technological restructuring. It is well known that in female industries, such as textiles, clothing, electronics, food, and beverages, wages are usually lower than in other industries.

What is the impact of new technologies on women's jobs? While technological progress over the years has widened women's employment opportunities in the modern sector, it has had the effect of frequently displacing them into low-skilled and low-status occupations. This trend is illustrated by the commerce, finance, and services sectors where their employment at first expanded enormously but may now be affected in two ways: those who are already employed may lose the jobs or see the content of their jobs change, while those who are looking for jobs may not find one corresponding to their qualifications. This situation, combined with high rates of unemployment, may cause serious setbacks to the emancipation of women through work. It appears that even in newer industries, such as electronics, the dynamics of technological change require higher levels of technical skills, generally not accessible to women. In plants located in several industrial estates and export processing zones, young, inexperienced rural women are considered to be the best choice, since they are believed to be more patient and diligent and to have keener eyesight and more nimble fingers than men.

In developing countries lack of skills leads women to seek employment as domestic servants, an occupation in which they are often exploited and which offers low wages and uncertain and long hours, with no paid leave or other social benefits. Other occupations in which women find themselves are those of barmaids, hostesses, and receptionists, which are outside the reach of labour regulations. Sometimes young girls under the minimum age of admission to employment work as domestic servants or entertainers under harsh conditions and often without adequate pay, food, or shelter.

The number of women working in offices and commerce varies from country to country. In developing countries secretaries and teachers are still occupational categories filled by both men and women. There is, however, a trend for these occupations to become more feminised. This is true of first-grade teachers in Asia and secondary-level teachers in Africa, where the number of women occupying such posts rose from 22 to 29 percent and from 25 to 33 percent respectively between 1975 and 1980. Community, social, and health services in many countries show a high concentration of women since welfare services are considered to be a female sphere of activity. But even in these occupations women hold jobs in the lower echelons, while the higher echelons are almost exclusively occupied by men. This is particularly true of the health sector where women are usually nurses, etc., but not hospital managers, surgeons, or research technicians.

There are occupations, however, in which there is a neat division of labour between men and women. For example, it is mainly women who are engaged in the retail trade of certain African and Asian countries, while men dominate the wholesale trade and commerce.

In the public service sector women usually have reasonable opportunities to reach responsible positions, owing to the scope of labour legislation and other regulations. Although their numbers are still very small, in some countries they work in ministries of health, education, and social affairs at intermediate levels and in various government departments and agencies.

EXHIBIT VI.4. Women in the Workplace

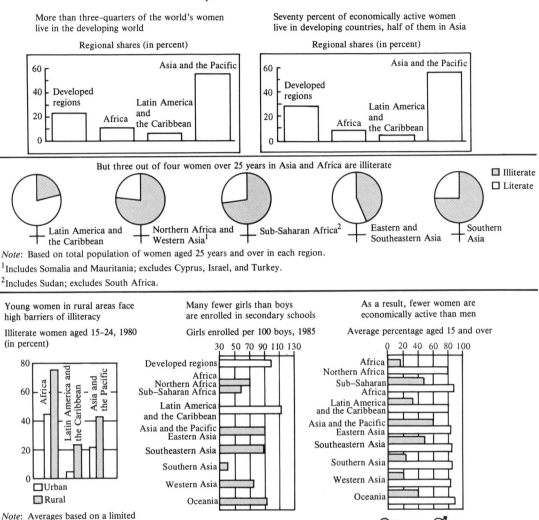

More than three-quarters of the world's women live in the developing world

Regional shares (in percent)

Seventy percent of economically active women live in developing countries, half of them in Asia

Regional shares (in percent)

But three out of four women over 25 years in Asia and Africa are illiterate

Latin America and the Caribbean — Northern Africa and Western Asia[1] — Sub-Saharan Africa[2] — Eastern and Southeastern Asia — Southern Asia

□ Illiterate
□ Literate

Note: Based on total population of women aged 25 years and over in each region.

[1] Includes Somalia and Mauritania; excludes Cyprus, Israel, and Turkey.

[2] Includes Sudan; excludes South Africa.

Young women in rural areas face high barriers of illiteracy

Illiterate women aged 15–24, 1980 (in percent)

Many fewer girls than boys are enrolled in secondary schools

Girls enrolled per 100 boys, 1985

As a result, fewer women are economically active than men

Average percentage aged 15 and over

Note: Averages based on a limited number of countries in each region for census years around 1980.

♀ Women   ♂ Men

About 70 percent of the economically active women in the world live in developing countries. In most cases, they work longer hours than men. Official employment statistics, however, do not capture work done in the household or in family-run agricultural or other subsistence activities. The gaps between women and men's economic participation remain wide, reflecting fewer educational opportunities, social restrictions, and market imperfections.

Source: "Women in the Workplace in Developing Countries," *Finance & Development* (June 1992), p. 44.

EXHIBIT VI.5. Women in Development

	Health and Welfare						Education							
	Under 5 Mortality Rate (per 1,000 live births)		Life Expectancy at Birth (years)				Maternal Mortality (per 100,000 live births) 1988	Percentage of Cohort Persisting to Grade 4				Females per 100 Males			
			Female		Male			Female		Male		Primary		Secondary	
	Female 1991	Male 1991	1970	1991	1970	1991		1970	1986	1970	1986	1970	1990	1970	1990
Low-income economies	96	104	54	58	53	61	308	—	—	—	—	—	78	—	65
China and India	75	80	57	60	57	64	115	—	—	—	—	—	79	—	65
Other low-income	135	148	47	57	46	54	587	65	66	74	70	61	76	44	66
Middle-income economies	44	54	62	71	58	65	107	78	87	76	90	86	91	94	104
Lower-middle-income	50	60	61	69	57	64	111	79	87	80	88	80	90	89	104
Upper-middle-income	36	46	64	72	59	65	104	75	—	70	94	94	95	101	102
Low- and middle-income	80	89	56	63	54	62	238	61	76	64	80	70	81	60	73
Sub-Saharan Africa	167	186	45	52	42	49	686	66	71	69	72	60	76	40	67
East Asia and Pacific	46	58	60	66	58	66	195	—	78	—	82	—	88	—	75
South Asia	129	127	48	59	50	59	444	45	—	48	—	55	69	38	54
Europe and Central Asia	28	35	69	74	64	66	60	90	97	92	98	89	94	137	143
Middle East and North Africa	73	84	54	65	52	63	151	83	90	87	92	54	79	41	72
Latin America and Caribbean	48	58	63	71	58	65	162	66	76	60	85	96	97	101	103
Severely indebted	55	66	62	69	58	64	171	75	80	73	89	87	88	109	115
High-income economies	8	11	75	80	68	73	—	95	98	93	97	96	95	95	100
OECD members	8	11	75	80	68	73	—	95	98	93	97	96	95	95	100

Source: World Bank, *World Development Report 1993* (1993), pp. 300–301.

EXHIBIT VI.6. Female–Male Gaps

	Females as Percentage of Males (see *note*)								
HDI Rank	Life Expectancy 1990	Population 1990	Literacy 1970	Literacy 1990	Mean Years of Schooling 1990	Primary Enrollment 1960	Primary Enrollment 1988–90	Secondary Enrollment 1988–90	Tertiary Enrollment 1988–90	Labor Force 1990
---	---	---	---	---	---	---	---	---	---	---
High Human Development	110	100	90	98	86	95	100	99	80	42
Barbados	107	109	—	—	93	—	98	92	—	92
Hong Kong	107	94	71	—	63	85	99	106	56	57
Cyprus	107	101	—	—	86	—	100	102	114	60
Uruguay	109	103	100	99	110	100	98	—	114	45
Trinidad and Tobago	107	101	94	—	101	98	100	104	68	38
Korea, Rep. of	109	100	86	94	61	90	100	97	53	51
Chile	110	102	98	100	92	96	92	108	82	45
Costa Rica	106	98	99	101	97	98	100	105	68	40
Singapore	108	97	60	—	66	93	100	104	—	64
Argentina	110	102	98	100	105	101	107	113	117	27
Venezuela	109	98	90	103	97	100	103	—	91	27
Kuwait	106	76	65	87	79	78	98	94	129	16
Mexico	110	100	88	94	96	94	97	102	76	46
Qatar	107	60	—	—	93	—	98	112	—	8
Medium Human Development	105	96	59	80	65	83	99	82	57	66
Excluding China	105	99	—	87	75	—	95	88	75	54
Mauritius	108	102	77	—	68	90	102	100	52	54
Malaysia	106	98	68	81	91	77	100	105	95	45
Bahrain	106	73	—	84	67	—	98	101	—	11
Colombia	109	99	96	98	106	100	103	119	108	69
Seychelles	—	101	—	—	92	—	99	100	—	74
Suriname	107	102	—	100	92	—	100	119	113	41
United Arab Emirates	106	48	29	—	101	—	100	114	—	7
Panama	106	97	100	100	106	96	106	109	—	37
Jamaica	106	101	101	100	97	101	98	111	75	45
Brazil	109	101	91	97	94	96	—	90	100	54
Fiji	107	99	—	—	83	—	101	104	57	23
Turkey	105	95	49	79	50	64	93	64	55	49
Thailand	106	99	84	96	76	90	—	97	—	88
Cuba	105	97	101	98	103	100	99	112	—	46
Syrian Arab Rep.	106	98	33	—	60	44	93	72	72	18
Saudi Arabia	106	84	13	66	26	—	81	75	73	8
South Africa	110	101	—	—	90	90	—	—	—	50
Sri Lanka	106	99	81	89	80	90	100	107	71	59
Libyan Arab Jamahiriya	106	91	22	67	23	26	90	—	—	10
Ecuador	107	99	91	95	92	91	98	104	68	43
Paraguay	107	97	88	96	88	86	99	107	88	70
Korea, Dem. Rep. of	110	101	—	—	63	—	—	100	—	85
Philippines	106	99	96	99	89	95	98	104	—	59
Tunisia	103	98	39	76	41	49	91	80	67	15
Oman	106	91	—	—	22	—	94	81	80	9
Peru	106	99	74	86	80	75	96	—	24	49
Iraq	103	96	36	71	69	38	87	64	64	6
Dominican Rep.	107	97	94	96	87	99	100	—	—	17
Jordan	106	95	45	79	66	63	—	—	—	11
Mongolia	104	99	85	—	95	99	103	110	—	83
China	105	94	—	73	60	—	100	77	50	76
Lebanon	106	106	73	83	66	94	92	71	44	37

(*continued*)

EXHIBIT VI.6. (*continued*)

	Females as Percentage of Males (see *note*)								
HDI Rank	Life Expectancy 1990	Population 1990	Literacy 1970	Literacy 1990	Mean Years of Schooling 1990	Primary Enrollment 1960	Primary Enrollment 1988–90	Secondary Enrollment 1988–90	Tertiary Enrollment 1988–90	Labor Force 1990
---	---	---	---	---	---	---	---	---	---	---
Iran, Islamic Rep. of	101	97	43	67	68	48	91	73	45	21
Botswana	111	109	—	78	97	—	106	—	76	55
Guyana	109	99	—	98	91	—	100	105	76	27
Algeria	103	100	28	65	18	67	88	80	44	5
Indonesia	106	101	64	85	58	67	96	84	—	66
Gabon	107	103	51	66	33	—	—	—	41	61
El Salvador	111	104	87	92	98	—	103	100	73	81
Nicaragua	104	100	98	—	110	102	104	—	121	51
Guatemala	108	98	73	75	86	78	85	68	—	34
Cape Verde	103	112	—	—	39	—	95	100	—	41
Viet Nam	107	104	—	91	59	—	94	93	28	88
Honduras	107	98	91	94	93	99	106	—	65	22
Swaziland	107	103	—	—	82	—	105	96	68	67
Morocco	106	100	29	62	36	40	68	70	59	26
Lesotho	117	108	—	—	—	—	119	—	—	78
Zimbabwe	106	102	75	82	40	—	100	85	36	54
Bolivia	109	103	68	83	60	64	90	84	—	31
Myanmar	106	101	67	81	72	85	98	92	—	60
Egypt	104	97	40	54	42	65	79	75	53	12
Congo	110	103	38	63	35	51	—	—	20	64
Kenya	107	100	43	—	42	47	96	70	45	67
Madagascar	106	102	77	83	65	78	98	90	82	66
Papua New Guinea	103	93	62	58	50	12	85	63	38	64
Zambia	104	103	56	81	45	67	98	56	37	40
Ghana	107	101	42	73	46	48	81	65	26	67
Pakistan	100	92	37	45	25	28	55	45	41	13
Cameroon	106	103	40	64	33	49	86	68	—	42
India	101	93	43	55	34	50	97	61	47	34
Côte d'Ivoire	107	97	38	60	31	35	—	44	27	52
Haiti	106	104	65	80	63	84	100	95	35	67
Tanzania, U. Rep of	107	102	38	—	45	55	104	80	33	93
Comoros	102	102	—	—	65	—	83	75	—	69
Zaire	107	102	36	73	33	36	79	50	—	56
Lao People's Dem. Rep.	106	99	76	—	59	47	80	68	50	81
Nigeria	107	102	40	63	26	59	93	77	38	25
Yemen	101	108	15	50	18	—	—	20	—	15
Liberia	105	98	30	58	26	40	—	55	31	44
Togo	107	102	26	54	31	38	68	30	15	58
Uganda	107	102	58	56	41	—	88	44	36	71
Bangladesh	99	94	33	47	30	39	88	50	22	7
Cambodia	106	101	—	46	71	—	—	—	—	64
Rwanda	107	102	49	58	31	—	100	67	20	92
Senegal	104	102	28	48	29	—	75	52	26	35
Ethiopia	107	102	—	—	43	27	75	71	23	71
Nepal	98	95	13	35	32	5	51	40	—	51
Malawi	103	103	43	—	46	—	95	50	27	72
Burundi	107	104	34	65	33	33	84	67	33	—
Equatorial Guinea	107	103	—	—	20	—	—	—	—	56
Central African Rep.	111	106	23	48	32	23	65	35	20	86
Mozambique	107	103	48	47	54	60	82	44	33	92
Sudan	105	99	21	27	45	40	71	74	68	41

EXHIBIT VI.6. (*continued*)

								Tertiary	
						Primary		Enroll-	
	Life				Mean	Enrollment		ment	Labor
	Expec-	Popu-	Literacy		Years of			Secondary	1988–	Force
	tancy	lation			Schooling			Enrollment	90	1990
HDI Rank	1990	1990	1970	1990	1990	1960	1988–90	1988–90		
Bhutan	97	93	—	—	32	—	65	29	—	48
Angola	107	103	44	51	52	—	82	—	15	64
Mauritania	107	102	—	45	29	23	70	45	14	28
Benin	107	103	35	49	29	39	52	38	15	31
Djibouti	107	98	—	—	33	—	73	67	—	—
Guinea-Bissau	108	105	—	48	27	—	55	44	—	72
Chad	107	103	10	42	31	14	44	25	11	21
Somalia	107	110	20	39	31	—	57	58	22	64
Gambia	108	103	—	41	23	—	73	45	—	69
Mali	107	106	36	59	27	43	58	44	14	20
Niger	107	102	33	82	40	43	61	44	17	89
Burkina Faso	107	102	23	32	54	42	64	56	27	96
Afghanistan	102	94	15	32	12	13	52	45	18	9
Sierra Leone	108	104	44	37	26	—	75	57	20	49
Guinea	102	102	33	38	20	36	50	36	12	43
All developing countries	104	96	54	72	58	61	94	74	51	52
Least-developed countries	104	100	38	58	43	44	81	58	28	48
Sub-Saharan Africa	107	102	42	64	46	52	85	64	32	55
Industrial countries	110	106	—	—	99	—	—	—	—	77
World	106	99	—	—	72	—	—	—	—	56

Note: All figures are expressed in relation to the male average, which is indexed to equal 100. The smaller the figure the bigger the gap, the closer the figure to 100 the smaller the gap, and a figure above 100 indicates that the female average is higher than the male.

Source: United Nations Development Programme, *Human Development Report 1993* (1993), pp. 152–53.

VI.D.2. Women's Share of Poverty*

The relative intensity of women's poverty is apparent from data on: (1) the income of households that are headed by women, and (2) the productivity and earnings of women's work in developing countries. This selection reviews the evidence related to these measures and describes some of the factors that explain why income tends to be lowest in women-headed households and why women's work is less productive than men's work and the lowest paid.

*From Mayra Buvinic and Margaret A. Lycette, "Women, Poverty and Development in the Third World," in John P. Lewis, ed., *Strengthening the Poor: What Have We Learned?* (Overseas Development Council, 1989), pp. 150–56, 160–61. © 1989. Reprinted by permission from Transaction Publishers.

The Poverty of Women-Headed Households

The incidence of households headed by women is increasing rapidly in the Third World. In Africa in the 1980s, the seasonal migration of males seeking work abroad or in domestic urban labor markets has resulted in large numbers of rural households headed by "left behind" women. From one-third to one-half of all rural households are at any one time headed by women in, for example, Botswana, Kenya, and Zambia. In the Arab, Islamic countries of North Africa, the male exodus has created women-headed households on a large scale, even though this household category is scarcely recognized in the applicable family law. In Latin America and in the Caribbean region, steady rural-to-urban migration of young women since the 1960s—combined with marital abandonment and unstable unions—has led to a heavy incidence of households headed by women in the urban areas.

The available data show that in rural Africa, in the Commonwealth Caribbean territories, and in urban Latin America, women-headed households are poorer than those jointly headed or headed by men. In Latin America, comparative analyses of the earnings of household heads show that the type of occupation, rather than age or education, explains most of the differential earnings between male and female heads. Female-headed households also are poorer because they have fewer secondary earners and more dependents to support than male-headed households. The pattern is the same in the English-speaking Caribbean. Similarly, in Africa, comparisons of male and female household heads reveal no significant differences as to age and education. Instead, women-headed households are poorer because they have fewer resident working members than male-headed households, but more dependents and smaller landholdings. It is also true that these households are much less likely to have access to productive services such as agricultural extension and credit for more explicitly gender reasons. In any event, in Latin America, the Caribbean, and Africa, female-headed households are on average distinctly worse off.

The situation in Asia is more hopeful in that poverty does not seem to be concentrated on women-headed households. Evidence from India, Nepal, Sri Lanka, Taiwan, and peninsular Malaysia indicated that women-headed households are not found disproportionately among the bottom deciles of the household distributions of per capita income and expenditure. This is probably due to the fact that in Asia—in contrast to Africa and Latin America—few women of prime reproductive age have sole responsibility for the care of young children and the extended family household is more common. Even in Asia, however, a substantial number of women, often widows, do head households, especially among the lower castes.

Women's Earnings

Women-headed households are not the only cases of poverty among women—nor should they be the only ones targeted for gender-oriented interventions. Women in male- and jointly-headed households contribute to family income through both unremunerated home labor and production for income, and the low compensation some of them receive keeps their households' incomes in the poverty zone.

To a large extent, the poverty of women (including heads of households) is related to the type of work women do and the meager returns they obtain for it. Their lower earnings are a direct function of their limited access to capital and modern technologies. Women perform low-productivity, labor-intensive work both as homemakers and income earners. The result is overwork and low pay for women and harder times for their families.

Moreover, the poorer the country, the more hours women work. In parts of East Africa, for example, women work sixteen hours a day doing housework, caring for children, preparing food, and raising 60–80 percent of the food for the family. In Burkina Faso, women have only a little more than one hour a day in which to perform personal care, undertake community responsibilities, and engage in leisure activities. In fact, in all regions women devote significantly more time than men to a combination of work for income and home maintenance, food preparation, and childcare. As the demand for child-rearing time and for cash income increases over the household life cycle, women's work hours increase and leisure decreases. The burdens of poverty are aggravated when women, out of need, seek work in the marketplace and, because of their lack of assets, undertake low-productivity work in agriculture, in the informal non-ag-

TABLE 1. 1980 Distribution of Economically Active Population by Sector (percentage)

	Agriculture		Industry		Services	
	Males	Females	Males	Females	Males	Females
Latin America and Caribbean	38	15	28	20	34	66
Asia	63	71	17	13	21	16
Africa	64	78	15	6	21	17

Source: International Labour Office, *Economically Active Population, 1950–2025*, Vols. I, II, III, and V (Geneva: ILO, 1986).

ricultural sector, or in the lowest paid sectors of the modern economy.

In agriculture, because of limited access to credit and modern technologies and services, women's work is labor-intensive and yields very low economic returns. This has been documented for countries as disparate as Cameroon, Indonesia, and Peru. Women wage laborers in agriculture are hired for lower-paid agricultural tasks and/or are paid less than men for similar work. In Sri Lanka they receive only 66–75 percent of the male wage, while in Honduras they are paid about 70 percent of the male wage for performing the same tasks in tobacco cultivation.

In industry and services, women tend to be clustered in low-skilled jobs with little potential for training or advancement. While the proportion of women among unskilled industrial workers is less than 30 percent in developed countries, it is higher than 50 percent in some Asian and African countries. In Latin American countries, women workers tend to be concentrated in lower-status occupations in the service sector rather than in industry. In Brazil, Chile, and Peru, for example, over 50 percent of economically active urban women work in services—a low-wage sector in those countries.

Unable to gain better-paid, formal sector employment, increasing numbers of women have turned to self-employment in the informal sector—either as a supplement to formal sector earnings or as their sole source of support. In much of the Third World, the informal sector rivals formal employment as a source of jobs for both men and women. In Bombay and Jakarta, for example, as well as in many African and Latin American cities, 50 to 60 percent of the labor force is employed in the informal sector, which is often the fastest-growing segment of the economy. Informal sector employment tends to be labor-intensive and to have low output per worker. This is reflected in the close association between informal employment and lower average earnings, particularly for women. In Kenya in 1978, for example, 41 percent of informally employed women—compared with 13.8 percent of men—had incomes of less than 199 shillings. In Bolivia, 48 percent of the self-employed in La Paz in 1983 were women, and their average weekly earnings were 70 percent of those of men.

Even if much of women's increased participation in product and labor markets yields low economic returns, it often makes a crucial difference to family well-being.

The Economic Contributions of Poor Women

Three indicators of the importance of women's earnings in low-income developing-country households are their proportional representation in household budgets, their role in promoting child nutritional status, and their importance in periods of economic crisis.

Women's Earnings in Low-Income Households

Studies have repeatedly shown that the earnings of adult women are proportionately more important in poor families than among the better off. In Indonesia, women and girls of poor landless families, unlike those of upper-income families, devote almost as much time to wage labor as do men and boys. In the Peruvian Sierra, women from landless peasant households provide 35 percent of the total number of family labor days devoted to agricultural production, while women from the middle and rich peasantry provide only 21 percent. Moreover, it is mainly the women in poor near-landless and smallholder households who resort to wage labor or artisan activities to supplement family incomes; in so doing, they are adversely affected by the differential returns to male and female labor.

Women's Earnings and Child Nutrition

Joanne Leslie's 1987 critical review of fifty empirical studies on the relationship between women's market work, infant feeding practices, and child nutrition demonstrates that children of higher-income-earning mothers are nutritionally better off than children of lower-income earners. Efforts to raise women's incomes are critical to the provision of high-quality foods for infants and children.

In the case of women heads of household it is possible that the additional meager income from market work may not compensate for the time lost in child (and self) care, especially since these women may have little access to alternative child caretakers. Nevertheless, evidence for rural Africa suggests that children may actually be nutritionally better off in households headed by women. This is largely because women heads of household have more control over income, and resources controlled by women are more likely to be allocated to family food expenditures. In Kenya, for example, female-headed households (controlled for land size and household composition) allocate a greater proportion of income toward supplying high-calorie foods than do male-headed households.

Women's Earnings in Periods of Economic Adversity

As happened during the Great Depression in the United States, adverse economic conditions in developing economies in the early 1980s seem to have increased the participation of poor women in formal and informal labor markets to help compensate for the loss in real family incomes. In rural Africa, poorer women farmers and nearly landless women have responded to economic contraction and food insecurity by increasing the time they devote to farming marginal lands and to low-productivity informal sector activities.

In Latin America, during the economic crises of the early 1980s, women's labor force participation rates generally increased more than those of men, leveling off or declining during periods of relative economic recovery. In Chile, for example, despite a long-term downward trend in women's labor force participation, women's activity rates in the lowest quintile of household incomes increased sharply—from 18 percent to 22.4 percent—during the economic crisis of 1974–75. Over the same period, the participation rates of women in the higher quintiles of the income distribution declined.

From the foregoing, it is clear that attempts to expand women's economic opportunities and increase their earnings should be a preferred anti-poverty strategy. The next sections examine problems such efforts must overcome and make some recommendations for policy reform.

Constraints on Gender-Related Reforms

Five major constraints have to be addressed in poverty–alleviation strategies that are intended to focus in whole or in part on the particular economic and social needs of women.

1. Perhaps the most important of these constraints is the virtually universal responsibility of women for household production chores such as childcare, food preparation, and provision of water and fuel-wood or other sources of cooking fuel. The dual burden of home labor and production for cash income has far-reaching implications for women's ability to invest the time often required to participate in and benefit from development programs.

2. Women's educational attainment in developing countries is severely limited, both relative to men and in absolute terms, in most world regions. Only in Latin America are there virtually identical enrollment rates for girls and boys through the secondary school level. Even in this region, however, functional literacy and numeracy rates among women—especially in rural areas—are still low. Until the educational imbalance between women and men is reduced, it will be impossible for adequate numbers of women to be trained for skilled occupations or to participate in development programs that depend on participants' ability to read and write.

3. Cultural dictates regarding the sexual division of labor in agriculture, formal employment, and, perhaps to a somewhat smaller degree, informal employment, can effectively bar women's participation in what often are the more lucrative areas of economic activity. Such dictates are reflected in, and in turn contribute to, biases regarding the extent, quality, and type of education available to women. Other biases regarding, for example, the types and levels of women's asset ownership and the "protection" of women, must also be dealt with in the design of many development programs, as such cultural factors often determine when and in what circumstances women can attend a training center or meet collateral conditions for loans.

4. Some of the restrictive cultural norms are enshrined in laws. In many countries, laws prohibit a woman's participation in education or family planning programs without the consent of her husband or father. More important, laws regarding title to land or housing can determine whether or not women—even women who head households—are able to participate in housing or credit programs; and protective labor laws may result in women being denied the chance to work and be paid for overtime or to work at all in certain occupations in which late night shifts are common.

5. Because of the factors cited, women are over-represented in the most marginally productive occupations and are among the smallest operators and producers. The scale of women's economic activities, in and of itself, increases the difficulty of reaching women through development programs.

These constraints translate into sectoral policy and program concerns and point to the need for alternative approaches in poverty–alleviation programs that hope to incorporate women. For example, women who operate micro-enterprises face particular constraints in access to credit. First, they may lack access to information about credit programs, especially when the latter are sponsored by organizations to which women do not belong. Because women are less educated than men, they are less likely to be able to fill out loan application forms. Collateral requirements, based on land or property ownership, are another serious constraint, since women seldom hold title to such assets. And in loan programs that accept business ownership as collateral, women may miss out because their businesses are too small or are not formally registered.

Women farmers typically face similar problems. Lack of title to land can block their access to agricultural credit, services, and inputs. In addition, women farmers rarely have direct contact with agricultural extension agents; and when they are reached, their limited education may prevent them from using agricultural information effectively. A study of six rural Peruvian communities revealed that 88 percent of women farmers had never been offered any agricultural extension services or advice, although 67 percent expressed strong interest in agricultural and livestock training.

Women's access to vocational training is also inhibited by many factors. Low-income and rural women especially are often precluded from participation in such programs by educational prerequisites, timing conflicts between instruction hours and inflexible work and family responsibilities, as well as distance and lack of cheap transport.

Moreover, when women do gain access to training, the effectiveness of the programs often is diminished by sex-biased curricula. Women's training typically concentrates in such traditionally female areas as cosmetology, hairdressing, and typing, while men predominate in such higher-paying areas as machine tool operation and motor vehicle mechanics.

Finally, because of their household responsibilities, women choose courses of short duration, which generally do not lead to high-paying jobs. In Argentina, for example, a recent survey found that 95 percent of the students in short-term training programs were women, while 92 percent of those in long-term training were men.

Conclusions and Recommendations

Given the degree of poverty among women in developing countries and the importance of their economic contributions to households, it is clear that anti-poverty strategies must be designed to address the social, legal, and economic constraints that women face.

An effective strategy for accomplishing this goal should include, first, a focus on women themselves rather than on women as members of households or families. Because there are critical differences in the types of work men and women perform, and in the ways in which they utilize income received, development interventions aimed at the household or family are not effective in alleviating women's poverty nor, in most cases, that of the children for whom women are almost universally responsible. Conversely, programs focused on women, when they are effective in raising women's productivity and income, produce benefits for family well-being.

Micro-enterprise interventions have been successful in reaching women largely because they have been designed to improve entrepreneurial, rather than family, income. Agriculture projects, however, must be reoriented to smallholders and should rely on a farming systems approach that takes into account women's roles as farmers and resource managers. Improvements in women's education and training will depend on the introduction of flexible class timing, incentives for parents to release girls from home production, and the removal of traditional biases regarding "appropriate" training for women.

At the policy level, the need to consider gender implications is becoming increasingly clear. Structural adjustment and other policy reform programs worldwide have produced a number of unforeseen problems because the role of women in various economic activities was not taken into account. To be effective, such reforms must be structured to assist women, not only men, to respond to price and other incentives. Similarly, broader changes in legal, financial, and educational systems must be undertaken in order to genuinely enhance women's social and economic contributions to development in the long term. There is a need to examine carefully, for instance, the ways in which legal inheritance patterns or protective labor legislation can reinforce women's disadvantaged economic position. Financial policies that encourage biases against, or reduce the profitability of, the types of borrowing that poor women seek must be revamped in order to maximize the productivity of women's work. And educational policies and funding must be changed to reflect the very high social and economic returns to women's primary education and literacy.

In essence, policymakers and development practitioners must consider gender differences, and the implications of development interventions for women, at each stage of policy and project development and for all social and economic sectors. Failure to do so may mean not only bypassing women in poverty–alleviation efforts, but perhaps even increasing their relative poverty.

VI.D.3. Market Gender Discrimination*

Most of the literature on discrimination focuses on the labor market. The most commonly deployed technique, the earnings function, is well suited to show one type of discrimination, namely, differentially low pay for the same characteristics. However, this is perhaps the less important aspect of labor market gender discrimination. The more important is differentially poor access. Evidence on this requires logistic techniques and sampling frames based upon households rather than employers. One such study, for rural Tanzania, found extreme discrimination in access to non-farm wage employment, which was the highest return activity. Access was determined largely by education, age, and gender: a 36-year-old man with secondary education had a three-in-four chance of such employment, whereas a woman of the same age and education had half of that chance. With completed primary education she had only a quarter of the chance, and with partial primary or less she had only one-fifth of the chance. This declension suggests that discrimination may apply differentially at different levels of education. Thus general expansion of the education system may reduce the aggregate incidence of discrimination even if the educational expansion is not targetted to women.

Since the rural non-agricultural labor market commonly contains a large public sector, discrimination is the outcome of government recruitment policies. In turn, this may reflect the use of public sector employment as part of a patronage system rather than its being a competitive entry based upon job-related characteristics. Women may because of their low status in society be badly represented in the lobby for patronage.

In urban areas, the labor market is probably the main arena of discrimination. However, in rural areas, non-agricultural wage employment can usually only be available to a minority of women because it is only available to a minority of men. Rather, it is the savings, credit, and financial markets where discrimination is more important because these constrain the earning capacities of women in agricultural self-employment.

Savings and Credit

Women are severely disadvantaged in the credit market: they usually do not own marketable land rights and hence have no collateral, and if subordinates in the household may have no capacity to establish reputations for creditworthiness as independent agents. Formal credit programs are usually channeled to household heads, and are commonly based on non-food crops in which men tend to specialise. It is very hard to see how these obstacles in the credit market can be overcome, except in the case of female-headed households. For this group, who have the capacity to build reputations, formal credit programs could be monitored to see whether discrimination is occurring. Where it is, it should be a relatively simple matter for a public credit program to be redirected to them as a target group.

However, where women are in male-headed households, which is the majority, the alternative is probably to rely upon the savings market. The latter suffers none of the problems intrinsic to the credit market: dependents can hold individual rights to financial assets. Once such assets are accumulated they fulfil the same functions as a credit line, namely, liquidity and the capacity to finance lumpy investments. It is notable that whereas men predominate as borrowers in both the formal and informal rural credit market, women predominate in the informal savings market (both as savers and even as lenders in many cases). A particularly interesting manifestation of this is the savings club. In this arrange-

*From Paul Collier, *Women in Developing Countries*, World Bank, Policy Research Working Paper 129 (December 1988), pp. 3–11. Reprinted by permission.

ment a group of women agree to make regular payments into a common fund, the whole sum being distributed on each occasion to the members of the group in turn, the sequence being determined by lot. This offers two advantages over individual savings: first, it enables any scale economies in expenditure to be reaped earlier, and secondly, the social pressure to make contributions enforces savings behaviour against both temporary lapses on the part of the saver and pressure on the woman from other claimants upon assets. The latter may be particularly difficult to resist because of the dependent status of the woman. To bring out the implications, public interventions in rural financial markets have overwhelmingly been on credit rather than the savings side of the market. Yet we have suggested that the former is intrinsically male biased, whereas the latter is far more likely to be gender neutral. Since the savings market can serve as a substitute for credit, it is therefore likely to be female biased. The neglect of the rural savings market by public programs would be less important were the informal savings market in a position to provide an adequate service. However, this is often not the case. First, due to problems of the high co-variance of withdrawals, informal savings institutions rarely develop (hence money lenders are far more common than deposit takers). Secondly, because of foreign exchange and interest rate controls, formal deposit-taking institutions are not in a position to offer a secure and positive real return upon assets to depositors, despite such returns being available on the world financial market. Thirdly, if as we have suggested, contractual savings schemes (which both compel saving and limit the capacity to make withdrawals) would be popular, this requires a degree of contractual enforcement and continuity more suited to formal than informal agencies. The design of rural formal savings schemes attractive to women is a priority because it contributes on several different fronts. Savings can finance long-term investment in the sectors in which women specialise, thereby rectifying a current misallocation of capital and possibly increasing the overall savings rate. They also provide a cushion for temporary negative shocks and a means of profiting in a sustained way from positive ones. Finally, when women command assets their status and bargaining position is improved, and financial assets being new they are not bound by the conventions which often restrict the major real assets, land and livestock, to male ownership.

Role Models

In rural Africa formal wage employment, non-food crops, and improved livestock are generally innovations of this century. The economy is in disequilibrium in the sense that the rates of return to factors differ systematically among activities. Typically, food production is at the bottom of this hierarchy and formal wage employment and new-technique agricultural investments are at the top. Women are a minority towards the top of the hierarchy and a majority at the bottom. Economic change in rural Africa is to a considerable extent a process of taking up these disequilibrium opportunities by switching into the higher return activities.

Women are at a disadvantage in this process: Bevan et al. (1986) establish that controlling for a wide range of other characteristics, female-headed households are radically less likely to adopt tree crops and improved livestock. Although this is partly due to discrimination, it appears also to be because of the enormous power of role models.

Bevan et al. demonstrated that a "copying effect" is decisive in the entry into new, high-return activities. The peasant population has access to a very restricted stream of trustworthy information, chiefly its own social network. This network is defined by family and spatial proximity. If this social network is indeed the chief determinant of economic innovation then the very fact that women are under-represented in high-return activities creates a powerful role model for its perpetuation. The externalities, which the copying effect constitute, provide a case for temporary positive discrimination to establish a countervailing role model.

The copying effect works both on states and on decisions. That is, in deciding to enter a new activity people are influenced both by the number of other people already in the activity and by the number of other people who have recently decided to enter it. Bevan et al. find that the copying effect is much more pronounced for decisions than for states: that is, the decisions currently being made are much more influential than past decisions. Hence, encouraging one woman to enter a high-return activity may have the same inducement to other women to follow as that provided to men by two men who are already in the activity. This is hopeful because it suggests that although role models are important, their inertial properties can be overcome.

Since gender is only one of the dimensions on which actors identify themselves, and hence appropriate role models, the copying effect can be enhanced by concentrating change among similar women (for example, geographically proximate, young, educated women).

Asymmetric Rights and Obligations

To some extent the household can be viewed as a set of implicit contracts which generate reciprocal rights and obligations. Typically, women incur obligations to grow food crops for subsistence, to gather fuel and water, to cook, and to rear children. In return, the man will provide land and will meet the cash needs of the household. This allocation is commonly unequal—women work much harder than men. This is clearly the case in much of rural Africa as measured by hours of work. It may also be inefficient, labor and land being imperfectly allocated between activities. Returns to factors are generally radically higher in non-food activities, consistent with the hypothesis that women work excessively on food crops because they cannot secure the land for, or would forfeit part of the income from non-food activities. Specialisation is not confined to food versus non-food crops. For example, in Kenya tea picking tends to be women's work. The adoption of tea was found to be significantly effected by the gender composition of the household labour endowment: the more female labor the more likely was the household to adopt the crop. Conversely in coffee, which tends to be a man's crop, adoption was encouraged only by additional male labor. A constant set of asymmetric rights and obligations may give rise to variable material circumstances. First, there may be asymmetric vulnerability—at times of crisis women may suffer relative to men. For example, work by Vaughan on famine in Malawi shows that men took the opportunity to out-migrate, leaving women with a collapse in subsistence production and a reduced command over cash to purchase food in the market. Women may be especially vulnerable to unanticipated rapid changes associated with slumps and rapid structural adjustment. If so this is worrying since the burden of adjustment costs should not, on equity grounds, be borne by an initially disadvantaged group. Further, since women spend disproportionately upon children, an adjustment that involves short-term costs and long-term gains (as most do), may inflict upon a cohort of children an intertemporal redistribution of consumption which is undesirable (because low but temporary levels of consumption in children may give rise to permanent effects). Secondly, changes in circumstances may make a given set of rights and obligations increasingly unequal or increasingly inefficient. For example, the emphasis upon technical progress and extension in non-food activities relative to food increases the returns to male labor relative to female labor, and factor allocations become less appropriate because of the restrictions upon substitution possibilities. As the returns to non-food activities rise, female labor and land constrained to food production represent an increasing misallocation.

However, this very specialisation by function makes it relatively easy to target programs for women (much easier than for poor households). For example, rural water, fuel, and health services are all pro-women. Water fetching is an arduous and time-consuming activity undertaken almost exclusively by women. Piped water is in effect the supply of leisure to women. Wood gathering for fuel is also a time-consuming female activity. The growing scarcity of such wood reflects the absence of private property rights which, if they are to be created, would most sensibly be vested in women. Reforestation programs have generally been targeted at men. The pricing of firewood substitutes such as kerosene is also, therefore, a woman's issue.

Reference

Bevan, D. L., et al. (1986). *Trade Shocks in Controlled Economies* (London: Oxford University Press).

VI.D.4. Missing Women*

In Europe and North America women tend to outnumber men. For example, in the United Kingdom, France, and the United States the ratio of women to men exceeds 1.05. In many Third World countries, however, especially in Asia and north Africa, the female:male ratio may be as low as 0.95 (Egypt), 0.94 (Bangladesh, China, and west Asia), 0.93 (India), or even 0.90 (Pakistan). These differences are relevant to an

*From Amartya Sen, "Missing Women," *British Medical Journal* 304 (1992): 587–88. Reprinted by permission.

assessment of female inequality across the world.[1]

Everywhere about 5 percent more boys than girls are born. But women are hardier than men and, given similar care, survive better at all ages—including in utero. There are other causes for this preponderance of women—for example, some remaining impact of the deaths of men in the last world war and more cigarette smoking and violent deaths among men. But even taking these into account, women would still outnumber men if given similar care.[2]

Social factors must therefore explain the low female:male ratios in Asian and north African countries. These countries would have millions more women if they showed the female:male ratios of Europe and the United States.[3] Calculated on this basis, China is missing more than 50 million women.

Using European or American ratios may not, however, be appropriate. Because of lower female mortality in Europe and America the female:male ratio rises gradually with age. A lower ratio would therefore be expected in Asia and north Africa partly because of a lower life expectancy and higher fertility rate. There are several ways of adjusting for this. One is to adopt the female:male ratios of Sub-Saharan Africa, where there is little female disadvantage in terms of relative mortality but where life expectancy is no higher and fertility rates no lower than those in Asia and north Africa. Using the Sub-Saharan ratio of 1.022 yields an estimate of 44 million missing women in China, 37 million in India, and a total of more than 100 million worldwide.[4]

Using population models based on Western demographic experience, it is possible to esti-

mate roughly how many women there would be without any female disadvantage in survival, given the actual life expectancy and the fertility rates in these countries. Coale estimates 29 million missing women in China, 23 million in India, and an overall total of 60 million for selected countries.[5] Though lower, these numbers are still enormous.

Why is overall mortality for females higher than that for males in these countries? Consider India, where age specific mortality for females consistently exceeds that for males until the fourth decade. Although the excess mortality at childbearing age may be partly due to material mortality, obviously no such explanation is possible for female disadvantage in survival in infancy and childhood. Despite occasional distressing accounts of female infanticide, this could not explain the extra mortality or its age distribution. The comparative neglect of female health and nutrition, especially—but not exclusively—during childhood, would seem the prime suspect. Considerable direct evidence exists of neglect of female children in terms of health care, admission to hospitals, and even feeding.[6]

Even though the position in India has been more extensively studied than that in other countries, similar evidence of relative neglect of the health and nutrition of female children may be found in other countries in Asia and north Africa. In China some evidence suggests that the extent of neglect may have increased sharply in recent years, particularly since compulsory restrictions on the size of families were introduced in some parts of the country in the late 1970s. There are also some new, ominous signs in China, such as a substantial increase in the reported ratio of male to female births—quite out of line with the rest of the world. It could quite possibly indicate ''hiding'' of newborn female children (to avoid the rigours of compulsory restriction on the size of the family), but it could, no less plausibly, reflect a higher female infant mortality—whether or not induced (with new births and new deaths both going unreported).

What causes the relative neglect of females, and how can it be changed? Possible influences

[1]A. K. Sen, *Resources, Values and Development* (1984), pp. 346–85, and ''Women's Survival as a Development Problem,'' *Bulletin of the American Academy of Arts and Sciences* 43 (1989): 14–29; J. Kynch, ''How Many Woman Are Enough? Sex Ratios and the Right to Life,'' in *Third World Affairs 1985*, ed. A. Gauhar (1985), pp. 156–72; B. Harriss and E. Watson, ''The Sex Ratio in South Asia,'' in *Geography of Gender in the Third World*, ed. J. H. Momson and J. Townsend (1987), pp. 85–115; J. Drèze and A. K. Sen, *Hunger and Public Action* (1989), pp. 50–59, 221–25; A. J. Coale, ''Excess Female Mortality and the Balance of the Sexes in the Population: An Estimate of the Number of 'Missing Females,' '' *Population and Development Review* 17 (1991): 517–23.

[2]I. Waldron, ''The Role of Genetic and Biological Factors in Sex Differences in Mortality,'' in *Sex Differences in Mortality*, ed. A. D. Lopez and L. T. Ruzicka (1983).

[3]Sen, ''Women's Survival as a Development Problem.''

[4]Drèze and Sen, *Hunger and Public Action.*

[5]Coale, ''Excess Female Mortality and the Balance of the Sexes in the Population.''

[6]L. Chen, E. Huq, and S. D'Souza, ''Sex Bias in the Family Allocation of Food and Health Care in Rural Bangladesh,'' *Population and Development Review* 7 (1981): 55–70; A. K. Sen, *Commodities and Capabilities* (1985), pp. 81–104.

include traditional cultures and values. But some economic links have also emerged, and some connections between economic status and social standing have been identified. For example, the ability to earn an outside income through paid employment seems to enhance the social standing of a woman (which is the case in Sub-Saharan Africa). This makes her contribution to the prosperity of the family more visible. Also, being less dependent on others, she has more voice. The higher status of women also affects ideas on the female child's "due." Secondly, education, especially female literacy, may make a substantial difference. Thirdly, women's economic rights (for example, land ownership and inheritance) may be important.[7] Public policy can influence all of these.

The Indian state of Kerala provides an illuminating exception to the prevailing experience.

It has the most developed school education system in India, which dates from the early nineteenth century, with strongly supportive state policies in the "native kingdoms" of Travancore and Cochin.[8] Adult literacy rate is now over 90 percent. Property inheritance passes through the female line for an influential part of the community (the Nairs). Many women participate in "gainful" economic activities. Kerala also has an extensive health care system, which has been built up through public policy. Even though Kerala is one of the poorer Indian states, life expectancy at birth there now exceeds 73 years for women and 67 years for men.

The female:male ratio of the Kerala population is now around 1.04—similar to that in Europe and America (and most unlike that in the rest of India, Bangladesh, Pakistan, China, west Asia, and north Africa). It seems that the "missing women" may be rescuable, after all, by public policy.

[7]E. Boserup, *Women's Role in Economic Development* (1970), pp. 15–154; A. K. Sen, "Gender and Cooperative Conflict," in *Persistent Inequalities*, ed. I. Tinker (1990), pp. 123–49.

[8]Drèze and Sen, *Hunger and Public Action.*

Comment: Gender-Aware Analysis

Numerous gender studies indicate that economic analysis that is aware of gendered relationships can provide a better understanding of the development process and a better understanding of policies required to diminish gender inequality. See Diane Elson, "Gender-Aware Analysis and Development Economics," *Journal of International Development* 5 (1993), and Diane Elson, ed., *Male Bias in the Development Process* (1991).

Also of special significance are Janet Momsen and Vivian Kinnaird, *Different Plans, Different Voices* (1993); Caroline O. N. Moser, *Gender Planning and Development* (1993); John Humphrey, *Gender and Work in the Third World* (1987); Esther Boserup, *Women's Role in Economic Development* (1970); K. Young, ed., *Of Marriage and the Market* (1984); N. Long, ed., *Family and Work in Rural Societies* (1984); J. Nash and P. Fernandes-Kelly, *Women, Men and the International Division of Labor* (1983); and S. Joekes, *Women in the World Economy* (1987).

A number of empirical studies focus on gender asymmetry in intrahousehold activities—distribution of food, health, education. See Mark M. Pitt et al., "Productivity, Health, and Inequality in the Intrahousehold Distribution of Food in Low-Income Countries," *American Economic Review* (December 1990); Jere Behrman, "Intrahousehold Allocation of Nutrients in Rural India," *Oxford Economic Papers* (March 1988); Jere Behrman and Barbara Wolfe, "How Does Mothers' Schooling Affect Family Health, Nutrition, Medical Care Usage, and Household Sanitation?" *Journal of Econometrics* 36 (1987); and Duncan Thomas, "Intra-Household Resource Allocation," *Journal of Human Resources* (Fall 1990).

Gender studies are especially prominent in analyzing women's role in agriculture. They examine how the division of labor by task, field, and product, as well as how different people's access to land and to each other's labor, affect choices of crop and technology. See Uma Lele, "Women and Structural Transformation," *Economic Development and Cultural Change* (January 1986); C. D. Deere, "The Division of Labor by Sex in Agriculture," *Economic Development and Cultural Change* (July 1982); Amartya Sen, "Gender and Cooperative Conflicts" in *Persistent Inequalities: Women and World Development,* ed. I. Tinker (1990); and Ann Whitehead, *Female Farmers in Africa* (1990).

VI.E. NUTRITION AND HEALTH

VI.E.1. Nutrition Actions*

It may be fair at this point to offer the following conclusions about the nutrition problem:

- Malnutrition is a problem of major proportions.
- The nutritional condition of the poor is no better than it was a decade ago. In many countries it is worse.
- The nutrition problem is not likely to be resolved in most countries within a generation by increasing incomes and agricultural production.
- The basic problem is food-energy insufficiency, sometimes complicated by deficiencies of specific nutrients.
- The principal victims are the very poor, especially the rural poor. Most governments are not reaching them with the benefits of nutrition; few have central ministries with the outreach to do so.

Commonly expressed goals to eradicate malnutrition in the near future are unrealistic. The aim should be to overcome malnutrition in those areas, forms, and population groups in which it exerts the greatest drag on development. The problem exists in almost all countries, but within countries it differs significantly among various income groups, occupations, and regions. Malnutrition in Northeast Brazil, for example, is as severe as it is in parts of South Asia. The largest problem in sheer numbers is the Indian subcontinent. The largest problem by proportion of population in need is in Sahelian Africa, Bangladesh, and parts of Central America. In most parts of the world, supply of food has kept ahead of population growth. In Sub-Saharan Africa, however, food production per capita has been declining for a decade. Life expectancy is fifteen years less than in Asia and may well become worse.

The need for nutritional help exists among people of all ages and both sexes, not just small children and pregnant and lactating women. The problem is particularly serious among families of landless agricultural laborers, farmers with small landholdings that rural development programs do not reach, small-scale fishermen, and the urban unemployed. Together they constitute more than half the malnourished in most countries. Their nutritional condition reflects inadequacies in the availability of food, in economic and sometimes physical access to the food that is available, in knowledge of the best way to use the available resources, and in health practices that affect biological use of the food that is consumed.

Accordingly, nutrition efforts should be designed to expand food supplies—increasing production and reducing food losses—in ways that will benefit the poor, with attention focused on what is grown, who grows it, and what is stored; to increase the incomes of the poor, to improve their access to food by improving the marketing system and adjusting price policies in ways that benefit consumers without creating a disincentive to producers and by setting up special feeding programs; to try through education to bring about changes in food preferences, in the distribution of food within families, and in hygiene; to improve health and environmental conditions—water, sanitation, immunization, and management of diarrhea—and to attack specific problems of micronutrient deficiencies with mass-dose capsules or through fortification of food staples. Some changes can best—or perhaps only—be brought about through changes in government policies; others can be attacked directly through nutrition projects.

The effectiveness of different nutrition efforts and the relative importance of various determinants of malnutrition under differing conditions are now better understood than they were five years ago. Although increasing income is fundamental to increasing food consumption, for example, it is now seen to be less efficient than lowering food prices. From tightly controlled field studies it has been learned that, in addition to equity benefits, increasing the amount of food consumed and improving nutrition in other ways can significantly increase the weights and heights of total populations of children and improve their nutritional status—or at least prevent or retard its rate of deterioration. It is possible to suggest what it costs through nutrition ser-

*From Alan Berg, *Malnourished People: A Policy View* (Washington, D.C., 1981), pp. 47–51. Reprinted by permission.

vices to avert death at an early age, to avert a day of illness, to gain an extra centimeter in growth, and to increase psychomotor development scores by a percentage point. Even some general effects of broad nutrition programs can be predicted.

Priorities

Despite the high degree of variability in nutritional needs among countries and in the causes of and appropriate responses to those needs, there are certain strategies that merit high priority in most countries. Accelerated growth in the incomes of the poor and—with few exceptions—in food production continue to be of primary importance. Attention needs to be given to the development of nutrition-oriented agricultural production policies and programs. And to ensure that food reaches those in need, food-demand programs, including the strong possibility in many instances of food subsidies, are required. Broad programs, such as general consumer food subsidies, may under some circumstances be as effective in reaching target groups as narrow efforts, such as institutional feeding programs designed to reach children of preschool age. Clearly, however, subsidy programs should concentrate on low-income groups instead of all income groups, on regional rather than countrywide programs, and on seasonal rather than year-round aid. Most of the larger developing countries already have sizable subsidy programs. Concentration should be on increasing their effect on nutrition, improving their efficiency in the process.

These are new areas of emphasis that can complement the well-known direct programs— nutrition education, fortification of staples with micronutrients, incorporation of nutrition-related actions into health services. The priorities that public officials assign to these various actions will depend on their countries' nutrition problems and the causes of them, the distribution of malnutrition between rural and urban areas, the extent to which the rural malnourished are small-farm families, the probable cost-effectiveness of possible programs, the institutional strength and funding capacity to mount programs, and political constraints.

The actions selected should have the aim of causing a specific improvement in specific nutritional deficiencies of a specific population within a stated period. They should be well defined as to content, costs, timing, location, and means of execution. When information to determine all this is not sufficient, projects can be developed for laying the groundwork. Action should not be limited to the gathering of data, but every operational program should include a track for evaluation and for learning from experience. Nutrition work in a country with an information base and experience in nutrition programs, such as Costa Rica, India, or the Philippines, would be very different from work in a country that had previously given little attention to nutrition.

The complexity of the nutrition problem and the multiplicity of potential nutrition actions should not be allowed to dictate complex projects. Projects should be broadly conceived with regard to content, but they should not be expected to address the many factors that affect nutritional status. Complex projects have generally been found difficult to implement effectively. Whenever it is feasible, there should be a sharp focus on a small number of critically needed actions.

Nutrition actions should be designed in ways that limit the need for managerial skills, of which many countries have a shortage. Similarly, there needs to be a clear focal point for administration of projects—multiministerial coordinating mechanisms have not proved to be particularly promising in accelerating actions. Generally a single agency should be made responsible for nutrition projects—whether an agriculture, health, or social welfare ministry, or a planning agency will depend on the nature of the project and the practices and preferences of government.

Nutrition in Agriculture

In countries where actions involving agriculture can make a significant contribution to meeting chronic needs in nutrition—urban as well as rural—specific agriculture projects designed to have an effect on nutrition should be considered. Nutrition should also be inserted as an explicit objective in agricultural and rural development projects aimed at improving the well-being of low-income groups whenever it is feasible. Malnutrition sometimes is used as a justification for such projects, but nutrition goals are not explicitly included in project objectives, and any nutritional gains occur largely by coincidence. Improvements in nutrition must be accepted as an important objective of these projects and the costs of possible actions must be taken into account. Nutrition actions should not be undertaken if their negative effects on other project goals would more than offset the gains from other actions. But modest reorientation of project designs can sometimes have significant nutritional effects without causing unacceptable changes in the achievement of other goals. When benefits of various goals are conflicting, the tradeoffs among the various goals should be weighed.

In certain agricultural and urban projects the addition of nutrition objectives might improve project design. The importance of nutrition to objectives and design will differ among projects. In Nepal, for example, a rural development project was based on an understanding of the way food consumption in the region was related to need; designation of project components, including the selection of crops, flowed from this understanding. A project in the Southern Highlands in Papua New Guinea, involving a shift from subsistence crops to cash crops, was modified to provide extension services that would help increase production in family food gardens and to include other assurances that the modernization effort would not be nutritionally negative. In Malaysia the design for a resettlement project in south Kelantan provided means for settlers to meet their nutritional needs during the first seven years, before rubber trees could be tapped. The government thus withheld a portion of the land for food crops, helped to build and stock community fish ponds, and provided nutrition education.

Often the steps required to incorporate nutritional goals are relatively easy to plan and implement—as, for example, in the choice of crops to emphasize in agricultural research projects—and need not be administratively or analytically complex. . . .

Nutrition in Health

The interaction of malnutrition and infection has a far more serious effect on individuals than the combined effect of the two working independently. Consequently, the effects of nutrition actions and health programs undertaken simultaneously are greater than the sum of their effects on the same populations would be if the actions were undertaken separately. Since integration of nutrition with health services is a particularly efficient way of using limited resources, improved nutrition should be considered an explicit objective in all relevant health work. Problems associated with acute forms of malnutrition and vitamin and mineral deficiencies can be much more productively attacked through health services than can the low levels of performance associated with chronic food deprivation. . . .

VI.E.2. Health Policy*

Despite remarkable improvements, enormous health problems remain. Absolute levels of mortality in developing countries remain unacceptably high: child mortality rates are about ten times higher than those in the established market economies. If death rates among children in poor countries were reduced to those prevailing in the rich countries, 11 million fewer children would die each year. Almost half of these preventable deaths are a result of diarrheal and respiratory illness, exacerbated by malnutrition. In addition, every year 7 million adults die of conditions that could be inexpensively prevented or cured; tuberculosis alone causes 2 million of these

*From World Bank, *World Development Report 1993* (New York: World Bank by Oxford University Press, 1993), pp. 1–8. Reprinted by permission.

deaths. About 400,000 women die from the direct complications of pregnancy and childbirth. Maternal mortality ratios are, on average, thirty times as high in developing countries as in high-income countries.

Although health has improved even in the poorest countries, the pace of progress has been uneven. In 1960 in Ghana and Indonesia about one child in five died before reaching age 5—a child mortality rate typical of many developing countries. By 1990 Indonesia's rate had dropped to about one-half the 1960 level, but Ghana's had fallen only slightly. Table 1 provides a summary of regional progress in mortality reduction between 1975 and 1990.

In addition to premature mortality, a substantial portion of the burden of disease consists of disability, ranging from polio-related paralysis to blindness to the suffering brought about by severe psychosis. To measure the burden of disease, this Report uses the disability-adjusted life year (DALY), a measure that combines healthy life years lost because of premature mortality with those lost as a result of disability.

There is huge variation in per person loss of DALYs across regions, mainly because of differences in premature mortality; regional differences in loss of DALYs as a result of disability are much smaller. The total loss of DALYs is referred to as the global burden of disease.

The world is facing serious new health challenges. By 2000 the growing toll from acquired immune deficiency syndrome (AIDS) in developing countries could easily rise to more than 1.8 million deaths annually, erasing decades of hard-won reductions in mortality. The malaria parasite's increased resistance to available drugs could lead to a doubling of malaria deaths, to nearly 2 million a year within a decade. Rapid progress in reducing child mortality and fertility rates will create new demands on health care systems as the aging of populations brings to the fore costly noncommunicable diseases of adults and the elderly. Tobacco-related deaths from heart disease and cancers alone are likely to double by the first decade of the next century, to 2 million a year, and, if present smoking patterns continue, they will grow to more than 12 million

a year in developing countries in the second quarter of the next century.

Health Systems and Their Problems

Although health services are only one factor in explaining past successes, the importance of their role in the developing world is not in doubt. Public health measures brought about the eradication of smallpox and have been central to the reduction in deaths caused by vaccine-preventable childhood diseases. Expanded and improved clinical care has saved millions of lives from infectious diseases and injuries. But there are also major problems with health systems that, if not resolved, will hamper progress in reducing the burden of premature mortality and disability and frustrate efforts to respond to new health challenges and emerging disease threats.

• *Misallocation.* Public money is spent on health interventions of low cost-effectiveness, such as surgery for most cancers, at the same time that critical and highly cost-effective interventions, such as treatment of tuberculosis and sexually transmitted diseases (STDs), remain underfunded. In some countries a single teaching hospital can absorb 20 percent or more of the budget of the ministry of health, even though almost all cost-effective interventions are best delivered at lower-level facilities.

TABLE 1. Population, Economic Indicators, and Progress in Health by Demographic Region, 1975–90

	Population, 1990 (millions)	Deaths, 1990 (millions)	Income per Capita		Child Mortality		Life Expectancy at Birth (years)	
Region			Dollars, 1990	Growth Rate, 1975–90 (percent per year)	1975	1990	1975	1990
Sub-Saharan Africa	510	7.9	510	−1.0	212	175	48	52
India	850	9.3	360	2.5	195	127	53	58
China	1,134	8.9	370	7.4	85	43	56	69
Other Asia and islands	683	5.5	1,320	4.6	135	97	56	62
Latin America and the Caribbean	444	3.0	2,190	−0.1	104	60	62	70
Middle Eastern crescent	503	4.4	1,720	−1.3	174	111	52	61
Demographically developing group[a]	4,123	39.1	900	3.0	152	106	56	63
World	5,267	50.0	4,000	1.2	135	96	60	65

Note: Child mortality is the probability of dying between birth and age 5, expressed per 1,000 live births; life expectancy at birth is the average number of years that a person would expect to live at the prevailing age-specific mortality rates.

[a]The countries of the demographic regions Sub-Saharan Africa, India, China, Other Asia and islands, Latin America and the Caribbean, and Middle Eastern crescent.

Source: For income per capita, World Bank data.

• *Inequity.* The poor lack access to basic health services and receive low-quality care. Government spending for health goes disproportionately to the affluent in the form of free or below-cost care in sophisticated public tertiary care hospitals and subsidies to private and public insurance.

• *Inefficiency.* Much of the money spent on health is wasted: brand-name pharmaceuticals are purchased instead of generic drugs, health workers are badly deployed and supervised, and hospital beds are underutilized.

• *Exploding costs.* In some middle-income developing countries health care expenditures are growing much faster than income. Increasing numbers of general physicians and specialists, the availability of new medical technologies, and expanding health insurance linked to fee-for-service payments together generate a rapidly growing demand for costly tests, procedures, and treatments.

World health spending—and thus also the potential for misallocation, waste, and inequitable distribution of resources—is huge. For the world as a whole in 1990, public and private expenditure on health services was about $1,700 billion, or 8 percent of total world product. High-income countries spent almost 90 percent of this amount, for an average of $1,500 per person. The United States alone consumed 41 percent of the global total—more than 12 percent of its gross national product (GNP). Developing countries spent about $170 billion, or 4 percent of their GNP, for an average of $41 per person— less than one-thirtieth the amount spent by rich countries.

In the *low-income countries* government hospitals and clinics, which account for the greatest part of the modern medical care provided, are often inefficient, suffering from highly centralized decision-making, wide fluctuations in budgetary allocations, and poor motivation of facility managers and health care workers. Private providers—mainly religious nongovernmental organizations (NGOs) in Africa and private doctors and unlicensed practitioners in South Asia—are often more technically efficient than the public sector and offer a service that is perceived to be of higher quality, but they are not supported by government policies. In low-income countries the poor often lose out in health because public spending in the sector is heavily skewed toward high-cost hospital services that disproportionately benefit better-off urban groups. In Indonesia, despite concerted government efforts in the 1980s to improve health services for the poor, government subsidies to health for the richest 10 percent of households in 1990 were still almost three times the subsidies going to the poorest 10 percent of Indonesians.

In *middle-income countries* governments frequently subsidize insurance that protects only the relatively wealthy—a small, affluent minority in the case of private insurance in South Africa and Zimbabwe and, in Latin America, the larger industrial labor force covered by compulsory public insurance (so-called social insurance). The bulk of the population, especially the poor, relies heavily on out-of-pocket payments and on government services that may be largely inaccessible to them. In Peru, for example, more than 60 percent of the poor have to travel for more than an hour to obtain primary health care, as compared with less than 3 percent of the better-off. The quality of care is also low: drugs and equipment are in short supply, patient waiting times are long and medical consultations are short; and misdiagnoses and inappropriate treatment are common. . . .

The Roles of the Government and of the Market in Health

Three rationales for a major government role in the health sector should guide the reform of health systems.

• Many health-related services such as information and control of contagious disease are *public goods.* One person's use of health information does not leave less available for others to consume; one person cannot benefit from control of malaria-carrying mosquitoes while another person in the same area is excluded. Because private markets alone provide too little of the public goods crucial for health, government involvement is necessary to increase the supply of these goods. Other health services have large *externalities*: consumption by one individual affects others. Immunizing a child slows transmission of measles and other diseases, conferring a positive externality. Polluters and drunk drivers create negative health externalities. Governments need to encourage behaviors that carry positive externalities and to discourage those with negative externalities.

• Provision of cost-effective health services to the poor is an effective and socially acceptable approach to *poverty reduction.* Most countries view access to basic health care as a human right. This perspective is embodied in the goal, "Health for All by the Year 2000," of the conference held by the World Health Organization (WHO) and the United Nations Children's Fund (UNICEF) at Alma-Ata in 1978, which launched today's primary health care movement. Private markets will not give the poor adequate access to essential clinical services or the insurance often needed to pay for such services. Public finance of essential clinical care is thus justified to alleviate poverty. Such public funding can take several forms: subsidies to private providers and NGOs that serve the poor; vouchers that the poor can take to a provider of their choice; and free or below-cost delivery of public services to the poor.

• Government action may be needed to compensate for problems generated by *uncertainty* and *insurance market failure.* The great uncertainties surrounding the probability of illness and the efficacy of care give rise both to strong demand for insurance and to shortcomings in the operation of private markets. One reason why markets may work poorly is that variations in health risk create incentives for insurance companies to refuse to insure the very people who most need health insurance—those who are already sick or are likely to become ill. A second has to do with "moral hazard"; insurance reduces the incentives for individuals to avoid risk and expense by prudent behavior and can create both incentives and opportunities for doctors and hospitals to give patients more care than they need. A third has to do with the asymmetry in information between provider and patient concerning the outcomes of intervention; providers advise patients on choice of treatment, and when the providers' income is linked to this advice, excessive treatment can result. As a consequence of these last two considerations, in unregulated private markets costs escalate without appreciable health gains to the patient. Governments have an important role to play in regulating privately provided health insurance, or in mandating alternatives such as social insurance, in order to ensure widespread coverage and hold down costs.

If governments do intervene, they must do so intelligently, or they risk exacerbating the very problems they are trying to solve. When gov-

ernments become directly involved in the health sector—by providing public health programs or financing essential clinical services for the poor—policymakers face difficult decisions concerning the allocation of public resources. For any given amount of total spending, taxpayers and, in some countries, donors want to see maximum health gain for the money spent. An important source of guidance for achieving value for money in health spending is a measure of the cost-effectiveness of different health interventions and medical procedures—that is, the ratio of costs to health benefits (DALYs gained).

Until recently, little has been done to apply cost-effectiveness analysis to health. This is, in part, because it is difficult. Cost and effectiveness data on health interventions are often weak. Costs vary between countries and can rise or fall sharply as a service is expanded. Some groups of interventions are provided jointly, and their costs are shared. Nonetheless, cost-effectiveness analysis is already demonstrating its usefulness as a tool for choosing among possible health interventions in individual countries and for addressing specific health problems such as the spread of AIDS.

Just because a particular intervention is cost-effective does not mean that public funds should be spent on it. Households can buy health care with their own money and, when well informed, may do this better than governments can do it for them. But households also seek value for money, and governments, by making information about cost-effectiveness available, can often help improve the decisions of private consumers, providers, and insurers.

Government Policies for Achieving Health for All

This Report focuses primarily on the relation between policy choices, both inside and outside the health sector, and health outcomes, especially for the poor.

• Since overall economic growth—particularly poverty-reducing growth—and education are central to good health, governments need to pursue sound macroeconomic policies that emphasize reduction of poverty. They also need to expand basic schooling, especially for girls, because the way in which households, particularly mothers, use information and financial resources to shape their dietary, fertility, health care, and other life-style choices has a powerful influence on the health of household members.

• Governments in developing countries should spend far less—on average, about 50 percent less—than they now do on less cost-effective interventions and instead double or triple spending on basic public health programs such as immunizations and AIDS prevention and on essential clinical services. A minimum package of essential clinical services would include sick-child care, family planning, prenatal and delivery care, and treatment for tuberculosis and STDs. Low-income countries would have to redirect current public spending for health and increase expenditures (by government, donors, and patients) to meet needs for public health and the minimum package of essential clinical services for their populations; less reallocation would be needed in middle-income countries. Tertiary care and less cost-effective services will continue, but public subsidies to them, if they mainly benefit the wealthy, should be phased out during a transitional period.

• Because competition can improve quality and drive down costs, governments should foster competition and diversity in the supply of health services and inputs, particularly drugs, supplies, and equipment. This could include, where feasible, private supply of health care services paid for by governments or social insurance. There is also considerable scope for improving the quality and efficiency of government health services through a combination of decentralization, performance-based incentives for managers and clinicians, and related training and development of management systems. Exposing the public sector to competition with private suppliers can help to spur such improvements. Strong government regulation is also crucial. . . .

Improving the Economic Environment for Healthy Households

Advances in income and education have allowed households almost everywhere to improve their health. In the 1980s, even in countries in which average incomes fell, death rates of children under age 5 declined by almost 30 percent. But the child mortality rate fell more than twice as much in countries in which aver-age incomes rose by more than 1 percent a year. Economic policies conducive to sustained growth are thus among the most important measures governments can take to improve their citizens' health.

Of these economic policies, increasing the income of those in poverty is the most efficacious for improving health. The reason is that the poor are most likely to spend additional income in ways that enhance their health: improving their diet, obtaining safe water, and upgrading sanitation and housing. And the poor have the greatest remaining health needs. Government policies that promote equity and growth together will therefore be better for health than those that promote growth alone.

In the 1980s many countries undertook macroeconomic stabilization and adjustment programs designed to deal with severe economic imbalances and move the countries onto sustainable growth paths. Such adjustment is clearly needed for long-run health gains. But during the transitional period, and especially in the earliest adjustment programs, recession and cuts in public spending slowed improvements in health. This effect was less than originally feared, however—in part because earlier expenditures for improving health and education had enduring effects. As a result of this experience, most countries' adjustment programs today try to rationalize overall government spending while maintaining cost-effective expenditures in health and education. Despite these improvements, much is still to be learned about more efficient ways of carrying out stabilization and adjustment programs while protecting the poor.

Policies to expand schooling are also crucial for promoting health. People who have had more schooling seek and utilize health information more effectively than those with little or no schooling. This means that rapid expansion of educational opportunities—in part by setting a high minimum standard of schooling (say, six full years) for all—is a cost-effective way of improving health. Education of girls and women is particularly beneficial to household health because it is largely women who buy and prepare food, maintain a clean home, care for children and the elderly, and initiate contacts with the health system. Beyond education, government policies that support the rights and economic opportunities of women also contribute to overall household well-being and better health.

EXHIBIT VI.7. Good Policies Matter

Life Expectancies and Health Expenditures in Selected Countries

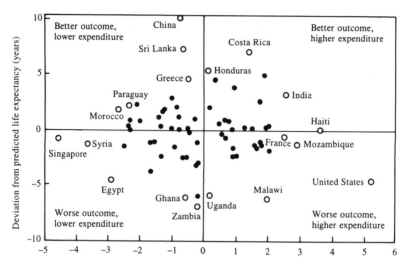

Deviation from predicted percentage of GDP spent on health

Differences in health spending are an obvious starting point in the search for why some countries have better health levels than others. But as this chart shows, health spending alone cannot explain the discrepancies—nor can income and education, or even spending, income, and schooling taken together.

The vertical axis shows how far life expectancy in a country differs from the value predicted on the basis of that country's income and average schooling. France, Haiti, Singapore, and Syria have almost exactly the life expectancy predicted. China, Costa Rica, Honduras, and Sri Lanka all achieve five years or more of life beyond what would be expected. Egypt, Ghana, Malawi, Uganda, the United States, and Zambia all have a life expectancy about five years lower than expected.

The horizontal axis shows how far total health spending differs from the value predicted by income and education. Egypt, Morocco, Paraguay, Singapore, and Syria spend relatively little. France, Haiti, India, Mozambique, and the United States spend more than expected.

At any level of income and education, higher health spending should yield better health, all else being equal. But there is no evidence of such a relation. Countries are scattered in all quadrants. The countries that appear in the upper-left quadrant obtain better health for less money. China, for instance, spends a full percentage point less of its GNP on health than other countries at the same stage of development but obtains nearly ten years of additional life expectancy. The United States is another extreme case, spending 5 percent more of GNP than predicted to achieve several years less of life expectancy than would be typical for its high income and educational level.

So why do some countries have better health levels than others? The missing link looks to be the quality of a government's health policy.

Source: Dean T. Jamison, ''Investing in Health,'' *Finance & Development* (September 1993), p. 4.

VI.F. EDUCATION

VI.F.1. Investment in Human Capital—Note

Although the objective of adding to the stock of physical capital has dominated investment discussions, it has now become evident that a high priority must also be assigned to investment in human capital.

Many studies of economic growth in advanced countries confirm the importance of nonmaterial investment. These statistical investigations indicate that output has increased at a higher rate than can be explained by an increase in only the inputs of labor and physical capital. The "residual" difference between the rate of increase in output and the rate of increase in physical capital and labor encompasses many "unidentified factors," but a prominent element is the improvement in the quality of inputs. Although some of this progress may be incorporated in physical capital, the improvements in intangible human qualities are more significant.

For purposes of measurement, capital formation is usually identified with the net increase of land, structures, durable equipment, commodity stocks, and foreign claims. But the capital stock should be interpreted more broadly to include the body of knowledge possessed by the population and the capacity and training of the population to use it effectively. Expenditures on education and training, improvement of health, and research contribute to productivity by raising the quality of the population, and these outlays yield a continuing return in the future. If these expenditures are considered as capital expenditures, then the proportion of capital formation in national income in the rich countries would be much larger than is conventionally indicated in national accounts that treat these expenditures under the flow of goods to ultimate consumers rather than under capital. But since poor countries do not make many such investments in the formation of human capital, this broad interpretation of capital would not increase significantly the proportion of their national incomes devoted to capital formation.

While investment in human beings has been a major source of growth in advanced countries, the negligible amount of human investment in underdeveloped countries has done little to extend the capacity of the people to meet the challenge of accelerated development. The characteristic of "economic backwardness" is still manifest in several particular forms:[1] low labor efficiency, factor immobility, limited specialization in occupations and in trade, a deficient supply of entrepreneurship, and customary values and traditional social institutions that minimize the incentives for economic change. The slow growth in knowledge is an especially severe restraint to progress. The economic quality of the population remains low when there is little knowledge of the natural resources that are available, the alternative production techniques that are possible, the necessary skills, the existing market conditions and opportunities, and the institutions that might be created to favor economizing effort and economic rationality. An improvement in the quality of the "human factor" is, then, as essential as investment in physical capital. An advance in knowledge and the diffusion of new ideas and objectives are necessary to remove economic backwardness and instill the human abilities and motivations that are more favorable to economic achievement. Although investment in material capital may indirectly achieve some lessening of the economic backwardness of the human resources, the direct and more decisive means is through investment in human beings.

Emphasizing the weight that should be given to the growth in the quality of human resources, Theodore Schultz illustrates the possible implications of the quality component:

Suppose there were an economy with the land and physical reproducible capital including the available techniques of production that we now possess in the United States, but which attempted to function under the following restraints: there would be no person available who had any on-the-job experience, none who had any schooling, no one who had any information about the economy except of his locality, each individual would be bound to his locality, and the average life span of people would be only forty years. Surely, production would fall castastrophically. It is

---

[1] Hla Myint, "An Interpretation of Economic Backwardness," *Oxford Economic Papers* (June 1954), pp. 132–63.

certain that there would be both low output and extraordinary rigidity of economic organization until the capabilities of the people were raised markedly by investing in them. Let me now take a Bunyan-like step and suppose a set of human resources with as many but no more capabilities per man than existed as of 1900 or even as of 1929 in the United States. The adverse effects on production in either case would undoubtedly be large. To continue the speculations, suppose that by some miracle India, or some other low-income country like India, were to acquire as it were overnight a set of natural resources, equipment, and structures including techniques of production comparable per person to ours—what could they do with them, given the existing skills and knowledge of the people? Surely the imbalance between the stock of human and non-human capital would be tremendous.[2]

Recent experience with attempts to accumulate physical capital at a rapid rate in poor countries bears out the necessity of due attention to human capital. It has become evident that the effective use of physical capital itself is dependent on human capital. If there is underinvestment in human capital, the rate at which additional physical capital can be productively utilized will be limited, since technical, professional, and administrative people are needed to make effective use of material capital. In many newly developed countries, the absorptive capacity for physical capital has proved to be low because the extension of human capabilities has failed to keep pace with the accumulation of physical capital.[3]

While the case for investment in human resources is gaining wider acceptance, the means of attaining an increase in this type of investment have still received only superficial consideration compared with the intensive investigations that have been made of the problems of investment in physical goods.

It is not difficult to identify the more important categories of activities that improve human capabilities. As Schultz suggests, a typical list would be

(1) health facilities and services, broadly conceived to include all expenditures that affect the life expec-

tancy, strength and stamina, and the vigor and vitality of a people; (2) on-the-job training, including old-style apprenticeship organized by firms; (3) formally organized education at the elementary, secondary, and higher levels; (4) study programs for adults that are not organized by firms, including extension programs notably in agriculture; (5) migration of individuals and families to adjust to changing job opportunities.[4]

Underlying each of these activities, however, are a number of questions that should be studied more seriously.[5] At the outset, the problem of measurement presents several difficulties: Is it possible to separate the consumption and the investment parts of expenditures on these activities? Can the particular resources entering into each of these components be identified and measured? And can the rate of return on investment in education be compared with the rate of return on investment in some other alternative use? As yet, no completely satisfactory empirical procedure for answering these questions has been devised. Although a few studies have recently made noteworthy steps in the direction of measuring some consequences of an increase in tangible capital,[6] no empirical study of investment in human capital is yet free from some arbitrary elements, and more statistical evidence is needed.

Another problem of particular importance to a country engaged in development programming is to determine at what phase of development the formation of intangible capital is most significant. It can be argued that a high rate of increase in the demand for improvements in the quality of inputs appears only at a fairly advanced phase of development. The early industrialization in western Europe, for example, appears to have been accomplished without requiring as prerequisites marked improvements in skills and knowledge and health of workers.[7] And the contribution of education to American

[2]Theodore W. Schultz, "Reflections on Investment in Man," *Journal of Political Economy*, Supplement (October 1962): 2–3.

[3]For strong arguments that "the experience of planning seems to suggest that knowledge (and certainly not investment resources) is the most important scarce factor in underdeveloped countries with otherwise favorable social climate," see B. Horvat, "The Optimum Rate of Investment," *Economic Journal* (December 1958): 751–53.

[4]Theodore W. Schultz, "Investment in Human Capital in Poor Countries," in *Foreign Trade and Human Capital*, ed. P. D. Zook (1962), pp. 3–4, 11–12.

[5]The remainder of our discussion concentrates on education and training. For a consideration of human-capital formation through health services, see Selma J. Mushkin, "Health as an Investment," *Journal of Political Economy*, Supplement (October 1962): 129–57.

[6]For example, Mary Jean Bowman, "Human Capital: Concepts and Measures," in *Money, Growth, and Methodology, Essays in Honor of Johan Akerman* (1961), pp. 146–68.

[7]Schultz, "Investment in Human Capital," pp. 3–4, 11–12.

growth has been most pronounced in the more recent decades, while capital investment was more important in earlier decades.[8] Unlike the earlier historical situation, however, it may now be necessary to have a relatively high level of skill and much more knowledge to take advantage of the more complex equipment and techniques that may be obtained from advanced countries.

There are additional questions to be raised concerning what types of education should be emphasized, to what degree, and how soon. Some economists have such questions in mind when they criticize—from the viewpoint of the economic, although not social or moral, value—proposals for mass education or extensive systems of higher education in newly developing nations. They contend that these countries do not yet have an effective demand for large numbers of educated workers; it will take considerable time to raise the presently limited absorptive capacity of the economy for educated persons; and a poor country cannot afford to pay for as much education as can rich countries.[9] Since educational outlays compete for resources that have an alternative use in directly productive investment, it is essential to determine the proportion of national income that should be devoted to education. And within the education system itself it is necessary to establish priorities for the various possible forms of education and training.

From the standpoint of accelerating development, the immediate requirements may call for emphasis on vocational and technical training and adult education rather than on a greatly expanded system of formal education. Considering its high cost and the problems of absorption that it raises, even universal primary education is questionable. W. Arthur Lewis expresses such skepticism in the following comments on African proposals:

The limited absorptive capacity of most West African economies today—especially owing to the backwardness of agriculture—makes frustration and dislocation inevitable if more than 50 percent of children enter school. This, coupled with the high cost due to the high ratio of teachers' salaries to average national

income, and with the time it takes to train large numbers of teachers properly, has taught some African countries to proceed with caution; to set the goal of universal schooling twenty years ahead or more, rather than the ten years ahead or less associated with the first flush of independence movements. Such a decision is regarded as highly controversial by those for whom literacy is a universal human right irrespective of cost. . . . On the other hand, considering that in most African territories less than 25 per cent of children aged six to fourteen are in school, a goal of 50 per cent within ten years may be held to constitute revolutionary progress.[10]

More immediately serious than the lack of universal primary education is the deficiency in secondary education. The most critical manpower requirement tends to be for people with a secondary education who can be managers, administrators, professional technicians (scientists, engineers, agronomists, doctors, economists, accountants), or subprofessional technical personnel (agricultural assistants, technical supervisors, nurses, engineering assistants, bookkeepers). Lewis characterizes the products of secondary schools as

the officers and noncommissioned officers of an economic and social system. A small percentage goes on to university education, but the numbers required from the university are so small that the average country of up to five million inhabitants could manage tolerably well without a university of its own. Absence of secondary schools, however, is an enormous handicap. . . . The middle and upper ranks of business consist almost entirely of secondary school products, and these products are also the backbone of public administration.[11]

Also deserving of high priority is the infusion of new skills and knowledge into the agricultural sector. In order to achieve a system of modern agriculture, the quality of labor in agriculture has to be improved as an input in its own right and to allow the use of better forms of nonhuman capital (equipment, seeds, insecticides). In many countries that have experienced substantial increases in agricultural production, the key factor has not been new land or land that is superior for agriculture; nor has it been mainly the addition of reproducible capital. More importantly, the agricultural transformation has been based predominantly on new skills and useful knowledge required to develop a modern ag-

[8]Edward F. Denison, ''Education, Economic Growth, and Gaps in Information,'' *Journal of Political Economy* (October 1962): 127.

[9]These arguments are cogently presented by W. Arthur Lewis, ''Education and Economic Development,'' *International Social Science Journal* 14, no. 4 (1962): 685–99, and Thomas Balogh, ''Misconceived Educational Programmes in Africa,'' *Universities Quarterly* (June 1962): 243–49.

[10]Lewis, ''Education and Economic Development,'' p. 689.

[11]Ibid., pp. 688–90.

riculture.[12] Educational facilities for agriculture may also provide a way of encouraging rural school-leavers to take up work in the rural sector rather than migrating to the towns, and the special training of young school-leavers may allow them to act as the agents for introducing new and improved agricultural techniques.

For the broader problems of educational requirements, the making of "manpower surveys" may furnish a useful basis for determining the principal skill shortages and the types of training activities to be emphasized. At least for the short term, the provision of agricultural extension services, training in mechanical and technical skills, and training in supervisory and administrative skills may contribute the most to fulfilling manpower requirements. After overcoming the immediate bottlenecks of scarce personnel in specific key occupations, the education system should then be devised to provide a balance among general education, prevocational preparation, and vocational education and training.

We may conclude that the recent attention to investment in human capital should prove salutary in cautioning against an overemphasis on physical capital, to the neglect of the more intangible factors. When considered for a poor country, however, investment in human capital calls for new approaches and special emphases that differ from those in advanced economies. An extensive system of formal education is a commendable objective, but it must necessarily be a distant objective. Instead of attempting to imitate the educational system of an advanced country, newly developing countries may more suitably concentrate, at least in the early phases of their development programs, on methods of informal education and on the objectives of functional education. These efforts are less time consuming, less costly, and more directly related to manpower requirements than is a formal educational system. As such, they are likely to prove more effective in improving the economic quality of human resources.

[12]Schultz, "Investment in Human Capital," p. 9.

Comment: Human-Capital Theory

References to the literature on human-capital theory are included in a number of selections in this chapter. In contrast to the early emphasis on the accumulation of physical capital, Schultz called attention to the need for investment in human capital in order to increase productivity and income. See Theodore W. Schultz, "Investment in Human Capital," *American Economic Review* (January 1961). Subsequent studies have provided a strong empirical base for the theory through analysis of rates of return to investment in human capital, the production function approach to the causes of growth, and comparative cross-country studies of investment in human resources.

For surveys of the subject, see M. J. Bowman, "The Human Investment Revolution in Economic Thought," *Sociology of Education* (1966); Mark Blaug, "Human Capital Theory: A Slightly Jaundiced Survey," *Journal of Economic Literature* (September 1976); and A. P. Thirwall, *Growth and Development,* 2nd ed. (1978), chaps. 2, 4. An illuminating analysis is also presented by M. FG. Scott, "The Contribution of Investment to Growth," *Scottish Journal of Political Economy* (November 1981). Scott concludes that investment, both human and material, accounts for all, or virtually all, growth in output per worker when investment is properly interpreted.

VI.F.2. Educational Investment*

The educational product, in the context of economic development . . . not only includes the components of education usually distinguished as consumption (i.e., enjoyment of the fuller life

*From Richard A. Musgrave, "Notes on Educational Investment in Developing Nations," in OECD Study Group in the Economics of Education, *Financing of Education for Economic Growth* (Paris, 1966), pp. 31–39. Reprinted by permission.

permitted by education) and as direct investment (with the gains accruing "internally" in the form of increased earnings to the educated person), but also education as investment in the functioning of the economic and social system at large. These latter gains accrue "externally," not only to those in whom the educational input is invested, but also to other members of the community.

The theory of investment planning may be

looked at from the micro or macro level. In macro terms, the problem is to determine the alternative growth path available to the economy, assuming the best structure of capital formation to apply in each case, and then to choose the optimum path on the basis of the community's time preference. In micro terms, the problem is one of rating alternative investment projects and of deciding which one is to be included within a given level of overall capital formation. There is no reason why investment in human resources by education should not be included in such an analysis. However, education investment has certain characteristics—quite apart from the previously noted factor of externality—which pose special problems and should be noted at the outset.

Characteristics of Educational Investment

The product of education outlays, to begin with, carries joint features of consumption and investment. For this reason, the share of resources allocated to education cannot be considered wholly an investment outlay. The consumption component has to compete with alternative forms of consumption, while the investment component must compete with alternative forms of capital formation. To the extent that the two parts are inseparable, the proper allocation of resources to education should leave the rate of return thereon (computed as ratio of the present value of additional earnings to investment cost) below that of alternative investments which do not carry joint consumption components.

This distinction between the consumption and capital formation aspects of education outlays, however, is somewhat misleading. The consumption product of education may be divided into current consumption (the delights of attending school) and the future consumption (the ability to appreciate life more fully later on). Since the latter is much the major element, the consumption component is largely in the nature of a durable consumer good and hence investment. The essential distinction, thus, is not between the consumption and investment aspects of education output, but between education investment which generates imputed income (the fuller life later on) and education investment which generates increased factor earnings to the labour supplied by the educated person.

What weight is to be given to the two components in the development context, and how is this to be reflected in the pattern of the education programme? Recent writers have pointed to the extension of secondary education as being the primary goal of education policy in countries with a low level of educational capital stock, with extension of elementary education and technical training at the subsequent level of capital stock, and expansion of higher education at a more advanced stage.[1] While this priority is derived from the projected needs for various types of skill and training, it also suggests that the imputed-income component of the education mix tends to be of particularly great importance at the early stages.

Secondly, investment in education is characterized by a gestation period which is substantially longer than that of many other types of capital formation. Indeed, education seems the time-consuming, Boehm-Bawerkian type of investment par excellence. Periods of ten to twenty years may be involved, depending on how far the education process is carried, and even longer spans must be allowed for if teacher-training is taken into consideration. Even though certain skills may be acquired fairly rapidly, especially if a previous foundation is laid, the educational capital stock cannot be changed quickly, particularly for the more advanced type of education. This introduces a constraint in investment planning and demands a correspondingly longer planning horizon which in turn points to the need for a public policy guidance seen in the context of a long-term development perspective, if not development plan.

A similar consideration relates to a further feature of investment in education, that is, the relatively long useful life of the education asset. Considerations of returns over, say, a thirty-year period, lends great weight to the importance of the discount factor in assessing the relative productivity of investment in education. Since the useful life for competing investments tends frequently to be shorter, the relative case for investment in education is low if the appropriate rate of discount is high. Thus, the selection of the appropriate rate of discount is of particular importance in assessing the proper share for education in total capital formation. There being no developed capital markets which provide a clear indicator of this rate, its determination becomes essentially a matter of public policy. Investments should be ranked by a present value

[1]See Frederick Harbison and Charles A. Myers, *Education, Manpower and Economic Growth*, New York, 1964, Chapters 4–6.

rather than an internal rate of return criteria. Moreover, there may well be a difference between the government's and the private investor's evaluation of present, relative to future, needs. To the extent that public policy takes a longer view, it will also tend to require a larger share for education in investment outlays.

The relatively long, useful life, moreover, makes it necessary that the type of education be chosen in order to meet future demands in particular skills. This applies less to general and elementary education, which lays a more flexible basis, but becomes of great importance for specialized and technical types of training that do not permit easy conversion. As already noted, educational planning in the context of a longer-term development view is essential.

Finally, a word regarding the resource cost of education. Recent discussions of the economics of education[2] emphasize, and rightly so, that this cost not only includes teachers' salaries, buildings and equipment, but also the opportunity cost of lost income on the part of the student. Depending on the structure of the developing country, this latter component may be of varying significance. Where there is a general surplus of labour supply, the opportunity cost of forgone earnings will be small or non-existent. Under other conditions, customary use of child labour may produce the opposite situation. While the former is the more typical case, other components of education cost (school teachers' salaries in particular) tend to be relatively high in underdeveloped countries.[3] Even though the income stream from a given factor input into education will be large (educated workers are needed to take advantage of modern techniques, and education is highly complementary to other types of capital formation) the rate of return on educational investments (relative to that on other investments) is therefore not as high as suggested by the income stream alone.

Externalities

The standard procedure for determining the value of investment in education is to estimate the future stream of incremental earnings which accrue to the student, and to discount it to obtain the present value. This present value is then related to the cost of investment in obtaining the rate of return. This procedure excludes additions to output which accrue externally and to the benefit of others rather than to the educated person alone. Such oversight may be acceptable in assessing the value of education for a developed economy, but hardly for the underdeveloped country, where external benefits constitute a substantial part of the total gain.

Perhaps the most important aspect of the external benefits of education lies in the change in the social and cultural climate, incident to the widening of horizons, which education entails. As has been pointed out many times, such a change is an essential condition of success for many developing nations. At the same time, this benefit result is not an automatic consequence of education at large, but only of the proper type, quality and quantity of education. Supply of professional people who cannot be absorbed into appropriate positions may readily become an external dis-economy and source of instability.

As noted previously, different types of investments in the early stages of development tend to be highly complementary, and this holds par excellence for the proper combination of investment in education and capital equipment. Without a capable labour force modern capital equipment cannot be operated, and it is precisely the access to superior techniques that is the one hopeful factor in the development picture. Now it is true that the existence of such complementarity need not, per se, constitute an externality which would fail to be recorded in a perfectly functioning pricing system. If tractors can be substituted for oxen only if trained drivers are available, this will be reflected in corresponding higher wages for the driver. The trouble, however, lies in the fact that in an economy where there are as yet no tractors, the supply of drivers is unlikely to be forthcoming, and vice versa. The generation of growth (whether "balanced" in an overall Nurkse sense or not) requires a concerted effort to provide a chain of investments, thereby reducing the risks of individual investments and making it possible for an investment programme to succeed where individual investments would fail.

This necessity for investment planning exists even for investments which, given the necessary supply of entrepreneurial talent, would be appropriately undertaken privately. It exists par excellence for investment in education. Left to

[2]For a survey of this literature, see Chapter I in William J. Bowen, *Economic Aspects of Education,* Princeton, 1964.

[3]See W. Arthur Lewis, "Priorities for Educational Expansion," *Policy Conference on Economic Growth and Investment in Education,* OECD, Washington, 1961, Part III, p. 37.

household decisions, neither the market knowledge, foresight or financial requirements are present which are needed to secure adequate supplies. This is especially the case in underdeveloped countries where the whole attitude towards education has to overcome conventional barriers and become reoriented to the development process. . . .

Sensible education targets, therefore, must be developed by considering the needs of the particular economy and the demands posed by its specific plans. This raises a question of the rate at which the system needs to, or can absorb additional supplies of educated manpower. Arthur Lewis stresses the fact that absorption capacity is limited by the high cost of education in developing countries. To quote:

The main limitation on the absorption of the educated in poor countries is their high price, relative to average national output per head. . . . In consequence, all production . . . which depends on using educated people is much more expensive, in relation to national income, in poor than in rich countries. The poor countries may need the educated more than the rich, but they can even less afford to pay for or absorb large numbers. . . . In the long run, the situation adjusts itself because the premium for education diminishes as the number of educated increases. . . . As the premium for education falls, the market for the educated may widen enormously.

And he further notes that

to give eight years of primary education to every child would cost at current prices about 0.8 per cent of national income in the USA, 1.7 per cent in Jamaica, 2.8 per cent in Ghana and 4.0 per cent in Nigeria. The main reason for this difference is that, while the average salary of a primary school teacher is less than one and a half times per capita national income in the USA, a primary school teacher gets three times per capita national income in Jamaica, five times in Ghana, and seven times in Nigeria.[4]

The fact that school teachers' wages are high relative to average wages in the underdeveloped country need not mean that the absorptive capacity, as we understand it, is low. The rate of return on education equals the ratio of present value of wages, or earnings due to education, to the cost of producing it. The high relative wage of the educated person may merely express the extreme scarcity of the education factor, and

hence its ability to command a high return at the given cost of producing it. The high wage might be an indicator of under- rather than over-supply, as demand may prove elastic if only increased supplies could be made available. At the same time, the cost of producing education may be high at early stages of development, relative to that of producing other capital goods, say tractors. If so, the rate of return on education (relative to that on tractors) will not be as high as suggested by the high income stream (wages) accruing to the educated factor alone. The cost of producing education must be lowered before increased investment in education is profitable. This, however, is subject to the previously noted condition that education is highly complementary to other forms of capital formation.

In addition to genuine scarcity, the high salaries demanded for work in positions requiring education reflect conventional factors and the desire to absorb the status previously held by the colonial official. As a result, there is frequently a "minimum wage structure" for high-level work which exceeds the economic return on such work, and prices educated services out of the market. Such rigidities need to be broken down to permit an effective education policy, and to the extent that they are permitted to prevail, appropriate allowance must be made in formulating realistic education targets. A policy which results in a supply of education that cannot be absorbed is obviously inefficient.

A further aspect of the cost problem which deserves special attention is the extent to which the educational effort involves a need for foreign exchange. Capital formation in the developing countries is frequently limited by the fact that capital goods cannot be produced at home, and that the foreign exchange available for acquiring them abroad is scarce. The question arises whether investment in education is more or less capital intensive than are other, and to some extent alternative, forms of capital formation. The answer depends on the level of education. While the exchange component of elementary education cost tends to be relatively low, it rises at the middle level, and for higher education it becomes extremely high. At later stages, this pattern may fit the needs and resources of the country but at the earlier stages, where emphasis is on middle-level education, the match tends to be an unfortunate one and points to the need for an all-out effort in domestic teacher-training.

Priorities

The matter of educational priorities is obviously of vital importance. Unless the right kind of education is provided, setting overall targets has little meaning. Educated people who are unable to find suitable jobs, not only fail to add to the national product but become a source of political instability. Since the cost of various types of education (primary versus secondary versus advanced; liberal arts versus technical, and so forth) differs greatly, the very setting of overall targets has to be derived from the structural composition of the education supply.

Comment: Education and Development

The World Bank's *Education Sector Policy Paper* (1980) concludes that "studies have shown that economic returns on investment in education seem, in most instances, to exceed returns on alternative kinds of investment, and that developing countries obtain higher returns than the developed ones."

For an extensive bibliography on education and development see Mark Blaug, ed., *Economics of Education,* vols. 1 and 2 (1968, 1969). Several writings by Theodore W. Schultz are highly instructive on the role of education in development: "Capital Formation by Education," *Journal of Political Economy* (December 1960); "Education and Economic Growth," in *Social Forces Influencing American Education,* ed. N. B. Henry (1961); and "Investment in Human Capital in Poor Countries," in *Foreign Trade and Human Capital,* ed. P. D. Zook (1962). "Investment in Human Beings," the special supplement of the *Journal of Political Economy* (October 1962), also contains a number of pertinent papers covering particular aspects of the problem.

For a comprehensive survey of the state of knowledge about the effects of education on income, see Timothy King, ed., "Education and Income," *World Bank Staff Working Paper,* no. 402 (July 1980).

A critique of social cost–benefit analysis in educational planning is offered by G. S. Fields, "Assessing Educational Progress and Commitment," *Report for the U.S. Agency for International Development* (October 1978). See also World Bank, *Education* (1980); Ronald Dore, *The Diploma Disease* (1976); Marcelo Selowsky, "On the Measurement of Education's Contribution to Growth," *Quarterly Journal of Economics* (August 1969); and Dean T. Jamison and Lawrence J. Lau, *Farmer Education and Farm Efficiency* (1981).

Also informative are Marcelo Selowsky, "A Note on Preschool-age Investment in Human Capital in Developing Countries," *Economic Development and Cultural Change* (July 1976); M. R. Rosenzweig and R. E. Evenson, "Fertility, Schooling and the Economic Contribution of Children in Rural India," *Econometrica* (July 1977); George Psacharopoulos, "Returns to Education: An Updated International Comparison," *Comparative Education* (1981); Christopher Colclough, "The Impact of Primary Schooling on Economic Development: A Review of the Evidence," *World Development* (March 1982); World Bank, *Education in Sub-Saharan Africa* (1988); Lawrence H. Summers, *Investing in All the People,* World Bank, Policy Research Working Paper 905 (May 1992); and Elizabeth M. King and M. Anne Hill, *Women's Education in Developing Countries: Barriers, Benefits and Policies* (1993).

Comment: Education and the Success Stories

The East Asian success stories have been based not on an abundance of natural resources but on their human resources. All the fast developers have invested heavily in education. The quality of education and extent of schooling and training in East Asian countries have markedly increased in the course of their development. By 1960, just before South Korea's economic "take-off," 90 percent of children were already completing primary school, and over one-third were going on to secondary education. Korea's achievement is notable in universalizing primary education at an earlier stage than any other developing country. Secondary and university enrollment have also grown rapidly.

Exhibits VI.8 and VI.9 present a stylized summary of the results of regressing primary and secondary enrollment rates on per capita income for more than 90 developing countries in 1965 and 1987.

Also striking is the decline in the gender gap (male versus female) in enrollment rates at the primary and secondary levels. By 1987, the East Asian countries had all achieved universal primary education for girls, virtually eliminating the gender gap at that level. In contrast, substantial gender gaps still persist in some 40 low-income countries to almost the same degree as in 1965.

The education of girls is especially important—not only because the private returns to education are similar for women and men, but because the social benefits from educating girls are high.

EXHIBIT VI.8. Cross-Economy Regression for Primary Enrollment Rates, 1965 and 1987

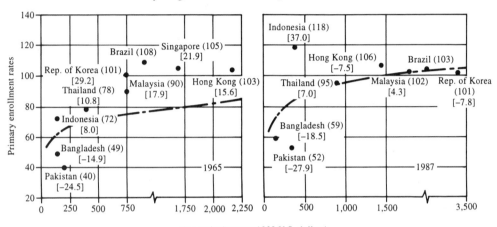

Per capita income (1988 U.S. dollars)

Note: Figures in parentheses are enrollment rates; bracketed numbers show residuals.
Source: World Bank, *East Asian Miracle* (1993), p. 45.

EXHIBIT VI.9. Cross-Economy Regression for Secondary Enrollment Rates, 1965 and 1987

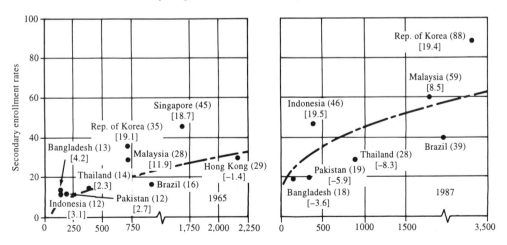

Per capita income (in 1988 U.S. dollars)

Note: Figures in parentheses are enrollment rates; bracketed numbers show residuals.
Source: World Bank, *East Asian Miracle* (1993), p. 46.

VI.F.3. Economic Impact of Education*

In this paper I review the evidence on the economic impact of education produced in the past thirty years and compile a number of lessons from the literature that might be useful to policy makers. And since no field is without controversy, I also review the major debates that have surrounded human capital theory and its applications.

The Evidence

The evidence on the economic impact of education can be divided into two distinct types: micro and macro.

Micro

If expenditure on education is a kind of investment leading to the formation of human capital, either for the individual or for society at large, one should be able to estimate the rate of return to this investment. In its most simplified form, the rate of return to investment in education (r) can be estimated by dividing the permanent annual benefits stream due to education ($Y_1 - Y_0$) by the cost of obtaining such education ($Y_0 + C_1$),

$$r = \frac{(Y_1 - Y_0)}{S(Y_0 + C_1)}$$

In this case Y_1 and Y_0 could refer to the mean earnings of workers who are literate and illiterate, respectively, S to the number of years of schooling it takes for someone to become literate, and C_1 to the annual cost of keeping someone in school. Note the appearance of Y_0 in the denominator of the expression, representing the opportunity cost of attending school rather than working in the labor market.

There are several ways to examine rates of return to education: by whether the returns refer to the individual investor or to society at large, namely, the private or social rate of return; by the country's level of economic development; by the type of curriculum—say, general or vocational secondary education; by type of economic sector the worker is in, say, modern wage employment or self-employment; and by gender.

Hundreds of studies have been conducted in the past thirty years on the profitability of investment in education in a large number of countries across the dimensions cited above (for a summary see Psacharopoulos 1985). Figures 1 and 2 offer an impressionistic summary of the results of these studies. The figures are impressionistic in the sense that I want the reader to focus on the structure of the returns to education rather than the exact percentage points represented by the vertical axes. As a point of reference I give an illustrative 10 percent opportunity cost of capital or alternative discount rate. This might be more realistic in a developed country than in a developing country, although the 10 percent rate could be defended in a developing country setting if the country could borrow internationally for investment in education at this interest rate.

The first notable result of the application of rate of return studies to education is that the rates are not far off the yield of more conventional investments. The returns to investment in education in advanced industrial countries are roughly the same as those of investment in physical capital. By contrast, the returns to education in developing countries stand at a much higher level relative to industrial countries. This reflects both the continuing scarcity of human capital in poorer countries and barriers to the allocation of funds to human capital investment, so that the returns to any kind of capital (physical or human) equalize at the margin.

A typical pattern, found since the early days of rate of return estimation in education, is that returns decline by level of schooling. Thus, returns to primary education are higher relative to returns to secondary education, and the latter are higher than returns to university education. This finding, corroborated in study after study, has fundamental policy implications.

Another result worth noting is the difference between social and private rates of return. Because of the public subsidization of education in all parts of the world, private rates are typically several percentage points higher than social rates of return. By definition, the cost in a private rate-

*From George Psacharopoulos, *The Economic Impact of Education: Lessons for Policymakers* (San Francisco: ICS Press, 1991), pp. 8–15. Reprinted by permission.

FIGURE 1. The returns to investment in education by level and country type.

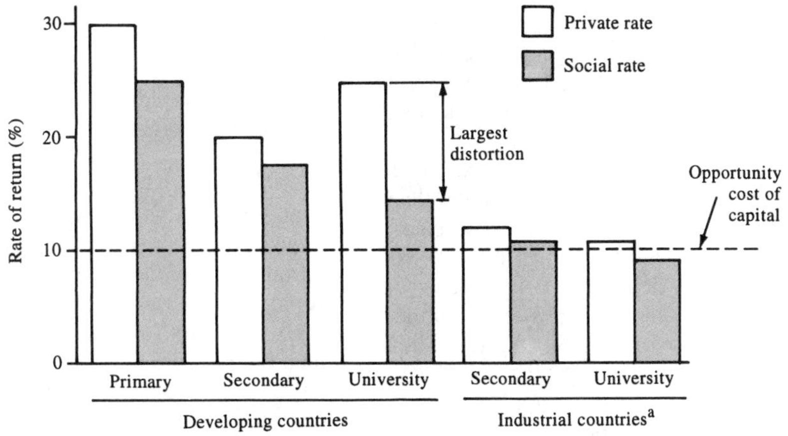

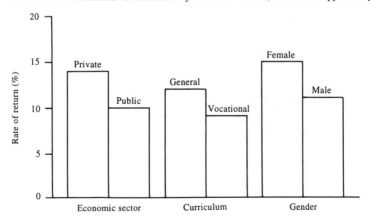

^aThe rate of return for primary education in industrial countries is undefined because of universal enrollment at this level of schooling.

Source: Based on Psacharopoulos 1985.

of-return estimation refers only to what the individual pays out of his or her pocket, whereas the cost in a social rate of return estimation refers to the full resource cost of someone attending school. The distortion incurred by the public subsidization of education means that, in some instances, individuals will find it profitable to pursue education to a given level whereas, from the point of view of society, this investment is not profitable. The maximum distortion between the private and the social rates refers to education at the university level. This level is more heavily subsidized in most countries relative to any other level.

Figure 2 presents three additional rate-of-return patterns that have been found in studies in many countries, irrespective of whether the rate of return is social or private. The first comparison shows that the return to education is typically higher in the private or competitive sector

FIGURE 2. The returns to education by economic sector, curriculum type, and gender.

Source: Based on Psacharopoulos 1985.

than in the public sector. It is well known that the public pay structure is very compressed, leading to a lower rate of return relative to estimates based on earnings in the private sector, where there is no limit to rewards. To the extent that private sector earnings truly approximate a worker's productivity, rates of return based on earnings in the competitive sector provide a better fix for the scarcity of human capital than rates of return based on civil service pay scales. The latter, however, are very important for explaining the private behavior of individuals in seeking different levels and types of education. Given the dominance of the public sector in hiring university graduates in any kind of country, a private rate-of-return estimation using civil service data is very appropriate, if not a must, in understanding the demand for university education. However, a private earnings base would be more appropriate for setting priorities for educational investment in a given country.

The second pattern in Figure 2 provides a well documented yet highly counterintuitive finding: within a given level of education, say, secondary schooling or university education, the more general the curriculum the higher the returns to education. This startling finding is due to two factors. First, the unit cost of vocational education, at any level, is higher than that of general education, because of the more specialized faculty and equipment that vocational education entails. Second, graduates of general programs are more flexible in fitting a wide spectrum of occupations—and perhaps are more easily trained on the job—than graduates of vocational programs that are earmarked to enter a particular occupation (to put it at the extreme, mechanical watch repairers).

The last pattern presented in Figure 2 refers to the worker's gender. Investment in the education of females often yields a higher rate of return than investment in the education of males. This finding could also be considered counterintuitive, in the sense that males typically earn much more than females. One must remember that the rate of return to investment in education is a *relative* concept, comparing the *difference* between more- and less-educated workers with the cost of their education. A major component of the cost is the forgone earnings of the worker while studying, which can lead to a higher rate of return for females than for males.

Macro

If investment in education yields returns at the individual or social level, this must be reflected at the level of the economy. Growth accounting in the post-World War II period was based on the so-called aggregate production function.

$$\text{Output} = f(\text{Land, Labor, Capital}),$$

expressing a country's output (measured by gross domestic product) as a function of the traditional triad of factors of production: land, measured in terms of cultivated area; labor, measured in terms of the number of persons or man-hours worked; and capital, measured in terms of the value of the physical plant in operation. Fitting the above relationship to time-series data for the United States left a huge unexplained residual, named "the coefficient of our ignorance." Output grew much faster than increases in the traditional factors of production could account for. Relabeling the residual "technical change" was simply begging the question "what determines technical change?"

It was then that Schultz (1961) and Denison (1967), using computationally different although conceptually similar approaches, introduced the quality of labor or human capital into the traditional production function. Schultz, for example, plugged in the amount of investment represented by expenditures on education and explained a great part of the previously puzzling residual. The macro approach has been replicated by others over the past thirty years with similar results.[1]

Figure 3 shows that in Africa, investment in education explains nearly twice the proportion of economic growth that it does in more affluent Europe and North America. This macro result essentially replicates the rate-of-return structure by country type presented above, given that human capital is much scarcer in the poorer countries.

Beyond the results cited above, which have been generated by econometricians, economic historians took a stab at the matter by taking a much longer-term view than sophisticated statistical analysis permits. Thus it has been established that bouts of long-term economic growth were preceded by increases in the population's literacy level. The examples of Japan and Korea are the classic cases in which an educated pop-

[1]For a review see Psacharopoulos (1984).

FIGURE 3. The contribution of education to economic growth by continent.

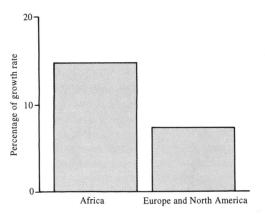

Source: Based on Psacharopoulos 1984.

ulation base has provided the necessary infrastructure for industrial advances to take place at a later date (see Saxonhouse 1977 and Easterlin 1981).

Wider Social Impact

Beyond the above "strict" or monetary impact of education, investment in human beings also has many other social values. Some come under the heading of externalities—namely, values captured by persons other than the individual investor. Others are labeled "nonmarket effects" (for a superb account of this see Haveman and Wolfe 1984). And others are simply means or mechanisms by which the overall impact of education is realized.

When a person becomes literate, this person will enjoy a higher lifetime consumption path, according to statistics for a large number of countries. Others will also benefit if the country has a more literate population—through lower transaction costs than if they were dealing with illiterates, for example.

Many educated females may choose not to participate in the labor force. This does not mean, however, that such females are not more productive (relative to their less educated counterparts) in the variety of goods and services produced within the household that are not readily marketable. For example, they may provide better sanitation conditions for all members of the family and more nutritional meals. Such effects should be counted as part of the social impact of education.

Education increases the opportunity cost to a woman staying in the household and induces her to participate in the labor market. This contributes to overall efficiency in the economy to the extent that her market wage is higher than her implicit, shadow wage of being engaged in household activities.

Migration is an illustrative example of the means by which the returns to education are realized. To the extent that education makes the worker aware of employment opportunities elsewhere, or simply makes him or her employable in other contexts, it will instigate a more efficient allocation of labor to the most productive uses.

Health status is a very important part of human well-being. Several studies have shown that literacy and other measures of education are more closely correlated with life expectancy than per capita income is. The mechanism of this relationship is that education helps determine both the level of knowledge about how to combat disease and the ease with which it can be transmitted and utilized (Cochrane, O'Hara, and Leslie 1980).

The relationship between education and fertility is a very complex one, although most observers would agree that the link is negative—that increased literacy and school attendance in general delay marriage and increase the opportunity cost of having children. Consequently, families desire and have fewer children. This has been clearly demonstrated in urban areas on a global scale (see Cochrane 1979).

Last but not least, another often mentioned wider effect of education is that of having a more informed body of consumers and a literate electorate, leading to democratic government.

References

Cochrane, S. H. (1979). *Fertility and Education: What Do We Really Know?* Baltimore: Johns Hopkins University Press.

Cochrane, S. H., D. O'Hara, and J. Leslie (1980). *The Effects of Education on Health.* Staff Working Paper no. 405. Washington, D.C.: World Bank.

Denison, E. F. (1967). *Why Growth Rates Differ?* Washington D.C.: Brookings Institution.

Easterlin, R. (1981). "Why Isn't the Whole World Developed?" *Journal of Economic History* 41 (March): 1–19.

Haveman, R. H., and B. Wolfe (1984). "Schooling and Economic Well-being: The Role of Nonmarket Effects." *Journal of Human Resources* 19: 377–407.

Psacharopoulos, G. (1984). "The Contribution of Education to Economic Growth: International Comparisons." In J. W. Kendrick, ed., *International Comparisons of Productivity and Causes of the Slowdown.* New York: Ballinger, pp. 335–60.

——— (1985). "Returns to Education: A Further International Update and Implications." *Journal of Human Resources* 20 (Fall): 583–604.

Saxonhouse, G. R. (1977). "Productivity Change and Labor Absorption in Japanese Cotton Spinning, 1881–1935." *Quarterly Journal of Economics* 91: 195–200.

Schultz, T. W. (1961). "Education and Economic Growth." In N. B. Henry, ed., *Social Forces Influencing American Education.* Chicago: University of Chicago Press.

CHAPTER VII

Industrialization and Agriculture: 1

This chapter focuses on industrialization strategy, but it should be read in conjunction with Chapter VIII, on agricultural strategy. For a development program cannot afford to emphasize industrialization at the expense of agricultural development. The role of industrialization is now being reappraised. It is not a question of concentrating resources on industry or on agriculture—as alternatives. Rather, it is increasingly evident that the mutually supportive interactions between agriculture and industry should receive prime attention. Sections VII.A and VII.E are therefore important in providing background and a transition for Chapter VIII.

Instead of earlier policies of high-cost industrialization by means of import substitution, which involved an output mix and choice of techniques that conflicted with other development objectives, there is now the advocacy of a more appropriate type of export-oriented industrialization. As a corollary of this shift, the old dispute about whether to give priority to industry or to agriculture is not a real issue.

The question instead is how to achieve concurrently both agricultural and industrial development. Section VII.A considers this question in terms of the structural transformation of a developing economy. The structural transformation over time from a low-income, agrarian rural economy to an industrial urban economy with higher per capita income involves the phenomena of industrialization, agricultural change, migration, and urbanization. As discussed in VII.A.1, there are some uniform features in the "normal" pattern of structural change. Agricultural transformation involves a relative decline in the agricultural sector, but absolute levels of agricultural output and employment will rise throughout much of the process of structural transformation. At the structural transformation turning point, the rural labor force will fall in absolute size.

Section VII.B indicates that industrialization offers substantial dynamic benefits that are important for changing the traditional structure of the less developed economy. The advocacy of industrialization may be particularly compelling for primary export countries that confront problems of a lagging export demand while having to provide employment for a rapidly increasing labor force. Systematic support is given to the industrialization argument in Paul Rosenstein-Rodan's emphasis on the external economies to be realized through industrialization, and his advocacy of a "big push" in the form of a high minimum amount of industrial investment in order to jump over the economic obstacles to development (VII.B.1).

In the early postwar period of development economics, there was considerable discussion of "balanced growth" versus "unbalanced growth" approaches to investment. By emphasizing that investment decisions are mutually reinforcing and that overall supply "creates its own demand," the balanced growth doctrine had considerable appeal as a means of initiating development. Critics of the doctrine, however, argued that a poor country does not have the capacity to attain balanced investment over a wide range of industries and that, moreover, the method of balanced growth cannot bring about as high a rate of development as can unbalanced growth. Instead of striving for balanced investment, proponents of unbalanced growth advocated the creation of strategic imbalances that would set up stimuli and pressures that are needed to induce investment decisions.

As expressed by Albert O. Hirschman, "our aim must be to keep alive rather than eliminate the disequilibria of which profits and losses are symptoms in a competitive economy. If the economy is to be kept moving ahead, the task of development policy is to maintain tensions, disproportions, and disequilibria."[1]

According to this view, the central task of a development strategy is to overcome the lack of decision-taking actions in the economy; for this purpose, unbalanced growth is necessary to induce investment decisions and thereby economize on the less developed economy's principal scarce resource—genuine decision making.

It has now become clear that the phrases "balanced growth" and "unbalanced growth" initially caught on too readily and that each approach has been overdrawn. Instead of seeking to generalize either approach, we should more appropriately look to the conditions under which each can claim some validity. It may be concluded that while a newly developing country should aim at balance as an investment criterion, this objective will be attained initially only by following in most cases a policy of unbalanced investment. In operational terms, the crucial question has become how to determine the proper sequence of investment decisions in order to create the proper amount of imbalance in the right activities. Relevant for this strategy is the concept of "linkages," as discussed by Hirschman in selection VII.B.2.

Section VII.B also focuses on recent experience with industrialization strategies that have been based on import substitution (VII.B.4) and on export substitution (VII.B.5). Policies that have encouraged industrialization through import controls and tariff protection have at the same time adversely taxed agricultural production and exports. To redress the previous bias in favor of import substitution, emphasis is now being given to the positive relationships between exports and industrialization. Several reasons are offered for the superiority of industrialization via export substitution. (Chapter IX will offer a more detailed analysis of export-led development.)

Beyond trade policy, government's role in promoting industrial development is examined more extensively—first analytically in VII.B.3 and then with policy guidelines in VII.B.6.

Technological progress, as discussed in Section VII.C, is central to the industrialization process. What is "appropriate technology" (VII.C.1)? What is the correct choice of technique (VII.C.2)? What is the significance of technology transfer (VII.C.3)? The answers that a country gives to these questions will have considerable impact on the pace and pattern of its industrialization.

Recently, with the growing criticism of state-owned enterprises (SOEs), there has been considerable effort to privatize. Selection VII.D.1 provides a guide to privatization policy.

Finally, the relationships between agriculture and industry are outlined in Section VII.E. The view that agriculture can serve as a resource reservoir for industry is examined, but the shift in focus now is on the mutual interactions between industry and agriculture. Without agricultural development, as formulated in the next chapter, there cannot be the realization of a positive industrial program, as outlined in this chapter.

---

[1]Albert O. Hirschman, *The Strategy of Economic Development* (1958), p. 66.

VII.A. STRUCTURAL TRANSFORMATION

VII.A.1. Modeling Structural Transformation*

The present study attempts to provide a uniform analysis of the principal changes in economic structure that normally accompany economic growth. The focus is on the major features of resource mobilization and allocation, particularly those aspects needed to sustain further growth and therefore of primary interest for policy. By treating these aspects in a uniform econometric framework, it is possible to provide a consistent description of a number of interrelated types of structural change and also to identify systematic differences in development patterns among countries that are following different development strategies.

The starting point for this study is the pioneering work of Simon Kuznets, who first demonstrated the value of quantitative intercountry analysis of economic structures.[1] . . . With the benefit of the great increase in data that has taken place over the past decade, we are able to compare cross-country and time-series estimates and to establish some useful relationships between them.

The establishment of a more uniform and comprehensive description of structural change opens up the possibility of identifying countries that have been following similar development strategies. The choice of a development strategy is affected not only by the structural characteristics of the economy but also by the government's social objectives and willingness to use various policy instruments. Our analysis leads to the identification of three main patterns of resource allocation: *large country, balanced allocation; small country, primary specialization; small country, industry specialization.* By comparing countries that are following similar

development patterns, it is possible to derive more valid performance standards and also compare the policies chosen by countries under similar conditions.

Conceptual Framework

In general terms, a development pattern may be defined as a systematic variation in any significant aspect of the economic or social structure associated with a rising level of income or other index of development. Although some variation with the income level is observable in almost all structural features, we are primarily interested in those structural changes that are needed to achieve sustained increases in per capita income. Since one can rarely prove that a given aspect of development is logically "necessary," we start with those for which a plausible case can be made on empirical grounds.

Kuznets's approach to the identification and measurement of development patterns is largely inductive. Starting with the elements of the national accounts that are recorded in a number of countries, he measures the changes in the composition of consumption, production, trade, and other aggregates as income rises. His observations are either for individual advanced countries over time or for groups of countries classified by income level. In this way he achieves comparable measures of development patterns both among countries and over time.

This form of analysis is further developed by examining some of the underlying growth processes that generate the observed development patterns. General models of structural change applicable to all countries can be derived from the following types of assumptions:

1. Similar variation in the composition of consumer demand with rising per capita income, dominated by a decline in the share of foodstuffs and a rise in the share of manufactured goods;
2. Accumulation of capital—both physical and human—at a rate exceeding the growth of the labor force;

*From Hollis Chenery and Moshe Syrquin, *Patterns of Development 1950–1970* (New York: World Bank by Oxford University Press, 1975), pp. 3–11. Reprinted by permission.

[1] In a series of ten articles published in the journal *Economic Development and Cultural Change* (1956–67), Kuznets analyzed the intercountry variation in the principal components of the gross national product (GNP) and compared these results with historical changes in the developed countries over the past century or more.

3. Access of all countries to similar technology;
4. Access to international trade and capital inflows.

These basic aspects of consumer demand, technology, and trade change over time as a result of technological progress, population growth, the rising level of world income, and consequent changes in trading conditions and the supply of external capital. Rather than ignore the existence of such changes, we will estimate time trends in all structural relations during the postwar period.

Any attempt to identify the causes of structural change is complicated by the fact that supply and demand factors often interact. For example, one of the most fundamental development patterns—the shift from agriculture to industry—is promoted by the change in the composition of internal demand, by the rising level of skills, and by international shifts in comparative advantage. When the level of per capita income is the only explanatory variable used in a regression equation, it will incorporate elements of all of these factors in a single income effect. This combined relationship can be broken down, however, by allowing for independent variation in some of the elements, such as trade patterns, which depend on resource endowments and government policies as well as on the level of income.

A major objective of this study will be to separate the effects of universal factors affecting all countries from particular characteristics such as natural endowments or government policies. To the extent that this objective is achieved, each aspect of a country's development pattern, such as the observed rise in saving or in the level of industry, can be described in terms of three components: (a) the normal effect of universal factors which are related to the level of income; (b) the effect of other general factors such as market size or natural resources over which the government has little or no control; (c) the effects of the country's individual history, its political and social objectives, and the particular policies the government has followed to achieve them. Our primary concern here is the identification of the uniform factors (a) and (b) which affect all countries. Since these typically account for well over half the observed variation among countries in most structural characteristics, the effects of factors specific to a given country can be more readily evaluated after allowing for the uniform elements in each development pattern.

In order to separate universal factors from characteristics that are specific to individual countries, this study tries to establish testable links between empirically derived development patterns and the deductive results of development theory. In some cases the links between theory and observation are fairly simple and lead directly to causal statements as to the nature of the underlying process. For example, Arthur Lewis's dual economy theory (1954) predicts that the share of saving in GNP will rise due to the more rapid growth of the modern, capitalistic sector with its higher saving potential—a prediction that has been borne out by subsequent experience. This type of relationship between a structural characteristic such as saving and the level of income is defined here as a development process.

Engel's law provides a second example of a universal development process. It specifies that the income elasticity of demand for food is less than unity, implying that the share of food in total consumption will fall as the level of income rises. When combined with other development processes, such as the accumulation of capital and skills with rising income, Engel's law also helps to explain the observed patterns of industrialization.

For the present study we have selected ten basic processes that appear to be essential features of development in all countries. One test of essentiality is provided by economic theory. It is virtually impossible to construct a disaggregated model of long-term growth in which there is not some shift of resources from primary production to industry, a rise in the ratio of capital to labor, and a systematic change in the composition of imports and exports. To study these processes on the basis of intercountry data the compositions of domestic demand, trade, and production are taken as the units of analysis.

There is a second type of income-related change for which the available evidence suggests considerable uniformity but for which there is as yet no well-defined body of theory. Examples of such processes include the growth of the public sector's share in income and expenditure, the movement of population from rural to urban locations, and the demographic transition that results in a lowering of both death and birth rates. Since these processes have strong claims to be considered both universal and essential on the basis of the experience of more advanced countries, they are included in the present study.

The ten basic processes to be analyzed are listed in Table 1. They are defined by twenty-

TABLE 1. Structural Characteristics Analyzed

Dependent Variable	Symbol	Basic Regression	
		Number of Countries	Number of Observations
Accumulation Processes			
1. *Investment*			
a. Gross domestic saving as percent of GDP	S	93	1,432
b. Gross domestic investment as percent of GDP	I	93	1,432
c. Capital inflow (net import of goods and services) as percent of GDP	F	93	1,432
2. *Government revenue*			
a. Government revenue as percent of GDP	GR	89	1,111
b. Tax revenue as percent of GDP	TR	89	1,111
3. *Education*			
a. Education expenditure by government as percent of GDP	$EDEXP$	100	794
b. Primary and secondary school enrollment ratio	$SCHEN$	101	433
Resource Allocation Processes			
4. *Structure of domestic demand*			
a. Gross domestic investment as percent of GDP	I	93	1,432
b. Private consumption as percent of GDP	C	94	1,508
c. Government consumption as percent of GDP	G	94	1,508
d. Food consumption as percent of GDP	C_f	52	642
5. *Structure of production*			
a. Primary output as percent of GDP	V_p	89	1,325
b. Industry output as percent of GDP	V_m	89	1,325
c. Utilities output as percent of GDP	V_u	89	1,325
d. Services output as percent of GDP	V_s	89	1,325
6. *Structure of trade*			
a. Exports as percent of GDP	E	93	1,432
b. Primary exports as percent of GDP	E_p	88	413
c. Manufactured exports as percent of GDP	E_m	88	413
d. Services exports as percent of GDP	E_s	88	413
e. Imports as percent of GDP	M	93	1,432
Demographic and Distributional Processes			
7. *Labor allocation*			
a. Share of primary labor	L_p	72	165
b. Share of industry labor	L_m	72	165
c. Share of service labor	L_s	72	165
8. *Urbanization*			
Urban percent of total population	URB	90	317
9. *Demographic transition*			
a. Birth rate	BR	83	213
b. Death rate	DR	83	213
10. *Income distribution*			
a. Share of highest 20 percent	$DIST$	55	66
b. Share of lowest 40 percent	$DIST$	55	66

seven variables for which data are available for a large number of countries. The processes and the variables used to measure them represent a compromise among four desiderata: theoretical significance, universality, data availability, and policy relevance.

Taken together these ten processes describe different dimensions of the overall structural transformation of a poor country into a rich one. Single dimensions of the transformation—such as industrialization or urbanization—are often used to symbolize the whole set of development processes. It is more useful to consider them as separate processes of change, however, since they may proceed at different rates even though all are highly correlated.

Before attempting to measure these processes it is useful to consider some of their common characteristics. Long time series of almost any of these variables for the presently developed countries usually show a period of fairly rapid change followed by deceleration and in some cases even a reversal of the direction of change. Among less developed countries that have grown substantially over the past fifty years, it is often possible to identify a period in which the rate of change has accelerated following an earlier period of little structural change. Taken together, these observations suggest that an s-shaped curve, characterized by an upper and lower asymptote, will generally represent the major features of the structural transformation.

For almost all of the development processes considered here the existence of an upper and lower asymptote is virtually a logical necessity. No economy can continue to exist without minimal levels of investment, government revenue, or food consumption. It is equally necessary that there should be an upper limit to the share of each of these components in total income. For other processes, such as industrialization or urbanization, the lower limit may be close to zero but there is an equally strong case for an upper asymptote. Since structural discontinuities may be ruled out, a logistic curve, which describes a gradual transition from one limit to the other, illustrates the type of function needed for the analysis of these transitional processes.

Econometric Procedure and Data

Since we are concerned with interrelated changes in the structure of the whole economy, the model implicit in our analysis is one of general equilibrium. Simplified versions of such a model have been used for historical analysis of structural change in a number of countries. Although these models are not directly applicable to intercountry analysis, they do suggest the nature of the interdependent changes in resource allocation which underlie the major development patterns.

The regression equations proposed for the description of development processes can be thought of as reduced forms of a more detailed general equilibrium system. In the simplest case, we can imagine that the observed patterns of resource allocation are produced by only two of the factors suggested above: changes in demand with rising income and differences in trade patterns, resulting from variations in market size as well as changes in factor proportions. On these assumptions, an interindustry model yields solutions for levels of consumption, production, and trade by sector as a function of the level of per capita gross domestic product (GDP) and population. Such a model also provides a basis for interpreting the direct and indirect effects of other exogenous variables, such as natural resources and capital inflow.

To deal statistically with the problem of interdependence among processes we will first include as exogenous variables only the income level and population of the country, since these affect virtually all processes. This specification permits a uniform analysis of all aspects of structural change. The resulting descriptions provide a basis for studying the interdependent changes in demand and resource allocation in a consistent framework.

The basic hypothesis underlying this set of statistical estimates is that development processes occur with sufficient uniformity among countries to produce a consistent pattern of change in resource allocation, factor use, and other structural features as the level of per capita income rises. The statistical analysis is designed to explore various aspects of this general hypothesis:

1. The extent of variation in each structural feature with changes in the income level;
2. The range of income over which each process shows the most pronounced change;
3. The effect on each process of other key variables;
4. Differences between time series and intercountry relations;
5. The major sources of differences in development patterns and the nature of their effects.

VII.A.2. Elements of Structural Transformation*

The mechanism of economic progress in farming is the same one that operates in every other sector of the economy. That mechanism is *specialization*. Not only is there specialization along specific crop lines among farmers, but a host of functions formerly carried out by the household is transferred to specialist producers. Increasing division of labor in all economic activity brings with it the opportunity to use machinery whose power, speed, and precision multiplies the yield of human effort. Specialization not only makes possible the introduction of capital equipment, it facilitates changes to better organization and more productive technologies. The result is augmented productivity of land and capital as well as of labor. As these processes get under way, households shift along the continuum from self-sufficiency to dependence upon markets for disposal of their production, for purchase of their raw materials, for opportunities to hire labor and work for wages, for investments and loans, and for other goods and services.

Structural transformation at the sectoral level results from movement toward specialization and market participation at the producer level. Specialization means that new manufacturing and service activities emerge. Formerly small sectors—education, health, financial services— are greatly enlarged. The most dominant change, however, is the proportionate decline in the agricultural sector and the rise of the manufacturing sector. This is in part the result of greater demand for nonagricultural goods with rising incomes, but the more fundamental cause is the transfer of function from generalist producers in the countryside to specialist firms in the towns.

Thus, in countries at the lower end of the income scale, members of rural households devote 35 to 50 percent of their time to nonfarm tasks. Gradually such tasks as the making of clothing, utensils, furniture, weapons, jewelry, the processing of crops into food, the construction of buildings and boats are turned over to specialist producers. . . .

High-productivity agriculture entrains indus-trialization directly; it also fosters it indirectly since the specialized services, differentiated market networks, and financial institutions that serve farming simultaneously lead to increased efficiency in various manufacturing and service activities. Moreover, the roads and other rural infrastructure built initially to facilitate expanded agricultural production also foster the growth of rural nonfarm activities.

Patterns of Structural Transformation

Structural transformation accompanying rising per capita income can be considered along two dimensions, changing output shares and reallocation of the labor force. In both dimensions, structural transformation is characterized by *relative* decline in the agricultural sector. But absolute levels of agricultural output and employment will rise throughout much of the prolonged process of structural transformation.

Changing Output Shares

For Tanzania, agriculture accounts for 50–60 percent of GDP (Table 1). As productivity and income increase, that share will decline sharply. The parallel rise in manufacturing as the most dynamic sector, until a middle income level is attained, progresses from 5–8 percent and rises to 30–35 percent; thereafter it diminishes as the share of educational, governmental, and professional services continue to expand in high-income post-industrial societies. Whatever the particular propellant that drives the growth process, every developing country traverses this common pathway of structural change. . . .

The natural resource effect on GDP shares is reflected in the make-up of exports. As a country develops, its comparative advantage evolves from resource-intensive commodities to labor-intensive products and finally to capital and skill-intensive goods. While the natural endowment strongly influences the level and composition of exports for virtually all countries with *a*bundant *r*ural *l*abor (CARLs), the impact is most powerful for mineral exporters: the enlarged "Other" category in Table 1 for Nigeria, Indonesia, and Malaysia (16–31 percent) is attributable to their petroleum income. Just how important natural resources can be in determin-

*From Thomas P. Tomich, Peter Kilby, and Bruce F. Johnston, *Transforming Agrarian Economies: Opportunities Seized, Opportunities Missed* (Ithaca: Cornell University Press, 1995), chap. 2, passim. Reprinted by permission.

TABLE 1. Selected Measures of Structural Transformation, 1990

	GNP Per Capita (1990 US$)	Share in GDP (percent)			
		Agriculture	Manufacturing	Services	Other[a]
Tanzania	110	59	10	29	2
Bangladesh	210	38	9	46	6
Nigeria	290	36	7	25	31
India	350	31	19	40	10
Kenya	370	28	11	51	10
China	370	27	38	31	4
Indonesia	570	22	20	38	20
Egypt	600	17	16	53	13
Colombia	1,260	17	21	51	11
Thailand	1,420	12	26	48	13
Malaysia	2,320	21[b]	19[b]	44[b]	16[b]
Mexico	2,490	9	23	61	7
Brazil	2,680	10	26	51	13
Taiwan	7,954	4	34	54	8
United States	21,790	2[c]	17[c]	69[c]	12[c]
Japan	25,430	3	28	56	13

[a]"Other" is comprised of electricity, water, gas, construction, and mining.
[b]For the year 1984.
[c]For the year 1989.

Sources: World Bank, *World Development Report 1992;* FAO, *Production Yearbook 1990;* Council for Economic Planning and Development, *Industry of Free China,* Vol. 74, 1993.

ing the level and composition of GDP has been made transparent by the volatility of energy prices. With the precipitate fall in the price of oil and reduced petroleum production by 1988, Nigeria's per capita output had fallen to one third its 1980 high of $1,040, with an ensuing "expansion" of its agricultural share from 27 to 34 percent—and all this with no change in the underlying productivity of domestic factors of production.

In sum, within the broad confines of a common pattern of structural transformation that accompanies the growth in per capita income, there is considerable variation around the trend, some of a permanent nature and some transitory. . . .

Changing Labor Shares

The changing allocation of labor broadly tracks that of output. The share of agricultural labor falls continuously but over a wider range—from 70–80 percent to 2–6 percent. Hence, measured output per agricultural worker is below the national average until late in structural transformation. The larger the agricultural

sector, the greater the deviation below that national average output.

Employment shares of all other sectors increase. Initially, manufacturing accounts for a large chunk of nonfarm jobs. As per capita incomes increase, manufacturing shows the highest growth in productivity, which means fewer jobs per unit of output growth than other nonfarm sectors. This low employment elasticity is mainly the result of increasing capital intensity, which in turn results from a changing mix of industrial products and greater mechanization in existing lines. Policies that avoid subsidies and keep the discipline of comparative advantage in the choice of new industry can significantly raise employment elasticity.

What about employment in other nonfarm sectors? It grows at a faster rate than in manufacturing. Growth in demand is biased toward those where productivity is below the sector average. In construction, there is a shift to labor-intensive urban dwellings and away from ports, bridges, and roads. In trade, the shift is to retail services and away from less labor-using wholesaling and storage. As the extended family declines and more women enter the labor force, there is a shift from home-supplied to market-

TABLE 2. Selected Measures of Structural Transformation, 1990

	Share of the Labor Force in Agriculture (percent)	Agricultural Output		Labor Force Participation[a] (percent)
		Per Capita (1990 US$)	Per Farm Worker (1990 US$)	
Tanzania	81	53	140	48
Bangladesh	69	75	376	29
Nigeria	65	116	473	38
India	67	92	364	40*
Kenya	77	89	279	41
China	68	88	219	60
Indonesia	49	127	666	43*
Egypt	41	110	981	28
Colombia	27	208	2,379	32
Thailand	64	179	524	56**
Malaysia	32	—	—	42
Mexico	30	238	2,256	35
Brazil	24	281	3,156	37
Taiwan	13	318	6,043	59
United States	2	367[b]	30,969[b]	44
Japan	6	600	18,475	53

[a]Labor force participation measures the proportion of the agricultural population that is economically active, as estimated by the FAO. Where no asterisk appears, the participation rate is approximately the same for both the agricultural and the nonagricultural population. One asterisk indicates the former exceeds the nonagricultural participation rate by 4 to 6 percentage points; two asterisks indicate 8 percentage points difference.

[b]For the year 1988.

Sources: World Bank, *World Development Report 1992;* FAO, *Production Yearbook 1990;* Council for Economic Planning and Development, *Industry of Free China,* Vol. 74, 1993.

supplied personal services—restaurants, domestic services, household repair.

Farming provides the main source of livelihood for over half the population until per capita incomes reach $600–800. And, as seen in Table 2, per capita output in agriculture tends to rise, despite an ever-shrinking portion of the workforce. This flows from the extraordinary advance in measured output per worker: from a low starting point, productivity growth is more rapid in agriculture than in any other sector. . . .

The Hidden Extent of Rural Nonfarm Activities

Until recently, the rural economy was equated with the agricultural economy. The primary function of rural households was thought to be production of food, fiber, and livestock for the home market and one or more crops for export. Household members might be engaged in limited agricultural processing, transporting, and marketing. This conventional view was derived, however, from census statistics that understate rural nonfarm activities. Censuses classify indi-

viduals by primary occupation only; other activities are ignored. Moreover, the classification of rural areas as urban (especially the small rural towns that are the hub for much rural nonfarm activity) also understates the importance of nonagricultural pursuits in rural areas. . . .

The size of the rural nonfarm sector has, until quite recently, been severely underestimated in CARLs. This has occurred because of occupational classification procedures employed in population censuses and because of the way the rural-urban boundary has been drawn. The sector is large and diverse. It plays a major role in augmenting rural welfare and can be a significant ingredient in advancing structural transformation. Finally, implied in the underestimation of the nonfarm labor force is an overestimation of that devoted to agricultural pursuits.

Natural Resource Endowments Matter Less

In low per-capita-income countries, natural resource endowment has important effects on the relative contribution of different sectors to

GDP, on the type of productive stimuli at work in the economy, and on savings and foreign exchange. Labor, land, and natural resources are the original factors of production. In early development, when the supply of the "produced factor" (capital) is modest and technology rudimentary, natural resource endowment figures large in national output. Later, new technology, capital accumulation, and international trade progressively free the tight relationship between output and resource inputs. Hence, for Holland and Japan, meager natural resources are not now a serious handicap to increases in per capita output.

Without the right policies, even the richest endowment of natural resources will not lead to structural transformation. Indonesia's success depended heavily on macroeconomic policies, and Nigeria's failure on the lack of agricultural development during the oil-boom years of the 1970s.

Institutional Aspects of Structural Transformation

The division of labor among producers cannot proceed without the development of institutions to coordinate their activities. Efficient, competitive markets integrate increasingly specialized producers and consumers of a variety of goods and services. And during structural transformation, markets for labor, land, capital, and financial services multiply in number and in size, with a proliferation of services to buyers and sellers.

Labor Markets

The development of labor markets accommodates differentiation in two directions: specialization by commodity and by skill. In subsistence, household labor produces many items for family consumption. As more goods are purchased on the market, the range of crops and crafts is narrowed. Concurrently, as various functions are transferred out of the household, the nonfarm rural economy begins to emerge, with labor supplied under apprenticeship and for wages.

In some areas, the earliest rural labor market emerges in plantations and mines, and in seasonal jobs in cotton ginneries, rice mills, and canneries. In agriculture, the evolution of a permanent labor force is determined by agricultural development, land ownership, and tenure arrangements. Finally, development of efficient urban labor markets depends on transportation, urban housing, and job information, as well as education.

Labor markets do not just reallocate workers. Wage and salary differences play a central role in the formation of *human capital*—that is, skills and broader characteristics, such as health, that raise the productivity of people. Without human capital to bind together complex technology and organization, structural transformation cannot be sustained.

The development of labor skills is dependent upon other inputs besides pecuniary incentives—education, both general and technical, employer policies, and traditions. Given reasonable education and training, supplies of technical skills respond to market-generated wage premiums. Supervisory and managerial skills are more influenced by sociological factors, and tend to develop at a slower pace.

Financial Markets

By increasing the incentive to save and the profitability of investment, financial markets help to raise the level of physical capital formation. They shift investable resources from one sector to another, from areas of limited growth to those of rapid expansion. Efficient financial markets also augment national product and consumer welfare by financing more current business transactions and allowing households more freedom in the timing of big expenditures.

In the subsistence economy, investment is limited by the ability and willingness to save—that is, the household labor time that can be diverted from production for current consumption and from non-economic activities. Saving and investment are thus mutually constraining. With monetization and development of a market for debt, savings and investment separate, and the geographic boundaries in which investable resources can be mobilized are extended.

Initially, in most CARLs, risks are great, competition among lenders is slight, and transaction costs are high. The result: interest rates are high (40 to 100 percent a year) and only the distressed borrow. With economic development, the real cost of lending falls and competition increases.

Technical Change and Productivity Growth

The evolution of markets that accompanies structural transformation makes three principal contributions to raising per capita national product. First, markets draw into productive use land, labor, and entrepreneurship that might otherwise go untapped. Second, since competitive pricing creates incentives to allocate resources to areas where their return is highest, output per worker tends to increase as a result of the efficient resource allocation. Third, the operation of financial markets results in a more rapid increase in the stock of capital available to assist individual laborers, augmenting their productivity.

There is another set of factors which raises long-term productivity. "Technical change" encompasses the interconnected elements of new technology, augmented labor skills, and improved organization efficiency.

When research and development become institutionalized, much of the increase in factor productivity comes from applied research that results in specific products or production techniques that fit prevailing factor prices, technical conditions, and consumer tastes. In the past, technical progress was slow and evolutionary, relying on the accidental discovery or the inspired experiments of many small producers. Such was agricultural change in nineteenth-century America and Japan.

Technical progress in today's CARLs is different. Advances come from drawing on existing knowledge in high-income countries. Such transfers of applied technology are easiest when the improvement is embodied in the whole product, such as sharper tools or electronic calculators. It becomes more difficult when the improvement depends on new skills, restructured organization, and altered relationships with other economic agents.

Elements of Social Change

The proliferation of firms and public institutions, the emergence of new technologies and marketing relationships, and the changing individual behavior bring changes to the traditional social structure. The general direction of that change is toward ever greater differentiation of social roles and institutions, as well as new methods of social integration. One example: the role of village elders is gradually taken over by lawyers, judges, legislators, and family counselors. Some of the new mechanisms of integration are elections, political parties, professional associations, and consumer organizations.

From Rural to Urban

The differences between agriculture and industry in the organization of production and in the technologies employed have profound implications for social change. The modernization of agriculture—while it entails the same increased use of capital equipment, purchased inputs, and technical knowledge as industry—does not alter the sequential division of labor imposed by nature nor alter the social organization of the family farm. In striking contrast, the shift from craft production to large-scale manufacturing means migration to a new place, new society, and new way of working.

Policy Implications of Structural Transformation

Specialization and technological change are the driving forces that transform an agrarian economy into a diversified economy. Although agriculture predominates in early structural transformation, recent research shows that a diverse nonfarm sector also figures large in the unspecialized rural economy of CARLs. In the near term, development strategies for agriculture and rural nonfarm activities are as important for CARLs as industrial strategy is for the "newly industrialized countries" at a later stage of structural transformation.

CARLs cannot eliminate mass poverty without structural transformation, but there is a wide range of successful paths to higher productivity. A country's policy choices matter more than endowments of land, oil, timber, and other natural resources. Without the right policies, even the richest in natural resources cannot sustain productivity growth. With them, they can.

But the "right" policies also depend on a country's stage of structural transformation. So, for CARLs, what does the policy dictum "getting prices right" mean, while markets for land, labor, and capital, as well as commodities, are evolving? There is no simple, single answer. Commodity market imperfections arising, for example, from poor transport, infrastructure, and communications raise the costs and risks of trade, so inhibiting exchange of commodities among regions and in the world market.

CARLs embody the most powerful arguments for and against intervention in markets. And since the evolution of economic institutions, including markets, is both a cause and a consequence of structural transformation, the scope and limits of government policy vary throughout the long process of structural transformation. The plethora of plausible market imperfections, combined with expanding public expectations following social and political change, often pro-pel governments toward intervention. Yet limited government capacity and inevitable tensions accompanying political development easily subvert the original intent of intervention.

Comment: Empirical Research on Structural Change

The process of structural transformation has been analyzed in quantitative terms through techniques such as input–output analysis, computable general equilibrium models, cross-country comparisons, and time series. Most notable are the econometric studies of long-term changes in economic structure by Hollis Chenery and Moshe Syrquin: *Patterns of Development, 1950–1970* (1975); Hollis Chenery, Sherman Robinson, and Moshe Syrquin, *Industrialization and Growth: A Comparative Study* (1986); "Three Decades of Industrialization," *World Bank Economic Review* (May 1989).

The last study analyzes data from 108 countries during the period 1950 to 1983 and defines the range of structural transformation in 1980 U.S. dollars as the interval from $300 to $4,000 per capita GNP. The evidence from this study suggest that uniformity of the structural transformation is robust. One of the most uniform features in the process of structural change is the change in final demand: the share of private consumption in GDP declines with a rising level of income, the share of investment rises, and the trade deficit declines. The composition of foreign trade also changes: the share of manufactures in exports tends to increase fairly steadily. In domestic production, the share of value added in agriculture declines during the transformation process while manufacturing, construction, and utilities double their share, and the share of the service sector rises by about 50 percent. At the per capita income level of $1,500 (1980 dollars), the rising share of industrial output surpasses the declining share of the agricultural sector.

Exhibits VII.1 and VII.2, based on Chenery and Syrquin's 1975 study, show similar changes, but over the earlier 1950 to 1970 interval from $70 to $1,500 in 1964 dollars.

EXHIBIT VII.1. Transformation of Demand

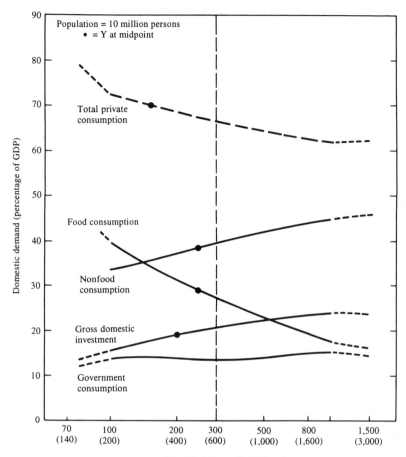

Per capita GNP in 1964 U.S. dollars (1976 dollars in parentheses)

Source: Hollis Chenery and Moshe Syrquin, *Patterns of Development, 1950–1970*
(1975), fig. 4.

EXHIBIT VII.2. Transformation of Production

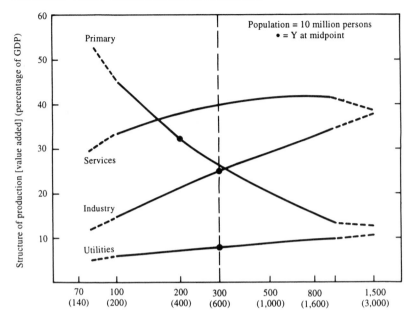

Per capita GNP in 1964 U.S. dollars (1976 dollars in parentheses)

Source: Hollis Chenery and Moshe Syrquin, *Patterns of Development, 1950–1970* (1975), fig. 5.

EXHIBIT VII.3. Trade Patterns for Three Groups of Countries

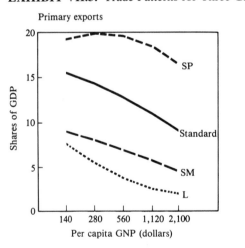

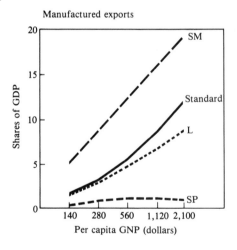

Key: L: large country pattern
SM: small, manufacturing-oriented country pattern
SP: small, primary-oriented country patttern

From a cross-country model, a standard pattern of industrialization is defined corresponding to average demand and trade patterns at each level of income, with population size and capital inflow held constant. A major source of industrialization is the transformation of international trade—the decline in primary exports and rise in manufactured exports according to type of country (see key). This Exhibit compares the estimated export pattern in each type of country with the standard pattern derived from the pooled regression for all countries. According to type of country, there are important variations in the role of trade in industrialization.

EXHIBIT VII.4. Growth of Production

	GDP		Agriculture		Industry		Manufacturing		Services	
	\
Average Annual Growth Rate (percent)									
	1970–80	1980–91	1970–80	1980–91	1970–80	1980–91	1970–80	1980–91	1970–80	1980–91
Low- and middle-income economies	5.3	3.3	2.7	2.8	—	3.3	—	—	6.2	3.5
Sub-Saharan Africa	4.0	2.1	1.5	1.8	5.3	2.0	3.5	—	5.5	2.5
East Asia and Pacific	6.6	7.7	3.1	4.3	9.4	9.4	10.5	10.6	7.1	8.6
South Asia	3.5	5.4	1.8	3.3	4.6	6.4	4.6	6.7	4.7	6.6
Middle East and North Africa	5.2	2.1	4.2	3.6	3.2	0.9		3.5	7.2	2.1
Latin America and Caribbean	5.5	1.7	3.5	1.9	6.1	1.4	8.0	1.3	6.1	2.0
Severely indebted	6.1	1.7	3.8	1.5	6.7	1.4	8.2	2.0	6.4	2.2

Note: Percentages are weighted averages.

Source: World Bank, *World Development Report 1993* (1993), p. 241

VII.B. PROMOTING INDUSTRIALIZATION

VII.B.1. External Economies and Industrialization*

An institutional framework different from the present one is clearly necessary for the successful carrying out of industrialisation in international depressed areas. In what follows arguments are submitted tending to show why the whole of the industry to be created is to be treated and planned like one huge firm or trust.

The first task of industrialisation is to provide for training and "skilling" of labour which is to transform Eastern European peasants into full-time or part-time industrial workers. The automatism of *laissez-faire* never worked properly in that field. It broke down because it is not profitable for a private entrepreneur to invest in training labour. There are no mortgages on workers—an entrepreneur who invests in training workers may lose capital if these workers contract with another firm. Although not a good investment for a private firm, it is the best investment for the State. It is also a good investment for the bulk of industries to be created when taken as a whole, although it may represent irrecoverable costs for a smaller unit. It constitutes an important instance of the Pigovian divergence between "private and social marginal net product" where the latter is greater than the former. Training facilities (including transport and housing) of one million workers per annum would involve costs of certainly more than £100 million per annum—a sum which may be too great to be borne by the State (of the Eastern European national economy) if taken *apart* from the costs of the 50 percent participation in its own "Eastern European Industrial Trust" that we shall propose. It should be counted as capital investment in the Eastern European Industrial Trust (EEIT).

That is not, however, the most important reason in favour of such a large investment unit.

Complementarity of different industries pro-vides the most important set of arguments in favor of a large-scale planned industrialisation. In order to illustrate the issues involved, let us adopt the somewhat roundabout method of analysing two examples. Let us assume that 20,000 unemployed workers in Eastern and South-Eastern Europe are taken from the land and put into a large shoe factory. They receive wages substantially higher than their previous meagre income *in natura*. It would be impossible to put them into industry at their previous income standard, because they need more foodstuffs than they had in their agrarian semi-unemployed existence, because these foodstuffs have to be transported to towns, and because the workers have to pay for housing accommodation. If these workers spent all their wages on shoes, a market for the products of their enterprise would arise representing an expansion which does not disturb the pre-existing market, and 90 percent of the problem (assuming 10 percent profit) would be solved. The trouble is that the workers will not spend all their wages on shoes. If, instead, one million unemployed workers were taken from the land and put, not into one industry, but into a whole series of industries which produce the bulk of the goods on which the workers would spend their wages, what was not true in the case of one shoe factory would become true in the case of a whole system of industries: it would create its own additional market, thus realising an expansion of world output with the minimum disturbance of the world markets. The industries producing the bulk of the wage goods can therefore be said to be complementary. The planned creation of such a complementary system reduces the risk of not being able to sell, and, since risk can be considered as cost, it reduces costs. It is in this sense a special case of "external economies."

It may be added that, while in the highly developed and rich countries with their more variegated needs it is difficult to assess the prospective demand of the population, it is not as difficult to foresee on what the formerly unemployed workers would spend their wages in regions where a low standard of living obtains.

*From Paul N. Rosenstein-Rodan, "Problems of Industrialisation of Eastern and South-Eastern Europe," *Economic Journal,* June–September 1943, pp. 204–7; "Notes on the Theory of the 'Big Push,'" in Howard S. Ellis (ed.), *Economic Development for Latin America,* Macmillan and Co. Ltd., London; St. Martin's Press, New York, 1961, pp. 57–58, 60–62, 65–66. Reprinted by permission.

Two other types of "external economies" will arise when a system of different industries is created. First, the strictly Marshallian economies external to a firm within a growing industry. The same applies, however (secondly), to economies external to one industry due to the growth of other industries. It is usually tacitly assumed that the divergence between the "private and social marginal net product" is not very considerable. This assumption may be too optimistic even in the case of a crystallized mature competitive economy. It is certainly not true in the case of fundamental structural changes in the international depressed areas. External economies may there be of the same order of magnitude as profits which appear on the profit and loss account of the enterprise.

The existing institutions of international and national investment do not take advantage of external economies. There is no incentive within their framework for many investments which are profitable in terms of "social marginal net product," but do not appear profitable in terms of "private marginal net product." The main driving-force of investment is the profit expectation of an individual entrepreneur which is based on experience of the past. Experience of the past is partly irrelevant, however, where the whole economic structure of a region is to be changed. An individual entrepreneur's knowledge of the market is bound to be insufficient in this case because he cannot have all the data that would be available to the planning board of an EEIT. His subjective risk estimate is bound to be considerably higher than the objective risk. If the industrialisation of international depressed areas were to rely entirely on the normal incentive of private entrepreneurs, the process would not only be very much slower, the rate of investment smaller and (consequently) the national income lower, but the whole economic structure of the region would be different. Investment would be distributed in different proportions between different industries, the final equilibrium would be below the optimum which a large EEIT could achieve. In the international capital market the existing institutions are mostly used to invest in, or to grant credit to, single enterprises. It might easily happen that any one enterprise would not be profitable enough to guarantee payment of sufficient interest or dividends out of its own profits. But the creation of such an enterprise, for example, production of electric power, may create new investment opportunities and profits elsewhere, for example, in an electrical equip-

ment industry. If we create a sufficiently large investment unit by including all the new industries of the region, external economies will become internal profits out of which dividends may be paid easily.

Professor Allyn Young's celebrated example elucidates our problem. He assumed that a Tube line was to be built in a district and that an accurate estimate was made of costs and receipts. It was found that the rate of profit would be below the usual rate of yield on investments obtainable elsewhere. The project was found not profitable and was abandoned. Another enterprising company bought up the land and houses along the proposed Tube line and was then able to build the line. Although the receipts from the passenger traffic would not pay a sufficient rate of profit, the capital appreciation on the houses and land more than made up the deficiency. Thus the project was realised; the Tube line was built. The problem is: Is it desirable—that is, does it lend to an optimum allocation of resources and maximization of national income— that this form of capital gain (external economy) be included as an item in the calculus of profitability, or is it not? Allyn Young hints that it is not desirable because the capital appreciation of houses and land along the Tube line due to an influx of people from other districts has an uncompensated counterpart in a capital depreciation of houses and land in districts out of which people moved into the Tube-line district. Agricultural land in Eastern and South-Eastern Europe will, however, not depreciate when the agrarian excess of population moves out. In this case external economies should be included in the calculus of profitability.

. . .

"There is a minimum level of resources that must be devoted to . . . a development program if it is to have any chance of success. Launching a country into self-sustaining growth is a little like getting an airplane off the ground. There is a critical ground speed which must be passed before the craft can become airborne. . . . "[1] Proceeding "bit by bit" will not add up in its effects to the sum total of the single bits. A minimum quantum of investment is a necessary, though not sufficient, condition of success. This,

[1]Massachusetts Institute of Technology, Center for International Studies, *The Objectives of United States Economic Assistance Programs* (1957), p. 70.

in a nutshell, is the contention of the theory of the big push.

This theory seems to contradict the conclusions of the traditional static equilibrium theory and to reverse its famous motto *natura non facit saltum.* It does so for three reasons. First, it is based on a set of more realistic assumptions of certain indivisibilities and "nonappropriabilities" in the production functions even on the level of static equilibrium theory. These indivisibilities give rise to increasing returns and to technological external economies. Second, in dealing with problems of growth this theory examines the path toward equilibrium, not the conditions at a point of equilibrium only. At a point of static equilibrium net investment is zero. The theory of growth is very largely a theory of investment. Moreover, the allocation of investment—unlike the allocation of given stocks of consumer goods (equilibrium of consumption), or of producers' goods (equilibrium of production)—necessarily occurs in an imperfect market, that is, a market on which prices do not signal all the information required for an optimum solution.[2] Given an imperfect investment market, pecuniary external economies have the same effect in the theory of growth as technological external economies. They are a cause of a possible divergence between the private and the social marginal net product. Since pecuniary, unlike technological, external economies are all-pervading and frequent, the price mechanism does not neccessarily put the economy on an optimum path. Therefore, additional signalling devices apart from market prices are required. Many economists, including the author, believe that these additional signals can be provided by programming. Third, in addition to the risk phenomena and imperfections characterizing the investment equilibrium, markets in under-developed countries are even more imperfect than in developed countries. The price mechanism in such imperfect markets does not provide the signals which guide a perfectly competitive economy towards an optimum position. . . .

Indivisibilities of inputs, processes, or outputs give rise to increasing returns, that is, economies of scale, and may require a high optimum size of a firm. This is not a very important obstacle to development since with some exceptions (for instance in Central America) there is usually sufficient demand, even in small, poor countries, for at least one optimum scale firm in many industries. There may be room, however, only for one or a few firms with the obvious danger of monopolistic markets.

As Allyn Young pointed out, increasing returns accrue to a firm not only with the growth of its size but also with the growth of the industry and with the growth of the industrial system as a whole. Greater specialization and better use of resources become possible when growth helps to overcome indivisibilities generating pecuniary external economies. The range of increasing returns seems to be very wide indeed.[3]

Social overhead capital is the most important instance of indivisibility and hence of external economies on the supply side. Its services are indirectly productive and become available only after long gestation periods. Its most important products are investment opportunities created in other industries. Social overhead capital comprises all those basic industries like power, transport, or communications which must precede the more quickly yielding, directly productive investments and which constitute the framework or infrastructure and the overhead costs of the economy as a whole. Its installations are characterized by a sizeable initial lump and low variable costs. Since the minimum size in these basic industries is large, excess capacity will be unavoidable over the initial period in under-developed countries.[4] In addition, there is also an irreducible minimum industry mix of different public utilities, so that an under-developed country will have to invest between 30–40 percent of its total investment in these channels. Since over-all vision is required as well as a correct

[2]See P. N. Rosenstein-Rodan, "Programming in Theory and in Italian Practice," in Massachusetts Institute of Technology, Center for International Studies, *Investment Criteria and Economic Growth* (1955).

[3]The capital-output ratio in the United States has fallen over the last eighty years from around 4:1 to around 3:1, while income per head, wage-rates, and the relative importance of heavy industry were rising. This is due to technical progress (change in production functions), increasing returns on balance (increasing returns prevailing over decreasing returns), and to the rising demand for labour-intensive services characteristic of high-income economies. It is my conviction that increasing returns played a considerable part in it.

[4]We may distinguish in fact between the developmental social overhead capital which provides for a hoped for but uncertain future demand and the rehabilitation social overhead capital which caters to an unsatisfied demand of the past. The first with its excess capacity will necessarily have a big sectoral capital-output ratio (10–15:1); the second, through breaking bottlenecks, has a certain high indirect productivity and a much lower capital-output ratio.

appraisal of future development, programming is undoubtedly required in this lumpy field. Normal market mechanisms will not provide an optimum supply.

Social overhead capital is characterized by four indivisibilites. First, it is indivisible (irreversible) in time. In must precede other directly productive investments. Second, its equipment has high minimum durability. Lesser durability is either technically impossible or much less efficient. For this and other reasons it is very lumpy. Third, it has long gestation periods. Fourth, an irreducible minimum social overhead capital industry mix is a condition for getting off the dead-end.

Because of these indivisibilities and because service of social overhead capital cannot be imported, a high initial investment in social overhead capital must either precede or be known to be certainly available in order to pave the way for additional more quickly yielding directly productive investments. This indivisibility of social overhead capital constitutes one of the main obstacles to development of under-developed countries.

Relatively few investments are made in the small market of an under-developed country. If all investment projects were independent (which they are not) and if their number grew, the risk of each investment project would decline by simple actuarial rules. The lower marginal risk of each investment dose (or project) would lead to either higher or cheaper credit facilities and these would thus constitute internal economies. In reality, however, various investment decisions are not independent. Investment projects have high risks because of uncertainty as to whether their products will find a market.

Let us restate our old example, at first for a closed economy. If a hundred workers who were previously in disguised unemployment (so that the marginal productivity of their labour was equal to zero) in an under-developed country are put into a shoe factory, their wages will constitute additional income. If the newly employed workers spend all of their additional income on the shoes they produce, the shoe factory will find a market and will succeed. In fact, however, they will not spend all of their additional income on shoes. There is no easy solution of creating an additional market in this way. The risk of not finding a market reduces the incentive to invest, and the shoe factory investment project will probably be abandoned. Let us vary the example. Instead of putting a hundred previously un-

employed workers in one shoe factory, let us put ten thousand workers in one hundred factories and farms which between them will produce the bulk of the wage-goods on which the newly employed workers will spend their wages. What was not true in the case of one single shoe factory will become true for the complementary system of one hundred factories and farms. The new producers will be each other's customers and will verify Says' Law by creating an additional market. The complementarity of demand will reduce the risk of not finding a market. Reducing such interdependent risks naturally increases the incentives to invest. . . .

A high minimum quantum of investment requires a high volume of savings, which is difficult to achieve in low income, under-developed countries. There is a way out of this vicious circle. In the first stage when income is increased due to an increase in investment which mobilizes additional latent resources, mechanisms must be provided which assure that in the second stage the marginal rate of saving is very much higher than the average rate of saving. Adam Smith's dictum that frugality is a virtue and prodigality a vice has to be adapted to a situation of growing income. Economic history does not show that the proportion saved from the increase in income was higher than the previous average rate of saving.

A zero (or very low) price elasticity of the supply of saving and a high income elasticity of saving thus constitute the third indivisibility.

These three indivisibilities and the external economies to which they give rise, plus the external economies of training labour, form the characteristic pattern of models of growth of under-developed countries.

The economic factors discussed so far give only the necessary, but not the sufficient, conditions of growth. A big push seems to be required to jump over the economic obstacles to development. There may be finally a phenomenon of indivisibility in the vigour and drive required for a successful development policy. Isolated and small efforts may not add up to a sufficient impact on growth. An atmosphere of development may only arise with a minimum speed or size of investment. Our knowledge of psychology is far too deficient to theorize about this phenomenon. This does not make it a less important factor. It may well constitute the difference between necessary and sufficient conditions for success.

VII.B.2. Linkage Effects and Industrialization*

[T]wo inducement mechanisms may be considered to be at work within the directly productive activities (DPA) sector:

1. The input-provision, derived demand, or *backward linkage effects,* that is, every non-primary economic activity, will induce attempts to supply through domestic production the inputs needed in that activity.
2. The output-utilization or *forward linkage effects,* that is, every activity that does not by its nature cater exclusively to final demands, will induce attempts to utilize its outputs as inputs in some new activities.

Development policy must attempt to enlist these well-known backward and forward effects; but it can do so only if there is some knowledge as to how different economic activities "score" with respect to these effects. Ordinarily economists have been content with general references to the advantages of external economies, complementarities, cumulative causation, etc. But no systematic effort has been made to describe how the development path ought to be modified so as to maximize these advantages even though the existence of input-output statistics supplies us with a few tools for an analysis of this kind.

First, a further note on the linkage concept itself. What do we imply when we speak of the linkage effects emanating from industry *A* toward industry *B?* Language can be quite ambiguous here, for we may have in mind the potential *importance* of the linkage effect in terms of, say, the net output of new industries that might be called forth; or we may mean the *strength* of the effect, that is, the probability that these industries will actually come into being. The total effect could be measured by the sum of the products of these two elements; in other words, if the establishment of industry *W* may lead, through linkage effects, to the establishment of *n* additional industries with net outputs equal to x_i ($i = 1, 2, \ldots n$) and if the probability that each one of these industries will actually be set up as a result of the establishment of industry *W* is p_i

($i = 1, 2, \ldots n$), then the total linkage effect of industry *W* is equal to

$$\sum_{l}^{n} x_i p_i$$

The probabilities can be interpreted as measuring the strength of the stimulus that is set up. For backward linkage, this strength can be roughly measured as follows: suppose industry *W* requires annual inputs of $y_i, y_2 \ldots y_n$ and suppose that the minimum economic size (in terms of annual productive capacity) of firms that would turn out these inputs is equal to $a_1, a_2 \ldots a_n$; then the strength of the stimulus or the probability that the setting up of industry *W* will lead to the setting up of industries producing the inputs is equal to the ratio of the *y*'s to the *a*'s.[1] Minimum economic size is not a technical concept, but is defined in economic terms relative to normal profits and efficient foreign suppliers. In other words, it is the size at which the domestic firm will be able both to secure normal profits and to compete with existing foreign suppliers, taking into account locational advantages *and* disadvantages as well as, perhaps, some infant industry protection. In this way comparative cost conditions are automatically taken into account.[2]

In the case of forward linkage, an interpretation of the *p*'s is less straightforward. The concept of economic size is not helpful here, since the size of the market for the industries that might be brought into being through forward linkage does not depend on their suppliers. A clue can perhaps be found in the importance of the articles produced by industry *W* as inputs for the output of the to-be-linked industry. If these

---

[1]The ratio is to be defined as having a ceiling of 1, i.e., the value of the ratio is equal to unity, whenever the *y*'s are equal to *or larger than* the *a*'s. Note also that the *y*'s are equivalent to the gross output of the new industries or firms in physical terms whereas the *x*'s are their net outputs in value terms.

[2]Data on the economic size of plants in different industries would be the starting point for determining minimum economic size in different countries. Research in this area in relation to economic development is surprisingly scant, except for the pioneering article of K. A. Bohr, "Investment Criteria for Manufacturing Industries in Underdeveloped Countries," *Review of Economics and Statistics,* Vol. 36 (May 1954), pp. 157–66.

---

*From Albert O. Hirschman, *The Strategy of Economic Development,* New Haven, Yale University Press, 1958, pp. 100-4, 109-13; reprint, Boulder, Colo.: Westview Press. Reprinted by permission.

inputs are a very small fraction of the industry's eventual output, then their domestic availability is not likely to be an important factor in calling forth that industry. If, on the other hand, these articles are subjected to few further manufacturing operations, then the strength of the forward stimulus is likely to be substantial, provided demand is sufficient to justify domestic production.

In these cases, then, importance and strength—the x's and the p's—of the linkage effect are inversely correlated. Industries where the x's are small and the p's large are sometimes aptly called "satellite" industries. They are almost unfailingly established in the wake of industry W but are of minor importance in comparison to that industry. Thus defined, satellite industries can be established through backward or forward linkage. In the case of cement, for instance, the manufacture of multi-wall bags for packing purposes, represents backward linkage while the establishment of a cement block industry represents satellite formation through forward linkage. A satellite industry usually has the following characteristics:

1. It enjoys a strong location advantage from proximity to the master industry;
2. it uses as principal input an output or by-product of the master industry without subjecting it to elaborate transformation, or its principal output is a—usually minor—input of the master industry; and
3. its minimum economic size is smaller than that of the master industry.

While satellite industries are almost certain to be established once the master industry is in place, the establishment of industry W also results in stimuli toward the setting up of nonsatellite industries. In these cases, the strength of the stimulus is infinitely weaker, but the stake is far bigger. Examples of such a situation are the stimulus that the setting up of a multi-wall bag factory gives toward the creation of pulp and paper industry or, for the case of forward linkage, the stimulus given by the establishment of an iron and steel industry to all the metal-fabrication industries. Here the establishment of one industry is a contributing factor which by itself is quite unlikely to result in the creation of the others; but when we speak of external economies and complementarities, we think at least as much of these uncertain linkages as of the far more certain, but also far less significant, satellites with which any industry of a certain size surrounds itself. The weakness of the stimulus in the case of nonsatellites can be explained by the absence of the three factors that define satellites. Linkage is reduced to the fact that an input of the newly established industry is an output of the to-be-created industry or vice versa, but the established industry would not be the principal customer or supplier of the to-be-created industry; in fact, particularly in cases of backward linkage, minimum economic size of the to-be-created industry would frequently be larger than that of the industry where the linkage originates.[3]

In spite of the importance of the nonsatellite type of linkage, it seems necessary to provide for some arbitrary cut-off point for small probabilities. It is all very well to say that the establishment of a brewery sends out a stimulus in the direction of a paper industry because of the labels needed for the beer bottles, but by itself this stimulus is not likely ever to lead to the setting up of a paper mill. Thus, if we consider *in isolation* the linkage effects exclusively of the beer industry on further industrial or agricultural development, we should consider only those stimuli whose probability exceeds a certain critical value, say one-half.[4]

If we proceed in this way, the joint linkage effects of two industries, say beer and cement, considered as a unit, are likely to be larger than the sum of their individual linkage effects, since some of the xp products which are omitted in computing the individual effects because the p's are below the critical value will exceed this value if added together for both industries. Here we have an argument in favor of multiple development that we would consider convincing were it not that our principal argument against it is concerned with its feasibility rather than with its desirability.

The fact that the linkage effects of two industries viewed in combination are larger than

---

[3]To the extent that the minimum economic size of an industry is larger the farther away one moves from the finished consumer or producer goods stage. This is, of course, by no means universally true as is shown, e.g., by the large minimum size of the motor vehicles makers.

[4]It is a good rule of thumb that an industry can properly be established in an underdeveloped but developing country as soon as existing demand is equal to one-half of the economic size of the plant as defined above. The additional demand needed to justify the investment can be expected to come from the growth of existing demand and from the development of new demand through forward linkage, once the plant is in existence.

the sum of the linkage effects of each industry in isolation helps to account for the cumulative character of development. When industry *A* is first set up, its satellites will soon follow; but when industry *B* is subsequently established, this may help to bring into existence not only its own satellites but some firms which neither *A* nor *B* in isolation could have called forth. And with *C* coming into play some firms will follow that require the combined stimuli not only of *B* and *C* but of *A, B,* and *C*. This mechanism may go far toward explaining the *acceleration* of industrial growth which is so conspicuous during the first stages of a country's development.

Backward Linkage at Work

The lack of interdependence and linkage is of course one of the most typical characteristics of underdeveloped economies. If we had homogeneous input-output statistics for all countries, it would certainly be instructive to rank countries according to the proportion of intersectoral transactions to total output; it is likely that this ranking would exhibit a close correlation with both income per capita and with the percentage of the population occupied in manufacturing.

Agriculture in general, and subsistence agriculture in particular, are of course characterized by the scarcity of linkage effects. By definition, all *primary* production should exclude any substantial degree of backward linkage although the introduction of modern methods does bring with it considerable outside purchases of seeds, fertilizers, insecticides, and other current inputs, not to speak of machines and vehicles. We may say that the more primitive the agricultural and mining activities, the more truly primary they are.

Forward linkage effects are also weak in agriculture and mining. A large proportion of agricultural output is destined directly for consumption or export; another important part is subjected to some processing industries that can be characterized as satellite inasmuch as the value added by them to the agricultural product (milling of wheat, rice, coffee, etc.) is small relative to the value of the product itself. Only a comparatively small fraction of total agricultural output of underdeveloped countries receives elaborate processing, which usually takes place abroad.

The case for inferiority of agriculture to manufacturing has most frequently been argued on grounds of comparative productivity. While this case has been shown not to be entirely convincing, agriculture certainly stands convicted on the count of its lack of direct stimulus to the setting up of new activities through linkage effects: the superiority of manufacturing in this respect is crushing. This may yet be the most important reason militating against any complete specialization of underdeveloped countries in primary production.

The grudge against what has become known as the "enclave" type of development is due to this ability of primary products from mines, wells, and plantations to slip out of a country without leaving much of a trace in the rest of the economy. Naturally hostility to the profits earned by foreign companies plays an important role in such attitudes; but the absence of direct linkage effects of primary production for export lends these views a plausibility that they do not have in the case of foreign investment in manufacturing. I say plausibility rather than validity, for while as such the primary production activities leading to exports may exert few developmental effects, they do finance imports which can become very powerful agents of development as we shall see below.

Since interdependence in the input-output sense is so largely the result of industrialization, we must now attempt to trace the various ways in which manufacturing and the accompanying linkage effects make their appearance. In this connection, we shall utilize another one of Chenery's findings, namely that more than ninety percent of all input-output flows can usually be arranged in a triangular pattern. Circularity—that is, the fact that coal is needed for steel-making and steel for coal mining—is undoubtedly present in the structure of a country's production, but apparently to a much smaller degree than would be suspected upon looking at an input-output table that has not been "triangularized." In other words, there is no compelling *technological* requirement for the simultaneous setting up of various industries, an interesting complement to our case against the existence of such a requirement on economic grounds.

In a triangular arrangement of the input-output matrix, there is a "last" sector whose output goes entirely to final demand and which takes in inputs from a number of other sectors; the second-to-last sector sells its output to final demand and to the last sector and buys inputs from some or all other sectors except from the "last"; and so on, until we come to the "first" sector whose output goes to all the subsequent sectors and possibly also to final demand, but which does not use any inputs from other sectors.

Industrialization can of course *start* only with industries that deliver to final demand, since *ex hypothesi* no market exists as yet for intermediate goods. This means that it will be possible to set up only two kinds of industries:

1. those that transform domestic or imported primary products into goods needed by final demands;
2. those that transform imported semimanufactures into goods needed by final demands.

To the pioneer industrial countries only the first course was open, and this explains the towering importance of a few industries (textiles, iron and steel, pottery) during the early stages of the Industrial Revolution. In today's underdeveloped countries the textiles, food processing, and construction materials industries based on local materials are still of great importance, but, to a very significant extent, industrialization is penetrating these countries in the second manner, through plants that perform the "final touches" on almost-finished *industrial* products imported from abroad. Examples are the many converting, assembly, and mixing plants, the pharmaceutical laboratories, the metal-fabricating industries, and many others. This trend has many advantages: it often provides an investment outlet for small amounts of capital that might not easily become available for ventures which require the pooling of the resources of many investors, and it makes it possible to start industrial undertakings without the heavy risk that comes in underdeveloped countries from having to rely on the output of unreliable domestic producers.

In this way underdeveloped countries often set up "last" industries first—that is, these are "last" industries considering the input-output flow of the advanced countries: what in these countries are inputs from the other sectors are replaced in underdeveloped countries by imports. Such industries could be termed "enclave import industries," in analogy to the enclave export activities that were previously mentioned. For here again we have an undertaking that at least in its beginning is antiseptically linkage-free; materials are imported from abroad, some value is added to them through mixing, assembling, packaging, etc., and the finished product is rushed to the final consumers. The enclave nature of these industries is sometimes emphasized by the location of the plant at a point as close as possible to the most convenient port of arrival of the imported materials, and again this type of venture has proven particularly attractive to foreign capital—many of the branch plants owned by foreign corporations specialize in this kind of operation.

But there is a considerable difference between the enclave export and enclave import activities. The former have great trouble in breaking out of the enclave situation. Usually some forward linkage effects can be utilized—ores and cane sugar can be refined before being shipped. But the scope for such operations is strictly limited. With respect to import enclave industries, the situation is radically different: they set up backward linkage effects of practically infinite range and depth.

Comment: Linkages

Albert O. Hirschman has broadened his linkages approach in an important paper, "A Generalized Linkage Approach to Development, with Special Reference to Staples," in *Essays on Economic Development and Cultural Change in Honor of Bert Hoselitz*, ed. Manning Nash (1977). This paper goes beyond production linkages of the input–output character to consider consumption and fiscal linkages. The analysis is applied to export-led growth based on staple exports.

Comment: Industrialization and the "Big Push" Revisited

In the early postwar period, when development plans were being formulated by emerging nations, a case for deliberate industrialization was built on the notions of the "big push" and "balanced growth." As in VII.B.1, where he emphasized external economies and indivisibilities in production, Rosenstein-Rodan argued for a big push. He maintained that although no one industry might be profitable alone, if several industries adopted increasing returns technology simultaneously, they could each create demand for each other's output, and the industrialization program could then be profitable.

Ragner Nurkse also argued for industrialization in terms of balanced growth—the synchronized application of capital to a wide range of industries:

> An increase in production over a wide range of consumables, so proportioned as to correspond with the pattern of consumers' preferences does create its own demand. . . . A frontal attack—a wave of capital investments in a number of different industries—can economically succeed while any substantial application of capital by an individual entrepreneur in any particular industry may be blocked or discouraged by the limitations of the preexisting market. . . . [T]hrough the application of capital over a wide range of activities, the general level of economic activity is raised and the size of the market enlarged. . . . [Balanced growth] is a means of getting out of the rut, a means of stepping up the rate of growth when the external forces of advance through trade expansion and foreign capital are sluggish or inoperative.[1]

Recently the big push argument has been refined in the context of an imperfectly competitive economy in which industries have large fixed costs but generate pecuniary external economies. Through demand spillovers to other firms, an industrial firm can then raise the size of other firms' markets even if the first firm itself is not profitable. The big push is associated with multiple equilibria of the economy, and industrialization on a broad front can move the economy from a traditional cottage-type production equilibrium to a modern industrial equilibrium. Through a big push, the limitations of the small size of the domestic market are overcome, provided that there are increasing returns, demand spillovers, and pecuniary externalities are created. This situation may be especially important for stimulating investment in infrastructure that has high fixed costs.

For modeling of the big push in an imperfectly competitive economy, see Kevin M. Murphy, Andrei Shleifer, and Robert W. Vishny, "Industrialization and the Big Push," *Journal of Political Economy* (October 1989).

In "Toward a Counter-Counterrevolution in Development Theory," *World Bank Economic Review Supplement* (1992), Paul Krugman has also revived the big push argument by noting that economies of scale at the level of the individual plant can translate into increasing returns at the aggregate level through pecuniary external economies.

Linkages, as discussed by Hirschman in VII.B.2, can also lead to complementarity among industries. Hirschman focuses, however, on a few strategic industries instead of an economywide big push.

Although the "new trade theory" and "new growth theory" are being used to support a big push and balanced growth, see criticisms by Joseph Stiglitz, "Comment on Krugman," *World Bank Economic Review Supplement* (1992).

---

[1]Ragnar Nurkse, *Problems of Capital Formation in Underdeveloped Countries* (1953), pp. 10, 13–15, and "The Conflict between 'Balanced Growth' and International Specialization," *Lectures on Economic Development* (1958): 171–72.

VII.B.3. Welfare Economics of Industry Promotion*

Governments have various objectives in their promotion of specific industries. Subsidies may be used to foster development in certain regions of a country, to transfer income to certain disadvantaged groups within society, to augment national prestige, and so on. Economic analysis has little to say about the appropriate weights that should be placed on these objectives relative to that of maximising the size of the overall economic pie. Accordingly, economists tend to concentrate on efficiency arguments for policy interventions. I shall not deviate from this traditional course here.

A Framework for Analysis

In welfare economics, industry performance is often judged by comparing the benefits generated by an industry with those that would be created if the same resources were deployed elsewhere in the economy. In such "surplus" analysis, market values are used to measure the

*From Gene M. Grossman, "Promoting New Industrial Activities," OECD Economic Studies, no. 14 (Spring 1990): 89–96, 118–19. Reprinted by permission.

opportunity cost of the resources that are consumed or released by the industry under consideration. Strictly speaking, the validity of this procedure requires that policy-induced resource reallocations not be so large as to alter the prices of primary inputs that are determined on economywide factor markets.

Three components of industry surplus are distinguished, according to the identity of the potential beneficiaries. *Producer surplus* is the excess of the value of the output of an industry over the opportunity cost of the resources that are used up in production. This surplus may accrue to several different agents. Returns to capital in excess of the "normal" rate (i.e., the amount the capital could earn by being deployed elsewhere) constitute surplus for the owners of the capital. Wages paid to workers in excess of the "normal" rate (i.e., the amount the workers could receive in employment elsewhere) also constitute surplus. Owners of resources that have special value in a particular industry (e.g., the owner of land with characteristics especially suitable for growing grapes or the owner of a patent for an idea especially suitable for producing a particular product) derive surplus in the form of rents to their scarce but industry-specific inputs.

Consumer surplus is the excess of the "enjoyment" that consumers derive from purchasing a certain amount of some good over the cost of those purchases. The former concept is made operational by asking what is the maximal amount that the consumers would be willing to pay for each successive unit acquired. If the consumer is able to purchase the unit in the marketplace for less than this maximal amount, the difference is imputed to total industry surplus.

The government derives surplus from any *revenues* it collects from an industry. In cases where subsidies are paid out by the government, this component of total surplus is negative. The government is included in the welfare calculus because, if an industry is to be supported, funds must ultimately be raised from domestic citizens through one form of taxation or another. The cost of a subsidy is at least as large as the payment that is made, and may be larger if the government must (as is typically the case) collect revenues by some method that imposes an efficiency burden on society. There remains the question of how these surplus components ought to be aggregated. The appropriate weights reflect societal concerns for equity. Lacking contextual information on who are the relevant actors and

what is their claim to governmental attention, it is common for economists to weight all components equally. The resulting measure then reflects the contribution of the industry in question to the aggregate surplus generated in the economy. Sometimes government revenues are given a weight greater than one, in recognition of the fact that real-world taxes always distort economic decision making. . . . I shall not make any such explicit adjustments here, but only point out that any case that emerges for government subsidies must be tempered to reflect the "excess burden" of raising the necessary funds.

The following formula expresses total industry surplus:

$$W = u[(p+z)x - S(x)] - n(f-v)$$
$$+ [U(c) - pc] - (p-p^*)e - znx - nv \quad (1)$$

where

W is total surplus generated by an industry;

n is the number of "representative" firms in the industry;

x is the level of output of a typical domestic firm;

p is the price paid by home consumers;

z is the subsidy (if any) to producers per unit of output;

$S(x)$ is the social opportunity cost of the resources used to produce x, net of any fixed costs of entering the industry;

f is the social cost of the resources needed for entry (assumed to equal private cost of entry);

v is the lump-sum subsidy (if any) to producers to induce entry;

c is the level of domestic consumption;

$U(c)$ is the (gross) consumer benefit from consuming an amount c;

p^* is the international price of the industry's output (in local currency); and

$e = nx - c$ is net exports (net imports if negative).

The first two terms measure producer surplus. They incorporate total industry revenue (including government subsidies) minus the social cost of the resources used up in entry and in operation. The third term is consumer surplus. The last three terms reflect the cost of export subsidies (or the revenue from import tariffs, if p exceeds p^* and e is negative), of output subsidies, and of entry-inducing subsidies that help to cover fixed costs, respectively.

Government intervention typically alters many or all of the magnitudes on the right-hand side of equation (1). The various channels through which policy might affect social welfare can be identified by asking how W varies with its determinants. This exercise proves useful for classifying the different arguments that have been made in favour of government support for specific industries.

Equation (1) implies the following expression for the total change in W, denoted ΔW (the symbol "Δ" will be used to mean the "change in"), that results from changes in the magnitudes of the various economically determined variables:

$$\Delta W = W_x \Delta x + W_n \Delta n + W_p \Delta p$$
$$+ W_c \Delta c + W_e \Delta e + W_{p^*} \Delta p^* \quad (2)$$

where W_x is the rate at which welfare changes with a change in output per firm x, W_n is the rate at which welfare changes with a change in the number of firms n, etc. The expressions for these rates of change can be derived from (1). The term $Wp\Delta p$ vanishes, because $W_p = nx - c - e = 0$. Intuitively, a change in the domestic price of an item, everything else constant, affects only the distribution of income between producers, consumers, and the government, but not the efficiency with which resources are allocated. The remaining terms in (2) can be expressed as the sum of seven distinct components. I shall list them here and describe them briefly. A more detailed discussion of each is reserved until later, when the particular arguments for intervention are reviewed. The components of ΔW are:

(i) $n[p - m(x)]\Delta x$; where $m(x)$ is the private cost to a typical manufacturer of producing one more unit of output, or the "private marginal cost." This term has been referred to as the *profit-capture effect*. It arises in oligopolistic environments (where prices are above marginal cost) anytime policy induces firms to change their levels of output. The output changes alter firms' (net-of-subsidy) profits and thus total industry surplus.

(ii) $n[m(x) - s(x)]\Delta x$; where $s(x)$ is the social cost of the resources used by a firm in producing one more unit of output, or the "social marginal cost." This is an *externality effect*, which arises when policy induces a

change in resource use in situations where the amount that firms pay for their inputs deviates from their true opportunity cost to society. Such a divergence between private and social resource costs obtains when firms do not enjoy all the benefits or bear all the costs of their actions.

(iii) $[px - M(x) - f]\Delta n$; where $M(x)$ is the total private cost to a firm from producing x units of output net of any fixed cost of entry f. This term represents the *profits-from-entry effect*, reflecting the excess of the operating profits earned by new firms that are induced by policy to enter over the private cost of that entry.

(iv) $[M(x) - S(x)]\Delta n$. This is the *externality-from-entry*. When the number of firms in the industry changes, this term measures the extent to which the private costs of production borne by the new firms exceed the social costs. It is similar to the externality effect in (ii), except that it arises when policy induces entry by new firms rather than (or in addition to) expansion by existing firms.

(v) $(p - p^*)\Delta e$. This is the *volume-of-trade effect*. Goods sold to or purchased from an external market have an opportunity cost p^*. In the presence of trade policies, the domestic price will differ from this opportunity cost. Then policies that alter the volume of trade have implications for efficiency, because domestic decisions are based on prices that differ from true international opportunity costs.

(vi) $e\Delta p^*$. This *terms-of-trade effect* reflects the welfare gain that accrues to a country when its exports command a higher price on world markets, or when it is able to purchase its imports more cheaply. Policies that induce an expansion of exports generally cause the world price of the export good to fall, and so contribute a negative component to industry surplus on this account. By analogy, policies that contract imports impart a positive effect if the country is large enough in relation to world markets to substantially affect the world price of its import good.

(vii) $[u(c - p]\Delta c$; where $u(c)$ is the benefit consumers derive from consuming one more unit of a commodity after c units have already been consumed. This *consumer-surplus effect* measures the societal gain from any expansion in consumption of the good in question.

Surplus analysis is used to check the logical consistency of various arguments for government intervention and to evaluate specific policy proposals. The advantage of this framework is that it catalogues all the different channels through which policy might affect the efficiency with which resources are allocated. A change in policy will, in general, invoke several component effects. Policy analysis then requires a comparison of their relative sizes. I shall proceed to describe a number of situations that frequently arise in the course of discussing modern, "high-technology" industries, and then use surplus analysis to elucidate the arguments for and against government intervention.

The Orthodox Argument Against Industry Promotion

It is useful to begin by demonstrating how the current framework yields the conventional economists' wisdom against industry promotion when markets are "well functioning" and competitive. This exercise will illustrate why the various assumptions of the competitive paradigm are critical to the *laissez faire* policy conclusion.

The competitive paradigm assumes the absence of any barriers to entry and that individual domestic firms are so small relative to the size of the world industry that they neglect their individual influences on the ultimate market price of their output. In these circumstances, free entry drives "excess" profits (profits in excess of those needed to cover fixed entry costs) to zero. Producers receive $p+z$ for each unit of their output and collect revenues equal to $(p+z)x$. Then zero excess profits implies $(p+z)x = M(x) + f$. Also, each firm produces up to the point where marginal cost $m(x)$ equals the price $p+z$ that it receives. Then term (i) reduces to $-nz\Delta x$ and (iii) reduces to $-zx\Delta n$. The first of these is negative if an output subsidy ($z>0$) is used to promote industry expansion by existing firms ($\Delta x>0$). This is because the resources used to expand output have opportunity cost m, but create output in the targeted industry with value p. Since m exceeds p by the amount of the subsidy, the use of the resources in the targeted industry is inefficient. By similar reasoning, the second term is negative if an output subsidy is used to

induce entry ($\Delta n>0$). Then the value of the output created by the new firms does not justify the resources used by them.

Well-functioning markets are defined, in this context, by (inter alia) the absence of externalities. So terms (ii) and (iv) vanish in the orthodox analysis by assumption. Term (vii) also is not present in this case, because each consumer selects an optimal level of purchases by setting the price of the last unit just equal to its marginal value (i.e., $u(c) = p$). All that remains are terms (v) and (vi). If a subsidy is used to stimulate exports ($\Delta e>0$), domestic price p will exceed the world price p^* by the amount of the subsidy, and so term (v) will be negative. Finally, there is the terms-of-trade effect. Both output subsidies and export subsidies serve to expand the amount that the home country sells on world markets, and thereby push the world price downward ($\Delta p^*<0$). If the home country is a net exporter of the good in question ($e>0$), this fall in world price is detrimental to the country's national welfare.

For exporting industries, output and trade subsidies generate only negative components in the surplus analysis. Thus, industry promotion by either measure can only reduce welfare in the orthodox economic setting. With perfect competition, small firms, and no externalities, market prices give producers the appropriate signals for efficient resource allocation. Government support causes resources to be used in an industry beyond the point where the marginal social benefit justifies the marginal opportunity cost. And, to the extent that the terms of trade deteriorate, the presence of international trade only strengthens the argument against the promotion of domestic industries.

Market Distortions and the Theory of the Second Best

For the most part, the new literature in support of government targeting has been cast in an economic environment where markets do not function perfectly. This is not surprising, in the light of the attributes of the industries that are the focus of this literature. Nearly all of these characteristics imply some departure from the orthodox paradigm.

The arguments that arise fall within the purview of "the general theory of the second best." This theory argues that, for every market distortion, there exists some targeted policy remedy that most directly corrects for the market failure. This policy tool is optimal in each case, because it does not create any additional by-product distortions. However, if the designated policy remedy is not available to the government for political or other reasons, alternatives may exist that indirectly attain some of the same efficiency benefits. In many cases, industry-wide subsidies fall into this latter category. Since general support for an industry represents a blunt form of intervention, such support rarely redresses the market failure in a targeted way. Thus, in the case of each market imperfection it is necessary to ask not only whether export or output subsidies might enhance economic performance, but also whether and which other approaches might be available for achieving even greater efficiency in the ultimate allocation of resources. . . .

Several common themes emerge from the analysis. First, arguments in favour of government subsidies to particular new activities rest on detailed qualitative descriptions of the marketplace and often on specific parameters that describe conditions there. These arguments do not apply across the board. . . . The nature of the problem makes case-by-case analysis unavoidable.

Second, output subsidies and trade policies often are not the proper instruments for correcting the most common market imperfections. These policy tools are simply too blunt for effecting the needed market corrections, inasmuch as they fail to differentiate among the types of firms that they support and fail to attract to the industry especially those resources that are underprovided by the market. When market activity is too low relative to an efficient outcome, it is because the active and potentially active firms fail to appropriate all the benefits from some aspect of their operation. Corrective government policy should be targeted to the particular activity that generates positive spillovers, and should not merely encourage firms to produce more output. Only if the externalities are a by-product of production *per se* will output subsidies be the policy instrument of choice. In all other cases such intervention will at best provide benefits that are less than might otherwise be attained, and at worst will fail to promote the desirable objective at all.

Third, policies that require government revenue should only be invoked when the potential efficiency gains outweigh the costs of raising the necessary funds. When lump-sum taxes are available to the government, a dollar of revenue can be raised at a dollar of social cost, and then targeted subsidies ought to be invoked whenever their direct impact on the allocation of resources is positive. But real world taxes are far from lump sum in nature. Empirical research has established the existence of a non-negligible excess burden in raising government revenue. Such research suggests that governments ought to pursue a conservative bias in their use of subsidies.

Fourth, few of the valid arguments for intervention rely explicitly on the existence of international competition. Where growth of some new activity is too slow, it often is so for the world as a whole. Rarely does the national identity of the new firms matter for the argument. The exceptions to this rule are arguments in favour of strategic promotion of domestic interests in their competition with foreign rivals. These arguments have been shown to be especially sensitive to the details of market structure and conduct and to rely on information that the government is not likely to have at its disposal. Moreover, strategic interventions seek gain at the expense of trade partners, and so invite retaliation. When countries head down this road, mutually harmful subsidies or protection can easily be the outcome. Countries may need on occasion to invoke strategic trade policies to safeguard their interests, but the ultimate goal in all cases ought to be a co-operative outcome in which all parties desist from pursuit of strategic gains.

One last caveat is in order. In any public policy program the parties that stand to benefit from government support have more than ample incentive to plead the merits of their own cases. The success of an industrial policy program hinges as much on the protection that it builds into the process to prevent it from being co-opted by interested parties as it does on the ability of economists and policy makers to identify market failures and to propose appropriate remedies under idealised analytical conditions. The potential societal gains from an activist policy can easily be sacrificed if opportunities for wasteful rent seeking are created or if the criteria for selection become the political clout of the applicant rather than the economic merits of the case.

VII.B.4. Industrialization via Import Substitution—Note

In many LDCs—especially in Latin America and Asia—the production of consumer goods in substitution for imports has had considerable appeal as the dominant strategy of industrialization. Given an existing demand for imported consumer goods, it was simple to base the postwar rationale for industrialization on the home replacement of these finished goods (in most industries by importing components and engaging in the final assemblying process, in the hope of proceeding to "industrialize from the top downward" through the ultimate production of the intermediate products and capital goods). Besides allowing the home replacement of an existing market, import substitution had considerable appeal by virtue of the common belief that it would help meet the developing country's balance-of-payments problem.

Although the widespread pursuit of import substitution has in practice been based mainly on the objectives of industrialization and balance-of-payments support, the policy has been rationalized by a number of protectionist arguments. Proponents of industrial protectionism have adduced several special arguments in the context of development—arguments that should be considered more seriously than the usual simple assertions about a "natural" inferiority of agriculture or the supposed necessity of industrialization to achieve a rising level of income.

Support for import replacement comes partly from an appeal to the experience of industrialized countries. Historical studies of some countries show not only that the share of industrial output rises with development, but also that the growth of industries based on import substitution accounts for a large proportion of the total rise in industry.[1] It is also true that "much of the recent economic history of some rapidly developing underdeveloped countries can be written in terms of industrialization working its way backward from the 'final touches' stage to domestic production of intermediate, and finally to that of basic, industrial materials."[2] At first, the country may import semifinished materials and perform domestically the "final touches" of converting or assembling the almost-finished industrial imports into final products. Later on, with the growth in demand for the final product, a point may be reached at which the import demand for intermediate components and basic goods is sufficiently high to warrant investment in their production at home; the market has become sufficiently large to reach a domestic production threshold.[3]

As with any interpretation of historical development, however, it is one thing to determine what has happened to make the course of development in one country a "success story" and quite another to infer from this experience that the same result could now be induced more rapidly in another country through deliberate policy measures. The historical evidence on the contribution of import substitution to industrialization applies to only some countries; in other countries, the replacement of imports was not significant. Moreover, we should recognize that the rise of industry through import replacement was due in large part to systematic changes in supply conditions, not simply to a change in the composition of demand with rising income.[4] The changes in factor supply—especially the growth in capital stock per worker and the increase in education and skills of all kinds—were instrumental in causing a systematic shift in comparative advantage as per capita income rose. But for a presently underdeveloped country, there is no reason to expect that a tariff on industrial imports would cause the supplies of capital, human skills, and natural resources to change in a way that would favor the substitution of domestic production for imports. The changes in supply conditions that occurred in other countries cannot now be duplicated simply by a policy of industrial protection.

Nor is industrial protection justified by reference to the historical pattern of industrialization working its way backward from the "final touches" stage to domestic production of formerly imported materials. On the contrary,

[1]For evidence, see H. B. Chenery, "Patterns of Industrial Growth," *American Economic Review* (September 1960): 639–41, 651.

[2]A. O. Hirschman, *The Strategy of Economic Development* (1958), p. 112.

[3]Ibid., p. 114.

[4]Chenery, "Patterns of Industrial Growth," pp. 624–25, 628–29, 644.

this pattern demonstrates that it is the growth of imports that subsequently induces domestic production; in offering proof that a market exists, the imports can fulfill the important function of demand formation and demand reconnaisance for the country's entrepreneurs, and the imports can act as a catalytic agent that will bring some of the country's underemployed resources together in order to exploit the opportunities they have revealed.[5] For the objective of eventually replacing imports with domestic production, it would thus be self-defeating to restrict imports at too early a stage and thereby forgo the awakening and inducing effects that imports have on industrialization.[6] An increase in imports—not their restriction—is the effective way to prepare the ground for the eventual creation of an import-replacing industry. Only after the domestic industry has been established can the country afford to dispense with the "creative" role played by imports, and only then would there be a case for protection of the domestic industry.

Although in promoting the demand for import substitutes, restrictions on imports allow the country to by-pass the difficulties of having to build up internal demand simultaneously with supply,[7] such a protective commercial policy is designed merely to replace imports; this in itself is no guarantee of cumulative growth. Even though industrialization may be initiated through import substitution, there remains the problem of sustaining the industrialization momentum beyond the point of import replacement.

Another special argument for industrialization via import substitution rests on the contention that a peripheral country's demand for industrial imports increases much more rapidly than does the foreign demand for its exports, so that the country must supply all those industrial products that cannot be imported in view of the relatively slow growth of its exports. If we accept the contentions that there is disparity in the income elasticities of demand for imports and exports, that the industrial imports are essential and must be either imported or produced at home, and that the country has no other means of increasing its capacity to import, then there is *prima facie* a case for industrial protection to encourage import substitutes. What is relevant for individual primary exporting countries, however, is not the overall income elasticity of demand for primary products, but the prospects for their individual exports. It is unreasonable to believe that export prospects are equally unfavorable for foodstuffs, minerals, and raw materials, or for all commodities in each of these broad categories.

Moreover, although the elasticity of demand for a commodity may be low on world markets, it may be high for the commodity from a particular source of supply. Nor can the future demand of industrial countries for imports be inferred simply from their income elasticity of demand for imports. Their import requirements will also depend on their growth rates in income (a high growth rate may offset a low income elasticity of demand), on shifts of the long-term supply elasticities within the industrial countries (domestic output of certain minerals and fuels, for example, has not kept pace with demand, so that import requirements are rising relatively to income growth), and on the degree of liberalization in the importing countries' commercial policies. Without undertaking individual commodity and country studies, it is therefore difficult to gauge the applicability of the argument for industrialization because of a weak export position.

We should also allow for the fact that a developing country's capacity to import industrial products will depend not only on its export earnings, but also on the inflow of foreign capital, changes in the terms of trade, and the capacity to replace other imports (such as foodstuffs and raw materials) with domestic production. To the extent that these other factors may raise the capacity to import industrial products, there is less need for industrial protection.

The case is also weakened if in attempting to offset the limited demand for exports, the policy of import substitution should, in turn, give rise to limitations on the supply side and deter exports. Such a worsening of the export situation may occur when the country's scarce financial and human resources are concentrated on industrialization, resources are diverted from the export sector, home consumption limits the available export supply, or the industrialization program is inflationary.

Another facet of the argument for replacing industrial imports with domestic production is related to the objective of expanding employment outside of agriculture. It may be contended that industrialization is necessary to provide em-

---

[5]Hirschman, *Strategy of Economic Development,* p. 123.

[6]Ibid., p. 124.

[7]See Gunnar Myrdal, *An International Economy* (1956), p. 276.

ployment opportunities for the presently under-employed, to absorb manpower that would otherwise become redundant when agricultural productivity rises through the adoption of more advanced techniques, and to take up the increase in the size of the labor force as population grows.

The promotion of new employment opportunities is certainly a crucial component of development programming, and in this connection there is considerable point to the emphasis on industrialization. The relevant questions here, however, are whether investment should be directed toward import-replacing industries, and whether industrial protectionism is the most appropriate policy for facilitating the expansion of nonagricultural employment.

A policy of industrialization through import substitution must also be compared with a policy of gradually inducing industrialization through agricultural improvement, or promoting industry through the production of manufactured exports (as discussed in section IX.B). There is also a tendency to exaggerate the amount of employment that could be provided by substituting home manufacture for imports; as country studies show, the direct employment that can be provided by replacing imports with domestic manufacture is generally limited for a poor country.

Further, it can be questioned whether industrialization through protection is the best remedy for underemployment. The effect of surplus labor in agriculture is low productivity, but the remedy for this is capital formation, not industrialization as such. Although the surplus labor constitutes an "investible surplus," this surplus can be applied in various investment outlets, and we cannot simply conclude that the optimum resource use is in import-competing industries.

We should also recognize that policies other than protection might be more effective in stimulating labor mobility. When occupational mobility is restricted by institutional and cultural barriers, the supply responses to the price and income stimuli of protection are necessarily weak, and extra-economic measures are required in such forms as education and training, land-tenure reforms, and policies that foster cultural change. Finally, we must distinguish between the mere availability of surplus laborers and their actual transference into productive employment as efficient and fully committed industrial workers. This raises all the complex problems

of creating and disciplining an industrial labor force.[8]

A more sophisticated version of the employment argument is that industry should be protected by a tariff in order to offset the effects of an excessively high wage rate for labor in the importable manufacturing industries.[9] It is claimed that the wage differential between the agricultural and the industrial sectors overvalues labor for the industrial sector in the sense that industrial wage rates exceed the social opportunity costs of employing more labor in industry. This may be due to the alleged fact that industrial wages are based on agricultural earnings, which are determined by the average product of labor in agriculture rather than by the marginal product of labor, which is lower (compare the discussion of Lewis's model in Note III.B.1); or it may be due to market imperfections that make the gap between agricultural and industrial wages greater than can be accounted for by "net advantages" between agricultural and industrial work. In either case, there is a distortion in the labor market that raises the private cost of labor in industry above its social opportunity cost (the marginal product of labor in agriculture). This results in an inefficient allocation of labor between agriculture and industry and understates the profitability of transforming agriculture into manufactures.[10] It is therefore concluded that protection of manufacturing industry may increase real income above the free-trade level by making the relative price of manufactures higher

[8]See W. Galenson, ed., *Labor and Economic Development* (1959), and W. E. Moore and A. S. Feidman, eds., *Labor Commitment and Social Change in Developing Areas* (1960).

[9]For a detailed analysis of this argument, see E. E. Hagen, "An Economic Justification for Protection," *Quarterly Journal of Economics* (November 1958); J. Bhagwati, "The Theory of Comparative Advantage in the Context of Underdevelopment and Growth," *Pakistan Development Review* (Autumn 1962): 342–45; and J. Bhagwati and V. K. Ramaswami, "Domestic Distortions, Tariffs and the Theory of Optimum Subsidy," *Journal of Political Economy* (February 1963): 44–50.

[10]In technical terms, the wage differential against industry causes the feasible production possibility curve to be drawn inward within the maximum attainable production possibility curve based on a uniform wage. It also makes the commodity price ratio diverge from the domestic rate of transformation, so that the optpimum conditions characterized by the equality of the foreign rate of transformation, domestic rate of transformation in production, and domestic rate of substitution in consumption are violated in the free-trade case. See Bhagwati and Ramaswami, "Domestic Distortions," pp. 48–49.

and facilitating the redistribution of labor from agriculture to import-competing industries.

This conclusion, however, can be criticized in several respects. Insofar as it is concerned with absorbing underemployed agricultural labor into import-competing industries, this aspect of the argument is subject to the same qualifications raised previously for the general argument of expanding employment through industrial protection. More pointedly, with regard to the alleged distortion in the labor market, it can be questioned whether the mere existence of a differential between industrial and agricultural wages is proof of a distortion. To the extent that the wage differential might be explained entirely by rational considerations of differences in costs and preferences between industrial and agricultural work, there is no genuine distortion.[11] Considering the other possible reason for a distortion in the labor market—that industrial wages are related to agricultural earnings, but these earnings exceed the marginal productivity of agricultural labor—we must recognize that this result is based on the assumption of surplus agricultural labor and the ability of the worker to receive the average product because the supply of labor is the family, which works on its own account and not for wages. This consideration is not relevant, however, for thinly populated countries or for plantation labor. And regarding the concept of surplus labor and any estimate of its extent, we should recall all the reservations discussed in our earlier analysis of the labor surplus economy (section III.A).

Even if we assume, however, that the wage differential does represent a genuine distortion, we must still recognize that the effects of this distortion may be better offset by domestic policies than by a tariff on industrial imports. The difficulty with protection by a tariff is that it seeks to remedy the distortion by affecting foreign trade, whereas the distortion is in a domestic factor market.[12] In this case, a policy of subsidization of production of the import-competing commodity, or of taxation of agricultural production, would be superior to a tariff.[13] A policy of subsidization on the use of labor in the import-competing industry, or a tax on its use in agriculture, would be an even better solution; since it directly eliminates the wage differential, this policy yields a higher real income than would a tariff, and an even higher real income than can be attained by tax-cum-subsidy on domestic production.[14] A tariff on industrial imports is thus the least effective way of offsetting a distortion in the labor market.

Although we have so far been skeptical about the validity of protectionist arguments for import substitution, there remain two arguments that have more merit: the infant industry case, and the attraction of foreign investment argument.[15] Temporary tariff protection of an infant industry is generally accepted as a valid policy for establishing an industry that would eventually be able to produce at lower costs and compete favorably with foreign producers. Nonetheless, to justify government intervention, it is not sufficient to anticipate solely the realization of internal economies of scale. For if the future

[11]For a list of conditions under which wage differentials do not represent a genuine distortion, see ibid., pp. 47–48.

[12]A tariff could make the foreign and domestic rates of transformation equal, but it destroys the equality between the domestic rate of substitution and the foreign rate of transformation.

[13]A policy of subsidization or taxation of domestic products could equate the domestic and foreign rates of transformation and the domestic rate of substitution. But since it does not eliminate the inefficiency of labor-use induced by the excessive wage differential, it achieves this equality along the production possibility curve that is within the maximum attainable production possibility curve.

[14]A policy of tax-cum-subsidy on the use of labor could achieve the equality of the domestic rate of transformation, foreign rate of transformation, and domestic rate of substitution, and it can do this along the maximum attainable production possibility curve. For in this case, the wage differential against the industrial sector is directly removed, and both the inefficiency in labor allocation and the divergence of commodity prices from opportunity costs are simultaneously eliminated.

[15]We omit the more general external economies argument and the terms-of-trade case for protection. These arguments are analytically correct, but are not among the most relevant for import substitution in a poor country. The external economies argument merges with the balanced growth doctrine. There is, moreover, no *a priori* reason why—among all possible alternative investment opportunities—we should expect the net external economies to be greatest in import-competing industries. And, again, a policy of tax-cum-subsidy on domestic production may be shown to be superior to a tariff. See Bhagwati and Ramaswami, "Domestic Distortions," pp. 45–47.

Although it is possible that a nation may succeed in improving its terms of trade by switching production from exportables to import substitutes, this policy has little practical relevance for poor countries that cannot exercise sufficient monopoly or monopsony power in foreign trade.

benefits were to accrue only to the firm, the investment might then still be made by a private firm without protection, insofar as the firm can cover its earlier costs of growth out of its later profits. Protection should instead be based on the condition that the social rate of return exceeds the private rate of return on the investment. The social benefit is likely to exceed the private benefit in an infant industry for two special reasons that are particularly relevant for a newly developing country: the knowledge of new industrial production techniques acquired in the protected industry may also be shared with other producers, and the training of the labor force may also redound to the benefit of other employers. When external economies are present, social benefits will exceed private benefits, and market forces would not yield the social optimum output. To gain the additional benefits, government aid may then be advocated.

It should be realized, however, that protection causes society to bear not only the losses that would be incurred by the industry during its period of infancy, but also the cost of consumption in the form of higher priced import substitutes during this period. The ultimate saving in costs, therefore, ought to be sufficient to compensate the community for the excess costs during the "growing up" period.

Finally, when the social rate of return exceeds the private, the preferable policy, in a way analogous to the other cases of domestic distortions, would be a direct subsidy on facilities to further the "learning process" of new production methods, or provisions by the government for the training of labor. These subsidies are superior to a protective tariff, since they avoid the intermediate loss to consumption that occurs with protection.

Protection may, however, be an effective policy for fostering an import-replacing industry when its successful establishment depends on the acquisition of better technical knowledge and experience. For when the country imposes prohibitive tariffs, or other import restrictions, against foreign manufactures, the foreign manufacturer may be induced to escape the import controls against its product by establishing a branch plant or subsidiary behind the tariff wall. Although the protection would have little effect in attracting supply-oriented industries, the inducement may be significant for the creation of "tariff factories" in market-oriented industries. It may be particularly effective in encouraging

the final stages of manufacture and assembly of parts within the tariff-imposing country when there is an import duty on finished goods, while raw materials or intermediate goods remain untaxed. This assumes, of course, that a sufficiently high domestic demand exists for the product of the tariff factory. And in determining whether the attraction of additional private foreign capital provides a net gain, we must again recall the earlier discussion about the various costs and benefits of foreign capital.

From this appraisal of the various protection arguments, we may conclude that they must be highly qualified, the costs of protection not underestimated, and superior alternative policies not overlooked. Beyond these analytic considerations, the actual experience of many developing countries with industrial protectionist policies confirms the conclusion that developing countries are likely to overemphasize the scope for replacement of industrial imports. A policy of import-substitution industrialization becomes increasingly difficult to follow beyond the consumer-goods phase because with each successive import-substitution activity through the intermediate and capital-goods phases, the capital intensity of import-substitution projects rises, resulting in a larger import content of investment. On the demand side, the projects tend to require increasingly large domestic markets for the achievement of a minimum efficient scale of production.[16]

The limitations and deleterious effects that have resulted in practice from actual import-substitution policies will be discussed in greater detail in Chapter IX. We may simply note now that in many instances, the protectionist policies have resulted in higher prices, a domestic product of inferior quality, excess capacity in the import-competing industries, and a restraint of agricultural output and exports. A number of country studies can now document the contention that overinvestment has occurred in import-replacing industry.

In some countries, the promotion of import substitutes through tariff rates that escalate with the degree of processing (low on imported intermediate goods and high on final goods) has actually resulted in negative value added. Although high protection of final goods makes pro-

[16]David Felix, "The Dilemma of Import Substitution—Argentina," in *Development Policy—Theory and Practice,* ed. Gustav F. Papanek (1968), pp. 60–61.

duction of the import substitute privately profitable in local currency, the value of inputs at world prices exceeds the value of the final product at world prices; the process of import substitution is socially inefficient.

The actual process of import substitution not only has been inefficient in resource use, but also has often intensified the foreign-exchange constraint. At the same time as policies have subsidized import replacement, they have inhibited expansion of exports, but there has not been a net saving of imports because the replacement of finished import commodities has required heavy imports of fuels, industrial materials, and capital goods, as well as foodstuffs in cases where agricultural development has also suffered.

After a period of import-substitution industrialization, the problems of maldistribution of income and unemployment have also become more serious than they were in the first place. The use of subsidies, overvalued exchange rates, the rationing of underpriced import licenses, high levels of effective protection, and loans at negative real interest rates have induced the production of import substitutes by capital-intensive, labor-saving methods and have resulted in industrial profits in the sheltered sector and high industrial wages for a labor elite, aggravating inequalities in income distribution. As noted repeatedly, employment creation in the urban import-replacement industrial sector has not kept pace with the rural–urban migration, and the unemployment problem has been aggravated by the transfer of the rural underemployed into open unemployment and underemployment in the urban sector.

Country studies provide some supporting evidence for the disenchantment with industrialization via import substitution, and at the same time they reinforce our conclusion that an LDC must now focus on the possibilities of inducing a gradual process of industrialization through agricultural development, and on the potential industrialization through the export of manufactured products. Having realized the limitations of an inward-looking strategy of industrialization, many LDCs have in fact recently changed their emphasis and are now seeking measures that will promote industrialization through the substitution of exports of processed primary products, semimanufactures, and manufactures for exports of primary commodities.

Comment: Critique of ISI

The strategy of development via import-substitution industrialization (ISI) has been critically examined by many economists. For an analysis of theoretical issues and empirical results, see B. Balassa, *The Structure of Protection in Developing Countries* (1971); M. Bruno, "The Optimal Selection of Export Promoting and Import Substituting Projects," in United Nations, *Planning the External Sector* (1967), and "Optimal Patterns of Trade and Development," *Review of Economics and Statistics* (November 1967); A. O. Hirschman, "The Political Economy of Import Substituting Industrialization," *Quarterly Journal of Economics* (February 1968); K. H. Raj and A. K. Sen, "Alternative Patterns of Growth Under Conditions of Stagnant Export Earnings," *Oxford Economic Papers* (February 1961); H. Bruton, "The Import Substitution Strategy of Economic Development," *Pakistan Development Review* (Summer 1970); I. M. D. Little, T. Scitovsky, and M. FG. Scott, *Industry and Trade in Some Developing Countries* (1970), chaps. 2 and 3; Hollis Chenery, "Comparative Advantage and Development Policy," *American Economic Review* (March 1961); Joel Bergsman, "Commercial Policy, Allocative Efficiency and 'X-efficiency,'"*Quarterly Journal of Economics* (August 1974); I. M. D. Little, "Import Controls and Exports in Developing Countries," *Finance & Development* (September 1970); J. Bhagwati, *Anatomy and Consequences of Trade Control Regimes* (1978); and Anne O, Krueger, *Foreign Trade Regimes and Economic Development: Liberalization Attempts and Consequences* (1978), and "Trade Policies in Developing Countries," in *Handbook of International Economics,* ed. R. W. Jones and P. B. Kenen (1984).

VII.B.5. Industrialization via Export Substitution—Note

In contrast with industrialization via import substitution, there is an increasing interest in the potentialities of an industrialization strategy that emphasizes export substitution. "Export substitution" is the export of nontraditional products, such as processed primary products, semimanufactures, and manufactured goods, rather than the traditional export of primary products. Other selections have already indicated how some countries have reduced the share of traditional exports in total exports while diversifying into new exports made up largely of manufactured goods (see selection I.C.1).

This Note considers why the export-substitution process has some distinct advantages over the import-substitution process. It might be thought that in terms of relaxing a country's foreign-exchange constraint, a unit of foreign exchange saved by import substitution is equivalent to a unit of foreign exchange earned by export substitution. But there are other indirect effects and dynamic considerations in favor of export substitution.

First, the domestic resource cost of earning a unit of foreign exchange tends to be less than the domestic resource cost of saving a unit of foreign exchange. This means that the resources used in import substitution could have earned a greater amount of foreign exchange through export expansion than the foreign exchange saved in import substitution, which relies on high effective rates of protection. Even though the import substitution is profitable in local currency because of the high protection, the economic costs in terms of real resource used is excessive. The value of exports that could be produced with a given use of scarce factors is greater than the value of imports that could be replaced.

Moreover, to the extent that it rests on exogenous world demand, the process of industrialization through export substitution is not limited to the narrow domestic market, as is the import-substitution process. A developing economy must overcome the diseconomies of small size. And as classical economists have emphasized, "the division of labor is limited by the extent of the market." If a country can export to a world market, it can enjoy economies of scale, learning effects, and the competitive gains

of X-efficiency.[1] "X-efficiency" refers to forces that intensify motivation and competition that result in lower cost curves for the firm.

Furthermore, a pro-trade strategy may also attract foreign direct investment. An inflow of foreign capital to support export substitution is not dependent on home market protection but is induced by considerations of efficiency on the side of resource costs. Foreign investment for export substitution also tends to have more linkages to agriculture when it involves the processing of primary products. It also upgrades labor skills when it involves the production of labor-intensive manufactures.

Besides private foreign investment, other sources of foreign capital—such as commercial banks that syndicate Eurocurrency loans to the LDCs—may be more willing to lend to a country that promotes exports. This is because the debt-servicing problem is eased when the country has increasing export revenue, and the ratio of debt servicing to export revenue is falling.

Most important, export substitution contributes more than does import substitution to the objectives of greater employment and improvement in the distribution of income. Being labor intensive in production technique and dependent on the demand of worldwide markets, the nontraditional exports may absorb more labor than import replacement. They may also reduce the cost of employment in terms of the complementary use of scarce factors of capital and imported inputs.

Export substitution also indirectly aids employment creation in the urban industrial sector by avoiding an agricultural bottleneck that would otherwise handicap urban industrial employment. By exporting manufactures and semimanufactures, the developing countries are able to import agricultural goods and thereby keep the real wage low, as expressed in terms of industrial goods. If, on the contrary, there is a slow growth of agricultural production, and the price of agricultural goods rises relative to that of in-

---

[1]Harvey Leibenstein, *General X-Efficiency Theory and Economic Development* (1978).

dustrial goods, the real wage in terms of industrial goods will rise. This, in turn, will induce a substitution of capital for labor and reduce profit margins, thereby causing savings to decline and the rate of capital formation to decrease. Industrial employment will thereby be adversely affected.[2]

The evidence from the past three decades does show that the range of labor-intensive manufactures exported from LDCs has indeed widened, and the number of LDCs engaged in export substitution has increased. In conformity with hypotheses about export-based development, the evidence indicates that export growth rates explain a significant portion of the variance in income growth rates, which cannot be explained by the growth in primary inputs; that generally the greatest increase in the GNP of various LDCs is better correlated with exports than with any other variables; that the higher-income LDCs have a higher ratio of exports to GDP and a faster rate of growth; and that the higher rate of growth is correlated with a more diversified export base.

Export-oriented industrializaton has led to superior development performance in a number of countries, of which the East Asian NICs are prime examples. By undertaking policies that remove the bias against exports and make it as profitable to produce for export as for the domestic market, these countries achieved dynamic gains from trade. They overcame the diseconomies of being small countries and realized dynamic efficiency in their mobilization and allocation of resources. Evidence of increasing dynamic efficiency appeared in the greater utilization of plant capacity, the realization of economies of scale, a declining incremental capital–output ratio, the gains of X-efficiency, higher saving ratios, the transfer of factors to activities with higher marginal productivities, greater total factor productivity, and the overcoming of organizational dualism.[3]

Recognizing the potential for a new industrialization strategy, an increasing number of LDCs desire to promote nontraditional exports. Chapter IX outlines various policy measures in support of a strategy of export-oriented industrialization.

The new industrialization strategy has not, however, gone unchallenged. Some analysts interpret the promotion of labor-intensive processes and component manufacturing as the replacement of a nineteenth-century "plantation society" with the twentieth-century creation of a "branch plant society," as involving undue bargaining power in favor of the foreign enterprise, or as resulting in an unequal international distribution of the gains from trade and investment. Thus Helleiner cautions about the dependence effects:

Export-oriented labour-intensive industries selling to multinational firms, and totally unintegrated with the rest of the economies in which they are located, would seem to combine some of the most disagreeable features of outward orientation and foreign investment. Particularly where there are "export processing zones," the manufactured export sector constitutes an "enclave"—an "output of the mother country"—in as real a sense as any foreign-owned mine ever did. These disagreeable features, moreover, are combined in a manner which leaves the host country with a minimum of bargaining advantage.

Not only is the export manufacturing activity extraordinarily "foot-loose," dependent as it is on neither local resources nor local markets, but it is also likely to bind the host country both to sources of inputs and to market outlets over which it has an absolute minimum of control. Bargaining strength is likely to be considerably less for a country manufacturing components or undertaking middle-stage processing than it is even for a raw material exporter. . . . Production for export within the multinational firm may indeed be a means for acquiring a share of the expanding markets in products for which world demand is income-elastic; but it may render the host country exceptionally "dependent" upon powerful foreign actors; foreign firms and/or governments may be in a strong position to influence the host countries' policies—both external and domestic—either directly or through their employees or local suppliers where they dominate so utterly particular sectors of their economies. The fundamental problem with this dependency relationship is that continuation or further development in the field of these manufactured exports is subject to the decision of foreign firms over which the host countries can have extraordinarily little influence—decisions over plant location, new product development, choice of techniques, market allocations, etc. One might therefore sensibly hesitate before committing oneself overly in this direction.[4]

[2]Countries have adjusted to agricultural stagnation by expanding food imports by means of labor-intensive industrial exports. Contemporary examples are Korea and Taiwan, while historical cases include the repeal of the Corn Laws in the United Kingdom and Japanese food imports from its colonies after 1900.

[3]For an elaboration, see section IX.B.2.

[4]G. K. Helleiner, "Manufacturing for Export, Multinational Firms and Economic Development," *World Development* (July 1973): 17.

To the extent that export substitution rests on foreign investment by vertically integrated transnational firms, it has been criticized by Vaitsos as constituting only "shallow development." Vaitsos analyzes the export-substitution activities of transnational enterprises:

The basic attraction offered by developing countries to such export activities by transnational firms is obviously due to the very low wages of unskilled labor in such countries given minimum productivity rates. . . .

The development of this type of international sourcing by transnational firms has important repercussions for developing countries. Their comparative advantage in this case rests in specializing in unskilled labor whose wages have to stay comparatively low while importing a package of inputs (both physical and intangibles) from abroad. Since skills and technology, capital, components and other goods are mobile internationally while unskilled labor is not (or is preferred not to be, due to the heavy social costs involved), transnational firms will be induced to intensify such international sourcing, diversifying their sources of unskilled labor among different developing countries to assure a continuous availability of supply, or the products of that input.

The "shallowness" of such a development process is a result of the following reasons. The type of labor utilized represents generally the weakest and less organized part of the labor class, thus limiting possibilities for increasing labor returns unless a general shortage of labor takes place in the country, in which case opportunity cost considerations arise for the host economy. If wages increase foreign investors will tend to shift to other countries since their locational interests stem from the existence of low wages given some minimum productivity levels. The training necessary for local labor in such activities is generally very small, limiting spill-over effects. Of critical importance is the absence of marketing knowhow effects for the host country since the goods traded are within the captive markets of affiliates. Final product promotion is handled abroad by the foreign centers of decision making.

The concentration on low wage, unskilled-labor-intensive, export promoting activities has been compared to the older enclave structures in the extractive industry. The basic difference between them, though, is that in the former the foreign investor is not very much captive once he has committed his activities in a country since the investment is very low, the shifting of activities to other nations is easy to undertake since there is no uniqueness in the local supply of inputs and the tapping of local resources did not imply the expensive discovery of previously unknown resources (as in the extractive sector). Thus, the possibility of enhancing the bargaining power of the host government to share in a more equitable distribution of the surplus involved is minimal or non-existent.[5]

From these quotations, it is clear that the issues raised by a strategy of industrialization via export substitution are controversial. They cannot be resolved in isolation. The efficacy of this industrialization strategy depends on the performance of foreign investment, relations between multinational enterprises and host countries, and the trade policies of the developed importing countries. This topic should therefore be considered in conjunction with those discussed in the selections in section V.E and in Chapter IX.

---

[5]Constantine V. Vaitsos, "Employment Effects of Foreign Direct Investments," in *Employment in Developing Nations*, ed. Edgar O. Edwards (1974), pp. 339–41.

Comment: Small Manufacturing Enterprises

The promotion of small enterprises is often believed to have a special role in industrial policy—for example, in facilitating the efficient use of labor and other factors of production. But analyses based on data from India and Colombia found that small firms are not reliably more labor intensive than their larger counterparts, and they are not consistently more technically efficient in their use of resources. See I. M. D. Little, "Small Manufacturing Enterprises in Developing Countries," *World Bank Economic Review* (January 1987).

For other studies, see I. M. D. Little, Dipak Mazumdar, and John M. Page, *Small Manufacturing Enterprises: A Comparative Analysis of India and Other Economies* (1987); Mariluz Cortes, Albert Berry, and Ashfaq Ishaq, *Success in Small and Medium-Scale Enterprises: The Evidence from Colombia* (1987); and Dennis Anderson, "Small Industry in Developing Countries," *World Development* (November 1982).

Comment: Industrialization and the Environment

The World Bank's *World Development Report on Development and the Environment* (1992) argues that to protect the natural environment, the objective should not be to produce less, but rather to produce differently. The report demonstrates that there is no linear relationship between economic activity and environmental damage. Instead, the relationship between industrialization and the environment depends on four factors: structure (goods produced), efficiency (inputs per unit of output), substitution (ability to substitute for scarce resources), and technology and management (environmental damage per unit of input or output).

To avoid environmental market failure, the report advocates the introduction of proper incentives to check industrial pollution and to utilize proper technological means for improving the environmental performance of many industrial activities (Chapter 6). Industries in developing countries also have the advantage of making new investments rather than replacing old equipment. Each new investment offers an opportunity to incorporate cost-effective pollution control and low-waste processes.

See also Paul R. Portney, ed., *Public Policies for Environmental Protection* (1990); Theodore Panayotou, *Green Markets* (1993); and David W. Pearce and Jeremy J. Warford, *World Without End: Economics, Environment, and Sustainable Development* (1993).

VII.B.6. Government Interventions for Industrial Development*

Over the past four decades or so, most developing countries have mounted sustained efforts to build up modern manufacturing industries. They have experienced dramatic successes (as in the newly industrializing economies, NIEs, of East Asia) as well as dismal failures (as in much of Sub-Saharan Africa). Many factors have contributed to this highly uneven record. Countries started (around the 1950s) from very different points on the industrial scale, some with well-established manufacturing bases, others with rudimentary manufacturing facilities (and little of the skills, institutions, and infrastructure that go with industry). They were exposed to very different external economic environments and managed their macroeconomic policies with differing degrees of success. Political and natural events were conducive to some countries' development efforts and not to others.

Even if these differences are taken into account, there remains considerable variation in the *efficiency* with which industrialization has been carried out. Industrial success depends not only on the ability to buy the capital goods and know-how needed. It depends also on the ability to absorb and efficiently deploy the new technologies, adapt it to local conditions, improve upon it, and ultimately create new knowledge, what may collectively be termed "technological or industrial dynamism." The real difference between the successful industrializers and others

lies in this dynamism. Technological dynamism enables even resource-poor countries to invest their scarce resources effectively, enter export markets and substitute efficiently for imports, diversify their industrial and export structures, and make manufacturing lead sustained structural transformation. What accounts for the uneven distribution of technological dynamism among developing countries?

The dominant explanation in the current literature is that industrial success is due to outward-oriented trade strategies. Such strategies are usually taken to involve, not just equal incentives to sell abroad as at home, but also "liberal" economic policies: low and uniform protection to domestic industries, free flows of foreign technologies and capital, investment patterns governed by market incentives, the absence of measures to promote local technologies or capacities, and unrestrained domestic competition. This "liberal" interpretation of recent industrial experience leads to strong policy recommendations: reduce government interventions, especially in trade, liberalize direct investment and technology flows, promote internal competition, restructure or privatize enterprises, remove controls on the financial sector, and so on (generally described as "getting prices right"). The ideal role left for the government is the minimalist one, to provide physical infrastructure and set the legal rules of the game.

This paper argues that while export orientation (in the sense of providing neutral incentives between foreign and domestic markets) is desirable, the experience of successful industrializers does not support the minimalist government role

*From Sanjaya Lall and Gerog Kell, "Industrial Development in Developing Countries and the Role of Government Interventions," *Banca Nazionale del Lavoro Quarterly Review* (September 1991): 271–76, 291–92. Reprinted by permission.

prescribed. On the contrary, the most successful industrializers have been dynamic precisely because they [governments] intervened heavily in the process of building up technological capabilities. Their interventions were both "functional" (to strengthen market forces without favouring particular activities) and "selective" (to promote particular activities or firms over others), though the extent and choice of intervention varied greatly. It is suggested that both sorts of intervention are necessary to overcome market failures associated with the liberal paradigm of optimal free markets. The nature of interventions needed may vary with the stage of development and national objectives, and with the ability of governments to mount interventions, but the need to intervene remains. This leads to very different policy implications from the undifferentiated "liberal" solutions now being imposed on a wide spectrum of developing countries.

The Determinants of Industrial Dynamism

A country's technological dynamism in manufacturing has many elements. These can be grouped under two headings: first, the capabilities of its individual manufacturing enterprise; and second, the interactions between individual manufacturers and between them and the supporting environment. Firm-level capabilities consist of the skills, knowledge, and institutional coherence which enable a manufacturer to do three things: first, to identify and engineer viable projects, purchase the relevant technology and capital goods, execute the investment efficiently (or "investment capabilities"); second, to master the process and product technology, achieve efficient levels of quality, maintenance and operating procedures, adapt the technologies to local materials and customer needs, improve the technology over time, and diversify, innovate, and add to the technological base ("production capabilities"); and third, to establish efficient flows of knowledge and information with suppliers, customers, consultants, and science and technology institutions ("linkage capabilities").

Some of these capabilities can be acquired by an enterprise "ready made" from the market. However, most of the skills needed to handle new technologies do not exist in developing countries and have to be acquired by the firm. Once skills are created, an enterprise has to blend them together effectively in an institutional sense. All this entails a conscious (and often prolonged and expensive) process of training, acquiring new information, experimentation, and interaction with other agents. Thus, even gaining mastery of a given technology is a "learning process" in developing countries, requiring effort and investment at all levels of operation. Different firms achieve different levels of efficiency depending on their learning investments, the skills available on labour markets, and the support provided externally. Technological mastery shades into improvement and, as the firm matures, into innovation (with formal R&D becoming prominent), but technological dynamism in essence is a process of constant capability building in every aspect of manufacturing activity.

As with any investment, that in acquiring capabilities is conditioned by incentives arising in the markets facing firms. Two aspects need mention here. First, the macroeconomic environment has strong effects. Stability, growth, and a predictable policy structure are clearly conducive to investments in capability acquisition (just as they are to investments in physical capacity). A favourable growth setting also enables greater capability acquisition in a physical sense: enterprises have more opportunities and resources to repeat particular tasks and add to capacity.

Second, competition, both domestic and international, provides a powerful stimulant to technological dynamism. However, it is a double-edged sword: the full force of external competition from mature enterprises can prevent new entrants from acquiring a base of capabilities and so retard capability development. This is the "infant industry" case for protecting the learning period, theoretically justifiable when firms cannot finance the learning process (capital market failures), cannot appropriate all its benefits (externalities), or underinvest in learning because they are risk-averse or unable to predict the outcome (information failure or "learning to learn" phenomena). Protection is *not* justifiable, however, when the sources of high cost lie outside the firm, or when protection itself reduces incentives to invest in capability building: the mere existence of high costs that may come down over time does not in other words constitute a case for protection, though it may justify other forms of intervention (in developing capabilities, education, infrastructure, and the like).

Thus, *economically efficient protection* must be temporary (geared to the learning period of the relevant technology), selective (not too many activities being protected at one time and protection not being given to compensate for inefficiencies arising outside the firm), and counterbalanced by incentives to achieve world standards of performance (for instance, by making exporting attractive even when protecting domestic sales). Efficient interventions of this sort can be directed at whole sets of activities tightly interlinked by externalities (so constituting "strategic sectors") or, at the other extreme, at single selected enterprises (to reap economies of scale, firm size, or scope, or to internalize inefficient markets for capital, skills, or other inputs). At the same time, protection that is excessive, prolonged, wrongly targeted, and not supported by measures to reduce costs external to the protected activity, can lead to permanent "infants" that never mature to competitiveness in world markets. It is vital, in interpreting the development experience, to distinguish between economically selective and non-selective, non-economic interventions. This evidence, reviewed below, suggests that economically selective protection is necessary for entry and success in complex, technically demanding industrial activities.

Even given optimal incentive structures, firm-level technological development does not occur in isolation. It entails intense and continuous interaction with the industrial environment, which provides the human and financial resources needed for internal capability development; a dense network of products, services, and information flows, within which firms can specialize efficiently; and such "public goods" as standards, testing, basic R&D, and other forms of institutional support that enable firms to conduct in-house technical work effectively. Thus, national technological dynamism is more than the sum of individual enterprises capabilities: it is the synergy arising from the interaction of enterprises, markets, and a variety of institutions.

National technological dynamism is thus subject to policy interventions at three points.[1] First, in the *incentive structures* that induce enterprises to build up capabilities, requiring sound macro management and the provision of selective infant industry protection to activities with costly "learning" periods. Secondly, in the development of *capabilities* to respond to incentives, requiring interventions to develop the skill (education and training) base, to induce appropriate technology inflows, and to promote domestic R&D activity. Thirdly, in supporting a variety of *institutions* to facilitate the functioning of markets, in particular the flow of information and skills and the development of inter-industry linkages. Moreover, it is the complex interaction of these three factors that determines technological dynamism: simply providing incentives without building up capabilities or institutions, or *vice versa*, may be ineffective, even counterproductive. This simplified framework for analyzing the process of industrial development yields useful insights into recent experience. It also yields rich policy implications, sometimes quite different from the prevalent "liberal' orthodoxy. . . .

The most successful industrializers, the East Asian NIEs, have all intervened in support of industrialization. Hong Kong has intervened to provide a broad base of skills, excellent infrastructure, and institutional support of its industries. This low level of (essentially functional) intervention has enabled it to build a light, specialized, and efficient manufacturing base which, despite past dynamism, lacks technological depth and is, therefore, vulnerable to rising costs.[2] Korea, in contrast, has intervened very heavily, by protection, subsidies, and direct instruction, in incentives and factor markets and in technology transfer, and has succeeded in establishing probably the most competitive and advanced industrial structure among developing countries. The depth of this structure renders it far less vulnerable to rising labour costs. The structure, capabilities, and ownership of its industries largely reflect the pattern of strategic interventions undertaken to "pick winners" and promote them by a comprehensive battery of measures.

While interventions are necessary for sustained industrial development, however, not all interventions are efficient or desirable. Development experience is replete with cases of uneconomic interventions. Excessive, haphazard, across-the-board protection has bred, not

---

[1] See S. Lall, *Building Industrial Competitiveness in Developing Countries* (1990).

[2] Hong Kong has survived by rapidly shifting its manufacturing offshore, mainly to China, because it could not diversify into more complex activities at home. Its own manufactured exports are now growing much slower than its exports from other bases. A similar phenomenon is observable for low-tech small and medium enterprises in Taiwan. By contrast, the Korean *chaebol* are investing abroad mainly in sophisticated activities (and mainly in developed countries) to serve local markets, while upgrading into higher technology activities at home to cope with rising wages.

technological dynamism, but many "infant" industries that have never matured. The setting up of heavy industrial structures without providing the capabilities needed (i.e., an adequate skill or institutional base) has often led to inefficiency. Creating skills, on the other hand, without proper incentives has wasted human resources, while "getting prices right" without offering infant industry protection or institutional or skill back-up has led to industrial stagnation. Chile seems to be an example of poor industrial and manufactured export performance despite many years of "right" prices, outward orientation (with very low uniform tariffs), and high levels of skill, because of its lack of selective promotion of activities, firms, or supporting institutions, while African countries are examples of failure due mainly to lack of skills and institutions. The secret of success has been combining incentives with adequate capabilities and institutions, each supported by a proper mix of selective and functional interventions. The poor performers have often intervened in the wrong way, and many have intervened too much while some have intervened too little. This does not deny the need for interventions (of the right sort) in the future. What it does suggest is that the pattern of interventions be changed.

The proper mix of interventions varies over time and by national context. As markets and capabilities develop, the need for interventions declines and the mix changes. The availability of capabilities to design and implement interventions itself affects feasible policy options. These considerations lead to a very different set of recommendations, more differentiated and more directed to helping governments to intervene, than current orthodoxy.

VII.C. TECHNOLOGICAL PROGRESS

VII.C.1. Appropriate Technology*

Technology is often identified with the hardware of production—knowledge about machines and processes. Here a much broader definition is adopted, extending to all the ''skills, knowledge and procedures for making, using and doing useful things.'' Technology thus includes methods used in non-marketed activities as well as marketed ones. It includes the nature and specification of what is produced—the product design—as well as how it is produced. It encompasses managerial and marketing techniques as well as techniques directly involved in production. Technology extends to services—administration, education, banking and the law, for example—as well as to manufacturing and agriculture. A complete description of the technology in use in a country would include the organization of productive units in terms of scale and ownership. Although much of the discussion will be in terms of technological development in the hardware of technology, the wider definition is of importance since there are relationships between the hardware and the software—between, for example, mechanical process and managerial techniques and infrastructural services—which both determine the choice made in both spheres.

Technology consists of a series of techniques. The technology available to a particular country is all those techniques it knows about (or may with not too much difficulty obtain knowledge about) and could acquire, while the technology in use is that subset of techniques it *has* acquired. It must be noted that the technology available to a country cannot be identified with all known techniques: on the one hand weak communication may mean that a particular country only knows about part of the total methods known to the world as a whole. This can be an important limitation on technological choice. On the other hand, methods may be known but they may not be available because no one is pro-

ducing the machinery or other inputs required. This too limits technological choice.

The actual technology in use is thus circumscribed first by the nature of world technology, then by the availability to the country of known techniques, and finally by the choice made among those available. If the technology in use is thought to be inappropriate, it may be inappropriate because world technology is inappropriate, or because an inappropriate subset is available to the country, or because an inappropriate selection is made, or for some combination of the three reasons. Confusion is caused by failing to distinguish among the three.

Each technique is associated with a set of characteristics. These characteristics include the nature of the product, the resource use—of machinery, skilled and unskilled manpower, management, materials and energy inputs—the scale of production, the complementary products and services involved, etc. Any or all of these characteristics may be important in determining whether it is possible and/or desirable to adopt a particular technique in a particular country and the implications of so doing.

More formally, we may think of all the known techniques as $wT = \{Ta, Tb, Tc, Td \ldots Tn\}$ (where ''known'' means known to the world) as constituting world technology. For a particular country, the technology available for adoption is that subset of world technology known to the country in question *and* available. Say, $cT = \{\overline{Ta} \ldots \overline{Tn}\}$, where c denotes the country and the bar indicates that only techniques known to the country and available are included. Thus $cT \subset wT$.

Each of the techniques $Ta, Tb \ldots$ etc. is a vector consisting of a set of characteristics, ai, aii, aiii, bi, bii, biii. . . . Thus technology can be described in matrix form, with each column representing the characteristics of each technique, as shown in Table 1.

The technology in use in a particular country is that subset of the technology available to it that has been selected and introduced, or $uT = \{\overline{Ta} \ldots \overline{Tn}\}$ where $uT \subset cT \subset wT$.

The processes by which world technology is narrowed down to an actual set of techniques

*From Frances Stewart, *Technology and Underdevelopment,* 2nd ed., Macmillan, London and Basingstoke, 1977, pp. 1–3, and ''International Technology Transfer: Issues and Policy Options,'' *World Bank Staff Working Paper* No. 344, July 1979, pp. 78, 82–88. Reprinted by permission.

TABLE 1. Matrix of World Technology $= wT$

Characteristics	T_a	T_b	T_c	T_d	T_e
Product type					
Product nature					
Scale of production					
Material inputs					
Labor input:					
Skilled					
Unskilled					
Managerial input					
Investment requirements					

in use may be crudely described as shown in Figure 1.

The characteristics of technology are largely determined by the nature of the economies for which they are designed. The most significant determinants of the characteristics of new technology are the income levels, resource availability and costs in the society in and for which the technology is designed, the system of organization of production, and the nature of the technology in use in the society. In each of these respects, societies of advanced countries differ from those of poor countries. Consequently, technology designed to suit advanced countries tends to be ill adapted (or "inappropriate") to the conditions prevalent in poor countries. The transfer of such technology to poor societies tends, as a result, to cause various distortions and inefficiencies.

In discussing "characteristics" of technology, one should include all the relevant features which determine its resource use, productivity, and impact on production and consumption patterns. These features include the nature and design of the product, the scale and organizational system for which the technology is designed, its resource use, including capital and labor intensity, materials and fuel use, skill requirements, and the infrastructural and complementary inputs it requires. The traditional economist's characterization of techniques according to their capital or labor intensity forms only one, and quite often a relatively insignificant, aspect of the total characterization.

Techniques designed for modern advanced countries tend to produce high-income products, require high levels of investible resources per employee, high levels of education and skills, be of a large scale and require sophisticated management techniques, be associated with high levels of labor productivity, and be linked, through inputs and outputs, with the rest of the advanced technology system. If these techniques are transferred unmodified to LDCs, the result will be a concentration of resources, of savings and expenditure on human resources and infrastructure, on a small part of the economy. Incomes will tend to be concentrated in this area, leading to markets for the high-income products the system produces. Resources available in the low-income country will tend to be underutilized, including raw materials as well as labor.

Many of the well-established characteristics of the dual economy can be seen as following from the characteristics of advanced country technology: the capital-intensity of productive techniques, the heavy reliance on imported managers, skill deficiencies, un- and under-employment and a relative (often absolute) deprivation of the economy outside the modern sector. Only economies which are growing very rapidly and are selective about the choice of techniques and adept at modifying them are able to overcome this dualism, by absorbing a growing proportion of their workforce into the modern sector. South Korea and Taiwan provide the obvious examples. In other economies, dualistic tendencies have been partially offset by a deliberate attempt to protect the non-modern sector, providing it with resources and protected markets to prevent it being undermined by the modern sector. This is the policy of "walking on two legs" pursued most extensively by China (and to a less marked extent by India). In China employment expansion in the modern sector has been similar to that in many other developing economies, lagging well behind growth in output, while the tech-

FIGURE 1.

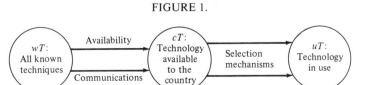

nology adopted has tended to be capital intensive. Overall employment policies have succeeded because of the absorption of labor in the agricultural and rural non-agricultural sectors.

There is a growing body of literature that questions the rather simplistic technological determinist argument advanced above. It is argued that in many industries a wide choice of efficient technologies has been established by empirical research. Recently, Pack has argued that countries could make significant gains at the macrolevel in terms of employment, output and savings, by policies leading to the adoption of the most appropriate techniques in existence.[1] It has long been established that there is considerable potential for labor intensity in ancillary processes, even if the core technology is more fixed. Old techniques from advanced countries offer more labor-intensive and small-scale alternatives than the most recent techniques. While this sort of argument supports the view that there is a wider range of choice than the completely determinist view implies, other considerations suggest that the potential for selecting labor-intensive techniques may be exaggerated by calculations based on the micro-case studies. In the first place, many of the studies show that considerations of product standards/characteristics may rule out the labor-intensive technologies. Secondly, the labor-intensive techniques are often only economic at small scale. Thirdly, entrepreneurs do not have information about the complete ''shelf'' of techniques in existence; their access to information about different techniques depends on their channels of information. There tends to be a bias in channels of information towards technology currently in use in the supplying countries—that is, the advanced countries. Appropriate techniques, which are often older techniques from advanced countries, or techniques recently developed in LDCs are less well promoted.

Fourthly, many of the studies neglect the determinants of choice or selection mechanisms. It is often assumed that the only relevant selection mechanism is the relative price of capital and labor, and that is in the control of government. In fact, the determinants of choice are far more complex. The nature and scale of the market is one critical determinant. Products sold on the international market or to high-income consumers may need to use the most recent technology in order to compete. Because scale of production and the nature of the market are of importance in determining choice of product and technique, the factors determining these are significant. Income distribution and trading strategy help determine the nature and scale of markets for different types of product. The distribution of investible resources between enterprises of different size and type is also of relevance. The very substantial wage differentials between enterprises of different sizes suggest that the real wage level may be outcome as well as (partial) cause of technological choice. Moreover, a number of recent studies of technological choice have shown that the most rational choices—both in terms of profit maximization and appropriateness of techniques—are somtimes rejected in favor of less profitable and less appropriate techniques. Thus investigation of the decision mechanisms involved is required if choice of technique is to be altered in a more appropriate direction.

Fifthly, the studies establishing a range of choice are essentially static, depicting the situation at the point in time when they were made. But the so-called ''shelf'' is moving as technical change proceeds, and some parts of the shelf are moving much faster than others. In particular, with the current world balance of Research and Development, the modern capital-intensive part of the shelf is moving forward, in terms of new products and efficiency of technique, as compared with the labor-intensive part; and the ''modern'' end is also getting increasingly capital-intensive, larger scale, and the products more sophisticated as incomes rise in the advanced countries. Thus while there may be scope for some push in the direction of labor intensity and other dimensions of appropriateness in some products, the aggregate effects are likely to be swamped by dynamic changes in the opposite direction.

More appropriate technology may be roughly defined as technology whose resource use is more in keeping with LDC resource availability, and whose products are more suited to low-income consumers. This means that more appropriate technology will be more labor-intensive, less skill-intensive, smaller scale, use more local materials, and produce simpler low-income products than most of advanced country technology currently being transferred to low-income countries. Technology may be more ap-

[1]Howard Pack, ''Technology and Employment: Constraints on Optimal Performance,'' in *Technology and Economic Development: A Realistic Perspective*, ed. Samuel M. Rosenblatt (1979).

propriate in one respect, and no more so in others; or more in some respects, less in others. It is then a matter of judgment as to whether it is to be preferred. More appropriate technology may be less efficient, either in the economic sense that it is less profitable (socially and/or privately), or in the stricter sense (which has been defined as technical inefficiency) that it uses more of all resources to produce the same output. If it is socially or technically inefficient as compared with the "inappropriate" alternative, then the economy would suffer from some output loss in adopting it. In such a situation it would only be worthwhile adopting if it were believed that learning effects would be such as to outweigh initial inefficiency, or that income distribution and similar effects are such as to outweigh the loss in output. If we assume that these effects may be incorporated into the measure of social efficiency (and that we can give some meaning to this concept), then an economy should only adopt more appropriate techniques if they can be shown to be socially efficient. In discussing ways in which appropriate technology can be promoted, it is assumed that what is in question is the promotion of socially efficient appropriate technology.

Broadly, one may distinguish two types of appropriate technology: appropriate technology for the "modern" sector, which consists in the adaptation of modern sector advanced country technologies in more labor-intensive directions; and appropriate technology for the traditional sector, which upgrades and improves traditional technologies.

Comment: Criteria of Technological Appropriateness

On the problem of "appropriate" technology, the following are noteworthy: "Technology" [special issue], *World Development* (March 1974); "Science and Technology in Development" [special issue], *Journal of Development Studies* (October 1972); G. K. Helleiner, "The Role of Multinational Corporations in the Less Developed Countries' Trade in Technology," *World Development* (April 1975); Paul Streeten, "Technology Gaps Between Rich and Poor Countries," *Scottish Journal of Political Economy* (November 1972); Jack Baranson, *Industrial Technologies for Developing Countries* (1969), and *Technology and the Multinationals* (1978); W. Berankek and G. Danis, *Science and Technology and Economic Development* (1978); A. K. Sen, *Employment, Technology and Development* (1975); Richard S. Eckaus, *Appropriate Technologies for Developing Countries* (1977); Robert Stobaugh and Louis T. Wells, Jr., *Technology Crossing Borders* (1984); Lawrence White, "The Evidence on Appropriate Factor Proportions in LDCs," *Economic Development and Cultural Change* (July 1980); A. S. Bhalla, *Toward Global Action on Appropriate Technology* (1979); C. Cooper, ed., *Science, Technology and Development* (1973); Frances Stewart, *Science, Technology and Underdevelopment* (1977); C. P. Timmer et al., *The Choice of Technology in Developing Countries* (1975); Charles Cooper, "Choice of Techniques and Technological Change as Problems in Political Economy," *International Social Science Journal* 14, no. 3 (1973); E. K. Y. Chen, *Multinational Corporations, Technology and Employment* (1982); A. C. Samli, *Technology Transfer* (1985); and R. J. Congdon, *Introduction for Appropriate Technology* (1977).

A series of reports by the United Nations Institute for Training and Research (UNITAR) is highly instructive, as are the Industrial Planning and Programming Series of the United Nations Industrial Development Organization (UNIDO) and the reports of UNCTAD.

Comment: Choice of Techniques by MNEs

We may raise three basic questions regarding the choice of technique by multinational enterprises: (1) whether the technologies used by multinationals are adaptable to the low-wage labor-abundant conditions in LDCs, (2) whether multinationals do in fact adapt the technologies they transfer, and (3) whether multinationals adapt better or worse than local firms. An excellent review of the literature addressed to these questions is presented by S. Lall, "Transnationals, Domestic Enterprises, and Industrial Structure in Host LDCs: A Survey," *Oxford Economic Papers* (July 1978), with an extensive bibliography. For empirical evidence on differences in the behavior of foreign subsidiaries and locally owned firms with regard to technology, marketing, trade, and wages, see Rhys Jenkins, "Comparing Foreign Subsidiaries and Local Firms in LDCs," *Journal of Development Studies* (January 1990).

Other significant references on this subject include Danny M. Leipziger, "Production Characteristics in Foreign Enclave and Domestic Manufacturing: The Case of India," *World Development* (April

1976); Frances Stewart and Jeffrey James, eds., *The Economics of New Technology in Developing Countries* (1982); and M. Fransman and K. King, eds., *Technological Capability in the Third World* (1984).

For additional readings on the micro-substitution possibilites in different industries in developing countries, see H. Pack, "The Substitution of Labor for Capital in Kenyan Manufacturing," *Economic Journal* (March 1976); Y. Rhee and L. Westphal, "A Microeconomic Investigation of Choice of Technology," *Journal of Development Economics* (September 1977); G. Ranis, "Industrial Technology Choice and Employment: A Review of Developing Country Evidence," *Intersciencia* (1977); L. J. White, "The Evidence on Appropriate Factor Proportions for Manufacturing in Less Developed Countries: A Survey," *Economic Development and Cultural Change* (October 1978); Gene M. Grossman and Assaj Razin, "Direct Foreign Investment and the Choice of Technique Under Uncertainty," *Oxford Economic Papers* (December 1985); and B. S. Chung and C. H. Lee, "The Choice of Production Techniques by Foreign and Local Firms in Korea," *Economic Development and Cultural Change* (October 1980).

Although these studies indicate a wide potential choice in both primary and secondary production operations and alternative commodity specifications, the empirical observation remains that the selections actually made in the developing countries still appear to be "inappropriate" by the standards discussed in the readings in this section. It is therefore necessary to analyze why the problem of inappropriate technology persists and what policy measures might be undertaken to overcome the obstacles to the use of appropriate technology.

Comment: Technological Capability

The way in which a developing country acquires "technological capability" is the subject of special study by C. J. Dahlman, B. Ross-Larson, and L. E. Westphal, "Managing Technological Development," *World Development* (June 1987):

> The central issue of technological development in the developing countries is not acquiring the capability to invent products and processes. It is acquiring the capability to use existing technology—to produce more efficiently, to establish better production facilities, and to use the experience gained in production and investment to adapt and improve the technology in use. The main way of doing this is to build on what can be obtained from abroad while developing local capabilities in areas where it makes the most sense. Since all capabilities cannot be developed simultaneously, and since the accumulation of any one capability takes time and experience, the sequence in which various capabilities are developed is crucial. And the required capabilities change as a firm or country matures, because of changes in existing capabilities and because of changes in market conditions.
>
> Since everything cannot be done at once, selectivity is at the heart of national policy for technological development. And since markets fail differently in different environments, the policies for government intervention have to be tailored to national and sector-specific circumstances. Whether new capabilities should be promoted in a sector depends on the relative costs and benefits of using local or foreign sources, now and in the future. How they should be promoted depends on the capabilities already accumulated in the industry and in related sectors. (p. 774)

See also Carl Dahlman and Larry Westphal, "The Transfer of Technology: Factors in the Acquisition of Technology," *Finance & Development* (December 1983), and "Technological Effort in Industrial Development—An Interpretative Survey of Recent Research," in *The Economics of New Technology in Developing Countries,* ed. Frances Stewart and Jeffrey James (1982); S. Lall, "Technological Capabilities and Industrialization," *World Development* (February 1992); and Martin Bell and Keith Pavitt, "Accumulating Technological Capability in Developing Countries," *World Bank Economic Review Supplement* (1992).

VII.C.2. Capital-Stretching Innovations*

First and foremost, it should be remembered that, unlike in an advanced country where technological change is viewed as rather automatic and routinized or as capable of being generated through R&D expenditures according to some rules of cost/benefit analysis, in the contemporary developing societies technological change cannot either be taken for granted or afforded through basic R&D allocations. In this situation, we cannot avoid the question of what, given the existence of a shelf of technology from abroad, is the pattern by which the typical less developed economy, in fact, manages to innovate. This question in turn forces us to look at least at the following dimensions more carefully: (1) the precise nature of that technology shelf, (2) the availability within the LDCs of required initial managerial and entrepreneurial capacity, and (3) the changing nature of that required managerial and entrepreneurial capacity in the course of transition to modern growth.

The technology shelf developed in the mature industrial economies abroad may be described by a set of unit activities following a smooth envelope curve as in Figure 1. A particular technology can be described by an L-shaped contour producing one unit of output with a given pair of capital and labor coefficients. The technology shelf is composed of the complete set of such activities or technologies which have been demonstrated to be feasible somewhere in the advanced countries at some historical point in time, including the present. Since there exists a number of technology-exporting countries—for example, the United States, Germany, the United Kingdom, and Japan—with continuous technological transfers among themselves as well as with the LDCs, it is not unreasonable to postulate the existence of a single technological shelf for the lending world as a whole. For example, unit technology A_0 may have been generated in Germany in 1920, A_1 in the United States in 1920, and A_2 in the United States in 1950. In other words, as we move to the left along the shelf we run into more "modern"

technology, that is, technology of more recent vintage and of higher capital intensity. As capital per head increases this means that the typical worker has learned to cooperate with more units of capital of increasing technical complexity. This capital-deepening process, in other words, is more complicated than the textbook version of "homogeneous" labor being equipped with more units of "homogeneous" capital.

At any point in time the typical LDC is, then, theoretically free to borrow a particular unit activity from anywhere along this shelf. What technology is chosen and what happens as an immediate and ultimate consequence of that choice, that is, what secondary processes and reactions are set off, is, of course, all part and parcel of the innovation process taken as a whole. The quality of the process, each step of the way, in turn depends on both the economic environment, that is, the nature of the relative price signals, and on the entrepreneurial, managerial, and skilled labor capacity of the borrower.

The role of innovation must therefore be seen as intimately related to the stage in which the developing economy finds itself. In other words, the role of technological change in output and

*From Gustav Ranis, "Industrial Sector Labor Absorption," *Economic Development and Cultural Change,* April 1973, pp. 392–97. Reprinted by permission.

FIGURE 1.

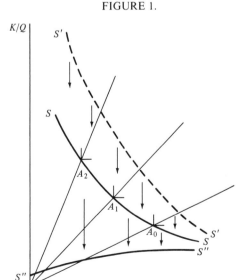

employment generation must be viewed as sensitive to the same discernible phases of growth as the economy moves in transition from open agrarianism to Kuznets's modern economic growth. In the first post-independence or import-substitution phase previously mentioned, an effort is made to increase the supply of domestic entrepreneurship and the economy's learning capacity, partly through the importation of people via aid but mainly through the system of protection established by government policies. In fact, the most reasonable explanation for the import-substitution syndrome is that it is a response to a real (or imagined) shortage of entrepreneurship and that it permits time, through informal learning by doing or more formal educational processes, for this entrepreneurial capacity to develop.

In terms of Figure 1, this means that, although the technological shelf may look as indicated by curve SS, the *actual* choices available to the developing country during the import-substitution phase are more aptly described by S'S'. In other words, due to the inadequate state of entrepreneurial capacity during the early postindependence period of physical controls, the efficiency of generating output per unit of capital in the borrowing country is likely to be substantially below that in the lending country. This is likely to be more true the more capital intensive the import, that is, the further removed from the cultural inheritance and experience of the borrower. Such technological imports are often accompanied by imported engineers, even managers and supervisors—adding up to what is called a "turn-key project." The most advanced and sophisticated technology can, of course, be made to "work," in the physical sense, even in the most backward developing economy. But a shiny new plant imbedded in a society many decades distant is bound to be substantially less efficient. This is true for a thousand direct reasons, such as the absence of even minimal skilled labor supplies, domestic subcontracting, and repair and maintenance possibilities, as well as for many more subtle sociological reasons which enter into the total milieu in which the plant is required to operate. The more sophisticated and removed from the rest of the economy is the technological transplant, the greater is the relative inefficiency, as indicated by the shape of the S'S' curve.

If and when the economy then moves away from the import-substitution phase and enters into the second phase of liberalization and export substitution, a second important, if unintentional, type of innovation is likely to appear, namely, a reduction in the extent of the inefficiency of the original transplanted technology. Call it X-efficiency if you like, but the cost of the pure transplantation is likely to be reduced, quite unintentionally, that is, largely as a result of factors external to the profit-maximizing behavior of the productive unit itself. This increase in productive efficiency over time will increase in quantitative significance as the import-substitution hothouse temperature is gradually turned down and a more competitive efficiency may be represented by the arrows tending, over time, to move S'S' back toward the original SS position.

Another more conscious and quantitatively more important type of innovation begins to gather importance during this same second phase of transition. This phenomenon may be called innovational assimilation—innovating "on top of" imported technology in the direction of using relatively more of the abundant unskilled labor supply. As the economy shifts from a natural-resource-based growth pattern in the import-substitution phase to a human-resource-based system in the export-substitution phase, there is an increasing sensitivity to the continuously changing factor endowment, first in terms of the efficient utilization of the domestic unskilled-labor force, and later in terms of the incorporation of growing domestic skills and ingenuity. In other words, the appropriate type of technology finally in place must be one in which not only the initial choice from the shelf but also the adaptations and adjustments consciously made thereafter, in response to changing domestic resource and capability constraints, play an important role.

The more liberalized the economy, in terms of the government's performing a catalytic role through the market by indirect means rather than trying to impose resource allocation by direct controls, the better the chances that the millions of dispersed decision makers can be induced, by the sheer force of profit maximization, to make the "right" decision. As the gap between shadow and market prices narrows—coupled with the expectation of continued labor surpluses for years to come—we would expect transplantation choices to become more flexible, that is, labor intensive. However, since shelf choices are likely to continue to be severely constrained—partly by a lack of illumination of substantial portions of it, partly by such institutional inhibitions as prestige, aid tying, and so forth—we can realistically expect relatively less benefits from liberalization to accrue in the transplantation process. On the other hand, we can expect much more from the assimilation type of innovational behavior which now tends, for the same reasons, to be more slanted in a labor-using direction. In the typical labor surplus type of economy—or one likely to become one over the next decade (as is probably the case in much of Africa)—all this means a much greater possibility for the efficient accomodation of pure labor services.[1] Whether this will lead to a sectoral output shift in favor of labor-intensive export commodities or a mix change predominantly addressed to the domestic market, of course, depends on, *ceteris paribus,* income elasticities of demand, the goverment's fiscal prowess, and the type (e.g., size) of the economy. Moreover, no strong generalization as to the relative importance of shifts in output mix versus changes in technology for given mixes is likely to be valid. It should be clear, however, that the important issue is that the search for innovation can now be considered a conscious activity of the individual entrepreneur and—given the combination of more realistic relative price signals after liberalization plus greater entrepreneurial capacity—that it is likely to be mainly directed toward various forms of indigenous capital stretching on top of the imported technology. Such capital stretching can be represented by a reduction in the capital coefficient per unit of output. The effective post-assimilation set of unit technologies, that is *after*

domestic assimilation, may thus be represented by curve $S''S''$ in Figure 1, with the strength of the indigenous labor-using innovative effort indicated by the amount of the "downward" shift in the capital coefficient.

It should be noted here that a negatively sloped technology shelf, for example, SS, representing pure technological transplantation, permits, as we move to the left, higher labor productivity levels, but only at increasing capital cost. In a country characterized by capital scarcity this may mean increased technical unemployment (à la Eckaus) and hence a lower value of per capita income for the economy—in spite of the higher level of labor productivity achieved. Domestic capital stretching, however, can materially affect that situation by enabling more workers to be employed per unit of the capital stock. If the post-assimilation unit technology set, $S''S''$, for example, is upward sloping from left to right, higher labor productivity levels become consistent with lower capital/output ratios.

In summary, once the overall policy setting has turned more favorable and permitted the economy to enter the second phase of transition, it is this indigenous capital-stretching capacity which I consider to be of the greatest importance—especially for the contemporary developing economy facing the formidable labor force explosion. . . . It is in this specific area also where the skepticism of planners, engineers, and aid officials generally is most pronounced—especially with respect to the full range of technological choice really available when all the dust has settled. Historical examples from the Japanese case, as well as contemporary evidence from Korea and Taiwan, permit us to demonstrate the existence and potential importance of such capital-stretching innovations for the labor surplus developing country.

---

[1] It is important to emphasize the word "efficient" since I am not concerned here with the, possibly also legitimate, objective of employment creation as a separate social goal, to be weighed against output growth.

VII.C.3. Technology Transfer*

Firms have several alternatives for obtaining new technology that, if mastered, yield a higher level of TFP for any given capital-labor ratio.

These alternatives include: (a) the purchase of new equipment; (b) direct foreign investment; (c) the purchase of technology licenses for domestic production of new products or the use of new processes; (d) the use of nonproprietary technology, including that obtained from purchasers of exports; (e) acquisition of knowledge from returning nationals who have been edu-

*From Howard Pack, "Technology Gaps between Industrial and Developing Countries: Are There Dividends for Latecomers?" *World Bank Economic Review Supplement* (1992): 295–99. Reprinted by permission.

cated or have worked in industrial countries and from nationals who remain in industrial countries; and (f) domestic research and development and efforts in reverse engineering.

All these possibilities, except for the research and development efforts, represent an attempt to move toward international best practice by transferring technologies available abroad. The research and development alternative may have an element of aiding the identification, modification, and absorption of foreign technology rather than generating a completely indigenous technology.

The Experience of Two Successful Asian Economies

This section describes some of the means by which two of the fastest-growing newly industrializing economies—Korea and Taiwan (China)—were able to shift toward an international production function.[1]

Korea and Taiwan (China)

Until the mid- to late 1970s neither Korea nor Taiwan (China) employed explicit technology policies. The main exceptions were the restrictions placed on direct foreign investment and a fairly perfunctory review of technology licensing agreements in Korea. The ability of the two countries to close the initial productivity gaps was a result of firms' responses to the incentives contained in national economic policies. Among these policies were: (a) the relative neutrality of the foreign trade regime with respect to profitability between domestic and foreign sales and the relatively low variance in protection across sectors; (b) export targeting in Korea and undervaluation of the real exchange rate in Taiwan (China) to encourage exports to a greater extent than would have been the case given the protection afforded to new industries in the domestic market; (c) a relatively undistorted labor market that, along with some movement toward market rates of interest (particularly in Taiwan, China), kept the wage-rental ratio closer to its scarcity value than in other developing countries.

The responses to these incentives led to a set of favorable but unintended technological consequences. For example, as a result of the rapid rates of export growth that these policies encouraged, there was a substantial inflow of nonproprietary technology, embodied in equipment and in the knowledge provided by customers (Westphal, Rhee, and Pursell 1981). This inflow was greater because exports and production increased most in older labor-intensive sectors in which technology from industrial countries was less protected. Technology and knowledge were relatively easy to acquire and absorb in these sectors even without a large stock of highly educated engineers. Much of the relevant information was based on mechanical knowledge rather than on electronic, biological, or chemical principles that would have required more formal education of employees.

Moreover, the machinery that was employed to manufacture the increased output was quite labor-intensive, in response to the low wage-rental ratio (Ranis 1979; Rhee and Westphal 1977). The simple equipment and the absence of continuous processing were conducive to minor innovations for increasing productivity, which were often suggested by blue-collar workers. Thus, the trade and factor price regimes were complementary and were conducive both to obtaining static gains in output and to fostering the move toward best practice. In this period, until the late 1970s, it is likely that much of the growth in productivity was the unplanned consequence of getting the prices right. Dollar and Sokoloff (1990) find that TFP growth in labor-intensive sectors in Korea exceeded that in the capital-intensive sectors. Technology policy was implicit in the standard economic policies, and technological learning complemented the conventional economic responses, stimulating further growth in production and exports as a consequence of reduced production costs.

In the 1970s a more explicit policy toward technology acquisition appeared. This policy differed in the two economies. In Korea the growth of large local firms was encouraged by the use of selected credit and other instruments. As domestic real wages increased and newer lower-wage competitors entered the international market, large Korean firms were encouraged to acquire the technological capacity to enter sectors that were more capital- and technology-intensive and to achieve best-practice productivity (Pack and Westphal 1986). Information about production technology in these more complex producer goods sectors was likely to be more closely guarded than in the consumer

[1]The evidence for the interpretations in this section is set forth in Dahlman and Sananikone (1990), Westphal, Rhee, and Pursell (1981), Pack and Westphal (1986), and Pack (1992).

goods industries, and importers in industrial countries were less likely to transfer such technology. The Korean government encouraged firms to obtain technology licenses, acquire advanced equipment, and engage in their own research and development.

In Taiwan (China) the transfer of knowledge in the consumer industries, in which the early export drive was concentrated, was similar to that in Korea (Pack 1992). As Taiwan entered newer areas, however, it did not encourage the growth of large-scale firms capable of substantial research and development. The industrial structure was characterized by many small firms, reflecting the prevalence of high interest rates and the limited use of selected credit directed to larger firms. Therefore Taiwan utilized central institutions such as the Industrial Technology Research Institute, as well as technology diffusion institutions such as the China Productivity Center, to introduce new technologies, develop new products and processes, diffuse knowledge of them, and scan international markets for both products and processes (see Dahlman and Sananikone 1990). Moreover, in the newest sectors the ability to attract back Taiwanese nationals or to utilize the knowledge of those who remain abroad has been critical (Pack 1992).

Efforts to obtain international knowledge will have lower payoffs if they are not accompanied by a growth in the stock of capital per worker. Capital, both physical and human, can be partly supplied by other countries in the form of direct foreign investment. The remarkable development of Singapore, for example, demonstrates the potency of externally provided capital and skills in facilitating a rapid movement to international best practice (Lim and Fong 1991). In the initial period of rapid growth of industrial productivity, Korea and Taiwan (China) benefited from both capital accumulation and the move toward international best practice.

It may be conjectured that the extent of the shift in the production function would have been less if the sectors in which exports grew had been those in which these countries were close to world best practice. In Chile, a more recent example of improved policies, TFP growth has been much slower. Part of the explanation for this may lie in its emphasis on primary exports, minerals, and agricultural products. It is likely that these sectors in Chile were much closer to international best practice than were the industrial growth sectors in Korea and Taiwan (China). Moreover, in some of the expanding

export sectors, such as electronics, the best-practice frontier was itself shifting rapidly, and the two Asian economies were able to take advantage of this. If these conjectures are correct, early proponents of import-substituting industrialization such as Singer and Prebisch may have been correct in their intuition of the dynamic (TFP growth) benefits of industrialization. They were mistaken, however, in their emphasis on import substitution rather than export growth as the process for realizing these benefits.

In both economies, people (and the knowledge they embody) who have been educated abroad return because of the high wages made possible by growing exports. Purely domestically oriented firms with smaller sales bases could not have offered sufficiently high wages to attract them. The newly acquired international knowledge was embedded in a framework conducive to efficiency. Competitive pressures led to a search within plants for better productivity performance. As a result, imported practices were improved, and purely domestic efforts were made to increase productivity.

The Interaction of Knowledge Acquisition, Investment, and Human Capital

Both Korea and Taiwan (China) invested extensively in education and in the accumulation of substantial physical capital. The ratio of investment to GDP increased from relatively low levels to more than 30 percent in the 1980s. Figure 1 elucidates the process. Initially the economy is at point A on production function f_0. As physical and human capital accumulation proceed, it moves to point E on production function f_1. The shift to the higher production function is realized because of the growing utilization of international best practice. Note, however, that

FIGURE 1.

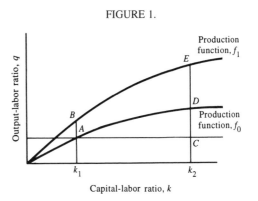

the benefit from this accumulation of knowledge would have been less—$AB < DE$—if capital per worker had not grown (Nelson 1973). Thus the size of the benefit from the growing import of knowledge and from local efforts to increase productivity depends on the stock of physical investment and skills complementing local unskilled labor.

References

Dahlman, Carl J., and Ousa Sananikone. 1990. "Technology Strategy in the Economy of Taiwan (China): Exploiting Foreign Linkages and Investing in Local Capability." World Bank, Industry and Energy Department, Washington, D.C.

Dollar, David, and Kenneth Sokoloff. 1990. "Patterns of Productivity Growth in South Korean Manufacturing Industries, 1963–1979." *Journal of Development Economics* 33: 309–27.

Lim, Linda Y. C., and Pang Eng Fong. 1991. *Foreign Direct Investment and Industrialization in Malaysia, Singapore, Taiwan, and Thailand.* Development Centre Studies. Paris: Organization for Economic Cooperation and Development.

Nelson, Richard R. 1973. "Recent Exercises in Growth Accounting: New Understanding or Dead End?" *American Economic Review* 73: 162–68.

Pack, Howard. 1992. "New Perspectives on Industrial Growth in Taiwan." In Gustav Ranis, ed., *Taiwan: From Developing to Mature Economy.* Boulder, Colo.: Westview.

Pack, Howard, and Larry E. Westphal. 1986. "Industrial Strategy and Technological Change: Theory versus Reality." *Journal of Development Economics* 22: 87–128.

Ranis, Gustav. 1979. "Industrial Development." In Walter Galenson, ed., *Economic Growth and Structural Change in Taiwan.* Ithaca, N.Y.: Cornell University Press.

Rhee, Yung W., and Larry E. Westphal. 1977. "A Microeconometric Investigation of Choice of Technique." *Journal of Development Economics* 4: 205–38.

Westphal, Larry E., Yung W. Rhee, and Garry G. Pursell. 1981. "Korean Industrial Competence: Where it Came From." World Bank Staff Working Paper no. 469, Washington, D.C.

VII.D. PRIVATIZATION

VII.D.1. Guide to Privatization Policy*

This paper focuses on a comparatively narrow set of issues, namely, those that arise when choosing state-owned enterprises (SOEs) for sale to the public. Specifically, the paper addresses three pivotal questions that arise in connection with such choices: Should the enterprise be sold? To whom should it be sold? At what price should it be sold?

Applying Project Analysis

Economists describe an approach that allows policymakers systematically to identify many of the key variables involved in addressing these questions (these ideas are presented in detail in Jones and others 1990). One cannot do justice to the scope and subtlety of their presentation in only a few pages, but its overall characteristics are clear. It draws heavily on the familiar concepts and assumptions of standard project analysis; at the same time, it shows marked sensitivity to the behavioral patterns of participants in imperfectly competitive markets.

State-owned enterprises, according to the authors' argument, can be valued in various ways. Two values in particular are critical when attempting to answer the three pivotal questions mentioned earlier.

The social value of the enterprise under continued government operation is one such critical value. The version of social value chosen by the authors is familiar enough to economists. In shorthand, it represents the discounted present value of the firm's real net output over time. This is not a figure that will actually have to be calculated; but it is a concept on which some critical figures that are calculated will depend.

The social value of the enterprise under private operation is a second key value. Once again, this figure need not be actually calculated, even though the concept itself may be critical.

The value of the firm under private operation is likely to be different from that under government operation for various reasons. The firm's static efficiency in private hands—as measured by the output it extracts from any given level of inputs—may prove to be higher than if the firm remained in state hands. And the capacity of private management for "dynamic entrepreneurship"—a catch-all term that picks up all the positive features of private ownership that static efficiency does not—could well add to the social yield. Moreover, the private buyers may conceivably extract some changes in the regulatory economic environment from the government that would add further to the real net output of the national economy, such as "getting the prices right," lowering trade barriers, and increasing credit availability.

The difference between these two values, according to the authors, will go a long way toward determining if an enterprise should be privatized. Indeed, if the social value of the firm in private hands would exceed its social value in government hands, the government might be rational if it gave the enterprise away to the private sector, perhaps even paying the private sector to take the enterprise over.

Guesses, Shrewd and Otherwise

What analysts and politicians need most of all is a crude scanning device, readily implemented, that will permit them to concentrate on the cases that offer promise of the largest salutary change. For that purpose, a single ranking measure, such as the difference between social value in private hands and social value in public hands, is likely to prove inferior to rankings on a number of different dimensions, rankings they can scan and weigh even in the absence of explicit additivity rules. The list that I find useful for this purpose reflects a multivalent approach to the choice of projects; one that acknowledges not only the relevance of expanding output through static efficiency increases and dynamic developments, but also the relevance of income distribution effects and cash generating effects.

*From Raymond Vernon, "A Technical Approach to Privatization Issues: Coupling Project Analysis with Rules of Thumb," in Ravi Ramamurti and Raymond Vernon, eds., *Privatization and Control of State-Owned Enterprises* (World Bank, 1991): 54–55, 65–72. Reprinted by permission.

The Static Efficiency Criterion

The object is to identify those cases in which static efficiency changes can produce the largest increase in the firm's output. Obviously any ranking of cases is bound to be highly subjective, because it depends on so many idiosyncratic factors. However, large firms are likely to produce more significant changes than small firms; and firms with internal processes that require difficult coordination, such as steel mills, are more likely to produce such results than firms with tightly packaged processes, such as hydroelectric power plants. Beyond such obvious criteria, the following illustrations, which are based on soft evidence from many different sources, may begin to provide a calibrating mechanism:

1. Some prospective privatization undertakings envisage no changes in management policies, in the structure of national markets, or in government regulations affecting those markets, as when the government proposes merely to sell off a minority interest in a natural monopoly such as a public utility. In that case, one possible source of increased efficiency may be the added capital provided by the private sector, assuming that the capital is in fact allocated to the plant and would not otherwise be available. If, for instance, a lack of working capital or inadequate plant size had been handicaps to achieving a high level of efficiency, such added capital could conceivably raise efficiency. On the whole, however, projects of this sort are not promising candidates for large efficiency increases.

2. Some privatization undertakings envision a change in the enterprise's management from public to private managers, while leaving the enterprise's monopoly position in local markets unaffected. This will occur, for instance, in the case of large enterprises that dominate the import-substituting industries of a developing country. In that case, efficiency increases will likely depend principally on the strength of the private managers' incentives for cutting costs. These in turn will depend on two factors: the nature of the market that the private firm confronts, and the nature of the regulatory pressures to which the firm is exposed. For instance, the incentive to cut costs will not be very strong if price changes can easily be passed on to buyers, as in the case of intermediate products. Nor will it be strong if the firm can easily influence the regulatory authority. In such cases, the expec-

tation of efficiency increases may still be stronger than in the first group of cases, but not substantially so.

3. In some instances, the privatization project contemplates not only a change in management, but concurrently, the end of a monopoly position for the state-owned enterprise and a shift to private competitive markets. Such cases usually offer greater promise of efficiency increases than cases 1 and 2.

4. The final case is that of the state-owned enterprise that has been operating in competitive markets, whether domestic or international. If the enterprise has been performing about as well as the domestic enterprises against which it has been pitted, the possibility of efficiency increases is presumptively not very high. If, however, the enterprise has been performing less well, the opportunity for efficiency increases may be as attractive as the cases mentioned in 3 above.

Obviously, the cases cited above do not represent all the available possibilities and are intended simply to illustrate the principal factors that are likely to provide a basis for an ordinal ranking. The underlying factors that have produced the relative rankings (changes in scale, shifts in management, changes in the structure of markets, and changes in government regulation), will be present in different combinations and will carry different weights. But a crude ordinal ranking for a limited number of large enterprises is likely to be possible.

Augmenting the Stock of Productive Resources

The productive resources that policymakers wish to augment, of course, are capital and human resources, notably management. Once again, a precise ranking of enterprises in terms of their likely contributions is infeasible, yet some guides to such a ranking are available.

Where domestic capital is concerned, augmentation will occur through either of two channels: through the importation or repatriation of capital from abroad, or through an increase in domestic savings at the expense of consumption or of capital exports. Not all equity offerings will appeal to the same type of buyer or require the same methods of distribution. Some may attract foreign buyers, some will not. Some may be distributed widely to relatively small purchasers, some to a single buyer. In the short run, these differences are likely to have different implications for domestic saving and for capital imports.

The longer-term effects of any given sale of equity in a state-owned enterprise upon the growth of capital will be harder to track. The problem arises because each sale is likely to have unique effects on efficiency and on income distribution, but the effects will be very complex. Where increases in efficiency are likely, increases in saving and investment are also likely; and where the income to investors can be expected to increase at the expense of households and labor, as through the exercise of monopoly power, a similar shift in saving and investment is likely to take place. But those savings may not remain in the country. Foreign owners may take their earnings home, while domestic owners may diversify their savings by shipping them abroad. In any case, the causal sequences associated with such shifts can be quite attenuated, producing uncertain outcomes. Still, analysts should not give up on the possibility that some crude rankings might be justifiable on this dimension as well.

Whether a given privatization project increases the supply of management in any country depends on the particular circumstances. In most developing countries, a market for managerial talent does not exist. Nevertheless, privatization can augment the national supply of management in at least two ways. When foreigners are allowed to acquire equity in state-owned enterprises, they may bring added management skills and management systems into the country. And when private domestic buyers take over the management of former state-owned enterprises, that step may enlarge the supply of management by ending a mismatch between the country's distribution of physical capital and the distribution of managerial capabilities.

The possibility of ending a mismatch is especially likely in developing countries in which the indigenous private sector has already been gaining strength. As long as the private sector was weak, governments have typically created state-owned enterprises to launch large-scale industrial projects. Over the years, the private business sector in some countries has grown in financial strength and managerial capabilities, reaching the stage in some cases at which its members may be ready to acquire and manage the state-owned enterprises involved (Aylen 1987 stresses this point).

The possibility exists, of course, that the private sector's acquisition of a public enterprise may do no more than divert the available managerial resources from one set of enterprises to another. The increase in managerial opportunities and compensation, however, should enhance the supply where a market for managers has begun to appear. Besides, the private managerial groups that have established themselves in developing countries such as Brazil, Korea, India, and Mexico frequently operate with some slack and with some capability to expand their managerial activities.

Here again, analysts will have an opportunity for a crude classification of privatization projects based on their analysis of the enlargement of the supply of management.

Income Distribution Effects

Different privatization projects are likely to affect the distribution of income in quite different ways, in terms of both magnitude and direction. State-owned enterprises that were buying their inputs and selling their outputs in competitive markets and were making an adequate profit will presumably continue to do so, thus their privatization will have little effect on the distribution of income. As a rule, however, the transition from state ownership to private ownership will be accompanied by some implicit or explicit changes in the conditions under which the firm acquires its inputs or sells its outputs, as well as changes associated with some relaxation of governmental policies relating to the firm's behavior. Once privatized, for instance, firms may be permitted to reduce their labor force, hold down wages, and increase prices.

Changes in governmental policies such as these may well be salutary, contributing to objectives already mentioned, such as an increase in static efficiency and an increase in productive resources; and in principle, analysts will already have taken such salutary consequences into account in the process of rating each project under each of those objectives. But the same changes will also affect the distribution of income, which presumably the country will wish to consider separately.

In some cases, the rankings generated by considering the relative income effects from privatizing given state-owned enterprises may point the decisionmaker in the same direction as the rankings generated by the efficiency factor and the resource augmentation factor. However, the various measures relating to a given state-owned enterprise under consideration for privatization could provide conflicting signals to decision-makers, requiring tradeoffs of one factor against another. I have no advice to offer on how that tradeoff function should be constructed. It is likely to prove highly sensitive, in any case, to the conditions prevailing in each country at a given time. But an explicit effort to marshall such ratings for a limited number of large firms should provide rich insights into the likely consequences of any given choice.

Short-Term Effects on Cash Flows to Government

When choosing enterprises for privatization, the short-run cash-flow effects may be thought of either as an objective or as a constraint. From the viewpoint of governments, they are likely to be seen as an objective; from the viewpoint of others, as a constraint. Note that those short-term cash flow effects can have consequences for both the efficiency objective and the resource augmentation objective, inasmuch as they represent the extent to which the government will have captured savings from the private domestic sector and drawn in the savings of foreigners in the process of selling the equity of a given state-owned enterprise. These same data will in any event have some considerable value in estimating whether the privatization process is likely to create some short-term monetary problems that require managing, such as the crowding out of the private sector or the expansion of the monetary base.

Technically, the challenge is to estimate the short-term cash-flow effects of each possible transaction, net of the flows that would have occurred if the equity or assets of the enterprise had remained in the public sector. Elements in the calculation include the sale price of the equity or assets, less the cash costs of preparing the enterprise or assets for sale, less the transaction costs, less the consideration received in forms other than cash (such as loans by the government to purchasers).

Remember that these same transactions will have medium-term and long-term effects as well, effects that result from changes in efficiency, in resource augmentation, and in income distribution. Eventually, those effects may prove more important for the government's cash-flow position than the short-run effects. However, they are likely to be so complex and uncertain in size and direction, and so remote from the

considerations of government officials, that for analysts to devote much time to their analysis will prove unprofitable.

Conclusions

The available data on state-owned enterprises do not conclusively demonstrate the validity of any sweeping generalizations about such enterprises, whether in terms of efficiency, resource augmentation, or income distribution. As a class, state-owned enterprises tend to be associated with negative cash flows to the public sector, at least as compared with private enterprises in similar fields. But these negative cash flows are due in part to policies on inputs and outputs that are the economic equivalent of transfer payments, such as the hiring of excess labor. Although in some cases, such negative cash flows may also be due to a lower level of efficiency than that of private enterprises performing the same business functions in the economy, the character and extent of those differences are not well documented. The income redistributing effects of the transfer payments are also not subject to easy generalization. Sometimes they appear to be egalitarian in direction; but at times they may penalize a poor agricultural sector in favor of an urban middle or upper class.

Accordingly, the economic basis for widespread programs of privatization, which ordinarily rests heavily on assumptions about efficiency, is not yet firmly developed. The transfer payment policies that many developing countries pursue through state-owned enterprises are probably quite uneconomic in many instances; but that issue could be addressed independently of the ownership issues.

If there is no solid basis for pressing for an unselective program of privatization, neither is there a basis for resisting such a program where governments are convinced that it is desirable. One danger in instituting such a program is the threat of high transaction costs, particularly costs in the form of the attention that such programs can demand from high-level policymakers and analysts. But there are ways to minimize those costs.

One approach is to refuse to address the three questions with which this paper began. Governments that are prepared to base their privatization programs on general conviction, for instance, could refuse to choose selectively among enterprises, could give away the shares by lottery or by per capita distribution rather than sell them, and could rely on the chance nature of the distribution or on various screening devices (supplemented perhaps by antitrust legislation) to avoid the risk that private monopolies might acquire an unwanted dominant position as a result of the distribution of the shares. Such policies would not transfer cash to the government sector, but a government that was sufficiently convinced of the superiority of private ownership to accept a nonselective program of privatization would presumably not see any great merit in capturing large dollops of the private sector's savings.

For governments that were unprepared to take such a broadside approach and eager to weed out selectively the state-owned enterprises whose privatization would serve their goals, some of the candidates for privatization might prove so obvious as to require no analysis. Some governments are so incapable of providing for the efficient management of their enterprises, and some enterprises are so notorious for their inefficiency, that almost any alternative to state ownership would be superior. Given the costs of analysis and the limits of its results, overintellectualizing the process of choice could be unwise.

Beyond such obvious cases, if a process of case-by-case selection is inescapable, the main drive should be to narrow the range of cases for analysis as rapidly and inexpensively as possible. In that case, the categories that are likely to be least promising are monopolistic enterprises that sell their products or services on domestic markets, and that use technologies that make few demands on management. Those that are likely to emerge at the top of the priority list are relatively large state-owned enterprises that are operating poorly in competitive markets when compared with private firms in the same markets. Such enterprises may merit the detailed level of scrutiny suggested in this discussion.

References

Aylen, Jonathan. 1987. "Privatization in Developing Countries." *Lloyd's Bank Review* 163 (January): 15–30.

Jones, Leroy P., Pankaj Tandon, and Ingo Vogelsang. 1990. *Selling Public Enterprises: A Cost–Benefit Methodology.* Cambridge, Mass.: MIT Press.

Comment: State-Owned Enterprises and Privatization

For a variety of reasons—not only economic, but also historical, ideological, and sociopolitical—governments of LDCs have often relied on public enterprise to try to achieve their development goals. In many LDCs, state-owned enterprises (SOEs) account for 10 to 40 percent of GDP. The major economic reasons for establishing state-owned enterprises have been to mobilize savings, create employment, provide public goods, and invest in large-scale capital-intensive projects that are natural monopolies or are subject to economies of scale or are especially risky for private investors.

There has, however, been growing concern about the performance of SOEs. One reason is that SOEs make large and growing claims on the budget and may resort to external debt for financing. In a number of countries, the public-enterprise deficit has been identified as a proximate cause of excessive credit creation, leading to monetary expansion, price inflation, and, ultimately, balance-of-payments pressures. SOEs also often undertake policies of controlling prices of public services, food grains, and other basic wage goods, which often prevent the public enterprises from covering their costs, with corresponding fiscal and monetary repercussions. For an elaboration of these macroeconomic aspects of SOEs, see Robert H. Floyd et al., *Public Enterprise in Mixed Economies: Some Macroeconomic Aspects* (1984).

At the micro level, there is also much concern about efficiency in production, profitable investment decisions, and nondistorting pricing policies. Various ways of improving SOE efficiency are now being emphasized—from the provision of systems for monitoring and evaluating performance to the sale of state-owned enterprises and promotion of privatization programs. On problems of management and control, see World Bank, *World Development Report, 1983* (1983), chap. 8.

Other instructive references are Deepak Lal, "Public Enterprises," in *Policies for Industrial Progress in Developing Countries*, ed. John Cody, Helen Hughes, and David Wall (1980); Leroy P. Jones, *Public Enterprise in Less Developed Countries* (1982); Tony Killick, "Role of the Public Sector in the Industrialization of African Developing Countries," *Industry and Development* (1985); Malcolm Gillis, "Role of State Enterprises in Economic Development," *Social Research* (Summer 1980);

George Yarrow, "Privatization in Theory and Practice," *Economic Policy* (April 1984); and Gabriel Roth, *Private Provision of Public Services in Developing Countries* (1987).

In recent years, there have been numerous cases of privatizing state-owned enterprises—in terms of either ownership or management—in an effort to improve their efficiency and reduce their financial burden on the government's budget. For an appraisal of these cases, see Steve H. Hanks, ed., *Privatization and Development* (1987); Paul Cook and Colin Kirkpatrick, eds., *Privatization in LDCs* (1988); John Vickers and George Yarrow, *Privatization: An Economic Analysis* (1988); William Glade, ed., *Privatization of Public Enterprises in Latin America* (1991); Mary Shirley and John Nellis, *Public Enterprise Reform: Lessons of Experience* (1991); Sunita Kikeri et al., *Privatization: The Lessons of Experience* (1992); Leroy Jones et al., *Selling Public Enterprises: A Cost–Benefit Methodology* (1990); and Paul H. Boeker, ed., *Latin America's Turnaround: Privatization, Foreign Investment and Growth* (1993).

The study by Vickers and Yarrow (1988) is especially instructive in demonstrating how ownership of a firm will have significant effects on its behavior and performance, since changes in property rights will alter the structure of incentives faced by decision makers in the firm.

VII.E. AGRICULTURE–INDUSTRY INTERACTIONS

VII.E.1. Industrialization and Agricultural Development*

This selection focuses on what is generally the most important of the connections between industrialization and other sectors—the relationship with agriculture.

Agricultural economists usually analyze the role of agriculture in economic development in the context of models of closed economies. Foreign trade is absent, and final demand linkages and input-output relations ensure a perfect complementarity in production between agriculture and industry. International trade theorists, on the other hand, caution that when trade intervenes, demand interrelationships need not imply supply complementarities. Exports and imports may be large enough to offset the relation between domestic demand and domestic supply of major commodities. In the stylized view of agricultural economists, industry and agriculture produce only goods for domestic absorption which for one reason or another cannot be subject to international trade. In the simplified vision of international trade theorists, all agricultural and industrial goods are internationally traded. Empirically, the first view aptly describes the economy of large countries, but the second has more applicability to countries of less than 15 million population, in which imports typically are 40 percent or more of the total supply of commodity consumption.

The position taken here is midway between the models of international trade theorists and the agricultural economists. [When we deal] with food supply, agricultural production is assumed not to be subject to international trade, whereas industrial commodities can be freely imported and exported. The analysis is conducted in terms of a dual economy where agriculture provides the growing urban sector with both workers and wage goods. Attention is focused on the problem of producing an agricultural surplus for the urban market and on the connections between economic growth and the

agricultural terms of trade. [When we deal] with export agriculture, the roles are reversed: agricultural output is a traded commodity and industry a producer of domestic goods. Industrialization and export agriculture are discussed in terms of a simplified analysis of a foreign exchange-constrained economy, in which the industrial sector neither exports nor competes with imports. The discussion centers on the consequences for the pattern and rate of economic growth of the developing economy of a "squeeze" on agriculture through foreign exchange controls.

The purpose of these semi-open models is not to discuss the advantages or disadvantages of food self-sufficiency or autarkic industrialization, but rather to inquire into the policy issues that arise under such empirically relevant scenarios.

The difficulties associated with policies relying solely on the price mechanism to promote a "virtuous circle" of interactions between industry and agriculture are reviewed in the third and final section.

Industrialization and the Food Supply

In this section, two-sector models are used to study the interrelationships between industry and agriculture. While historically labor market linkages have been perhaps the first connection between the two, product markets eventually became the dominant focus of their interaction, as described below. The need to provide food for the growing urban labor force gives rise to so-called marketed surplus problems. Here these are analyzed in the context of the Soviet and the Japanese experiences. . . .

The Dual Growth Models

The relationships between subsistence agriculture and manufacturing industry rarely fit the enclave growth model in which a modern export sector develops by importing labor, capital, food, and raw materials, with traditional agriculture remaining as a purely subsistence ac-

*From Edmar L. Bacha, "Industrialization and Agricultural Development," in John Cody et al. (eds.), *Policies for Industrial Progress in Developing Countries* (London, Oxford University Press, 1980), pp. 259–61, 263–66, 268–72. Reprinted by permission.

tivity without any connection to the growth of manufacturing. Foreign-controlled plantation economies approximated this enclave model, as did some highly capital-intensive, foreign-dominated mining operations, until developing countries began to appropriate the economic rents accruing to such operations.

The first connection between agriculture and industry is established by the use of an unskilled labor force from agriculture in the industrial sector and its ancillary service activities. A stylized view of the labor market relationships between town and country in the early stages of economic development runs as follows. Industry is a labor-using activity which can draw freely from a pool of surplus agricultural labor. These labor resources are made available to industry at a constant wage in terms of industrial goods. Economic growth is defined as the transfer of labor from subsistence agriculture to market-oriented industry. Implicitly, industry is defined as everything that is modern and growing, and agriculture everything that is traditional and stagnant. Intersectoral product flow are ignored because of two assumptions: (1) extended family systems in the rural sector supply urban workers with the required wage goods through nonmarket channels: or (2) wage goods are imported at constant prices in terms of domestic industrial goods.

Both assumptions are untenable. The latter leaves open the question of where the modern sector is going to obtain the foreign exchange to pay for the wage goods; it does not recognize that, culturally, wage goods may be specific to the local economy and hence not available from foreign sources; and it ignores that governments are usually adamantly opposed to letting a significant fraction of basic food consumption be imported from abroad.

The assumption that migrant workers provide for their own subsistence through informal rural connections is equivalent to saying that the terms of trade between agriculture and industry remain constant as workers move from country to town. The equivalence would follow because under fixed terms of trade it can be assumed that the urban wage is fixed in terms of industrial goods. In fact, the urban wage consists of a bundle of wage goods in which agricultural, not industrial, products predominate. The terms of trade will remain constant as labor is withdrawn from agriculture only if (1) the marginal product of labor in agriculture is zero, so that total agricultural output remains constant in spite of the labor transfer, and (2) the migrant worker consumes the same amount of agricultural goods as when he was a rural dweller. The second assumption ignores transport and commercialization costs, which are important, as well as the eventual need for a higher industrial wage to induce workers to migrate. The zero marginal productivity assumption has been the object of a long and heated debate in the development literature, with many experts suggesting that this is an acceptable presumption only for clearly overpopulated rural areas.

In the absence of informal subsistence mechanisms, the need to provide food for the industrial labor force establishes a product market relationship between agriculture and industry. As industrial employment grows and income per capita expands, the urban demand for agricultural products increases.

If it can indeed be presumed that under these conditions the terms of trade will not change, the policy implication is clear—policymakers need worry only about industrial growth. Agriculture will respond swiftly to the increasing urban demand by making better use of its partially idle labor and land resources.

There is a problem with the assumption that market-oriented agricultural growth is constrained only by lack of demand and that, if urban demand materializes, rural output will respond along a highly price-elastic supply curve. Historically this has been the case in only a few countries, and they had strongly market-oriented agricultural production. Several Southeast and East Asian countries, some African countries, and such areas in Latin America as Argentina and southern Brazil fit this pattern. In other countries the "benign neglect" of agriculture and even active policies were unable to avoid the grave difficulties that occasioned the voluminous literature on the marketed surplus problem.

The Marketed Surplus

The important question is how to guarantee a continuous supply of agricultural goods to the growing urban sector. The neoclassical answer is simple: raise agricultural prices. But this would mean paying more for farm products and would leave less resources for industrial accumulation. The higher the volume of industrial goods that has to be put aside to pay for agricultural inputs (both wage goods and raw materials), the lower will be the volume of industrial goods that can be added to the capital stock of the modern sector.

The Soviet industrialization debate of the 1920s showed the dilemma is particularly acute in the case of a crash industrialization program. The issue was further complicated in the USSR because agriculture was based on private peasant farming, whereas industry was state-owned and run. Under these conditions, as Preobrazhensky noted, "an exchange of the smaller quantity of labor of the [socialist] economic system for the greater quantity of labor of the [nonsocialist] economic system" was needed to secure a rapid industrial advance from the low initial base.[1] This famous "law of primitive socialist accumulation" stands for the whole set of government market controls which serve one purpose: to bring about a shift of resources from the private to the socialized sector over and above the share the latter could obtain as a result of the operation of competitive economic relations.

The trouble with this scheme is that the relationships between a modern industrial sector and a backward peasant agricultural sector are not symmetrical. Food is indispensable for industry, while the peasants' need for industrial products is secondary, if not superfluous. Faced with dwindling supplies of industrial goods and increasing claims for their own products, peasants may simply refuse to play the game and step back to a closed subsistence economy. This was the situation in the USSR. The price squeeze that resulted from a policy of holding down food prices was met by the peasants' massive withdrawal from the market, which threatened to bring the Soviet economy to the brink of disaster. Stalin's solution was to step up forced collectivization of the peasantry. Through state farming, he managed to break the peasants' veto power over his decision on economic policy and so managed to industrialize peasant Russia. However, the human costs were enormous (Preobrazhensky himself died in the great purge of 1937), and long-term agricultural productivity growth became, and still is, a bottleneck in Soviet economic development. The lesson seems to be that developing countries not contemplating forced output by the rural sector will find it difficult to follow Preobrazhensky's recommendation to further industrialization by reducing the relative prices of agricultural products.

For an example of how to resolve the terms of trade dilemma, agricultural economists point to Japan from the Meiji revolution to World War I. Despite its meager endowment of land, Japan's agricultural and industrial development went forward concurrently. Farm output expanded within the existing framework of small-scale agriculture with remarkably low demands on foreign exchange resources. The major factors responsible for the high rate of growth in agricultural output were the increased productivity and greater utilization of existing land and labor made possible by the diffusion of new technology. While it has been argued that this process did not require major capital inputs, the Meiji period did see substantial investment in rural infrastructure. It is, however, true that rural-to-urban capital flows occurred. A policy of high land taxes was adopted, which drew a substantial share of the increased agricultural productivity for investment in the industrial infrastructure, while avoiding the disincentive effects of the Soviet experience before collectivization.

It is moot whether a similar option exists for contemporary developing countries. More important now are institutional and organizational reform, infrastructural investments, and research and development, all highly complementary inputs in the creation of new production potentials in agriculture. The complementarity between infrastructure investments and investment in research and development raises a serious question about the validity of the assumption that primary emphasis on scientific progress can provide a relatively inexpensive route to rapid growth of agricultural production during the early stages of development.

Where modernization of agriculture requires heavy initial investments, it is not possible a priori to anticipate the direction of intersectoral capital flows between agriculture and industry in a process of concurrent economic growth. But is not this question of intersectoral financial flows just a red herring? Should agriculture and industry be analyzed as separate entities, as if they were two independent countries? The answer might be in the affirmative in the USSR of the 1920s, where a socialized industrial sector confronted an antagonistic peasant society. But it should not be true for planning processes in politically integrated developing countries if planners are concerned with the welfare of the country as a whole rather than with the interests of specific social groups within it.

What this means is that, in principle, the sectoral location of an investment activity should not be an issue in planned investment decisions. However, the planning process of many devel-

[1]Evgeny Preobrazhensky, *The New Economics* (London, Oxford University Press, 1965), p. 91.

oping countries has been characterized by a considerable degree of urban bias. Agriculture is often treated as inherently low in productivity, industry as high in productivity. Empirical misconceptions, ideological biases, and class interests mingle together to explain such an anti-rural attitude. Policy measures are sometimes designed to deliver subsidized inputs, credits, and extension activities to farmers to mitigate such bias, but in practice these measures largely tend to benefit medium- and large-scale farmers. This policymaking pattern has been criticized as one of the main reasons economic growth in developing countries since World War II has failed to reach the poorer groups in the population.

A pro-rural strategy has been advocated in its stead as part of a broad reconsideration of the development problem. The reasoning behind this is simple enough. Most of the poor are in the countryside. Given current rates of rural population growth and likely rates of urban labor absorption, it is argued that the poor will remain in the rural sector for a long time. If alleviation of poverty is the main objective of development policy, then it follows that the problem should be attacked at its root, without waiting for an eventual absorption of most of the labor force in the modern urban sector. Measures should be adopted to increase the productivity and income of the rural poor even if they result in less resources for urban industrial capital accumulation, which mostly benefits the middle- and upper-income groups. Such a strategy is of course in sharp contrast to the industrialization-first doctrine with which this analysis for the interactions between agriculture and industry began.

Industrialization and Export Agriculture

Viewed from the intersectoral perspective, the main difference between the analyses of the last section and those of this section lies in a redefinition of the role of agriculture. Earlier, it was described as that of supplying industry with food. Here its output is foreign exchange.

To facilitate the discussion, consider the case of a developing country with a budding, fully protected domestic-market-oriented industrial sector, the material inputs of which are indirectly supplied by domestic agriculture through the export of primary products to the rest of the world. The relevant policy issues are illustrated by reference to the historical experiences of Brazil and Argentina since the 1930s.

A triangular trade pattern is established between agriculture, industry, and the rest of the world, which can be visualized from the Brazilian growth process from the 1930s to the early 1960s. Agriculture (A) sells coffee to the world (W) and buys manufactured products from industry (I), which in turn acquires capital goods from foreign markets. (These relationships are illustrated in Figure 1.) In its role of foreign exchange supplier, agriculture in fact functions as the machine-producing sector of the economy. For the sake of the argument, take the dollar prices of coffee and imported machines to be given and assume that coffee production depends only on a specific input—say, land—the growth of which is exogenously determined. How can the growth rate of domestic industry be raised under these conditions?

One clear possibility is to increase the cruzeiro price of manufactures relative to the cruzeiro price of machines. If this is done, the industrial sector will have more of its own product—say, cement—left over after paying for the machines and can add that to its capital stock. In practice, the relative price change can be done by freezing the cruzeiro-dollar exchange rate at a time when the internal price of manufactures is being raised by domestic inflation. This certainly happened in Brazil from the immediate postwar period to the early 1960s. In fact, the price twist was carried to such an extreme that, by the end of the 1950s, the purchasing power of a unit of domestic industrial goods in terms of imported machinery was two and a half times higher than in the late 1940s. As the exchange rate lags behind industrial prices to increase the purchasing power of domestic manufactures over imports, the domestic price ratio of coffee to manufactures goes down.

FIGURE 1. The trade pattern between agriculture, industry, and the rest of the world.

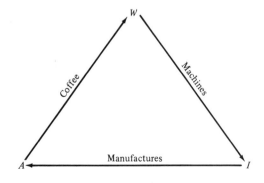

Domestic inflation increases the prices of industrial goods, while the cruzeiro price of coffee, under given world coffee prices, accompanies the more sluggish growth of the cruzeiro-dollar exchange rate.

This method of increasing industrial capital accumulation raises several issues. First, the assumption that the external terms of trade (the dollar price of coffee divided by the dollar price of machines) are given does not fit the facts. The amount of coffee exported by Brazil does affect the international coffee prices.

Second, the quantity of coffee that Brazilian farmers produce is a function of the domestic terms of trade (cruzeiro price of coffee divided by the cruzeiro price of manufactures). Abundant empirical evidence on the supply response of Brazilian coffee farmers indicates that the quantity produced cannot be taken as exogenously determined. Coffee production is a profit-making activity that shares with other sectors the available endowments of labor and capital. In the context of the two-sector model under discussion, this means that as the relative price changes, there is some substitution in production between coffee and manufactures. Again, this is true for agricultural production more generally.

Third, while a surplus is generated for the industrial sector through the relative price twist, the conclusion cannot be drawn that this surplus will be invested productively. It may be wasted as conspicuous consumption or else embodied in a form—say, cement—with very low marginal productivity indeed.

Consider the first two issues together. Since Brazil has a monopoly power in the international coffee market, it follows that up to a point it is to its advantage to turn the domestic terms of trade against the coffee sector in order to reduce exports and raise world coffee prices. In the determination of the optimal price policy from the national point of view, attention has to be paid to the fact that the long-run foreign demand curve is more price elastic than the corresponding short-run relation. As a consequence, to keep competition at bay and foreign consumers loyal, the optimal price will be found at a lower level than that which would maximize short-run earnings. Thus if a country has a monopoly power in international trade, turning relative domestic prices against exports would be, up to a point, not a squeeze on agriculture but a squeeze on foreigners. The latter could be justified in terms of national welfare.

Argentina more than Brazil provides a pure case where industrial development was achieved by a squeeze on domestic export agriculture. Trade policies similar to those applied in Brazil were followed from the early 1940s to the mid-1950s. Argentina was certainly an important supplier of meat, wool, and grains in the world market, but, from a long-run perspective, foreign demand price elasticities for Argentinian products were high enough to justify the assumption of given world prices.

The degree of price discrimination in Argentina in favor of industry and against agriculture can be gauged by the evolution of the purchasing power of domestic manufactures over imports, as previously defined. According to Diaz-Alejandro, this quotient increased by an average of 54 percent between 1930–39 and 1945–55. Diaz-Alejandro submits that Argentina's slippage behind other countries of recent settlement since the 1930s was causally associated with the price shifts and related economic policies. He reasons, in terms of the relationships shown in Figure 1, that the industrial sector in Argentina during this period would be better described as a home-goods sector than as a truly import-substituting sector. Cement, for example, is not exported, and domestically it is only a poor substitute for imported machines. But this home-goods sector expands by drawing resources away from export agriculture, causing a reduction in the supply of foreign exchange to the economy. Additional investment in the industrial sector can only take the form of cement, to continue the example, because foreign exchange is not available to convert domestic savings into imported machines. Because cement substitutes poorly for machines, the incremental capital-output ratio is very high. Diaz-Alejandro concludes that in an economy with a severe foreign exchange bottleneck, not even a gross saving of 20 percent, as was the case in Argentina, will bring rapid growth. Under such conditions, the transformation of savings into tangible machinery and equipment becomes a difficult task.

From this example, it would appear that for most developing countries the capacity to transform smoothly ex ante savings propensities into nonconstruction capital goods requires either expansion of foreign exchange earnings or a balanced, in-depth program of industrialization.

VII.E.2. Complementarity of Industry and Agriculture*

The case for rapid industrialisation in the West Indies rests chiefly on over-population. The islands already carry a larger population than agriculture can absorb, and populations are growing at rates of from 1.5 to 2.0 percent per annum. It is, therefore, urgent to create new opportunities for employment off the land. . . .

However carefully the peasant may work his holding in staple crops—and, of course, at present he is very backward—he cannot make 2 or 3 acres yield him a reasonable standard of living. He cannot get from 2 or 3 acres even the 6 shillings a day or more which he hopes to earn in the town, so that it is not at all surprising that there is a continual drift to the towns. If peasant agriculture is to be put on its feet, the number of peasants must be reduced drastically, in relation to the land that they now occupy, so that each family may be able to have a reasonable acreage (more equipment to work the land will also be needed). . . .

In a word, if West Indian agriculture is to yield a decent standard of living, the number engaged in the present acreage must be drastically reduced—it must be something like halved, if current expectations of what is reasonable are to be fulfilled. But this is not practicable unless new employments can be found for those who would be displaced in the process. Until new employments can be created, mechanisation and other increased use of capital equipment will be a doubtful boon, and major improvements in peasant agriculture will be impossible. . . .

If this impression is right, then agriculture in the islands will yield a decent standard of living only if the numbers engaged in it are drastically reduced, and this will be possible only if new employments can be created outside agriculture. The creation of new industries is an essential part of a programme for agricultural improvement.

This is not generally realized. There are still people who discuss industrialisation as if it were an *alternative* to agricultural improvement. In countries where agriculture is not carrying surplus population, industry and agriculture are alternatives. New Zealand, on the one hand, or England on the other, have to weigh carefully the respective merits of industry and agriculture, and to decide on relative emphases. But this approach is without meaning in the West Indian islands. There is no choice to be made between industry and agriculture. The islands need as large an agriculture as possible, and, if they could even get more people into agriculture, without reducing output per head, then so much the better. But, even when they are employing in agriculture the maximum number that agriculture will absorb at a reasonable standard of living, there will still be a large surplus of labour, and even the greatest expansion of industry which is conceivable within the next twenty years will not create a labour shortage in agriculture. It is not the case that agriculture cannot continue to develop if industry is developed. Exactly the opposite is true: agriculture cannot be put on to a basis where it will yield a reasonable standard of living unless new jobs are created off the land. . . .

Two propositions follow from this. The first is that, if the West Indian market is itself to support a large manufacturing industry, then the standard of living must first be greatly increased. The way to increase the standard of living, as we have already seen, is to make it possible for each worker to have at his disposal the produce of a large acreage; i.e., greatly to reduce the number of persons in agriculture per 1,000 acres, without reducing the total output of agriculture. But this, as we have also seen, means putting more persons into manufacturing industry. Thus the full complementarity of industry and agriculture stands revealed. If agriculture is to give a higher standard of living, then industry must be developed. But equally, if industry is to be developed, then agriculture must give a higher standard of living, in order to provide a demand for manufactures. The agricultural and the industrial revolutions thus reinforce each other, and neither can go very far unless the other is occurring at the same time. Those who speak as if the choice in the West Indies lay between agricultural development and industrial development have failed completely to understand the problem.

*From W. Arthur Lewis, ''The Industrialisation of the British West Indies,'' *Caribbean Economic Review* (May 1950), pp. 1, 6–7, 16–17, 38. Reprinted by permission.

The second proposition is that manufacturing industries cannot provide employment for an extra 120,000 in the next ten years unless the islands start to export manufactures to outside destinations. Neither their own growing demands, nor the replacement of imports, can provide a large enough market. The domestic market for manufactures is too small to support more than a fraction of what is needed. For, at the present standard of living, the local demand is for food, rather than for manufactures.

Now, if the islands were not short of good, cultivable land, the conclusion would be to put the surplus population on to the land to grow this food. Since they are short of land, they will have to depend for their food supplies increasingly on importing food, and on putting people instead into producing manufactures which will be exported to pay for imported food. . . .

The islands cannot be industrialised to anything like the extent that is necessary without a considerable inflow of foreign capital and capitalists, and a period of wooing and fawning upon such people. Foreign capital is needed because industrialisation is a frightfully expensive business quite beyond the resources of the islands. Light industries, based on imported materials, will require, say £600 of capital or more, for each person employed, and heavy industries, using local materials, may easily demand £2,000 per head. To provide employment for 100,000 persons calls for an investment in manufacturing alone (i.e., excluding all the subsidiary activities that will bring employment up to 400,000) of something like £130,000,000. There is no prospect of the West Indies providing such a sum out of its own savings; it must be borrowed abroad. Then, some people may say, let it be borrowed by the government. Let the government set up the factories, and hire foreign technicians to run them. It is very doubtful if the governments could raise any such sum on their own credit. But even if they could, and even if they were able to hire technicians, the problem would still not be solved. For successful industrialisation on a big scale is possible only if the islands can export manufactures. And, since it is difficult and expensive to break into a foreign market by building up new distribution outlets, this is most likely to succeed if the islands concentrate on inviting manufacturers who are already well established in foreign markets. If an industry is to supply only the local West Indian market, it is quite feasible for the government to start and run it. But those industries which are to try to sell in Latin America, or in the United States, or in England, are better left to foreign capitalists.

VII.E.3. Overcoming the Weakness of Agriculture*

Agriculture has been the weakest link in the development chain. Industry in LDCs has grown at around 7 percent per annum, the number of children in school has multiplied by four, the domestic savings ratio has risen by three percentage points—the picture is everywhere bright until one turns to agriculture, where the dominant fact is that, in LDCs as a whole, food production has failed to keep pace with the demand for food, thereby causing or aggravating a whole series of other problems.

The basic reasons for this failure are well known, so I will list but not dwell on them.

The first has been fast population growth. Population has grown at around 2.5 percent per annum, and per capita demand has pushed the growth of total demand well beyond three percent, while output has grown at significantly less than 3 percent, turning what used to be an export surplus into an import surplus of food.

Second, the technological revolution in tropical food production has only just begun, research in the colonial days having been confined almost but not exclusively to commercial crops exportable to the world market. We have made spectacular progress with maize, wheat for subtropical conditions, and rice for areas of controlled irrigation, but have still far to go with other rice, with sorghums, and millets, and with livestock management.

Third, even where there is new technology to impart, the agricultural extension services and

*From Sir W. Arthur Lewis, "Development Strategy in a Limping World Economy," The Elmhurst Lecture, The International Conference of Agricultural Economists, Banff, Canada, September 3–12, 1979 (processed), pp. 2–9. Reprinted by permission.

the network for supplying modern inputs to the farmer—especially seeds, fertilisers and pesticides, are gravely deficient, and in many areas virtually non-existent.

Fourth, investment in rural infrastructure is inadequate. Road systems have improved immensely, and the penetration of the countryside by buses and trucks is altering the patterns of rural life. But not enough has been invested in irrigation, or in storage facilities.

Fifth, everyone speaks in favour of land reform, but very few governments have done it in any of its various forms, whether distributing land to the landless, or converting from rental to ownership tenures, or fixing rental ceilings. The case for some sort of land reform remains unquestionable from the standpoint of justice; the case from the standpoint of its effects on production is now stated with greater sophistication, recognising the extent to which higher output is tied to improved technology, extension and investment. Indeed several writers now speak not of land reform but of "the land reform package," to distinguish what they see as good land reform from bad land reform.

And finally to complete our list of factors that have inhibited agricultural output we must add poor terms of trade. The prices of agricultural commodities in world trade fell throughout the 1950s and most of the 1960s, while industrial prices rose all the time. This was anomalous, since prosperity usually improves agriculture's terms of trade. The basic factor was the enormous increase in agricultural productivity in the United States, resulting in the build up of stocks of cereals; since agricultural commodities compete with each other either on the demand side or on the supply side, this depressed all other agricultural prices. Add to this that in several LDCs governments wanted to keep farm revenues low, whether by imposing taxes on exportable crops, or by placing price ceilings on food for the domestic market. This is at first sight a curious phenomenon. One would expect that farm populations, being more than half the nation (in most cases), would carry enough political clout to be able to defend themselves against such measures—and would on the contrary be manipulating the terms of trade in their favour, but this is not automatic. European farmers were doing this at the end of the nineteenth century, but the contemporaneous efforts of American farmers—though they were still in the majority—were a failure.

Let me now turn from the causes of the low level of agricultural output in the LDCs to some of its effects. Agricultural failure is not the sole cause of the problems I shall mention, but makes in each case a significant contribution.

Take first the probability that inequality of the income distribution has increased along with recent growth. This is not a novel phenomenon. Increased inequality is inherent in the classical system of economics because population growth keeps labour income down while profits and rents increase. Given the long and strident debate between economic historians as to what happened to the European living standards in the first half of the century, no modern economist should have assumed that economic growth would automatically raise the incomes of those at the lower end of the scale. Rapid population growth has also played its negative role in our day, restraining the wage level and farm income per head. Since the majority of the labour force in LDCs consists of farm people, who also have the lowest incomes, the standard of living of the great bulk of the population can be raised only by raising farm income. Discussions of the effects of growth on income distribution or income distribution on growth lead nowhere unless farm income is at the centre of the alleged relationship.

The worst effects of population growth combined with technological standstill are to be seen in the arid zones of the tropical world, where some 500 million people live, especially along the fringes of the African and Asian deserts. There we have the largest concentration of human poverty; the numbers continue to grow rapidly; and we have not yet had the technological breakthrough in dry farming that might promise higher productivity. To raise the living standards of these hundreds of millions is the greatest challenge to those who work for development.

Consider next the huge flow of migrants from the countryside into the towns. Central to this of course is the growth of population. Relatively under-populated countries can cope with population growth by opening up new land, as has been happening over much of Africa, but in less favoured countries population growth means smaller farms, more landless labourers and lower output per head. Unless a green revolution is set in motion, the natural reaction of farmers caught in this situation is to put pressure on the young to migrate to the cities, which they will do if the cities show signs of expanding employment. This is not a complete solution. The towns cannot provide employment for the whole of the natural increase in the countryside, not to speak of women now also leaving the family tasks and seeking wage employment; so unemployment mounts. The government is also trapped. The towns exert great pressure for expansion of the public services—of water, bus transport, schools, hospitals, and so on—eating up more funds than exist, and leaving nothing to spend in the countryside. So the differential in amenities between town and country widens all the more, and the stream of migrants is increased. Unemployment in the towns cannot be ended by spending more in the towns. The basic solution is rather to make the countryside economically viable, with a larger cultivated area, with rising productivity on the farms, more rural industry, and better social amenities.

Note "the larger cultivated area." Development economists have been mesmerized by European experience into assuming that the development process always involves a decline in the number of persons in agriculture. This is true of relative decline, but it extends to an absolute decline only in the later stages of development. For example, around 1850 in Western Europe the agricultural population was only 50 percent of the whole, and the rate of natural increase about one and a quarter percent. So the agricultural population would decline absolutely if the non-agricultural population grew at over 2.5 percent per year. Whereas with 70 percent in agriculture and a rate of natural increase of 2.5 percent, an absolute decline of the agricultural labour force requires non-agricultural employment to expand at 8.3 percent per annum, which it cannot do.

An increase in the absolute numbers engaged in agriculture is therefore an essential item in coping with the current flood of population. The fact that the green revolution in cereals is labour-intensive helps, especially if the natural propensity of the more enterprising farmers to invest in labour saving machinery can be restrained. But there is no escaping the need to bring more land under cultivation, by opening up roads, irrigation, terracing, drainage, and other investment in infrastructure. Some governments are actively engaged in colonisation schemes of this sort, which, if highly planned to meet modern standards, are costly and troublesome. The subject is neglected in our textbooks. It needs more research and experimentation, leading to action.

A third consequence of the weakness of agriculture is that it is one of the reasons why so many LDCs have had balance of payments troubles, have incurred large external debts, or have found themselves defaulting on their obligations. It is not just that a larger output would earn more foreign exchange, or save on food imports. Indirectly it would reduce urbanization, the high cost of which is the prime cause of their needing so much capital and having to borrow so much. Also, in countries suffering from the two-gap disease, it would facilitate the translation of domestic saving into foreign exchange.

A fourth and final consequence of the weakness of agriculture has been to inhibit the growth of manufacturing industry because of the farmers' low purchasing power. The physical output of LDC commercial export crops grew rapidly, aided on the supply side by the expansion of internal transport, and on the demand side by the unusually rapid growth of the developed countries. But the prices at which these commodities sold were poor; exports are a small part of agricultural output, so their prices are linked on the supply side to the price of food, which as we saw earlier, was depressed by American surpluses. The individual LDC can do well out of exporting agricultural raw materials or tropical beverages; but for the group of LDCs as a whole the elasticity of supply of these commodities is so high, at prices yielding roughly the same incomes as domestic food production, that the factoral terms of trade stay much the same despite increases in demand or improvements in technology. The road to riches does not run in these directions.

At the same time farm incomes from domestic production were also low, for reasons which we have already considered. So import substitution of manufactures, which was the starting point of industrialization, was limited by the narrowness of the domestic market. LDCs soon discovered that if industry is to grow at 7 percent per annum, in the face of a peasantry with only a small marketable surplus, industry must look to foreign markets. By the year 1970 this lesson had been learnt, and nearly every LDC has begun exporting some manufactures to developed countries. Unfortunately this range was very narrow, dominated by textiles and clothing; broadening only as the protests and restrictions of MDCs forced the more advanced LDCs into light metals, electronics and other fields. The

LDC effort was clearly successful, since LDC exports of manufactures were growing at 10 percent a year, despite the barriers erected by the MDCs. Whether world trade will revive, and if so whether LDC exports of manufactures will again grow at 10 percent, are crucial questions for LDC development strategy.... But no matter how they may be answered, it will be to the advantage of LDCs to raise their agricultural productivity, since this would simultaneously raise the living standards of their farmers, create a domestic market for their manufactures, and improve their terms of trade.

CHAPTER VIII

Industrialization and Agriculture: 2

If, as was stated in the last chapter, "agriculture has been the weakest link in the development chain," then we must in this chapter emphasize policies that will promote the important role that agriculture must play in the structural transformation of a developing economy. Agriculture must be viewed not merely as a source of surpluses to support industrialization, but also as a dynamic source of growth, employment, and better distribution of income.

Agricultural conditions should not constrain development. Agricultural progress is essential to provide food for a growing nonagricultural labor force, raw materials for industrial production, and savings and tax revenue to support development of the rest of the economy; to earn more foreign exchange (or save foreign exchange when primary products are imported); and to provide a growing market for domestic manufactures. As the theme of section VIII.A emphasizes, the intersectoral relations between agriculture and industry will determine the course of structural transformation in a developing economy. If in the long run, there is to be a diminishing share of agriculture in output, there first must be in the short run successful policies of agricultural development to facilitate this transformation. It is essential to eliminate urban bias that hinders agricultural progress (VIII.A.3).

There have recently been a number of advances in analyzing the microeconomics of the rural sector. Section VIII.B examines the organization of labor, land, and credit markets. Special attention is given to the interlinking of these markets. Selection VIII.B.5 interprets the decision making of members of rural households as the maximization behavior of a "household-firm."

As discussed in section VIII.C, the design of an agricultural strategy must take into account policies that relate to subsidies and taxes, tariffs and quotas, price-stabilization programs and expenditure programs. The effects of government intervention in agricultural pricing have become a major concern to development economists. This concern is directed to an analysis of the interrelationships among agricultural prices and resource allocation, incentives, income distribution, and employment. A number of studies present evidence that agricultural-pricing policies have had an adverse effect on (1) the gap between rural and urban income; (2) the incentive to produce food and export crops; (3) the ability of governments to establish and maintain food reserves; and (4) employment opportunities in farming, processing, and rural industries. More attention is also being given to relative food prices as important determinants of change in the relative and absolute real income of low-income people.

For most of the developing countries, rural development on a massive scale will be needed for decades. But the progress of rural development will be crucially dependent on the outcome of the green revolution, measures of land reform, land settlement at the extensive margin, new forms of rural institutions, and various special programs designed to increase the productivity and incomes of the rural poor.

While the green revolution provides a potential for increasing farm output by technical innovations that increase the productivity of labor and land, it is necessary—from the standpoint of labor absorption—to realize the advantages of a labor-using and yield-increasing strategy of agricultural development. In this connection, the transformation of Japanese agriculture is instructive. The ''Japanese model'' has three important characteristics: first, agricultural output has been increased within the unchanged organizational framework of the existing small-scale farming system. This was possible because of increases in the productivity of the scarce resources of capital and foreign exchange. Second, the bulk of the nation's farmers have been involved in increases in agricultural productivity associated with the use of improved varieties of seeds, fertilizers, and other current inputs; technological progress of this type has continually been the source of greater agricultural productivity. Third, agricultural and industrial development have moved forward together in a process of ''concurrent'' growth.[1]

Emphasis is therefore placed in selection VIII.C.4 on the relevance of a ''unimodal strategy,'' such as occurred historically in the Japanese pattern of a small-scale farming system and the participation of the bulk of the nation's farmers in the increase of agricultural productivity. Such a strategy, however, must also be linked to changes in the land-tenure system, technological development in agriculture, and persistent concern with the effects on employment generation.

Higher per capita output must be realized. But to do this, a number of policies are required, as is discussed in the selections in section VIII.C. It is necessary to use more ''modern'' inputs per unit of land, while also providing for an increasing total use of labor. There must be continual, institutionalized technological change and improved incentives for farm producers, especially through pricing policies that do not overvalue inputs to farmers while undervaluing their output. Better distribution of ownership or access to productive resources is also required, especially for small landholders, and the distribution of income must be improved.

The final selection (VIII.C.5) outlines priorities for countries with abundant rural labor.

---

[1]Kazushi Ohkawa and Bruce F. Johnston, ''The Transferability of the Japanese Pattern of Modernizing Traditional Agriculture,'' in *The Role of Agriculture in Economic Development*, ed. Erik Thorbecke (1969), pp. 277–78.

VIII.A. IMPORTANCE OF AGRICULTURE

VIII.A.1. Agriculture's Contribution to Development—Note

Ever since at least the time of Ricardo, the "theology" of development has emphasized that agricultural progress contributes to the support of greater productivity throughout the economy. In his *Principles of Political Economy and Taxation,* Ricardo viewed the problem of diminishing returns in agriculture as crucial. He believed that a limitation on the growth of agricultural output sets the upper limit to the growth of the nonagricultural sector and to capital formation for economic expansion.

It is now customary to summarize in four ways how greater agricultural productivity and output contribute to an economy's development: (1) by supplying foodstuffs and raw materials to other expanding sectors in the economy; (2) by providing an "investable surplus" of savings and taxes to support investment in another expanding sector; (3) by selling for cash a "marketable surplus" that will raise the demand of the rural population for products of other expanding sectors; and (4) by relaxing the foreign-exchange constraint by earning foreign exchange through exports or by saving foreign exchange through import substitution.

Kuznets summarizes these contributions as the "market contribution" and the "factor contribution":

A given sector makes a contribution to an economy when it provides opportunities for other sectors to emerge, or for the economy as a whole to participate in international trade and other international economic flows. We designate this contribution the market type because the given sector provides such opportunities by offering part of its product on domestic or foreign markets in exchange for goods produced by the other sectors, at home or abroad. . . .

Thus agriculture makes a market contribution to economic growth by (1) purchasing some production items from other sectors at home or abroad; (2) selling some of its product, not only to pay for the purchases listed under (1) but also to purchase consumer goods from other sectors or from abroad, or to dispose of the product in any way other than consumption within the sector. In all these ways, agriculture makes it feasible for other sectors to emerge and grow and for international flows to develop; just as these other sectors and the international flows make it feasible for the agricultural sector to operate more efficiently as a

producing unit and use its product more effectively as a consuming unit.[1]

The "factor contribution" occurs when there is a transfer or loan of resources from the given sector to others. Thus if agriculture itself grows, it makes a product contribution; if it trades with others, it renders a market contribution; if it transfers resources to other sectors, these resources being productive factors, it makes a *factor* contribution.[2]

In this traditional interpretation, the development process is viewed as one of structural transformation from an economy in which agricultural employment and output dominate to a decline in the share of the labor force in agriculture and a decrease in the share of agriculture in GNP. But this structural transformation is itself dependent on agricultural progress. Industrial development will be cut short by lack of agricultural progress—unless the economy is in the exceptional situation of being able to export manufactures for imports of foodstuffs and raw materials (for example, Hong Kong). In Lewis's dual-sector model, we saw that if food supplies to the modern sector do not keep up with the modern sector's demand for labor, the modern sector will have to consume a larger share of its output in feeding its labor force, and this will leave a smaller surplus for capital accumulation. More generally, it is widely believed that "both in concept and in practice it is possible for the agricultural sector to make large net transfers of resources to other sectors. If these transfers are used productively, the rate of economic growth can be accelerated."[3]

Agriculture's contribution of foodstuffs—the "wage good" in classical terminology—is clear. If the labor force for manufacturing or another expanding sector is drawn from ag-

[1]Simon Kuznets, *Economic Growth and Structure* (1965), pp. 244–45.

[2]Ibid., p. 250.

[3]John W. Mellor, "Accelerated Growth in Agricultural Production and the Intersectoral Transfer of Resources," *Economic Development and Cultural Change* (October 1973): 5.

riculture, the new workers must "take their lunch" with them when they leave the rural sector. A growing urban labor force must be supported by an expanding supply of foodstuffs. A growing population must also be supported with increased food supplies. The annual rate of increase in demand for food is given by $D = p + \eta g$, where p and g are the rate of growth of population and per capita income, and η is the income elasticity of demand for agricultural products.[4] As indicated by Johnston and Mellor,[5] not only are there high rates of population growth in the LDCs, but the income elasticity of demand for food in these countries is considerably higher than in high-income countries—probably on the order of 0.6 or higher in the low-income countries, as compared with 0.2 or 0.3 in Western Europe, the United States, and Canada. A given rate of increase in per capita income therefore has a considerably stronger impact on the demand for agricultural products in the low-income countries than in the economically advanced countries.

Through the transfer of capital and labor to nonfarm activities, agriculture may also provide an investable surplus. The transfer of labor has been repeatedly discussed in the context of the Lewis model and needs no further attention here. But it should be noted that agriculture can be a source of capital formation in ways other than the simple lending of voluntary savings. There may be a compulsory transfer from agriculture for the benefit of other sectors, ordinarily through taxation in which the burden on agriculture is greater than the governmental services provided to agriculture. Kuznets remarks:

The measurement of such forced contributions of agriculture to economic growth is not easy; the incidence of some indirect taxes is difficult to ascertain and the allocation of government expenditures in terms of benefits to agriculture and to economic growth elsewhere is far from simple. But this factor contribution by agriculture was clearly quite large in the early phases of economic growth in some countries. Thus in Japan in the last two decades of the nineteenth century the land tax was over 80 percent of central government taxation, and the direct tax ratio to income produced was between 12 and 22 percent in agriculture, compared with from 2 to 3 percent in the nonagricultural sectors. Forced extraction of sur-

plus from agriculture by taxation, confiscation, and other measures also probably financed a considerable part of industrialization in the Soviet Union. Indeed, one of the crucial problems of modern economic growth is how to extract from the product of agriculture a surplus for the financing of capital formation for industrial growth without at the same time blighting the growth of agriculture, under conditions where no easy *quid pro quo* for such surplus is available within the country. It is only the open economy, with access to the markets of the more highly developed countries, both for goods and for capital loans, that can minimize this painful task of initial capital accumulation.[6]

Another way of transferring resources from the agricultural to the nonagricultural sectors is by the government turning the terms of trade against agriculture by imposing price controls on agricultural products by taxation, or by using multiple exchange rates that discriminate against agriculture. If the improvement in the terms of trade in the nonagricultural sectors raises nonagricultural incomes, and the beneficiaries save at a higher marginal rate than the decreased agricultural incomes, aggregate saving rates will increase, and agriculture will have made a net contribution to total saving in an indirect manner. Selection VIII.A.2 gives some indication of what has actually occurred in recent years by way of income transfers from agriculture.

A "marketable surplus" from agriculture is needed not only to provide the wage good to industry, but also to widen the home market for the industrial products. The demand for industrial products depends on growth of farm cash income, unless the country can export its growing industrial output. Barring unlimited export possibilities, and with 70 to 90 percent of the home market in the rural sector, the nature of rural demand will affect the growth of nonfarm employment and output. Increased agricultural productivity, a growing marketable surplus, and rising real income are necessary to raise the rural sector's demand for industrial output.

Finally, agriculture may be a major source of foreign exchange. It is clear that agricultural exports dominate in a country's early phase of development. But also important in relaxing the foreign-exchange constraint is the possibility in several developing countries of saving foreign exchange by replacing imports of foodstuffs with home production. Export promotion and import substitution are activities not only for the industrial sector, but also for agriculture.

[4]Kazushi Ohkawa, "Economic Growth and Agriculture," *Annuals Hitotsubashi Academy* (October 1956): 45–60.

[5]Bruce F. Johnston and John W. Mellor, "The Role of Agriculture in Economic Development," *American Economic Review* (September 1961): 571–81.

[6]Kuznets, *Economic Growth and Structure*, pp. 250–51.

Considering these various contributions of agriculture, development economists have insisted that if there is to be in the longer run a structural transformation in output and labor force, there must first be in the short run "successful policies of agricultural development" to facilitate this transformation. But what specifically do "successful policies of agricultural development" entail? And is the purpose of agricultural development simply to underwrite the expansion of nonagricultural sectors—even at the expense of an "agricultural squeeze"? Now, in view of the emphasis on absolute poverty and the employment problem, is it not necessary to concentrate on agricultural development for the sake of employment and a diminution in inequality? Even though the long-term objective is structural transformation—the absorption of a larger fraction of the rural population in new income-earning opportunities—there remains the complex problem of the timing of this transformation and the intertemporal sequence of policies to accomplish it. The lessons of recent history have shown that an "urban bias" can discriminate against agriculture;[7] and that the net outflow of resources from agriculture may be excessive. Not only may there be an inefficient use of the resources transferred to the nonagricultural sectors, but the transfer may itself be at the expense of more employment and higher income in the agricultural sector. Should not the "growth-promoting interactions between agriculture and industrial development" mean more than that agricultural development should have simply instrumental value for industrial development?

In the early years of development planning, Viner wisely anticipated the answer to this question:

Let us suppose that *real* incomes are lower in agriculture than in industry, and that by tariff protection or subsidies industry can be made to expand and to draw workers from the country into the cities. Is this sound economic policy?

The correct answer depends on why *per capita* real incomes are lower in agriculture than in manufacturing. There may be urban exploitation of agriculture, through monopolistic pricing by employers, or through labour monopolies in the factories which by forcing wages up force up also the prices which the agricultural population has to pay for urban products and services—including government services.

The tariff, supported as providing better employment opportunities for the agricultural population, may itself be a major instrument whereby agricultural real incomes are depressed. Government may also operate to depress agricultural real incomes by imposing its taxes, mainly or largely, directly or indirectly, on agriculture, and directing its expenditures mainly to the benefit of the urban population. Even though the rural population may have lower *per capita* incomes than the urban, it may nevertheless be the only economically healthy part of the population, the only part which gives good value to the community in exchange for what it gets from the community. Where the situation is one—as it often is—of urban exploitation of the rural population, to propose as a remedy the further subsidization of urban industry as a means of drawing rural workers to the city is equivalent to proposing to remedy the exploitation of worker bees also to drones. It is obvious that it can work at all only as long as there still remain worker bees in the fields to be exploited.

The refutation of bad argument does not necessarily refute the conclusions reached by such argument. It is not my position that the path to economic progress is not, for many countries and even for most countries, by way of industrialization and urbanization. I have in fact conceded that as any country or any region becomes more prosperous it will normally tend to increase the ratio of its population which is non-agricultural. My position is a different one, and I will now state it frankly and positively for the first time. The real problem in poor countries is not agriculture as such, or the absence of manufactures as such, but poverty and backwardness, poor agriculture, or poor agriculture and poor manufacturing. The remedy is to remove the basic causes of the poverty and backwardness. This is as true in principle, and probably nearly as true in practice, for industrialized countries as for predominantly agricultural countries.

Misallocation of resources as between agriculture and manufactures is probably rarely a major cause of poverty and backwardness, except where government, through tariffs, discriminatory taxation and expenditure policies, and failure to provide on a regionally non-discriminatory pattern facilities for education, health promotion, and technical training, is itself responsible for this misallocation. Where there is such government-induced misallocation, it is today more likely to consist of the diversion of agrarian-produced resources to the support of parasitic cities than of overinvestment of resources in primary industries and in workers in such industries.

Economic improvement may call for greater industrialization, but this should be a natural growth, appropriately facilitated by government but not maintained under hot-house conditions. In many countries, the most promising field for rapid economic development lies in agriculture, and the measures needed are primarily such as will promote health, general ed-

---

[7]Michael Lipton, "Strategy for Agriculture: Urban Bias and Rural Planning," in *The Crisis of Indian Planning,* ed. Paul Streeten and Michael Lipton (1968).

ucation, technical training, better transportation facilities, and cheap rural credit for productive use. There are no inherent advantages of manufacturing over agriculture, or, for that matter, of agriculture over manufacturing. It is only arbitrarily in fact that the line separating the two can be drawn. The choice between expansion of agriculture and expansion of manufactures can for the most part best be left to the free decisions of capitalists, entrepreneurs, and workers. To the extent that there is need for government decision, it should be made on rational grounds, in the light of considerations of costs and of comparative returns from alternative allocations of scarce national resources, human and material. If direction is accepted from maxims and arbitrary dogmas and prejudices, from unsubstantiated and incredible natural laws of the inherent inferiority of one type of industry over another, then it is highly probable that the result will be the squandering of resources so scanty in supply that they need to be carefully husbanded, and the sore disappointment of the wishes of the great masses of population crying to be relieved of their crushing poverty.[8]

The emphasis on agricultural development now is not only for its instrumental value in sustaining expansion elsewhere in the nonagricultural sectors, but also for its own absorption of labor and its own increase of real income among the rural-poverty target groups of the small farmers and the landless laborers.

[8]Jacob Viner, *International Trade and Economic Development* (1953), pp. 51–53.

VIII.A.2. Role of Peasant Agriculture*

As in many parts of low-income Asia, such as Nepal, Sri Lanka, India, Bangladesh, and Thailand, in Africa concern for economic development is primarily a concern about agricultural and rural development. Between 80 and 90 percent of the nearly 400 million people in Sub-Saharan Africa live in rural areas. Most derive their subsistence from meager crop and livestock production and survive on annual per capita incomes of less than U.S. $150. Although production is geared largely to subsistence, the rural sector is also the major source of food for urban consumption and of raw materials for exports and for domestic manufacturing. Except in a few mineral-producing countries such as Zaire, Zambia, and Nigeria, agriculture constitutes the largest income-generating sector, contributing up to 40 percent of the gross national product of many African countries. Between 70 and 80 percent of the annual export earnings of many countries is derived from three to six agricultural commodities. Direct and indirect taxes on agriculture are the most important sources of government revenues. Although the estate sector is an important producer of marketed surpluses of certain crops in certain countries, a major share of the total production and marketed surplus nevertheless comes from the smallholder sector. Not only is broad-based agricultural development thus crucial for increasing incomes, employment, and export earnings, but raising the incomes of the rural poor is essential for raising government revenues and creating a domestic market for the goods and services produced in a growing urban manufacturing sector.

The "Modernization Now" Approach

Rhetoric and plan documents in almost all African countries make reference to the key role of the agricultural and rural sector in Africa's modernization. Since the disastrous drought of 1973–74 self-sufficiency in food has become a major objective, often supported by donor-financed projects. The need for increasing export earnings is also being recognized more urgently, the balance-of-payments difficulties having grown with the rising cost of imported energy and manufactured goods. Despite the growing awareness and the increased number of projects, however, unlike in Asia, there is not yet the basic conviction among many African policy makers that the smallholder agricultural sector can and will have to be the engine of broad-based

*From Uma Lele, "Rural Africa: Modernization, Equity, and Long-Term Development," in Carl K. Eicher and John M. Staatz (eds.), *Agricultural Development in the Third World*, The Johns Hopkins University Press, Baltimore, 1984, pp. 438–44. Reprinted by permission.

economic development and eventual modernization.

Modernization is taken to mean mainly industrialization and the commercialization of agriculture, largely through mechanized, large-scale farming. The fluctuating prices of primary exports explain the desire to industrialize, as does the relative ease of setting up factories and state farms compared with the organizationally far more demanding development of peasant agriculture. In its broadest sense the objective of modernization is, of course, shared extensively throughout the developing world. It is the short time perspective of the African expectations that poses a problem, especially given the much poorer institutional and trained manpower base that Africa inherited at independence.

The frequently noted perception of peasant agriculture as a "holding sector" is, however, by no means unique to Africa. At an earlier stage, India's first five-year plan (1951–56) incorporated community development and promotion of cottage and small-scale industry essentially as stopgap arrangements to ensure rural welfare and employment until industrialization could absorb the growing pool of surplus agricultural labor. The more dynamic development strategy, oriented toward small-farmer productivity, which is now being implemented successfully in many parts of India came into ascendancy only in the mid-1960s, with technological change made possible by the new high-yield cereals. In Africa the view of agriculture as a holding sector and the "Modernization Now" strategy have had many of the same consequences for the development of peasant agriculture in more free-enterprise, growth-oriented Nigeria and Zambia as in Ethiopia and Tanzania, which show greater concern about income distribution and class formation.

Government Investment in Agriculture

Planning the use of government finances for agricultural development is, of course, not easy for most African countries because of great fluctuations in their export earnings. Their bureaucracies are less experienced than those of their Asian counterparts, which experience similar fluctuations in earnings. Lately their ability to plan has been further eroded, as has that of other developing countries, by the declining purchasing power of their export earnings, as import prices of oil and industrial goods have soared. In constant dollars, the purchasing power of exports from fourteen principal countries in Africa fell by about 40 percent from 1973 to 1980.

Even within these all too obvious constraints, however, far fewer resources are plowed back into agriculture by most African countries than would seem justified. Intercountry comparisons are exceedingly difficult, owing to definitional data, and other measurement problems, but in the 1970s around 10 percent or less of the planned development expenditure was allocated to the agricultural sectors in Kenya and Mali, compared with 31 percent in India during its first five-year plan in 1951 and 20 percent of the much larger absolute investment in the subsequent three plans. In Zambia the total agricultural budget may have decreased in real terms by an annual average of slightly over 9 percent in the late 1970s, reflecting general budgetary cuts. Malawi is one of the few exceptions in Africa; it appears to have allocated close to 30 percent of the known planned public expenditures to agriculture. However, even there, because of the more favorable tax, wage, and pricing policies toward the estate sector, large-scale production has grown at an annual rate of close to 17 percent since 1968, with 70 percent of the share in exports. The corresponding production increase in the smallholder sector has been only 3 percent a year, even though services to peasant agriculture generally operate far more effectively in Malawi than in several neighboring African countries.

Large-scale farming per se is far less important a portion of total production or exports in Tanzania than in Malawi. However, government policies of "villagization" of peasant producers, combined with pronouncements of the need for cooperative cultivation and actual haphazard attempts to introduce it, have had an adverse effect on smallholder incentives and production. Several other seemingly well-motivated government initiatives to raise peasant productivity have ended up being poorly implemented. These have led, for instance, to unrealistically high production and input-use targets, the consequent indiscriminate promotion of fertilizer use, and discouragement of interplanting of crops (which is traditionally done by peasants to reduce risks of crop failure) as not being "modern." These government initiatives, combined with unreliable provision of agricultural extension, credit, and output marketing, rather than enabling producers to raise overall agricultural productivity, have resulted in producers responding mainly to changing relative prices of food and export crops. The failed government initiatives have in turn led to an increased official tendency to look toward large-scale mechanized and irrigated production to guarantee food and export surpluses. Like Tanzania, many other countries have already invested or have plans to invest substantial resources in large-scale state farms, but the record of public-sector farming is very poor throughout Africa, and large subsidies are required for these operations.

Irrigation will have to become important ultimately, as the vast, less costly possibilities of increasing production under rain-fed conditions begin to be exhausted. For the short run, however, in most of Africa there is not the complex institutional and managerial capacity to operate irrigation systems indigenously. The frequently costly rehabilitation (at five thousand to fifteen thousand dollars per hectare) being undertaken in many of the existing schemes illustrates the problem.

Incentives to Peasant Producers

Peasant agriculture is highly taxed by fixing low prices for its products and by overvaluing the national currencies vis-à-vis those of importing countries. Agricultural taxation helps keep urban food prices low and finances modernization through many capital-intensive investments, such as construction of new capital cities, stadiums, manufacturing and processing plants, and airports. Agriculture is, of course, the most important sector and hence has to be the major source of revenue. However, traditionally it was taxed because peasants were perceived as irrational, lazy, and unresponsive to price incentives. The resulting tax practices were inherited by independent governments from colonial administrations. Evidence of producer response has mounted, however. In turn, relative official producer prices of food and export crops have been changed in many countries in the last decade, first in order to achieve food self-sufficiency and more recently to promote exports. Relative prices have in fact been easier for governments to influence than technology or quality of services. Thus, while the composition of food and export crops has changed, overall productivity has stagnated. The producer's share in the total net market value of the output has frequently remained very low.

Again, the inadequate recognition of producer incentives is by no means confined to Africa. Theodore W. Schultz's *Transforming Tradi-*

tional Agriculture, which included examination of the peasant irrationality hypothesis, was prompted by similar observations in developing Asia in the early post-independence period. In Asia these attitudes, trends, and perceptions have been muted, however. In fact, an articulate pro-agriculture lobby has been created within most governments in Asia. What accounts for these differences? In comparison with Africa (with a few exceptions, such as Kenya), in most of Asia there has been greater overt discussion of policy issues, both domestically and between domestic and outside scholars. More widespread formal education and training of policy makers and administrators in Asia has been helpful, as has their greater exposure to the farming communities through longer practical work experience. New technological possibilities and increased use of purchased inputs have also changed the perspective on price incentives. Now several rural development projects in Africa have gradually begun to produce a similar cadre of knowledgeable Africans in several countries, but their numbers are small because of government and donor policies to be described later.

A large part of the agricultural budget in many countries is spent on subsidies—over 70 percent in Zambia. But contrary to general opinion, many of the subsidies provided in the agricultural sectors in the hope of increasing overall peasant production do not compensate effectively for high rates of taxation. For instance, fertilizer subsidies frequently only help alleviate the high cost of production or inefficient domestic fertilizer plants or the high cost of their local distribution. General subsidies on interest rates and inputs largely benefit the already better-off commercial farmers. A policy followed in many African countries of uniform pricing of output, involving complex cross-subsidies of transport and other handling costs across regions, has achieved regional equity, especially where few attractive enterprises exist, but has discouraged crop specialization to exploit different natural resources among regions.

Input and Output Marketing

Input and output marketing and processing facilities are almost always operated by semiautonomous government or parastatal agencies or by largely government-initiated cooperatives on a monopoly basis. Public marketing agencies tend to be high-cost operations because of overstaffing, poor financial control and accountability, and inexperienced mangement. If an informal traditional market operates, it is only tolerated rather than helped to improve. Frequently it is actively discouraged. The eviction of largely Asian-dominated trade through Operation Maduka in Tanzania and the massive expulsion of Asians in Uganda illustrate the point. A strong desire to abolish exploitation of nationals by other races is understandable, even if such exploitation is imputed rather than real. But even Nigeria, which has a buoyant, largely indigenous small-scale traditional trading sector, adopted a policy of public-sector monopoly of the distribution of fertilizer. Tanzania has similarly discouraged its own enterprising tribes from trading, among other things by instituting some four hundred parastatals and over eight thousand village cooperatives, which are expected to provide most of the public services.

Some of these same policies are followed for almost the same political and bureaucratic reasons in most Asian countries, but the consequences there are far less severe. The degree of government control is more limited, there is greater administrative capacity to exercise it, and there has been more development of private institutions and transport and communication networks. In Africa, inputs are more frequently late, inadequately labeled and packaged, and in wrong combinations. Marketed surpluses are often not picked up on time, first payments to farmers are inordinately late, promised second payments rarely materialize, and damages to crops in storage and handling are extensive. Discouragement of private retail trade has affected rural supply of even the most basic day-to-day necessities in some countries, thus further reducing incentives for producers to consume, save, or invest. Institutional pluralism needs to be given major consideration as an element of development strategy in Africa.

Agricultural Research, Extension, Training, and Social Services

Whereas there is indiscriminate government intervention in some areas of policy, there is neglect of others, for instance, agricultural research, extension, and development of trained manpower. This neglect is due partly to inadequate recognition of the importance of these services and of the time required to establish effective institutions and delivery systems and partly to preoccupation with politically more expedi-

tious short-run objectives. The role of donors in this regard should not be underrated. The diversion of scarce financial and manpower resources to purposes that the private sector could well be allowed to serve is also a handicap.

Because of the inadequate provision of recurrent resources, the research, extension, and training facilities that do exist are frequently underfinanced and poorly maintained. As President Nyerere observed in his famous speech "The Arusha Declaration: Ten Years After," the pressure to maintain and even expand public-sector employment is so high that the wage bill is difficult to control. Consequently, there are not enough public funds for transport allowances for field staff to carry out research trials and extension demonstrations nor for spare parts, maintenance and operation of stores, processing facilities, research stations, vehicles, and roads. The general situation is one of ill-trained, unmotivated, unsupervised, and demoralized field staff in many sectors. Of course there are notable exceptions, such as the Kenya Tea Development Authority and the Agricultural Marketing Corporation in Malawi. Inadequacy and depletion of capital and government services over time are far more severe in areas where donor projects do not exist, inasmuch as these areas do not benefit from priority budgetary allocations. But the implementation of budgets also needs to be improved, as frequently even the resources allocated are not spent.

Social services suffer from many of the same problems. For example, lack or poor quality of water supply in many rural areas of Africa leads to ill health. Time spent in fetching water reduces time available for agricultural activities. Lack of health facilities similarly reduces labor productivity in agriculture. Absence of primary education results in limited access to services and employment opportunities in towns. Demand for social services is therefore widespread throughout Africa. On the other hand, public resources to pay the recurrent costs of providing social services are generally too limited to permit blanket coverage. Either a high degree of selectivity or greater direct cost recovery is therefore required in the provision of such services. As many *harambee* (''self-help'') schemes in Kenya illustrate, rural people are glad to contribute their own resources, provided the services are responsive to precise local demands and reliable, low-cost delivery is assured. Tanzania's example indicates, however, that for a combination of welfare and political reasons, governments refrain from cost recovery and genuine local involvement in planning and implementation. Tanzania's policy of universal provision of services through central financing has undoubtedly achieved results in some areas. According to official data, the proportion of the eligible population enrolled in primary schools went up from 28 percent in 1960 to over 90 percent in the late 1970s. The ratio of population with access to safe water has gone up from 13 percent in 1960 to about 40 percent in the 1970s. To a lesser extent, most African countries have expanded coverage of social services in a similar way, but the overall result is still inadequately financed services, with substantial demands on government resources.

Government objectives of modernization also exacerbate manpower shortages in the traditional sector. The low status of the traditional rural sector and the unattractive living conditions and facilities, in contrast to the urban or the large-scale agricultural sector, often deter qualified nationals from serving the needs of peasant agriculture. On the other hand, demand for education in Africa is one of the strongest in the developing world. The governments have allocated substantial portions of their own resources to education, with different emphases on primary and higher education, depending on their ideology. Because Tanzania has largely emphasized primary education, the enrollment ratio in secondary schools in Tanzania only went up from 2 percent at independence to 4 percent by the late 1970s, and from nearly zero to 0.3 percent in higher education. The shortage of middle- and higher-level technical and administrative manpower is consequently extremely severe. In Kenya, budgetary allocations to secondary and higher education have been expanding more rapidly, and private-sector expansion is permitted more liberally. As a result, 18 percent of the eligible population is enrolled in secondary schools and 1 percent is in higher education. Even then, middle- and higher-level manpower shortages are considerable, especially in technical fields such as accountancy, financial aid and physical resources management, agronomy, plant breeding, and mechanical and civil engineering. On a unit basis, skilled labor in African countries typically costs between three and ten times as much as in many Asian countries. And, of course, not nearly enough scientists are available even to rehabilitate, let alone to expand, the national research systems in Africa.

To summarize, the "Modernization Now" objective and the consequent national policies, investment priorities, and attitudes toward smallholder agriculture explain the poor performance of the agricultural and rural sectors in many African countries. In contrast, the Asian and, to a very limited extent, the African experience indicate that greater trained manpower, combined with longer developmental experience by nationals, leads to a better time perspective on modernization and more support of peasant agriculture.

EXHIBIT VIII.1. Food Production Per Capita: Average Growth Rate, 1979–91

Country	Food Production Per Capita (average growth rate; 1979–81 = 100), 1979–91
Argentina	−0.6
Bangladesh	−0.6
Brazil	1.7
China	3.0
Chile	1.5
Dominican Republic	−2.6
Ecuador	0.0
Guatemala	−0.7
Haiti	−1.2
Honduras	−1.6
India	1.6
Indonesia	2.2
Jamaica	−0.5
Kenya	0.5
Malaysia	4.1
Mexico	0.2
Nicaragua	−5.1
Niger	−3.4
Peru	−0.6
Philippines	−1.9
Thailand	0.5
Venezuela	0.0

Source: World Bank, *World Development Report 1993* (1993), pp. 244–45.

Comment: Food, Hunger, Famine

Can developing countries attain levels of food consumption that will ensure adequate nutrition even for the lowest deciles in their income distribution? To guarantee adequate nutrition, agricultural development must be concerned simultaneously with the rate of increase in food production and the means by which production is increased. Unless a country's "pattern" of agricultural development facilitates the absorption of a large segment of the rural labor force into productive employment, even a large increase in food output will leave many households with inadequate access to food supplies.

Rather than being a race between food and population, the food equation is to be viewed as a dynamic balance in individual countries between food supply and food demand that depends on complex relationships among a number of variables. Equilibrium in this vital food equation can range from a low one—a small increase in food supplies and little purchasing power in the hands of the poor— to high levels of each. The level at which the food supply–food demand equation is balanced is largely dependent on the design and implementation of a country's development strategy, especially as it influences the rate of expansion of employment.

These views are presented in detail in John W. Mellor and Bruce F. Johnston, "The World Food Equation: Interrelations Among Development, Employment, and Food Consumption," *Journal of Economic Literature* (June 1984).

There is now deeper understanding of the causes and consequences of hunger and famine. The cause is not so much deficient food output as it is the absence of "entitlements" and the lack of "capability" for poor people without the financial means or political influence. This understanding follows from Sen's analysis in section I.A and is elaborated in Jean Drèze and Amartya Sen, *Hunger and Public Action* (1989).

Drèze and Sen also submit that capability and nutritional requirements encompass more than food intake—health care, basic education, clean drinking water, sewage, and adequate shelter. They point out that most of those who die in famines succumb to disease, not to starvation. Gender bias is also a cause.

Analyzing the Great Bengal Famine of 1943 and more recent famines in Bangladesh and Ethiopia, Sen has shown that it was not the decline in available food that was the major cause of famine. In Bengal, military expenditures in urban areas and the consequent inflation in food prices were responsible. Especially hard hit were landless agricultural laborers and self-employed rural artisans whose incomes lagged behind the inflation. When a threat of famine arises, relief works to provide employment and real purchasing power to the poorest can do much to avert famine. See A. K. Sen, *Poverty and Famines* (1981).

As demonstrated by India, famines can be averted, even in the event of harvest failure, by targeted and timely employment programs, direct relief to the unemployable, and careful use of food reserves. Drèze and Sen note that, in contrast to China, India's democratic political system and free press induced government action to avert famine. They contrast India, which has eliminated famine but retained chronic hunger, with China, which has reduced chronic undernutrition but has suffered famines.

For estimates of hunger and its causes and consequences, see also D. Gale Johnson and G. Edward Schuch, eds., *Role of Markets in the World Food Economy* (1983); Nicole Ball, *World Hunger* (1981); A. Macbean, "Achieving Food Security," in *Current Issues in Development Economics*, ed. U. N. Balasutramanyam and S. Lall (1991), chap. 4; and Paul Streeten, "Hunger," in *Equity and Efficiency in Economic Development*, ed. Donald J. Savoie and Irving Brecher (1992).

VIII.A.3. Urban Bias*

The most important class conflict in the poor countries of the world today is not between labour and capital. Nor is it between foreign and national interests. It is between the rural classes and the urban classes. The rural sector contains most of the poverty, and most of the low-cost sources of potential advance; but the urban sec-

*From Michael Lipton, *Why Poor People Stay Poor*, 1977, Gower Publishing Limited. Reprinted by permission.

tor contains most of the articulateness, organisation and power. So the urban classes have been able to "win" most of the rounds of the struggle with the countryside; but in so doing they have made the development process needlessly slow and unfair. Scarce land, which might grow millets and beansprouts for hungry villagers, instead produces a trickle of costly calories from meat and milk, which few except the urban rich (who have ample protein anyway) can afford. Scarce investment, instead of going into water-pumps to grow rice, is wasted on urban motorways. Scarce human skills design and administer, not clean village wells and agricultural extension services, but world boxing championships in showpiece stadia. Resource allocations, within the city and the village as well as between them, reflect urban priorities rather than equity or efficiency. The damage has been increased by misguided ideological imports, liberal and Marxian, and by the town's success in buying off part of the rural elite, thus transferring most of the costs of the process to the rural poor.

The disparity between urban and rural welfare is much greater in poor countries now than it was in rich countries during their early development. . . . This huge welfare gap is demonstrably inefficient, as well as inequitable. . . . It persists mainly because less than 20 percent of investment for development has gone to the agricultural sector . . . although over 65 percent of the people of less-developed countries (LDCs), and over 80 percent of the really poor who live on $1 a week each or less, depend for a living on agriculture. The proportion of skilled people who support development—doctors, bankers, engineers—going to rural areas has been lower still; and the rural-urban imbalances have in general been even greater than those between agriculture and industry. Moreover, in most LDCs, governments have taken numerous measures with the unhappy side-effect of accentuating rural-urban disparities: their own allocation of public expenditure and taxation; measures raising the price of industrial production relative to farm production, thus encouraging private rural saving to flow into industrial investment because the value of industrial output has been artificially boosted; and educational facilities encouraging bright villagers to train in cities for urban jobs.

Such processes have been extremely inefficient. For instance, the impact on output of $1 of carefully selected investment is in most countries two to three times as high in agriculture as elsewhere yet public policy and private market power have combined to push domestic savings and foreign aid into non-agricultural uses. The process has also been inequitable. Agriculture starts with about one-third the income per head of the rest of the economy, so that the people who depend on it should in equity receive special attention not special mulcting. Finally, the misallocation between sectors has created a needless and acute conflict between efficiency and equity. In agriculture the poor farmer with little land is usually efficient in his use of both land and capital, whereas power, construction and industry often do best in big, capital-intensive units; and rural income and power, while far from equal, are less unequal then in the cities. So concentration on urban development and neglect of agriculture have pushed resources away from activities where they can help growth *and* benefit the poor, and towards activities where they do either of these, if at all, at the expense of the other.

Urban bias also increases inefficiency and inequity *within* the sectors. Poor farmers have little land and much underused family labour. Hence they tend to complement any extra developmental resources received—pumpsets, fertilisers, virgin land—with much more extra labour than do large farmers. Poor farmers thus tend to get most output from such extra resources (as well as needing the extra income most). But rich farmers (because they sell their extra output to the cities instead of eating it themselves, and because they are likely to use much of their extra income to support urban investment) are naturally favoured by urban-biased policies; it is they, not the efficient small farmers, who get the cheap loans and the fertiliser subsidies. The patterns of allocation and distribution within the cities are damaged too. Farm inputs are produced inefficiently, instead of imported, and the farmer has to pay, even if the price is nominally "subsidised." . . . The processing of farm outputs, notably grain milling, is shifted into big urban units and the profits are no longer reinvested in agriculture. And equalisation between classes inside the cities becomes more risky, because the investment-starved farm sector might prove unable to deliver the food that a better-off urban mass would seek to buy.

Moreover, income in poor countries is usually more equally distributed within the rural sector than within the urban sector. Since income creates the power to distribute extra income, therefore, a policy that concentrates on raising income in the urban sector will worsen inequalities in two ways: by transferring not only from poor to rich, but also from more equal to less equal. Concentration on urban enrichment is triply inequitable: because countryfolk start poorer; because such concentration allots rural resources largely to the rural rich (who sell food to the cities); and because the great inequality of power *within* the towns renders urban resources especially likely to go to the resident elites.

However, urban bias does not rest on a conspiracy, but on convergent interests. Industrialists, urban workers, even big farmers *all*
benefit if agriculture gets squeezed, provided its
few resources are steered, heavily subsidised, to
the big farmer, to produce cheap food and raw
materials for the cities. Nobody conspires; all
the powerful are satisfied; the labour-intensive
small farmer stays efficient, poor and powerless,
and had better shut up. Meanwhile, the economist, often in the blinkers of industrial deter-
minism, congratulates all concerned on reso-
lutely extracting an agricultural surplus to
finance industrialisation. Conspiracy? Who
needs conspiracy?

Thirdly, how far does the urban bias thesis go
towards an agricultural or rural emphasis? It was
noted that there is a rather low limit to the shifts
than *can* swiftly be made in allocations of key
resources like doctors or savings between huge,
structured areas of economic life like agriculture
and industry. In the longer run, if the arguments
of this section are right, how high do they push
the allocations that should go to agriculture in
poor countries: from the typical 20 percent of
various sorts of scarce resource (for the poorest
two-thirds of the people, who are also those normally using scarce resources more efficiently, as
will be shown) up to 50 percent, or 70 percent,
or (absurdly) 100 percent? Clearly the answer
will differ according to the resource being reallocated, the length of time for the reallocation,
and the national situation under review. The optimal extra proportion of doctors for rural India,
of investment for rural Peru, and of increase in
farm prices for rural Nigeria will naturally differ.
However, it remains true that pressures exist to
set all these levels far below their optima. To
acquire the right to advise against letting children go naked in winter, do I need to prescribe
the ideal designs of babies' bonnets?

Linked to the question "Is there a limit to the
share of resources agriculture ought to get?" is
a more fundamental question. Does the need for
a high share of rural resources last for ever?
Does not development imply a move out of agriculture and away from villages? Since all developed countries have a very high proportion
of resources outside agriculture, can it make
sense for underdeveloped countries to push
more resources *into* agriculture? And—a related
question—as a poor country develops, does it
not approach the British or U.S. style of farming,
where it is workers rather than machines or land
that are scarce, so that the concentration of farm

resources upon big labour-saving farms begins
to make more sense?

The best way to look at this question is to
posit four stages in the analysis of policy in a
developing country towards agriculture. Stage I
is to advocate leaving farming alone, allowing it
few resources, taxing it heavily if possible, and
getting its outputs cheaply to finance industrial
development, which has top priority. This belief
often rests on such comfortable assumptions as
that agricultural growth is ensured by rapid technical change; does not require or cannot absorb
investment; and can be directed to the poor
while the rich farmers alone are squeezed to provide the surpluses. Such a squeeze on agriculture
was overtly Stalin's policy, and in effect (though
much more humanely) the policy of the Second
Indian Plan (1956–61) as articulated by Mahal-
anobis, its chief architect. The bridge between
the two was the economic analysis of Preobrazhensky and Feldman. The underlying argument, that it is better to make machines than to
make consumer goods, especially if one can
make machines to make machines, ignores both
the possible case for international specialisation,
and the decided inefficiency of using scarce resources to do the right thing at the wrong time.

The second stage in policy for rural development usually arises out of the failures of Stage
I. In Stage II, policy-makers argue that agriculture cannot be safely neglected if it is adequately
to provide workers, materials, markets and saving to industry. Hence a lot of resources need to
be put into those parts of agriculture (mainly big
farms, though this is seldom stated openly) that
supply industry with raw materials, and industrial workers with food. That is the stage that
many poor countries have reached in their official pronouncements, and some in their actual
decisions. Stage II is still permeated by urban
bias, because the farm sector is allocated resources not mainly to raise economic welfare,
but because, and insofar as, it uses the resources
to feed urban-industrial growth. Development of
the rural sector is advocated, but not for the people who live and work there.

In Stage III, the argument shifts. It is realised
that, so long as resources are concentrated on
big farmers to provide urban inputs, those resources will neither relieve need nor—because
big farmers use little labour per acre—be used
very productively. So the sequence is taken one
step further back. It is recognised, not only (as
in Stage II) that efficient industrialisation is unlikely without major growth in rural inputs, but

also (and this is the distinctive contribution of Stage III) that such growth cannot be achieved efficiently or equitably—or maybe at all—on the basis of immediately "extracting surplus." Stage III therefore involves accepting the need for a transformation of the *mass* rural sector, through major resource inputs, *prior* to substantial industrialisation, except insofar as such industrialisation is a more efficient way than (say) imports of providing the mass rural sector with farm requirements or processing facilities. For development to "march on two legs," the best foot must be put forward first.

It is at Stage III that I stop. I do not believe that poor countries should "stay agricultural" in order to develop, let alone instead of developing. The argument that neither the carrying capacity of the land, nor the market for farm products, is such as to permit the masses in poor countries to reach high levels of living without a major shift to non-farm activities seems conclusive. The existence of a Stage IV must be recognised, however. Stage IV is the belief that industrialism degrades; that one should keep rural for ever. This is attractive to some people in poor countries because it marks a total rejection of imitativeness. Neither Western nor Soviet industrialism, but a "national path," is advocated. Other people, notably in rich countries, argue that environmental factors preclude an industrialised world where all consume at U.S. levels; that there would be too little of one or more key minerals, or that the use of so much energy would disastrously damage the world's air, water, climate or other aspects of the ecosystem. . . .

The learning process, needed for modern industrialisation, is sometimes long; but it is fallacious for a nation, comprising above all a promising but overwhelmingly underdeveloped agriculture, to conclude that, in order to begin the process of learning, a general attack on numerous branches of industrial activity should be initiated. A far better strategy is to concentrate first upon high-yielding mass rural development, supported (partly for learning's sake) by such selective ancillary industry as rural development makes viable. Rapid industrialisation on a broad front, doomed to self-strangulation for want of the wage goods and savings capacity that only a developed agricultural sector can provide, is likely to discredit industrialisation itself.

The arguments for rapid general industrialisation, prior to or alongside agricultural development, assume against most of the evidence that such a sequence is likely to succeed. But no national self-esteem, no learning-by-doing, no jam tomorrow, can come from a mass of false starts. If you wish for industrialisation, prepare to develop agriculture.

Comment: Rural–Urban Terms of Trade

For a discussion of methods chosen to test the urban-bias thesis and a critical examination of the evidence, see Michael Lipton, "Urban Bias Revisited," *Journal of Development Studies* (April 1984).

Highly relevant to urban bias are the rural–urban terms of trade as determined by government policies that influence the output and input prices for agriculture and the output and input prices for the urban industrial sector. The terms of trade for the rural sector are an indication of the profitability of agriculture and the purchasing power of agricultural income. To the extent that the types of government interventions reflect urban bias, the terms-of-trade level for the rural sector will be more unfavorable than a market-determined level in the absence of government intervention.

The following are instructive on the terms of trade manipulation and resource transfer from agriculture: G. T. Brown, "Agricultural Pricing Policies in Developing Countries," in *Distortion of Agricultural Incentives,* ed. Theodore W. Schultz (1978); A. K. Dixit, "Marketable Surplus and Dualistic Development," *Journal of Economic Theory* (August 1969); and R. K. Sah and J. E. Stiglitz, "The Economics of Price Scissors," *American Economic Review* (March 1984), and "Price Scissors and the Structure of the Economy," *Quarterly Journal of Economics* (February 1987). Also relevant is selection VIII.C.3.

EXHIBIT VIII.2. Rural and Urban Poverty in the 1980s

Region and Country	Rural Population as Percentage of Total	Rural Poor as Percentage of Total	Infant Mortality (per thousand live births)		Access to Safe Water (percentage of population)	
			Rural	Urban	Rural	Urban
Sub-Saharan Africa						
Côte d'Ivoire	57	86	121	70	10	30
Ghana	65	80	87	67	39	93
Kenya	80	96	59	57	21	61
Asia						
India	77	79	105	57	50	76
Indonesia	73	91	74	57	36	43
Malaysia	62	80	—	—	76	96
Philippines	60	67	55	42	54	49
Thailand	70	80	43	28	66	56
Latin America						
Guatemala	59	66	85	65	26	89
Mexico	31	37	79	29	51	79
Panama	50	59	28	22	63	100
Peru	44	52	101	54	17	73
Venezuela	15	20	—	—	80	80

Source: World Bank, *World Development Report 1990* (1990), p. 31.

Comment: The Rural–Urban Divide

Critics of the formulation of "urban bias" contend that the pattern of rural–urban relations is not the prime cause of slow economic growth or of continuing mass poverty. They further argue that the rural–urban dichotomy has been asked to bear too heavy a burden, that there is considerable overlap between and differentiation within the two sectors, and that the complexities of actual patterns of political action beyond an urban-biased coalition are ignored. See John Harriss and Mick Moore, eds., "Development and the Rural–Urban Divide" [special issue], *Journal of Development Studies* (April 1984). In this same issue, Michael Lipton defends his formulation of urban bias against the major criticisms.

Also relevant is Robert Bates's theory of urban bias for tropical Africa: *Markets and States in Tropical Africa* (1981). Compare also the symposium "Robert Bates, Rational Choice and the Political Economy of Development in Africa," *World Development* (June 1993).

Comment: Green Revolution

Studies of the green revolution include T. T. Poleman and D. K. Freebairn, eds., *Food, Population, and Employment: The Impact of the Green Revolution* (1973); Clive Bell, "The Acquisition of Agricultural Technology," *Journal of Development Studies* (October 1972); Bruce F. Johnston and J. Cownie, "The Seed-Fertilizer Revolution and Labor Force Absorption," *America Economic Review* (September 1969); John W. Mellor, *The New Economics of Growth* (1976); C. Wharton, "The Green Revolution: Cornucopia or Pandora's Box?" *Foreign Affairs* (April 1969); W. Ladejinsky, *Agrarian Reform as Unfinished Business* (1978); and Walter P. Falcon, "The Green Revolution: Second-Generation Problems," *American Journal of Agricultural Economics* (December 1978).

Radical political economists have argued that the green revolution's technology tends to be monopolized by large commercial farmers who have better access to new information and better financial capacity. A large profit resulting from the exclusive adoption of modern varieties of technology by large farmers stimulates them to enlarge their operational holdings by consolidating the farms of small nonadopters through purchase or tenant eviction. As a result, polarization of rural communities into large commercial farmers and landless proletariat is promoted. See Harry M. Cleaver, "The Contradictions of the Green Revolution," *American Economic Review* (May 1972); Ali M. S. Fatami, "The

Green Revolution: An Appraisal,'' *Monthly Review* (June 1972); Keith Griffin, *The Political Economy of Agrarian Change* (1974); and Richard Grabowski, "The Implications of an Induced Innovation Model," *Economic Development and Cultural Change* (July 1979), and "Reply," *Economic Development and Cultural Change* (October 1981).

The green revolution is also often compared with the "Japanese model" of increases in agricultural productivity associated with the use of improved seed varieties, fertilizers, implements, and other complementary inputs within the framework of Japan's small-scale farming system. For a comparative study of Japan's experience and what has been brought about by the green revolution, see Kazushi Ohkawa, *Differential Structure and Agriculture—Essays on Dualistic Growth* (1972).

Experience with the green revolution has been mixed, with differential growth rates of agriculture in different countries or in agriculture in different regions within the same country. This has been because of differences in the availability of inputs, extent of information, and attitude toward risks.

For an appraisal of the recent history of high-yielding cereals, see Michael Lipton with Richard Longhhurst, *New Seeds and Poor People* (1989). This study examines the impact of the new varieties on the poor and claims that the increases in food supplies have had little impact on the nutrition of the poor and on their poverty.

VIII.B. MICROECONOMICS OF THE RURAL SECTOR

VIII.B.1. Theory of Rural Organization*

There are a wide variety of institutional arrangements observed in different LDCs. One set that has been of long-standing interest to economists is sharecropping. Earlier views of sharecropping held that it was an inefficient form of economic organization: the worker received less than the value of his marginal product, and thus he had insufficient incentives to exert effort. The question was, how could such a seemingly inefficient form of economic organization have survived for so long (and why should it be such a prevalent form of economic organization at so many different places at different times?). For those who believe in even a modicum of economic rationality, some explanation had to be found.

One explanation that comes to mind is that peasants are more risk averse than landlords; if workers rented the land from the landlords, they would have to bear all of the risk. Though workers' risk aversion is undoubtedly of importance, it cannot be the entire explanation: there are alternative (and perhaps more effective) risk-sharing arrangements. In particular, in the wage system, the landlord bears all of the risk, the worker none. Any degree of risk sharing between the landlord and the worker can be attained by the worker dividing his time between working as a wage-laborer and working on his own or rented land.

The other central part of the explanation of sharecropping is that it provides an effective incentive system in the presence of costly supervision. Since in a wage system, the worker's compensation is not directly related to his output, the landlord must spend resources to ensure that the worker actual works. In a sharecropping system, since the worker's pay depends directly on his output, he has some incentives to work. The incentives may not be as strong as they would if he owned the land (since he receives, say, only half the product); but that is not the relevant alternative. Sharecropping thus represents a compromise between the rental system, in which incentives are "correct" but all the risk is borne by the worker, and the wage system, in which the landlord who is in a better position to bear risk, bears all the risk but in which effort can only be sustained through expenditures on supervision. This new view (Stiglitz, 1974) turns the traditional criticism of sharecropping on its head: it is precisely because of its incentive properties, relative to the relevant alternative, the wage system, that the sharecropping system is employed.

The contention that the rental system provides correct incentives is, however, not quite correct. The rental system provides correct incentives for effort decisions. But tenants make many decisions other than those involving effort; they make decisions concerning the choice of technique, the use of fertilizer, the timing of harvest, etc. These decisions affect the riskiness of the outcomes. For instance, many of the high-yielding seed varieties have a higher mean output, but a greater sensitivity to rainfall. Whenever there is a finite probability of default (that is, the tenant not paying the promised rent), then tenants may not have, with the rental system, the correct incentives with respect to these decisions. Of course, with unlimited liability, the worker could be made to bear all of the costs. But since the tenant might be unable to pay his rent even if he had undertaken all of the "right" decisions, and since it is often difficult to ascertain whether the individual took "unnecessary" risks, most societies are reluctant to grant unlimited liability, or to use extreme measures like debtor prisons, to ensure that individuals do not take unnecessary risks. Hence, in effect, part of the costs of risk taking by the tenant is borne by the landlord. With sharecropping, both the landlord and the tenant face the same risks.

Thus, sharecropping can be viewed as an institution which has developed in response to (a) risk aversion on the part of workers; (b) the limited ability (or desire) to force the tenant to pay back rents when he is clearly unable to do so; and (c) the limited ability to monitor the actions of the tenant (or the high costs of doing so).

*From Joseph E. Stiglitz, "The New Development Economics," *World Development* 14, no. 2 (1986): 258–61. Reprinted by permission from Elsevier Science Ltd., Oxford, England.

The general theory has been extended in a number of directions, only three of which I can discuss here: cost sharing, interlinkage, and technical change.

In many situations, there are other important inputs besides labor and land, such as bullocks or fertilizer. How should these inputs be paid for? Clearly, if the worker pays all of the costs, but receives only a fraction of the benefits, he will have an insufficient incentive to supply these other inputs. Cost sharing is a proposed remedy. If the worker receives 50 percent of the output, and pays 50 percent of the cost, it would appear that he has the correct incentives: both benefits and costs have been cut in half.

But in fact, though cost shares equal to output shares are common, they are far from universal. How do we explain these deviations from what seems both a simple, reasonable rule, and a rule which ensures economic efficiency? To find the answer, we again return to our general theoretical framework, which focuses on the role of imperfect information. First, it is clear that the landlord may want the tenant to supply more fertilizer than he would with a 50–50 rule, if increasing the fertilizer increases the marginal product of labor, and thus induces the worker to work harder. Remember, the central problem of the landlord is that he cannot directly control the actions of his worker; he must induce them to work hard. The reason that sharecropping was employed was to provide these additional incentives.

But if a cost-sharing arrangement can be implemented, it means that the expenditures can be monitored; and if the expenditures can be monitored, there is no necessity for engaging in cost sharing; rather the terms of the contract could simply specify the levels of various inputs. But workers typically have more information about current circumstances than the landlord (in the fashionable technical jargon, we say there is an asymmetry of information). A contract which specifies the level of inputs cannot adapt to the changing circumstances. Cost-sharing contracts provide the ability and incentives for these adaptations, and thus are more efficient contracts than contracts which simply specified the level of inputs.

Another aspect of economic organization in many LDCs is the interlinkage of markets: the landlord may also supply credit (and he may also supply food and inputs as well). How can we explain this interlinkage? Some have claimed that it is simply another way that landlords ex-ploit their workers. We shall comment later on these alternative explanations. For now, we simply note that our general theory can explain the prevalence of interlinkage (both under competitive and noncompetitive circumstances). We have repeatedly noted the problem of the landlord in inducing the worker both to work hard and to make the "correct" decisions from his point of view (with respect to choice of technique, etc.). Exactly analogous problems arise with respect to lenders. Their concern is that the borrower will default on the loan. The probability of a default depends in part on the actions taken by the borrower. The actions of the tenant-borrower thus affect both the lender and the landlord. Note too that the terms of the contract with the landlord will affect the lender, and vice versa: if the landlord can, for instance, reduce the probability of default by supplying more fertilizer, the lender is better off. The actions of the borrower (both with respect to the effort and the choice of technique) may be affected by the individual's indebtedness, so that the landlord's (expected) income may be affected by the amount (and terms) of indebtedness. There appear to be clear and possibly significant externalities between the actions of the landlord and the actions of the lender. Whenever there are such externalities, a natural market solution is to internalize the externality, and that is precisely what the interlinkage of markets does.

Thus, interlinkage is motivated by the desire for economic efficiency, not necessarily by the desire for further exploitation of the worker.

Interlinkage has, in turn, been linked to the incentives landlords have for resisting profitable innovations. Bhaduri has argued, for instance, that landlords-cum-creditors may resist innovations, because innovations reduce the demand for credit, and thus the income which they receive in their capacity as creditors. Braverman and Stiglitz have shown that there is no presumption that innovations result in a reduction in the demand for credit. Credit is used to smooth income across periods, and under quite plausible conditions, innovations may either increase or decrease the aggregate demand for credit. But they argue further that what happens to the demand for credit is beside the point.

The central question is simply whether the innovation moves the economically relevant utilities possibilities schedule outward or inward. The utilities possibilities schedule gives the maximum level of (expected) utility to one group (the landlord) given the level of (expected) utility of the other (the workers). The economically relevant utilities possibilities curve takes into account the information problems which have been the center of our discussion thus far, for instance, the fact that with sharecropping, individuals' incentives are different from what they would be with costless monitoring. The utilities possibilities schedule with costless monitoring might move one way, the economically relevant utilities possibilities schedule the other. Thus, for instance, there are innovations which, at each level of input, increase the output, but which, at the same time, exacerbate the incentives–monitoring problem. Such innovations would not be socially desirable. Landlords would resist such innovations, as well they should, though from an "engineering" point of view, such innovations might look desirable.

The consequences of interlinkage for the adoption of innovations, within this perspective, are ambiguous. There are innovations which would be adopted with interlinkage, but would not without it, and conversely; but the effect of the innovation on the demand for credit does not seem to play a central role.

Though the landlord correctly worries about the incentive–monitoring consequences of an innovation, one should not jump to the conclusions either that the landlords collectively make decisions which maximize their own welfare, or that the landlord always makes the socially efficient decision. The landlord, within a competitive environment, will adopt an innovation if at current prices (terms of contracts, etc.) it is profitable for him to do so. Of course, when all the landlords adopt the innovation, prices (terms of contracts) will change, and they may change in such a way that landlords are adversely affected. In a competitive environment landlords cannot resist innovations simply because it is disadvantageous to them to do so. (By contrast, if they are in a "monopoly" position, they will not wish to resist such innovations, since presumably they will be able to capture all the surplus associated with the innovation.)

But just as the market allocation is not constrained Pareto efficient (even assuming a perfectly competitive economy) whenever there are problems of moral hazard, so too the market decisions concerning innovation are not constrained Pareto efficient. (We use the term *constrained Pareto efficient* to remind us that we are accounting for the limitations on information; we have not assumed the government has any

information other than that possessed by private individuals.) Though in principle there exist government interventions which (accounting for the costs of information) could make everyone better off, whether such Pareto-improving interventions are likely to emerge from the political process remains a moot question.

Alternative Theories

In this section, I wish to present in summary form what I view to be the major competing approaches to understanding the organization of economic activity in the rural sector.

In many respects, I see my view as lying between other more extreme views. In one, the peasant is viewed as rational, working in an environment with reasonably complete information and complete and competitive markets. In this view, then, the differences between LDCs and more developed countries lies not so much in the difference between sophisticated, maximizing farmers and uneducated rule-bound peasants, as it does in differences in the economic environments, the goods produced by these economies, their endowments, and how their endowments are used to produce goods. In this view, sharecropping is a rational response to the problems of risk sharing; but there is less concern about the incentive problems than I have expressed; with perfect information and perfect enforceability of contracts, the sharecropping contract can enforce the desired level of labor supply and the choice of technique which is efficient. These theories have had little to say about some of the other phenomena which I have discussed: interlinkage, technical change, cost sharing. Interlinkage might be explained in terms of the advantages in transactions costs, but if transactions costs were central, one should only have observed simple cost-sharing rules (with cost share equalling output share).

By contrast, there are those who view the peasant as irrational, with his behavior dictated by customs and institutions which may have served a useful function at some previous time but no longer do so. This approach (which I shall refer to, somewhat loosely, as the institutional–historical approach) may attempt to describe the kinds of LDCs in which there is sharecropping, interlinkage, or cost sharing. It may attempt to relate current practices to earlier practices. In particular, the institutional–historical approach may identify particular historical events which lead to the establishment of the sharecropping system, or to the development of the credit system. But this leaves largely unanswered the question of why so many LDCs developed similar institutional structures, or why in some countries cost shares equal output shares, while in others the two differ. More fundamentally, a theory must explain how earlier practices developed; and to provide an explanation of these, one has to have recourse to one of the other theories. Thus, by itself, the institutional–historical approach is incomplete.

Still a third view emphasizes the departures from competitiveness in the rural sector, and the consequent ability of the landlords to exploit the workers. In some cases, workers are tied to their land; legal constraints may put the landlord in a position to exploit the worker. But in the absence of these legal constraints, one has to explain how the landlords exercise their allegedly coercive powers. In many LDCs there is a well-developed labor market. Many landlords need laborers at harvest time and at planting time. The worker chooses for whom he will work. It is important to recognize that the exploitation hypothesis fails to explain the mechanisms by which, in situations where there are many landlords, they exercise their exploitative power. More generally, it fails to explain variations in the degree of exploitation over time and across countries. The fact that wages are low is not necessarily evidence of exploitation: the competitive market will yield low wages when the value of the marginal product of labor is low.

The exploitation hypothesis also fails to explain the detailed structure of rural organization: why cost shares are the way they are, or why (or how) landlords who can exploit their workers use the credit market to gain further exploitative capacity.

There may be some grain of truth in all these approaches. Important instances of currently dysfunctional institutions and customs can clearly be identified. Institutional structures clearly to not adapt instantaneously to changed circumstances. Yet, as social scientists, our objective is to identify the systematical components, the regularities of social behavior, to look for general principles underlying a variety of phenomena. It is useful to describe the institutions found in the rural sector of LDCs, but description is not enough.

Therefore, I view the rationality hypothesis as a convenient starting point, a simple and general principle with which to understand economic behavior. Important instances of departures from rationality may well be observed. As social scientists, our objective is to look for *systematic* departures. Some systematic departures have been noted, for instance in the work of Tversky, in individuals' judgments of probabilities, particularly of small probability events; but as Binswanger's 1978 study has noted, departures from the theory appear less important in "important" decisions than in less important decisions. Many of the seeming departures from "rationality" that have been noted can be interpreted as "rational" decision-making in the presence of imperfect information.

I also view the competitiveness hypothesis as a convenient starting point. Many of the central phenomena of interest can be explained without recourse to the exploitation hypothesis. Some degree of imperfect competition is not inconsistent with the imperfect information paradigm: the imperfect information paradigm provides part of the explanation for the absence of perfect competition; it can help identify situations where the landlords may be in a better position to exploit the workers. Moreover, to the extent that imperfect information limits the extent to which even a monopoly landlord can extract surplus from his workers, the imperfect information paradigm can provide insights into how he can increase his monopoly profits. The theory of interlinkage we have developed can thus be applied to the behavior of a monopolist landlord.

There is one other approach that has received some attention that is, in fact, closely related to the one I have advocated: the transactions cost approach, which attempts to explicate economic relations by focusing on transactions costs. Information costs are an important part of transactions costs (though information problems arise in other contexts as well). My reservations concerning the transactions cost approach lie in its lack of specificity: while the information paradigm provides a well-defined structure which allows one to derive clear propositions concerning, for instance, the design of contracts, the transactions cost paradigm does not. Thus, the transactions cost approach might provide some insight into why cost sharing is employed, but not into the terms of the cost-sharing agreement. The transactions cost paradigm might say that economies of scope provide an explanation for why the landlord also supplies credit, but it does not provide insights into when the landlord-cum-creditor would subsidize credit, or when he would "tax" it. Moreover, while the information paradigm identifies parameters which affect the magnitude of the externalities between land-lords and creditors, and thus enables, in princi-ple, the identification of circumstances under which interlinkage is more likely to be observed, the transactions cost paradigm can do little more than to say that there are circumstances in which the diseconomies of scope exceed the econo-mies, and in these circumstances there will not be interlinkage.

References

Bhaduri, A. (1973). "Agricultural Backward-ness Under Semi-Feudalism." *Economic Journal* (March): 120–37.

Binswanger, H. P. (1978b). "Attitudes Towards Risk: Implications and Psychological The-ories of an Experiment in Rural India." Yale University Economic Growth Center DP 286.

Braverman, A., and J. E. Stiglitz (1982). "Sharecropping and the Interlinking of Agrarian Markets." *American Economic Review* (September): 695–715.

Stiglitz, J. E. (1974). "Alternative Theories of Wage Determination and Unemployment in LDCs: The Labor Turnover Model. *Quarterly Journal of Economics* 87 (May): 194–227.

Tversky, A. (1969). "Intransitivity of Prefer-ences." Psychological Review 76: 31–48.

VIII.B.2. Labor Contractual Arrangements*

In a world of perfect markets for all factors of production (including credit and insurance), a person's annual income would simply represent the employment of his or her factor endowments valued at the market rate per unit. In such a world, the initial distribution of endowments among people—for given tastes and aggregate quantities of each factor—would uniquely de-termine the distribution of income among peo-ple. Moreover, production—total output—would be not only maximal but unrelated to the distribution of factor ownership. Production techniques would be identical on all farms fac-ing the same market environment and operating the same quality of land; for example, because output and employment per acre would be un-related to farm size, barring scale economies, productive efficiency could not be improved by a rearrangement of factor uses or distributions. To explain labor earnings in a world of perfect markets with a given distribution of endow-ments requires that one explain the returns to each factor (wage rates, rent), a task for which the competitive supply-demand model has proved a powerful tool. The failure of one or

more markets, however, would have important implications for the distribution of earnings and productive efficiency and would probably mean that more complex models would be required to understand earnings determination. An im-portant, unresolved question is whether such models can outpredict the simpler, competitive models when only some markets are imperfect or absent.

Attention to market failure, however, is im-portant not only for understanding the de-termination of earnings and the achievement of productive efficiency. It may also help us to un-derstand the existence of and changes in the la-bor market's many and diverse institutional ar-rangements—different types of contracts and labor recruitment strategies and the interlinking of labor and one or more factors of production within one transaction. Indeed, because of the general nonindependence, or interrelatedness, of all factor markets, market failures anywhere in the rural sector may have a significant effect on labor market earnings or arrangements even if the market for labor operates perfectly. In these circumstances, explaining earnings requires in-formation beyond the determination of wages and labor supply.

In the rural economy, it is a fact that some labor is combined with land, not by the tem-porary sale of labor services but by the tem-porary acquisition of land. It is clear that the

*From Hans P. Binswanger and Mark R. Rosenzweig, *Contractual Arrangements, Employment and Wages in Ru-ral Labor Markets: A Critical Review*, Agricultural Devel-opment Council, 1981, pp. 3–4, 21–27. Reprinted by per-mission.

terms and arrangements associated with the market for land have a significant effect on the earnings of rural households and the production of aggregate output. . . . [This raises] two primary issues: First, what are the efficiency characteristics of a contract that provides laborers with a share of total agricultural output, an important contractual arrangement in the rural economy? Second, how do the welfare levels or earnings of such sharecroppers compare with those of laborers who work only for wages—that is, what determines the contractual terms?

Recent Tenancy Models

If the sales market for land is absent or involves very high transaction costs, landowners can hire all cooperating factors of production, including bullocks and management, in quantities that are optimal for their own land. Landowners can then rent out any nonland factors owned that are in excess of these optimal quantities. Productive efficiency—that is, equal factor ratios on all farms with land of equal quality—can still be achieved. Thus the absence of a sales market for land is not sufficient to force the use of tenancy. However, the institution of tenancy and the market for tenancies do substitute for the sales market. When there are no scale economies, at least one other factor market must be absent before the temporary rental of land becomes a necessary tool to achieve the most efficient factor ratios for all factors of production and all agents. The absent or incomplete markets (which involve high risks or high transaction costs) may be those for insurance, family labor, bullocks, or managerial skills. . . .

Cheung's (1968, 1969) work set the stage for the recent sharecropping literature in terms of the major reasons for share tenancy and the major issues to be addressed. His work both attacked the negative efficiency (incentive) implication of sharecropping and broadened the scope of inquiry of the sharecropping literature to include discussion of the manner in which size of tenancy and share of crop are determined. All writers from Cheung onward have regarded both tenancy size and share level as endogenous to a particular model, while they have taken the wage rate as exogenously given. Contractual terms, but not the wage rate, are thus determined by economic forces, and the equilibrium solution to the contract choice problem involves maximization by both landlord and worker. The worker's equilibrium requires that "of the set of

contracts available in the economy, there [exist] none which the individual worker prefers to the one which he has" (Stiglitz, 1974, p. 222). And landlord equilibrium implies that "there exists no subset [of the available contracts] which the landlord prefers to the subset which he employs" (ibid.).

Cheung also assigned *risk* and *risk aversion* a much larger role in determining share tenancy than others have accorded them. He did not include them, however, in his formal model. Clearly, under a wage labor system all the risks of cultivation are borne by the owner-cultivator; owner-cultivator income is the residual after payment of production costs at fixed wages. Under a fixed-rate tenancy, tenants bear all the risk since their income is the residual after payment of a fixed rent. Under share tenancy, however, the risk is divided between tenant and owner in proportion to the crop share of each.

As Jaynes (1979) has shown, however, Cheung's model achieves its efficiency outcome because it simply assumes away two problems—the negative incentives of sharing and the difficulty of monitoring effort. If these problems did not exist, we would not observe share tenancy. Thus Cheung must indeed introduce risk, risk aversion, and transaction costs in order to explain the existence of the contracts his formal model explores under conditions in which such sources of market imperfections do not exist.

With respect to risk aversion motivation for sharecropping, Newbery (1975) and Reid (1976) have shown that, with constant returns to scale, sharecropping provides no risk-sharing benefits that landlord and worker could not achieve by dividing a plot of land "into two subplots, one of which is rented out at a fixed rental R and the other is operated by the landlord who hires labor at a wage W" (Newbery and Stiglitz, 1979, p. 314). Thus a model in the Cheungian tradition— that is, one without problems of worker incentives—does not explain the existence of share tenancy, even in the presence of production risk and risk aversion. Sharecropping can, however, be a means of risk avoidance under more complex characterizations of risk. Newbery and Stiglitz (1979) have demonstrated that with a second independent source of risk, such as wage rate risk in the labor market, share contracts are superior to a mixture of wage and fixed-rent contracts. If there are no incentive (monitoring) problems or economies of scale but there are multiple sources of risk, the sharecropping contract acts as the necessary instrument to achieve productive efficiency; that is, it prevents rather than creates an inefficient allocation of resources.

Another class of tenancy models focuses on the costliness of labor supervision as a cause of sharecropping—the *Marshallian inefficiency.* One of Stiglitz's (1974) models assumes costly supervision: the landlord sets the size of the tenancy just like the share, taking into account the impact of tenancy size on the tenant's input decision. The landlord can prevent the tenant from renting any other land or from working for wages, or he can include these restrictions in the contract and monitor and enforce them. The landlord thus has an extra control instrument and can, by means of maximization, control the contractual terms in such a way as to limit the tenant to his or her reservation utility—that is, the wage rate. Of course, given the effort monitoring problem, productive efficiency cannot be achieved in this model.

Braverman and Srinivasan (1979) have extended the Stiglitz model of costly supervision so as to allow tenant and landlord to engage in a simultaneous share-cum-credit contract, the credit being used for the tenant's consumption. Such a tied contract becomes superior to an untied contract if the landlord has access to credit from third parties at lower rates of interest than the tenant can obtain. The landlord sets four contractual terms: crop share, tenancy size, rate of interest to be charged the tenant, and proportion of credit requirements that the tenant borrows from the landlord. Given that the landlord has two extra instruments available, the landlord can almost always hold the tenant to the utility level the latter would obtain as a wage laborer. As a result, policies like tenancy reform or provision of credit to tenants at lower than market rates cannot improve the tenant's utility level. Nothing less than land redistribution, intervention in several markets, or rising alternative wage levels can improve tenants' welfare.

In the models discussed, costly supervision arises because of imperfect information. Information is asymmetrically distributed between landlord and tenant because only the tenant can know how much effort he or she will provide; the landlord cannot know this at sufficiently low cost. And a central planner, who shares the landlord's lack of information, cannot improve on the existing allocation. Such improvement can be achieved only if the central planner has cheaper means of monitoring effort than the landlord, which, in agriculture, is not likely. Al-

ternatively, the central planner will have to redistribute land to tenants in order to overcome their inability to buy land in the land market, which inability has led to their status as tenants. Such a policy, however, will also improve efficiency in a decentralized economy. As long as the underlying constraints on information or land transfer remain in place, the share tenancy equilibrium achieved is optimal with respect to these constraints; that is, it is a second best optimum, relative to the set of informational constraints assumed in the model. This point is an important recurrent theme in the literature.

A problem that the models we have discussed so far fail to address explicitly is the coexistence in the same region of all forms of contracts: owner cultivation, share contracts, and fixed rent contracts. Moreover, *tenancy ladders* appear to be important in both developed and developing countries: workers first become sharecroppers, then fixed-rent tenants, and finally acquire land of their own.

There are three explanations for the coexistence of tenurial contractural arrangements: (1) differences in risk aversion, (2) screening of workers of different quality, and (3) market imperfections for inputs other than labor. But differential risk aversion cannot account for the tenancy ladder, since there is little reason to expect the same person to become completely risk neutral as he or she becomes older, even if the person accumulates assets. It must be recognized, therefore, that workers differ in other respects, such as ability, management skills, and capital endowments.

If productivity per hour of work differs among otherwise homogeneous workers but the productivity differences are known only to the workers and cannot be observed by the landlord without cost, landowners or workers face a screening cost. In this case, Hallagan (1978) and, independently, Newbery and Stiglitz (1979) have shown that the choice of contract conveys information about workers' perception of their abilities. "Individuals who believe they are most productive [as workers] will choose the rental contract; individuals who believe they are very unproductive will choose the wage contract and those in between will choose the share contract" (Newbery and Stiglitz, 1979, p. 323). Each class of workers prefers its respective contract. Utility levels for the more able workers are higher than the levels they could achieve in a labor market without screening. Again, since information is asymmetrically distributed between landlord and workers, productive efficiency cannot be achieved. The implicit screening by means of contract choice again represents a second best improvement in efficiency over the situation without tenancy contracts. This model leads to coexistence of contracts but not to a tenancy ladder unless workers move to higher efficiency classes as they grow older.

The clearest route to the tenancy ladder, the social differentiation of laborers, and different types of tenants is through absent markets or imperfect markets for inputs other than labor.

References

Braverman, Avishay, and T. N. Srinivasan. Conference Paper, "Agrarian Reforms in Developing Rural Economies Characterized by Interlinked Credit and Tenancy Markets," 1979.

Cheung, S. N. S. *The Theory of Share Tenancy* (Chicago: University of Chicago Press, 1969).

Cheung, S. N. S. "Private Property Rights and Sharecropping," *Journal of Political Economy*, Vol. 76, 1968, pp. 1117–1122.

Hallagan, W. "Self-selection by Contractual Choice and the Theory of Sharecropping," *Bell Journal of Economics*, Vol. 9, 1978, pp. 344–54.

Jaynes, Gerald D. Conference Paper, "Economic Theory and Land Tenure," 1979.

Newbery, D. M. G. "The Choice of Rental Contracts in Peasant Agriculture" in Lloyd G. Reynolds (ed.), *Agriculture in Development Theory* (New Haven: Yale University Press, 1975).

Newbery, D. M. G., and J. E. Stiglitz. "Sharecropping, Risk Sharing and the Importance of Imperfect Information" in James A. Roumasset, Jean Marc Boussard, and Inderjit Singh (eds.), *Risk, Uncertainty, and Agricultural Development* (College, Laguna, Philippines and New York: Southeast Asian Regional Center for Graduate Study and Research in Agriculture and Agricultural Development Council, 1979).

Reid, Joseph D., Jr. "Sharecropping and Agricultural Uncertainty," *Economic Development and Cultural Change*, Vol. 24, 1976, pp. 549–76.

Stiglitz, Joseph E. "Incentives and Risk Sharing in Agriculture," *Review of Economic Studies*, Vol. 41, 1974, 209–56.

Comment: Contractual Choice Models

The macro dual-economy models with labor surplus (as discussed in Chapter III) take land distribution as exogenously given and are concerned with long-term trends of real rural wages. These models, however, do not analyze behavioral and institutional features of the rural sector. In contrast, the recent formulations of contractual choice theories of rural markets allow for a land-rental or -sale market and focus on the principles of a supply–demand, competitive model. They take the wage rate as exogenously given, while concentrating on land- and credit-market transactions. The contractual choice models have the merits of clarifying the efficiency and equity implications of contracts and of identifying the causes of the market imperfections that lead to the contracts. They also emphasize the need to analyze all the major markets—land, labor, credit—as being interlocking factor markets. Frequently, a landlord and tenant enter into several transactions at the same time—land renting, wage-labor hiring, production and consumption credit, cost sharing of purchased inputs, marketing of output—as part of the interlinked contact encompassing several markets. Policy intervention must recognize the interrelatedness of the rural factor markets.

The characteristics of land and labor contracts in agrarian economies help to explain why the decentralized system of small-scale family firms continues to be the dominant mode of production, rather than the emergence of hierarchical internal organizations such as the industrial firm. Contractual arrangements among independent farm-operators, laborers, and landlords are substituted for the large internal organizations. These arrangements are analyzed by Yujiro Hayami and Keijiro Otsuka, *The Economics of Contract Choice* (1993)—a study that aims for a "general theory of agrarian contracts," in which land tenancy and labor employment are modeled together as substitutes along a continuous spectrum of contract choice. The theory is applicable to the mode of peasant production, but not to large-scale farms or plantations specializing in the export of tropical cash crops.

A number of studies attempt to model institutions in agrarian economies—particularly the economics of sharecropping and the phenomena of interlocking factor markets. Of special interest are P. K. Bardhan and T. N. Srinivasan, "Cropsharing Tenancy in Agriculture," *American Economic Review*

(March 1971); Clive Bell, "Alternative Theories of Sharecropping," *Journal of Development Studies* (July 1977); D. M. G. Newbery, "Risk-Sharing, Sharecropping, and Uncertain Labor Markets," *Review of Economic Studies* (October 1977); A. Braverman and T. N. Srinivasan, "Credit and Sharecropping in Agrarian Societies," *Journal of Development Economics* (December 1981); A. Braverman and J. E. Stiglitz, "Sharecropping and the Interlinking of Agrarian Markets," *American Economic Review* (September 1982); Hans P. Binswanger and Mark R. Rosenzweig, *Contractual Arrangements, Employment, and Wages in Rural Labor Markets in Asia* (1984); and P. K. Bardhan, ed., *The Economic Theory of Agrarian Institutions* (1989).

VIII.B.3. Land Tenure*

If we compare the different forms of land tenure, three distinct patterns emerge, and we can say that from the standpoint of economic analysis there are really three distinct problems of reform. We can leave out some land systems altogether as irrelevant to our subject—the peasant systems, in which land ownership is more or less equally distributed, and communal tenure systems, in which the land is communally owned (mainly prevalent in Africa). These may need other types of reform—reforms of the agrarian structure—but they do not need redistribution of ownership. We can concentrate on the land systems in which the large estate is the predominant form of tenure.

We must, however, distinguish sharply between the different types of large estate. One of the great difficulties in the study of this subject is that we have no accepted vocabulary. Much confusion arises from lack of precise terminology. "Large estate" itself is an ambiguous term, referring to at least three different forms of tenure and three different types of economic organisation. The three types are:

1. The type of ownership characteristic of Asian countries, in which the land holding is only a property and not a large farm or large producing unit. The property is leased in small units to tenant cultivators, either on the basis of money rent or on a basis of sharecropping rents.
2. The large estate, characteristic of South European countries and of Latin America, which is both a large property and a large enterprise.

This type of estate is managed by salaried officials and worked by labourers and people of indeterminate status, squatters or share-croppers. Estates of this kind are usually extensively cultivated, or used as cattle ranges. We may call them latifundia, since this is the term used in the countries where they prevail; they are the direct descendants of the slave-tilled ranches of the Roman Empire.

3. Plantation estates. These are also both large properties and large enterprises. They are usually owned by a company with foreign capital and foreign management, though estates of a plantation type may also be found in private ownership. The methods of cultivation are usually intensive.

Many countries have agrarian structures which include estates of two or even three of these types. The land system of Egypt in certain features resembles the Asian form of ownership, while in other features it is a plantation system.

These forms of ownership and enterprise have very little in common with the types of large-scale farming found in advanced countries, that is, in countries with an industrialised economy and commercialised agriculture. The Asian system is found principally in subsistence economies, while latifundia and plantations produce mainly for export.

From the standpoint of economic analysis, the most obvious feature of all these types of ownership is the existence of an institutional monopoly. In Asian countries, where demographic pressure is high, the level of rents is determined not by the fertility of the land, but by the fertility of human beings. Land is a scarce factor of production, and would command a high price in terms of its produce, whatever the system of land tenure. The existence of institutional monopoly allows the landowner to raise rents to

---

*From Doreen Warriner, *Land Reform and Economic Development,* National Bank of Egypt Fiftieth Anniversary Commemoration Lectures, Cairo, 1955, Lecture II. (Corrected version reprinted in Carl Eicher and Lawrence Witt [eds.], *Agriculture in Economic Development,* New York, McGraw-Hill, 1964, pp. 280–90.) Reprinted by permission.

a still higher level. In latifundian systems and in plantation systems, the estate owner is a monopoly buyer of labour, controlling the use of land rather than its price, and he uses his monopoly power to keep wages low.

The main economic argument for land reform is the need for securing a more equal distribution of income by eliminating these monopoly elements. In the first case the aim is to reduce the price for the use of land, that is, a reduction in rents, and in the second case, the aim is to subdivide big holdings and secure a fuller use of land, an increased demand for labour, and higher wages for the farm worker.

But, it may be objected, will not this redistribution of ownership reduce productivity by dividing up efficient large estates? If we wish to use this argument, we must consider in what sense these estates are to be regarded as efficient. The theory of the firm is always difficult to apply in agriculture, and as far as the under-developed countries are concerned, it seems to have very limited application.

The argument that the division of large agricultural enterprises will cause a decline in productivity is true on two assumptions: (1) that there is competition between the factors of production and (2) that there are economies of large scale production. These assumptions are generally valid in industrialised countries. In England, for example, a large farm has generally become large because it is a more efficient producer, that is, it produces at lower costs; it can compete more effectively for the factors of production and combine them more efficiently, using more capital and using it more fully; it can also use more efficient management and more specialised labour. In such conditions there is a presumption that the size of farms is more or less adjusted to an optimum scale of output for certain types of farming. This optimum scale of output is difficult to define precisely, and in practice means the minimum area needed to utilise power-driven machinery. . . .

When we try to apply this argument about the scale of production to the under-developed countries, we shall find that over a very wide range of conditions it has no validity at all. In Asian land system, large estates are not large producing units. Land reform in such systems simply means the transfer of ownership from the landowner to the cultivator of the existing small holding. The size of the farm is not affected, for there are no large farms. When the Governments of India and Pakistan speak of "uneconomic farms," they mean farms which fall below a subsistence minimum, not below a technical optimum. Nor does the argument about efficient large estates apply generally to latifundian systems. The haciendas in Mexico and many of the latifundia in Southern Italy were not efficient large estates on any standard. They wasted both land and labour.

So generally speaking, the argument about "efficient large estates" does not seem to apply to the first type or the second type of estates which we have distinguished. It does seem to apply to plantation estates which use intensive methods of cultivation and modern methods. Every plantation system is a special case. Where there is reason to believe that sub-division of the estate would lead to a decline in production, then the monopoly effect on labour must be tackled by a policy for raising wages, and taxing profits to secure reinvestment in other types of farming producing for local needs. Or the estate may be divided with safeguards for maintaining efficiency, as under the Egyptian Land Reform. . . .

Several other arguments used against land reform are false because they are based on projections of conditions in advanced countries, and do not take these basic differences into account. One argument frequently encountered in international discussions is that because tenancy works very well in England there can be no reason for Asian countries to abolish tenancy by redistribution of ownership: what they need is legislation to improve the security of tenure for tenants. This argument overlooks the monopoly influence in Asian countries. It is true that tenancy works well in England, because the conditions of tenancy are regulated by law, and also because land is only one of the many forms of holding wealth. If a landowner attempts to take too high a rent, the tenant will prefer to invest his capital in other ways. But in Asian conditions tenancy laws will never suffice to counteract the effects of monopoly ownership.

Another argument of this kind is that there is no need for expropriation by compulsion. This argument runs as follows: "If governments wish to encourage ownership, they can do this by giving tenants special credit facilities enabling them to buy their holdings. In Switzerland (or Denmark or Sweden) the land system has evolved itself by gradual adjustment to modern conditions, and Asian countries should therefore adjust their systems gradually, without drastic legislation to expropriate owners of land." The logical fallacy in this argument is obvious. In advanced countries, an improvement in the economic position of agriculture will enable the tenant to buy his land, and special credit facilities can encourage the acquisition of ownership. In the United States, the proportion of ownership to tenancy rises when agriculture is prosperous, and special legislation aids farm purchase. In European countries, particularly in Scandinavia, governments have helped tenants to become owners by giving them easy credit terms. But in Asian countries, the market price of land is too high in terms of what it produces to allow the tenant to purchase his land. If agriculture becomes more prosperous, either as a result of higher prices or better harvests, the share-cropping tenant will not be able to buy his holding, because the landlord benefits equally from the increased income, and the tenant's position in relation to the landlord has not improved. There is no price which the tenant can afford to pay which the landlord will be willing to accept. If the tenant is to acquire ownership, the price of land must be fixed at a level which he can pay, and this will inevitably be much lower than the market value of the land. All land reforms involve expropriation to some extent for this reason.

In economic terms, there can be no ground for paying compensation at all, since the existing prices of land are monopoly prices. The price that is actually fixed in reform legislation is determined by political bargaining power.

We can conclude therefore that the existence of institutional monopoly creates a strong argument for land reform on the ground of equalizing incomes. We can conclude that in Asian systems and in latifundian systems the redistribution of ownership will not have adverse effects on production through the division of efficient large units, though in plantation systems sub-division may have bad effects, and other ways of equalizing incomes may have to be used.

These arguments, however, tell us nothing about the positive effects of reform on development. They are negative arguments which show it will not do harm. If we are to consider the effects on economic development, this is not enough, and it is the investment aspect that must be considered.

The general economic argument for land reform as distinct from the social argument for more equality is that these systems of ownership give rise to large incomes which are not reinvested in production. They give rise also to social attitudes inimical to investment. Landowners spend conspicuously; buy more land; or invest in urban house property; or lend at extortionate rates of interest to cultivators for nonproductive purposes. This argument applies with great force to Asian tenancy systems and to latifundian systems. It does not apply generally to plantation systems. These may have bad social consequences, but whatever their defects may be, failure to invest productively is not one of them, or not generally one. (There are exceptions where plantations keep land out of cultivation, and these systems cause trouble.)

In general, the land systems of Asia and Latin America are strong deterrents to investment and aggravate the shortage of capital by draining capital from agriculture. They undervalue the future. The land owners' preference for land as a form of holding wealth can be explained simply as a result of the secure and high return on capital which results from institutional monopoly. . . .

The crucial question is whether land reform—the change to small ownership—will give better results in the future. Can it promote more investment? . . .

All we can say as to the investment effect is that results depend mainly on what can be done to give inducements to invest, through special credit facilities and special forms of village organisation. We cannot say that reform will *cause* more investment: but we can certainly say that it is a condition, for without more income in the hands of the cultivator, no investment programme for agriculture is likely to have much effect.

Can we say anything about the production effects of reform, when there is actually sub-division of the land?

Here too we can only say that results will depend on how far the new owners can intensify farming, either by the use of more labour on the land, or by the use of more labour and more capital. . . .

Comment: Land Reform

The case for a small-farm or reformed agricultural system claims several advantages—more employment, more equitable distribution of income, and a wider home market for the manufacturing sector. But the case for smallholdings must also address itself to other requirements. It is essential to consider the effects of land reform on agricultural production, both for exports and for increasing food production. Capital formation is also necessary in both agricultural and industrial sectors. And efficiency must be achieved, as well as employment and equity.

The economic gains to be had from a radical modification of land-tenure patterns appear to be greatest during periods when rapid technical changes are opening up new production possibilities that are inhibited by existing tenure relationships. See Yujiro Hayami and Vernon W. Ruttan, *Agricultural Development: An International Perspective* (1971). In view of the technical revolution in grain production and the explosive rate of growth in the agricultural labor force, the authors conclude that the payoff to tenure reforms, involving a shift from share tenure, plantation, and collective tenure systems to smallholder owner-operator systems, may be greatly increased in the future.

On the need for reform in connection with the development of agriculture, see Peter Dorner, *Land Reform and Economic Development* (1972); Louis J. Walinsky, ed., *Agrarian Reform as Unfinished Business* (1977); Albert Berry and William Cline, *Agrarian Structure and Productivity in Developing Countries* (1979); and Alain de Janvry, "The Role of Land Reform in Economic Development," *American Journal of Agricultural Economics* (May 1981).

VIII.B.4. Rural Credit Markets*

Until recently conventional wisdom held that imposing low ceilings on interest rates and allocating massive amounts of credit to rural financial markets would speed rural development and improve income distribution. But by and large policies directed along these lines have failed. Indeed, most often they have made matters worse. Low interest rate ceilings provide income transfers to loan recipients, distorting the real price ratio of investment opportunities by undervaluing the real cost of capital in different sectors. To the standard cost of distorted resource allocation, add the specific costs and consequences of implementing credit programs in rural financial markets for the full measure of impact. The record overwhelmingly shows credit programs' objectives have not been met.

These credit policy failures can be attributed to basic flaws intrinsic to formal rural credit markets out of which arise persistent problems as described in Table 1.

Informal lending was once the only form credit took in rural settings. Evidence suggests that as farm size increases, private credit sources, village moneylenders and pawnbrokers, chit funds with an array of implicit interest rates, and friends or relatives grow less important than banks. With the implementation of development plans, official lending complements but clearly does not supersede informal sources.

Sample surveys supply the information on the extent of informal lending practices. They indicate that its volume is far greater than that of organized institutions. It is characterized by a much shorter processing time, better screening techniques or enforcement devices (noted in the lower default rate), and higher interest rates, with a median around 50 percent and a variance much higher than institutionalized credit rate.

The lower delinquency rates reported in informal credit sources are to a large extent due to better assessment of creditworthiness, ability to exert social pressure for repayment, and the frequent practice of tying (interlinking) credit contracts with other input or output contracts. Documentation of the use and characteristics of the latter practice is quite extensive. Sharecropping contracts are quite often interlinked with credit contracts. . . . Credit contracts between landlords and tenants are often in the form of production loans and tied to the purchase of fertilizer, seeds, and other forms of capital with different tenants paying different interest rates on their loans. These interlinkage practices have been viewed as a way to address the adverse selection problem and the moral hazard problem indigenous to these markets.

Two approaches have been put forward in the past to explain why landlords (employers) transact with their tenants (workers) in credit. They are: (1) reduction of transaction costs and (2) exploitation of weaker agents by more powerful ones. Though both have merits under certain cir-

*From A. Braverman and J. L. Gausch, "Rural Credit Markets and Institutions in Developing Countries: Lessons for Policy Analysis from Practice and Modern Theory," *World Development*, Vol. 14, Nos. 10/11 (October/November 1986), pp. 1253–55, 1257, 1260–62. Reprinted by permission from Elsevier Science Ltd., Oxford, England.

TABLE 1. Characteristics of Rural Financial Markets

Basic Flaws

Weakness of competitive forces.

Weak legal enforcement of contracts.

Corruption and lack of accountability in institutions, patronage and income transfer practices, which are partly due to poorly designed or non-existent incentive mechanisms to induce accountability on both sides of the market.

Significant information problems and uncertainty regarding the ability of borrowers to meet future loan obligations.

Inability to monitor the use of funds.

Lack of collateral often due to land tenure arrangements or ill-defined property rights (e.g. parts of Africa).

Lack of coherent financial savings mobilization program.

Higher opportunity cost of capital in other sectors because of interest rate ceilings.

Persistent Problems

Credit loans to wealthy farmers, small farmers rationed out of the credit market.

Loans for agricultural programs diverted to non-agricultural uses.

Credit policies that encourage consumption and discourage savings.

The term structure of agricultural loans contracts or fails to expand.

Low adoption rates of cost-saving technologies in agriculture and in financial services.

Low recovery rate.

Significant distortions in the optimal allocation of resources across markets.

Extensive use of interlinking credit contracts with labor and land contracts.

---

cumstances, they fail to explain such interlinkages under a wider range of circumstances. In particular, they do not pay attention to the particular information structure. Even though information costs are part of the transaction cost, it is essential to specify them in order to explain the details of the contractual equilibrium, for example, why some landlords may subsidize tenants' credit while others charge their tenants higher interest rates. The exploitation theory fails to explain why monopolist landlords choosing tenants (workers) from a pool of the "reserve army of the unemployed" need any extra instrument (credit) for exploitation beyond the rental (tenant) or wage (worker) contract.

The modern theory of contractual equilibrium under imperfect information focuses on the moral hazard and adverse selection features commonly found in rural developing economies. The "moral hazard" features as pertaining to the interlinking credit with labor and land contracts are:

a. Individuals are not paid on the basis of their input (effort) in general since this is not observable and they often do not rent land for a fixed sum since that imposes too much risk on them. Hence the contractual arrangements involve at least some form of sharecropping; as a result, tenants do not obtain the full marginal product of their efforts.

b. The landlord cannot completely specify the actions to be taken by the tenant: the tenant has considerable discretion both with respect to the allocation and level of effort, and the choice of production technique. Some of these decisions may be easily monitored by the landlord, but there are others, perhaps equally important, for which the cost of monitoring would be very high.

The tenant's considerable discretion over his own actions combined with their significant impact on the landlord's expected profits—have some further implications. In particular, the landlord has an incentive to *induce* tenants to behave as he wishes. This is attempted through influencing the amount and terms of credit the tenant borrows and by the goods he can purchase and the prices he pays.

The behavior affected includes the effort supplied by the tenant and the choice of technique (risk distribution) applied by him. For instance, if the landlord makes credit less expensive, under reasonable conditions the tenant will be induced to borrow more. If there are severe penalties associated with default (e.g., bonded labor), the tenant will then need to work harder to avoid this contingency.

Similarly the landlord may observe that his tenants are employing techniques of production which are too safe; the landlord's income might be increased if his tenants were willing to employ techniques with higher means and higher variances. He may note that his tenants are acting in a particularly risk-averse manner because of the consequences of defaulting on outstanding loans. To change their behavior, the landlord may require that his tenants only borrow from him. He may charge them interest above the market rate in order to induce them to limit their borrowing, and at the same time he may offer a tenancy contract which is much more attractive in some other dimensions. Such a phenomenon prevails both in competitive and non-competitive environments and shifts the utilities possibilities frontier. Since interlinking is really the internalization of the externality from the credit to the labor/land markets in the absence of a complete set of markets, the utilities possibilities frontier moves outward while the distribution effects of interlinkage are ambiguous. The rationale for interlinkage becomes even stronger where law or custom restricts certain contractual arrangements, for example usury laws or floors on tenants' crop shares.

Another rationale for interlinking is the "adverse selection" effect, where interlinking credit and tenancy contracts may screen the high-ability from the low-ability types. . . .

Braverman and Stiglitz have shown that there is no presumption that innovation results either in a reduction or in an increase in tenants' demand for credit. Whether the demand for credit itself is increased or decreased depends critically on both how the technical change affects the probability distribution of yields and on tenants' utility functions. The presence of interlinkage between credit and land markets does not preclude either resistance to or encouragement of the adoption of technological innovations. Either is possible. In some cases, it might actually encourage the adoption of some technologies which otherwise would not be adopted, even though the innovation itself reduces tenants' demand for credit.

As explained before, the amount borrowed affects the landlord's return (through its effect both on the tenants' effort and on his decisions concerning choices of technique), and conversely, the terms of the landlord's contract affect returns to the lender (through its effect on the likelihood of default). Interlinkage was a method by which these "externalities" could be internalized. What then concerns the landlord-cum-lender is the total impact of the innovation on his income; the decomposition of his income into a return as a lender, or return as a landlord, has no particular significance. So it becomes clear that the impact of an innovation on a landlord-cum-lender may be quite different from the impact of the same innovation on a landlord who does not control the borrowing activities of his tenants. . . .

VIII.B.5. Agricultural Household Models*

Efforts to predict the consequences of agricultural policies are often confounded by the complex behavioral interactions characteristic of semicommercialized, rural economies. Most

*From Inderjit Singh, Lyn Squire, and John Strauss, "A Survey of Agricultural Household Models: Recent Findings and Policy Implications," *World Bank Economic Review*, Vol. 1, No. 1, September 1986, pp.149–50, 152–54. Reprinted by permission.

households in agricultural areas produce partly for sale and partly for own-consumption. They also purchase some of their inputs—such as fertilizer and labor—and provide some inputs—such as family labor—from their own resources. Any change in the policies governing agricultural activities will therefore affect not only production but also consumption and labor supply.

Agricultural household models are designed to capture these interactions in a theoretically consistent fashion and in a manner that allows empirical applications so that the consequences of policy interventions can be illuminated. The existence of such models would enable the analyst to examine the consequences of policy in three dimensions.

First, one could examine the effects of alternative policies on the well-being of representative agricultural households. Well-being may be interpreted here to mean household income or some other measure such as nutritional status. For example, in examining the effect of a policy designed to provide cheap food for urban consumers, an agricultural household model would allow the analyst to assess the costs to farmers of depressed producer prices. The nutritional benefits for the urban population may be more than offset by the reduced nutritional status of the rural population that results from lower farm incomes.

Second, an understanding of the behavior of agricultural households would shed light on the spillover effects of government policies on other segments of the rural population. For example, since most investment strategies are designed to increase production, their primary impact is on the incomes of agricultural households. As a result, rural investment strategies may not reach landless households or households engaged in nonagricultural activities. A model that incorporates total labor demand and family labor supply, however, would allow the analyst to explore the effects of investment policy on the demand for hired labor and hence on the rural labor market and the incomes of landless households. Similarly, a model that incorporates consumer behavior would allow the analyst to explore the consequences of increased profits for agricultural households on the demand for products and services provided by nonagricultural, rural households. Since the demand for nonagricultural commodities is often thought to be much more responsive to an increase in income than the demand for agricultural staples, this spillover effect may well be important.

Third, governments are interested in the performance of the agricultural sector from a more macroeconomic perspective. For example, agriculture is often an important source of revenue for the public budget and a major earner of foreign exchange. In assessing the effects of pricing policy on the budget or the balance of payments, the government is obliged to consider how agricultural households will alter their production and consumption in response to changes in prices. A reduction in export taxes, for example, may increase earnings of foreign exchange and budget revenues if households market enough additional production. Since agricultural household models capture both consumption and production behavior, they are an appropriate vehicle for examining the effect of pricing policy on marketed surplus and hence on foreign exchange earnings and budget revenues.

The importance of agricultural households in the total population and the significance of sector policies combine to make the behavior of agricultural households an area warranting thorough theoretical and empirical investigation.

Modeling the Agricultural Household

In general, any analysis of the consumption or labor supply of agricultural households has to account for the interdependence of household production and consumption. Agricultural households combine the household and the firm, two fundamental units of microeconomic analysis. When the household is a price taker in all markets, for all commodities which it both consumes and produces, optimal household production can be determined independent of leisure and consumption choices. Then, given the maximum income level derived from profit-maximizing production, family labor supply and commodity consumption decisions can be made.

Given this sequential decisionmaking, the appropriate analytical framework is a recursive model with profit- and utility-maximizing components. Empirical analysis of both household consumption and production becomes considerably more tractable in a recursive model, which as a result has been used by most (but not all) empirical analyses.

In this section, a prototype static model is developed. (A more detailed treatment with derivations is found in Strauss, 1986.) For any production cycle, the household is assumed to maximize a utility function:

$$U = U(X_a, X_m, X_l) \qquad (1)$$

where the commodities are an agricultural staple (X_a), a market-purchased good (X_m), and leisure (X_l). Utility is maximized subject to a cash income constraint:

$$p_m X_m = p_a(Q_a - X_a) - p_l(L - F) - p_v V + E$$

where p_m and p_a are the prices of the market-purchased commodity and the staple, respectively; Q_a is the household's production of the staple (so that $Q_a - X_a$ is its marketed surplus); p_l is the market wage; L is total labor input; F is family labor input (so that $L - F$, if positive, is hired labor and, if negative, is off-farm labor); V is a variable input (for example, fertilizer); p_v is the variable input's market price; and E is any nonlabor, nonfarm income.

The household also faces a time constraint; it cannot allocate more time to leisure, on-farm production, or off-farm employment than the total time available to the household:

$$X_l + F = T$$

where T is the total stock of household time. It also faces a production constraint or production technology that depicts the relationship between inputs and farm output:

$$Q_a = Q(L,V,A,K)$$

where A is the household's fixed quantity of land and K is its fixed stock of capital.

In this presentation, various complexities are omitted. For example, the possibility of more than one crop is ignored. In addition, it is assumed that family labor and hired labor are perfect substitutes and can be added directly. Production is also assumed to be riskless. Finally, and perhaps most importantly, it is assumed that the four prices in the model—$p_a, p_m, p_v,$ and p_l—are not affected by actions of the household. That is, the household is assumed to be a price taker in the four markets; as seen below, this will result in a recursive model.

The three constraints on household behavior can be collapsed into a single constraint. Substituting the production constraint into the cash income constraint for Q_a and substituting the time constraint into the cash income constraint for F yields a single constraint:

$$p_mX_m + p_aX_a + p_lX_l = p_lT + \pi + E \quad (2)$$

where $\pi = p_aQ_a (L,V,A,K) - p_lL - p_vV$ and is a measure of farm profits. In this equation, the left-hand side shows total household "expenditure" on three items: the market-purchased commodity, the household's "purchase" of its own output, and the household's "purchase" of its own time in the form of leisure. The right-hand side is a development of Becker's concept of full income, in which the value of the stock of time (p_lT) owned by the household is explicitly recorded, as is any labor income. The extension for agricultural households is the inclusion of a measure of farm profits, $p_aQ_a - p_lL - p_vV$,

with all labor valued at the market wage, this being a consequence of the assumption of price-taking behavior in the labor market. Equations 1 and 2 are the core of all the studies of agricultural households reported in this article.

Equations 1 and 2 reveal that the household can choose the levels of consumption for the three commodities, the total labor input, and the fertilizer input into agricultural production. Maximization of household utility subject to the single constraint yields the following first-order conditions:

$$p_a \frac{\partial Q_a}{\partial L} = p_l \quad (3a)$$

$$p_a \frac{\partial Q_a}{\partial V} = p_v \quad (3b)$$

$$\frac{\partial U/\partial X_a}{\partial U/\partial X_m} = \frac{p_a}{p_m} \quad (4a)$$

$$\frac{\partial U/\partial X_l}{\partial U_l\partial X_m} = \frac{p_l}{p_m} \quad (4b)$$

plus the constraint. Equations 3a and 3b show that the household will equate the marginal revenue products for labor and fertilizer to their respective market prices. An important attribute of these two equations is that they contain only two endogenous variables, L and V. The other endogenous variables, X_m, X_a, and X_l, do not appear and do not, therefore, influence the household's choice of L or V (provided second-order conditions are met). Accordingly, farm labor and fertilizer demand can be determined as a function of prices (p_a, p_l and p_v), the technological parameters of the production function, and the fixed area of land and quantity of capital. Since equations 3a and 3b depict the standard conditions for profit maximization, it can be concluded that the household's production decisions are consistent with profit maximization and independent of the household's utility function.

The maximized value of profits can be substituted into equation 2 to yield:

$$p_mX_m + p_aX_a + p_lX_l = Y^* \quad (5)$$

where Y^* is the value of full income associated with profit-maximizing behavior. Equations 4a, 4b, and 5 can be thought of as the first-order conditions of a second maximization. That is, having first maximized profits (see equations 3a and 3b), the household then maximizes utility subject to its (maximized) value of full income.

Equations 4a, 4b, and 5 can then be solved to obtain the demand equations for X_m, X_a, and X_l as functions of prices (p_m, p_a, p_l) and full income (Y^*). This demonstrates, given the assumptions made about markets, that even though the household's production and consumption decisions may be simultaneous in time, they can be modeled recursively (Nakajima, 1969; Jorgenson and Lau, 1969).

The presence of farm profits in equation 5 demonstrates the principal message of the farm household literature—that farm technology, quantities of fixed inputs, and prices of variable inputs and outputs affect consumption decisions. The reverse, however, is not true provided the model is recursive. Preferences, prices of consumption commodities, and income do not affect production decisions; therefore, output supply responds positively to own price at all times because of the quasi-convexity assumption on the production function. However, for consumption commodities (X_a) which are also produced by the household (Q_a), own-price effects are

$$\frac{dX_a}{dp_a} = \frac{\partial X_a}{\partial p_a}\bigg|Y^* + \frac{\partial X_a}{\partial Y^*}\frac{\partial Y^*}{\partial p_a} \qquad (6)$$

The first term on the right-hand side of this expression is the standard result of consumer demand theory and, for a normal good, is negative. The second term captures the "profit effect," which occurs when a rise in the price of the staple increases farm profits and hence full income. Applying the envelope theorem to equation 6,

$$\frac{\partial Y^*}{\partial p_a} dp_a = \frac{\partial \pi}{\partial p_a} dp_a = Q_a dp_a \qquad (7)$$

that is, the profit effect equals output times the price increase and therefore is unambiguously positive. The positive effect of an increase in profits (and hence farm income), an effect totally ignored in traditional models of demand, will definitely dampen and may outweigh the negative effect of both income and substitution in standard consumer demand theory. The presence of the profit effect is a direct consequence of the joint treatment of production and consumption decisions.

References

Jorgenson, Dale, and Lawrence Lau. 1969. "An Economic Theory of Agricultural Household Behavior." Paper presented at Fourth Far Eastern Meeting of Econometric Society.

Nakajima, Chihiro. 1969. "Subsistence and Commercial Family Farms: Some Theoretical Models of Subjecture Equilibrium." In C. F. Wharton, Jr., ed., *Subsistence Agriculture and Economic Development*. Chicago: Aldine.

Strauss, John. 1986. "The Theory and Comparative Statics of Agricultural Household Models: A General Approach." In I. J. Singh, L. Squire, and J. Strauss, eds., *Agricultural Household Models: Extensions, Applications, and Policy*. Baltimore, Md.: Johns Hopkins University Press.

Comment: Supply Functions and Price Responsiveness

A number of empirical studies offer evidence on the positive supply elasticity of agricultural production in response to price incentives. An excellent summary of empirical estimates of supply elasticities is presented by Hossein Askari and John T. Cummings, *Agricultural Supply Response: A Survey of the Econometric Evidence* (1976). See also Raj Krishna, "Agricultural Price Policy and Economic Development," in *Agricultural Development and Economic Growth,* ed. Herman M. Southworth and Bruce F. Johnston (1967); Theodore W. Schultz, ed., *Distortions of Agricultural Incentives* (1978); Walter Falcon, "Farmer Response to Price in a Subsistence Economy," *American Economic Review, Papers and Proceedings* (May 1964); and K. Bardhan, "Price and Output Response of Marketed Surplus of Foodgrains," *American Journal of Agricultural Economics* (February 1970).

Considering the efficiency of farmer decision making, several studies have examined the allocational behavior of peasant producers from the viewpoint of efficiency across farm size groups, risk, pricing policy, credit, and marketing. See Theodore W. Schultz, *Transforming Traditional Agriculture* (1964); Amartya K. Sen, "Peasants and Dualism With or Without Surplus Labor," *Journal of Political Economy* (October 1966); D. W. Hopper, "Allocational Efficiency in Traditional Indian Agriculture," *Journal of Farm Economics* (August 1965); Michael Lipton, "The Theory of the Optimizing Peasant,"

Journal of Development Studies (August 1968); and M. Schluter and T. Mount, ''Some Management Objectives of the Peasant Farmer,'' *Journal of Development Studies* (August 1977).

In an important study, *Palanpur: The Economy of an Indian Village* (1982), C. J. Bliss and N. H. Stern examine whether farmers' decisions about inputs and outputs can be explained by an optimizing model (whether farmers are rational profit- or utility-maximizing agents) and whether sharecropping tenancy is inefficient.

Comment: Rural Labor Markets

Unlike urban labor markets, the rural labor markets display some special characteristics of a less developed economy. The operation of rural labor markets depends on how the rural economy is organized—whether there are simple family farms, extended families, landless laborers, sharecroppers, or plantations and estates. In a large part of the rural economy, the household represents both the demand for and supply of labor, as analyzed in producer–consumer household models (see (VIII.B.5).

A special characteristic in a poor economy is the relation between productivity and consumption. Employers may realize that health and nutrition can influence productivity in agriculture. They may therefore pay more than the minimum wage at which labor is available because the extra consumption from the higher wages will raise the worker's productivity sufficiently to offset the cost of the extra wages. This it the ''efficiency wage hypothesis'' outlined by Joseph Stiglitz, ''The Efficiency Wage Hypothesis, Surplus Labor, and the Distribution of Income in LDCs,'' *Oxford Economic Papers* (July 1976), and Christopher Bliss and Nicholas Stern, ''Productivity, Wages, and Nutrition: Parts I and II,'' *Journal of Development Economics* (December 1978).

The fact that better nutrition can improve the efficiency of labor and raise farm productivity explains why wages in a competitive labor market may not fall even when labor is in surplus and there is unemployment. For empirical evidence that the nutrient intake does affect labor productivity, see John Strauss, ''Does Better Nutrition Raise Farm Productivity?'' *Journal of Political Economy* (April 1986); Christopher Bliss and Nicholas Stern, ''Productivity, Wages and Nutrition, Part II: Some Observations,'' *Journal of Development Economics* (December 1978); and Amil B. Deolaikar, ''Nutrition and Labor Productivity in Agriculture: Estimates for Rural South India,'' *Review of Economics and Statistics* (August 1988). Bliss and Stern found that the efficiency wage hypothesis explains why landless laborers in India are paid more than landed, and permanent laborers more than casual.

Another theory that explains why employers may pay more than the minimum required to hire labor is the ''labor-turnover model.'' By raising the wage, the employer reduces turnover. This theory is elaborated by Joseph Stiglitz, ''Alternative Theories of Wage Determination and Unemployment in LDCs: The Labor Turnover Model,'' *Quarterly Journal of Economics* (May 1974).

We should also recognize that there is not only agricultural production in the rural economy, but also nonagricultural activities. The sale of labor time by households is frequently in joint supply to both agricultural and nonagricultural activities. East Asian experience is especially impressive in showing a strong positive relationship between the achievement of dynamic balanced rural growth and success in a country's overall development effort. Moreover, the rural industrial sector may expand over time—from household and village enterprises to food processing plants and small factories using modern technologies. See Gustav Ranis and Frances Stewart, ''Rural Non-agricultural Activities in Development,'' *Journal of Development Economics* (February 1993).

Beyond any static and microanalysis of labor markets, we have to consider the macrodynamics of the intersectoral labor markets. Over the longer term, there is extensive rural–urban migration, as we discussed in Chapter III. Associated with this migration is the persistence of an urban–rural wage gap dualism within the rural–urban wage structure (see section III.C).

Among the many illuminating studies of the rural labor market are Rizwanul Islam, ed., *Rural Industrialization and Employment in Asia* (1982); Paul Collier and Deepak Lal, *Labor and Poverty in Kenya: 1900–1980* (1986); Paul Collier et al., *Labour and Poverty in Rural Tanzania* (1986); and Mark R. Rosenzweig, ''Labor Markets in Low Income Countries,'' in *Handbook of Development Economics*, ed. Hollis Chenery and T. N. Srinivasan (1988), vol. 1, chap. 15.

Comment: Women in Rural Areas

Women play an important role in household decision making and management of food crop production. This is especially true in Sub-Saharan Africa, where subsistence farming is essentially a female activity, and women are the primary laborers on small farms. If farm production is to be improved in Africa, it will be necessary to utilize African women farmers by giving them access to inputs and providing the incentives to produce. Given the large number of women in agriculture, this improvement is necessary for at least the next decade or so. In the longer run, however, female farming may decline with agricultural intensification (lower land–person ratio), technological change, and Western-funded development projects that tend to limit women's access to inputs.

See Christina H. Gladwin and Della McMillan, "Is a Turnaround in Africa Possible Without Helping African Women to Farm?" *Economic Development and Cultural Change* (January 1989); and Jacqueline Ashby, *Invisible Farmers: Women and Crisis in Agriculture* (1981); and Jean Due and Rebecca Summary, "Constraints to Women and Development in Africa," *Journal of Modern African Studies* (March 1982).

Women also constitute a substantial part of the rural labor force in the Caribbean, Asia, and Latin America. See selection VI.D.1.

Comment: Induced Technical and Institutional Change

Hayami and Ruttan have presented an "induced innovation" model to explain growth in agricultural productivity:

> The model attempts to make more explicit the process by which technical and institutional changes are induced through the responses of farmers, agribusiness entrepreneurs, scientists, and public administrators to resource endowments and to changes in the supply and demand of factors and products.
>
> The state of relative endowments and accumulation of the two primary resources, land and labor, is a critical element in determining a viable pattern of technical change in agriculture. Agriculture is characterized by much stronger constraints of land on production than most other sectors of the economy. Agricultural growth may be viewed as a process of easing the constraints on production imposed by inelastic supplies of land and labor. Depending on the relative scarcity of land and labor, technical change embodied in new and more productive inputs may be induced primarily either (a) to save labor or (b) to save land.
>
> The nonagricultural sector plays an important role in this process. It absorbs labor from agriculture. And it supplies to agriculture the modern technical inputs that can be substituted for land and labor in agricultural production.
>
> The critical element in this process is an effective system of market and non-market information linkages among farmers, public research institutions, private agricultural supply firms, and political and bureaucratic entrepreneurs. It is hypothesized that the proper functioning of such interactions is a key to success in the generation of the unique pattern of technical change necessary for agricultural development in any developing economy.[1]

According to the theory of induced technical innovation, progress in agricultural technology is largely an endogenous phenomenon. As formulated by Hayami and Ruttan, the theory states that the high price associated with a scarce factor of production (e.g., land) induces farmers to choose technologies that conserve the scarce factor. A rise in the price of land relative to the price of labor induces the substitution of labor for land. Or mechanization relaxes labor constraints. Or new high-yield seeds and fertilizer relax land constraints. But the advance in technology is itself a function of institutional innovation. Therefore, farmers exert political pressure to induce institutional innovations that will advance technological change (e.g., by public research institutions or institutions of land reform). Shifts in the demand for institutional change are thus induced by changes in relative factor supply and technical change.

Evidence in support of the Hayami–Ruttan theory, however, has been questioned: see Michael Lipton with Richard Longhurst, *New Seeds and Poor People* (1989). Lipton and Longhurst also place more emphasis on the need for a global research and planning apparatus that will give more attention to the effects of modern agricultural technologies on the poor. In particular, they argue that research must focus not only on increasing output, but also on generating employment, on provision of cheap calories, and on the "full social systemic influences" of any new seed or technology.

Recognizing some special characteristics of the institutional structure of an agrarian economy, Bra-

[1]Yujiro Hayami and Vernon W. Ruttan, *Agricultural Development: An International Perspective*, rev. ed. (1985), pp. 4–5; for a detailed exposition, see also Vernon W. Ruttan, "Innovation and Agricultural Development," *World Development* (September 1989).

verman and Stiglitz have presented another interpretation of technological innovation in agriculture. They investigate two common beliefs: that landlords have used their control over the means of production to direct the development and adoption of technologies that have increased their own welfare at the expense of workers; and that interlinkage between credit and tenancy markets provides an impetus to the resistance of innovations: innovations that make tenants better off reduce their demand for loans, and thereby make landlords—as creditors—worse off.

Those who apply purely competitive models dismiss these beliefs, arguing that if an economy is competitive these results would not occur.

Braverman and Stiglitz, however, point out that, contrary to the competitive model in many LDCs, sharecropping contracts are widely employed, widespread unemployment prevails, and there is not the full set of risk and capital markets required by the competitive paradigm.

Under these different institutional conditions Braverman and Stiglitz conclude that

   (i) landlords may wish to—and can—resist innovations which unambiguously increase production whenever sharecropping contracts are employed.

  (ii) conversely, landlords may adopt innovations which not only lower the welfare of workers, but even lower net national product.

 (iii) the presence of interlinkage may, indeed, affect the adoption of a new technology; however, the reason for this is only partly related to the effect of innovations on tenants' borrowing. Indeed, innovations may increase as well as decrease the tenants' demand for borrowing.[2]

[2]Avishay Braverman and Joseph Stiglitz, "Landlords, Tenants and Technological Innovations," *Journal of Development Economics* (October 1986): 313–32; see also selection VIII.B.1.

VIII.C. DESIGNING AN AGRICULTURAL STRATEGY

VIII.C.1. The Agricultural Transformation*

Several main lessons have been learned in the last two decades about the functioning of the agricultural sector and its potential role in the development process: the emergence of the agricultural sector into a general equilibrium perspective; the recognition of the importance of macroeconomic policy for agricultural performance; the necessity (and feasibility because of the potential for technical change) of rapid economic growth to deal with the human welfare concerns that stem from poverty and hunger; and the superior performance of trade- and market-oriented systems in achieving this growth. These lessons do not define a single strategic approach to agricultural development, however. In fact, three sharply different paths would seem to be open for appropriate policies toward agriculture that view development of the sector as a means to an end—as part of the effort to speed the overall process of development—rather than as an end in itself.

The Alternatives

The first path has parallels to the philosophy of the 1950s, in which benign neglect of agricultural policy was thought to be sufficient for stimulating the process of economic growth. This perspective grows out of the recognition of the role of well-functioning markets and decision makers operating in a world of "rational expectations." In this view, most policy is irrelevant to farmers in more than a very transitory sense, and this is especially true of price policy. . . .

In this world, agricultural incomes are determined by employment opportunities outside agriculture, the agricultural sector *must* decline in proportional output terms and absolutely in the labor force, and the long-run decline in basic agricultural commodity prices due to technical change simply emphasizes that society is best

served by getting resources out of agriculture as rapidly as possible. Although the clearest case for this view of the world is in the OECD countries, a host of middle-income countries, and even some quite poor countries, are also facing the problem of declining real incomes in the agricultural sector under the impact of rapid technical change domestically and lower world prices for the resulting output. This perspective is obviously consistent with the view that open economies will show better performance than those with substantial trade barriers.

A sharply different path has been sketched by Mellor and Johnston (1984). Building on their earlier stress on balanced growth (1961), Johnston and Mellor call for an "interrelated strategy" that improves nutrition in one dimension while it fosters the broader growth process in the other. The approach calls for a major role of government in strategic design and program implementation, a role that is in marked contrast with the free-market approach sketched out above.

We have, therefore, emphasized that improvements in nutrition [one of Mellor and Johnston's key objectives for agricultural development] require a *set of interacting forces:* accelerated growth in agriculture; wage goods production; a strategy of development that structures demand towards high employment content goods and services; increased employment; and increased effective demand for food on the part of the poor. Agricultural growth not only satisfies the need for food to meet nutritional requirements (which is the other side of the wage-goods coin), but fosters a favorable employment-oriented demand structure as well. Agriculture's role in generating a structure of demand, favorable to rapid growth in employment, is central. (pp. 567–68, emphasis added)

Mellor and Johnston go on to summarize their earlier argument that agriculture can play this multiplicity of roles only if a unimodel development strategy is followed, that is, one in which a broad base of smallholders are the central focus of agricultural research and extension services and the recipient of the bulk of receipts from agricultural sales. The authors see the dualism inherent in bimodel strategies—those placing modernization efforts primarily on

*From C. Peter Timmer, "The Agricultural Transformation," in *Handbook of Development Economics*, Vol. I, H. Chenery and T. N. Srinivasan (eds.), Elsevier Science Publishers, North Holland Publishing Company, Amsterdam, 1988, pp. 321–28. Reprinted by permission.

large, "progressive" farms while neglecting the "backward" smallholders—as the major obstacle to putting their set of interacting forces in motion.

The most common barrier to the interrelated strategy indicated is pronounced dualism in capital allocations—too much to industry and the unproductive elements of the private sector rather than to agriculture, and to capital intensive elements within those, as well as to large-scale and therefore capital-intensive allocations within agriculture. The outcome of the strategy will depend upon national-level decisions about macroeconomic policies, exchange rates, interest rates, and investment allocations among sectors and regions, not just within agriculture itself. Indeed, the whole strategy fails if it is viewed simply as the responsibility of agriculture ministries. (Mellor and Johnston, 1984, p. 568)

This interrelated strategy must be directed by government planners; there is relatively little concern or role for the private sector, other than small farmers. The analysis leading to the strategy remains heavily influenced by closed economy considerations, and little attention is given to either domestic marketing activities or their relationship to international markets. Three key elements are suggested as essential to meeting all objectives of agricultural development— massive investment in human capital through nutrition, health, and family planning services in the countryside, creation of the complex, rural organizational structures seen in Japan and Taiwan that provide services to small farmers while also serving as a voice for their interests, and investment in rapid technical change appropriate to these small farmers in order to raise agricultural output and rural incomes simultaneously.

Notably missing in this list of key elements is significant concern for the structure of incentives for agriculture relative to industry or for the country's tradables relative to foreign competitors. Although it is realized that the macroeconomic setting is no doubt important to agriculture, it remains outside the scope of appropriate strategy for agricultural development. Not surprisingly, given the argument in Johnston and Clark (1982), the intellectual foundation for this strategy lies in rural development, not in a vision of agriculture linked to the macro economy and world markets by powerful market mechanisms. It is this latter vision which provides the third potential path for agricultural development strategy for the rest of the 1980s and into the 1990s.

The third approach contrasts with both the "free market" and "interrelated strategy" approaches. It calls for government policy interventions into market outcomes but uses markets and the private marketing sector as the vehicle for those policy interventions. This "market policy" approach recognizes widespread "market failures" in agriculture as well as extensive "government failures" in implementation of economic tasks. The strategic dilemma is how to cope with segmented rural capital and labor markets, poorly functioning land markets, the welfare consequences of sharp instability of prices in commodity markets, the pervasive lack of information about current and future events in most rural economies, and the sheer absence of many important markets, especially for future contingencies involving yield or price risks. One powerful lesson of the postwar development record is that direct government interventions to correct market failures frequently make matters worse by inhibiting whatever market responses were possible in the initial circumstances, without providing greater output or more efficient utilization of resources. The agricultural sector in particular is vulnerable to well-intended but poorly conceived and managed state organizations that attempt a wide array of direct economic activities, including monopoly control of input supplies, capital-intensive state farms, and mandated control over crop marketing and processing. As Bates (1981) has demonstrated, these direct controls and agencies have a strong political economy rationale for a government that tries to reward its supporters and centralize power and resources in the hands of the state (see also Lipton, 1977).

The answer to the dilemma over making matters worse, in this approach, is to gain a much clearer understanding of the necessary interaction between the public and private sectors. . . . Political objectives for the performance of agriculture—its capacity to feed the population regularly and cheaply, or its ability to provide fair incomes to farmers caught in the pressures of successful structural transformation—are inevitable and, in some long-run sense, highly desirable.

The "market policy" path argues that these objectives are best served by making carefully considered interventions into the prices determined in markets, not by leaving markets alone or by striving to reach the objectives through direct activities by the government. If the "free market'' approach incurs heavy political costs as markets relentlessly redistribute incomes to the winners in the course of economic development, and the ''interrelated strategy'' incurs heavy managerial and administrative costs as the government plays an active and direct economic role, the ''market policy'' approach incurs heavy analytical costs.

These analytical costs come from the need to understand each country's path of structural change, the workings of factor and commodity markets, and the potential impact of macro and commodity price interventions on these markets and ultimately on the structural path itself. It requires that government intervention be based on an empirical understanding of economic responses to a change in policy and the political repercussions from them. There is an important role for models in illuminating where to look for these responses, but the models themselves cannot provide the answers. This is especially true as attempts are made to build into the models the response of policy itself to changes in the economic environment. Such endogenous policy models may reveal some of the historical factors that accounted for policy shifts, but they seldom provide a sense of when the degrees of freedom for policy initiative are about to expand. Frequently, this is in times of crisis. Policy makers often embark on bold experiments in such times, and the payoff would be very high if sufficient analytical understanding already existed in order to anticipate the response to a policy change.

Agricultural Policy and Structural Change

Hayami and Ruttan (1985) have asked why agricultural growth has not been faster and more evenly spread around the world:

We indicated that the basic factor underlying poor performance was neither the meager endowment of natural resources nor the lack of technological potential to increase output from the available resources at a sufficiently rapid pace to meet the growth of demand. The major constraint limiting agricultural development was identified as the policies that impeded rather than induced appropriate technical and insti-

tutional innovations. As a result, the gap widened between the potential and the actual productive capacities of LDC agriculture. (p. 416)

This perspective, with its emphasis on the relationship between policy and agriculture's role in structural change, has provided the organizing theme for this selection. The progression of topics has followed from understanding why the agricultural sector is different from the industrial and service sectors and how the differences condition the nature of effective policy interventions. The factors needed for inducing the agricultural transformation, to ''get agriculture moving,'' involves a complex mix of appropriate new technology, flexible rural institutions, and a market orientation that offers farmers material rewards for the physical effort they expend in their fields and households and for the risks they face from both nature and markets.

References

Bates, Robert H. 1981. *Markets and States in Tropical Africa: The Political Basis of Agricultural Policies.* Berkeley: University of California Press.

Hayami, Yujiro, and Vernon Ruttan. 1985. *Agricultural Development: An International Perspective* (revised and expanded edition). Baltimore and London: Johns Hopkins University Press.

Johnston, Bruce F., and William C. Clark. 1982. *Redesigning Rural Development: A Strategic Perspective.* Baltimore and London: Johns Hopkins University Press.

Johnston, Bruce F., and John W. Mellor. 1961. ''The Role of Agriculture in Economic Development,'' *American Economic Review* 51, no. 4: 566–93.

Lipton, Michael. 1977. *Why Poor People Stay Poor: Urban Bias in World Development.* Cambridge, Mass.: Harvard University Press.

Mellor, John W., and Bruce F. Johnston. 1984. ''The World Food Equation: Inter-relations Among Development, Employment, and Food Consumption.'' *Journal of Economic Literature* 22: 531–74.

EXHIBIT VIII.3. Changing Environments for Agriculture's Contribution to Economic Growth

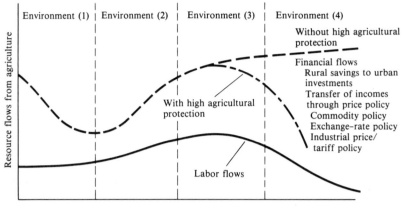

Policy settings (1) "Getting Agriculture Moving"—institutional change; new technology; structure of markets and incentives; significant investments in rural infrastructure. (2) "Agriculture as a Contributor to Growth"—establish market links with industry; technology and incentives to create a healthy agricultural sector; improve factor markets to mobilize rural responses. (3) "Integrating Agriculture into the Macro Economy"—declining share of food in urban budgets; push to make agriculture efficient; shift resources out, but substantial income-distribution problems from lagging rural labor productivity. (4) "Agriculture in Industrial Economies"—small share of food commodities in consumer budgets; income distribution a political issue; unemployment in industrial sector creates pressures to keep labor in agriculture; environmental concerns and "way-of-life" issues.

Source: C. Peter Timmer, "The Agricultural Transformation," Harvard Institute for International Development, Discussion Paper, no. 223 (March 1986), p. 8.

Comment: Agricultural Strategies

The four environments depicted in Exhibit VIII.3 correspond to (1) Arthur T. Mosher, *Getting Agriculture Moving* (1966); (2) Bruce F. Johnston and John W. Mellor, "The Role of Agriculture in Economic Development," *American Economic Review* (September 1961); (3) Theodore W. Schultz, *Transforming Traditional Agriculture* (1964); and (4) D. Gale Johnson, *World Agriculture in Disarray* (1973).

Other major studies of strategies of agricultural development may be consulted. Especially informative are Bruce F. Johnston and Peter Kilby, *Agriculture and Structural Transformation* (1975); John W. Mellor, *Economics of Agricultural Dvelopment,* 2nd ed. (1974); Yujiro Hayami and Vernon W. Ruttan, *Agricultural Development: An International Perspective*, rev. ed. (1986); Uma J. Lele, *The Design of Rural Development: Lessons from Africa* (1975); Bruce F. Johnston and William C. Clark, *Redesigning Rural Development: A Strategic Perspective* (1982); C. Peter Timmer, Walter P. Falcon, and Scott R. Pearson, *Food Policy Analysis* (1983); C. Peter Timmer, "The Agricultural Transformation," in *Handbook of Development Economics*, ed. Hollis Chenery and T. N. Srinivasan (1988), vol. 1, chap. 8; Carl K. Eicher, *Agricultural Development in the Third World*, 2nd ed. (1990); and Thomas P. Tomich, Peter Kilby, and Bruce F. Johnston, *Transforming Agrarian Economies: Opportunities Seized, Opportunities Missed* (1995).

VIII.C.2. Evaluation of Government Intervention*

What are the legitimate reasons for government intervention in agricultural markets? In particular, what makes the market's own allocation either inefficient or otherwise "unacceptable"? There is a standard litany of such reasons; five are relevant to agriculture.

1. *Incomplete markets in insurance futures and credit.* Farmers cannot get complete insurance against the big (output and price) risks they face. Rural credit markets, like agricultural insurance markets, are notoriously imperfect. Farmers' access to credit is limited, if they can obtain it at all. They often have to pay usurious interest rates, though this may have something to do with the likelihood of default.[1]

2. *Public goods and increasing returns.* These provide the justification for governments to finance water projects. In some cases, the marginal cost of using irrigated water, once the dam has been built, is relatively low, and the cost of monitoring water usage is relatively high. Water projects therefore satisfy both the criteria of pure public goods. The provision of water is almost always a natural monopoly, and a common (though not universal) response to such monopolies is production by government.

3. *Imperfect information.* Government supply of information can be thought of as a type of public good. (Where the government ascertains what crops grow best in a particular area, the information is best described as a local public good.) However, disseminating information is costly, and the benefits accrue mainly to those who receive it. So it is probably wrong to think of agricultural extension as a pure public service. It may be justified, however, by the next category of market failure.

4. *Externalities.* The successful adoption of a new technology by one farmer conveys valuable information to his neighbors and hence gives them a significant externality. The existence of this externality has been used to justify subsidies for farmers to adopt new technologies.

5. *Income distribution.* Perhaps the most important reason for government intervention in agriculture is concern with the distribution of income generated by free markets. Given the initial holdings of assets, this distribution need not, and often does not, satisfy society's ethical judgments. In particular, it may result in significant numbers of people having unacceptably low incomes or supplies of food. This suggests the government should design programs that increase the incomes of small farmers—and, for urban dwellers, a program of food subsidies.

Though this list provides various rationales for government action, the link between them and actual government policies may be tenuous. Thus, measures aimed at reducing risk (like price stabilization programs) may actually increase the riskiness of farmers' income, and they often entail large subsidies. Though government policies may be defended in terms of helping the small farmer, the main beneficiaries may be large farmers. And though governments may claim that their policies redistribute income, the net impact of the programs may be regressive.

Critics of government programs thus claim that market failures are matched by a corresponding list of government failures. The fact that markets face certain problems does not in itself justify government intervention; it only identifies the potential area for it. This caveat is particularly important in any assessment of public remedies for those market failures affected by imperfect information (for instance, imper-

---

*From Joseph E. Stiglitz, "Some Theoretical Aspects of Agricultural Policies," *World Bank Research Observer*, Vol. 2, No. 1 (January 1987), pp. 43–47, 49, 51. Reprinted by permission.

[1]Insurance markets are notoriously bad in many contexts other than agricultural markets. Particular problems in agricultural markets are adverse selection and moral hazard: the farmer is likely to be better informed about the hazards he faces than the insurer (this is referred to as the adverse selection problem); and there are actions the farmer can take that affect output (or, more generally, the insurance companies' expected liability; this is referred to as the moral hazard problem). Thus, though the farmer cannot affect whether there is a hailstorm, he can affect the losses he incurs if one happens, by taking precautionary action. Adverse selection and moral hazard problems need to be taken into account in the design of insurance contracts.

Government policies that ignore adverse selection and moral hazard may exacerbate the problems. Thus, government stabilization programs may induce farmers to increase their production of risky crops, thus imposing a greater cost on government than it would otherwise have to face.

fect credit markets), since the government is likely to face similar problems if it intervenes.[2]

To understand the nature of government interventions in agricultural markets, one must approach the problem from the perspective of the *second best*. Whether government or market failures are of greater importance may differ from country to country, and this will crucially affect the nature of the appropriate government policy. Failure to recognize this fact has given rise to much of the controversy over state intervention. Simplistic views—such as "governments should not intervene in free markets"— or even the more sophisticated view (based on optimal tax theory for developed countries) that "government should not impose trade taxes" become inappropriate once it is recognized that the government has limited instruments for collecting revenue (thus, some distortionary taxation is necessary) and for redistributing income (so that the surest way of improving the lot of the rural poor may be through trade taxes). But the prescription that the government use trade taxes to redistribute income may be inappropriate when the redistributive impact of trade taxes is likely to be regressive.

An analysis of the appropriate policy for a particular country must therefore begin by specifying the reasons for market failure and the instruments the government can use to remedy it. The role of general theories is to identify the circumstances under which one kind of policy is more likely to be appropriate, thereby developing a taxonomy for analyzing policies in different countries. The models for specific countries help to frame the policy discussion. They enable one to establish whether the source of disagreement over policy is differences in objectives (welfare weights associated with different groups or between current generations and future generations); or differences in views about the structure of the economy; or differences in views about the values of key parameters.

The following sections organize the evaluation of alternative policies around several themes: risk, credit, dynamic effects.

Risk

Most economists acknowledge that farmers face significant risks and have only limited op-

portunity to avoid them through insurance and other markets. However, appropriate remedies are the subject of theoretical and practical disagreement.

What is of crucial importance to farmers is stabilizing their *income*, not stabilizing the prices of their produce. If price and quantity are negatively correlated, stabilizing prices may actually exacerbate the fluctuations in income.

Some economists favor the use of futures markets. These have the advantage of allowing a farmer to choose how much of his crop to sell forward, to "adapt" the extent of price stabilization to his own circumstances and preferences. But futures markets have two important drawbacks. First, they involve bigger transactions costs than those price stabilization schemes that work through the market. To the extent that such schemes serve to stabilize incomes, they do so without any farmer taking special action for himself. Second, to the extent that crop sizes are uncertain, no farmer can completely hedge his position unless he purchases crop insurance (which in general is unavailable). These disadvantages are not necessarily as bad as those produced by schemes in which the government does not stabilize the market price, but makes separate agreements with different farmers to buy given amounts of a crop at a guaranteed price.

Despite their transactions costs, futures markets dominate most types of price stabilization schemes. The intuitive reason is that futures markets allow the farmer to choose how much he wishes to divest himself of price risk. However, even in developed countries in which futures markets exist, farmers have not (at least until recently) used these markets to any significant extent. Thus, it remains an open question whether futures markets could be an effective way of sparing small farmers from risks.

If governments decide to stabilize prices, they have several ways to do so. They can, for instance, use buffer stocks, which can be operated according to various rules. Perfect price stability is, in essence, impossible. Even simple rules, such as setting a band within which prices can move, are not immune to speculative attack. The only generally feasible rules involve prices being a function of the size of the current stock; as the amount in storage decreases, the government allows the price to rise.

The limited calculations done so far suggest that the welfare gains from well-designed rules may be significantly greater than those from cer-

---

[2]Indeed, the problems associated with distinguishing between good and bad borrowers and of monitoring the actions of borrowers enhance the scope for political abuse within subsidized credit schemes.

tain simple rules, such as keeping prices within a band (even if that were possible). Indeed, questions may be raised about the significance of the latter gains altogether (Newbery and Stiglitz, 1982). As for buffer stocks, a major criticism is that it is usually more efficient to store general purchasing power than specific commodities—that is, to use savings and reserves—except when transport and transactions costs are large.

Another way for governments to try to affect price variability is to impose trade restrictions. These may have marked transactional advantages over other forms of price stabilization, though they may be less effective in stabilizing incomes. It is now widely recognized that, in the presence of uncertainty (and with limited governmental ability to respond to changing circumstances), quotas and tariffs are not interchangeable. Tariffs do not insulate a country from foreign-induced price fluctuations, but quotas may do so. Quotas are particularly effective when the source of price fluctuations is neither domestic demand nor supply; they can then completely insulate the producers from foreign shocks (at the cost, of course, of preventing a country from taking full advantage of its current comparative advantage). Quotas are also effective in the extreme case in which the only source of variability is domestic output; they then serve to raise prices whenever farmers are suffering from lower volume. Even in these circumstances, however, it is not clear that the gains from reducing risk exceed the costs of failing to take advantage of temporary comparative advantage. The calculations depend partly on supply responses.

With any price stabilization scheme, supply responses are a major uncertainty. How do farmers react to a reduction in risk? And to what extent do a government's price stabilization programs serve simply to replace the stabilizing (arbitrage) activities of the private sector? Little empirical work has been done on either of these issues, though the effects can clearly be large: some countries have had to restrict their farmers' production so as to limit the costs of government programs.

Though there often is a role for government intervention to reduce the risks faced by farmers, many of the programs justified on these grounds serve more to redistribute income than to stabilize it. Indeed, in some instances, they may actually increase the variability of income. The appeal of these programs may lie in the way that they conceal the size and allocation of subsidies.

Were the subsidies provided more openly, they might not be politically acceptable.

Credit

It is a common observation that farmers in developing countries are unable to obtain credit, or that they can do so only at usurious interest rates. This is not, in itself, evidence of a market failure. Interest rates will be high if the probability of default is high—which is indeed often the case. At the same time, the fact that there is imperfect information on the credit risks of different individuals (the adverse selection problem) and on the actions of those individuals (the moral hazard problem) means that the market equilibrium is not, in general, (constrained) Pareto efficient.

Nonetheless, government policies to boost credit for farmers need to take account of these adverse selection and moral hazard problems. The government is usually in no better (indeed, often worse) position for gathering information on the varying probabilities of default. Furthermore, a government credit program that involves some discretion in the granting of loans also contains scope for giving subsidies to particular individuals: whenever a "high-risk" farmer is granted a loan for which the interest rate has not been increased accordingly, he is obtaining an implicit subsidy. It is naturally difficult for an outsider to judge whether a subsidy has been granted; precisely for this reason, such programs are open to abuse.

Dynamic Effects

A justification for subsidizing inputs has to do with the adoption of new technologies. If peasants were perfectly rational and risk markets were perfect, then farmers would adopt the new technology if it increased their expected utility. No government subsidy would be needed.

Reality is different: risk markets are imperfect, and peasants are risk averse. Moreover, technologies that are riskier, but offer higher returns, yield more tax revenue for the government. Thus, the government has a real interest in encouraging the adoption of such technologies. If such technologies use a lot of fertilizer, for example, then a fertilizer subsidy may be an effective way of encouraging the adoption of the riskier technologies.

There is an added (and rather distinct) justification for governments to encourage the use of new technologies: when one farmer tries a new technology, he conveys a large amount of information to his neighbors. The presence of these informational externalities implies that farmers will have insufficient incentives for trying new technologies; the solution is to levy corrective (Pigovian) taxes or to provide subsidies.

The conflict between these dynamic efficiency objectives and distributional considerations raises a familiar problem. The farmers that are least risk averse are likely to be the large ones, so they are likely to be willing to try the new technology. Thus, subsidies for those who introduce the new technology are likely to be regressive. (The effect may be exacerbated if the new technologies are also capital intensive, and the larger farmers have easier access to capital markets or can borrow at lower interest rates.)

References

Newbery, David N., and Joseph E. Stiglitz. 1981. *The Theory of Commodity Price Stabilization.* London: Oxford University Press.

Newbery, David N., and Joseph E. Stiglitz. 1982. "Optimal Stockpiling Rules." *Oxford Economic Papers* 34, no. 3 (November): 403–27.

VIII.C.3. Price Policy Analysis*

In market economies nearly all government economic policies influence the rural-urban terms of trade, defined roughly as the price of food crops relative to the prices of goods and services, including consumer products and farm inputs, purchased by farmers growing food crops. The rural-urban terms of trade is a major factor determining incentives to increase agricultural output while simultaneously signaling consumers about the relative costs of food. For convenience and clarity, the terms of trade will be called the "food parity price." This term is a reminder that farm incentives can be raised in two ways: higher output prices or lower input prices (or lower prices for consumer goods that farmers purchase with their incomes).

The food parity price is principally influenced by two sets of policies: foreign exchange rate, interest rate, and wage rate policies; and the subsidy and trade policies that drive a wedge between the world price of a product (output or input) and its domestic price. These price policies are illustrated here with food crops in mind, although the reasoning applies equally well to manufactured goods or agricultural inputs, such as fertilizer.

Price policies are judged by their effects on the four food policy objectives—promoting economic efficiency and hence faster growth of income, distributing incomes more equally, guaranteeing adequate nutritional status for all people, and providing security of food supplies. Empirical analysis of a policy requires measurement of the size as well as the likely direction of its impact. In addition, the weights given by governments to the several objectives and the constraints on choice of policy, including international repercussions, determine the actual feasibility and efficacy of a price policy.

Each price policy uses a subsidy or a trade restriction to cause the domestic producer or consumer price, or both, to differ from the world price. A simple consumer subsidy causes both producers and consumers to face lower prices than those in the world market. A specific producer price subsidy can raise the farmers' decision price above world levels while leaving the consumer price at the world price. In the absence of specific policy intervention, the domestic price and world price for a commodity will be the same for both producers and consumers.

A price policy intervention has an impact on the four food policy objectives in the following ways: it affects economic growth by the extent of efficiency losses; income distribution by the direction of income transfers; food security by increases or decreases in quantities traded internationally; and nutritional status by the income transfers price policies effect to or from consumers. (The differential impact on poor consumers of food price changes is not captured within this analytical framework.) The effect of the policy on the food parity price itself depends on

*From C. Peter Timmer, Walter P. Falcon, and Scott R. Pearson, *Food Policy Analysis,* The Johns Hopkins University Press, Baltimore, 1983, pp. 190–96. Reprinted by permission.

whether the policy is applied to a food crop or to a manufactured product purchased by farmers and on whether the policy raises or lowers the domestic price of the commodity. A subsidy on rice imports lowers the food parity price by reducing the food price. A subsidy on fertilizer raises the food parity price by lowering the cost of an important input for food crop production.

Subsidy Policy

A consumer subsidy on importables—goods for which domestic supplies are less than domestic demand in the absence of price policy—is a common price policy intervention in developing countries. Subsidizing rice imports, for example, causes the domestic price of rice for both consumers and producers to be less than the world price. As a result, the quantity of rice produced domestically declines, the amount consumed locally increases, and rice imports are greater than before the subsidy was introduced. The government must use budget resources to lower the price of rice, and this makes consumers better off. In this short-run, static model, when consumers gain, however, the producers of rice lose because their production, sales, and profits are reduced because of the lower price of rice. In effect, producers are forced to transfer income to consumers. A subsidy on rice imports also causes the food parity price to fall because the domestic rice price is reduced.

All four effects of subsidy policy—on quantities, transfers, efficiency losses, and the food parity price—are shown in Figure 1. The initial situation, before the subsidy policy, has the domestic price equal to the world price, and so domestic supply is Q_1 and domestic demand is Q_3, with imports making up the difference $(Q_3 - Q_1)$. When the government introduces a subsidy on rice prices, thus lowering the domestic price below the world price by $P_w - P_d$, demand increases to Q_4 and domestic supply drops to Q_2, both because of lower prices. The import gap widens to $Q_4 - Q_2$.

The government must pay a budget subsidy on all imported rice since the world price is higher than the domestic price. The total subsidy is $(P_w - P_d) \cdot (Q_4 - Q_2)$, or the per unit subsidy times total imports. This amount shows up in Figure 1 as the rectangle BEHG. The rest of the subsidy is paid implicitly by farmers because of the lower price they receive. Their income transfer to consumers is equal to the unit subsidy times total production, or rectangle ABGF, plus

the profits lost by reducing output, the triangle BCG. It is clear that the total economic costs of the subsidy policy are much larger than just the cost of the budget subsidy itself.

Although consumers clearly benefit by this price subsidy on rice, their total gain is less than the sum of the budget subsidy and implicit transfer from farmers. The difference is due to the efficiency losses caused by the price distortions introduced by the wedge between domestic and international rice prices. In this example, there are efficiency losses in both the producing and consuming sectors.

The production efficiency losses are measured by the dotted triangle BCG. Because domestic resources can be used to produce rice more cheaply than the opportunity cost of imports as long as the domestic supply curve is below the world price, the triangle between the world price, the domestic price, and the domestic supply curve is an area of wasted resources. The cost of this waste is paid by the budget, but no commensurate gains accrue to consumers.

On the consumer side, the demand curve represents the price consumers are willing to pay for each quantity; so a lower price produces benefits for consumers who were willing to pay a higher price but no longer have to. This consumer surplus is reflected by the area under the demand curve but above the consumer price. In Figure 1 the increase in consumer surplus is measured by the quadrilateral figure ADHF. The government budget subsidies needed to move the domestic price from P_w to P_d are greater than the gain in consumer surplus that comes from the lower prices. The consumption efficiency loss is shown by the triangle DEH.

One last lesson is apparent from the figure. The country using subsidies to provide consumers with imported rice at prices lower than those in the international market has reduced the degree of food self-sufficiency achieved relative to what would have occurred with free trade. An entirely different result would come from restricting imports and causing domestic rice prices to rise above world levels. If pursued far enough, a policy of pushing up rice prices could result in self-sufficiency for the country illustrated in Figure 1. In fact, if domestic rice prices were maintained at P_s, the country would exactly reach self-sufficiency, with domestic rice consumption just equaling domestic production. The point is not that pursuing such self-sufficiency is a good or a bad policy, but rather that any policy debate about food self-sufficiency

FIGURE 1. Effects of a subsidy policy on a consumer import, rice.

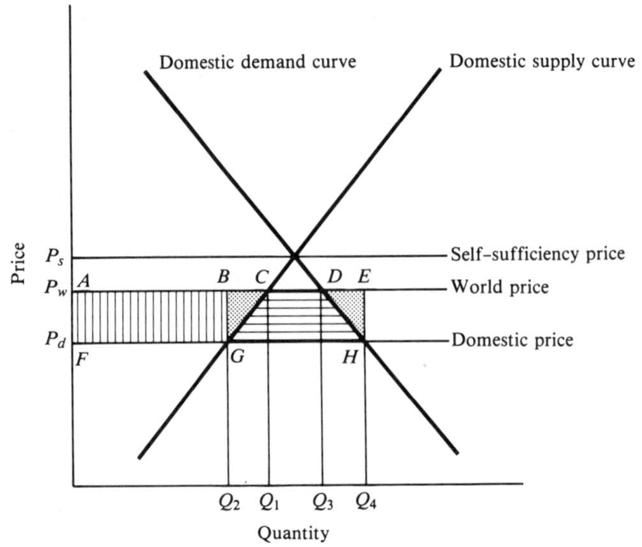

can be conducted only in the context of the domestic price environment relative to world prices. Self-sufficiency at price P_s could be a bitter policy victory if it reduces food consumption and displaces the production of other important agricultural commodities.

Trade Restrictions

Trade policies that place restrictions on the flow of imports or exports of a commodity can be analyzed by using diagrams similar to Figure 1. A trade restriction can be applied to either the price or the quantity of the commodity to reduce the amount traded internationally and to drive a wedge between the world price and the domestic price. For imports, the trade policy imposes either a per unit tariff (import tax) or a quantitative restriction (import quota) to limit the quantity imported and raise the domestic price above the world price. Likewise, trade policy for exports limits the quantity exported through imposition of either a per unit export tax or an export quota, and the result is to cause the domestic price to be lower than the world price.

If, for example, a trade policy restricts imports of textiles through imposition of a tariff, producers of textiles gain because the domestic price rises above the world price. In response to higher local textile prices, production expands, consumption declines, and the quantity of imports is reduced. Since the domestic price is raised, consumers transfer income to producers

and to the government budget because of the duties paid on imports. As with the consumer subsidy on rice, efficiency losses occur in both production and consumption because the policy-adjusted price is higher than the world price, which represents the actual opportunity costs of imports. A tariff on textiles reduces the food parity price because textile prices rise for farmers, thus increasing the price index of manufactured items purchased by farmers. Hence the relative food parity price falls.

Effects of Price Policies

Price policies can be classified into six categories:

Policies Benefiting Producers	Policies Benefiting Consumers
Subsidy Policies	
Producer subsidies on importables	Consumer subsidies on importables
Producer subsidies on exportables	Consumer subsidies on exportables
Trade Policies	
Restrictions on imports	Restrictions on exports

Each price policy can be analyzed graphically (as in Figure 1) to determine the impact on quantities produced, consumed, and traded; on income transfers among producers, consumers, and the budget; and on efficiency losses in production and consumption. The results of these analyses are shown in Table 1, which summa-

TABLE 1. Summary of Effects of Price Policies

Type of Policy	Quantity (increase, no change, or decrease)			Transfer (gains, no change, or losses)			Efficiency Loss (incurred or no change)	
	Production	Consumption	Trade	Producers	Consumers	Budget	Production	Consumption
Producer subsidy on importables	+	0	−	+	0	−	X	0
Producer subsidy on exportables	+	−	+	+	−	−	X	X
Consumer subsidy on importables	−	+	+	−	+	−	X	X
Consumer subsidy on exportables	0	+	−	0	+	−	0	X
Restrictions on imports	+	−	−	+	−	+	X	X
Restrictions on exports	−	+	−	−	+	+	X	X

Note: X indicates an efficiency loss is incurred.

rizes the impact of each price policy and reveals several important effects of price policy interventions.

In the short-run, static world of this analysis all price policy interventions incur efficiency losses in either production or consumption relative to an international price standard. The only exception is when a price policy intervention specifically offsets an existing source of static inefficiency, such as a divergence between public and private profitability that occurs because of externalities or economies of scale. Most policies have efficiency losses in both production and consumption. Long-run efficiency gains are possible if the subsidies call forth dynamic forces leading to technical change or the maturation of infant industries, but these forces are not automatic. In many circumstances the short-run efficiency losses have tended to accumulate and widen the distortions in the economy.

A government uses food price policy to bring about basic changes in the food system. Incentive prices can encourage production, discourage consumption, and reduce imports. Alternatively, food subsidies can reduce production, increase consumption, and increase imports. All price policies have opposite (or at least neutral) effects on production and consumption. To increase both the production and consumption of food would require maintaining a dual price policy involving subsidies to both producers and consumers. . . .

All price policies have an impact on quantities traded internationally since, by definition, the policies apply only to tradable commodities. The welfare effects of price policies for nontradables are difficult to measure because of the absence of an international price standard of comparison. Table 1 shows that most price policies reduce trade. This tendency is related to the pervasive efficiency losses incurred by price policies. Because trade leads to gains in economic efficiency through better allocation of productive resources, policies that reduce trade will likely incur efficiency losses.

The allocative effects of price policies on quantities produced, consumed, and traded have corresponding income distribution effects that occur as transfers are made among producers, consumers, and the budget. The full incidence of such transfers can be understood only in the context of the burden of raising tax revenues for the budget, but the direct gains to producers and consumers, before taxes are netted out, are shown in Table 1. Transfers to producers and consumers tend to mirror the effects on quantities produced and consumed. More important, all subsidy policies incur negative budget transfers while trade restrictions earn the government a budget surplus. Such budget losses or gains are only a part of the total economic transfers occasioned by price policy, and frequently only a tiny part if traded quantities are small relative to total domestic production and consumption. The implicit transfers between producers and consumers are often the most important aspects of food price policy and yet are the least visible.

For some purposes of food policy, knowing the direction of policy effects is enough. In most situations the actual measurement is required. Demand and supply elasticities permit the empirical analysis of trade, transfer, and efficiency effects. Because of the static nature of this analysis, these measured effects reflect short-run adjustments only. The dynamic adjustments of the food system to long-run price distortions are at least as important, as is the disaggregated welfare impact relative to the average impact reflected in this analysis. Income and price elasticities for each income class are necessary to disaggregate the impact on the poor of the various subsidy and trade policies. Typically the nonfarm poor will be disproportionately benefited by price policies that lower food prices and transfer income to consumers at large and will be disproportionately hurt by higher food prices and income transfers to farmers, at least in the short run. Price policies designed for efficiency and more rapid growth of farm output will have a dynamic side effect of creating more jobs in rural areas and probably in urban areas as well.

The policy problem is one of finding mechanisms to protect the food intake of poor urban and rural landless consumers while the dynamic growth process has time to build momentum. . . .

While food subsidies that favor consumers can operate within the general price policy environment created by trade and subsidy policies with respect to international border prices, specific subsidies targeted to reach poor urban and rural landless consumers are likely to be implemented through the marketing system. The mutual interaction of food subsidies and the marketing system can be analyzed with the same tools that were used for supply and demand analysis and for determining the effects of trade and subsidy policies.

Subsidies and the Food Price Dilemma

Both socialist and capitalist economies use a variety of subsidies to protect their producers and consumers from the full brunt of the food price dilemma. Developed countries with highly productive farmers often end up paying huge price subsidies to prevent their productivity from driving many farmers into bankruptcy. Developing countries use subsidies to their consumers to allow small household budgets to be stretched just a bit further, thus saving some of the very poor from the brink of starvation itself. Socialist economies often face the food price dilemma directly by attempting to maintain entirely separate and unconnected prices for producers and consumers. This requires that the state carry out all of the functions of the marketing system.

Some countries have managed these respective tasks quite efficiently and have equitable food distribution and vigorous food producing sectors to show for it. Hungary and Costa Rica are examples. Others have been trapped by the size of budget deficits or by the lack of information and the inability to make appropriate allocative decisions. The failure is characteristic of bureaucratic behavior in the absence of markets where price formation takes place.

Comment: Agricultural Pricing Policy

A five-volume research project, *The Political Economy of Agricultural Pricing Policy* (1991–92), sponsored by the World Bank, presents some significant findings on the experience of 18 developing countries.

The project provides systematic estimates of the degree of price discrimination against agriculture within individual countries and explains how it changed over time; determines how this intervention affected such key variables as foreign exchange earnings, agricultural output, and income distribution; and offers further insight into the political economy of agricultural pricing policy through a study of the motivations of policy makers, the economic and political factors determining the degree of agricultural intervention, and the attempts to reform unsuccessful policies.

The main findings of the comparative study of agricultural price interventions are

- The indirect tax on agriculture from industrial protection and macroeconomic policies was about 22 percent on average for the eighteen countries over 1960–85—nearly three times the direct tax from agricultural pricing policies (about 8 percent). The total tax (direct plus indirect) was thus 30 percent.
- Industrial protection policies taxed agriculture more than did real overvaluation of the exchange rate.
- High taxation of agriculture was associated with low growth in agriculture—and low growth in the economy.
- The transfers out of agriculture have been enormous. The net effect of total (direct plus indirect) interventions averaged 46 percent of agricultural gross domestic product (GDP) from 1960 to 1984. These transfers ranged from 2 percent for the protectors (Korea and Portugal) to 140 percent of actual agricultural GDP in Sub-Saharan African countries. Such enormous transfers must have severely depressed private investment and growth in agriculture.
- Surprisingly, most countries protected importables. On average, the direct protection of importables was about 18 percent and the direct taxation of exportables about 16 percent, for an average impact on the relative price of importables to exportables of about 40 percent. These distortions within agriculture increased between the early 1960s and mid-1980s.
- Direct price policies stabilized domestic agricultural prices relative to world prices, with an average reduction in variability of 25 percent and even more when world prices were highly volatile. Indirect policies contributed little, if anything, to price stability.
- Public investment in agriculture did not compensate for adverse price policies.
- The effect of removing agricultural price interventions is not regressive. In most countries, removing direct (or total) interventions changed the real incomes of the poorer urban and rural groups by less than 5 percent (up or down). More often than not, the rural poor gained from the removal of the interventions.
- The contribution of agriculture to fiscal revenues has fallen over time and is on average small.[1]

[1]World Bank, *The Political Economy of Agricultural Pricing Policy* (1992), vol. 4, pp. 199–200.

It is concluded:

> Discrimination against agriculture in developing countries has generally been pronounced. It has been more extreme the more ideologically committed those influencing policy have been to the notions of modernization through industrialization and import substitution; it has been more extreme where agricultural production consists predominantly of traditional exportable commodities; and it has been more extreme when agricultural interests have not been part of the governing coalition.
>
> Indirect discrimination against agriculture through trade regime and exchange rate policies is generally of greater importance than direct discrimination. Interestingly, however, most major reforms of direct agricultural pricing policies have been carried out in conjunction with major reforms of the overall trade and payments regimes.[2]

[2]Ibid., vol. 5, p. 139.

Comment: Rural Environmental Policy

Agricultural policy must also be concerned with the future exploitation of land, forest, water, and fisheries. To reduce the pressure to absorb more natural resources, rural environmental policy should seek to increase the yields of those resources that are already in use. Extensive growth of agriculture, however, is likely to be necessary in addition to agricultural intensification. The World Bank therefore concludes that improvement in resource management will have to include three essential components:

- A recognition of the true value of natural resources. Failure to accept that natural resources are ultimately in finite supply, and divergences in the private and social costs of resource exploitation, are root cause of many environmental problems: erosion of deforested hill slopes, releases of carbon dioxide by land-clearing fires, and losses of biological diversity as a result of poorly controlled logging.
- Institutions that match responsibility for resource management with accountability for results. The public sector will inevitably retain responsibility for allocating some of the most sensitive natural resources; it will often own them and will sometimes manage them. Governments need to make sure that those who use natural resources bear the full costs of doing so. But when public institutions are themselves directly involved in production, that rarely happens.
- Better knowledge of the extent, quality, and potential of the resource base. At present, emerging constraints that confront resource management are often poorly understood; research is hampered by inadequate funding. In addition to developing new knowledge and techniques, there is a need to accelerate the diffusion of existing technology that can expand output in environmentally sound ways.[1]

For an extensive bibliography on environmental management, see World Bank, *World Development Report, 1992* (1992), pp. 183–91.

[1]World Bank, *World Development Report, 1992* (1992), p. 136.

VIII.C.4. The Case for a Unimodal Strategy*

The historical experience in a number of countries, and the recent technical breakthroughs of the Green Revolution, justify major emphasis on increases in factor productivity. It is, however, the experience of Japan and Taiwan that is es-

*From Bruce F. Johnston, "Criteria for the Design of Agricultural Development Strategies," *Food Research Institute Studies in Agricultural Economics, Trade, and Development*, Vol. 11, No. 1, 1972, pp. 35–37, 42–54. Copyright 1972 by the Board of Trustees of Leland Stanford Junior University.

pecially useful in demonstrating that an *appropriate* sequence of innovations based on modern scientific knowledge and experimental methods makes possible an expansion path for the agricultural sector that is characterized by large increases in factor productivity *throughout* the agricultural sector. Such a strategy enables a widening fraction of the working population in agriculture to be associated with increasingly productive technologies, based mainly on expanded use of purchased inputs that are divisible and neutral to scale. It is because the new inputs of seed and fertilizer, that are the essence of the Green Revolution, are complementary to the large amounts of labor and land already committed to agriculture that these increases in factor productivity can have such a large impact on total farm output. At the same time, by involving an increasing large fraction of the rural population in the process of technical change, such a strategy means that the fruits of economic progress are widely shared.

The Choice Between Unimodal and Bimodal Agricultural Strategies

The most fundamental issue of agricultural strategy faced by the late developing countries is to choose between a bimodal strategy whereby resources are concentrated within a subsector of large, capital-intensive units or a unimodal strategy which seeks to encourage a more progressive and wider diffusion of technical innovations adapted to the factor proportions of the sector as a whole. The essential distinction between the two approaches is that the unimodal strategy emphasizes sequences of innovations that are highly divisible and largely scale-neutral. These are innovations that can be used efficiently by small-scale farmers and adopted progressively. A unimodal approach does not mean that all farmers or all agricultural regions would adopt innovations and expand output at uniform rates. Rather it means that the type of innovations emphasized are appropriate to a progressive pattern of adoption in the twofold sense that there will be progressive diffusion of innovations within particular areas and extension of the benefits of technical change to new areas as changes in environmental conditions, notably irrigation facilities, or improved market opportunities or changes in the nature of the innovations available enable farmers in new areas to participate in the process of modernization. Although a bimodal strategy entails a much more rapid adoption of a wider range of modern technologies, this is necessarily confined to a small fraction of farm units because of the structure of economies in which commercial demand is small in relation to a farm labor force that still represents some 60 to 80 percent of the working population.

The late developing countries face a wide choice of farm equipment embodying large investments in research and development activity in the economically advanced countries. The performance characteristics of these machines are impressive, and representatives of the major manufacturing firms in the economically advanced countries are experienced and skillful in demonstrating their equipment. And they now have added incentive to promote sales in the developing countries to more fully utilize their plant capacity which is large relative to domestic demand (mainly a replacement demand since the period of rapid expansion of tractors and tractor-drawn equipment in the developed countries has ended). The availability of credit under bilateral and international aid programs temporarily eliminates the foreign exchange constraint to acquiring such equipment; and when such loans are readily available it may even appear to be an attractive means of increasing the availability of resources—in the short run. Within developing countries there is often considerable enthusiasm for the latest in modern technologies. But little attention is given to research and development activity and support services to promote the manufacture and wide use of simple, inexpensive equipment of good design, low import content, and suited to the factor proportions prevailing in countries where labor is relatively abundant and capital scarce. . . .

Under a bimodal strategy frontier firms with their high capital to labor ratio would account for the bulk of commercial production and would have the cash income required to make extensive use of purchased inputs. Inasmuch as the schedule of aggregate commercial demand for agricultural products is inelastic and its rightward shift over time is essentially a function of the rate of structural transformation, to concentrate resources within a subsector of agriculture inevitably implies a reduction in the ability of farm households outside that subsector to adopt new purchased inputs and technologies. In addition, the high foreign exchange content of many of the capital inputs employed in the frontier sector implies a reduction in the amount of foreign exchange available for imported inputs for other farm firms (or for other sectors). It is, of course, because of these purchasing power and foreign exchange constraints that it is impossible for the agricultural sector as a whole to pursue a crash modernization strategy. It might be argued that a proper farm credit program could eliminate the purchasing power constraint, but the availability of credit (assuming that repayment takes place) merely alters the shape of the time horizon over which the constraint operates. And capital and government revenue are such scarce resources in a developing country that government subsidy programs are not feasible means of escaping from this constraint. In brief, bimodal and unimodal strategies are to a considerable extent mutually exclusive.

Under the bimodal approach the divergence between the factor intensities and the technical efficiency of "best" and average firms is likely to become progressively greater as agricultural transformation takes place. Moreover, both the initial and subsequent divergences between the technologies used in the two sectors are likely to be accentuated because the factor prices, including the price of imported capital equipment, faced by the modern sector in contemporary developing countries typically diverge from social opportunity cost. This divergence is obvious when subsidized credit is made available on a rationed basis to large farmers and when equipment can be imported with a zero or low tariff at an official exchange rate that is overvalued. In addition, the large-scale farmers depend on hired labor rather than unpaid family labor. The wages paid hired labor may be determined by minimum wage legislation, and even without a statutory minimum the price of hired labor is characteristically higher than the opportunity cost of labor to small farm units. . . .

Under the unimodal strategy with its emphasis on highly divisible and scale-neutral innovations, the best firms in the agrarian sector display essentially the same factor intensities as average firms. Interfarm differences in performance will be large, especially during transitional periods as farmers are learning how to use new inputs efficiently, but this will reflect mainly differences in output per unit of input rather than major differences in factor proportions. Inasmuch as the expansion path for the agricultural sector associated with a unimodal strategy implies a level of capital intensity and foreign exchange requirements that are compatible with a late developing country's economic structure, more firms within the agricultural sector are able to expand their use of fertilizer and the other divisible inputs that dominate purchases under this strategy. Thus, the diffusion of innovations and associated inputs will be more broadly based, and the divergence in factor intensities between frontier firms and average firms will be moderate.

Although the foregoing has emphasized the contrast in the pattern of technical change, it is apparent that the two strategies will have significantly different impacts on many dimensions of economic and social change. Most obvious are the differences in the nature of demand for farm inputs, but the structure of rural demand for consumer goods will also be very different under a unimodal as compared to a bimodal strategy.

A major difference in income distribution is to be expected because of the likelihood that under a bimodal strategy the difficult problem of absorbing a rapidly growing labor force into productive employment would be exacerbated whereas under a unimodal strategy there is a good prospect that the rate of increase in demand for labor would be more rapid than the growth of the labor force. Underemployment and unemployment would thus be reduced as a result of wide participation of the rural population in improved income-earning opportunities. This improvement in income opportunities available to members of the rural work force would result in part from increased earnings as hired labor since rising demand for labor would tend to raise wage rates and the number of days of work available during the year for landless laborers and for very small farmers whose incomes derive to a considerable extent from work on farms that are above average size.

Most important, however, would be the increased incomes earned by farm households cultivating their own or rented land. The extent to which tenants would be able to share in the increased productivity resulting from yield-increasing innovations will be determined by forces related to land reform as an aspect of broadly based improvements in the welfare of the rural population. Basically, however, it will depend upon the rate of growth of the rural population of working age seeking a livelihood in farming or in nonfarm activities relative to the rate of expansion of income-earning opportunities. The latter will be influenced strongly by the demand on the part of landowners for labor "hired" indirectly as laborers on owner-operated farms.

The Multiple Objectives of an Agricultural Strategy

In the paragraphs that follow I comment briefly on some of the reasons why the design of an efficient strategy for agriculture should be guided by explicit consideration of four major objectives of an agricultural strategy and the interrelationships among them. . . .

Contributions to overall economic growth and structural transformation. It is conventional when considering agriculture's role in economic development to catalog a number of specific "contributions." Several of these contributions imply a net transfer of factors of production out of the agricultural sector as the process of structural transformation takes place. Typically the farm sector provides foreign exchange, public and private investment resources, and labor to the more rapidly expanding sectors of the economy as well as increased supplies of food and raw materials to support a growing urban population and manufacturing sector.

These contributions are, of course, synonymous with the increased sectoral interdependence that characterizes a developing economy. Outward labor migration and increased farm purchasing power are synchronized with the growing importance of commodity flows between agriculture and other sectors: a flow of food and raw materials out of agriculture and a return flow of farm inputs and consumer goods from the manufacturing sector. Tertiary activities of government, transport, marketing and other service industries expand to meet the needs of individual sectors and to facilitate the linkages between them.

Agricultural exports have special significance here for two reasons. First, in countries that have experienced little structural transformation there are usually few alternative means of meeting the growing demands for foreign exchange that characterize a developing economy. Secondly, expanded production for export makes it possible to enlarge farm cash incomes when the domestic market for purchased food is still very small, and at the same time it provides a stimulus and the means to establish some of the physical infrastructure and institutions that are necessary for the creation of a national, market-oriented economy.

The structure of rural demand for farm inputs associated with alternative agricultural strategies exerts an important influence on the growth of local manufacturing as well as on the pattern of productivity advance within agriculture. I emphasize the composition of this demand because the capacity of the agricultural sector to purchase inputs from other sectors is powerfully constrained by the proportion of the population living outside agriculture. Pathological growth of population in urban areas only loosely related to the growth of off-farm employment opportunities is a conspicuous and distressing feature of many of the contemporary less developed countries, but basically this growth of urban population depends on the transformation of a country's occupational structure that is a concomitant of economic growth.

The nature of the linkages between agriculture and the local manufacturing sector and the seriousness of foreign exchange and investment constraints on development will be influenced significantly by the structure of rural demand for both inputs and consumer goods. Because of their differential effects on the sequence of innovations and on rural income distribution, a bimodal and a unimodal strategy will differ greatly in their aggregate capital and foreign exchange requirements.

The more capital-intensive bimodal strategy emphasizes rapid adoption of mechanical innovations such as tractors along with chemical fertilizers and other inputs essential for increasing crop yields. Even if that type of machinery is manufactured locally, the foreign exchange requirements for capital equipment and for components are high, and the production processes require a high level of technical sophistication, large plants, and capital-intensive technologies.

The unimodal strategy with its emphasis on mechanical innovations of lower technical sophistication and foreign exchange content, such as improved bullock implements and low-lift pumps, appears to offer greater promise for the development of local manufacturing which is less demanding in its technical requirements and which is characterized by lower capital-labor ratios and lower foreign exchange content. On the basis of experience in Japan and Taiwan as well as an analysis of the nature of the supply response to the two patterns of demand, it seems clear that a unimodal strategy will have a much more favorable impact on the growth of output and especially on the growth of employment in local manufacturing and supporting service industries. The reasons cannot be pursued here except to note the wider diffusion of opportunities to develop entrepreneurial and technical skills through "learning by doing" that leads to increasing competence in manufacturing. Progress in metalworking and in the domestic manufacture of capital goods are especially significant because they are necessary to the creation of an industrial sector adapted to the factor proportions of a late developing economy.

Increasing farm productivity and output. The differences in farm productivity between modern and traditional agriculture are, of course, to be attributed mainly to their use of widely different technologies. Those differences in turn are based on large differences in their use of fixed and working capital and associated differences in their investments in human resources that affect the level and efficiency of agricultural research and other supporting services as well as the knowledge, skills, and innovativeness of the farm population.

The importance of distinguishing between inputs and innovations that are mainly instrumental in increasing output per acre and those that make it possible for each farm worker to cultivate a larger area has already been noted. Biological and chemical innovations increase agricultural productivity mainly through increasing yields per acre. In general the effect on yield of farm mechanization *per se* is slight, although certain mechanical innovations, notably tubewells and low-lift pumps may be highly complementary to yield-increasing innovations. Indeed, for some high-yielding varieties, especially rice, an ample and reliable supply of water is a necessary precondition for realizing the genetic potential of the new varieties. This distinction between yield-increasing and labor-saving innovations is significant because the relative emphasis given to these two types of innovations largely determines whether development of agriculture will follow a unimodal or bimodal pattern.

The thrust of a unimodal strategy is to encourage general diffusion of yield-increasing innovations and such mechanical innovations as are complementary with the new seed-fertilizer technology. The bimodal strategy emphasizes simultaneous adoption of innovations that increase substantially the amount of land which individual cultivators can efficiently work in addition to the yield-increasing innovations emphasized in the unimodal approach.

For reasons discussed above, it is not possible for developing countries to pursue the unimodal and bimodal options simultaneously. In placing emphasis on reinforcing success within a subsector of large and capital-intensive farms, a bimodal strategy may have an advantage in maximizing the rate of increase in the short run because it bypasses the problems and costs associated with involving a large fraction of the farm population in the modernization process. In a longer view, however, a unimodal strategy appears to be more efficient, especially in minimizing requirements for the scarce resources of foreign exchange and loanable funds.

Policies and programs to ensure that the seed-fertilizer revolution is exploited as widely and as fully as possible are clearly of central impor-

tance. This emphasizes the importance of adaptive research and of training and extension programs to promote further diffusion of new varieties and to narrow the gap between yields at the farm level and the potential yields obtainable. Investments in infrastructure and in land and water development required to provide environmental conditions favorable to the introduction of more productive technologies are also priority needs. . . .

The distribution of land ownership and, more particularly, the size distribution of operational units are highly important factors influencing the choice of technique and the factor proportions that characterize the expansion path of the agricultural sector. Both are influenced by policies and practices affecting land tenure which are discussed in the following section.

Achieving broadly based improvement in the welfare of the rural population. In a longer term view substantial improvement in the welfare of the rural population depends upon the process of structural change which, inter alia, makes possible a reduction in the absolute size of the rural population, a large increase in commercial demand for farm products, and large increases in the capital-labor ratio in agriculture. There are, however, some more direct relationships between strategies for agriculture and the improvement of rural welfare that need to be considered.

Rural works programs are probably the more frequently discussed measure aimed directly at improving the welfare of the poorest segments of the farm population. There is much to be said for such programs as a means of providing supplemental employment and income to the most disadvantaged members of the rural population and at the same time building infrastructure important to agriculture and other sectors. But because of the organizational problems and particularly the severe fiscal constraints that characterize a developing country, it seems doubtful whether this approach can have a very substantial effect on underemployment and unemployment in rural areas. . . .

Other programs also merit attention because they offer the promise of substantial benefits relative to their cost, and some of them can also make a substantial contribution to the expansion of output by improving the health and productivity of the rural population. Public health programs such as malaria control are notable examples. The success of such programs is, of course, a major factor underlying the population explosion and the urgent need for policies and programs that will have both direct and indirect effects in encouraging the spread of family planning. Nutritional programs also deserve attention. The effects on well-being of increased farm productivity and incomes can be enhanced considerably if diet changes are informed by practical programs of nutrition education. . . .

Although it is foolhardy to attempt to treat the complex and controversial subject of land tenure in a few paragraphs, the positive and negative effects on rural welfare of land reform programs cannot be ignored. In Asia the land tenure situation is dominated by the fact that the area of arable land is small relative to the large and growing farm population entirely or mainly dependent on agriculture for their livelihood. One implication of this, which is distressing but beyond dispute, is that for the agricultural sector as a whole in these countries the average farm size will become even smaller—or at least that the number of agricultural workers per acre of arable land will continue to increase for several decades until a structural transformation turning point is reached.

It is sometimes argued that because of the connection between size of holding and choice of technique, redistributive land reform is a necessary condition for a unimodal strategy. Indeed it is even claimed that the success of unimodal strategies in Japan and Taiwan is attributable to their postwar land reforms, notwithstanding the fact that in both countries the basic pattern of progressive modernization of small-scale, labor-intensive, but technically progressive farm units was established long before World War II.

I am persuaded that an effectively implemented land reform program that brings about a more equal distribution of landed wealth will not only contribute to the goal of equity but will also tend to facilitate low-cost expansion of farm output based primarily on yield-increasing innovations. Although such a program would appear to be desirable, there is reason to believe that for a good many Asian countries it is not a likely outcome. It therefore seems important to emphasize that historical evidence and logic both contradict the view that in the absence of land reform the pattern of agricultural development will inevitably accentuate the problems of rural underemployment and unemployment and the inequality of income distribution.

The critical factor determining the choice of technique and factor proportions in agriculture is the size distribution of operational (management) units rather than ownership units. Past ex-

perience, for example in prewar Japan and Taiwan, demonstrates that a highly skewed pattern of land ownership is not incompatible with a unimodal size distribution of operational units. To a considerable extent the widespread condemnation of tenancy, particularly of share tenancy, seems to stem from a tendency to confuse what is really a symptom with the root cause of the miserable existence that is the plight of so many tenant households in underdeveloped countries. The fact that tenants are prepared to accept rental arrangements that leave them such a meager residual income is fundamentally a consequence of the extreme lack of alternative income-earning opportunities. The proposition, briefly stated, is that bargaining between landowners and tenants will tend to result in equilibrium arrangements with respect to the rental share, the amount of land rented to individual tenants, the cropping pattern and other farm practices, and sharing of expenses of inputs. These arrangements will tend to maximize the landowner's rental income subject to the constraint that a tenant and members of his household must obtain residual income that represents a ''wage'' approximately equal to his best alternative earnings or they will not enter into the agreement. To the extent that the proposition is valid, it means that improvement in the welfare of tenants must depend primarily on improving the income-earning opportunities available, including the possibility of enlarging their own holdings by redistributive land reform as well as the increase in demand for labor within and outside agriculture.

The advantages of organizing agricultural production primarily on the basis of small-scale units appropriate to the unfavorable man-land ratios that characterize the agricultural sector in late developing countries are enhanced by the new technical possibilities resulting from the seed-fertilizer revolution. Although those advantages are to a considerable extent a function of the size of operational units, there are some specific advantages of owner cultivation related to productivity considerations as well as the more obvious effects on income distribution. Although in principle investments in land improvement that are profitable will be made by the landowner, by the tenant, or under some joint agreement, the division of responsibility in decision-making is likely to delay or prevent investments even though they would be to the advantage of both parties. Owner cultivation also avoids the difficulties that arise when landlords, responding to higher yields, raise the percentage share of output that they demand as rent. But if redistributive land reform is not a realistic possibility, widespread renting of land seems clearly preferable to the further concentration of land in large operational units and the bimodal pattern which is thereby accentuated.

Facilitating the processes of social modernization by encouraging widespread attitudinal and behavioral changes. The spread of economic and technical change among the rural population, buttressed by a network of institutions and communication links, undoubtedly has significant effects on the process of social modernization that go beyond their effects on economic growth. It seems likely that the broad impact of a unimodal strategy would have favorable effects in three areas important to this process of social change. First, the wide diffusion of familiarity with the calculation of costs and returns and of opportunities to acquire managerial experience would appear to provide a favorable environment for the training and recruitment of entrepreneurs. The same would apply, of course, to the wider diffusion of learning experiences in manufacturing which is associated with a unimodal strategy.

Secondly, a broadly based approach to agricultural development seems likely to generate strong support for rural education as well as the institutions more directly related to promoting increased agricultural productivity. It is sometimes argued that large-scale, highly commercialized farm enterprises are easier to tax than millions of small units. Because of the power structure maintained or created by a bimodal

strategy, however, the greater administrative convenience may in practice mean very little. The fact that public education, and especially rural education, in most of South America seems to lag behind progress in other developing countries where average incomes are considerably lower seems to provide some support for this generalization.

Thirdly, and most important, the reduction in birthrates in the countryside, resulting from spontaneous changes in attitudes and behavior as well as behavioral changes induced by government population programs, are likely to be more widespread and have a greater effect on the national birthrate under a unimodal than a bimodal strategy. For reasons examined earlier, the bulk of the population in the late developing countries is going to be in the agricultural sector for several decades or more. Under those circumstances rapid reduction in a country's birthrate to bring it into tolerable balance with a sharply reduced death rate cannot be achieved unless family planning spreads in the countryside as well as in towns and cities. It seems probable that reasonably rapid changes in this domain of behavior are more likely to take place if the dynamic processes of economic and technical change affect a large fraction of a rural population involved to an increasing extent in formal and informal education and communication networks (including mass media). It also seems likely that the wider spread of improved income and educational opportunities will affect motivations in ways favorable to the practice of family planning. . . .

VIII.C.5. Strategic Priorities for Agriculture*

The focus here has been on CARLs (countries with abundant rural labor), because their distinctive characteristics strongly influence the choice of development strategies. In all CARLs, the need to simultaneously expand jobs and labor productivity in agriculture is a fundamental (and unavoidable) challenge. For most CARLs,

*From Thomas P. Tomich, Peter Kilby, and Bruce F. Johnston, *Transforming Agrarian Economies: Opportunities Seized, Opportunities Missed* (Ithaca: Cornell University Press, 1995), Conclusion. Reprinted by permission.

agriculture's dominant share of the workforce is reinforced by rapid population growth of 2–4 percent a year, compounding the difficulty of changing the occupational composition of the labor force. In an agrarian economy, even with rapid expansion in industrial and service jobs, the proportion of the agricultural labor force will fall only slowly. And for years (often decades), the absolute size of the farm workforce will grow. So, CARLs can eliminate widespread hunger and mass poverty only with a structural transformation and a demographic transition.

The shortage of physical and human capital in CARLs is associated with underdeveloped markets, with the weak capacity of government to provide services, and with the low productive efficiency of firms. Although agriculture predominates in the early stages of structural transformation, a diverse nonfarm sector also figures strongly in the unspecialized rural economy of CARLs. So, development strategies for agriculture and rural nonfarm activities are as important to CARLs as those for industry strategy are to the newly industrialized countries, at a later stage of structural transformation.

Differing natural resource endowments are one cause of different patterns of agricultural development, as shown in Japan and the United States. But policy choices matter more for the growth of productivity than do endowments of land, petroleum, or whatever. Since the evolution of markets and other economic institutions is both a cause and a consequence of structural transformation, the scope (and limits) of government policy vary throughout the long process of development. The ''right'' policies thus depend on the stage of structural transformation. Market imperfections and high public expectations often propel governments toward interventions. But limited governmental capacity along with the inevitable tensions accompanying political development can easily subvert those interventions. CARLs face a policy double bind: they have the greatest need for public initiative but the least capacity to design appropriate policies and to finance and implement them. Hence, the crucial need to identify priorities. . . .

The long-term results derive not from a grand strategic design but from the concrete policy choices governing our ''Six I's'': innovations, inputs, incentives, infrastructure, institutions, and initiative. Is agricultural research oriented toward the development of divisible *innovations*—that is, ones that can be used efficiently by small-scale units to complement, rather than displace, abundant labor? Is the allocation of scarce *inputs* handled by market-clearing prices, which give producers equal access, or are they rationed administratively in a way that gives privileged access to individuals with influence and wealth? Do price and marketing policies for agricultural products provide adequate *incentives* for efficient productivity growth? Does the design of public irrigation and the layout of the road network favor large farms over small ones, as in Mexico? Or does investment in rural *infrastructure* foster broad-based growth of rural out-

put and employment—farm and nonfarm—as in Taiwan? Are extension programs and other support *institutions* directed toward widespread adoption of innovations? Has the policy environment enabled farmers and other entrepreneurs to perceive and seize opportunities? Has government favored constructive public *initiatives*, such as the People's Bank in Indonesia? Or are they ill-advised initiatives, such as Mexico's Uxpanapa Project and land-rental ceilings designed to aid tenants but that encourage landlords to evict tenants and engage in mechanized cultivation of large farms? . . .

The Right Priorities

The crucial requirement for agricultural development is to create a favorable environment so that many individuals and firms perceive and seize opportunities. Changing conditions mean new opportunities, while many earlier initiatives will no longer be profitable. Thus the ability to learn from experience is crucial to avoid repeating costly mistakes and to reallocate resources to seize new opportunities.

Although individual firms often try to increase profits by stifling competition and the flow of information, they rarely succeed—except when the state is ''captured'' sufficiently to protect the monopoly of privileged firms. With that important caveat, markets are highly efficient not only in the transmission of information but also for the *discovery* of emerging opportunities.

Even so, new opportunities depend on the supporting role of government. Experience has shown the critical importance of public goods—education, agricultural research, rural infrastructure, public health, macroeconomic stability, and prices that reflect the scarcity value of resources. But it is too easy to expand the list of essential objectives that a CARL ''must'' achieve. Their severe constraints mean that priority should go to elements of development strategy that are necessary either to accelerate broad-based development or to complement it. . . .

The following strategic notions can help guide policymakers in reaching consensus on strategic priorities in CARLs:

As long as the opportunity cost of labor is low, broad-based productivity growth involving the majority of farms (which inevitably are small) is more efficient and provides more rural employ-

ment opportunities than a dualistic strategy aimed at a subsector of large farms. A broad-based agricultural strategy has important advantages for CARLs since they need to simultaneously expand jobs *and* raise labor productivity until they reach their structural transformation turning points.

The "Six I's"—innovations, inputs, incentives, infrastructure, institutions, and initiative—that are crucial to a broad-based agricultural strategy also promote expansion of rural non-farm activities. A successful broad-based agricultural strategy provides cash income and a pattern of demand that promotes growth in the rural non-farm economy. Furthermore, the rural infrastructure to serve agriculture (especially roads, electric power, communication, and market places in towns of 5,000 to 30,000 inhabitants) also lowers costs and expands opportunities for rural non-farm enterprises.

Policies favoring a subset of large farms can cause dramatic shifts toward a bimodal agrarian structure. Aside from redistributive land reform, policies that favor a unimodal agrarian structure work slowly. Thus, the advantages a unimodal agrarian structure holds for CARLs in terms of rural employment generation through mutually reinforcing agriculture-industry interactions are hard to obtain and easy to lose.

Macroeconomic policies can have an even more powerful effect on agricultural incentives than sectoral policies. The basic elements of sound macroeconomic policy—exchange rates near equilibrium, positive real interest rates near the opportunity cost of capital, and prudent fiscal policies—are essential to creating an environment conducive to broad-based development. Overvalued exchange rates and subsidized interest rates favor large enterprises over small

farms and firms. Control of the government budget is necessary to sustain funding of rural infrastructure, agricultural research, and social programs.

Some direct measures to enhance rural welfare complement agricultural development and accelerate structural transformation; others do not. Investments in human capital—especially rural primary education—have come to be regarded as important elements of successful agricultural development strategies. Selective public health interventions aimed at infants, pre-school children, and their mothers can improve child survival and maternal health at very low cost. They also are associated with rapid fertility decline, thereby hastening the structural transformation turning point. Consequently, these also deserve priority. . . .

Government's comparative advantage lies in provision of essential public goods and services. Minimizing the role of public agencies in commercial or productive activities is essential in CARLs because of the severe constraints they face. As a consequence, the first claim on scarce public finances and administrative capacities must go to those goods and services that will not be supplied adequately by the private sector. There is some scope for public sector initiative to catalyze or facilitate activities that are essentially commercial, but identifying and acting on these opportunities for public initiative is perhaps the most difficult strategic element.

The art of effective development strategies includes not only identifying government priorities but also sequencing activities in order to seize emerging opportunities. Chance will favor those policymakers who can recognize emerging opportunities—and who are prepared to act.

CHAPTER IX

Trade and Development

Countries must pursue their national development within the context of the world economy. Chapter V considered the effects of international capital movements and the transmission of technology on a country's development. Now we consider the ways in which international trade may contribute to development.

The central issue is whether there is a conflict between market-determined comparative advantage and the acceleration of development—whether in pursuing the gains from trade (as in neoclassical trade theory), a country might limit its intertemporal attainment of the gains from growth. Materials in section IX.A present opposing views on this issue. The significance of dynamic comparative advantage is emphasized (IX.A.1).

Some economists argue that the accrual of the gains from trade is biased in favor of the advanced industrial countries, that foreign trade has inhibited industrial development in the poorer nations, and that—contrary to what would be expected from neoclassical trade doctrine—free trade has in reality accentuated international inequalities. In contrast, others maintain the traditional position that foreign trade can contribute substantially to the development of primary-exporting countries and that the gains from international specialization merge with the gains from growth. A more eclectic approach, discussed in Note IX.A.4, attempts to identify the various conditions that favor—or inhibit—a process of export-led development.

As analyzed in section IX.B, the rate and structural pattern of a country's development will be influenced by whether the country's trade regime biases the allocation of resources toward import substitutes or is neutral and does not favor production for the domestic market over export promotion.

In theory, import substitution might be advocated on the basis of a reasoned consideration of how protectionism might improve the country's terms of trade, raise its savings ratio, take account of external economies, or overcome distortions in its dualistic labor market. In reality, however, import substitution has been practiced for other reasons. In particular, the persistent shortage of foreign exchange has dominated considerations of trade policy, and protectionist policies have been much more in the nature of ad hoc responses to recurrent balance-of-payments crises. The results of import-substitution industrialization (ISI) strategy, however, have been disappointing in most countries. The policies have not succeeded in reducing the foreign-exchange constraint; indeed, in some cases, it can be claimed that import-substitution policies have actually intensified the shortage. Nor have the policies of import replacement succeeded in achieving any widespread degree of industrialization beyond the immediate replacement of the final imported consumer goods. Nor has there been the expected progression from import replacement to production for export markets (as in the earlier Japanese case). Nor has industrial protection been an effective means of ameliorating the labor absorption problem. Nonetheless, import-substitution policies have become self-justifying in LDCs as their trade gap has widened, and countries have resorted to yet another round of import restrictions to meet the balance-of-payments problem. These disappointing results of import substitution in practice are reviewed in section IX.B.

The adverse effects of inward-looking policies have led to a shift of emphasis away from import substitution to export promotion, particularly of semimanufactured and manufactured exports. The policy lessons from the experience of the newly industrializing countries (NICs) are especially instructive, as is discussed in IX.B.3 and IX.B.4. Policies of trade liberalization have become essential for export promotion, and the problems associated with liberalization programs are examined in selections IX.B.6 and IX.B.7.

"New" trade theory concentrates on noncompetitive market structure and increasing returns to scale. This theory raises somewhat controversial questions as to its relevance for LDCs. Does it provide new insights for determining the pattern of trade? Does it provide new arguments for trade activism? Section IX.B and especially IX.B.4 consider these questions.

Although the new trade theory focuses on the microfoundations of trade, macroeconomic policies also affect the pattern of trade and trade policy. Selections IX.B.6 and IX.B.7 analyze the macro aspects of trade liberalization and the importance of competitive real exchange rates.

Although countries are now placing special emphasis on the potential for the export of manufactures, problems associated with the export of primary products also require urgent attention. As outlined in section IX.C., recession and inflation from the major industrial nations are transmitted to the developing countries through the international commodity markets. The impact of commodity market instability is of much concern to primary-product exporters. If commodity market instability has adverse effects on a country's development, how can such instability best be overcome or offset?

Moreover, developing countries seek not merely greater trade volume, but also trade at higher export prices. Both international commodity agreements for primary products and tariff preferences for manufactured exports have the objective of improving the LDCs' terms of trade by raising export prices, thereby effecting a transfer of real resources from consumers in developed countries to producers in LDCs. Note IX.C.2 discusses how the character of trade in primary products might be changed through the use of "producer power" and the establishment of international commodity agreements.

Proposals for regional integration, as a means of lessening the dependence on primary exports and accelerating development, have also gained increasing favor. With slower growth in the more developed countries (MDCs) and the slowdown of trade between the LDCs and the MDCs, there is now more consideration of how inter–LDC trade might be promoted. Note IX.D appraises the contributions that regional integration, in the form of a customs union or free trade area, might make to the development of its member nations.

IX.A. GAINS FROM TRADE VERSUS GAINS FROM GROWTH

IX.A.1. Dynamic Comparative Advantage—Note

What determines the commodities and services that a country will export or import? Why did the composition of exports from Japan change from raw silk and tea in the nineteenth century to textiles in the 1890s, to metals and machinery after World War II, and then on to capital-intensive and knowledge-intensive exports? Why in the course of two decades have exports from Taiwan changed from mushrooms to electronics? How can we predict the future exports and imports of a country?

The answers relate to the fundamental forces that determine a country's comparative advantage. The principle of comparative advantage has held pride of place in economic thought ever since the English economist David Ricardo enumerated it in 1817. In a simple illustration, under free trade, of what would determine trade between England and Portugal in wine and cloth, Ricardo focused on the relative differences in labor productivity in producing wine and cloth in England and Portugal. Even though Portugal is more productive ("better") than England in both wine and cloth, giving Portugal an absolute advantage in both wine and cloth, its labor is relatively more productive ("more better") in wine than in cloth. Portugal therefore has a comparative advantage in wine. England is less productive in both wine and cloth (absolute disadvantage), but has the lesser disadvantage—or comparative advantage—in cloth. In essence, technological differences between England and Portugal result in relative productivity differences that allow a basis for mutually profitable trade between the countries.

In a free market–price system, Portugal would then export wine and import cloth, while England exports cloth and imports wine. As a result, both countries can consume their importable commodity at a lower cost than if each country tried to produce each commodity for itself. The fundamental principle is that exports are the indirect means for securing the importable at a lower cost than if the country tried to produce the importable commodity directly at home. Specialization according to comparative advantage results in an efficient international division of labor, giving each country a higher real national income than it would have with no trade.

Comparative advantage is not simply a nineteenth-century principle. It has been refined and generalized to modern conditions. Recognizing all the factors of production that may be inputs, one element in the modern theory of comparative advantage focuses on factor proportions in the production of different products in different countries. The Swedish economist Bertil Ohlin emphasized that the basic determinant of a country's comparative advantage is relative factor endowment—that is, its relative factor supplies of natural resources, labor, and capital (the inputs necessary for production). Each country is endowed with different relative supplies of these factors of production. If a country's relatively abundant factor is labor, then wages will be relatively low, and the price of commodities that are also labor-intensive in their production will also be low. The country will then have a comparative advantage in labor-intensive products. Thus the Philippines exports labor-intensive products such as textiles, clothing, and footwear; Indonesia exports natural resource–intensive products such as oil and timber; the United States exports capital-intensive products such as chemicals, machinery, and aircraft.

Even if all other elements of production and consumption were identical for all countries, there would still be a basis for profitable international trade as long as the countries have different relative factor endowments. The differences in relative factor endowments—with some countries being relatively abundant in labor, while others are relatively abundant in capital or natural resources—are sufficient to give differences in costs and prices, thereby forming a basis for international trade. Beyond these minimum differences, however, other differences also contribute to a country's comparative advantage. These differences may be in technology, the quality of factors of production, economies of scale, or in consumption patterns.

The differences in resource endowments of labor, capital, and natural resources among nations account for the pattern of interindustry trade—the exchange of food (land intensive) or textiles (labor intensive) for machinery (capital intensive). A growing proportion of international trade—about one-fourth of world trade—is, however, intraindustry trade—for example, the exchange of automobiles for automobiles or office machines for office machines. The trade of manufactures against manufactures—accounting for 60 percent of world trade—is closely related to differences in technology among countries and economies of scale in production. Differences in skills, R&D, and innovations in new products are also highly correlated with differences in technology and economies of scale.

Dynamic Comparative Advantage

Nations have a comparative advantage in industries in which their firms gain a lead in technology, thereby allowing the creation of new products or product improvement. Innovations based on new technology initially gives a country a temporary monopoly position and easy access to foreign markets. For a period of time, the innovating industry may enjoy an export monopoly as long as there is an "imitation lag" in other countries. But eventually the technological gap is narrowed, the imitation lag is overcome, and other countries may then acquire a comparative advantage in the product.

More generally, a product life cycle occurs. This cycle is based not only on technology, but also on the changing mix of other inputs in production at different stages of the product's life. As depicted in Exhibit IX.1, a product moves over time from being a new product to being eventually a mature standardized product.

The determinants of the trade structure may change so much over time that a country that initially imported a product begins to substitute home-competing production for the import, becomes more efficient in its import-substitution production, and eventually acquires a comparative advantage for the mature product. This is the other side of the product cycle—what Japanese economists call the "catching-up product cycle." Overseas producers may then actually begin to export the "old" product to third countries and to the first country, which has lost its initial comparative advantage. A global product life cycle can thus occur over several country markets. For example, the production and export of TV sets from the United States gave way to imports from Japan and then from South Korea and Taiwan.

As the technological gap narrows and the imitation lag shortens, so too does the product gap. As the comparative advantage in the mix of input requirements changes over the product's life cycle, so does the comparative advantage of producing the product in one country rather than another. Through technological change, there is a continually changing international division of labor. Changes in comparative advantage can be expected to be even more rapid in the future as technological progress accelerates, imitation lags shorten, and product life cycles speed up.

The product cycle explains how comparative advantage of a new product is first acquired in the advanced economy and then transmitted to less developed economies through trade and investment. The catching-up process in the less developed describes the sequence from imports to import substitution and eventual exportation of the standardized product as domestic costs reach the international competitive cost threshold. As one country acquires new comparative advantages in products with different input requirements, other countries "in the queue" move into a competitive position in the earlier products: for example, South Korea and Taiwan become more competitive with Japan in the more labor-intensive products, while Japan moves on to the more skill- and knowledge-intensive products.

The product life cycle model explains some changes in comparative advantage. More generally, comparative advantage changes as a country's factor endowment changes. Over time, a country that is initially labor abundant may become relatively labor scarce; a country that is capital scarce may become more plentifully endowed with capital. South Korea and Taiwan, for example, have now reached a situation in which labor is relatively scarce and inexpensive labor has disappeared. At the same time, capital has been accumulated, and more of the country's exports reflect capital intensity.

Over time, as it develops, a country tends to proceed up a ladder of comparative advantage—from initially exporting commodities that are resource-intensive (sugar or rice) to commodities that are unskilled labor–intensive (textiles) to semiskilled and skilled labor–intensive (electronics) to capital-intensive (machines), and finally to knowledge-intensive (computers, robotic equipment) (Exhibit IX.2).

The upward movement is from exports that embody basic factors, such as natural resources and unskilled or semiskilled labor, to exports that embody more advanced and specialized factors such as modern digital data communications infrastructure, highly educated and skilled personnel, and R&D activities. The basic factors are passively inherited or created with relatively modest or unsophisticated investment. But the basic factors dominate only the lower rungs of the ladder with Ricardo-type and Ohlin-type goods that are based on "natural" comparative advantage. The advanced factors that dominate the top rungs of the ladder must be upgraded or created over time through considerable investment in human and physical capital in order to create comparative advantage in differentiated products and proprietary production technology.[1] The industries at the upper rungs of the ladder are often in imperfect competition and are subject to economies of scale.[2] They are Porter-type and Krugman-type goods, based on "created" comparative advantage.

Ladder and Queue

As Exhibit IX.2 illustrates, countries normally enter world markets by exporting natural resource–intensive exports (oil, jute, sugar) and then climb over time to higher rungs on the ladder of comparative advantage. As the early comers climb the ladder, latecomers to the queue can occupy the vacant rungs. For example, as Japan has proceeded up the ladder, Korea has come behind it—first exporting primary products in the late 1950s, subsequently moving upscale to textiles and plywood in the 1960s, and then to iron and steel products and electrical machinery in the 1970s.

Taiwan has also moved rapidly up the ladder. The government now encourages the substitution of machines for labor and is letting labor-intensive and low-tech factories close or move offshore. Firms are moving toward high technology and higher-value products.[3]

While Japan proceeds up the ladder of comparative advantage, it is now being followed by the Asian NICs (Taiwan, South Korea, Hong Kong, and Singapore). (See Exhibit IX.2.) Accordingly, Japan now imports more of the labor-intensive, low price–like manufactures (footwear, watches, radios, and TVs) from the latecomers to development. As the upper-tier country moves on to specialization in the more sophisticated products, the lower-tier countries also expand their exports of the lower-technology products to the markets of third countries. Japan's labor cost advantage in textiles and consumer electronics has long since been lost to South Korea and Hong Kong. The Asian NICs export textiles and the simpler consumer electronic products to North America and Europe as Japan specializes in even higher-technology exports.

As the Asian NICs, in turn, move up the ladder of comparative advantage, their former positions on the lower rungs of the ladder are being taken by those behind them in the queue—Thailand, Malaysia, Indonesia, and the Philippines. Thailand and Malaysia, in particular, have in recent years gained impressive footholds in export markets for manufactures.

---

[1]Michael E. Porter, *The Competitive Advantage of Nations* (1990), p. 77.

[2]Paul Krugman, "Scale Economies, Product Differentiation and the Pattern of Trade," *American Economic Review* 70 (1980): 950–59.

[3]For example, Microelectronics Technology, Inc., was making components for microwave receiving equipment; now it makes complete systems for ships. Inventa Electronics Co., which made almost-disposable calculators, now builds personal computers. And Vidar-Sun Moon Star Co., which used to produce electronic parts, now makes mobile phones and digital microwave radios (*Wall Street Journal*, June 1, 1991, p. 1).

EXHIBIT IX.1. Product Life Cycle and Trade

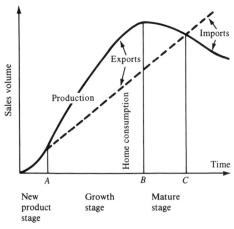

Stages of product development

A country may initially innovate and then, after time *A*, become an exporter of a new product. After time *B*, the innovating country loses its comparative advantage when the product becomes standardized and foreign countries compete with the innovating country's exports. Finally, after time *C*, the innovating country becomes an importer of the product.

EXHIBIT IX.2. Ladder of Comparative Advantage

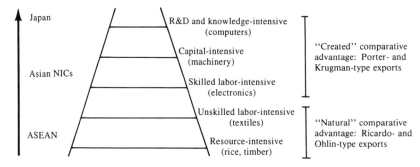

IX.A.2. Trade as an "Engine of Growth"—Note

An overriding issue in the relations between trade and development is the ultimate question of whether there is a conflict between the gains from trade and the gains from growth.[1] Can foreign trade have a propulsive role in the development of a country? Or, on the contrary, are the dictates of comparative advantage incompatible with the requirements of accelerated development?

The orthodox interpretation as expounded by classical and neoclassical economists is that foreign trade can be a propelling force in development. Adam Smith's model of foreign trade postulates the existence of idle land and labor before a country is opened to world markets. The excess resources are used to produce a surplus of goods for export, and trade thereby "vents" a surplus productive capacity that would otherwise be unused. In Smith's words,

[1]This Note is an abbreviated version of Gerald M. Meier, "External Trade and Internal Development," in *Colonialism in Africa, 1870–1960,* vol. 4, *The Economics of Colonialism,* ed. Peter Duignan and L. H. Gann (1975). See also Gerald M. Meier, *The International Economics of Development* (1968), chap. 8.

Between whatever places foreign trade is carried on, they all of them derive two distinct benefits from it. It carries out that surplus part of the produce of their land and labour for which there is no demand among them, and brings back in return for it something else for which there is a demand. It gives a value to their superfluities, by exchanging them for something else, which may satisfy a part of their wants, and increase their enjoyments. By means of it, the narrowness of the home market does not hinder the division of labour in any particular branch of art or manufacture from being carried to the highest perfection. By opening a more extensive market for whatever part of the produce of their labour may exceed the home consumption, it encourages them to improve its production powers, and to augment its annual produce to the utmost, and thereby to increase the real revenue and wealth of the society.[2]

This idea of "vent for surplus" assumes that resources are not fully employed prior to trade, and that exports are increased without a decrease in domestic production, with the result that trade raises the level of economic activity.

More generally, classical economists considered comparative advantage as determining the pattern of trade. Not the use of surplus resources but the reallocation of resources allowed trade to benefit a country by promoting a more efficient international allocation of resources. Without any increase in resources or technological change, every trading country is able to enjoy a higher real income by specializing in production according to its comparative advantage and trading. The exports have instrumental significance as the intermediate goods used for the "indirect production" of imports: exports allow the country to "buy" imports on more favorable terms than if produced directly at home. The gain from trade is on the import side, and it is significant that the gains are also mutual, realized by all the trading countries. By specializing in commodities for which its costs are comparatively lowest, a trading nation would, in Ricardo's words, increase "the sum of commodities and mass of enjoyments"; in modern jargon, trade optimizes production.

Although specialization according to comparative advantage yields the direct benefits of international exchange, there are in addition dynamic aspects of trade that are relevant for the growth-transmitting effects of trade above and beyond the static gains. Classical and neoclassical economists did not make the dynamic aspects of trade central to their thought; but to the extent that they did consider the effects of trade on development, they saw no conflict between a country's conformity with its comparative advantage and the acceleration of its development. Indeed, John Stuart Mill stated that trade, according to comparative advantage, results in a "more efficient employment of the productive forces of the world," and that this might be considered the "direct economical advantage of foreign trade. But there are, besides, indirect effects, which must be counted as benefits of a high order." A most important "indirect" dynamic benefit, according to Mill, is

the tendency of every extension of the market to improve the processes of production. A country which produces for a larger market than its own, can introduce a more extended division of labour, can make greater use of machinery, and is more likely to make inventions and improvements in the processes of production.

Widening the extent of the market, inducing innovations, and increasing productivity through foreign trade allow a country to overcome the diseconomies of being small.

Another important consideration, according to Mill, "principally applicable to an early age of industrial advancement," is that

a people may be in a quiescent, indolent, uncultivated state, with all their tastes either fully satisfied or entirely undeveloped, and they may fail to put forth the whole of their productive energies for want of any sufficient object of desire. The opening of a foreign trade, by making them acquainted with new objects, or tempting them by the easier acquisition of things which they had not previously thought attainable, sometimes works a sort of industrial revolution in a country whose resources were previously undeveloped for want of energy and ambition in the people: inducing those who were satisfied with scanty comforts and little work, to work harder for the gratification of their new tastes, and even to save, and accumulate capital, for still more complete satisfaction of those tastes at a future time.[3]

[2] Adam Smith, *An Inquiry into the Nature and Causes of the Wealth of Nations,* ed. Edwin Cannan (1937), p. 415. For more detailed discussion of Smith's theory, see Hla Myint, "The Classical Theory of International Trade and the Underdeveloped Countries," *Economic Journal,* 68 (1958): 317–31. Myint indicates that Smith's concept of surplus productive capacity is not merely a matter of surplus land by itself but surplus land combined with surplus labor; and the surplus labor is then linked with his concept of "unproductive labor" (p. 323). This interpretation allows Smith's vent-for-surplus model of trade and growth to be consistent with W. Arthur Lewis's model of development with unlimited supplies of labor. See Richard E. Caves, "Vent for Surplus' Models of Trade and Growth," in *Trade, Growth, and the Balance of Payments: Essays in Honor of Gottfried Haberler,* ed. R. E. Baldwin et al. (1965).

[3] John Stuart Mill, *Principles of Political Economy,* 2 vols. (1848), vol. 2, book 3, sec. 5, chap. 17.

Further, Mill stated that trade benefits the less developed countries through

the introduction of foreign arts, which raises the returns derivable from additional capital to a rate corresponding to the low strength of accumulation; and the importation of foreign capital which renders the increase of production no longer exclusively dependent on the thrift or providence of the inhabitants themselves, while it places before them a stimulating example, and by instilling new ideas and breaking the chain of habit, if not by improving the actual condition of the population, tends to create in them new wants, increased ambition, and greater thought for the future.[4]

The indirect benefits of trade on development are therefore of three kinds: (1) those that widen the extent of the market, induce innovations, and increase productivity; (2) those that increase savings and capital accumulation; and (3) those that have an educative effect in instilling new wants and tastes and in transferring technology, skills, and entrepreneurship. This emphasis is on the supply side of the development process—the opportunity that trade gives a poor country to remove domestic shortages, to overcome the diseconomies of the small size of its domestic market, and to accelerate the "learning rate" of its economy.

For these several reasons, the traditional conclusion has been that the gains from trade do not result in merely a once-over change in resource allocation, but are continually merging with the gains from development: international trade transforms existing production functions and increases the productivity of the economy over time. If trade increases the capacity for development, then the larger the volume of trade, the greater should be the potential for development.

More recently, various export-based models of growth have been formulated to present a macrodynamic view of how an economy's growth can be determined by expansion in its exports. One version of the export-based model is that of the staple theory of growth.

The term "staple" designates a raw material or resource-intensive commodity occupying a dominant position in the country's exports. It has a structural similarity to the vent-for-surplus view insofar as "surplus" resources initially exist and are subsequently exported. It also has some affinity with Lewis's model of development with an unlimited supply of labor when the surplus to be vented through trade is one of labor and not natural resources.

The staple theory postulates that with the discovery of a primary product in which the country has a comparative advantage, or with an increase in the demand for its comparative advantage commodity, there is an expansion of a resource-based export commodity; this, in turn, induces higher rates of growth of aggregate and *per capita* income. Previously idle or undiscovered resources are brought into use, creating a return to these resources and being consistent with venting a surplus through trade. The export of a primary product also has effects on the rest of the economy through diminishing underemployment or unemployment, inducing a higher rate of domestic saving and investment, attracting an inflow of factor inputs into the expanding export sector, and establishing links with other sectors of the economy. Although the rise in exports is induced by greater demand, there are supply responses within the economy that increase the productivity of the exporting economy.

The staple theory has some relation also to Rostow's leading-sector analysis insofar as the staple-export sector may be the leading sector of the economy, growing more rapidly and propelling the rest of the economy along with its growth. In Rostow's analysis, however, a primary-producing sector can be a leading sector only if it also involves processing of the primary product.

A more general analysis of the effects of trade on the rate of growth has been considered by Corden.[5] Instead of the "demand-motored" model of the staple theory, Corden analyzes a "supply-motored" model that emphasizes growth in factor supplies and productivity. After a country is opened to world trade, five effects may be distinguished. First is the "impact effect," corresponding to the static gain from trade: current real income is raised. Then there may be the "capital-accumulation effect": an increase in capital accumulation results when parts of the static gain are invested. This amounts to a transfer of real income from the present to the future instead of an increase in present consumption. Third may be the "substitution effect," which may result from a possible fall in the relative price of investment goods to

[4]Ibid., vol. 1, book 1, sec. 1, chap. 13.

[5]W. Max Corden, "The Effects of Trade on the Rate of Growth," in *Trade, Balance of Payments and Growth*, ed. Jagdish N. Bhagwati et al. (1971).

consumption goods if investment goods are import intensive. This would lead to an increase in the ratio of investment to consumption and an increase in the rate of growth. The fourth possibility is an "income-distribution effect": there will be a shift in income toward the factors that are used intensively in the production of exports. If the savings propensities differ between sectors or factors, this will have an effect on the overall savings propensity and hence on capital accumulation. Finally, there is the "factor-weight effect," which considers the relative productivity of capital and labor and recognizes that if the rate of growth of output is a weighted average of capital and labor growth rates (with a constant returns-to-scale aggregate production function), then if exports rise, and exports use the faster-growing factor of production, the rate of growth of exports will rise more rapidly. All these effects are cumulative and intensify the increase in real income over time as a result of opening a country to foreign trade.

The positive view of trade and development thus emphasizes the direct gain that comes from international specialization plus the additional support to a country's development through a number of spread effects within the domestic economy.

Comment: Criticism of Neoclassical Trade Theory

Critics of the view that trade will transmit development often deny the relevance of the conclusions of neoclassical trade theory. Some claim that the theory of comparative advantage is static and misses the essence of change in the development process. But the conclusions derived from the theory of comparative advantage need not be limited to a "cross-section" view and a given once-for-all set of conditions. The comparative cost doctrine still has validity among countries undergoing differential rates of development. For a simple exposition of how to incorporate different types of factor growth, technological progress, and changes in the structure of demand into the neoclassical theory of comparative advantage, see G. M. Meier, *International Trade and Development* (1963), chap. 2. For some illustrations of the changing international division of labor, see Bela Balassa, "A 'Stages' Approach to Comparative Advantage," in *Economic Growth and Resources,* vol. 5, *National and International Issues,* ed. Irma Adelman (1979).

Another criticism is directed against the "factor-price equalization theorem" derived from neoclassical theory. This theorem states that, under certain conditions, free trade is a perfect substitute for complete international mobility of factors and is sufficient to equalize, in the trading countries, not only the prices of products, but also the prices of factors. Against this proposition, however, critics argue that, in reality, the international distribution of income has become more unequal. Some, like Myrdal, would contrapose against the factor-price equalization theorem a theory of "cumulative causation," or a cumulative process engendered by international trade away from equilibrium in factor proportions and factor prices.

This criticism is, however, highly overdrawn. The critics attribute much more importance to the theorem than did its expositors, who recognized its highly restrictive assumptions and hence never maintained that equalization will actually occur. The very special set of assumptions are identical production functions in all countries, constant returns to scale in the production of each commodity, and perfectly competitive factor and product markets. Insofar as these restrictive conditions have been violated in reality, it should not be surprising that factor returns have not been equalized between rich and poor countries. See P. A. Samuelson, "International Factor-Price Equalization Once Again," *Economic Journal* (June 1949).

Although the factor-price equalization theorem cannot be claimed to be a valid empirical generalization, the fundamental contention of neoclassical trade theory does hold: the real income of each country will be higher with trade than without trade.

Contrary to the neoclassical version of mutually beneficial trade, some critics argue, as does Myrdal in selection IX.A.3, that differences in economic structure among countries bias the gains from trade in favor of the technologically advanced and industrialized countries and against the poor countries.

IX.A.3. Trade as a Mechanism of International Inequality*

Contrary to what the equilibrium theory of international trade would seem to suggest, the play of the market forces does not work towards equality in the renumerations to factors of production and, consequently, in incomes. If left to take its own course, economic development is a process of circular and cumulative causation which tends to award its favours to those who are already well endowed and even to thwart the efforts of those who happen to live in regions that are lagging behind. The backsetting effects of economic expansion in other regions dominate the more powerfully, the poorer a country is.

Within the national boundaries of the richer countries an integration process has taken place: on a higher level of economic development expansionary momentum tends to spread more effectively to other localities and regions than those where starts happen to have been made and successfully sustained; and inequality has there also been mitigated through interferences in the play of the market forces by organised society. In a few highly advanced countries—comprising only about one-sixth of the population in the non-Soviet world—this national integration process is now being carried forward towards a very high level of equality of opportunity to all, wherever, and in whatever circumstances they happen to be born. These countries are approaching a national harmony of interest which, because of the role played by state policies, has to be characterized as a ''created harmony''; and this has increasingly sustained also their further economic development.

Outside this small group of highly developed and progressive countries, all other countries are in various degrees poorer and mostly also less progressive economically. In a rather close correlation to their poverty they are ridden by internal economic inequalities, which also tend to weaken the effectiveness of their democratic systems of government in the cases where they are not under one form or another of oligarchic or forthright dictatorial rule.

The relations between relative lack of national economic integration and relative economic backwardness run, according to my hypothesis of circular cumulative causation, both ways. With a low level of economic development follow low levels of social mobility, communications, popular education and national sharing in beliefs and valuations, which imply greater impediments to the spread effects of expansionary momentum; at the same time the poorer states have for much the same reasons and because of the very fact of existing internal inequalities often been less democratic and, in any case, they have, because they are poorer, been up against narrower financial and, at bottom, psychological limitations on policies seeking to equalise opportunities. Inequality of opportunities has, on the other hand, contributed to preserving a low ''quality'' of their factors of production and a low ''effectiveness'' in their production efforts, to use the classical terms, and this has hampered their economic development.

On the international as on the national level trade does not by itself necessarily work for equality. A widening of markets strengthens often on the first hand the progressive countries whose manufacturing industries have the lead and are already fortified in surroundings of external economies, while the under-developed countries are in continuous danger of seeing even what they have of industry and, in particular, their small scale industry and handicrafts outcompeted by cheap imports from the industrial countries, if they do not protect them. . . .

If international trade did not stimulate manufacturing industry in the under-developed countries but instead robbed them of what they had of old-established crafts, it did promote the production of primary products, and such production, employing mostly unskilled labour, came to constitute the basis for the bulk of their exports. In these lines, however, they often meet inelastic demands in the export market, often also a demand trend which is not rising very rapidly, and excessive price fluctuations. When, furthermore, population is rapidly rising while the larger part of it lives at, or near, the subsistence level—which means that there is no scarcity of common labour—any technological improvement in their export production tends to confer the advantages from the cheapening of

*From Gunnar Myrdal, *Development and Underdevelopment,* National Bank of Egypt Fiftieth Anniversary Commemoration Lectures, Cairo, 1956, pp. 47–51. Reprinted by permission.

production to the importing countries. Because of inelastic demands the result will often not even be a very great enlargement of the markets and of production and employment. In any case the wages and the export returns per unit of product will tend to remain low as the supply of unskilled labour is almost unlimited.

The advice—and assistance—which the poor countries receive from the rich is even nowadays often directed towards increasing their production of primary goods for export. The advice is certainly given in good faith and it may even be rational from the short term point of view of each under-developed country seen in isolation. Under a broader perspective and from a longer term point of view, what would be rational is above all to increase productivity, incomes and living standards in the larger agricultural subsistence sectors, so as to raise the supply price of labour, and in manufacturing industry. This would engender economic development and raise incomes *per capita*. But trade by itself does not lead to such a development; it rather tends to have backsetting effects and to strengthen the forces maintaining stagnation or regression. Economic development has to be brought about by policy interferences which, however, are not under our purview at this stage of the argument when we are analysing only the effects of the play of the market forces.

Neither can the capital movements be relied upon to counteract international inequalities between the countries which are here in question. Under the circumstances described, capital will, on the whole, shun the under-developed countries, particularly as the advanced countries themselves are rapidly developing further and can offer their owners of capital both good profits and security.

There has, in fact, never been much of a capital movement to the countries which today we call under-developed, even in earlier times—except tiny streams to the economic enclaves, mainly devoted to export production of primary products which, however, usually were so profitable to their owners that they rapidly became self-supporting so far as investment capital was concerned and, in addition, the considerably larger but still relatively small investments in railways and other public utilities which had their security in the political controls held by colonial governments. The bulk of European overseas capital exports went to the settlements in the free spaces in the temperate zones which were becoming populated by emigration from Europe. After the collapse of the international capital market in the early 'thirties, which has not been remedied, and later the breakdown of the colonial system, which had given security to the foreign investor, it would be almost against nature if capital in large quantities were voluntarily to seek its way to under-developed countries in order to play a role in their economic development.

True, capital in these countries is scarce. But the need for it does not represent an effective demand in the capital market. Rather, if there were no exchange controls and if, at the same time, there were no elements in their national development policies securing high profits for capital—i.e., if the forces in the capital market were given unhampered play—capitalists in under-developed countries would be exporting their capital. Even with such controls and policies in existence, there is actually a steady capital flight going on from under-developed countries, which in a realistic analysis should be counted against what there is of capital inflow to these countries.

Labour migration, finally, can safely be counted out as a factor of importance for international economic adjustment as between under-developed and developed countries. The population pressure in most under-developed countries implies, of course, that they do not need immigration. . . . Emigration from these countries would instead be the natural thing. For various reasons emigration could, however, not be much of a real aid to economic development, even if it were possible.

And the whole world is since the First World War gradually settling down to a situation where immigrants are not welcomed almost anywhere from wherever they come; people have pretty well to stay in the country where they are born, except for touristing by those who can afford it. And so far as the larger part of the under-developed world is concerned, where people are "coloured" according to the definition in the advanced countries, emigration is usually stopped altogether by the colour bar as defined by the legislation, or in the administration, of the countries which are white-dominated and at the same time better off economically.

If left unregulated, international trade and capital mvoements would thus often be the media through which the economic progress in the advanced countries would have backsetting effects in the under-developed world, and their mode of operation would be very much the same as it is in the circular cumulation of causes in the development process within a single country. ... Internationally, these effects will, however, dominate the outcome much more, as the countervailing spread effects of expansionary momentum are so very much weaker. Differences in legislation, administration and *mores* generally, in language, in basic valuations and beliefs, in levels of living, production capacities and facilities, etc. make the national boundaries effective barriers to the spread to a degree which no demarcation lines within one country approach.

Even more important as impediments to the spread effects of expansionary momentum from abroad than the boundaries and everything they stand for is, however, the very fact of great poverty and weak spread effects within the under-

developed countries themselves. Where, for instance, international trade and shipping actually do transform the immediate surroundings of a port to a centre of economic expansion, which happens almost everywhere in the world, the expansionary momentum usually does not spread out to other regions of the country, which tend to remain backward if the forces in the markets are left free to take their course. Basically, the weak spread effects as between countries are thus for the larger part only a reflection of the weak spread effects within the under-developed countries themselves.

Under these circumstances the forces in the markets will in a cumulative way tend to cause ever greater international inequalities between countries as to their level of economic development and average national income *per capita*.

Comment: Terms of Trade and Unequal Exchange

During the 1950s and 1960s, the United Nation's Economic Commission for Latin America (ECLA) was influential in formulating ideas on development that contradicted orthodox, neoclassical thought. In doing so, ECLA was in many respects a precursor of the dependency school and also the North–South dialogue.

The main ECLA document is entitled *The Economic Development of Latin America and Its Principal Problems* (1950). ECLA publications offer a critique of the neoclassical theory of trade and emphasize the tendency of international trade to reproduce the inequality among nations through relations between the center and the periphery. Special emphasis is given to the consequences of differential technical progress and the worsening of the periphery's terms of trade.

The terms-of-trade issue remains very much alive—despite the many critical questions raised about the empirical evidence, its welfare significance, and policy implications. The Singer–Prebisch thesis on the alleged tendency of the long-term movement in terms of trade to be against developing countries is still prominent in discussions of gains from trade. For an account of the emergence of this thesis, see Joseph Love, "Raúl Prebisch and the Origins of the Doctrine of Unequal Exchange," *Latin American Research Review* (November 1980). The thesis is reexamined by John T. Cuddington, "Long-run Trends in 26 Primary Commodity Prices," *Journal of Development Economics* (October 1992).

The empirical evidence for the postwar period has been reviewed by John Spraos, *Inequalising Trade?* (1983), and D. Sapsford, "The Statistical Debate on the Net Barter Terms of Trade Between Primary Commodities and Manufactures," *Economic Journal* (September 1985). See also H. W. Singer, "The Terms-of-Trade Controversy and the Evolution of Soft Financing," and Bela Balassa, "Comment," in *Pioneers in Development,* ed. Gerald M. Meier and Dudley Seers (1984) For a comprehensive study and extensive bibliography, see Dimitris Diakosavvas and Pasquale L. Scandizzo, "Trends in the Terms of Trade of Primary Products, 1900–1982: The Controversy and Its Origins," *Economic Development and Cultural Change* (January 1991).

The theory of "unequal exchange" as presented in A. Emmanuel, *Unequal Exchange: A Study of the Imperialism of Trade* (1972), stems from Marxist theory and contends that there is a transfer of reinvestable surplus (surplus value) from the low-wage developing country to the high-wage industrial country via the terms of trade. Trade is believed to be unequal to the "South" because its terms of trade are lower than they would be under a Pareto efficient trade arrangement, which would allow perfect international labor mobility. This argument relates to the absolute level of the terms of trade rather than to secular deterioration or cyclical fluctuations. For a discussion of Emmanuel's analysis, see Edmar L. Bacha, "An Interpretation of Unequal Exchange from Prebisch–Singer to Emmanuel," *Journal of Development Economics* (December 1978). Another Marxist analysis of unequal exchange is offered by Samir Amin in three works: *Accumulation on a World Scale* (1974), *Unequal Development* (1976), and *Imperialism and Unequal Development* (1977). A more technical, non-Marxist model of "unequal development" is presented by Paul Krugman, "Trade, Accumulation, and Uneven Development," *Journal of Development Economics* (April 1981).

For other discussions of the alleged bias in the gains from trade in favor of industrialized countries, see Sheila Smith and John Toye, "Three Stories About Trade and Poor Economies," *Journal of Development Studies* (October 1979); David Evans and Parvin Alizadeh, "Trade, Industrialization, and the Visible Hand," *Journal of Development Studies* (October 1984); and David Evans, "Alternative Perspectives on Trade and Development," in *Handbook of Development Economics*, vol. 2, ed. Hollis Chenery and T. N. Srinivasan (1989).

IX.A.4. Conditions of Export-Led Development—Note

The foregoing materials raise a central question: Under what conditions can a process of export-induced development follow on an expansion of the export sector? How can export expansion also act as an engine of domestic development? Notwithstanding the possibility of lagging exports in more recent decades, most of the underdeveloped countries have experienced long periods of export growth. In most cases, after a country was exposed to the world economy, its exports grew markedly in volume and in variety. Yet, despite their secular rise, exports in many countries have not acted as a key propulsive sector, driving the rest of the economy forward. Although the classical belief that development can be transmitted through trade has been confirmed by the experience of some countries that are now among the richest in the world, trade has not had a similar stimulating effect for countries that have remained underdeveloped. Why has not the growth in exports in these countries carried over to other sectors and led to more widespread development in the domestic economy?

As noted above, some critics of the classical position contend that the very forces of international trade have been responsible for inhibiting development. They argue that the development of the export sector by foreign capital has created a "dual economy," in which production has been export-biased, and the resultant pattern of resource utilization has deterred development. This argument, however, tends to contrast the pattern of resource utilization that actually occurred with some other ideal pattern. More relevant is a comparison between the actual pattern and the allocation that would have occurred in the absence of the capital inflow. There is little foundation to the assertion that if there had been no foreign investment, a poor country would have generated more domestic investment, or that in the absence of foreign entrepreneurs, the supply of domestic entrepreneurs would have been larger. Contrary to what is often implied by the critics of foreign investment, the real choice was not between employing the resources in the export sector or in domestic production, but between giving employment to the surplus resources in export production or leaving them idle.[1] It is difficult to substantiate the argument that foreign investment was competitive with home investment, or that the utilization of resources in the export sector was at the expense of home production.

Another contention is that trade has impeded development by the "demonstration effect": the international demonstration of higher consumption standards in more developed countries has allegedly raised the propensity to consume in the less developed countries and reduced attainable saving rates. By stimulating the desire to consume, however, the international demonstration effect may also have operated on incentives and been instrumental in increasing the supply of effort and productive services—especially between the subsistence sector and the exchange economy.[2] This positive effect on the side of fac-

[1] See Hla Myint, "The Gains from International Trade and the Backward Countries," *Review of Economic Studies* 22, no. 58 (1954–55) and "The 'Classical Theory' of International Trade and the Under-developed Countries," *Economic Journal* (June 1958): 317–37.

[2] For an instructive analysis of the general process by which the money economy has developed through expansion of export production induced by the growth of new wants for imported consumers' goods, see Hla Myint, *The Economics of Developing Countires* (1964), chaps. 1–5.

tor supply may have more than offset any negative effect on saving.

More serious is the argument that international market forces have transferred income from the poor to the rich nations through a deterioration in the terms of trade of the less developed countries. The significance of this argument is also overdrawn, and it can be questioned on both theoretical and empirical grounds. The alleged trend is not based on the measurement of prices within the poor countries, but on inferences from the United Kingdom's commodity terms of trade or the terms of trade between primary products and manufactured products.[3] This does not provide a sufficiently strong statistical foundation for any adequate generalization about the terms of trade of poor countries. The import-price index conceals the heterogeneous price movements within and among the broad categories of foodstuffs, raw materials, and minerals; no allowance is made for changes in the quality of exports and imports; there is inadequate consideration of new commodities; and the recorded terms of trade are not corrected for the substantial decline in transportation costs. The introduction of new products and qualitative improvements have been greater in manufactured than in primary products, and a large proportion of the fall in British prices of primary products can be attributed to the great decline in inward freight rates. The simple use of the "inverse" of the United Kingdom's terms of trade to indicate the terms of trade of primary-producing countries involves therefore a systematic bias that makes changes appear more unfavorable to the primary-exporting countries than they actually were.

Even if it were true that the less developed countries experienced a secular deterioration in their commodity terms of trade, the question would still remain whether this constituted a significant obstacle to their development. The answer depends on what caused the deterioration and whether the country's factoral terms of trade and income terms also deteriorated. If the deterioration in the commodity terms is due to increased productivity in the export sector, the single-factoral terms of trade (commodity terms corrected for changes in productivity in produc-

ing exports) can improve at the same time. As long as productivity in its export industries is increasing more rapidly than export prices are falling, the country's real income can rise despite the deterioration in the commodity terms of trade; when its factoral terms improve, the country benefits from the ability to obtain a greater quantity of imports per unit of factors embodied in its exports. Also possible is an improvement in the country's income terms of trade (commodity terms multiplied by quantity of exports) at the same time as its commodity terms deteriorate. The country's capacity to import is then greater, and this will ease development efforts. When due weight is given to the increase in productivity in export production and the rise in export volume, it would appear that the single-factoral terms and income terms of trade actually improved for many poor countries, notwithstanding any possible deterioration in their commodity terms of trade.

Having rejected the view that international trade operated as a mechanism of international inequality, we must look to other factors for an understanding of why trade has not had a more stimulating effect in under-developed countries. If the export sector is to be a propelling force in development, it is essential that the export sector not remain an enclave, separate from the rest of the economy; instead, an integrated process should be established, diffusing stimuli from the export sector and creating responses elsewhere in the economy. A more convincing explanation of why export-led development has occurred in some countries, but not in others, would therefore distinguish the differential effects of the integrative process by focusing on the varying strength of the stimuli in different countries from their exports and on the different response mechanisms within the exporting countries.[4]

Different export commodities will provide different stimuli, according to the technological characteristics of their production. The nature of the export good's production function has an influence on the extent of other secondary changes elsewhere in the economy, beyond the primary increase in export output. With the use of different input coefficients to produce different types of export commodities, there will be different rates of learning and different linkage ef-

[3]United Nations, Department of Economic Affairs, *Relative Prices of Exports and Imports of Under-Developed Countries* (1949), pp. 7, 13–24; W. A. Lewis, "World Production, Prices, and Trade, 1870–1960," *The Manchester School* (May 1952): 118.

[4]The following paragraphs draw on Gerald M. Meier, "External Trade and Internal Development," in *Colonialism in Africa, 1870–1960*, vol. 4, *The Economics of Colonialism*, ed. Peter Duignan and L. H. Gann (1975).

fects. The degree to which the various exports are processed is highly significant in the determination of external economies associated with the learning process; the processing of primary-product exports by modern methods is likely to benefit other activities through the spread of technical knowledge, training of labor, demonstration of new production techniques that might be adapted elsewhere in the economy, and acquisition of organizational and supervisory skills.

In contrast, growth of the export sector will have a negligible carry-over if the techniques of production in the export sector are the same as those already in use in other sectors, or if the expansion of the export sector occurs by a simple widening of production without any change in production functions. If the introduction or expansion of export crops involves simple methods of production that do not differ markedly from the traditional techniques already used in subsistence agriculture, the stimulus to development will clearly be less than if the growth in exports entails the introduction of new skills and more productive recombinations of factors of production. More favorable linkages may stem from exports that require skilled labor than from those using unskilled labor. The influence of skill requirements may operate in various ways: greater incentives for capital formation may be provided through education; on-the-job training in the export sector may be disseminated at little real cost through the movement of workers into other sectors or occupations; skilled workers may be a source of entrepreneurship; skilled workers may save more of their wage incomes than unskilled workers.[5] The level of entrepreneurial skill induced by the development of an export is also highly significant. The level will be expanded if the development of the export commodity offers significant challenge and instills abilities usable in other sectors, but is not so high as to require the importing of a transient class of skilled managerial labor.

Although the processing of a primary product provides forward linkages in the sense that the output of one sector becomes an input for another sector, it is also important to have backward linkages. When some exports grow, they provide a strong stimulus for expansion in the input-supplying industries elsewhere in the economy. These backward linkages may be in agriculture or in other industries supplying inputs to the expanding export sector, or in social overhead capital. The importance of linkages has been stressed by Hirschman.[6]

The notion is emphasized also by Perroux, who refers to a developing enterprise as a "motor unit" when it increases its demands on its suppliers for raw materials or communicates new techniques to another enterprise. The "induction effect" that the motor unit exerts on another unit may be considered in two components that frequently occur in combination: (1) a dimension effect that is the augmentation of demand by one enterprise to another by increasing its supply; and (2) an innovation effect that introduces an innovation that for a given quantity of factors of production yields the same quantity of production at a lower price and/or of a better quality. When a motor unit is interlinked with its environment, Perroux refers to a growth pole or a development pole.[7] The emphasis on generating new skills, innovations in the export sector or other sectors linked to exports, and technical change is important in determining the learning rate of the economy.

Beyond this, the nature of the production function of the export commodity will also determine the distribution of income and, in turn, the pattern of local demand and impact on local employment. The use of different factor combinations affects the distribution of income in the sense that the relative shares of profits, wages, interest, and rent will vary according to the labor intensity or capital intensity of the export production and the nature of its organization—whether it is mining, plantation agriculture, or peasant farming. If the internal distribution of the export income favors groups with a higher propensity to consume domestic goods than to import, the resultant distribution of income will be more effective in raising the demand for home-produced products; to the extent that these home-produced products are labor intensive, there will be more of an impact on employment. In contrast, if income is distributed to those who have a higher propensity to import,

[5]Richard E. Caves, "Export-led Growth and the New Economic History," in *Trade, Balance of Payments and Growth*, ed. Jagdish N. Bhagwati et al. (1971).

[6]Albert O. Hirschman, *The Strategy of Economic Development* (1958), chap. 9.

[7]François Perroux, "Multinational Investment and the Analysis of Development and Integration Poles," in Inter-American Development Bank, *Multinational Investment in the Economic Development and Integration of Latin America* (1968), pp. 99–103.

the leakage through consumption of imported goods will be greater. If income increments go to those who are likely to save large portions, the export sector may also make a greater contribution to the financing of growth in other sectors.

If the export commodity is subject to substantial economies of scale in its production, this will tend to imply large capital requirements for the establishment of enterprises, and hence extra regional or foreign borrowing. This may then lead to an outward flow of profits instead of providing profit income for local reinvestment. But this is only part of the impact of the foreign investment. For a full appraisal, it would be necessary to consider all the benefits and costs of the foreign investment. And they, too, will vary according to the nature of the export sector in which the foreign investment occurs.

Finally, the repercussions from exports will also differ according to the degree of fluctuation in export proceeds. Disruptions in the flow of foreign-exchange receipts make the development process discontinuous; the greater the degree of instability, the more difficult it is to maintain steady employment, because there will be disturbing effects on real income, government revenue, capital formation, resource allocation, and the capacity to import according to the degree of amplitude of fluctuation in foreign-exchange receipts. To the extent that different exports vary in their degree of fluctuation and in revenue earned and retained at home, their repercussions on the domestic economy will also differ. Depending on the various characteristics of the country's export, we may thus infer how the strength of the integrative process, in terms of the stimulus from exports, will differ among countries.

In summary, we would normally expect the stimulating forces of the integrative process to be stronger under the following conditions: the higher the growth-rate of the export sector, the greater is the direct impact of the export sector on employment and personal income, the more the expansion of exports has a ''learning effect'' in terms of increasing productivity and instilling new skills, the more the export sector is supplied through domestic inputs instead of imports, the more the distribution of export income favors those with a marginal propensity to consume domestic goods instead of imports, the more productive is the investment resulting from any saving of export income, the more extensive are the externalities and linkages connected with the export sector, and the more stable are the export receipts that are retained at home. Some exports fulfill these conditions more readily than others, and countries specializing in these exports will enjoy greater opportunities for development.

Even with a strong stimulus from exports, however, the transmission of growth from the export base to the rest of the economy will still be contingent on other conditions in the economy. The weak penetrative power of exports in underdeveloped countries can be explained not only by a possibly weak stimulus from a particular type of export, but also by the host of domestic impediments that limit the transmission of the gains from exports to other sectors even when the stimulus may be strong.

After analyzing the character of a country's export base for an indication of the strength of the stimulus to development provided by its export commodities, we must go on to examine the strength of the response or diffusion mechanism within the domestic economy for evidence of how receptive the domestic economy is to the stimulus from exports. The strength of the integrative process, in terms of the response mechanism to the export stimulus, will depend on the extent of market imperfections in the domestic economy and on noneconomic barriers in the general environment. The integrative forces are stronger under the following conditions: the more developed the infrastructure of the economy, the more developed are market institutions, the more extensive is the development of human resources, the less are the price distortions that affect resource allocations, and the greater is the capacity to bear risks. Our view of the carry-over should stress not only the mechanical linkages, but also a more evolutionary (and hence biological rather than mechanical) analogy that recognizes societal responses. What matters is not simply the creation of modern enterprise or modern sectors, but also modernization as a process. This involves physical production or mechanical linkages as well as a change in socioeconomic traits throughout the society, and an intangible atmosphere that relates to changes in values, in character, in attitudes, in the learning of new behavior patterns, and in institutions.

In sum, the effects of a strong integrative process will be the following: (1) an acceleration in the learning rate of the economy; (2) an enrichment of the economic and social infrastructure (transportation, public services, health, education); (3) an expansion of the supply of entrepreneurship (and a managerial and administrative class); and (4) a mobilization of a larger surplus above consumption in the form of taxation and saving. These effects constitute the country's development foundations. Once these foundations have been laid, the country's economy can be more readily transformed through diversification in primary production and the service industries, new commodity exports, and industrialization via efficient import substitution and export substitution.

It follows that if a more extensive carry-over from exports is to be achieved, it is necessary to remove the domestic impediments that cut short the stimulus from exports. Many of the policy recommendations in this book refer to the need for diminishing the economy's organizational dualism (selection III.B.4)—reducing the fragmentation and compartmentalization of the economy by overcoming the narrow and isolated markets, ignorance of technological possibilities, limited infrastructure, and slow rate of human-resource development. To accomplish this, alternative forms of economic and social organization are required, and policy measures must aim at diminishing the prevalance of semi-monopolistic and monopolistic practices, removing restraints on land tenure and land use, deepening financial markets, and increasing investment in economic and social infrastructure.

IX.B. TRADE STRATEGY

IX.B.1. Inward-Oriented Strategies*

Industrial development generally begins in response to domestic demand generated in the primary sector that also provides investible funds for manufacturing industries. Demand for industrial products and investible savings represent possible uses of the surplus generated in agriculture, or in mining. The surplus is generated as primary output comes to exceed subsistence needs and, more often than not, it is associated with export expansion.

At the same time, the effects of primary exports on industrial development depend to a considerable extent on input-output relationships and on the disposition of incomes generated in the export sector. Infrastructure in the form of ports, railways, and roads are often important inputs for primary exports, and their availability may contribute to the development of industrial activities.

The disposition of incomes generated in the export sector is affected by ownership conditions. In the case of foreign ownership, a substantial part of the surplus may be repatriated, albeit taxing the earnings of foreign capital does add to domestic incomes. There are leakages in the form of investing and spending abroad, as well as consuming imported luxuries, in the case of domestic ownership in a system of plantation-type agriculture and large-scale mining, too. And, as Douglas North noted, plantation owners have little incentive to finance human investment in the form of general education.

By contrast, in cases when family-size farms predominate, demand is generated for the necessities and the conveniences of life as well as for education. Such demand contributes to the development of domestic industry that enjoys "natural" protection from imports in the form of transportation costs. It further contributes to the accumulation of human capital that finds use in manufacturing industries.

The process of industrial development may be accelerated if natural protection is complemented by tariff or quota protection. This last point, in turn, leads me to the discussion of the next step in the industrialization process: the first, or "easy" stage of import substitution.

The First Stage of Import Substitution

With the exception of Britain at the time of the Industrial Revolution, and, more recently, Hong Kong, all present-day industrial and developing countries protected their incipient manufacturing industries producing for domestic markets. There were differences, however, as regards the rate and the form of protection. While the industrial countries of today relied on relatively low tariffs, a number of present-day developing countries applied high tariffs or quantitative restrictions that limited, or even excluded, competition from imports.

At the same time, high protection discriminates against exports through the explicit or implicit taxation of export activities. Explicit taxation may take the form of export taxes while implicit taxation occurs as a result of the effects of protection on the exchange rate. The higher the rate of protection, the lower will be the exchange rate necessary to ensure equilibrium in the balance of payments, and the lower the amount of domestic currency exporters receive per unit of foreign exchange earned.

The adverse effects of high protection are exemplified in the case of Ghana, where import prohibitions encouraged inefficient, high-cost production in manufacturing industries: taxes on the main export crop, cocoa, discouraged its production, and other crops were adversely affected by the unfavorable exchange rate. Ghana's neighbor, the Ivory Coast, in turn, followed a policy encouraging the development of both primary and manufacturing activities. As a result, it increased its share in cocoa exports, developed new primary exports, and expanded manufacturing industries.

Differences in the policies applied may largely explain that, between 1960 and 1978, per capita incomes fell from $430 to $390 in Ghana, in terms of 1978 prices, as compared to an increase from $540 to $840 in the Ivory Coast. This has occurred notwithstanding the fact that the two countries have similar natural resource

*From Bela Balassa, *The Process of Industrial Development and Alternative Development Strategies,* Princeton University, International Finance Section, Essays in International Finance, no. 141 (December 1980), pp. 4–11. Reprinted by permission.

endowments and, at the time of independence, Ghana had the advantage of a higher educational level and an indigenous civil service corps.

Indeed, there is no need for high protection at the first stage of import substitution, entailing the replacement of the imports of nondurable consumer goods, such as clothing, shoes, and household goods, and of their inputs, such as textile fabrics, leather and wood, by domestic production, since these commodities suit the conditions existing in developing countries that are at the beginning of the industrialization process. The commodities in question are intensive in unskilled labor; the efficient scale of output is relatively low and costs do not rise substantially at lower output levels; production does not involve the use of sophisticated technology; and a network of suppliers of parts, components, and accessories is not required for efficient operations.

The relative advantages of developing countries in these commodities explain the frequent references made to the "easy" stage of import substitution. At the same time, to the extent that the domestic production of these commodities generates external economies in the form of labor training, the development of entrepreneurship, and the spread of technology, there is an argument for moderate infant industry protection or promotion.

The Choice of Second-Stage Import Substitution

In the course of first-stage import substitution, domestic production will rise more rapidly than domestic consumption, since it not only provides for increases in consumption but also replaces imports. The rate of growth of output will however decline to that of consumption, once the process of import substitution has been completed.

Maintaining high industrial growth rates, then, necessitates turning to the exportation of manufactured goods or moving to second-stage import substitution. This choice, in fact, represents alternative industrial development strategies that may be applied after the completion of the first stage of import substitution.

Second-stage import substitution was undertaken in the postwar period in several Latin American countries, some South Asian countries, in particular India, as well as in the European socialist countries. In Latin America, it responded to the ideas of Raúl Prebisch, in whose view adverse foreign market conditions for primary exports and lack of competitiveness in manufactured exports would not permit developing countries to attain high rates of economic growth by relying on export production. Rather, Prebisch suggested that these countries should expand their manufacturing industries oriented towards domestic markets. This purpose was to be served by industrial protection that was said to bring additional benefits through improvements in the terms of trade.

Similar ideas were expressed by Gunnar Myrdal. Myrdal influenced the policies followed by India, which were also affected by the example of the Soviet Union that chose an autarkical pattern of industrial development. And, the European socialist countries faithfully imitated the Soviet example; they attempted to reproduce the Soviet pattern in the framework of much smaller domestic markets and also lacking the natural resource base of the Soviet Union.

Second-stage import substitution involves the replacement of the imports of intermediate goods and producer and consumer durables by domestic production. These commodities have rather different characteristics from those replaced at the first stage. Intermediate goods, such as petrochemicals and steel, tend to be highly capital-intensive. They are also subject to important economies of scale, with efficient plant size being large compared to the domestic needs of most developing countries and costs rising rapidly at lower output levels. Moreover, the margin of processing is relatively small and organizational and technical inefficiences may contribute to high costs.

Producer durables, such as machinery, and consumer durables, such as automobiles and refrigerators, are also subject to economies of scale. But, in these industries, economies of scale relate not so much to plant size as to horizontal and to vertical specialization, entailing reductions in product variety and the manufacture of parts, components, and accessories on an efficient scale in separate plants.

Reducing product variety will permit longer production runs that lower production costs through improvements in manufacturing efficiency along the "learning curve," savings in expenses incurred in moving from one operation to another, and the use of special-purpose machinery. Horizontal specialization is however limited by the smallness of domestic markets in the developing countries. Similar conclusions apply to vertical specialization that leads to cost reductions through the subdivision of the production process among plants of efficient size.

Given the relative scarcity of physical and human capital in developing countries that completed the first stage of import substitution, they are at a disadvantage in the manufacture of highly physical capital-intensive intermediate goods and skill-intensive producer and consumer durables. In limiting the scope for the exploitation of economies of scale, the relatively small size of their national markets also contributes to high domestic costs in these countries. At the same time, net foreign exchange savings tend to be small because of the need for importing materials and machinery.

The domestic resource cost ratio relates the domestic resource cost of production, in terms of the labor, capital, and natural resources utilized, to net foreign exchange savings (in the case of import substitution) or net foreign exchange earnings (in the case of exports). In the absence of serious distortions in factor markets, the domestic resource cost (DRC) ratio will be low for exported commodities. It is also relatively low for consumer nondurables and their inputs, in the production of which developing countries have a comparative advantage. However, for the reasons noted beforehand, DRC ratios tend to be high in the manufacture of intermediate goods and producer and consumer durables.

Correspondingly, the establishment of these industries to serve narrow domestic markets is predicated on high protection. Also, rates of protection may need to be raised as countries "travel up the staircase," represented by DRC ratios, in embarking on the production of commodities that less and less conform to their comparative advantage. This will occur as goods produced at earlier stages have come to saturate domestic markets. High protection, in turn, discriminates against manufactured and primary exports and against primary activities in general.

Characteristics of Inward-Oriented Development Strategies

In the postwar period, several capitalist countries in Latin America and in South Asia and the socialist countries of Central and Eastern Europe adopted inward-oriented industrial development strategies, entailing second-stage import substitution. Capitalist countries generally utilized a mixture of tariffs and import controls to protect their industries whereas socialist countries relied on import prohibitions and on industry level planning.

Notwithstanding differences in the measures applied, the principal characteristics of the industrial development strategies applied in the two groups of countries show considerable similarities. To begin with, while the infant industry argument calls for temporary protection until industries become internationally competitive, in both groups of countries protection was regarded as permanent. Also, in all the countries concerned, there was a tendency towards what a Latin American economist aptly described as "import substitution at any cost."

Furthermore, in all the countries concerned, there were considerable variations in rates of explicit and implicit protection among industrial activities. This was the case, first of all, as continued import substitution involved undertaking activities with increasingly high domestic costs per unit of foreign exchange saved. In capitalist countries, the generally uncritical acceptance of demands for protection contributed to this result, when, in the absence of price comparisons, the protective effects of quantitative restrictions could not even be established. In socialist countries, the stated objective was to limit imports to commodities that could not be produced domestically, or were not available in sufficient quantities, and no attempt was made to examine the implicit protection the pursuit of this objective entailed.

In both groups of countries, the neglect of intraindustry relationships further increased the dispersion of protection rates on value added in processing, or effective protection, with adverse effects on economic efficiency. In Argentina, high tariffs imposed on caustic soda at the request of a would-be producer made the theretofore thriving soap exports unprofitable. In Hungary, the high cost of domestic steel, based largely on imported iron ore and coking coals, raised costs for steel-using industries and large investments in the steel industry delayed the substitution of aluminum for steel, although Hungary had considerable bauxite reserves.

Countries applying inward-oriented industrial development strategies were further characterized by the prevalence of sellers' markets. In capitalist countries, the size of national markets limited the possibilities for domestic competition in industries established at the second stage of import substitution while import competition was practically excluded by high protection. In socialist countries, the system of central planning applied did not permit competition among domestic firms or from imports and buyers had no choice among domestic producers or access to imported commodities.

The existence of sellers' markets provides little inducement for catering to the users' needs. In the case of industrial users, it led to backward integration as producers undertook the manufacture of parts, components, and accessories in order to minimize supply difficulties. This outcome, observed in capitalist as well as in socialist countries, led to higher costs, since economies of scale were forgone.

Also, in sellers' markets, firms had little incentive to improve productivity. In capitalist countries, monopolies and oligopolies assumed importance, and the oligopolists often aimed at the maintenance of market shares while refraining from actions that would invoke retaliation. In socialist countries, the existence of assured outlets and the emphasis on short-term objectives on the part of managers discouraged technological change.

The managers' emphasis on short-term objectives in socialist countries had to do with uncertainty as to the planners' future intentions. In capitalist countries, fluctuations in real exchange rates (nominal exchange rates, adjusted for changes in inflation rates at home and abroad) created uncertainty for business decisions. These fluctuations, resulting from intermittent devaluations in the face of rapid domestic inflation, aggravated the existing bias against exports as the domestic currency equivalent of export earnings varied with the devaluations, the timing of which was uncertain.

In countries engaging in second-stage import substitution, distortions were further apparent in the valuation of time. In capitalist countries, negative real interest rates adversely affected domestic savings, encouraged self-investment, including inventory accumulation, at low returns, and provided inducements for the transfer of funds abroad. Negative interest rates also necessitated credit rationing that generally favored import-substituting investments, whether it was done by the banks or by the government. In the first case, the lower risk of investments in production for domestic as compared to export markets gave rise to such a result; in the second case, it reflected government priorities. Finally, in socialist countries, ideological considerations led to the exclusion of interest rates as a charge for capital and as an element in the evaluation of investment projects.

There was also a tendency to underprice public utilities in countries following an inward-oriented strategy, either because of low interest charges in these capital-intensive activities or as a result of a conscious decision. The underpricing of utilities benefited, in particular, energy-intensive industries and promoted the use of capital.

In general, in moving to the second stage of import substitution, countries applying inward-oriented development strategies de-emphasized the role of prices. In socialist countries, resources were in large part allocated centrally in physical terms; in capitalist countries, output and input prices were distorted and reliance was placed on non-price measures of import restrictions and credit allocation.

Effects on Exports and on Economic Growth

The discrimination in favor of import substitution and against exports did not permit the development of manufactured exports in countries engaging in second-stage import substitution behind high protection. There were also adverse developments in primary exports as low prices for producers and for consumers reduced the exportable surplus by discouraging production and encouraging consumption.

In fact, rather than improvements in the external terms of trade that were supposed to result, turning the internal terms of trade against primary activities led to a decline in export market shares in the countries in question. Decreases in market shares were especially pronounced in cereals, meat, oilseeds, and nonferrous metals, benefiting developed countries, in particular, the United States, Canada, and Australia. . . .

The slowdown in the growth of primary exports and the lack of emergence of manufactured exports did not provide the foreign exchange necessary for rapid economic growth in countries pursuing inward-oriented industrial development strategies. The situation was aggravated as net import savings declined because of the increased need for foreign materials, machinery, and technological know how. As a result, economic growth was increasingly constrained by limitations in the availability of foreign exchange, and intermittent foreign exchange crises occurred as attempts were made to expand the economy at rates exceeding that permitted by the growth of export earnings.

Also, the savings constraint became increasingly binding as high-cost, capital-intensive production at second-stage import substitution raised capital-output ratios, requiring ever-increasing savings ratios to maintain rates of economic growth at earlier levels. At the same time, the loss of incomes due to the high cost of protection reduced the volume of available savings and, in capitalist countries, negative interest rates contributed to the outflow of funds.

In several developing countries, the cost of protection is estimated to have reached 6–7 percent of the gross national product. At the same time, there is evidence that the rate of growth of total factor productivity was lower in countries engaging in second-stage import substitution than in the industrial countries. Rather than reducing the economic distance vis-à-vis the industrial countries that infant industry protection was supposed to promote, then, there was a tendency for this lag to increase over time.

Comment: ERP and DRCs

Given a structure of tariff rates that escalates according to the degree of processing, there can be a difference between the nominal tariff rate on the final commodity and the effective rate of protection (ERP) given to the process of adding domestic value to imported inputs. The ERP shows the percentage increase in value added as a result of protection over the value added that would prevail under free trade. For example, if a nominal tariff on a final product (clothing) is 25 percent but there is no tariff on the imported intermediate input (cloth), and domestic value added is one-half of the final price, then the ERP on the domestic activity of processing the cloth, the intermediate input, into the final commodity is 50 percent. In other words, the tariff structure allows domestic factors of production to be 50 percent less efficient or to have 50 percent higher payments than foreign competitors. Only if the nominal rate of protection on the final product is equal to the rate on the input will the effective rate be equal to the nominal rate. Otherwise, a decrease in the tariff on inputs or an increase in the nominal tariff rate on the final product will increase the ERP. When an import-substitution industry is given a high nominal tariff on the finished product but low tariffs on its imported inputs, then the ERP is high and resources will be attracted to that sheltered industry if its ERP is higher than that of some other industries.

There may also be, however, distortions in factor prices that would bias the allocation of resources away from what would occur in a well-functioning competitive market. To obtain a better measure of the additional domestic resources employed per unit of value added, or output in protected industries, some analysts convert their estimates of effective protection into estimates of domestic resource costs (DRCs). This is done by adjusting estimates of inputs of primary factors of production (usually capital or labor) to reflect shadow prices rather than market prices.

The DRC formula is

$$DRC = \frac{\text{value added at domestic prices in local currency}}{\text{value added at world prices in foreign currency}}$$

If for a particular investment in an import substitute (or an export) this ratio is below the official foreign-exchange rate, the country could save (or earn) foreign exchange through this investment, convert the foreign exchange into local currency at the official exchange rate, cover the costs of production, and retain a surplus in local currency. If this ratio exceeds 1, the opportunity cost of domestic factors in terms of foreign exchange is greater than the value added at world prices by these factors.

If factor markets were competitive, DRC estimates would be identical to ERP estimates plus 1, since the ERP measures the excess domestic value added as a fraction of international value added, while the DRC measure gives total value added as a fraction of international value added. Usually, the ERP gives a better indication of the incentives created by the trade regime, whereas DRCs provide a better estimate of the cost of the regime. For a more detailed explanation, see Anne O. Krueger, "Trade Policies in Developing Countries," in *International Trade: Surveys of Theory and Policy,* ed. R. W. Jones (1986), and Michael Bruno, "Domestic Resource Costs and Effective Protection," *Journal of Political Economy* (January–February 1972).

Comment: Infant-Industry Protection

The essence of the infant-industry argument rests on "dynamic learning effects" that will allow an industry that is not currently competitive to achieve comparative advantage after a temporary period of protection. Properly stated, three conditions are necessary for infant-industry protection.

1. Technological externalities are generated that are non capturable by the protected industry.
2. The protection is limited in time.
3. The protection allows the industry to generate a sufficient decrease in economic costs so that the initial excess costs of the industry will be repaid with an economic rate of return equal to that earned on other investments.

If the first condition is not fulfilled, the private market should be able to yield an efficient allocation unless capital markets are imperfect or information is inadequate, so that risks are overestimated. Infant-industry protection is justified not by the fact that there are losses until the infant grows up, but by the fact of externalities associated with the learning process. The second condition guarantees that the industry is not protected from infancy to geriatric or even senile stages. And the third condition ensures that the expected benefit is sufficiently great to offset, in present value terms, the current costs of the policy required to produce the benefit.

If free trade is not optimal because of the presence of externalities and the possibility of lower costs over time, what, then, are the optimal policy instruments for protecting the infant industry? The normative theory of international-trade policy has established that the best policy is a production subsidy aimed at the source of the distortion. This is preferable to a tariff, which, in turn, is preferable to a quantitative restriction.

Although market failure justifies the protection, under certain types of market failure, the best policy may not be a production subsidy. If the learning experience results in dynamic internal economies in which the learning benefits remain wholly within the firm, the market failure may be in the imperfection of the capital market that makes the financing of such investment difficult or too expensive because the capital market is biased against this type of "invisible" investment in human capital, or because the rate of interest for all long-term investment is too high as a result of private myopia. In this case, the best policy is to improve the capital market directly; a subsidy to the activity that gives rise to the learning benefits is second best, while farther down the hierarchy is a general ouput subsidy to the industry and, finally, a tariff.

Another case might involve dynamic external economies created by the labor training carried out by a firm, which is not able to retain the workers it has trained. In a perfect market situation, the learning effects would be internalized: the workers would accept low wages during the learning stage, financing themselves by borrowing with recoupment through subsequent mobility. But if the capital market is imperfect or if there are rigidities in wage determination, this may not be possible. Again, best policy is to improve the capital market; the second-best policy is to provide financing for or subsidization of the labor training, while subsidization of the firm's output is farther down the policy hierarchy.

For elaboration of the infant-industry argument, see R. E. Baldwin, "The Case Against Infant-Industry Tariff Protection," *Journal of Political Economy* (May–June 1969); W. M. Corden, "Normative Theory of International Trade," in *Handbook of International Economics,* vol. 1, ed. R. W. Jones and P. B. Kenen (1984); and G. M. Meier, "Infant Industry," in *The New Palgrave Dictionary of Economics* (1987).

The "new trade theory" that focuses on imperfect competition and economies of scale has also given rise to a type of infant-industry argument. See Paul Krugman, "Import Protection as Export Promotion: International Competition in the Presence of Oligopoly and Economies of Scale," in *Monopolistic Competition and International Trade,* ed. H. Kierzkowski (1984).

The argument is that temporary tariff protection or a subsidy to a domestic industry may allow the infant industry to grow through the scale effect and eventually achieve a competitive position in export markets. As with other aspects of the new trade theory, however, the relevance of this type of infant-industry protection is questionable when the size of the home market is small, there are not economies of scale for primary products, there is free entry to the industry, governments retaliate, or there is corruption and political patronage in the setting of government policy. So that the argument is simply a veil for crude protectionism (as Krugman notes).

The next selection (IX.B.2) considers other arguments for protection or intervention that have emerged from the new trade theory.

IX.B.2. New Protectionist Arguments*

A whole host of arguments for intervention/protection have emerged from the new trade theories. Inevitably, given the structure of the underlying models, many of the arguments are model-specific and not robust to variations in these assumptions. Since many of the arguments are likely to have limited applicability in the context of most LDCs, we will concentrate on the two arguments which have circulated most widely, and which some commentators have claimed may have applicability in the context of LDCs. These are the external economies and rent-snatching arguments.

External Economies

The first of these arguments is predicated on the assumption of positive externalities—that is, beneficial spillover effects in an industry. Where such external economies are important significant benefits go unpriced, reliance on the market is likely to result in underprovision of the good or service in question. Now the idea of externalities being an important market imperfection necessitating government intervention to counter the distortion is not a new one; economists have long accepted the validity of such a case.

What, then, is "new" about the external economy argument in the new theories? Basically, this: there are many human capital-intensive, knowledge-based industries/sectors, which are potentially strategically important, which may make this particular line of argument more widely applicable than hitherto thought. The sectors most often mentioned in this regard are information technology, semiconductors, artifi-

cial intelligence, and biotechnology. These are industries where learning effects are crucially important, and where the benefits from investment are spread widely in society. There may be first-mover disadvantages: even where investment takes place, the industry size could be suboptimal due to externalities (in other words, an insufficient number of firms will enter the industry); if overseas producers enjoy the benefits of government support for their activities while home firms do not, this will provide them with a strategic advantage in both the home *and* overseas market—import protection results in export promotion (Krugman, 1984). Government support allows the firm to expand output and thereby move down its scale curve. As a result, average costs fall providing it with a competitive advantage at home and abroad. For any one, or some combination, of these reasons, it can be argued that government should intervene to promote the industry in question.

It can be argued that the knowledge-based, human capital-intensive industries which analysts have in mind are crucial sectors in the development process in LDCs in general, and NICs in particular. Moreover, the success with which new technology is absorbed has a crucial bearing on comparative advantage. Some LDCs and NICs have already established an international presence in such activities. Korea, for instance, not only assembles microprocessors, but also manufactures semiconductors. Moreover, Korean manufacturers reportedly have research programmes under way to establish a presence in the next generation of semiconductors.

India has established an international market presence in the provision of software services. In both cases these activities confer wider benefits on society at large; in the Korean case, the rapid evolution of the industry to one where it can conceive of competing at the frontier may, it can be argued, be attributable (at least in part) to government support for the industry. Such

*From David Greenaway, "New Trade Theories and Developing Countries," in V. N. Balasubramanyam and S. Lall, eds., *Current Issues in Development Economics* (London: Macmillan, 1992), pp. 159–69. Reprinted by permission.

support should therefore be more widely available in LDCs. The validity of this line of argument will be considered later.

Rent-Snatching

The so-called rent-snatching argument is, superficially at least, a new argument for protection arising from the work of Brander and Spencer (1984). As we shall see, however, it too has a familiar ring to it. This argument begins with the existence of rents, or supernormal profits, in a market. The simple theory of monopoly tells us that we can expect to find rents in highly concentrated markets. This is well known and empirical evidence suggests that rents are indeed a common feature of highly concentrated markets.

What do rents have to do with protection? After all intuition suggests that the presence of rents in domestic markets most probably provides a case for trade liberalisation—competition from imports is a very effective mechanism for constraining the market power of a domestic monopolist. This is one mechanism by which rents are dissipated in a competitive economy. More generally, one could argue that so long as governments ensure that barriers to entry do not arise, there is no need to worry about rents, the market takes care of the problem.

Suppose, however, that rents cannot be competed away. There may be circumstances where this is the case; production technology may be such that the market can support only a small number of producers operating profitably. Call this number n. If entry occurs and we have $n + 1$ producers, *all* make losses. This could be the case in technologically advanced sectors where product development costs are enormous, and learning economies important. Sunk costs and learning economies create a market structure which is naturally duopolistic or oligopolistic. If such a market were confined within given national frontiers then regulation could be used to secure some of the rents. Suppose, however, that the relevant market is international. In these circumstances intervention could be used to redistribute rents from one country to another.

The basic idea behind this kind of intervention is quite simple. Suppose we have an international market which can support only one firm operating profitably. Suppose further that there are two potential entrants to this market, A and B. Which one of them will survive depends upon the outcome of the competitive process. In duopoly situations, outcomes are difficult to predict

because of the problems created by strategic interdependence. In the simplest of game theoretic settings where the firms behave according to Cournot rules, Brander and Spencer (1982) demonstrate how government intervention can have a decisive impact on the eventual equilibrium. Thus, the government of the country in which ''A'' resides could provide its firm with a production subsidy which ensures that whatever firm B does, A survives operating profitably. Whereas both A and B make losses if both enter in the absence of intervention, with intervention only B makes losses if both enter. The subsidy therefore allows A to pre-commit itself to production whatever B does. Clearly this increases the probability that A will be the successful survivor. If this were so, rents will accrue to the home country which exceed the value of the subsidy. The intervention has succeeded in redistributing income internationally, raising real income in A, and lowering real income in B.

It can be argued that where LDCs have the opportunity to enter markets with these kinds of characteristics, governments should be willing to consider intervention as a basis for helping the firms in question to pre-commit. Baldwin and Flam (1989) have argued that just this kind of intervention has been successfully implemented by Brazil in the market for 30–40-seater aircraft where its national producer (Brazilia) competes with firms from industrialised countries—Saab from Sweden and De Havilland from Canada.

The applicability of these new arguments for protection/intervention in LDCs can be evaluated in two ways, first by considering how applicable the new trade theories are to the explanation of trade flows in LDCs; second, in light of this, by evaluating the intrinsic merit of the arguments themselves.

Assessment of the relevance of the new theories to LDCs requires identification of the widespread presence of scale economies and product differentiation. This, however, is easier said than done. One can, however, get some idea of the existence of these characteristics by evaluating the extent of intra-industry trade (IIT) in these countries.

To summarise then on empirical evidence: it would seen that IIT is less important in developing countries than in industrialised countries, as we would anticipate from economic theory. However, it is of growing importance in the trade of NICs. Among non-NICs some portion of what is recorded as IIT is trade in primary products and foodstuffs; by contrast, recorded IIT in NICs appears to be predominantly trade in intermediates and finished manufactures produced by relatively capital-intensive methods. Finally, the evidence suggests that as industrialisation proceeds and *per capita* income rises, IIT becomes increasingly prevalent. This clearly suggests that this is a phenomenon which will become more important in the trade of developing countries.

What, then, is the relevance of the new trade theories to developing countries? The new trade theories provide us with a framework for systematically incorporating factors like scale economies and product differentiation into models of trade. This is important since we know these to be common features of the real world. Both theory and evidence relating to IIT suggest that these tend to be characteristics of the markets for manufactures. We would not therefore expect these determinants to be of paramount importance in the trade of the least developed LDCs. By contrast, we would expect them to become more important as industrialisation proceeds. Empirical evidence suggests that this is indeed the case. The new trade theories do have an increasingly important part to play in explaining the direction and commodity composition of the trade of the more developed developing countries (i.e., the NICs), and will have an increasingly important part to play in the future determination of the direction and commodity composition of those economies which are currently non-NIC developing countries.

This being so, what is the relevance of the new theories for protection? Are they likely to provide a widely applicable justification for intervention in LDCs? The answer to this is probably not, for several reasons. First, the new arguments for protection suggest that there may be net benefits from protection in particular circumstances. These circumstances are, to say the least, specific, particularly in the case of rent-snatching intervention. Notwithstanding the fact that one empirical analysis suggests gains from rent-snatching in a NIC (Baldwin and Flam, 1989, the market for 30–40 seater commuter aircraft), this argument is probably wholly irrelevant to the vast majority of developing countries. In fact, a cynic would say that this particular argument has been custom built for the aerospace industry. External economies, the other argument for protection, may however be a more prevalent feature of the real world. But

as earlier analysis has demonstrated, these typically do not provide a justification for protection, but for some other form of intervention (such as R&D or training subsidies). Moreover, these arguments ignore the more general benefits of free trade. A number of studies have now addressed the issue of the gains from free trade in an imperfect competition setting (albeit in the context of industrialised countries). Many of these studies suggest that the gains from trade in a setting of imperfect competition may be significantly in excess of those typically associated with the "conventional" gains from trade— largely due to the influence of scale economies.

A second set of reasons for being cautious about these new arguments for protection revolves around political economy factors. For example, how does one identify sectors where the most important external economies exist, or where the greatest potential for rent-snatching is available? This is a serious practical problem, and since many developing countries do not have a happy record when it comes to picking winners, it is a problem which is not to be taken lightly. In addition, the evolution of protectionist regimes in many developing countries confirms that demonstration effects are extremely influential. One may find that many industries claim potential external economies, or a potential for rent-snatching.

Governments do not always find it easy to resist such pressures. Moreover, once protection support is granted, it may not result in industry expansion, but rather in higher rents to the industry incumbents. The prevalence of rent-seeking behaviour in many developing countries suggests that this is certainly a realistic possibility. Rent-seeking, as we know, serves to increase the costs of protection.

Overall, then, there are compelling reasons for doubting whether the new arguments for strategic protection are likely to be widely applicable in developing countries. There are grounds for suspecting that they may provide another case for intervention which simply serves to encourage rent-seeking behaviour, and incrementalism in the formation of policy. Since a growing amount of evidence suggests that this kind of policy posture is damaging to economic performance, this gives grounds for caution. Note, however, that this is *not* to argue that there are no convincing arguments at all for *intervention* in developing countries; there no doubt are such arguments. Of the new arguments one, rent-snatching, does not add to the list of persuasive arguments; the other, external econo- mies in knowledge-based–human capital- intensive infant industries may do. When it does, however, it is likely to provide a case for some kind of intervention other than protection.

References

Baldwin, Richard E., and Harry Flam (1989). "Strategic Trade Policies in the Market for 30–40 Seat Commuter Aircraft." Institute for International Economic Studies, University of Stockholm, Seminar Paper no. 431.

Brander, J. A., and B. J. Spencer (1982). "International R&D Rivalry and Industrial Strategy." *Review of Economic Studies* 50: 707–22.

Brander, J. A., and B. J. Spencer (1984). "Tariff Protection and Imperfect Competition." In H. Kierzkowski, ed., *Monopolistic Competition and International Trade* (Oxford).

Krugman, P. R. (1984). "Import Protection as Export Promotion." In H. Kierzkowski, ed., *Monopolistic Competition and International Trade* (Oxford).

Comment: New Trade Theory and LDCs

A number of studies consider the relevance of the "new trade theories" for developing countries. The features of increasing returns to scale and noncompetitive market structure have, as noted in previous selections, caused some analysts to favor an active industrial policy. While some also use new trade theory in advocating some forms of protection, others argue that the case for trade liberalization is by no means weakened by the new theory.

For a variety of views, see T. N. Srinivasan, "Recent Theories of Imperfect Competition and International Trade: Any Implications for Development Strategy?" *Indian Economic Review* (1989); Paul Krugman, "New Trade Theory and the Less Developed Countries," in *Debt, Stabilization, and Development,* ed. Guillermo Calvo et al. (1989); D. Rodrick, "Imperfect Competition, Scale Economies, and Trade Policy in Developing Countries," in *Trade Policy Issues and Empirical Analysis,* ed. R. E. Baldwin (1988); Christopher Bliss, "The New Trade Theory and Economic Policy," *Oxford Review of Economic Policy* (1987); and Frances Stewart, "Recent Theories of International Trade: Some Implications for the South," in *Monopolistic Competition and International Trade,* ed. H. Kierzkowski (1984).

IX.B.3. Superiority of Export-Oriented Policies*

My topic is the question: what difference does the set of commercial policies chosen by a developing country make to its rate of economic growth?

Turning first to theory, there are many static propositions but few useful theorems about the effects of alternative trade policies on growth. Clearly there are gains to be achieved through trade in the development process.

To be sure, once the assumption that there are only two goods is abandoned, theory suggests

*From Anne O. Krueger, "Trade Policy as an Input to Development," *American Economic Review, Papers and Proceedings* (May 1980), pp. 288–92. Reprinted by permission.

that activity in production of tradables should be undertaken to the point where the international marginal rate of transformation (IMRT) equals the domestic marginal rate of transformation (DMRT), with no production in lines where domestic opportunity cost exceeds the international price ratio. An allocation of resources satisfying this criterion would be optimal in the absence of any dynamic considerations.

Theory does not, however, indicate how many activities are likely to be undertaken. Nor does it suggest the relative importance of exporting and import-competing activities in an optimum allocation, or how that allocation would change with growth. Worse yet, there is nothing in theory to indicate why a deviation from the optimum should affect the rate of economic growth. Most growth models suggest that there are once-and-for-all losses arising from nonoptimal policies with lower levels of income resulting from them but no change in growth rates.

Turning from theory to practice, developing countries' trade-policies have fallen into two distinct categories. One group of developing countries has adopted trade policies which diverge from the optimality criterion, often by a large amount, by protecting their domestic industries. These "import substitution" policies have been employed to stimulate domestic production on the theory that nonagricultural sectors must grow at a rate above the rate of growth of domestic demand, and can do so only insofar as additional production substitutes for imports. The other category, "export promotion," has consisted of encouragement to exports, usually beyond the extent that would conform to the IMRT = DMRT criterion. Countries adopting an export-oriented trade strategy have generally experienced rapid growth of traditional exports, but even more rapid growth of nontraditional exports.

Experience has been that growth performance has been more satisfactory under export promotion strategies than under import-substitution strategies. While it is impossible to specify a particular model of growth process that will simultaneously satisfy all observers, the relationship between export performance and growth is sufficiently strong that it seems to bear up under many different specifications of the relationship. It has been tested over many countries for: (1) rates of growth of real GNP and of exports; (2) for real GNP net of exports and exports; and (3) for rates of growth of GNP as a function of rate of capital formation, aid receipts, and export growth. Time-series and cross-section data have been pooled, so that deviations of countries' growth rates from their trends have been estimated as a function of the growth of export earnings. In all of these specifications, rate of growth of exports has turned out to be a highly significant variable. While the "success stories" of Korea, Taiwan, and Brazil are well known, there are enough other observations, both for different time periods in the same country (as for example Turkey and the Philippines) and of countries (including on the positive side Ivory Coast, Colombia, and Malaysia and on the negative side India, Argentina, and Egypt), so that there is little doubt about the link between export performance and growth rates.

Moreover, it seems clear the export perfor-mance is a function in large part of governmental policies. While an export promotion strategy will not always be successful in generating more export growth (especially if policies affecting the domestic market are inappropriate), certainly policies adopted to encourage import substitution, especially when they include overvalued exchange rates and quantitative restrictions upon imports, retard the growth of exports. . . .

The central question, then, is why such a difference in growth performance should be associated with export promotion contrasted with import substitution. There are three major hypotheses, and each undoubtedly contains some explanatory power. . . .

The first hypothesis is that technological-economic factors imply an overwhelming superiority for development through export promotion. These factors include such phenomena as minimum efficient size of plant, increasing returns to scale, indivisibilities in the production process, and the necessity for competition. According to this hypothesis, failure to take advantage of the opportunities to exploit these phenomena through trade significantly impairs the attainable rate of growth. A second hypothesis is that differences in growth rates have resulted, not from the choice of trade strategy per se, but rather from excesses in the ways in which import substitution policies were administered. The third hypothesis is that policies adopted in pursuit of an export promotion strategy are generally far closer to an optimum, both in the DMRT = IMRT sense and with respect to the domestic market, than are those adopted under import substitution. Under this interpretation, the role of trade policy is to constrain policymakers in such a way that they do not impede the growth rate as much as they otherwise would.

Both the first and second hypotheses are consistent with the notion that the nonagricultural sector of most developing countries is, in some sense, an "infant industry," and requires some stimulus for growth. The third, by contrast, essentially takes the negative view, that markets would function well and provide satisfactory growth if only policymakers would abstain from counter-productive intervention.

The first hypothesis really amounts to an assertion that the gains from trade, especially for developing countries, are so sizable that the losses associated with import substitution significantly reduce the rate of return on factor accumulation. On the negative side, domestic markets are extremely small in most developing countries, and attempts to replace imports result in the construction of plants of less-than-efficient minimum size, while simultaneously generating an oligopolistic or monopolistic market structure. As import substitution proceeds, new activities are increasingly capital intensive and inefficiencies from below-minimum-efficient size increase. On the positive side, so the argument runs, export promotion permits entrepreneurs to base their plans on whatever size plant seems appropriate: size of domestic market is no longer a virtually binding constraint, as it is when the activity is profitable only because of very high rates of effective protection. Moreover, monopoly positions arise less frequently under export promotion, as exporters face competition from abroad as well as from other domestic producers.

Export promotion may also be more efficient in permitting rapid expansion of profitable activities; by contrast, under import substitution, most activities are constrained to expanding at approximately the same rate: inefficient firms and sectors expand approximately as rapidly as efficient ones. In this view, potential export lines consist of a number of industrial products (girls' sneakers, wigs, tennis rackets, engine parts, plywood, and so on) and it is as much a matter of the right entrepreneur, and the right specialized product, as choosing the "right industry" that is necessary for rapid growth. To be sure, factor proportions and comparative advantage may result in greater profitability of relatively labor-using industries, but the basic notion is that there are thousands of industrial products, and that, among relatively labor-intensive activities, the ones which will develop into exports will be those in which there are firms with good management and an ability to utilize factors of production efficiently.

A final aspect of the technology-related view of the advantages of export promotion has to do with factor proportions. Given the vast disparity in capital-labor ratios of the industrial sectors of the developed and developing countries, the opportunity for trade represents a means for shifting the demand for labor outward more rapidly than the import-substitution strategy permits. If there are differences of, say, two-to-one and six-to-one in capital-labor ratios between activities at the prevailing wage-rental ratio, while the rate of capital accumulation is the binding constraint on expansion of employment in the urban sector, an allocation of additional capital to the labor-intensive activity for export will permit an upward shift in the demand for labor three times

as great as that which would occur if import substitution dictates the start of the more capital-intensive activity. To be sure, the expectation is that the more rapid rate of growth of demand for industrial labor would drive up the urban wage once the demand for labor was rising more rapidly than the labor force, but this is precisely a desired outcome of policy. . . .

The second hypothesis focuses upon the costs of import substitution policies as in fact carried out, and suggests that alternative means of achieving import substitution might have avoided them. According to this view, the failure of import substitution resulted from the excesses of the particular ways in which domestic industries were encouraged: extreme currency overvaluation combined with quantitative restrictions provided the equivalent of prohibitive tariff protection; techniques of allocating import licenses were employed which prevented competition among domestic firms and rewarded entrepreneurs for license-getting abilities rather than their cost-minimizing performance; and excessive and detailed quantitative controls were employed over many aspects of economic activity. One of the costs was the failure of export earnings to grow as much as they would have under "better" import-substitution policies; that in turn led to "stop-go" patterns with their attendant costs. Simultaneously, the emerging "foreign exchange bottleneck" had both direct and indirect impacts upon the structure and growth of the economy. In particular, efforts at "import substitution" stopped being geared toward development of economic new industries, and became focused upon "foreign exchange saving," often in highly irrational and indiscriminate ways, which further distorted the system.

The third view denies the need for any bias toward exports and implicitly or explicitly asserts that growth would be optimal in the absence of intervention. A bias toward exports is therefore better than one toward import-substitutes only because policies are less distortive. In this view, an export-oriented strategy imposes constraints on policymakers, both in what they can attempt to do, and in making them aware of the costs of mistakes. Policymakers receive feedback in a relatively short time period as to the costs of their policies. Also, it is infeasible to rely upon quantitative controls: the international price, at least, cannot be administered and to that extent, more generalized forms of incentive, including a relatively realistic exchange rate, must be employed. Indeed, it is argued that incentives cannot be as biased toward export promotion as they can be toward import substitution. This is precisely because to do so would require either export subsidization (whose costs would be immediately evident through the drain on the budget) or such a degree of currency undervaluation that a current account surplus would absorb much of the country's savings potential.

According to this third line of argument, constraints upon policymakers go well beyond the inability to impose too great a bias toward exports. For example, it is virtually impossible to administer any highly protective system for intermediate and capital goods imports if exporters are expected to compete in international markets: they must be permitted ready access to imported raw materials, intermediate goods, and capital equipment. To impose any comprehensive system of licensing or controls would entail delays and other costs, inconsistent with the export strategy. Thus, the commitment to an export-oriented development strategy implies a fairly liberal and efficient trade regime, and thus prevents paperwork, delays, bureaucratic regulation, and other costs that can arise under import substitution. This in turn limits the restrictions that can be imposed on capital account. More generally, under an export promotion strategy, there is an international market in the background: it functions as a constraint upon economic behavior, both of entrepreneurs and of government officials, and simultaneously provides feedback to them as to the success or failure of policies in terms of their objectives.

Undoubtedly, all three approaches to the differential in economic performance contain elements of truth. There are export opportunities that are passed up under import substitution where indivisibilities or increasing returns within a range would permit sizable gains in output. There are also high-cost import substitution activities which, if never undertaken, would have freed resources for considerably more productive use, even within an import-substitution strategy. Likewise, the international market has served to constrain policymakers and induce them to abandon uneconomic policies sooner than they otherwise would have done. Knowledge is not yet far enough advanced to determine the relative importance of the alternatives. It will not be until we have far more information than is currently available about the order of magnitude of indivisibilities and minimum size plant contrasted with size of markets in LDCs, and also about the determinants of politicians' and bureaucrats' behavior. Moreover, it is certain that the primary sources of growth are internal, and that there is no magic formula, or single policy change, that can by itself account meaningfully for differences in economic performance.

Nonetheless, experience has clearly demonstrated the importance of access to international markets in providing a means of permitting more rapid growth than would otherwise be feasible. Given the enormous difficulties and costs of achieving the institutional and other changes that economic growth requires, it is probable that trade policy changes have a higher rate of return to LDCs than most other feasible policy changes. It is, of course, to be hoped that protectionist pressures in the developed countries do not result in fewer opportunities for the LDCs. If such protectionist measures are taken, they will lower the rate of return to outward-oriented trade strategies. They will however, for the foreseeable future, still leave that rate distinctly above the returns from a policy of persisting with inward-oriented growth.

EXHIBIT IX.3. Exports of Goods and Services, Developing Countries, 1990 (percentage)

	Total Exports of Goods and Services	
	Developing Countries	World
Developing countries	**100.0**	**20.3**
By Region		
Africa	9.9	2.0
Asia	52.7	10.7
Middle East and Europe	20.9	4.2
Western Hemisphere	16.5	3.4
Sub-Saharan Africa	3.3	0.7
Four newly industrializing Asian economies	32.2	6.6
By Predominant Export		
Fuel	27.1	5.5
Nonfuel exports	72.9	14.8
Manufactures	51.4	10.4
Primary products	7.8	1.6
Agricultural products	5.3	1.1
Minerals	2.5	0.5
Services and private transfers	4.3	0.9
Diversified export base	9.4	1.9

Source: International Monetary Fund, *World Economic Outlook* (May 1993), p. 122.

EXHIBIT IX.4. Merchandise Exports, Various Developing Countries, 1970–91

Country	Merchandise Exports (millions of dollars) 1991	Average Annual Growth Rate (percent) 1970–80	Average Annual Growth Rate (percent) 1980–91
Taiwan	76,090	15.6	11.0
China	72,875	8.7	11.5
Korea, Rep. of	71,672	23.5	12.2
Singapore	58,871	4.2	8.9
Malaysia	34,300	4.8	10.9
Brazil	31,610	8.5	4.3
Hong Kong	29,738	9.7	4.4
Indonesia	28,997	7.2	4.5
Thailand	28,324	10.3	14.4
Mexico	27,120	13.5	3.5
India	17,664	4.3	7.4
Venezuela	15,127	−11.6	0.1
Turkey	13,594	4.3	7.2
Argentina	11,975	7.1	2.1
Philippines	8,754	6.0	3.3
Peru	3,307	3.3	1.1
Ecuador	2,957	12.5	4.8
Sri Lanka	2,629	2.0	6.3
Costa Rica	1,490	5.2	4.6
Guatemala	1,202	5.7	−0.7
Mauritius	1,193	3.8	9.9
Jamaica	1,081	−1.7	0.8
Ghana	992	−6.3	5.2

Source: World Bank, *World Development Report, 1993* (1993), pp. 264–65.

EXHIBIT IX.5. Ratio of Total Trade to GDP

Economy/Region	1970	1980	1985	1988
HPAEs				
Hong Kong	1.50	1.52	1.78	2.82
Indonesia	0.25	0.46	0.38	0.42
Korea, Rep. of	0.32	0.63	0.66	0.66
Japan	0.19	0.25	0.23	0.11
Malaysia	0.89	1.00	0.85	1.09
Singapore	2.12	3.70	2.77	3.47
Taiwan, China	0.53	0.95	0.82	0.90
Thailand	0.28	0.49	0.44	0.35
Sub-Saharan Africa	0.24	0.30	0.27	0.45
South Asia	0.11	0.17	0.16	0.19
Latin America and Caribbean	0.20	0.25	0.22	0.23

Note: Total trade = value of exports and value of imports divided by gross domestic product.

Source: World Bank, *East Asian Miracle* (1993), p. 39.

Comment: Dynamic Gains from Exports

Why should various indicators of development—real GNP, real per capita income, employment, income distribution, nonmonetary indicators—be superior in countries that follow export promotion instead of import promotion? Neoclassical trade theory, based on the static gains from trade, can provide only part of the answer. For what must be explained is not merely the neoclassical once-over change to a higher level of real income as a result of following comparative advantage. More significantly, it is necessary to explain the higher rate of growth in income over time.

In terms of favorable effects on resource allocation, an export-oriented industrialization strategy may result in not simply a once-for-all improvement in allocation according to the country's comparative advantage in international trade, but more importantly in the realization of dynamic benefits. While a reallocation of resources in conformity with comparative advantage can raise the level of income, the dynamic gains are significant in increasing the rate of growth in income.

There may be increased utilization of plant capacity, realization of economies of scale, the creation of employment through export of labor-intensive products, a multiplier effect that gives rise to increased demand for intermediate inputs and increased demand by consumers, and growth in total factor productivity. Marginal factor productivities in export-oriented industries also tend to be significantly higher than in the nonexport-oriented industries. The difference seems to derive, in part, from intersectoral beneficial externalities generated by the export sector.

Most important may be the realization of dynamic efficiency in the sense of a fall in the incremental capital–output ratio, the realization of "X-efficiency," the extension of informational efficiency, enjoyment of external economies, and of "learning-by-doing" effects. Considering the last, there is evidence that the faster export output grows, the faster is the growth in productivity. This is because of economies of scale, higher investment embodying capital of a more productive vintage, and a faster pace of innovation in products and processes.

As noted by classical economists (IX.A.2), many of the dynamic gains stem from the trade in ideas and the educative effect associated with exports. Mill's perceptive observation that ''the introduction of foreign arts'' and ''the importation of foreign capital raise the returns derivable from additional capital'' (IX.A.2) has been validated in the experience of the NICs. For these countries, exports have facilitated their move toward international-best technologies with a resultant growth in TFP.[1]

The ability of the NICs to tap world technology has been an important benefit of exports. Because the international markets for technology and knowledge are imperfect (markets do not exist or are monopolized), exporting helps to overcome some imperfections and permits access to international best-practice technology through other mechanisms. These include importation of new equipment (for producing exports and paid for by export revenue), export-oriented foreign direct investment, better bargaining power for licensing technology, information from purchases of exports, knowledge from returning nationals, and domestic research devoted to exports.

As export growth leads to dynamic efficiency, it also reduces what Myint terms ''organizational dualism'' (recall III.B.4). By overcoming indivisibilities and filling in the gaps in the organizational framework of the traditional sector, the expansion of exports may be able to shift the production feasibility curve upward. Beyond this, organizational dualism is reduced through a decline in the costs of transactions, transportation, information, and administration. The improved effectiveness of the domestic economic organization allows the exporting country to take advantage of external economic opportunities in the form of international trade, foreign investment, technological adaptation, and ideas from abroad. There is institutional adaptation to realize the potential comparative advantage in trade. The mutual interaction between economic policies and economic institutions results in improvement of the organization of production, more effective incentives, and a strengthening of markets. Dynamic efficiency is realized as diseconomies of a small economy are overcome, the transformation capacity of the economy widens, and the learning rate of the economy accelerates. The integrative process that we discussed in Note IX.A.4 is stronger in terms of stimulus and diffusion from the export sector.

Whereas proponents of the old export pessimism could criticize neoclassical trade theory and assert that the dynamic gains from import-substitution industrialization (ISI) would outweigh the possible static costs of protection, it is more likely that the dynamic gains are far superior for export promotion. The case for development through trade can actually be expressed in stronger terms than in its neo-classical version.[2]

As noted earlier, several empirical studies demonstrate that exports contribute to the rate of growth of GDP by more than simply the change in the volume of exports. Explanations of these observations have concentrated on various beneficial aspects of competing in the world market: greater utilization of plant capacity, economies of scale, incentives to technological improvements, training of higher quality labor, and internationally competitive management.

Econometric analysis supports the view that export-oriented policies bring the economy closer to an optimal allocation of resources; social marginal productivities also are significantly higher in the export sector than in the nonexport sectors. For such an analysis, see Gershon Feder, ''On Exports and Economic Growth,'' *Journal of Development Economics* (February–April 1982).

A number of studies indicate that the creation of employment is greater from export expansion than from import substitution; see, for example, Larry E. Westphal, ''The Republic of Korea's Experience with Export-Led Industrial Development,'' *World Development* 6, no. 3 (1978), and Anne O. Krueger, ''Alternative Trade Strategies and Employment in LDCs,'' *American Economic Review* (May 1978). Employment rises with a switch to a more labor-intensive mode of production in exportables and with an expansion in the capital stock. For elaboration, see Anne O. Krueger et al., *Trade and Employment in Developing Countries, I. Individual Studies* (1981).

For empirical evidence that export expansion is positively correlated and import substitution is negatively correlated with changes in total factor productivity, see Nieko Nishimizu and Sherman

---

[1]World Bank, *East Asian Miracle* (1993), pp. 316–24.

[2]Hla Myint, ''Neo-classical Development Analysis,'' in *Pioneers in Development*, ed. Gerald M. Meier, 2nd ser. (1987), pp. 109–10, 126–30.

Robinson, "Trade Policies and Productivity Change in Semi-industrialized Countries," *Journal of Development Economics* (September–October 1984). Also, David Dollar, "Outward-Oriented Developing Economies Do Grow More Rapidly: Evidence from 95 LDCs, 1976–1986," *Economic Development and Cultural Change* (April 1992).

IX.B.4. Export Promotion: Lessons of Experience—Note

An increasing number of countries have promoted their manufactured exports and reached the status of newly industrializing countries (NICs) or semi-industrialized countries (SICs). Outstanding performers have been South Korea, Taiwan, Hong Kong, Singapore, and Brazil. The record of some of these "success stories" has been noted in Chapter I. They have achieved the promotion of industry through an outward-looking policy rather than through the protection of an inward-looking industrial structure. These countries exemplify the structural transformation of an open dualistic economy. As successful export performers, they demonstrate that this transformation involves a substantial rise in the share of manufacturing in GNP and a significant shift away from dependence on primary exports toward manufactured goods as a source of foreign exchange. There is considerable evidence that success in promoting manufactured exports is critical to the course of industrial development.[1]

What are some of the lessons to be learned from the experience of these countries and the manner in which they promoted the export of their manufactured goods?

On the demand side, conditions were highly favorable during the 1950s and 1960s until the slowing down of growth in the world economy after 1973. The earlier two decades were unique for the high rate of growth in the more developed countries (MDCs)—a historical record period—and for the growth in world trade. The demand for imports was high and rising in the MDCs, and the high growth rate of the MDCs fostered trade liberalization and weakened the case for protection. Of course, as growth occurs in the MDCs, their pattern of demand has to match the actual or potential comparative advantage of the exporting LDCs to create oppor-

tunities for exports. This is likely to be more true for exports of manufactured goods than of primary products.

On the supply side, however, the LDCs varied in their international competitiveness and in their capacity to take advantage of export markets. In large part, the differences in performance are to be explained by differences in governmental policies—especially as related to the entire set of policies that determined the foreign-trade regime and the bias between import substitution and export promotion in the different countries. To promote exports, governmental policies have to accomplish an outward-oriented policy shift that removes the bias in favor of import substitution. As long as an import-substitution bias exists, exports will suffer from the implicit taxation and quantitative restrictions, from the cost of inputs being above free-trade prices, and from the diversion of resources to the sheltered and capital-intensive import-substitution industries.

When government policies are biased against exports in favor of import substitution, the effective exchange rate for imports (EER_m) is higher than the effective exchange rate for exports (EER_x). The term EER_m equals the number of units of domestic currency that would be paid for a dollar's worth of imports, taking into account tariffs, surcharges, interest on advance deposits, and other measures that affect the price of imports. The term EER_x is defined as the number of units of domestic currency that can be obtained for a dollar's worth of exports, taking into account export duties, subsidies, special exchange rates, input subsidies related to exports, and other financial and tax measures that affect the price of exports.

An outward-looking policy shift must reduce the bias against exports by changing the ratio of EER_x to EER_m from less than unity to equal to unity. This is illustrated in Figure 1, where the international price ratio changes from PP under a foreign-trade regime that is biased in favor of

[1]See Hollis B. Chenery, "Interactions Between Industrialization and Exports," *American Economic Review* (May 1980): 281–87.

FIGURE 1. Definition of import-substituting and export-promoting strategies.

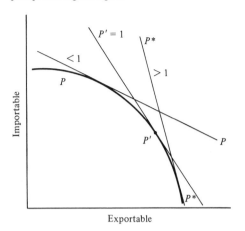

Source: Adapted from J. Bhagwati, *Anatomy and Consequences of Exchange Control Regimes* (1978), p. 208.

import substitution to $P'P'$ in a regime that is neutral and represents free-trade conditions. The policy objective should be to remove the bias against exports and establish an unbiased "free-trade" regime for exports. If the regime were to raise the ratio of EER_x to EER_m above unity ($P*P*$), it would be oversubsidizing exports and protecting exports instead of promoting exports by simply removing the bias against exports and establishing a neutral trade regime.

There is evidence that oversubsidization of exports is less likely to occur than oversubsidization of import substitution. This is because an export-promotion regime usually begins after a preceding period of import substitution that has been so biased against exports that incentives for exports can be considerable before they reach a point of over-subsidizing exports. Moreover, export-promoting measures tend to rely on price incentives, while import-substitution regimes are usually administered through quantitative controls that are characterized by considerable dispersion and unpredictability. Export-promotion measures are also subject to more public scrutiny to the extent that they involve budgetary measures rather than quantitative restrictions. Exporting firms must also face price and quality competition in international markets, and the exporting firms are more likely to realize economies of scale than are import-substitution industries producing for only a narrow domestic market. Although an outward-oriented industrial development strategy does not

mean favoring exports over import substitution, it does mean that similar incentives are provided to production for domestic and for export markets. The creation of such a free-trade regime for exports provides incentives that improve export performance. A devaluation of the country's overvalued exchange rate will stimulate the demand for the country's exports. If, at the same time, tariffs and quantitative restrictions are removed from imports, the devaluation will be compensated on the import side.

If the EER_m is initially greater than EER_x, the exchange rates can be realigned by raising their EER_x. This can be done through a number of policy measures that increase gross export receipts, reduce the cost of exports, or reduce profit tax liability through such measures as export exchange rates, subsidies to export value, tax and duty concessions, foreign-exchange retention schemes, and preferential credits.

Much of the export success of South Korea, Singapore, and Taiwan has been written in terms of policy reforms. In South Korea, for example, various export-promotion schemes have been followed: tariff exemptions on imports of raw materials and spare parts, tariff and tax exemptions granted to domestic suppliers of exporting firms, domestic indirect tax exemptions, lower direct taxes on income earned in exporting, accelerated depreciation allowances, import entitlement linked to exports, reduced public-utility rates, monopoly rights granted in new export markets, credit subsidies through lower interest rates, and automatic access to bank loans for the working capital needed for all export production.[2] When these incentives are included in the computation of the EER_x, the effective exchange rate becomes considerably higher than the nominal or official exchange rate. (In 1975, for example, Korea's official exchange rate was 485 won per U.S. dollar, but when export subsidies were added, the EER_x became 566 won per dollar.)

Although the countries entered the first easy stage of import substitution (selection IX.B.1), they departed fairly early from reliance on ISI strategy and instead adopted policies that brought their economies closer to a neutral free-trade regime. Import substitution was not com-

[2]Larry E. Westphal, "The Republic of Korea's Experience with Export-Led Industrial Development," *World Development* 6, no. 3 (1978); Yung Whee Rhee et al., *Korea's Competitive Edge* (1984); Vittoria Corbo et al., *Export-Oriented Development Strategies* (1985).

pletely excluded, but protection and tax inducements for infant industries were highly selective, small in number, not overdone, and continually monitored over time. It was assured that infant industries would be privately and socially profitable in the medium, although not always in the short, run. And although imports destined for the domestic market were subject to tariffs and quantitative controls, the system of controls on these imports was rationalized and thereby converted from a mechanism of socially unproductive rent-seeking into an instrument of industrial protection.

The selected industries confronted export targets, and their performance was judged by their export record. The firms had to improve their productivity in order to export. While judging potential comparative advantage and intervening on behalf of these infant industries, government intervention did not constrain the pursuit of comparative advantage in well-established industries. When other industries were excessively crowded out of markets for labor and capital in Korea in the late 1970s by the demand of targeted infant industries, the interventionist policies were reversed.[3]

The country's technological capability was also expanded through licensing of foreign technology, but at the same time "home" technology was being developed to conform to local factor endowments. Education and training upgraded skills, and the capital–labor ratios used in production were kept consistent with factor endowments. Aid for research and development and for technological development has now become less industry-specific and more general and functional for the entire economy.

South Korea also did not hesitate to undertake periodic devaluations that ensured that domestic inflation did not result in overvaluation of the real exchange rate for exports.

These incentives guaranteed that in the manufacturing sector, on average, exports and import substitution received similar treatment. Nor was there discrimination against primary exports and primary production in general.

Experience also shows that these export incentives will not be effective unless the policies can be expected to last for the duration of investments in the export sector. A long-term commitment to these measures is essential; the political and economic risks can be reduced only if there is policy consistency and stability. As happened in South Korea, government plans must have credibility, assuring exporters of the permanence of government policies designed to remove the disincentives to exporting and keeping production for export as profitable as that for the domestic market.

Despite the concentration on trade-policy reform, the transition to a liberalized unbiased trade regime has proved difficult for a number of countries. Economists have proposed that a country start with a compensated devaluation— that is, a devaluation coupled with the removal of quotas and tariffs in order to bring the exchange rate to its long-run equilibrium level and to adjust tariffs and export subsidies so that domestic relative prices remain the same.

As a first step, quotas should be replaced by tariffs to allow price incentives. The next step should be to reduce both the variance in effective rates of protection and the home-market bias, including additional liberalization, variance reduction, and bias reduction. But the transition period to the liberalized trade regime will take a number of years, and a successful transition requires a whole sequence of changes over several years.

Once a country succeeds in shifting to an outward-oriented policy, it must continue to follow monetary and fiscal policies that will avoid inflation. For if inflation were to ensue, the domestic currency would again become overvalued in terms of foreign currency, and tariffs and quantitative restrictions would be reimposed. A combination of protection for domestic sale of final goods and a declining real effective exchange rate or the purchasing-power-parity-adjusted effective exchange rate (say, EER_x deflated by general consumer prices) will make it less profitable, relatively and absolutely, to export than to sell domestically.

At the micro level, the competitiveness of export firms will depend on their cost competitiveness and product or nonprice competitiveness. Cost competitiveness is determined by factor productivity, factor prices, factor proportions, and location relative to export markets. Especially significant is the relationship between wages and labor productivity for the labor-intensive exports that tend to dominate in the early period of export promotion. Although money wages in the LDC may be low, exports will not be competitive if the efficiency of labor is so low that the wage costs per unit of output are actually

[3]Larry E. Westphal, "Industrial Policy in an Export-Propelled Economy: Lessons from South Korea's Experience," *Journal of Economic Perspectives* (Summer 1990): 41–59.

high. Product competitiveness will also depend on such nonprice determinants of export success as design, quality control, punctuality in delivery, and service. A close relationship with Western trading companies has often helped to improve models and design and to overcome marketing problems.

Furthermore, the supply of entrepreneurship is obviously important in improving both cost competitiveness and product competitiveness. There has not, however, been a uniform need for foreign entrepreneurship or the resources of the multinational enterprise. In South Korea and Taiwan, for example, only a small percentage of the exports is produced by firms with any foreign equity participation. Nor has it always been necessary to first produce for the home demand before being able to export. For a number of countries exporting manufactures, the new export industries have been quite different from their old import-substitution industries.

IX.B.5. Taiwan's Trade Strategy*

Development policy in Taiwan, China, has consisted of five stages in which the government has implemented comprehensive but changing policy packages. Throughout, low inflation and macroeconomic stability have been a foundation for growth-enhancing policy initiatives, and since the late 1950s, export growth has also been a fundamental goal.

Land Reform and Reconstruction (1949–52)

When the Taiwanese authorities took over in 1949, one of their first initiatives was an ambitious land reform program. The program fostered social and political stability and increased agricultural production. Greater agricultural output provided raw materials for exports and earned foreign exchange to fund imports of machinery, equipment, and industrial raw materials. These in turn helped to make possible subsequent export-led rapid development.

Import-Substituting Industrialization (1953–57)

During the second stage, the government attempted to develop industry as the base for economic self-sufficiency. The government invested heavily in infrastructure, expanding transportation and power networks built by the Japanese; U.S. aid was an important source of finance, funding 49 percent of public investment in infrastructure. Extensive quantitative restrictions and high tariff rates shielded domestic consumer goods from foreign competition. To take advantage of abundant labor, the government subsidized some light industries, particularly textiles. Consumer goods industries such as textiles, apparel, wood and leather products, and bicycles developed very rapidly. By the end of the 1950s, industrial production had doubled. However, the costs of import substitution increased over time. By stimulating the import of capital and intermediate goods while penalizing exports, import substitution contributed to a growing trade deficit, financed largely by U.S. aid. As the small domestic market became saturated, overall growth declined, from 9 percent in the early 1950s to 6.5 percent in the mid-1950s.

Export Promotion (1958–72)

Anticipating the termination of U.S. aid and hence a need to obtain foreign exchange, the government shifted to a policy of outward orientation and export promotion. Starting in 1958 it adopted a series of measures aimed at promoting exports and foreign investment. A multiple exchange rate system was replaced with a unitary rate, and appreciation was avoided. Tariffs and import controls were gradually reduced, especially for inputs to export. In addition, the Bank of Taiwan, China, offered low-interest loans to exporters. The government also hired the Stanford Research Institute to identify promising industries for export promotion and development. On the basis of Taiwan, China's comparative advantage in low-cost labor and existing technical capabilities, the institute chose plastics, synthetic fibers, and electronic components. Other industries subsequently promoted

*From World Bank, *East Asian Miracle* (1993), pp. 131–34. Reprinted by permission.

included apparel, consumer electronics, home appliances, watches, and clocks. Direct foreign investment (DFI) played a catalytic role during this period and replaced U.S. aid as the main source of foreign capital. Although DFI was only 6 percent of gross capital formation in the 1960s, nearly 80 percent of it went into manufacturing. More important, DFI facilitated technology and skill transfers, leading to much improvement in quality and the diversification of industries.

The impact of these measures was dramatic. Exports, which had grown less than 12 percent annually between 1953–62, grew 28 percent a year between 1963–72, rising from 123 million to almost 3 billion dollars. The transition from import substitution to export promotion was the most important policy change in Taiwan, China's economic development. It shifted the economy from a relatively closed to an open economic system and exposed it to the forces of international competition and technological change.

Industrial Consolidation and New Export Growth (1973–80)

As the 1970s progressed, internal and external challenges threatened the continuation of export-led growth. The rapid manufacturing increases of the 1960s strained transportation, electricity, and communications systems. The island suffered profound external setbacks. More important, Taiwan, China's light manufacturing industries faced new competition from lower-wage producers abroad. As foreign investors rushed to the newly opened mainland Chinese market, international confidence in Taiwan, China's economy declined. The 1973–74 oil crisis had dramatic repercussions for the Taiwanese economy. Real GNP grew only 1.2 percent in 1974 and inflation climbed to 47 percent, while exports declined in real terms by about 7 percent.

Beginning in 1973, the government chose a more self-reliant development strategy based on industrial consolidation and renewed export growth. Once again, it turned to foreign experts and commissioned the U.S. management firm of Arthur D. Little to find solutions to the economic crisis. Based on Taiwan, China's economic needs and capabilities, the Americans recommended heavy investments in infrastructure, industrial upgrading, and secondary import substitution. A government plan incorporating the recommendations focused on development of capital-intensive, heavy, and petrochemical industries to increase production of raw materials and intermediates for the use of export industries. The government also launched ten major public sector projects, at a total cost of 8 billion dollars, to revitalize the economy and remove bottlenecks to economic growth. These included highways, railroads, airports, and construction of nuclear power plants.

High Technology and Modernization (1981–   )

As it entered its fourth decade, Taiwan, China confronted a challenging domestic and international environment. The spectacular growth of the 1960s and early 1970s sputtered to just below 7 percent in the late 1970s. Taiwan, China's continued integration into the world economy revealed structural weaknesses, particularly the financial system's inability to match the increasing demands of industrialization and external trade. Externally, Taiwan, China's persistent trade surpluses with major trading partners led to growing protectionism. In the later half of the 1980s, Taiwan's exports faced an additional loss of competitiveness due to the appreciation of the Taiwan, China dollar and rapidly rising wages. Manufacturing wages rose, undercutting Taiwan, China's advantage, and local firms moved production overseas. As in other first-generation East Asian NIEs, Taiwan, China manufacturers were squeezed between lower-wage NIEs in traditional, labor-intensive manufacturing on the one hand, and high-technology products from industrial economies on the other.

Once again, the government moved to restructure the economy. After extensive consultations with domestic and foreign advisers, the government decided to focus on high-technology industries: information, biotechnology, electro-optics, machinery and precision instruments, and environmental technology industries. The shift to a high-technology economy has necessitated the close coordination of industrial, financial, science and technology, and human resources policies. In 1984, the government revised laws to provide tax incentives for manufacturers who allocate a percentage of their revenues to research and development (R&D). Incentives were given to industry to diversify and improve production techniques. The government encouraged the establishment of venture-capital firms and revised university curricula to strengthen science, mathematics, engineering, and computer education. It began to recruit technical manpower from abroad by offering competitive salaries to former Taiwan, China residents living overseas.

In addition, in 1985 the government launched fourteen major infrastructure projects, including expansion of the energy, telecommunications, and transportation networks and development of water resources and national parks. The government's development plan for 1991–96 calls for 330 billion dollars in public sector projects. To support these efforts, the government has adopted an overall strategy of economic liberalization and internationalization, including the lifting of foreign exchange controls.

While it is too early to assess these policies fully, a few observations are possible. A growing number of small, high-technology firms produce increasingly sophisticated and higher-value-added products. For most firms, however, the transition to hi-tech industries has been difficult. On one hand, the rapid rate of technological change and rising protectionism in industrial economies make it increasingly difficult to obtain advanced technology. On the other, the small-scale structure of industry is not conducive to the costly investments in R&D and skills-training needed to shift toward high technology. As a result, most Taiwan, China manufacturers are still assembling imported high-tech components.

Comment: New Export Pessimism

Successful as the newly industrializing countries were in promoting exports of manufactures during the past three decades, there is now a resurgence of export pessimism. If the old export pessimism focused on dim prospects for primary-product exports and led to an ISI strategy, the new export pessimism is skeptical about the potential of exports of manufactures from additional NICs. The new export pessimism rests on the belief that the countries that have been able to follow export-led industrialization have done so because of favorable initial conditions that cannot be replicated elsewhere, and on the assertion that future demand will not support exports from additional developing countries. W. R. Cline has asked, "Can the East Asian Model of Development be Generalized?" *World Development* (February 1982). W. Arthur Lewis has also expressed concern about the slowing down in the growth of world trade; see W. A. Lewis, "The Slowing Down of the Engine of Growth," *American Economic Review* (September 1980).

If the success of the East Asian countries is attributed to unusually favorable initial conditions, both domestically and externally, rather than to good policies, then pessimism about other countries' ability to repeat the East Asian success might be justified. But the lesson of the NICs is that effective demand management and efficient supply-oriented policies have been the strategic variables accounting for successful development performance. As Gustav Ranis notes in "Equity with Growth in Taiwan: How Special Is the Special Case?" *World Development* (January 1978) we must differentiate between those elements of "non-transferability" that relate to obstacles "in nature" and those that relate to obstacles "in man." The latter obstacles can be overcome by institutional choices and the political process. Appropriate measures need not be confined to any one country. The lessons of the NICs can be transferred to other countries by the creation and extension of social, economic, and political institutions and mechanisms that promote the mobilization and efficient allocation of resources and an increase in total factor productivity.

Focusing on the constraint of external demand, some invoke the fallacy of composition to maintain that it is impossible to generalize the experience of the East Asian NICs. If many other developing countries reach the same high ratio of exports to GDP as have the NICs, would not the market be saturated? And would not their terms of trade deteriorate?

It is, however, unreasonable to expect that all countries would export at the same time and at the same rate and with the same range of exports. It is characteristic of the export of manufactures that the manufactured goods become ever more diversified. Empirical studies have shown that intraindustry trade through horizontal specialization has increased and that the extent of intraindustry trade conducted by industrialized countries has grown much more rapidly with the developing countries than with other industrialized countries. See Bela Balassa, "Comments," in *Trade Policy in the 1980s,* ed. W. R. Cline (1983). There appears to be wide scope for horizontal specialization or intraindustry specialization.

Moreover, the ever-changing structure of comparative costs allows a country to proceed up the ladder of comparative advantage from specialization in resource-intensive exports, to unskilled labor–intensive exports, to skilled labor–intensive exports, to capital-intensive exports, to knowledge-intensive exports. And as a given country moves up the ladder, another country in the queue is able to follow it up another rung on the ladder. Thus as Japan has risen on the ladder, the East Asian NICs have become major suppliers of Japan's former exports. Now, as the Asian NICs proceed through the various stages of comparative advantage, there is room for other nations—Thailand, Malaysia, Indonesia, and the Philippines—to take over the markets vacated by the earlier exporting countries. Recall selection IX.A.1.

The pessimists may also be giving too much emphasis to the external-demand constraint. It is true that 1945 to 1973 was indeed a unique historical period of growth in world real GNP and an even higher rate of growth in world exports, but even during the slower period of growth since 1973, the Asian NICs have been able to expand exports at a highly credible rate. They have done so by remaining competitive on the supply side, thereby contradicting the commonly held belief that the export growth of LDCs depends on income growth in MDCs. Thus a study by J. Riedel—"Trade as an Engine of Growth in Developing Countries, Revisited," *Economic Journal* (March 1984)—emphasizes supply conditions in the developing countries rather than external-demand factors as the principal determinants of a developing country's export performance in manufactures.

So, too, does an econometric study by Love suggest that export performance in most countries is relatively more sensitive to domestic factors, particularly the ability to compete in world markets, than to other factors; see J. Love, "External Market Conditions, Competitiveness, Diversification and LDC's Exports," *Journal of Development Economics* (December 1984).

It should also be realized that the developing countries now supply only some 3 percent of the manufactured goods consumed by the developed countries. There is a large potential for greater import penetration. Moreover, trade among the developing countries themselves accounts for less than 20 percent of the exports of LDCs that are not members of the Organization of Petroleum Exporting Countries (OPEC). There is also considerable potential for inter–LDC trade.

For an instructive overview of the issue, see Helen Hughes, ed., *The Dangers of Export Pessimism* (1992).

IX.B.6. Trade Policy Reform*

The number of countries that have experimented seriously with trade reform is limited. This limited progress reflects a number of problems—real or perceived—in the transition from inward to outward orientation. The transition means that some activities become more profitable and others less so. Often it is protected manufacturing activities whose profitability is most threatened. The more inward-oriented the original policies, the greater these shifts—and the costs associated with them—will be. The pattern of transition may need to be designed to suit specific national situations.

• The more rapid and fundamental the policy changes, the greater the immediate benefits to the economy. But there is also a greater likelihood that more people will face transitional costs as workers are displaced from old jobs and firms abandon old activities.

• As some activities or occupations become less remunerative, resistance to policy change will emerge. Those who are threatened will use political means to obstruct reform.

• Trade policy reform is closely related to reform of other economic policies. In particular, the exchange rate and the way domestic inflation affects it in real terms are crucial to competitiveness in import-replacing and export activities. In turn these are influenced by domestic fiscal, monetary, and credit policies and by policies affecting capital flows.

All these problems of transition make the design of policy reform important. How can policies best be selected, phased, and sequenced to gain the benefits of reform as quickly as possible while minimizing transitional costs and political resistance?

*From World Bank, *World Development Report, 1987* (1987), pp. 95, 109–12. Reprinted by permission.

The Design of Trade Policy Reform

Reform in the conventional instruments of trade policy can be discussed under three headings: replacing quantitative restrictions with tariffs, reforming tariff protection, and the direct promotion of exports.

Replacing Quantitative Restrictions with Tariffs

It is broadly accepted that moving from nontariff barriers to tariffs is a move toward a more open trade policy. This is so for two reasons. First, tariffs are generally less protective than quantitative restrictions (although it is possible to have tariffs set so high that they prohibit imports). Second, a tariff is a price instrument, not a quantity instrument. As a result, tariffs are more ''transparent''—changes in foreign prices feed through more readily to the domestic economy. Quotas, by contrast, uncouple national economies from the world economy. For example, in India cotton is protected by quantitative restrictions, and textile producers are required to use Indian cotton. As a result, movements in the price of this crucial raw material are not always related to those of world cotton prices, which determine the cost of this input to competitors. It is therefore difficult for Indian producers to commit themselves to production for export: the conditions under which they have to compete are unpredictable.

In many cases a shift from quotas to tariffs has been a key element in the early stages of trade policy reform. Sometimes it has been the only element. For example, Israel's first and second phases of reform focused on imports and consisted of the gradual removal of quotas and their replacement with tariffs. Greece's first reforms removed almost all quotas and replaced them with tariffs which were for the most part lower than the tariff equivalent of the quotas.

The evidence of similar episodes strongly suggests that this shift in the form of protection was highly beneficial. Often, not only did the economy's growth speed up following such shifts, but even in the sectors whose protection had been lowered, production increased as firms began to operate in a less restrictive and more transparent regime. This suggests that in an economy in which trade is regulated largely by quantitative restrictions—and this is true for most economies in which trade is severely restricted—a liberalization policy should start with a shift from the use of quotas to the use of tariffs, even if it means very high tariffs. . . .

Reforming Tariffs

The movement toward greater neutrality has two dimensions: the lowering of the average level of protection and the reduction in the average dispersion, or variance, of protection. If the dispersion of tariffs is not reduced as the tariff average is reduced, the tariff structure may not become more neutral. Indeed, a reform that reduces tariffs on intermediate and capital goods but leaves intact those on final outputs could *increase* effective protection—the level of protection afforded to domestic value added—even though it *reduced* the average level of tariffs.

Of course, it is possible to reduce at the same time both the average level of tariffs and their dispersion. Governments have approached the task in several ways: an equiproportional cut in all tariffs, an equiproportional reduction of the excess of each tariff over some target level, higher proportional reductions of higher tariffs, or some combination of these and other methods. As a rule, simple schemes widely applied work better than case-by-case and fine-tuning methods. Some tariff reforms have attempted to target the effective, rather than the nominal, rate of protection (the Philippine reforms of 1981–85 are an example). This is unnecessarily complicated and may misfire anyway because of measurement problems.

Many economists favor the so-called concertina approach to tariff cutting. First, all tariffs above a certain ceiling are lowered to that ceiling; next, all tariffs above a new, lower ceiling are lowered to that ceiling; and so on. This should yield the lowest adjustment costs without leading to inadvertent increases in effective protection. Chile's tariff reductions in the 1970s more or less followed this scheme.

Lessons about the amount of time necessary to eliminate quantitative restrictions and tariffs are difficult to draw. Some reforms have taken a long time—Korea and the countries of southern Europe, for instance, have still not completed their reforms after at least two decades. Fewer have been completed within the medium term—the process lasted five years in Chile, for example. But none have been fully implemented over the short term. There is no obvious relationship between the length of the period of policy reform and its chances of success. But the apparently low adjustment costs in most trade reforms, together with the danger that lengthier reforms will be less credible, are arguments for faster reform. . . .

Direct Promotion of Exports

The logic of trade liberalization is that the tariffs should be as low as possible. As long as the average tariff is not zero, an element of discrimination against exports remains (unless they are equivalently subsidized). Chile's reforms achieved a uniform tariff of 10 percent with no exceptions. Later, this was revised, and Chile ended up with a uniform tariff of 20 percent, which left a mild discrimination against exports, but not enough to prevent export growth. The experience of Brazil and the Philippines shows that export growth can be achieved in the presence of significant import protection, as long as governments can prevent the real exchange rate from appreciating.

Where significant import protection remains, governments might consider offsetting the discrimination against exports with administrative measures to provide imported inputs at world prices or with subsidies. Directly promoting exports in this way may also help to form a constituency for continued protection. But it may come to be seen as a long-term alternative to further import liberalization. This appears to have been the case in Pakistan and, in the 1970s at least, in the Philippines.

Direct export promotion is a difficult alternative to cuts in import protection. It raises administrative problems and often requires significant budgetary resources. Like any other selective intervention, it will also encourage rent seeking. Above all, the risk of GATT disputes and of countervailing duties in importing countries has made direct export promotion increasingly unattractive.

The Lessons of Trade Liberalization

Trade policy reform is complicated. It is closely linked to liberalization in capital, labor, and domestic product markets and to macroeconomic policy. It is partly a political process, in which credibility and expectations play an important role. Feasible policy choices may differ from country to country, and reform may be vulnerable to changes in the international environment. Because of this complexity, there is no single optimal path to reform. But there are, nonetheless, lessons to be drawn from previous attempts.

- Trade liberalization must involve large shifts of resources, but it has not always raised unemployment by as much as is commonly supposed.
- Strong and decisive reforms have carried greater credibility and have been better sustained than more timid reforms.
- Replacing quantitative restrictions with tariffs is a useful first stage of trade liberalization.
- Providing a realistic real exchange rate is vital to the successful introduction of trade reform. Keeping it stable is essential if the reform is to be sustained. All this requires a macroeconomic policy that manages inflation and the nominal exchange rate so as to keep domestic costs in line with world prices.
- The scope for successful trade liberalization depends on complementary reforms in the domestic economy—especially in financial and labor markets.

Comment: Overvalued Exchange Rates and Trade Balance

Trade policy is frequently influenced by a country's foreign-exchange rate. An overvalued exchange rate has an anti-export bias. Moreover, if a country's exchange rate is overvalued and its current account deficit is not being financed by an inflow of foreign capital and foreign-exchange reserves are low, the government is likely to resort to import controls. Although economists may recommend other policies to correct the payments imbalance, governments only too often resort to trade restrictions to ration the excess demand for foreign exchange. If import restrictions are later to be removed, devaluation may be necessary to enable an offsetting trade liberalization. Without devaluation, the reduction in tariffs or quotas will worsen the balance of payments. The next selection (IX.B.7) explains the relationship between trade liberalization and exchange rates. As background, we review the simple analytics of foreign-exchange markets.

Ordinary supply and demand analysis applies to foreign-exchange markets. The only peculiarity is that we express the price of one currency in terms of another currency. In Exhibit IX.6, the price of foreign exchange is on the vertical axis, expressed as the number of units of domestic currency (d)

per unit of foreign currency (f). On the horizontal axis is represented the quantity of foreign exchange (f) demanded and supplied. The view is from the d-country. Going up the vertical axis, the d-currency depreciates—more units of d are offered per unit of f. Correspondingly, there is an appreciation of the f-currency as we go up the vertical axis. When the d currency depreciates, the prices of imports from f country increase in terms of d. We would, therefore, expect the quantity demanded of f-currency to decrease as the d-currency depreciates. As the d-currency appreciates (going down the vertical axis), the prices of imports from f-country become lower in terms of d. We would, therefore, expect a greater quantity of f-currency to be demanded. The demand curve for foreign currency DD_f therefore slopes down to the right, as in Exhibit IX.6. What lies behind DD_f are all the transactions that give rise to payments from d-country to f-country for the import of goods, services, and financial assets (ordinary payments above the line).

The supply of f-currency is derived from transactions for goods, services, and financial assets above the line that give rise to receipts in the d-currency. The supply of f is the flip side of the demand for imports that must be paid for in d-currency. If the f-currency appreciates and the d-currency depreciates, the price of imports from d-country will fall in terms of f-currency. We would then expect a greater quantity of f to be supplied. Conversely, a lower quantity of f will be supplied when the f-currency depreciates (d appreciates). The supply curve for f-currency, therefore, slopes up to the right as represented by SS_f in Exhibit IX.6.

If there is a free market in foreign exchange, the market would establish a market-clearing exchange rate where the quantity demanded of f equals the quantity supplied of f. In Exhibit IX.6, this would give a market-clearing exchange rate of $1.80d{:}1f$.

If now domestic investment rises, or domestic saving falls, or there is an increase in government expenditure, or a fall in tax revenue, then the national income of the d-country would increase and there would be a greater demand for imports from the f-country. At each and every exchange rate, then, the d-country would demand a greater quantity of f-currency. This demand is represented in Exhibit IX.6 by a shift of the demand curve from DD_f to $D'D'_f$.

If the exchange rate is held by central bank intervention, there will be excess demand for foreign exchange represented by the amount GP in Exhibit IX.6. To hold the rate, the central bank will have to fill the foreign-exchange gap of GP with the sale of reserves of f, in effect, increasing the supply of f from SS_f to $S'S'_f$. Even though there is now a regime of flexible exchange rates, intervention is common by central monetary authorities in order to defend the existing rate by selling or purchasing reserves.

If the monetary authority intervenes to hold the rate, as in Exhibit IX.6, then the rate remains overvalued. If demand and supply were allowed to operate freely in this foreign-exchange market, the rate would go to $1.90d$ to $1f$. If, however, the rate is held, how can we tell that the rate is overvalued? Some economists would want to calculate "purchasing power parity" to determine this—that is, compare the domestic cost relative to foreign cost for a given basket of goods. More directly, it is possible to judge an exchange rate as being overvalued if the central bank continues to lose reserves in an attempt to hold the rate, or if the country has to borrow capital from overseas in order to fill the gap GP (these are induced compensatory capital flows below the line), or if the country has to license foreign exchange, or impose tariffs and quantitative restrictions in order to restrict the demand for foreign exchange. All these would indicate that the exchange rate is inappropriate compared with a market-clearing rate.

The "real exchange rate" is frequently used as an indicator of the need for depreciation. The real exchange rate can be calculated by comparing the relative costs of manufactures in two countries, or an alternative measure is to compare wage levels within the country with those abroad, adjusted for productivity. When the real exchange rate appreciates, balance-of-payments difficulties may lie ahead because imports rise and exports fall. The larger the increase in domestic costs relative to foreign costs, the more likely it is that a currency depreciation will be necessary. Falling reserves are another indicator of depreciation to follow. The reserves can fall because of a current account deficit, or because there is capital flight from the domestic currency toward foreign currencies that are expected to appreciate.

To avoid import restrictions, the country's real exchange rate must be at a level that will maintain international competitiveness. Domestic inflation must be offset by currency depreciation (an increase in the real exchange rate). Not only are changes in the nominal exchange rate necessary to support trade liberalization, but so too are restrained fiscal and monetary policies that do not cause inflation. If, however, the real exchange rate falls substantially (the currency appreciates), it is difficult to maintain a liberal trade regime because import prices fall and export prices rise in terms of foreign exchange and the country encounters a payments imbalance.

EXHIBIT IX.6. Foreign Exchange Market

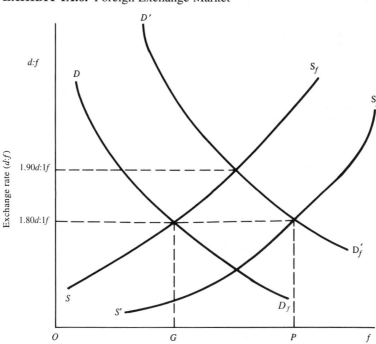

Quantity of foreign exchange (f)

Note: d: domestic currency; f: foreign currency.

Viewed from the "d-country," demand for and supply of foreign exchange are initially given by DD_f and SS_f. If demand now rises to $D'D'_f$, but the central bank holds the exchange rate of 1.80d:1f, d's currency is overvalued. The excess demand for foreign exchange is then likely to be controlled by import restrictions.

IX.B.7. Trade Liberalization and Exchange Rates*

The most important point about large-scale unilateral trade liberalization is that it must be associated with real devaluation if the current account is not to deteriorate and if the employment losses in protected import-substituting industries are to be compensated by employment gains elsewhere, especially in export industries. Nor-

*From W. Max Corden, "Protection and Liberalization: A Review of Analytical Issues," *IMF Occasional Paper 54* (August 1987), pp. 19–23. Reprinted by permission.

mally nominal devaluation will be needed to bring about the required real devaluation. A liberalization program must, therefore, be part of a policy package which includes exchange rate adjustment. The appropriate exchange rate adjustment will be hard to judge in advance, but it is important to bear in mind that the longer-run equilibrium real exchange rate does depend on the degree of trade liberalization.

The question is often asked where the extra jobs would come from when liberalization brings about employment losses in highly protected import-competing industries. In a general context of growth, liberalization may lead not to absolute losses in employment in these industries but rather to a reduced rate of growth. But the question is relevant even in that case.

In the main, the extra jobs will be generated by the real depreciation which is part of the policy package. It will make exporting more profitable and also improve competitiveness of import-competing industries. Some import substitution may become economic that was previously uneconomic—and hence generate extra employment. Those import-competing industries which had received low protection, or none at all, will benefit.

Industries that use imported inputs that were not readily available before liberalization or that used inputs produced locally at high cost owing to protection will find that their costs have fallen and may expand employment. Against this must be set the higher costs of imports resulting from the devaluation, which will affect some industries adversely. In addition, the improvement in resource allocation in the tradable sector as a whole is likely to increase real national income, leading to more consumption spending and hence employment generation in domestic industries producing for the home market. The higher real incomes will yield more tax revenue and so improve the fiscal balance. If tax rates are reduced to restore the initial fiscal balance, increased private consumption or investment will generate extra jobs, or alternatively, increased government expenditure financed by the higher tax revenue would do so.

The sequencing of liberalization and the associated exchange rate adjustment is also a matter of some complexity. A choice, essentially political, has to be made between gradualism and sudden measures, and how much advance announcement there should be. The longer the period between the announcement of a credible program of liberalization and the actual changes in tariffs and quotas, the easier it is for protected industries to make the necessary adjustments and for potential gainers—notably export industries—to gear up for expansion. But the announcement has to be credible. On the other hand, it has been argued that the longer the lag between the formal commitment to a program and its actual implementation, the greater the opportunity for interest groups to slow up or even halt liberalization and the more likely it is

that expectations about the credibility of the authorities' intentions will be undermined.

The exchange rate should be adjusted early even at the cost of generating temporarily excess profits in export industries and in import-competing industries that are not protected. The beneficial effects of depreciation on exports are likely to develop with a lag, while an increase in imports resulting from liberalization could be quite quick. A firm, credible assurance that a program of liberalization will be followed should discourage the flow of resources out of nontradables into highly protected industries during the transitional period when the protected industries are excessively profitable because the exchange rate has already been devalued while the liberalization process is not complete.

Is a time of balance of payments difficulties the right time to liberalize trade? This important issue arises currently and needs to be considered in relation to International Monetary Fund programs. It is, of course, not possible to resolve this issue here or arrive at conclusions appropriate for all countries but some considerations can be set out.

From the narrow but popular partial view it certainly appears to be the wrong time. Traditionally, a balance of payments crisis has led to the imposition or tightening of import restrictions since it is noneconomists' common sense that when imports are too high in relation to exports the proper policy is to restrict imports.

Two immediate answers can be given. First, liberalization will allow, possibly for the first time, the ready availability of cheap imported inputs required for exports. This aspect of liberalization would improve the balance of payments by raising exports even if the exchange rate stayed constant. There may be a lag before all the benefits come through since it takes time to expand exports, find new markets, and so on, but at least there is a favorable and direct balance of payments effect.

The more important answer is that the alternative to import restrictions is not to do nothing but to depreciate the exchange rate. Hence one is back to the choice already highlighted several times in this paper between two "switching" devices, one of which discriminates between imports and in favor of import substitution relative to export expansion, while the other—exchange rate adjustment—is nondiscriminatory. The improvement in the current account requires both a reduction in aggregate spending and depreciation of the exchange rate to switch demand from foreign toward home-produced goods and, within the latter, toward tradables. If there is simultaneously some liberalization of imports, even more depreciation is required.

Restrictions may be so widespread, complex, and dislocating that their removal can have fairly immediate beneficial effects on incentives and output. This would particularly be so when imported inputs for manufacturing production with export potential are subject to licensing. It would then also become easier to solve the balance of payments problem, because an increase in supply would modify the extent of the reduction in aggregate demand required, and hence reduce the painfulness of the required adjustment.

In other cases the beneficial effects of removing restrictions combined with adequate devaluation would only show up in the medium run, as new investment is directed into more productive channels, rent seeking declines, and so on. In the short run, liberalization associated with exchange rate adjustment may give rise to dislocations and to localized or industry-specific unemployment as profitability of some industries declines while that of others improves. The question then arises whether the short-run problems of liberalization should be added to the problems involved in bringing about the reduction in real expenditures needed for restoring macroeconomic stability.

In considering whether to liberalize at a time of balance of payments crisis it is then a matter of trading off additional short-term problems against medium- or long-run benefits; there may be short-run adjustment costs, and the short-run problems these engender may be harder to bear when at the same time the needs of the balance of payments call for a major reduction in aggregate spending. Liberalization may also risk being unjustly blamed for the many problems—including often unemployment—caused by the need to reduce spending in order to improve the balance of payments. On the other hand, some countries seem to have continuous balance of payments difficulties which have underlying structural causes and call for longer-term measures to increase output, as well as appropriate adjustment of demand to available resources, domestic and foreign. In these cases it may be best to focus on supply-side measures—including liberalization designed to improve resource allocation, reduce rent seeking and so on.

Finally, trade liberalization might be attempted when a country suffers from high inflation. Countries may certainly have balance of payments problems without at the same time suffering from high inflation, and may also, though less commonly, suffer from high inflation without having a balance of payments problem. For a country to sustain inflation higher than that of its trading partners without a balance of payments problem emerging, the nominal exchange rate would need to be continuously or frequently depreciated. Normally high inflation is associated with many distortions, notably an exchange rate that is not adjusted sufficiently so that it becomes overvalued, nominal interest rates that are too low owing to controls of various kinds, and import controls designed to compensate for the failure to adjust the exchange rate sufficiently.

The question arises whether trade liberalization is possible if the fundamental factors causing high inflation (usually a high budget deficit financed by money creation) are not eliminated. The answer has to be that it is technically possible provided the nominal exchange rate is depreciated even more than it needs to be to compensate for the inflation. If there is continued high inflation, as well as a current account deficit that has to be reduced, the addition of trade liberalization to the policy program will require continuous nominal depreciation to compensate for continuous inflation, and in addition nominal depreciation to bring about sufficient real devaluation. The real devaluation must be large enough both to improve the current account as required (to switch expenditure from foreign toward home-produced goods and to switch the pattern of output from nontradables toward tradables) and to compensate for the employment and current account effects of trade liberalization. In addition, real expenditure must, of course, be reduced.

In practice high-inflation countries have often failed to depreciate their currencies sufficiently, and high inflation gives rise to the distortions mentioned above. These are caused essentially by attempts to deal with symptoms rather than causes—to control interest rates, prices, imports and so on. It is then important to tackle the fundamental causes, and either to associate liberalization with a credible and adequate inflation stabilization program or even to make the attainment of reasonable stabilization a precondition for substantial trade liberalization.

Capital Market and Trade Liberalization

For the more usual cases, where exchange rates can be altered, a matter that has been much discussed has been the relationship between trade liberalization and capital market liberalization. This discussion has been stimulated by the experiences of Argentina, Chile, and Uruguay where some liberalization of both kinds took place in various orders. In Argentina capital market liberalization (for a limited period) came first and in Chile trade liberalization.

It is clear that one kind of liberalization is possible without the other. Some countries have very open capital markets but restrictive trade regimes while others have extensive international capital controls but relatively free trade. Among industrial countries during the Bretton Woods era controls on international capital movements were the norm while trade was progressively liberalized, and this has also been true until very recently within the European Community. It is striking that in recent years the tendency to increased protection or protectionist pressures in some major industrial countries has coincided with the rapid growth of the international capital market and a general tendency to capital market liberalization.

There are three important links between the two kinds of liberalization.

First, capital market liberalization involving the freeing of domestic interest rates and the removal of controls on inward and outward capital flows may lead to greater capital inflows than before. Not only would removal of controls on inflows, including direct investment, encourage this, but removal of controls on outflows (provided the liberalization is expected to last and economic conditions support the policy thrust) might also, since it would reduce the risk that capital cannot be repatriated. With more foreign capital available domestically it is then particularly desirable that the relative profitability of domestic industries gives a true indication of social profitability, so that investment is directed in optimal directions. Hence some trade liberalization should ideally precede capital market liberalization if the existing protection system is very distorting.

The need to get the signals right also applies when new investment is wholly domestically financed, but the argument is strengthened when major capital inflows are in prospect. It is unfortunate if foreign capital flows primarily into heavily protected industries so that low benefits to the country result, and possibly there could be a social loss, the local consumers of the protected products in effect subsidizing foreign capital. In addition, foreign companies become yet another interest group in support of maintaining protection.

Second, the process of capital market liberalization is likely to affect the real exchange rate, possibly quite sharply for a limited period, as a portfolio adjustment takes place. If domestic interest rates had been held down by controls and are now raised, capital will flow in, or at least there will be pressures in that direction. This effect will be strengthened if investors' perceptions of the security (and opportunity to repatriate) of investment in the country improve. The nominal exchange rate and, with it, the real rate may then appreciate. The exchange rate may, of course, depreciate if the portfolio adjustment involves net capital outflow, which might occur if controls on outflows were initially severe or if decontrol were expected to be temporary. But the more common experience has been for the exchange rate to appreciate consequent upon financial liberalization.

If the real exchange rate appreciates, this will make trade liberalization inconsistent with current account balance. The adverse effects of appreciation on import-competing industries will intensify the effect of the trade liberalization. Of course the real appreciation caused by capital market liberalization will be temporary, but it does create problems. Furthermore, the appreciation will render exporting less instead of more profitable.

If capital tends to flow out after financial liberalization, the exchange rate will move in the right direction for the current account (by depreciating) but it will overshoot, since the extent of depreciation required for the current account to be maintained with trade liberalization is less than that required for a temporary current account surplus to accommodate capital outflow.

Third, if the capital market has already been liberalized, trade liberalization, or even just the expectation of it, may give rise to capital movements which then affect the exchange rate.

One possibility is that depreciation comes to be expected—since, as noted earlier, it would eventually be required if the current account is not to change once trade liberalization takes place. Hence the exchange rate depreciates in advance of actual trade liberalization. As also noted above, this might be desirable, bearing in mind that export expansion will be required and is likely to take time. But the opposite possibility must also be allowed for.

The acceptance of proposals for trade liberalization, possibly combined with other structural reforms, may make local and foreign investors more ''bullish'' about the economy, expecting higher and more secure profits. Hence the tendency will be for capital to flow in and for the exchange rate to appreciate. This is similar to the effect discussed above where the capital inflow and the appreciation were caused by capital market liberalization. In the present case the capital market is already liberalized and the same effect results from expectations stimulated by trade liberalization and other structural reforms. In both cases the appreciation can create problems by making industries producing tradable goods in general less profitable at a time when industries that are losing their protection will suffer a loss of profitability in any case while export industries need to become more profitable.

To sum up, opening the domestic capital market to the world market is likely to make it more difficult to manage the exchange rate. The rate will be put under capital-market-determined pressures, and this presents problems if it is desired to fine tune the exchange rate as part of a major trade liberalization exercise. On the other hand, there seems little reason to slow down capital market liberalization if trade liberalization is piecemeal and gradual. Furthermore, sometimes capital market liberalization may be inevitable because of the breakdown or high administrative costs of controls.

One might also note the case where the nominal exchange rate is fixed or, at least, the more common case where there is some degree of intervention designed to moderate exchange rate changes. If capital market liberalization or trade liberalization stimulates capital inflow, as seems quite possible, there will then be a buildup of reserves and, if the effects are not sterilized, a domestic monetary expansion, and hence domestic inflationary effects. In the latter case there would be a real appreciation with the same kinds of adverse effects already discussed. If the capital movements are short term it will clearly be desirable for the monetary effects to be sterilized.

The problem would be greater if the net effect of capital market liberalization and of the expectation of trade liberalization (and hence of eventual devaluation) were for capital to flow out rather than in. The reserves will then decline, and—if the exchange rate regime is not changed—the balance of payments situation may then inhibit the trade liberalization process.

A similar difficulty can arise when an import liberalization is not expected to last—when a government has not succeeded in making the program credible to private traders. Imports may then flood in, in expectation of the reimposition of quotas. An immediate, though temporary, balance of payments problem will then be created. If depreciation of the exchange rate is ruled out, a tightening-up of monetary policy may be needed in all these cases.

Comment: Stabilization-cum-Liberalization Programs

Stabilization-cum-liberalization programs involve the liberalization of external trade, decontrol of domestic financial markets, and liberalization of capital flows from abroad. The timing and sequencing of these liberalization measures have differed among countries. But more attention to the sequencing of policies is essential for the success of the program. As Bruno observes,

Economic theory tells us that a fully liberalized economy is most probably Pareto superior to a heavily controlled economy. It can also tell us something about the advantages of certain departures from full liberalization in some markets. However, theory tells us virtually nothing about optimal transition paths from a distorted system to one that is more liberalized. Unfortunately, this is the most important problem for any successful reform. The study of actual cases may, however, eventually lead to theoretical insights on optimal transition paths or the kind of economic policies that should accompany the process of transition.

Should all markets be liberalized at the same time? If they cannot, can one say anything about the sequencing of market liberalization? . . . A major distinction should be drawn between the real and the financial sides of opening up. No general case can be made against the opening up of the current account. The most successful development histories are those in which a country very early on switched from an import-substitution-led towards an export-led development strategy. There are problems of adjustment speed and of what kind of investment and/or trade policy should be adopted in the transition, but there is little doubt, from a pure efficiency point of view, as to the wisdom of opening up the real side of the economy, as quickly as is consistent with the other major social objectives. Moreover, there seems to be substantial evidence attesting to productivity gains coming from the trade liberalization process.

The liberalization of financial markets has turned out to be much more problematic. There are obvious efficiency gains to be obtained when a country moves from a repressed capital market, with negative real interest rates, to one which is less regulated. In practice, however, various factors caused real interest rates to rise to excessively high levels. This, coupled with the opening up to foreign capital inflows, proved disastrous. The issue of credibility is clearly at the heart of the success or failure of any reform. Even the most drastic reforms take time to be implemented and to work themselves out. The behavior of economic agents is dictated by their perception of the future, which incorporates the government's present and expected behavior as a key input. Thus, the maintenance of high government deficits will be inconsistent with the announced slowing down of the rate of devaluation as an anti-inflationary device (the case of Argentina). Not only will prices be slow in coming down, if at all, thus bringing about a real appreciation, with consequences to the current account, but the expected large devaluation will force capital flight today. Like the building up of real assets, credibility formation is an asymmetric process. Once eroded, credibility is very hard to restore.[1]

Several studies attempt to distill the lessons from the reform undertaken in various countries. From the experiences of Argentina, Chile, and Uruguay, some observers conclude that for countries with annual inflation rates of 25 percent or more, anti-inflation stabilization programs should precede liberalization. This is because inflation reduces substantially the information content of relative prices, and the main aim of liberalization is to adjust relative prices in accordance with economic costs. Stabilization is also necessary because successful liberalization depends on credibility and on a stable and competitive real exchange rate. These objectives cannot be fulfilled when inflation is rapid. See Anne O. Krueger, *Foreign Trade Regimes and Economic Development: Liberalization Attempts and Consequences* (1978); R. Dornbusch, "Stabilization Policies in Developing Countries: What Have We Learned?" *World Development* (September 1982); S. Fischer, "Issues in Medium-term Macroeconomic Adjustment," *World Bank Research Observer* (July 1986); Michael Mussa, "Macroeconomic Policy and Trade Liberalization: Some Guidelines," *World Bank Research Observer* (January 1987); Vittorio Corbo and Jaime de Melo, "Lessons from the Southern Cone Policy Reforms," *World Bank Research Observer* (July 1987); and Dani Rodrik, "The Limits of Trade Policy Reform in Developing Countries," *Journal of Economic Perspectives* (Winter 1992).

A major eight-volume research project has reviewed the experience of 18 countries with respect to policy prescriptions for successful implementation of liberalization policies: Michael Michaely et al., *Liberalizing Foreign Trade*, vol. 7 (1990). It is concluded that the successful programs of trade reform had certain elements in common: momentum, reduced quantitative restrictions, competitive real exchange rates, prudent macroeconomic policies, proper sequencing of reform (trade liberalization should precede capital-market liberalization), and political stability.

[1]Michael Bruno, "The Reforms and Macroeconomic Adjustments," *World Development* (August 1985): 867–69.

IX.C. TRADE IN PRIMARY PRODUCTS

IX.C.1. Impact of Agricultural Protection*

Industrial countries' agricultural policies may be aimed at solving domestic problems, but their effects spill over onto the rest of the world. By expanding output and depressing domestic demand, their policies reduce world prices and distort the relative prices of agricultural and manufactured goods. By granting special trading privileges to remedy some of the harm, industrial countries can make matters worse. And by destabilizing international markets, their farm policies can amplify rather than dampen commodity price fluctuations.

Supply and Price Effects

How much agricultural policies in industrial countries depress world prices depends on four things: the level of protection, the extent to which domestic surpluses lead to reduced imports or subsidized exports, the share of world output and consumption accounted for by the industrial countries, and the responsiveness of supply and demand to price changes in the world markets.

Agricultural prices and costs are the key to the profitability of investment in agriculture. In industrial countries, resources are diverted from other sectors to agriculture. In developing countries, which face low world prices for agricultural products but nonetheless tax domestic production, resources are diverted from agriculture to industry. As a result, agricultural production is favored in industrial countries, even though in some of them the costs of production are higher than in many developing countries. This makes developing countries export less and import more, even though they could become—if they are not already—efficient producers by making investments to acquire the necessary technology. The longer agricultural protection is maintained in industrial countries, the more damaging it will be to the world economy.

The impact of agricultural protection differs from one developing country to another. It de-

pends on whether the country is a net importer or exporter of each product. Exporters of commodities that are in surplus in the industrial countries are most vulnerable. In contrast, net food importers benefit from the low world prices caused by current policies, and at first sight it may appear that they would lose from liberalization. But this need not be so if they liberalize their domestic policies and allow domestic production to substitute for imports. Moreover, some developing countries would be able to increase their exports or become exporters for the first time.

The rate of protection varies among agricultural products. So protection not only depresses the overall level of world prices, but also distorts relative prices among agricultural products. Prices for the most highly protected products— dairy products, beef, and sugar—are depressed more than prices of other agricultural products. These distorted prices make the use of resources in world agriculture even less efficient. If Japan were to reduce its protection of rice of the varieties in which other Asian countries have a comparative advantage, they could produce more.

Differing rates of protection hit developing countries especially hard when the rate of protection is higher for processed agricultural products than for unprocessed ones. Tariffs in industrial countries are higher for wheat flour, pasta, cheese, and poultry than they are for wheat, milk, or feed grains. As a result, industrial countries export larger quantities, and import smaller quantities, of processed goods than of the related raw materials.

Subsidies and Trade Preferences

Some industrial countries have to give subsidies to sell crops on world markets. Developing countries' competitiveness, therefore, depends less on their own efficiency than on political decisions in industrial countries. And their ability to compete may be undermined at any time by increased export subsidies on industrial countries' exports. Even when industrial

*From World Bank, *World Development Report, 1986* (1986), pp. 123–27. Reprinted by permission.

countries appear to provide developing ones with market opportunities, the gains may not last. High grain prices in the EC created new markets for feed grain substitutes such as cassava, corn gluten feed, and citrus pellets. But China, Indonesia, and Thailand, which produce cassava, had to sign "voluntary" export restraint agreements.

When a high-cost importing country becomes an exporter, potential gains from trade are wasted. The losses are often made worse by the special trade preferences that industrial countries grant to developing ones in the hope of mitigating these distortions. In some cases, industrial countries which produce an exportable surplus of a crop have to import it under the trade preference scheme. The EC imports dairy products from New Zealand and beef from some African, Caribbean, and Pacific countries. These trade flows raise income in the exporting countries which are part of the preference scheme, but importers and potential exporters outside the scheme suffer greater losses. Increases in production costs and transport and other marketing costs account for the net worldwide loss.

Destabilization of World Markets

Most industrial countries hold domestic consumer prices relatively constant when world market prices change. A shortfall in world output will not affect demand in a country which insulates its domestic markets. But someone's consumption must be reduced. And if some countries refuse to cut their consumption, others must reduce theirs disproportionately. To ration the world output, world prices have to rise by more. If meat consumption and demand for feed grains were allowed to change with world market prices, cereal prices would fluctuate less—thus reducing the risk of food shortages in developing countries.

The price changes caused by sudden supply or demand shocks can be absorbed by commodity stockpiles. In theory, world prices could be stabilized even if most countries insulated their markets, as long as countries or private individuals that operated on the free market held big enough stocks. But the more countries insulate their economies, the greater the size of the stockpiles needed. One study of fourteen regions found that stocks had to be eight times larger if the regions completely insulated their economies than if they allowed free trade. The cost of the extra stocks indicates one source of gain from liberalization. For crops that can be grown under a wide variety of conditions at similar costs, important gains from trade arise from temporary trade flows as each country's yield varies from year to year. Policies that insulate domestic markets sacrifice these gains.

Decisions to build up or release stocks are often made not by private traders but by governments. As in developing countries, governments in industrial countries determine the size of public stockpiles according to how much money is available from the budget or in response to other political pressures rather than by the size of stockpile needed for stabilization purposes. In the mid-1970s some countries built up stocks when they should have been releasing them, and this made the world food crisis worse.

Counting the Costs of Protection

Because of the distortions in every trading country, the whole world would be better off if industrial countries were to stop protecting their farmers and liberalize agricultural trade. But by how much? Recent studies have made some progress in quantifying the gains from liberalization.

The effects of trade and policy liberalization can be observed when trade or domestic policies are liberalized. Unfortunately, liberalization experiments are rare. Estimates of multilateral or global liberalization can be made only with the aid of simulation models.

IX.C.2. International Resource Bargaining—Note

The control of the price of oil by the Organization of Petroleum Exporting Countries (OPEC) has posed in dramatic form the question of whether the exercise of "producer power" in commodities can be generalized to other primary producers. Can there be additional producer monopoly agreements that effectively control future supplies or prices of minerals, food, and other primary products in order to create artificial scarcities and raise export prices above competitive market levels? Is oil a special commodity, or can effective producer power be exercised also for bauxite, copper, tin, phosphates, coffee, tea, rubber, and other primary products?

The answers to these questions rest in the outcome of a complex process of international resource bargaining. But we might identify various conditions in this process that will determine the relative bargaining strengths of different producing and consuming countries. First, primary production in the LDCs must be disaggregated—at the least, into such categories as oil, nonfuel minerals, tropical agricultural products, and cereals. Second, it should be recognized that market intervention can assume various forms: a cartel of exporters that takes collusive action to set production and export quotas or to raise export prices; one producer acting as a price leader, with others following; or export controls over the flow of exports through imposition of quantitative limitations or export taxes. Whether a particular form of market intervention will be successful in raising the export price and revenue for a particular primary product will depend essentially on the existence of three conditions: (1) a dominant position by a producer country in export markets or the capacity for effective collusion by a group of producer nations; (2) an inelastic demand for the product in consumer countries; and (3) a low elasticity of supply of alternative materials for consumer countries.

The economic prospects for successful market intervention must ultimately be determined by detailed econometric studies on an individual commodity basis.[1]

The major purpose of the cartel might be interpreted as the improvement in the producing country's terms of trade—more precisely, not simply the commodity terms of trade P_x/P_m but the income terms of trade $(P_x Q_x)/P_m$, where P_x is an export price index, Q_x is an export volume index, and P_m is an import price index. This is an attempt to raise the primary country's share in the gains from trade and to increase its "capacity to import" (Q_m) derived from a given Q_x (as distinguished from the capacity to import

based on a capital inflow). Thus issues of international distributional equity and the size of a country's development program (as determined by the foreign-exchange constraint) become intertwined with the process of international resource bargaining.

But to the extent that cartels and other measures to control export prices succeed, they impose real costs on the international community by inducing the production of costlier sources of supply, aggravating inflationary pressures, slowing down the rate of growth in consuming countries, and inviting retaliatory measures.

The deleterious effects on the "Fourth World" countries that are in the "resource-poor" category—that is, agricultural countries without mineral resources—should be of special concern to the international community. The problem of acquiring minerals (and the derivatives of fertilizer and foodstuffs) at a price they can afford is a major handicap to the realization of development plans in resource-poor developing countries. Special arrangements that will provide these countries with the means of financing these imports or with additional export revenue may impose additional costs on the world economy.

It is also noteworthy that most primary products are actually produced in high-income countries. At the same time as several rich countries are substantial exporters of primary products, some poor countries are heavy importers of foodstuffs and industrial raw materials. Price-raising commodity agreements would therefore not offer a straightforward transfer of resources from rich to poor countries. On the contrary, as Richard Cooper notes, they would generate

a quite arbitrary distribution of gains and losses among both developed and less developed countries. Moreover, the less developed countries that would benefit tend to be those that are better off; with minor exceptions, the poorest countries would not benefit, and often would lose, from raising commodity prices. Such an action would thus not contribute much to the alleviation of world poverty.[2]

From the standpoint of world economic welfare, the policies of trade liberalization, additional aid, and foreign investment (with a benefit–cost ratio greater than unity) are first-best, in comparison with cartels and related price-fix-

---

[1] Political prospects are as crucial as economic prospects, but they are not amenable to such systematic empirical study. That is why the problem of international resource bargaining might be characterized more aptly as a problem of international resource *diplomacy.*

[2] Richard N. Cooper, "Developed Country Reactions to Calls for a NIEO," in *Toward a New Strategy for Development.* A Rothko Chapel Colloquium (1979), p. 259.

ing undertakings that have costly side effects and are hence second-best as policies for increasing the gains from trade and raising the capacity to import.

The discussion of the control of trade in primary products has raised other issues that deserve attention. The use of export controls that impede access to supplies imposes costs on the world economy that are similar to those of import controls. But the General Agreement on Tariffs and Trade (GATT) has been concerned with only the latter.

International commodity agreements are also frequently proposed to reduce price fluctuations and stabilize foreign-exchange earnings. The two most common instruments are international buffer stocks and export quotas. The fundamental argument for internationally controlled buffer stocks is that changes in private stocks and/or national government stocks are suboptimal because these stocks fail to distribute production and consumption through time in a Pareto optimal fashion. Thus there is excessive variability in commodity prices. The extreme variability in prices may also cause large swings in national income and can have macroeconomic effects on both exporting and importing nations, causing inflation and unemployment and retardation of growth. By stabilizing price by means of buffer stocks, it is believed, other desirable outcomes follow: reduction of risks to producers and users of the commodites, reduced instability in foreign-exchange earnings and in producers' incomes, government revenues, increased investment and growth. The ultimate objectives, however, may not be achieved even if stabilization of prices is successful. This is because fluctuations in real terms will remain for most countries because of supply variability, import price variability, and currency variations.

Moreover, the history of attempts to maintain international commodity agreements has been a dismal one. The agreements usually break down. Difficulties arise over what to do about excess production. Either production controls have to be introduced, or national stocks must be created. If stocks are created, the financial burden is shifted directly to the government of the exporting nations instead of being shared with consuming nations. If production is controlled, other costs arise in the form of misallocation of resources and restriction of output of individual farms and mines, thereby causing unemployment in groups that are already poor.[3]

Finally, the problem of international resource bargaining relates to two other issues, discussed in Chapters V and VII. Another objective of the exercise of "commodity power" is to increase the domestic value added from the primary commodity by inducing domestic processing of the commodity (bauxite into alumina, crude oil into refined petroleum products, and so on). This relates to the process of industrialization through export substitution. An additional objective is to exercise more national control over foreign investment in primary products and to capture more of the rents from that investment. This relates to the problem of private foreign investment.

Thus the exercise of "producer power" raises not just one issue—that of improvement in the terms of trade—but also other related issues: (1) the stability of export prices and foreign-exchange receipts in order to increase the developing country's capacity to import; (2) the domestic processing of primary commodities; and (3) an increase in the benefit–cost ratio of foreign investment. For the long-run period that is relevant to the outcome of development programs, the resolution of these other issues may well be more crucial than the short-run use of "producer power" to improve the terms of trade.

---

[3]For a more detailed analysis, see Alastair MacBean and Duc Tin Nguyen, "International Commodity Agreements: Shadow and Substance," *World Development* (May 1987): 575–90.

EXHIBIT IX.7. Concentration of Primary
Exports, 1991

| Country | Percentage Share of Merchandise Exports | |
	Fuels, Minerals, and Metals	Other Primary Commodities
Tanzania	5	84
Ethiopia	3	94
Uganda	4	95
Madagascar	8	85
Sierra Leone	34	33
Malawi	0	96
India	8	19
Kenya	16	64
Nigeria	96	3
China	9	15
Ghana	15	84
Nicaragua	2	86
Sri Lanka	1	34
Honduras	5	89
Indonesia	43	16
Egypt, Arab Rep.	40	20
Zimbabwe	17	51
Bolivia	74	21
Côte d'Ivoire	11	79
Philippines	9	20
Guatemala	2	70
Ecuador	43	55
Peru	52	30
Colombia	29	38
Paraguay	0	89
Jamaica	17	27
Thailand	2	32
Taiwan	2	6
Costa Rica	2	72
Chile	50	35
Venezuela	86	2
Argentina	8	64
Uruguay	1	59
Brazil	16	28
Mexico	41	14
Trinidad and Tobago	65	6
Korea, Rep. of	3	4
Hong Kong	2	3
Singapore	18	8

Source: World Bank, *World Development Report, 1993* (1993),
pp. 268–69.

Comment: The Commodity Problem

The feasibility of international arrangements to stabilize commodity prices is highly dependent on the characteristics of individual commodity markets. For different commodities, see Walter P. Falcon and Eric A. Monke, "International Trade in Rice," *Food Research Institute Studies* 17, no. 3 (1979–80), and "International Maize and Wheat Improvement Center," *World Wheat Facts and Trends* (1981). The problems associated with buffer stocks are analyzed by Shlomo Reutlinger, "Evaluating Wheat Buffer Stocks," *American Journal of Farm Economics* (February 1976); Anne E. Peck, "Implications of Private Storage of Grains for Buffer Stock Schemes to Stabilize Prices,'' *Food Research Institute Studies* 16, no. 3 (1977–78); and David M. G. Newbery and Joseph E. Stiglitz, *The Theory of Commodity Price Stabilization: A Study in the Economics of Risk* (1981).

For a discussion of conditions that support monopolistic collusive behavior, see E. Stern and W. Tims, ''The Relative Bargaining Strengths of the Developing Countries, '' *American Journal of Agricultural Economics* (May 1975).

A special issue of *World Development* (May 1987) is devoted to ''Primary Commodities in the World Economy: Problems and Policies.''

For the responses of countries to international prices of primary commodity exports, see M. Gersovitz and C. H. Paxson, *The Economies of Africa and the Prices of Their Exports* (1990), chap. 5, and J. Cuddington, ''Commodity Export Booms in Developing Countries,'' *World Bank Research Observer* (July 1989).

IX.D. REGIONAL INTEGRATION AND DEVELOPMENT—NOTE

There have been several efforts to secure economic integration among developing countries. Most notable are the Latin American Free Trade Association (LAFTA), the Central American Common Market (CACM), the Andean Common Market (ACM), the Caribbean Community (CARICOM), the East African Community (EAC), and the Association of Southeast Asian Nations (ASEAN). These integration schemes, however, have generally not lived up to expectation, and most have undergone major modifications. Problems have generally been encountered in determining the scope for profitable specialization, the creation or strengthening of appropriate production structures, and the equitable distribution of the benefits of integration among member countries.

The possibilities for South–South cooperation are now being considered more seriously—whether in deference to Lewis's concern about the slow growth of the MDCs, or to other implications of dependence, delinking, and collective self-reliance. A major effort at South–South cooperation could come from regional integration schemes. As a close student of the North–South dialogue observes,

The weakness of most proposals for South-South cooperation has been that they tended to build grand designs on the basis of an aggregated, mythical South. . . . It may be far more productive to follow up on avenues of cooperation on a regional or sub-regional level and in certain specific areas of action. The perspective for cooperation may often be functional and geopolitical, rather than global and "idealized."[1]

Various degrees of integration are possible, but most interest centers on the potential role of customs unions and free-trade areas. Although both a customs union and a free-trade area provide for across-the-board trade liberalization for all or most products among the member countries, a customs union also adopts a common external tariff.

At a level less general than a customs union or free-trade association, regional integration might be directed simply toward "sectoral integration"—that is, the removal of trade restrictions on only a selected list of commodities, or the treatment of the problems of some one industry as a whole on a regional basis.

Beyond free trade in goods, a more comprehensive economic union might allow for the free movement of factors of production, a common monetary system, and the coordination of economic policies among the member countries. It is still unrealistic to expect this of developing countries; therefore, we will be concerned here with the implications of only free trade in goods.

As a basis for appraising specific proposals, we consider in this Note the benefits that might be derived from economic groupings among developing countries and the difficulties that are likely to be encountered in their formation.

Advocates of an economic union believe that its formation will accelerate the development of the member countries by (1) stimulating the establishment and expansion of manufacturing industries on a more rational basis, (2) increasing the gains from trade, and (3) providing benefits from intensified competition.

We have seen that many countries have adopted a policy of deliberate import substitution in consumer goods. When each country restricts its imports, however, and attempts to substitute home production, industrialization becomes unduly compartmentalized, and the uneconomic multiplication of import-competing industries is wasteful. In contrast, if manufacturing industry can be encouraged in the context of a customs union or free-trade area, it may attain a higher level of productivity than results from industrial protection in each country. Greater specialization within the region can increase the share of exports and imports in manufacturing and reduce the excessive number of products manufactured in an excessive number of protected firms.

To reach an efficient scale of output, a modern manufacturing plant may have to produce a larger output than the low level of home demand in a single underdeveloped country can absorb. By pooling markets through the removal of internal trade barriers, a free-trade union might thus provide a sufficiently wide export market to make economies of scale realizable. Within a union, secondary industry can become more ef-

---

[1]Mahbub ul-Haq, "Beyond the Slogan of South–South Cooperation," in *Dialogue for a New Order,* ed. Khadija Haq (1981).

ficient as specialization occurs in the member country that acquires a comparative advantage. At the same time, the other constituent countries may now replace their manufactures imported from outside the union and thereby be able to spend a higher proportion of their foreign exchange on outside imports that are essential but cannot be produced efficiently within the union. A more rational pattern of production and trade within the region may therefore be an important result of integration.

It is frequently argued that because of similiar levels and patterns of consumption in the LDCs, there should be more scope for inter–LDC trade than for trade with developed countries. As Frances Stewart states,

Consumption patterns among South (i.e., developing) countries should be much more similar to each other than those of North (i.e., developed) countries: the sort of goods—for consumption and investment—developed for one country in the South should be more appropriate, both for production and consumption, to other South countries than to North products they currently import. . . . A coordinated policy to encourage South-South trade would provide the South innovators with the markets they require, and hence, in the end, would be likely to prove self-justifying.[2]

The extension of the market, together with the inducement to get behind the external tariff wall, may also be particularly effective in attracting direct private foreign investment in manufacturing. And over time, there is the further possibility that new industries can become increasingly competitive on world markets and eventually be able to export manufactured goods to nonmember countries. But this depends first on establishing a sufficiently wide market within the union to allow operation of a manufacturing industry on a large enough scale.

An expansion of trade among the member countries is also expected to result from the removal of trade barriers. If this takes the form of replacing high-cost producers within the region by lower cost producers, the effect is one of "trade creation."[3] The gains from trade are then increased, since the international division of labor is improved as resources shift into more efficient production. But some of the intraunion trade may merely replace trade that formerly occurred between members and nonmembers. When the formation of an economic union has this "trade-diverting" effect, the international division of labor will be worsened if the outside source of supply is actually a low-cost source, and its product now becomes higher priced within the union because of the external tariff. In this case, there is an uneconomic diversion of output from the low-cost outside source to the high-cost supplier within the union, and the gains from trade are diminished.

In considering whether trade creation or trade diversion is likely to dominate in a particular union, we have to take into account the preunion level of tariff rates among the members, the level of the postunion external tariff compared with the preunion tariff levels of each member country, the elasticities of demand for the imports on which duties are reduced, and the elasticities of supply of exports from the members and foreign sources. Conditions are more propitious for trade creation when each member's preunion duties are high on the others' products, the members are initially similar in the products they produce but different in the pattern of relative prices at which they produce them, the external tariff of the union is low compared with the preunion tariff levels of the members, and the production within the union of commodities that are substitutes for outside imports can be undertaken at a lower cost.

The formation of a free-trade union might also result in an improvement—or at least the forestalling of a deterioration—in the region's commodity terms of trade. This is possible if there is a reduction in the supply of exports from the union, or the demand by members of the union is reduced for imports from outside, or the bargaining power of the members in trade negotiations is strengthened. But unless the members of the union are the chief suppliers on the world market or constitute a large part of the world market for their imports, they are unlikely to be able to exercise sufficient monopolistic or monopsonistic power to influence their terms of trade by raising duties on their trade with the outside world or by inducing outsiders to supply their goods more cheaply. Moreover, when free trade is confined to only the region, there is the risk of retaliation through the formation of other economic blocs. A union may thereby inhibit the realization of the more extensive gains from the "universal" approach to free trade.

Finally, regional integration might be beneficial in encouraging competition among the

[2]Frances Stewart, "The Direction of International Trade: Gains and Losses for the Third World," in *A World Divided*, ed. Gerald K. Helleiner (1976), pp. 98–99.

[3]Jacob Viner, *The Customs Union Issue* (1950), pp. 48–52.

member countries. Technical efficiency in existing industries might then be improved as marginal firms are forced to reduce their costs, resources are reallocated from less efficient to more efficient firms, and monopolies that had been established behind tariff walls are no longer in a sheltered position. Further, the stimulation of competition within each country not only may yield a better utilization of given resources, but also may raise the rate of growth of productive resources. This may result from stronger incentives to adopt new methods of production, to replace obsolete equipment more rapidly, and to innovate more rapidly with more and better investment.

In practice, however, a number of objections have been raised against proposals for regional integration, and actual negotiations have encountered serious difficulties. As is true for a union among even advanced countries, political problems take precedence, nations will guard against a sacrifice of their sovereignty, and the administration of the union may be extremely complex. For underdeveloped countries, these problems tend to be especially acute, since many have only recently gained political independence, newly established national governments may be excessively concerned with their own national interests and needs, and the administrative requirements may be beyond their present capacity. Aside from the political and administrative difficulties, there are several economic objections to a union.

To begin with, it may be argued that the case for an economic union is in reality weak when the constituent countries have not yet established many industries. Limitations on the supply side may be more of a deterrent to the creation of an industry than is the narrow market on the side of demand. If production conditions do not also improve, the mere extension of the consumer market will not be sufficient to create industries. Moreover, when manufacturing industry is at only a rudimentary stage in the member countries, there is not much scope for eliminating high-cost manufacturers within the region. Nor is there much scope for realizing the benefits of increased competition when there are not yet similar ranges of rival products, produced under different cost conditions, in the several member nations. A union will not cause substantial improvement in the utilization of resources unless industries have already been established but need wider markets than the national economy can provide for the realization of economies of scale, and the member countries have been protecting the same kinds of industry, but have markedly different ratios of factor efficiency in these industries to factor efficiency in nonprotected branches of production.

It has been pointed out that the case for a union is strongest among countries that have little foreign trade in proportion to their domestic production, but conduct a high proportion of their foreign trade with one another.[4] When these conditions prevail, there is less possibility for introducing, within each member country, a distortion of the price relation between goods from other member countries and goods from outside the union, and more of a possibility for eliminating any distortion by tariffs of the price relations between domestic goods and imports from other member countries. There is therefore greater likelihood that the union will improve the use of resources and raise real income.

A union among underdeveloped countries, however, is unlikely to conform to these conditions. The ratio of foreign trade to domestic production is generally high for these countries, and the actual volume of intraregional trade is normally only a small proportion of the region's total foreign trade. The gain from regional integration would therefore be small. The basic difficulty is that, with existing trade patterns, the formation of a union is likely to cause a considerable amount of wasteful "trade diversion." Over the long run, comparative costs and trade patterns may change, and economies of scale may give rise to competitive advantages as development proceeds, so that the scope for "trade creation" will become greater within the union. But the immediate gain is small, and the long-run prospects for the creation of new trade are not likely to influence current decisions to join a union.

The case for regional preferential trading arrangements is stronger than that for a general preference scheme if the regional arrangement allows the avoidance of trade diversion. GATT (Article 24) insists that tariffs among members of a customs union or free-trade area be reduced to zero; it can be demonstrated, however, that in some cases, less trade diversion will result if the members reduce their internal tariffs below the

---

[4]R. G. Lipsey, "The Theory of Customs Unions: A General Survey," *Economic Journal* (September 1960): 507–9. This conclusion rests, however, on the assumption that there are no production economies of large scale.

external tariff but not necessarily to zero.[5] In this respect, a partial preferential arrangement has merit.

Besides the possibility of "trade diversion," other undesirable consequences may result from a union. The member countries are unlikely to benefit equally, and some members may feel that others are gaining at their expense. A country may have a strong comparative advantage in only primary products and will sell to other members only goods that it could as readily export to outside countries. At the same time, the location of manufacturing industry and ancillary activities may become localized within one member country, and "polarization" results. Other members may then contend that if they too had been able to adopt tariff protection against their partners, they would have also been able to attract industry. A nonindustrialized member country may further complain that in buying from an industrialized partner, instead of importing from the outside, it is losing revenue equal to the duty on outside manufactures. And, with a common external tariff, member countries no longer have the discretionary power to use variations in the tariff for the purpose of adjusting their national revenues to their own requirements. The internal strains that arise from uneven development among the member countries may thus make it extremely difficult to preserve a regional grouping. As one study states,

Surprising as it may appear to some, one of the main obstacles lies in the *differences* among the developing countries which form a union. These disparities of size and stage of economic development cause problems so far as the equitable sharing of costs and benefits are concerned. In fact, this emphasis on "equity" might well prove the rock on which all such schemes founder. If indeed customs unions are instituted to take advantage of a larger market, to shift production to optimum localities and, in general, to stimulate economic efficiency, *some* sectors in *some* geographical areas will undoubtedly be adversely affected. Theoretically, it should be possible, if the customs union leads to a rate of growth higher than would otherwise have been the case, to compensate the losers *and* have a net surplus. But the technical implementation of compensation schemes is fraught with practical difficulties.

Basically, what has to be provided for the disadvantaged members, if they are to stay in the union, is one or more of the following preferential measures:

1. Balance-of-payments support through financial institutions of the union or external institutions (e.g.,

the IMF). A credit system organised by a Regional Payments Union (perhaps initially funded externally) might be one way by which countries could be assisted if *intra*-union trade were to lead to balance-of-payments problems.
2. Fiscal policy support measures. Import duties, particularly for small countries, often form a large part of total government revenue. These are slated to disappear with the union and so alternative fiscal means must be developed for substituting lost receipts. Fiscal policy may also have to be used to encourage new industry to locate in the disadvantaged member but, of course, if this means a *permanent* subsidy, the advantage of the customs union is lost.
3. Commercial policy might be especially geared to the needs of the least developed of the group. For example, a longer transition period to the zero tariff situation might be provided for.
4. Credits for new investment.[6]

The most important lesson to be learned from efforts at regional integration is that, if the potential benefits of integration are to be fully realized, the regional association must be a strong one and must be capable of coordinating trade policies, including exchange-rate policy, among the member countries, and must provide some means for an equitable distribution of the costs and benefits among the members. Most proposals for regional integration do not yet show promise of sufficient cohesion and policy coordination.

Although a comprehensive form of free-trade area or full customs union may not yet be practicable for most of the developing countries, there are still substantial advantages that can be derived from more ad hoc functional types of regional cooperation short of comprehensive integration. Measures of "partial integration" may help to avoid the costs of "micro-states" and national development along compartmentalized lines. In particular, the complementary development of specific industries through a regional investment policy has considerable potential. The realization of markets of sufficient size, avoidance of duplication, and better location of projects might result. There are a few outstanding examples of multinational investment projects, and there should be scope for many more.

It is also possible for more to be accomplished by way of partial liberalization of regional trade for certain products or sectors. Countries might

[5]Ibid., pp. 506–7; W. M. Corden, *Recent Developments in the Theory of International Trade* (1965), p. 54.

[6]Derek T. Healey, *Integration Schemes Among Developing Countries: A Survey.* Sixth Conference of Economists (1977), pp. 31–32.

identify specific sectors or individual products for which they could commit themselves not to erect trade barriers with one another. Products that are not yet fabricated in a particular group— that is, new products for the region—might be singled out as a particularly suitable object of such a commitment, especially if supplemented by some commitments regarding a regional investment policy.

A regional agreement might also be effective in bargaining over the entry of foreign investment and the import of technology into the region. Instead of individual countries having to engage in their own bargaining with the foreign investor or foreign supplier of technology, a regional bargaining unit may have more power and may be able to harmonize conditions of entry to greater advantage for the recipient members.

Finally, an important area of regional co-operation—and one that could be used to support other areas—is that of channeling aid through regional integration banks or development corporations. The more this is done, the more influential might the regional institutions be in promoting the regional investment policies and regional trade liberalization policies that are necessary to avoid uncoordinated duplicative national development policies.

Until the risks of joining a free-trade union are diminished, this less ambitious approach involving efforts to secure sectoral integration may be the most feasible alternative. Even though a customs union may be the ultimate objective, it will still be a sizable accomplishment in the immediate future to secure the mutually supporting measures of regional investment policies, regional trade liberalization, and regional aid institutions.

CHAPTER X

Markets, Government, and Policy

All the preceding chapters have had some relevance for development policy making. But only too often the policy maker has remained exogenous, and the "state" has been assumed to pursue the public interest or Pareto efficiency. The state and the actual process of policy making have remained in black boxes. In this final chapter we therefore want to take a more systematic and summary look at the advantages and disadvantages of relying on markets or state economic activity.

First, we shall summarize in section X.A a number of "policy lessons" and policy prescriptions that some leading development economists have presented on the basis of their interpretation of the development record. The theme of defining the proper role of the government as development policy maker runs through the policy recommendations in selections X.A.1 to X.A.5.

The next two sections provide some analytical principles by which to evaluate the policies advocated in X.A. Section X.B examines more closely the case for relying on the market-price system. In support of the market, it can be argued that the objections to the price system are relatively unimportant compared with the essential functions of the market and that the disadvantages of detailed planning by a central authority are far more serious than the deficiencies of the market system. The market is extremely valuable in the context of development as an administrative instrument that is relatively cheap to operate, as is discussed in selection X.B.1. For this reason and others outlined in section X.B, development policy might be better devoted to improving and strengthening the market system than to supplanting the market with detailed administrative controls. Government interventions, however, may still be necessary to remedy the pervasiveness of "new market failures" (X.B.2) and to make markets work more effectively (X.B.3).

Section X.C considers the issue of the optimal character and level of government intervention. Government interventions can range from simply having the state establish property rights and rules of the game to providing infrastructure and macrostabilization policies and on to more detailed micro-interventions, with central planning at the other end of the spectrum. Of particular interest to developing countries is the practice of social benefit–cost analysis in project appraisal (X.C.3). So too is the issue of industrial policy that divides economists between those who advocate policies that would lead or govern the market and those who would only follow the market or intervene with only "market friendly" measures.

The policy lessons summarized in selections X.A.1 to X.A.4 would now be generally subscribed to by mainstream development economists. And yet these policy lessons are not heeded by many governments in the less developed world. Why is the policy advice of development economists not listened to? Is the state a spearhead of development or is it concerned with the allocation of rents? Is it a strong state or a weak state? Is it an instrument for creating markets or for opposing markets? Is policy the outcome of conflicting interests? Does economic analysis really determine policy outcomes? To answer these questions, the selections in section X.D follow the "new political economy" and attempt to endogenize the policy maker and to analyze the political process in neoclassical economic terms. The selections apply elements of the new political economy to explain government failure in import substitution (X.D.3), agriculture (X.D.4), and fiscal policy (X.D.5).

Insofar as the new political economy may appear overly narrow and formalistic, Note X.E incorporates some elements of the older tradition of political economy in considering the ultimate question of improving the quality of development policy making. Developing countries need to avoid both market failure and government failure. Given this task, the economics that we have studied in this book is certainly the economics that really matters. But development economics should matter more. To this end, the final Note offers some suggestions on how development economists can be more influential in meeting the challenge of development.

X.A. POLICY PRESCRIPTIONS

X.A.1. Policy Reform Packages*

"Economic reform" is a broad term, encompassing different strategies and policy approaches to economic development. The following definitions help to relate the various concepts to one another:

1. *Economic reform:* Changes in government policy, institutional structure, or administrative procedures designed to alter economic activity and improve performance.
2. *Stabilization:* Correction of imbalances in foreign payments, government budgets, and the money supply, with the aim of controlling inflation and otherwise reducing macroeconomic instability.
3. *Structural adjustment:* Reforms aimed at changing the structure of production (towards tradable goods) and consumption (towards nontradable goods) and increasing the efficiency and flexibility of the economy. Stabilization is generally considered a precondition of longer-term structural adjustment policies.
4. *Outward-looking (-oriented) strategy:* A complex of policies in which export expansion is the engine of economic growth and development. Policies in this strategy can employ market forces or government interventions, but have in common the establishment of incentives for export growth (and efficient import substitution), with pivotal domestic prices closely related to world prices. Structural adjustment is often designed to achieve an outward-looking economy.
5. *Liberalization or deregulation:* A subset of structural adjustment, dealing with removal of government interventions of all kinds: price controls, quantity restrictions, investment and import licensing, and other barriers to entry.
6. *Privatization:* The sale of government-owned corporations to private investors and the contracting of formerly governmental functions to private agents.
7. *Budget rationalization:* Reforms to bring government's resources more closely into balance and to make them more productive in support of economic growth.
8. *Institutional reform:* Changes in government (and sometimes private) institutions that make it possible for economic reforms to work, predominantly involving shifts away from administered controls towards mechanisms that support private activity.

The Neoclassical Case for Reform

The genesis of the case for economic reform, especially the liberalization agenda, is the neoclassical paradigm of competitive markets. In its strong form, the theory of competitive markets requires small firms or economic agents, none of which has any power to control prices; no externalities, and no government intervention. Under these ideal conditions, the value of output is determined jointly and automatically by the buyers (consumers) and sellers (producers) of goods, services, and factors of production (land, labor, capital). Higher prices create higher returns to factors of production, including future workers and investment, which therefore move into activities that create the greatest value. Competition among producers, whether from home or abroad, forces them to use factors as productively as they can, or else fail. Static efficiency is achieved, in the sense that at any time, returns to factors of production (rents, wages, interest, and profits) are maximized, as is consumers' satisfaction.

If time is added to the neoclassical model, the idealized system can also maximize income growth. Investment in both human and physical capital is then treated explicitly and is allocated to the highest productivity uses. New technologies, broadly defined to include new ways of doing old things, raise productivity and attract investable resources. Modern growth theory, which began with Solow's 1956 article, is based on a highly aggregated form of this neoclassical model.

In real economies, markets deviate from this idealized model in a number of ways. First,

*From Michael Roemer and Steven C. Radelet, "Macroeconomic Reform in Developing Countries," in Dwight H. Perkins and Michael Roemer, eds., *Reforming Economic Systems in Developing Countries* (Harvard Institute for International Development, May 1991), pp. 56–59, 67–69, 71–73, 79–80. Reprinted by permission.

some firms gain market power, defined as the ability to influence prices and raise profits within limits by restricting output. These monopolies and oligopolies can arise either through market forces, as economies of scale encourage larger size, or through policies that protect large firms from international or even domestic competition. Second, external costs of production, such as pollution or the overuse of natural resources like forests, are borne by society at large but not by firms. Because firms do not pay the full cost, they produce more than society considers optimal. Third, and conversely, firms underinvest when some benefits, available to society at large, cannot be realized by the firm that creates the benefits. Irrigation schemes that combine flood control and recreational facilities provide such external benefits, as do firms that train new workers who later leave to work elsewhere.

Fourth, quantum changes in economic structure that may eventually enhance growth, such as the development of heavy industry, may never be profitable in markets that necessarily reflect current structure and discourage infant industries. Fifth, in developing countries, market institutions are themselves poorly developed and do not function efficiently; indeed, large segments of the population are excluded from some important markets. Sixth, governments may have policy goals, especially concerned with self-sufficiency, income distribution, and poverty alleviation, that are not well served by markets.

Neoclassical economics prescribes corrections for some of these market failures. Monopolies can be regulated or forced to compete with imported goods. Firms can be taxed or subsidized, and in some cases regulated, to correct for external costs or benefits. Infant industries can be protected or subsidized until they mature and become competitive. Governments can promote private institutions to improve market performance. Government itself can invest in infrastructure that supports private activity. Though distributional goals sometimes conflict with productivity and growth, especially in the short term, interventions can often be designed to mute such conflicts in the medium to long term.

When interventions are necessary to correct for market failure, neoclassical economics suggests a set of priorities: (1) try first to improve or enhance the way markets work by providing infrastructure and promoting market institutions; (2) prefer market-based mechanisms, such as taxes, subsidies, and administered prices, over

quantity controls, such as import bans or credit allocations; and (3) when regulations are necessary, use them sparingly and target them carefully. Thus, neoclassical economics accepts the need for some intervention, including some regulation, to overcome market failure and achieve optimal outcomes.

However, governments in developing (and many industrial) countries have often intervened to a much greater degree than these neoclassical guidelines suggest. For a variety of reasons, including attempts to correct for market failures, enhance growth, and improve income distribution, governments control and frequently distort foreign exchange rates, interest rates, wages, prices of essential commodities (especially food), the quantity of imports, credit allocations, and many other market variables. Governments also enter directly into production, establishing firms that are insulated from the rigors of market competition. Although such interventions may sometimes succeed, typical interventions are either poorly designed to achieve government's goals or poorly implemented.

Any regulation establishes incentives for rent seeking and corruption, as private agents try to circumvent the rules and civil servants gain the ability to earn income from their administration of regulations. When government actions become more important than market forces in determining incomes, economic agents have less incentive to produce efficiently and instead concentrate on seeking governmental favors. Interventions of this magnitude almost always work against productivity and economic growth. For these reasons, interventions often work against the distributional and other policy aims they are meant to achieve. . . .

Structural Adjustment

With a stabilization program in place, the next task is to undertake reforms to restructure the economy for economic growth. A complete reform package, derived from the neoclassical paradigm, contains five components:

1. freeing markets to determine prices ("letting markets work");
2. adjusting controlled prices to scarcity values ("getting prices right");
3. shifting resources from government into private hands (privatization);
4. rationalizing government's remaining role in development (budget rationalization); and

5. reforming institutions to carry out government's new role.

The crux of neoclassical reform is to free markets as completely as possible to equate supply and demand, thus allowing prices to reflect opportunity costs. Transactions made under these prices would move goods and factors towards maximum output and an optimal rate of growth. Governments would intervene only to improve markets by regulating monopolies, taxing or subsidizing external costs and benefits, protecting infant industries, investing in infrastructure, and developing new market institutions.

Even the staunchest advocates of reform accept that some prices will be controlled by governments, especially exchange rates, possibly interest rates, and the prices of basic foods. But price controls should be kept to a minimum and in no case ought governments control quantities. Controlled prices should be adjusted to reflect real scarcities or opportunity costs of goods, services, factors of production, and time. In this way, controlled prices can approximate free market prices. Oskar Lange (1938) suggested this as a means of managing socialist economies, with managers instructed to maximize profits under government-determined prices.

The rationale for freeing markets, as already discussed, is to introduce a greater degree of competition and flexibility into all aspects of economic activity (Fischer 1986). Government controls over quantities, such as import controls and credit allocations, work against competitive markets because allocations depend on the administrative competence and, often, on the favors of government regulators rather than on the ability of firms to compete. Such controls almost always result in rent seeking and bribery, so that the reward structure favors political skills rather than entrepreneurial and managerial skills.

In small economies, it is unrealistic to expect domestic competition in all fields, especially those involving modern industry, much of which is characterized by economies of scale or scope, rapid technological change, product differentiation on the basis of quality, and large-scale international competition. Thus, the freeing of markets is not a call for a Smithian world of atomistic competition. However, when domestic competition is limited, it is crucial that international competition be present, either through easily available, competitive imports or through export markets. This is where the outward-looking strategy comes in: whatever the degree of competition in the home market, an open economy ensures international competition, providing the stimulus for productivity gains that are necessary for sustained growth. It also requires that at least certain prices be close to opportunity costs as determined by world markets and domestic scarcities: exchange rates, prices of importable and exportable goods, and preferably wages, interest rates, and the prices of nontradables that are important in the cost structure of firms producing for export.

The agenda for the first two components of market reform—letting markets work and getting prices right–dates to at least 1970, with the publication of Little, Scitovsky, and Scott's comparative study, *Industry and Trade in Some Developing Countries*. Several later contributions reaffirm the program. Its main elements include:

1. trade reform: eliminating controls over imports, reducing tariff levels, achieving a more uniform tariff structure, and subsidizing nontraditional exports;
2. reducing restrictions on foreign investment;
3. adjusting the exchange rate to establish and then to maintain the profitability of more export industries and to compensate for part of the reduction in protection from competing goods;
4. financial reform: adjusting interest rates to levels above the rate of inflation, in order to eliminate the excess demand for credit, or, preferably, freeing credit markets to determine interest rates, and promoting new credit instruments and institutions;
5. removing minimum wage controls and other regulations that artificially increase labor costs, or at least permitting inflation to erode the real value of these costs;
6. freeing or at least adjusting prices on farm products to encourage investment and increased productivity in agriculture; and
7. generally eliminating controls over prices and otherwise reducing regulations that inhibit market behavior.

Market reforms are expected to raise the productivity of private activities. But price signals alone will not be enough (Chenery et al. 1986; Streeten 1987). To take advantage of a more effective private sector, reform packages include as a third component the shift of resources from government to private hands. "Privatization," which encompasses the sale of government-owned firms to private investors and the contracting of government services to private firms, is one part of this reform. Of possibly greater importance is the reduction of government deficits, advocated for macroeconomic stabilization, but also as a means of reducing government's drain on private saving to finance the deficit. A complementary approach would focus government services and investments increasingly on support of the private sector, emphasizing infrastructure development, agricultural research and extension, credit institutions, health, and education.

The fourth component of reform packages is the rationalization of government's remaining activities. Not only must resources be shifted into private hands, but those left to government need to be used more efficiently, a process sometimes called "budget rationalization." Project appraisal and other techniques are employed to channel more resources into activities with the highest returns. When investment funds are in short supply, those available must be channeled to fewer investments so that projects can be completed and brought into use quickly. Government corporations should be held more accountable by limiting their borrowing or establishing performance contracts with government. The first call on revenues should be to finance the operating and maintenance costs of completed projects and existing government facilities (World Bank 1984). Rationalization also means a reduction in government's own work force, or at least in its rate of hiring. For obvious reasons, this is seldom accomplished.

For governments used to widespread interventions, these reforms suggest fundamental changes in the way government—and sometimes private—agencies operate. The fifth component of structural adjustment is the reform of institutions to carry out government's new economic role. For example, import liberalization requires the licensing authority to be dismantled and the customs authority to be made more efficient and honest; financial market reform includes the creation of new financial instruments and new institutions; and efficient infrastructure investment may be helped by decentralization of government activities and the upgrading of disbursed planning and implementing agencies. Success in economic reform often depends heavily on the completion of complex institutional reforms.

Sequencing Reforms

Although it is easy to distinguish stabilization from structural adjustment in principle, it is nearly impossible to disentangle them in practice. There are enough common elements to make this division artificial: exchange rate devaluation, interest rate increases, reductions in food subsidies, higher charges for services supplied by government enterprises, and so forth. Although stabilization may be a prerequisite for structural adjustment, there is usually a very short interval, if any, between implementation of these two aspects of reform. When the two are considered together, the interesting questions deal with the sequencing of policies contained in the two packages. It is to this frontier of economic theory that we now turn.

Until recently the literature on economic reform has been conducted in comparative static terms. Neoclassical theory tells us that a liberalized economy is more efficient (and thus productive) than a controlled economy. "However, theory tells us virtually nothing about optimal transition paths from a distorted system to one that is more fully liberalized. Unfortunately, this is the most important problem for any successful reform" (Bruno 1985). The theory of the second best tells us that partial reforms—the adjustment of only some prices or the removal of some controls—does not necessarily lead to overall gains in efficiency and welfare. The path to comprehensive reform is likely to pass through phases of lower average incomes as well as shifts in the distribution of income. Experience with liberalization in Latin America suggests that even a feasible, never mind optimal, sequencing of stabilization and reform measures can be elusive (Corbo and de Melo 1985). Virtually all the literature on sequencing derives from Latin America, where severe macroeconomic imbalances, rooted deeply in political and social patterns, have been attacked by comprehensive packages of stabilization and liberalization. Chile is the extreme and most studied case, with considerable literature on Argentina, Uruguay, Brazil, and, to a lesser extent, Bolivia, Mexico, and Peru.

The sequencing issue is a highly technical one. Our intention here is only to impart some of the flavor of the problem and to illustrate two basic points about economic reform. First, even at the general level of technical macroeconomic analysis, stabilization and structural adjustment programs are complex and fragile. The sequencing of measures and their predicted outcomes are difficult to explain to decision makers, indeed are often counterintuitive. On some issues, there is no settled judgment among economists. And much depends on the economic history, structure, and expected response of the particular economy.

Second, the ramifications of sequencing for income distribution and political acceptability, both discussed later, can be substantial. Comprehensive packages of stabilization and reform are not for the timid. Implementation of these packages requires robust but nimble governments, capable of experimenting with the economy under political pressure. It is not surprising that only a handful of governments have tried to implement comprehensive reform programs, and few have been totally successful.

The sequencing problem has been framed as succinctly as possible by Sebastian Edwards (1987), and this account follows his. Begin with the classic unbalanced, distorted economy characterized by high inflation, large budgetary deficits substantially financed by money creation, controlled interest rates, high tariffs, and controls on foreign capital flows. Edwards is describing Latin American countries, especially Chile. If this were Africa, we would start with lower inflation, but add controls over imports and an overvalued exchange rate. With many possible reforms, there are many possible conflicts in sequencing.

If reform is to adjust the structure of the economy, it is essential that land, labor, and capital can be moved from one use to another. This in turn requires the early liberalization of factor markets, especially those for labor and credit (Krueger 1984). The dynamic East Asian exporters enjoyed highly flexible labor markets, with market-determined wages. The Korean government did control the credit market, but used credit allocation to shift resources towards export industries (Scitovsky 1985).

If domestic credit markets are liberalized early in the reform and if lenders, not trusting the efficacy of stabilization, anticipate renewed inflation, then interest rates will shoot up, as they did in the Southern Cone reforms of the 1970s and 1980s. Should controls over foreign capital also be relaxed, both foreign and domestic investors will borrow abroad to finance investment in the country, because high domestic interest rates make peso loans much more expensive

than dollar loans. The inflow of foreign capital adds to the money supply, exacerbating inflation and the interest rate differential that caused the problem in the first place. This was Chile's particular problem, repeated in other Latin American countries, and it led to increasing concentration of ownership as those with access to foreign capital bought out other firms (Foxley and Whitehead 1980; Edwards 1987).

A real depreciation of the currency—devaluation in excess of the rate of inflation—is central to promoting exports and liberalizing imports. But when controls over foreign capital are reduced, or if a large aid package supports the reform program, the inflow of capital will cause the currency to appreciate in real terms, squeezing the profitability of producers of exports and import substitutes. Attempts by Southern Cone countries to control inflation by limiting the rate of nominal devaluation of the exchange rate also reduced the profitability of exporting and contributed to the failure of several reform programs (Corbo and de Melo 1985; Edwards 1987).

Sequencing problems affect sectoral strategies as well. Import liberalization and tariff reform are mostly aimed at increasing the productivity of manufacturing. If import controls are important, it will be easier to relax them while tariffs are still high enough to protect the affected industries. This sequence has the advantage of moving first to a price-based system of protection. However, the conversion can take a long time (Michaely 1986). Moreover, the rationalization of tariffs then becomes more difficult because quantitative controls no longer mask the reduction of tariff protection. Tariffs on imported inputs are sometimes reduced before duties on competing imports to make industry more competitive, but this increases effective protection and makes future tariff cuts on competing imports more difficult.

Whatever their sequence, trade reforms typically involve major changes in the way institutions, such as the customs and import licensing authorities, work and take years to implement. During this period, if foreign capital controls are relaxed before the import regime is thoroughly rationalized, then private investment will be channeled into some inefficient industries whose eventual decline is one of the aims of the reform program (Corbo and de Melo 1985; Edwards 1987).

Agricultural productivity and food security often require that prices of domestically produced foods be raised from controlled levels. But if this is done before the exchange rate has been devalued, resources may move out of export crops into food crops, contrary to comparative advantage and hence contrary to government's goals for macroeconomic productivity and growth (Krueger 1984).

Very few clear rules survive from the literature on sequencing. Stabilization survives intact as a prerequisite for liberalizing reforms, as does the critical importance of a near-equilibrium exchange rate. One implication of the literature—though still subject to debate—is that the deregulation of foreign capital probably ought to be delayed until trade and domestic capital market reforms have been put in place and domestic interest rates have settled down to levels consistent with international rates. Other prescriptions are much more tentative and depend more on particular circumstances.

Conclusion

From this review of the literature on economic reform in developing countries, a few points emerge as crucial to understanding why economic reform is desirable, how it can be made to work, and why it often fails.

First, reform is desirable because freer markets introduce more competition, which is believed to spur growth in productivity and hence in incomes. Economists believe that competition enhances productivity because first principles of neoclassical economics strongly suggest it and because there is empirical evidence to support it, although this evidence is based on a few cases rather than comprehensive cross-country data.

Second, the agenda for reform, though extensive, has attracted a wide consensus among development economists and practitioners. Because competition is the crucial ingredient of reform and the strongest dose of competition is likely to come from outside the economy, the reform agenda is closely associated with the outward-looking or export-oriented strategy of development.

Third, the major doubts about the reform agenda are those of implementation: With such a large agenda, how much can be done, in what order, and how soon? Reform programs are technically complex, with many opportunities to make fatal mistakes. Experience offers few convincing general lessons about the sequencing, timing, and magnitude of reform measures. Differing country circumstances demand tailor-made programs, which increase the chances for error.

Fourth, over several years a well-implemented reform should raise average income. Despite popular belief to the contrary, evidence is mixed that stabilization and structural adjustment necessarily lower incomes in the short run, especially if the correct (though difficult) comparison is made with the situation as it would have been without reform.

Fifth, reform ought to improve the income distribution in many circumstances, especially in Africa and Asia where economies are characterized by small farmers and a labor surplus. But in the most successful reforming countries in East Asia, reform has probably had a marginal impact on income equality, compared with the impact of war and land reform. And in Latin America it appears that stabilization may concentrate incomes.

Sixth, even if reform does raise income and equalize it, losses are likely to be concentrated among the most powerful groups in the society, who have both motive and means to thwart structural adjustment. This is especially true in clientelistic regimes, whose main support comes from favorites of the regime who benefit enormously from the controls that are a principal target of structural adjustment.

Finally, technical complexity and political fragility make it much easier to explain why reforms fail than why they succeed. Yet reforms do succeed, not only in East Asia, but in some unexpected places such as Indonesia, Bangladesh, Bolivia, and, increasingly, in some African countries. Research on reform can make its greatest contribution by explaining how these programs have worked.

References

Bruno, Michael. 1985. ''The Reforms and Macroeconomic Adjustments: Introduction.'' *World Development* 13, no. 8: 867–69.

Chenery, Hollis, Jeffery Lewis, Jaime de Melo, and Sherman Robinson. 1986. ''Alternative Routes to Development.'' In Hollis Chenery, Sherman Robinson, and Moshe Syrquin, eds., *Industrialization and Growth: A Comparative Study.* Washington, D.C.: World Bank, pp. 311–47.

Corbo, Vittorio, and Jaime de Melo. 1985. ''Overview and Summary.'' *World Development* 13, no. 8: 863–66.

Edwards, Sebastian. 1987. "Sequencing Economic Liberalization in Developing Countries." *Finance and Development* (March): 26–29.

Fischer, Stanley. 1986. "Issues in Medium-Term Macroeconomic Adjustment." *World Bank Research Observer* 1, no. 2 (July): 163–82.

Foxley, Alejandro, and Laurence Whitehead. 1980. "Economic Stabilization in Latin America: Political Dimensions." *World Development* 8, no. 11: 823–32.

Krueger, Anne O. 1984. "Problems of Liberalization." In Arnold C. Harberger, ed., *World Economic Growth*. San Francisco: Institute for Contemporary Studies, pp. 403–23.

Lange, Oskar. 1938. "On the Economic Theory of Socialism." In B. Lippincott, ed., *On the Economic Theory of Socialism*. Minneapolis: University of Minnesota Press, pp. 55–143.

Little, Ian, Tibor Scitovsky, and Maurice Scott. 1970. *Industry and Trade in Some Developing Countries: A Comparative Study.* London: Oxford University Press.

Michaely, Michael. 1986. "The Timing and Sequencing of a Trade Liberalization Policy." In Armeane M. Choksi and Demetrius Papageorgiou, eds., *Economic Liberalization in Developing Countries.* New York: Basil Blackwell, pp. 41–59.

Scitovsky, Tibor. 1985. "Economic Development in Taiwan and South Korea: 1965–1981." *Food Research Institute Studies* 19, no. 3: 215–64.

Streeten, Paul. 1987. "Structural Adjustment: A Survey of the Issues and Options." *World Development* 15, no. 12: 1469–82.

World Bank. 1984. *Toward Sustained Development in Sub-Saharan Africa.* Washington, D.C.: World Bank.

X.A.2. Policies for Economic Development*

At the end of a decade in which many developing countries have seen economic regress rather than progress and in which the formerly socialist economies for the most part turned away from central planning toward a market-oriented approach, there appears to be more agreement on the policies needed to produce growth and economic development than at any time in the post-World War II period. It remains to be seen whether the moment is more than fleeting. But it is certainly a good time to attempt to set out a mainstream, pragmatic view of what those policies are and of the uncertainties that surround the basic market- and outward-oriented approach to development.

In this paper we summarize the consensus views of the major economic policies needed to generate economic growth and development, consider issues that cut across these policy areas, and then provide brief concluding comments.

*From Stanley Fischer and Vinod Thomas, "Policies for Economic Development," *American Journal of Agricultural Economics* (August 1990): 809–13. Reprinted by permission.

Consensus Views in Major Policy Areas

Policies conducive to economic development in three broad areas are an appropriate macroeconomic framework, the right set of sectoral policies and investments, and integration of the domestic economy into the world economy.

Getting the Macroeconomic Framework Right

Economic development is unlikely to occur unless policies produce a stable macroeconomic environment in which inflation remains reasonably low, the real exchange rate is competitive and stable, and foreign exchange and debt crises are avoided.

Fiscal Policy. Tax rate and expenditure policies of government, including the composition of government spending, are the government's major microeconomic tools for affecting the allocation of resources. Beyond these microeconomic effects, fiscal policy is increasingly seen as the key to successful macroeconomic policy because, in its macro impacts, it has direct effects on the current allocation of resources, and because all methods of financing budget deficits have potentially adverse macroeconomic consequences when used to excess.

Given private saving, fiscal deficits displace private domestic investment or cause current account deficits. Thus, unless private saving responds fully to public sector deficits—and there is little reason to think it does—reduction of the fiscal deficit is likely to improve the current account and, perhaps after a period of adjustment, increase investment.

Fiscal deficits can be financed by printing money, by running down foreign-exchange reserves, and by borrowing, at home or abroad. Each of these methods of financing can be used on a small scale (and in the case of running down foreign-exchange reserves, on a transitory basis), but each is likely to have seriously adverse consequences if used on a major scale. Printing (high-powered) money is inflationary; running down foreign-exchange reserves leads to a foreign-exchange crisis; domestic borrowing can lead to higher real interest rates and an unstable domestic fiscal situation; and excessive foreign borrowing can lead to an external debt crisis.

While the conclusion is that fiscal moderation is the key to macroeconomic stability, this does not mean a zero deficit is optimal: a country that is growing fast can afford to run a larger deficit than one that is growing slowly; a country with a higher saving rate can run a given deficit for longer than a country with a lower saving rate. Fiscal moderation must be judged by the projected path of the debt (the sum of internal and external debt) to GNP ratio, and of the inflation rate and external balance. On the whole, inadequate fiscal policies remain a central factor behind the macroeconomic instability and poor performance of many developing countries.

The Exchange Rate. The second key to a sound macro framework is the exchange rate; it plays two roles in economic policy. First, the level of the real exchange rate is crucial to the development of the domestic economy: it establishes market incentives to export and the level of protection for domestic industries. Second, stability of the nominal exchange rate is one potential monetary anchor and a powerful anti-inflationary factor. When an economy operates with a fixed nominal exchange rate, the quantity of money becomes endogenous. This simplifies the job of the monetary authority; but, as experience shows, it frequently leads to a host of foreign exchange controls.

The two roles of the exchange rate sometimes clash: governments afraid of inflation hold the nominal exchange rate constant or devalue it too slowly, with the result that the domestic currency appreciates, and—with a lag—the current account goes into crisis. When the monetary anchor and trade incentive roles of the exchange rate conflict, the monetary anchor should be pulled up first and attention turned to the underlying source of inflationary pressure, typically the budget. Intermediate steps, such as a crawling peg, in conjunction with appropriate fiscal policy can provide some monetary stability without tending to produce an overvalued currency.

Investment, Saving, and Growth. Investment and saving ratios in rapidly growing economies are typically higher than those in stagnating economies. It is further clear that sustained growth will not resume in Sub-Saharan Africa and Latin America until investment ratios there rise significantly. The rise in the real interest rate in the 1980s reduces the possibilities of financing investment from abroad; economic growth in the 1990s will have to be largely domestically financed. The surest way to increase domestic saving is to increase government saving, that is, to reduce the government budget deficit. The emphasis in the 1980s was on the importance of positive real interest rates for development. The emphasis is appropriate when the real interest rate is significantly negative, as it frequently is in high inflation economies: negative real interest rates appear to reduce saving and impair the efficiency of the financial system by reducing the share of saving that is intermediated through financial institutions. But once the real interest rate is positive, or nearly so, there is little empirical or theoretical reason to believe that further increases will increase saving.

Responding to Shocks. Emphasis on the stability of the macroeconomic framework should not obscure the importance of the ability of the government to adjust macroeconomic policy quickly to external and internal shocks. Fiscal and monetary policy, and the exchange rate, may have to change rapidly when external conditions change; the more successful governments recognize change and respond to it. The need for flexibility is especially great for economies whose external earnings fluctuate a great deal, typically because they are dependent on earnings from one or a few primary commodities.

Sectoral Policies: Projects and Beyond

Macroeconomic policies for stability and growth usually need to be underpinned by appropriate sectoral policies to obtain a satisfactory supply response. Sectoral policies include investment decisions, pricing and regulatory policies, and institutional development.

Investments in agriculture, industry, infrastructure, and human resources have long formed the core of development efforts. The traditional approach was to pursue development projects in these sectors with the aid of project analysis of benefits and costs. The effectiveness of the investments, however, depends on the policy environment affecting the sector and the degree of institutional development.

Sectoral Priorities and Investments. Although there is no universal prescription for sectoral priorities for development, development usually requires increases in agricultural productivity permitting an increasing share of the labor force to contribute to industrial production. Accordingly, development is usually accompanied by an increasing share of industry in output. Human resource development is both an independent goal of development and an essential instrument of economic progress.

Unprecedented rates of population growth in the post-World War II period have contributed to low or negative per capita income growth in much of Africa, Asia, and for some time in China and India. Despite significant political opposition within the United States, international agencies have sought to assist governments to reduce population growth. Success to date has been limited, but there have recently been encouraging signs from some African countries, where population growth rates appear to be turning down as a result of government educational programs and the provision of contraceptives. Reducing the rate of population growth remains a priority of development policy in many developing countries.

Sectoral Policies and Strategy. The emphasis on the centrality of sectoral and macroeconomic policies to the success of projects has strength-ened in recent years, along with the recognition that policies are of independent importance to sectoral performance. Measures to bring domestic relative prices closer to international levels and to establish a relatively neutral macroeconomic framework are often essential to enhancing sectoral performance. In agriculture, for example, incentives were historically suppressed by agricultural taxes. Perhaps more important, macroeconomic policies resulting in overvalued exchange rates have translated into heavy (often unintended) taxation of that sector. Adjustment programs in the 1980s have therefore focussed on both macroeconomic policies (exchange rate, import protection) and sectoral pricing policies (eliminating price controls on agricultural output, for example). Concurrently, many programs have also attempted to reduce the rather ineffective input subsidies in agriculture while improving the delivery of inputs and services.

The consensus is converging to the view that macroeconomic and sectoral pricing and regulatory policies should be relatively neutral, that governments should move away from interventions designed to favor particular industries, regions, or factors of production. However, moving toward neutrality may require active transitional government policies, for instance in restructuring public enterprises or the financial system (see also the next section). It also remains true that an active government investment program in the sectors, especially physical infrastructure and human resource development and technology, is essential to development.

Integrating with the World Economy

The most successful performers of recent decades have been the newly industrializing economies, characterized by their relative openness and links with the world economy. To maintain these links, they have had to remain competitive in a rapidly changing world environment. Common to successful competition strategies is the reduction or elimination of discrimination against tradables—permitting exports and efficient import substitutes to be produced on a similar footing with nontradables.

However, such neutrality in the trade regime has been approached through different routes. Some successful reformers have substantially liberalized their trade restrictions (Chile, Mexico), others have intervened to offset existing biases against exports (Korea, Taiwan), and still others have done both (Indonesia, Turkey). Government controls have been especially prevalent in the area of capital flows in many countries. Interventions to encourage new technologies and to industrialize have also paid off on occasion.

Commercial Policy Reforms. Developing countries are more open, and their trade regimes are more efficient than a decade ago. They have substantially reformed their exchange rate and export policies. They also have increased the efficiency of their import regimes by switching from quantitative restrictions to tariffs. But reductions in the levels of nominal and effective protection have been more limited than is generally believed.

Most countries that have implemented trade policy reforms have won long-term economic gains. The policy changes and additional financing under adjustment programs have both been associated with moderate improvements in output and export growth. However, supply response to changes in relative prices associated with the trade reforms has been limited in many countries. The main constraints on the supply response have been restrictive domestic regulations and inefficient public enterprise policies; growing protectionism in industrial countries; doubts about the permanence of the reforms; and inadequate institutions, infrastructure, and entrepreneurial and managerial capacity in the reforming country.

Issues Spanning Policy Areas

There are several issues that span policy areas. These include sustainable development, both country-specific and global environmental sustainability, and social, political, and economic sustainability of adjustment programs. Other issues include poverty alleviation and the balance between both public and private sectors.

Sustainable Development

Two issues fall under this heading. The first is environmental sustainability, which has both a country-specific and global aspects. One fear is that in many countries development is taking place by exploiting and destroying much of the resource base, and that such development is accordingly not sustainable. The presumption is that two-way links exist between growth and the environment: certain growth policies are consis-

tent with environmental protection, and environmental care in turn contributes to sustained growth. But knowledge of the tradeoffs between measured growth and environmental protection must increase. At the same time, simple steps to prevent environmental damage, such as environmental assessments for all projects, are already being implemented.

Global environmental issues pose more difficult problems. If global warming is taking place, it is largely the result of current and past economic activities of the now-industrialized countries. If measures are put in place to reduce global environmental damage, the issue of burden sharing between developing and industrialized countries—as well as among all countries—will pose major political difficulties.

A second sustainability issue is whether the adjustment programs of many countries are socially, politically, and economically sustainable. Adjustment is more likely to be socially sustainable if the poor are protected during the process of adjustment. Political sustainability may depend on how adjustment affects the segment of population with political clout. In general, adjustment is more likely to be sustainable the sooner it shows economic results. One reason to provide external financing during the adjustment process is temporarily to reduce the extent of cuts in expenditures and in imports that would otherwise have been necessary.

Poverty Alleviation

Although the purpose of economic development is to reduce poverty, poverty alleviation is a separate goal of policy in developing as well as industrialized economies. Specific policies, such as targeted food subsidy and health programs, can be used to protect the poor and reduce poverty, even during adjustment. Bolivia's experiment with the Emergency Social Fund and Ghana's Program of Actions to Mitigate the Social Cost of Adjustment are examples. These are temporary measures (three years in Bolivia and two in Ghana). More fundamentally, education and other social programs can be designed to reduce poverty, even though in many countries social spending helps mainly the middle and upper classes. More effective and better targeted public expenditures are needed. Sometimes it would help to correct mistargeting of existing public social expenditures, for example, by reducing public funding of education and curative health care expenditures.

The Balance Between Public and Private Sectors

The new consensus on development policy places greater stress than before on the central role of markets, and on the private sector (in some countries, the informal private sector) as the engine of growth. The role of the public sector is seen as the creation of a favorable enabling environment for economic activity. The enabling environment consists of the legal, institutional, and policy framework within which economic agents operate.

A government that creates a favorable enabling environment has a large role to play, for instance in ensuring the provision of infrastructure, including social services, such as poverty alleviation, basic education, and access to health care; public security; a stable macroeconomic framework; and an efficient fiscal and regulatory system.

The most difficult question about the role of the government is whether it should take an active part in promoting particular industries, that is, whether it should pursue an industrial policy. Some successful elements of an active policy are clear: export development and assistance in marketing, information, technology, and know-how. Expanding manufactured exports requires sustained efforts on both macroeconomic and microeconomic levels. Japan, Korea, and Taiwan have paid attention to the many nonprice requirements of export development. For a period of time, they also pursued export development while maintaining a certain degree of import protection.

Outstanding Issues

General agreement on the policies needed to produce growth and economic development will remain only if the currently agreed upon policies produce growth and development. Seen in that light, the challenges, particularly from Africa and Latin America, and most recently from the reforming socialist economies, are formidable. In many cases, the problems are analytic, for instance, how to sequence the adjustment of a heavily distorted economy with macroeconomic and external imbalances to the market-oriented structure that its policy makers seek. In other cases, the problems are political: countries with infrastructure and analytic capacity lack the political ability to implement changes that are generally recognized to be desirable. This is not a problem only for developing countries. In other countries, inadequate human capital and institutional framework constrain development. It is essential to recognize that the problems of development differ from country to country, and that each country's policies have to fit its own structure while still recognizing the realities of the world economy in which it operates.

There are also deep questions about the role of external funding and the international development agencies. It is often argued that countries would have done better if left to their own devices and forced to confront their budget constraints earlier and harder. One can agree with this judgment for some countries, but not for most. Nonetheless, it is essential to recognize that an important goal of development is for countries to reach the stage at which they manage their own affairs.

X.A.3. Principal "Lessons"*

Following are some widely shared conclusions of policy professionals about the principal "lessons" associated with successful growth policy:

1. *Avoid false technicism in economic policymaking.* Too often, and in too many

*From Arnold C. Harberger (ed.), *Economic Policy and Economic Growth*, International Center for Economic Growth, San Francisco, 1984, pp. 9–16. Reprinted by permission.

countries, the task of economic planning has been conceived as that of making projections (predictions) of future economic progress. Sometimes these predictions have been elaborated in incredible detail, to the point of projecting the output of individual industries five or ten years into the future. Such exercises simply have not paid off. They have been a waste of good talent and money. They have distracted able people from the more important task of attacking real economic policy problems; and, to make things worse, they have generally been wide of the mark—often corrupted by commingling with political promises and propaganda.

2. *Keep budgets under adequate control.* Budgets need not be balanced, but there are severe limits to the budget deficits that can be incurred with relative impunity. Somewhere along the line, budgetary authorities must learn to say no to spending requests, and standing behind them, governments must learn to resist pressures to spend more. The time for governments and budgetary authorities to take their stand is clearly *before* budgetary discipline has broken down. Some bending and yielding there will (and probably must) always be, but once authorities have caved in too many times, it is as if a dam had broken, and they will be overwhelmed by a flood of requests from newly hopeful solicitants.

3. *Keep inflationary pressures under reasonable control.* To encourage economic development in a small country, the optimal policy may be to live with the ongoing rate of inflation in the world economy. However, if, for whatever reason, a higher rate must be accepted, it should be kept both moderate and steady.

Most of the major inflations in the postwar period have had their roots in excessive fiscal deficits (see the previous point), which the governments could only finance by resort to the printing press. This was true in Argentina, Chile, and Indonesia in the 1960s, and in the recent eruptions of inflationary forces in Africa. But it is also possible to unleash very dramatic inflationary forces by printing money in order to grant credit to the private sector—as occurred in Uruguay for more than two decades, and in Brazil for about a decade beginning in the mid-1960s.

Inflation undermines growth in two ways. First, it disturbs the most basic process whereby relative prices guide resources from lower-valued to higher-valued uses. In fact, the very essence of growth occurs as resource investments are made in situations featuring high relative output prices (benefits) and low input prices (costs). The key to the process is clear signals about relative prices. Inflation, on the other hand—especially when it is unsteady and thus unanticipated—disturbs those signals by obscuring the differences between *relative* and *absolute* price rises.

A second problem with inflation results from rewarding people for estimating the correct inflation rate—and thus making money from people who guess either too low or too high. Guessing the inflation rate does nothing to make the economy grow, and inflation thus diverts productive resources to non-productive purposes.

Finally, inflation tends, especially when it is unanticipated and unindexed, to generate capricious transfers of wealth among economic sectors and groups. This breaks the link between earnings and effort, and has been known to cause violent political upheavals sparked by the embittered losers.

4. *Take advantage of international trade.* It may be that most policy professionals, deep down, are free traders at heart. But this is not the way they speak in policy forums: on such a politically incandescent topic as protectionism, the professional's credibility with different groups depends on discretion. Thus, rather than openly celebrating free trade, modern policy professionals tend to emphasize the strategic choice between a relatively open versus a relatively closed economy.

The relatively open economy implies high imports and high exports relative to GDP. The relatively closed one implies the reverse: low imports (because of import restrictions) and low exports. Restrictions on imports act also as indirect restrictions on exports by causing changes in exchange rates, thus raising the prices of exported goods. The underlying reason for this process is that imports must ultimately be paid for by exports; and if you limit one, you thus necessarily limit the other. Protecting imports thus *dis*-protects exports, distorting the most efficient allocation of resources as protection of relatively less efficient import-competing industries diverts resources (capital and labor) from more efficient export industries. In our study, Taiwan presents the most vivid picture of advantages from liberalizing trade restrictions. With liberalization in the early 1950s, a veritable explosion of trade occurred over the next two and a half decades, increasing the dollar volume of Taiwan's exports 200 times between 1954 and 1980.

The policy professional's task at this stage is to moderate these distortions, to avoid reducing the volume of trade very seriously below its potential.

5. *Some types and patterns of trade restrictions are far worse than others.* Economists' understanding of restrictive processes took a giant step forward in the 1960s with the development of the concept of "effective protection." It was found, among other things, that the same tariff on a final product can imply incredibly different

amounts of effective protection, depending on how important are imported inputs into the productive process and on how they are taxed. The only sure way to guarantee against catastrophic variations in rates of effective protection—even with moderate-looking rates of nominal protection on final products—is to make the rate of nominal protection uniform across all final products. This obviously means including raw materials and capital goods in the list of commodities subject to the uniform rate of protection. Even goods that are not produced in the country, and perhaps never can be, should still be subject to the uniform rate so as to keep "honest" the degree of effective protection granted to products in which they are inputs. For only when all *nominal* rates of protection are equal are all *effective* rates equal to this same nominal rate. Only a given uniform rate of tariff can automatically avoid capricious and distorting variations in the effective rates of protection actually achieved. Modification of tariff schedules in the direction of greater equality is thus one of the most important reforms advocated by professionals.

6. *If import restrictions become excessive, and reducing them directly is politically impossible, mount an indirect attack on the problem by increasing incentives to export*—helping to compensate for the anti-export bias that comes with restrictions on imports. The most natural instrument for encouraging exports is to rebate at the border indirect taxes incurred during production. Such rebating is explicitly approved by the General Agreement on Tariffs and Trade (GATT) and has been implemented in whole or in past by many countries.

Other devices for encouraging exports include rebate of direct taxes and even (more drastic still) direct subsidies. (Although not approved by GATT, the latter have been used by some countries and are justified up to a point on purely economic grounds). Obviously, when this neutralizing device has been fully implemented, further use of it ceases to be a corrective and becomes a new source of distortion.

7. *Make tax systems simple, easy to administer, and (as much as possible) neutral and non-distorting with respect to resource allocation.* The best tax for accomplishing all three of these purposes is the value-added tax. First introduced in France in the early 1950s, this tax has come to be the most important source of revenue in close to half the non-Communist world. Its neutrality, perhaps its most distinctive

attribute, results from the fact that as goods pass through successive stages of production, they are taxed only on the value added at each successive stage. Thus, by the time they take shape as final products, each element or component of the final product has been taxed only once. This tax is a great improvement over the sales tax system it replaced in many countries—avoiding taxation of full value at each stage of the productive chain. This obviously ended up taxing the value added of the early stages several times, and also generated strong artificial incentives toward vertical integration of productive processes.

8. *Avoid excessive income tax rates.* There is little economic justification for rates exceeding 50 percent of any kind of income. Such rates distort behavior and create large disincentives to economic activity, while yielding little revenue. In general policy professionals favor careful and prudent design of tax systems, paying special attention to (a) allowing business firms a proper recovery of capital (for tax purposes) over the economic life of an asset, and (b) preventing inflation from grossly distorting the calculation of income for tax purposes, and of the consequent tax liability.

9. *Avoid excessive use of tax incentives to achieve particular objectives.* Such incentives have been especially common in a number of Third World countries. The Brazilian law favoring investment in the northeast and in Amazonia is a good example. Under this law, a firm in another region that owes the government 1,000 in corporation income tax can take 500 of this and invest it in an approved project in the northeast, and end up paying only 500 in tax. In truth, the firm would be investing money that would otherwise belong to the government; but the firm would have claim to the income produced. Note that the firm would be better off making the investment even if it ended up extracting only 200 or 300 in return—i.e., even if it makes very bad, money-losing investments.

Another case was an investment tax credit at the incredible rate of 30 percent, which was in effect in Bolivia in the mid-1970s. Under this law, a firm could invest 1,000 yet have only 700 of "its" money involved. The remaining 300 would otherwise have gone to the government as taxes. Such a firm would probably be quite content if the investment produced a relatively quick return of 900 (viewed in light of "its" capital-at-risk of 700); yet the investment would be a disaster from an economic point of view

(900 of return on a 1,000 investment). All investment tax credit schemes share this basic flaw. It was more obvious in the Bolivian case because of the very high 30 percent rate at which the tax credit was granted.

10. *Use price and wage controls sparingly, if at all.* They are rarely (if ever) justified on strictly economic grounds, so at the very least they repesent a situation of non-economic objectives impinging on strictly economic goals, tending to frustrate achievement of the latter. Price and wage controls tend in particular to vitiate the crucial signaling role that prices are supposed to play—moving resources from lower-valued to higher-valued uses. High prices should reflect scarcity and attract resources to the activity in question; low prices should reflect abundance and help keep unwanted additional resources away. Most price controls reflect efforts to keep prices low in the face of scarcity, or—what often amounts to much the same thing—to perpetuate prices which used to prevail, in the face of drastically changed circumstances. The typical consequences of price controls in such situations are (a) production, responding to the signal of a low controlled price, fails to increase and may even decline in the face of scarcity; and (b) black markets emerge, frustrating for at least some buyers the efforts of government to keep prices low. Little good has ever come from government ventures into the swamp of price and wage controls.

11. *Quotas, licenses, and similar quantitative restrictions* on output, imports, exports, and other economic variables are often found in tandem with efforts at price control of various types. Once again, only rarely can a cogent economic justification be found for such practices; for this reason policy professionals view them with great suspicion. In general, such restrictions almost automatically indicate that resort is being had to some criterion other than price for rationing the limited supply among contending demanders. This gives easy scope for favoritism, which in practice can (and often does) readily degenerate into corruption. These evils are then added to the fact that such quantitative controls almost invariably reduce economic efficiency.

12. *Policy professionals tend to take a rather technical view of the problems associated with public-sector enterprises.* The professionals have typically seen too much of the world to take a dogmatically ideological position in connection with public enterprises. Some public enterprises, they know, have succeeded, while others have compiled records that no one will ever envy. The differences between the successes and the failures, it seems, can best be summarized by saying that public enterprises have succeeded on the whole when their governments allowed them to behave like enterprises. If the government is intent on using public-sector enterprises as vehicles to pursue other non-economic goals, then almost inevitably their success as economic entities is put in peril. The ways are countless in which governments have encroached on the economic functions of their enterprises. They have artificially kept down the prices of the goods and services that public enterprises sell. This is dramatically true for electricity, gas, and telephone companies, as well as other public utilities, often with the consequence that the companies, deprived of funds by low rates, were unable to maintain the quality of service. They have required the enterprises to pay above-market prices for inputs—most particularly for manual (blue-collar) workers, but also often for materials, via rules that preclude the enterprises from seeking least-cost sources on the international market. They have also set maximum salaries (usually related to those of high government officials) that were far below those prevailing in the private marketplace for major business executives. If under those circumstances public enterprises succeed in attracting managers comparable to those of similar private enterprises, it is only because some particularly dedicated people are willing to make major personal financial sacrifices. In addition, many public-sector enterprises are routinely precluded from taking the tough decisions that often make the difference between viability and failure—to shut down a product line, to close a plant, to lay off workers when demand falls.

Policy professionals know that all of the above possibilities represent threats to the economic viability and success of public-sector enterprises. Thus they realize that the public-sector enterprises are at an inherent disadvantage in the search for economic efficiency vis-à-vis private enterprises. Nevertheless, a number of public enterprises—in a goodly number of different countries—have somehow managed to surmount these obstacles and turn in good, at times even outstanding, economic performances. These successes have been achieved only through some sort of (at least tacit) understanding between the enterprise and the government, to the effect that the enterprise will not be forced or pressed to behave in an anti-economic fashion. Policy professionals hold up these cases as models for the rest.

13. *Finally, make the borderlines of public-sector and private-sector activity clear and well-defined. When the two compete in a given area, the same rules should govern their operations.* Arbitrary or capricious confiscations, without due compensation, tend to produce a typical and understandable reaction. In sectors that consider themselves threatened (even if confiscation has not yet occurred), private owners immediately tend to disinvest. Saving rates fall and capital tends to flow overseas, usually in a clandestine manner (via black markets in currency, under-invoicing of exports, overinvoicing of imports, and analogous maneuvers). Multiple examples exist of this counterproductive reaction. Rarely

has a country ended up being the real gainer as the result of arbitrary and insufficiently compensated confiscation. . . .

Most developing countries have public-sector enterprises scattered widely, almost throughout the industrial complex. In these cases, the professionals' rule is clear: let the public and the private sector compete freely, under the same tax laws, the same regulations, the same rules. And, in the worst cases, if a public-sector enterprise cannot compete (a) let it go under, (b) bail it out by just enough to keep it alive, but (c) never let it outcompete legitimate private enterprises, simply by undercutting prices and making losses that are then financed out of the public treasury.

X.A.4. Interaction of State and Markets*

In creating the best environment for changes in productivity to take place, governments must look carefully at how the state and markets interact. The four critical areas—human resources, the domestic economy, the international economy, and macroeconomic policy—are interrelated, and because of such links, if handled properly, promise to render disproportionate benefits. For example, a relatively undistorted domestic economy rewards those who build up their human capital more generously than does a distorted one, and microeconomic efficiency makes it easier to keep inflation low.

Investment in People

Improving people's education and health is key to economic performance, and therefore, to development. Increasing the quantity and quality of investments in people thus rightly forms a central part of the development agenda. But markets in developing countries cannot be relied upon to provide people—especially the poor—with adequate education, health care, nutrition, and family planning.

Many governments are investing far too little in human development with predictable results;

in Brazil and Pakistan rapid growth alone was insufficient to improve the social indicators, such as life expectancy, literacy, and infant mortality. In Chile and Jamaica, however, investments in people improved these indicators, even in periods of slow growth. These varying country experiences show that different levels of investments in human resource development and their quality have strongly contributed to these differences.

Competitive Microeconomy

Domestic and external competition has very often spurred innovation, the diffusion of technology, and an efficient use of resources. Japan, the Republic of Korea, Singapore, the United States, and Europe's most successful economies have all established global competitive advantage through the rigors of competition. Conversely, in much of the developing world, systems of industrial licensing, restrictions on entry and exit, inappropriate legal codes concerning bankruptcy and employment, inadequate property rights, and price controls have all weakened the forces of competition and held back technological change and the growth of productivity.

An efficient domestic economy also requires public goods of correspondingly high quality. These include, most fundamentally, a regulatory framework to ensure competition, and legal and

*From Vinod Thomas, "Lessons from Economic Development," *Finance & Development* (September 1991): 7–9. Reprinted by permission.

property rights that are both clearly defined and conscientiously protected. In addition, investment in infrastructure, such as irrigation and roads, which provide high returns, is essential.

Global Links

When international flows of goods, services, capital, labor, and technology have expanded quickly, the pace of economic advance has been rapid. Openness to trade, investment, and ideas has been critical in encouraging domestic producers to cut costs by introducing new technologies and to develop new and better products. The positive effect of import competition on firms, for instance, in Chile, Mexico, and Turkey, and greater competition in export markets on firms in Brazil, Japan, and the Republic of Korea confirm the decisive contribution to efficiency that the external economy can make. Removing barriers to international trade means that a country's own population is not a constraint to achieving economies of scale. Singapore, with a population of about 2.7 million, exports about $35 billion worth of manufactured goods annually—nearly twice as much as does Brazil with a population of about 147 million, or three times as much as Mexico with a population of about 85 million.

The international flow of technology has taken many forms: foreign investment; foreign education; technical assistance; the licensing of patented processes; the transmission of knowledge through labor flows and exposure to foreign goods markets; and technology embodied in imports of capital, equipment, and intermediate inputs. Policies to promote these flows include greater openness to investment and to trade in goods and services, as well as appropriate education and on-the-job training. Nontariff barriers, which are especially distorting, need to be phased out, and tariffs reduced, often substantially.

Stable Macroeconomy

A stable macroeconomic foundation is one of the most important public goods that governments can provide. When government spending has expanded too far, the result has often been large deficits, excessive borrowing or monetary expansion, and problems in the financial sector. These have been quickly followed by inflation, chronic overvaluation of the currency, and losses of export competitiveness. Excessive bor-

rowing can also lead to domestic and external debt problems and the crowding out of private investment. Strengthening the confidence of the private sector is now a basic component of efforts to spur renewed growth and generate employment in several countries with previous experience of macroeconomic stability, including Argentina, Bolivia, Ghana, the Philippines, and Turkey.

A government can maintain a prudent fiscal policy by looking carefully at the division of economic tasks between the government and the private sector. That is desirable in any case. In reappraising their spending priorities, implementing tax reform, reforming the financial sector, privatizing state-owned enterprises, and using charges to recover the cost of some state-provided services, governments can meet the goals of microeconomic efficiency and macroeconomic stability at the same time.

Rethinking the State

The experience in fostering investments and better policies suggests how governments and markets can interact most productively as well as avoid costly conflicts. Put simply, governments need to do less in those areas where markets work, or can be made to work, reasonably well. Governments need to let domestic and international competition flourish. At the same time, governments need to do more in areas where markets cannot be relied upon. Above all, this means investing in people, building social and physical infrastructure, and protecting the environment. It also requires a strengthening of political and economic institutions and more efficient policies for income redistribution and growth.

It has often been argued that a democratic polity makes economic development more difficult to achieve. Reform almost always comes at the expense of certain vested interests, and macroeconomic stabilization usually means at least a temporary rise in unemployment: the claim has been that only authoritarian governments can make such hard choices. This is patently false. Evidence from large samples of countries offers no support at all for the view that individual freedoms hold growth back. Neither does it endorse the notion that authoritarian governments, on average, show greater promise for achieving rapid growth. Looking beyond growth to the other elements of economic development, the lesson of experience is clear: political freedoms and civil liberties—such as a free press and the free flow of information—seem to be associated with progress in health and education in large groups of countries.

Clearly, economic policies are not chosen in a vacuum. All but the most repressive governments need to retain a measure of popular support for their actions. Often this support has been bought with an assortment of damaging policy interventions (such as high tariffs, currency overvaluation, and industrial licensing), as well as corruption and wasteful public spending. One of the most questionable categories of public spending is that on the military. In many countries it is well in excess of the combined public expenditures on education and health.

Governments sometimes intervene in the market to address political instability and other political constraints. But the result is that, all too often, the combination of pervasive distortions and predatory states leads to development disasters. A vicious circle of harmful interventions entrenches special interests. Reversing this process requires political will and a political commitment to development.

Institutional development also assists in political and economic progress. The establishment of a well-functioning legal system and judiciary, and of secure property rights, is essential. Reform of the public sector is a priority in many countries. That includes civil service reform, rationalizing public expenditures, reforming state-owned enterprises, and privatization. Related economic reforms include better delivery of public goods, supervision of banks, and legislation for financial development. Strengthening these institutions will increase the quality of governance and the capacity of the state to implement development policy and enable society to establish checks and balances.

Experience also suggests that a relatively equitable distribution of income and assets broadens the base of political support for difficult changes. But caution is needed. Redistribution through distorting prices (such as subsidized credit) can be damaging, and the benefits often go to the less needy. Many of the policies recommended are expected to tilt the distribution of income in favor of the poor.

Finally, economic reform itself is an essential means for strengthening market and state institutions and achieving development. What are the lessons on the nature of economic reform? Swift reforms help to neutralize the resistance of interest groups opposed to change; at the same time, more gradual reforms may allow time to address their concerns. Countries such as Chile, Ghana, Indonesia, the Republic of Korea, and Mexico show that packages of comprehensive reform, with at least some bold changes made at the start of the program, are more likely to succeed, whereas the social cost of not reforming rapidly can be very great, as Argentina, Côte d'Ivoire, Peru, countries in Eastern Europe, and others discovered in the 1980s. There is no single formula for success, but swift and comprehensive reforms—with strong, accompanying measures to reduce poverty and protect the environment directly—will usually be the right way forward.

X.A.5. Neo-Structuralist Agenda for Development*

From a specifically Latin American perspective, the present advocates of neo-structuralism affirm that the main economic problems and the underdevelopment still prevalent in our countries are due not so much to distortions induced by economic policies as to historical causes of an endogenous and structural nature. In the opinion of Rosales (1988), the truth of this theory is revealed in three crucial characteristics of the Latin American economy at the end of the 1980s: (a) a continuing pattern of external insertion which, given the trends in international trade and the international financial system, leads to an impoverishing specialization; (b) the predominance of an uncoordinated production apparatus, which is vulnerable and highly heterogeneous, concentrates technical progress, and is incapable of absorbing productively the growth of the labour force; (c) the persistence of

*From Osvaldo Sunkel and Gustavo Zuleta,'' Neo-Structuralism versus Neo-Liberalism in the 1990s,'' *CEPAL Review*, no. 42 (December 1990): 41–43, 45–46. Reprinted by permission.

a very concentrated and exclusive income distribution, which reveals the system's incapacity to reduce poverty.

Consequently, our countries must do more than carry out marginal adjustments to the change curve—a reflection of their exclusive preoccupation with the efficient allocation of productive factors. They must generate a dynamic process that gradually moves the economy towards the curve of production possibilities and continuously and accumulatively pushes this curve towards new productive frontiers. In particular, this movement must be capable of generating a dynamic insertion into the international economy and of responding to the need to increase the production of the poorer sectors. Hence growth demands more than a policy of liberalization designed to promote correct prices for an optimum allocation of productive factors in a static situation and in conditions of an extremely unequal distribution of income. On the contrary, the interplay of the market should be significantly complemented by dynamic action on the part of the State. Apart from its classical functions (public property, macroeconomic equilibria, equity), the State should include within the range of its administrative capacity: (a) the promotion or simulation of markets that are lacking (long-term capital markets, currency futures markets); (b) the strengthening of incomplete markets (technology market); (c) the elimination or reduction of structural distortions (the asymmetrical character of external insertion, heterogeneity of the productive structure, the concentration of property, the fragmentation of the capital and labour markets); (d) the elimination of, or compensation for, the more important defects in the market arising from output at different scales; (e) externalities and the learning process (in the industrial or external sector), among others.

These are the basic policy guidelines behind recent efforts to present a renewed strategic proposal for the recovery and consolidation of development in Latin America (ECLAC, 1990; Sunkel, ed., 1990). In line with the initial neo-structuralist analysis, both alternatives provide concrete propositions for shaping a productive structure that allows for dynamic growth, ensures an efficient insertion of our countries in the world economy, increases the generation of productive employment, and reduces structural heterogeneity. In this way, income distribution will be enhanced and the extreme poverty of most Latin Americans will be alleviated.

As regards the general guidelines outlined by Sunkel, the strategy of development "from within" seeks to take up once again and go beyond Prebisch's original challenge to industrialize. The aim is to generate an endogenous accumulation process that absorbs and generates technical advances, including the use of foreign private investment. This process will give a country its own decision-making capacity for dynamic growth. Such a strategic concept is not biased *a priori* in favour of import substitution, which would ultimately lead it into a blind alley. On the contrary, this proposal leaves open the options to orient industrialization from within to the priority domestic and external markets which are more promising for the long-term development strategy. In these markets our countries already have or can acquire levels of relative excellence which would guarantee them a solid insertion into the world economy.

In other words, it is not so much a question of demand. What is vital is a dynamic effort on the supply side: accumulation, quality, flexibility; the combination and efficient use of productive resources; the deliberate incorporation of technical progress, innovation, and creativity; organizational capacity, social harmony, and discipline; frugal private and public consumption and emphasis on national savings; and the acquisition of the capacity to insert the national economy dynamically into the world economy. In short, our countries must make a deliberate effort "from within," with the active participation of the State and private economic agents, to achieve self-sustained development.

Some elements of ECLAC's proposal for changing production patterns with social equity (1990) come very close to this conception. Development "from within" is clearly identified with the criterion of genuine competitiveness which seeks to progress from the "perishable income" derived from natural resources to the "dynamic income" derived from the incorporation of technical progress into productive activity. Likewise, both proposals stress the systematic character of this competitiveness, and therefore, the integral effort demanded by a dynamic insertion into world markets. They recognize that in the economies that compete in those markets the individual firm is integrated into a broad network of linkages with the educational system, with the technological, energy and transport infrastructure, with employer-worker relations, with public and private institutions, and with the financial system.

Another important element in both proposals is the commitment to re-establish and maintain basic macroeconomic equilibria as a necessary condition for achieving the sustainability of the development process. One of the ways of doing this is to reduce external transfers as debt service. However, such a reduction will be insufficient if it is not accompanied by domestic stabilization policies which regain control of fiscal accounts (including increased public revenues and not just reduced expenditures), and which serve as a guide for expectations through a suitable management of prices and income in order to minimize the recessive impact of greater fiscal discipline. Adjustment policies should stimulate the reallocation of resources towards the production of tradeable goods with particularly strong incentives during the first few years, especially for exports. In the interests of social efficiency, the adjustment should be gradual; in the case of high inflation, shock policies are more appropriate and inevitable. In practice this approach differs from the traditional recommendations of the International Monetary Fund, which are usually too drastic as regards adjustment and too gradualist as regards inflation (Ramos, 1990).

An essential objective which affects every aspect of the neo-structuralist agenda for development is to achieve equity and social justice and to strengthen democratic institutions. In the context of the constraints imposed by the economic crisis, top priority must be given to problems of extreme poverty and to policies designed to alleviate and eradicate it once and for all. Once back on the road to stable growth, basic medium- and long-term changes to achieve greater equity can be introduced to overcome the high degree of heterogeneity prevalent in the productive structure.

For this purpose, the State must concentrate on three priority aims: (a) to minimize the impact of external shocks on the poorer and more vulnerable groups by supporting their production and productivity as well as their income levels and social services; (b) to lower the costs of relocating manpower associated with the structural reforms inherent in the adjustment; (c) to facilitate the eradication of poverty and the excessive concentration of income and wealth, once growth has been recovered (Lustig, 1990). Also, in order to improve the functioning of the labour markets and the absorption of manpower, it is imperative to adopt a new strategy that takes serious account of the informal sector. As a re-

sult of the recent crisis, this sector has expanded and contains a high concentration of poor people. There is increasing evidence that only a small amount of resources is needed to promote their activity. There are two schools of thought on this point, which are not necessarily contradictory, but have a different emphasis and involve different proposals. The first attempts to solve the structural problems affecting the existence, duration, and operation of the informal sector; the second deals with the institutional aspects and centres its analysis primarily on the current juridical order, transferring the cause of the problem, in a certain sense, from the structural to the juridical level (Tokman, 1990). . . .

The Renovation of the State

Today the State is clearly overwhelmed by demands and its financial position is weak, especially after the debt crisis. Governments have had serious difficulties in fulfilling their basic economic functions of supervising macroeconomic equilibria, promoting equity, and avoiding stagnation with regard to foreign exchange, savings, and investment. The neo-structuralists recognize many of these problems and, following a pragmatic approach and using the lessons of experience, are seeking to build a consensus as regards the new role of the State.

According to this consensus, where the question is not so much the size of the State as its capacity for management and concerted action, its main economic function can be defined as follows: it must formulate a strategic vision of the development process; it must reorder and maintain economic incentives and relative prices in a manner coherent with this strategy; and through constructive dialogue and concerted action, it must ensure that all social and political sectors are committed to this strategy. A State efficiently organized in this way around a central function, that is, a State based on concerted action, would represent a new stage in Latin American development, characterized by an emerging democracy and the need to adjust the development strategy.

Considering these necessary adaptations and redefinitions, the neo-structuralists maintain that the role of the State needs to be strengthened in its classical functions (providing public goods, maintaining macroeconomic equilibria and equity, etc.); in its basic functions (minimum transport and communications infrastructure, health care, housing, education, etc.); and in its auxiliary functions (support for structural competitiveness of the economy by promoting or simulating markets not yet in existence, development of the scientific and technological infrastructure, elimination of or compensation for the defects of the market, etc.). These functions are more important than its entrepreneurial and productive functions which were critical in the past but today are less necessary. The State should reorganize its finances, especially by consolidating its sources of revenues through tax reform. As for expenditures, it must establish investment priorities and rationalize the public investment programme, it must also reduce subsidies, except for those that are truly redistributive. Actions to increase the efficiency of public enterprises are also important. For example, the State must limit their objectives to those that are productive. It must make them more competitive by granting them greater financial and managerial autonomy, by allowing them to charge prices similar to those of a private enterprise, by fixing "social" prices only in a limited and exceptional fashion, by subcontracting and inviting bids for auxiliary services, and by privatizing "non-strategic" productive enterprises.

Given the need for development "from within" for the support of an efficient State, it is essential that an optimal strategy for intervention should be designed. Neo-structuralism emphasizes the following elements for such a strategy.

First, since the administrative resources of the public sector are limited, its actions cannot attempt to attack the innumerable distortions of the economy, but only the most important ones. Therefore, priorities must be established for State intervention.

A second and urgent requisite is to decentralize and depoliticize public administration, since the more conflicts are resolved by the political system (as opposed to the market), or on a central level (as opposed to regional or local governments), the greater the burden of social demands on the central government, all of which creates problems for and overwhelms its capacity for action. Thus, if it can decentralize and depoliticize conflicts, this will help in an indirect but real way to reduce the overload and improve its efficiency. This rule is obviously not valid in the case of those defects and conflicts which would be poorly resolved on decentralized levels or by the market.

Finally, another important issue is that of providing institutional counterweights to asymmetrical pressure in favour of intervention. Since those who benefit from an increase of intervention are few (those who exert pressure) and those who benefit from reducing it are many (and therefore exert less pressure), intervention has a unidirectional character: it tends to increase rather than diminish. Therefore, automatic mechanisms should be created which anticipate this situation and which serve as counterweights. For example, a policy of differentiated tariffs will produce growing and rising disparities between sectors; tariffs not only become different but they also have a higher average value. Thus, when a differentiated policy is established, an average tariff can be established: every time one tariff rises, another one has to be lowered in compensation. This provides a kind of institutional counterweight against a natural rising trend.

References

ECLAC (Economic Commission for Latin America and the Caribbean) (1961). *Economic Development Planning and International Co-operation* (E/CN.12/682/Rev. 1). Santiago, Chile, June. United Nations publication, Sales no. 61.II.G.6.

ECLAC (1990). *Changing Production Patterns with Social Equity* (LC/G.1601[SES.23/4]). Santiago, Chile, March. United Nations publication, Sales no. E.90.II.G.6.

Lustig, N. (1988). "Del estructuralismo al neoestructuralismo: la búsqueda de un paradigma heterodoxo." *Colleción Estudios CIEPLAN*, no. 23, Santiago, Chile, Corporación de Invetigaciones Económicas para Latinoamérica (CIEPLAN), March.

Lustig, N. (1994). "Equidad y desarrollo." In O. Sunkel, ed., *El desarrollo desde dentro: un enfoque neoestructuralista para América Latina.* Mexico City: Fondo de Cultura Económica, México Serie Lecturas.

Ramos, J. (1984). "Estabilización y liberalización económica en el Cono Sur." Estudios e Informes de la CEPAL series, no. 38 (E/CEPAL/G.13), Santiago, Chile, August. United Nations publication, Sales no. S.84.II.G.11.

Ramos, J. (1994). "Equilibrios macroeconómicos y desarrollo." In O. Sunkel, ed., *El desarrollo desde dentro: un enfoque neoestructuralista para América Latina.* Mexico City: Fondo de Cultura Económica, México Serie Lecturas.

Rosales, O. (1988). ''Balance y renovación en el paradigma estructuralista del desarrollo latinoamericano.'' *CEPAL Review*, no. 34 (LC/G.1521-P), Santiago, Chile, April.

Sunkel, O., ed. (1994). *El desarrollo desde dentro: un enforque neoestructuralista para América Latina.* Mexico City: Fondo de Cultura Económica, México Serie Lecturas.

Tokman, V. (1994). ''Mercados del trabajo y empleo en el pensamiento económico latin-americano.'' In O. Sunkel, ed., *El desarrollo desde dentro: un enforque neoestructuralista para América Latina.* Mexico City: Fondo de Cultura Económica, México Serie Lecturas.

X.B. MARKET FORCES AND DEVELOPMENT

X.B.1. The Market Mechanism as an Instrument of Development*

In recent times, there has been a retreat both in economic theory and in economic policy from the nineteenth-century ideal of the unfettered market as a principle of economic organization. But the economic pros and cons of this retreat have been fully debated, and the economist consequently has a great deal to say about the relative merits of the market as contrasted with other methods of economic organization, and the circumstances appropriate to each.

The subject of planning and the market in economic development is, therefore, one which falls definitely within the field of the economist. Before I go on to discuss it, I must define more precisely what I mean by it. "Planning and the market" may be interpreted in two different ways. First, it may refer to the contrast between direction of the economy by Government and the policy of *laissez-faire*. This is not my subject, though in a wider philosophical and historical context of it offers much to discuss. For example, though *laissez-faire* and direction are often regarded as opposites, if one looks to the history of economic development one finds (as Professor Easterbrook has shown[1]) that economic development is almost invariably a process in which planning and direction on the one hand and freedom of enterprise on the other play their part, and are mixed. There is almost no case in which economic development has been entirely planned or entirely unplanned. The usual pattern is one of some framework of control by Government, within which the entrepreneur provides his services—a mixture of bureaucracy and enterprise, in which bureaucracy takes care

of the major risks of development and enterprise faces and overcomes the minor ones. Another relevant point that Easterbrook makes is that an economy which succeeds in finding a formula for growth tends to repeat that pattern after it has become inappropriate. For example, Britain has gone on trying to work the internationally-oriented pattern for her nineteenth-century development; Russia has been very successful in developing heavy industry but has not yet solved the problem of agriculture.

The alternative interpretation takes planning, in the sense of a general direction of the economy, as an established principle, and considers the market as an alternative to other and more direct means of detailed control. Given the general framework of economic planning, there is still a choice between two alternative methods of looking after the details. One is by direct detailed planning by a central authority, the other is by leaving the working out of details as far as possible to the operation of the market. (There is a third alternative, in which the Government is itself the entrepreneur and investor, which I shall consider later.)

This alternative interpretation is the one I shall be using: I shall discuss the question of the market mechanism as against detailed planning as an instrument of economic development. I should like to make it clear from the start that I am going to make a strong case for the market, as the preferable instrument of economic development, on two main grounds. The first is that the achievement of the desired results by control methods is likely to be especially difficult and inefficient in an underdeveloped economy; at this point I should like to remind you that a large part of Adam Smith's argument for *laissez-faire* was the inefficiency and corruption he saw in the Governments of his time. The second is that the remedies for the main fault which can be found with the use of the market mechanism, its undesirable social effects, are luxuries which underdeveloped countries cannot afford to indulge in if they are really serious about attaining a high rate of development. In particular, there is likely to be a conflict between rapid growth and an

*Reprinted by permission of the publishers from *Money, Trade and Economic Growth* by Harry G. Johnson, Cambridge, Mass.: Harvard University Press, pp. 152–53, 156–59, 160–63. Copyright © 1962, 1964 by George Allen & Unwin Ltd.

[1]Professor Easterbrook's analysis was presented in the Marshall Lectures at Cambridge University in the spring of 1956. Unfortunately these lectures have not been published, but some of the ideas are available in W. T. Easterbrook, "Long Period Comparative Study: Some Historical Cases," *Journal of Economic History*, XVII, No. 4 (December 1957), pp. 571–95.

equitable distribution of income; and a poor country anxious to develop would probably be well advised not to worry too much about the distribution of income.

I am going to make a fairly strong case for the market, because the market figures relatively little in the literature of economic development, and the theoretical analysis which economics has developed in relation to markets is often overlooked or disregarded. . . .

I now want to recapitulate briefly the various economic functions of the market and the price system as a method of economic organization. I shall be brief, as the argument is a familiar one.

In the first place, the market rations supplies of consumer goods among consumers; this rationing is governed by the willingness of consumers to pay, and provided the distribution of income is acceptable it is a socially efficient process. Secondly, the market directs the allocation of production between commodities, according to the criterion of maximum profit, which, on the same assumption, corresponds to social usefulness. Thirdly, the market allocates the different factors of production among their various uses, according to the criterion of maximizing their incomes. Fourthly, it governs the relative quantities of specific types of labour and capital equipment made available. Fifthly, it distributes income between the factors of production and therefore between individuals. Thus it solves all the economic problems of allocation of scarce means among alternative ends.

These are static functions; but the market also serves in various ways to provide incentives to economic growth. Thus the availability of goods through the market stimulates the consumer to seek to increase his income; and access to the market provides an opportunity for inventors of new goods and technical improvements to profit from their exploitation. Moreover, the market serves particularly to provide an incentive to the accumulation of capital of all kinds; first to the accumulation of personal capital in the form of trained skill, since such skill earns a higher reward; and second to the accumulation of material capital, since such capital earns an income.

The argument, then, is that a properly functioning market system would tend to stimulate both economic efficiency and economic growth. And it is important to note that the market does this automatically, while it requires no big administrative apparatus, no central decision-making, and very little policing other than the provision of a legal system for the enforcement of contracts.

All this sounds very impressive; but it is clearly not the whole of the story. What, then, are the objections to the market, how serious are they, and what should be done about them in the context of economic development? I shall discuss these questions in some detail. But first I shall state briefly the central theme of my discussion. It is that in many cases the objections to the market can be overcome by reforming specific markets, so as to bring them closer to the ideal type of market; and that to overcome other objections to the market may be very expensive and may not prove to be worthwhile—in other words, the defects of the market mechanism may on balance be more tolerable than they look at first sight.

Now, what are the objections to the market? They can, I think, be classified into two main types. One type of objection is that the market does not perform its functions properly. The other type of objection is that the results produced by the functioning of the market are undesirable in themselves.

I begin with the first type of objection, that the market does not perform its functions properly. Here it is useful to draw a distinction between two quite different sorts of cases—those in which the market operates imperfectly, and those in which a perfectly functioning market would not produce the best results.

Imperfect operation of the market in an underdeveloped country may be attributable to ignorance, in the sense of lack of familiarity with market mechanisms and of awareness of relevant information, or to the prevalence of other modes of behaviour than the rational maximization of returns from effort. In the first case, the appropriate Governmental policy would seem to me to be, not to assume from the market the responsibility for allocative decisions, but to disseminate the knowledge and information required to make the market work efficiently and provide the education required to use it. The second case implies a more fundamental obstacle, not only to the use of the market but also to economic development itself, and suggests that successful economic development requires a basic change in social psychology. To my mind, it raises a serious question of fact. Is it really true that people in underdeveloped countries are strangers to the idea of maximizing gains? The idea that they are is very common in the literature and policy-making of economic development; one of its manifestations is the implicit assumption that both supplies and demands are completely price-inelastic. I am very sceptical about this, partly because of Bauer's work and partly because at least some of the actions of Governments in underdeveloped areas presuppose that even the poorest producers are susceptible to price incentives. I personally do not think one is justified in assuming as a general proposition that ignorance and illiteracy necessarily imply that men are not interested in making money. If it is true, there will be serious difficulties in the way of economic development; but again, the appropriate Governmental policy would seem to be to educate the people in the practice of rational economic behavior.

Even if the market functions perfectly, it will not produce the best possible results by its own criteria if there is a difference between social and private benefit or cost. This type of case may be particularly relevant to economic development; it includes the case of increasing returns to scale, and can be extended to include the possibility that technical progress or capital accumulation tend to proceed more rapidly in industry than in agriculture. But it raises an immediate question of fact—whether divergences between social and private benefit or cost are numerous and important or not. This is an important question, but one on which we do not know very much for certain. The theory of increasing returns is logically intriguing, but the influence of increasing returns still has to be disentangled from that of technical progress in historical growth. Again, it is a fact that few advanced countries are not industrial; but this by itself does not establish the wisdom of a policy of forced industrialization in an underdeveloped country. Aside from the question of fact, the existence of divergences between social and private returns does not necessarily indicate a need for the government to replace the market mechanism; instead, the operation of the market can be perfected by the use of appropriate taxes and subsidies to offset any divergences between social and private returns.

I now turn to the second type of objection to the market, the point of which is not that the market does not work in the way it should, but that the results produced are undesirable in themselves. Here, I think, there are two major objections to the market. The first is that the income distribution produced by the market is unjust and socially undesirable. The distribution of income through the market depends on the wealth and talents of different individuals, and on their individual skill in seeing a profitable opportunity of employing their money or labour. If they make a wise or lucky choice, they may obtain a much higher income. The objection is that this method of determining the distribution of income is not just. But it you attempt to intervene in the distribution of income, you immediately encounter the problem that such intervention interferes with the efficiency of the market system. If people are not allowed to enjoy the income they could obtain by their decisions, their decisions in turn will be affected, and the efficiency of the system will be impaired. There is, therefore, a conflict between economic efficiency and social justice. The extent and importance of this conflict is likely to vary according to the state of economic development. The more advanced a country is, the more likely are its citizens to have consciences about the distribution of income, and to accept the high taxation necessary to correct it without disastrously altering their behaviour; and on the other hand, the higher the level of income reached, the less serious will be any slowing down of the rate of growth brought about by redistribution policies. An advanced country can afford to sacrifice some growth for the sake of social justice. But the cost of greater equality may be great to any economy at a low level of economic development that wishes to grow rapidly, particularly as it is evident that historically the great bursts of economic growth have been associated with the prospect and the result of big windfall gains; it would therefore seem unwise for a country anxious to enjoy rapid growth to insist too strongly on policies aimed at ensuring economic equality and a just income distribution. I should add that the problem may not be in fact as serious as I have made it out to be, since in the course of time rapid growth tends in various ways to promote a more equal distribution of wealth. . . .

I have been discussing the objection to the results of the market system on the grounds that it produces an undesirable distribution of income. A second objection of the same sort is that the free market will not produce as high a rate of growth as is desirable. I think there is a strong case for this objection, because people's actions in regard to saving and investment depend very much on their guesses about the future. Now people are likely to know their own current requirements better than the Government. But the requirements of the future have to be looked at not from the individual or family point of view or that of the nation as a collection of individuals, but from the point of view of the ongoing society. The needs of society in the future, many economists agree, tend to be underprovided for by the free market.

Even if the conclusion that state action is desirable to raise the rate of growth is accepted, this conclusion nevertheless does not carry with it a number of corollaries which are often attached to it. In particular, it does not necessarily imply that the state ought to undertake development saving and investment itself. Private enterprise may be more efficient than the Government in constructing and operating enterprises, so that the best policy may be to stimulate private enterprise by tax concessions, subsidies, and the provision of cheap credit. Similarly, it may be preferable to stimulate private saving by offering high interest rates, rather than by forcing savings into the hands of the state by taxation or inflation. One argument against a policy of low interest rates and forced saving is that it may in the long run contribute to the inequality of income distribution. The reason is that the poor or small savers are mainly confined to low-yielding fixed-interest investments, directly or indirectly in Government debt, because these are safe and easily available, whereas the larger savers can invest their money in higher-yielding stocks and shares or directly in profitable enterprises. There is, therefore, an opportunity here for Government both to stimulate saving for development and to improve the distribution of income.

There is another reason for being wary of the proposition that the state should undertake development investment itself—the danger that if the Government undertakes investment itself, especially if its administrators are not too clear on their objectives, the result will be the creation of vested industrial interests inimical to further development, and resistant to technical change.

To summarize the foregoing argument from the point of view of development policy, it seems to me that much of development planning could usefully be devoted to the improvement and strengthening of the market system. This does not imply the acceptance of all the results of *laissez-faire,* especially with respect to the rate of growth; but there are reasons for thinking that too much emphasis on a fair or ethical distribution of income can be an obstacle to rapid growth.

The argument I have presented has been concerned mainly with one side of the case for the market. The other side concerns the costs and difficulties of controls, in terms of the manpower costs of the administration they require, and their effects in creating profit opportunities which bring windfall gains to some members of the community and create incentives to evasion which in turn require policing of the controls. I have touched on that side of the argument sufficiently frequently to make it unnecessary to elaborate on it further.

Instead, I shall comment briefly on international markets in relation to economic development, since so far I have been implicitly concerned with internal markets. Economic development planning inevitably has a strong autarkic bias, by reason both of its motivation and of the limitation of the scope of control to the national economy. Nevertheless, international trade can play an important part in stimulating and facilitating the development process. Access to foreign markets for exports can permit an economy with a limited domestic market to exploit economies of scale, and the potentiality of such exports can serve as a powerful attraction for foreign capital and enterprise. Similarly, the capacity to import provided by exports can give a developing economy immediate access to the products of advanced technology, without obliging it to go through the long and perhaps costly process of developing domestic production facilities. Economic nationalism and excessive fear of the risks of international trade, by fostering aversion to exploiting the advantages of the international market, can therefore retard economic development unnecessarily.

One further comment on the international aspects of the market and economic development seems to me worth making. Discussion of the international side of development has been mostly concerned with commodity trade and commercial policy. But in fact one of the most important ways in which the world market system is imperfect is with respect to the international mobility of capital and labour. The problem of international capital movements has received a fair amount of attention, labour mobility and immobility much less. Now, the process of economic development in the past, especially in the nineteenth century, was characterized by vast movements, not only of capital, but also of labour, about the world. The mass movement of labour between countries has now been more or less shut off by the growth of nationalism. I believe it is important to recognize this restriction on international competition, and its implications for programmes of economic development. It means—looking at the world economy as a whole—that the solution to the problem of maximizing world output cannot be approached directly, by bringing labour, capital, technology, and natural resources together at the most efficient location; instead, the other productive factors have to be brought to the labour. To a large extent, "the economic development of underdeveloped countries" is a second-best policy,[2] in which gifts of capital and technical training by advanced to underdeveloped countries are a compensation for the unwillingness of the former to consider the alternative way of improving the labour to resources

ratio, movement of the labour to the resources. The fact that development is a second-best policy in this respect may impose severe limitations on its efficiency and rapidity.

To conclude, I have been concerned with the role of the market in economic development; and I have aimed at stressing the economic functions of the market, in automatically taking decisions about various kinds of allocations of economic resources, and the place in economic development programmes of improvements in market organization and methods. I have been advocating, not a policy of *laissez-faire,* but recognition of the market as an administrative instrument that is relatively cheap to operate and may therefore be efficient in spite of objectionable features of its operations. The general assumption on which I have been arguing is that economic development is a process of co-operation between the state and private enterprise, and that the problem is to devise the best possible mixture.

[2]See J. E. Meade, *The Theory of International Economic Policy, Volume II: Trade and Welfare,* London, 1955, and R. G. Lipsey and Kelvin Lancaster, "The General Theory of Second Best," *Review of Economic Studies,* XXIV (1), No. 63 (1956–57), pp. 11–33.

X.B.2. Market Failures—Note

In neoclassical analysis, the "Fundamental Theorem of Welfare Economics" establishes a set of conditions under which a perfectly operating market economy leads to a Pareto-efficient allocation of resources (i.e., it is impossible to make some individual better off without making some other individual worse off). This ideal model is contradicted in reality, however, by the existence of market failures. Indeed, for an LDC, many would interpret the state of underdevelopment as being in large measure synonymous with pervasive market failure. We should therefore identify market failures, determine which failures can be remedied with government interventions, and which cannot, and how markets might be made to operate more efficiently.

The list of market failures includes public goods (free riders cannot be excluded and it is undesirable to exclude), externalities (nonappropriability of benefits or no liability for costs), monopolies (especially natural monopolies, such as public utilities that are subject to increasing returns to scale), merit goods (education, health), and distribution of income (equity).

Market failure can exist in various forms:

1. The market does not function properly—the case of market imperfections.

2. The market result is incorrect—the case of externalities.
3. No market exists for the relevant activity—the case of public goods.
4. The market yields undesirable results in terms of objectives other than resource allocation.

In these cases of market failure, market prices do not exist, do not reflect the true value of what they are pricing, or are irrelevant.

A variety of market imperfections can reduce the efficiency of private market performance. The properties of efficiency in resource allocation and Pareto optimality of distribution, which characterize a competitive equilibrium, depend on the existence of a competitive set of markets. But an underdeveloped economy is to some extent an "empty economy" with an incomplete set of markets. Moreover, unlike perfectly competitive markets, a market may be deficient in the provision of information, subject to lags in adjustment, or characterized by insufficient competition among firms.

In addition, "new market failures" are analyzed in modern microtheory. Stiglitz, for instance, emphasizes informational imperfections and incomplete markets (universal contingent commodity markets do not exist). He states that

risk and information imperfections are even more pervasive within LDCs than in developed economies. With this recognition has gone [sic] a changed perception of the efficiency of a market economy. The "Fundamental Theorem of Welfare Economics," the theorem which tried to give precision to Adam Smith's invisible-hand conjecture, has been shown to be far more restrictive than was previously realized: Greenwald and Stiglitz (1986, 1988) have shown that the economy is essentially always constrained Pareto inefficient.[1]

By being "constrained Pareto inefficient," Stiglitz means that in economies in which markets are incomplete or in which information is imperfect—that is, all economies—there almost always exists some form of quite limited government intervention (e.g., taxes and subsidies, which respect the limitations on markets and information), which is Pareto improving.[2] The term *constrained Pareto efficiency* is used to remind us that in making the comparison between decentralized markets and government interventions, the government is assumed to be subjected to the same kinds of informational and incomplete market constraints that face the private sector.

The new market failures are significant in going beyond the traditional list of market failures that were viewed as exceptions to the general rule that decentralized markets lead to efficient allocation. In the new view of market failures, the presumption is reversed. It is only under exceptional circumstances that markets are efficient. According to Stiglitz, "this makes the analysis of the appropriate role of government far more difficult; the issue becomes one not of identifying market failures, for these are pervasive in the economy, but of identifying *large* market failures where there is scope for welfare-enhancing government interventions."[3]

[1]Joseph E. Stiglitz, "Alternative Tactics and Strategies for Economic Development," in *New Directions in Development Economics*, ed. A. K. Dutt and K. P. Jameson (1992). See also B. Greenwald and J. E. Stiglitz, "Externalities in Economies with Imperfect Information and Incomplete Markets," *Quarterly Journal of Economics* 101 (1986): 229–56, and "Pareto Inefficiency of Market Economies," *American Economic Review* 78 (1988): 351–55.

[2]Joseph E. Stiglitz, "Financial Markets and Development," *Oxford Review of Economic Policy* (Winter 1989): 61.

[3]Joseph E. Stiglitz, "On the Economic Role of the State," in *The Economic Role of the State*, ed. Arnold Heertje (1990), pp. 38–39.

If information is inadequate or inaccurate, market signaling will not be read or correctly interpreted by agents in the market. A certain resource allocation will occur, but it will differ from the efficient allocation based on adequate and accurate information. It can then be argued that it is in the public interest to have the government correct these informational deficiencies. The scope for the provision of public information is wide in a developing economy—from agricultural extension services to technical assistance to information on world-market opportunities.

Time lags also impede the efficient working of the market. While resources might respond to market signals, they may do so only after an unduly long delay. To accelerate the supply response to a rise in price, for example, the government may want to undertake policies to stimulate supply. This action is especially relevant for overcoming factor immobility, by means of training and educational measures and other policies designed to reduce barriers to entry in an occupation or industry. After acquiring information about a market opportunity, the economic agent must be willing and able to act on this information. To fulfill these conditions more speedily, the government in a developing country may have to undertake policies to overcome the fragmentation or segmentation of markets and improve the operation of markets. And yet while these market imperfections may prompt government intervention, it is necessary to weigh the costs of arbitrary direct administrative controls and to ensure that they do not exacerbate an already fragmented economy.

After identifying the existence of a market failure, we need to determine how to remedy it—by what type of government policy or by what measures to improve the market's operation. If there is to be government intervention, it is necessary to recognize that alternative policies may be possible to correct the market failure. Some interventions may operate indirectly through the price mechanism (taxes, subsidies), while others operate directly through quantitative controls, bureaucratic orders, direct production.

The alternative policies will have different effects. There is normally a hierarchy of policies, ranging from the "first best" to second best to third best to -nth best. For example, if an import-competing industry is truly an infant industry that creates external economies, then the industry can be protected either by a quota on imports, a tariff, or a subsidy. The quota is third best (a direct quantitative control that paralyzes the price system); a tariff is second best (price distortion with consumption loss while producers gain); a subsidy to the production activity that creates the externality is first best (achieves producer gain without consumption loss and is directed specifically to remedying the market failure).

We should note that government production is by no means the first-best method of correcting market failure. Even for a natural monopoly, indirect control through regulation, taxation, or government competition may be superior to having the government assume direct production.

In the following selections, we should try to assess the various effects of alternative forms of intervention. We should also keep in mind that informational problems and incomplete markets also confront governments in their policy making. Finally, although market failure may provide a rationale for public policy intervention, this is only a necessary—not a sufficient—condition for policy formulation. The realized inadequacies of market outcomes must be compared with the potential inadequacies of nonmarket efforts to ameliorate them: market failure must be weighed against government failure. The issue then is whether imperfect markets are really inferior to imperfect governments.

X.B.3. Steps to Making Markets Work*

Thus far, this essay has made two simple points. First, developing countries' economies are dominated by a wide variety of bureaucratic controls. Second, there may be reason to believe that the existing degree of bureaucratic control in many developing countries is detrimental to high productivity growth and hence to a rapid increase in per capita national product. It follows that growth could be accelerated either by increasing the role of market forces or by improving management of bureaucratic controls. But how is this to be done in practice? The popular notion that all that needs to be done is to abolish state controls or privatize the economy does not come close to capturing the many changes that are required.

The Steps to Making Markets Work

There are four components to a market system, and all four must be in place before one can speak of a system where market forces predominate. Three of these components are commonly discussed in the economics literature. The fourth component, the profit motive which compels producers to respond to market forces, is usually taken for granted, but should not be. . . .

The four components of a well-functioning market system are described below.

(1) Goods must be available for purchase and sale on the market. Items allocated through official licensing procedures or government-determined quotas are not distributed through the market.

(2) Prices on these markets must reflect true relative scarcities in the economy. In no economy will this condition hold for all products, but there is some point where prices are so distorted that bureaucratic commands may be a more efficient allocation mechanism than markets. Where that tipping point is will vary from country to country depending in part on the skills possessed by the bureaucrats responsible for making such allocations.

(3) The markets must be competitive. Much of economics is concerned with how price distortions in a static context lead to departures from efficient allocation (Pareto optimality). Most attempts to measure the gains from improving static allocative efficiency, however, come up with quite small numbers. Simulations with computable general equilibrium models of a major across-the-board elimination of trade restrictions, for example, result in static efficiency gains ranging from 1.8 percent of GDP if high elasticities of substitution are assumed, to 2.9 percent of GDP if low elasticities of substitution are assumed. . . .

*From Dwight H. Perkins, ''Economic Systems Reform in Developing Countries,'' in Dwight H. Perkins and Michael Roemer, eds., *Reforming Economic Systems in Developing Countries* (Harvard Institute for International Development, May 1991), pp. 33–41. Reprinted by permission.

Whatever one thinks of the assumptions underlying these simulations, they clearly do not explain more than a small part of why some countries grow rapidly and others do not. National growth rates can vary by as much as 5 to 8 percent a year. Even after eliminating differences in rates of capital formation, the residual or productivity growth between nations can range from negative rates to 4 percent a year and more.

One plausible hypothesis is that it is competition that plays a major role in generating these productivity gains. The gains from competition come not so much from better allocative efficiency, but because of better X-efficiency. Competition forces entrepreneurs to be constantly on the lookout for better ways of doing things rather than relaxing behind a state-guaranteed market monopoly. At this time, however, this possible relationship between competition and high productivity growth remains a hypothesis. There is no theoretical argument that establishes unequivocally such a connection, and empirical studies to date have not done so either.

(4) Those who make decisions on markets, notably producers, must behave according to the rules of the market. Specifically, they must pursue profit maximization or some goal that approximates profit maximization. Furthermore, the pursuit of profits must take place through efforts to cut enterprise production costs or increase sales. Profits generated by manipulating the bureaucracy to grant the enterprise favors violate the rules of market behavior and move one toward the bureaucratic command system. Economists typically take the appropriate kind of profit maximization for granted. The reality of many bureaucracy-dominated developing economies is that decision rules by producers do not come close to approximating those required by well-functioning markets. Changing these rules is one of the greatest challenges to the effective introduction of efficient markets.

The four components and how they relate to current efforts in developing countries to increase and improve the functioning of markets will be discussed one by one, but in reality, substantial progress must be made on all four before any one of them will produce the desired results.

(1) For socialist countries such as China, it is possible to speak in concrete terms about the share of inputs and outputs that are distributed through the government allocation bureaucracy versus those distributed through the market. In China, for example, material inputs supplied through the market to state enterprises rose from 16 to 27 percent of total inputs supplied during the early phase of reform in 1984–85.

For most developing countries, however, measuring the share of industrial inputs supplied through market mechanisms is a complex task. A critical area for many developing countries is how imports are handled. Are they imported by trading companies and sold to the highest bidder, or does the state issue import licenses to those it deems to have priority? When a state firm is the sole producer of an important input such as electricity or steel and demand for that input is greater than the supply, does the state firm raise its prices so that the market clears? Or is the firm expected to allocate its output to users on the basis of state-set priorities or some other administrative mechanism?

The issue of bureaucratic control applies mainly to modern sector inputs that are in chronically short supply. Surplus inputs are likely to be freely available to whoever will purchase them. Most developing countries, however, have balance-of-payments problems, which means that most imports face excess demand situations. Imports in turn are often the main source of equipment for plant expansion and for key intermediate inputs. If enterprises regularly bid openly for licenses to import these shortage items, allocation would still be through the market, but how many countries allocate import licenses in this way? Currency devaluation may also alleviate a balance-of-payments disequilibrium that then allows the free import of industrial inputs, but the number of developing countries with overvalued exchange rates is legion.

Among nontraded goods, electric power is often in short supply relative to demand. If shortages of electric power are combined with shortages of imports and both are allocated in accordance with government priorities, enterprise success will depend critically on receiving a high enough priority. Those who do receive priority in allocation will have a substantial cushion against failure. Those who do not are likely to go out of business.

(2) The issue of ''getting the prices right'' is such a central part of the economics literature that only the most cursory treatment is called for here to put the subject in its proper context with respect to this essay.

Much of the literature on price distortions deals with agriculture and the impact on consumers. These are important subjects, but are not central to the discussion here. Even when agricultural and consumer prices are highly distorted, allocation is still through the market. Given the numbers of farmers and consumers, rationed allocation through bureaucratic channels is very difficult for a developing nation to implement. Even the Chinese in the prereform era relied on the market for the allocation of many, although not all, of these goods. In other developing countries there are times when key farm inputs such as chemical fertilizer are in short supply and governments are tempted to allocate these supplies through channels they control, but the results are usually disastrous and soon abandoned.

The central issue here has to do with setting prices of investment goods and intermediate inputs for industry and of the output of industry. How large are the distortions typically found in developing countries in these sectors? The discussion of international comparisons of prices would suggest that these distortions are often substantial. Even in export-oriented Korea the departures from international prices for most domestic outputs appear to be very large. . . .

Given the magnitude of the distortions in domestic industrial input prices caused by trade policies, a case might be made that bureaucratic allocation is necessary in order to overcome these distortions. But bureaucratic intervention, for the most part, caused the distortions in the first place, and further intervention is as likely to reinforce as to offset the original distortions.

(3) Competition, or the lack thereof, is also primarily a problem for the industrial sector, particularly sectors with large enterprises. Farmers cannot form cartels, and most rural trade is competitive despite widespread popular feelings that such is not the case.

In many industries in developing countries, vigorous competition is the exception rather than the norm. Again, import restrictions often stifle competition in two separate ways. First, quotas on imports or outright prohibitions effectively insulate domestic producers from competition from producers abroad. Second, the government administration of key investment and intermediate goods has the effect of creating or reinforcing domestic cartels. When imports are allocated through quotas and licensing arrangements, the simplest procedure is to make allocations on the basis of existing capacity, essentially the same criteria used in most cartel agreements.

Bureaucracies, it should be noted, abhor competition. Competition is by nature disorderly, and bureaucracies are not well constituted to deal with disorder. The better a bureaucracy functions, the more likely it is to impose "order" on the markets it controls, and orderly marketing is another name for suppression of competition.

(4) Economists assume that enterprise managers are rational utility maximizers and that this assumption of rationality ensures that the firm will pursue profits. Risk, uncertainty, and incomplete information will modify how profit maximization is pursued, but the underlying goal remains.

In a world of extensive state ownership and bureaucratic control over both private and public sectors, enterprises may be pursuing success criteria that are not even indirectly related to profit maximization. There are two general reasons why success criteria for enterprise managers often have little to do with profits.

First, enterprise managers in state-owned firms are typically selected by politicians or high government civil servants. The criteria for selection are frequently political. The enterprise controls jobs and funds, and the nation's political leaders want to be sure that those jobs and funds are used to support the party in power. The heads of large parastatals in Africa and Asia are even more powerful politicians than many cabinet ministers. Pertamina in Indonesia or the National Cereals Produce Board in Kenya are two important but not unusual cases in point. Individuals picked as managers because of their political skills and connections will define success in their parastatal management job in terms of how that job can be used to further their political ambitions. Only rarely will profit maximization be the logical route to political success.

Private firms with boards of directors who represent the firms' owners are only partly insulated from these political pressures. If controls by government determine whether an enterprise will succeed or fail, a board of directors will appoint managers who can elicit the desired kinds of government support. In many cases, government regulators will simply leave the government to take high-paying jobs in the firms that they previously had regulated. . . .

A second reason why enterprises in a bureaucratic system pay little attention to raising profits through cutting costs or increasing sales has to do with the ease with which some enterprises can escape financial trouble. In the terminology of socialist economics this condition is referred to as the "soft budget constraint." In developing countries the phenomenon occurs with great frequency.

One reason for the prevalence of the "soft budget constraint" is that governments are reluctant to allow large enterprises to fail. In China a bankruptcy law was put forward with great fanfare, but two years later the law was still used on a trial basis and only one major enterprise had actually declared bankruptcy. Bankruptcy of a large firm throws many workers out of a job, and those workers, particularly in state-owned enterprises, may have powerful political allies. Bankruptcy of an enterprise built with government subsidies behind a wall of protectionist legislation, Krakatoa Steel in Indonesia for example, would be politically embarrassing or worse for the politicians and government officials who supported the idea in the first place. From the political perspective of these officials, it is usually easier to perpetuate the mistake by reinforcing the subsidies and the wall of protection than it is to acknowledge failure. For small enterprises and for individual farmers, on the other hand, the consequences of bankruptcy are of little political significance unless small enterprise and farm failures become widespread.

A second reason for the "soft budget constraint" facing many large modern enterprises in developing countries is the way bank loans to these firms are handled. China, again, is an extreme example of a widespread phenomenon. In China, as in most Soviet-style economies, the banks make loans at interest rates far below market levels. More important, these banks are virtually required to provide a firm with credit for any activity that is in conformity with the state plan. Government and banking rules are written to ensure that banks will always have enough money on hand to meet these needs. The fact that an enterprise may be running at a loss and is unable to pay back past loans is not a reason for refusing to tender new credits. . . .

Banking reform, therefore, is one way of eliminating the soft budget constraint. If the banks are cut loose from government subsidies and forced to survive on their commercial skills, soft loans will gradually disappear to be reduced to manageable proportions. Manufacturing enterprises, unable to cover chronic losses, will be forced to bring their costs under control or fail. Interest rates will tend to rise toward market clearing levels because banks will want the added income. Higher interest rates will reduce

or eliminate credit rationing by banks, and government officials will no longer be in a position to provide banks with "advice" on who should receive rationed credit. Thus, a thoroughgoing banking reform accomplishes much more than just allowing banks to approach a state Pareto optimum allocation of credit. A major bureaucratic lever or control over industrial and other enterprises is eliminated, and pressure is felt throughout the modern sector to improve performance and profits in order to ensure survival.

If the budget constraint facing the modern large-scale sector is not hardened, then firms will not behave in accordance with the rules of the market. If market rules are not followed, getting the prices right will not help much. Competition between firms will also be reduced or eliminated. In short, markets will not work well, and productivity growth will be slowed.

Privatization

A centerpiece of reform efforts in the 1980s is and was the pressure brought by the international agencies and USAID to privatize many formerly public activities. A look at privatization from the point of view of the above analysis is a useful way of highlighting what is and is not important in the way of reform, if the objective is to make markets work and achieve higher productivity growth. Privatization (and its opposite, socialization), of course, may not be carried out with the goal of higher productivity growth in mind at all. Privatization versus socialization is often an argument over the distribution of power between different ethnic groups or between the bureaucracy and private industrialists. Ideologies of various sorts also play an important role. Here, however, we are only interested in whether privatization leads to changes consistent with what it takes to make competitive markets work and achieve higher productivity.

Is privatization either a necessary or a sufficient condition for achieving the elimination of bureaucratic controls over the proper functioning of markets? It is certainly not a sufficient condition. A public steel mill or oil refinery sold to private sources but allowed to retain a domestic market monopoly and receive highly subsidized bank credit won't necessarily change its behavior. Success still depends primarily on support from the government. It is probably true generally that government is less willing to subsidize the private sector than it is state-owned enterprises directly under government control, but how much less willing will vary depending on the political and personal interests of the government officials involved. On average, private firms face harder budget constraints than public firms, but the difference is in degree, not in kind.

Is privatization a necessary condition? The theory of market socialism makes it clear that there is no logical flaw in the view that state enterprises can behave in accordance with market criteria. The early theorists, however, assumed that enterprise managers would behave as they were supposed to if ordered to maximize profits. Few today are so naive as to believe that this is all that is required. The objective function of state enterprise managers includes many elements other than profits, and getting rid of most of these other elements can be very difficult because political and bureaucratic goals will often be in conflict with the requirements of economic efficiency. The key, as above, is to break the connection between the government bureaucracy and the enterprise, and privatization will often help toward that goal. But there are also examples of efficient state enterprises that have managed to achieve a degree of independence of the government bureaucracy comparable to that of much of the private sector.

Many of the reforms that really matter for making markets work apply whether the enterprises involved are public or private. Creation of an independent commercial banking system that must survive without infusions of government money will tighten the budget constraints for all enterprises, not just the banks or the private sector. Devaluation of an overvalued currency to a level that makes broad-based trade liberalization possible will create competition for domestic enterprises, public as well as private. Trade liberalization will also break an important level of bureaucratic control over these enterprises, again public as well as private. Investment licensing procedures may be one area where bureaucratic control is tighter over the private sector than over public investment. In any case, eliminating or regularizing and speeding up the licensing procedures is likely to improve productivity in both sectors. Promoting small-scale industry may be desirable in part because competition among small firms is likely to be vigorous and the budget constraints they face hard; also, small-scale firms are usually, though not always, private.

There is nothing unusual or surprising in this list of reforms. If there is a departure from the normal shopping list of market-oriented economists, it is in the analysis of what these reforms are designed to accomplish. Markets are excellent vehicles for promoting decentralized decision making and vigorous competition. Closer approximations of static Pareto optimality are also useful, but it is doubtful that the improvements in allocative efficiency involved account for growth rate differentials of 4 or 5 percent *per year*. Put differently, it is possible to conceive of a situation, however unreal in practice, where all traded goods prices were set at world price levels but each private enterprise was given a government guaranteed monopoly of the domestic market, easy access to credit to cover losses, and prohibition on imports of competitive items. Alternatively, a system with distorted prices (because of uneven tariffs), but with vigorous competition both domestically and internationally between private and public firms, and domestic commercial credit available only on hard terms, is also conceivable. The question raised here is which of these systems would be most likely to produce the highest rate of growth in productivity? It is unlikely to be the former of these two extreme choices.

Government's Role in Making Markets Work

Many involved in the discussion of government's role in making markets work have argued that the government bureaucracy should get out of the task of manipulating enterprises through direct and discretionary controls in order to make state-owned enterprises, where they exist, behave in accordance with market rules. There are important areas, however, even in a market economy, where the government's role is essential to making markets work efficiently. Market-oriented reforms require that governments do these tasks well. . . .

One area where government must function well if markets are to work is in control of key macroeconomic variables, notably inflation and balance-of-payments disequilibrium. This is an empirically based statement, not a theoretical one. In theory, markets could function well in the presence of rapid increases in prices. In practice there is some level of inflation that each nation finds politically intolerable. That level may be 50 percent a year or more, as in parts of Latin America, or it may be 10 percent or less, as in China. Whatever the level, once it is passed, government will be tempted to impose price controls, and price controls will lead to queues and other forms of informal rationing. Informal rationing will be deemed inconvenient and inefficient, and the government will take steps to introduce formal controls over distribution, in effect undermining what was left of the market system and replacing it with bureaucratic allocation mechanisms.

Balance-of-payments disequilibrium caused by inflation is similar. If the currency is not devalued fast enough to match domestic price increases of traded goods, imports outstrip exports, causing a foreign-exchange shortage. The typical response to a foreign-exchange crisis in the developing world is to tighten import quotas, and the economy is rapidly on the way back to a world of bureaucratic control. Devaluation might make such controls unnecessary, but devaluation is not always politically feasible even when the economic need is clear.

All governments are responsible for collecting taxes, and all governments perform some regulatory functions. How these tasks are carried out can have a fundamental impact on whether markets function well or not. From the standpoint of making markets work, the important step is to remove as much discretion as possible from the tax and regulatory authorities. Discretionary authority in the hands of tax and regulatory officials is a common means of achieving bureaucratic control over the direction of the economy, taking that control away from the market. Discretionary authority also leads to delays, and delays are often artificially generated in order to elicit bribes. In effect, private bureaucratic agendas in this situation replace both market forces and public command direction of the economy.

X.C. GOVERNMENT INTERVENTIONS

X.C.1. Role of the State*

The Role of the State

Early writers on development, governments of recently independent developing countries, and many Western countries facing reconstruction after World War II saw a major role for the state in the production process. Behind these judgements were a pessimism about the market's ability to deliver economic change in key dimensions with the speed deemed necessary. . . . More recently the pendulum has swung the other way with a sizeable fraction of the herd of both politicians and economists charging in the direction of minimalist government, privatisation, and so on. I shall argue, on the basis of theory, of rights, and of experience, that the state's role should not be minimal. The state's emphasis, however, should not be on production. It should rather be on health, education, protection of the poor, infrastructure, and providing the right environment for entrepreneurial activity to flourish. When we add to the list basic administration, law and order, and defence, we see that a substantial fraction of GDP will be involved. It should be emphasised that the organisation and finance of this expenditure can take many forms, particularly concerning the tier of government and the relationship between government and community, but the discussion of these important issues would take us too far afield.

I begin with a brief review of what standard microeconomic theory has to say about market and government failures. First note that it would be a mistake to see the issue of the role of the state in terms of finding an appropriate balance along a single dimension such as the fraction of productive capacity owned by the state. Many activities and institutions have public and private aspects to them and many of the crucial policy issues involve finding an effective integration of the market and the government.

Five groups of arguments for state intervention in the economy may be distinguished:

(i) market failure, which may arise from many possible sources including externalities,

missing markets, increasing returns, public goods, and imperfect information;

(ii) a concern to prevent or reduce poverty and/or to improve income distribution;

(iii) the assertion of rights to certain facilities or goods such as education, health, and housing;

(iv) paternalism (relating, for example, to education, pensions, and drugs); and

(v) the rights of future generations (including some concerns relevant to the environment).

The first two groups of arguments arise from standard welfare economics but the others arise rather differently. Strands from all five provide grounds for government action for both developed and developing countries although they are perhaps stronger for the latter. Together they point fairly directly to particular areas of government expenditure, notably education, health, social support, and the environment.

There is a further substantial role for government in improving market functioning and private sector activity through such measures as building infrastructure, providing a regulatory and legislative framework which allows competition to work effectively, and intervening selectively in industry and agriculture. The market failure arguments are especially persuasive concerning infrastructure, where increasing returns, public goods, and externalities can all be of considerable importance. The arguments therefore help identify important areas for state activity, but, as we have remarked, the case for direct state activity in the production of ordinary producer and consumer goods such as steel, cars, shoes, or ice cream does not appear to be strong, at least from the perspectives included here.

Until now, we have assumed implicitly that the government is well intentioned, well informed, and competent. Governments, however, may be craven or manipulated, they may be very badly informed, and they may be incompetent. In recent years much of the profession seems to have swung towards an emphasis on government failures in contrast to market failures (see, for example, the symposium in the June 1990 issue of the *Journal of Economic Perspectives*, in particular, Krueger 1990), and this shift in the

*From Nicholas Stern, ''Public Policy and the Economics of Development,'' *European Economic Review* 35 (1991): 250–57. Reprinted by permission.

climate of opinion has gone hand-in-hand with the reduction of government activities in a number of countries, although it is not clear that it is economic analysis that has led the way. There is no doubt, however, that failures of government are indeed important and are particularly severe for developing nations.

In the recent past there has been substantial attention in development economics given to the generation by government action (including quotas, prohibitions, restrictions, and the like) of rent-seeking and unproductive activities. It has been argued that this type of economic loss associated with government activity can be very large, relative to traditional calculations of deadweight losses (usually associated with government action in the form of taxes) of the "triangle" variety (or suitable general equilibrium generalisations) which have often been viewed as quite small (1% or so of GNP is a common figure for these losses).

Rent-seeking is no doubt important, but in my judgement the empirical evidence on its magnitude has been weak. Attempts, however insecure, to measure the size of rents are generally far more secure than estimates of the resources used in the pursuit of those rents. Those resources are usually estimated simply by the magnitude of the rents themselves. This rests on the rather dubious assumption that the competition for rents take place in a manner which is perfect in an important sense. Indeed, one of the complaints about the generation of rents is precisely that they are allocated in ways which favour certain groups (such as close relations of the President) and the market for them is not competitive. While this causes aggravation, it may imply that efficiency losses are much smaller than the rents themselves. The effects, however, of the creation of special privileges for certain groups by government may be rather more pernicious and long-term than is portrayed in the simple static descriptions embodied in the arguments just described. Rent-seeking is not limited to developing countries, of course. The New Yorkers see Washington as the rent-seeking capital of the world and the Milanese have a similar view of Rome.

Let us now turn to an examination of empirical evidence. Consideration of the expenditure figures shown in Table 1 indicates that health and social security receive relatively less attention in developing than in industrial nations while defence and general public services show a greater share. It is reasonable to ask why it is

that industrial countries attach greater (proportional) weight to social security expenditures when problems of poverty are clearly far greater in developing nations. One can also argue that the share of expenditure on infrastructure (proxied by Transport and Communications in Table 1) is too low given its backward state in many LDCs and its central role in generating growth and aiding market functioning. There appears to be considerable scope for alteration of the composition of expenditures in order to improve living standards and market functioning in developing countries. In support of this view evidence is provided on the impact of various types of interventions drawn from a wide range of countries.

Health and Nutrition

The performance of China and Sri Lanka in reducing mortality rates and increasing life expectancy has been outstanding in relation to their incomes. This high performance appears largely to have been the result of public action. I shall describe some central elements briefly. China's life expectancy of 70 and infant mortality rate of 31 per thousand may be compared with India's of 58 and 97, respectively. It seems reasonable to relate this to the extensive social support system in China. Through, in large part, a strong focus on the food supply and distribution system China has attained a high level of food consumption per capita (2,630 daily calories per person in 1986) as compared with India at 2,238 (*World Development Report 1990*, table 28). In 1984 there were 1,000 people per physician in China as compared with 2,520 in India and much greater attention was paid to maternal and child health care and support of the elderly.

Aggregate income would not appear to be the main issue here. Brazil with an income per capita of $2,160 (conventionally measured), as compared with $330 for China, has only managed a life expectancy of 65 and an infant mortality rate of 61, and the gains in life expectancy and infant mortality rate in China were achieved prior to the very rapid growth since the reforms began in 1979. The crude comparisons of aggregates understates the achievements of China's support system. Whereas China provides a fairly universal system of support, reaching all parts of the country, coverage in India and Brazil is haphazard. For example, the poorest part of Brazil, the north-east which contains most of the country's poor (but only a quarter of the popu-

TABLE 1. Central Government Expenditures by Type (percent total expenditure, 1986–87)

Area	General Public Services	Defense	Education	Health	Social Security	Transport and Communication	Other Economic Services	Other	Central Expenditures (% GDP)
Industrial	8.05	7.34	8.45	9.61	37.71	5.12	7.15	16.57	31.46
Developing	16.94	11.97	14.11	6.21	12.60	7.19	16.04	14.94	25.40
Africa	18.54	8.85	15.97	5.51	8.25	7.12	17.49	18.27	25.63
Asia	17.87	12.99	14.39	5.18	7.14	11.23	19.41	11.79	19.89
Europe	16.88	13.63	7.26	6.26	23.07	6.53	21.18	5.19	29.15
Middle East	13.29	26.69	12.54	4.85	13.22	3.71	11.06	14.64	33.12
Western Hemisphere	16.09	7.53	13.98	8.32	18.77	6.80	11.88	16.63	25.04

Source: International Monetary Fund, *Government Finance Statistics Yearbook* (1989).

lation) receives few social services. Indeed, Brazil's population per physician (1,080) and food consumption per capita (2,656 calories) are similar to China's but the distribution is much worse. The distribution of services probably plays a major part in explaining the higher life expectancy and lower infant mortality rate—the weak and the old in China receive much better support than in most developing countries. Further, China has placed a great emphasis on preventive measures including education, the provision of pure water supply, and adequate sanitation.

The explanation behind Sri Lanka's outstanding performance is similar to that of China although Sri Lanka's advance came rather earlier (primarily prior to 1960). The subsidised rice system was introduced in 1942 and the promotion of primary education goes back to the early part of this century (see Drèze and Sen 1990, chap. 12). Like China, Sri Lanka has long had an emphasis on public health—a particularly important example being the eradication of malaria. Chile reduced its infant mortality from 103 per thousand in 1965 to 20 per thousand in 1988 in large part as a result of reforms begun in the early 1970s, including an expansion of primary health care with an emphasis on vulnerable groups (World Bank 1990, chap. 5).

Improved health and nutrition are important in their own right. They may also improve economic performance and there are a number of cases from, for example, Indonesia, Kenya, and India (see Berg 1987, chap. 6) where it has been claimed that improved nutrition in manual workers led to higher productivity.

Protection of Living Standards

To a major extent the reduction of age-specific mortality rates and the lengthening of life expectancy are achieved by protecting the poor from death and illness by, for example, providing clean water, adequate sanitation, and ensuring that they can obtain food. The protection of health and nutrition constitutes a central aspect of social support in developing countries. Over the last ten years or so we have come to understand much more about how protection can be provided (see, for example, Sen 1981, Drèze and Sen 1990, and Ahmad, Drèze, Hills, and Sen 1991). These authors have argued persuasively for careful integration of public action with the market. An important example is the employment-based famine prevention and poverty re-

duction schemes which have been effective where applied in India throughout this century— see Drèze (1988). The Employment Guarantee Scheme in Maharastra, as well as providing longer-term support, was also effective in meeting the threat of famine in the early 1970s. The cash-for-work element in these schemes embodies both the self-selection device of presentation for work and the provision of purchasing power to buy food. Markets seem effective in ensuring that the supply becomes available to meet the demand. Cash allows that demand to manifest itself.

Education

We have already discussed the Barro (1989a, b) results relating growth rates to human capital measured in terms of education. The *World Development Report 1990* (chap. 5) reports similar statistical relationships (although between the level of the real GDP and average years of education—Box 5.2) plus estimates of social returns to primary education in Sub-Saharan Africa (16%), Asia (27%), and Latin America 26%) based on Psacharopoulos (1985).

Infrastructure

Looking back over the World Bank's successes and failures (as seen through the eyes of its Operation Evaluation Department) in different areas of activity, Pohl and Mihaljek (1989) found investments in roads and irrigation to have been particularly productive. The *World Development Report 1990* (p. 85) indicates an economic rate of return, on average, for agricultural infrastructural projects of 17 percent. The *World Development Report 1987* noted a study of the Indian economy that put the costs of power cuts in the mid-1970s at 2 percent of GDP. In Bangladesh a study of sixteen villages found that those which had benefitted from public programmes for infrastructure (roads, power, and so on) displayed an increase in average household income approaching one-third (*World Development Report 1990*, p. 60). . . .

The Environment for Economic Activity

Health, education, and infrastructure all play a critical role in the economic environment. So too does competition. Indeed one of the critical lessons of the British privatisation experience has been that competition seems to be of greater importance than whether an industry is publicly or privately owned (see Vickers and Yarrow 1988). A number of discussions of agriculture and the environment in Africa (for example, Platteau 1990) point to the importance of the establishment of clear property rights if investment and land development are to be encouraged. A similar interpretation may be attached to the substantial negative effect of political instability on growth in the Barro analysis. Reynolds (1983), in a study of comparative growth from a perspective of 100 years or so, suggests that the single most important explanatory variable is "political organisation and the administrative competence of government" (p. 978).

The role of government in encouraging private industry can involve much more than defining property rights and promoting a competitive environment.... To take some examples from developing countries which have exhibited rapid growth, the government has been very actively involved in channeling credit to selected industries in South Korea, Singapore, and Taiwan. It is interesting that in most of the countries just cited the strategies have involved neither the command economy nor the free market. In some cases international trade has been substantially less than free. One should not view the apparent collapse of the Eastern European economies and the success of Hong Kong together with the (strong) evidence on the beneficial effects of trade-oriented strategies (see, for example, Papageorgiou et al. 1990) as establishing an overwhelming case for minimalist government and a free trade policy. Looking to agriculture we see that governments, such as those of Mexico, India, and Indonesia, have been very influential in developing and disseminating the new technologies that created what is sometimes called "the green revolution." Economic coordination and the encouragement of new ideas and adoption do seem to be areas where the state can play a productive role in assisting the market.

References

Ahmed, E., J. P. Drèze, J. Hills, and A. K. Sen, eds. (1991). *Social Security in Developing Countries.* Oxford: Oxford University Press.

Barro, R. J. (1989a). "Economic Growth in a Cross Section of Countries." National Bureau of Economic Research, Working Paper no. 3120, September.

Barro, R. J. (1989b). "Economic Growth in a Cross Section of Countries." University of Rochester, Working Paper no. 201, September.

Berg, A. (1987). *Malnutrition: What Can Be Done? Lessons from World Bank Experience.* Baltimore: Johns Hopkins University Press.

Drèze, J. P. (1988). "Famine Prevention in India." Development Economics Research Programme Discussion Paper no. 3 (London School of Economics) February.

Drèze, J. P., and A. K. Sen. (1990). *Hunger and Public Action.* Oxford: Oxford University Press.

International Monetary Fund. (1989). *Government Finance Statistics Yearbook,* vol. 13 (Washington, D.C.: International Monetary Fund).

Krueger, A. O. (1990). "Government Failures in Development." *Journal of Economic Perspectives* 4: 9–24.

Papageorgiou, D., M. Michaely, and A. M. Choksi (1990). *Liberalizing Foreign Trade.* Oxford: Basil Blackwell for the World Bank.

Platteau, J. Ph. (1990). *Land Reform and Structural Adjustment in Sub-Saharan Africa: Controversies and Guidelines.* Report prepared for the Food and Agricultural Organisation, August.

Pohl, G., and D. Mihaljek. (1989). *Project Evaluation in Practice: Uncertainty at the World Bank.* Economic Advisory Staff, The World Bank.

Psacharopoulos, G. (1985). "Returns to Education: A Further International Update and Implications." *Journal of Human Resources* 20: 583–604.

Reynolds, J. (1983). "The Spread of Economic Growth to the Third World, 1850–1980. *Journal of Economic Literature* 21: 941–80.

Sen, A. K. (1981). *Poverty and Famines.* Oxford: Oxford University Press.

Vickers, J., and G. Yarrow. (1988). *Privatisation: An Economic Analysis.* Cambridge, Mass.: MIT Press.

World Bank. (1987, 1990). *World Development Report.* Oxford: Oxford University Press/ World Bank.

X.C.2. The State and Industrial Strategy*

Industrial strategies can follow three broad lines—proactive state guidance of the economy, *laissez faire*, and a middle way.

The proactive industrializing state has fallen from fashion in recent years, especially in its traditional central planning attire. With party cadres calling the shots throughout the system under guidance from the top, planning did aid industrialization in big countries with simple economics and strong states—the Soviet Union in the 1930s and China two decades later. However, when production processes become more interlinked and technically harder to organize and consumers grow more sophisticated, absence of personal freedom and room for initiative handicaps adoption of new techniques and products, braking productivity growth. A rule-bound, rent-seeking bureaucracy becomes an additional fetter on change. The current wave of reforms in (ex?) socialist nations is aimed precisely at removing these obstacles to modern economic growth.

Proactive guidance can also take the form of widespread, intense industrial targeting. Such policies have been practiced with some success by the NICs in both their import-substitution and export-promotion phases. However, they fit less well into an economy that is small, open, and lacks industrial sophistication. In such a context, public participation in, but not direction of, the economy runs naturally between the free market and centrally planned extremes. This road was taken by small country development "success cases" such as those in East Asia since World War II and in European social democracies after the turn of the century. For the reasons just discussed, elements of the strategies appropriate to large and small countries are best described through empirical generalizations rather than the abstract model used by neoclassical economic theory. They include the following:

(1) Even with successfully interventionist strategies, the government generally guides but does not directly manage decentralized, market-responsive decision making at the firm level. Especially in developing economies where middle-level cadres are weak, highly able people to do the guiding from the top of both the state and key enterprises are essential. There do not have to be large forces of "planners," but they need political backing, which in turn rests upon effective state mediation among interest groups. Guidance takes place through continual consultation among the state and producer, export and labor organizations. It may be centralized as in the famous presidential Blue House export targeting in Korea or in MITI in Japan, or more widely spread as around the development banks, planning ministry, and producers' organizations in Brazil. The point is that flexible, institutionally appropriate channels are created.

(2) Through the consultation process there is feedback from producers to the state, which centralizes information and selectively shares it among firms. National solidarity and an ideology of growth sanction such bureaucratic transgressions of the rules of market game. If such forces do not coalesce behind an industrialization push, it is much more likely to fail.

(3) The state also provides venture capital for new enterprises, often at highly favorable interest rates. This is a form of lending that traditional, garden-variety banks are usually not willing to undertake. Development banks, if aggressive, can play a key role in providing venture capital and long-term investment finance in general. Their project search and identification procedures have to take place at the micro level—among the 20,000 commodities in the seven-digit SITC. Economists' two-digit level computations of effective protection rates and domestic resource costs are not of great use in identifying potentially profitable niches and sources of productivity growth in detail. Market knowledge and intuition are essential to the decision process. A publicly backed private sector is the institution best suited to carry it out.

(4) Targeting is universal, with the state giving support to "thrust industries." However, in success cases, incentives can be (and are) withdrawn if firms do not meet performance criteria such as export expansion or incorporation of best-practice techniques. When scale economies are possible, protection plus barriers to entry through firm licensing may be combined. If too many producers are in an already protected mar-

*From Helen Shapiro and Lance Taylor, "The State and Industrial Strategy," *World Development* 18, no. 6 (1990): 874–76. Reprinted by permission from Elsevier Science Ltd., Oxford, England.

ket, cost reductions due to rising output volume at the firm level may never be realized unless the state or a large private sector agent brings about consolidation. For an industry starting *ab initio*, the relative merits of a quota *cum* licensing and a tariff regime have to be weighed; the former may only be essential when an existing sector has to be rationalized.

(5) The most effective incentives depend on context. Some drain and others add revenue to the treasury, and this dimension must be weighed. Some are administratively difficult, provide especially strong incentives for rent-seeking, etc. Large countries on an import-substitute-then-export (ISTE) path may opt for a Brazil-type "law of similars," banning any imports that compete closely with items produced at home; smaller economies might suffocate under such blanket provisions, but then they have to manage detailed import tariffs or quotas. Cheap credit is often an effective, easily administered incentive, but the government has to have the power (and the will) to cut it off if firms do not satisfy performance criteria.

(6) The criteria themselves should be straightforward and transparent—exports and technical advance. More theoretical considerations such as potential economies of scale may be used in selecting industries for targeting, but firms should perform according to simpler rules. "White elephants" grazing happily on state subsidies are not permitted to thrive in a well-run economy. In many cases, the monsters' pale hue is due to poor management, which can be changed. In situations where a bad investment decision was initially made or a good one was overtaken by external competition (e.g., Swedish shipyards), the government accepts an obligation to retain and reemploy workers discharged in white elephant liquidations. Rapid overall growth lets this sort of transition hurt less.

(7) The issue of who bears the costs of the policies just sketched must be addressed. Vicious DUP [Directly Unproductive Profit-Seeking] circles involving the government and specific social groups can always appear—a successfully industrializing state will cut such knots and with luck compensate the losers from the fruits of productivity growth (e.g., Korean real wages rise less rapidly than productivity, but they do rise). External circumstances may make interventionist strategies more feasible in some contexts than others. A government that is fiscally constrained because it pays interest on ex-

ternal debt has few degrees of freedom; indeed, pushing exports via domestic recession to transfer resources abroad may distort the whole economic system. Successful growth may be impossible in debtor economies without reduced payments, in which case foreign institutions would pay part of the adjustment cost.

(8) There is often division of control, implicit or regulated through licensing, of sectoral production among national public and private enterprises and sometimes transnational corporations (or TNCs). Public enterprises do best in infrastructure, "base" industries, and sectors like oil and high-tech services in which, largely for social reasons, labor and management come to share a strong ethos of performance. Parastatals become bureaucratized and do poorly in sectors where performance depends on complex product and process changes; private enterprise often does a better job of keeping up.

(9) "Infrastructure" broadly construed includes health and education. Small European countries specializing in high productivity exports, Korea, and Japan all score high on indicators such as ratios of technical people to the overall population, student scores on international science examinations, and overall well-being of their residents. The educational system in many economically successful nations is geared more toward high average performance than individual brilliance.

(10) In the rich small countries and the NICs synergy between state and private sector extends to capital formation. Public investment often does not crowd out private investment from its assigned sectors, but in fact crowds it in. The implication is that state investment programs should be designed to raise productivity in both the public and private sectors. A state-directed phase of growth is not likely to end successfully unless private institutions appear to sustain high investment levels and generate and channel savings flows to finance them.

(11) Orthodox economic theory suggests that distortions should just be avoided—in practice this recommendation reduces to little more than common sense. Successful industrializers hold distortions in line, but their efforts in this direction should not be exaggerated. The NICs are not models of *laissez faire*; nor were the generations of successful economies preceding them. Long-term, large divergences from market signals are costly; in a shorter run they may stimulate entrepreneurship and productivity growth. Neoclassical theory mostly gives static alloca-

tion rules. They boil down to a list of ''don'ts,'' useful curbs to exuberance in decision making but secondary to dynamic processes of change.

Summary and Conclusions

The early optimism of development economics was misplaced—in the competence of the state, in the effectiveness of its interventions, in the independence of the national growth project from international trade, technology, and capital markets. In contrast to their predecessors, the legacy of 1980s vintage development economists will be documentation of imperfect policy making. The operating assumption of imperfect markets has been replaced by the presumed inevitability of imperfect states. Many have concluded that the former is the lesser of two evils, the implication being that governments should get out of development altogether.

The difficulty with this largely neoclassical recommendation is that its attempt to frame the question of the role of the state as a choice between evils is fundamentally flawed. This perspective only reinforces the profession's tendency to view economics and politics as distinct spheres. When economists finally discovered the state, they found it wanting and tried to reason it away. In the new neoclassical synthesis, the political and economic sciences are once again divorced.

But the state cannot be dismissed so easily. As we have noted repeatedly, virtually all cases of successful economic development have involved state intervention and improvisation of an industrial strategy. Mainstream economists deny this reality, arguing that no political ar-rangement can exist under which the state's actions will not be vitiated by DUP. But on the other hand, they want that state to act by disengaging itself from the economy. A much more sophisticated political economy is required, to *explain* and not just postulate the relationship between state and society.

Beyond these theoretical issues, changing conditions also have to be recognized. Constraints on public action have become more binding in recent years. Both foreign debt obligations and policy pressures such as International Monetary Fund and World Bank conditionality impose limits and generate internal political realignments. Fiscal costs of subsidies become more irksome at the same time as globalization of industrial activity makes it harder to attract foreign investment simply to serve an internal, albeit protected, market.

The general lesson to be learned from experience is that there are no bags of policy tricks that work regardless of context. However, that does not mean the policy decisions are contingent only on internal and external political and economic conditions of individual countries. Comparative analysis helps explain *why* particular strategies perform well or poorly in particular contexts. We have seen that successful industrial strategies have respected the boundary conditions limiting economies in which they were applied, and have incorporated the context-dependent structures discussed above. They were also flexible and adaptive. By describing boundaries and institutional dynamics within a consistent framework, we have attempted to move the intellectual debate about the state's role in development toward a synthesis that policy makers can use.

EXHIBIT X.1. Market Failure and State Intervention

Reasons for Market Failure

(i) Markets may be monopolised or oligopolistic.

(ii) There may be externalities.

(iii) There may be increasing returns to scale.

(iv) Some markets, particularly insurance and futures markets, cannot be perfect and, indeed, may not exist.

(v) Markets may adjust slowly or imprecisely because information may move slowly or marketing institutions may be inflexible.

(vi) Individuals or enterprises may adjust slowly.

(vii) Individuals or enterprises may be badly informed about products, prices, their production possibilities, and so on.

(viii) Individuals may not act so as to maximise anything, either implicitly or explicitly.

(ix) Government taxation is unavoidable and will not, or cannot, take a form which allows efficiency.

Some Problems of State Intervention

(i) Individuals may know more about their own preferences and circumstances than the government.

(ii) Government planning may increase risk by pointing everyone in the same direction—governments may make bigger mistakes than markets.

(iii) Government planning may be more rigid and inflexible than private decision-making since complex decision-making machinery may be involved in government.

(iv) Governments may be incapable of administering detailed plans.

(v) Government controls may prevent private sector individual initiative if there are many bureaucratic obstacles.

(vi) Organisations and individuals require incentives to work, innovate, control costs, and allocate efficiently and the discipline and rewards of the market cannot easily be replicated within public enterprises and organisations.

(vii) Different levels and parts of government may be poorly coordinated in the absence of the equilibrating signals provided by the market, particularly where groups or regions with different interests are involved.

(viii) Markets place constraints on what can be achieved by government, for example, resale of commodities on black markets and activities in the informal sector can disrupt rationing or other non-linear pricing or taxation schemes. This is the general problem of "incentive compatibility."

(ix) Controls create resource-using activities to influence those controls through lobbying and corruption—often called rent-seeking or directly unproductive activities in the literature.

(x) Planning may be manipulated by privileged and powerful groups which act in their own interests and further, planning creates groups with a vested interest in planning, for example, bureaucrats or industrialists who obtain protected positions.

(xi) Governments may be dominated by narrow interest groups interested in their own welfare and sometimes actively hostile to large sections of the population. Planning may intensify their power.

Source: Nicholas Stern, "The Economics of Development," *Economic Journal* (September 1989), p. 616. Reprinted by permission.

Comment: Development Planning

Beginning in the early 1950s with India's first Five-Year Plan, many countries attempted to formulate a central plan for their economy's development. General introductions to development planning were provided by Maurice Dobb, *An Essay on Economic Growth and Planning* (1960); W. Arthur Lewis, *Development Planning* (1966); Jan Tinbergen, *Development Planning* (1967); K. Griffin and J. Enos, *Planning Development* (1971); and Michael P. Todaro, *Development Planning* (1971).

In the 1970s and 1980s, however, the failures of central planning were more widely recognized. Deficiencies in the formulation and especially the implementation of development plans became acute. One critic of the practice of development planning lists the following causes of poor plan performance:

1. Deficiencies in the plans: they tend to be over-ambitious; to be based upon inappropriately specified macro-models; to be insufficiently specific about policies and projects; to overlook important non-economic considerations; to fail to incorporate adequate administrative provision for their own implementation.

2. Inadequate resources: incomplete and unreliable data; too few economists and other planning personnel.

3. Unanticipated dislocations to domestic economic activity: adverse movements in the terms of trade; irregular flows of development aid; unplanned changes in the private sector.

4. Institutional weaknesses: failures to locate the planning agency appropriately in the machinery of government; failures of communication between planners, administrators, and their political masters; the importation of institutional arrangements unsuited to local circumstances.

5. Failings on the part of the administrative civil service: cumbersome bureaucratic procedures; excessive caution and resistance to innovations; personal and departmental rivalries; lack of concern with economic considerations. (Finance Ministries are a particularly frequent target, often said to undermine the planning agency by resisting the co-ordination of plans and budgets.)[1]

See also S. Chakravarty, "Development Planning: A Reappraisal," *Cambridge Journal of Economics* (March 1991).

Among the numerous country studies of development planning, of particular interest are those related to India: S. Chakravarty, *Development Planning: The Indian Experience* (1987); B. S. Minhas, "Objectives and Policy Frame of the Fourth Indian Plan," in *The Crisis in Planning*, vol. 2, ed. Mike Faber and Dudley Seers (1972); J. Bhagwati and P. Desai, *India—Planning for Industrialization* (1970); and P. Bardhan, *The Political Economy of Development in India* (1984).

[1]Tony Killick, "The Possibilities of Development Planning," *Oxford Economic Papers* (July 1976): 164.

Comment: Governing the Market

Although many developing countries have abandoned central planning of a comprehensive character, an active public sector still exercises substantial influence in most countries. Of special interest—and subject to varying interpretations—is the role of government in the high-performing economies of Asia. Some neoclassical economists read the success of these economies as having been the result of the "invisible hand"—little government intervention and neutral incentives across activities that promote allocative efficiency. A revisionist view, however, sees the visible hand of government in "picking winners," protecting infant industries, and promoting exports.

The latter view is presented by Robert Wade, *Governing the Market: Economic Theory and the Role of Government in East Asian Industrialization* (1990). He rejects the claims of those who interpret the East Asian story as a vindication of either free-market principles or the confinement of government intervention only to promoting exports and correcting market failures. Equally, he disputes those who maintain that it all resulted from government intervention. Instead of "market supremacy," Wade's interpretation emphasizes "government leadership"—that is,

> a synergistic connection between a public system and mostly private market system, outputs of each becoming inputs for the other, with the government setting rules and influencing decision-making in the private sector in line with its view of an appropriate industrial and trade profile for the economy. Through this mechanism, the advantages of markets (decentralization, rivalry, diversity and multiple experiments) have been combined with the advantages of partially insulating producers from the instabilities of free markets and of stimulating investment in certain industries selected by government as important for the economy's future growth. This combination has improved upon the results of free markets.[1]

Wade concludes that

> a necessary but not sufficient condition for more rapid industrialization is state deployment of a range of industrial promotion policies, including ones to intensify the growth of selected industries within the national territory. This is not to say that effectiveness increases with the sheer amount of intervention, nor that it increases the more the state imposes its will on society, ignoring other groups. State effectiveness is a function of the range of options, given by the number and force of policy instruments, and the flexibility with which those policy instruments are used. Flexibility means that the capacity to intervene, as given by the number and force of policy instruments, is used to varying degrees, more in some industries than in others at any one time, and more in one industry at some times than at others, always with an eye on the costs of interventions in political as well as economic terms.[2]

What distinguishes the use of state power in the high-performing economies is that government intervened in accordance with market opportunities, national economic management was independent

[1]Robert Wade, *Governing the Market: Economic Theory and the Role of Government in East Asian Industrialization* (1990), p. 5.

[2]Ibid., pp. 370–71.

of interest groups, government was capable of undertaking an entire set of appropriate policies (especially monetary and fiscal as well as industrial), government and business had close consultations, and policy instruments were used promotionally rather than restrictively.

From the experience of the high-performing economies, we can conclude that the most important questions about the role of the state are not how large should be the public sector or how much government intervention there should be, but rather what kind of intervention. What can government do best? And in what types of policy instruments does government have a comparative advantage? Answers do not point to a minimalist state, but rather to a shift from policies of planning and control to policies that work through markets. See Tony Killick, *A Reaction Too Far* (1990), pp. 27–32.

A similar interpretation of market friendly interventionism is given by Christopher Colclough and James Manor. The problem is not "too much government" but too much of government doing the wrong things. "The task is to dismantle the disabling state . . . [and] . . . establish the enabling state."[3]

Being realistic, we should endorse the conclusion of Dwight Perkins:

> Making markets work is a much more complex process than slogans such as "getting the prices right," "privatization," or "getting rid of controls" would imply. Making markets work involves fundamental changes in enterprise behavior in most cases and substantial changes in the way government itself carries out its functions. Finally, most developing nations are never going to be willing to turn as much over to the market as, say, Hong Kong. Nonmarket controls or hierarchical commands will continue to play a major role in many sectors of most economies. Reform, therefore, is not just a matter of getting rid of such commands. A high growth economy must learn to make both the market and the bureaucracy perform efficiently.[4]

[3]Christopher Colclough and James Manor, eds., *States or Markets?* (1991), pp. 276–77.
[4]Dwight H. Perkins, *Reforming Economic Systems in Developing Countries* (1991), p. 45.

X.C.3. Social Benefit–Cost Analysis—Note

When investment resources are as scarce as they are in a poor country, the rational allocation of capital is clearly of the greatest importance. How can a developing country be assured that the resources used in a given investment project would not have any better alternative use in terms of the country's objectives? To answer this question is to appraise projects in terms of social benefit–cost analysis. Using this analysis, national governments can guide the pattern of investment either by their direct investment in the public sector or by controls on private investment.

To provide rational guidance, the government must compare and evaluate alternative projects in terms of their contribution to the development objectives of the nation. An international lending agency, such as the World Bank, or a regional development bank must also engage in project appraisal. Moreover, a private foreign investor may have to negotiate with a host government over the real worth of the foreign investment to the host economy (recall selection V.E.3). Social benefit–cost analysis is therefore extensively practiced in developing countries.

A private firm typically invests according to commercial profitability, based on its calculation of a financial internal rate of return or the net present value (NPV) of the investment based on private benefits (cash inflows) and private costs (cash outflows). But national economic profitability (social profitability) may be quite different from private commercial profitability. Social benefits and costs may differ from the firm's benefits and costs. Some of the benefits or costs may have no market price (for example, externalities or public goods). Some market prices may be less than ideal (for example, monopoly or oligopolistic pricing, undervaluation of such merit wants as education or health). And many market prices may be distorted through government policies affecting wages, foreign-exchange rates, and interest rates, and through the divergences caused by taxes, subsidies, tariffs, quotas, and price controls. Moreover, dualism—especially organizational dualism with high transaction costs and limited information—obviates the law of one price and the clearing of all markets. To the extent that a developing economy is characterized by these market imperfections and is a disequilibrium system, market price will not reflect marginal social value and marginal social costs.

A "first-best" economy would fulfill the marginal conditions of perfectly competitive equilibrium in all product and factor markets, with no uncertainty, no externalities, and a given income distribution. The perfectly competitive solution to resource allocation would then be equivalent to a Pareto-efficient allocation, reached by voluntary exchange in a market-price system. Market prices of goods and factors would equate and equal the marginal social cost (MSC) of producing and the marginal social value (MSV) of using the relevant goods and factors. For a marginal investment project, the values of outputs and inputs at market prices would then provide the correct values to be used in calculating the NPV of the project. Economic costs and benefits would not differ from financial costs and benefits, and calculations of private commercial profitability would then be equivalent to social economic profitability.

Once conditions in a developing economy diverge from those of the ideal first-best world, however, we enter a second-best world—a world in which the development practitioner must live. The development economist must be concerned with the existence of monopolies, taxes and subsidies, externalities, and price distortions. When market prices are not honest prices, reflecting real value, or prices do not exist for public goods or do not value the social benefit of merit wants, then the market prices will no longer equate and equal the MSC and the MSV of the commodities.

To remove price distortions, neutral fiscal devices of lump-sum taxes and subsidies would constitute the best remedial policies, restoring the equivalence of the MSC and the MSV with market price. But this is not feasible and is rarely undertaken. The problem, then, is to correct for the price distortions in the practice of project appraisal through shadow pricing, using a cost–benefit analysis based on imputed values—that is, on the real economic values of costs and benefits—instead of relying on the market-price data used in calculating private commercial profitability. The divergence between the MSC and the MSV has to be taken as a constraint, and the shadow prices corresponding to this constrained,

or "second-best," welfare optimum will need to be computed. Shadow pricing involves "efficiency" prices, and the calculation of a project's rate of return proceeds from the internal rate of *financial* return to the internal rate of *economic* return. Similarly, calculations of the projects NPV proceed onward from the discounted value of private net benefits (private receipts minus private costs) to the value of social net benefits (social benefit minus social cost), discounted at a social rate of discount.

If project analysis is to make its maximum contribution to a better allocation of resources, it should proceed through a sequence of seven steps: (1) project identification, (2) technical-feasibility studies (scale and technique), (3) financial appraisal (discount of cash flow analysis to determine financial internal rate of return or present value), (4) specification of the project's time streams of social benefits and social costs, (5) use of shadow prices to value the various benefits and costs at economic or "efficiency" prices, (6) choice of social rate of discount for discounting future streams of benefits and costs, and (7) selection of a decision rule for accepting or rejecting projects.

The fifth step is especially important. The concept of a social benefit or social cost has meaning only in relation to the objectives of the country's development program. Various objectives might be relevant: higher consumption or real income; better distribution of consumption or income; employment; national prestige or independence; changes in skills, attitudes, and institutions. Because project appraisal in the context of a development plan is an exercise in constrained maximization, the choice of the objective function and the selection of the relevant constraints are crucial. The shadow price of a given resource is the increase in the maximum value of the objective function where *ceteris paribus* the economy is endowed with a unit more of the resource. As such, it is the "marginal product" of the resource, the "product" being reflected in the value of the objective function. The choice of shadow prices will therefore depend on the objective function and the nature of the constraints that the economy faces.

We may illustrate the choice of shadow prices for two crucial prices—the wage rate and the foreign-exchange rate. When a dual wage structure exists and surplus labor and unemployment are prominent (recall Chapter III), it is necessary to shadow price the major input of labor. What is the real economic cost of "producing" an input of labor in a project?

Consider the following effects of employing labor and their implications for shadow pricing labor:

1. If the labor had previously been employed, there is the opportunity cost of the foregone marginal product of labor in the best alternative use. The shadow wage rate (SWR) should cover this cost.

If, however, labor comes to the modern sector from the disguised unemployed in the traditional sector, where the average product of labor is greater than its marginal product, and the market wage in the modern sector must equal or exceed this average product, then the SWR will be less than the market wage.

2. If, however, the labor had previously been unemployed, there is the disutility of effort in working instead of having leisure time. But public policy is unlikely to deem this a social cost, and the SWR would ignore it.

3. The attraction of a wage-paying job may cause excessive migration from the traditional sector to the wage-paying project. This, in turn, puts pressure on infrastructure and housing, thereby requiring more public investment. To avoid this, a higher SWR may be used to diminish the demand for labor.

4. When labor is employed, consumption will increase. If public policy puts a premium on savings over current consumption, then the SWR would be raised above the market wage, again in order to decrease the demand for labor. If, however, the government favors the redistribution of income to low-income labor, it would shadow price labor at a lower level.

In view of the effects of hiring labor, it is common in project appraisal to use a SWR for unskilled and semiskilled labor that is less than the market wage, but to raise the SWR of skilled labor who are in scarce supply. For example, in shadow pricing labor for an aluminum mill in China, World Bank analysts shadow priced manual workers at one-half actual market wages, engineers at four times the actual wage, and managerial and administrative staff at their actual wages.

A developing country's foreign-exchange rate is frequently overvalued. An investment project's net present economic value must then be adjusted by an appropriate premium, to reflect the fact that foreign exchange is actually more valuable than indicated by the nominal or official exchange rate (OER). The country's excess demand for foreign exchange is usually being suppressed by tariffs and quotas on imports. The value of traded goods is then understated relative to nontraded goods. A first-best remedial policy would be depreciation of the domestic currency relative to foreign currencies. Failing this policy, however, a second-best policy of using a shadow exchange rate (SER) is necessary to adjust traded items upward by translating their foreign-currency values into domestic-currency values by means of the SER.

The standard conversion factor (SCF) converts domestic prices to border prices in terms of domestic currency.

$$\begin{aligned} SCF &= OER/SER \\ &= 1/\text{Premium on Foreign Exchange.} \end{aligned} \quad (1)$$

A simple formula for calculating an average SER is

$$SER = OER \left[\frac{(M + T_M) + (X + S_X)}{M + X} \right] \quad (2)$$

where

M = c.i.f. value of imports
X = f.o.b. value of exports
T_m = import tax revenues
S_x = export subsidies.

This figure in brackets constitutes the premium to be attached to foreign exchange.

Consider the following example. If $M = 20{,}000$ and $T_m = 9320$, then the average tariff = 46 percent $(29{,}320/20{,}000 = 1.46)$.

If $X = 21{,}000$ and $S_x = 6300$, the average subsidy equals 30 percent $(27{,}300/21{,}000 = 1.30)$.

This is equivalent to a de facto 38 percent average devaluation:

$$\frac{9320 + 6300}{20{,}000 + 21{,}000}$$

Or the premium on foreign exchange = 1.38.

In accord with equation (2), the SER then equals OER $\times$ 1.38. And in accord with equation (1), the SCF = 1/1.38 = 0.72—that is, to translate domestic prices into border prices one would reduce them to 72 percent of their stated amount.

If the OER equals 2 units of domestic currency for one unit of foreign currency $(2d{:}1f)$, then the SER = OER/SCF = 2/0.72 = 2.77d:

1f. The SER then adjusts traded items upward by translating the foreign currency values into local currency values by means of the exchange rate of 2.77d:1f. By valuing foreign exchange more highly than the OER, the SER gives a higher NPV to any project that increases exports or reduces imports.

In practice, shadow prices can be only "ap-proximately right," given the complexity of objectives and constraints in any actual economy. Nonetheless, although the perfectionist may be left unsatisfied, the practice of project appraisal is an improvement over simple reliance on calculations of private commercial profitability, when prices are as distorted as they are in a less developed country.

Comment: Shadow Prices

The leading sources on project appraisal techniques are United Nations Industrial Development Organization (UNIDO), *Guidelines for Project Evaluation* (1972), reinterpreted by John R. Hansen, *Guide to Practical Project Appraisal: Social Benefit–Cost Analysis in Developing Countries* (1978), and I. M. D. Little and J. A. Mirrlees, *Project Appraisal and Planning for Developing Countries* (1974).

For a more detailed analysis of shadow exchange rates, see Edmar Bacha and Lance Taylor, "Foreign Exchange Shadow Prices: A Critical Review of Current Theories," *Quarterly Journal of Economics* (May 1971); Bela Balassa, "Estimating the Shadow Price of Foreign Exchange in Project Appraisal," *Oxford Economic Papers* (July 1974); and M. FG. Scott, "How to Use and Estimate Shadow Exchange Rates," *Oxford Economic Papers* (July 1974).

Shadow wage rates are analyzed by Deepak Lal, "Disutility of Effort, Migration and the Shadow Wage Rate," *Oxford Economic Papers* (March 1973), and D. Mazumdar, "The Rural–Urban Wage Gap, Migration, and the Shadow Wage," *World Bank Staff Working Paper*, no. 197 (1974).

Shadow interest rates are discussed by M. S. Feldstein, "The Social Time Preference Discount Rate in Cost–Benefit Analysis," *Economic Journal* (June 1964); Charles R. Blitzer, "On the Social Rate of Discount and Price of Capital in Cost–Benefit Analysis," *World Bank Staff Working Paper*, no. 144 (1972); and Deepak Lal, "On Estimating Certain Inter-temporal Parameters for Project Analysis" (World Bank, 1973, processed).

Elements of risk and uncertainty in project appraisal are examined by Shlomo Reutlinger, "Techniques for Project Appraisal Under Uncertainty," *World Bank Staff Occasional Paper*, no. 10 (1970), and Louis Y. Pouliquen, "Risk Analysis in Project Appraisal," *World Bank Staff Occasional Paper*, no. 11 (1970).

Also useful are I. M. D. Little and M. FG. Scott, *Using Shadow Prices* (1976); M. FG. Scott et al., *Project Appraisal in Practice* (1976); and Arnold C. Harberger, *Project Evaluation* (1976).

One of the most complex aspects of the exercise of project appraisal is the precise identification of the project evaluator's areas of control. This will affect the nature of the exercise that the evaluator has to solve and the shadow prices that will be relevant in the evaluation. How one assesses the government's ability to control different policies will alter markedly the nature of the appropriate shadow prices that are selected in project appraisal. This is illustrated, especially in the choice of shadow wage rates, by Amartya K. Sen, "Control Areas and Accounting Prices," *Economic Journal* (March 1972). To determine the appropriate shadow price of labor, Sen emphasizes that it is important for the project evaluator to consider the extent of influence that the government exercises over such relevant variables as the premium on savings over consumption, weights based on income distributional considerations, the valuation of efforts by the peasant family and laborers, and the impact of employment creation on migration.

X.D. POLITICAL ECONOMY OF GOVERNMENT FAILURE

X.D.1. Neoclassical Political Economy*

A curious facet of neoclassical [competitive equilibrium] is that it is "institution free" in that it does not explicitly refer to any state. However, a complete set of smoothly functioning commodity, factor, insurance and capital markets is presumed. Above all, it is presumed that producer and consumer decisions, particularly those involving trades across time, space or conditions of nature, are taken with full confidence that the parties to a trade will fulfill their obligations. Thus, contracts will be observed or at the very least a mechanism for enforcing contracts is implicit. Some view this feature as a strength rather than a weakness, in the sense that the informationally efficient decentralization of decisions brought about by price-guided allocations can, in principle, be exploited by a capitalist or a socialist state. Others argue that the state itself is an actor in the scene rather than an impartial enforcer of contracts.

In the dominant stream of development literature, the assigned role for the state extends beyond maintaining law and order and enforcing contracts. The argument is familiar. Because of pervasive externalities and increasing returns, some markets fail and others such as insurance and capital markets either do not exist or do not function well because of, among others, moral hazards and adverse selections. The very existence of markets and other vital institutions can be viewed as the availabilty of a public good, in the sense that their "use" by one agent does not reduce their potential use by other agents. And for well-known reasons, including the "free-rider" problem, most public goods will be underprovided if left to private decisions. However, it was believed that a well-informed government motivated solely by social welfare can correct all these market failures through appropriate intervention and also provide public goods. Further, such government intervention will also promote distributional justice. And the

literature is full of sophisticated analyses and recommendations in regard to optimal taxation of income and wealth, import tariffs, and taxes or subsidies on commodity inputs, outputs and primary factors. It is hard to say whether governments of developing countries were influenced by this advice. But it is a fact that they intervened massively. More often than not, these interventions either proved to be ineffective or worse than the disease of market failure that they were meant to cure.

From a somewhat different perspective, some students of the economies of developed countries began focusing attention on the interaction between public policies and private lobbies and interest groups. An important element of this analytical effort is an attempt to understand why some economies grow faster than others.[1] This is of particular interest from the viewpoint of economic development of developing countries. Equally relevant is the contribution of some economic historians to this research on the theory of three important institutions, viz., *property rights* that describe and circumscribe individual and group incentives, the *state* that formulates and enforces these rights, and *ideology* that relates to different perceptions of and reactions to the same change in objective situations by individuals. Independently of this, students of international trade interested in the continuing strength of protectionism in developed countries and the cost of inward-oriented import-substituting industrialization policies in developing countries also began analyzing the impact of lobbies on the creation and sustenance of protection and on the competition for the "rents" so created.

Neoclassical Political Economy

Colander christened this area of research Neoclassical Political Economy. He distinguished

---

*From T. N. Srinivasan, "Neoclassical Political Economy, the State, and Economic Development," *Asian Development Review*, Vol. 3, No. 2 (1985), pp. 40–45. Reprinted by permission.

[1]D. C. Mueller, *The Political Ecomony of Growth* (New Haven: Yale University Press, 1983); and M. Olson, *The Rise and Decline of Nations* (New Haven: Yale University Press, 1982).

it from neoclassical economics by its assumption that the state, far from being "an exogenous force, trying to do good . . . is at least partially endogenous and the policies it institutes will reflect vested interests in society."[2] Such a view of the state is not particularly new and goes back to Marx, if not earlier. What is new and interesting in the analysis of neoclassical political economists is their application of the standard tools of individual optimization to lobbies and interest groups. It turns out that the benign Smithian metaphor of the "invisible hand" guiding self-interested individuals to achieve social good has to be replaced by Magee's colorful metaphor of the "invisible foot" symbolizing the welfare-reducing effects of competitive self-interested behavior in the political arena over redistribution.[3]

The three major stands of this literature are: (i) the collective choice analysis of Olson and his associates; (ii) the public choice school of Buchanan, Tullock and their followers; and (iii) the international trade and development school of Bhagwati and Srinivasan, Brock and Magee, Findlay and Wellisz, Krueger, Mayer and Wilson. The contributions of economic historians led by North, while not belonging to this genre, address some of the same set of issues. Also noteworthy is the work of Assar Lindbeck on "endogenous politicians."

Olson observes that even though a group of individuals or firms had some interest in common and can be expected to organize and lobby for that interest, in the absence of special arrangements or circumstances, rational individuals will not act in their group interest.[4] The reason is that the services of such a lobby, like those of a state, are "public goods" such that their provision to *anyone* in the group means provision to *everyone*. This results in each rational individual trying to be a "free-rider" by contributing nothing to the group while enjoying the fruits of the contributions of others. Of course, it follows that "if there is only voluntary and rational individual behavior, then for the most part neither governments nor lobbies and cartels will exist, unless individuals support them for some reason *other* than the collective goods they provide."[5] However, since governments and lobbies obviously exist, the reason for their existence has to be sought elsewhere. Governments have monopoly over coercion and force and to levy taxes. The existence of large private organizations depends on whether they can institute a set of *selective incentives,* that is, an incentive that applies selectively to individuals depending on whether they contribute to the provision of the collective good. Small groups *can* engage in collective action without selective incentives. The reason is that in small groups bargaining is feasible and not unduly costly. Therefore, bargaining among members can lead to a group-optimal outcome, even though to begin with, benefits of an individual contribution are shared by the entire group.

Olson draws several implications from his analysis, of which those relating to "distributional coalitions" are of particular interest. These coalitions are "overwhelmingly oriented to struggles over the distribution of income and wealth rather than to the production of additional output."[6] The "free-rider" argument extended to organizations suggests that a typical lobby in a society is more likely to be a narrow special interest group or distributional coalition since the benefits of any resources spent by the group to *expand* the society's output have to be shared with the rest of society, while the benefits of the same resources spent on redistributing society's output in its favor accrue entirely to the group. Stable societies with unchanged boundaries are likely to accumulate more such coalitions over time; these coalitions make decisions more slowly than their members, slow down a society's capacity to introduce technical change and adapt quickly to changing conditions, and lower the rate of economic growth.[7] And the accumulation of such coalitions inevitably increases the role of government and the complexity of regulations.

[2]D. Colander, ed., *Neo-Classical Political Economy* (Cambridge: Ballinger Publishing Co., 1984), p. 2.

[3]S. Magee, "The Theory of Endogenous Tariffs," in D. Colander, ed., *Neo-Classical Political Economy* (Cambridge: Ballinger Publishing Co., 1984), chap. 3.

[4]M. Olson, *The Logic of Collective Action* (Cambridge, Mass.: Harvard University Press, 1965); and M. Olson, *The Rise and Decline of Nations.*

[5]M. Olson, *The Rise and Decline of Nations,* pp. 19–20.

[6]Ibid., p. 44.

[7]One has to be careful about drawing conclusions in regard to growth. A resource diversion to non-productive lobbying per se need not slow down growth. That is, a society can be operating inside its production possibility frontier at each time-point because of the diversion, yet it can grow as fast as another in which there is no such diversion. Olson's argument depends on the effect of the activities of distributional conditions on the *growth process.*

An implication of Olson's analysis is that since distributional coalitions such as cartels can operate through markets, and not only by influencing government policy, laissez-faire per se would not be sufficient to counter them, at least in a closed economy, although a free trade policy in an open economy is an effective cartel buster. However, distributional coalitions that congeal into social classes and castes are not easily countered this way. The distributional coalitions operating at all levels will slow down growth and redistribute national product, not necessarily to the poor.

Neoclassical economic theory presumes that the only social loss associated with a distortion introduced by a policy is the deadweight loss associated with it. For instance, the loss due to an import tariff imposed by a country which cannot influence its terms of trade is equated to the value of the resources that could be saved by abolishing the tariff while assuring the consumers their post-tariff level of welfare. On the other hand, as Buchanan of the public choice school put it, the loss is not confined only to the deadweight loss. For it to be so, the only response of producers and consumers to the tariff must be to shift their production and consumption patterns.[8] But in fact a person or group that is differentially affected, favorably or unfavorably, by a government may: (i) engage in *lobbying efforts* to institute or repeal it; (ii) engage *directly in politics* to secure access to decision-making power; and (iii) *shift resources* into or out of the affected activity. Resources may be employed at all three levels simultaneously while the traditional deadweight loss calculation is confined only to the last level. The analysis of all such activities falls under the rubric of public choice theory that is concerned with non-market decision-making. It "shifts attention to interactions and to institutions outside of and beyond the confined competitive market process, while applying essentially the same tools as those applied to interactions within the process."[9] Activities, legal and illegal, such as tax avoidance, tax evasion, and smuggling, are also covered by the analysis.

The essential feature of all these activities is that while they are rational and not wasteful from a private viewpoint they are often socially wasteful. The important policy implication drawn by Buchanan is that "so long as governmental action is restricted largely, if not entirely, to protecting individual rights, persons and property, and enforcing voluntarily negotiated private contracts, the market process dominates economic behavior and ensures that any economic rents that appear will be dissipated by the force of competitive entry. Furthermore, the prospects for economic rents enhance the dynamic process of development, growth and orderly change. If, however, governmental action moves significantly beyond the limits defined by the minimal or protective state, if government commences, as it has done on a sweeping scale, to interfere in the market adjustment process, the tendency toward the erosion or dissipation of rents is countered and may be shortly blocked."[10] If political allocation is to be undertaken without giving rise to rent seeking, then such allocation has to be done without creating differential advantages to some groups and, more important, a credible precommitment not to depart in future from such an allocation procedure needs to be given. This suggests that such a scheme will be more difficult to implement the larger is the size of government and the extent and scope of its intervention.

The approach of North and his fellow economic historians to the evolution of the state is also based on the importance of the structure of property rights which in their view "causes growth or stagnation or economic decline" depending on its efficiency.[11] In a "neutral" state, property rights that would emerge from competition would be efficient relative to the existing constraints of technology, information costs and uncertainty, efficiency presumably being identified with the minimization of transaction costs. In postulating a "neutral" state thereby allowing it a role and level of activity, this school differs from the extreme that is sometimes attributed to the public choice and rent-seeking schools, namely, the belief that the state is nothing more than a gigantic redistributive machine! But in the real world, the state is not "neutral" and the emerging property rights would reflect the tension "between the desires of rulers of the state, on the one hand and efforts of the parties to exchange to reduce transaction costs on the other."[12] The state emerges as a

[8]J. M. Buchanan, "Rent Seeking and Profit Seeking," in J. M. Buchanan, R. D. Tollison, and G. Tullock, eds., *Toward a Theory of Rent-Seeking Society* (College Station: Texan A&M University Press, 1980).

[9]Ibid., p. 14.

[10]Ibid., p. 9.

[11]D. C. North, *Structure and Change in Economic History* (New York: Norton & Co., 1981), p. 17.

[12]Ibid., p. 18.

monopolistic provider of protection and justice because these activities are subject to indivisibility and increasing returns to scale. It attempts to maximize revenue acting as a discriminating monopolist in setting property rights, subject only to the constraint that it does not force its constituents to other available means of assuring themselves the same services. Since the revenue potential will in general increase with the production potential of the economy, the state will also attempt to devise a structure of property rights that will reduce transaction costs and hence raise output. Yet the structure that maximizes state revenue need not coincide with the one that maximizes output and growth. Lal, for instance, argues that successive empires in North India were essentially predatory revenue-maximizing states and each fell when it attempted to extract more than the maximum natural "rent" that the system could provide.[13]

In modeling the politico-economic institution of the state and the structure of property rights as a result of a trade-off between revenue maximization and minimization of transaction costs, North's theory differs from an interest-group modeling of the political system *à la* Buchanan et al. and the collective choice approach of Olson. Also, North differs from others in assigning, along with Marx, an important role for ideology. In his scheme, ideology combats the "free-rider" problem. The individual incentive to ride free is tempered if he or she considers the institution (of which he or she is a member) to be legitimate. And legitimacy is an ideological evaluation. It leads individuals to obey rules and law, even if such obedience is not in their narrow private interest, because of an ideological conviction as to the legitimacy of the institution imposing the rules and laws. Thus, an ideology is successful only to the extent it mitigates, if not eliminates, the "free-rider" problem by acting as "an economizing device by which individuals come to terms with their environment" and come to acquire "a 'world view' so that decision making is simplified."[14] The degree of success of a particular ideology in deterring an individual from riding free will depend on the extent to which his or her perception about the "fairness" of the world (an important aspect of which is the perceived fairness of the income distribution) is consistent with the moral and ethical judgments that the ideology inculcates. In particular, an individual will change his currently held ideological perspective if his experience consistently runs counter to it. An implication of this is that when there is a dominant ideology and its tenets are consistent with behavior that promotes rapid economic development, such development will occur. A pluralistic society, such as India, with many competing ideologies is placed at a disadvantage in this respect compared with, for example, the Republic of China or the Republic of Korea.

Let me briefly sum up the discussion. The dominant view of the early development literature that a benevolent state, acting solely in the societal interest, and equipped with needed information, knowledge and policy instruments, can intervene in an optimal way to correct any market failure and launch a society along the road to self-sustained and rapid development turned out to be much too optimistic, if not completely out of touch with the realities. Instead, the state is seen to be pushed and pulled by lobbies and interest groups that are mostly interested in redistribution rather than growth and development. State interventions *intended* at best to improve the efficiency of resource allocation and channel it in socially desired directions and *at worst* by creating fairly small deadweight losses due to distortions may instead end up diverting resources to a significant extent from production to "rent seeking."

[13]D. Lal, *The Political Economy of the Predatory State,* Discussion Paper DRD 105, Development Research Department (Washington, D.C.: World Bank, 1984).

[14]North, p. 49.

X.D.2. Rent-Seeking and DUP Activities—Note

When a government intervenes by imposing physical quantitative controls over imports or by licensing investment in capacity creation and expansion, these restrictions give rise to rents in various forms, and people often compete for these unearned profits. The imposition of a quantitative restriction on imports, for example, raises the prices of imports and gives a rent to the importer who is able to secure a license for the limited quantity of imports. The importable goods can be sold at a premium as the market price becomes greater than the world price. There is a redistribution of income from consumers of the importable to the importer with the property right of the import license. The rent seekers compete in various ways, some of which are perfectly legal; but other methods involve bribery, corruption, smuggling, and black markets.

The rent-seeking activity—the use of time and resources to secure the import license—has no social value. In the importer's attempt to capture the restriction-created rents, there is an opportunity cost as real resources are used in lobbying or other rent-seeking activities that produce no greater supply of the restricted quantity. As importers engage in activities to receive the favor of government, resources that go into the rent-seeking activities are diverted from other productive activities. Although the rent-seeking activity is rational in terms of self-interest, it is socially wasteful. The marginal social product of the rent-seeking activity is less than the private marginal product, and the activity should be limited.

Consider Figure 1. In the free-trade situation, the price of the importable would be P_f, and the supply of imports from abroad would be given by the perfectly elastic supply curve S_f (a small-country case in which the country cannot influence its terms of trade). In the free-trade situation, OH would be produced at home, and HM—the excess demand—imported from abroad at the price of P_f. If the government im-

poses a quantitative restriction on imports equal to a quota in the amount HQ, then the total supply available to the economy is composed of $S + S_f'$, where the distance between S and $S + S_f'$ is equivalent to the quota HQ at all price levels. As a result of the quota, the price of the importable rises to P_q. Domestic producers of the competing importable gain. The government may gain revenue if it sells import licenses equivalent to the quota. But consumers lose through the higher price and smaller amount of consumption of the importable. It can be shown that there is a net welfare loss insofar as the decrease in consumer surplus is greater than any increase in producer surplus plus government revenue.

In addition to this net welfare loss, there is a loss if rent-seeking activity occurs in order to gain the import licenses and earn the premium on imports. The rent seeking entails cost in addition to the production and consumption costs of the quota. The additional production cost of the rent seeking itself may be estimated as equal to the value of the rents. Because a tariff can always be found that is equivalent to a quota in bringing about the same increase in price from P_f to P_q, the rents can be calculated as the rent per unit of imports—that is, the tariff equivalent—times the amount imported. Empirical evidence for a number of countries indicates that the value of rents associated with import licenses can be relatively large. Prevention of loss from rent seeking can be achieved only by restricting entry into the activity for which a rent has been created. But enforcement of laws against illicit forms of rent seeking itself involves costs.

Anne Krueger analyzes how different licensing practices of governments give rise to rents and the ways in which rent seeking is competitive with a resultant dead-weight welfare loss.[1] Jagdish Bhagwati extended the analysis to the general concept of directly unproductive, profit-seeking (DUP) activities, which yield pecuniary returns but produce no goods or services. This concept can cover "premium seeking" from industrial or import licenses, "revenue seeking" and "tariff seeking" from protectionist tariffs, tariff evasion or smuggling, and "monopoly seeking."[2]

FIGURE 1.

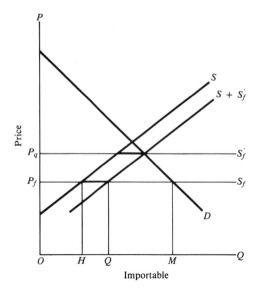

Importable

[1] Anne O. Krueger, "The Political Economy of the Rent-seeking Society," *American Economic Review* (June 1974).

[2] Jagdish Bhagwati, "Directly Unproductive, Profit-Seeking (DUP) Activities," *Journal of Political Economy* (October 1982); Jagdish Bhagwati, Richard A. Brecher, and T. N. Srinivasan, "DUP Activities and Economic Theory," in *Neo-classical Political Economy*, ed. D. C. Colander (1984).

X.D.3. Political Economy of Import Substitution*

Our concern here is with the "political economy" of import substitution. We will try to consider what constellation of social and political forces induces the state to establish a trade and payments regime oriented toward import substitution. Since it is manufactured goods that are usually the target for such strategies the issue becomes one of the promotion of industrialization behind a wall of implicit or explicit protection.

Once again it is convenient to begin with the experience of Latin America, where the process has been going on for longer than in the much more newly independent Asian and African countries, and where a sophisticated literature on the political economy aspects has grown up.

Despite several earlier attempts, particularly in Mexico and Brazil, it was not until the Great Depression of the thirties that industrialization in Latin America got substantially under way. The massive adverse shift in the terms of trade against primary products gave a market incentive to reallocate existing resources toward the domestic production of imported manufactures, particularly in the more labor-intensive and less technically sophisticated lines. The countries with larger domestic markets, such as Brazil and Mexico, naturally went furthest in this direction. This tendency was reinforced during the Second World War when trade channels were disrupted for a considerable time. When the world economy started to function normally again the terms of trade for primary products had vastly improved and much of the earlier industrialization might have now become uneconomic. Not surprisingly, however, the gains made were consolidated by protective measures, and additional more ambitious attempts at further industrialization were also undertaken.

These economic trends produced a shift in the rural-urban balance of the population, creating a mass of urban workers who had not hitherto been part of the political process. In Western Europe the political expression of this class was through mass-based political parties that entered the legislative arena and successfully struggled for the adoption of a welfare state and full employment policies. In Latin America the process took the form of "cooptation from above" rather than "pressure from below." Charismatic politicians, such as Getulio Vargas in Brazil and Juan Peron in Argentina adopted policies that catered to the interests of these new groups while retaining political power in their own hands in conformity with the Latin tradition of a dominant executive even when coming to power in popular elections, as was the case with both Peron and Vargas. The term "populism" has been coined to denote this political phase in Latin American history. . . .

The success of such regimes would naturally be judged on the basis of the extent to which they were able to "deliver the goods." The only two sources available were redistribution from the old elite, the "agro-export oligarchy" of cattle ranchers and coffee planters, and development, which in practice meant industrialization based on import substitution. Peron's policy of low internal purchase prices for beef and wheat provided the masses with cheap "bread," while Evita of course helped with the "circuses." The consequences were that the supply of exportables from the productive rural sector shrank drastically, while internal relative prices shifted in favor of the establishment of domestic industry. The intense nationalist fervor associated with the regime resulted in the use of substantial foreign exchange reserves for the nationalization with compensation of extensive public utilities, which also meant a reduced ability to deal with the inevitable balance of payments pressures of the "populist" program. The crisis finally led to the fall and exile of Peron in 1955.

In Brazil Vargas, and after him Kubitschek, were much more pragmatic and less confrontational in their political style. Rather than sharply pitting one group against another, as Peron did with the urban masses and the agro-exporting interests, they attempted to forge cooperative alliances between all of the organized segments of the population. Economic performance, particularly in exports, was thus much better in Brazil than in Argentina. The supply of coffee and other agricultural exports was not sharply cut, since there was some attempt to maintain price incentives. The state also generally seems to

*From Ronald Findlay, "Trade, Development and the State," Economic Growth Center, Yale University, 25th Anniversary Symposium, April 1986, pp. 11–18, processed. Reprinted by permission.

have put more into the industrialization drive with massive investments in social overhead, steel and other "heavy industry" sectors. The presence of an elastic labor supply from the large subsistence or traditional sector also helped. As several commentators have noted, Brazil fits well into the Veblen–Gerschenkron model of a "great spurt," with the state playing an active promotional role in the development process, albeit in conjunction with local entrepreneurs and multinationals.

Latin American development has tended to be marked by "cycles," in which a boom in investment and employment is started, with rising real wages and consumption, and industrialization stimulated by a regime that discriminates against exports. The inevitable balance of payments crisis then requires a period of austerity, with the IMF supervising the swallowing of the bitter medicine. . . .

How is the "import substitution syndrome" to be accounted for? One approach, in line with Keynes' famous quote, is to stress the influence of ideas, of some particular "defunct economist," from whose thoughts a "madman in authority distills his frenzy." . . . My own view is that ideas *per se* are not the exogenous force that Keynes makes them out to be. I prefer to proceed from "interests," with particular groups or leaders selecting those ideas that serve them best from the "menu" currently available. Thus I do not believe that any amount of lectures on neoclassical economics will induce protectionists to see the errors of their ways and to reform.

But how do we go from particular interests to protection, which must of necessity be a national policy? One possible model is to conceive of the state as an inert "black box," which can however be prodded into doing something for a particular interest, say setting a tariff, if enough resources are devoted to influencing it in that direction by the concerned parties. Other groups may of course wish to block this, which they can if they in turn are prepared to spend enough on lobbying activities. This process can be modelled *à la* Cournot, with each group making the optimal political input for itself, given what the other is doing, with equilibrium established at the tariff level corresponding to political inputs by each faction given by the intersection of their respective "reaction functions." . . .

By contrast, the tradition not only in Latin America but throughout the developing world is for a strong executive, heir to the all-powerful colonial governors and viceroys of the past, with

their control augmented by the communications technology of the twentieth century. Thus instead of a Madisonian struggle between factions within well-defined rules of the game involving checks and balances, we have a case of the "autonomy of the state," a situation in which the "ruler" is to a large extent able to implement his own "agenda" of action, constrained only by the availability of domestic and external resources.

The "autonomy of the state" need not be a mere piece of Hegelian mysticism. After all Hegel himself had the perfectly concrete nineteenth-century Prussian state in mind, in which the king could exercise almost absolute power, with the bureaucracy as a "universal class" suspended above the petty concern of "civil society." It is not surprising that several Latin American social scientists have put forward a model of the "bureaucratic authoritarian" state reminiscent of this Hegelian one, with a faceless junta instead of an individual "strong man" at the apex of the pyramid, exercising power through, and in the interest of, the military and civilian bureaucracy itself. The self-imposed tasks of the regime are "national security," with its concomitant of "internal order," and "development," which serves both as an end in itself and, if successful, as a means to further expansion of the role of the state, and therefore of the bureaucracy itself. The Parkinson-Niskanen model of departmental or corporate bureaucracy can be applied to the state as a whole, to produce the concept of a particular type of "Leviathan," a Frankenstein monster in which the entities such as army and civil service, ostensibly created to serve the "people's will," instead arrogate to themselves the task of defining the goals of the state, which they make to coincide with their own.

The only constraint on the Leviathan's appetite for the pursuit of what it sees as its "tasks" is revenue. Given the well-known difficulties attendant upon collection of corporate and personal income and other direct taxes in developing countries, particularly in Latin America, one is left largely with taxes of one sort or another on foreign trade and of course, the inflation tax. The stubborn persistence of inflationary cycles in the Latin American context is proof that the process is driven by something more deep-seated than governmental ignorance of the quantity theory of money. Indeed, it may be that a "rational" government will systematically use the inflationary tax to fleece its own populace. Once powerful inflationary forces have been generated it is almost impossible to prevent them from distorting the structure of relative prices. If adjustment of the exchange rate tends to lag, as it generally does, a bias is introduced against tradable goods. Quantitative import restrictions imposed to stem the loss of foreign exchange reserves tilt relative prices against exportables within the tradable sector itself. Combined with high maximum revenue tariffs and export taxes, also imposed to satisfy the Leviathan's appetite for revenue, the outcome can be very heavy discrimination against exports, in short the "import substitution syndrome," which thus appears in this analysis as a by-product of the revenue- or expenditure-maximizing activities of the Leviathan.

Urban manufacturing interests would of course be delighted with this outcome, since it provides the market incentive for investment and profits on their part. Since the resultant structure of industrialization is likely to be haphazard, leaving all sorts of gaps, there are likely to be calls for "coordination," "rationalization," "deepening," etc. The end result of all this is of course that there are more "tasks" for the bureaucracy to perform—and so on and so on and so on. Democratic reformers, who complain that various sections of the masses are being impoverished, may also have their criticisms answered by yet more distortionary schemes ostensibly designed to protect the living standards of the poor and deprived but in reality further reducing real national income.

The military is always a key component of the bureaucracy and, for a number of obvious reasons, its influence will be to encourage the more extravagant aspects of the import substitution syndrome. For one thing, there is the "national defense" argument for self-sufficiency in armaments, which leads to the demand for domestic production of the necessary metallurgical and chemical inputs. Military intellectuals and staff officers also tend to be fascinated with technology for its own sake regardless of the humdrum economic criterion of cost-effectiveness.

X.D.4. Political Economy of Agricultural Policy*

Governments in Africa intervene in agricultural markets in characteristic ways. They tend to lower the prices offered for agricultural commodities. They tend to increase the prices which farmers must pay for the goods they buy for consumption purposes. And although African governments subsidize the prices that farmers pay for the goods they use in farming, the benefits of these subsidies are appropriated by the rich few—the small minority of large-scale farmers.

There are other characteristics of patterns of government market intervention. Insofar as African governments seek increased farm production, their policies are project-based rather than price-based. Insofar as they employ prices to strengthen production incentives, they tend to encourage production by lowering the prices of inputs (i.e., by lowering costs) rather than by increasing the prices of products (i.e., by increasing revenues). A last characteristic is that governments intervene in ways that promote inefficiency; they create major price distortions, reduce competition in markets, and invest in poorly conceived agricultural projects. In all of these behaviors, it should be stressed, the conduct of African governments resembles the conduct of governments in other parts of the world.

The Regulation of Commodity Markets

It is useful to distinguish between two kinds of agricultural commodities: food crops, many of which could be directly consumed on the farm, and cash crops, few of which are directly consumable and which are instead marketed as a source of cash income. Many cash crops are in fact exported; they provide not only a source of cash incomes for farm families but also a source of foreign exchange for the national economies of Africa.

*Reprinted by permission of Westview Press from "Governments and Agricultural Markets in Africa" by Robert H. Bates, *The Role of Markets in the World Food Economy*, edited by D. Gale Johnson and G. Edward Schuh. © Westview Press, Boulder, Colorado, 1983.

Export Crops

An important feature of the African economies is the nature of the marketing systems employed for the purchase and exportation of cash crops. The crops are grown by private farm families, but they are then sold through official, state-controlled marketing channels. At the local level, these channels may take the form of licensed agents or registered private buyers; they may also take the form of cooperative societies or farmers' associations. But the regulated nature of the marketing system is clearly revealed in the fact that these primary purchasing agencies can in most cases sell to but one purchaser: a state-owned body, commonly known as a marketing board. . . .

Upon independence, many African governments found themselves the inheritors of bureaucracies that held a legal monopoly over the purchase and export of commodities in the most valuable sector of their domestic economies. These new states possessed extremely powerful instruments of market intervention. They could purchase export crops at an administratively set, low domestic price; they could then market these crops at the prevailing world price; and they could accumulate the revenues generated by the difference between the domestic and world prices for these commodities.

Government Taxation. Initially, the revenues accumulated by the marketing boards were to be kept in the form of price assistance funds and used for the benefit of the farmers. At times of low international prices, they were to be employed to support domestic prices and so shelter the farmers from the vagaries of the world market. In the case of the Western Nigerian marketing board, for example, 70 percent of the board's revenues were to be retained for such purposes. But commitments to employ the funds for the benefit of the farmers proved short-lived. They were overborn by ambitions to implement development programs and by political pressures brought to bear upon governments from nonagricultural sectors of the economy. . . .

The movement from an instrument of price stabilization, largely for the benefit of farmers, to an instrument of taxation, with the diversion of revenues to nonfarm sectors, can be seen as well in changes in the pricing formulas employed by the marketing boards. Insofar as the boards were employed to stabilize producer prices, the domestic prices—i.e., the price offered the farmers—should have moved independently of the world prices; moreover, a policy of price stabilization implies that domestic prices should have at times exceeded world prices, as the marketing board attempted to protect farmers from falls in the world price. But investigations clearly suggest that what was being stabilized was not the domestic price but rather the difference between the domestic and world price, i.e. the tax on the farmers' income.

Food Crops

African governments also intervene in the market for food crops. And, once again, they tend to do so in ways that lower the price of agricultural commodities.

Price Controls. One way in which African governments attempt to secure low-priced food is by instructing bureaucracies to purchase food crops at government-mandated prices. A recent study by the U.S. Department of Agriculture examined the marketing systems for food crops in Africa and discovered a high incidence of government market intervention. In the case of three of the food crops studied, in over 50 percent of the countries in which the crop was grown, the government had imposed a system of producer price controls; in over 20 percent the government maintained an official monopsony for the purchase of that food crop.

Projects. In order to keep food prices low, governments take additional measures. In particular, they attempt to increase food supplies, either by importing food or by investing in food production projects.

Foreign exchange is scarce. Especially since the rise of petroleum prices, the cost of imports is high. To conserve foreign exchange, African governments therefore attempt to become self-sufficient in food. But they seek to do so within the context of a low-price policy; and therefore invest in projects that will yield increased food production.

In some cases, governments turn public institutions into food production units: youth league and prison farms provide illustrative cases. In other instances, they invest in large-scale efforts to furnish scarce factors of production. In Africa, water is commonly scarce and governments invest heavily in river basin development schemes and irrigation projects. Capital equipment is also scarce; by purchasing and operating farm machinery, governments attempt to promote farm production. Some governments invest in projects to provide particular crops; rice production in the case of Kenya, for example, or wheat production in the case of Tanzania. In other instances, governments divert large portions of their capital budgets to the financing of food production schemes.

Nonbureaucratic Forms of Intervention

Thus far I have emphasized direct forms of government intervention. But there is an equally important, less direct form of intervention: the overvaluation of the domestic currency.

Most governments in Africa maintain an overvalued currency. One result is to lower the prices received by the exporters of cash crops. For a given dollar earned abroad, the exporters of cash crops receive fewer units of the domestic currency. In part, overvaluation also inflicts losses on governments; deriving a portion of their revenues from taxes levied by the marketing boards, the governments command less domestic purchasing power as a result of overvaluation. But because their instruments of taxation are monopolistic agencies, African governments are able to transfer much of the burden of overvaluation: they pass it on to farmers in the form of lower prices.

In addition to lowering the earnings of export agriculture, overvaluation lowers the prices paid for foreign imports. This is, of course, part of the rationale for a policy of overvaluation: it cheapens the costs of importing plant, machinery and other capital equipment needed to build the base for a nascent industrial sector. But things other than plant and equipment can be imported, and among these other commodities is food. As a consequence of overvaluation, African food producers face higher levels of competition from foreign food stuffs. In search of low-priced food, African governments do little to protect their domestic food markets from foreign products—whose prices have artificially been lowered as a consequence of public policies.

Industrial Goods

In the markets for the crops they produce, African farmers therefore face a variety of government policies that serve to lower farm prices. In the markets for the goods they consume, however, they face a highly contrasting situation: they confront consumer prices that are supported by government policy.

In promoting industrial development, African governments adopt commercial policies that shelter local industries from foreign competition. To some degree, they impose tariff barriers between the local and international markets. To an even greater extent, they employ quantitative restrictions. Quotas, import licenses, and permits to acquire and use foreign exchange: all are employed to conserve foreign exchange on the one hand, while on the other hand they protect the domestic market for local industries. In connection with the maintenance of overvalued currencies, these trade barriers create incentives for investors to import capital equipment and to manufacture goods domestically that formerly had been imported from abroad.

Not only do government policies shelter industries from low-cost foreign competition; they shelter them from domestic competition as well. In part, protection from domestic competition is a by-product of protection from foreign competition. The policy of allocating licenses to import in conformity with historic market shares provides an example. The limitation of competition results from other policies as well. In exchange for commitments to invest, governments guarantee periods of freedom from competition. Moreover, governments tend to favor larger projects; seeking infusions of scarce capital, they tend to back those proposals that promise the largest capital investments. Given the small markets typical of most African nations, the result is that investors create plants whose output represents a very large fraction of the domestic market; a small number of firms thus come to dominate the industry. Lastly, particularly where state enterprises are concerned, governments sometimes confer virtual monopoly rights upon particular enterprises. The consequence of all these measures is to shelter industries from domestic competition.

Discussion

Governments intervene in the market for products in an effort to lower prices. They adopt policies that tend to raise the price of the goods farmers buy. And while they attempt to lower the costs of farm inputs, the benefits of this policy are experienced by a small minority of the richer farmers. Agricultural policies in Africa thus tend to be adverse to the interests of most producers.

We may accept for the moment the premise that states act as agencies for maximizing the social welfare. Nonetheless, we are left with the fact that this premise is not very useful, particularly when applied to food policy, for it yields little by way of predictive power. To secure social objectives, governments can choose among a wide variety of policy instruments; and knowledge of the public objectives of a program often does not allow us to predict or to explain the particular policy instrument chosen to implement it.

For example, an important objective of African governments is to increase food supplies. To secure greater supplies, governments could offer higher prices for food or invest the same amount of resources in food production projects. There is every reason to believe that the former is a more efficient way of securing the objective. But governments in Africa systematically prefer project-based policies to price-based policies.

To strengthen the incentives for food production, African governments can increase the price of farm products or subsidize the costs of farm implements. Either would result in higher profits for producers. But governments prefer the latter policy.

To increase output, African governments finance food production programs. But given the level of resources devoted to these programs, they often create too many projects; the programs then fail because resources have been spread too thin. Such behavior is nonsensical, given the social objectives of the program.

To take a last example: In the face of shortages, governments can either allow prices to rise or they can maintain lower prices while imposing quotas. In a variety of markets of significance to agricultural producers African governments choose to ration. They exhibit a systematic preference for the use of this technique—a preference that cannot readily be accounted for in terms of their development objectives.

A major problem with an approach that tries to explain agricultural policies in terms of the social objectives of governments, then, is that the social objectives underlying a policy program rarely determine the particular form the policies assume. The approach thus yields little predictive power. There is a second major difficulty. Insofar as this approach does make predictions, they are often wrong.

This problem is disclosed by the self-defeating nature of many government policies. To secure cheaper food, for example, governments lower prices to producers; but this only creates shortages which lead to *higher* food prices. To increase resources with which to finance programs of development, governments increase agricultural taxes; but this leads to declines in production and to shortfalls in public finances and foreign exchange. And to secure rapid development, governments seek to transfer resources from agriculture to industry; but this set of policies has instead led to reduced rates of growth and to economic stagnation.

The policy instruments chosen to secure social objectives are thus often inconsistent with the attainment of these objectives. The approach thus makes false predictions and it should therefore be rejected. And yet the choices of governments are clearly stable; despite undermining their own goals, governments continue to employ these policy instruments. Some kind of explanation is required, and other kinds of theories must therefore be explored.

There are other grounds for rejecting the development economics approach to the explanation of governmental behavior. One is that the approach assumes autonomy on the part of governments: they are viewed as having the capability of making meaningful choices. It could be that domestic forces impose binding constraints on governments in the developing areas; alternatively, their position in the international political economy may offer them a highly impoverished menu of alternatives. In either case, it would make little sense to view governments as possessing the capacity for making choices. Another basis for rejecting this approach is that it posits benign motives for governments. In contrast to welfare economists, political scientists like myself view governments as possessing their own private agendas, and regard it as the duty of all who bear a commitment to the public interest to make it in the private interest of governments to do the same. Quite apart from philosophic predisposition, however, recent experiences in Africa and elsewhere make it clear that the preference of governments often bears little correspondence to any idealization of the public interest. Rather, governments engage in bureaucratic accumulation and act so as to enhance the wealth and power of those who derive their incomes from the public sector; they also act on behalf of private factions, be they social classes, military cliques, or ethnic groups. They engage in economic redistribution, often from the poor to the rich and at the expense of economic

growth. These are central themes in policy formation in Africa and their prominence serves to
discredit any approach based on a conviction
that governments are agencies of the public interest.

Pluralist Theory

The pluralist approach views public policy as
the outcome of political pressures exerted by
members of the domestic economy, i.e., by local
groups seeking the satisfaction of their private
interests from political action.

Particularly in the area of food price policy,
this approach has much to recommend it. Put
bluntly, food policy in Africa appears to represent a form of political settlement designed to
bring peaceful relations between African governments and their urban constituents. It is a settlement whose costs tend to be borne by the
farmers.

Urban consumers in Africa constitute a vigi-
lant and potent pressure group demanding low-
priced food. Because they are poor, they spend
much of their income on food; most studies suggest that urban consumers in Africa spend between 50 and 60 percent of their incomes on
food. Changes in the price of food therefore
have a major impact on the economic well-being
of urban dwellers in Africa, and this group pays
close attention to the issue of food prices.

Urban consumers are potent because they are
geographically concentrated and strategically located. Because of their geographic concentration, they can quickly be organized; because
they control such basic services as transport,
communications, and public services, they can
impose deprivations on others. They are therefore influential. Urban unrest forms a significant
prelude to changes of governments in Africa,
and the cost and availability of food supplies is
a significant factor promoting urban unrest.

It is not only the worker who cares about food
prices. Employers care about food prices because food is a wages good; with higher food
prices, wages rise and, all else being equal, profits fall. Governments care about food prices not
only because they are employers in their own
right but also because as owners of industries
and promoters of industrial development programs they seek to protect industrial profits. Indicative of the significance of these interests is
that the unit that sets agricultural prices often
resides not in the Ministry of Agriculture but in
the Ministry of Commerce or Finance.

When urban unrest begins among food consumers, political discontent often rapidly
spreads to upper echelons of the polity: to those
whose incomes come from profits, not wages,
and to those in charge of major bureaucracies.
Political regimes that are unable to supply low-
cost food are seen as dangerously incompetent
and as failing to protect the interests of key elements of the social order. In alliance with the
urban masses, influential elites are likely to shift
their political loyalties and to replace those in
power. Thus it was that protests over food shortages and rising prices in Ghana in 1972 formed
a critical prelude to the coup that unseated Busia
and led to the period of political maneuvers and
flux that threatened to overthrow the government of Arap Moi in Kenya in 1980.

It is ironic but true that among those governments most committed to low-cost food are
the ''radical'' governments in Africa. Despite
their stress on economic equality, they impose
lower prices on the commodity from which the
poorest of the poor—the peasant farmers—derive their incomes. A major reason for their behavior is that they are deeply committed to rapid
industrialization: moreover, they are deeply
committed to higher real wages for urban workers and have deep institutional ties to organized
labor.

We can thus understand the demand for low-
cost food. Its origins lie in the urban areas. It is
supported by governments, both out of political
necessity and, on the part of more radical ones,
out of ideological preference. It arises because
food is a major staple and higher prices for such
staples threaten the real value of wages *and* profits. . . .

Governments as Agencies that Seek to Retain Power

Nonetheless, the pluralist explanation is also
incomplete. Its primary virtue is that it helps to
account for the essentially draconian pricing
policies adopted by African governments. Its
primary limitation is that it fails to explain how
governments get away with these policies. How,
in nations where the majority of the population
are farmers and the majority of the resources are
held in agriculture, are governments able to succeed in implementing policies that violate the
interests of most farmers? In search of answers
to this question, another approach is needed: one
that looks at agriculture programs as part of a
repertoire of devices employed by African gov-

ernments in their efforts to secure political control over their rural populations and thus to remain in power.

Organizing a Rural Constituency

We have already seen that adopting policies in support of higher prices for agricultural commodities would be politically costly to African governments. It is important to note that this stance would generate few political benefits as well. From a political point of view, conferring higher prices offers few attractions for politicians, for the benefits would be enjoyed by rural opponents and supporters alike. The benefits could not be restricted exclusively to the faithful and withheld from the politically disloyal. Pricing policies therefore cannot be employed by politicians to organize political followings in the countryside.

Project-based policies, however, suffer less from this liability. Officials can exercise discretion in locating projects; they can also exercise discretion in staffing them. This allows them to bestow benefits selectively upon those whose political support they desire. Politicians are therefore more likely to be attracted to project-based policies as a measure of rural development.

Disorganizing the Rural Opposition

We have seen that government policies are often aimed at establishing low prices for agricultural products. Particularly in the market for cash crops, governments maintain monopsonistic agencies and use their market power to lower product prices, thereby imposing deprivations on all producers. What is interesting, however, is that they return a portion of the resources they exact to selected members of the farm community. Some of the earnings taxed from farmers are returned to a privileged few in the form of subsidies for farm inputs. While imposing collective deprivations, governments thus confer selective benefits. The benefits serve as "side payments": they compensate selected members of the rural sector for the losses they sustain as a consequence of the governments' programs. They thereby make it in the private interests of particular members of the rural sector to abide by policies that are harmful to rural dwellers as a whole. By so doing, they secure the defection of favored farmers from a potential rural opposition and insure their adherence to a governing coalition that implements agricultural programs harmful to farming as a whole.

We have already noted that agricultural producers are both subsidized and taxed. What is of concern at this point is the use of subsidy programs for political purposes. In northern Ghana in the late 1970s, for example, subsidized credit was given to large-scale, mechanized producers who were close allies of the ruling military government.

In conferring selective benefits in the markets for farm inputs while imposing collective deprivations in the markets for products, governments secure the deference of a privileged few to programs that are harmful to the interests of most farmers. By politicizing their farm programs and making access to their benefits contingent upon political loyalty, governments secure acquiescence to those in power and compliance with their policies. The political efficacy of these measures is underscored by targeting the large producers who have the most to gain from a change in pricing policy, and who might otherwise provide the "natural leadership" for efforts on the part of farmers to alter the agricultural policies of their governments.

Markets as Instruments
of Political Organization

As part of their development programs, African governments intervene in markets to alter prices. At least in the short run, market intervention establishes disequilibrium prices, i.e., prices at which demand exceeds supply. Such prices artificially induce scarcities, and the allocation of these scarce resources through regulated market channels becomes a significant source of political power. Regulated markets can be used to organize political support and to perpetuate governments in power.

As we have seen, in the markets for agricultural products public monopsonies depress the price of commodities below the market price. Those in charge of the market can then bestow the right of entry; persons given access to the market can reap excess profits and owe their special fortunes to the favor of those in charge. Members of the Cocoa Marketing Board in Ghana, for example, frequently allowed private trading on the part of persons whose political backing they wished to secure.

Disequilibrium product prices also facilitate political control by yielding the capacity to *disorganize* those most hurt by the measure: the farmers themselves. For a portion of the gains, the bureaucrat in charge of the market can turn a blind eye while farmers make sales at market-clearing prices. The structure of regulation vests legal powers in the bureaucrats; the farmers have no right to make such sales. Only by securing an individual exception to the general rule can the farmer gain access to the market-clearing price. Within the framework established by marketing policy, the farmers thus do best by securing individual exceptions. The capacity for discretion therefore allows the bureaucrat to separate the individual interests of particular producers from the interests of their class, and collective organization on the part of rural producers becomes more difficult. In addition, the structure of regulations creates for the government essential elements of political power. By allowing exceptions to the rules, the bureaucracy grants favors; by threatening to enforce the rules, it threatens sanctions. Market regulations thus become a source of political control, and this, in a sense, is most true when they are regularly breached.

Governments establish disequilibrium prices in the markets for inputs as well; the result, once again, is the enhancement of their capacity for political control. When they lower the price of inputs, private sources furnish lesser quantities, users demand greater quantities, and the result is excess demand. One consequence is that the inputs acquire new value; the administratively created shortage creates an economic premium for those who acquire them. Another is that, at the mandated price, the market cannot allocate the inputs; they are in short supply. Rather than being allocated through a pricing system, they must be rationed. Those in charge of the regulated market thereby acquire the capacity to exercise discretion and to confer special benefits upon those whose favor they desire.

Comment: Urban versus Rural Interests

The new political economy would explain a great deal of government policy making in terms of the balance of power between urban and rural interests in a developing country. This balance of power is relevant for the government's relative emphasis on industry or agriculture, trade strategies, liberalization programs, and stabilization programs. The effects of alternative policies can be analyzed in terms of their impact on intersectoral resource shifts and their income-distributional effects. Thus Jeffrey Sachs has suggested that

> distributional effects provide some clues as to why the Latin American countries have chosen to rely on an overvalued currency, a large service sector, and a small export sector, while the Asian economies have lived with the reverse. I believe that long term differences in the balance of power between urban and rural interests helped to account for much of the discrepancy. To a first approximation, the Latin American governments—whether civilian or military, right wing or left wing—find their most important constituencies among urban workers and capitalists. For decades, the agricultural sector has been relatively weak, though certainly not powerless, almost everywhere in Latin America, with peasants only loosely organized and, with some exceptions, large scale agricultural interests unable to hold decisive sway. Moreover, political unrest is most dangerous in the cities, so that urban interests must be bought off first in difficult periods. Interestingly, the opposite seems to be true in most of East Asia. Governments there, whether Japanese colonial rulers before World War II or nationalist governments, have felt the pressing need to win support of, or at least to appease, the rural sector.[1]

From a political-economy perspective, Michael Lipton has also analyzed how resources are being allocated in an urban-biased way; see selection VIII.A.3.

For other instructive analyses of conflicting urban and rural interests, see R. H. Bates, *Essays on the Political Economy of Rural Africa* (1983), and *States and Markets in Tropical Africa* (1981); C. Peter Timmer, Walter P. Falcon, and Scott R. J. Pearson, *Food Policy Analysis* (1983); Peter Timmer, *Getting Prices Right* (1987); Raymond F. Hopkins et al., eds., *Food, Politics and Agricultural Development* (1979); Merilee Grindle, *State and Countryside* (1986); and Avishay Braverman and Ravi Kanbur, "Urban Bias and the Political Economy of Agricultural Reform," *World Development* (September 1987).

[1] Jeffrey D. Sachs, "External Debt and Macroeconomic Performance in Latin America and East Asia," *Brookings Papers on Economic Activity* (1985): 523.

X.D.5. Political Economy of Economic Liberalization*

With the growing importance of International Monetary Fund (IMF) stabilization and World Bank structural adjustment programs, there has been concern about the proper sequencing of the standard stabilization cum liberalization measures contained in these packages. In particular, there is grave concern at the very mixed and in some cases disastrous effects of liberalization attempts on incomes and employment in the Southern Cone of Latin America in the late 1970s and early 1980s. Much of the existing discussion of the order of liberalization is conducted within the traditional technocratic framework,[1] which seeks to determine the welfare-cost-minimizing deployment of policies in the standard stabilization and adjustment packages. Not surprisingly, no clear-cut answers are possible to the unavoidably second best welfare questions that arise.

In this essay I take issue with this emerging consensus on the order of liberalization. I argue that it is based on an implausible model of the attributes and behavior of the State and its citizens, and I suggest that a different, positive "political economy" approach may be more useful in answering questions concerning the sequencing and timing of measures of economic liberalization. . . .

One of the paradoxical dynamic effects of the past dirigisme of many countries in the developing world (as, of course, in some developed countries) has been that attempts to exercise political control over ever-increasing areas of economic life have often led, after a certain stage, to a diminution of the government's effective areas of control as private agents find numerous ways of avoiding them. What concerns us is the empirical observation that there appears to be a sort of "Laffer curve" of government intervention, so that after a certain stage, increased government intervention, instead of increasing the area of government control, diminishes it. It is rare for liberalization to follow some intellectual

conversion of policymakers who, having seen the errors of their ways, seek to find a second best welfare maximizing transition from a controlled to a market economy. Rather, various measures of economic liberalization and/or stabilization are most often sought in order to reassert government control over the economy. It is important to determine the *costs to the State* of *not* liberalizing the economy. For sustained liberalization to be undertaken, these must be greater than the apparent costs of liberalization, namely, the inevitable political pressures which will follow from the changes in distributional rewards and rents which are entailed in any measure of liberalization.[2] This subsection elaborates on these points.

A major motivation for liberalization from the viewpoint of many States in the developing world lies in an attempt to regain control over an economy which seems to be less and less amenable to the usual means of government control. Usually the most important symptom of this malaise is a creeping but chronic fiscal crisis (also reflected sometimes but not always in a balance of payments crisis), which has in different forms beset most economies—including developed ones—in the last decade. . . . Its origins lie in the creation of politically determined "entitlements" to current and future income streams for various groups in the economy (the deserving poor; industrial labor; regional interests; old age pensioners; infant, declining, or sick industries—to name just a few). As these entitlements are implicit or explicit subsidies to particular groups, they have to be paid for by implicit or explicit taxation of other groups in the economy. However justifiable on grounds of

*From Deepak Lal, "The Political Economy of Economic Liberalization," *World Bank Economic Review*, Vol. 1, No. 2 (January 1987), pp. 273–74, 281–85. Reprinted by permission.

[1]This assumes a benevolent and well informed government maximizing a social welfare function subject to resource and technological constraints.

[2]One could, following the "State as pressure group" school of political economy, seek to explain the move to liberalization as resulting from a new pressure group equilibrium. But this model of political economy relies on political institutions corresponding to those in Western democracies. Its applicability to the varied authoritarian regimes in the developing world would seem to be limited. Hence my attempt to explain why a developing world government which is *relatively* (but not completely) immune to democratic pressure group activity would seek to liberalize its economy. Another way of making this point is that instead of considering the State to be a passive transmitter of pressure group activity, one looks upon it as an autonomous agent with its own goals.

social welfare, the gradual expansion of this "transfer State" leads to some surprising dynamic consequences.

The gradual expansion of politically determined entitlements creates specific "property rights." The accompanying tax burden to finance them leads at some stage to generalized tax resistance, avoidance, and evasion and to the gradual but inevitable growth of the parallel or underground economy. This has been the case with both developed and developing countries in the past decade. Faced with inelastic or declining revenues but burgeoning expenditure commitments, incipient or actual fiscal deficits become chronic. These can only be financed by three means: domestic borrowing, external borrowing, or levying of the inflation tax.

Many countries, particularly those in Latin America, have tried all three—with dire consequences. Domestic borrowing to close the fiscal gap may crowd out private investment . . . and diminish the future growth of income—and thus the future tax base. The fiscal deficit may be financed by foreign borrowing for a time, particularly as in the mid-1970s, when real interest rates were low and even negative. But this form of financing is inherently unstable. The debt service ratio can become unviable if, as in the late 1970s, world interest rates rise and the ability of the economies to generate the requisite export and fiscal surpluses to service the higher interest costs of publicly guaranteed debt is limited. This is often due to policy-induced distortions inhibiting exports—for example, the maintenance of overvalued exchange rates and high and differentiated effective rates of protection which are an indirect tax on exports—and the difficulty in generating fiscal surpluses to match the interest on the debt. Thereupon, foreign lending can abruptly cease, leading to the kind of "debt crisis" which has plagued Latin America in the 1980s. The third way of financing the deficit, through the use of the inflation tax, is also unviable over the medium run, for it promotes a further growth of the parallel economy and a substitution of some indirect or direct form of foreign currency based assets for domestic money as a store of value. The tax base for levying the inflation tax thus shrinks rapidly.

With taxes being evaded, with domestic and foreign credit virtually at an end, and with private agents having adjusted to inflation to evade the inflation tax, the government finds its fiscal control of the economy vanishing. The growth of entitlements, moreover, reduces the *discre-*

tionary funds available to the government, and it is discretionary funds which give the government power. It may not even be able to garner enough resources to pay the functionaries required to perform the classical State functions of providing law and order, defense, and essential infrastructure. This dynamic process whereby the expansion of the transfer State leads to the unexpected and very un-Marxian withering away of the State has rarely reached its full denouement, although in some Latin American countries it may be close.

But well before things come to such a dire pass, attempts are usually made to regain government control. Two responses by the government are possible—an illiberal and a liberal one. The former (which is rarely observed) consists of a further tightening and more stringent enforcement of direct controls. Tanzania provides an example of this response. If this tightening is effective, and the private utility of after-tax income received from legal productive activity declines to the level at which untaxed subsistence activities are preferable, however, producers may seek to escape the controls by ceasing to produce the taxed commodities altogether. The tightening and enforcement of controls could lead to an implosion of the economy. The government might then find that as producers return to untaxable subsistence activities, the very production base over which it seeks control has shrunk or disappeared.

The more usual response is to regain a degree of fiscal control through some liberalization of controls on the economy. Typically, however, these liberalization attempts are half-hearted and include some tax reform, monetary contraction, and some measures of export promotion. Their aim is to raise the economy's growth rate as well as the yield from whatever taxes are still being paid and to improve the debt service ratio in the hope that this will lead to a resumption of voluntary foreign lending. But unless the underlying fiscal problem (which is largely that of unsustainable public expenditure commitments) has been tackled, these liberalization attempts have usually been aborted.

Without a commitment to reducing unviable levels of entitlements, the liberalization attempts have tended to worsen the fiscal situation. With the lowering of tax rates and lags in supply response, revenues do not rise and may even fall initially. The necessary reductions in money supply to contain inflation reduce the limited seigniorage previously being extracted. Government unwillingness to allow either public or private enterprises to fail entails absorbing the deficits of public enterprises as well as any newly sick units taken over, as the liberalization exerts competitive pressure on unviable firms. Moreover, where liberalization has been accompanied by large public or private capital inflows (often to finance the public sector deficit), there has been an appreciation of the real exchange rate sometimes accompanied by inflationary pressures arising from inappropriate nominal exchange rate policies. This appreciation thwarts potential export growth, so that as capital inflows diminish, the incipient fiscal deficit is only again reflected in a chronic balance of payments problem which the government then seeks to control in the old unviable ways—and the liberalization process is reversed.

The above patterns have been observed in a large number of countries which have attempted to liberalize in the 1970s. The major lesson to be drawn is that liberalization is often undertaken to gain fiscal control, but if nothing is done to rescind unsustainable public expenditure entitlements a stabilization cum balance of payments crisis eventually emerges which undermines the attempt to liberalize the economy. It would thus seem that a sine qua non of a sustainable liberalization attempt must be the prior establishment of fiscal control through a reduction of unsustainable public expenditure commitments. The stabilization of the economy no less than any prospective liberalization also entails a willingness to overcome the resistance of those whose entitlements will be rescinded.

The *political* problem governments most usually face when considering economic liberalization is that the pressures from the potential losers from the liberalization tend to antedate the support which will subsequently be provided by all those who gain. As can be readily shown, under many circumstances there will be losers in the short run from the changes in relative prices and/or disabsorption flowing from stabilization and structural adjustment programs, particularly those whose relative returns on sector specific human and physical capital fall as a result of these changes. If the liberalization is sustained, however, it is likely to yield higher and more efficient growth in income, which will benefit most groups in the economy. Given the government's own rate of discount (which may be much higher than that of society), even if the resulting purely technocratic economic welfare integral is positive, policymakers may still be reluctant to undertake the reforms if they feel uncertain about their ability to survive the political pressures during the transition.

Comment: Politics of Stabilization

Rescheduling of international debt, conditional assistance from the IMF, and structural adjustment loans from the World Bank—as well as a government's own program to stabilize its economy—often require painful economic adjustments, with losses to some in the community. Domestic political forces are therefore influential in determining the success or failure of stabilization programs. On the political sustainability of adjustment and stabilization programs, see Joan Nelson, "The Politics of Stabilization," in *Adjustment Crisis in the Third World,* ed. Richard E. Feinberg and Valeriana Kallab (1984); John Sheahan, "Market-Oriented Economic Policies and Political Repression in Latin America," *Economic Development and Cultural Change* (January 1980); Stephan Haggard, "The Politics of Adjustment: Lessons from the IMF's Extended Fund Facility," *International Organization* (Summer 1985); Miles Kahler, ed., *The Politics of International Debt* (1986); and Joan M. Nelson, ed., *Economic Crisis and Policy Choice* (1990).

Comment: The Older Political Economy

The new political economy adopts a more formal approach based on a neoclassical economic view of politics. The older—but broader—approach to the political-economy aspects of government policy making can be found in Warren F. Ilchman and Norman T. Uphoff, *The Political Economy of Change* (1971); Guillermo O'Donnell, *Modernization and Bureaucratic Authoritarianism* (1979); Albert O. Hirschman, *Essays in Trespassing* (1980); Bruce F. Johnston and William C. Clark, *Redesigning Rural Development: A Strategic Perspective* (1982); Henry Bruton, "The Search for Development Economics," *World Development* (October–November 1985); John M. Cohen, Merilee S. Grindle, and S. Tjip Walker, "Foreign Aid and Conditions Precedent: Political and Bureaucratic Dimensions," *World Development* (December 1985); Miriles S. Grindle and John W. Thomas, *Public Choices and Policy Change* (1991).

X.E. IMPROVING THE QUALITY OF POLICY MAKING—NOTE

We began our study with the challenge of development (Chapter I). After all the discussion in the preceding chapters, we are left with the question of why the success stories of development have been so limited. Accomplishments there have certainly been, but the development record also reveals too many disappointments (section I.C). For the future, we must concentrate on remedial action to overcome the disappointments of the past. We have emphasized that nations remain poor because of inappropriate policies and that the super constraint relates to national economic management (I.D). The ultimate challenge now is to improve the quality of policy making. How can strategies and tactics improve? How can better policies be devised and the process of policy making be made more effective?

Better policies depend in the first instance on better ideas. A former chief economist of the World Bank has noted that a 0.2 of 1 percent increase in total factor productivity in developing countries would contribute more to their GDP growth than an additional $100 billion of capital invested at historical rates of return. This suggests that what will make the greatest difference for development are good policies, well implemented, and not simply the transfer of resources.[1] Throughout this book we have presented a host of ideas to accelerate development. A greater degree of understanding, however, is still needed in at least three fundamental areas before there can be a more intelligent basis for development policy making. One area is that of the "unexplained residual factor" (recall II.B.2). To the extent that our knowledge of the sources of economic development remains inadequate, we must also remain ignorant of relevant policy variables. Even if we were to succeed in disaggregating the residual into recognizable elements (such as advances in technical, managerial, and organizational knowledge), it is still difficult to specify exactly how these elements are to yield to policies. Many policies that we have considered bear on the supply of inputs, but it is a more difficult challenge to devise and implement policies to promote the income-raising forces constituting the residual.

More research is also needed to assess the impact of population growth on development performance (VI.C). The consequences of reducing population growth are likely to vary according to the policies by which the reduction is achieved and according to specific countries. The intense need for accelerated development stems from the projection that over the next two decades the developing world will account for 95 percent of labor force growth, but for less than 15 percent of capital investment.[2]

If we are to improve our understanding of the two problem areas of the residual factor and population growth, we must also be able to evaluate more thoroughly the noneconomic factors in the development process. It is now stating the obvious to say that economic, social, and political changes are interrelated. Nonetheless, we do not yet know under what conditions and by what mechanisms it is possible to have the types of sociocultural and political change that will be most favorable for development. If policy makers cannot identify the functional relationships between economic and noneconomic factors and their quantitative significance, how can they determine whether to operate on economic incentives, attitudes, organizational structure, social relations, or any of the many other factors that connect economic and noneconomic change? The future success of economic policy making may depend on a better understanding of how to achieve social and political transformations.

Knowledge of political conditions is especially important to achieve improvements in policy making. For reform in economic policy making also depends on political reform. Issues of "governance" are now to the fore. By "governance" is meant more than the elimination of corruption or more effective administration. What is wanted is the avoidance of nonmarket failure in government policy making. Even if economists do have ideas for appropriate policies—even if they do agree on what has gone wrong and how to put it right—will government policy makers listen to them? In previous chapters, there has been repeated criticism of import-

---

[1]Lawrence Summers, "Research Challenges for Development Economists," *Finance & Development* (September 1993): 3.

[2]Ibid., p. 5.

substitution industrialization and advocacy of liberalization of the foreign-trade regime, and yet governments still turn to import substitution and maintain a bias against exports. Economists emphasize the need for rural development, and yet governments perpetuate their urban bias. Economists recommend stabilization programs, but inflation remains recurrent and governments practice stop-go measures.

Many are the reasons why the economists' policy advice is often ignored. Among these reasons, the following tend to be prevalent in developing countries.

The policy makers' objective may not be efficiency, but rising employment (and hence a mistaken reliance on import-substitution industrialization), lower prices out of a consideration for "welfare" (and hence distortions through subsidies), and a more equitable distribution of income and wealth (and hence government expenditures and deficits).

Policy makers may also have to adopt a third- or fourth-best policy because they cannot solve other problems when there are multiple objectives. For example, import substitution may be followed because the government encounters a balance-of-payments crisis, or it is believed to be the easiest route to industrialization, or because it portends a decrease in external dependence. The policy maker lives within a constrained policy triangle, at one vertex of which is accelerated development; at the second vertex, external balance; and at the third vertex, freer trade. The three objectives cannot be achieved simultaneously. In favor of accelerated development, the policy maker therefore often adopts a third- or fourth-best policy with respect to trade and balance-of-payments.

The new political economy (NPE) also attempts to explain why such government failures occur.[3] It attempts to endogenize the policy maker and policy changes over time by applying the rational choice concepts of neoclassical economic analysis to political markets and political phenomena. It maintains that rational self-interested choice principles with respect to goals and instruments shape the decisions of politicians, bureaucrats, and administrators. If the concept of self-interest or self-goal choice is relevant in the political arena, then the neoclassical techniques of maximizing behavior, minimization, and optimization apply. Hence, marginal analysis and equilibrium outcomes can be applied to political preference functions, political resources, and political constraints to explain why governments do what they do.

This approach differs from the usual linear-type analysis of policy formation. As depicted in Figure 1, the linear approach views the economist as offering predictions and prescriptions to the policy maker, who in turn exercises a policy choice that is implemented with a resultant policy outcome. And in offering prescriptions the economist is guided by some notion of the public interest, generally based on welfare economics. For the economist, the policy maker is a platonic guardian.

If, however, the process of policy formation is interpreted more broadly, and from the viewpoint of the new political economy more realistically, then there are other forces impinging on the policy maker and determining policy choice. In Figure 1, these other forces are categorized as being (I) "society centered" or (II) "state centered."[4] The society-centered forces provide societal inputs to a passive government, and the policy choice is a dependent variable. The demand from society creates the supply of policy. Thus, I.A represents inputs from classes whether in Marxist, neo-Marxist, or dependency theory; I.B represents the interest groups of pluralist theory and public choice theory; I.C denotes political parties and voters.

The state-centered approach, category II, views the state as having its own objectives. The state is autonomous, and policy elites are active. In this case, II.A represents the technocratic approach of a benevolent government that is devoted to the national welfare. II.B represents bureaucratic politics; II.C denotes forces acting on the policy maker on behalf of state interests. Being rational choice political economists, the new political economists reject explanations of policy making based on I.A and II.A. Instead they focus on I.B, I.C, II.B, and II.C.

[3]The following discussion of the "new political economy" and government failure is adapted from G. M. Meier, "The New Political Economy and Policy Reform," *Journal of International Development* 65, no. 4 (1993): 382–88. For a more detailed analysis, see G. M. Meier, ed., *Politics and Policymaking in Developing Countries* (1991).

Other relevant studies of government failure and policy reform are Merilee S. Grindle and John W. Thomas, *Public Choices and Policy Change* (1991); Anne Krueger, "Government Failures in Development," *Journal of Economic Literature* (Summer 1990); Dwight H. Perkins and Michael Roemer, *Reforming Economic Systems in Developing Countries* (1991); Dani Rodrik, "The Positive Economics of Policy Reform," *American Economic Review* (May 1993); and John Williamson, ed., *The Political Economy of Policy Reform* (1993).

[4]See Grindle and Thomas, *Public Choices and Policy Change*, chap. 2.

FIGURE 1. The policy formation process.

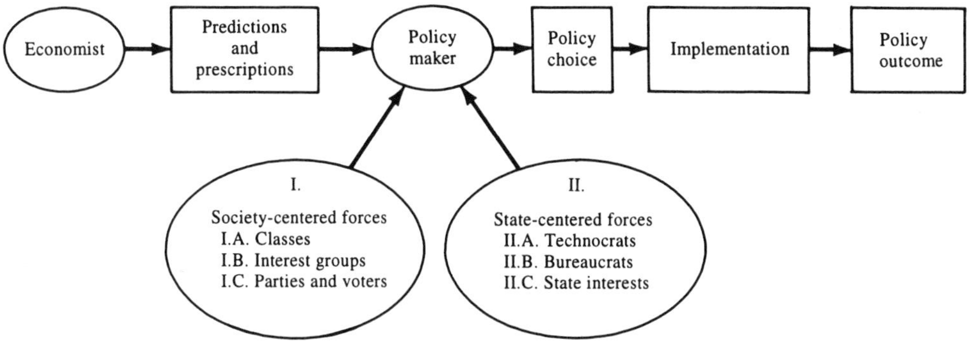

Recognizing these forces, the NPE no longer views government as composed of platonic guardians, acting benevolently in seeking the public interest. While neoclassical economists refer to the public interest, a social welfare function, Pareto efficiency, or first-best policies, the new political economists now refer to the Leviathan state, bureaucratic state, or factional state.

Whether a Leviathan, bureaucratic, or factional model of the state is used, the thrust of the NPE is that an underdeveloped economy has commonly given rise to an overextended state and to a negative or exploitative state. This implication appears in writings on price distortions (rent-seeking and directly unproductive profit-seeking activities), state-owned enterprises (patronage and bureaucracy), financial repression (politicized credit allocation and cheap credit to supporters), agricultural markets (pro-urban bias), inflation (populism), tariffs, and quotas (lobbying).

Although the NPE can provide insights into some instances of government failure, it is overgeneralizing to maintain that all policy making can be explained in terms of rational choice self-interest models. Indeed, no single universal characterization of political behavior is possible. Instead of a unitary state, there is in reality an aggregation of preferences. Moreover, at times, altruism or some sense of the social good may be more operative than self-interest. Other social-psychological elements enter into decision making, especially when "bounded rationality" prevails.[5] Nor should insights from the old political economy be ignored: historical tradition, social structure, ideologies, and institutions can

all influence policy decisions at the expense of rational choice models. And at times economic rationality can take precedence over political rationality.

Besides the positive analysis of the NPE, can the NPE also have predictive and normative value in promoting policy reform? The NPE is most robust in illuminating instances of government failure *ex post*. Its attention to policy reform *ex ante* has been almost negligible. The relative neglect in advocating political change for purposes of economic reform is because the NPE implies a minimal state. As Grindle states, the NPE "is weakened as an approach to understanding policymaking in developing countries and as a policy analytic tool by the assumption that politics is a negative factor in attempting to get policies right."[6] In contrast, politics should not be viewed as "a spanner in the economic works, but as the central means through which societies seek to resolve conflict over issues of distribution and values. In such a perspective, politically rational behaviour would not be viewed as a constraint on the achievement of collectively beneficial public policy."[7]

To achieve an improvement in the quality of policy making does not mean a resort to either centralized planning or the laissez faire of a minimalist state. For each of these types of national economic management, the disadvantages outweigh the advantages. What is needed instead is the avoidance of both market failure and government failure. While correcting market failure, national economic management must restrict government to doing only what government can

---

[5]H. Simon, "A Behavioral Model of Rational Choice," in *Models of Man: Social and Rational*, ed. H. A. Simon, (1957), pp. 241–60.

[6]M. Grindle, "The Limitations of the New Political Economy: Positive Economics and Negative Politics," in *Politics and Policymaking in Developing Countries*, ed. Meier, p. 44.

[7]Ibid., p. 45.

do better than the private sector. For an LDC, this may still mean a strong state with a limited agenda but a legitimate range of government intervention.[8] An even-handed reading of selections in X.B and X.C should give a proper balance to the private and public sectors. The ultimate issue is the quality of government policy making and the role of politics in determining that quality.

Considering policy reform, what type of political regime might be considered most effective? Do democratic or authoritarian regimes do better?

The empirical evidence is inconclusive. In part this is because the empirical evidence itself suffers from methodological problems of designating a political typology and measurement of relevant indices. Other reasons, however, also explain the indeterminacy. The strength of the state may matter more than the type of political regimes in the state. The role of the state in Latin American countries also differs markedly from the role in a newly independent country. Although some may believe that an authoritarian political regime possesses powers favorable to the initiation of development, there may come a time when an authoritarian regime becomes dysfunctional.[9] Moreover, democratic regimes have been no worse at controlling fiscal deficits than have authoritarian regimes.[10]

Generalization is also impossible because regimes differ as to their effect not only on long-term development but also on particular micro-, sectoral, and macro-policies. Some types of regimes are more favorable for appropriate policy making in some areas, while others may be more appropriate in different policy areas.

Although we cannot generalize on what type of political regime is best for development, we can conclude that political instability matters even though instability is not connected with any particular type of political regime. The empirical evidence confirms that political instability hinders development. We can also generalize that markets seem to be a necessary but not sufficient condition for democracy, in so far as the decentralization of power in markets prevents a political monopoly. The more democratic countries also tend to spend less on security and defense and more on health, education, and agriculture.[11]

Another generalization is that policy reform depends on the emergence of a domestic constituency that blames economic hardship on past policies.[12] More significant than the strength of the state is the quality of statecraft, that is, the quality of policy decisions, their credibility, their transparency, and the administrative capacity to implement the policies.

Most important for policy reform is an understanding of what causes the successes of government policy. The NPE ignores what Grindle calls the critical moments, the turning points when policy changes occur: for example, from import-substituting policies to export promotion, from inflationary policies to successful stabilization, from financial repression to financial liberalization. Grindle rejects the notion that change depends on the introduction of enlightened technocrats or statespeople who are somehow liberated from the pursuit of self-interest and thus able to see beyond short-term goals to long-term public interests. She states that ''in the general context of negative politics predicted by neoclassical political economists, change is explained exogenously by benign leadership or disinterested advice.''[13] A contrasting view sees change emerging through a more constructive role for the political process, a role that emphasizes such political values as

the compromise of conflicting interests, the search for more equitable solutions to public problems, the achievement of social and political stability based on a reasonable set of rules about how collective problems are best resolved, the creation of public trust based on a shared sense of legitimate authority, the search for basic consensus on the nature of the public interest, the definition of an agreed-upon role for government to perform.[14]

---

[8]For recent advocacy, see P. Streeten, ''Markets and States: Against Minimalism,'' *World Development* (August 1993); Tony Killick, *A Reaction Too Far* (1990); John P. Lewis, ''Government and National Economic Development,'' in *A World to Make*, ed. Francis X. Sutton (1990); and Christopher Colclough and James Manor, eds., *States or Markets?* (1991).

[9]J. Manor, *Rethinking Third World Politics* (1991), p. 274.

[10]J. Healey, R. Ketley, and M. Robinson, ''Political Regimes and Economic Policy Patterns in Developing Countries, 1978–88,'' Working Paper no. 67, Overseas Development Institute (1992).

[11]J. Healy and M. Robinson, *Democracy, Governance, and Economic Policy* (1992).

[12]P. Collier, ''From Critic to Secular God: The World Bank in Africa,'' *African Affairs* (1991): 112.

[13]Grindle, ''Limitations of the New Political Economy,'' p. 5

[14]Ibid., p. 67.

Others have looked to catastrophic learning experiences or dramatic performance failures as the explanation of change to more appropriate policies. Lal's interpretation of the change from inflationary policies to stabilization programs incorporates this approach.[15] A government may liberalize its economy during a crisis to regain control when the growth of the "transfer state" has led to generalized tax resistance, avoidance, or evasions. The "withering of the state" occurs as parallel markets arise to erode state control; dramatic policy change is then necessary.

Similarly, Ranis hypothesizes

that relatively linear policy change occurs not when the role of government atrophies but when government actions become explicit rather than implicit. Policy oscillation occurs when covert policies adopted for short-term political convenience self-destruct because of the unexpected and delayed adverse effects on some groups whose income is being transferred in the absence of a clear political consensus.[16]

Ranis and Fei have observed that the liberalization process may result from "a natural organizational evolution, companion to the transition toward the epoch of modern economic growth. As the economy becomes increasingly complex, sooner or later the idea seems to surface that command by political forces is cumbersome and that economic decisions must be decentralized in order to achieve economic efficiency."[17]

The general problem in explaining "turning points" is to determine what are the forces that induce political innovations. Policy reform requires political entrepreneurship. But a theory of political entrepreneurship is not to be found in the NPE. Actual experience may thus itself be more telling than the economist's prescriptions. As Bhagwati observes: "Many developing countries learned [the policy lessons] the hard way; by following import-substituting industrialization (ISI) policies too long and seeing the fortunate few pursuing the export promotion (EP) strategy do much better. Perhaps learning by others' doing and one's own undoing is the most common form of education."[18] There is indeed an international demonstration effect in government policies, and governments may be tempted to emulate policies that have been demonstrated as successful in other countries. Under international leverage through the elites of the World Bank, IMF, or OECD there may also be considerable persuasion to import measures of policy reform.

In the past, the critical movements and turning points have normally involved what Hirschman calls "pressing" problems. In examining what types of problems are placed on the government's agenda, which problems become privileged ones that receive the government's attention, Hirschman distinguishes between "pressing" problems and autonomously "chosen" problems.[19] Pressing problems are those "that are forced on the policymakers through pressure from injured or interested outside parties." Chosen problems are those that decision makers "have picked out of thin air" as a result of their own perceptions and preferences. Pressing problems are generally those in which a perception of crisis is apparent; the undertaking of policy reform involving large innovative changes tends to be induced by pressing problems. But we must now ask: Do economists exercise sufficient influences over these large innovative changes?

We began by assuming that economists do have the knowledge to put things right. However, this will be for situations susceptible to ordinary economic analysis. Such situations occur in a policy space characterized by incremental policy changes involving chosen problems. They are subject to more technical analysis and hence a "low" degree of politics (i.e., politics-as-usual). They involve an instrumental type of rationality (i.e., technical policy instruments as the means to achieve policy objectives). The perspective is from a society-centered type of policy (with government as a clearinghouse or broker among interest groups). And institutions are given or ignored. See the northwest quadrant in Figure 2, representative of ordinary economic analysis with a high understanding by economists of the policy-making process.

In contrast, when economists have to deal with situations involving large, innovative pol-

[15]D. Lal, "The Political Economy of Economic Liberalization," *World Bank Economic Review* (January 1987): 273–300.

[16]G. Ranis, "The Political Economy of Development Policy Change," in *Politics and Policymaking in Developing Countries*, ed. Meier, pp. 74–75.

[17]G. Ranis and J. C. H. Fei, "Development Economics: What Next?" in *The State of Development Economics*, ed. G. Ranis and P. Schultz (1988), p. 108.

[18]J. Bhagwati, "Export-Promoting Trade Strategy," *World Bank Research Observer* (1988): 41.

[19]A. O. Hirschman, *Journeys Toward Progress* (1963), pp. 229–35.

icy changes, they are called upon to advise in a political economy context in which the economist has a lower understanding of the policy-making process. In this policy space (see the southeast quadrant in Figure 2), the problems are pressing problems. They are not amenable to as much technical analysis but instead are highly politicized. The rationality involved is of a constitutive type. That is, decisions have to be made about how decisions are to be made: a constitution is needed and an institutional context for decision making has to be established. The policy-making process is more state centered. And institutional structures need to change.

If economists are to become more influential in advising on how to correct nonmarket failures and overcome resistance to policy reform, they will have to give more attention to the policy situations represented by the southeast quadrant in Figure 2. It is especially necessary to make policy changes transparent by identifying the distribution of not only the economic, but also the political, costs and benefits of policy changes, and by identifying the gainers and losers. To promote policy reform, it is then necessary to examine possible ways to compensate the losers, discover the possibilities for building supportive coalitions, and consider the scope for alternative institutional arrangements. It is especially important to insulate policy makers from rent-seekers and interest groups so that

government can give more attention to the efficiency of the economy and less to distribution for favor-seeking groups.

The upshot is that the giving of economic advice should not be viewed as merely a technical exercise; instead, it must be integrated with knowledge of the country's political process. To determine the feasibility and desirability of various policy reforms, economists need first to acquire knowledge of the underlying reasons for government failure. The NPE, although still new, may help economists do this in some countries at some times. The relationship, however, between the economist's knowledge, economic policy, and development performance still remains more elusive than it should. We still need more insights from both the old and the new political economy in order to better understand the causes of differential development performance and how to institute policy reform. Going beyond the limitations of formal rational choice models, a richer analysis might be achieved by incorporating some concepts of the old political economy, such as nationalism, power, ideology, class, and relationship between the state and society. Future research may provide a synthesis of the old and new political economy that will point up the possibilities of policy changes including more political variables and a more favorable view of the political process.

So, too, is more research needed to under-

FIGURE 2. Different policy situations.

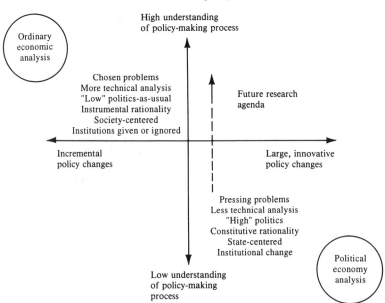

stand the nature of institutional change and its effect on development performance. In doing this, more attention should focus on markets, property rights, formation of contracts, information problems, organizational change, and incentives. These concepts from the new institutional economics may also enrich the old and new political economy.

From this more comprehensive view of the policy-making process in practice, economists might be in a better position to advise on how to correct nonmarket failure and overcome re- sistance to policy reform. It is to be hoped that future research may allow the next generation of development economists to achieve greater understanding of pressing problems that are less tractable to technical analysis, more politicized, involve issues of constitutive rationality, and require institutional change. As analysts of development policy making, they may then move upward from the southeast quadrant of Figure 2 to the northeast quadrant, where they will exercise more influence in meeting the challenge of development.

INDEX

Absolute poverty, 3, 5, 28–30, 266
Agriculture: as constraint, 65; contribution of, to
  development, 397–400; interactions of, with
  industry, 385–94; and international trade, 501–6;
  new political economy explanation of, 569–75;
  policy implications of, 337–38, 431–51; pricing
  policies for, 395, 438–44; role of peasants in,
  400–404; and structural transformation, 333–41;
  unimodal strategy for, 444–50. *See also* Green
  revolution; Industrialization; Urban bias
Analytical perspectives, 86–106
Arrow, Kenneth, 102

Bacha, Edmar L., 385–89
Backwardness, 72–74
Balance of payments, 174, 213, 216, 242–44, 249–50.
  See also External debt; Foreign-exchange gap;
  Policies
Balanced growth, 87, 327
Balassa, Bela, 470–74
Bardhan, Pranab, 103–6
Bates, Robert H., 569–75
"Big push," 86–87, 327, 343–44, 349–50
Binswanger, Hans P., 415–18
Birdsall, Nancy, 279–82
Bliss, Christopher, 90
Bruno, Michael, 499–500
Burki, Shahid Javed, 55–58
Buvinic, Mayra, 295–300

Capabilities, 9, 11–12
Capital flight, 191–92, 210, 216–17
Capital formation. *See* Investment
Capital-stretching innovations, 373–75
Cardoso, Fernando Henrique, 108–9
Chenery, Hollis, 23–24, 95–99, 329–32
Child labor, 285
China, development of, 55–59
Clark, J. M., 102
Classical economic analysis, 74–75, 276
Classical growth theory, 89–90
Collier, Paul, 210–12, 300–302
Colonialism, 62–63
Comparative advantage, 453, 455–61. *See also* Trade
Conditionality, 230

Constraints, 64–66
Contracts in agrarian economies, 415–19
Contractual choice models, 416–18
Corden, W. Max, 198, 495–99
Country risk matrix, 243–44. *See also* External debt
Cross-country comparisons, 59–61
Culture, 78–79, 83–84. *See also* Korea; Success
  stories; Taiwan

Debt-servicing problem. *See* External debt
Demand-following finance, 202–4
Dependency, 107–11
Development: financing of, 167–212, 213–63;
  measurement of, 13–17; planning, 556–57. *See
  also* New political economy; Policies; State
Directly unproductive, profit-seeking (DUP) activities,
  566
Disequilibrium growth, 97–98
Disguised unemployment, 117–20, 124. *See also*
  Surplus labor
Distributional weights, 23–24
Domestic resource cost, 474
Dornbusch, Rudiger, 239–40
DRC. *See* Domestic resource cost
Dualism: financial, 131–35; organizational, 80, 132–39,
  484; technological, 129–31, 139; versions of,
  129–39; wage, 131, 136–37. *See also* Dual-sector
  model; Lewis, W. Arthur; Myint, Hla
Dual-sector model, 117–19, 121–28, 137, 153–59,
  385–86
Dynamic comparative advantage, 455–58
Dynamic gains from trade, 459–60, 483–85. *See also*
  Export-led development; Trade

Easterlin, Richard, 62
Econometric default functions, 244
Economic development: historical perspectives on,
  69–85 (*see also* Stages); meaning of, 7–9; as
  subject, 67, 86–90. *See also* Development:
  measurement of
Education, 266–67, 269; characteristics of, 316–25;
  economic impact of, 322–25; and externalities,
  318–20; as investment in human capital, 313–16,
  551; and success stories, 320–21. *See also* Human
  capital

Effective exchange rates for imports and exports, 485–87
Effective rate of protection, 474
Endogenous growth theory. *See* New growth theory
Entitlements, 9, 11–12
Entrepreneurship, 273–75
Environment, 30–32, 231–32, 363–64, 444
ERP. *See* Effective rate of protection
Exchange rates, overvalued, 493–95. *See also* Balance of payments; Foreign exchange, as constraint
Export-led development, 327, 361–63, 453–54, 465–69, 479–88. *See also* Industrialization; Success stories; Trade
Exports. *See* Balance of payments; Industrialization; Statistics; Trade
External debt: and country risk analysis, 241–43; and growth, 239–40; and policies to reduce, 186, 244–46; problems of, 214, 233–35; statistics on, 235–39

Famine, 404–5
Financial constraint, 209. *See also* Financial repression
Financial Institutions, 167–68, 190–91, 193, 210–12. *See also* Financial repression; Money markets
Financial liberalization, 208–12. *See also* Financial repression
Financial repression, 190–91, 193, 204–9
Financing of development: domestic sources for, 167–212; external sources for, 169, 213–63. *See also* Investment
Fischer, Stanley, 239–40, 521–25
Food: and population, 276; supplies of, 276, 305, 385–86, 404–5. *See also* Agriculture; Famine; Hunger; Nutrition
Foreign aid: case for, 221–22; criticism of, 224; effects of, 224–26; improvement in, 226–29
Foreign exchange, as constraint, 64, 215–16. *See also* Balance of payments; Exchange rates, overvalued
Foreign-exchange gap, 213, 215–16
Fry, Maxwell, 209

Gender analysis, 287–304. *See also* Women
Gerschenkron, Alexander, 72–74, 204
Gini coefficient, 17, 20, 34
Government failure. *See* New political economy; Policies: reform of
Green revolution, 396, 409–10
Greenaway, David, 476–79
Grindle, Merilee, 580–82
Growth: balanced, 87, 327; sources of, 92–96; unbalanced, 87, 327

Harberger, Arnold C., 91–93, 525–29
Hayami–Ruttan theory, 429–30, 433
HDI. *See* Human Development Index
Health, 305–12, 549–51
Helleiner, G. K., 362
Hirschman, Albert O., 63, 346–49
Household models, 424–27
Household savings, 192–93

Human capital, 64, 265, 269–74, 285; theory of, 316. *See also* Human resources; Investment; Knowledge; Population
Human development, balance sheet of, 4
Human Development Index (HDI), 9–11
Human resources: as constraint, 64; and education, 313–26; and knowledge, 265, 313; women as, 287–304. *See also* Gender analysis; Human capital; Nutrition; Population
Hunger, 404–5. *See also* Food; Nutrition

ICOR. *See* Incremental capital–output ratio
IMF. *See* International Monetary Fund
Import substitution, 155–56, 327, 355–60, 368–78, 453–54, 470–74, 567–69. *See also* Industrialization; New political economy; Trade
Imports. *See* Balance of payments; Industrialization; Statistics; Trade
Incentives, problems with, 99–101
Income distribution, 5, 17–23, 33–34, 39–40
Incremental capital–output ratio, 164–66
Induced innovation model, 429–30
Industrialization: and export-orientation, 327, 361–63; and external economies, 342–45; historical analysis of, 72–74, 82; and import substitution, 327, 355–60; interactions of, with agriculture, 327, 385–94; linkage effects of, 346–49; strategy of, 553–58; and structural transformation, 329–38; and technological progress, 327, 368–78. *See also* "Big push"; Policies
Industry, promotion of, 350–54, 364–67. *See also* Industrialization
Inequality. *See* Income distribution
Infant industry, protection of, 475–76. *See also* Import substitution; Trade
Inflation, 174–85, 576–78
Informal sector, 146–51
Information, 201–2, 211–12; analysis of, 99–101, 414
Initial conditions, 49–50, 63
Institutions, 80, 104–6. *See also* New institutional economics
Interest rates, 38–39, 199–202, 210–11. *See also* Financial institutions; Financial repression; Money markets
International commodity agreements, 454
International Monetary Fund, 184–87, 229–30
Inverted-U hypothesis, 20–22. *See also* Kuznets, Simon
Investment: in neoclassical analysis, 91–93; requirements for, 163–66; sources of financing of, 167–73; in stages of growth, 69–72; in success stories, 42. *See also* Human Capital; Industrialization; Neoclassical economics; Savings
Inward orientation. *See* Import substitution

Johnson, Harry G., 269–72, 536–40
Johnston, Bruce F., 333–38, 444–51

Kaldor, Nicholas, 168, 194
Kilby, Peter, 333–38, 450–51

Killick, Tony, 51–52
Knowledge, 102–3, 265. *See also* Human Capital; New growth theory
Korea, development of, 33–42. *See also* Success stories
Krueger, Anne O., 88, 479–82
Krugman, Paul, 245–46, 350
Kuznets, Simon, 20–22, 69, 82, 397–98

Labor force: contractual arrangements with, 415–18; growth of, 5; in rural labor markets, 428. *See also* Migration; Urban labor markets; Women
Lal, Deepak, 576–78
Lall, Sanjaya, 364–67
Land reform, 35–36, 421–22
Land tenure, 419–21
Landes, David S., 74–79
Latin America, development of, 40–46
Leibenstein, Harvey, 273–75
Lele, Uma, 400–404
Lewis, W. Arthur, 121–28, 156–57, 163–64, 188, 390–94
Linkages, 346–49
Lipton, Michael, 405–9
Livingstone, Ian, 150–51
Lorenz curve, 17, 19–20

Malnutrition, 3–4, 55. *See also* Health; Nutrition
Market economy, 36–38. *See also* Neoclassical economics; Policies
Market failures, 211, 540–42, 546. *See also* New market failures; State
Markets, interlinkage of, 412–13. *See also* Market failures; Neoclassical economics; Policies; Privatization
Marshall, Alfred, 265
Marxian analysis, 70–71, 76–77, 106. *See also* Dependency
McKinnon, Ronald I., 204–8
Migration: econometric studies of, 145–46; and employment, 156–58; Todaro model of, 140–45; and urbanization, 140–44
Missing components, 63
Modern sector, 125–28. *See also* Dual-sector model; Lewis, W. Arthur
Monetarism, 183–84
Money markets, 199–202
Multinational enterprises, 256–59, 363, 371–72
Myint, Hla, 132–39
Myrdal, Gunnar, 462–64

Naya, Seiji, 42–45
Neoclassical economics, 87–89, 90–93, 96, 137–38, 515–17. *See also* Analytical perspectives; Policies: reform of
Neoclassical political economy. *See* New political economy
Neostructuralism, 110–11; agenda of 531–34
New export pessimism, 490–91
New growth theory, 102–3
New institutional economics, 103–6

New market failures, 101–2. *See also* Market failures; New political economy; Policies: reform of
New political economy: characteristics of, 562–65, 579–85; as explanation of agricultural policy, 569–75; of fiscal crisis, 576–78; of import substitution, 567–69; and rent-seeking, 565–66. *See also* Policies; State
New trade theory, 454, 476–79
North, Douglass C., 80
Nurkse, Ragnar, 87, 117–19, 163, 350
Nutrition, 305–7, 549–51

Obstacles, 63–64, 83
Organizational dualism, 80, 132–39, 484
Outward orientation. *See* Export-led development

Pack, Howard, 375–78
Patrick, Hugh T., 202–4
Penrose, Edith, 261
Perkins, Dwight H., 542–47, 558
Policies: agricultural, 337–38, 431–51; appropriate, 64–66; from dependency theory, 109–10; early advocacy, 86–88; educational, 313–25; environmental, 31–32; and financial systems, 210–12; health, 307–13; and IMF, 184–87; lessons of, 52–55, 485–90; 525–29; nutrition, 305–7; political economy of, 42; reform of, 515–29, 582–85 (*see also* New political economy); taxation, 196–97; trade, 491–500
Political risk analysis, 262–63. *See also* Country risk matrix
Population: growth of, 277–82; and poverty, 276–79; pressures of, 82–83, 266; quality of, 266 (*see also* Human Development Index; Quality of life, statistics on); revisionist view of, 286; statistics on, 282–84. *See also* Human resources
Poverty, measures of, 25–29; vicious circle of, 163. *See also* Absolute poverty
Price distortions, 87–88, 155, 558–61. *See also* Policies; Project appraisal; Shadow prices
Primary products. *See* Agriculture; Producer power; Trade
Private foreign investment: benefit–cost analysis of, 247–54; and multinationals, 256–58; negotiation of, 259–63; potential for, 214, 247; statistics on, 254–55
Privatization, 379–84, 545–46
Producer power, 454, 502–4
Product life cycle, 456–58
Production function, 91–94
Project appraisal, 558–61
Protection. *See* Import substitution; Infant industry, protection of; Trade
Purchasing power parities, 5, 13, 17–19, 186

Quality of life, statistics on, 3–4, 8–9. *See also* Education; Health; Human Development Index; Nutrition

Ranis, Gustav, 373–75, 583
Redundant labor, 128
Regional integration, 507–11
Rent-seeking, 477–78, 565–66. *See also* New political economy
Residual, 91. *See also* Total Factor Productivity
Resource gap, 215–16. *See also* Balance of payments; Savings
Reynolds, Lloyd, 62–63
Roemer, Michael, 515–20
Romer, Paul M., 103
Rosenstein-Rodan, Paul N., 342–49
Rosenzweig, Mark R., 415–18
Rostow, W. W., 69–72, 81
Rural credit, 193, 300–301; markets for, 422–24
Rural development. *See* Agriculture
Rural financial markets, characteristics of, 423
Rural sector: microeconomics of, 411–30; organization of, 411–15. *See also* Agriculture; Dualism
Rural–urban terms of trade, 408

Sachs, Jeffrey, 575
Savings: as constraint, 64–66; private, 188–93; as resources for financing investment, 167–68, 170–73; statistics on, 217–19. *See also* Financing of development; Household savings; Investment; Resource gap
Schultz, Theodore, 265
Scitovsky, Tibor, 33–39
Sen, Amartya, 9, 11–12, 119–20, 302–4
Sequencing reforms, 518–20
Shadow prices, 141, 559–61
Shapiro, Helen, 553–55
Sharecropping, 411–16
Smith, Adam, 89–90, 163
Social benefit–cost analysis, 558–61
Solow, Robert, 102–3
Srinivasan, T. N., 562–65
Stabilization policy, 184–87, 212, 577–778. *See also* Policies
Stages, 69–72
Stark, Oded, 145–46
State, 513–14, 529–31, 533–34, 548–58, 580–82. *See also* New political economy
State-owned enterprises, 383–84. *See also* Privatization
Statistics: on balance of payments, 213–19; as basic indicators, 14–16, 50–51; as comparative indicators, 47, 58, 60–61; on education, 321, 323, 325; on exports and imports, 482–83, 505; on external debt, 235–39; on external financing, 220–23; on female–male gaps, 293–96; financial, 206–7; on foreign direct investment, 254–55; on government expenditures, 550; on government revenue, 195; on growth rates, 33; on health, 308, 312; on human development, 4, 10–11; on income, 18–19, 25; on income distribution, 23, 34; on inflation, 183; on investment, 217–19; on population, 146, 282–84, 308; on poverty, 25, 27–28, 409; on private foreign investment, 254–55; on savings, 217–19; as social indicators,

34; on sources of growth, 94–95; on structural transformation, 334–35, 339–41; on structure of demand, 170–73; on women, 291–95
Stern, Nicholas, 13–17, 194–97, 548–55
Stewart, Frances, 368–71
Stiglitz, Joseph E., 99–102, 411–15, 435–38
Streeten, Paul P., 84
Structural adjustment, 516–18
Structural analysis, 87, 95–99, 183–84. *See also* Dependency
Structural transformation, 98–99, 327, 329–41. *See also* Dual-sector model
Sub-Saharan Africa, development of, 46–55
Success stories, 42
Summers, Lawrence, 52–55
Sunkel, Osvaldo, 108, 531–34
Supply-leading finance, 202–4
Surplus labor, 117–25, 137
Syrquin, Moshe, 329–32

Taiwan, development of, 33–39. *See also* Success stories
Take-off, 71–72. *See also* Stages
Taxation, 167–69, 194–98
Taylor, Lance, 553–55
Technological progress, 78, 84, 91
Technology: appropriate, 368–71; transfer of, 375–78
Tenancy, models of, 416–18
Thomas, Vinod, 521–25, 529–31
Timmer, C. Peter, 431–33, 438–43
Todaro, Michael P., 140–45
Tomich, Thomas P., 333–38, 450–51
Total Factor Productivity, 93–94
Trade: gains from, 453, 458–61, 465–69, 483–85; and international inequalities, 453, 462–65; liberalization of, 495–500; and neoclassical theory, 461, 484; policy reform, 491–500; in primary products, 501–6; regional integration of, 507–11; Taiwan's strategy of, 488–90; terms of, 464–65. *See also* Comparative advantage; Export-led development; Import substitution
Traditional sector, 125–28. *See also* Dual-sector model; Lewis, W. Arthur
Transaction costs, 80, 103–5, 414–15, 422

ul-Haq, Mahbub, 507–11
Unbalanced growth, 87, 327
Unemployment, problem of, 141, 156–59
Unimodal strategy, 444–50
Urban bias, 399, 405–9, 575
Urban labor markets, 143–44, 151–55. *See also* Informal sector; Migration

Values, *See* Culture
Vent-for-surplus, 458–59
Vernon, Raymond, 379–83
Viner, Jacob, 399–400

Wade, Robert, 557–58
Wage gap, 151–52. *See also* Migration; Todaro, Michael P.; Urban labor markets

Wai, U Tun, 199–202
Warriner, Doreen, 419–21
Williamson, Jeffrey, 21–22, 142–44
Women: earnings of, 296–98; female–male gaps, 293–96; and gender discrimination, 300–302; and gender-related reforms, 298–300; in labor force, 28, 287–91, 296–97, 428–29; and market discrimination, 300–302; missing number of, 302–4; share of poverty of, 295–300
World Bank, 229–30

X-efficiency, 361, 483

Young, Allyn, 343–44